D1238273

HEBREW-ENGLISH EDITION OF
THE BABYLONIAN TALMUD

SEDER ZERA'IM

BERAKOTH

תלמוד בבלי

מסכת

ברכות

עם פירוש רש״י ותוספות
ובצירוף תרגום ופירוש והערות באנגלית

על ידי
משה סימון

בעריכת
יחזקאל (איזידור) אפשטיין

דפוס שונצין
שנת להחז״ר העטר״ה ל׳ושנה לפ״ק
לונדון

HEBREW-ENGLISH EDITION OF
THE BABYLONIAN TALMUD

BERAKOTH

TRANSLATED INTO ENGLISH
WITH NOTES, GLOSSARY AND INDICES BY
MAURICE SIMON, M.A.

UNDER THE EDITORSHIP OF
RABBI DR I. EPSTEIN, B.A., PH.D., D.LIT.

FOREWORD BY
DR J. H. HERTZ
LATE CHIEF RABBI OF THE BRITISH EMPIRE

INTRODUCTION BY
THE EDITOR

LONDON
THE SONCINO PRESS
1960

PUBLISHERS' NOTE

In publishing this HEBREW-ENGLISH EDITION of BERAKOTH, The Soncino Press has made available for the first time, the complete Tractate Berakoth based on the Wilna Talmud with each unabridged Hebrew page facing the corresponding English translation of the Soncino Talmud.

This first volume in the series has been published to facilitate the easier reference to the original text by scholars and students.

The Publishers express their appreciation of the co-operation received from S. Goldman-Otzar Hasefarim Inc. publishers of *Otzar Hasefarim Talmud Bavli*, New York, 1958.

© THE SONCINO PRESS LTD. 1960
ALL RIGHTS RESERVED INCLUDING THE RIGHT TO
REPRODUCE THIS BOOK OR PARTS THEREOF IN ANY FORM

FOREWORD

BY

THE VERY REV. THE CHIEF RABBI

Dr J. H. HERTZ

The Talmud is the product of Palestine, the land of the Bible, and of Mesopotamia, the cradle of civilisation. The beginnings of Talmudic literature date back to the time of the Babylonian Exile in the sixth pre-Christian century, before the Roman Republic had yet come into existence. When, a thousand years later, the Babylonian Talmud assumed final codified form in the year 500 after the Christian era, the Western Roman Empire had ceased to be. That millenium opens with the downfall of Babylon as a world-power; it covers the rise, decline and fall of Persia, Greece and Rome; and it witnesses the spread of Christianity and the disappearance of Paganism in Western and Near Eastern lands.

I

The Babylonian Exile is a momentous period in the history of humanity—and especially so in that of Israel. During that Exile, Israel found itself. It not only rediscovered the Torah and made it the rule of life, but under its influence new religious institutions, such as the synagogue, i.e., congregational worship without priest or ritual, came into existence—one of the most far-reaching spiritual achievements in the whole history of Religion. At the re-establishment of the Jewish Commonwealth, Ezra the *Sofer*, or Scribe, in the year 444 B.C.E. formally proclaimed the Torah the civil and religious law of the new Commonwealth. He brought with him all the oral traditions that were taught in the Exile, and he dealt with the new issues that confronted the struggling community in that same spirit which had created the synagogue. His successors, called after him *Soferim* ('Scribes'), otherwise known as the 'Men of the Great Assembly', continued his work. Their teachings and ordinances received the sanction of popular practice, and came to be looked upon as *halachah*, literally, 'the trodden path', the clear religious guidance to the Israelite in the way he should go. When the Men of the Great Assembly were no more, the Sanhedrin of Jerusalem took their place. The delight of all those generations was in the Law of the Lord, and in His Law did they meditate day and night. When their exposition followed the verses of Scripture, it was called *Midrash;* and when such exposition followed the various precepts, it was known as *Mishnah*. Academies arose for systematic cultivation of this New Learning, as well as for the assiduous gathering of the oral traditions current from times immemorial concerning the proper observance of the commandments of the Torah. This movement for the intensive study of Scripture did not pass unchallenged. The aristocratic and official element of the population—later known as the Sadducees—unhesitatingly declared every law that was not specifically written in the Torah to be a dangerous and reprehensible innovation. The opposition of the Sadducees only gave an additional impetus to the spread of the Oral Law by the Scribes, later known as the Pharisees. What they sought was the full and inexhaustible revelation which God had made. The knowledge of the contents of that revelation, they held, was to be found in the first instance in the Written Text of the Pentateuch; but the revelation, the real Torah, was the *meaning* of that Written Text, the Divine thought therein disclosed, as unfolded in ever greater richness of detail by successive generations of devoted teachers. 'Apart from the direct intercourse of prayer,' says Herford, 'the study of Torah was the way of closest approach to God; it might be called the Pharisaic form of the Beatific Vision. To study Torah was to think God's thoughts after Him, as Kepler said.'

The product of the feverish activity of the Pharisaic schools threatened to become too unwieldy to be retained by unassisted memory. For all this teaching was *oral*, and was not to be written down. The first effort at arrangement of the traditional material into a system, was made in the first pre-Christian century by Hillel. He is the best known of all the rabbis, renowned for his enunciation of the Golden Rule, 'Whatsoever is hateful unto thee, do it not to thy fellow; this is the whole Torah, the rest is but commentary.' He was the embodiment of meekness and humanity. 'Love peace, and pursue peace, love thy fellow-creatures and bring them near to the Torah,' was his motto. He popularised seven exegetical rules for the interpretation of the Torah—e.g., the rules of inference, and analogy—by which the immanent meaning of Scripture might better be brought out; and he divided the mass of traditions that in his day constituted the Oral Law into the six main Orders, which division was accepted by all his successors.

Of the 150 *Tannaim*, or 'teachers', who may be called the architects of the spiritual edifice which in its completed form is known as the Mishnah, it is necessary to mention three more besides Hillel. These are Joḥanan ben Zakkai, Rabbi Akiba, and Rabbi Judah the Prince. Joḥanan ben Zakkai was the youngest of Hillel's disciples. By his Academy at Jabneh, he rescued Judaism from the shipwreck of the Roman destruction that overwhelmed the Jewish nation in the year 70. Jabneh became the rallying-ground of Jewish Learning and the centre of Jewish spiritual life. Like nearly every one of the rabbis, he earned his bread by manual labour. Judaism, he held, could outlive its political organism; and charity and love of men replaced the Sacrificial Service. 'A good heart', he declared, was the most important thing in life.

In the following generation, Akiba was the author of a collection of traditional laws out of which the Mishnah actually grew. He was the greatest among the rabbis of his own and of succeeding times, the man of whom—as the legend says—even Moses was for a moment jealous when in a vision he was given a glimpse of the distant future. His keen and penetrating intellect enabled him to find a Biblical basis for every provision of the Oral Law. Romance illumines the early life of this great rabbi and mystic. In 132 he died a martyr's death for his God and People. On the day that Akiba died was born R. Judah the Prince, also called simply 'Rabbi'. He was a descendant of Hillel in the seventh generation, and a man of uncommon ability, wide culture and lofty virtue. As Patriarch—spiritual ruler of his generation—he made it his aim to ensure unity of religious observance by the establishment of one Code of undisputed authority. He, therefore, surveyed anew the whole aggregation of ordinances that had accumulated with the centuries, sifting and arranging, abridging and amplifying; and often incorporating the opinions of earlier teachers in exactly the form in which he had received them. Thus the Mishnah is not cast in a single mould. It is a composite work. Perhaps for this reason also it displaced all rival collections of traditional law, and soon attained to canonical authority.

We do not know the precise year in which Rabbi applied the

finishing touches to his work. Late in life he undertook a complete revision of his Mishnah, probably in the year 220 A.C.E. In this, its final form, the Mishnah consists of six Orders:

1) *Zera'im,* agricultural laws, has eleven tractates, the first of which (Berakoth) deals with Prayer;

2) *Mo'ed,* laws concerning the festivals and fasts, has twelve tractates;

3) *Nashim,* seven tractates dealing with laws relating to woman and family life;

4) *Neziḳin,* the tractates on civil and criminal jurisprudence (including the Pirke Aboth);

5) *Ḳodoshim,* eleven tractates of laws in connection with the Sanctuary and food laws;

6) *Ṭoharoth,* twelve tractates on the laws of clean and unclean; —altogether sixty-three tractates. Each tractate (*massechta*) is again subdivided into *perakim* (chapters), of which the total number is five hundred and twenty-three.

Concerning the exact time at which the Mishnah was committed to writing, diversity of opinion has prevailed among eminent Jewish authorities during the last nine centuries. Sherira Gaon, Rashi, Luzzatto, Rapoport and Graetz hold that Rabbi arranged the Mishnah in his own mind without the help of pen or parchment; delivered it in his Academy, the same in form and contents as it stands to-day; and thus transmitted it by *word of mouth* to his disciples. These again delivered it to succeeding generations. It was thus orally preserved with verbal accuracy down to the time when the Academies sank in importance, and the teachers of the day found it necessary to fix the existing stock of traditions in writing, some time in the 8th or 9th century. Opposed to this opinion, we have other authorities no less eminent, who maintain that Rabbi himself wrote out the Mishnah in full. Among them are Yehudah Hallevi, Maimonides and Abarbanel; Weiss, Geiger and Fränkel.

The language of the Mishnah is Neo-Hebrew, a natural development from Biblical Hebrew; a living speech and not an artificial language (like Latin in the Middle Ages), as has been maintained by some. Its vocabulary and idiom bear the stamp of colloquial usage. Being a record of sayings and oral discussions of men of the people on the manifold activities of life, there is in it a large admixture of Aramaic, Greek and also Latin terms.

The oldest manuscript copies of the Mishnah, are in Parma (13th century), Cambridge (on which the Jerusalem Talmud is said to be based), and New York (vocalised fragments, 10th or 11th century). The first printed edition appeared in Naples (1492), with the commentary of Maimonides. The current editions of to-day are accompanied by commentaries of Obadiah di Bertinoro of the 15th century, and Yomtob Lipman Heller of the 17th century. The Mishnah has often been translated; the latest version being in English by Canon Danby. A critical edition of the Mishnah, however, is a task for the future.

II

The comprehensive commentary on the Mishnah that forms the second and far larger portion of the Talmud is called the Gemara. The Gemara, which word came to denote 'teaching', explains the terms and subject-matter of the Mishnah; seeks to elucidate difficulties and harmonise discrepant statements; to refer anonymous decisions to their proper authors in the Mishnah, or in the parallel compilations of Tannaitic teachings contemporary with the Mishnah in which the same subject is treated; and to determine to what extent they are in agreement. Finally, it reports in full the controversies that took place in the Palestinian or Babylonian Academies concerning these subjects.

But the Gemara is more than a mere commentary. In it are sedulously gathered, without any reference to their connection with the Mishnah, whatever utterances had for centuries dropped from the lips of the Masters; whatever Tradition preserved concerning them or their actions; whatever bears directly, or even distantly, upon the great subjects of religion, life, and conduct. In addition, therefore, to legal discussions and enactments on every aspect of Jewish duty, whether it be ceremonial, civic, or moral, it contains homiletical exegesis of Scripture; moral maxims, popular proverbs, prayers, parables, fables, tales; accounts of manners and customs, Jewish and non-Jewish; facts and fancies of science by the learned; Jewish and heathen folklore, and all the wisdom and unwisdom of the unlearned. This vast and complex material occurs throughout the Gemara, as the name of an author, a casual quotation from Scripture, or some other accident in thought or style started a new association in ideas.

The Talmud itself classifies its component elements either as *Halachah* or *Haggadah*. Emanuel Deutsch describes the one as emanating from the brain, the other from the heart; the one prose, the other poetry; the one carrying with it all those mental faculties that manifest themselves in arguing, investigating, comparing, developing; the other springing from the realms of fancy, of imagination, feeling, humour:

> *Beautiful old stories,*
> *Tales of angels, fairy legends,*
> *Stilly histories of martyrs,*
> *Festal songs and words of wisdom;*
> *Hyperboles, most quaint it may be,*
> *Yet replete with strength and fire*
> *And faith—how they gleam,*
> *And glow and glitter!*

as Heine has it.

Halachah, as we have seen, means 'the trodden path', rule of life, religious guidance. To it belong all laws and regulations that bear upon Jewish conduct. These include the ritual, the civil, criminal, and ethical laws. Everything else is embraced under the term *Haggadah;* literally, 'talk', 'that which is narrated', 'delivered in a discourse'. This again can be subdivided into various groups. We have dogmatical *Haggadah,* treating of God's attributes and providence, creation, revelation, Messianic times, and the Hereafter. The historical *Haggadah* brings traditions and legends concerning the heroes and events in national or universal history, from Adam to Alexander of Macedon, Titus and Hadrian. It is legend pure and simple. Its aim is not so much to give the facts concerning the righteous and unrighteous makers of history, as the moral that may be pointed from the tales that adorn their honour or dishonour. That some of the folklore element in the *Haggadah,* some of the customs depicted or *obiter dicta* reported, are repugnant to Western taste need not be denied. 'The greatest fault to be found with those who wrote down such passages,' says Schechter, 'is that they did not observe the wise rule of Dr Johnson who said to Boswell on a certain occasion, "Let us get serious, for there comes a fool". And the fools unfortunately did come, in the shape of certain Jewish commentators and Christian controversialists, who took as serious things which were only the expression of a momentary impulse, or represented the opinion of some isolated individual, or were meant simply as a piece of humorous by-play, calculated to enliven the interest of a languid audience.' In spite of the fact that the *Haggadah* contains parables of infinite beauty and enshrines sayings of eternal worth, it must be remembered that the *Haggadah* consists of mere individual utterances that possess no general and binding authority.

III

There are two Gemaras—one elaborated in the Academies of Babylon, the other in Palestine. Strictly speaking, the current name for the latter, 'the Jerusalem Talmud', is incorrect, as after the destruction of the Temple no Academy existed in Jerusalem. It was Tiberias that was the principal seat of rabbinic learning, till the closing of the Palestinian schools in the 4th century.

The principal Teachers (now called *Amoraim*, 'expounders') of the Palestinian Talmud are Rabbis Joḥanan and Abbahu.

Joḥanan (d. 279) was in his early youth a disciple of R. Judah the Prince. He made his Academy at Tiberias the principal seat of learning in the Holy Land, and for a long time he was erroneously held to be editor of the Palestinian Gemara. The following saying of this illustrious *Amora* is typical of the man: 'When the Egyptians were drowning in the Red Sea, the angels in Heaven were about to break forth in songs of jubilation. God silenced them with the words, My creatures are perishing, and ye are ready to sing!'

Abbahu of Caesarea was a man of wealth, general culture and influence with the Roman authorities. He was a skilful defender of his Faith against Christian attacks. 'Be of the persecuted not of the persecutors,' was his maxim. He put forward the bold notion of successive creations—the idea later taken up by the Jewish Mystics that prior to the existence of the present universe, certain formless worlds issued from the Fountain of existence and then vanished, like sparks from a red-hot iron beaten by a hammer.

The oppression in Palestine under the first Christian emperors led to the extinction of the Patriarchate and to the closing of the Schools in the year 425. The discussions in these Schools were never formally edited. It seems that the Palestinian Gemara originally extended over the whole of the Mishnah; but owing to the adverse circumstances of the time, much of it has been irretrievably lost.

Its *halachic* portions are marked by calm and temperate discussion, free from the dialectic subtleties which characterise the Babylonian Talmud. Its *Haggadah* is also purer, more rational, though less attractive and poetical, than the *Haggadah* in Babylonia. The Palestinian Talmud, written in a Syriac dialect little known by later generations, was for many centuries almost forgotten by Jewry. Its legal decisions were at no time deemed to possess validity, if opposed by the Babylonian Talmud. It was first printed in Venice in 1523. Fränkel's classical *Introduction to the Jerusalem Talmud* appeared in 1859. There is a French translation of the Palestinian Talmud by M. Schwab.

IV

When we come to the Babylonian Gemara, we are dealing with what most people understand when they speak or write of the Talmud. Its birthplace, Babylonia, was an autonomous Jewish centre for a longer period than any other land; namely, from soon after 586 before the Christian era to the year 1040 after the Christian era—1626 years; from the days of Cyrus down to the age of the Mongol conquerors!

For a long time it was held that the language in which the Babylonian Talmud was written defied grammatical formulation. This is now seen to be nothing but prejudice. Eminent grammarians have discovered its laws, and have determined its place in the scheme of Semitic languages. Its philological side was treated nearly a thousand years ago in the Talmudic Lexicon (*Aruch*) of Asher ben Jeḥiel, and has been completed by the labours of Levy, Kohut and Jastrow in the last century. The style of the Babylonian Talmud is mostly one of pregnant brevity and succinctness. It is at no time 'easy reading'. Elliptical expression is a constantly recurring feature, and whole sentences are often indicated by a single word. In the discussions, question and answer are closely interwoven, and there is an entire absence of demarcation between them. Hard thinking and closest attention are required under the personal guidance of an experienced scholar, or of an elaborate written exposition of the argument, for the discussion to be followed, or the context understood. And that understanding cannot be gained by the aid of Grammar or Lexicon alone. Even a student who has a fair knowledge of Hebrew and Aramaic, but has not been initiated into the Talmud by Traditional Jewish guides, will find it impossible to *decipher* a page! A great philologist who was also a Talmudist has rightly declared: 'Suppose the teaching of the Talmud suddenly interrupted during the life of a generation; the tradition once lost, it would be well-nigh impossible to recover it.'

Of the thousand and more *Amoraim* mentioned by name, we select Rab and Samuel, and R. Ashi and Rabina. Rab and Samuel, born in Babylonia, went to the Holy Land to sit at the feet of Judah the Prince, and brought back to their home country the Mishnah, the authorised Code of the Oral Law. In the year 219, Rab founded an Academy at Sura, and it continued to flourish for eight centuries. 'The commandments of the Torah were given to purify the life of man,' was one of his sayings. Life in Hereafter, he taught, was not mere passivity, for 'there is no rest for the righteous. They ever proceed from strength to strength in this world and in the world to come, where they rejoice in the radiance of the Divine Presence.' 'Since the Exile,' he declares, 'the Shechinah mourns, and God prays: Be it My will that in My dealings with My children My mercy overcome My justice.' Some of the sublimest portions of the New Year Liturgy are attributed to Rab.

Samuel of Nehardea, his companion—a physician and astronomer—was an epoch-maker in Judaism. He laid down the principle, based on an utterance of Jeremiah the Prophet, that has enabled Jews to live and serve in non-Jewish countries. *Dina d'malchutha dina,* he ruled; i.e., 'in all civil matters, the law of the land is to us Divine Law.'

Of the other two names, Ashi, who died in 427 and was for fifty-two years head of the Sura Academy, combined a vast memory with extraordinary mental orderliness, that enabled him to systematise the bewildering mass of Talmudic material and prepare it for codification. Such codification was finally effected by Rabina, who died in the year 499. He is the author of the concluding paragraph of the Amidah: 'Guard my tongue from evil and my lips from speaking guile; and to such as curse me let my soul be dumb, yea, let my soul be unto all as the dust.' Many tractates seem to have been edited by various *Amoraim* before the time of Ashi and Rabina. As in the case of the Mishnah, it is a moot point whether Ashi and Rabina *wrote* down the Babylonian Gemara, or only arranged it orally. The latter is the view of Rashi, and, in modern times, of Luzzatto; both of them place the writing of the Gemara two centuries later. Other scholars, however, deem it a matter of absolute impossibility that so vast a literature, and one, too, full of such intricate controversies, should for some two centuries have been *orally* arranged, fixed and transmitted with perfect accuracy.

The Babylonian Talmud is about four times as large as that of Palestine. It contains 5894 folio pages, usually printed in twelve large volumes, the pagination of which is kept uniform in all editions. Only thirty-six of the sixty-three Mishnaic tractates are commented on in the Babylonian Talmud. However, most of the subject matter of the omitted tractates is dealt with in the Gemara of other tractates.

A voluminous work like the Babylonian Gemara, passing through the hands of numberless copyists, could not have remained free from errors. Fifty years ago, Rabbinowicz collected variants to the current Text, and examined it in the light of manuscripts, especially of the Munich MS. which covers the whole Talmud and dates from the year 1334. Alas, that that is the *only* complete MS. of the Talmud in existence; due to the bigotry of the medieval popes, who often consigned whole cartloads of Talmud MSS. to the flames. After the invention of printing, stupid and over-zealous censors not only expunged the few passages that refer to the Founder of Christianity, but also many others which they in their ignorance looked upon as disguised attacks upon their religion. Only one edition of the Talmud has escaped defacement at the hands of the censors, having been printed in Holland.

V

We now proceed to the history of the Talmud. What the Pentateuch had been to the *Tannaim* of the Mishnah, the Mishnah to the *Amoraim*, the Talmud became to the ages following its close. The Sabureans ('Opinion-givers') in the sixth century, and the Geonim ('Excellencies') in the succeeding century, made some slight additions to it. Then the demand for simplification and explanation began to make itself felt. The principal decisions of the Talmud were classified in the order of the 613 commandments; and the *halachic* portions were separated from the *Haggadah*, and printed by themselves. Later, explanatory glosses were written to the Text of the various tractates. Greatest of all these attempts, and to this day absolutely indispensable for the understanding of the Talmud, is the commentary of R. Solomon Yitzchaki, known as Rashi, of Troyes, in France. Rashi was born in the year 1040, the same year when the Exilarchate was extinguished in Babylon. His commentary is a masterpiece of brevity, precision and clearness. 'He has two of the greatest and rarest gifts of a commentator; the instinct to discern precisely the point at which explanation is necessary, and the art of giving or indicating the needed help in the fewest words' (G. F. Moore).

The French rabbis of the 12th and 13th century continued the clarification of the Talmud by their glosses, known as Tosafoth. These Tosafoth, together with Rashi's commentary, are printed in all regular editions of the Talmud. In the meantime, the genius of Maimonides illumined the Mishnah by his Arabic commentary; and by his gigantic undertaking called *Mishneh Torah*, or *Yad Hachazakah*, written in clear neo-Hebrew, he succeeded in introducing logical order and classification into the Talmudic labyrinth. In 1567, R. Joseph Caro produced the *Shulchan Aruch*, in which all the religious and civil laws of Jewish life still in force at the present-day are classified according to subjects. This work, annotated by R. Moses Isserles of Cracow in 1571, is the last authoritative codification of the *Halachah*, and has in turn called forth many commentaries and super-commentaries.

During all these centuries, the non-Jewish attitude to the Talmud remained one of implacable hostility. 'Ever since the Talmud came into existence—almost before it existed in a palpable shape—it has been treated much like a human being,' says Emanuel Deutsch. 'It has been proscribed, and imprisoned, and burnt, a hundred times over. Kings and emperors, popes and anti-popes, vied with each other in hurling anathemas and bulls and edicts of wholesale confiscation and conflagration against this luckless book. We remember but one sensible exception in this Babel of manifestos. Clement V in 1307, before condemning the book, wished to know something of it and there was no one to tell him. Whereupon he proposed that chairs be founded for Hebrew, Chaldee, and Arabic as the three tongues nearest to the idiom of the Talmud in the Universities of Paris, Salamanca, Bologna, and Oxford. In time, he hoped, one of these Universities might be able to produce a translation of this mysterious book. Need we say that this consummation never came to pass? The more expeditious process of destruction was resorted to again and again and again, not merely in the single cities of Italy, and France, but throughout the entire Holy Roman Empire.'

John Reuchlin, the great Humanist, was the first to maintain that, even if the Talmud contained attacks on Christianity, it would be best to answer them. 'Burning,' he said, 'is but a ruffianly argument.' Defence of Jewish books and saving them from destruction by hysterical bigots became the battle-cry of all those who stood for religious freedom. And it is not accidental that in the same year in which the first printed edition of the whole Babylonian Talmud appeared, in 1520, Luther burned the Papal bull at Wittenberg. Then followed two centuries of feverish activity among Christian divines to become masters in Talmudic lore—not always for the pure love of learning. It was only in our time that non-Jewish scholars like George Foot Moore in America, Travers Herford in England, and Wuensche and Strack in pre-Nazi Germany, have fallen under the spell of Rabbinic studies for their own sake, and recognised their indispensableness for the elucidation of fundamental problems in the world of Religion. A translation of the entire Babylonian Talmud in German, together with the original in the Text of the Venice 1520 edition, was undertaken by L. Goldschmidt in 1897 and is now almost completed.

A unique theory of the religious life is fully elaborated in the Talmudic scheme. Religion in the Talmud attempts to penetrate the whole of human life with the sense of law and right. Nothing human is in its eyes mean or trivial; everything is regulated and sanctified by religion. Religious precept and duty accompany man from his earliest years to the grave and beyond it. They guide his desires and actions at every moment. Food and sleep, civic duty and family life—all are under discipline of the Torah, a discipline accepted freely and joyfully. While every religion attempts such regulation, the Talmudic system represents this striving of the religious idea in its perfection. 'In our eyes,' says Arsène Darmsteter, 'this is its greatest title to the respect and consideration of thinkers. In Judaism we have thus the completest, and consequently the most perfect, expression of the religious idea.' The late I. Zangwill describes the Judaism of the Rabbis as 'a code which left the intellect and the emotions free to speculate and wonder, to produce philosophy and poetry, but which fettered the will, leaving the spirit free to transcend the law in love and self-sacrifice, but not to fall below it; so that even those Philistines who for religion—the music of life—had no ear, should at least be kept sane and strong and mechanically moral, centres of happiness to themselves and channels for a finer posterity. They should be kept from playing wrong notes and jarring chords, if they could not give us sonatas and symphonies of their own.'

Enough has been said to show that the Talmud is not an ordinary literary work. It bears no resemblance to any single literary production, but forms a world of its own that must be judged according to its own laws. The ancient Hebrew metaphor which speaks of the 'ocean of the Talmud', is helpful to the understanding of its nature. The Talmud is indeed an ocean, vast in extent, unfathomable in depth, with an ocean-like sense of immensity and movement about it. Its great broad surface is at times smooth and calm, at others disturbed by waves of argument and breakers of discussion, stormy with assertion and refutation. And like the ocean, it swarms with a thousand varied forms of life. It is as difficult to say what is not in it as what is. He who would navigate securely this sea of the Talmud must be familiar with the compass and the rudder, i.e., its language and modes of thought; and have the guidance of an experienced master, if he is to gather the precious stores of knowledge and inspiration enshrined in its indestructible pages.

This is not the place to speak of the influence of the Talmud; how throughout the centuries of persecution and darkness, it saved Israel from intellectual and moral degradation. My purpose is merely to give a brief presentation of the Talmud as a book. I shall therefore conclude with the words of I. Abrahams. 'The Talmud,' he says, 'is one of the great books of the world. Rabbinism was a sequel to the Bible; and if, like all sequels, it was unequal to its original, it nevertheless shares its greatness. The works of all Jews up to the modern period were the sequel to this sequel. Through them all may be detected the unifying principle that literature in its truest sense includes life itself; that intellect is the handmaid to conscience; and that the best books are those which best teach men how to live. The maxim, *Righteousness delivers from death,* applies to books as well as to men. A literature whose consistent theme is Righteousness, is immortal.'

* * *

A reliable English translation of the whole Babylonian Talmud has long been looked forward to by scholars. This expectation is beginning to be realised by the publication of the Soncino edition of the Order Neziḳin.

The translation is based on the Text of the Wilna Talmud, corrected where necessary in the light of variants from MSS. and other printed editions. All the censored passages reappear in the Text or in the Notes. The Notes bring the essence of the classical interpretations, clarify the argument, explain technical expressions, and show in what sense the Biblical verses quoted are to be understood. Wherever possible, place-names are identified, historical and archaeological allusions elucidated, and their parallels in the life of contemporary nations traced.

This notable achievement is due to the quite extraordinary erudition of the Editor, Rabbi Dr I. Epstein, assisted by his staff of scholarly translators. The Editor's Prefatory Note gives some indication of his colossal task. Aside from planning the scope and character of the work, the Editor fixed the Text, controlled the translation and interpretation, as well as the introductions and glossaries to the various parts, and supplied the greater portion of the 'cultural' notes.

The Publishers too have done their share in the undertaking conscientiously and efficiently. With the result, that never before has there appeared a translation of the Order Neziḳin as helpful to the student as these volumes of the Soncino edition of the Babylonian Talmud in English.

J. H. HERTZ

London, Chanukah 5695
2 December 1934

INTRODUCTION TO THE SONCINO HEBREW-ENGLISH EDITION OF THE BABYLONIAN TALMUD

BY

THE EDITOR

The very best translation, it has been said, is only a book about a book. It cannot tell us quite what the author said. In order to discover this, we have to go back to the original itself. That is why it is always well worth studying the original alongside any translation in which its thoughts and teachings are reproduced and presented. Such is the consideration that prompted The Soncino Press to undertake the publication of a series of volumes of Talmudic tractates in which the Soncino translation will appear facing each corresponding page of the unabridged Hebrew and Aramaic original text; and the present volume containing the Tractate Berakoth is the first in the series.

The Publishers have been encouraged in this, their new and ambitious venture by the conspicuous position which the Soncino Talmud has established for itself among Talmudic students throughout the English-speaking world. Contrary to the opinion expressed over and over again that the Talmud, which for centuries had formed an integral part of the Jewish educational system, was destined to become extinct or at best a subject of remote and specialist study even among observant Jews, we are witnessing today a remarkable revival of interest in the Talmud, alike in Israel and the Diaspora, even in quarters where hitherto it had been entirely neglected. More and more do Jewish schools and colleges include Talmud as a subject of instruction, and the number of adult groups meeting regularly for the study of the Talmud is steadily increasing everywhere. In present-day Israel tens of thousands of sets of Talmuds are being sold annually. Noteworthy in this connection is the *Daf Yomi* (Daily Talmudic Folio), instituted in 1929 at the instance of the late Rabbi Meir Shapiro (1887-1933), of Lublin, and adopted by a large number of lay Orthodox Jews in many parts of the globe as their daily lectionary. Significant too is the growing tendency in Jewish elementary schools everywhere to feed the mind of the child with stories from the Talmud, and to make increasing use of its *aggadah* to instil in him a high ethic and loyalty to Jewish traditions and ideals.

The causes of this revival are many and varied. Among them must be included the recognition at last of the Talmud as a unique preservative force of Judaism, and of its importance as constituting the 'Humanities' of Hebraism, which no Jew with a claim to Jewish culture can afford to ignore. Another powerful contributory factor is the restoration of the Jewish polity, which has given to the Talmud a new significance. Many of the Talmudic laws which had fallen into disuse by reason of the fall of the Jewish State about 2,000 years ago, particularly those relating to the *jus* and agriculture, are once more coming into their own; and it is to the Talmud that the builders of the new social order in Israel are turning more and more for light and guidance in their manifold and stupendous tasks. Nor can we underrate the distinct contribution to this revival made by the Soncino translation in having made the Talmud accessible to many an English reader to whom it would otherwise have remained a closed book; and this Hebrew-English edition, which is designed to facilitate easier reference to the original text, by scholar and student alike, should help to bring to even wider circles the knowledge of that unique repository of inspired law and exalted faith which is the Talmud.

This brief Introduction cannot close without a tribute to the translator of the Tractate Berakoth, the late Maurice Simon, who departed from our midst at the age of 81 in 1955. Mr Simon had been the closest of my collaborators in the preparation of the Soncino Talmud. This enabled me to appreciate his outstanding intellectual as well as his more personal qualities. A stylist of the first order, he was able by means of a happy turn of phrase to make clear the meaning of the most difficult Rabbinic text to all those who cared to know and to learn. Humble and modest, without the slightest trace of vanity and envy, he was endowed with that rarest of virtues praised by the Rabbis: 'a good eye'. It was this 'good eye' which lay behind much of the 'silent service' he rendered in many directions without any desire for self-advertisement or reward, particularly in connection with the Soncino Talmud. An eternal student, 'whose soul was wedded to the Torah,' he left an enduring monument and 'an everlasting name that shall not be cut off' (Isaiah LVI, 5).

Apart from the Editor's Introduction to Seder Zera'im, the present volume includes the Foreword by the late Chief Rabbi, Dr J. H. Hertz, which appeared originally in the Baba Kamma volume of the Soncino Talmud.

The Publishers have maintained the consistently high standard of type, paper, binding and format associated with the Soncino Press, and by this publication have placed the English-speaking Jewries throughout the world still more in their debt.

I. EPSTEIN

Sivan, 5720.
May, 1960.

INTRODUCTION TO *SEDER ZERA'IM*

BY

a THE EDITOR[1]

GENERAL CHARACTER AND CONTENTS

Zera'im ('Seeds'), the name given to the first of the six 'Orders' into which the Talmud is divided, deals principally with the agricultural laws of the Torah in both their religious and social aspects. It sets forth and elaborates the Biblical precepts relating to the rights of the poor and of the priests and levites to the produce of the harvest, as well as the rules and regulations which concern the tillage, cultivation and sowing of fields, gardens and orchards. These laws are digested in ten tractates, each of which deals with a separate aspect of the general subject which gives the 'Order' its name. To them is prefixed the Tractate Berakoth, which has for its theme the daily prayers and worship of the Jew.

The 'Order' thus comprises 11 tractates, arranged in the separate printed editions of the Mishnah in the following sequence:

(1) BERAKOTH ('Benedictions'): Deals with the prayer and worship of Israel; the regulations relating to the main components of the daily prayers; and the forms of thanksgiving or 'grace' to be recited over food and on sundry occasions. 9 Chapters.

(2) PE'AH ('Corner'): Treats of the laws of the corners of the field which must be left to the poor and other dues assigned to them in accordance with Lev. XIX, 9f; XXIII, 22; and Deut. XXIV, 19-21. 8 Chapters.

(3) DEMAI ('Doubtful'): Treats of produce concerning which there is a doubt whether or not the tithes have been set aside from it. 7 Chapters.

(4) KIL'AYIM ('Mixtures'): Deals with the prohibition of mixture in plants, animals and garments set forth in Lev. XIX, 19, and Deut. XXII, 9-11. 9 Chapters.

(5) SHEBI'ITH ('Seventh'): Discusses the regulations concerning the rest to be given to the land and the release of debts in the sabbatical year *(Shemiṭṭah)*. See Ex. XXIII, 11; Lev. XXV, 2-7; and Deut. XV, 1-11. 10 Chapters.

(6) TERUMOTH ('Heave Offerings'): Sets forth the laws regarding the portion of the harvest assigned to the priest in accordance with Num. XVIII 12. 11 Chapters.

(7) MA'ASEROTH ('Tithes'): Has for its theme the 'first tithe' which must be given annually to the levite from the produce of the harvest according to Lev. XXVII, 30-33; and Num. XVIII, 21-24. 5 Chapters.

(8) MA'ASER SHENI ('Second Tithe'): Details the rules of the 'second tithe' set aside in the first, second, fourth and sixth years of the septennate in accordance with Deut. XIV, 22ff. 5 Chapters.

(9) ḤALLAH ('Dough'): Deals with the rules concerning the portion of the dough which must be given to the priest. See Num. XV, 20-21. 4 Chapters.

(10) 'ORLAH ('Uncircumcision', *sc.* of trees): Deals with the prohibition of the use of the fruit of the young trees during the first three years, and the rules for its treatment in the fourth year. See Lev. XIX, 23-24. 3 Chapters.

(11) BIKKURIM ('First Fruits'): Gives the regulations concerning the offering of the first fruits in the Temple (see Deut. XXVI, 1ff.), and includes an account of the accompanying ceremony. 3 Chapters.

This sequence is followed practically in all the printed and manuscript editions of the Mishnah and Talmud. The only notable exception is the Munich MS. which places Berakoth between Mo'ed b and Nashim.[1] This, however, seems to have been due more to technical reasons than to a deliberate departure from the recognised sequence. Several attempts have been made to explain the sequence c of the tractates in the Seder,[1] but none is very convincing. There is no doubt that there were several determining factors, of which the order in which the laws appear in the Pentateuch was one, and the number of chapters in the tractate was another; whilst another probable factor was the frequency with which the matters treated in the respective tractates occurred.[2]

FUNDAMENTAL CONCEPT OF SEDER ZERA'IM

Seder Zera'im is designated in one place in the Talmud by the term *Emunah*.[3] This designation provides the answer to the question how regulations regarding worship and prayer came to be grouped with agricultural laws[4], and at the same time the reason for the priority given to Berakoth in this 'Order'.

The Hebrew word *Emunah* has a two-fold connotation—theological and human. It signifies alike faith—trust—in God, and faithfulness—honesty, integrity—in human relations. These two concepts of *Emunah* do not conflict with each other; on the contrary, they complement and supplement each other. In Judaism, unlike other religions, faith is not some mystic quality charged with supernatural powers capable of winning divine favour and grace. Faith is a dynamic, a motive for faithfulness, and is of value only in so far as it is productive of faithful action; nor is there any faithful action that is not rooted in faith in God. The man of faithfulness is an *Ish Emunah*, and the man of faith is a *Ba'al Emunah*. For it is the man of the highest faith in God who is the man of the greatest faithfulness in his dealings with his fellow man; and it is only the man of faithfulness who can truly be considered a man of faith.

The application to the agricultural laws of the signification of *Emunah* as *faith* is aptly explained by the Midrash in its exposition of Psalm XIX, 8. '"*The testimony of the Lord is faithful* (trustworthy)"—this refers to Seder Zera'im, for man has faith (trust) in the Life d of the World and sows.'[1] Man, that is to say, has faith in the divine governance of the world and in the regularity of the natural world order which God has established in His Universe, and sows with the assurance of reaping.

On the other hand, the term *Emunah* as applied to the 'Order' has also been interpreted in the sense of *faithfulness*. Thus Rashi[2] says that the 'Order' is called *Emunah* because the fulfilment of its precepts is a mark of man's faithfulness in his social relations. Man observes these laws, and pays the poor and the priests and levites their respective dues, because he is a man of faithfulness.

Here, too, faith and faithfulness combine to form an indissoluble unity. The man of faith will carry out these observances with faith-

a (1) A general Introduction to the Talmud by the late Chief Rabbi Dr J. H. Hertz, appears in the Baba Ḳamma volume of Seder Neziḳin.

b (1) See H. L. Strack, *Introduction to the Talmud and Midrash* (English ed.) pp. 253 and 366. Another minor divergence is found in Kauffmann's Mishnah Codex in which Ma'aseroth and Ma'aser Sheni change places; see *op. cit.* p. 366.

c (1) See Maimonides, *Introduction to Seder Zera'im;* Solomon Sirillos's Introduction to his *Commentary on Seder Zera'im of the Jerusalem Talmud;* and Z. Frankel, *Darke ha-Mishnah*, p. 257. (2) See H. L. Strack, *op. cit.* pp. 26-8. (3) Shab. 31*a*. (4) Cf. Strack, *op. cit.*, p. 27: 'Berakoth is alien to Zera'im'.

d (1) *Midrash Tehillim.* a.l. (2) On Shab. 31*a*, a.l.

fulness; whilst the faithfulness with which he performs his duties is a test of his faith.

The reason for this close connection of faith and faithfulness in the carrying out of these observances is not far to seek. Faith in the 'Life of the World', if held with conviction, implies the recognition of God as the owner of the earth. In virtue of this principle the earth as well as all the gifts of Nature can never become altogether private property. It is handed out in trust to man who by the sweat of his brow extracts its produce. He has the right and the duty to apply his labour to the land; but this does not constitute it *his*. He must always recognise that *'To the Lord belongs the earth, and the fulness thereof'* (Psalm XXIV, 1). Whatever rights man has in the earth and its produce are derived from God, and are subject to the overruling consideration that He alone has the ultimate ownership of the land. It follows from this as a corollary that all God's children are entitled to a share in the land, as their common heritage. The landowner, therefore, while enjoying the reward of his toil and stewardship must recognise that others too have a right to live and that he has a duty to enable them to live. It was these common human rights, flowing from the idea of divine ownership of the earth, which the Torah sought to safeguard by the provisions it made under various laws for the benefit of the poor. When a field is harvested
a the corners *(Pe'ah)* are to be left uncut; a sheaf[1] forgotten in the field by the owner (*Shikḥah*) is not to be reclaimed; the gleanings of cornfields *(Leḳeṭ)* and vineyards *(Pereṭ)*[2] which fall to the ground in harvesting are not to be picked up; nor are the defective clusters of grapes *('Oleloth)*[3] to be gathered. A special tithe (*Ma'aser 'Oni*) has in addition to be set aside every three years and laid up in towns and villages for distribution. All these parts of the harvest belong to the poor as their prescriptive rights in the common heritage assigned to them by the divine owner.[4]

It is in the same spirit that the laws of the Sabbatical year *(Shemiṭṭah)* were ordained. Designed to confirm the landless poor in their right to live, *'the Sabbath of solemn rest for the land, a Sabbath unto the Lord'* (Lev. XXV, 4) helped at the same time to teach that the produce of the earth must not be regarded as the exclusive private property of a selected class, but is part of a common divine heritage in which the poor, the alien, the slave, and even animals have a share.

The idea of the divine ownership of the land was likewise suggested by the biblical prohibition regarding the mixture of seeds *(Kil'ayim)*. While this and similar laws are designated as *'Statutes'* (Lev. XIX, 19), for which no reason has been revealed, there is no question that underlying them is the idea that the earth belongs to God, and that man has no right to interfere with the appointed order of things or violate the *'Statutes'* God has established in His physical universe for ever and ever.[5]

The recognition of the divine ownership of the earth is likewise enforced by the command regarding the first fruits *(Bikkurim)*. 'The object of this precept,' writes Aaron Halevi, 'is to instil in man the belief that all he has, he holds from the Lord of the Universe.'[6] This too, according to Naḥmanides, is the significance of the prohibition of the fruit of young trees in the first three years (*'Orlah*), and the laws regarding them in the fourth year. This precept, in his view, is closely connected with that of the first fruits. The fruit in the first three years is stunted in growth and hence unfit for the offering to
b God which alone releases it for human use.[1]

The same motive equally underlies the gifts to be made to the priest — the heave-offering *(Terumah)*, and the portion of the dough (*Ḥallah*), and to the levite — the tithe *(Ma'aser)*. In the words of Rabbi Aaron Halevi, 'Since corn and wine and oil constitute the main staple food of human beings and the whole world belongs to God, it is fitting that man should be mindful of his Creator, in enjoying the blessings wherewith He blessed him, and set aside, in His name, a portion thereof, giving it to His ministers who occupy themselves all the time with "heavenly work", before he himself derives benefit from the produce.'[2]

Faith in the divine ownership of the earth is thus implicit in the agricultural laws of the 'Order' and is the all-inspiring motive for the fulfilment of them in faithfulness; and it is this faith which constitutes the very heart of Jewish prayer and worship, to which Berakoth is devoted. For what is the *Shema'*, which forms the opening theme of the Tractate, but the grand affirmation of Israel's faith in God's ownership of the world — His mastery over life and Nature — with His consequent claim upon human service, devotion and love? Similarly the *'Amidah*, the Jewish daily Prayer *par excellence*, covering the whole range of human needs — physical, mental, and spiritual — is grounded on faith in God's ownership of the Universe, wherein He has power to do as He wills, and to meet the needs of man in prayer. And likewise those benedictions prescribed for various occasions, such as for partaking of food or for enjoying other gifts of Nature, are uttered in grateful acknowledgment to their divine Owner. This is how the Rabbis of the Talmud understood the significance of these ancient benedictions instituted by the spiritual Fathers of Israel. There is nothing sacramental about them; they are but expressions of thanks to God for personal enjoyments and benefits. Noteworthy in this connection is the Talmudic dictum, 'He who enjoys aught in this world without benedition is as though
c he robbed God.'[1] The world is God's and whatever is therein is His; and it is only after making acknowledgment to the divine Owner that man has the right to put to personal use what he has received at His hands.

With faith in divine ownership as the common basic concept, the relevancy of Berakoth in Zera'im becomes evident; nor could there be any fitter introduction to the 'Order' than that tractate from which there breathes the spirit of faith.

It is also to this basic concept that Zera'im owes its pride of place as the opening Seder of the Talmud. Faith is after all the very pivot of the Jewish religion, and it was only natural for the 'Order' which has Faith as its underlying principle to form the prelude, with the *Shema'* leading, to that authoritative guide of Jewish life and action which is the Talmud.[2]

THE AGRICULTURAL LAWS AND OUR TIMES

Berakoth is the only tractate in this 'Order' which has Gemara in both the Babylonian and Palestinian versions. The other tractates have Palestinian Gemara only, as the laws with which they deal are with a few exceptions restricted to the Holy Land. This is in conformity with the well-known principle that all the religious commandments that depend on the soil apply only in the Holy Land.[3] The reason for this reservation is apparently because the conception of divine ownership basic to these commandments has no relevance

a (1) Or at most two sheaves; see Pe'ah, VI, 5. *Shikḥah* applies also to fruit trees, see Ḥul. 131*b*. (2) *Pereṭ* applies only to grapes, and corresponds to *Leḳeṭ* in grain, see Ḥul. 131*b* and Maimonides, *Yad, Mattenoth Aniyim*, I. 7. (3) Lit., 'child clusters', applies only to grapes. (4) See Menaḥem b. Moses ha-Babli, *Ta'ame ha-Mizwoth*, 97 and Isaiah Hurwitz, *Shene Luḥoth ha-Berith, Torah she-bi-kethab, Ḳedoshim*. (5) Moses Naḥmanides, *Commentary on Pentateuch*, Lev. XIX, 19; See also Josephus, *Antiquities*, IV, 8, 20. (6) *Sefer ha-Ḥinnuk*, Precept 106.

b (1) Moses Naḥmanides, *op. cit.*, Lev. XIX, 23. See also Josephus, *op. cit.* IV, 8. 19. (2) *Sefer ha-Ḥinnuk*, Precept 507.

c (1) Ber. 35*b*. (2) Cf. Marginal Gloss. in Maimonides' *Introduction to Zera'im* in the name of Isaiah di Trani (The Elder): '"The beginning of wisdom is the fear of the Lord," and for this reason our holy teachers begun the Order of the Mishnah with the Unity of God and the acceptance of the yoke of His kingdom and of the Torah and precepts, evening and morning.' (3) See Ḳid. 36*b*.

to conditions in which the Jewish tenancy of the land is not derived directly from its divine Owner. An exception is the law of the 'mixed
a species', which in some of its aspects is valid also outside Palestine,[1] as the underlying idea of not interfering with the natural order appointed by God in His Cosmos is of universal application.

Since the fall of the Hebrew State, many of the precepts, particularly those connected with the Temple, such as the priestly portion and the tithe, have lost their biblical force, though rabbinically they are still binding to a certain degree[2] and are observed by religious settlements in the New Yishuv.[3] The transformation of the national economy consequent upon the loss of Israel's political independence has likewise affected the harvesting laws, reducing their observance to a mere token.[4] As to the *Shemittah*, the question of its present-day validity has been the subject of much controversy among post-Talmudic authorities, giving rise to a variety of opinions. Some there are who hold that the *Shemittah* still retains its full biblical force;[5] others would deprive it of all validity;[6] whilst others again insist on its observance, though only as part of Rabbinic legislation.[7] The point at issue is the dependence of the *Shemittah* on the Jubilee. It is the accepted Rabbinic view that the Jubilee is bound up with the territorial integrity of the Jewish State on both sides of the Jordan; and that accordingly its observance came to an end with the cessation of the Hebrew polity.[8] This being the case, the dependence of the *Shemittah* on the Jubilee, would mean that its laws are no longer applicable nowadays. Its non-dependence, on the other hand, would mean that the *Shemittah* may well remain in force, even though the Jubilee had become obsolete. Here is no place to enter into a discussion of the complicated *Halachic* problems involved; but from the point of view of human relations, to make the *Shemittah* dependent on the Jubilee, would impart to it a political connotation not applicable to our own days; while its non-dependence would bring it into the category of those socio-moral Laws of the Torah which have not lost their significance even for our times.

In practice the Jewish Communities that maintained themselves in the Holy Land throughout the centuries following the destruc-
b tion of the Temple continued to adhere to the *Shemittah* laws.[1] But since the rise of the New Judea with agriculture as the basis of its economy, the observance of the *Shemittah* has become a burning question, urgently demanding a solution. In the early stages of the *Chovevei Zion* Movement, the fear that the observance of the *Shemittah* might jeopardise the existence of the struggling colonists impelled Rabbinic authorities to devise measures for overcoming the hardships involved in its operation. With the approach of the *Shemittah* year 5649 (1888-1889), Rabbi Isaac Elhanan Spektor of Kovno (1817-1896), the foremost rabbinical authority of his age, relying on the view that the *Shemittah* nowadays is only of Rabbinic origin, sanctioned the nominal sale of the land to a non-Jew and the employment of non-Jewish labourers during the *Shemittah*.[2] This device met with strong opposition on the part of a number of rabbis, such as Joshua Loeb Diskin (1818-1898) and Samuel Salant (1816-1911), both of Jerusalem.[3] A staunch defender of the measure advocated by Rabbi Spektor was Rabbi A. I. Kook (1865-1935), who wrote a brilliant work on the subject under the title שבת הארץ.[4] He, too, was not without his opponents, of whom the most prominent was Rabbi Jacob David Willowsky of Slutsk, commonly known as the Ridbaz (1845-1913). At present most of the religious settlements in Palestine avail themselves of Rabbi Spektor's concessions, though a few adopt the more rigorous attitude and, at a great sacrifice, observe the *Shemittah* in all its details.[5]

The gradual restoration of the Hebrew polity, which is taking shape before our eyes, after a submergence of almost 2.000 years, gives to the study of this 'Order' more than an mere academic or antiquarian interest. It is yet too early to foretell the form in which these agricultural laws of the Torah will find their embodiment in the economic, political and social structure of the Jewish State that is slowly coming into being. But the occupation of mind and heart with these laws must surely help to foster those social ideals which should be the distinguishing mark of the new civilisation the Jewish people are resolved to plant on the hills of Judea, and by which alone
c it can be preserved.[1]

And not for the Jewish people alone. The humanitarian implications, for all times, of these early biblical measures are obvious. The same motives as inspired the social legislation of the Torah will to-day prompt any ethical being to apply the sense of duty to his daily tasks. He will recognise that whatever he has he holds from God, and that his claim to possession of property is justified only by the opportunity it provides for service to his fellow-man. With this principle as his mainspring of action, he will strive to turn his vocation and his talents, as well as other gifts that fall to him by good fortune, into a contribution to the common weal. This is a lesson the importance of which for our times cannot be overestimated; for it is only insofar as humanity will assimilate these ideals to all the complexity of its material problems that it can hope to witness the realisation of its millenial dreams of universal peace and happiness.

METHOD AND SCOPE

TEXT. The Text for this edition is in the main that of the Wilna Romm Edition. Note has, however, been taken of the most important variants of manuscript and printed editions some of which have been adopted in the main body of the translation, the reason for such preference being generally explained or indicated in the Notes. All the censored passages appear either in the text or in the Notes.

TRANSLATION. The translation aims at reproducing in clear and lucid English the central meaning of the original text. It is true some translators will be found to have been less literal than others, but in checking and controlling *every line* of the work, the Editor has endeavoured not to lose sight of the main aim of the translation. Words and passages not occurring in the original are placed in square brackets.

NOTES. The main purpose of these is to elucidate the translation by making clear the course of the arguments, explaining allusions and technical expressions, thus providing a running commentary on the text. With this in view resort has been made to the standard Hebrew commentators, Rashi, the Tosafists,

a (1) See Kid. 39*b*. (2) See Maimonides, *Terumoth*, I, 26. (3) See A. I. Kook, *Mishpat Kohen*, Responsa 29-57. For the procedure to be followed in setting aside the priestly portion and tithes, see Responsum 35. (4) See Israel of Shklow, *Pe'ath ha-Shulhan* (ed. Luncz), p. 22*a*. (5) Maimonides, *Shemittah we-Yobeloth*, IV, 25, according to *Kesef Mishneh*. (6) Zerahia ha-Levi, *Sefer ha-Terumoth*, Sha'ar 85. (7) Tosaf. 'Ar. 32*b* s.v. '*Manu*', and Eliezer of Metz, *Sefer Yere'im*, 187. (8) See 'Ar. 32*b*; *Sifra*, *Behar*, II, 3.

b (1) See Israel of Shklow, *op. cit.*, pp. 103*a*, 104*b*-107*b*. (2) See A. Benzion Shurin, *Rabbi Isaac Elchanan's Attitude towards the New Settlement in Palestine*, *Talpioth* (N.Y.) III, pp. 58ff. (3) See *J.E.* p. 607. (4) First edition, Jerusalem 1910; 2nd ed. revised and enlarged, Jerusalem, 1937. See also A. I. Kook, *Mishpat Kohen*, Responsa 58-88, and I. M. Blumenfeld, *Ma'asé Rab*, *Sinai*, 1937, pp. 316. For texts of deeds of sale, see *Mishpat Kohen*, pp. 162-166. (5) See correspondence of Rabbi A. I. Kook, with the I.C.A., pleading on behalf of their Jewish employees who refused to work on *Shemittah*, in *Sinai*, 1937, pp. 104f. As to *Shemittah Kesafim* (release of money debts), opinions vary whether it applies at all to-day, even rabbinically. It is, nevertheless, being widely observed in Palestine, and to some extent also outside, and resort is accordingly made to the *Prozbul* enactment of Hillel which is designed to overcome the effects of this *Shemittah* law. See Shebi'ith X, 4.

c (1) A special institute under the name of '*Midrash Bene Zion*' has been established in Jerusalem in which the study of agricultural laws of the Torah is being assiduously pursued. A brief digest of these laws is given in the Calendar of the Institute for the year 5708 (1947-8).

Asheri, Alfasi, Maimonides, Maharsha, the glosses of BaḤ, Rashal, Strashun, the Wilna Gaon, etc.[1] Advantage has also been taken of the results of modern scholarship, such as represented by the names of Graetz, Bacher, Weiss, Halevy, Levy, Kohut, Jastrow, Obermeyer, Klein and Büchler,—happily still with us—Krauss, Ginzberg, and Herford among others, in dealing with matters of general cultural interest with which the Talmud teems—historical, geographical, archaeological, philological and social.

GLOSSARY AND INDICES. Each tractate is equipped with a Glossary wherein recurring technical terms are fully explained, thus obviating the necessity of explaining them afresh each time they appear in the text. To this have been added a Scriptural Index and a General Index of contents.

In the presentation of the tractates the following principles have also been adopted:

(i) The Mishnah and the words of the Mishnah recurring and commented upon in the Gemara are printed in capitals.

(ii) תנן introducing a Mishnah cited in the Gemara, is rendered 'we have learnt'.

(iii) תניא introducing a Baraitha, is rendered 'it has been (or was) taught'.

(iv) תנו רבנן introducing a Tannaitic teaching, is rendered 'Our Rabbis taught'.

(v) Where an Amora cites a Tannaitic teaching the word 'learnt' is used, e.g., תני רב יוסף, 'R. Joseph learnt'.

(vi) The word tanna designating a teacher of the Amoraic period (v. Glos.) is written with a small 't'.

(vii) A distinction is made between ... הלכה כ referring to a Tannaitic ruling and ... הלכתא כ which refers to the ruling of an Amora, the former being rendered 'the *halachah* is ...' and the latter, 'the law is ...'

(viii) R. stands either for Rabbi designating a Palestinian teacher or Rab designating a Babylonian teacher, except in the case of the frequently recurring Rab Judah where the title 'Rab' has been written in full to distinguish him from the Tanna of the same name.

(ix) רחמנא, lit., 'The Merciful One', has been rendered 'the Divine Law' in cases where the literal rendering may appear somewhat incongruous to the English ear.

(x) Biblical verses appear in italics except for the emphasized word or words in the quotation which appear in Roman characters.

(1) These names are referred to more fully in the list of Abbreviations at the end of each tractate.

(xi) No particular English version of the Bible is followed, as the Talmud has its own method of exegesis and its own way of understanding Biblical verses which it cites. Where, however, there is a radical departure from the English versions, the rendering of a recognized English version is indicated in the Notes. References to chapter and verse are those of the Massoretic Hebrew text.

(xii) Any answer to a question is preceded by a dash (—), except where the question and the answer form part of one and the same argument.

(xiii) Inverted commas are used sparingly, that is, where they are deemed essential or in dialogues.

(xiv) The archaic second person 'thou', 'thee' etc. is employed only in *Haggadic* passages or where it is necessary to distinguish it from the plural 'you', 'yours', etc.

(xv) The usual English spelling is retained in proper names in vogue like Simeon, Isaac, Akiba, as well as in words like *halachah, Shechinah, shechitah*, etc. which have almost passed into the English language. The transliteration employed for other Hebrew words is given at the end of each tractate.

(xvi) It might also be pointed out for the benefit of the student that the recurring phrases 'Come and hear:' and 'An objection was raised:' or 'He objected:' introduce Tannaitic teachings, the two latter in contradiction, the former either in support or contradiction of a particular view expressed by an Amora.

ACKNOWLEDGMENTS

I desire once again to express my grateful thanks to all the translators and collaborators of Seder Zera'im, and to pay a tribute to Mr. Jacob Davidson, the Governing Director of the Soncino Press for the care with which he has seen through the Press the volumes of this 'Order'.

In conclusion, on behalf of all those of us who have been closely associated with this publication, I offer the traditional prayer.

יהי רצון מלפניך ד׳ אלהינו כשם שעזרתנו לסיים סדר זרעים כן תעזרנו להתחיל סדרים אחרים ולסיימם.

May it be Thy will, O Lord our God, even as Thou hast helped us to complete the Seder Zera'im, so to help us to begin other 'Orders', and complete them.

I. EPSTEIN

Jews' College, London.
7th Kislev, 5708.
20th November, 1947.

INTRODUCTION TO BERAKOTH

The Tractate Berakoth ('Benedictions') consists of nine chapters of which only the last four are concerned with benedictions proper. The first three contain the rules for the recital of the *shema'*, the next two those for the recital of the *tefillah*. The Tractate first lays down the hours within which the *shema'* must be recited first in the evening and then in the morning — preferably in the synagogue — and then specifies a number of conditions for its recital and the persons who are exempt from reciting it. Incidentally the conditions under which the Torah may be studied and the tefillin worn are also discussed. The recital of the *tefillah* is then dealt with on similar lines and its wording is discussed. Chapter six first enunciates the principle that before partaking of any kind of food one must recite a benediction, and then lays down the form of blessing for various kinds of foodstuffs. Chapter seven deals specifically with grace before and after meals, and table etiquette generally, particularly *zimmun* or the invitation to join in the grace. Chapter eight lays down the rules for the washing of the hands in connection with a meal, grace over the wine-cup, and the *habdalah* on the termination of the Sabbath. Chapter nine formulates the benedictions to be uttered on a large number of special occasions.

Berakoth contains more Aggada in proportion to its length than any other tractate. The long Chapter nine is mostly aggadic, and is notable for a lenghty excursus on the interpretation of dreams. Another striking piece of Aggada is the account of the quarrel between Rabban Gamaliel and R. Joshua in Chapter four. Chapter six throws great light on the dietary of the Jews in Babylon, while Chapter eight shows that the table customs of Jews in Palestine were largely modelled on those of the Romans.

For some reason which is not obvious Berakoth is included in the 'Order' of Zera'im, or Seeds. In complete editions of the Talmud it has always been placed first in the sequence of tractates. The reason for this is no doubt — as suggested by Maimonides — that the precepts with which it deals — the recital of the *shema'* and the *tefillah* and the benedictions — are among the first which claim the attention of the Jew in his daily life, and are also among the first taught to the Jewish child. Containing as it does few passages of legal casuistry, Berakoth is among the easiest of the tractates, and on this account and because of its wealth of Aggada it is perhaps the most suitable with which to commence the study of the Talmud.

MAURICE SIMON

The Indices of this Tractate have been compiled by Dr. Judah J. Slotki, M. A.

PREFATORY NOTE BY THE EDITOR

The Editor desires to state that the translation of the several tractates, and the notes thereon, are the work of the individual contributors and that he has not attempted to secure general uniformity in style or mode of rendering. He has, nevertheless, revised and supplemented, at his own discretion, their interpretation and elucidation of the original text, and has himself added the footnotes in square brackets containing alternative explanations and matter of historical and geographical interest.

ISIDORE EPSTEIN

מסכת
ברכות

BERAKOTH

CHAPTER I

MISHNAH. [2*a*] FROM WHAT TIME MAY ONE RECITE THE SHEMA' IN THE EVENING? FROM THE TIME THAT THE PRIESTS
a ENTER [THEIR HOUSES] IN ORDER TO EAT THEIR TERUMAH[1] UNTIL THE END OF THE FIRST WATCH.[2] THESE ARE THE WORDS OF R. ELIEZER. THE SAGES SAY: UNTIL MIDNIGHT. R. GAMALIEL SAYS: UNTIL THE DAWN COMES UP.[3] ONCE IT HAPPENED THAT HIS[4] SONS CAME HOME [LATE] FROM A WEDDING FEAST AND THEY SAID TO HIM: WE HAVE NOT YET RECITED THE [EVENING] SHEMA'. HE SAID TO THEM: IF THE DAWN HAS NOT YET COME UP YOU ARE STILL BOUND TO RECITE. AND NOT IN RESPECT TO THIS ALONE DID THEY SO DECIDE, BUT WHEREVER THE SAGES SAY 'UNTIL MIDNIGHT', THE PRECEPT MAY BE PERFORMED UNTIL THE DAWN COMES UP. THE PRECEPT OF BURNING THE FAT AND THE [SACRIFICIAL] PIECES, TOO, MAY BE PERFORMED TILL THE DAWN COMES UP.[5] SIMILARLY, ALL [THE OFFERINGS] THAT ARE TO BE EATEN WITHIN ONE DAY MAY LAWFULLY BE CONSUMED TILL THE COMING UP OF THE DAWN. WHY THEN DID THE SAGES SAY 'UNTIL MIDNIGHT'? IN ORDER TO KEEP A MAN FAR FROM TRANSGRESSION.

GEMARA. On what does the Tanna base himself that he com-
b mences: FROM WHAT TIME?[1] Furthermore, why does he deal first with the evening [*Shema'*]? Let him begin with the morning [*Shema'*]!—The Tanna bases himself on the Scripture, where it is written [*And thou shalt recite them*] . . . *when thou liest down and when thou risest up*,[2] and he states [the oral law] thus: When does the time of the recital of the *Shema'* of lying down begin? When the priests enter to eat their *terumah*.[3] And if you like, I can answer: He learns [the precedence of the evening] from the account of the creation of the world, where it is written, *And there was evening and there was morning, one day*.[4] Why then does he teach in the sequel: THE MORNING [SHEMA'] IS PRECEDED BY TWO BENEDICTIONS AND FOLLOWED BY ONE. THE EVENING [SHEMA'] IS PRECEDED BY TWO BENEDICTIONS AND FOLLOWED BY TWO?[5] Let him there, too, mention the evening [*Shema'*] first?—The Tanna commences with the evening [*Shema'*], and proceeds then to the morning [*Shema'*]. While dealing with the morning [*Shema'*], he expounds all the matters relating to it, and then he returns again to the matters relating to the evening [*Shema'*].

The Master said: FROM THE TIME THAT THE PRIESTS ENTER TO EAT THEIR 'TERUMAH'. When do the priests eat *terumah?* From the time of the appearance of the stars. Let him then say: 'From the time of the appearance of the stars'?—This very thing he wants to teach us, in passing, that the priests may eat *terumah* from the time of the appearance of the stars. And he also wants to teach us that the expiatory offering is not indispensable,[6] as it has been taught:[7] *And when the sun sets* we—ṭaher,[8] the setting of the sun is indispensable [as a condition of his fitness] to eat *terumah*, but the expiatory offering is not indispensable to enable him to eat *terumah*. But how do you know that these words *'and the sun sets'* mean the setting of the sun, and this *'we-ṭaher'* means that the day clears away? [2*b*] It means perhaps: And when the

a (1) If the priests have become ritually unclean, they are not permitted to eat *terumah*, to which a certain holiness attaches, till they have taken a bath and the sun has set. (2) I.e., until either a fourth or a third of the night has passed. V. *infra* 3*a*. (3) Maim: about one and one fifth hours before actual sunrise. V. Pes. 93*b*. (4) R. Gamaliel's. (5) This sentence is parenthetical. It is nowhere laid down that the burning of the fat etc. is permitted only till midnight. It is mentioned here in order to inform us that wherever the time fixed for the performance of a duty is the night, it expires at the rise of the dawn (Rashi).

b (1) I.e., where is it stated in the Law that the recital of the *Shema'* is prescribed at all? (2) Deut. VI, 7. (3) This answers also the second question, as the Bible mentions first the recital of the evening time. (4) Gen. I, 5. (5) *Infra* 11*a*. (6) For the eating of *terumah* even where it is necessary to complete the purification rites, v. Ker. II, 1. (7) Sifra, *Emor*. (8) Lev. XXII, 7. This can be rendered as E.V.: 'he (*the man*) *is clean*', or it (the day) is clean (clear), as understood now by the Gemara.

מאימתי

מאימתי קורין את שמע בערבין ^א^משעה שהכהנים נכנסים לאכול בתרומתן עד סוף האשמורה הראשונה דברי ר' אליעזר וחכמים אומרים ^ב^עד חצות רבן גמליאל אומר ^ג^עד שיעלה עמוד השחר מעשה ובאו בניו מבית המשתה אמרו לו לא קרינו את שמע אמר להם אם לא עלה עמוד השחר חייבין אתם לקרות ולא זו בלבד אמרו אלא *כל מה שאמרו חכמים עד חצות מצותו עד שיעלה עמוד השחר *^ד^הקטר חלבים ואברים מצותן עד שיעלה עמוד השחר ^ה^וכל *הנאכלים ליום אחד מצותן עד שיעלה עמוד השחר אם כן למה אמרו חכמים עד חצות כדי להרחיק אדם מן העבירה: **גמ'** *תנא היכא קאי דקתני מאימתי ותו מאי שנא דתני בערבית ברישא לתני דשחרית ברישא תנא אקרא קאי *דכתיב °בשכבך ובקומך והכי קתני זמן קריאת שמע דשכיבה אימת משעה שהכהנים נכנסין לאכול בתרומתן ואי בעית אימא יליף מברייתו של עולם. דכתיב °ויהי ערב ויהי בקר יום אחד אי הכי סיפא *דקתני ^ו^בשחר מברך שתים לפניה ואחת לאחריה בערב מברך שתים לפניה ושתים לאחריה לתני דערבית ברישא תנא פתח בערבית והדר תני בשחרית עד דקאי בשחרית פריש מילי דשחרית והדר פריש מילי דערבית: אמר מר משעה שהכהנים נכנסים לאכול בתרומתן מכדי כהנים אימת קא אכלי תרומה משעת צאת הככבים לתני משעת צאת הככבים מלתא אגב אורחיה קמשמע לן *כהנים אימת קא אכלי בתרומה משעת צאת הככבים והא קמ"ל דכפרה לא מעכבא *כדתניא °ובא השמש וטהר ^ז^ביאת שמשו מעכבתו מלאכול בתרומה ואין כפרתו מעכבתו מלאכול בתרומה *וממאי דהאי ובא השמש ביאת השמש והאי וטהר טהר יומא דילמא

תורה אור: דברי' ו · ראשי' א · ויקרא כב

רש"י

מאימתי קורין את שמע בערבין. משעה שהכהנים נכנסים לאכול בתרומתן. כהנים שנטמאו וטבלו והעריב שמשן והגיע עתם לאכול בתרומה: עד סוף האשמורה הראשונה. שליש הלילה כדמפרש בגמרא (דף ג.) ומשם ואילך עבר זמן דלא מקרי תו זמן שכיבה ולא קרינן ביה בשכבך. ומקמי הכי נמי לאו זמן שכיבה לפיכך הקורא קודם לכן לא יצא ידי חובתו. אם כן למה קורין אותה בבית הכנסת כדי לעמוד בתפלה מתוך דברי תורה. והכי תניא בברייתא בברכות ירושלמי. ולפיכך חובה עלינו לקרותה משתחשך. ובקריאת פרשה ראשונה שאדם קורא על מטתו יצא: עד שיעלה עמוד השחר. שכל הלילה קרוי זמן שכיבה: הקטר חלבים ואברים. של קרבנות שנזרק דמן ביום: מצותן. להעלות כל הלילה ואינן נפסלים בלינה עד שיעלה עמוד השחר והן למטה מן המזבח דכתיב (שמות לד) ולא ילין לבקר: חלבים. של כל קרבנות: אברים. של עולה: וכל הנאכלים ליום אחד. כגון חטאת ואשם וכבשי עצרת ומנחות ותודה: מצותן. זמן אכילתן: עד שיעלה עמוד השחר. והוא מביאן להיות נותר דכתיב בתודה (ויקרא ז) לא יניח ממנו עד בקר וכלם מתודה ילמדו: אם כן למה אמרו חכמים עד חצות. בקריאת שמע ובאכילת קדשים: כדי להרחיק אדם מן העבירה. ואסרום באכילה קודם זמנן כדי שלא יבא לאכלן לאחר עמוד השחר ויתחייב כרת. וכן בקריאת שמע לזרז את האדם שלא יאמר יש לי עוד שהות ובתוך כך יעלה עמוד השחר ועבר לו הזמן. והקטר חלבים דקתני הכא לא אמרו בו חכמים עד חצות כלל ולא נקט להו הכא אלא להודיע שכל דבר הנוהג בלילה כשר כל הלילה. והכי נמי תנן בפרק שני דמגילה (דף כ' ב') כל הלילה כשר לקצירת העומר ולהקטר חלבים ואברים: **גמ'** היכא קאי. מהיכא קא סליק דתנא ביה חובת קריאת שמע שהתחיל לשאול כאן זמן הקריאה: אקרא קאי. ושם למד חובת הקריאה: ואי בעית אימא. הא דתנא ערבין ברישא יליף מברייתו של עולם: והדר תנא בשחרית. מאימתי קורין את שמע בשחרית: משעת צאת הככבים. שהוא גמר ביאת השמש כדיליף לקמן (עמוד ב'):

דילמא

תוספות

מאימתי קורין וכו'. פי' רש"י ואנן היכי קרינן מבעוד יום ואין אנו ממתינין לצאת הככבים כדמפרש בגמרא. על כן פי' רש"י שקריאת שמע שעל המטה עיקר והיא לאחר צאת הככבים. והכי איתא בירושלמי אם קרא קודם לכן לא יצא. וא"כ למה אנו מתפללין ק"ש בבית הכנסת כדי לעמוד בתפלה מתוך דברי תורה. תימה לפירושו והלא אין העולם רגילין לקרות סמוך לשכיבה אלא פרשה ראשונה (לקמן דף ס':) ואם כן שלש פרשיות היה לו לקרות. ועוד קשה דצריך לברך בקריאת שמע שתים לפניה ושתים לאחריה בערבית. ועוד דאותה קריאת שמע סמוך למטה אינה אלא בשביל המזיקין כדאמר בסמוך (דף ה.) ואם תלמיד חכם הוא אינו צריך. ועוד קשה דאם כן פסקינן כר' יהושע בן לוי דאמר תפלות באמצע תקנום פי' באמצע בין שני קריאת שמע בין קריאת שמע של שחרית ובין קריאת שמע של ערבית. ואנן קיימא לן כר' יוחנן דאמר לקמן (דף ד':) איזהו בן העולם הבא זה הסומך גאולה של ערבית לתפלה. לכן פי' ר"ת דאדרבה קריאת שמע של בית הכנסת עיקר. וא"ת היאך אנו קורין כל כך מבעוד יום. וי"ל דקי"ל כר' יהודה דאמר בפרק תפלת השחר (דף כו.) דזמן תפלת מנחה עד פלג המנחה דהיינו אחד עשר שעות פחות רביע ומיד כשיכלה זמן המנחה מתחיל זמן ערבית. ואם תאמר היאך אנו מתפללין תפלת מנחה סמוך לחשכה ואפילו לאחר פלג המנחה. יש לומר דקיימא לן כרבנן דאמרי זמן תפלת המנחה עד הערב ואמרינן לקמן (דף כז.) השתא דלא אתמר הלכתא לא כמר ולא כמר דעבד כמר עבד ודעבד כמר עבד. מ"מ קשיא דהוי כתרי קולי דסתרן אהדדי שהרי מאיזה טעם אנו מתפללין ערבית מיד לאחר פלג המנחה משום דקיימא לן דשעת המנחה כלה כדברי ר' יהודה ומיד הוי זמן ערבית ובזמן התפלה עצמה לא קיימא לן כר' יהודה אלא כרבנן. על כן אומר ר"י דודאי קריאת שמע של בית הכנסת עיקר ואנו שמתפללין ערבית מבעוד יום סבירא לן כהני תנאי דגמרא דאמרי משעה שקדש היום וגם משעה שבני אדם נכנסין להסב דהיינו סעודת ע"ש והיא היתה מבעוד יום ומאותה שעה הוי זמן תפלה. וגם ראי' (לקמן פ"ד דף כז ב') דרב הוי מצלי של שבת בערב שבת ומסתמא גם היה קורא קריאת שמע. מכל אותן הראיות משמע דקריאת שמע של בית הכנס' היא עיקר. והא דקאמר בירושלמי למה היו קורין בבית הכנסת וכו' אומר רבינו תם שהיו רגילין לקרות ק"ש קודם תפלתם כמו שאנו רגילין לומר אשרי תחלה ואותה ק"ש אינה אלא לעמוד בתפלה מתוך דברי תורה. ומכאן נראה מי שקורא קריאת שמע על מטתו שאין לברך. וגם אינו צריך לקרות אלא פרשה ראשונה:

לתני דשחרית ברישא. כדאשכחן בתמיד דכתיב של בקר תחלה:

אי הכי סיפא דקתני שחרית ברישא. אי אמרת בשלמא דסמיך אקרא דבשכבך אם כן אינו מקפיד קרא אלא אקריאת שמע. אלא אי אמרת דסמיך אקרא דברייתו של עולם אם כן קפיד אכל מילי אם כן סיפא דקתני וכו':

מברך ב' לפניה וכו'. (ירושלמי) וז' ברכות הוו כנגד שבע ביום הללתיך (תהלים קיט). ולא קא חשיב יראו עינינו. דההיא ברכה תקנו רבנן כדי להמתין חביריהם בבית הכנסת. ודוקא בבה"כ שלהם שהיו עומדים בשדה והם מסוכנים מן המזיקין אבל בבתי כנסיות שלנו אין צריכין להמתין לחביריהם אלא בלילה:

והא קמ"ל דכפרה לא מעכבא. ואם תאמר הא תנינא חדא זימנא במסכת נגעים (פ' יד) ומייתי לה בהערל (דף עד ב') העריב שמשו אוכל בתרומה. וי"ל דרגילות של משניות לאשמועינן בקוצר אף למה שמפורש כבר *:

דילמא

עין משפט נר מצוה

א אמיי' פ"א מהלכות ק"ש הלכה ט' סמ"ג עשין יח טור וש"ע א"ח סי' רלה סעיף א'

ב בג מיי' וסמ"ג שם טוש"ע שם סעיף ג'

[*ע' תוס' זבחי' כז: ד"ה להרחיק]

ג דמיי' פ"ד מהלכות מעשה קרבנות הלכה ב' סמ"ג עשין קכג

ד המיי' פ"י שם הל' ח'

ה ומיי' פ"א מהלכות ק"ש הלכה ה' סמ"ג עשין י"ח טור וש"ע א"ח סימן כח ובסימן רלו סעיף א'

ו זמיי' פ"ז מה' תרומות הל' ב'

מסורת הש"ס

מגילה דף כ: · מכילתא דר"י פ' בא · פסחים דף סח ב · [מגילה כ:] · [תענית ב.] · [ע' תוס' לקמן כא. ותוס' סוטה לב: ד"ה ורבי] · לקמן דף יא. · כלים פר' א' נגעים פר' יד · ת"כ פ' אמור יבמות דף עד: · [עיין ג' הגאונים בספר המאור] · [וע' תוס' זבחים כח. ד"ה אמר ותוס' מנחות לג. ד"ה הכל]

תורה אור

דילמא ביאת אורו הוא ומאי וטהר טהר גברא אמ׳ רבה בר רב שילא אם כן לימא קרא ויטהר ומאי וטהר טהר יומא כדאמרי אינשי איערב שמשא ואדכי יומא במערבא הא דרב׳ בר רב שיל׳ לא שמיע להו ובעו לה מבעיא האי ובא השמש ביאת שמשו הוא ומאי וטהר טהר יומא או דילמא ביאת אורו הוא ומאי וטהר טהר גברא והדר פשטו לה מבריתא מדקתני בבריתא סימן לדבר צאת הככבים שמע מינ׳ ביאת שמשו הוא ומאי וטהר טהר יומא: אמר מר משעה שהכהנים נכנסין לאכול בתרומתן ורמינהי מאימתי קורין את שמע בערבין משהעני נכנס לאכול פתו במלח עד שעה שעומד ליפטר מתוך סעודתו סיפא ודאי פליגא אמתניתין רישא מי לימא פליגא אמתניתין לא עני וכהן חד שעור׳ הוא ורמינהי *מאימתי מתחילין לקרות קרית שמע בערבית משעה שבני אדם נכנסין לאכול פתן *בערבי שבתות דברי ר׳ מאיר וחכמים אומרים משעה שהכהנים זכאין לאכול בתרומתן סימן לדבר צאת הככבי׳ ואע״פי שאין ראיה לדבר זכר לדבר שנאמר °ואנחנו עושים במלאכה והצים מחזיקים ברמחים מעלות השחר עד צאת הכוכבים ואומר °והיו לנו *הלילה משמר והיום מלאכה *מאי ואומר וכי תימא מכי ערבא שמשא ליליא הוא ואינהו דמחשכי ומקדמי תא שמע והיו לנו הלילה משמר והיום מלאכה קא סלקא דעתך דעני ובני אדם חד שעורא הוא ואי אמרת עני וכהן חד שעורא הוא חכמים היינו רבי מאיר אלא שמע מינה עני שעורא לחוד וכהן שעורא לחוד לא עני וכהן חד שעורא הוא ועני ובני אדם לאו חד שעורא הוא ועני וכהן חד שעורא הוא ורמינהי מאימתי מתחילין לקרות שמע בערבין משעה שקדש היום בערבי שבתות דברי ר׳ אליעזר. ר׳ יהושע אומר משעה שהכהנים מטוהרים לאכול בתרומתן ר׳ מאיר אומר משעה שהכהנים טובלין לאכול בתרומתן אמר ליה ר׳ יהודה והלא כהנים מבעוד יום הם טובלים רבי חנינא אומר משעה שעני נכנס לאכול פתו במלח רבי אחאי ואמרי לה ר׳ אחא אומר משעה שרוב בני אדם נכנסין להסב ואי אמרת עני וכהן חד שעורא הוא רבי חנינא היינו רבי יהושע אלא לאו שמע מינה שעורא דעני לחוד ושעורא דכהן לחוד שמע מינה הי מינייהו מאוחר מסתברא דעני מאוחר דאי אמרת דעני מוקדם ר׳ חנינא היינו רבי אליעזר אלא לאו שמע מינה דעני מאוחר שמע מינה: אמר מר אמר ליה רבי יהודה והלא כהנים מבעוד יום הם טובלים שפיר קאמר ליה רבי יהודה לרבי מאיר ורבי מאיר הכי קאמר ליה מי סברת דאנא אבין השמשות דידך קא אמינא. אנא בין השמשות דרבי יוסי קא אמינא דאמר *רבי יוסי בין השמשות כהרף עין זה נכנס וזה יוצא ואי אפשר לעמוד עליו

קשיא

נחמי׳ ד

שם

דילמא ביאת אורו. שיאור השמש ביום השמיני ויטהר האיש עצמו בהבאת קרבנותיו ואחר יאכל: אם כן. דהאי קרא וטהר לשון לווי הוא לימא קרא ויטהר מאי וטהר: אדכי. לשון עבר כתפנה מן העולם השמש: מבריתא. דקתני לקמן בשמעתין משעה שהכהנים נכנסים לאכול בתרומתן וראיה לדבר צאת הככבים ש״מ אין כפרתן מעכבתן: משהעני. שאין לו נר להדליק בסעודתו: סיפא ודאי פליגא אמתניתין. דקתני הכא עד שעה שעומד ליפטר מתוך הסעודה והיינו לא כרבי אליעזר ולא כרבנן ולא כרבן גמליאל. דדרים ובשכבך תחלת זמן שכיבה ובמתניתין תנן עד סוף האשמורה הראשונה: עני וכהן. עני כל לילותיו וכהן נמי לאכול בתרומה: חד שעורא הוא. לצאת הככבים: בערבי שבתות. ממהרין לסעודה שהכל מוכן: שאין ראיה לדבר. שהיום כלה בצאת הככבים זכר לדבר איכא: דמחשכי. ועושין מלאכה בלילה משקיעת החמה עד צאת הככבים: ומקדמי. ומשכימין קודם היום דאימא יום לא הוי עד הנץ החמה והם מקדימין מעלות השחר דהוי כמו מהלך ה׳ מילין (פסחים ד׳ צג:): ת״ש והיו לנו הלילה משמר. מדקאמר והיום מלאכה אלמא האי דעבד מעלות השחר עד צאת הככבים יממא הוא. וזכר לדבר איכא דכל עת מלאכה קורא הכתוב יום: קס״ד. רוב בני אדם היינו עניים *כלו׳ בני אדם בערבי שבתות ועניים בימות החול חד שעורא הוא: משעה שקדש היום בערבי שבתות. היינו בין השמשות ספק יום ספק לילה וכיון דספק הוא קדש היום מספק: משעה שהכהנים טובלים. היינו קודם בין השמשות כדי שיהא להם קודם בין השמשות הערב שמש והכי אמרינן בבמה מדליקין (דף לה.) דזמן הטבילה קודם בין השמשות מעט: והלא כהנים מבעוד יום טובלים. רבי יהודה לטעמיה דאמר בבמה מדליקין *בין השמשות כדי מהלך חצי מיל קודם צאת הככבים קרוי בין השמשות הוי ספק הלכך טביל׳ דמקמי הכי מבעוד יום הוא ולאו זמן שכיבה הוא ולקמן מפרש מאי אהדר לי׳ רבי מאיר: נכנסין להסב. אית דאמרי בימות החול ואית דאמרי בשבתות מכל מקום מאוחר הוא (לכולם): והי מינייהו מאוחר. (לכול׳) דעני או דכהן: ה״ג אי ס״ד דעני קודם רבי חנינא היינו רבי אליעזר: בין השמשות דר׳ יהודה מהלך חצי מיל לפני צאת הככבים ודר׳ יוסי כהרף עין לפני צאת הככבים ור׳ מאיר כרבי יוסי ס״ל וכי טביל מקמי הכי סמוך לחשיכ׳ הוא וזמן שכיב׳ קרינן ביה:

קשיא

דילמא ביאת אורו הוא. פירש רש״י עד שיזרח אורו של יום השמיני ומאי וטהר טהר גברא שיטהר האיש בהבאת קרבנותיו. ותימה לפירושו לפרוך אההיא דהערל (דף עד:) דהעריב שמשו אוכל בתרומה וכו׳ מכלן דביאת שמשו הוא. ועוד היכי מצי למימר דמיירי בזריחה דאי בזריחה הוא הוה מצי למכתב בקרא וזרח השמש וטהר כמו מזרח השמש (במדבר כא) או לשון יציאה כמו השמש יצא על הארץ (בראשית יט) ונקט בקרא ובא השמש אלמא דהיינו שקיעת החמה. ועוד דבסמוך קא מבעיא ליה האי ובא השמש אי ביאת אורו הוא ופשיט מברייתא וזכר לדבר וכו׳. תפשוט ממתניתין [דנגעים פ״יד] העריב שמשו אוכל בתרומה אלמא דהיינו ביאת שמש. וי״ל דהכי פירושו מאי דהאי ובא השמש ועהר ביאת שמש הוא ממש ומאי וטהר טהר יומא דהיינו צאת הככבים דלמא ביאת אורו הוא דהיינו תחלתה של שקיעת החמה והוא תחלת הכנסתו ברקיע ועדיין יש שהות *ביום חמש מילין עד צאת הככבים ומאי וטהר טהר גברא. והשתא למתניתין דהערל לא קשה מידי דמצי למימר העריב שמשו דהתם היינו ביאת אורו. ואף מהתם לא תפשוט דהיינו צאת הככבים. משום הכי אצטריך לאתויי הכא הברייתא דצאת הככבי׳:

אם כן לימא קרא ויטהר. אע״ג דבכמה מקומות כתיב וטהר. התם ליכא למיטעי אבל הכא דאיכא למיטעי הוה ליה למכתב ויטהר:

משעה שהעני נכנס לאכול פתו במלח. תימה עני גופי׳ מתי יתפלל דהא אמרת זמן אכילתו היינו זמן קריאת שמע וכיון שבא זמן ק״ש אסור להתחיל בסעודה עד שיתפלל ברישא כדתניא לקמן (ד׳ ד׳:) וקורא קריאת שמע ומתפלל ואוכל פתו ומברך וכל העובר על דברי חכמים חייב מיתה. ויש לומר דזמן תפלה הוי קודם לזמן סעודה דלאו דוקא משעני נכנס לאכול אלא פורתא מעיקרא קאמר שעד שיכינו לו סעודתו יקרא ויתפלל:

אע״פ שאין ראיה לדבר. ראיה גמורה איכא דהא לא מיירי התם לענין קריאת שמע*:

ואי ס״ד דעני קדים רבי חנינא היינו ר׳ אליעזר. ולא מצי למימר דעני קדים לקדוש היום או קדוש היום קדים לשעורא דעני. דלא מסתברא לחלק כל כך בשעורי זמן שכיבה דכל זמנים הללו אית ביה:

אמר ליה ר׳ יהודה והלא כהנים מבעוד יום הם טובלים. תימה תיקשי ליה לנפשיה שהרי פלג המנחה מבעוד יום היא והוא אומר (לקמן דף כו.) מיד כשיעבור פלג המנחה הוי זמן תפלת ערבית. ויש לומר דלדידיה לא קשיא דלא דריש בשכבך ובקומך אבל לרבנן דדרשינן קשיא דאינו זמן שכיבה:

קשיא

מסורת הש״ס

תוספת׳ ברכות פרק א׳

[*ר״ל בעניים בימות החול או שסיפה גי׳ רש״י בגמ׳ קס״ד רוב בני אדם היינו עניים ורש״י מפרש כלומר וכו׳]

מגילה דף כ׳ ב׳ ושם

מכילתא דר״י פר׳ בא פסחים פ״ח:

[לד: ע״ש היטיב וע׳ רש״י נדה נג. ד״ה ב״ה]

רש״א מ״ז

רש״ל מ״ז

[שבת דף לד: נדה נג.]

[כלאי׳ פסחים צג:]

(ירו׳ גרס בלילי׳)

(נוסח ירו׳ והיה בה״א למשמר למלאכה בל׳)

[וע׳ בתוס׳ מגילה כ: ד״ה והי׳]

sun [of the next morning] appears, and *we-ṭaher* means the man
a becomes clean?[1]—Rabbah son of R. Shila explains: In that case, the text would have to read *weyiṭhar*.[2] What is the meaning of *we-ṭaher?*[3] The day clears away, conformably to the common expression, The sun has set and the day has cleared away. This explanation of Rabbah son of R. Shila was unknown in the West,[4] and they raised the question: This *'and the sun sets'*, does it mean the real setting of the sun, and *'we-ṭaher'* means the day clears away? Or does it perhaps mean the appearance of the sun, and *we-ṭaher* means the man becomes clean? They solved it from a Baraitha, it being stated in a Baraitha: The sign of the thing is the appearance of the stars. Hence you learn that it is the setting of the sun [which makes him clean] and the meaning of *we-ṭaher* is the clearing away of the day.

The Master said: FROM THE TIME THAT THE PRIESTS ENTER TO EAT THEIR 'TERUMAH'. They pointed to a contradiction [from the following]: From what time may one recite the *Shema'* in the evening? From the time that the poor man[5] comes [home] to eat his bread with salt till he rises from his meal. The last clause certainly contradicts the Mishnah. Does the first clause also contradict the Mishnah?—No. The poor man and the priest have one and the same time.

They pointed to a contradiction [from the following]: From what time may one begin to recite the *Shema'* in the evening? From the time that the people come [home] to eat their meal on a Sabbath eve. These are the words of R. Meir. But the Sages say: From the time that the priests are entitled to eat their *terumah*. A sign for the matter is the appearance of the stars. And though there is no real proof of it,[6] there is a hint for it. For it is written: *So we wrought in the work: and half of them held the spears from the rise*
b *of the dawn till the appearance of the stars.*[1] And it says further: *That in the night they may be a guard to us, and may labour in the day.*[2] (Why this second citation?[3]—If you object and say that the night really begins with the setting of the sun, but that they left late and came early, [I shall reply]: Come and hear [the other verse]: *'That in the night they may be a guard to us, and may labour in the* day'). Now it is assumed that the 'poor man' and 'the people' have the same time [for their evening meal.][4] And if you say that the poor man and the priest also have the same time, then the Sages would be saying the same thing as R. Meir? Hence you must conclude that the poor man has one time and the priest has another time?—No; the 'poor man' and the priest have the same time, but the 'poor man' and the 'people' have not the same time.

But have the 'poor man' and the priest really the same time? They pointed to a contradiction [from the following]: From what time may one begin to recite the *Shema'* in the evening? From the time that the [Sabbath] day becomes hallowed on the Sabbath eve. These are the words of R. Eliezer. R. Joshua says: From the time that the priests are ritually clean to eat their *terumah*. R. Meir says: From the time that the priests take their ritual bath in order to eat their *terumah*. (Said R. Judah to him: When the priests take their ritual bath it is still day-time!)[5] R. Ḥanina says: From the time that the poor man comes [home] to eat his bread with salt. R. Aḥai (some say: R. Aḥa), says: From the time that most people come home to sit down to their meal. Now, if you say that the poor man and the priest have the same time, then R. Ḥanina and R. Joshua would be saying the same thing? From this you must conclude, must you not, that the poor man has one time and the priest has another time.—Draw indeed that conclusion!

Which of them is later?—It is reasonable to conclude that the 'poor man' is later. For if you say that the 'poor man' is earlier,
c R. Ḥanina would be saying the same thing as R. Eliezer.[1] Hence you must conclude that the poor man is later, must you not?—Draw indeed that conclusion.

The Master said:[2] 'R. Judah said to him: When the priests take their ritual bath it is still day-time!' The objection of R. Judah to R. Meir seems well founded?—R. Meir may reply as follows: Do you think that I am referring to the twilight [as defined] by you?[3] I am referring to the twilight [as defined] by R. Jose. For R. Jose says: The twilight is like the twinkling of an eye. This[4] enters and that[5] departs, and one cannot exactly fix it.[6] [*3a*] There

a (1) Through his sin-offering. (2) The verb being in the future. (3) Which may be taken as a past tense, the *waw* not being conversive. (4) In the Palestinian schools. (5) Who cannot afford an artificial light. (6) That the day ends with the appearance of the stars.

b (1) Neh. IV, 15. (2) Ibid. 16. (3) The first verse seems to afford ample proof. (4) I.e., the time the 'poor man' mentioned in the first Baraitha comes home to take his evening meal is indentical with that at which people generally come to eat their meals on Sabbath eve. (5) And not even twilight, v. Shab. 35*a*.

c (1) Tosef. points out that the ground for this statement is not clear. (2) In the Baraitha just quoted. (3) According to which definition it lasts as long as it takes to walk half a *mil*, v. Shab. 34*b*. (4) The evening. (5) The day. (6) And consequently the priests may bathe at twilight as defined by R. Jose since it is still day, and one may also read at that time the *Shema'* since it is practically night.

is a contradiction between R. Meir [of one Baraitha][7] and R. Meir [of the last Baraitha]?[8]—Yes, two Tannaim transmit different versions of R. Meir's opinion. There is a contradiction between R. Eliezer [of the last Baraitha][9] and R. Eliezer [of the Mishnah]?[10]—Yes, two Tannaim[11] transmit two different versions of R. Eliezer's opinion. If you wish I can say: The first clause of the Mishnah[12] is not R. Eliezer's.[13]

UNTIL THE END OF THE FIRST WATCH. What opinion does R. Eliezer hold? If he holds that the night has three watches, let him say: Till four hours [in the night]. And if he holds that the night has four watches, let him say: Till three hours?—He holds indeed, that the night has three watches, but he wants to teach us that there are watches in heaven[14] as well as on earth. For it has been taught: R. Eliezer says: The night has three watches, and at each watch the Holy One, blessed be He, sits and roars like a lion. For it is written: *The Lord does roar from on high, and raise*
a *His voice from His holy habitation; 'roaring He doth roar'*[1] *because of his fold.* And the sign of the thing is:[2] In the first watch, the ass brays; in the second, the dogs bark; in the third, the child sucks from the breast of his mother, and the woman talks with her husband. What does R. Eliezer understand [by the word *watch*]? Does he mean the beginning of the watches? The beginning of the first watch needs no sign, it is the twilight! Does he mean the end of the watches? The end of the last watch needs no sign, it is the dawn of the day! He, therefore, must think of the end of the first watch, of the beginning of the last watch, and of the midst of the middle watch. If you like I can say: He refers to the end of all the watches. And if you object that the last watch needs no sign, [I reply] that it may be of use for the recital of the *Shema'*, and for a man who sleeps in a dark room[3] and does not know when the time of the recital arrives. When the woman talks with her husband and the child sucks from the breast of the mother, let him rise and recite.

R. Isaac b. Samuel says in the name of Rab: The night has three watches, and at each watch the Holy One, blessed be He, sits and roars like a lion and says: Woe to the children, on account of whose sins I destroyed My house and burnt My temple and exiled them among the nations of the world.

It has been taught: R. Jose says, I was once travelling on the road, and I entered into one of the ruins of Jerusalem in order to pray. Elijah of blessed memory appeared and waited for me at the door till I finished my prayer.[4] After I finished my prayer, he said to me: Peace be with you, my master! and I replied: Peace be with you, my master and teacher! And he said to me: My son, why did you go into this ruin? I replied: To pray. He said to me: You ought to have prayed on the road. I replied: I feared lest passers-by might interrupt me. He said to me: You ought to have said an abbreviated prayer.[5] Thus I then learned from him three things: One must not go into a ruin; one may say the prayer on the road; and if one does say his prayer on the road, he recites an abbreviated prayer. He further said to me: My son, what sound did you hear in this ruin? I replied: I heard a divine voice, cooing like a dove, and saying: Woe to the children, on account of whose sins I destroyed My house and burnt My temple and exiled them among the nations of the world! And he said to me: By your life and by your head! Not in this moment alone does it so exclaim, but thrice each day does it exclaim thus! And more than that, whenever the Israelites go into the synagogues and schoolhouses and respond: 'May His great name
b be blessed!'[1] the Holy One, blessed be He, shakes His head and says: Happy is the king who is thus praised in this house! Woe[2] to the father who had to banish his children, and woe to the children who had to be banished from the table of their father!

Our Rabbis taught: there are three reasons why one must not go into a ruin: because of suspicion,[3] of falling debris and of demons.—[It states] *'Because of suspicion'*.[4] It would be sufficient to say,

(7) Where he says: When people come home for their Sabbath-meal, which is after twilight. (8) Which fixes a time which is before twilight. (9) Which fixes sunset as the time-standard. (10) Which fixes as time-standard, the appearance of the stars (when priests enter to eat *terumah*). (11) V. Glos. (12) Where the beginning of the time is fixed. (13) R. Eliezer's ruling being merely with reference to the *terminus ad quem*. (14) Among the ministering angels.

a (1) So literally. Thus 'roaring' is mentioned three times in the text. (2) I.e., of each watch. (3) That has no windows to admit the daylight. (4) The *Tefillah*, v. Glos. (5) V. *infra* 29a.

b (1) The principal congregational response in the doxology, the *Kaddish* v. *P.B.* p. 37. (2) V. *D.S.* cur. edd.; what is there for the father. (3) That a woman may be waiting for him there. (4) The Gemara now proceeds to explain why all the three reasons must be mentioned.

תורה אור

קשיא דרבי מאיר אדר' מאיר תרי תנאי אליבא דרבי מאיר קשיא דרבי אליעזר אדרבי אליעזר תרי תנאי אליבא דרבי אליעזר ואיבעית אימא רישא לאו ר' אליעזר היא: עד סוף האשמורה: מאי קסבר ר' אליעזר אי קסבר שלש משמרות הוי הלילה לימא עד ארבע שעות ואי קסבר ארבע משמרות הוי הלילה לימא עד שלש שעות לעולם קסבר שלש משמרות הוי הלילה והא קמשמע לן דאיכא משמרות ברקיעא *ואיכא משמרות בארעא דתניא ר' אליעזר אומר שלש משמרות הוי הלילה ועל כל משמר ומשמר יושב הקב"ה ושואג כארי שנאמר °ה' ממרום ישאג וממעון קדשו יתן קולו שאוג ישאג על נוהו וסימן לדבר משמרה ראשונה חמור נוער שנייה כלבים צועקים שלישית תינוק יונק משדי אמו ואשה מספרת עם בעלה מאי קא חשיב ר' אליעזר אי תחלת משמרות קא חשיב תחלת משמרה ראשונה סימנא למה לי אורתא הוא אי סוף משמרות קא חשיב סוף משמרה אחרונה למה לי סימנא יממא הוא אלא חשיב סוף משמרה ראשונה ותחלת משמרה אחרונה ואמצעית דאמצעיתא ואי בעית אימא כלהו סוף משמרות קא חשיב וכי תימא אחרונה לא צריך למאי נפקא מינה למקרי קריאת שמע למאן דגני בבית אפל ולא ידע זמן קריאת שמע אימת כיון דאשה מספרת עם בעלה ותינוק יונק משדי אמו ליקום וליקרי: *אמר רב יצחק בר שמואל משמיה דרב שלש משמרות הוי הלילה ועל כל משמר ומשמר יושב הקב"ה ושואג כארי ואומר אוי לבנים שבעונותיהם החרבתי את ביתי ושרפתי את היכלי והגליתים לבין אומות העולם תניא אמר רבי יוסי פעם אחת הייתי מהלך בדרך ונכנסתי לחורבה אחת מחורבות ירושלים להתפלל בא אליהו זכור לטוב ושמר לי על הפתח (והמתין לי) עד שסיימתי תפלתי לאחר שסיימתי תפלתי אמר לי שלום עליך רבי ואמרתי לו שלום עליך רבי ומורי ואמר לי בני מפני מה נכנסת לחורבה זו אמרתי לו להתפלל ואמר לי היה לך להתפלל בדרך ואמרתי לו מתיירא הייתי שמא יפסיקו *בי עוברי דרכים ואמר לי היה לך להתפלל תפלה קצרה באותה שעה למדתי ממנו שלשה דברים למדתי שאין נכנסים לחורבה ולמדתי שמתפללין בדרך ולמדתי שהמתפלל בדרך מתפלל תפלה קצרה ואמר לי בני מה קול שמעת בחורבה זו ואמרתי לו שמעתי בת *קול שמנהמת כיונה ואומרת אוי לבנים שבעונותיהם החרבתי את ביתי ושרפתי את היכלי והגליתים לבין האומות ואמר לי חייך וחיי ראשך לא שעה זו בלבד אומרת כך אלא בכל יום ויום שלש פעמים אומרת כך ולא זו בלבד אלא בשעה שישראל נכנסין לבתי כנסיות ולבתי מדרשות ועונין יהא *שמיה הגדול מבורך הקב"ה מנענע ראשו ואומר אשרי המלך שמקלסין אותו בביתו כך מה לו לאב שהגלה את בניו ואוי להם לבנים שגלו מעל שלחן אביהם: תנו רבנן מפני שלשה דברים אין נכנסין לחורבה מפני חשד מפני המפולת ומפני המזיקן מפני חשד ותיפוק ליה משום מפולת

בחדתי

רש"י

קשיא דרבי מאיר אדרבי מאיר. לעיל אמר משעה שבני אדם נכנסין לאכול פתן בערבי שבתו' והוא שיעור מאוחר משל כהן והכא אמר משעת טבילה שהיא קודם בין השמשות: קשיא דר' אליעזר. דברייתא אדר' אליעזר דמתני': ואיבעית אימא רישא דמתני' לאו רבי אליעזר היא. והא דקתני דברי רבי אליעזר אסוף הזמן קאי דקאמר עד סוף האשמורה הראשונה. ופליגי רבנן עלי' ואמרי עד חצות. דר' אליעזר דריש בשכבך זמן התחלת שכיבה שבני אדם הולכים לשכב זה קודם וזה מאוחר. ורבנן דרשי כל זמן שכיבה דהיינו כל הלילה אלא שעשו סייג לדבר ואמרו עד חצו' ורבן גמליאל לית ליה ההוא סייג: מאי קסבר כו'. הוה ליה לומר זמן הניכר: אי קסבר. דפליגי תנאי לקמן בהא מילתא איכא מאן דאמר ג' משמרות הוי הלילה במשמרות עבודת המלאכים ושיר שלהם נחלק לשלשה חלקי' ראשונה לכת אחת שניה לכת אחרת שלישית לכת שלישית. ואיכא מאן דאמר ארבע משמרות הוי הלילה: והא קמ"ל. כשנתן לך סימן זמן הקריאה בסוף האשמורת ולא פירש לך סימן מפור' למדך שיש היכר לכל אדם בדבר דכי היכי דאיכא ברקיע: ישאג שאוג ישאג. הרי ג': ואשה מספרת עם בעלה. כבר הגיע קרוב ליום ובני אדם מתעוררים משנתן והשוכבים יחד מספרים זה עם זה: מאי קא חשיב. סימנים הללו שנתן למשמרות הארץ היכן נתנו. בתחלת האשמורות או בסופן: אורתא הוא. לאת הכוכבים: ושמר. והמתין כמו לא יאמר אדם לחברו שמור לי בלד ע"א פלוני'. (סנהדרין דף סג:) ובב"ק בפ' החובל (דף צ:) שומרת ועומדת על פתח חצרה. וכן ואביו שמר את הדבר. (בראשית לז) שומר אמונים (ישעי' כו): תפלה קצרה. [הביננו] ולקמן מפרש לה בפ' תפלת השחר (דף כט.): אשרי המלך שמקלסין אותו בביתו כך. אשרי כל זמן שהיה קלוס זה בתוך בית המקדש: מפני חשד. שלא יאמרו זונה מוכנת לו שם: ומפני המפולת. שחומת החורבה רעועה ומסוכן הוא פן תפול החומ' עליו: תיפוק ליה. כלומר למה לנו ג' טעמים לדבר א' הרי די באחת מהן אם לא בא ללמדך שיש שעות שאין הטעם הזה וצריך להכיא בשביל זה:

בחדתי

תוספות

קשיא דר' מאיר אדרבי מאיר. דלא מצי למימר בשעה שבני אדם נכנסין וכהן חד שעורא הוא דאם כן רבי מאיר היינו רבי אחאי לפי' רש"י שפי' שרוב בני אדם נכנסין להסב דהיינו בע"ש. [וגם] כן לא מסתברא למימר דבני אד' ממהרין כ"כ בערבי שבתות כמו בזמן שהכהנים טובלין דהיינו מבעוד יום קודם הערב שמש:

קשיא דר' אליעזר אדרבי אליעזר. דלא מצי למימר משקדש היום וכהנים נכנסין לאכול בתרומתן חד שיעורא הוא. דאם כן רבי אליעזר היינו ר' יהושע:

למאן דגני בבית אפל. וא"ת והלא רבי אליעזר בעי (לקמן דף ט:) עד שיכיר בין תכלת לכרתי בק"ש של שחרית. וי"ל מ"מ כיון שידע מתי יעלה עמוד השחר. קודם שיקום ויזמן עצמו כבר הגיע אותו עת:

היה לך להתפלל תפלה קצרה. לכאור' משמע שאין זה הביננו. דהא קא בעי לקמן (פ"ד ד' ל.) מאי איכא בין הביננו לתפלה קצרה. א"כ לפירוש הקונ' שפיר' בכאן דהיינו הביננו קשה. אלא ע"כ היינו תפלה אחריתא כדמפר' לקמן [דף כט:] צרכי עמך מרובים וכו'. וגם על זה קשה דלקמן אמרינן שאין לומר תפלת של צרכי עמך אלא במקום סכנה. ורבי יוסי לא הוה במקום סכנה פי' במקום לסטים ודהשיב לו שמא יפסיקו בי עוברי דרכים ולא השיב שמא יהרגוני לסטים. ונראה לי כפ"ה תפלה קצרה דהכא היינו הביננו. ואע"ג דלייט עלה אביי *אמאן דמתפלל הביננו. היינו דוקא בעיר אבל בשדה מותר. והא דאמרי' לקמן מאי איכא בין הביננו לתפל' קצרה. הכי קאמר בין תפלה קצרה דאמר בפ' תפלת השחר (דף כט:) כגון צרכי עמך וכו'. אבל ודאי תפלה קצרה דהכא ל"ל הביננו:

ועונין יהא שמיה הגדול מבורך. מכאן יש לסתור מה שפירש במחזור ויטרי יהא שמיה רבא שזו תפלה שאנו מתפללין שימלא שמו כדכתיב (שמות יז) כי יד על כס יה שלא יהא שמו שלם וכסאו שלם עד שימחה זרעו של עמלק. ופירושו כך יהא שמי"ה שם יה רבא כלומר שאנו מתפללין שיהא שמו גדול ושלם. ומבורך לעולם הוי תפלה אחרת כלומר ומבורך לעה"ב. וזה לא נראה מדקאמ' הכא יהא שמיה הגדול מבורך משמע דתפלה אחת היא ואינו רוצה לומר שיהא שמו גדול ושלם אלא יהא שמו הגדול מבורך. וגם מה שאומרים העולם לכך אומרי' קדיש בלשון ארמי' לפי שתפלה נאה ושבח גדול היא על כן נתקן בלשון תרגו' *שלא יבינו המלאכים ויהיו מתקנאין בנו. וזה אינו נראה שהרי כמה תפלות יפות שהם בלשון עברי. אלא נראה כדאמרינן בסוף סוטה (ד' מט.) אין העולם מתקיים אלא אקדושא דסדרא ואיהא שמיה רבא דבתר אגדתא. שהיו רגילין לומר קדיש אחר הדרשה ושם היו עמי הארצות ולא היו מבינין כולם לשון הקדש. לכך תקנוהו בלשון תרגום שהיו הכל מבינים שזה היה לשונם:

במקומן

עין משפט נר מצוה

ז א טור וש"ע א"ח סימן א סעיף ב ג

ח ב טור א"ח סימן נו

ט ג מיי' פ"ה מה' תפלה הלכה ו' ופי"ב מה' רוצח ושמירת נפש הלכה ו סמג עשין יט ועשין עט טוש"ע א"ח סי' נ סעיף ו

[ג' רש"ל. ורש"א גר' א"כ]

גי' הרא"ש כי היכא דאיכא

ירמיה כה

גי' הרא"ש א"ר שמואל בר נחמ'

רש"ל

בר"ף ל"ג

[לקמן כט. וע"ש תוס' ד"ה לייט]

רש"א יפסיקוני

קול הברה [ועיין תוס' סנהדרין מח. ד"ה בת קול]

ג' רש"א שמו

[כדאי' שבת יב: וסוטה לג.]

עין משפט נר מצוה

[מי שמתו יג:]

י

א מיי' פרק יג מהלכות אבילות הל' ט סמג עשין ב טור ושו"ע י"ד סימן שדמ סעיף יז שייך לעיל

[וע' תוס' סנהד' עז. ד"ה אחרי']

במקומן חיישינן. פירוש שידוע שרגילין שם המזיקין והשיא דלעיל דבתרי ופריצי ליכא משום מזיקין איירי בסתם שאין רגילין:

אין אומרים בפני המת אלא דבריו של מת. ופסק רב אלפס* משום רב האי דוקא דברי תורה אבל דברים דעלמא לית לן בה ודוקא בארבע אמות שלו:

רוח צפונית מנשבת. פי' לבדה דהא אמרי' בפרק לא יחפור (ב"ב דף כה.) שהיא מנשבת עם כל אחד ואחד:

*__ואתא__ אידו ואמר כחצות. ואם תאמר מ"מ לימא בחצות כמו שאמרו לו מן השמים דהא אמת אמרו לו וי"ל שלא רצה לומר להם דבר שלא היה יכול להראות ולהוכיח אם ישאלו לו:

אין הבור מתמלא מחוליתו. פירש רש"י אם יחפור ויחזור בו עפרו לא יהא מלא *ותימה דאין הנדון דומה לראיה שהרי לא היה אומר להם אלא ליטול מן העשירים וליתן לעניים ואם היה מלוה ליטול מן העניים ולחזור וליתן להם אז היה דומה למשל. ומפרש ר"ת מחוליתו מנביעתו כלומר אין הבור מתמלא מן המים הנובעים בו ובתוספתא יש אין הבור מתמלא מחוליתו אלא אם כן מושכין לו מים מצד אחר ור"י פירש שאם תחפור מצד זה ותניח מצד אחר לא תמלא שמה שנותן כאן חסר כאן כמו כן מה שנוטל מן העשירים יתחסר מן העשירים:

בניהו

תורה אור

בחדתי ותיפוק ליה משום מזיקין בתרי אי בתרתי חשד נמי ליכא בתרי ופריצי מפני המפולת ותיפוק ליה משום חשד ומזיקין בתרי וכשרי מפני המזיקין ותיפוק ליה מפני חשד ומפולת בחורבה חדתי ובתרי וכשרי אי בתרי מזיקין נמי ליכא במקומן חיישינן ואי בעית אימא לעולם בחד ובחורבה חדתי דקאי בדברא דהתם משום חשד ליכא דהא אשה בדברא לא שכיח' ומשום מזיקין איכא: *ת"ר ארבע משמרות הוי *הלילה דברי רבי רבי נתן אומר שלש מ"ט דר' נתן דכתיב °ויבא גדעון ומאה איש אשר אתו בקצה המחנה ראש האשמורת התיכונה תנא אין תיכונה אלא שיש לפניה ולאחריה ורבי מאי תיכונה אחת מן התיכונה שבתיכונות ור' נתן מי כתיב תיכונה שבתיכונות תיכונה כתיב מ"ט דרבי אמר ר' זריקא אמר רבי אמי אמר ר' יהושע בן לוי כתוב אחד אומר °חצות לילה אקום להודות לך על משפטי צדקך וכתוב אחד אומר °קדמו עיני אשמורות הא כיצד ארבע משמרות הוי הלילה ור' נתן סבר לה כרבי יהושע *דתנן רבי יהושע אומר עד שלש שעות שכן דרך מלכים לעמוד בשלש שעות שית דליליא ותרתי דיממא הוו להו שתי משמרות רב אשי אמר משמרה ופלגא נמי משמרות קרו להו: ואמר רבי זריקא אמר רבי אמי אמר רבי יהושע בן לוי [א]אין *אומרין בפני המת אלא דבריו של מת אמר רבי אבא בר כהנא לא אמרן אלא בדברי תורה אבל מילי דעלמא לית לן בה ואיכא דאמרי אמר רבי אבא בר כהנא לא אמרן אלא [אפי'] בדברי תורה וכ"ש מילי דעלמא: ודוד בפלגא דליליא הוה קאי מאורתא הוה קאי דכתיב °קדמתי בנשף ואשועה ומאי דהאי נשף אורתא הוא דכתיב °בנשף בערב יום באישון לילה ואפילה אמר רבי אושעיא אמר רבי אחא הכי קאמר (דוד) מעולם לא עבר עלי חצות לילה בשינה רבי זירא אומר עד חצות לילה היה מתנמנם *כסוס מכאן אילך היה מתגבר כארי רב אשי אמר עד חצות לילה היה עוסק בדברי תורה מכאן ואילך בשירות ותשבחות ונשף אורתא הוא הא נשף צפרא הוא דכתיב °ויכם דוד מהנשף ועד הערב למחרתם מאי לאו מצפרא ועד לילה לא מאורתא ועד אורתא אי הכי לכתוב מהנשף ועד הנשף או מהערב ועד הערב אלא אמר רבא תרי נשפי הוו נשף ליליא ואתי יממא נשף יממא ואתי ליליא ודוד מי הוה ידע פלגא דליליא אימת השתא משה רבינו לא הוה ידע דכתיב °כחצות הלילה אני יוצא בתוך מצרים מאי כחצות אילימ' דאמר ליה קודשא בריך הוא כחצות *מי איכא ספיקא קמי שמיא אלא דאמר ליה (למחר) בחצות (כי השתא) ואתא אידו ואמר כחצות אלמא מספקא ליה ודוד הוה ידע דוד סימנא הוה ליה *דאמר רב אחא בר ביזנא א"ר שמעון חסידא כנור היה תלוי למעלה *ממטתו של דוד וכיון שהגיע חצות לילה בא רוח צפונית ונושבת בו ומנגן מאליו מיד היה עומד ועוסק בתורה עד שעלה עמוד השחר כיון שעלה עמוד השחר נכנסו חכמי ישראל אצלו אמרו לו אדונינו המלך עמך ישראל צריכין פרנסה אמר להם לכו והתפרנסו זה מזה אמרו לו אין הקומץ משביע את הארי *ואין הבור מתמלא *מחוליתו אמר להם לכו ופשטו ידיכם בגדוד מיד יועצי' באחיתופל ונמלכין בסנהדרין ושואלין באורים ותומים אמר רב יוסף מאי קראה (דכתיב) °ואחרי אחיתופל בניהו בן יהוידע ואביתר ושר צבא למלך יואב אחיתופל זה יועץ וכן הוא אומר °ועצת אחיתופל אשר יעץ בימים ההם כאשר ישאל (איש) בדבר האלהים

בניהו

שופטים ז — תהלים קיט — שם — שם — משלי ז' — ש"א ל — שמות יא — (ירושלמי גרס כנגד חלונותיו) — ד"ה א כז — שמואל ב טז

[*פי' עפר שע"פ הבור וי"מ מעפר שחופרין מן הבור אינו מתמלא עד שמוסיף בו עפר אחר ערוך ערך חליא]

בחדתי. שנפלה מחדש שהחומה שלה נפלה ועודנה בחזקתה: חשד נמי ליכא. דתנן (במסכת קדושין דף פ:) אבל אשה מתיחדת עם ב' אנשים: בתרי ופריצי. דאמרינן התם לא שנו אלא בכשרים: במקומן חיישינן. במקום שהם מצויין תדיר חיישינן אפלו בתרי: בדברא. בשדה: קדמו עיני אשמורות. אלמא חצות לילה שהיה דוד עומד שתי משמרות יש בהם: ור' נתן. אמר לך האי קדמו עיני אשמורות דקאמר דוד קדמו לשאר מלכים קאמ' שדרכן לעמוד בשלש שעות ביום בתחלת שעה שלישית: שית דליליא. מחצות לילה הוו שש שעות: ותרתי דיממא. שאר מלכים ישנים הוו להו תרתי משמרות של שמונה שעות: אלא לדבר הלכה. אסור לספר לפניו שהכל חייבים לספר בהן והמת דומם והוה ליה לועג לרש חרף עושהו (משלי יז): אבל מילי דעלמא. שאין גנאי למתים בהן לית לן בה: מאורתא. מתחלת הלילה: בנשף בערב יום. בהעריב היום קרוי נשף: ה"ק. קרא דחצות לילה: מעולם לא עבר עלי חצות לילה בשינה. שקודם לכן הייתי עומד: מתנמנם כסוס. עוסק בתורה כשהוא מתנמנם כסוס הזה שאינו נרדם לעולם אלא מתנמנם ונעור תמיד: בשירות ותשבחות. והכי מפרש בהדיא קרא להודות לך וגו': למחרתם. ליום מחרת של הכאתם שם: ה"ג אי הכי לכתוב מהנשף ועד הנשף או מהערב ועד הערב אלא אמר רב אשי תרי נשפי הוו: נשף יממא. קפץ ועלה כמו ליכשף מדוכתיה (מגילה ד' ג.) וכמו האי בוקא דאטמא דשף מדוכתיה טרפה (חולין דף כד.): ואתא אידו ואמר כחצות. לפי שלא היה יודע לכוין השעה ולהעמיד דבריו בשעת המאורע: כנור היה תלוי למעלה ממטתו. ונקביו לצד צפון כיון שהגיע חצות הלילה רוח צפונית מנשבת בו דאמר מר (בב"ב ד' כה.) ארבע רוחות מנשבות בכל יום ויום שש שעות ראשונות של יום מנשבת רוח מזרחית מהלוך החמה ושש אחרונות רוח דרומית ובתחלת הלילה רוח מערבית *ובחצות הלילה רוח צפונית: אין הבור מתמלא מחוליתו. העוקר חוליא מבור כרוי וחוזר ומשליכו לתוכו אינו מתמלא בכך אף כאן אם אין אתה מכין לעניים שבנו מזונות ממקום אחר אין אנו יכולין לפרנסם משל עצמנו: יועצים באחיתופל. איזה הדרך ילכו והיאך יציבו מצב ומשחית ועכשיי מארב מלחמה: ונמלכים בסנהדרין. נוטלין מהם רשות כדי שיתפללו עליהם: ושואלים באורים ותומים. אם יצליחו: ה"ג מאי קראה ואחרי אחיתופל בניהו בן יהוידע ואביתר ושר צבא למלך יואב אחיתופל זה יועץ: בניהו

מסורת הש"ס

תוספתא ברכות פ"א (ירושלמי מוסיף ד אשמורות ביום)

לקמן דף ט:

שמחות פ"ג

[סוכה כו:]

*עיין רש"י יבמות עב. ד"ה עת רצון מלתא היא

גיטין ו:

סנהדרין פ"ק ד' ט"ז:

לקמן דף כט.

because of falling debris'?—[3b] When the ruin is new.[5] But it would be sufficient to say: 'because of demons'?—When there are two people.[6] If there are two people, then there is no suspicion either?—When both are licentious [there is suspicion].—[It states] 'Because of falling debris'. It would be sufficient to say: 'because of suspicion and demons'?—When there are two decent people. [It states] *'Because of demons'*. It would be sufficient to say; 'because of suspicion and falling debris'?—When there are two decent people going into a new ruin. But if there are two, then there is no danger of demons either?—In their haunt there is danger. If you like I can say, indeed the reference is to one man and to a new ruin which was situated in the fields; in which case there is no suspicion, for a woman would not be found in the fields, but the danger of demons does exist.

Our Rabbis taught: The night has four watches. These are the words of Rabbi. R. Nathan says: Three. What is the reason of R. Nathan?—It is written: *So Gideon, and the hundred men that were with him, came into the outermost part of the camp in the beginning of the*
a *middle watch.*[1] And one taught: Under *'middle'* is to be understood only something which is preceded by one and followed by one. And Rabbi?[2]—*'The middle'* means: one of the middle ones. And R. Nathan?—Not 'one of the middle ones' is written, but *'the middle'* is written. What is Rabbi's reason?—R. Zeriḳa, in the name of R. Joshua b. Levi, says: One verse reads, *At midnight do I rise to give thanks unto Thee because of Thy righteous ordinances.*[3] And another verse reads: *Mine eyes forestall the watches.*[4] How is this?[5]—[This is possible only if] the night has four watches. And R. Nathan?—He is of the opinion of R. Joshua, as we have learnt: R. Joshua says: until the third hour, for such is the custom of kings, to rise in the third hour.[6] Six hours of the night and two hours of the day amount to two watches.[7] R. Ashi says: One watch and a half are also spoken of as *'watches'*. (R. Zeriḳa further said, in the name of R. Ammi in the name of R. Joshua b. Levi: One may discuss in the presence of a dead body only things relating to the dead. R. Abba b. Kahana says: This refers only to religious matters,[8] but as for worldly matter there is no harm. Another version is: R. Abba b. Kahana says: This refers *even* to religious matters. How much more so to worldly matters!)

But did David rise at midnight? [Surely] he rose with the evening dusk? For it is written: *I rose with the* neshef *and cried.*[9] And how do you know that this word *neshef* means the evening? It is written: *In the* neshef, *in the evening of the day, in the blackness of night and the*
b *darkness!*[1]—R. Oshaia, in the name of R. Aḥa, replies: David said: Midnight never passed me by in my sleep. R. Zera says: Till midnight he used to slumber like a horse,[2] from thence on he rose with the energy of a lion. R. Ashi says: Till midnight he studied the Torah, from thence on he recited songs and praises. But does *neshef* mean the evening? Surely *neshef* means the morning? For it is written: *And David slew them from the* 'neshef' *to the evening* 'ereb *of the next day,*[3] and does not this mean, from the *'morning dawn'* to the evening?—No. [It means:] from the [one] eventide to the [next] eventide. If so, let him write: From *neshef* to *neshef*, or from *'ereb* to *'ereb*?—Rather, said Raba: There are two kinds of *neshef:* [the morning *neshef*], when the evening disappears [*nashaf*] and the morning arrives,[4] [and the evening *neshef*], when the day disappears [*nashaf*] and the evening arrives.[5]

But did David know the exact time of midnight? Even our teacher Moses did not know it! For it is written: *About midnight I will go out into the midst of Egypt.*[6] Why 'about *midnight*'? Shall we say that the Holy One, blessed be He, said to him: 'About *midnight'?* Can there be any doubt in the mind of God?[7] Hence we must say that God told him 'at *midnight*', and he came and said: 'About *midnight*'. Hence he [Moses] was in doubt; can David then have known it?—David had a sign. For so said R. Aḥa b. Bizana in the name of R. Simeon the Pious: A harp was hanging above David's bed. As soon as midnight arrived, a North wind came and blew upon it and it played of itself. He arose immediately and studied the Torah till the break of dawn. After the break of dawn the wise men of Israel came in to see him and said to him: Our lord, the King, Israel your people require sustenance! He said to them: Let them go out and make a living one from the other.[8] They said to him: A handful cannot satisfy a lion, nor can a pit be filled up
c with its own clods.[1] He said to them: Then go out in troops and attack [the enemy for plunder]. They at once took counsel with Ahithofel and consulted the Sanhedrin and questioned the *Urim* and *Tummim.*[2] R. Joseph says: What verse [may be cited in support of this]? *And after Ahithofel was Jehoiada, the son of Benaiah,*[3] *and Abiathar; and the captain of the King's host was Joab.*[4] *'Ahithofel'*, this was the counsellor. And so it is said: *Now the counsel of Ahithofel, which he counselled in those days, was as if a man inquired of the word*

(5) So that there is no danger of falling debris. (6) The assumption is that where two are together there is no danger of an attack by demons.

a (1) Judg. VII, 19. (2) How does he explain the term *middle?* (3) Ps. CXIX, 62. (4) Ibid. 148. (5) That somebody may rise at *midnight* and still have *two* watches before him, the minimum of the plural *'watches'* being two. (6) V. *infra 9b*. With reference to the morning *Shema*'. (7) Since the day for royal personages begins at eight a.m. that is with the third hour when they rise. David by rising at midnight forestalled them by eight hours, i.e., two watches each having four hours. (8) Lit., 'words of Torah'. It would show disrespect for the dead. (9) Ibid. 147. E.V. *'dawn'*.

b (1) Prov. VII, 9. (2) That has a very light sleep, v. Suk. *26a*. (3) I Sam. XXX, 17. (4) *Neshef* in this case denoting 'dawn'. (5) *Neshef* in this case denoting 'dusk'. (6) Ex. XI, 4. (7) Lit., 'heaven'. (8) Let the rich support the poor.

c (1) We cannot be self-supporting to supply all our needs, any more than a handful can satisfy a lion, or the soil taken out of a pit fill its cavity. (2) The divine oracle of the High Priest's breast-plate. (3) The text here has 'Benaiah, the son of Jehoiada', who is mentioned in II Sam. XX, 23. (4) I Chron. XXVII, 34.

of God.[5] [4a] *'Benaiah the son of Jehoiada'*, this means the Sanhedrin. *'And Abiathar'*,[6] these are the *Urim* and *Tummim*. And so it says: *And Benaiah the son of Jehoiada was over the Kerethi and Pelethi.*[7] Why are they[8] called *'Kerethi'* and *'Pelethi'*? *Kerethi*, because their words are decisive [*korethim*]; *Pelethi*, because they are distinguished [*mufla'im*] through their words. And then comes *'the captain of the King's host Joab'*. R. Isaac b. Adda says: (Some say, R. Isaac the son of Addi says) Which verse?[9] *Awake, my glory; awake, psaltery and harp; I will awake the dawn.*[10]

R. Zera says:[11] Moses certainly knew and David, too, knew [the exact time of midnight]. Since David knew, why did he need the harp? That he might wake from his sleep. Since Moses knew, why did he say 'about *midnight*'?—Moses thought that the astrologers of Pharaoh might make a mistake, and then they would say that Moses was a liar. For so a Master said: Let thy tongue acquire the habit of saying, 'I know not', lest thou be led to falsehoods [lying]. R. Ashi says: It[12] was at midnight of the night of the thirteenth passing into the fourteenth [of Nisan], and thus said Moses to Israel: The Holy One, blessed be He, said: Tomorrow
a [at the hour] *like*[1] the midnight of to-night, I will go out into the midst of Egypt.

A prayer of David . . . Keep my soul, for I am pious.[2] Levi and R. Isaac:[3] The one says, Thus spoke David before the Holy One, blessed be He; Master of the world, am I not pious? All the kings of the East and the West sleep to the third hour [of the day], but I, *at midnight I rise to give thanks unto Thee.*[4] The other one says: Thus spoke David before the Holy One, blessed be He: Master of the world, am I not pious? All the kings of the East and the West sit with all their pomp among their company, whereas my hands are soiled with the blood [of menstruation], with the foetus and the placenta, in order to declare a woman clean for her husband.[5] And what is more, in all that I do I consult my teacher, Mephibosheth, and I say to him: My teacher Mephibosheth, is my decision right? Did I correctly convict, correctly acquit, correctly declare clean, correctly declare unclean? And I am not ashamed [to ask]. R. Joshua, the son of R. Iddi, says: Which verse [may be cited in support]? *And I recite Thy testimonies before kings and am not ashamed.*[6] A Tanna taught: His name was not Mephibosheth. And why then was he called Mephibosheth? Because he humiliated[7] David in the *Halachah*. Therefore was David worthy of the privilege that Kileab[8] should issue from him. R. Joḥanan said: His name was not Kileab but Daniel. Why then was he called Kileab? Because he humiliated [*maklim*] Mephibosheth [*ab*][9] in the *Halachah*. And concerning him Solomon said in his wisdom: *My son, if thy heart be wise, my heart will be glad, even mine.*[10] And he said further: *My son, be wise, and make my heart glad, that I may answer him that taunteth me.*[11]

But how could David call himself pious? It is not written: *I am*
b *not sure* [lule] *to see the good reward of the Lord in the land of the living;*[1] and a Tanna taught in the name of R. Jose: Why are there dots upon the world *'lule'*?[2] David spoke before the Holy One, blessed be He: 'Master of the world, I am sure that you will pay a good reward to the righteous in the world to come, but I do not know whether I shall have a share in it'?[3] [He was afraid that] some sin might cause [his exclusion].[4] This conforms to the following saying of R. Jacob b. Iddi. For R. Jacob b. Iddi pointed to a contradiction. One verse reads: *And behold, I am with thee, and will keep thee whithersoever thou goest,*[5] and the other verse reads: *Then Jacob was greatly afraid!*[6] [The answer is that] he thought that some sin might cause [God's promise not to be fulfilled]. Similarly it has been taught: *Till Thy people pass over, O Lord, till the people pass over that Thou hast gotten.*[7] *'Till Thy people pass over, O Lord'*: this is the first entry [into the Land]. *'Till the people pass over that Thou hast gotten'*: this is the second entry. Hence the Sages say: The intention was to perform a miracle for Israel[8] in the days of Ezra, even as it was performed for them in the days of Joshua bin Nun,[9] but sin caused [the miracle to be withheld].[10]

THE SAGES SAY: UNTIL MIDNIGHT. Whose view did the Sages adopt?[11] If it is R. Eliezer's view, then let them express themselves in the same way as R. Eliezer? [4b] If it is R. Gamaliel's view, let

(5) II Sam. XVI, 23. (6) He was the High Priest of David. (7) II Sam. XX, 23. (8) The Sanhedrin (Rashi). The Tosafists, however, refer this to the *Urim* and *Tummim*. (9) May be cited in support of the story of David's harp. (10) Ps. LVII 9. (11) Here the Gemara resumes the discussion of the question raised above as to how it is possible that David knew something which Moses did not know. (12) The incident of Ex. XI, 4.

a (1) The particle *ka* being rendered 'like' and not 'about'. (2) Ps. LXXXVI, 1-2. (3) Offer different homiletical interpretations. (4) Ibid. CXIX, 62. (5) The restrictions of Lev. XII, 2ff do not apply to all cases of abortion nor is all discharge treated as menstrual, and David is represented as occupying himself with deciding such questions instead of with feasting. MS.M. omits 'blood'. (6) Ps. CXIX, 46. (7) The homiletical interpretation of the name is, *Out of my mouth humiliation*. (8) Cf. II Sam. III, 3. (9) Lit., 'father', a teacher. (10) Prov. XXIII, 15. (11) Ibid. XXVII, 11.

b (1) Ps. XXVII, 13. (2) The dots are interpreted as meaning that he was not quite sure. (3) Hence you see that he was not so sure of his piety. (4) This is the reply to the question. David was quite sure of his general pious character, but he feared that his sins might exclude him from the reward etc. (5) Gen. XXVIII, 15. (6) Ibid. XXXII, 8. The contradiction lies in the fact that Jacob was afraid in spite of having God's promise. (7) Ex. XV, 16. (8) Lit. 'the Israelites were worthy to have a miracle performed for them'. (9) When they entered victoriously. (10) And they entered only as subjects of Cyrus. (11) According to the Gemara, R. Eliezer and R. Gamaliel differ in the interpretation of the Bible words, *'And when thou liest down'*. R. Eliezer explains them to mean, when you *go to bed;* hence he says that the time expires at the end of the first watch. R. Gamaliel understands them to mean, when you *sleep;* hence he fixes the whole night as the time of the recital.

תורה אור

בניהו בן יהוידע זה סנהדרין ואביתר אלו אורים ותומים וכן הוא אומר °ובניהו בן יהוידע על הכרתי ועל הפלתי ולמה נקרא שמם כרתי ופלתי כרתי שכורתים דבריהם פלתי שמופלאים בדבריהם* ואחר כך שר צבא למלך יואב אמר רב יצחק בר אדא ואמרי לה אמר רב יצחק בריה דרב אידי מאי קראה °עורה כבודי עורה הנבל וכנור אעירה שחר. ר' זירא אמר משה לעולם הוה ידע ודוד נמי הוה ידע וכיון דדוד הוה ידע כנור למה ליה לאתעורי משנתיה וכיון דמשה הוה ידע למה ליה למימר כחצות משה קסבר שמא יטעו אצטגניני פרעה ויאמרו משה בדאי הוא דאמר מר *למד לשונך לומר איני יודע שמא תתבדה ותאחז רב אשי אמר בפלגא אורתא דתליסר נגהי ארבסר הוה קאי והכי קאמר משה לישראל אמר הקב"ה למחר *כחצות הלילה כי האידנא אני יוצא בתוך מצרים: °לדוד שמרה נפשי כי חסיד אני לוי ור' יצחק חד אמר כך אמר דוד לפני הקדוש ברוך הוא רבונו של עולם לא חסיד אני שכל מלכי מזרח ומערב ישנים עד שלש שעות. ואני °חצות לילה אקום להודות לך ואידך כך אמר דוד לפני הקדוש ברוך הוא רבונו של עולם לא חסיד אני שכל מלכי מזרח ומערב יושבים אגודות אגודות בכבודם ואני ידי מלוכלכות בדם ובשפיר ובשליא כדי לטהר אשה לבעלה ולא עוד אלא כל מה שאני עושה אני נמלך במפיבשת רבי ואומר לו מפיבשת רבי יפה דנתי יפה חייבתי יפה זכיתי יפה טהרתי יפה טמאתי ולא בשתי אמר ר' יהושע בריה דרב אידי מאי קראה °ואדברה בעדותיך נגד מלכים ולא אבוש תנא לא מפיבשת שמו אלא איש *בשת שמו ולמה נקרא שמו מפיבשת שהיה מבייש פני דוד בהלכה לפיכך זכה דוד ויצא ממנו כלאב ואמר ר' יוחנן לא כלאב שמו אלא דניאל שמו ולמה נקרא שמו כלאב שהיה מכלים פני מפיבשת בהלכה ועליו אמר שלמה בחכמתו °בני אם חכם לבך ישמח לבי גם אני ואומר °חכם בני ושמח לבי ואשיבה חורפי דבר ודוד מי קרי לנפשי' חסיד והכתיב °לולא האמנתי לראות בטוב ה' בארץ חיים ותנא משמיה דרבי יוסי למה נקוד על לולא אמר דוד לפני הקב"ה רבונו של עולם מובטח אני בך שאתה משלם שכר טוב לצדיקים לעתיד לבא אבל איני יודע אם יש לי חלק בינידם אם לאו שמא יגרום החטא *כדר' יעקב בר אידי דר' יעקב בר אידי רמי כתיב °והנה אנכי עמך ושמרתיך בכל אשר תלך וכתיב °ויירא יעקב מאד אמר שמא יגרום החטא *כדתניא °עד יעבור עמך ה' עד יעבור עם זו קנית עד יעבור עמך ה' זו ביאה ראשונה עד יעבור עם זו קנית זו ביאה שניה מכאן אמרו חכמים ראוים היו ישראל ליעשות להם נס בימי עזרא כדרך שנעשה להם בימי יהושע בן נון אלא שגרם החטא: וחכמים אומרים עד חצות. חכמים כמאן סבירא להו אי כר' אליעזר סבירא להו לימרו כר' אליעזר ואי

שמואל ב' כ' · תהלי' נז · שם פו · שם · שם קיט · שם · משלי כג כז · תהלי' כז · בראשית כח · שם לב · שמות טו

רש"י

בניהו בן יהוידע זה סנהדרין. שהיה אב בית דין: וכן הוא אומר ובניהו בן יהוידע על הכרתי ועל הפלתי. ראשון וקודם להם שבתחילה נוטלים רשות ואחר כך שואלים אם יצליחו: ואביתר אלו אורים ותומים. שכל ימי דוד היה נשאל באביתר עד מלחמות אבשלום שנשאל אביתר ולא עלתה לו ונשאל לצדוק ועלתה לו כדאמרינן בסדר עולם ונסתלק אז מן הכהונה: שכורתים את דבריהם. שאומרים דברים קצובים וגמורים שלא יפחתו ולא יוסיפו: שר צבא למלך יואב. להוליך אנשי המלחמה: מאי קראה. דכנור היה תלוי למעלה ממטתו ומעוררו: עורה כבודי. אל תתכבדי בשינה כשאר מלכים: אעירה שחר. שאר מלכים השחר מעוררן ואני אעורר את השחר: שמא יטעו אצטגניני פרעה. אם אני יודע לכוין השעה הם אינם יודעים לכוין השעה וקודם שיגיע חצות יהו סבורים שהגיע ועדיין לא באה המכה ויאמרו משה בדאי הוא הלכך טוב לאחוז לשון איני יודע: דאמר מר. במסכת דרך ארץ: ותאחז. תהא נאחז ונכשל בדבריך: תליסר נגהי ארבסר. ליל שעבר שלשה עשר ולמחרת יגיע ארבעה עשר: ידי מלוכלכות בדם. שהנשים מראות לו דם נדה אם טמא אם טהור שיש מראות דם טהור באשה (נדה יט:): ובשפיר. הוא עור הולד שהעלמות והגידים והבשר נבראים בתוכו. ויש שפיר שהאשה יושבת עליו ימי טומאה וימי טהרה ואיזה זה המרוקם ובמסכת נדה (דף כד:) מפרש לה. ויש שפיר מלא מים ודם שאינו חשוב ולד ליישב עליו טומאת יולדת וימי טהרה: ובשליא. דתנן (שם כו.) אין שליא בלא ולד והוא כמין כיס שהולד שוכב בתוכה וקורין ויסטי"דור בלע"ז ותניא (שם) אין שליא פחותה מטפח ותחלתה כחוט של ערב וסופה כתורמוס והיו מביאין אותה לפניו לראות אם יש בה כשיעור ואם עשויה כדת שליא שנחזיקנה שהיה ולד בתוכה וטמאה ותשב עליו ימי טומאה וטהרה אם לאו: זכיתי וחייבתי. שייך בדיני ממונות ודיני נפשות: טמאתי וטהרתי. בהלכות טומאה וטהרה: מפיבשת. [מפי בושת] בדברי הלכה היוצאין מפיו היה בושת לדוד. שפעמים שהיה טועה והוא אומר לו טעית: לפיכך. בזכות שהיה דוד מקטין עצמו זכה ויצא ממנו כלאב: אלא דניאל שמו. במקום אחד אומר (שמואל ב ג) ומשנהו כלאב לאביגיל אשת נבל וגו' ובמקום אחר אומר והשני דניאל לאביגיל בדברי הימים (א' ג'): שהיה מכלים פני מפיבושת. כל אב מכלים את הרב שהיה אב בהוראות: לולא האמנתי לראות בטוב ה'. כבר עדודי מילאתך כמו שנאמר כי גרשוני היום מהסתפח בנחלת ה' לאמר לך עבוד וכו' (שמואל א כו): נקוד על לולא. לדרוש את הנקודה שהיא ממעטת את משמעות הכתוב לומר שלא דבר ברור היה לו לראות בטוב ה'. לולא לשון אם לא כמו לולי אלהי אבי וגו' היה לי (בראשית לא): שמא יגרום החטא. תירוצא הוא לעולם מוחזק בידו שהוא חסיד וזה שספק בידו אם יראה בטוב ה' לפי שהיה ירא שמא יחטא ויגרום החטא מלראות בטוב: ויירא יעקב. שמא אחר הבטחה חטאתי וכדתניא שהחטא גורם שאין ההבטחה מתקיימת: ביאה ראשונה. שבאו בימי יהושע: ביאה שניה. כשעלו מגלות בבל בימי עזרא: ראויים היו ליעשות להם נס. לבוא ביד רמה: אלא שגרם החטא. ולא הלכו אלא ברשות כורש וכל ימי מלכי פרס כשנשתעבדו להם לכורש ולאחשורוש ולדריוש האחרון: חכמים כמאן סבירא להו. במשמעות בשכבך האמור בתורה: אי כרבי אליעזר ס"ל. דאית ליה בשכבך כל זמן שבני אדם עוסקין לילך ולשכב זה מקדים וזה מאחר: לימרו כרבי אליעזר. דאמר סוף האשמורה הראשונה דודאי כל שדעתו לישן כבר שכב וישן: ואי

תוספות

בניהו זה סנהדרין. מסברא אומר כן. אביתר אלו אורים ותומים וכן הוא אומר ובניהו בן יהוידע על הכרתי ועל הפלתי כלומר היה קודם להם אם כן אורים ותומים היו אחר בניהו. א"כ אביתר שהזכיר אחר בניהו היינו אורים ותומים כך פירש רש"י. ותימה לפירושו פשיטא דאביתר כהן היה בימי דוד שלא היה כהן אחר שכולם נהרגו בנוב עיר הכהנים ולמה צריך ראיה עליה. ועוד לגירסת הקונטרס בניהו בן יהוידע אין זה הפסוק בשום מקום. לכך מפרש רבינו תם כדאיתא בדברי הימים *אחרי אחיתופל יהוידע בן בניהו זה סנהדרין וכן הוא אומר ובניהו בן יהוידע על הכרתי ועל הפלתי ופירש רבינו תם דכרתי ופלתי היינו סנהדרין שכורתין דבריהם לאמתן ופלתי שמופלאים בהוראה כמו מופלא שבבית דין. ואם תאמר היכי פשיט יהוידע בן בניהו מבניהו בן יהוידע. ויש לומר דמסתמא ממלא מקום אביו היה וכי היכי דאביו היה מסנהדרין גם הוא *היה מהם: וקורא

[וכ"ה בערוך ערך אחר]

[וע' בתוספות סנהדרין טז: ד"ה ואחרי]

מסורת הש"ס

ס"א ולמה נקרא שמם אורים שמאירין את דבריהם תומי' שמשלימי' את דבריהם ועיין ביומא ע"ג:

מס' דרך ארץ זוטא פ"ג:

פי' שדבר עמו בחלות ואמר למחר כי השתא ולפ"ז לא קשה קושי' התוספת לעיל

עיין בפ' הערל דף עט. בתוספ' דגרס ר"ת אלא אים בעל שמו וע"ש

חלק ד' לח: ע"ש

ג"ז שם סוטה ד' לו.

ואי כרבן גמליאל סבירא להו לימרו כרבן גמליאל לעולם כרבן גמליאל סבירא להו והא דקא אמרי עד חצות כדי להרחיק את האדם מן העבירה כדתניא חכמים עשו סייג לדבריהם [א]כדי שלא יהא אדם בא מן השדה בערב ואומר אלך לביתי ואוכל קימעא ואשתה קימעא ואישן קימעא ואחר כך אקרא קריאת שמע ואתפלל וחוטפתו שינה ונמצא ישן כל הלילה אבל אדם בא מן השדה בערב נכנס לבית הכנסת אם רגיל לקרות קורא ואם רגיל לשנות שונה וקורא קריאת שמע ומתפלל ואוכל פתו ומברך *וכל העובר על דברי חכמים חייב מיתה מאי שנא בכל דוכתא דלא קתני חייב מיתה ומאי שנא הכא דקתני חייב מיתה אי בעית אימא משום דאיכא אונס שינה ואי בעית אימא לאפוקי ממאן דאמר *תפלת ערבית רשות קא משמע לן דחובה: אמר מר קורא קריאת שמע ומתפלל מסייע ליה לרבי יוחנן *דאמר רבי יוחנן [ב]איזהו בן העולם הבא זה הסומך גאולה לתפלה של ערבית: רבי יהושע בן לוי אומר תפלות באמצע תקנום במאי קא מפלגי *אי בעית אימא קרא אי בעית אימא סברא אי בעית אימא סברא דרבי יוחנן סבר גאולה מאורתא נמי הוי אלא גאולה מעלייתא לא הויא אלא עד צפרא ור' יהושע בן לוי סבר כיון דלא הויא אלא מצפרא לא הוי גאולה מעלייתא ואי בעית אימא קרא ושניהם מקרא אחד דרשו דכתיב °בשכבך ובקומך רבי יוחנן סבר מקיש שכיבה לקימה מה קימה קריאת שמע ואחר כך תפלה אף שכיבה נמי קריאת שמע ואחר כך תפלה רבי יהושע בן לוי סבר מקיש שכיבה לקימה מה קימה קריאת שמע סמוך למטתו אף שכיבה נמי קריאת שמע סמוך למטתו מתיב מר בריה דרבינא *בערב מברך שתים לפניה ושתים לאחריה ואי אמרת בעי לסמוך הא לא קא סמך גאולה לתפלה דהא בעי למימר השכיבנו אמרי כיון דתקינו רבנן השכיבנו כגאולה אריכתא דמיא דאי לא תימא הכי שחרית היכי מצי סמיך והא *אמר ר' יוחנן [ג]בתחלה אומר °ה' שפתי תפתח ולבסוף [ד]הוא אומר °יהיו לרצון אמרי פי אלא התם כיון דתקינו רבנן למימר ה' שפתי תפתח כתפלה אריכתא דמיא הכא נמי כיון דתקינו רבנן למימר השכיבנו כגאולה אריכתא דמיא: אמר רבי אלעזר *אמר רבי אבינא [ה]כל האומר °תהלה לדוד בכל יום ג' פעמים מובטח לו שהוא בן העולם הבא מאי טעמא אילימא משום דאתיא באל"ף בי"ת נימא °אשרי תמימי דרך דאתיא בתמניא *אפין אלא משום דאית ביה °פותח את ידך נימא *הלל הגדול דכתיב ביה °נותן לחם לכל בשר אלא משום דאית ביה תרתי אמר רבי יוחנן מפני מה לא נאמרה נו"ן באשרי מפני שיש בה מפלתן של שונאי ישראל דכתיב °נפלה לא תוסיף קום בתולת ישראל במערבא מתרצי לה הכי נפלה ולא תוסיף לנפול עוד קום בתולת ישראל אמר רב נחמן בר יצחק אפילו הכי חזר דוד וסמכן ברוח הקודש שנ' °סומך ה' לכל הנופלים: אמר רבי אלעזר בר אבינא גדול מה שנאמר במיכאל יותר ממה שנאמר בגבריאל דאלו במיכאל כתיב °ויעף אלי אחד מן השרפים ואלו גבי גבריאל כתיב °והאיש גבריאל אשר ראיתי בחזון בתחלה מועף ביעף וגו' מאי משמע דהאי אחד מיכאל הוא אמר רבי יוחנן אתיא אחד אחד כתיב הכא ויעף אלי אחד מן השרפים וכתיב התם °והנה מיכאל אחד (מן) השרים הראשונים בא לעזרני תנא מיכאל באחת גבריאל בשתים אליהו בארבע ומלאך המות בשמנה ובשעת המגפה באחת: אמר רבי יהושע בן לוי אף על פי שקרא אדם קריאת שמע בבית הכנסת [ו]מצוה לקרות על מטתו א"ר *יוסי מאי קראה °רגזו ואל תחטאו אמרו בלבבכם על משכבכם ודומו סלה ואמר רב נחמן

אם

ואי כרבן גמליאל סבירא להו. דמשמע ליה בשכבך כל זמן שבני אדם שוכבים ויש בכלל הזה כל הלילה: לימרו כרבן גמליאל. עד עמוד השחר: מן העבירה. שמא יסמוך על שהות שיש לו כדתניא: קימעא. מעט: משום אונס שינה. התוקפתו לעבור על דברי חכמים החקקו להזהירו יותר: ממאן דאמר. לקמן בפרק תפלת השחר (ד' כז:): אמר מר קורא קריאת שמע. של ערבית תחלה ואחר כך מתפלל: מסייע ליה לרבי יוחנן. דאמר ערבי' נמי קריאת שמע ואחר כך תפלה כדי שיסמוך גאולה לתפלה. ודלא כרבי יהושע בן לוי דאמר תפלה ואחר כך קריאת שמע: זה הסומך. וכל שכן דשחרית דעיקר גאולת מצרים בשחרית הית' כדכתיב ממחר' הפסח יצאו בני ישראל (במדבר לג) וסמיכת גאולה לתפלה רמזה דוד בספר תהלים דכתיב ה' צורי וגואלי (תהלים יט) וסמיך ליה יענך ה' ביום צרה (שם כ) ואמרינן בברכות ירושלמי מי שאינו סומך גאולה לתפלה למה הוא דומה לאוהבו של מלך שבא ודפק על פתחו של מלך יצא המלך ומצאו שהפליג אף הוא הפליג. אלא יהיה אדם מקרב להקדוש ברוך הוא אליו ומרצהו בתשבחות וקלוסין של יציאת מצרים והוא מתקרב אליו ובעודו קרוב אליו יש לו לתבוע צרכיו: באמצע תקנום. בין שני קריאת שמע תקנו כל תפלות של יום דקא סבר תפלת ערבית קודמת לקריאת שמע: גאולה. מאורתא לא הוי הלכך גאולה דאורתא לא חשיבא לאהדורי עלה סמיכת תפלה: מה קימה קריאת שמע ואחר כך תפלה. דבשחרית כולהו מודו דבעי מסמך: שלש פעמים. כנגד שלש תפלות: דאית ביה תרתי. דאתי באלף בי"ת ויש בו שבח הכנת מזון לכל חי: אפילו הכי. אף על פי שהפסיק נו"ן מפני נפילה שבה ולא אבה לרומזה חזר ורמז סמיכת הנפילה תיכף לה: ויעף אלי. בפריחה אחת ולא הרגיע בינתים: מועף ביעף. שתי פריחות: באחת. בפריחה אחת: אמרו בלבבכם. אמרו מה שכתוב על לבבך (דברים ו): על משכבכם. שנאמר ובשכבך (שם) ודומו בשינה אחרי כן: ואם

וקורא קריאת שמע ומתפלל. מכאן משמע שמשעה שהגיע זמן קריאת שמע של לילה שאין לו לאכול סעודה עד שיקרא קריאת שמע ויתפלל ערבית:

אמר רבי יוחנן איזהו בן העולם הבא וכו'. ואנו שאומרים יראו עינינו ופסוקים אחרים אחר השכיבנו נראה הואיל ותקינו להו רבנן ה"ל כגאולה אריכתא דתקינו לומר זה שבתוך כך יתפלל חברו גם הוא ולא ילך מבה"כ עד שיגמור כל אחד תפלתו. וגם יש באותם פסוקים שמנה עשרה אזכרות כנגד י"ח ברכות דשמונה עשרה. ואגב שתקנו לומר אותם פסוקים תקנו לומר חתימה של יראו עינינו. והלכה כרבי יוחנן דברייתא מסייע ליה וכן פוסק ה"ג ואם כן יש ליזהר שלא לספר בין גאולה דערבית לי"ח. ומיהו בסדר רב עמרם פירש מה שאנו אומרים קדיש בין גאולה לתפלת ערבית לאשמועינן דלא בעינן מסמך גאולה דערבית לתפלה משום דתפלת ערבית רשות. ולא נהירא [דאם כן] רבי יוחנן סבירא ליה תפלת ערבית חובה דפלוגתא היא *דרב ורבי יוחנן והלכה כרבי יוחנן: ונכון להחמיר ולהזהר מלספר בינתים. ואי תימא קשיא הלכתא אהלכתא דקיימא לן תפלת ערבית רשות והכא פסקינן כרבי יוחנן צריך לומר דאפילו אי סובר רבי יוחנן כרב דאמר רשות היא מכל מקום מחייב לסמוך. אם כן גם לנו יש לסמוך:

הא

עין משפט נר מצוה

יא [א]מיי' פ"ו מה' תפלה הלכה ז טור וש"ע א"ח סי' רלה סעי' ב

יב [ב]מיי' פ"ז שם הלכה יח סמג עשין יט טור א"ח סימן רלה וטוש"ע א"ח סי' רלו סעיף ב

יג [ג]מיי' פ"ב שם הלכה ט סמג שם טור וש"ע א"ח סימן קיא סעיף א [לקמן כז: כפי שנדפס שם בלד הגליון וע"ע תוס' שם ד"ה והלכתא]

יד [ד]מיי' וסמג שם טוש"ע א"ח ס' קכב סעיף ב

טו [ה]מיי' פ"ז שם הלכה יב יז יח סמג עשין יט טוש"ע א"ח סי' נא סעי' ז [ורב אלפס פ' אין עומדין דף כו.]

טז [ו]מיי' פ"ו שם הלכה ב טוש"ע א"ח סי' רלט סעי' א

מסורת הש"ס

[עירובין ד"א:]

[לקמן כז: שבת ט:]

לקמן ט:

[יבמות לה: קדושי' לה: ב"ב ח: ט. ע"ז לד: סנהדרי' ל. שבועות דב: ע"ש בתוס' זבחים ב. ז: מנחות ב. יו: עג: חולין קי"מ: תמול' ל.]

לקמן יא:

לקמן ט:

[בע"י וברב אלפס אי' בר אבינא ובזה נכון מאמר הסמוך ול"ל שם וא"כ. אלעזר]

[פסחים קיח]

תורה אור

דברי' ו

תהל' נא

שם יט ו

תהלים קמה

נ"א אלפין

שם קיט קמה

תהלים קלו:

עמוס ה

תהלים קמה

ישעיה ו

דניאל ט

שם י

תהלים ד

נ"ל רב אסי או רב יוסף

them express themselves in the same way as R. Gamaliel?—In reality it is R. Gamaliel's view that they adopted, and their reason for saying, UNTIL MIDNIGHT is to keep a man far from transgression. For so it has been taught: The Sages made a fence for their words so that a man, on returning home from the field in the evening, should not say: I shall go home, eat a little, drink a little, sleep a little, and then I shall recite the *Shema'* and the *Tefillah,* and meanwhile, sleep may overpower him, and as a result he will sleep the whole night. Rather should a man, when returning home from the field in the evening, go to the synagogue. If he is used to read the Bible, let him read the Bible, and if he is used to repeat the Mishnah, let him repeat the Mishnah, and then let him recite the *Shema'* and say the *Tefillah,* [go home] and eat his meal and say the Grace. And whosoever transgresses the words of the Sages deserves to die. Why this difference that, in other cases, they do not say 'he deserves to die', and here they do say 'he deserves to die'?—If you wish, I can say because here there is danger of sleep overpowering him. Or, if you wish, I can say because they want to exclude the opinion of those who say that the evening
a prayer is only voluntary.[1] Therefore they teach us that it is obligatory.

The Master said:[2] 'Let him recite *Shema'* and say the *Tefillah*'. This accords with the view of R. Johanan.[3] For R. Johanan says: Who inherits the world to come? The one who follows the *Ge'ullah*[4] immediately with the evening *Tefillah.* R. Joshua b. Levi says: The *Tefilloth* were arranged to be said in the middle.[5] What is the ground of their difference?—If you like, I can say it is [the interpretation of] a verse, and if you like, I can say that they reason differently. For R. Johanan argues: Though the complete deliverance from Egypt took place in the morning time only,[6] there was
b also some kind of deliverance in the evening;[1] whereas R. Joshua b. Levi argues that since the real deliverance happened in the morning [that of the evening] was no proper deliverance.[2] 'Or if you like, I can say it is [the interpretation of] a verse'. And both interpret one and the same verse, [viz.,] *When thou liest down and when thou risest up.*[3] R. Johanan argues: There is here an analogy between lying down and rising. Just as [at the time of] rising, recital of *Shema'* precedes *Tefillah,* so also [at the time of] lying down, recital of *Shema'* precedes *Tefillah.* R. Joshua b. Levi argues [differently]: There is here an analogy between lying down and rising. Just as [at the time of] rising, the recital of *Shema'* is next to [rising from] bed,[4] so also [at the time of] lying down, recital of *Shema'* must be next to [getting into] bed.[5]

Mar b. Rabina raised an objection. In the evening, two benedictions precede and two benedictions follow the *Shema'*.[6] Now, if you say he has to join *Ge'ullah* with *Tefillah,* behold he does not do so, for he has to say [in between], 'Let us rest'?[7]—I reply: Since the Rabbis ordained the benediction, 'Let us rest', it is as if it were a long *Ge'ullah.* For, if you do not admit that, how can he join in the morning, seeing that R. Johanan says: In the beginning [of the *Tefillah*] one has to say: *O Lord, open Thou my lips* [etc.],[8] and at the end one has to say: *Let the words of my mouth be acceptable?*[9] [The only explanation] there [is that] since the Rabbis ordained that *O Lord, open Thou my lips* should be said, it is like a long *Tefillah.*[10] Here, too, since the Rabbis ordained that 'Let us rest' should be said, it is like a long *Ge'ullah.*

R. Eleazar b. Abina says: Whoever recites [the psalm] *Praise of David*[11] three times daily, is sure to inherit[12] the world to come. What is the reason? Shall I say it is because it has an alphabetical arrangement? Then let him recite, *Happy are they that are upright*
c *in the way,*[1] which has an eightfold alphabetical arrangement. Again, is it because it contains [the verse], *Thou openest Thy hand [and satisfiest every living thing with favour]?*[2] Then let him recite the great *Hallel,*[3] where it is written: *Who giveth food to all flesh!*[4]—Rather, [the reason is] because it contains both.[5] R. Johanan says: Why is there no *nun* in *Ashre?*[6] Because the fall of Israel's enemies[7] begins with it. For it is written: *Fallen is*[8] *the virgin of Israel, she shall no more rise.*[9] (In the West[10] this verse is thus interpreted: *She is fallen, but she shall no more fall. Rise, O virgin of Israel).* R. Nahman b. Isaac says: Even so, David refers to it by inspiration[11] and promises them an uplifting. For it is written: *The Lord upholdeth all that fall.*[12]

R. Eleazar b. Abina said furthermore: Greater is [the achievement] ascribed to Michael than that ascribed to Gabriel. For of Michael it is written: *Then flew unto me one of the Seraphim,*[13] whereas of Gabriel it is written: *The man Gabriel whom I had seen in the vision at the beginning, being caused to fly in a flight* etc.[14] How do you know that this [word] *'one'* [of the Seraphim] means Michael?—R. Johanan says: By an analogy from [the words] *'one', 'one'.* Here it is written: *Then flew unto me* one *of the Seraphim;* and in another place it is written: *But, lo, Michael,* one *of the chief princes, came to help me.*[15] A Tanna taught: Michael [reaches his goal] in one [flight], Gabriel in two, Elijah in four, and the Angel of Death in eight. In the time of plague, however, [the Angel of Death, too, reaches his goal] in one.

R. Joshua b. Levi says: Though a man has recited the *Shema'* in the synagogue, it is a religious act to recite it again upon his bed. R. Assi says: Which verse [may be cited in support]? *Tremble and sin not; commune with your own heart* upon your bed, *and be still,*

a (1) V. *infra* 27b. (2) In the Baraitha just quoted. (3) That in the evening, too, the *Shema'* has to precede the *Tefillah.* (4) The benediction for the deliverance from Egypt (v. *P.B.* p. 99). It follows the *Shema'* and precedes the *Tefillah.* (5) Between the two *Shema'* recitals. In the morning the *Tefillah* follows, and in the evening it precedes the *Shema'*. (6) As it says, *On the morrow of the Passover the children of Israel went forth* (Num. XXXIII, 3).

b (1) Hence even in the evening *Ge'ullah* must be joined closely to *Tefillah.* (2) Hence in the evening the *Ge'ullah* must not be joined closely to *Tefillah.* (3) Deut. VI, 7. (4) I.e., it is the first prayer said on rising from the bed. (5) I.e., it is the last prayer said before going to bed. (6) V. *infra* 11a. (7) This is the second benediction, to be said in the evening between *Ge'ullah* and *Tefillah,* v. *P.B.* p. 99. The prayer, 'Blessed be the Lord for evermore' that follows the second benediction is a later addition. (8) Ps. LI, 17. This verse said in introduction to the *Tefillah* ought to be considered an interruption. (9) Ps. XIX, 15. (10) I.e., part of the *Tefillah.* (11) I.e., Ps. CXLV. (12) Lit., 'that he is a son of'.

c (1) Ps. CXIX. (2) Ibid. CXLV, 16. (3) I.e., Ibid. CXXXVI. On *Hallel,* v. Glos. (4) Ibid. v. 25. (5) The alphabetical arrangement and the sixteenth verse, dealing with God's merciful provision for all living things. (6) This is Psalm CXLV, which is arranged alphabetically, save that the verse beginning with the letter *nun* (N) is missing. (7) Euphemistic for Israel. (8) Heb. נפלה. (9) Amos V, 2. (10) Palestine. V. *supra* 2b, n. a4. (11) Lit., 'the Holy Spirit'. The meaning is, David knew by inspiration that Amos was going to prophesy the downfall of Israel, and he refers to that verse and prophesies their being raised up again, though their downfall is not mentioned by David. (12) Ps. CXLV, 14. (13) Isa. VI, 6. (14) Dan. IX, 21. The meaning is: Michael covered the distance in one flight, without any stop, whereas Gabriel had to make two flights, resting in between. This is inferred from the fact that the word *fly* occurs twice. (15) Ibid. X, 13.

a *Selah.*[1] R. Naḥman, however, says: [5a] If he is a scholar, then it is not necessary. Abaye says: Even a scholar should recite one verse of supplication, as for instance: *Into Thy hand I commit my spirit. Thou hast redeemed me, O Lord, Thou God of truth.*[2]

R. Levi b. Ḥama says in the name of R. Simeon b. Laḳish: A man should always incite the good impulse [in his soul][3] to fight against the evil impulse. For it is written: *Tremble and sin not.*[4] If he subdues it, well and good. If not, let him study the Torah. For it is written: *'Commune with your own heart'.*[5] If he subdues it, well and good. If not, let him recite the *Shema'*. For it is written: *'Upon your bed'.* If he subdues it, well and good. If not, let him remind himself of the day of death. For it is written: *'And be still, Selah'.*

R. Levi b. Ḥama says further in the name of R. Simeon b. Laḳish: What is the meaning of the verse: *And I will give thee the tables of stone, and the law and the commandment, which I have written that thou mayest teach them?*[6] *'Tables of stone'*: these are the ten commandments; *'the law'*: this is the Pentateuch; *'the commandment'*: this is the Mishnah; *'which I have written'*: these are the Prophets and the Hagiographa; *'that thou mayest teach them'*: this is the Gemara.[7] It teaches [us] that all these things were given to Moses on Sinai.

R. Isaac says: If one recites the *Shema'* upon his bed, it is as though he held a two-edged sword in his hand.[8] For it is said: *Let the high praises of God be in their mouth, and a two-edged sword in*
b *their hand.*[1] How does it indicate this?—Mar Zutra, (some say, R. Ashi) says: [The lesson is] from the preceding verse. For it is written: *Let the saints exult in glory, let them sing for joy upon their beds,*[2] and then it is written: *Let the high praises of God be in their mouth, and a two-edged sword in their hand.* R. Isaac says further: If one recites the *Shema'* upon his bed, the demons keep away from him. For it is said: *And the sons of* reshef[3] *fly* ['uf] *upward.*[4] The word *'uf* refers only to the Torah, as it is written: *Wilt thou cause thine eyes to close* [hata'if][5] *upon it? It is gone.*[6] And *'reshef'* refers only to the demons, as it is said: *The wasting of hunger, and the devouring of the* reshef [*fiery bolt*] *and bitter destruction.*[7] R. Simeon b. Laḳish says: If one studies the Torah, painful sufferings are kept away from him. For it is said: *And the sons of* reshef *fly upward.* The word *'uf* refers only to the Torah, as it is written: *'Wilt thou cause thine eyes to close upon it? It is gone'.* And *'reshef'* refers only to painful sufferings, as it is said: *'The wasting of hunger, and the devouring of the* reshef [*fiery bolt*]. R. Joḥanan said to him: This[8] is known even to school children.[9] For it is said: *And He said: If thou wilt diligently hearken to the voice of the Lord thy God, and wilt do that which is right in His eyes, and wilt give ear to His commandments, and keep all His statutes, I will put none of the diseases upon thee which I have put upon the Egyptians; for I am the Lord that healeth thee.*[10] Rather [should you say]: If one has the opportunity to study the Torah and does not study it, the Holy One, blessed be He, visits him with ugly and painful sufferings which stir him up. For it is said: *I was dumb with silence, I kept silence from the good thing, and my pain was stirred up.*[11] *'The good thing'* refers only to the Torah, as it is said: *For I give you* good *doctrine; forsake ye not My teaching.*[12]

R. Zera (some say, R. Ḥanina b. Papa) says: Come and see how the way of human beings differs from the way of the Holy One, blessed be He. It is the way of human beings that when a
c man sells[1] a valuable object to his fellow, the seller grieves and the buyer rejoices. The Holy One, blessed be He, however, is different. He gave the Torah to Israel and rejoiced. For it is said: *For I give you good doctrine; forsake ye not My teaching.*

Raba (some say, R. Ḥisda) says: If a man sees that painful sufferings visit him, let him examine his conduct. For it is said: *Let us search and try our ways, and return unto the Lord.*[2] If he examines and finds nothing [objectionable], let him attribute it to the neglect of the study of the Torah. For it is said: *Happy is the man whom Thou chastenest, O Lord, and teachest out of Thy law.*[3] If he did attribute it [thus], and still did not find [this to be the cause], let him be sure that these are chastenings of love. For it is said: *For whom the Lord loveth He correcteth.*[4]

Raba, in the name of R. Saḥorah, in the name of R. Huna, says: If the Holy One, blessed be He, is pleased with a man, he crushes him with painful sufferings. For it is said: *And the Lord was pleased with* [*him, hence*] *he crushed him by disease.*[5] Now, you might think that this is so even if he did not accept them with love. Therefore it is said: *To see if his soul would offer itself in restitution.*[6] Even as the trespass-offering must be brought by consent, so also the sufferings must be endured with consent. And if he did accept them, what is his reward? *He will see his seed, prolong his days.*[7] And more than that, his knowledge [of the Torah] will endure with him. For it is said: *The purpose of the Lord will prosper in his hand.*[8]

R. Jacob b. Idi and R. Aḥa b. Ḥanina differ with regard to the following: The one says: Chastenings of love are such as do not involve the intermission of study of the Torah. For it is said: *Happy is the man whom Thou chastenest, O Lord, and teachest out of Thy law.*[9] And the other one says: Chastenings of love are such as do not involve the intermission of prayer. For it is said: *Blessed*
d *be God, Who hath not turned away my prayer, nor His mercy from me.*[1] R. Abba the son of R. Ḥiyya b. Abba said to them: Thus said R. Ḥiyya b. Abba in the name of R. Joḥanan: Both of them are chastenings of love. For it is said: *For whom the Lord loveth He correcteth.*[2] Why then does it say: *'And teachest him out of Thy law'?* Do not read *telammedennu*, [Thou teachest him] but *telammedenu*, [Thou teachest us]. Thou teachest us this thing out of Thy law as a conclusion *a fortiori* from the law concerning tooth and eye.[3] Tooth and eye are only one limb of the man, and still [if they are hurt], the slave obtains thereby his freedom. How much more so with painful sufferings which torment the whole body of a man! And this agrees with a saying of R. Simeon b. Laḳish. For R. Simeon b. Laḳish said: The word *'covenant'* is mentioned in connection with salt, and the word *'covenant'* is mentioned in connection with sufferings: the word *'covenant'* is mentioned in connection with salt, as it is written: *Neither shalt thou suffer the salt of the covenant of thy God to be lacking.*[4] And the word *'covenant'* is mentioned in connection with sufferings, as it is written: *These are the words of the covenant.*[5] Even as in the covenant mentioned in connection with salt, the salt lends a sweet taste to the meat, so also in the covenant mentioned in connection with sufferings, the sufferings wash away all the sins of a man.

It has been taught: R. Simeon b. Yoḥai says: The Holy One, blessed be He, gave Israel three precious gifts, and all of them were given only through sufferings. These are: The Torah, the Land of Israel and the world to come. Whence do we know this of the Torah?—Because it is said: *Happy is the man whom Thou chastenest, O Lord, and teachest him out of Thy law.*[6] Whence of the Land of Israel? —Because it is written: *As a man chasteneth his son, so the Lord thy God chasteneth thee,*[7] and after that it is written: *For the Lord thy God bringeth thee into a good land.*[8] Whence of the world to come?— Because it is written: *For the commandment is a lamp, and the teaching*
e *is light, and reproofs of* sufferings *are the way of life.*[1]

A Tanna recited before R. Joḥanan the following: If a man busies

a (1) Ps. IV, 5. (2) Ibid. XXXI, 6. (3) In the Talmud the good impulses and evil impulses of a man are personified as two genii or spirits dwelling in his soul, the one prompting him to do good things and the other one to do wicked things. The meaning of this saying here is that a man has always to make an effort and to fight against the evil instincts. (4) Ibid. IV, 5. The word רגזו is translated, not as *tremble*, but as *fight, incite to fight*. (5) Ibid. (6) Ex. XXIV, 12. (7) MS.M. Talmud, v. B.M., Sonc. ed., p. 206, n. 6. (8) To protect him against the demons.

b (1) Ps. CXLIX, 6. (2) Ibid. v. 5. (3) E.V. *'sparks'*. (4) Job V, 7. (5) I.e., if thou neglect it (the Torah). E.V. *'Wilt thou set thine eyes etc.'*. (6) Prov.

ואם תלמיד חכם הוא. שרגיל במשנתו לחזור על גרסתו תמיד דיו בכך: ירגיז יצר טוב. שיעשה מלחמה עם יצר הרע: ודומו סלה. יום הדומיה הוא יום המות שהוא דומיה עולמית: זה מקרא. חומש שמצוה לקרות בתורה: זו משנה. שיתעסקו במשנה: זה גמרא. סברת טעמי המשניות שממנו יוצאה הוראה. אבל המורים הוראה מן המשנה נקראו מבלי העולם במסכת סוטה (דף כב.): כאלו אוחז חרב של שתי פיות בידו. להרוג את המזיקין: מאי משמע. דבקריאת שמע: התעיף עיניך בו. אם תכפל ותסגור עיניך בתורה היא משתכחת ממך: ובני רשף יגביהו עוף. העוף מסתלקת ממך: קטב מרירי. זה שם שד הצהרים במסכת פסחים (דף קיא:): ולחומי רשף. כתיב בין רעב למזיקין כדרש לפניו ולאחריו יסורין ומזיקין: אפילו תינוקות של בית רבן יודעים. שהתורה מגינה שלמדין מספר חומש אם שמוע תשמע כל המחלה אשר שמתי וגומר ואפילו הקטנים שלא הגיעו לספר איוב כבר למדו:

החשתי מטוב. מן התורה: וכאבי נעכר. מכה עכורה: המוכר עצב. שפירש היינו דבר חשוב כזה ומתוך דוחקו מכרו: ושמח. שהרי הקב"ה מזהירם מלעזוב אותה ומשבחה לפניהם בלקח טוב אחר שנתנה להם: פשפש ולא מצא. לא מצא עבירה בידו שבשבילה לראויין יסורין הללו לבא: אשרי הגבר אשר תיסרנו יה ומתורתך תלמדנו. שבשביל יסורין לריך אדם לבא לידי תלמוד תורה: יסורין של אהבה. הקב"ה מייסרו בעולם הזה בלא שום עון כדי להרבות שכרו בעולם הבא יותר מכדי זכיותיו: וה' חפץ דכאו החלי. מי שהקב"ה חפץ בו מחלהו ביסורין: אשם. קרבן: נפשו. מדעתו: דבר זה. שאשרי אדם תיסרנו יה: מתורתך תלמדנו. כלומר מתורתך אנו למדין אותו: ונאמר ברית ביסורין דכתיב אלה דברי הברית. אחר הקללות כאמור במשנה תורה: אף יסורין ממרקין כל עונותיו של אדם. גרסינן: ודרך חיים. חיי העולם הבא הויין לו תוכחות מוסר לאדם:

תורה אור

אם תלמיד חכם הוא אין צריך אמר אביי אף תלמיד חכם מיבעי ליה למימר חד פסוקא דרחמי כגון °בידך אפקיד רוחי פדיתה אותי ה' אל אמת: אמר רבי לוי בר חמא אמר רבי שמעון בן לקיש לעולם ירגיז אדם יצר טוב על יצר הרע שנאמר °רגזו ואל תחטאו אם נצחו מוטב ואם לאו יעסוק בתורה שנאמר אמרו בלבבכם. אם נצחו מוטב ואם לאו יקרא ק"ש שנאמר על משכבכם אם נצחו מוטב ואם לאו יזכור לו יום המיתה שנאמר ודמו סלה: ואמר רבי לוי בר חמא אמר ר' שמעון בן לקיש מאי דכתיב °ואתנה לך את לחת האבן והתורה והמצוה אשר כתבתי להורתם לוחות אלו עשרת הדברות תורה זה מקרא והמצוה זו משנה אשר כתבתי אלו נביאים וכתובים להורתם זה גמרא מלמד *שכולם נתנו למשה מסיני: אמר ר' *יצחק כל הקורא ק"ש על מטתו כאלו אוחז חרב של שתי פיות בידו שנאמר °רוממות אל בגרונם וחרב פיפיות בידם מאי משמע אמר מר זוטרא ואיתימא רב אשי מרישא דעניינא דכתיב °יעלזו חסידים בכבוד ירננו על משכבותם וכתיב בתריה רוממות אל בגרונם וחרב פיפיות בידם: ואמר רבי יצחק כל הקורא קרית שמע על מטתו מזיקין בדילין הימנו שנאמר °ובני רשף יגביהו עוף ואין עוף אלא תורה שנאמר °התעיף עיניך בו ואיננו ואין רשף אלא מזיקין שנאמר °מזי רעב ולחומי רשף וקטב מרירי אמר רבי שמעון בן לקיש כל העוסק בתורה יסורין בדילין הימנו שנאמר ובני רשף יגביהו עוף ואין עוף אלא תורה שנאמר התעיף עיניך בו ואיננו ואין רשף אלא יסורין שנאמר *מזי רעב ולחומי רשף אמר ליה ר' יוחנן *הא אפילו תינוקות של בית רבן יודעין אותו שנאמר °ויאמר אם שמוע תשמע לקול ה' אלהיך והישר בעיניו תעשה והאזנת למצותיו ושמרת כל חקיו כל המחלה אשר שמתי במצרים לא אשים עליך כי אני ה' רופאיך אלא כל שאפשר לו לעסוק בתורה ואינו עוסק הקב"ה מביא עליו יסורין מכוערין ועוכרין אותו שנא' °נאלמתי דומיה החשיתי מטוב וכאבי נעכר *ואין טוב אלא תורה שנאמר °כי לקח טוב נתתי לכם תורתי אל תעזובו: א"ר זירא ואיתימא רבי חנינא בר פפא בא וראה שלא כמדת הקב"ה מדת בשר ודם מדת בשר ודם אדם מוכר חפץ לחבירו מוכר עצב ולוקח שמח אבל הקב"ה אינו כן נתן להם תורה לישראל ושמח שנאמר כי לקח טוב נתתי לכם תורתי אל תעזובו: אמר רבא ואיתימא רב חסדא אם רואה אדם שיסורין באין עליו יפשפש במעשיו שנאמר °נחפשה דרכינו ונחקורה *ונשובה עד ה' *פשפש ולא מצא יתלה בבטול תורה שנ' °אשרי הגבר אשר תיסרנו יה ומתורתך תלמדנו ואם תלה ולא מצא בידוע שיסורין של אהבה הם שנאמר °כי את אשר יאהב ה' יוכיח: אמר רבא אמר רב סחורה אמר רב הונא כל שהקדוש ב"ה חפץ בו מדכאו ביסורין שנאמר °וה' חפץ דכאו החלי יכול אפילו לא קבלם מאהבה ת"ל °אם תשים אשם נפשו מה אשם לדעת אף יסורין לדעת ואם קבלם מה שכרו °יראה זרע יאריך ימים ולא עוד אלא שתלמודו מתקיים בידו שנ' °וחפץ ה' בידו יצלח. פליגי בה רבי יעקב בר אידי ור' אחא בר חנינא חד אמר אלו הם יסורין של אהבה כל שאין בהן בטול תורה שנאמר אשרי הגבר אשר תיסרנו יה ומתורתך תלמדנו וחד אמר אלו הם יסורין של אהבה כל שאין בהן בטול תפלה שנאמר °ברוך אלהים אשר לא הסיר תפלתי וחסדו מאתי אמר להו רבי אבא בריה דרבי חייא בר אבא הכי *אמר רבי חייא בר אבא אמר ר' יוחנן אלו ואלו יסורין של אהבה הן שנאמר כי את אשר יאהב ה' יוכיח אלא מה ת"ל ומתורתך תלמדנו אל תקרי °תלמדנו אלא תלמדנו דבר זה מתורתך תלמדנו ק"ו משן ועין מה שן ועין שהן אחד מאבריו של אדם עבד יוצא בהן לחרות יסורין שממרקין כל גופו של אדם על אחת כמה וכמה והיינו דרבי שמעון בן לקיש דאמר רשב"ל נאמר ברית במלח ונאמר ברית ביסורין נאמר ברית במלח דכתיב °ולא תשבית מלח ברית ונאמ' ברית ביסורין דכתי' °אלה דברי הברית מה ברית האמור במלח מלח ממתקת את הבשר אף ברית האמור ביסורין יסורין ממרקין כל עונותיו של אדם: °תניא רבי שמעון בן יוחאי אומר ג' מתנות טובות נתן הקב"ה לישראל וכולן לא נתנן אלא על ידי יסורין אלו הן תורה וארץ ישראל והעולם הבא תורה מנין שנאמר אשרי הגבר אשר תיסרנו יה ומתורתך תלמדנו ארץ ישראל דכתיב °כי כאשר ייסר איש את בנו ה' אלהיך מיסרך וכתיב בתריה כי ה' אלהיך מביאך אל ארץ טובה העולם הבא דכתיב °כי נר מצוה ותורה אור ודרך חיים תוכחות מוסר: תני תנא קמיה דרבי יוחנן כל העוסק בתורה ובגמילות חסדים

ובנים וקובר

תהלי' לא; שם ד'; שמות כד; תהלים קמ"ט; שם; איוב ה; משלי כג; דברים לב; שמות טו; תהלים לט; משלי ד; איכה ג; תהלים לד; משלי ג; ישעיה נ"ג; שם; שם; תהלים ס; כ"ל הדל"ית בקמול אלא בליר"י; ויקרא ב; דברים כח; מכילתא סוף פר' יתרו וספרי פ' ואתחנן; דברים ח; משלי ו

[ע' מגיל' יט:] גי' הרי"ף והרא"ש ר' אלעזר; [גיטין דע. חולין פח:]; [לקמן מח: ע"ז: יט: מנחו' כג: אבות פ"ו]; ס"א פשפש ומלא יעשה תשובה שנאמר ונשובה; [יתכן להיות הכי א"ר אבא א"ר יוחנן אלו וכו' וע' מ"ק כג.]

XXIII, 5. (7) Deut. XXXII, 24. (8) That the Torah is a protection against painful disease. (9) Who study the Pentateuch, where it is plainly said. (10) Ex. XV, 26. (11) Ps. XXXIX, 3. E.V. '*I held my peace, had no comfort, and my pain was held in check*'. (12) Prov. IV, 2.

c (1) Out of poverty and not for business. (2) Lam. III, 40. (3) Ps. XCIV, 12. (4) Prov. III, 12. (5) Isa. LIII, 10. (6) Ibid. The Hebrew word for 'restitution' is *asham* which means also 'trespass-offering'. (7) Ibid. (8) Ibid. (9) Ps. XCIV, 12.

d (1) Ps. LXVI, 20. (2) Prov. III 12. (3) V. Ex. XXI, 26, 27. If the master knocks out the tooth or eye of his slave, then the slave has to be set free. (4) Lev. II, 13. (5) Deut. XXVIII, 69. These words refer to the chapter dealing with the sufferings of Israel. (6) Ps. XCIV, 12. (7) Deut. VIII, 5. (8) Ibid. v. 7.

e (1) Prov. VI, 23.

וקובר את בניו מוחלין לו על כל עונותיו אמר ליה רבי יוחנן בשלמא תורה וגמילות חסדים דכתיב °בחסד ואמת יכופר עון חסד זו גמילות חסדים שנאמר °רודף צדקה וחסד ימצא חיים צדקה וכבוד *אמת זו תורה שנאמר °אמת קנה ואל תמכור אלא קובר את בניו מנין תנא ליה ההוא סבא משום ר' שמעון בן יוחאי אתיא עון עון כתיב הכא בחסד ואמת יכופר עון וכתיב התם °ומשלם עון אבות אל חיק בניהם אמר רבי יוחנן נגעים ובנים אינן יסורין של אהבה ונגעים לא והתניא כל מי שיש בו אחד מארבעה מראות נגעים הללו אינן אלא מזבח כפרה מזבח כפרה הוו יסורין של אהבה לא הוו ואי בעית אימא *הא לן והא להו ואי בעית אימ' הא בצנעא הא בפרהסיא: ובנים לא היכי דמי אילימא דהוי ליה ומתו והא *אמר ר' יוחנן דין גרמא דעשיראה ביר אלא הא דלא הוו ליה כלל והא דהוו ליה ומתו: רבי חייא בר אבא חלש על לגביה רבי יוחנן א"ל חביבין עליך יסורין א"ל לא הן ולא שכרן א"ל הב לי ידך יהב ליה ידיה ואוקמיה רבי יוחנן חלש על לגביה ר' חנינא אמר ליה חביבין עליך יסורין אמר ליה לא הן ולא שכרן א"ל הב לי ידך יהב ליה ידיה ואוקמיה אמאי לוקים רבי יוחנן לנפשיה אמרי *אין חבוש מתיר עצמו מבית האסורים רבי *אליעזר חלש על לגביה רבי יוחנן חזא דהוה קא גני בבית אפל גלייה לדרעיה ונפל נהורא חזייה דהוה קא בכי רבי *אליעזר אמר ליה אמאי קא בכית אי משום תורה דלא אפשת *שנינו אחד המרבה ואחד הממעיט ובלבד שיכוין לבו לשמים ואי משום מזוני לא כל אדם זוכה לשתי שלחנות *אי משום בני דין גרמא דעשיראה ביר א"ל להאי שופרא דבלי בעפרא קא בכינא א"ל על דא ודאי קא בכית ובכו תרוייהו אדהכי והכי א"ל חביבין עליך יסורים א"ל לא הן ולא שכרן א"ל הב לי ידך יהב ליה ידיה ואוקמיה רב הונא תקיפו ליה ארבע מאה דני דחמרא על לגביה רב יהוד' אחוה דרב סלא חסידא ורבנן ואמרי לה רב אדא בר אהבה ורבנן ואמרו ליה לעיין מר במיליה אמר להו ומי חשידנא בעיניכו אמרו ליה מי חשיד הקב"ה דעביד דינא בלא דינא אמר להו אי איכא מאן דשמיע עלי מלתא לימא אמרו ליה הכי שמיע לן דלא יהיב מר שבישא לאריסיה אמר להו מי קא שביק לי מידי מיניה הא קא גניב לי כולי אמרו ליה היינו דאמרי אינשי בתר גנבא גנוב וטעמיה טעים אמר להו קבילנא עלי דיהיבנא ליה איכא דאמרי הדר חלא והוה חמרא ואיכא דאמרי אייקר חלא ואיזדבן בדמי דחמרא: תניא אבא בנימין אומר על שני דברים הייתי מצטער כל ימי על תפלתי שתהא לפני מטתי ועל מטתי שתהא נתונה בין צפון לדרום על תפלתי שתהא לפני מטתי מאי לפני מטתי אילימא לפני מטתי ממש והאמר רב יהודה אמר רב ואיתימא ריב"ל מנין למתפלל שלא יהא דבר חוצץ בינו לבין הקיר שנאמר °ויסב חזקיהו פניו אל הקיר ויתפלל לא תימא לפני מטתי אלא אימא סמוך למטתי ועל מטתי שתהא נתונה בין צפון לדרום דא"ר חמא בר' חנינא אמר רבי יצחק כל הנותן מטתו בין צפון לדרום הויין ליה בנים זכרים שנאמר °וצפונך תמלא בטנם ישבעו בנים רב נחמן בר יצחק אמר אף אין אשתו מפלת נפלים כתיב הכא וצפונך תמלא בטנם וכתיב התם °וימלאו ימיה ללדת והנה תומים בבטנה: תניא אבא בנימין אומר שנים שנכנסו להתפלל וקדם אחד מהם להתפלל ולא המתין את חבירו ויצא טורפין לו תפלתו בפניו שנאמר °טורף נפשו באפו הלמענך תעזב ארץ ולא עוד אלא שגורם לשכינה שתסתלק מישראל שנאמר °ויעתק צור ממקומו ואין צור אלא הקב"ה שנאמר °צור ילדך תשי ואם המתין לו מה שכרו

אמר

תורה אור

משלי טז; שם כא; שם כג; ירמי' לב; ישעיה לח; תהלים יז; בראשית כה; איוב יח; שם; דברים לב

רש"י

ובנים. קא סלקא דעתי' הקובר את בניו: ארבע מראות. שאת ותולדתה בהרת ותולדתה. בהרת עזה כשלג שניה לה כסיד ההיכל. שאת כצמר לבן שניה לה כקרום ביצה: הא לן והא להו. בא"י שערי חומה מקודשות בה ומצורע טעון שילוח חולה להן אינן יסורין של אהבה. בבל שאינן טעונין שילוח והן מזבח כפרה הוו יסורין של אהבה: בצנעא. תחת בגדיו: דין גרמא דעשיראה ביר. זה עצם של בן עשירי שמת לו: ביר. כמו בר. וצר עצם *פחות מכשעורה ממנו בסודרו לעגמת נפש. וגברא רבא כר"י לא באו לו יסורין שאינן של אהבה: דהוו ליה בנים ומתו. הוו להו יסורין של אהבה שהאבלות מכפרת על עונותיו: גלייה. ר' יוחנן לדרעי': נפל נהורא. שהיה בשרו מבהיק שיפה היה מאד כדאמרי' בב"מ בהשוכר את הפועלים (דף פד.): אי משום תורה. שלא למדת הרבה כרצונך: אחד המרבה ואחד הממעיט. לענין קרבנות שנוי' בשלהי מנחות (דף ק"י.) נאמר בעולת בהמה ריח ניחוח ובמנחה ריח ניחוח ללמדך שאחד המרבה וכו': אי משום מזוני. שאינך עשיר: על דא ודאי קא בכית. ע"ז ודאי יש לך לבכות: דני. חביות: תקיפו. החמיצו: ליעיין מר במיליה. יפשפש במעשיו: אי איכא דשמיע עלי מלתא לימא. אם יש בכם ששמע עלי דבר שאני צריך לחזור בי יודיעני: שבישא. חלקו בזמורות הגפן שחותכין מהן בשעת הזמיר ותנא (בב"מ דף קג.) כשם שחולקין ביין כך חולקין בזמורות ובקנים. שריגם מתרגמינן שבישין (בראשית מ'): מי שביק לי מידי מניה. וכי אינו חשוד בעיניכם שהוא גונב לי הרבה יותר מחלקו: בתר גנבא גנוב כו'. הגונב מהגנב אף הוא טועם טעם גנבה: סמוך למטתי. כל ימי נזהרתי שלא לעשות מלאכה ושלא לעסוק בתורה כשעמדתי ממטתי עד שאקרא ק"ש ואתפלל: צפון לדרום. ראשה ומרגלותיה זה לצפון וזה לדרום. ונראה בעיני שהשכינה במזרח או במערב לפיכך נכון להסב דרך תשמיש לרוחות אחרות: וצפונך. לשון צפון וסיפא דקרא ישבעו בנים: תמלא בטנם. תמלא ימי הריונם: טורף נפשו באפו. לך אומר אשר גרמת לך לטרוף את נפשך בפניך ומה היא הנפש זו תפלה כמו שנאמר ואשפוך את נפשי לפני ה' (שמואל א' א'): הלמענך תעזוב ארץ. וכי סבור היית שבשבילך שיצאת תסתלק השכינה ויעזוב את חבירך המתפלל לפניו:

לו

תוספות

הא לן והא להו. פירש רש"י לבני ארץ ישראל שצריכין שילוח חוץ לשלש מחנות לא היו יסורין של אהבה. ותימה דשילוח מחנות לא היה נוהג אלא בזמן שהיובל נוהג ובתי ערי חומה. וביומי האמוראין לא היה היובל נוהג כדאמרינן במסכת גיטין (פ"ד דף לו.) והילך היה מדבר ר' יוחנן מדבר שלא היה נוהג בימיו. וי"מ הא לן והא להו לענין טומאה שנזהרין בארץ ישראל ולא בבבל:

והאמר רבי יוחנן דין גרמא דעשיראה ביר. פרש"י דלאדם חשוב כרבי יוחנן מסתמא לא היו אלא יסורין של אהבה. ותימה דהא מסיק דהיכא דלא הוו ליה בנים כלל לא הוו יסורין של אהבה והרי כמה צדיקים שלא היו להם בנים. ואי משום בנות רבי יוחנן נמי הוו ליה בנות בפרק בתרא דקדושין (דף עא:) ונראה לפרש דהכי פריך והאמר ר' יוחנן דין גרמא וכו' אלמא מדהוה רגיל לנחם אחרים בכך שמע מינה דהוו יסורין של אהבה. אבל אינו תלוי בכך שהצדיקים עצמם פעמים מעונים ביסורין:

*ה"ג לא כל אדם זוכה לשתי שלחנות. אבל אין לגרוס אין אדם זוכה דהא כמה צדיקים זוכין לשתי שלחנות כגון רבי *וכדאמרינן בפרק בתרא דהוריות (דף י:):

דינא בלא דינא. הרבה צדיקים יש שלוקין בגופם ובממונם אלא הם היו יודעים שלא היה נותן שבישא לאריסי' והיו רוצים לרמוז לו שלא יעשה עוד:

שלא יהא דבר חוצץ בינו לבין הקיר. אבל מלתא דקביעא כגון ארון ותיבה אין זה הפסק אבל מטה נראה שאין זה קבוע:

אלא אימא סמוך למטתי. שלא היה עושה מלאכה עד שיתפלל. ורש"י פירש אפילו ללמוד שאסור ללמוד קודם תפלה. ולא ידעתי מנא ליה. אבל ראיה דשרי ללמוד קודם דלקמן בפרק שני (דף יד:) אמרינ' דרב מקדים ומשי ידיה ומברך ומתני פרקיה וקרי ק"ש כי מטא זמן ק"ש וכו':

כל הנותן מטתו בין צפון לדרום וכו'. ולא בין מזרח למערב. ודוקא כשישן עם אשתו. מפני שהשכינה מצויה בין מזרח למערב והיה הדבר גנאי לשכב אצל אשתו מפני התשמיש וכן משמע ממוכחי קראי:

המתפלל

עין משפט נר מצוה

יז
א מיי' פ"ז מה' בית הבחירה הל' ט טוש"ע א"ח סימן ג סעיף ו ובסי' רמ סעיף יז
[*ע"ז ד: תורה דכתיב וכו'.]

יח
ב מיי' פ"ה מהל' תפלה הל' ו סמג עשין יט טוש"ע א"ח סי' צ סעיף כ"א

יט
ג מיי' פ"ו שם הלכה ד טוש"ע א"ח סימן פט סעיף ו

וכ"ה במס' ד"א זוט' פ"ד

[ב"מ פה.]

כ
ד מיי' פ"ט שם הלכה יא סמג עשין יט טוש"ע א"ח סי' צ סעי' טו

[וע' תוס' נדה ס. ד"ה ולאמר]

מסורת הש"ס

[בערוך ערך גרם פי' שהוא עצם שן הוי דאינו מטמא וכ"כ הכתב"ס בב"ב קטו.]

[לקמן יד. וש"נ]

בבא בתרא קיו.

[נדרים ז: סנהד' לה.]

לקמן יז. מנחות קי. [שבת לו. יומא מב. שבועו' טו.]

himself in the study of the Torah and in acts of charity [5b] and [nonetheless] buries his children,[2] all his sins are forgiven him. R. Joḥanan said to him: I grant you Torah and acts of charity, for it is written: *By mercy and truth iniquity is expiated.*[3] *'Mercy'* is acts of charity, for it is said: *He that followeth after righteousness and mercy findeth life, prosperity and honour.*[4] *'Truth'* is Torah, for it is said: *Buy the truth and sell it not.*[5] But how do you know [what you say about] the one who buries his children?—A certain Elder [thereupon] recited to him in the name of R. Simeon b. Yoḥai: It is concluded from the analogy in the use of the word *'iniquity'*. Here it is written: *By mercy and truth* iniquity *is expiated.* And elsewhere it is written: *And who recompenseth the* iniquity *of the fathers into the bosom of their children.*[6]

R. Joḥanan says: Leprosy and [the lack of] children are not chastisements of love. But is leprosy not a chastisement of love? Is it not taught: If a man has one of these four symptoms of leprosy,[7] it is nothing else but an altar of atonement?—They are an altar of atonement, but they are not chastisements of love. If you like, I can say: This [teaching of the Baraitha] is ours [in Babylonia], and that [saying of R. Joḥanan] is theirs [in Palestine].[8] If you like, I can say: This [teaching of the Baraitha] refers to hidden [leprosy], that [saying of R. Joḥanan] refers to a case of visible [leprosy]. But is [the lack of] children not a chastisement of love? How is this to be understood? Shall I say that he had children and they died? Did not R. Joḥanan himself say: This is the bone of my tenth son?[9]—Rather [say then] that the former saying refers to one who never had children, the latter to one who had children and lost them.

R. Ḥiyya b. Abba fell ill and R. Joḥanan went in to visit him. He said to him: Are your sufferings welcome to you? He replied:
a Neither they nor their reward.[1] He said to him: Give me your hand. He gave him his hand and he[2] raised him.

R. Joḥanan once fell ill and R. Ḥanina went in to visit him. He said to him: Are your sufferings welcome to you? He replied: Neither they nor their reward. He said to him: Give me your hand. He gave him his hand and he raised him. Why could not R. Joḥanan raise himself?[3]—They replied: The prisoner cannot free himself from jail.[4]

R. Eleazar fell ill and R. Joḥanan went in to visit him. He noticed that he was lying in a dark room,[5] and he bared his arm and light radiated from it.[6] Thereupon he noticed that R. Eleazar was weeping, and he said to him: Why do you weep? Is it because you did not study enough Torah? Surely we learnt: The one who sacrifices much and the one who sacrifices little have the same merit, provided that the heart is directed to heaven.[7] Is it perhaps lack of sustenance? Not everybody has the privilege to enjoy two tables.[8] Is it perhaps because of [the lack of] children? This is the bone of my tenth son!—He replied to him: I am weeping on account of this beauty[9] that is going to rot in the earth. He said to him: On that account you surely have a reason to weep; and they both wept. In the meanwhile he said to him: Are your sufferings welcome to you?—He replied: Neither they nor their reward. He said to him: Give me your hand, and he gave him his hand and he raised him.

Once four hundred jars of wine belonging to R. Huna turned sour. Rab Judah, the brother of R. Sala the Pious, and the other scholars (some say: R. Adda b. Ahaba and the other scholars) went in to visit him and said to him: The master ought to examine
b his actions.[1] He said to them: Am I suspect in your eyes? They replied: Is the Holy One, blessed be He, suspect of punishing without justice?—He said to them: If somebody has heard of anything against me, let him speak out. They replied: We have heard that the master does not give his tenant his [lawful share in the] vine twigs. He replied: Does he leave me any? He steals them all! They said to him: That is exactly what the proverb says:[2] If you steal from a thief you also have a taste of it![3] He said to them: I pledge myself to give it to him [in the future]. Some report that thereupon the vinegar became wine again; others that the vinegar went up so high that it was sold for the same price as wine.

It has been taught: Abba Benjamin says, All my life I took great pains about two things: that my prayer should be before my bed and that my bed should be placed north and south. 'That my prayer should be before my bed'. What is the meaning of 'before my bed'? Is it perhaps literally *in front of my bed?* Has not Rab Judah said in the name of Rab (some say, in the name of R. Joshua b. Levi): How do you know that when one prays there should be nothing interposing between him and the wall? Because it says: *Then Hezekiah turned his face to the wall and prayed?*[4]—Do not read 'before my bed', but 'near[5] my bed'. 'And that my bed should be placed north and south'. For R. Ḥama b. R. Ḥanina said in the name of R. Isaac: Whosoever places his bed north and south will have male children, as it says: *And whose belly Thou fillest with Thy* treasure,[6] *who have* sons in *plenty.*[7] R. Naḥman b. Isaac says: His wife also will not miscarry. Here it is written: *And whose belly* Thou fillest *with Thy treasure,* and elsewhere it is written: *And when her*
c *days to be delivered* were fulfilled, *behold there were twins in her womb.*[1]

It has been taught: Abba Benjamin says, When two people enter [a Synagogue] to pray, and one of them finishes his prayer first and does not wait for the other but leaves,[2] his prayer is torn up before his face.[3] For it is written: *Thou that tearest thyself in thine anger, shall the earth be forsaken for thee?*[4] And more than that, he causes the Divine Presence to remove itself from Israel. For it says *Or shall the rock be removed out of its place?*[5] And *'rock'* is nothing else than the Holy One, blessed be He, as it says: *Of the Rock that begot thee thou wast unmindful.*[6] And if he does wait, what is his

(2) An allusion to R. Joḥanan himself, who was a great scholar and a charitable man, and was bereft of his children. (3) Ibid. XVI, 6. (4) Ibid. XXI, 21. (5) Ibid. XXIII, 23. (6) Jer. XXXII, 18. (7) Which are enumerated in Mishnah Nega'im I, 1. (8) In Palestine where a leprous person had to be isolated outside the city (cf. Lev. XIII, 46), leprosy was not regarded as 'chastisements of love' owing to the severity of the treatment involved. (9) Who died in his lifetime. The Gemara deduces from that saying that he regarded the death of children as a chastisement of love. Aruch understands this to have been a tooth of the last of his sons which he preserved and used to show to people who suffered bereavement in order to induce in them a spirit of resignation such as he himself had in his successive bereavements.

a (1) The implication is that if one lovingly acquiesces in his sufferings, his reward in the world to come is very great. (2) R. Joḥanan. He cured him by the touch of his hand. (3) If he could cure R. Ḥiyya b. Abba, why could not he cure himself? (4) And the patient cannot cure himself. (5) R. Eleazar was a poor man and lived in a room without windows. (6) R. Joḥanan was supposed to be so beautiful that a light radiated from his body, v. B.M. 84*a*. (7) Men. 110*b*. (8) Learning and wealth. Or perhaps, this world and the next. (9) I.e., the beautiful body of yours.

b (1) You may perhaps have deserved your misfortune through some sin. (2) Lit., 'what people say'. (3) Even if your tenant is a thief this does not free you from giving him his lawful share. (4) Isa. XXXVIII, 2. (5) Near in time. He used to pray immediately after rising. (6) The word צפונך may mean *treasure* and also *north*. (7) Ps. XVII, 14.

c (1) Gen. XXV, 24. (2) The synagogues were outside the town and it was dangerous to remain alone. (3) I.e., rejected. (4) Job. XVIII, 4. The homiletical interpretation of the verse is: 'Your prayer will be thrown into your face, if on your account the earth or synagogue is forsaken'. (5) Ibid. (6) Deut. XXXII, 18.

reward?—[6a] R. Jose b. R. Ḥanina says: He is rewarded with the blessings enumerated in the following verse: *Oh that thou wouldest hearken to My commandments! Then would thy peace be as a river, and thy righteousness as the waves of the sea; Thy seed also would be as the sand, and the offspring of thy body like the grains thereof* etc.[7]

It has been taught: Abba Benjamin says, If the eye had the power to see them, no creature could endure the demons. Abaye says: They are more numerous than we are and they surround us like the ridge round a field. R. Huna says: Every one among us has a thousand on his left hand and ten thousand on his right hand.[8] Raba says: The crushing in the *Kallah*[9] lectures comes from them.[10] Fatigue in the knees comes from them. The wearing out of the clothes of the scholars is due to their rubbing against them. The bruising of the feet comes from them. If one wants to discover them,[11] let him take sifted ashes and sprinkle around his bed, and in the morning he will see something like the footprints of a cock. If one wishes to see them, let him take the after-birth of a black she-cat, the offspring of a black she-cat, the first-born of a first-born, let him roast it in fire and grind it to powder, and then let him put some into his eye, and he will see them. Let him also pour it into
a an iron tube and seal it with an iron signet that they[1] should not steal it from him. Let him also close his mouth, lest he come to harm. R. Bibi b. Abaye did so,[2] saw them and came to harm. The scholars, however, prayed for him and he recovered.

It has been taught: Abba Benjamin says: A man's prayer is heard [by God] only in the Synagogue. For it is said: *To hearken unto the song and to the prayer.*[3] The prayer is to be recited where there is song.[4] Rabin b. R. Adda says in the name of R. Isaac: How do you know that the Holy One, blessed be He, is to be found in the Synagogue? For it is said: *God standeth in the congregation of God.*[5] And how do you know that if ten people pray together the Divine Presence is with them? For it is said: '*God standeth in the congregation of God*'.[6] And how do you know that if three are sitting as a court of judges the Divine Presence is with them? For it is said: *In the midst of the judges He judgeth.*[7] And how do you know that if two are sitting and studying the Torah together the Divine Presence is with them? For it is said: *Then they that feared the Lord spoke one with another;*[8] *and the Lord hearkened and heard, and a book of remembrance was written before Him, for them that feared the Lord and that thought upon His name.*[9] (What does it mean: '*And that thought upon His name*'?—R. Ashi[10] says: If a man thought to fulfil a commandment and he did not do it, because he was prevented by force or accident, then the Scripture credits it to him as if he had performed it.) And how do you know that even if one man sits and studies the Torah the Divine Presence is with him? For it is said: *In every place where I cause My name to be*
b *mentioned I will come unto thee and bless thee.*[1] Now, since [the Divine Presence is] even with one man, why is it necessary to mention two?[2]—The words of two are written down in the book of remembrance, the words of one are not written down in the book of remembrance. Since this is the case with two, why mention three?—I might think [the dispensing of] justice is only for making peace, and the Divine Presence does not come [to participate]. Therefore he teaches us that justice also is Torah. Since it is the case with three, why mention ten?—To [a gathering of] ten the Divine Presence comes first, to three, it comes only after they sit down.

R. Abin[3] son of R. Ada in the name of R. Isaac says [further]: How do you know that the Holy One, blessed be He, puts on *tefillin*?[4] For it is said: *The Lord hath sworn by His right hand, and by the arm of His strength.*[5] '*By His right hand*': this is the Torah; for it is said: *At His right hand was a fiery law unto them.*[6] '*And by the arm of his strength*': this is the *tefillin*; as it is said: *The Lord will give strength unto His people.*[7] And how do you know that the *tefillin* are a strength to Israel? For it is written: *And all the peoples of the earth shall see that the name of the Lord is called upon thee, and they shall be afraid of thee,*[8] and it has been taught: R. Eliezer the Great says: This refers to the *tefillin* of the head.[9]

R. Naḥman b. Isaac said to R. Ḥiyya b. Abin: What is written in the *tefillin* of the Lord of the Universe?—He replied to him: *And who is like Thy people Israel, a nation one in the earth.*[10] Does, then, the Holy One, blessed be He, sing the praises of Israel?—Yes, for it is written: *Thou hast avouched the Lord this day . . . and the Lord hath avouched thee this day.*[11] The Holy One, blessed be He, said to Israel: You have made me a unique entity[12] in the world, and I shall make you a unique entity in the world. 'You have made me a unique entity in the world', as it is said: *Hear, O Israel, the Lord*
c *our God, the Lord is one.*[1] 'And I shall make you a unique entity in the world', as it is said: *And who is like Thy people Israel, a nation one in the earth.*[2] R. Aḥa b. Raba said to R. Ashi: This accounts for one case, what about the other cases?[3]—He replied to him: [They contain the following verses]: *For what great nation is there,* etc.; *And what great nation is there,* etc.;[4] *Happy art thou, O Israel,* etc.;[5] *Or hath God assayed,* etc.;[6] and *To make thee high above all nations.*[7] If so, there would be too many cases?—Hence [you must say]: *For what great nation is there,* and *And what great nation is there,* which are similar, are in one case; *Happy art thou, O Israel,* and *Who is like Thy people,* in one case; *Or hath God assayed,* in one case; and *To make thee high,* in one case. [6b] And all these verses are written on [the *tefillin* of] His arm.

(7) Isa. XLVIII, 18, 19. (8) Cf. Ps. XCI, 7 which verse is quoted in some editions. (9) The Assemblies of Babylonian students during the months of Elul and Adar, v. Glos. (10) For really the lectures are not overcrowded. (11) MS.M.: their footprints.

a (1) The demons. (2) He put the powder into his eye. (3) I Kings VIII, 28. (4) The song of the community and of the officiating Cantor. (5) Ps. LXXXII, 1. (6) And a congregation consists of not less than ten, v. Sanh. 2*b*. (7) Ibid. A *Beth din* consists of three. (8) A phrase denoting two. (9) Mal. III, 16. (10) MS.M.: R. Assi. This remark is made in passing by the editor of the Gemara, R. Ashi. Hence the reading 'R. Ashi' as given by the editions, seems to be correct.

b (1) Ex. XX, 21. The lesson is derived from the use of the singular 'thee'. (2) This question is asked by the Gemara apropos of Rabin's statement. (3) The same as the Rabin mentioned above. (4) Phylacteries, v. Glos. (5) Isa. LXII, 8. (6) Deut. XXXIII, 2. (7) Ps. XXIX, 11. (8) Deut. XXVIII, 10. (9) The *tefillin* of the arm are covered by the sleeves. (10) I Chron. XVII, 21. (11) Deut. XXVI, 17, 18. (12) So the Aruch. Jastrow, however, translates חטיבה 'the only object of your love'.

c (1) Deut. VI, 4. (2) I Chron. XVII, 21. (3) The *tefillin* of the head has four cases. (4) Deut. IV, 7, 8. (5) Ibid. XXXIII, 29. (6) Ibid. IV, 34. (7) Ibid. XXVI, 19.

תורה אור

אמר רבי יוסי ברבי חנינא זוכה לברכות הללו שנאמר °לוא הקשבת למצותי ויהי כנהר שלומך וצדקתך כגלי הים ויהי כחול זרעך וצאצאי מעיך וגו': תניא אבא בנימין אומר אלמלא נתנה רשות לעין לראות אין כל בריה יכולה לעמוד מפני המזיקין אמר אביי אינהו נפישי מינן וקיימי עלן כי כסלא לאוגיא אמר רב הונא כל חד וחד מינן אלפא משמאליה ורבבתא מימיניה *אמר רבא האי דוחקא דהוי בכלה מינייהו הוי הני ברכי דשלהי מינייהו הני מאני דרבנן דבלו מחופיא דידהו הני כרעי דמנקפא מינייהו האי מאן דבעי למידע להו לייתי קיטמא נהילא ונהדר אפורייא ובצפרא חזי כי כרעי דתרנגולא האי מאן דבעי למחזינהו ליתי *שלייתא דשונרתא אוכמתא בת אוכמתא בוכרתא בת בוכרתא ולקליה בנורא ולשחקיה ולימלי עיניה מיניה וחזי להו ולשדייה בגובתא דפרזלא ולחתמיה בגושפנקא דפרזלא דילמא גנבי מיניה ולחתום פומיה כי היכי דלא ליתזק רב ביבי בר אביי עבד הכי חזא ואתזק בעו רבנן רחמי עליה ואתסי: תניא אבא בנימין אומר *אין תפלה של אדם נשמעת אלא בבית הכנסת שנאמר °לשמוע אל הרנה ואל התפלה במקום רנה שם תהא תפלה אמר רבין בר רב אדא אמר רבי יצחק מנין שהקב"ה מצוי בבית הכנסת. שנאמר °אלהים נצב בעדת אל ומנין לעשרה שמתפללין ששכינה עמהם שנאמר אלהים נצב בעדת אל *ומנין לשלשה שיושבין בדין ששכינה עמהם שנאמר °בקרב אלהים ישפוט ומנין לשנים שיושבים ועוסקין בתורה ששכינה עמהם שנאמר °אז נדברו יראי ה' איש אל רעהו ויקשב ה' וגו' *מאי °ולחושבי שמו אמר רב אשי חשב אדם לעשות מצוה ונאנס ולא עשאה מעלה עליו הכתוב כאלו עשאה ומנין שאפילו אחד שיושב ועוסק בתורה ששכינה עמו שנאמר °בכל המקום אשר אזכיר את שמי אבוא אליך וברכתיך וכי מאחר דאפילו חד תרי מבעיא תרי מכתבן מלייהו בספר הזכרונות חד לא מכתבן מליה בספר הזכרונות וכי מאחר דאפילו תרי תלתא מבעיא מהו דתימא דינא שלמא בעלמא הוא ולא אתיא שכינה קמ"ל דדינא נמי היינו תורה וכי מאחר דאפילו תלתא עשרה מבעיא עשרה קדמה שכינה ואתיא תלתא עד דיתבי: אמר רב אבין בר רב אדא אמר רבי יצחק מנין שהקב"ה מניח תפילין שנאמר °נשבע ה' בימינו ובזרוע עוזו בימינו זו תורה שנאמר °מימינו אש דת למו ובזרוע עוזו אלו תפילין שנאמר °ה' עוז לעמו יתן ומנין שהתפילין עוז הם לישראל דכתיב °וראו כל עמי הארץ כי שם ה' נקרא עליך ויראו ממך *ותניא רבי אליעזר הגדול אומר אלו תפילין שבראש א"ל רב נחמן בר יצחק לרב חייא בר אבין הני תפילין דמרי עלמא מה כתיב בהו א"ל °ומי כעמך ישראל גוי אחד בארץ ומי משתבח קודשא בריך הוא בשבחייהו דישראל אין דכתיב °את ה' האמרת היום (וכתיב) וה' האמירך היום *אמר להם הקב"ה לישראל אתם עשיתוני חטיבה אחת בעולם ואני אעשה אתכם *חטיבה אחת בעולם אתם עשיתוני חטיבה אחת בעולם שנאמר °שמע ישראל ה' אלהינו ה' אחד ואני אעשה אתכם חטיבה אחת בעולם שנאמר ומי כעמך ישראל גוי אחד בארץ אמר ליה רב אחא בריה דרבא לרב אשי תינח בחד ביתא בשאר בתי מאי אמר ליה °כי מי גוי גדול ומי גוי גדול °אשריך ישראל °או הנסה אלהים °ולתתך עליון אי הכי נפישי להו טובי בתי אלא כי מי גוי גדול ומי גוי גדול דדמיין להדדי בחד ביתא אשריך ישראל ומי כעמך ישראל בחד ביתא או הנסה אלהים בחד ביתא ולתתך עליון בחד ביתא וכולהו

לוא הקשבת. לשון התחנה היא: למצותי. בשביל מצותי אשר צויתי לגמול חסד: לראות. כל השדין העומדים לפניו: כי כסלא לאוגיא. כשולת חפירה המקפת האוגיא שעושין תחת הגפנים כמו ששנינו (מועד קטן דף ב.) אין עושין אוגיות לגפנים לאסוף שם מים להשקות הגפן. כסלא הוא תלם של מענה המקפת סביב סביב את תל האוגיא והגפן נטוע בתל ובריש נדרים (דף ו ב') הדין אוגיא להוי פאה: האי דוחקא דכלה. פעמים שבני אדם יושבים רווחים ביום השבת שבאין לשמוע דרשה ודומה להם כיושבים דחוקים: הני ברכי דשלהי. ברכים עייפים: מאני דרבנן דבלו. בגדי התלמידים שבלים מהר והם אינם בני מלאכה שיבלו בגדיה': מחופיא דידהו. באין המזיקים ויושבין אצלם ומתחככי' בהם. חופיא לשון חופף ומפספס [שבת דף כ:] פר"ייר בלעז: שלייתא דשונרתא. שליית הולד של חתול נקבה: בוכרתא. הבכורה לאמה: בת בוכרתא. ואף אמה היתה בכור': ולימלי עיניה מיניה. ישים ממנה מעט בעיניו. כל לשון נתינה בעין קורהו בלשון גמרא לשון מלוי לפי שדבר מועט הוא מלא: גובתא דפרזלא. קנה חלול של ברזל: ולחתמי'. לקנה: בגושפנקא דפרזלא. בחותם של ברזל דמזידי דלייר וחתים לית להו רשותא כדאמרי' בכל הבשר בשחיטת חולין (דף קה ב'): במקום רנה. בבית הכנסת ששם אומרים הצבור שירות ותושבחות בנעימת קול ערב: בעדת אל. בבית מועד שלו: ומנין לעשרה וכו'. עדה קרויה בעשרה שנאמר עד מתי לעדה הרעה הזאת (במדבר יד) יצאו יהושע וכלב: בקרב אלהים ישפוט. ואין בית דין קרוים אלהים אלא בג' בפ"ב דסנהדרין (דף ג ב'): ויקשב ה'. ממתין להם שם: אשר אזכיר את שמי. אשר יזכר שמי על מצותי ודברי: אבא אליך. לשון יחיד הוא: מכתבן מלייהו. כדכתיב ויכתב ספר זכרון לפניו (סיפא דקרא): קדמ' שכינה ואתיא. קודם שיהיו כלם העשרה: נצב בעדת אל. מעיקר' משמע: עד דיתבי. כדכתי' ישפוט בשעת המשפט: עוז לעמו. ומנין שהתפילין עוז הם לישראל דכתיב וראו וגו' ויראו ממך: מה כתיב בהו. בשלמא בתפילין דידן כתיב שמע (דברים ו) והיה אם שמוע (שם יא) קדש לי כל בכור (שמות יג) והיה כי יביאך (שם) פרשיות שנצטוו בהם לשום זכרון מצותיו של הקב"ה אות ונכון להם לישראל אלא בדידי' מאי כתיב בהו: האמרת. לשון חשיבות ושבח כמו יתאמרו כל פועלי און (תהלים צד) ישתבחו: בשאר בתי מאי. שהרי ארבעה בתים הם: וכולהו

---

*המתפלל ולא המתין את חבירו טורפין לו וכו'. פירש ר"ת דזה היה להם בבתי כנסיות שלהם שהיו בשדה ולכך בלילה יש להמתין. והר"י היה מאחר תפלתו ומאריך עד שילכו כלם ואם בתוך כך היה שום אדם בא בבית הכנסת היה מעיין בספר עד שגמרו תפלתם. ונראה להחמיר אף לנו:

כי כסלא לאוגיא. כעין תלמים המקיפין את הערוגה כדאמרי' בריש נדרים (דף ו ב') הדין אוגיא להוי פאה:

חד לא מכתבן מיליה בספר זכרונות. כלומ' עם אחרים. אבל בספר לבדו נכתבין כדאמרי' וכל מעשיך בספר נכתבים (אבות פרק ב) כ"ש מדה טובה:

אלו תפילין שבראש. לפי שיש בה רוב' של שם שדי שהשי"ן כתוב' בקמט שבבתים והד"לת ברצועות. ותימא מסכת פרק במה מדליקין (דף כח ב') דקאמר מן המותר בפיך. ולא מפיק רצועות מתורת ה' בפיך. ועוד דבפ' בתרא דמגלה (דף כו ב') קרי לרצוע' תשמישי קדושה בעלמא. אלא י"ל אלו תפילין שבראש לפי שהן בגבהו של ראש ונראין דשייך בהו וראו. אבל תפילין של יד מכוסין דכתיב (שמות יג) לך לאות על ידך *ולא לאחרים לאות:

מי כעמך ישראל. זה שיסד הפייטן (ביו' א' דפסח) עוטפ' כלילו גדלי:

אחורי בית הכנסת. פי' רש"י כל פתחי בתי כנסיות היו למזרח *ואחוריהם למערב וזה המתפלל אחורי בית הכנסת ואינו מחזיר פניו לבית הכנסת נרא' ככופר במי שהצבור מתפללין לפניו. ולא נהירא דאדרבה בדאהדר אפיה לבית הכנסת מיחזי כשתי רשויות שהקהל מתפללין למערב והוא מתפלל כנגדם למזרח. ע"כ נראה אחורי בית הכנסת מי שהוא אחורי העם במזרח והעם משתחוים למערב ולהכי קאמר ולא מהדר אפיה כו'. ודוקא הם שהיה מנהגם להתפלל למערב. אבל אנו מתפללים למזרח שאנו במערבו של א"י וכתי' והתפללו אליך דרך ארצם (מלכים א ח') ונראה כמו שפירש להם לצד מערב תפרש לנו לצד מזרח:

שאלמלא

עין משפט נר מצוה

כא אמיי' פ"ח מהלכו' תפלה הל' א' סמג עשין יט טוש"ע א"ח סי' צ סעיף ט

מסורת הש"ס

ש"א שנאמ' יפול מצדך אלף ורבבה מימינך [וכ"ה הגי' בילקוט ובע"י]

בערוך גרס סילתא וכן הגי' שבת קלד. סליתא דאימי'

[ע' תוס' סוכה יג. ד"ה בשלש]

שבת סג. קדושין מ.

לקמן כז. מנחו' לה: [מגילה טז: סוטה יז. חולין פט.]

[וע"ע תוס' שבת סב. ד"ה ש"ין ותו' עירובין לז. ד"ה קשר ומגילה כו: ד"ה תשמישי ותוס' מנחו' לה: ד"ה אלו]

*עיי' פירש"י ברי"ף ועיי' רש"א

חגיגה ג. [פי' ליור אחד בעולם כלומר דבר הניכר שאין כמותו ערוך בערך אמר]

תורה אור: ישעיה מח; מלכים א' ח; תהלים פב; שם; מלאכי ג; שם; שמות כ; ישעיה סב; דברים לג; תהלים כט; דברים כח; ד"ה א' יז; דברים כו; שם ו; שם ד; שם לג; שם כו

וכולהו כתיבי באדרעיה. אמר רבין בר רב אדא אמר רבי יצחק כל הרגיל לבא לבית הכנסת ולא בא יום אחד הקב"ה משאיל בו שנאמר °מי בכם ירא ה' שומע בקול עבדו אשר הלך חשכים ואין נוגה לו אם לדבר מצוה הלך נוגה לו ואם לדבר הרשות הלך אין נוגה לו יבטח בשם ה' מאי טעמא משום דהוה ליה לבטוח בשם ה' ולא בטח: אמר רבי יוחנן בשעה שהקב"ה בא בבית הכנסת ולא מצא בה עשרה מיד הוא כועס שנאמר °מדוע באתי ואין איש קראתי ואין עונה אמר רבי חלבו אמר רב הונא ᵃכל הקובע *מקום לתפלתו אלהי אברהם בעזרו וכשמת אומרים לו אי עניו אי חסיד מתלמידיו של אברהם אבינו ואברהם אבינו מנא לן דקבע מקום דכתיב °וישכם אברהם בבקר אל המקום אשר עמד שם *ואין עמידה אלא תפלה שנאמר °ויעמד פנחס ויפלל: אמר רבי חלבו אמר רב הונא ᵇהיוצא מבית הכנסת אל יפסיע פסיעה גסה אמר אביי לא אמרן אלא למיפק אבל למיעל מצוה למרהט שנאמר °נרדפה לדעת את ה' אמר רבי זירא מריש כי הוה חזינא להו לרבנן דקא רהטי לפרקא בשבתא אמינא קא מחליין רבנן שבתא כיון דשמענא להא דרבי תנחום אמר ר' יהושע בן לוי לעולם ᶜירוץ אדם לדבר הלכה ואפי' בשבת שנאמר °אחרי ה' ילכו כאריה ישאג וגו' אנא נמי רהיטנא: אמר רבי זירא אגרא דפרקא רהטא אמר אביי אגרא דכלה דוחקא אמר רבא אגרא דשמעתא סברא אמר רב פפא אגרא דבי *טמיא שתיקותא אמר מר זוטרא אגרא דתעניתא צדקתא אמר רב ששת ᵈאגרא דהספדא דלויי אמר רב אשי אגרא דבי הלולי מילי: *אמר רב הונא ᵉכל המתפלל אחורי בית הכנסת נקרא רשע שנאמר °סביב רשעים יתהלכון: אמר אביי לא אמרן אלא דלא מהדר אפיה לבי כנישתא אבל מהדר אפיה לבי כנישתא לית לן בה: ההוא גברא דקא *מצלי אחורי בי כנישתא ולא מהדר אפיה לבי כנישתא חלף *אליהו חזייה אידמי ליה כטייעא אמר ליה *כדו בר קיימת קמיה מרך שלף ספסרא וקטליה אמר ליה ההוא מרבנן לרב ביבי בר אביי ואמרי לה רב ביבי לרב נחמן בר יצחק מאי °כרום זלות לבני אדם אמר ליה אלו דברים שעומדים ברומו של עולם ובני אדם מזלזלין בהן ר' יוחנן ורבי אלעזר דאמרי תרווייהו כיון שנצטרך אדם לבריות פניו משתנות ככרום שנאמר כרום זלות לבני אדם מאי כרום כי אתא רב דימי אמר עוף אחד יש בכרכי הים וכרום שמו וכיון שחמה זורחת *מתהפך לכמה גוונין רבי אמי ורבי אסי דאמרי תרווייהו כאלו נדון בשני דינים אש ומים שנאמר °הרכבת אנוש לראשנו באנו באש ובמים ואמר רבי חלבו אמר רב הונא ᶠלעולם יהא אדם זהיר בתפלת המנחה שהרי אליהו לא נענה אלא בתפלת המנחה שנאמר °ויהי בעלות המנחה ויגש אליהו הנביא ויאמר וגו' *ענני ה' ענני שתרד אש מן השמים ועננו שלא יאמרו מעשה כשפים הם רבי יוחנן אמר אף בתפלת ערבית שנאמר °תכון תפלתי קטורת לפניך משאת כפי מנחת ערב רב נחמן בר יצחק אמר אף תפלת שחרית שנאמר °ה' בקר תשמע קולי בקר אערך לך ואצפה: ואמר רבי חלבו אמר רב הונא כל הנהנה מסעודת חתן ואינו משמחו עובר בחמשה קולות שנאמר °קול ששון וקול שמחה קול חתן וקול כלה קול אומרים הודו את ה' צבאות ואם משמחו מה שכרו אמר רבי יהושע בן לוי זוכה לתורה שנתנה בחמשה קולות שנאמר °ויהי ביום השלישי בהיות הבקר ויהי קולות וברקים וענן כבד על ההר וקול שופר וגומר ויהי קול השופר וגומר והאלהים יעננו בקול איני והא כתיב °וכל העם רואים את הקולות אותן קולות דקודם מתן תורה הוו רבי אבהו אמר כאלו הקריב תודה שנאמר °מביאים תודה בית ה' רב נחמן בר יצחק אמר כאלו בנה אחת מחורבות ירושלים שנאמר °כי אשיב את שבות הארץ כבראשונה אמר ה': ואמר רבי חלבו אמר רב הונא כל אדם שיש בו יראת שמים דבריו נשמעין שנאמר °סוף דבר הכל נשמע את האלהים ירא וגומר מאי °כי זה כל האדם *אמר ר' אלעזר אמר הקב"ה כל העולם כולו לא נברא אלא בשביל זה רבי אבא בר כהנא אמר שקול זה כנגד כל העולם כולו *רבי שמעון בן עזאי אומר ואמרי לה רבי שמעון בן זומא אומר כל העולם כולו לא נברא אלא לצוות לזה: ואמר רבי חלבו אמר רב הונא כל שיודע בחבר שהוא רגיל ליתן לו שלום יקדים לו שלום שנאמר °בקש שלום ורדפהו ואם נתן לו ולא החזיר נקרא גזלן שנאמר °ואתם בערתם הכרם גזלת העני בבתיכם: אמר

וכולהו כתיבי באדרעי'. כל הכתובי' הללו כתובים בזרוע בבית א' שאותן של יד אינן אלא בית אחד כדאמרי' במנחות (דף לד:) וכל הפרשיות כתובות בו: משאיל בו. מה טיבו של פלוני למה לא בא: ירא ה'. שהיה רגיל לבא אליו: אשר הלך חשכים ואין נוגה לו. אשר עתה הלך למקום חשך אשר ימנע עצמו מלהשכים לפתחי: ואין עונה. שיעור שיוכלו לענות דבר קדושה: אלהי אברהם. שקבע מקום לתפלתו: בעזרו. כדרך שהיה עוזר לאברהם: אל יפסיע פסיעה גסה. לפי שנראה בעצמו שעכוב בית הכנסת דומ' עליו כמשוי: נרדפה. לשון מרוצה משמע שהרודף רץ: לפרקא. לשמוע הדרשה: מחליין רבנן שבתא. דאמר מר (שבת דף קיג:) אסור לפסוע פסיעה גסה בשבת שנאמר אם תשיב משבת רגליך: אגרא דפרקא. עיקר קבול שכר הבריות הרצים לשמוע דרשה מפי חכם היא שכר המרוצה. שהרי רובם אינם מבינים להעמיד גרסא ולומר שמועה מפי רבן לאחר זמן שיקבלו שכר לימוד: אגרא דכלה. שבת שלפני הרגל שהכל נאספין לשמוע הלכות הרגל: אגרא דשמעתא סבר'. שהוא יגע וטורח ומחשב להבין טעמו של דבר: אגרא דתעניתא צדקתא. שנותנין צדקה לערב לפרנסת העניים *שהתענו היום: דלויי. להרים קול בלשון נהי ועגמת נפש שיבכו השומעים:

מילי. לשמח החתן בדברים: אחורי בית הכנסת. כל פתחי בית הכנסת היו במזרח והכי תניא בתוספתא דמגילה (פרק ג') מעין מקדש ומשכן פניהם למערב ואחוריהם למזרח והמתפלל אחורי בית הכנסת ואינו מחזיר פניו לבית הכנסת נראה ככופר במי שהצבור מתפללין לפניו והא דרב הונא מוקי לה אביי בדלא מהדר אפיה לבי כנישת': חלף ההוא טייעא. סוחר ערבי: כדו בר*. כדו שתי. בר רשות כי הא דאמרינן בסוכה (דף מה:) הא דעיילי בבר: כרום זלות. סיפיה דקרא דלעיל: דברים שעומדים ברומו של עול'. כגון תפלה שעולה למעלה: כיון שנצטרך אדם לבריות. הוא זל בעיניהם: לראשנו. להיות רוכב בנו דמתרגמינן כרוכב (שמו' כב) כרשיא: עובר בחמשה קולות. מזלזל בחמשה קולות שבירך בהן הקב"ה את ישראל: אותן קולות דקודם מתן תורה הוו. הנך קולות בתראי הייכו הנך דאיירי בהו לעיל וקאמר דכראשון היו ואע"פ שהקול איכו נראה זה נראה: מביאים תודה בית ה'. כי אשיב את שבות וגומר סיפיה דקרא דחמשה קולות דלעיל הוא: בשביל זה. שיברא זה: לצוות. שלו"ן בלע"ז: גזלת העני. והלא אף גזלת העשיר גזלה היא אלא גזלת העני שאין לו כלום לגזול ממנו אלא שלא להשיב על שלומו:

תורה אור

ישעיה נ · שם · בראשי' יט · תהלי' קו · הושע ו · נענע · שם יא · בית אבל י"א בית עלמות של מתים · תהלים יב · ס"א ההוא טייעא חזי' א"ל כדו [גי' הערוך כדובר] · ס"א ועליו · שם סו · מלכים א יח · [לקמן ט:] · תהלים קמא · שם ה · ירמיה לג · שמות יט · שם כ · ירמיה לג · שם · קהלת יב · שם · [שבת ל:] · תהלים לד · ישעיה ג

מסורת הש"ם: כדו בר כשתי לשויות כ"כ ברש"י בעין יעקב · ע"ל ז: · [לקמן כו:]

עין משפט נר מצוה

כב ᵃמיי' פ"ה מהל' תפלה הלכה ו סמג עשין יט טוש"ע א"ח סי' צ סעי' יט

כג ᵇבמיי' פ"ח שם הל' ג ופכ"ד מה' שבת הל' ה' סמג עשין יב יט טוש"ע א"ח סי' צ סעי' יב ובסי' רנ סעי' א [רב אלפס כאן ובשבת פרק ע"ו]

כד ᵈטור וש"ע י"ד סי' שדמ סעיף א

כה ᵉמיי' פ"ו מהל' תפלה הל' ו' סמג עשין יט טוש"ע א"ח סי' צ סעי' ז [ע' סנהד' לה: וברש"י שם]

כו ᶠטור א"ח סי' רלב

גי' הרי"ף והרא"ש וא"ר חלבו

[ע' תוספו' עירובין יח: ד"ה ולא אחורי] תהלים יב

[שבת שם איתא שמעון בן עזאי וע' ברטנורה כפ"ד דאבות וכס"י קידושין מע: ד"ה בן עזאי]

b (1) Ps. XII, 9. (2) MS.M.: An Arab passed by and saw him. (3) V. Jast. Rashi: 'As if there were two powers'. (4) Ibid. (5) Lit., 'standing on the highest point of the world'. (6) He interprets, 'When the exalted things (*kerum*) are reviled among the sons of men'. The reference is to Prayer. (7) The meaning is: In the distant countries lying across the sea. (8) Lewysohn, *Zoologie*, p. 183 identifies the bird with the 'bird of Paradise'. (9) Ps. LXVI, 12.

c (1) I Kings XVIII, 36, 37. (2) Ps. CXLI, 2. (3) Ibid. V, 4. (4) Jer. XXXIII, 11. (5) Lit., 'voices'. The plural is counted as two. (6) Ex. XIX, 16, 19. (7) There were not only five, but *seven* voices. (8) Ibid. XX, 15. Cf. n. 5. (9) One who felicitates the bridegroom. (10) Jer. XXXIII, 11. (11) Ibid.

d (1) Eccl. XII, 13. He interprets: 'Everything is heard, if you fear God'. (2) [MS.M.: If one is used to greet his neighbour and fails to do so a single day, he transgresses the injunction *'Seek peace, etc.'*] (3) Ps. XXXIV, 15. (4) Isa. III, 14. (5) Ibid. LVI, 7. Lit., 'In the house of My prayer'. (6) I.e., not exact the full penalty from them. (7) Lit., 'crown of God'.

Rabin son of R. Adda in the name of R. Isaac says [further]: If a man is accustomed to attend Synagogue [daily] and one day does not go, the Holy One, blessed be He, makes inquiry about him. For it is said: *Who is among you that feareth the Lord, that obeyeth the voice of His servant, and now walketh in darkness and hath no light?*[8] [And still] if he absented himself on account of some religious purpose, he shall have light. But if he absented himself on account of a worldly purpose, he shall have no light. *Let him trust in the name of the Lord.*[9] Why?[10] Because he ought to have trusted in the name of the Lord and he did not trust.

R. Joḥanan says: Whenever the Holy One, blessed be He, comes into a Synagogue and does not find ten persons there,[11] He becomes angry at once.[12] For it is said: *Wherefore, when I came, was there no man? When I called, was there no answer?*[13]

R. Ḥelbo, in the name of R. Huna, says: Whosoever has a fixed place for his prayer has the God of Abraham as his helper. And
a when he dies, people will say of him: Where is the pious man,[1] where is the humble man,[2] one of the disciples of our father Abraham!—How do we know that our father Abraham had a fixed place [for his prayer]? For it is written: *And Abraham got up early in the morning to the place where he had stood.*[3] And 'standing' means nothing else but prayer. For it is said: *Then stood up Phinehas and prayed.*[4]

R. Ḥelbo, in the name of R. Huna, says [further]: When a man leaves the Synagogue, he should not take large steps. Abaye says: This is only when one goes *from* the Synagogue, but when one goes *to* the Synagogue, it is a pious deed to run. For it is said: *Let us run to know the Lord.*[5] R. Zera says: At first when I saw the scholars running to the lecture on a Sabbath day, I thought that they were desecrating the Sabbath.[6] But since I have heard the saying of R. Tanḥum in the name of R. Joshua b. Levi: A man should always, even on a Sabbath, run to listen to the word of *Halachah*, as it is said: *They shall walk after the Lord, who shall roar like a lion*,[7] I also run. R. Zera says: The merit of attending a lecture lies in the running. Abaye says: The merit of attending the *Kallah* sessions[8] lies in the crush. Raba says: The merit of repeating a tradition lies in [improving] the understanding of it. R. Papa says: The merit of attending a house of mourning lies in the silence observed. Mar Zuṭra says: The merit of a fast day lies in the charity dispensed. R. Shesheth says: The merit of a funeral oration lies in raising the voice.[9] R. Ashi says: The merit of at tending a wedding lies in the words [of congratulation addressed to the bride and bridegroom].[10]

R. Huna says: Whosoever prays at the rear of a Synagogue is
b called wicked. For it is said: *The wicked walk round about.*[1] Abaye says: This only applies where he does not turn his face towards the Synagogue, but if he does turn his face towards the Synagogue there is no objection to it. There was once a man who prayed at the rear of a Synagogue and did not turn his face towards the Synagogue. Elijah passed by and appeared to him in the guise of an Arabian[2] merchant. He said to him: Are you standing with your back to your Master?[3] and drew his sword and slew him.

One of the scholars said to R. Bibi b. Abaye (some say: R. Bibi said to R. Naḥman b. Isaac): What is the meaning of: *When vileness is exalted among the sons of men?*[4] He replied to him: These are the things of supreme importance[5] which nevertheless people neglect.[6] R. Joḥanan and R. Eliezer both interpret: As soon as a man needs the support of his fellow-creatures his face changes colour like the *kerum*, as it is said: '*As the* kerum *is to be reviled among the sons of men*'. What is the '*kerum*'? When R. Dimi came [from Palestine] he said: There is a bird in the coast towns[7] whose name is *kerum*, and as soon as the sun shines upon it it changes into several colours.[8] R. Ammi and R. Assi both say: [When a man needs the support of his fellow-beings] it is as if he were punished with two [opposite] punishments, with fire and water. For it is said: *When Thou hast caused men to ride over our heads, we went through fire and through water.*[9]

R. Ḥelbo further said in the name of R. Huna: A man should always take special care about the afternoon-prayer. For even Elijah was favourably heard only while offering his afternoon-prayer. For it is said: *And it came to pass at the time of the offering of the evening offering, that Elijah the prophet came near and said . . .*
c *Hear me, O Lord, hear me.*[1] '*Hear me*', that the fire may descend from heaven, and '*hear me*', that they may not say it is the work of sorcery. R. Joḥanan says: [Special care should be taken] also about the evening-prayer. For it is said: *Let my prayer be set forth as incense before Thee, the lifting up of my hands as the evening sacrifice.*[2] R. Naḥman b. Isaac says: [Special care should be taken] also about the morning-prayer. For it is said: *O Lord, in the morning shalt Thou hear my voice; in the morning will I order my prayer unto Thee, and will look forward.*[3]

R. Ḥelbo further said in the name of R. Huna: Whosoever partakes of the wedding meal of a bridegroom and does not felicitate him does violence to 'the five voices' mentioned in the verse: *The voice of joy and the voice of gladness, the voice of the bridegroom and the voice of the bride, the voice of them that say, Give thanks to the Lord of Hosts.*[4] And if he does gladden him what is his reward?—R. Joshua b. Levi said: He is privileged to acquire [the knowledge of] the Torah which was given with five voices. For it is said: *And it came to pass on the third day, when it was morning, that there were* thunders[5] *and lightnings and a thick cloud upon the mount, and* the voice of a horn . . . *and when* the voice of the horn *waxed louder . . . Moses spoke and God answered him* by a voice.[6] (This is not so![7] For it is written: *And all the people perceived the thunderings?*[8]—These voices were before the revelation of the Torah.) R. Abbahu says: It is as if he[9] had sacrificed a thanksgiving offering. For it is said: *Even of them that bring offerings of thanksgiving into the house of the Lord.*[10] R. Naḥman b. Isaac says: It is as if he had restored one of the ruins of Jerusalem. For it is said: *For I will cause the captivity of the land to return as at the first, saith the Lord.*[11]

R. Ḥelbo further said in the name of R. Huna: If one is filled with the fear of God his words are listened to. For it is said: *The end of the matter, all having been heard: fear God, and keep his command-*
d *ments, for this is the whole man.*[1] What means, '*For this is the whole man*'?—R. Eleazar says: The Holy One, blessed be He, says: The whole world was created for his sake only. R. Abba b. Kahana says: He is equal in value to the whole world. R. Simeon b. 'Azzai says (some say, R. Simon b. Zoma says): The whole world was created as a satellite for him.

R. Ḥelbo further said in the name of R. Huna: If one knows that his friend is used to greet him, let him greet him first.[2] For it is said: *Seek peace and pursue it.*[3] And if his friend greets him and he does not return the greeting he is called a robber. For it is said: *It is ye that have eaten up the vineyard; the spoil of the poor is in your houses.*[4]

(8) Isa. L, 10. (9) Ibid. (10) Has he no light. (11) The number required for a public service. (12) In the absence of a quorum of ten, a number of important features in the service are omitted. (13) *Sc.* the congregational responses. Isa. L, 2.

a (1) *Aliter:* Alas, the pious man (is no more)! (2) Cf. previous note. (3) Gen. XIX, 27. (4) Ps. CVI, 30. (5) Hos. VI, 3. (6) It is forbidden to take large steps on the Sabbath, v. Shab. 113*b*. (7) Hos. XI, 10. The text continues: *For he shall roar, and the children shall come hurrying* (E.V. '*trembling*'). (8) V. Glos. (9) I.e., in the loud lamentation of the listeners. (10) These aphorisms are intended to bring home the lesson that the real merit of doing certain things lies not in themselves, but in their concomitants. For instance, the people running to the lectures do not benefit by the lectures, as they do not understand them. However they will be rewarded for enduring the rush and crush. The mechanical repetition of a tradition has no value if you do not try to understand it better. The merit of a fast day lies not in the fasting but in giving charity to the poor people, that they may have something to eat, etc.

[7a] R. Joḥanan says in the name of R. Jose: How do we know that the Holy One, blessed be He, says prayers? Because it says: *Even them will I bring to My holy mountain and make them joyful in My house of prayer.*[5] It is not said, 'their prayer', but *'My prayer'*; hence [you learn] that the Holy One, blessed be He, says prayers. What does He pray?—R. Zuṭra b. Tobi said in the name of Rab: 'May it be My will that My mercy may suppress My anger, and that My mercy may prevail over My [other] attributes, so that I may deal with My children in the attribute of mercy and, on their behalf, stop short of the limit of strict justice'.[6] It was taught: R. Ishmael b. Elisha says: I once entered into the innermost part [of the Sanctuary] to offer incense and saw Akathriel Jah,[7] the Lord of Hosts, seated upon a high and exalted throne. He said to me: Ishmael, My son, bless Me! I replied: May it be Thy will that Thy mercy may suppress Thy anger and Thy mercy may prevail over Thy other attributes, so that Thou mayest deal with Thy children according to the attribute of mercy and mayest, on their behalf, stop short of the limit of strict justice! And He nodded to me with His head. Here we learn [incidentally] that the blessing of an ordinary man must not be considered lightly in your eyes.

R. Joḥanan further said in the name of R. Jose: How do you know that we must not try to placate a man in the time of his
a anger? For it is written: *My face will go and I will give thee rest.*[1] The Holy One, blessed be He, said to Moses: Wait till My countenance of wrath shall have passed away and then I shall give thee rest. But is anger then a mood of the Holy One, blessed be He?—Yes. For it has been taught:[2] *A God that hath indignation every day.*[3] And how long does this indignation last? One moment. And how long is one moment? One fifty-eight thousand eight hundred and eighty-eighth part of an hour. And no creature has ever been able to fix precisely this moment except the wicked Balaam, of whom it is written: *He knoweth the knowledge of the Most High.*[4] Now, he did not even know the mind of his animal; how then could he know the mind of the Most High? The meaning is, therefore, only that he knew how to fix precisely this moment in which the Holy One, blessed be He, is angry. And this is just what the prophet said to Israel: *O my people, remember now what Balak king of Moab devised, and what Balaam the son of Beor answered him . . . that ye may know the righteous acts of the Lord.*[5] What means *'That ye may know the righteous acts of the Lord'?*—R. Eleazar says: The Holy One, blessed be He, said to Israel: See now, how many righteous acts I performed for you in not being angry in the days of the wicked Balaam. For had I been angry, not one remnant would have been left of the enemies of Israel.[6] And this too is the meaning of what Balaam said to Balak: *How shall I curse, whom God hath not cursed? And how shall I execrate, whom the Lord hath not execrated?*[7] This teaches us that He was not angry all these days. And how long does His anger last? One moment. And how long is one moment? R. Abin (some say R. Abina) says: As long as it takes to say *Rega'*.[8] And how do you know that He is angry one moment? For it is said: *For His anger is but for a moment* [rega'], *His favor is for a lifetime.*[9] Or if you prefer you may infer it from the following verse:
b *Hide thyself for a little moment until the indignation be overpast.*[1] And when is He angry?—Abaye says: In [one moment of] those first three hours of the day, when the comb of the cock is white and it stands on one foot. Why, in each hour it stands thus [on one foot]?[2]—In each other hour it has red streaks, but in this moment it has no red streaks at all.

In the neighbourhood of R. Joshua b. Levi there was a Sadducee[3] who used to annoy him very much with [his interpretations of] texts. One day the Rabbi took a cock, placed it between the legs of his bed and watched it. He thought: When this moment arrives I shall curse him. When the moment arrived he was dozing. [On waking up][4] he said: We learn from this that it is not proper to act in such a way. It is written: *And His tender mercies are over all His works.*[5] And it is further written: *Neither is it good for the righteous to punish.*[6] It was taught in the name of R. Meir: At the time when the sun rises and all the kings of the East and West put their crowns upon their heads and bow down to the sun, the Holy One, blessed be He, becomes at once angry.

R. Joḥanan further said in the name of R. Jose: Better is one self-reproach in the heart of a man than many stripes, for it is said: *And she shall run after her lovers . . . then shall she say,*[7] *I shall go and return to my first husband; for then was it better with me than now.*[8] R. Simon b. Laḳish says: It is better than a hundred stripes, for it is said: *A rebuke entereth deeper into a man of understanding than a hundred stripes into a fool.*[9]

R. Joḥanan further said in the name of R. Jose: Three things did Moses ask of the Holy One, blessed be He, and they were granted to him. He asked that the Divine Presence should rest upon Israel, and it was granted to him. For it is said: *Is it not in that Thou goest with us* [*so that we are distinguished, I and Thy people, from all the people that are upon the face of the earth*].[10] He asked that the Divine Presence should not rest upon the idolaters, and it was granted to him. For it is said: *'So that we are distinguished, I and Thy people'*. He asked that He should show him the ways of the Holy One, blessed be He, and it was granted to him. For it is said:
c *Show me now Thy ways.*[1] Moses said before Him: Lord of the Universe, why is it that some righteous men prosper and others are in adversity, some wicked men prosper and others are in adversity? He replied to him: Moses, the righteous man who prospers is the righteous man the son of a righteous man; the righteous man who is in adversity is a righteous man the son of a wicked man. The wicked man who prospers is a wicked man son of a righteous man; the wicked man who is in adversity is a wicked man son of a wicked man.

The Master said above: 'The righteous man who prospers is a righteous man son of a righteous man; the righteous man who is in adversity is a righteous man son of a wicked man'. But this is not so! For, lo, one verse says: *Visiting the iniquity of the fathers upon the children,*[2] and another verse says: *Neither shall the children be put to death for the fathers.*[3] And a contradiction was pointed out between these two verses, and the answer was given that there is no contradiction. The one verse deals with children who continue in the same course as their fathers, and the other verse with children who do not continue in the course of their fathers!—[You must] therefore [say that] the Lord said thus to Moses: A righteous man who prospers is a perfectly righteous man; the righteous man who is in adversity is not a perfectly righteous man. The wicked man who prospers is not a perfectly wicked man; the wicked man who is in adversity is a perfectly wicked man. Now this [saying of R. Joḥanan][4] is in opposition to the saying of R. Meir. For R. Meir said: only two [requests] were granted to him, and one was not granted to him. For it is said: *And I will be gracious to whom I will be gracious,* although he may not deserve it, *And I will show mercy on whom I will show mercy,*[5] although he may not deserve it.[6]

And He said, Thou canst not see My face.[7] A Tanna taught in the name of R. Joshua v. Ḳorḥah: The Holy One, blessed be He, spoke thus to Moses: When I wanted, you did not want [to see
d My face][1] now that you want, I do not want.—This is in opposition to [the interpretation of this verse by] R. Samuel b. Naḥmani in the name of R. Jonathan. For R. Samuel b. Naḥmani said in the name of R. Jonathan: As a reward of three [pious acts][2] Moses was privileged to obtain three [favours]. In reward of *'And Moses hid his face'*, he obtained the brightness of his face.[3] In reward of *'For he was afraid'*, he obtained the privilege that *They were afraid to come nigh him.*[4] In reward of *'To look upon God'*, he obtained *The similitude of the Lord doth he behold.*[5]

And I will take away My hand, and thou shalt see My back.[6] R. Ḥama b. Bizana said in the name of R. Simon the Pious: This teaches us that the Holy One, blessed be He, showed Moses the knot of the *tefillin*.[7]

R. Joḥanan further said in the name of R. Jose: No word of blessing that issued from the mouth of the Holy One, blessed be He, even if based upon a condition, was ever withdrawn by Him. How do we know this? From our teacher Moses. For it is said: *Let me alone, that I may destroy them, and blot out their name from under heaven; and I will make of thee a nation mightier and greater than they.*[8] Though Moses prayed that this might be mercifully averted and it was cancelled, [the blessing] was nevertheless fulfilled towards his children. For it is said: *The sons of Moses: Gershom and Eliezer . . . And the sons of Eliezer were Rehabia the chief . . . and the sons of Rehabiah were very many.*[9] And R. Joseph learnt: They were more than sixty myriads. This is to be learnt from two occurrences of the term 'manifold'. Here it is written: *were very many,* and elsewhere it is written: *And the children of Israel were very fruitful and increased abundantly, and became very many.*[10]

תורה אור

א"ר יוחנן משום ר' יוסי מניין שהקב"ה מתפלל שנא' °והביאותים אל הר קדשי ושמחתים בבית תפלתי תפלתם לא נאמר אלא תפלתי מכאן שהקב"ה מתפלל מאי מצלי אמר רב זוטרא בר טוביא אמר רב יה"ר מלפני שיכבשו רחמי את כעסי ויגולו רחמי על מדותי ואתנהג עם בני במדת רחמים ואכנס להם *לפנים משורת הדין תניא א"ר ישמעאל בן אלישע פעם אחת נכנסתי להקטיר קטרת לפני ולפנים וראיתי אכתריאל יה ה' צבאות שהוא יושב על כסא רם ונשא ואמר לי ישמעאל בני ברכני אמרתי לו יהר"מ שיכבשו רחמיך את כעסך ויגולו רחמיך על מדותיך ותתנהג עם בניך במדת הרחמים ותכנס להם לפנים משורת הדין ונענע לי בראשו וקמ"ל *שלא תהא ברכת הדיוט קלה בעיניך: וא"ר יוחנן משום ר' יוסי מנין *שאין מרצין לו לאדם בשעת כעסו דכתיב °פני ילכו והניחותי לך אמר לו הקב"ה למשה המתן לי עד שיעברו פנים של זעם ואניח לך ומי איכא רתחא קמיה דקודשא בריך הוא אין *דתניא °ואל זועם בכל יום וכמה זעמו רגע וכמה רגע אחד *מחמשת רבוא ושמונת אלפים ושמנה מאות ושמנים ושמנה בשעה וזו היא רגע *ואין כל בריה יכולה לכוין אותה שעה חוץ מבלעם הרשע דכתיב ביה °ויודע דעת עליון *השתא דעת בהמתו לא הוה ידע דעת עליון הוה ידע אלא מלמד שהיה יודע לכוין אותה שעה שהקב"ה כועס בה והיינו דאמר להו נביא לישראל °עמי זכר נא מה יעץ בלק מלך מואב וגו' מאי °למען דעת צדקות ה' א"ר אלעזר אמר להן הקב"ה לישראל דעו כמה צדקות עשיתי עמכם שלא כעסתי בימי בלעם הרשע שאלמלי *כעסתי לא נשתייר משונאיהם של ישראל שריד ופליט והיינו דקא"ל בלעם לבלק °מה אקוב לא קבה אל ומה אזעום לא זעם ה' מלמד שכל אותם הימים לא זעם: וכמה זעמו רגע וכמה רגע א"ר אבין ואיתימא רבי אבינא רגע כמימריה ומנא לן דרגע רתח שנאמר °כי רגע באפו חיים ברצונו ואב"א מהכא °חבי כמעט רגע עד יעבור זעם ואימת רתח אמר אביי בהנך תלת שעי קמייתא כי חוורא כרבלתא דתרנגולא וקאי אחד כרעא כל שעתא ושעתא נמי קאי הכי כל שעתא אית ביה שורייקי סומקי בההיא שעתא לית ביה שורייקי סומקי ההוא צדוקי דהוה בשבבותיה דר' יהושע בן לוי הוה קא מצער ליה טובא בקראי יומא חד שקל תרנגולא ואוקמיה בין כרעיה דערסא ועיין ביה סבר כי מטא ההיא שעתא אלטייה כי מטא ההיא שעתא ניים אמר ש"מ לאו אורח ארעא למעבד הכי °ורחמיו על כל מעשיו כתיב וכתיב °גם ענוש לצדיק לא טוב תנא משמיה דרבי מאיר בשעה שהחמה זורחת וכל מלכי מזרח ומערב מניחים כתריהם בראשיהם ומשתחוים לחמה מיד כועס הקב"ה: וא"ר יוחנן משום רבי יוסי טובה מרדות אחת בלבו של אדם יותר מכמה מלקיות שנאמר °ורדפה את מאהביה וגו' ואמרה אלכה ואשובה אל אישי הראשון כי טוב לי אז מעתה וריש לקיש אמר יותר ממאה מלקיות שנאמר °תחת גערה במבין מהכות כסיל מאה: וא"ר יוחנן משום רבי יוסי שלשה דברים בקש משה מלפני הקב"ה ונתן לו בקש שתשרה שכינה על ישראל ונתן לו שנאמר °הלא בלכתך עמנו *בקש שלא תשרה שכינה על אומות העולם ונתן לו שנאמר °ונפלינו אני ועמך בקש להודיעו דרכיו של הב"ה ונתן לו שנאמר °הודיעני נא את דרכיך אמר לפניו רבונו של עולם מפני מה יש צדיק וטוב לו ויש צדיק ורע לו יש רשע וטוב לו יש רשע ורע לו אמר לו משה צדיק וטוב לו צדיק בן צדיק צדיק ורע לו צדיק בן רשע רשע וטוב לו רשע בן צדיק רשע ורע לו רשע בן רשע: אמר מר צדיק וטוב לו צדיק בן צדיק צדיק ורע לו צדיק בן רשע איני והא כתיב °פוקד עון אבות על בנים וכתיב °*ובנים לא יומתו על אבות *ורמינן קראי אהדדי ומשנינן לא קשיא הא כשאוחזים מעשה אבותיהם בידיהם הא כשאין אוחזין מעשה אבותיהם בידיהם אלא הכי קא"ל צדיק וטוב לו צדיק גמור צדיק ורע לו צדיק שאינו גמור רשע וטוב לו רשע שאינו גמור רשע ורע לו רשע גמור ופליגא דר' מאיר דא"ר מאיר שתים נתנו לו ואחת לא נתנו לו שנא' °וחנותי את אשר אחון אף על פי שאינו הגון °ורחמתי את אשר ארחם אע"פ שאינו הגון: °ויאמר לא תוכל לראות את פני תנא משמיה דר' יהושע בן קרחה כך א"ל הקב"ה למשה כשרציתי לא רצית עכשיו שאתה רוצה איני רוצה ופליגא דר' שמואל בר נחמני א"ר יונתן דא"ר שמואל בר נחמני א"ר יונתן בשכר שלש זכה לשלש בשכר °ויסתר משה פניו זכה לקלסתר פנים בשכר כי ירא זכה °וייראו מגשת אליו בשכר מהביט זכה °ותמונת ה' יביט °והסירותי את כפי וראית את אחורי אמר רב חנא בר ביזנא א"ר שמעון חסידא מלמד *שהראה הקב"ה למשה קשר של תפילין: וא"ר יוחנן משום ר' יוסי °כל דבור ודבור שיצא מפי הקב"ה לטובה אפילו על תנאי לא חזר בו מנא לן ממשה רבינו שנא' °הרף ממני ואשמידם וגו' ואעשה אותך לגוי עצום אע"ג דבעא משה רחמי עלה דמלתא ובטלה אפילו הכי אוקמה בזרעיה שנ' °בני משה גרשום ואליעזר ויהיו בני אליעזר רחביה הראש וגו' ובני רחביה רבו למעלה וגו' ותני רב יוסף למעלה מששים רבוא אתיא רביה רביה כתיב הכא רבו למעלה וכתיב התם °ובני ישראל פרו וישרצו וירבו:

אמר

מסורת הש"ס

נענע לי בראשו. כמוד' בברכתי ועונה אמן: דעת בהמתו לא הוה ידע. במסכת עבודה אלילים מפרש לה בפרק קמא: מאי קרא. דאף הוי כרגע דכתיב כי רגע באפו חיים ברצונו: בתלת שעי קמייתא. באחד מרגעי תלת שעות ראשונות: שורייקי. עיי"ש בלבן: לצדיק לא טוב. לענוש את הבריות: מרדות אחת. לשון רדוי והכנעה שאדם שם על לבו מאליו: ורדפה את מאהביה וגו'. וכשתראה שאין עוזר חשים על לבה לאמר אשובה אל אישי הראשון: תחת גערה במבין. תחת גערה באדם מבין טובה מהכות כסיל מאה. תחת הטעם למעלה תחת התי"ו ולא כמו אל תירא ואל תחת (דברים א) שטעמו בחי"ת אלא למעלה תחת התי"ו ראשון. לומר שהוא שם דבר שאי אפשר לפותרו לשון תפעל לומר תכניע את האדם אלא תכנע היא בעצמה. ולכך שינה את נקודתה לומר שהוא שם דבר: שלשה דברים בקש משה ונתן לו. שהרי לסוף שאלתו כתיב גם את הדבר הזה אשר דברת אעשה: להודיע דרכיו. מנהג מדת משפטיו כגון מפני מה צדיק וטוב לו רשע ורע לו צדיק ורע לו רשע וטוב לו: את אשר אחון. את אשר יכמרו רחמי עליו לשעה ואף על פי שאינו כדאי: כשרציתי. בסנה: לא רצית. שנאמר ויסתר משה פניו: ופליגא. דרבי יהושע בן קרחה. שמענישו על כך אדרבי שמואל שאמר קבל שכר על זה: לקלסתר פנים. כי קרן עור פניו: ותמונת ה' יביט. זה מראה אחורים כך שנויה בספרי (פר' בהעלותך) וקשר של תפילין מאחוריו הוא ואמרינן לעיל דקב"ה מניח תפילין:

אדני

שאלמלי כעסתי לא נשתייר וכו' ואם תאמר מה היה יכול לומר בשעת רגע. יש לומר כלם. אי נמי מאחר שהיה מתחיל קללתו באותה שעה היה מזיק אפילו לאחר כן:

ההוא צדוקי דהוה בשבבותיה דריב"ל כו' לאו אורח ארעא. אע"ג דהצדוקים והמוסרים מורידין ולא מעלין *הייני בידי אדם אבל בידי שמים לאו אורח ארעא להענישם ולהטרידם ולהורגם בידי שמים שלא כדרך בני אדם. ואי גרסינן הכא ע"א ניחא דקאמר התם הע"א ורועי בהמה דקה לא מעלין ולא מורידין*:

לא

עין משפט נר מצוה

כז אמיי' פ"ה מהלכ' דיעות הלכה ז

כח במיי' פ"י מהל' יסודי התורה הל' ד

[ע"ז כו:]

[ועיין בתוס' בע"ז ד: ד"ה ש"מ לאו כו']

יש גורסים שמונ' רבוא ויותר נכון למחוק הרבוא כלל ולגרוס שמונת אלפים שמונה מאות ופ"ח שמכוון כנגד פסוקי תורה [ירו' גרס ה' רבוא ר' אלפים ח' מאות ומ"ח]

עיי' תוס' מגלה כח. ד"ה אלמלא

[ב"ב נח:]

[ע' תוספ' כתובות כט. וע"ז לו: ד"ה דכתיב]

מנחות לה:

ישעיה נו; [לקמן מה: כתובות לז. ב"ק לט: ב"מ כד: ל:]; מגילה טו.; שמות לג; ע"א ד. ע"ש; תהלים ו; ס"א שאין; במדבר כד; שם. וחלק קה:; מיכה ו; שם; במדבר כג; תהלים ל; ישעיה כו; תהלים קמה; משלי יז; הושע ב; משלי יז; שמות לג; שם. שם; שם לד; דברים כד; סנהדרין כז:; שמות לג. שם; שם; שם ג; שמות לד; במדבר יב; שמות לג; דברים ט; ד"ה א כג; שמות א

(5) Ibid. LVI, 7. Lit., 'In the house of My prayer'. (6) I.e., not exact the full penalty from them. (7) Lit., 'crown of God'.

a (1) Ex. XXXIII, 14. (2) V. A.Z. 4*a*. (3) Ps. VII, 12. (4) Num. XXIV, 16. (5) Micah VI, 5. (6) Euphemism for Israel. (7) Num. XXIII, 8. (8) 'A moment'. (9) Ps. XXX, 6.

b (1) Isa. XXVI, 20. (2) A better reading is: 'its comb is thus (viz., white)'. (3) Var. lec. *Min*. v. Glos. (4) Added with MS.M. (5) Ps. CXLV, 9. (6) Prov. XVII, 26. (7) In her heart. (8) Hos. II, 9. (9) Prov. XVII, 10. (10) Ex. XXXIII, 16.

c (1) Ex. XXXIII, 13. (2) Ibid. XXXIV, 7. (3) Deut. XXIV, 16. (4) That all the three requests of Moses were granted. (5) Ex. XXXIII, 19. (6) And God's ways therefore cannot be known. (7) Ibid. v. 20.

d (1) At the burning bush, Ex. III, 6. (2) Mentioned in Ex. III, 6; (i) *And Moses hid his face;* (ii) *for he was afraid;* (iii) *to look upon God*. (3) Cf. Ex. XXXIV, 29–30. (4) Ibid. v. 30. (5) Num. XII, 8. (6) Ex. XXXIII, 23. (7) Worn at the back of the head. (8) Deut. IX, 14. This verse contains a curse and a blessing, the blessing being conditional upon the realization of the curse. (9) I Chron. XXIII, 15–17. (10) Ex. I, 7. And we know that they were about sixty myriads when leaving Egypt.

תורה אור

אמר רבי יוחנן משום רבי שמעון בן יוחי מיום שברא הקב"ה את העולם לא היה אדם שקראו להקב"ה אדון עד שבא אברהם וקראו [ה'] אדון שנא' °ויאמר אדני (*אלהים) במה אדע כי אירשנה אמר רב אף דניאל לא נענה אלא בשביל אברהם שנאמר °ועתה שמע אלהינו אל תפלת עבדך ואל תחנוניו והאר פניך על מקדשך השמם למען אדני למענך מבעי ליה אלא למען אברהם שקראך אדון: ואמר ר' יוחנן משום רבי שמעון בן יוחי מנין שאין מרצין לו לאדם בשעת כעסו שנא' °פני ילכו והניחותי לך: ואמר ר"י משום ר' שמעון בן יוחי מיום שברא הקב"ה את עולמו לא היה אדם שהודה להקב"ה עד שבאתה לאה והודתו שנאמר °הפעם אודה את ה': ראובן א"ר אלעזר אמרה לאה ראו מה בין בני לבן חמי דאלו בן חמי אף על גב דמדעתיה זבניה לבכירותי' דכתיב °וימכור את בכורתו ליעקב חזו מה כתיב ביה °וישטום עשו את יעקב וכתיב °ויאמר הכי קרא שמו יעקב ויעקבני זה פעמים וגו' ואלו בני אף על גב דעל כרחיה שקליה יוסף לבכירותיה מיניה דכתיב °ובחללו יצועי אביו נתנה בכורתו (לבני) [ל] יוסף אפי' הכי לא אקנא ביה דכתיב °וישמע ראובן ויצילהו מידם: רות *מאי רות אר"י שזכתה ויצא ממנה דוד שריוהו להקב"ה בשירות ותשבחות מנא לן דשמא גרים אמר ר' *אליעזר דאמר קרא °לכו חזו מפעלות ה' אשר שם שמות בארץ אל תקרי שמות אלא שמות: ואמר ר' יוחנן משום ר"ש בן יוחי קשה תרבות רעה בתוך ביתו של אדם יותר ממלחמת גוג ומגוג שנאמר °מזמור לדוד בברחו מפני אבשלום בנו וכתיב בתריה °ה' מה רבו צרי רבים קמים עלי ואלו גבי מלחמת גוג ומגוג כתיב °למה רגשו גוים ולאומים יהגו ריק ואלו מה רבו צרי לא כתיב: מזמור לדוד בברחו מפני אבשלום בנו מזמור לדוד קינה לדוד מבעי ליה אמר רבי שמעון בן *אבישלום משל למה הדבר דומה לאדם שיצא עליו שטר חוב קודם שפרעו היה עצב לאחר שפרעו שמח אף כן דוד כיון שאמר לו הקב"ה °הנני מקים עליך רעה מביתך היה עצב אמר שמא עבד או ממזר הוא דלא חייס עלי כיון דחזא דאבשלום הוא שמח משום הכי אמר מזמור*: *ואמר רבי יוחנן משום ר"ש בן יוחי מותר להתגרות ברשעים בעה"ז שנא' °עוזבי תורה יהללו רשע ושומרי תורה יתגרו בם תניא נמי הכי *ר' דוסתאי בר' מתון אומר מותר להתגרות ברשעים בעה"ז שנא' עוזבי תורה יהללו רשע וגו' ואם לחשך אדם לומר והא כתיב °אל תתחר במרעים אל תקנא בעושי עולה אמור לו מי שלבו נוקפו אומר כן אלא אל תתחר במרעים להיות כמרעים ואל תקנא בעושי עולה להיות כעושי עולה ואומר °אל יקנא לבך בחטאים כי אם ביראת ה' כל היום איני והאמר ר' יצחק אם ראית רשע שהשעה משחקת לו אל תתגרה בו שנא' °יחילו דרכיו בכל עת ולא עוד אלא שזוכה בדין שנא' °מרום משפטיך מנגדו ולא עוד אלא שרואה בצריו שנא' °כל צורריו יפיח בהם לא קשיא הא במילי דידיה הא במילי דשמיא ואיבע"א הא והא במילי דשמיא ול"ק הא ברשע שהשעה משחקת לו הא ברשע שאין השעה משחק' לו ואבע"א הא והא ברשע שהשעה משחקת לו ולא קשיא הא בצדיק גמור הא בצדיק שאינו גמור *דאמר רב הונא מאי דכתיב °למה תביט בוגדים תחריש בבלע רשע צדיק ממנו וכי רשע בולע צדיק והא כתיב °ה' לא יעזבנו בידו וכתיב °לא יאונה לצדיק כל און אלא צדיק ממנו בולע צדיק גמור אינו בולע ואיבעית אימא *שעה משחקת לו שאני: ואמר רבי יוחנן משום רבי שמעון בן יוחי כל הקובע מקום *לתפלתו אויביו נופלים תחתיו שנא' °ושמתי מקום לעמי לישראל ונטעתיו ושכן תחתיו ולא ירגז עוד ולא יוסיפו בני עולה לענותו כאשר בראשונה רב הונא רמי כתיב לענותו וכתיב *לכלותו בתחלה לענותו ולבסוף לכלותו: ואמר רבי יוחנן משום ר' שמעון בן יוחי גדולה שמושה של תורה יותר מלמודה שנאמר °פה אלישע בן שפט אשר יצק מים על ידי אליהו למד לא נאמר אלא יצק מלמד שגדולה שמושה יותר מלמודה: א"ל ר' יצחק לרב נחמן מאי טעמא לא אתי מר לבי כנישתא לצלויי אמר ליה לא יכילנא אמר ליה לכנפי למר עשרה וליצלי אמר ליה טריחא לי מלתא ולימא ליה מר לשלוחא דצבורא בעידנא דמצלי צבורא ליתי ולודעי למר אמר ליה מאי כולי האי דאמר רבי יוחנן משום

ר"ש בן יוחי   מאי

אדני אלהים. כתוב באל"ף דל"ת: הפעם אודה את ה'. לפי שראתה ברוח הקדש שיעקב מעמיד שני' עשר שבטים ולו ארבע נשים כיון שילדה בן רביעי הודית על חלקה שעלה יותר מן החשבון המגיע לה: ראו מה בין בני לבן חמי. על שם העתיד קראה שמו כדאמרינן לקמן שמא גרים: רות. שמואביה משום דאיירי בפירושי השמות נקט לה: למה רגשו גוים. מה תועלת להם אלמא דבר קל הוא בעיניו: מי שלבו נוקפו. שיראה מעבירות שבידו: אומר כן. מפרש אל תתחר במרעים אל תתקוטט והוא אינו כן אלא אל תתחר במרעים *להתגרות במעשיהם לומר אעשה כן גם אני: ואומר אל יקנא לבך בחטאים כי אם ביראת ה' כל היום. *אפשר לומר אל תתקוטט עם רשעים כי אם ביראת ה' יראי ה' אלא על כרחך אל יקנא לבך לעשות כמותן: יחילו. יצליחו. וחבירו על כן לא יחיל טובו (איוב כ): מרום משפטיך מנגדו. מסולקין דיניך ברחוק הימנו: יפיח בהם. בכפיחתו יהא דוח' אותם בקש: ושמתי מקום. סיפי' דקרא ולא יוסיפו בני עולה לענותו: כתיב לענותו. בספר שמואל: וכתיב לכלותו. בדברי הימים (א' יז): תחלה. כשבנה הבית נבנה על מנת שלא לענות עוד אויבים לישראל: ולבסוף. כשחטאו נגזר עליהם ענוי ותפלתם מגינה עליהם מן הכליון: לא יכילנא: תש כחי: עת

לא היה אדם שקראו להקב"ה אדון. וא"ת והא כתיב ברוך יי' אלהי שם (בראשית ט) ויש לומר דהתם אינו באלף דל"ת שהוא לשון אדנות. ואם תאמר אמאי לא מייתי קרא אדני (*אלהים) מה תתן לי (שם טו) שהוא כתוב קודם. ויש לומר שהפרשיות לא נאמרו כסדר ואין מוקדם ומאוחר בתורה וזה הפסוק דבין הבתרים היה קודם לכן. וכן נ"ל ע"כ שהרי אברהם היה בן שבעים שנה בברית בין הבתרים ואחר הדברים האלה (שם טו) כאומר אחר מלחמת המלכים כדפרש"י בפירוש חומש ובמלחמת המלכים היה בן ע"ג שנים שהרי כל הימים של סדום נ"ב שנים כדאמרינן בפרק קמא דשבת (דף יא.) לא מהם י"ב שנים שעבדו את כדרלעומר וי"ג שנים של מרידה ובשאר מיסובה כ"ו שנים שהיתה בשלוה ובהפיכתה היה אברהם בן צ"ט שנה שהרי היתה ההפיכה שנה אחת קודם שנולד יצחק לא מהם שמה ועשרים שנה למפרע של שלוה נמצא שבן ע"ג שנה היה במלחמת המלכים אם כן היתה פרשת בין הבתרים קודם לפרשת אחר הדברים שלש שנים ואותה פרשה מסיימת ויחשבה לו לצדקה ולכך הביא אותו פסוק דבמה אדע שהוא מוקדם. ומזה מיישב רשב"ם דבמקום אחד משמע שהיה לילה דכתיב וספור את הככבים (בראשית טו) ובתר הכי כתיב ויהי השמש לבא משמע שהיה יום אלא ודאי ש"מ דשני פרשיות הם ולאו בבת א' נאמרו ואין מוקדם ומאוחר בתורה: רב

מסורת הש"ס

ס"א להתלות

[ע' בפירש"י שבע"י]

בראשית טו · דניאל ט · שמות לג · בראשית כט · שם כה · שם כז · שם · ד"ה א ה · בראשית לו

[נ"ל אלעזר] תהלים מו · שם ג · שם. · שם ג · שמואל ב יב · מגילה דף ו: · משלי כח · מסכת דרך ארץ רבה פרק ג · תהלים לז · משלי כד · תהלים י · שם. · שם · מגילה שם · ב"מ ע. · חבקוק א · תהלים לז · משלי יב · כ"א לעמי · שמואל ב' ז · בספר שבדברי כתיב לבלותו · מלכים ב ג

[ה']

[נ"ב יד: ע"ש]

[ע' תוספ' יומא לח: ותוס' כתובות קד: ד"ה שני]

ס"א אמר קסם ברא דכתים על אבא

[פי' על זה תמלא בהכי"ף בע"י ועיין ילקוט תהלים יו"ד רמז תרמ"ע]

d (1) II Sam. VII, 10. (2) I Chron. XVII, 9. The Gemara read there לכלותו. Our masoretic text, however, reads לבלותו. The meaning is the same. (3) To act as the famulus of the teacher is even more meritorious than being his disciple. (4) II Kings III, 11. (5) Why does he not pray publicly with the congregation? (6) For physical reasons. (7) The Reader. (8) So that R. Naḥman might say his prayers at the same time as the congregation.

[7b] R. Johanan said [further] in the name of R. Simeon b. Yohai: From the day that the Holy One, blessed be He, created the world there was no man that called the Holy One, blessed be He, a *Lord*,[1] until Abraham came and called Him *Lord*. For it is said: *And he said, O Lord* [Adonai] *God, whereby shall I know that I shall inherit it?*[2] Rab said: Even Daniel was heard [in his prayer] only for the sake of Abraham. For it says: *Now therefore, O our God, hearken unto the prayer of Thy servant, and to his supplications, and cause Thy face to shine upon Thy sanctuary that is desolate, for the* Lord's *sake*.[3] He ought to have said: 'For Thy sake', but [he means]: For the sake of Abraham, who called Thee Lord.

R. Johanan further said in the name of R. Simeon b. Yohai: How do you know that we must not try to placate a man in the time of his anger? Because it is said: *My face will go and I will give thee rest*.[4]

R. Johanan further said in the name of R. Simeon b. Yohai: From the day that the Holy One, blessed be He, created His world there was no man that praised the Holy One, blessed be He, until Leah came and praised Him. For it is said: *This time will I praise the Lord*.[5]

Reuben. [What is the meaning of 'Reuben'?][6]—R. Eleazar said: Leah said: See the difference between[7] my son and the son of my father-in-law. The son of my father-in-law voluntarily sold his birthright, for it is written: *And he sold his birthright unto Jacob*.[8] And, nonetheless, behold, it is written of him: *And Esau hated Jacob*,[9] and it is also written: *And he said, is not he rightly named Jacob? for he hath supplanted me these two times*.[10] My son, however, although Joseph took his birthright from him against his will—as it is written: *But, for as much as he defiled his father's couch, his birthright was given unto the sons of Joseph*,[11]—was not jealous of him. For it is written: *And Reuben heard it, and delivered him out of their hand*.[12]

Ruth. What is the meaning of Ruth?—R. Johanan said: Because b she was privileged to be the ancestress of David, who saturated[1] the Holy One, blessed be He, with songs and hymns. How do we know that the name [of a person] has an effect [upon his life]?[2]—R. Eleazar said: Scripture says: *Come, behold the works of the Lord, who hath made* desolations *in the earth*.[3] Read not *shammoth*, ['desolations'], but *shemoth*, [names].

R. Johanan further said in the name of R. Simeon b. Yohai: A bad son[4] in a man's house is worse than the war of Gog and Magog. For it is said: *A Psalm of David, when he fled from Absalom his son*,[5] and it is written after that: *Lord, how many are mine adversaries become! Many are they that rise up against me*.[6] But in regard to the war of Gog and Magog it is written: *Why are the nations in an uproar? And why do the peoples mutter in vain*,[7] but, it is not written: *'How many are mine adversaries become!'*

'A Psalm of David, when he fled from Absalom his son'. *'A Psalm of David'?* He ought to have said: 'A Lamentation of David'! R. Simeon b. Abishalom said: A parable: To what is this to be compared? To a man who has a bond outstanding against him; until he pays it he worries[8] but after he has paid it, he rejoices. So was it with David. When the Holy One, blessed be He, said to him: *Behold, I will raise up evil against thee out of thine own house*,[9] he began worrying. He thought: it may be a slave or a bastard who will have no pity on me. When he saw that it was Absalom, he was glad, and therefore he said: *'A Psalm'*.

R. Johanan further said in the name of R. Simeon b. Yohai: It is permitted to contend with the wicked in this world. For it is said: *They that forsake the law praise the wicked, but such as keep the law contend with them*.[10] It has been taught to the same effect: R. Dosthai son of R. Mattun says: It is permitted to contend with the wicked in this world. For it is said: *'They that forsake the law praise the wicked*, etc.'—Should somebody whisper to you: But is it not written: *Contend not with evil-doers, neither be thou envious against them* c *that work unrighteousness*,[1] then you may tell him: Only one whose conscience smites[2] him says so. In fact, *'Contend not with evil-doers'*, means, to be like them; *'neither be thou envious against them that work unrighteousness'*, means, to be like them. And so it is said: *Let not thy heart envy sinners, but be in the fear of the Lord all the day*.[3] But this is not so! For R. Isaac said: If you see a wicked man upon whom fortune[4] is smiling, do not attack him. For it is said: *His ways prosper at all times*.[5] And more than that, he is victorious in the court of judgment; for it is said: *Thy judgments are far above out of his sight*.[6] And still more than that, he sees the discomfiture of his enemies; for it is said: *As for all his adversaries, he puffeth at them*.[7] There is no contradiction. The one [R. Isaac] speaks of his private affairs, the other one [R. Johanan] of matters of religion.[8] If you wish I can say: both speak of matters of religion, and still there is no contradiction. The one [R. Isaac] speaks of a wicked man upon whom fortune is smiling, the other one speaks of a wicked man upon whom fortune is not smiling. Or if you wish, I can say, both speak of a wicked man upon whom fortune is smiling, and still there is no contradiction. The one [R. Johanan] speaks of a perfectly righteous man, the other one of a man who is not perfectly righteous. For R. Huna said: What is the meaning of the verse: *Wherefore lookest Thou, when they deal treacherously, and holdest Thy peace, when the wicked swalloweth up the man that is more righteous than he?*[9] Can then the wicked swallow up the righteous? Is it not written: *The Lord will not leave him in his hand?*[10] And is it not written further: *There shall no mischief befall the righteous?*[11] [You must] therefore [say]: He swallows up the one who is only *'more righteous than he'*, but he cannot swallow up the perfectly righteous man. If you wish I can say: It is different when fortune is smiling upon him.

R. Johanan further said in the name of R. Simeon b. Yohai: If a man has a fixed place for his prayer, his enemies succumb to him. For it is said: *And I will appoint* a place *for My people Israel, and will plant them, that they may dwell in their own place, and be disquieted no more; neither shall the children of wickedness afflict them any more* d *as at the first*.[1] R. Huna pointed to a contradiction. [Here] it is written: *'To afflict them'*, and [elsewhere]: *To exterminate them?*[2] [The answer is]: First to afflict them and then to exterminate them.

R. Johanan further said in the name of R. Simeon b. Yohai: The service of the Torah is greater than the study thereof.[3] For it is said: *Here is Elisha the son of Shaphat, who poured water on the hands of Elijah*.[4] It is not said, *who learned*, but *who poured water*. This teaches that the service of the Torah is greater than the study thereof.

R. Isaac said to R. Nahman: Why does the Master not come to the Synagogue in order to pray?[5]—He said to him: I cannot.[6] He asked him: Let the Master gather ten people and pray with them [in his house]?—He answered: It is too much of a trouble for me. [He then said]: Let the Master ask the messenger of the congregation[7] to inform him of the time when the congregation prays?[8] He answered: Why all this [trouble]?—He said to him: For R. Johanan said in the name of R. Simeon b. Yohai: [8a]

a (1) In Hebrew: *Adon*. (2) Gen. XV, 8. (3) Dan. IX, 17. (4) Ex. XXXIII, 14. Cf. also *supra* 7a. (5) Gen. XXIX, 35. She implied that this had never been done before. (6) Words in brackets added from MS.M. This passage is suggested by the mention of Leah. (7) Reuben is explained as ראו בין, 'See the difference between'. (8) Ibid. XXV, 33. (9) Ibid. XXVII, 41. (10) Ibid. XXVII, 36. (11) I Chron. V, 1. (12) Gen. XXXVII, 21.

b (1) רות is derived from רוה to saturate. (2) Lit., 'causes', 'determines (one's destiny)'. (3) Ps. XLVI, 9. (4) Lit., 'training', 'upbringing'. (5) Ibid. III, 1. (6) Ibid. 2. (7) Ibid. II, 1. (8) MS.M.: To a man to whom it is said tomorrow a bill will be issued against you until he sees it . . . after he sees it etc. (9) II Sam. XII, 11. (10) Prov. XXVIII, 4.

c (1) Ps. XXXVII, 1. E.V. *'Fret not thyself'*. (2) Lit., 'whose heart knocks him'. (3) Prov. XXIII, 17. (4) Lit., 'the hour'. (5) Ps. X, 5. (6) Ibid. (7) Ibid. (8) You may fight him with regard to religious affairs, but not with regard to his private affairs. (9) Hab. I, 13. (10) Ps. XXXVII, 33. (11) Prov. XII, 21.

What is the meaning of the verse: *But as for me, let my prayer be made unto Thee, O Lord, in an acceptable time?*[9] When is the time acceptable? When the congregation prays. R. Jose b. R. Ḥanina says: [You learn it] from here: *Thus saith the Lord, In an acceptable time have I answered thee.*[10] R. Aḥa son of R. Ḥanina says: [You learn it] from here: *Behold, God despiseth not the mighty.*[11] And it is further written: *He hath redeemed my soul in peace so that none came*
a *nigh me; for they* were many *with me.*[1] It has been taught also to the same effect; R. Nathan says: How do we know that the Holy One, blessed be He, does not despise the prayer of the congregation? For it is said: '*Behold, God despiseth not the mighty*'. And it is further written: '*He hath redeemed my soul in peace so that none came nigh me,* etc.'. The Holy One, blessed be He, says: If a man occupies himself with the study of the Torah and with works of charity and prays with the congregation, I account it to him as if he had redeemed Me and My children from among the nations of the world.

Resh Laḳish said: Whosoever has a Synagogue in his town and does not go there in order to pray, is called an evil neighbour. For it is said: *Thus saith the Lord, as for all Mine evil neighbours, that touch the inheritance which I have caused My people Israel to inherit.*[2] And more than that, he brings exile upon himself and his children. For it is said: *Behold, I will pluck them up from off their land, and will pluck up the house of Judah from among them.*[3]

When they told R. Joḥanan[4] that there were old men in Babylon, he showed astonishment and said: Why, it is written: *That your days may be multiplied, and the days of your children, upon the land;*[5] but not outside the land [of Israel]! When they told him that they came early to the Synagogue and left it late, he said: That is what helps them. Even as R. Joshua b. Levi said to his children: Come early to the Synagogue and leave it late that you may live long. R. Aḥa son of R. Ḥanina says: Which verse [may be quoted in support of this]? *Happy is the man that hearkeneth to Me, watching daily at My gates, waiting at the posts of My doors,*[6] after which it is written: *For whoso findeth me findeth life.*[7] R. Ḥisda says: A man should always enter two doors into the Synagogue.[8] What is the meaning of 'two doors'? Say: The distance of two doors, and then pray.[9]

b *For this let every one that is godly pray unto Thee in the time of finding.*[1] R. Ḥanina says: '*In the time of finding*' refers to [the finding of] a wife. For it is said: *Whoso findeth a wife findeth a great good.*[2] In the West they used to ask a man who married a wife thus: *Maẓa* or *Moẓe?*[3] '*Maẓa*', for it is written: *Whoso findeth* [maẓa] *a wife findeth a great good*. '*Moẓe*', for it is written: *And I find* [moẓe] *more bitter than death the woman.*[4] R. Nathan says: '*In the time of finding*' refers to the [finding of] Torah. For it is said: *For whoso findeth me findeth life,* etc.[5] R. Naḥman b. Isaac said: '*In the time of finding*' refers to the [finding of] death. For it is said: *The issues of death.*[6] Similarly it has been taught: Nine hundred and three species of death were created in this world. For it is said: *The issues of death,* and the numerical value of *Toẓa'oth* is so. The worst of them is the croup, and the easiest of them is the kiss.[7] Croup is like a thorn in a ball of wool pulled out backwards.[8] Some people say: It is like [pulling] a rope through the loop-holes [of a ship].[9] [Death by a] kiss is like drawing a hair out of milk. R. Joḥanan said: '*In the time of finding*' refers to the [finding of a] grave. R. Ḥanina said: Which verse [may be quoted in support]? *Who rejoice unto exultation and are glad, when they can* find *the grave.*[10] Rabbah son of R. Shila said: Hence the proverb: A man should pray for peace even to the last clod of earth [thrown upon his grave]. Mar Zuṭra said: '*In the time of finding*', refers to the [finding of a] privy.[11] They said in the West: This [interpretation] of Mar Zuṭra is the best of all.

Raba said to Rafram b. Papa: Let the master please tell us some of those fine things that you said in the name of R. Ḥisda on matters relating to the Synagogue!—He replied: Thus said R. Ḥisda: What is the meaning of the verse: *The Lord loveth the gates of Zion* [Ziyyon]
c *more than all the dwellings of Jacob?*[1] The Lord loves the gates that are distinguished [*me-ẓuyanim*] through *Halachah* more than the Synagogues and Houses of study.[2] And this conforms with the following saying of R. Ḥiyya b. Ammi in the name of 'Ulla: Since the day that the Temple was destroyed, the Holy One, blessed be He, has nothing in this world but the four cubits of *Halachah* alone. So said also Abaye: At first I used to study in my house and pray in the Synagogue. Since I heard the saying of R. Ḥiyya b. Ammi in the name of 'Ulla: 'Since the day that the Temple was destroyed, the Holy One, blessed be He, has nothing in His world but the four cubits of *Halachah* alone', I pray only in the place where I study. R. Ammi and R. Assi, though they had thirteen Synagogues in Tiberias, prayed only between the pillars where they used to study.[3]

R. Ḥiyya b. Ammi further said in the name of 'Ulla: A man who lives from the labour [of his hands] is greater than the one who fears heaven.[4] For with regard to the one who fears heaven it is written: *Happy is the man that feareth the Lord,*[5] while with regard to the man who lives from his own work it is written: *When thou eatest the labour of thy hands, happy shalt thou be, and it shall be well with thee.*[6] '*Happy shalt thou be*', in this world, '*and it shall be well with thee*', in the world to come. But of the man that fears heaven it is not written: '*and it shall be well with thee*'.

R. Ḥiyya b. Ammi further said in the name of 'Ulla: A man should always live in the same town as his teacher. For as long as Shimei the son of Gera was alive Solomon did not marry the daughter of Pharaoh.[7]—But it has been taught that he should not live [in the same place]?—There is no contradiction. The former [speaks of a disciple] who is submissive to him, the other [of a disciple] who is not submissive.

R. Huna b. Judah in the name of R. Menaḥem in the name of R. Ammi said: What is the meaning of the verse: *And they that*
d *forsake the Lord shall be consumed?*[1] This refers to people who leave the Scroll of the Law [while it is being read from] and go out [from the Synagogue]. R. Abbahu used to go out between one reader and the next.[2] R. Papa raised the question: What of going out between verse and verse? It remains unanswered.—R. Shesheth used to turn his face to another side and study. He said: We [are busy] with ours, and they [are busy] with theirs.[3]

R. Huna b. Judah says in the name of R. Ammi: A man should always complete his *Parashoth* together with the congregation,[4] [reading] twice the Hebrew text and once the [Aramaic] Targum,

(9) Ps. LXIX, 14. (10) Isa. XLIX, 8. (11) Job. XXXVI, 5. I.e., the mighty and numerous people that pray to Him. E.V. *God is mighty and despiseth not any.*
a (1) Joining me in prayer. Ps. LV, 19. (E.V. 'for there were many that strove with me'.) (2) Jer. XII, 14. (3) Ibid. (4) Who was a Palestinian. (5) Deut. XI, 21. (6) Prov. VIII, 34. (7) Ibid. 35. (8) MS.M. adds: 'and then pray, for it is written: "*Waiting at the posts of My doors*".' (9) Were he to remain at the entrance, near the door, it would look as if he was anxious to leave.
b (1) Ps. XXXII, 6. (2) Prov. XVIII, 22. (3) Whereas the word *maẓa* is used in the Bible in connection with a good wife, the word *moẓe* is used in connection with a bad wife. (4) Eccl. VII, 26. (5) Prov. VIII, 35. (6) Ps. LXVIII, 21. תוצאות is translated 'findings'. (7) The Talmud refers to an easy death as the 'death by a kiss'. (8) And drawing the wool with it. (9) The friction being very great (Rashi). Jast.: Like the whirling waters at the entrance of a canal (when the sluicebars are raised). (10) Job. III, 22. (11) In Babylon, owing to the marshy character of the soil, privies were for the most part outside the town at some distance from the dwellings.
c (1) Ps. LXXXVII, 2. (2) *Beth Midrash* is here understood as the house of popular, *aggadic* lectures which, however, was not devoted to the study of *Halachah*. (3) In the Beth-hamidrash. (4) But for his living relies upon the support of other people. (5) Ps. CXII, 1. (6) Ibid. CXXVIII, 2. (7) The assumption is that he forbore to do so out of respect for his teacher.
d (1) Isa. I, 28. (2) I.e., when one portion was finished and before the next had commenced. (3) They are engaged in listening to the public reading and we, more profitably, with more advanced study. (4) I.e., recite (at home) the same weekly portion (*parashah*) from the Pentateuch.

מאי דכתיב °ואני תפלתי לך ה' עת רצון [א]אימתי *עת רצון בשעה שהצבור מתפללין רבי יוסי ברבי חנינא אמר מהכא °כה אמר ה' בעת רצון עניתיך רבי אחא ברבי חנינא אמר מהכא °הן אל כביר ולא ימאס וכתיב °פדה בשלום נפשי מקרב לי כי ברבים היו עמדי תניא נמי הכי רבי נתן אומר מנין שאין הקב"ה מואס בתפלתן של רבים שנאמר הן אל כביר ולא ימאס וכתיב פדה בשלום נפשי מקרב לי וגו' אמר הקב"ה כל העוסק בתורה ובגמילות חסדים ומתפלל עם הצבור מעלה אני עליו כאלו פדאני לי ולבני מבין אומות העולם: אמר ר"ל [ב]כל מי שיש לו בה"כ בעירו ואינו נכנס שם להתפלל נקרא שכן רע שנא' °כה אמר ה' על כל שכני הרעים הנוגעים בנחלה אשר הנחלתי את עמי את ישראל ולא עוד אלא שגורם גלות לו ולבניו שנא' °הנני נותשם מעל אדמתם ואת בית יהודה אתוש מתוכם: אמרו ליה לרבי יוחנן איכא סבי בבבל תמה ואמר °למען ירבו ימיכם וימי בניכם על האדמה כתיב אבל בחוצה לארץ לא כיון דאמרי ליה מקדמי ומחשכי לבי כנישתא אמר היינו דאהני להו כדאמר ר' יהושע בן לוי לבני' קדימו וחשיכו ועיילו לבי כנישתא כי היכי דתורכו חיי אמר רבי אחא ברבי חנינא מאי קראה °אשרי אדם שומע לי לשקוד על דלתותי יום יום לשמור מזוזות פתחי וכתיב בתריה כי מוצאי מצא חיים: אמר רב חסדא [ג]לעולם יכנס אדם *שני פתחים בבית הכנסת שני פתחים סלקא דעתך אלא אימא שיעור שני פתחים ואחר כך יתפלל: °על זאת יתפלל כל חסיד אליך לעת מצא אמר רבי חנינא לעת מצא זו אשה שנאמר °מצא אשה מצא טוב *במערבא כי נסיב איניש אתתא אמרי ליה הכי מצא או מוצא מצא דכתיב מצא אשה מצא טוב ויפק רצון מה' מוצא דכתיב °ומוצא אני מר ממות את האשה וגו' רבי נתן אומר לעת מצא זו תורה שנאמר °כי מצאי מצא חיים וגו' רב נחמן בר יצחק אמר לעת מצא זו מיתה שנאמר °למות תוצאות תניא נמי הכי תשע מאות ושלשה מיני מיתה נבראו בעולם שנאמר למות תוצאות תוצאות בגמטריא הכי הוו קשה שבכלן אסכרא ניחא שבכלן נשיקה אסכרא דמיא כחיזרא בגבבא דעמרא דלאחורי נשרא ואיכא דאמרי כפיטורי בפי ושט נשיקה דמיא כמשחל בניתא מחלבא רבי יוחנן אמר לעת מצא זו קבורה אמר ר' חנינא מאי קראה °השמחים אלי גיל ישישו כי ימצאו קבר אמר רבה בר רב שילא היינו דאמרי אינשי לבעי איניש רחמי אפילו עד זיבולא בתרייתא שלמא מר זוטרא אמר לעת מצא זה בית הכסא אמרי במערבא הא דמר זוטרא עדיפא מכלהו: אמר ליה רבא לרפרם בר פפא לימא לן מר מהני מילי מעלייתא דאמרת משמיה דרב חסדא במילי דבי כנישתא אמר ליה הכי אמר רב חסדא מאי דכתיב °אוהב ה' שערי ציון מכל משכנות יעקב אוהב ה' שערים המצויינים בהלכה יותר מבתי כנסיות ומבתי מדרשות והיינו דאמר רבי חייא בר אמי משמיה דעולא מיום שחרב בית המקדש אין לו להקב"ה בעולמו אלא ארבע אמות של הלכה בלבד *ואמר אביי מריש הוה גריסנא בגו ביתא ומצלינא בבי כנישתא כיון דשמענא להא דא"ר חייא בר אמי משמיה דעולא מיום שחרב בית המקדש אין לו להקב"ה בעולמו אלא ד' אמות של הלכה בלבד [ו]לא הוה מצלינא אלא היכא דגריסנא *רבי אמי ורבי אסי אע"ג דהוו להו תליסר בי כנישת' בטבריא לא מצלו אלא ביני עמודי היכא דהוו גרסי וא"ר חייא בר אמי משמיה דעולא גדול הנהנה מיגיעו יותר מירא שמים דאלו גבי ירא שמים כתיב °אשרי איש ירא את ה' ואלו גבי נהנה מיגיעו כתיב °יגיע כפיך כי תאכל אשריך וטוב לך *אשריך בעולם הזה וטוב לך לעולם הבא ולגבי ירא שמים וטוב לך לא כתיב ביה: וא"ר חייא בר אמי משמיה דעולא לעולם ידור אדם במקום רבו שכל זמן ששמעי בן גרא קיים לא נשא שלמה את בת פרעה והתניא אל ידור לא קשיא הא דכייף ליה הא דלא כייף ליה: אמר רב הונא בר יהודה א"ר מנחם אמר רבי אמי מאי דכתיב °ועזבי ה' יכלו [ז]זה המניח ספר תורה ויוצא [ח]רבי אבהו נפיק בין גברא לגברא בעי רב פפא [ט]בין פסוקא לפסוקא מהו תיקו רב ששת [י]מהדר אפיה וגריס אמר אנן בדידן ואינהו בדידהו: אמר רב הונא בר יהודה אמר רבי אמי [כ]לעולם ישלים אדם פרשיותיו עם הצבור שנים מקרא ואחד תרגום ואפילו

תורה אור: תהלי' סט; ישעי' מט; איוב לו; תהלים נה; ירמי' יב; שם; דברי' יא; משלי' ח; תהלים לב; משלי' יח; קהלת ז; משלי' ח; תהלים פח; איוב ג; תהלים פז; תהלים קיב; שם קכח; ישעיה א

רש"י

עת רצון. אלמא יש שעה שהיא של רצון: כביר לא ימאס. תפלת הרבים לא ימאס: מקרב לי. ממלחמות הבאות עלי: כי ברבים היו עמדי. שהתפללו עמי: פדה בשלום. זה שעסק בדברי שלום דהיינו תורה דכתיב וכל נתיבותיה שלום (משלי ג) וכן גמילות חסדים נמי שלום הוא שמתוך שגומל חסד בגופו לחבירו הוא מכיר שהוא אוהבו ובא לידי אחוה ושלום: הנני נותשם מעל אדמתם. סיפי' דקרא הוא: מקדמי. שחרית: מחשכי. ערבי' כלומר מאחרין בבית הכנסת: שיעור של שני פתחים. רוחב יכנס לפנים שלא ישב סמוך לפתח דנראה עליו כמשוי עכוב בית הכנסת ויהא מזומן סמוך לפתח לצאת: יתפלל לעת מצא. יתפלל שיהו מלויין לו כשיצטרך: לעת מצא זו מיתה. שימות במיתה יפה ונחה: אסכרא. איסטרנ"א כגולמכ"ע בלע"ז שבתוך הגוף: כחיזר' בגבבא דעמר' דלאחורי נשרא. כענפי הקוצים הסבוכים בגיזת הצמר כשאדם מנתק בחזקה ומשליך לאחור שאי אפשר שלא ינתק הצמר עמה: כפיטורי בפי ושט. יש אוקייאנוס יש בו מקומות שאינו מקבל ברזל ומחברין לוחי הספינה ע"י חבלים ועקלים שתוחבי' בנקביו ותוקעין אותו בדוחק לפי שהם גסין כמדת הנקב. פיטורי. חבלים דמתרגמינן ופיטורי ליצים (מלכים א ו) אטוכין. בפי ושט. הוא הנקב שהוא עגול כפי ושט: כמשחל בינית' מחלבא. כמושך נימת שער מתוך החלב: זיבולא בתריית' שלמא. שיהא לו שלום כל ימי חייו ואף ביום קבורתו עד השלכת עפר האחרונה שבכיסוי קבורתו. זיבולא. פלא"ה בלעז: לעת מצא זו בית הכסא. שיהא דר במקום שיש בית הכסא סמוך לו לפי שהיתה קרקע של בבל מצולת מים ואין יכולין לחפור שם חפירות והיו צריכין לצאת בשדות ולהתרחק מאד: המצויינים. ציון ואסיפת צבור: ביני עמודי. שבית המדרש בנוי עליהם מלמעלה: שכל זמן ששמעי בן גרא קיים כו' דסמוך למיתת שמעי כתיב ויתחתן שלמה את בת פרעה (מלכים א ג): הא דכייף ליה. אם כפוף הוא לרבו לקבל תוכחתו ידור אצלו. ואם לאו טוב להתרחק ממנו ויהי שוגג ואל יהי מזיד: מהדר אפיה וגריס. משנתו כשקורין ספר תורה: ישלים פרשיותיו. של כל שבת ושבת: ואפילו

תוספות

רב ששת מהדר אפיה וגריס. ואם תאמר והא אמרינן בסוטה (פ"ז ד' לט.) מאי דכתיב ובפתחו עמדו כל העם (נחמיה ח) כיון שנפתח ס"ת אסור לספר אפילו בדבר הלכה. ויש לומר התם איירי בקול רם כדי שלא יבטלו קול קריאת התורה והכא איירי בנחת והאי דקא מהדר אפיה רבותא משמע אע"ג דמהדר אפיה שנראה כמניח ספר תורה שפיר דמי והאי דאהדר אפיה כדי שיכוין גרסתו. ורב אלפס (מגילה פ"ד) כתב דה"ג ומפרשי דוקא שיש שם י' אחריני אז יכול ללמוד אבל אין שם עשרה כי אם עמו לא והכא איירי שהיו שם י' בלא הוא. ועוד תירץ האלפסי שאני רב ששת שתורתו אומנתו הוא ואכן מסתבר לן כי האי *תירוצא*:

שנים מקרא ואחד תרגום. י"מ והוא הדין ללועזות בלע"ז שלהן הוי כמו תרגום

מסורת הש"ס

[יומא סט: תענית כד: יבמות עב. סנה' סד.]

[ירו' פ"ד גרס לפנים משני דלתות]

[יבמות סג:]

[מגילה כט. וע"ש היטיב]

לקמן ד' ל:

[illegible] מ"א חולין מד:]

עין משפט נר מצוה

כט [א] מיי' פ"ח מהל' תפלה הל' א' סמ"ג עשין יט טוש"ע א"ח סי' צ' סעי' ט'

ל [ב] מיי' וסמ"ג שם טוש"ע א"ח סי' צ' סעי' י"א [וע' תוס' סוטה לט. ד"ה כיון]

לא [ג] מיי' שם הל' ג וסמ"ג שם טוש"ע א"ח שם סעי' כ'

לב [ד] מיי' שם הל' ג' וסמ"ג שם טוש"ע א"ח שם סעי' יח

לג [ה] מיי' פ' י"ב שם הל' ט'. סמ"ג שם טוש"ע א"ח סי' קמ"ו סעי' א'

לד [ו] טוש"ע שם סעי' ב [רב אלפס כאן ובפ' הקורא את המגילה דף רעג]

לה [ז] מיי' שם פ' י"ג הל' כה סמ"ג שם טוש"ע א"ח סי' רפ"ה סעי' א

עין משפט נר מצוה

בקדושין מט: המתרגם פסוק כצורתו

[גי' הערוך בערך כל סבר לאשלומינהו לכולהו פרשייתא דכלה במעלי יומא דכיפורי פי' הן שמונה פרשיות שקורין בד' שבתות שבאלול וד' שבתות שבאדר ומפני שהי' רב ביבי טרוד בחודש הכלה במס' דכלה לא הוה פנאי להשלים כל פרשה בשבתה]

לו
א מיי' פ"ו מהל' תפלה הל' ח סמ"ג עשין יט טוש"ע א"ח סי' צ' סעי' ח'

לז
ב מיי' פ"א מה' ק"ש הל' י יב סמ"ג עשין יח טוש"ע א"ח סי' נ"ח סעי' ג ד ה ובסי' רל"ה סעי' ד

תורה אור

ואפילו °עטרות ודיבון שכל המשלים פרשיותיו (במדבר לב) עם הצבור מאריכין לו ימיו ושנותיו רב ביבי בר אביי סבר לאשלומינהו לפרשייתא *דכולא שתא במעלי יומא דכפורא *תנא ליה חייא בר רב מדפתי כתיב °ועניתם את נפשותיכם (ויקרא כג) בתשעה לחדש בערב וכי בתשעה מתענין והלא בעשרה מתענין אלא לומר לך כל האוכל ושותה בתשיעי מעלה עליו הכתוב כאלו מתענה תשיעי ועשירי סבר לאקדומינהו אמר ליה ההוא סבא תנינא ובלבד שלא יקדים ושלא יאחר כדאמר להו רבי יהושע בן לוי לבני' אשלימו פרשיותייכו עם הצבור שנים מקרא ואחד תרגום והזהרו בורידין כרבי יהודה דתנן *ר' יהודה אומר עד שישחוט את הורידין והזהרו בזקן ששכח תלמודו מחמת אונסו דאמרינן *לוחות ושברי לוחות מונחות בארון: אמר להו רבא לבניה כשאתם חותכים בשר אל תחתכו על גב היד איכא דאמרי משום סכנה ואיכא דאמרי משום קלקול סעודה *ואל תשבו על מטת ארמית ואל תעברו אחורי בית הכנסת בשעה שהצבור מתפללין ואל תשבו על מטת ארמית א"ד לא תגנו בלא ק"ש ואיכא דאמרי דלא תנסבו גיורת' ואיכא דאמרי ארמית ממש ומשום מעשה דרב פפא *דרב פפא אזל לגבי ארמית הוציאה לו מטה אמרה לו שב אמר לה איני יושב עד שתגביהי את המטה הגביהה את המטה ומצאו שם תינוק מת מכאן אמרו חכמים אסור לישב על מטת ארמי' ואל תעברו אחורי בית הכנסת בשעה שהצבור מתפללין מסייע ליה לרבי יהושע בן לוי דאמר ר' יהושע בן לוי *אאסור לו לאדם שיעבור אחורי בית הכנסת בשעה שהצבור מתפללין אמר אביי ולא אמרן אלא דליכא פתחא אחרינא אבל איכא פתחא אחרינא לית לן בה ולא אמרן אלא דליכא בי כנישתא אחרינא אבל איכא בי כנישתא אחרינא לית לן בה ולא אמרן אלא דלא דרי טונא ולא רהיט ולא מנח תפילין אבל איכא חד מהנך לית לן בה: תניא אמר ר' עקיבא בשלשה דברים אוהב אני את המדיים כשחותכין את הבשר אין חותכין אלא על גבי השולחן כשנושקין אין נושקין אלא על גב היד וכשיועצין אין יועצין אלא בשדה אמר רב אדא בר אהבה מאי קראה °וישלח יעקב ויקרא לרחל וללאה (בראשית לא) השדה אל צאנו: תניא אמר רבן גמליאל בשלשה דברים אוהב אני את הפרסיים הן צנועין באכילתן וצנועין בבית הכסא וצנועין בדבר אחר: °אני צויתי (ישעיה יג) למקודשי תני רב יוסף אלו הפרסיים המקודשין ומזומנין לגיהנם: רבן גמליאל אומר וכו': אמר רב יהודה אמר שמואל הלכה כרבן גמליאל *תניא רבי שמעון בן יוחי אומר בפעמים שאדם קורא קריאת שמע שני פעמים בלילה אחת קודם שיעלה עמוד השחר ואחת לאחר שיעלה עמוד השחר ויוצא בהן ידי חובתו אחת של יום ואחת של לילה הא גופא קשיא אמרת פעמים שאדם קורא קריאת שמע שתי פעמים בלילה אלמא לאחר שיעלה עמוד השחר ליליא הוא והדר תני יוצא בהן ידי חובתו אחת של יום ואחת של לילה אלמא יממא הוא לא לעולם ליליא הוא והא דקרי ליה יום דאיכא אינשי דקיימי בההיא שעתה אמר רב אחא בר חנינא אמר רבי יהושע בן לוי הלכה כרבי שמעון בן יוחי איכא דמתני להא דרב אחא בר חנינא אהא דתניא ר"ש בן יוחי אומר משום רבי עקיבא, בפעמים שאדם קורא קריאת שמע שתי פעמים ביום אחת קודם הנץ החמה ואחת לאחר הנץ החמה ויוצא בהן ידי חובתו אחת של יום ואחת של לילה הא גופא קשיא אמרת פעמים שאדם קורא קריאת שמע שתי פעמים ביום אלמא קודם הנץ החמה יממא הוא והדר תני יוצא בהן ידי חובתו אחת של יום ואחת של לילה אלמא ליליא הוא

לא

רש"י

ואפי' עטרות ודיבון. שאין בו תרגום: מעלה עליו הכתוב וכו'. והכי קאמר קרא הכינו עצמיכם בתשעה לאדם לענוי המחרת והרי הוא בעיני כענוי היום: לאקדומינהו. לסדר כל הפרשיות בשבת אחת או בשתי שבתות: עד שישחוט את הורידין. כדי שיצא כל הדם ולא אמר כן אלא בעוף הואיל וצולהו כולו כאחד: מחמת אונסו. שחלה או שנטרד בדוחק מזונות הזהרו בו לכבדו: שברי לוחות מונחות בארון. דכתיב (דברים י) אשר שברת ושמת' בארון אף השברים שמים בארון: משום סכנה. שלא יקוץ ידו: משום קלקול סעודה. אף בחבורה קטנה יצא דם ויכלכך את המאכל וימאיס את המסובין: בלא ק"ש. שתהא מטתך דומה למטת ארמית: ארמי' ממש. על מטת ארמי': מעשה דרב פפא. שאמר' לו שב על המטה והיה בה מת מוטל עליה והיתה רוצה להעליל עליו ולומר שישב עליו והרגו: אסור לעבור וכו'. שנראה כמבריח עצמו מפתח בית הכנסת שבמזרח: על גב היד. את יד חברו הוא נושק ודרך חשיבו' הוא זה מפני הרוק: אלא בשדה. דאמרי אינשי אזנים לכותל: בדבר אחר. תשמיש: אני צויתי למקודשי. במפלת בבל כתיב אני צויתי את מלכי פרס ומדי לבא ולהשחיתה: ליליא הוא: עד הנץ החמה: דקיימי בההיא שעתא. הלכך זמן ק"ש דיום הוא דגבי ק"ש ובקומך כתיב והא קיימי:

והאי

תוספות

תרגום שמפרש לפעמים. כי כמו שהתרגום מפרש לע"ה כך הם מבינים מתוך הלעז. ולא נהירא שהרי התרגום מפרש במה שאין ללמוד מן העברי כדאשכחן *בכמה דוכתי דאמר רב יוסף (מגילה ד' ג.) אלמלא תרגום דהאי קרא לא ידענא מאי קאמר ע"כ אין לומר בשום לשון פעם שלישי' כי אם בלשון תרגום:

ואפי' עטרות ודיבון וכו'. פירש"י אפי' עטרות ודיבון שאין בו תרגום שצריך לקרותו ג"פ בעברי וקשה מאי נקט עטרות ודיבון שיש לו מכל מקום תרגום ירושלמי היה לו לומר לאוזן ושמעון או פסוקא אחריכא שאין בו תרגום כלל ויש לומר משום הכי נקט עטרות ודיבון אע"ג שאין בו תרגום ידוע אלא תרגום ירושלמי וצריך לקרות שלש פעמים העברי מכל מקום יותר טוב לקרות פעם שלישית בתרגום:

כאלו מתענה תשיעי ועשירי. ה"פ אם נצטוה להתענות יום ט'. והקשה רבינו שמואל ב"ר אהרן מיונבי"ל מאי קשיא ליה והא כתיב בראשון בארבעה עשר יום לחדש בערב תאכלו מצות (שמות יב) ואותו ערב ר"ל ערב של ט"ו הכא נמי נימא מאי ערב ערב של עשירי ויש לומר דשאני התם דכתיב תאכלו לבסוף דמשמע הכי בראשון בי"ד בלילה תאכלו מצות אבל הכא כתיב ועניתם קודם בערב דמשמע ועניתם מיד ביום התשיעי:

ישלים פרשיותיו עם הצבור. נראה דכל השבוע מכיון דמתחילין לקרות הפרשה דהיינו ממנחת שבת ואילך עד שבת הבאה נקראת עם הצבור ואף על גב דלענין גיטין לא נקרא קמי שבת אלא מרביעי ואילך (בפסחים דף קו.) והוו השלמה. במדרש ג' דברים צוה רבינו הקדוש לבניו בשעה שנפטר שלא תאכלו לחם בשבת עד שתגמרו כל הפרש' משמע דקודם אכילה צריך להשלימה ומיהו אם השלימה לאחר אכילה שפיר דמי. מ"מ מצוה מן המובחר קודם אכילה:

לא לעולם ליליא הוא. תימה אם כן ליתא רבותא שפעמים יש אדם קורא לאחר שיעלה עמוד השחר שני פעמים ויוצא בו משום שחרית ומשום ערבית יש לומר דהכי קאמר לעולם ליליא הוא בשאר מצות דבעינן בהו יום כמו תפילין וציצית אבל גבי ק"ש לא הואיל ואיכא אינשי דקיימי בההיא שעתא לאו זמן שכיבה הוא והאי דנקט לאחר שיעלה עמוד השחר לאו דוקא מיד הוא דהא צריך להמתין לכל הפחות שיעורא דמתניתין *עד שיכיר בין תכלת *לכרתי:

לעולם

לקמן ט:

[עוד להגיה לכאן]

מסורת הש"ס

פסחים סח: יומא פ"א: ר"ה ט.

חולין כז.

ב"ב יד: מנחות צ"ט.

ע"פ קיז:

[פסחי' שם וע"ש ברש"י וברשב"ם ול"ע גם בפירש"י דהכא]

לקמן דף ס"א.

בראשית לא

ישעיה יג

תוספתא פ"א

[8b] and even [such verses as] *Ataroth* and *Dibon*,[5] for if one completes his *Parashoth* together with the congregation, his days and years are prolonged. R. Bibi b. Abaye wanted to finish all the *Parashoth* of the whole year on the eve of the Day of Atonement. But Ḥiyya b. Rab of Difti[6] recited to him [the following Baraitha]: It is written: *And ye shall afflict your souls, in the ninth day of the month at even.*[7] Now, do we fast on the ninth? Why, we fast on the tenth! But this teaches you that if one eats and drinks on the ninth, Scripture accounts it to him as if he fasted on the ninth and tenth.[8] Thereupon he wanted to finish them in advance. But a certain Elder recited to him a Baraitha teaching: However, he should not read them in advance of nor later [than the congregation]. Even so did R. Joshua b. Levi say to his children: Complete your *Parashoth* together with the congregation, twice the Hebrew text and once Targum; be careful with the jugular veins to follow [the teaching of] R. Judah, as we have learnt: R. Judah says: He must cut through the jugular veins; and be careful [to respect] an old man who has
a forgotten his knowledge through no fault of his own,[1] for it was said: Both the whole tables and the fragments of the tables were placed in the Ark.[2]

Raba said to his children: When you are cutting meat, do not cut it upon your hand. (Some people say on account of danger;[3] and some in order not to spoil the meal.)[4] Do not sit upon the bed of an Aramaean woman, and do not pass behind a Synagogue when the congregation is praying. 'Do not sit upon the bed of an Aramaean woman'; some say that this means: Do not go to bed before reciting the *Shema'*;[5] some say it means: Do not marry a proselyte woman; and some say it means literally [the bed of] an Aramaean woman, and this rule was laid down because of what happened to R. Papa. For R. Papa once visited an Aramaean woman. She brought out a bed and said: Sit down. He said to her: I will not sit down until you raise the cover of the bed. She raised the cover and they found there a dead baby. Hence said the scholars: It is not permitted to sit down upon the bed of an Aramaean woman. 'And do not pass behind a Synagogue when the congregation is praying'; this supports the teaching of R. Joshua b. Levi. For R. Joshua b. Levi said: It is not permitted for a man to pass behind a Synagogue when the congregation is praying. Abaye said: This applies only when there is no other door, but when there is another door,[6] there is no objection. Furthermore, this applies only when there is no other Synagogue, but when there is another Synagogue, there is no objection. And furthermore, this applies only when he does not carry a burden, and does not run, and does not wear *tefillin*. But where one of these conditions is present there is no objection.

It has been taught: R. Akiba says: For three things I like the Medes: When they cut meat, they cut it only on the table; when they kiss, they kiss only the hand; and when they hold counsel, they do so only in the field. R. Adda b. Ahabah says: Which verse [may be quoted in support of the last]? *And Jacob sent and called*
b *Rachel and Leah* to the field *unto his flock*.[1] It has been taught: R. Gamaliel says: For three things do I like the Persians: They are temperate in their eating, modest in the privy, and chaste in another matter.[2] *I have commanded My consecrated ones*.[3] R. Joseph learnt: This refers to the Persians who are consecrated and destined for Gehinnom.[4]

R. GAMALIEL SAYS: UNTIL THE DAWN RISES. Rab Judah says in the name of Samuel: The *Halachah* is as laid down by R. Gamaliel. It was taught, R. Simeon b. Yoḥai says: Sometimes a man may recite the *Shema'* twice in the night, once before the dawn breaks and once after the dawn breaks, and thereby fulfil his duty once for the day and once for the night.

Now this is self-contradictory. You say: 'A man may sometimes recite the *Shema'* twice in the night', which shows that it is still night after the dawn breaks. And then you say: 'He thereby fulfils his duty once for the day and once for the night', which shows that it is daytime?—No! It is in reality night, but he calls it day because some people rise at that time. R. Aḥa b. Ḥanina said in the name of R. Joshua b. Levi: The *Halachah* is as stated by R. Simeon b. Yoḥai. Some people refer this [statement] of R. Aḥa b. Ḥanina to the following lesson,[5] which has been taught: R. Simeon b. Yoḥai says in the name of R. Akiba: Sometimes a man may recite the *Shema'* twice in the day-time, once before sunrise and once after sunrise, and thereby fulfil his duty once for the day and once for the night. Now this is self-contradictory. You say: 'A man may sometimes recite the *Shema'* twice in the daytime', which shows that before sunrise it is daytime, and then you state: 'He thereby fulfils his duty once for the day and once

(5) Num. XXXII, 3. Even strings of names which are left untranslated in the Targum should be recited in Hebrew and in the Aramaic version. (6) Dibtha on the Tigris. (7) Lev. XXIII, 32. (8) Therefore he should not devote the whole day to study.

a (1) I.e., as a result of illness or struggle for a livelihood. (2) V. B.B. 14*b*.

(3) Lest he should cut his hand. (4) With the blood that will ooze from the meat. (5) So that your bed should not be like that of an Aramaean. (6) By which he can enter and join in the prayers.

b (1) Gen. XXXI, 4. (2) In sexual matters. (3) Isa. XIII, 3. (4) R. Joseph experienced the persecution under Shapor II. (5) Which is most probably only another version of the previous one.

for the night', which shows that it is night?—[9a] No! It is in reality day, but he calls it night because some people go to bed at that time. R. Aha b. Hanina said in the name of R. Joshua b. Levi: The *Halachah* is as stated by R. Simeon who said in the name of R. Akiba. R. Zera says: However, he must not say [the
a prayer]: 'Cause us to lie down'.[1] When R. Isaac b. Joseph came [from Palestine], he said: This [tradition] of R. Aha b. Hanina in the name of R. Joshua b. Levi was not expressly said [by R. Joshua], but it was said [by R. Aha] by inference.[2] For it happened that a couple of scholars became drunk at the wedding feast of the son of R. Joshua b. Levi, and they came before R. Joshua b. Levi [before the rise of the sun] and he said: R. Simeon is a great enough authority to be relied on in a case of emergency.

IT ONCE HAPPENED THAT HIS SONS CAME HOME [LATE], etc. How is it that they had not heard before of this opinion of R. Gamaliel?—[They had heard], but they asked thus: Do the Rabbis join issue with you? For if so, where there is a controversy between an individual and a group, the *Halachah* follows the group. Or do the Rabbis agree with you [in substance], but they say: UNTIL MIDNIGHT, in order to keep a man far away from transgression?—He replied: The Rabbis do agree with me, and it is your duty [to recite the *Shema'*]. But they say, UNTIL MIDNIGHT, in order to keep a man far from transgression.

AND NOT IN RESPECT TO THIS ALONE DID THEY SO DECIDE, etc. But does R. Gamaliel say 'until midnight', that he should continue AND NOT IN RESPECT TO THIS ALONE DID THEY SO DECIDE?—That is what R. Gamaliel said to his sons: Even according to the Rabbis who say, 'UNTIL MIDNIGHT', the obligation continues until the dawn breaks, but the reason they said, 'UNTIL MIDNIGHT', was in order to keep a man far away from transgression.

THE BURNING OF THE FAT, etc. But [the Mishnah] does not mention the eating of the Passover offering. This would point to a contradiction [with the following Baraitha]: The duty of the recital of the *Shema'* in the evening, and of the *Hallel*[3] on the night of the Passover, and of the eating of the Passover sacrifice can be performed until the break of the dawn?—R. Joseph says: There is no contradiction. One statement [the Mishnah] conforms with the view of R. Eleazar b. Azariah, and the other with the view of R. Akiba. For it has been taught: *And they shall eat of the flesh*
b *in that night.*[1] R. Eleazar b. Azariah says: Here it is said: *'in that night'*, and further on it is said: *For I will go through the land of Egypt in that night.*[2] Just as the latter verse means until midnight, so also here it means until midnight. R. Akiba said to him: But it is also said: *Ye shall eat it in haste,*[3] which means: until the time of haste?[4] [Until the break of the dawn]. [Said R. Eleazar to him,][5] If that is so, why does it say: in the night? [R. Akiba answered,][5] Because I might think that it may be eaten in the daytime[6] like the sacrifices; therefore it is said: *'in the night'*, indicating that only in the night is it eaten and not in the day. We can understand why according to R. Eleazar b. Azariah, whose opinion is based on the *Gezerah shawah,*[7] the word *'that'* is necessary. But according to R. Akiba what is the purpose of this word *'that'*?[8]—It is there to exclude another night. For, since the Passover sacrifice is a sacrifice of minor sanctity and peace-offerings are sacrifices of minor sanctity, I might think that just as the peace-offerings are eaten for two days and one night so is also the Passover-offering eaten for two nights instead of the two days, and therefore it might be eaten for two nights and one day! Therefore it is said: *'in that night'*; in that night it is eaten, but it is not eaten in another night. And R. Eleazar b. Azariah?[9] He deduces it from the verse: *And ye shall let nothing of it remain until the morning.*[10] R. Akiba?—If [you deduced it] from there, I could say that *'morning'* refers to the second morning. And R. Eleazar?—He answers you: *'Morning'* generally means the first morning.

And [the controversy of] these Tannaim is like [the controversy of] the other Tannaim in the following Baraitha: *There thou shalt sacrifice the passover-offering at even, at the going down of the sun, at the*
c *season that thou camest forth out of Egypt.*[1] R. Eliezer says: *'At even'*,[2] you sacrifice; *'at sunset'*, you eat; and *'at the season that thou camest out of Egypt'*,[3] you must burn [the remainder]. R. Joshua says: *'At even'*, you sacrifice; *'at sunset'*, you eat; and how long do you continue to eat? Till *'the season that thou camest out of Egypt'*.

R. Abba said: All agree that when Israel was redeemed[4] from Egypt they were redeemed in the evening. For it is said: *The Lord thy God brought thee forth out of Egypt by night.*[5] But they did not actually leave Egypt till the daytime. For it is said: *On the morrow after the passover the children of Israel went out with a high hand.*[6] About what do they disagree?—About the time of the haste.[7] R. Eleazar b. Azariah says: What is meant by 'haste'? The haste of the Egyptians.[8] And R. Akiba says: It is the haste of Israel.[9] It has also been taught likewise: *'The Lord thy God brought thee forth out of Egypt by night.'* But did they leave in the night? Did not they in fact leave only in the morning, as it says: *'On the morrow after the passover the children of Israel went out with a high hand?* But this teaches that the redemption had already begun in the evening.

Speak now [na] *in the ears of the people*, etc.[10] In the school of R. Jannai they said: The word *'na'* means: I pray. The Holy One, blessed be He, said to Moses: I pray of thee, go and tell Israel, I pray of you to borrow from the Egyptians vessels of silver and

a (1) V. *P.B.* p. 99. This is essentially a night prayer. (2) From a decision of R. Joshua. (3) V. Glos.

b (1) Ex. XII, 8. (2) Ibid. 12. (3) Ibid. 11. (4) The hour of the break of dawn, when they hastened out of Egypt, v. Ex. XII, 22. (5) Inserted with MS.M. (6) I.e., during the very day on which it was slaughtered. (7) V. Glos. (8) The text should have simply stated 'in the night'. (9) How does *he* deduce this latter ruling? (10) Ibid. XII, 10.

c (1) Deut. XVI, 6. (2) In the afternoon. (3) At the break of dawn. Hence according to R. Eliezer, the time of eating extends only till midnight. (4) I.e., obtained permission to leave. (5) Ibid. XVI, 1. (6) Num. XXXIII, 3. (7) Which is the termination of the time when it is permitted to eat; v. Ex. XII, 11 and the Gemara above. (8) At midnight the Egyptians hastened to urge Israel to leave Egypt. (9) I.e., in the morning when the Israelites hastened to go out. (10) Ex. XI, 2.

לא לעולם יממא הוא והאי דקרו ליה ליליא דאיכא אינשי דגנו בההיא שעתא אמר רבי אחא ברבי חנינא אמר רבי יהושע בן לוי הלכה כרבי שמעון שאמר משום ר' עקיבא אמר ר' זירא ובלבד שלא יאמר השכיבנו כי אתא רב יצחק בר יוסף אמר הא דרבי אחא בר' חנינא אמר ריב"ל *לאו בפירוש אתמר [וע' תוס' יומא לז: ד"ה אמר] אלא מכללא אתמר דההוא זוגא דרבנן דאשתכור בהלולא דבריה דרבי יהושע בן לוי אתו לקמי' דריב"ל אמר *כדאי הוא ר"ש לסמוך עליו בשעת הדחק: מעשה שבאו בניו וכו' ועד השתא לא שמיע להו הא דר"ג הכי קאמרי ליה רבנן פליגי עילווך *ויחיד ורבים הלכה כרבים או דלמא רבנן כוותך סבירא להו והאי דקאמרי עד חצות כדי להרחיק אדם מן העבירה אמר להו רבנן כוותי סבירא להו וחייבין אתם והאי דקאמרו עד חצות כדי להרחיק אדם מן העבירה: ולא זו בלבד אמרו אלא וכו': ור"ג מי קאמר עד חצות דקתני ולא זו בלבד אמרו הכי קאמר להו ר"ג לבניה אפילו לרבנן דקאמרי עד חצות מצותה עד שיעלה עמוד השחר והאי דקא אמרי עד חצות כדי להרחיק אדם מן העבירה: הקטר חלבים וכו': *ואלו אכילת פסחים לא קתני ורמינהי ק"ש ערבית והלל בלילי פסחים ואכילת פסח מצותן עד שיעלה עמוד השחר אמר רב יוסף לא קשיא הא רבי אלעזר בן עזריה הא רבי עקיבא *דתניא °ואכלו את הבשר בלילה הזה (שמות יב) רבי אלעזר בן עזריה אומר נאמר כאן בלילה הזה ונאמר להלן °ועברתי בארץ מצרים בלילה הזה (שם) מה להלן עד חצות אף כאן עד חצות אמר ליה רבי עקיבא והלא כבר נאמר °בחפזון (שם) עד שעת חפזון א"כ מה תלמוד לומר בלילה יכול יהא נאכל כקדשים ביום תלמוד לומר בלילה בלילה הוא נאכל ולא ביום בשלמא לרבי אלעזר בן עזריה דאית ליה גזירה שוה אצטריך למכתב ליה הזה אלא לרבי עקיבא האי הזה מאי עביד ליה למעוטי לילה אחר הוא דאתא סד"א הואיל ופסח קדשים קלים ושלמים קדשים קלים מה שלמים נאכלין לב' ימים ולילה אחד אף פסח נאכל שתי לילות במקום ב' ימים ויהא נאכל לב' לילות ויום אחד קמ"ל בלילה הזה בלילה הזה הוא נאכל ואינו נאכל בלילה אחר ורבי אלעזר בן עזריה °מלא תותירו עד בקר (שם) נפקא ורבי עקיבא אי מהתם הוה אמינא מאי בקר בקר שני ורבי אלעזר אמר לך כל בקר בקר ראשון הוא והני תנאי כהני תנאי *דתניא °שם תזבח את הפסח בערב כבא השמש מועד צאתך ממצרים (דברי' טז) רבי אליעזר אומר בערב אתה זובח וכבא השמש אתה אוכל ומועד צאתך ממצרים אתה שורף רבי יהושע אומר בערב אתה זובח כבא השמש אתה אוכל ועד מתי אתה אוכל והולך עד מועד צאתך ממצרים אמר רבי אבא הכל מודים כשנגאלו ישראל ממצרים לא נגאלו אלא בערב שנאמר °הוציאך ה' אלהיך ממצרים לילה (שם) וכשיצאו לא יצאו אלא ביום שנאמר °ממחרת הפסח יצאו בני ישראל ביד רמה (במדב' לג) על מה נחלקו על שעת חפזון רבי אלעזר בן עזריה סבר מאי חפזון חפזון דמצרים ורבי עקיבא סבר מאי חפזון חפזון דישראל *תניא נמי הכי הוציאך ה' אלהיך ממצרים לילה וכי בלילה יצאו והלא לא יצאו אלא ביום שנאמר ממחרת הפסח יצאו בני ישראל ביד רמה אלא מלמד שהתחילה להם גאולה מבערב: °דבר נא באזני העם וגו' (שמות יא) אמרי דבי רבי ינאי *אין נא אלא לשון בקשה אמר ליה הקדוש ברוך הוא למשה בבקשה ממך לך ואמור להם לישראל בבקשה מכם שאלו ממצרים כלי כסף וכלי זהב שלא יאמר

אותו

תורה אור

רש"י

ודאי דקרו ליה ליליא. דקאמר יוצא בו קריאת שמע של לילה: משום דאיכא דגנו. וקרינא ביה ובשכבך: ובלבד שלא יאמר השכיבנו. הקורא ק"ש של לילה שחרית סמוך לעמוד השחר לא יאמר השכיבנו שאין עוד זמן תחלת שכיבה אלא זמן סוף שכיבה: דאשתכור. ושכרו ונרדמו עד לאחר עמוד השחר: בשעת הדחק. אבל שלא בשעת הדחק לא: הכי קא אמרי ליה. לרבן גמליאל ולא גרס אלא: רבנן פליגי עלך. כלומר מי פליגי רבנן עלך דהא דאמרי עד חצות דוקא קאמרי דלא משמע להו ובשכבך כל זמן שכיבה אלא כל זמן שדרך בני אדם להתעסק לילך ולשכב ומיהו בהא פליגי אדרבי אליעזר דאלו ר"א סבירא ליה זמן עסק שכיבה אינו אלא עד האשמורת הראשונה ולרבנן עד חצות ואת סבירא לך ובשכבך כל זמן שבני אדם שוכבים והיינו כל הלילה ויחיד ורבים הלכה כרבים: או דלמא כוותך סבירא להו. ומשמע להו ובשכבך כל זמן שכיבה והא דקאמרי עד חצות הרחקה הוא כדי לזרז ומיהו היכא דאתנים ולא קרא קודם חצות עדיין זמן חיובא הוא ומחייבי ונפקי ידי ק"ש בזמנו: כוותי סבירא להו. וחייבין אתם לקרות גרסינן ולא גרסינן מותרים דאפילו שלא בזמנו תנן (עמוד ב) הקורא מכאן ואילך לא הפסיד כאדם שקורא בתורה: שעת חפזון. שנחפזו לצאת והיינו עמוד השחר כדכתיב לא תצאו איש מפתח ביתו עד בקר (שמות יב): יכול יהא נאכל. כשאר קדשים ביום שחיטתו כדרך תודה שאף היא זמן אכילתה יום אחד ואוכל והולך כל יום שחיטתה והלילה עד הבקר כדין תודה דכתיב ביום קרבנו יאכל (ויקרא ז): מה שלמים נאכלין לשני ימים ולילה אחד. שביניהם דכתיב ביום זבחכם יאכל וממחרת (שם יט) אף פסח נמי הואיל ואינו נאכל אלא בלילה נוקים שני לילות במקום שני ימים דשלמי' ויהא נאכל בשני לילות ויום אחד לא שיאכלנו ביום אלא שיהא שהות זמן שלא יפסל באכילה בשביל המתנת היום ויאכלנו בלילה השני קמשמע לן: שם תזבח את הפסח בערב כבא השמש מועד צאתך ממצרים. הרי לך שלשה זמנים שאינם שוים. בערב כי ינטו צללי ערב היינו לאחר חצות שנסתלק' חמה מראש כל אדם ונוטה למערב. כבוא השמש. משחשכה. מועד צאתך ממצרים. בבקר. כיצד יתקיימו כולם. בערב לזמן שחיטה. כבוא השמש התחלת זמן אכילה. מועד צאתך זמן שריפה כלומר בבוקר הוא נעשה נותר שהגיע זמן שריפה אלא לפי שאין שורפין קדשים ביום טוב ממתינין לו עד בקר שני: עד מתי אתה אוכל. היינו כרבי עקיבא אבל לתנא קמא עד חצות לילה הוי זמן אכילה ותו לא דאי לא מאי בינייהו: הכל מודים. ר"ע גופיה מודה שהלילה מחצות ואילך היתה שעת חפזון דמצרים לשלחם מן הארץ: מערב נגאלו. נתנו להם רשות לצאת: חפזון דמצרים. מכת הבכורות שעל ידם נחפזו למהר לשלחם: חפזון דישראל. לא שמעו להם לצאת עד בקר:

אותו

תוספות

לעולם יממא הוא. ואם תאמר ליתני שתי פעמים קודם הנץ החמה והוי רבותא טפי דאפילו קודם הנץ הוי זמן דקריאת שמע של שחרית. ויש לומר כדפרשינן דהאי יממא לענין שאר מצות אבל לענין ק"ש הואיל ואיכא אינשי דגני לאו זמן קימה הוא. ותימה דקשיא דר"ע אדרבי עקיבא דהכא קאמר אחר הנץ ולקמן (עמוד ב) קאמר משיכיר בין חמור לערוד דהיינו אפילו קודם וי"ל דתרי תנאי אליבא דרבי עקיבא. אי נמי יש לומר יממא הוא אפילו גבי קריאת שמע דהא זמן קימה הוא והא דלא נקט שתי פעמי' קודם הנץ משום דבעי לאשמועינן שאינו יוצא בשל לילה אחר הנץ *:

ובלבד שלא יאמר השכיבנו. פי' בקונטרס אמילתא דר"ש בן יוחי דקורא קודם שיעלה עמוד השחר קאי. ונראה לי דאז ודאי זמן שכיבה הוא ומצי למימר השכיבנו. ועוד דהוה ליה למימר אמאי דסליק מיניה. ופי' השר מקוצי דקאי אקודם הנץ דסליק מיניה ולכך קאמר דלא מצי למימר השכיבנו דלאו זמן שכיבה הוא כיון שעלה כבר עמוד השחר אפילו קודם הנץ:

ר' אלעזר בן עזריה אומר נאמר כאן בלילה הזה וכו'. וא"ת היכי מצי למימר רבי אלעזר בן עזריה עד חצות והכתיב לא תותירו ממנו עד בקר (שמות יב) דמשמע עד בוקר מיהא מצי לאכלו. ויש לומר דמצי למימר דהכי קאמר לא תעשו דבר שיבא לידי נותר עד הבקר. שאם לא יהא נאכל עד חצות לא תוכל לאוכלו ולא לשורפו בלילה כדקא אמרינן* ביום אתה שורפו ואי אתה שורפו בלילה ואם כן ישאר עד הבקר:

אלא

עין משפט נר מצוה

לח א מיי' פ"א מה' ק"ש הלכה י סמג עשין י"ח טוש"ע א"ח סי' רלה סעיף ד

לט ב מיי' פ"ח מה' קרבן פסח הל' יד

[לקמן יא: שבת כט. לט: קמו: עירובין מו. לד. יבמו' ס: כתובו' פ': ב"ק כ: ב"מ לו: קא. ב"ב מ: קכו. קנה: שבועות כח. חולין לד. לה. קיא: מנחות ה:]

[וע' תוס' פסחי' פט. ד"ה דאלו] [פסחים ג'. זבחים נו:]

עירובין מו. גיטין יט. שבת מ"ה. נדה ו. מ"ח. [לקמן לז. שבת מ: קל: ביצה יח. יומא לו: יבמות מז. ב"ק קב. ע"ז ז. בכורות לז. נדה לז: מט.]

ע"פ קכ: מגילה כ. זבחים כז: מכילתא דר"י פר' בא

ספרי פרשת ראה

ספרי שם

[סוטה יוד: סנה' מג: פט:]

עין משפט נר מצוה

מ
א מיי' פ"א מהלכ' ק"ש הל' יא ופ"ד מה' תפילין הל' י סמג עשין י"ח טוש"ע א"ח סי' נח סעיף א ובסי' ל סעיף א

מא
ב מיי' פ"ז מה' תפלה הל' יז סמ"ג עשי' יט טוש"ע א"ח סי' סו סעי' ח וסי' קיא סעיף א [ע' תוס' סוטה יב. ע"ז כד:]

מב
ד מיי פ"ג מהל' אבל הל' י"ד טוש"ע א"ח סי' רכד סעי' ט [רב אלפס לקמן פ' הרואה דף מז:]

מג
ה סמ"ג עשין יט ט טוש"ע א"ח סי' רלו סעיף ב

(ירוש' גרס עד שהנץ החמה)

ע' תוס' מנחו' מג: ד"ה בין וכו' דמו פירש"י דהכא ופי' באופן אחר: [פי' קולין ע' תוס' סוכה מד: וע' תוס' יומא לז: סוף ד"ה אמר אביי]

אלא בין תכלת שבה ללבן שבה. פירש"י לצמר הצבוע תכלת ויש מקומות שלא עלה שם הצבע יפה. וקשה דאמרינן במנחות (פ"ד דף מ"ג:) ראה מצוה זו שזה תלויה מצוה אחרת ואיזו זו ק"ש כדתניא עד שיכיר בין תכלת ללבן ואי קאי אגיזת צמר אינה תלויה בציצית ועוד בלילה נמי פעמים יכולין לראות צמר שאינו צבוע כדרכו. ע"כ יש לפרש בין תכלת שבה בציצית שהיה קבוע בו תכלת וגם שני חוטין לבן ועושין בו חוליא של תכלת וחוליא של לבן: **אחרים** אומרים עד שיראה חברו וכו'. בירושלמי במה אנן קיימין אי ברגיל אפילו ברחוק טפי חכים ביה ואי בשאינו רגיל אפילו בקרוב לגביה לא חכים ביה. תפתר ברגיל ואינו רגיל כהדין אכסניא דאתי לקילין. וצריך לומר דהאי אחרים לאו רבי מאיר נינהו דהא ר"מ איירי לעיל מינייהו *: **לק"ש** כותיקין. תימה לעיל פסקינן כמאן דמתיר לאחר עמוד השחר מיד ולקמן פסקינן הלכה כר' יהושע דאמר עד ג' שעות והכא פסק אביי שהוא בתרא ואמר כותיקין ומשמ' דהכי הלכתא. וי"ל דודאי זמן ק"ש מתחיל לאחר עמוד השחר וזמנו עד ג' שעו' ומיהו מצוה מן המובחר כותיקין סמוך להנץ החמה כדי לסמוך גאולה לתפלה. ואפילו ותיקין נמי מודו לרבי יהושע שאם לא קרא קודם הנץ החמה דיכול לקרות עד שלש שעות ועל זה אנו סומכין. וכן בפרק מי שמתו (דף כב:) דקאמר בעל קרי ירד לטבול אם יכול לעלות ולקרות קודם הנץ וכו' ומסיק בגמרא (דף כה:) דילמא כר' יהושע וכותיקין כלומר מתני' דקתני קודם הנץ החמה כותיקין אלמא ותיקין נמי מודו לרבי יהושע שאין שעה עוברת עד שלש שעות. ומיהו קשה דאמרינן ביומא (פ"ג ד' לז: ושם) אף היא עשתה נברשת של זהב כיון שהחמה זורחת היו ניצוצות יוצאות הימנה והיו יודעין שהגיע הנץ החמה ובא זמן ק"ש של שחרית ומוקי לה התם בשאר עמא דירושלים אלמא משמע דעיקר זמן ק"ש לאחר הנץ החמה והא לא הוי כותיקין שהיו קורין קודם להנץ סמוך להנץ ויש לומר דאותו זמן הוקבע לצבור לפי שלא היו יכולין להקדים ולמהר כותיקין כי רוב בני אדם אינם יכולין לכוין אותה שעה: **כל** הסומך גאולה לתפלה אינו נזוק. וא"ת והלא כל העולם סומכין גאולה לתפלה ומאי רבותיה דרב ברונא דלא פסיק חוכא מפומיה ויש לומר דהכי קאמר כל הסומך גאולה לתפלה כותיקין שקורין ק"ש קודם הנץ ותפלה לאחר הנץ:

כל

תורה אור: בראשית טו; שמות יב; תהלים סח; שמות יב; שם ג; שם; מלכים א יח; שם; תהלים עב; תהלים קד

אותו צדיק °ועבדום וענו אותם קיים בהם ואחרי כן יצאו ברכוש גדול לא קיים בהם אמרו לו ולואי שנצא בעצמנו משל לאדם שהיה חבוש בבית האסורים והיו אומרים לו בני אדם מוציאין אותך למחר מבית האסורים ונותנין לך ממון הרבה ואומר להם בבקשה מכם הוציאוני היום ואיני מבקש כלום: °וישאלום א"ר אמי מלמד שהשאילום בעל כרחם. א"ד בעל כרחם דמצרים וא"ד בעל כרחם דישראל מ"ד בעל כרחם דמצרים דכתיב °ונות בית תחלק שלל מ"ד בעל כרחם דישראל משום משוי: °וינצלו את מצרים *א"ר אמי מלמד שעשאוה כמצודה שאין בה דגן ור"ל אמר עשאוה כמצולה שאין בה דגים: °אהיה אשר אהיה א"ל הקב"ה למשה לך אמור להם לישראל אני הייתי עמכם בשעבוד זה ואני אהיה עמכם בשעבוד מלכיות אמר לפניו רבש"ע דיה לצרה בשעתה א"ל הקב"ה לך אמור להם °אהיה שלחני אליכם °*ענני ה' ענני א"ר אבהו למה אמר אליהו ענני ב' פעמים מלמד שאמר אליהו לפני הקב"ה רבש"ע ענני שתרד אש מן השמים ותאכל כל אשר על המזבח ועננו שתסיח דעתם כדי שלא יאמרו מעשה כשפים הם שנ' °ואתה הסבות את לבם אחורנית:

מתני' *מאימתי קורין את שמע בשחרית משיכיר בין תכלת ללבן ר"א אומר בין תכלת לכרתי [*וגומר'] עד *הנץ החמה *ר' יהושע אומר עד ג' שעות שכן דרך מלכים לעמוד בג' שעות *הקורא מכאן ואילך לא הפסיד כאדם הקורא בתורה:

גמ' מאי בין תכלת ללבן אילימא בין גבבא דעמרא חיורא לגבבא דעמרא דתכלתא הא בליליא נמי מידע ידעי אלא *בין תכלת שבה ללבן שבה תניא ר"מ אומר משיכיר בין זאב לכלב ר"ע אומר בין חמור לערוד *ואחרים אומרים *משיראה את חברו רחוק ד' אמות ויכירנו אמר רב הונא הלכה כאחרים אמר אביי לתפילין כאחרים לק"ש כותיקין *דא"ר יוחנן ותיקין היו *גומרין אותה עם הנץ החמה תניא נמי הכי *ותיקין היו גומרין אותה עם הנץ החמה כדי שיסמוך גאולה לתפלה ונמצא מתפלל ביום א"ר זירא מאי קראה °ייראוך עם שמש ולפני ירח דור דורים העיד ר"י בן אליקים משום קהלא קדישא דבירושלים כל הסומך גאולה לתפלה אינו נזוק כל היום כולו אמר רבי זירא איני והא אנא סמכי ואיתזקי א"ל במאי איתזקת דאמטיית אסא לבי מלכא התם נמי מבעי לך למיהב אגרא למחזי אפי מלכא דא"ר יוחנן *לעולם ישתדל אדם לרוץ לקראת מלכי ישראל ולא לקראת מלכי ישראל בלבד אלא אפילו לקראת מלכי א"ה שאם יזכה יבחין בין מלכי ישראל למלכי א"ה א"ל רבי אלעא לעולא כי עיילת להתם שאיל בשלומא דרב ברונא אחי במעמד כל החבורה דאדם גדול הוא ושמח במצות זימנא חדא סמך גאולה לתפלה ולא פסיק חוכא מפומיה כוליה יומא היכי מצי סמיך והא א"ר יוחנן *בתחלה הוא אומר ה' שפתי תפתח ולבסוף הוא אומר יהיו לרצון אמרי פי וגו' אמר ר"א תהא בתפלה של ערבית והא א"ר יוחנן *איזהו בן העה"ב זהו הסומך גאולה של ערבית לתפלה של ערבית אלא אמר ר' אלעזר תהא בתפלת המנחה רב אשי אמר אפילו תימא אכולהו וכיון דקבעוה רבנן בתפלה כתפלה אריכתא דמיא דאי לא תימא הכי ערבית היכי מצי סמיך והא בעי למימר השכיבנו אלא *כיון דתקינו רבנן השכיבנו כגאולה אריכתא דמיא ה"נ כיון דקבעוה רבנן בתפלה כתפלה אריכתא דמיא מכדי האי יהיו לרצון אמרי פי משמע לבסוף ומשמע מעיקרא דבעינא למימר מ"ט תקנוהו רבנן לאחר י"ח ברכות לימרו מעיקרא אמר ר' יהודה בריה דר"ש בן פזי הואיל ולא אמרו דוד אלא לאחר י"ח פרשיות לפיכך תקינו רבנן לאחר י"ח ברכות הני י"ח י"ט הויין אשרי האיש ולמה רגשו גוים חדא פרשה היא דאמר ר' יהודה בריה דר"ש בן פזי ק"ג פרשיות אמר דוד ולא אמר הללויה עד שראה במפלתן של רשעים שנאמר °יתמו חטאים מן הארץ ורשעים עוד אינם ברכי נפשי את ה' הללויה הני ק"ג ק"ד הויין אלא ש"מ אשרי האיש ולמה רגשו גוים חדא פרשה היא דאמר רבי שמואל בר נחמני אמר רבי יוחנן

כל

אותו צדיק. אברהם: כמצודה שאין בה דגן. דרך ציידי עופות לזרוק דגן תחת מצודות כדי שיבאו עופות ונלכדין וכשאין בה דגן אין עוף פונה אליה כך ריקנו המצרים מכל ממונם. וינצלו תרגומו ורוקינו: כמצולה שאין בה דגים. כמו מצולות ים כלומר בתוך התהום אין מצויין דגים אלא על שפת הים היכא דאיכא מזון: דיה לצרה בשעתה. דיה לצרה שיתאוננו בה בשעה שתבא עליהם למה תדאיבם עכשיו בבשורה קשה שתסיח דעתם. מלבא בלבם מזמה של רשע להכחישני ולומר על ידי כשפים הבאתי האש הזאת: **מתני'** תכלת ירוק הוא וקרוב לצבע כרתי שקורין פור"יש: **גמ'** בין תכלת שבה ללבן שבה. גיזת צמר שצבעה תכלת ויש בה מקומות שלא עלה שם הצבע יפה: ערוד. חמור הבר: לתפילין. להניח תפילין שמצות הנחתן קודם קרית שמע בפרק שני (דף יד:): ותיקין. אנשים ענוים ומחבבין מצוה: מתפלל ביום. דהנץ החמה לדברי הכל יום הוא: מאי קראה. דמצוה להתפלל עם הנץ החמה: דכתיב ייראוך עם שמש וגו'. מתי מתיראין ממך כשמולכך מקבלים עליה' דהיינו מלכות שמים שמקבלים עליהם בק"ש: עם שמש. כלומר כשהשמש יוצא הייתו עם הנץ החמה: ולפני ירח. אף תפלת המנחה מצותה עם דמדומי חמה: שאם יזכה. לעה"ב לראות גדולתן של ישראל: יבחין. כמה הרבה גדולתן יותר על המלכות עכשיו: תהא. הא דרבי יוחנן בתפלת ערבית דלא חיישינן לסמוך גאולה לתפלה דגאולה ביממא הויא: דאמר רבי יהודה בריה דרבי שמעון גרסינן:

פתח

מסורת הש"ס: פסחים קיט. [וע"ש בתוס' ד"ה כמצודה]; [לעיל ו:]; [מנחות מג:]; [לעיל ב: לקמן כה: [פירש"י על זה תמצא לקמן יד:]; תוספתא פ"א; לקמן כה: כו.; תוספתא פ"א; תהלים עב; [לקמן יט: כח.]; לעיל ד:; ב"ב פס; [לעיל ד:]; תהלים קד

vessels of gold, so that [9b] this righteous man [Abraham] may not say: *And they shall serve them, and they shall afflict them*[11] He did fulfil for them, but *And afterward shall they come out with great substance*[12] He did not fulfil for them. They said to him: If only we could get out with our lives! A parable: [They were] like a man who was kept in prison and people told him: To-morrow, they will release you from the prison and give you plenty of money. And he answered them: I pray of you, let me go free to-day and I shall ask nothing more!

a *And they let them have what they asked.*[1] R. Ammi says: This teaches that they let them have it against their will. Some say, against the will of the Egyptians, and some say, against the will of the Israelites. Those that say 'against the will of the Egyptians' cite the verse: *And she that tarrieth at home divideth the spoil.*[2] Those that say: 'against the will of the Israelites', say it was because of the burden [of carrying it]. *And they despoiled Egypt.*[3] R. Ammi says: This teaches that they made it like a snare[4] without corn. Resh Lakish said: They made it like a pond without fish.

I am that I am.[5] The Holy One, blessed be He, said to Moses: Go and say to Israel: I was with you in this servitude, and I shall be with you in the servitude of the [other] kingdoms.[6] He said to Him: Lord of the Universe, sufficient is the evil in the time thereof! Thereupon the Holy One, blessed be He, said to him: Go and tell them: *I AM has sent me unto you.*[7]

Hear me, O Lord, hear me.[8] R. Abbahu said: Why did Elijah say twice: *'Hear me'?* This teaches that Elijah said before the Holy One, blessed be He: Lord of the Universe, *'hear me'*, that the fire may descend from heaven and consume everything that is upon the altar; and *'hear me'*, that Thou mayest turn their mind that they may not say that it was the work of sorcery. For it is said: *For Thou didst turn their heart backward.*[9]

MISHNAH. FROM WHAT TIME MAY ONE RECITE THE SHEMA' IN THE MORNING? FROM THE TIME THAT ONE CAN DISTINGUISH BETWEEN BLUE AND WHITE. R. ELIEZER SAYS: BETWEEN BLUE AND GREEN. AND HE HAS TIME TO FINISH UNTIL SUNRISE. R. JOSHUA SAYS: UNTIL THE THIRD HOUR OF THE DAY, FOR SUCH IS THE CUSTOM OF KINGS, TO RISE AT THE THIRD HOUR. IF ONE RECITES THE SHEMA' LATER HE LOSES NOTHING, BEING LIKE ONE WHO READS IN THE
b TORAH.[1]

GEMARA. What is the meaning of BETWEEN BLUE AND WHITE? Shall I say: between a lump of white wool and a lump of blue wool? This one may also distinguish in the night! It means rather: between the blue in it and the white in it.[2] It has been taught: R. Meir says: [The morning *Shema'* is read] from the time that one can distinguish between a wolf and a dog; R. Akiba says: Between an ass and a wild ass. Others say: From the time that one can distinguish his friend at a distance of four cubits. R. Huna says: The *halachah* is as stated by the 'Others'. Abaye says: In regard to the *tefillin,*[3] the *halachah* is as stated by the 'Others'; in regard to [the recital of] the *Shema'*, as practised by the *watikin.*[4] For R. Johanan said: The *watikin* used to finish it [the recital of the *Shema'*] with sunrise, in order to join the *ge'ullah* with the *tefillah,*[5] and say the *tefillah* in the daytime. R. Zera says: What text can be cited in support of this? *They shall fear Thee with the sun,*[6] *and so long as the moon throughout all generations.*[7] R. Jose b. Eliakim testified[8] in the name of the holy community of Jerusalem:[9] If one joins the *ge'ullah* to the *tefillah,* he will not meet with any mishap for the whole of the day. Said R. Zera: This is not so! For I did join, and did meet with a mishap. They asked him: What was your mishap? That you had to carry a myrtle branch into the king's palace?[10] That was no mishap, for in any case you would have had to pay something in order to see the king! For R. Johanan said: A man should always be eager to run to see the kings of Israel. And not only to see the kings of Israel, but also to see the kings of the
c Gentiles, so that, if he is found worthy,[1] he may be able to distinguish between the kings of Israel and the kings of the Gentiles.

R. Ela said to 'Ulla: When you go up there,[2] give my greeting to my brother R. Berona in the presence of the whole college, for he is a great man and rejoices to perform a precept [in the correct manner]. Once he succeeded in joining *ge'ullah* with *tefillah,*[3] and a smile did not leave his lips the whole day. How is it possible to join the two, seeing that R. Johanan has said:[4] At the beginning of the *tefillah* one has to say, *O, Lord, open Thou my lips,*[5] and at the end he has to say, *Let the words of my mouth be acceptable* etc.?[6]—R. Eleazar replied: This[7] must then refer to the *tefillah* of the evening. But has not R. Johanan said: Who is it that is destined for the world to come? One who joins the *ge'ullah* of the evening with the *tefillah* of the evening?—Rather said R. Eleazar: This must then refer to the *tefillah* of the afternoon. R. Ashi said: You may also say that it refers to all the *tefillahs,* but since the Rabbis instituted [these words][7] in the *tefillah,* the whole is considered one long *tefillah.* For if you do not admit this, how can he join in the evening, seeing that he has to say the benediction of *'Let us rest'?*[8] You must say then that, since the Rabbis ordained the saying of 'Let us rest', it is considered one long *ge'ullah.*[9] So here, since the Rabbis instituted these words in the *tefillah,* the whole is considered one long *tefillah.*

Seeing that this verse, *'Let the words of my mouth be acceptable* etc.' is suitable for recital either at the end or the beginning [of the *tefillah*], why did the Rabbis institute it at the end of the eighteen benedictions? Let it be recited at the beginning?—R. Judah the son of R. Simeon b. Pazzi said: Since David said it only after
d eighteen chapters [of the Psalms],[1] the Rabbis too enacted that it should be said after eighteen blessings. But those eighteen Psalms are really nineteen?—*'Happy is the man'* and *'Why are the nations in an uproar'*[2] form one chapter. For R. Judah the son of R. Simeon b. Pazzi said: David composed a hundred and three chapters [of Psalms], and he did not say *'Hallelujah'* until he saw the downfall of the wicked, as it says, *Let sinners cease out of the earth, and let the wicked be no more. Bless the Lord, O my soul. Hallelujah.*[3] Now are these a hundred and three? Are they not a hundred and four? You must assume therefore that *'Happy is the man'* and *'Why are the nations in an uproar'* form one chapter. For R. Samuel

(11) Gen. XV, 14. (12) Ibid.

a (1) Ex. XII, 36. (2) Ps. LXVIII, 13. (3) Ex. XII, 36. (4) For birds with corn for a lure. Var. lec.: like husks without grain, like a net without fish. (5) Ibid. III, 14. (6) Babylon and Rome. (7) Ibid. (8) I Kings XVIII, 37. (9) Ibid. Sc., from such a thought.

b (1) It is not a transgression. On the contrary, he has the ordinary merit of one who reads in the Torah, though he has not fulfilled the obligation of reading the *Shema'*. (2) In one and the same lump of wool which was dyed blue but had some white spots in it. *J.T.* refers it to the 'fringes' which contain a thread of blue and which are used when reading the *Shema'*. (3) I.e., the time for putting them on. MS.M. reads *Tefillah* (v. Glos.). (4) Lit., 'strong' (*sc.*, in piety), a title probably applied to certain men who, in the time of the Hasmonean kingdom, set an example of exceptional piety. Some identify them with the Essenes. (5) V. *supra* 4b. (6) I.e., when the sun rises. E.V. *'While the sun endureth'*. (7) Ps. LXXII, 5. (8) I.e., transmitted a tradition. (9) V. *J.E.* p. 226. (10) He was compelled to do some forced labour. V. *T.J.*

c (1) To live to the time of the restoration of the Jewish kingdom and to see the Jewish kings. (2) To Palestine. (3) Apparently this means, having read the *Shema'* after the manner of the *watikin*. V. Tosaf. ad loc. (4) V. *supra*, 4b. (5) Ps. LI, 17. (6) Ps. XIX, 15. (7) The recital of these extra verses at the beginning and end of the *tefillah*. (8) V. *supra*, 4b. (9) The benediction of 'Let us rest' also comes between *ge'ullah* and *tefillah*.

d (1) It comes at the end of Ps. XIX. (2) The opening verses of Pss. I and II. (3) Ibid. CIV, 35.

b. Naḥmani said in the name of R. Joḥanan: [10a]: Every chapter that was particularly dear to David he commenced with '*Happy*' and terminated with 'Happy'.[4] He began with 'Happy', as it is written, '*Happy is the man*', and he terminated with 'Happy', as it is written, '*happy are all they that take refuge in Him*'.[5]

There were once some highwaymen[6] in the neighbourhood of R. Meir who caused him a great deal of trouble. R. Meir accordingly prayed that they should die. His wife Beruria[7] said to him: How do you make out [that such a prayer should be permitted]? Because it is written Let *ḥatta'im* cease? Is it written *ḥot'im?*[8] It is written *ḥatta'im!*[9] Further, look at the end of the verse: *and let the wicked men be no more*. Since the sins will cease, there will be no more wicked men! Rather pray for them that they should repent, and there will be no more wicked. He did pray for them, and they repented.

A certain *Min*[10] said to Beruria: It is written: *Sing, O barren,*
a *thou that didst not bear*.[1] Because she did not bear is she to sing? She replied to him: You fool! Look at the end of the verse, where it is written, *For the children of the desolate shall be more than the children of the married wife, saith the Lord*.[2] But what then is the meaning of '*a barren that did not bear*'? Sing, O community of Israel, who resemblest a barren woman, for not having born children like you for Gehenna.

A certain *Min* said to R. Abbahu: It is written: *A Psalm of David when he fled from Absalom his son*.[3] And it is also written, *A miḥtam of David when he fled from Saul in the cave*.[4] Which event happened first? Did not the event of Saul happen first? Then let him write it first? He replied to him: For you who do not derive interpretations from juxtaposition, there is a difficulty, but for us who do derive interpretations from juxtaposition there is no difficulty. For R. Joḥanan said: How do we know from the Torah that juxtaposition counts? Because it says, *They are joined*[5] *for ever and ever, they are done in truth and uprightness*.[6] Why is the chapter of Absalom juxtaposed to the chapter of Gog and Magog?[7] So that if one should say to you, is it possible that a slave should rebel against his master,[8] you can reply to him: Is it possible that a son should rebel against his father? Yet this happened; and so this too [will happen].

R. Joḥanan said in the name of R. Simeon b. Yoḥai: What is the meaning of the verse, *She openeth her mouth with wisdom, and the law of kindness is on her tongue?*[9] To whom was Solomon alluding in this verse? He was alluding only to his father David who dwelt in five worlds and composed a psalm [for each of them]. He abode in his mother's womb, and broke into song, as it says, *Bless the Lord, O my soul, and all my inwards*[10] *bless His holy name*.[11] He came out into the open air and looked upon the stars and constellations and broke into song, as it says, *Bless the Lord, ye angels of His, ye mighty in strength that fulfil His word, hearkening unto the voice of His*
b *word. Bless the Lord, all ye His hosts*[1] etc. He sucked from his mother's bosom and looked on her breasts and broke into song, as it says, *Bless the Lord, O my soul, and forget not all His benefits*.[2] What means '*all His benefits*'?—R. Abbahu said: That He placed her breasts at the source of understanding.[3] For what reason is this?—Rab Judah said: So that he should not look upon the place of shame; R. Mattena said: So that he should not suck from a place that is foul. He saw the downfall of the wicked and broke into song, as it says, *Let sinners cease out of the earth and let the wicked be no more. Bless the Lord, O my soul, Hallelujah*.[4] He looked upon the day of death and broke into song, as it says, *Bless the Lord, O my soul. O Lord my God, Thou art very great, Thou art clothed with glory and majesty*.[5] How does this verse refer to the day of death?—Rabbah son of R. Shila said: We learn it from the end of the passage, where it is written: *Thou hidest Thy face, they vanish, Thou withdrawest their breath, they perish* etc.[6]

R. Shimi b. 'Uḳba (others say, Mar 'Uḳba) was often in the company of R. Simeon b. Pazzi, who[7] used to arrange *aggadahs* [and recite them] before R. Joḥanan. He[8] said to him: What is the meaning of the verse, *Bless the Lord, O my soul, and all that is within me bless His holy name?*[9]—He replied: Come and observe how the capacity of human beings falls short of the capacity of the Holy One, blessed be He. It is in the capacity of a human being to draw a figure on a wall, but he cannot invest it with breath and spirit, bowels and intestines. But the Holy One, blessed be He, is not so; He shapes one form in the midst of another, and invests it with breath and spirit, bowels and intestines. And that is what Hannah said: *There is none holy as the Lord, for there is none beside Thee, neither is there any ẓur* [*rock*] *like our God*.[10] What means, '*neither is there any ẓur like our God*'? There is no artist [*ẓayyar*] like our God. What means, '*For there is none beside Thee*'? R. Judah b. Menasiah said: Read not, There is none *bilteka*, but, There is none *lebalotheka* [to consume Thee]. For the nature of flesh and blood is not like that of the Holy One, blessed be He. It is the nature of flesh and blood to be outlived by its works, but the Holy One, blessed be
c He, outlives His works. He said to him:[1] What I meant to tell you is this: To whom did David refer in these five verses beginning with '*Bless the Lord, O my soul*'? He was alluding only to the Holy One, blessed be He, and to the soul. Just as the Holy One, blessed be He, fills the whole world, so the soul fills the body. Just as the Holy One, blessed be He, sees, but is not seen, so the soul sees but is not itself seen. Just as the Holy One, blessed be He, feeds the whole world, so the soul feeds the whole body. Just as the Holy One, blessed be He, is pure, so the soul is pure. Just as the Holy One, blessed be He, abides in the innermost precincts, so the soul abides in the innermost precincts. Let that which has these five qualities come and praise Him who has these five qualities.

R. Hamnuna said: What is the meaning of the verse, *Who is as the wise man? And who knoweth the interpretation* [pesher] *of a thing?*[2] Who is like the Holy One, blessed be He, who knew how to effect a reconciliation [*pesharah*] between two righteous men, Hezekiah and Isaiah? Hezekiah said: Let Isaiah come to me, for so we find that Elijah went to Ahab,[3] as it says, *And Elijah went to show himself unto Ahab*.[4] Isaiah said: Let Hezekiah come to me, for so we find that Jehoram son of Ahab went to Elisha.[5] What did the Holy One, blessed be He, do? He brought sufferings upon Hezekiah and then said to Isaiah, Go visit the sick. For so it says, *In those days was Hezekiah sick unto death. And Isaiah the prophet, son of Amoz, came to him and said unto him, Thus saith the Lord, Set thy house in order, for thou shalt die and not live*[6] etc. What is the meaning of '*thou shalt die and not live*'? Thou shalt die in this world and not live in the world to come. He said to him: Why so bad? He replied: Because you did not try to have children. He said: The reason was because I saw by the holy spirit that the children issuing from me would not be virtuous. He said to him: What have you to do with the secrets of the All-Merciful? You should have done what you were commanded, and let the Holy One, blessed be He, do that which pleases Him. He said to him: Then give me now your daughter; perhaps through your merit and mine combined virtuous
d children will issue from me. He replied:[1] The doom has already been decreed. Said the other: Son of Amoz, finish your prophecy and go. This tradition I have from the house of my ancestor:[2] Even if a sharp sword rests upon a man's neck he should not desist from prayer.[3] This saying is also recorded in the names of R. Joḥanan and R. Eleazar: Even if a sharp sword rests on a man's neck, he should not desist from prayer, as it says, *Though He*

(4) In point of fact this is the only one. V. Tosaf. a.l. (5) The last verse of Ps. II, which shows that according to R. Joḥanan Pss. I and II formed one psalm. (6) *Baryone*, a word of doubtful meaning. (7) Valeria. (8) Pres. part. of the verb *ḥata*, to sin. Hence meaning sinners. (9) Which can be read חֲטָאִים sins. M.T. vocalizes חַטָּאִים (sinners). (10) So MS.M. (v. Glos.) curr. edd.: Sadducee.

a (1) Isa. LIV, 1. (2) Apparently the point is that at present she is barren, but in the future she shall have many children. Probably Beruria was thinking of Rome as '*the married wife*' and Jerusalem as '*the desolate*'. (3) Ps. III, 1. (4) Ibid. LVII, 1. (5) Heb. *semukim*, the same word as for juxtaposed. E.V. '*established*'. (6) Ibid. CXI, 8. (7) Ps. II, which is supposed by the Rabbis to refer to the rebellion of Gog and Magog against God and the Messiah.

מסורת הש"ס

פתח באשרי וסיים באשרי. אלמא חדא היא דאשרי כל חוסי בו סיומא דלמה רגשו גוים הוא: בריוני. פריצים: חטאים כתיב. קרי ביה חוטאים שיכלה יצר הרע: שפיל. השפיל עלמך לסוף המקרא כל דבר שהוא בסוף קרי שפילו של דבר: סמוכים לעד לעולם. בדברי תורה כתיב [אחרי] נאמנים כל פקודיו סמוכים סמיכת כל פקודיו עשוים באמת וישר ולמוך ולא דבר רק: כלום יש עבד שמורד ברבו. ויצא להכחיש את דברי הנביא: אמור לו כלום יש בן כו'. והא חזינן הכא דהוה: הבא נמי הוה. סופיה להיות: ואמר שירה. כנגד כולם אמר שירה לכשסרתה רוח הקדש עליו: וכל קרבי. על שם קרבי אמו שדר בתוכן: מאי משמע. דעל יום המיתה נאמר: בא וראה כו'. הוא סבר דהכי בעי מאי שנא קרבים דנקט: חמשה ברכי נפשי. לעיל חשיב להו: מאי דכתיב מי כהחכם ומי יודע פשר דבר. משום דאיירי בקופה בסמיכת גאולה לתפלה נקט ליה: דהכי אשכחן דאזל אליהו לגבי אחאב. דכתיב וילך אליהו להראות אל אחאב: יהורם אזל לגבי אלישע. כשהלכו על מואב הוא ויהושפט (במלכים ב ג) ומתוך שלא היו הולכים זה אצל זה לא היה מוכיחו על שלא נשא אשה: כבשי דרחמנא. סתרים דהקב"ה כמו רישא בכבשא (חולין ד' לג:) בהטומ' האפר: נגזרה גזרה. שתמות: מקובלני מבית אבי אבא. דוד שראה את המלאך וחרבו שלופה בידו בסוף ספר שמואל (ב כד) ולא מנע עצמו מן הרחמים: אבי

תורה אור

כל פרשה שהיתה חביבה על דוד פתח בה באשרי וסיים בה באשרי פתח באשרי דכתיב
תהלים א °אשרי האיש וסיים באשרי דכתיב °אשרי
שם ב כל חוסי בו: הנהו בריוני דהוו בשבבותיה דרבי מאיר והוו קא מצערו ליה טובא הוה קא בעי רבי מאיר רחמי עלוידהו כי היכי דלימותו אמרה ליה ברוריה דביתהו מאי דעתך
שם קד משום דכתיב °יתמו חטאים מי כתיב חוטאים חטאים כתיב ועוד שפיל לסיפיה דקרא ורשעים עוד אינם כיון דיתמו חטאים ורשעים עוד אינם אלא בעי רחמי עלוידהו דלהדרו בתשובה ורשעים עוד אינם בעי רחמי עלוידהו והדרו בתשובה: אמר לה ההוא צדוקי לברוריה כתיב °רני עקרה
ישעיה נד לא ילדה משום דלא ילדה רני אמרה ליה שטיא שפיל לסיפיה דקרא דכתיב כי רבים בני שוממה מבני בעולה אמר ה' *אלא מאי עקרה לא ילדה רני כנסת ישראל שדומה לאשה עקרה שלא ילדה בנים לגיהנם כותייכו: אמר
תהלי' ג ליה ההוא צדוקי לרבי אבהו כתיב °מזמור לדוד בברחו מפני אבשלום בנו
שם נז וכתיב °לדוד מכתם בברחו מפני שאול במערה הי מעשה הוה ברישא מכדי מעשה שאול הוה ברישא לכתוב ברישא אמר ליה אתון דלא דרשיתון סמוכין
יבמות ד.
תהלים קיא קשיא לכו אנן דדרשינן סמוכין לא קשיא לן *דא"ר יוחנן סמוכין מן התורה מנין שנאמר °סמוכים לעד לעולם עשוים באמת וישר למה נסמכה פרשת אבשלום לפרשת גוג ומגוג שאם יאמר לך אדם כלום יש עבד שמורד ברבו אף אתה אמור לו כלום יש בן שמורד באביו אלא הוה הכא נמי הוה: אמר רבי יוחנן משום
משלי לא רבי שמעון בן יוחי מאי דכתיב °פיה פתחה בחכמה ותורת חסד על לשונה כנגד מי אמר שלמה מקרא זה
תהלים קג לא אמרו אלא כנגד דוד אביו שדר בחמשה עולמים ואמר שירה דר במעי אמו ואמר שירה שנאמר °ברכי
שם נפשי את ה' וכל קרבי את שם קדשו יצא לאויר העולם ונסתכל בככבים ובמזלות ואמר שירה שנאמר °ברכו ה' מלאכיו גבורי כח עושי דברו לשמוע בקול דברו ברכו ה' כל צבאיו וגומר ינק משדי אמו ונסתכל בדדיה
שם ואמר שירה שנאמר °ברכי נפשי את ה' ואל תשכחי כל גמוליו מאי כל גמוליו אמר רבי אבהו שעשה לה דדים במקום בינה טעמא מאי אמר (רבי) יהודה כדי שלא יסתכל במקום ערוה רב מתנא אמר כדי שלא
שם קד יינק ממקום הטנופת ראה במפלתן של רשעים ואמר שירה שנאמר °יתמו חטאים מן הארץ ורשעים עוד
שם אינם ברכי נפשי את ה' הללויה נסתכל ביום המיתה ואמר שירה שנאמר °ברכי נפשי את ה' ה' אלהי גדלת מאד הוד והדר לבשת מאי משמע דעל יום המיתה נאמר אמר רבה בר רב שילא מסיפא דעניינא דכתיב
שם °תסתיר פניך יבהלון תוסף רוחם יגועון וגומר רב שימי בר עוקבא ואמרי לה מר עוקבא הוה שכיח קמיה
שם קג דרבי שמעון בן פזי והוה מסדר אגדתא קמיה דר' יהושע בן לוי אמר ליה מאי דכתיב °ברכי נפשי את ה' וכל
מגילה יד. ע"ש קרבי את שם קדשו אמר ליה בא וראה שלא כמדת הקב"ה מדת בשר ודם *מדת בשר ודם צר צורה על גבי הכותל ואינו יכול להטיל בה רוח ונשמה קרבים ובני מעים והקב"ה אינו כן צר צורה בתוך צורה ומטיל
שמואל א' ב בה רוח ונשמה קרבים ובני מעים והיינו דאמרה חנה °אין קדוש כה' כי אין בלתך ואין צור כאלהינו מאי אין
מגילה יד. ע"ש סיע"ב צור כאלהינו אין צייר כאלהינו *מאי כי אין בלתך אמר רבי יהודה בר מנסיא אל תקרי כי אין בלתך אלא אין לבלותך שלא כמדת הקב"ה מדת בשר ודם מדת בשר ודם מעשה ידיו מבלין אותו והקב"ה מבלה מעשיו אמר ליה אנא הכי קא אמינא לך הני חמשה ברכי נפשי כנגד מי אמרן דוד לא אמרן אלא כנגד הקב"ה וכנגד נשמה מה הקב"ה מלא כל העולם אף נשמה מלאה את כל הגוף מה הקב"ה רואה ואינו נראה אף נשמה רואה ואינה נראית מה הקב"ה זן את כל העולם כולו אף נשמה זנה את כל הגוף מה הקב"ה טהור אף נשמה טהורה מה הקב"ה יושב בחדרי חדרים אף נשמה יושבת בחדרי חדרים יבא מי שיש בו חמשה
קהלת ח דברים הללו וישבח למי שיש בו ה' דברים הללו: אמר רב המנונא מאי דכתיב °מי כהחכם ומי יודע פשר דבר מי כהקב"ה שיודע לעשות פשרה בין שני צדיקים בין חזקיהו לישעיהו חזקיהו אמר ליתי ישעיהו גבאי
מלכים א' יח דהכי אשכחן באליהו דאזל לגבי אחאב (שנאמר °וילך אליהו להראות אל אחאב) ישעיהו אמר ליתי חזקיהו גבאי דהכי אשכחן ביהורם בן אחאב דאזל לגבי אלישע מה עשה הקב"ה הביא יסורים על חזקיהו ואמר לו
ישעיה לח לישעיהו לך ובקר את החולה שנאמר °בימים ההם חלה חזקיהו למות ויבא אליו ישעיהו בן אמוץ הנביא ויאמר [אליו] כה אמר ה' צבאות צו לביתך כי מת אתה ולא תחיה וגו' מאי כי מת אתה ולא תחיה מת אתה בעוה"ז ולא תחיה לעוה"ב א"ל מאי כולי האי א"ל משום דלא עסקת בפריה ורביה אמר ליה משום דחזאי לי ברוח הקדש דנפקי מינאי בנין דלא מעלו אמר ליה בהדי כבשי דרחמנא למה לך מאי דמפקדת אבעי לך למעבד ומה דניחא קמיה קודשא בריך הוא לעביד אמר ליה השתא הב לי ברתך אפשר דגרמא זכותא דידי ודידך ונפקי מינאי בני דמעלו אמר ליה כבר נגזרה עליך גזירה אמר ליה בן אמוץ כלה נבואתך וצא כך מקובלני מבית אבי אבא אפילו חרב חדה מונחת על צוארו של אדם אל ימנע עצמו מן הרחמים אתמר נמי רבי יוחנן ורבי (אליעזר) דאמרי
איוב יג תרוייהו אפילו חרב חדה מונחת על צוארו של אדם אל ימנע עצמו מן הרחמים שנאמר °הן יקטלני לו איחל

א"ר

כל פרשה שהיתה חביבה על דוד כו'. וא"ת מאי כל פרשה והא לא אשכחן שום פרשה אחרת שמתחלת באשרי ומסיימת באשרי אלא היא. ויש לומר דלאו דוקא פתח באשרי וסיים באשרי אלא חתימה מעין פתיחה כמו תהלה שפתח בתהלה וסיים בתהלה תהלת ה' ידבר פי וכן הרבה פרשיות שמתחילות בהללויה ומסיימות בהללויה: גדול

אלא מאי לא לד' עקרה רני כצ"ל רש"ל

[רב נ"ב]

[צ"ל אלעזר]

(8) *Sc.* the nations against God. (9) Prov. XXXI, 26. (10) I.e., his mother's womb. E.V. *'all that is within me'*. (11) Ps. CIII, 1.

b (1) Ps. CIII, 20, 21. (2) Ibid. 2. (3) I.e., the heart, (the seat of understanding). R. Abbahu connects the word *gemulaw* (his benefits) with *gamal* (weaned). (4) Ibid. CIV, 35. (5) Ibid. 1. (6) Ibid. 29. (7) Reading דהוה with MS.M. (8) R. Shimi or Mar 'Uḳba. (9) Ibid. CIII, 1. (10) I Sam. II, 2.

c (1) R. Shimi to R. Simeon b. Pazzi. (2) Eccl. VIII, 1. (3) The prophet went to the king. (4) I Kings XVIII, 2. (5) V. II Kings III, 12. (6) Isa. XXXVIII, 1.

d (1) Insert with MS.M. Behold I say to you *'Set thy house in order'*, and you say to me 'Give me now your daughter'. (2) David. (3) Cf. II Sam. XXIV, 17.

אבי אבא שחפה את ההיכל. שלמה: שגנז ספר רפואות. כדי שיבקשו רחמים: גירר עצמות אביו. לפי שהיה רשע בזהו ולא נהג בו כבוד בקבורתו להוליאו כהוגן במטות זהב וכסף: סתם מי גיחון. מי שלוח בדברי הימים (ב לב) ולמה כדי שלא ימלאו מלכי אשור מים לשתות ולא זהו גיחון הנהר הגדול דההוא לאו בארץ ישראל הוא אלא מעין קטן הוא סמוך לירושלים שנאמר והורדתם אותו אל גיחון (מלכים א א) ומתרגמינן ותחתון יתיה לשילוחא: עבר ניסן בניסן. הס"ד משנתקדש החדש לשם ניסן כמלך לעבר את השנה ועשאו אדר כמו שנאמר בדברי הימים (ב ל) ויועץ המלך (חזקיהו) לעשות הפסח בחודש השני: ביום שלשים של אדר. ואע"פ שלא נתקדש החדש שעדיין לא באו עדים: התולה בזכות עצמו. שאומר בתפלתו עשה לי בזכותי כגון חזקיהו שאמר זכר נא את אשר התהלכתי לפניך וגו': פרועה. מגולה שנטלה תקרה שלה: הרוצה ליהנות. משל אחרים: יהנה. ואין איסור בדבר: כאלישע. כמו שמלינו באלישע שנהנה: והרוצה שלא ליהנות. משל אחרים: אל יהנה. ואין בדבר לא משום גסות רוח ולא משום שנאה: כשמואל הרמתי. כמו שמלינו בשמואל הרמתי שלא רלה ליהנות: כי שם ביתו. לעיל מיניה כתיב והלך מדי שנה בשנה וסבב בית אל והגלגל והמלפה ושפט את ישראל וסמיך ליה ותשובתו הרמתה כי שם ביתו וכי איכי יודע ששם ביתו אלא אכולהו מקומות דקרא דלעיל מיניה קאי שבכל מקום שהיה הולך שם היה נושא כל כלי תשמישי בית עמו ואהל חכייתו שלא להנות מן אחרים: בהוד יפיה. בדדים: תפלה לעני. דרך עניות: יכוין את רגליו. זו אצל זו: ורגליהם רגל ישרה. כראין כרגל אחד: הקורא מכאן ואילך לא הפסיד. שהרי הוא כאדם שקורא אחת מכל הפרשיות שבתורה ואע"פ שלא יצא ידי ק"ש יש לו קבול שכר כעוסק בתורה:

מתני'. יטה. על לדו: בשכבך. דרך שכיבה: יעמוד. דכתיב ובקומך: כדרכו. או בקימה או בשכיבה או בישיבה או מהלך:

גמרא

תורה אור

גדול הקורא קריאת שמע בעונת' יותר מהעוסק בתורה. תימה אפי' תפלה נמי דהא אמרי' פ"ק דשבת (ד' יא.) כגון אנו מפסיקין בין לק"ש בין לתפלה. וי"ל דהכי קאמר יותר מהעוסק בתורה פעם אחרת שלא בשעת ק"ש. אבל העוסק בתורה בשעת קריאת שמע לא מיירי ואפילו לתפלה פוסק:

שנאמר

א"ר חנן אפי' בעל החלומות אומר לו לאדם למחר הוא מת אל ימנע עצמו מן הרחמים שנ' °כי ברוב חלומות והבלים ודברים הרבה כי את האלהים ירא מיד °ויסב חזקיהו פניו אל הקיר ויתפלל אל השם מאי קיר אמר רשב"ל מקירות לבו שנאמר °מעי מעי אוחילה קירות לבי וגו' רבי לוי אמר על עסקי הקיר אמר לפניו רבונו של עולם ומה שונמית שלא עשתה אלא קיר אחת קטנה החיית את בנה אבי אבא שחפה את ההיכל כולו בכסף ובזהב עאכ"ו °זכר נא את אשר התהלכתי לפניך באמת ובלב שלם והטוב בעיניך עשיתי מאי והטוב בעיניך עשיתי א"ר יהודה אמר רב שסמך גאולה לתפלה רבי לוי אמר שגנז ספר רפואות: ת"ר *ו' דברים עשה חזקיהו המלך על ג' הודו לו ועל ג' לא הודו לו על ג' הודו לו גנז ספר רפואות והודו לו כתת נחש הנחשת והודו לו גירר עצמות אביו על מטה של חבלים והודו לו ועל ג' לא הודו לו סתם מי גיחון *ולא הודו לו קצץ דלתות היכל ושגרם למלך אשור ולא הודו לו עבר ניסן בניסן ולא הודו לו ומי לית ליה לחזקיהו °החודש הזה לכם ראש חדשים *זה ניסן ואין אחר ניסן אלא טעה בדשמואל *דאמר שמואל אין מעברין את השנה ביום ל' של אדר הואיל וראוי לקובעו ניסן סבר הואיל וראוי לא אמרינן: א"ר יוחנן משום ר' יוסי בן זמרא כל התולה בזכות עצמו תולין לו בזכות אחרים וכל התולה בזכות אחרים תולין לו בזכות עצמו משה תלה בזכות אחרים שנאמר °זכור לאברהם ליצחק ולישראל עבדיך תלו לו בזכות עצמו שנאמר °ויאמר להשמידם לולי משה בחירו עמד בפרץ לפניו להשיב חמתו מהשחית חזקיהו תלה בזכות עצמו דכתיב זכר נא את אשר התהלכתי לפניך תלו לו בזכות אחרים שנאמר °וגנותי אל העיר הזאת להושיעה למעני ולמען דוד עבדי והיינו דריב"ל דאמר ריב"ל מ"ד °הנה לשלום מר לי מר אפילו בשעה ששיגר לו הקב"ה שלום מר הוא לו: °נעשה נא עליית קיר קטנה רב ושמואל חד אמר עלייה פרועה היתה וקירוה וחד אמר אכסדרה גדולה היתה וחלקוה לשנים בשלמא למ"ד אכסדרה היינו דכתיב קיר אלא למ"ד עלייה מאי קיר שקירוה בשלמא למאן דאמר עלייה היינו דכתיב עליית אלא למאן דאמר אכסדרה מאי עליית *מעולה שבבתים: ונשים לו שם מטה ושולחן וכסא ומנורה אמר אביי ואיתימא ר' יצחק הרוצה להנות יהנה כאלישע ושאינו רוצה להנות אל יהנה כשמואל הרמתי שנאמר °ותשובתו הרמתה כי שם ביתו וא"ר יוחנן *שכל מקום שהלך שם ביתו עמו: °ותאמר אל אישה הנה נא ידעתי כי איש אלהים קדוש הוא אמר ר' יוסי בר' חנינא מכאן שהאשה מכרת באורחין יותר מן האיש קדוש הוא מנא ידעה רב ושמואל חד אמר שלא ראתה זבוב עובר על שולחנו וחד אמר סדין של פשתן הציעה על מטתו ולא ראתה קרי עליו: קדוש הוא א"ר יוסי בר' חנינא הוא קדוש ומשרתו אינו קדוש (שנאמר) °ויגש גחזי להדפה א"ר יוסי בר' חנינא שאחזה בהוד יפיה: עובר עלינו תמיד א"ר יוסי בר' חנינא משום ראב"י כל המארח ת"ח בתוך ביתו ומהנהו מנכסיו מעלה עליו הכתוב כאלו מקריב תמידין: וא"ר יוסי בר' חנינא משום ראב"י *אל יעמוד אדם במקום גבוה ויתפלל אלא במקום נמוך ויתפלל שנאמר °ממעמקים קראתיך ה' תנ"ה *לא יעמוד אדם לא ע"ג כסא ולא ע"ג שרפרף ולא במקום גבוה ויתפלל אלא במקום נמוך ויתפלל לפי שאין גבהות לפני המקום שנאמר ממעמקים קראתיך ה' וכתיב °תפלה לעני כי יעטוף: וא"ר יוסי בר' חנינא משום ראב"י ^ג^המתפלל צריך שיכוין את רגליו שנאמר °ורגליהם רגל ישרה (א"ר יצחק א"ר יוחנן) ואמר רבי יוסי בר' חנינא משום ראב"י מ"ד °לא תאכלו על הדם ^ג^לא תאכלו קודם שתתפללו על דמכם (א"ד) א"ר יצחק *אמר רבי יוחנן א"ר יוסי בר' חנינא משום ראב"י כל האוכל ושותה ואח"כ מתפלל עליו הכתוב אומר °ואותי השלכת אחרי גויך אל תקרי גויך אלא גאיך אמר הקב"ה לאחר שנתגאה זה קבל עליו מלכות שמים: ר' יהושע אומר עד ג' שעות: אמר רב יהודה אמר שמואל ^ד^הלכה כר' יהושע: הקורא מכאן ואילך לא הפסיד: אמר רב הסדא אמר מר עוקבא ובלבד שלא יאמר יוצר אור מיתיבי הקורא מכאן ואילך לא הפסיד כאדם שהוא קורא בתורה אבל מברך הוא ב' לפניה ואחת לאחריה תיובתא דרב חסדא תיובתא איכא דאמרי א"ר חסדא אמר מר עוקבא מאי לא הפסיד שלא הפסיד ברכות תנ"ה ^ה^הקורא מכאן ואילך לא הפסיד כאדם שקורא בתורה אבל מברך הוא שתים לפניה ואחת לאחריה א"ר מני גדול הקורא ק"ש בעונתה יותר מהעוסק בתורה מדקתני הקורא מכאן ואילך לא הפסיד כאדם הקורא בתורה מכלל דקורא בעונתה עדיף: **מתני'** *ב"ש אומרים בערב כל אדם יטה ויקרא ובבוקר יעמוד שנאמר °ובשכבך ובקומך וב"ה אומרים ^ו^כל אדם *קורא כדרכו שנאמר ובלכתך בדרך א"כ למה נאמר ובשכבך ובקומך בשעה שבני אדם שוכבים ובשעה שבני אדם עומדים א"ר טרפון אני הייתי בא בדרך והטתי לקרות כדברי ב"ש וסכנתי בעצמי מפני הלסטים אמרו לו כדי היית לחוב בעצמך שעברת על דברי בית הלל:

גמרא

many words. (7) Isa. XXXVIII, 2. MS.M. adds: Finally he gave him his daughter (in marriage) and there issued from him Menasseh and Rabshakeh. One day he (Hezekiah) carried them on his shoulder to the Synagogue (Var. lec. to the house of learning) and one of them said, 'Father's bald head is good for breaking nuts on', while the other said, 'it is good for roasting fish on'. He thereupon threw them both on the ground and Rabshakeh was killed, but not Menasseh. He then applied to them the verse, *The instruments also of the churl are evil; he deviseth wicked devices.* (Isa. XXXII, 7).

a (1) Jer. IV, 19. (2) V. II Kings IV, 10. (3) King Solomon. (4) Isa. XXXVIII, 3. This comes in the prayer of Hezekiah. (5) V. *supra, 9b.* (6) A book containing remedies for various illnesses which Hezekiah hid from the public in order that people might pray for healing to God; v. *infra.* (7) V. Pes. 56a. (8) V. II Kings XVIII, 4. (9) Instead of giving him a royal burial. (10) Because Ahaz was a wicked man. (11) V. II Chron. XXXII, 30. (12) V. II Kings XVIII, 16. (13) V. II Chron. XXX, 2. (14) Ex. XII, 2. (15) I.e., a second Nisan must not be intercalated.

b (1) If the new moon is observed on it. (2) And he declared the month Adar Sheni (Second Adar). (3) Ex. XXXII, 13. (4) Ps. CVI, 23. (5) Isa. XXXVIII, 3. (6) Ibid. XXXVII 35. (7) Ibid. XXXVIII, 17. (8) Because it was not made to depend on his own merit. (9) II Kings IV, 10. (10) In the explanation of עלית קיר which means literally 'an upper chamber of (with) a wall'. (11) By means of a wall. (12) Lit., 'elevated'.

c (1) II Kings IV, 10. (2) There is no prohibition against this. (3) And this is not to be taken as a sign of pride or enmity. (4) I Sam. VII, 17. (5) I.e., he did not accept the hospitality of the people. R. Joḥanan takes the word 'there' to refer to all the places mentioned above. (6) II Kings IV, 9. (7) Ibid. 27. (8) Lit., 'the pride of her beauty', בהוד יפיה, a play on the word להדפה, '*to thrust her away*'. (9) Ibid. 9. (10) Which is also called *tamid*, lit., '*continually*'. (11) Ps. CXXX, 1. (12) Ibid. CII, 1.

d (1) I.e., close together and level. (2) Ezek. I, 7. (3) Lev. XIX, 26. (4) I.e., life. (5) I Kings XIV, 9. (6) The same Hebrew word may be translated 'behind' and 'after'. (7) The technical term for reciting the *Shema*'. (8) The first of the two introductory benedictions to the *Shema*'. V. *P.B.* p. 37. (9) If he who says later is as good, he who says at the proper time must be better.

e (1) Deut. VI, 7. (2) Ibid.

slay me, yet will I trust in Him.[4] [10b] ([Similarly] R. Ḥanan said: Even if the master of dreams[5] says to a man that on the morrow he will die, he should not desist from prayer, for so it says, *For in the multitude of dreams are vanities and also many words, but fear thou God*).[6] Thereupon straightway, *Hezekiah turned his face to the* kir [*wall*] *and prayed unto the Lord.*[7] What is the meaning of *'kir'?*— R. Simeon b. Laḳish said: [He prayed] from the innermost chambers [*kiroth*] of his heart, as it says, *My bowels, my bowels, I writhe*
a *in pain!* Kiroth [*The chambers*] *of my heart* etc.[1] R. Levi said: [He prayed] with reference to [another] *'kir'*. He said before Him: Sovereign of the Universe! The Shunammite woman made only one little chamber [on the roof] and Thou didst restore her son to life.[2] How much more so then me whose ancestor[3] overlaid the Temple with silver and gold! *Remember now, O Lord, I beseech Thee, how I have walked before Thee in truth and with a whole heart, and have done that which is good in Thy sight.*[4] What means, *'I have done that which is good in Thy sight'?*—Rab Judah says in the name of Rab: He joined the *ge'ullah* with the *tefillah*.[5] R. Levi said: He hid away the Book of Cures.[6]

Our Rabbis taught:[7] King Hezekiah did six things; of three of them they [the Rabbis] approved and of three they did not approve. Of three they approved: he hid away the Book of Cures; and they approved of it; he broke into pieces the brazen serpent,[8] and they approved of it; and he dragged the bones of his father [to the grave] on a bed of ropes,[9] and they approved of it.[10] Of three they did not approve: He stopped up the waters of Gihon,[11] and they did not approve of it; he cut off [the gold] from the doors of the Temple and sent it to the King of Assyria,[12] and they did not approve of it; and he intercalated the month of Nisan during Nisan,[13] and they did not approve of it. But did not Hezekiah accept the teaching: *This month shall be unto you the beginning of months:*[14] [this means] that this is Nisan and no other month shall be Nisan?[15]—He went wrong over the teaching enunciated by Samuel. For Samuel said: The year must not be declared a prolonged year on the thirtieth of Adar, since this day may
b possibly belong to Nisan;[1] and he thought: We do not pay heed to this possibility.[2]

R. Joḥanan said in the name of R. Jose b. Zimra: If a man makes his petition depend on his own merit, heaven makes it depend on the merit of others; and if he makes it depend on the merit of others, heaven makes it depend on his own merit. Moses made his petition depend on the merit of others, as it says, *Remember Abraham, Isaac and Israel Thy servants!*[3] and Scripture made it depend on his own merit, as it says, *Therefore He said that He would destroy them, had not Moses His chosen stood before Him in the breach to turn back His wrath, lest He should destroy them.*[4] Hezekiah made his petition depend on his own merit, as it is written: *Remember now, O Lord, I beseech Thee, how I have walked before Thee,*[5] and God made it depend on the merit of others, as it says, *For I will defend this city to save it, for Mine own sake and for My servant David's sake.*[6] And this agrees with R. Joshua b. Levi. For R. Joshua b. Levi said: What is the meaning of the verse, *Behold for my peace I had great bitterness?*[7] Even when the Holy One, blessed be He, sent him [the message of] peace it was bitter for him.[8]

Let us make, I pray thee, a little chamber on the roof.[9] Rab and Samuel differ.[10] One says: It was an open upper chamber, and they put a roof on it. The other says: It was a large verandah, and they divided it into two.[11] For him who says that it was a verandah, there is a good reason why the text says *kir* [wall]. But how does he who says that it was an upper chamber account for the word *kir?*—[It is used] because they put a roof on it [*kiruah*]. For him who says it was an upper chamber there is a good reason why the text uses the word *'aliyath* [upper chamber]. But how does he who says it was a verandah account for the word *'aliyath?*—It was the best [*me'ulla*][12] of the rooms.

And let us set for him there a bed, and a table, and a stool and a candle-
c *stick.*[1] Abaye (or as some say, R. Isaac) said: If one wants to benefit from the hospitality of another, he may benefit, as Elisha did;[2] and if he does not desire to benefit, he may refuse to do so, as Samuel the Ramathite did,[3] of whom we read, *And his return was to Ramah, for there was his house;*[4] and R. Joḥanan said: [This teaches that] wherever he travelled, his house was with him.[5]

And she said unto her husband: Behold now, I perceive that he is a holy man of God.[6] R. Jose b. Ḥanina said: You learn from this that a woman recognizes the character of a guest better than a man. *'A holy man'*. How did she know this?—Rab and Samuel gave different answers. One said: Because she never saw a fly pass by his table. The other said: She spread a sheet of linen over his bed, and she never saw a nocturnal pollution on it. *He is a holy* [*man*]. R. Jose son of R. Ḥanina said: *He* is holy, but his attendant is not holy. For so it says: *And Gehazi came near to thrust her away;*[7] R. Jose son of Ḥanina said: He seized her by the breast.[8]

That passeth by us continually.[9] R. Jose son of R. Ḥanina said in the name of R. Eliezer b. Jacob: If a man entertains a scholar in his house and lets him enjoy his possessions, Scripture accounts it to him as if he had sacrificed the daily burnt-offering.[10]

R. Jose son of Ḥanina further said in the name of R. Eliezer b. Jacob: A man should not stand on a high place when he prays, but he should pray in a lowly place, as it says; *Out of the depths have I called Thee, O Lord.*[11] It has been taught to the same effect: A man should not stand on a chair or on a footstool or on a high place to pray, but he should pray in a lowly place, since there is no elevation before God, and so it says, *'Out of the depths have I called Thee, O Lord'*, and it also says, *A prayer of the afflicted, when he fainteth.*[12]

R. Jose son of R. Ḥanina also said in the name of R. Eliezer b. Jacob: When one prays, he should place his feet in proper
d position,[1] as it says, *And their feet were straight feet.*[2]

R. Jose son of R. Ḥanina also said in the name of R. Eliezer b. Jacob: What is the meaning of the verse, *Ye shall not eat with the blood?*[3] Do not eat before ye have prayed for your blood.[4] R. Isaac said in the name of R. Joḥanan, who had it from R. Jose son of R. Ḥanina in the name of R. Eliezer b. Jacob: If one eats and drinks and then says his prayers, of him the Scripture says, *And hast cast Me behind thy back.*[5] Read not *gaweka* [thy back], but *geeka* [thy pride]. Says the Holy One, blessed be He: After[6] this one has exalted himself, he comes and accepts the kingdom of heaven![7]

R. JOSHUA SAYS: UNTIL THE THIRD HOUR. Rab Judah said in the name of Samuel: The *halachah* is as stated by R. Joshua.

HE WHO RECITES THE SHEMA' LATER LOSES NOTHING. R. Ḥisda said in the name of Mar 'Ukba: Provided he does not say the benediction of 'Who formest the light'.[8] An objection was raised from the statement: He who recites the *Shema'* later loses nothing; he is like one reading in the Torah, but he says two blessings before it and one after. Is not this a refutation of R. Ḥisda? It is [indeed] a refutation. Some there are who say: R. Ḥisda said in the name of Mar 'Ukba: What is the meaning of HE LOSES NOTHING? He does not lose the benedictions. It has been taught to the same effect: He who says the *Shema'* later loses nothing, being like one who reads from the Torah, but he says two blessings before and one after.

R. Mani said: He who recites the *Shema'* in its proper time is greater than he who studies the Torah.[9] For since it says, HE WHO SAYS LATER LOSES NOTHING, BEING LIKE A MAN WHO READS IN THE TORAH, we may conclude that one who recites the *Shema'* at its proper time is superior.

MISHNAH. BETH SHAMMAI SAY: IN THE EVENING EVERY MAN SHOULD RECLINE AND RECITE [THE SHEMA'], AND IN THE MORNING HE SHOULD STAND, AS IT SAYS, AND WHEN
e THOU LIEST DOWN AND WHEN THOU RISEST UP.[1] BETH HILLEL, HOWEVER, SAY THAT EVERY MAN SHOULD RECITE IN HIS OWN WAY, AS IT SAYS, AND WHEN THOU WALKEST BY THE WAY.[2] WHY THEN IS IT SAID, AND WHEN THOU LIEST DOWN AND WHEN THOU RISEST UP? [THIS MEANS], AT THE TIME WHEN PEOPLE LIE DOWN AND AT THE TIME WHEN PEOPLE RISE UP. R. TARFON SAID: I WAS ONCE WALKING BY THE WAY AND I RECLINED TO RECITE THE SHEMA' IN THE MANNER PRESCRIBED BY BETH SHAMMAI, AND I INCURRED DANGER FROM ROBBERS. THEY SAID TO HIM: YOU DESERVED TO COME TO HARM, BECAUSE YOU ACTED AGAINST THE OPINION OF BETH HILLEL.

(4) Job XIII, 15. (5) This seems to be simply a periphrasis for 'if a man is told in a dream'. Two explanations are then possible of what follows. (i) If he dreams and the dream so far comes true that a sword is placed on his neck, still he should pray. (ii) Even if he only dreams this, he should still pray etc. (R. Bezalel of Regensburg.) (6) Eccl. V, 6. Apparently this is how R. Ḥanan understands the verse. E.V. *Through the multitude and vanities there are also*

GEMARA. [11a] Beth Hillel cause no difficulty; they explain their own reason and the reason [why they reject the opinion] of Beth Shammai. But why do not Beth Shammai accept the view of Beth Hillel?—Beth Shammai can reply: If this is so,[3] let the text say, 'In the morning and in the evening'. Why does it say, '*When thou liest down and when thou risest up*'? To show that in the time of lying down there must be actual lying down, and in the time of rising up there must be actual rising up. And how do Beth Shammai explain the words '*And when thou walkest by the way*'?—They need it for the following, as has been taught: '*When thou sittest in thy house*':[4] this excludes a bridegroom. '*And when thou walkest by the way*': this excludes one who is occupied with the performance of a religious duty.[5] Hence they laid down that one who marries a virgin is free [from the obligation to say the *Shema'* in the evening] while one who marries a widow is bound.[6] How is
a the lesson[1] derived?—R. Papa said: [The circumstances must be] like a '*way*'. As a 'way' [journey] is optional, so whatever is optional [does not exempt from the obligation]. But does not the text treat [also] of one who is going to perform a religious duty, and even so the All Merciful said that he should recite?—If that were so, the All Merciful should have written [simply], 'While sitting and while walking'. What is the implication of *when* thou *sittest and when* thou *walkest*?—In the case of *thy* sitting and *thy* walking thou art under the obligation, but in the case of performing a religious duty thou art exempt. If that is so, one who marries a widow should also be exempt?—The one[2] is agitated, the other not. If a state of agitation is the ground, it would apply also the the case of his ship sinking at sea! And should you say, Quite so, why did R. Abba b. Zabda say in the name of Rab: A mourner is under obligation to perform all the precepts laid down in the Torah except that of the *tefillin*, because the term 'headtire' is applied to them, as it says, *Bind thy headtire upon thee*?[3]—In that case the agitation is over a religious duty, here it is over an optional matter.

And Beth Shammai?[4]—They require it to exclude persons on a religious mission.[5] And Beth Hillel?[6]—They reply: Incidentally it tells you that one recites also by the way.[7]

Our Rabbis taught: Beth Hillel say that one may recite the *Shema'* standing, one may recite it sitting, one may recite it reclining, one may recite it walking on the road, one may recite it at one's work. Once R. Ishmael and R. Eleazar b. Azariah were dining at the same place, and R. Ishmael was reclining while R. Eleazar was standing upright. When the time came for reciting the *Shema'*, R. Eleazar reclined and R. Ishmael stood upright. Said R. Eleazar b. Azariah to R. Ishmael: Brother Ishmael, I will tell you a parable. To what is this [our conduct] like? It is like that of a man to whom people say, You have a fine beard, and he replies, Let this go to
b meet the destroyers.[1] So now, with you: as long as I was upright you were reclining, and now that I recline you stand upright![2] He replied: I have acted according to the rule of Beth Hillel and you have acted according to the rule of Beth Shammai. And what is more, [I had to act thus], lest the disciples should see and fix the *halachah* so for future generations. What did he mean by 'what is more'? He meant: Should you argue that Beth Hillel also allow reclining, [I reply that] this is the case only where one was reclining from the first. Here, however, since at first you were upright and now you recline, they may say, This shows that they [both] are of the opinion of Beth Shammai, and perhaps the disciples will see and fix the *halachah* so for future generations.

R. Ezekiel learnt: If one follows the rule of Beth Shammai he does right, if one follows the rule of Beth Hillel he does right. R. Joseph said: If he follows the rule of Beth Shammai, his action is worthless, as we have learnt: If a man has his head and the greater part of his body in the *sukkah*[3] while the table is in the house, Beth Shammai declare his action void, while Beth Hillel declare it valid. Said Beth Hillel to Beth Shammai: Once the Elders of Beth Shammai and the Elders of Beth Hillel went to visit R. Johanan b. Ha-horanith, and they found him with his head and the greater part of his body in the *sukkah* while the table was in the house, and they made no objection. They replied: Do you bring a proof from this?[4] [The fact is that] they also said to him: If such has been your regular custom, you have never performed the precept of the *sukkah* in your lifetime.[5] R. Nahman b. Isaac said: One who follows the rule of Beth Shammai makes his life forfeit, as we have learnt: R. TARFON SAID: I WAS ONCE WALKING BY THE WAY AND I RECLINED TO RECITE THE SHEMA' IN THE MANNER PRESCRIBED BY BETH SHAMMAI, AND I INCURRED DANGER FROM ROBBERS. THEY SAID TO HIM: YOU DESERVED TO COME TO HARM, BECAUSE YOU ACTED AGAINST THE OPINION OF BETH HILLEL.

MISHNAH. IN THE MORNING TWO BLESSINGS ARE TO BE
c SAID BEFORE IT[1] AND ONE AFTER IT. IN THE EVENING TWO ARE SAID BEFORE IT AND TWO AFTER IT, ONE LONG AND ONE SHORT.[2] WHERE THEY [THE SAGES] LAID DOWN THAT A LONG ONE SHOULD BE SAID, IT IS NOT PERMITTED TO SAY A SHORT ONE. WHERE THEY ORDAINED A SHORT ONE A LONG ONE IS NOT PERMITTED. [A PRAYER] WHICH THEY ORDERED TO BE CONCLUDED [WITH A BENEDICTION][3] MUST NOT BE LEFT WITHOUT SUCH A CONCLUSION; ONE WHICH THEY ORDERED TO BE LEFT WITHOUT SUCH A CONCLUSION MUST NOT BE SO CONCLUDED.

(3) That only the time of the recital is meant. (4) Ibid. (5) This is the reading of MS.M., and this is the version found in Tosaf. Suk. 25a a.v. ובלכתך and elsewhere. Cur. edd. reverse the positions of 'bridegroom' and 'one who is occupied, etc.' (6) V. *infra*.

a (1) Relating to one who is occupied with the performance. (2) The one who marries a virgin is worried as to whether he shall find her really such. (3) Ezek. XXIV, 17. Ezekiel, though a mourner, was commanded exceptionally to wear his headtire, i.e., (as the Rabbis understand) *tefillin*, from which it is deduced that ordinarily a mourner does not do so. But the fact remains that worry as a rule does not exempt from the precepts. (4) How do they interpret the words '*and when thou walkest by the way*'? V. next note. (5) This seems to be a repetition of the question and answer given above and is best left out with MS.M. (6) How can they infer their view from this verse, seeing that it is required to exempt one who is occupied in performing a religious duty. (7) I.e., in his own way, as explained above.

b (1) As much as to say, I will have it cut off just to spite you. (2) As if to spite me. (3) V. Glos. (4) In respect of fulfilling the precept of the *sukkah*, v. Suk. 28a. (5) And since Beth Shammai invalidated action according to Beth Hillel, similarly Beth Hillel declared invalid action according to Beth Shammai.

c (1) *Sc.* the *Shema'*. (2) The reference is to the two that follow the evening *Shema'*. (3) I.e., with the words, Blessed art Thou, O Lord, etc.

תורה אור

גמ' בשלמא ב"ה קא מפרשי טעמייהו וטעמא דב"ש אלא ב"ש מ"ט לא אמרי כב"ה אמרי לך ב"ש א"כ נימא קרא *בבקר ובערב מאי בשכבך ובקומך בשעת שכיבה שכיבה ממש ובשעת קימה קימה ממש וב"ש האי ובלכתך בדרך מאי עביד להו ההוא מבעי' להו *לכדתניא בשבתך בביתך פרט *לעוסק במצוה ובלכתך בדרך פרט לחתן מכאן אמרו [א]הכונס את הבתולה פטור ואת האלמנה חייב מאי משמע אמר רב פפא כי דרך מה דרך רשות אף כל רשות מי לא עסקינן דקא אזיל לדבר מצוה ואפילו הכי אמר רחמנא לקרי א"כ לכתוב רחמנ' בשבת ובלכת מאי בשבתך ובלכתך בשבת דידך ובלכת דידך הוא דמחייבת הא דמצו' פטירת א"ה אפי' כונס את האלמנה נמי האי טריד והאי לא טריד אי משום טרדא אפי' טבעה ספינתו בים נמי וכי תימא ה"נ אלמא א"ר אבא בר זבדא אמר רב *אבל חייב בכל המצות האמורות בתורה [ב]חוץ מן התפילין שהרי נאמר בהם פאר שנא' (יחזקאל כד) פארך חבוש עליך התם טריד טרדא דמצוה הכא טריד טרדא דרשות *וב"ש ההוא מבעי להו פרט לשלוחי מצוה וב"ה אמרי ממילא ש"מ דאפי' בדרך נמי קרי: ת"ר ב"ה אומרים עומדין וקורין יושבין וקורין ומטין וקורין הולכין בדרך וקורין עושין במלאכתן וקורין *ומעשה ברבי ישמעאל ור' אלעזר בן עזריה שהיו מסובין במקום א' והיה רבי *ישמעאל מוטה ור' אלעזר בן עזריה זקוף כיון שהגיע זמן ק"ש הטה רבי אלעזר וזקף ר' ישמעאל א"ל ר' אלעזר בן עזריה לר' ישמעאל ישמעאל אחי אמשול לך משל למה הדבר דומה משל לאחד שאומרים לו זקנך מגודל אמר להם יהיה כנגד המשחיתים אף כך אתה כל זמן שאני זקוף אתה מוטה עכשיו כשאני הטתי אתה זקפת אמר לו אני עשיתי כדברי ב"ה ואתה עשית כדברי ב"ש ולא עוד אלא שמא יראו התלמידים ויקבעו הלכה לדורות מאי ולא עוד וכי תימא ב"ה נמי אית להו מטין הני מילי דמטה ואתא מעיקרא אבל הכא כיון דעד השתא הוית זקוף והשתא מוטה אמרי ש"מ כב"ש סבירא להו שמא יראו התלמידים ויקבעו הלכה לדורות: תני רב יחזקאל עשה כדברי ב"ש עשה כדברי ב"ה עשה רב יוסף אמר [ג]עשה כדברי ב"ש לא עשה ולא כלום דתנן *מי שהיה ראשו ורובו בסוכה ושלחנו בתוך הבית בית שמאי פוסלין ובית הילל מכשירין אמרו להם בית הילל לבית שמאי מעשה שהלכו זקני ב"ש וזקני ב"ה לבקר את ר' יוחנן בן החורני' מצאוהו שהיה ראשו ורובו בסכה ושלחנו בתוך הבית ולא אמרו לו כלום אמרו להם *משם ראיה אף הם אמרו לו א"כ היית נוהג לא קיימת מצות סוכה מימיך רב נחמן בר יצחק אמר עשה כדברי ב"ש חייב מיתה דתנן אמר ר"ט אני הייתי בא בדרך והטתי לקרו' כדברי ב"ש וסכנתי בעצמי מפני הלסטים אמרו לו כדאי היית לחוב בעצמך שעברת על דברי ב"ה: **מתני'** [ד]בשחר מברך שתים לפניה ואחת לאחריה ובערב מברך שתים לפניה ושתים לאחריה אחת ארוכה ואחת קצרה מקום שאמרו להאריך אינו רשאי לקצר לקצר אינו רשאי להאריך לחתום אינו רשאי שלא לחתום שלא לחתום אינו רשאי לחתום:

גמ' מאי מברך אמר ר' יעקב אמר ר' אושעיא יוצר

גמ' בשבתך בביתך פרט לעוסק במצוה. לקמיה מפרש מאי משמע: ובלכתך בדרך פרט לחתן. ואף על גב דחתן נמי עוסק במצוה הוא אי לאו קרא יתירה לא נפקא לן מקרא קמא דכיון דעוסק במצוה לא כתיב בקרא בהדיא אלא מיעוטא בעלמא הוא דקא דרשינן מביתך וממעטינן מינה עוסק במלאכת מצוה דאיכא טרדא אבל חתן דטרדא דמחשבה בעלמא הוא שמחשב על עסק בתולים אי לאו קרא יתירא לא אתמעוט: הכונס את הבתולה פטור. שטרוד במחשב' בעילת מצוה: מאי משמע. פרט לעוסק במצוה: כי דרך. בשבתך ובלכתך הקשו לדרך: מי לא עסקינן כו'. כלומר מכלן דבדרך רשות לחודא איירי קרא הא קרא דרך סתמא כתיב ומינלא משתמע נמי מניה דרך מצוה ואפילו הכי אמר רחמנא ליקרי: אי משום טרדא. דמחשבה פטרת ליה אפי' טבעה ספינתו נמי: אלמה א"ר אבא. כמו למה אמר אף ע"פ שטרוד בצערו חייב בכל המצות חוץ מן התפילין שנא' בהם פאר ליחזקאל פארך חבוש עליך וגו' וכיון דבעו פאר ואבל מתגולל בצערו בעפר אין זה פאר: טריד טרדא דמצוה. וכיון דאכן מיעוט בעלמא דרשינן פרט לחתן מסתייך אם ממעטת מינה טרדא דמצוה: וב"ה אמרי לך. כהי נמי דמקרא למדרש מיניה פרט לחתן אתא ממילא ש"מ בלכתך דידך הוא דמחייב אלמא בדרך נמי קרי: עוסקין במלאכתן וקורין. לקמן מוקמינן לה בפרק שני (דף יו.): הטה ר' אלעזר בן עזריה. כב"ש: לאחד שאמרו לו זקנך מגודל אמר להם יהיה זה כנגד המשחיתים. משל שלך דומה לאחד שאומרים לו זקנך נאה ומגודל והוא אומר להם הואיל וקלסתם אותו אף הוא יהיה כנגד המשחיתים הגדול הזה יהיה נתון לתער ולמספרים שאביא עליו ואשחיתנו: עכשיו שאני הטתי. הרי אני כמקלס את מעשיך שהיית מוטה ואתה נזקפת: ב"ה נמי אית להו מטין. דבמטין נמי שרו כדאמרינן לעיל מטין וקורין אבל עכשיו כיון דעד השתא היית זקוף ועכשיו הטית אם לא נזקפתי אני יראו התלמידים ויקבעו הלכה: לא קיימת כו'. וכי היכי דעשה כדברי ב"ה לא עשה ולא כלום לדברי ב"ש אף העושה כדברי ב"ש לא עשה ולא כלום לדברי ב"ה: **מתני'** בשחר מברך שתים וכו'. כדאמר בברכו' ירוש' שבע ברכות הללו על שם (תהלי' קיט) שבע ביום הללתיך: אחת ארוכה ואחת קצרה. אשתים לאחריה דערבית קאי (כ"א ארוכה אמת ואמונה קצרה השכיבנו): לחתום. בברוך: שלא לחתום. כגון ברכת הפירות ומצות: **גמ'** מאי מברך. שתים לפניה דשחר מאי ניהו: יוצר

שנאמר בהם פאר. פרש"י ואבל מעולל בעפר קרנו ואין נאה לתת פאר תחת אפר. וא"ת ולמה לי האי טעמא תיפוק ליה ונדאמר ליחזקאל פארך חבוש עליך מכלל דלכולי עלמא אסור. ותירץ השר מקוצי דלריך טעמא של רש"י כי היכי דלא נילף שאר מצות מתפילין מקל וחומר א"כ לריך טעמא דרש"י לחייבו לתפילין לאחר יום ראשון דלא שייך מעולל בעפר קרנו אלא ביום א' דוקא:

תני רב יחזקאל עשה כב"ש עשה ורב יוסף אמר עשה כב"ש לא עשה ולא כלום. וא"ת פשיטא דאין הלכה כמותן. ויש לומר הואיל וב"ש מחמירי' על האדם טפי וב"ה לא שייך לומר פשיטא דהא דעשה כב"ש לא עשה ולא כלום היינו היכא דב"ש מקילין וב"ה מחמירין אבל הכא בק"ש לא פסלי ב"ה דברי ב"ש. אבל תימה א"כ מה מייתי מסוכה כו' לא קיימת מצות סוכה כו' ופירש רש"י דכי היכי דמי שעשה כב"ה לא עשה ולא כלום לב"ש אף העושה כב"ש לא עשה ולא כלום לב"ה ומאי קא מדמית התם פסלי ב"ש לגמרי מה דמכשרי ב"ה אבל הכא קרא ק"ש כב"ש אליבא דב"ה יצא. ע"כ פירש הר"ר שמעיה דקא מדמה הכי מדקאמר לא קיימת אע"ג דמן הדין יצא שהרי ראשו ורובו בסוכה אינו אסור אלא גזירה שמא ימשך אחר שלחנו הה"נ גבי ק"ש אע"ג דמן הדין יצא בדיעבד כיון דלב"ה אין לכון כדאיתא במתניתין כדאי היית לחוב בעלמא הוי עשה כב"ש לב"ה לא עשה ולא כלום. [ועיין תוספת סוכה ג'. ד"ה דאמר]:

אחת ארוכה ואחת קצרה. פירש רש"י ארוכה אמת ואמונה קצרה השכיבנו. ותימה דהשכיבנו נמי ארוכה הרבה ותדע מדלא קא חשיב לה בתוספתא בהדי הקצרות ועוד פעמים שמאריכין הרבה בתוספות כמו אור יום הנף. ועוד אמת ואמונה פעמים שמקצרין בה מאד כדאמרי' לקמן למ"ד אין אומרין פרשת ציצית בלילה הוא קא מסיים מודים אנחנו לך שהוצאתנו ממצרים וכו' בפרק היה קורא (ד' יד:) ונראה לר"ת דהכל קאי באמת ואמונה אחת ארוכה ואחת קצרה כלומר בין יאריך בה בין יקצר בה כדלקמן וכן אשכחנא התם (יבמות ד' מח.) אחת ארוכות ואחת כשואות אחת בתולות ואחת בעולות:

מקום שאמרו לקצר. כגון בברכת פירות ובברכת המצות אין לו להאריך: ורבנן

עין משפט נר מצוה

נ
א מיימ' פ"ד מהלכ' ק"ש הל' א סמ"ג עשין יח טוש"ע א"ח סי' ע סעיף ב
[ע' רש"י ותוס' סוכה כה. ד"ה בלכתך וכו' דגרסו להיפך וכ"ה הגי' בתוספת' פ"א]

נא
ב מיימ' פ"ד מהלכ' תפילין הל' י"ג ופ"ד מהלכות אבילות הל' ט סמ"ג עשין ג' טוש"ע א"ח סי' לח סעי' ה טור ש"ע י"ד סי' שפח סעי' א

נב
ג טוש"ע א"ח סי' סג סעיף ג יש גורסי' ומוסיפי' בזה ע' רש"א בשם הילקוט וא"ל להגיה דכיון דלריכא ליה לב"ה למימר ממילא ש"מ ובהאי סבר' לחודי' שיטתי' נכון אבל זהו ודאי שמקשה על ב"ש ל"ל ב' פסוקי'

נג
ד מיימ' פ"א מהלכות ק"ש הל' ה' סמג עשין יח טוש"ע א"ח סי' נט וסי' רלו סעיף א

מסורת הש"ס

[בערב' ובבוקר כן יתכן להיות]

היה קורא יו. סוכה כה.

היה קורא יו: סוכה כה. מועד קטן טו. כתובות ו: שמחות פ"ו

תוספתא פ"א וספרי פרשת ואתחנן
* (בירוי הגי' בהפך ר"י במקום ראב"ע)

סוכה כ"ח. עירובין יג:

[שבת כט: וש"נ]

תורה אור

°יוצר אור ובורא חושך לימא יוצר אור ובורא נוגה כדכתיב קאמרינן אלא מעתה °עושה שלום ובורא רע מי קא אמרינן כדכתיב אלא כתיב רע וקרינן הכל *לישנא מעלי' הכא נמי לימא נוגה לישנא מעליא אלא אמר רבא *[א]כדי להזכיר מדת יום בלילה ומדת לילה ביום בשלמא מדת לילה ביום כדאמרינן יוצר אור ובורא חשך אלא מדת יום בלילה היכי משכחת לה אמר אביי גולל אור מפני חשך וחשך מפני אור ואידך מאי היא אמר רב יהודה אמר שמואל אהבה רבה וכן אורי ליה ר"א *לר' פדת בריה אהבה רבה תניא נמי הכי [ב]אין אומרים *אהבת עולם אלא אהבה רבה ורבנן אמרי אהבת עולם וכן הוא אומר °ואהבת עולם אהבתיך על כן משכתיך חסד א"ר יהודה אמר שמואל [ג]השכים לשנות עד שלא קרא ק"ש צריך לברך משקרא ק"ש אין צריך לברך שכבר נפטר באהבה רבה אמר רב הונא למקרא צריך לברך ולמדרש אין צריך לברך ור' אלעזר אמר למקרא ולמדרש צריך לברך למשנה א"צ לברך ורבי יוחנן אמר אף למשנה נמי צריך לברך [אבל לתלמוד אין צריך לברך] ורבא אמר [ד]אף לתלמוד צריך (לחזור) ולברך *דאמר רב חייא בר אשי זימנין סגיאין הוה קאימנא קמיה דרב לתנויי פרקין בספרא דבי רב הוה מקדים וקא משי ידיה ובריך ומתני לן פרקין מאי מברך א"ר יהודה אמר שמואל אשר קדשנו במצותיו וצונו לעסוק בדברי תורה ורבי יוחנן מסיים בה הכי *הערב נא ה' אלהינו את דברי תורתך בפינו ובפיפיות עמך בית ישראל ונהיה אנחנו וצאצאינו וצאצאי עמך בית ישראל כלנו יודעי שמך ועוסקי תורתך ברוך אתה ה' המלמד תורה לעמו ישראל ורב המנונ' אמר אשר בחר בנו מכל העמים ונתן לנו את תורתו ברוך אתה ה' נותן התורה אמר רב המנונ' זו היא מעולה שבברכות [ה]הלכך לימרינהו לכולהו תנן התם *[ו]אמר להם הממונה ברכו ברכה אחת והם ברכו וקראו עשרת הדברות שמע והיה אם שמוע ויאמר וברכו את העם ג' ברכות אמת ויציב ועבודה וברכת כהנים ובשבת מוסיפין ברכה אחת למשמר היוצא מאי ברכה אחת כי הא דרבי אבא ור' יוסי בר אבא אקלעו להדוא אתרא בעו מינייהו מאי ברכה אחת לא הוה בידייהו ואתו שיילוהו לרב מתנה לא הוה בידיה אתו שיילוהו לרב יהודה אמר להו הכי אמר שמואל אהבה רבה *ואמר רבי זריקא אמר ר' אמי אמר ר' שמעון בן לקיש יוצר אור כי אתא רב יצחק בר יוסף אמר הא דרבי זריקא *לאו בפירוש אתמר אלא מכללא אתמר דא"ר זריקא א"ר אמי אמר ר"ש בן לקיש זאת אומרת ברכות אין מעכבות זו את זו דאי אמרת בשלמא יוצר אור הוו אמרי היינו דברכות אין מעכבות זו את זו דלא קא אמרי אהבה רבה

אלא

ישעיה מה / שם / ירמיה לא / נ"ל לנמדרש / לעיל ע. וש"כ

יוצר אור ובורא חשך (עושה שלום ובורא רע). לקמיה מפרש היכי מאי היא דאלו ברכה דישתבח היכה מן המנין שהיא לאחרי פסוקי דזמרה כמו ברכת הלל ואומרים אותה קודם זמן ק"ש אם ירצו: כדכתיב קאמרינן. כתיב בקרא יוצר אור ובורא חשך עושה שלום ובורא רע: שכבר נפטר באהבה רבה. שיש בה מעין ברכת התורה ותן בלבנו להבין ולהשכיל לשמוע ללמוד וללמד לשמור ולעשות ולקיים את כל דברי תלמוד תורתך ותלמדם חקי רצונך: מדרש. הוא קרוב למקרא כגון מכילתא וספרא וספרי שהם מדרשי מקראות: *לגמרא אין צריך לברך. אפי' קודם אהבה רבה קאמר והכי מוכח מלתא *בפסח שני: אף לגמרא צריך לברך. שהוא עיקר התורה שממנו הוראה יוצאה. גמרא היינו סברת טעמי משנה ותירוצי משניות הסותרות זו את זו ותקוני מחסר': ומברך. ברכת התורה: ור' יוחנן מסיים בה הכי. דבעי פתיחה בברוך וחתימה בברוך: הערב נא ה' אלהינו. יערבו עלינו לעסוק בהם מאהבה: ברוך אתה ה' המלמד תורה לעמו ישראל גרסינן. ולא גרסינן למדני חקיך שאין זו ברכה והודאה על שעבר אלא לשון בקשה ודוד כי אמרה (בתהלים קיט) לא לשם ברכה אמרה אלא בלשון בקשה והכי קאמר ה' שאתה ברוך למדני חקיך: וזו היא מעולה שבברכות. שהודאה לפי שיש בה הודאה למקום וקילוס לתורה ולישראל: תנן התם. במסכת תמיד: אמר להם הממונה. והוא סגן הכהנים כדאיתא ביומא היינו סגן היינו ממונה (בפרק"י שם דף טו:): ברכו ברכה אחת. לקמן מפרש מאי היא ומן הברכו' שלפני קריאת שמע היא דהתם מסדר לכוליה סדר עבודת השחר וקאמר דלאחר שסדרו האברים ע"ג הכבש ומלחום ירדו ובאו להם ללשכת הגזית לקרות את שמע והדר תני אמר להם הממונה ברכו ברכה אחת והם ברכו וקראו עשרת הדברות: וברכו את העם. עם העם: ועבודה. בשביל העבודה שעשו היו מברכין אחריה רצה ה' אלהינו עבודת עמך ישראל ואשי ישראל ותפלתם תקבל ברצון ברוך המקבל עבודת עמו ישראל ברצון. אי נמי שאותך לבדך ביראה נעבוד: וברכת כהני'. לברך את העם ובשאר תפלה לא היה להם פנאי ואף זמן קריאת שמע לא הגיע כדאמר במסכת יומא (דף לז:) הקורא את שמע עם אנשי משמר ועם אנשי מעמד לא יצא לפי שאנשי משמר מקדימין כו': מוסיפין ברכה אחת. לקמן מפרש לה: למשמר היוצא. שהמשמרות מתחלפות ביום השבת כדאמרי' במסכ' סוכה (דף נו:) משמר היוצא עושה תמיד של שחר ומוספין ומשמר הנכנס עושה תמיד של בין הערבים ובזיכין: מאי ברכה אחת. דקתני ישא איזו מן הברכות הוא אומר: לאו בפירוש אתמר. לא שמע מפי ר"ל שאמר בפי' מאי ברכה א' יוצר אור: זאת אומרת. דקתני ברכו ברכה אחת:

אלא

[פסחים ג. וש"נ כמן יבמות יא: וש"נ] / [נ"ל בפרק שני דף יד:] / [ע'תוס' נדה ס. ד"ה ואמר] / נ"ל אהבה רבה אלא אהבת עולם וכ"ה גי' הרי"ף והרא"ש עיי' באורי הגאון מהרא"ו לא"ח סי' ס' סק"א / לקמן דף יד: / [ע' תוס' כתובות ח. ד"ה שהכל וע' תוס' לקמן מו. ד"ה כל הברכות ותוס' פסחים קד: ד"ה חוץ] / תמיד לב: / [אולי שגגת הדפוס היא]

ורבנן אמרי אהבת עולם וכו'. הלכך תקינו לומר בשחרית אהבה רבה ובערבית אהבת עולם:

שכבר נפטר באהבה רבה עד הלכך לימרינהו לכלהו. בירושלמי יש הא דאמרינן שכבר נפטר באהבה רבה והוא שׁשׁנה על אתר פירוש לאלתר שלמד מיד באותו מקום. ושאל להרב ר' יצחק כגון אנו שאין אנו לומדין מיד לאחר תפלת השחר שאנו טרודין והולכין כך בלא למוד עד אמצע היום או יותר אמאי אין אנו מברכין ברכת התורה פעם אחרת כשאנו מתחילין ללמוד. והשיב ר"י דלא קיימא לן כאותו ירושלמי הואיל וגמרא שלנו לא אמרו ואין צריך לאלתר ללמוד. ועוד אפילו לפי הירושלמי דוקא אהבה רבה דלא הוי עיקר ברכ' לברכת תורה דעיקר אהבה רבה לק"ש נתקן ובשביל היא אינו נפטר מברכת התורה אלא אם ילמוד מיד וגם לא יעשה הסח הדעת אבל ברכת בחר בנו וברכת לעסוק בדברי תורה שהן עיקר לברכת התורה פוטרות כל היום. וא"ת מאי שנא מסוכה שצריך לברך על כל סעודה וסעודה לישב בסוכה וי"ל דשאני תורה שאינו מייאש דעתו דכל שעה אדם מחויב ללמוד דכתיב והגית בו יומם ולילה והוי כמו יושב כל היום בלא הפסק אבל אכילה בסוכה יש שעה קבועה. וא"ת מפני מה אין אנו מברכין לישן בסוכה וי"ל דברכה דאכילה שמברכין לישב פוטרתו. א"נ משום שמא לא יישן והוי ברכ' לבטלה שהרי אין בידו לישן כל שעה שירצה. והיה אומר ר"ת כשאד' עומד ממטתו בלילה (בשחרית) ללמוד שא"צ לברך ברכת התורה מפני שברכת התורה של אתמול שהרי' פוטרת עד שחרית אחרת ולא נהירא. והצרפתים נהגו לומר פסוקים וברכת כהנים וגם אלו דברים שאין להם שיעור שהיא משנה (פ"א דפאה) ואלו דברים שאדם אוכל פירותיהן כו' שהיא *ברייתא (משכת שבת דף קכז.) מפני הירושלמי דבעי שילמוד על אתר. אבל אין צריך כמו שכתבתי כבר:

ה"ג בא"י המלמד תורה לעמו ישראל אבל לא גר' למדנו חקיך שאין זו ברכה אלא בקשה שאמר דוד:

וברכת כהנים. ואין זה דוכן שהרי לא היו עומדים לדוכן עד לאחר הקטרת אמורים דאמרי' בתענית (פ"ד ד' כו.) ג' פעמים ביום הכהנים נושאים כפיהם וכו' וא"כ הוה ליה למתני ד' פעמים אחד לפני הקטרה ואחד לאחר הקטר'. אלא בלא נשיאות כפים אמרו ברכת כהנים כמו שאנו אומרים:

ברכות אין מעכבות זו את זו. בירך את האחת ולא בירך את השניה נפקא מינה ידי חובתו בההיא שבירך ואין חברתה מעכבת לומר שאין זו מועלת בלא זו. ומהכא שמע ר' זריקא דס"ל לר"ל דהך ברכה אחת יוצר אור היא: דאי אמרת בשלמא יוצר אור הוו אמרי. ולא אהבה רבה ואף על גב דמטא ליה זמנה שאף בלילה ראוי לומר וכל שכן דכיון דאמר יוצר אור ודאי מטיא זמנה ואפילו הכי לא אמרי אלא יוצר אור ותו לא אמרי לה היינו דקאמר שמע מינה ברכות אין מעכבות זו את זו:

משום

עין משפט נר מצוה

נד [א]מיי' פ"א מהלכות ק"ש הל' ו' טוש"ע א"ח סי' נ"ט סעי' א

*[לקמן יב. ע"ש]

נה [ב]מיי' שם סמ"ג עשין יח טוש"ע א"ח סי' ס' סעי' א

נו [ג]מיימ' פ"ז מהלכ' תפלה הלכה י' טוש"ע א"ח סי' מז סעי' ז

נז [ד]מיי' שם טוש"ע שם סעיף ב

נח [ה]מיי' שם טוש"ע שם סעיף ה

נט [ו]מיי' פ"ו מהל' תמידין הלכה ד

[מימל' כ"נ]

GEMARA. What benedictions does one say [in the morning]? R. Jacob said in the name of R. Oshaia: [11*b*] '[Blessed art Thou] who formest light and createst darkness'.[4] Let him say rather: 'Who formest light and createst brightness'?—We keep the language of the Scripture.[5] If that is so, [what of the next words in the text], *Who makest peace and createst evil:* do we repeat them as they are written? It is written *'evil'* and we say 'all things' as a euphemism. Then here too let us say 'brightness' as a euphemism!—In fact, replied Raba, it is in order to mention the distinctive feature of the day in the night-time and the distinctive feature of the night in the day-time. It is correct that we mention the distinctive feature of the night in the day-time, as we say, 'Who a formest light and createst darkness'.[1] But where do you find the distinctive feature of the day mentioned in the night-time?—Abaye replied: [In the words,] 'Thou rollest away the light from before the darkness and the darkness from before the light'.[2]

Which is the other [benediction]?[3]—Rab Judah said in the name of Samuel: 'With abounding love'.[4] So also did R. Eleazar instruct his son R. Pedath [to say]: 'With abounding love'. It has been taught to the same effect: We do not say, 'With everlasting love', but 'With abounding love'. The Rabbis, however, say that 'With everlasting love'[5] is said; and so it is also said, *Yea, I have loved thee with an everlasting love; therefore with affection I have drawn thee.*[6]

Rab Juda said in the name of Samuel: If one rose early to study [the Torah] before he had recited the *Shema'*, he must say a benediction [over the study]. But if he had already recited the *Shema'*, he need not say a benediction, because he has already become quit by saying 'With abounding love'.[7]

R. Huna said: For the reading of Scripture it is necessary to say a benediction,[8] but for the study of the Midrash[9] no benediction is required. R. Eleazar, however, says that for both Scripture and Midrash a benediction is required, but not for the Mishnah. R. Johanan says that for the Mishnah also a benediction is required, [but not for the Talmud]. Raba said: For the Talmud also it is necessary to say a blessing. R. Ḥiyya b. Ashi said:[10] Many times did I stand before Rab to repeat our section in the Sifra of the School of Rab,[11] and he used first to wash his hands and say a blessing, and then go over our section with us.[12]

What benediction is said [before the study of the Torah]?—Rab Judah said in the name of Samuel: [Blessed art Thou . . .] who hast sanctified us by Thy commandments, and commanded b us to study the Torah.[1] R. Johanan used to conclude as follows:[2] 'Make pleasant, therefore, we beseech Thee, O Lord our God, the words of Thy Torah in our mouth and in the mouth of Thy people the house of Israel, so that we with our offspring and the offspring of Thy people the house of Israel may all know Thy name and study Thy Torah. Blessed art Thou, O Lord, who teachest Torah to Thy people Israel'.[3] R. Hamnuna said: '[Blessed art Thou . . .] who hast chosen us from all the nations and given us Thy Torah. Blessed art Thou, O Lord, who givest the Torah'.[4] R. Hamnuna said: This is the finest of the benedictions. Therefore let us say all of them.[5]

We have learnt elsewhere:[6] The deputy high priest[7] said to them [the priests], Say one benediction, and they said the benediction and recited the Ten Commandments, the *Shema'*, the section *'And it shall come to pass if ye hearken diligently'*, and *'And the Lord said'*,[8] and recited with the people three benedictions, viz., 'True and firm',[9] the benediction of the *'Abodah,*[10] and the priestly benediction.[11] On Sabbath they said an additional benediction for the outgoing watch.[12] Which is the 'one benediction' referred to above? The following will show. R. Abba and R. Jose came to a certain place the people of which asked them what was the 'one benediction' [referred to], and they could not tell them. They went and asked R. Mattena, and he also did not know. They then went and asked Rab Judah, who said to them: Thus did Samuel say: It means, 'With abounding love'. R. Zerika in the name of R. Ammi, who had it from R. Simeon b. Laḳish said: It is, 'Who formest light'. When R. Isaac b. Joseph came [from Palestine] he said: This statement of R. Zerika was not made explicitly [by R. Simeon b. Laḳish], but was inferred by him [from another statement]. For R. Zerika said in the name of R. c Ammi, who had it from R. Simeon b. Laḳish: This[1] shows that the recital of one blessing is not indispensable for that of the other. Now if you say that they used to recite 'Who formest the light', it is correct to infer that the recital of one blessing is not indispensable for that of the other, since they did not say, 'With abounding

(4) V. *P.B.* p. 37. (5) The words are a quotation from Isa. XLV, 7.
a (1) This formula is said only in the morning prayer. (2) V. *P.B.* p. 96. (3) Said before the morning *Shema'*. (4) V. *P.B.* p. 39. (5) In fact this blessing is now said in the evening. V. *P.B.* p. 96. (6) Jer. XXXI, 3. (7) This blessing contains a benediction over the Torah, v. *P.B.* p. 39. (8) In the morning, v. *P.B.* p. 4. (9) The exegetical midrashim of the Torah (Sifra, Sifre and Mekilta) are referred to. (10) So MS.M. Curr. edd., 'For R. Ḥiyya b. Ashi, etc.'. (11) *Sifra debe Rab*, an *halachic* Midrash on Leviticus, v. *J.E.* XI, p. 330. (12) This proves that over Midrash a benediction is required.
b (1) V. *P.B.* p. 4. (2) In order both to open and close with a benediction. (3) *P.B.* p. 4. (4) Ibid. (5) Alfasi and R. Asher have before these last words: R. Papa says. (6) Tamid 32*b*. (7) *Memuneh;* lit., 'the appointed one'; v. Yoma, Sonc. ed., p. 97, n. 3. (8) The second and third sections of the *Shema'*, Deut. XI, 13ff. and Num. XV, 37ff. V. *P.B.* p. 40ff. (9) V. *P.B.* p. 42. (10) The benediction commencing 'Accept, O Lord our God' in the *'Amidah*. V. *P.B.* p. 50. (11) V. *P.B.* p. 53. (12) The priestly watches in the Temple (which were twenty-four in number) were changed every week.
c (1) The fact that they said one blessing only.

love'. [12a] But if you say that they used to say, 'With abounding love', how can you infer that one blessing is not indispensable for the recital of the other? Perhaps the reason why they did not say, 'Who formest the light' was because the time for it had not yet arrived,[2] but when the time for it did arrive, they used to say it! And if this statement was made only as an inference, what does it matter?—If it was made only as an inference [I might refute it as follows]: In fact, they said, 'With abounding love', and when the time came for 'Who formest the light', they said that too. What then is the meaning of 'One blessing is not indispensable for the other'? The *order* of the blessings is not indispensable.

'They recited the Ten Commandments, the *Shema'*, the sections "*And it shall come to pass if ye diligently hearken*", and "*And the Lord said*", "True and firm", the '*Abodah*, and the priestly benediction'. Rab Judah said in the name of Samuel: Outside the Temple also people wanted to do the same,[3] but they were stopped on account of the insinuations of the *Minim*.[4] Similarly it has been taught: R. Nathan says, They sought to do the same outside the Temple,[5] but it had long been abolished on account of the insinuations of the *Minim*. Rabbah b. Bar Ḥanah[6] had an idea of instituting this
a in Sura,[1] but R. Ḥisda said to him, It had long been abolished on account of the insinuations of the *Minim*. Amemar had an idea of instituting it in Nehardea, but R. Ashi said to him, It had long been abolished on account of the insinuations of the *Minim*.

'On Sabbath they said an additional blessing on account of the outgoing watch'. What was this benediction?—R. Ḥelbo said: The outgoing watch said to the incoming one, May He who has caused His name to dwell in this house cause to dwell among you love and brotherhood and peace and friendship.

WHERE THEY ORDAINED THAT A LONG BENEDICTION SHOULD BE SAID. There is no question that where a man took up a cup of wine thinking that it was beer and commenced [with the intention to say the benediction] for beer but finished with that of wine, he has fulfilled his obligation. For even had he said the benediction, 'By whose word all things exist',[2] he would have fulfilled his duty, as we have learnt: 'In the case of all of them,[3] if he says, "By whose word all things exist", he has performed his obligation'.[4] But where he took up a cup of beer thinking it was wine and began [with the intention to say the benediction] for wine and finished with the benediction for beer, the question arises, do we judge his benediction according to its beginning or according to its ending?—Come and hear: 'In the morning, if one commenced with [the intention to say] "Who formest light" and finished with "Who bringest on the evening twilight",[5] he has not performed his obligation; if he commences [with the intention to say] "Who bringest on the evening twilight" and finished with "Who formest the light", he has performed his obligation. In the evening, if one commenced [with the intention to say] "Who bringest on the evening twilight" and finished with "Who formest the light", he has not performed his obligation; if he begins with [the intention to say] "Who formest the light" and closes with "Who bringest on the evening twilight", he has performed his obligation. The principle is that the final form is decisive'.—It is different there because [at the end] he says, 'Blessed art Thou
b who formest the luminaries'.[1] This would be a good argument for Rab who said that any blessing that does not contain the mention of God's name is no blessing.[2] But if we accept the view of R. Joḥanan who said that any blessing that does not contain a mention of the divine kingship is no blessing, what can be said?[3] Rather [we must reply]: Since Rabbah b. 'Ulla has said: So as to mention the distinctive quality of the day in the night-time and the distinctive feature of the night in the day-time,[4] [we may assume that] when he said a blessing [with the divine name] and with the kingship[5] in the beginning, he refers to both of them.[6]

Come and hear from the concluding clause: 'The principle is that the final form is decisive'. What further case is included by the words 'the principle is'? Is it not the one we have mentioned?[7]—No; it is to include bread and dates. How are we to understand this? Shall I say that he ate bread thinking that he was eating dates,[8] and commenced [with the intention of saying the benediction] for dates and finished [with the blessing for] bread? This is just the same thing!—No, this is required [for the case where] he ate dates thinking that he was eating bread, and he began with [the intention to say the blessing] for bread and finished with that of dates. In this case he has fulfilled his obligation; for even if he had concluded with the blessing for bread, he would also have fulfilled it. What is the reason?—Because dates also give
c sustenance.[1]

Raba b. Ḥinena the elder said in the name of Rab: If one omits to say 'True and firm'[2] in the morning and 'True and trustworthy'[3] in the evening, he has not performed his obligation; for it is said, *To declare Thy lovingkindness in the morning and Thy faithfulness in the night seasons*.[4]

Raba b. Ḥinena the elder also said in the name of Rab: In saying the *Tefillah*, when one bows,[5] one should bow at [the word] 'Blessed' and when returning to the upright position one should return at [the mention of] the Divine Name. Samuel said: What is Rab's reason for this?—Because it is written: *The Lord raiseth up them that are bowed down*.[6] An objection was raised from the verse, *And was bowed before My name?*[7]—Is it written, '*At* My name'? It is written, 'Before *My Name*'.[8] Samuel said to Ḥiyya the son of Rab: O, Son of the Law, come and I will tell you a fine saying enunciated by your father.[9] Thus said your father: When one bows, one should bow at 'Blessed', and when returning to the upright position, one should return at [the mention of] the Divine

(2) The priests of the watch used to say the *Shema'* before daybreak. V. *infra*. (3) To say the Ten Commandments before the *Shema'*. (4) That the Ten Commandments were the only valid part of the Torah. V. Glos. s.v. *Min*. (5) Lit., 'in the borders', 'outlying districts'. (6) MS.M. reads: 'Rabbah b. R. Huna', which is more correct; v *D.S.* a.l.

a (1) In Babylon, the seat of the famous School founded by Rab. (2) The blessing over all liquors except wine. V. *P.B.* p. 290. (3) Even wine. (4) V. *infra* 40a. (5) Instead of the morning formula 'Who formest light' he employed the evening formula, *P.B.* p. 96.

b (1) Which is the concluding formula of the morning benediction and is a complete blessing by itself. Hence we can disregard the beginning. The same is not the case with wine and beer where there was no benediction to rectify the error made at the beginning. (2) Which implies that if this condition is fulfilled, it is a blessing. (3) According to R. Joḥanan, since the concluding formula does not contain the words 'King of the Universe', it cannot be considered a complete benediction. (4) V. *supra* 11b. (5) The reference is to the introductory words 'who createst darkness' in the morning benediction and 'who rollest away light' in the evening benediction, which makes either of them appropriate for either morning or evening. These in turn are introduced by the formula making mention of Divine Kingship. (6) Hence in this case the beginning too was in order, but not in the case of wine and beer. (7) Of wine and beer. (8) The benediction after which is different from that after bread. V. *P.B.* p. 287 for the former and p. 280 for the latter.

c (1) Like bread, which is regarded as food *par excellence*. (2) V. *P.B.* p. 42. (3) V. ibid. p. 98. (4) Ps. XCII, 3. (5) One has to bow four times in the course of the *Tefillah:* at the beginning and end of the first benediction (v. *P.B.* p. 44) and at 'We give thanks unto Thee' (p. 51) and at the close of the last but one benediction (p. 53). (6) Ps. CXLVI, 8. (7) Mal. II, 5. E.V. '*And was afraid of My name*'. (8) I.e., before the mention of the name. (9) Samuel outlived Rab.

תורה אור

אלא א"א אהבה רבה הוו אמרי מאי ברכות אין מעכבות זו את זו דלמא האי דלא אמרי יוצא אור משום דלא מטא זמן יוצר אור וכי מטא זמן יוצר אור הוו אמרי *ואי מכללא מאי דאי מכללא לעולם אהבה רבה הוו אמרי וכי מטא זמן יוצר אור הוו אמרי ליה ומאי ברכות אין מעכבות זו את זו [א]סדר ברכות: וקורין עשרת הדברות שמע והיה אם שמוע ויאמר אמת ויציב ועבודה וברכת כהנים א"ר יהודה אמר שמואל אף בגבולין בקשו לקרות כן אלא שכבר בטלום מפני תרעומת המינין תנ"ה ר' נתן אומר בגבולין בקשו לקרות כן אלא שכבר בטלום מפני תרעומת המינין רבה בב"ח סבר למקבעינהו בסורא א"ל רב חסדא כבר בטלום מפני תרעומת המינין אמימר סבר למקבעינהו בנהרדעא א"ל רב אשי כבר בטלום מפני תרעומת המינין: ובשבת מוסיפין ברכה אחת למשמר היוצא מאי ברכה אחת א"ר חלבו [ב]משמר היוצא אומר למשמר הנכנס מי ששכן את שמו בבית הזה הוא ישכין ביניכם אהבה ואחוה ושלום וריעות: מקום שאמרו להאריך: פשיטא [ג]היכא דקא נקיט כסא דחמרא בידיה וקסבר דשכרא הוא ופתח ומברך אדעתא דשכרא וסיים בדחמרא יצא דאי נמי אם אמר שהכל נהיה בדברו יצא דהא *תנן על כולם אם אמר שנ"ב יצא אלא היכא דקא נקיט כסא דשכרא בידיה וקסבר דחמרא הוא פתח ובריך אדעתא דחמרא וסיים בדשכרא מאי בתר עיקר ברכה אזלינן או בתר חתימה אזלינן ת"ש [ד]שחרית פתח ביוצר אור וסיים במעריב ערבים לא יצא פתח במעריב ערבים וסיים ביוצר אור יצא ערבית פתח במעריב ערבים וסיים ביוצר אור לא יצא פתח ביוצר אור וסיים במעריב ערבים יצא כללו של דבר הכל הולך אחר החתום שאני התם דקאמר ברוך יוצר המאורות הניחא לרב *דאמר כל ברכה שאין בה הזכרת השם אינה ברכה שפיר אלא לרבי יוחנן דאמר כל ברכה שאין בה מלכות אינה ברכה מאי איכא למימר אלא כיון דאמר רבה בר עולא *כדי להזכיר מדת יום בלילה ומדת לילה ביום כי קאמר ברכה ומלכות מעיקרא אתרווייהו קאמר ת"ש מסיפא כללו של דבר הכל הולך אחר החתום כללו של דבר לאתויי מאי לאו לאתויי הא דאמרן לא לאתויי נהמא ותמרי ה"ד אילימא דאכל נהמא וקסבר דתמרי אכל ופתח אדעתא דתמרי וסיים בדנהמא היינו בעיין לא צריכא כגון דאכל תמרי וקסבר נהמא אכל ופתח בדנהמי וסיים בדתמרי [יצא] דאפילו סיים בדנהמי נמי יצא מ"ט דתמרי נמי מיזן זייני: אמר רבה בר חיננא סבא משמיה דרב [ה]כל שלא אמר אמת ויציב שחרית ואמת ואמונה ערבית לא יצא ידי חובתו שנאמר °להגיד בבוקר חסדך ואמונתך בלילות: ואמר רבה בר *חיננא משמיה דרב [ו]המתפלל כשהוא כורע כורע בברוך וכשהוא זוקף זוקף בשם אמר שמואל מ"ט דרב דכתיב °ה' זוקף כפופים מיתיבי °ומפני שמי נחת הוא מי כתיב בשמי מפני שמי כתיב א"ל *שמואל לחייא בר רב *בר אוריאן תא ואימא לך מילתא מעלייתא דאמר אבוך הכי אמר אבוך כשהוא כורע כורע בברוך כשהוא זוקף זוקף בשם

רב

אלא אי אמרת. הך ברכה דקאמר אהבה רבה היכי ש"מ דאין מעכבות זו את זו דלמא האי דלא אמרו יוצר אור משום דלא מטא זמניה הוא וכי מטא זמניה אמרי ליה ואף על גב דקרו אינהו ק"ש לא מטא זמניה כדאמרי' בעלמא [יומא לז:] הקורא את שמע עם אנשי משמר לא יצא שאנשי משמר מקדימין: ואי מכללא מאי. וכי אמר ליה מכללא מאי גריעותא איכא דאמר לאו בפירוש אמאי הא שפיר מצי למשמע מכללא דיוצר אור קא אמרי ומשכחן ליכא למשמע מהכא דלמא לעולם אימא לך אהבה רבה וכו': סדר ברכות. אם הקדים המאוחרות: בקשו. לקבוע עשרת הדברות בקריאת שמע: מפני תרעומת המינין. שלא יאמרו לעמי הארץ אין שאר תורה אמת ותדעו שאין קורין אלא מה שאמר הקב"ה ושמעו מפיו בסיני: המינין. עובדי ע"א: פתח בדשכרא וסיים בדחמרא. תחלת הברכה אמר ע"מ שהכל וכיון שהגיע למלך העולם נזכר שהוא יין ואמר פרי הגפן פשיטא לן דיצא דהא אפילו סיים כל הברכה כדעת פתיחתה ואמר שהכל יצא על היין דתנן וכו': אלא. קא מבעיא לן פתח אדעתא דחמרא כדי לסיים בפ"הג וכשהגיע למלך העולם נזכר שהוא שכר וסיים שהכל מהו: בתר עיקר ברכה אזלינן. ועיקר ברכה אדעתא דיין כאמרה והוי כמו שסיים ביין ואין ברכת היין מוציאה ידי ברכת שכר שאין השכר מן הגפן: פתח ביוצר אור. כלומר אדעתא דלימא יוצר אור: וסיים במעריב ערבים. כשאמר מלך העולם נזכר וסיים אשר בדברו מעריב ערבים: שאני התם וכו'. כלומר דלמא פתיחה איכא כלום והא דקתני יצא לפי שחוזר וחותם בה בברוך יוצר המאורו'. וע"י חתימתה קאמר דיצא *אלא בשהכל שאין חותם בה בברוך ופתיחתה אדעתא דבורא פרי הגפן הוא אימא דלא יצא: מאי איכא למימר. היכי נפיק משום חתימתה הא אין מלכות בחתימתה: ה"ג אלא כיון דאמר כו'. אלא לא תימא משום חתימתה יצא אלא פתיחתה כמי מעלייתא היא ולא תפשוט מיניה לאמרה ושכרא דלגבי ברכות ערבית ושחרית הוא דמצי למימר דכי פתח בזו וסיים בזו יצא דהא כי פתח בשחרי' אדעתא דמעריב ערבים הוה דעתיה לאדכורי בה מדת היום בלילה כגון גולל אור וכי פתח ערבית אדעתא דיוצר אור הוה דעתיה לאדכורי בה מדת לילה כגון ובורא חשך הלכך אדעתא דתרווייהו הואי: לאו לאתויי הא דאמרן. כגון שכרא וחמרא: היינו בעיין. דהא ברכת התמרים על העץ ועל פרי העץ איכא עולה לברכת הלחם ולי צ"ע) שעמת דהכל הולך אחר חתום ברכות הוא הדין לחמרא ושכרא: כל מי שלא אמר. ברכת אמת ויציב כמו שתקנוה וכן אמת ואמונה בערבית לא יצא: להגיד בבקר חסדך. וברכת אמת ויציב כולה על חסד שעשה עם אבותינו היא שהוציאם ממצרים ובקע להם הים והעבירם וברכת אמת ואמונה מדבר בה אף על העתידות שאנו מצפים שיקיים לנו הבטחתו ואמונתו לגאלנו מיד מלכים ומיד עריצים ולשום נפשנו בחיים ולהדריכנו על במות אויבינו כל אלה הנסים התדירים תמיד: כשהוא כורע. בהודאה ובאבות כורע בברוך וזוקף את עצמו כשהוא מזכיר את השם על שם ה' זוקף כפופים (תהלים קמו): נחת. לשון הכנעה:

משום דלא מטא זמן יוצר אור. דהכי דשחיטת התמיד משיעלה עמוד השחר פי' רש"י מיהו לא הוה שעה לומר יוצר אור כדאמר בהקורא ויכול לסבור הבריאה כותיקין*:

ברכה אחת למשמר היוצא וכו'. תימה קצת מאי היא הואיל ולית בה לא שם ולא מלכות:

פתח ואמר בא"י אלהינו מלך העולם והיה סבור שהיה יין והבין שהיה שכר ואחר שהבין שהיה שכר סיים שהכל:

לא לאתויי נהמא. ופירש רב אלפס הסתא דלא אפשיטא בעיין אזלינן לקולא ואפי' פתח בחמר' וסיים בשכרא יצא. ור"י היה אומר לחומרא דצריך לברך פעם אחרת. ומיהו היה אומר ר"ת אם היה יודע בברור שטעה בדבורו שאמר בורא פרי העץ תחת פרי הגפן דבתוך כדי דבור יכול לחזור בו. וכן בי"ט בחתימה של יום טוב אם טעה בין מקדש ישראל והזמנים ואמר מקדש השבת וחזר בתוך כדי דיבור יצא אחרי שהוא יודע שהוא י"ט. והקשה הר"ר יעקב מקינון מאי קא מבעיא ליה והא ודאי מלות אינן צריכות כונה והיה אומר הר"י דהיינו בשומע תפל' אחורי בית הכנסת ולא נתכוין לצאת אבל היכא דנתכוין לברך על היין ונמצא שכר לא מהני:

להגיד בבקר חסדך. חסד שהקב"ה עשה לנו במצרים. ואמונתך פירוש מדבר על העתיד שאנו מצפים שישמור הבטחתו ואמונתו ויגאלנו מיד המלכים ובסוף ברכה חוזר לגאולה דפרעה כדי לסמוך לגאל ישראל. א"כ ע"ד המדרש (רבה איכה ג) חדשים לבקרים רבה אמונתך שאדם מאמין ומפקיד רוחו בידו ומחזירה בלא יגיעה:

אמת ויציב וכו'. לא קאי על השכינה אלא קאי אהדבר הזה וכו' וכן איתא בהר"ס. ואיתא בירושלמי האי מרגניתא דלית ביה טימא פירוש שאין לה שומא כל מה שמשבח מתגני לה כדאמר לקמן (דף לג:) בהדא דפתח ואמר האל הגדול הגבור והנורא והיה מאריך הרבה וא"ל רבי חנינא סיימת לשבחי דמרך כי כל פה לא יוכל לספר שבחו:

כרע

בחזרא

א' בר אריא. בר אוריא ולא פי' רש"י כלום

עין משפט נר מצוה

[וע"ע תוס' יומא לז: ד"ה אמר אביי]

ס
[א]מיי' פ"א מה' ק"ש הל' ח טוש"ע א"ח סי' ס' סעי' ג

סא
[ב]מיי' פ"ו מה' תמידין הל' ד

סב
[ג]מיי' פ"ח מהל' ברכות הל' י"א סמ"ג עשין כז טוש"ע א"ח סי' ר"ט סעי' א ב

סג
[ד]מיי' פ"א מהל' ק"ש הל' ח' סמ"ג עשין יח טוש"ע א"ח סי' כ"ע סעי' ב

סד
[ה]מיי פ"א מהל' ק"ש הל' ז' טוש"ע א"ח סי' ס"ו סעי' י

סה
[ו]מיי' פ"ה מה' תפלה הל' י סמג עשין יג טוש"ע א"ח סי' קיג סעי' ז

[לעיל יא: ע"ש]

חיננא סבא כל"ל]

[בגיטין סב. וכן במנחו' כג. בר אוריין פירש"י בן תורה אכן ביומא עח. ובסוכה מג: בע"ז לא: ובחגיגה יד.

מסורת הש"ם

[שבת מ: יבמות ס: ב"ב קכה. חולין לד. לה. קיא.]

לקמן מ.

כ"א אבל

שם מ:

[חגיגה יד. ע"ש]

תילי' לג

שם קמו

שנ' מלאכי ב

רב ששת כי כרע כרע כחיזרא כי קא זקיף זקיף כחיויא: ואמר רבה בר חיננא סבא משמיה דרב כל השנה כולה אדם מתפלל האל הקדוש מלך אוהב צדקה ומשפט חוץ מעשרה ימים שבין ראש השנה ויום הכפורים שמתפלל המלך הקדוש והמלך המשפט ור"א אמר אפי' אמר האל הקדוש יצא שנא' ויגבה ה' צבאות במשפט והאל הקדוש נקדש בצדקה אימתי ויגבה ה' צבאות במשפט אלו י' ימים שמר"ה ועד יה"כ וקאמר האל הקדוש מאי הוי עלה אמר רב יוסף האל הקדוש ומלך אוהב צדקה ומשפט רבה אמר המלך הקדוש והמלך המשפט והלכתא כרבה: ואמר רבה בר חיננא סבא משמיה דרב כל שאפשר לו לבקש רחמים על חברו ואינו מבקש נקרא חוטא שנאמר גם אנכי חלילה לי מחטא לה' מחדול להתפלל בעדכם אמר רבא אם ת"ח הוא צריך שיחלה עצמו עליו מ"ט אילימא משום דכתיב ואין חולה מכם עלי וגולה את אזני דלמא מלך שאני אלא מהכא ואני בחלותם לבושי וגומר: ואמר רבה בר חיננא סבא משמיה דרב כל העושה דבר עבירה ומתבייש בו מוחלין לו על כל עונותיו שנאמר למען תזכרי ובושת ולא יהיה לך עוד פתחון פה מפני כלמתך (בכפרי לך לכל אשר עשית נאם ה' אלהים) דלמא צבור שאני אלא מהכא ויאמר שמואל אל שאול למה הרגזתני להעלות אותי ויאמר שאול צר לי מאד ופלשתים נלחמים בי *וה' סר מעלי ולא ענני עוד גם ביד הנביאים גם בחלומות ואקראה לך להודיעני מה אעשה ואלו אורים ותומים לא קאמר משום דקטליה לנוב עיר הכהנים ומנין דאחילו ליה מן שמיא שנא' ויאמר שמואל אל שאול מחר אתה ובניך עמי *ואמר ר' יוחנן עמי במחיצתי ורבנן אמרי מהכא והוקענום לה' בגבעת שאול בחיר ה' יצתה בת קול ואמרה בחיר ה': א"ר אבהו בן זוטרתי א"ר יהודה בר זבידא בקשו לקבוע פרשת בלק בק"ש ומפני מה לא קבעוה משום טורח צבור מ"ט אילימא משום דכתיב בה אל מוציאם ממצרים לימא פרשת רבית ופרשת משקלות דכתיב בהן יציאת מצרים אלא א"ר יוסי בר אבין משום דכתיב בה האי קרא *כרע שכב כארי וכלביא מי יקימנו ולימא האי פסוקא ותו לא גמירי כל פרשה דפסקה משה רבינו פסקינן *דלא פסקה משה רבינו לא פסקינן פרשת ציצית מפני מה קבעוה א"ר יהודה בר חביבא מפני שיש בה *חמשה דברים מצות ציצית יציאת מצרי' עול מצות ודעת מינים הרהור עבירה והרהור ע"א בשלמא הני תלת מפרשן עול מצות דכתיב וראיתם אותו וזכרתם את כל מצות ה' ציצית דכתיב ועשו להם ציצית וגומר יציאת מצרים דכתיב אשר הוצאתי וגו' אלא דעת מינים הרהור עבירה והרהור ע"א מנלן דתניא אחרי לבבכם זו מינות וכן הוא אומר אמר נבל בלבו אין אלהים אחרי עיניכם זה הרהור עבירה שנא' ויאמר שמשון אל אביו אותה קח לי כי היא ישרה בעיני אתם זונים זה הרהור ע"א וכן הוא אומר ויזנו אחרי הבעלים:

מתני' מזכירין יציאת מצרים בלילות *א"ר אלעזר בן עזריה *הרי אני כבן שבעים שנה ולא זכיתי שתאמר יציאת מצרים בלילות עד שדרשה *בן זומא שנאמר למען תזכור את יום צאתך מארץ מצרים כל ימי חייך ימי חייך הימים כל ימי חייך הלילות וחכמים אומרים ימי חייך העולם הזה כל ימי חייך להביא לימות המשיח:

גמ' *תניא אמר להם בן זומא לחכמים וכי מזכירין יציאת מצרים לימות המשיח והלא כבר נאמר הנה ימים באים נאם ה' ולא יאמרו עוד חי ה' אשר העלה את בני ישראל מארץ מצרים כי אם חי ה' אשר העלה ואשר הביא את זרע בית ישראל מארץ צפונה ומכל הארצות אשר הדחתים שם אמרו לו לא שתעקר יציאת מצרים ממקומה אלא שתהא שעבוד מלכיות עיקר ויציאת מצרים טפל לו כיוצא בו אתה אומר לא יקרא שמך עוד יעקב כי אם ישראל יהיה שמך

לא

רש"י

כחיזרא. שבט ביד אדם וחובטו כלפי מטה בבת אחת: זקיף כחיויא. בנחת ראשו תחלה ואח"כ גופו שלא תראה כריעתו עליו כמשוי: כחיויא. כנחש הזה כשהוא זוקף עצמו מגביה הראש תחלה ונזקף מעט מעט: המלך הקדוש. לפי שבימים הללו הוא מראה מלכותו לשפוט את העולם: המלך המשפט. כמו מלך המשפט. כמו נושאי הארון הברית (יהושע ג) כמו ארון הברית וכן המסגרות המכונות (מלכים ב טז) שהוא כמו מסגרות המכונות וכן העמק הפגרים (ירמיה לא) כמו עמק הפגרים: ה"ג. ואם תלמיד חכם הוא וצריך לרחמים צריך שיחלה עצמו עליו. אם ת"ח הוא זה שצריך לרחמים צריך שיחלה חבירו עצמו עליו: בחלותם. על דואג ואחיתופל הוא אומר שהיו ת"ח: למען תזכרי ובושת. סיפיה דקרא בכפרי לך את כל אשר עשית: גם בחלומות גם בנביאים. ולא א"ל גם באורים לפי שנתבייש ממנו שלא יאמר לו אתה גרמת לעצמך שלא נענית באורים ותומים לפי שהרגת את הכהנים: ורבנן. סברי מהכא שמעינן דאחילו לו: והוקענום. גבעונים אמרו לדוד בסוף ימיו שהיה רעב ג' שנים וישאל דוד בה' ויאמר ה' אל שאול ואל בית הדמים על אשר המית את הגבעונים שהרג את הכהנים שהיו מספיקים לגבעונים לחם ומים שהגבעונים נתנם יהושע חוטבי עצים ושואבי מים למזבח ויאמר דוד אל הגבעונים ובמה אכפר לכם וברכו את נחלת ה' והם אמרו לו יותן לנו שבעה אנשים מבניו והוקענום בגבעת שאול ובת קול יצאה וסיימה אחריהם בחיר ה' דודאי הם לא אמרו בחיר ה' שהרי לגנותו היו באין ולא לכבודו: פרשת רבית. אל תקח מאתו נשך ותרבית וגומר (ויקרא כה) וסמיך ליה יציאת מצרים: ופרשת משקלות. אבני צדק וגומר (ויקרא יט) סיפיה דקרא אשר הוצאתי אתכם וגומר: כרע שכב. דדמי לבשכבך ובקומך שהקב"ה שומרנו בשכבנו ובקומנו לשכב שלוים ושקטים כארי וכלביא: ולימא האי פסוקא. וליכא טורח לצבור: עול מצות. ועשיתם את כל מצותי: מינות. אותם ההופכים טעמי התורה למדרש טעות וע"א: וכן הוא אומר אמר נבל בלבו אין אלהים. ואין לך נבל מן ההופך דברי אלהים חיים:

מתני' מזכירין יציאת מצרים בלילות. פרשת ציצית בק"ש ואע"פ שאין לילה זמן ציצית דכתיב וראיתם אותו וזכרתם אומרים אותה בלילה מפני יציאת מצרים שבה: כבן שבעים שנה. כבר הייתי נראה זקן ולא זקן ממש שבאת עליו שיבה יום שהעבירו רבן גמליאל מנשיאותו ומינו רבי אלעזר בן עזריה נשיא כדאיתא לקמן בפרק תפלת השחר (ד' כח.) ואותו היום דרש בן זומא מקרא זה:

תוספות

כרע כחיזרא. ולקמן (דף כח:) אמרינן עד שיראה איסר וכו' לא סגי בכריעה לבד וראשו זקוף אלא בעי נמי שיכוף הראש וכן איתא בירושלמי דפרקין ובלבד שלא ישוח יותר מדאי. אמר רבי ירמיה ובלבד שלא יעשה כהדין חדרונא והיינו תרגום ירושלמי של גב (ויקרא יא) והלב כשהוא שוחה ראשו זקוף. ובר"ה ובי"כ שאנו שוחין כל שעה בתפלה צריך ליזהר שיגביה קודם שיסיים הברכה רק שיכרע בברוך ושיגביה מיד דאמרינן לקמן סוף אין עומדין (דף לד.) אם בא לשחות תחלת כל ברכה וסוף כל ברכה מלמדין אותו שלא ישחה:

והלכתא כוותיה דרבה. דצריך לחתום המלך הקדוש והמלך המשפט ואם לא אמר מחזירין אותו. וכן זכרנו ומי כמוך וכתוב לחיים ובספר חיים מחזירים אותו אם לא אמר. דכל המשנה ממטבע שטבעו חכמים אינו יוצא ידי חובתו. וכך פסק רבי' יהודה אם ספק לו אם אמר אם לא אמר מחזירים אותו כדאיתא בירושלמי דתענית פ"ק היה מתפלל ואינו יודע אם הזכיר טל ומטר ואם לאו כל שלשים יום בחזקת שלא למוד פירוש שלא אמר אלא כמו שהוא למוד עד עתה שלא אמר כן. אחר כן בחזקת שהזכיר והוא הדין לכל הדברים שצריך להזכיר כך הדין. וא"כ בעשרת ימי תשובה דליכא שלשים יום צריך לחזור. *ור"ח כתב דאין מחזירין אותו מכל אותן דברים דלא פסק בספר בפירוש והביא ראיה לדבריו:

בקשו לקבוע פרשת בלק בפרשת ק"ש ומפני מה לא קבעוה וכו'. איתא בירושלמי דאותן ג' פרשיות שתקנו בקריאת שמע לפי שבהן עשרת הדברות ועיין בו ותמצא הכל:

הדרן עלך מאימתי

עין משפט נר מצוה

סו א מיי' פ"ה מה' תפלה הל' יב טוש"ע א"ח סי' קי"ג סעי' ז

סז ב מיי' פ"ב שם הלכה יח סמ"ג עשין יט טוש"ע א"ח סי' קיח וסי' תקפב סעי' א

סח ג מיי' פ"א מה' ק"ש הל' ג

הגהות וציונים

נ"ל ור"מ כתב

[ואלהים]

גי' מהרש"א הן עם כלביא יקום עד יאכל טרף וכ"ה בהדי' בתנחומא

[לקמן כח.] מכילתא פ' בא פ"ו

מכילתא שם תוספת' פ"א

מסורת הש"ס

[עירובין כג:]

[תענית כז. מגילה כב.]

ספרי פר' ראה דברים טז

תורה אור

ישעי' ה; שמואל א יב; שם כב; תהלי' לה; יחזקאל טז; שמואל א כח; שם; שמואל ב כא; במדבר כג; שם כד; שם טו; תהלי' יד; שופטי' יד; שם ח; ירמיה כג; בראשית לה

Name. [12b] R. Shesheth, when he bowed, used to bend like a reed,[10] and when he raised himself, used to raise himself like a serpent.[11]

Raba b. Ḥinena the elder also said in the name of Rab: Throughout the year one says in the *Tefillah*, 'The holy God', and 'King who lovest righteousness and judgment',[12] except during the ten days between New Year and the Day of Atonement, when he says, 'The holy King' and 'The King of judgment'. R. Eleazar says: Even during these days, if he said, 'The holy God', he has performed his obligation, since it says, *But the Lord of Hosts is exalted*
a *through justice, and the holy God is sanctified through righteousness:*[1] When is the Lord of Hosts exalted through justice? In these ten days from New Year to the Day of Atonement; and none-the-less it says, 'the holy God'. What do we decide?[2]—R. Joseph said: 'The holy God' and 'The King who loves righteousness and judgment'; Rabbah said: 'The holy King' and 'The King of judgment'. The law is as laid down by Rabbah.

Raba b. Ḥinena the elder said further in the name of Rab: If one is in a position to pray on behalf of his fellow and does not do so, he is called a sinner, as it says, *Moreover as for me, far be it from me that I should sin against the Lord in ceasing to pray for you.*[3] Raba said: If [his fellow] is a scholar, he must pray for him even to the point of making himself ill. What is the ground for this? Shall I say, because it is written, *There is none of you that is sick for me or discloseth unto me?*[4] Perhaps the case of a king is different. It is in fact derived from here: *But as for me, when they*[5] *were sick, my clothing was sackcloth, I afflicted my soul with fasting.*[6]

Raba b. Ḥinena the elder further said in the name of Rab: If one commits a sin and is ashamed of it,[7] all his sins are forgiven him, as it says, *That thou mayest remember and be confounded, and never open thy mouth any more, because of thy shame; when I have forgiven thee all that thou hast done, saith the Lord God.*[8] Perhaps with a whole congregation the case is different?—Rather [we derive it] from here: *And Samuel said to Saul, Why hast thou disquieted me to bring me up? And Saul answered, I am sore distressed; for the Philistines make war against me, and God is departed from me, and answereth me no more, neither by prophets nor by dreams; therefore I called thee that thou mayest make known unto me what I shall do.*[9] But he does not mention the
b Urim and Thummim[1] because he had killed all [the people of] Nob, the city of the priests.[2] And how do we know that Heaven had forgiven him?— Because it says, *And Samuel said . . . Tomorrow shalt thou and thy sons be with me,*[3] and R. Johanan said: '*With me* means, in my compartment [in Paradise]. The Rabbis say [we learn it] from here: *We will hang them up unto the Lord in Gibeah of Saul, the chosen of the Lord.*[4] A divine voice came forth and proclaimed: *The chosen of the Lord.*[5]

R. Abbahu b. Zutrathi said in the name of R. Judah b. Zebida: They wanted to include the section of Balak[6] in the *Shema'*, but they did not do so because it would have meant too great a burden for the congregation.[7] Why [did they want to insert it]?—Because it contains the words, *God who brought them forth out of Egypt.*[8] Then let us say the section of usury[9] or of weights[10] in which the going forth from Egypt is mentioned?—Rather, said R. Jose b. Abin, [the reason is] because it contains the verse, *He couched, he lay down as a lion, and as a lioness; who shall rouse him up?*[11] Let us then say this one verse and no more?—We have a tradition that every section which our master, Moses, has divided off we may divide off, but that which our master, Moses, has not divided off, we may not divide off. Why did they include the section of fringes?[12] —R. Judah b. Ḥabiba said: Because it makes reference to five[13] things—the precept of fringes, the exodus from Egypt, the yoke of the commandments, [a warning against] the opinions of the *Minim*, and the hankering after sexual immorality and the hankering after idolatry. The first three we grant you are obvious: the yoke of the commandments, as it is written: *That ye may look upon it and remember all the commandments of the Lord;*[14] the fringes, as it is written:
c *That they make for themselves fringes;*[1] the exodus from Egypt, as it is written: *Who brought you out of the land of Egypt.*[2] But where do we find [warnings against] the opinions of the heretics, and the hankering after immorality and idolatry?—It has been taught: *After your own heart:*[3] this refers to heresy; and so it says, *The fool hath said in his heart, There is no God.*[4] *After your own eyes:*[3] this refers to the hankering after immorality; and so it says, *And Samson said to his father, Get her for me, for she is pleasing in my eyes.*[5] *After which ye use to go astray:*[3] this refers to the hankering after idolatry; and so it says, *And they went astray after the Baalim.*[6]

MISHNAH. THE EXODUS FROM EGYPT IS TO BE MENTIONED [IN THE SHEMA'] AT NIGHT-TIME. SAID R. ELEAZAR B. AZARIAH: BEHOLD I AM ABOUT[7] SEVENTY YEARS OLD,[7] AND I HAVE NEVER BEEN WORTHY TO [FIND A REASON] WHY THE EXODUS FROM EGYPT SHOULD BE MENTIONED AT NIGHT-TIME UNTIL BEN ZOMA EXPOUNDED IT: FOR IT SAYS: THAT THOU MAYEST REMEMBER THE DAY WHEN THOU CAMEST FORTH OUT OF THE LAND OF EGYPT ALL THE DAYS OF THY LIFE.[8] [HAD THE TEXT SAID,] 'THE DAYS OF THY LIFE' IT WOULD HAVE MEANT [ONLY] THE DAYS; BUT 'ALL THE DAYS OF THY LIFE' INCLUDES THE NIGHTS AS WELL. THE SAGES, HOWEVER, SAY: 'THE DAYS OF THY LIFE' REFERS TO THIS WORLD; 'ALL THE DAYS OF THY LIFE' IS TO ADD THE DAYS OF THE MESSIAH.

GEMARA. It has been taught: Ben Zoma said to the Sages: Will the Exodus from Egypt be mentioned in the days of the Messiah? Was it not long ago said: *Therefore behold the days come, saith the Lord, that they shall no more say: As the Lord liveth that brought up the children of Israel out of the land of Egypt; but, As the Lord liveth that brought up and that led the seed of the house of Israel out*
d *of the north country and from all the countries whither I had driven them?*[1] They replied: This does not mean that the mention of the exodus from Egypt shall be obliterated, but that the [deliverance from] subjection to the other kingdoms shall take the first place and the exodus from Egypt shall become secondary. Similarly you read: *Thy name shall not be called any more Jacob, but Israel shall be*

(10) I.e., sharply, all at once. (11) Showly and with effort. (12) In the third and twelfth benedictions respectively, v. *P.B.* pp. 45 and 48.

a (1) Isa. V, 16. (2) What should be said on the ten days of penitence. (3) I Sam. XII, 23. (4) With reference to Saul. I Sam. XXII, 8. E.V. '*that is sorry for me*'. (5) This is said to refer to Doeg and Ahitophel, who were scholars. (6) Ps. XXXV, 13. (7) I.e., conscience-stricken. (8) Ezek. XVI, 63. (9) I Sam. XXVIII, 15.

b (1) Though from v. 6 of this chapter it appears that he did consult the Urim. (2) And his silence shows that he was conscience-stricken. (3) I Sam. XXVIII, 16 and 19. (4) II Sam. XXI, 6. (5) And it was not the Gibeonites who said this. (6) Num. XXII-XXIV. (7) On account of its length. (8) Ibid. XXIII, 22. (9) Lev. XXV, 35-38. (10) Ibid. XIX, 36. (11) Num. XXIV, 9. The reason is that it mentions 'lying down' and 'rising up'. Tanhuma substitutes XXIII, 24. (12) Ibid. XV, 37-41. (13) Var. lec.: 'six', which seems more correct. (14) Ibid. XV, 39.

c (1) Num. XV, 38. (2) Ibid. 41. (3) Ibid. 39. (4) Ps. XIV, 1. (5) Judg. XIV, 3. (6) Ibid. VIII, 33. (7) Or, 'like one'. V. *infra*, 28a. (8) Deut. XVI, 3.

d (1) Jer. XXIII, 7, 8.

thy name.[2] [13a] This does not mean that the name Jacob shall be obliterated, but that Israel shall be the principal name and Jacob a secondary one. And so it says: *Remember ye not the former things, neither consider the things of old.*[3] *'Remember ye not the former things'*: this refers to the subjections to the other nations; *'Neither consider the things of old'*: this refers to the exodus from Egypt.

Behold I shall do a new thing; now shall it spring forth.[4] R. Joseph learnt: This refers to the war of Gog and Magog. A parable: To what is this like? To a man who was travelling on the road when he encountered a wolf and escaped from it, and he went along relating the affair of the wolf. He then encountered a lion and escaped from it, and went along relating the affair of the lion. He then encountered a snake and escaped from it, whereupon he forgot the two previous incidents and went along relating the affair of the snake. So with Israel: the later troubles make them forget the earlier ones.

Abram the same is Abraham.[5] At first he became a father to Aram [*Ab-Aram*] only, but in the end he became a father to the whole world.[6] [Similarly] Sarai is the same as Sarah. At first she became a princess to her own people, but later she became a princess to all the world.[7] Bar Ḳappara taught: Whoever calls Abraham Abram transgresses a positive precept, since it says, *Thy name shall be Abraham.*[8] R. Eliezer says: He transgresses a negative command,[9] since it says, *Neither shall thy name any more be called Abram.*[10] But if that is so, then the same should apply to one who calls Sarah Sarai?—In her case the Holy One, blessed be He, said to Abraham, *As for Sarai thy wife,* thou *shalt not call her Sarai,*
a *but Sarah shall her name be.*[1] But if that is so, the same should apply to one who calls Jacob Jacob?—There is a difference in his case, because Scripture restored it [the name Jacob] to him, as it is written: *And God spoke unto Israel in the visions of the night, and said, Jacob, Jacob.*[2] R. Jose b. Abin (or, as some say, R. Jose b. Zebida) cited in objection the following: *Thou art the Lord, the God who didst choose Abram!*[3]—The answer was given: There the prophet[4] is recounting the noble deeds of the All Merciful [and relates] that that was the case originally.

CHAPTER II

MISHNAH. IF ONE WAS READING IN THE TORAH [THE SECTION OF THE SHEMA'] WHEN THE TIME FOR ITS RECITAL ARRIVED, IF HE HAD THE INTENTION[1] HE HAS PERFORMED HIS OBLIGATION. IN THE BREAKS[2] ONE MAY GIVE GREETING OUT OF RESPECT[3] AND RETURN GREETING; IN THE MIDDLE [OF A SECTION] ONE MAY GIVE GREETING OUT OF FEAR[4] AND RETURN IT. SO R. MEIR. RABBI JUDAH SAYS: IN THE MIDDLE ONE MAY GIVE GREETING OUT OF FEAR AND RETURN IT OUT OF RESPECT, IN THE BREAKS ONE MAY GIVE GREETING OUT OF RESPECT AND RETURN GREETING TO ANYONE. THE BREAKS ARE AS FOLLOWS: BETWEEN THE FIRST BLESSING AND THE SECOND,[5] BETWEEN THE SECOND AND 'HEAR', BETWEEN 'HEAR' AND 'AND IT SHALL COME TO PASS', BETWEEN 'AND IT SHALL COME TO PASS' AND 'AND THE LORD SAID' AND BETWEEN 'AND THE LORD SAID' AND 'TRUE AND FIRM'.[6] RABBI JUDAH SAYS: BETWEEN 'AND THE LORD SAID' AND 'TRUE AND FIRM' ONE SHOULD NOT INTERRUPT.

R. JOSHUA B. KORḤAH SAID: WHY WAS THE SECTION OF 'HEAR' PLACED BEFORE THAT OF 'AND IT SHALL COME TO PASS'? SO THAT ONE SHOULD FIRST ACCEPT UPON HIMSELF THE YOKE OF THE KINGDOM OF HEAVEN[7] AND THEN TAKE UPON HIMSELF THE YOKE OF THE COMMANDMENTS.[8] WHY DOES THE SECTION OF 'AND IT SHALL COME TO PASS' COME BEFORE THAT OF 'AND THE LORD SAID'? BECAUSE [THE SECTION] 'AND IT SHALL COME TO PASS' IS APPLICABLE BOTH
c TO THE DAY AND TO THE NIGHT,[1] WHEREAS [THE SECTION] 'AND THE LORD SAID' IS APPLICABLE ONLY TO THE DAY.[2]

GEMARA. This[3] proves that precepts must be performed with intent.[4] [No, perhaps] what IF HE HAD THE INTENTION means is, if it was his intention to read the Scripture? 'To read'? But surely he is reading!—[The Mishnah may refer] to one who is reading [a scroll] in order to revise it.[5]

Our Rabbis taught: The *Shema'* must be recited as it is written.[6] So Rabbi. The Sages, however, say that it may be recited in any language. What is Rabbi's reason?—Scripture says: and they *shall be,*[7] implying, as they are they shall remain.[8] What is the reason of the Rabbis?—Scripture says *'hear'*,[9] implying, in any language that you understand.[10] Rabbi also must see that 'hear' is written?—He requires it [for the lesson]: Make your ear hear what your mouth utters.[11] The Rabbis, however, concur with the authority who says that even if he did not say it audibly he has performed his obligation. The Rabbis too must see that *'and they shall be'* is written?—They require this to teach that he must not say the words out of order. Whence does Rabbi derive the rule that he must not say the words out of order?—He derives it from the fact that the [text says] *'ha-debarim'* [the words] when it might have said simply *debarim* [words]. And the Rabbis?—They derive no lesson from the substitution of *ha-debarim* for *debarim.*

May we assume that Rabbi was of opinion that the whole Torah is allowed to be read in any language, since if you assume that it is allowed to be read only in the holy tongue, why the *'and they shall be'* written by the All-Merciful?—This was necessary, because
d *'hear'* is written.[1] May we assume that the Rabbis were of opinion that the whole Torah is allowed to be read only in the holy tongue, since if you assume that it is allowed to be read only in any language, why the *'hear'* written by the All-Merciful?—It is necessary because *'and they shall be'* is written.[2]

Our Rabbis taught: *'And they shall be'*.[3] This teaches that they must not be read backwards. *'These words upon thy heart'*.[3] Am I to say that the whole [first] section requires *kawanah?*[4] Therefore the text says *'these'*: up to this point *kawanah* is necessary, from this point *kawanah* is not necessary. So R. Eliezer. Said R. Akiba to

(2) Gen. XXXV, 10. (3) Isa. XLIII, 18. (4) Ibid. 19. (5) I Chron. I, 27. (6) As it says, *Behold I have made thee a father of a multitude of nations*, Gen. XVII, 5. (7) 'Sarai' means literally 'my princess', Sarah 'princess' simply. (8) Ibid. (9) Which is more serious. (10) Ibid.

(1) *Sc.* for you but not necessarily for others. Gen. XVII, 15. (2) Ibid. XLVI, 2. (3) Neh. IX, 7. (4) Nehemiah, so called because he was here speaking under the guidance of the holy spirit.

(1) This is explained in the Gemara. Lit., 'he directed his heart'. (2) Between the sections, as presently explained. (3) E.g., to a teacher. (4) To one who he is afraid will harm him if he does not give greeting, but not merely out of respect. (5) V. P.B. p. 39. (6) Ibid. p. 42. (7) By proclaiming the unity of God. (8) By saying the words, *if ye shall diligently hearken to all My commandments.*

c (1) Since it mentions all the commandments. (2) Since it mentions only the precept of fringes, which is not obligatory by night. (3) The words IF HE HAD INTENTION. (4) And not, as it were, accidentally. (5) And is not attending to the sense. (6) I.e., in the original language. (7) Deut. VI, 6. (8) Lit., 'in their being they shall be'. (9) Ibid. 4. (10) The Hebrew verb *shema'*, like the French *entendre*, means both 'hear' and 'understand'. (11) I.e., say it audibly.

d (1) And otherwise I might take this to imply, in any language. (2) Which otherwise I might take to imply, in the original only. (3) Deut. VI, 6. (4) The Hebrew word *kawanah* combines the meanings of attention and intention-attention to what is being said, intention to perform the commandment.

תורה אור

לא שיעקר יעקב ממקומו אלא ישראל עיקר ויעקב טפל לו וכן הוא אומר *אל תזכרו ראשונות וקדמוניות אל תתבוננו אל תזכרו ראשונות זה שעבוד מלכיות וקדמוניות אל תתבוננו זו *יציאת מצרים °הנני עושה חדשה עתה תצמח תני רב יוסף זו מלחמת גוג ומגוג *משל למה הדבר דומה לאדם שהיה מהלך בדרך ופגע בו *זאב וניצל ממנו והיה מספר והולך מעשה זאב פגע בו ארי וניצל ממנו והיה מספר והולך מעשה ארי פגע בו נחש וניצל ממנו שכח מעשה שניהם והיה מספר והולך מעשה נחש אף כך ישראל צרות אחרונות משכחות את הראשונות: °*אברם הוא אברהם בתחלה נעשה אב לארם ולבסוף נעשה אב לכל העולם כולו שרי היא שרה בתחלה נעשית שרי לאומתה ולבסוף נעשית שרה לכל העולם כולו: תני בר קפרא כל הקורא לאברהם אברם עובר בעשה שנאמר °והיה שמך אברהם רבי אליעזר אומר עובר בלאו שנאמר °ולא יקרא עוד שמך אברם אלא מעתה הקורא לשרה שרי הכא נמי התם קודשא בריך הוא אמר לאברהם °שרי אשתך לא תקרא את שמה שרי כי שרה שמה אלא מעתה הקורא ליעקב יעקב ה"נ שאני התם דהדר אהדרי' קרא דכתיב °ויאמר אלהים לישראל במראות הלילה ויאמר יעקב יעקב מתיב ר' יוסי בר אבין ואיתימא ר' יוסי בר זבידא °אתה הוא ה' האלהים אשר בחרת באברם א"ל התם נביא הוא דקא מסדר לשבחיה דרחמנא מה דהוה מעיקרא:

הדרן עלך מאימתי

*היה *קורא בתורה והגיע זמן המקרא אם כוון לבו יצא בפרקים שואל מפני הכבוד ומשיב ובאמצע שואל מפני היראה ומשיב דברי ר"מ רבי יהודה אומר *באמצע שואל מפני היראה ומשיב מפני הכבוד ובפרקים שואל מפני הכבוד ומשיב שלום לכל אדם *אלו הן בין הפרקים בין ברכה ראשונה לשניה בין שניה לשמע בין שמע לוהיה אם שמוע בין והיה אם שמוע לויאמר בין ויאמר לאמת ויציב רבי יהודה אומר *בין ויאמר לאמת ויציב לא יפסיק אמר רבי יהושע *בן קרחה *למה קדמה פרשת שמע לוהיה אם שמוע °כדי שיקבל עליו עול מלכות שמים תחלה ואח"כ מקבל עליו עול מצות והיה אם שמוע לויאמר שוהיה אם שמוע נוהג בין ביום ובין בלילה *ויאמר אינו נוהג אלא ביום בלבד: **גמ'** *ש"מ מצות צריכות כונה מאי אם כיון לבו לקרות והא קא קרי בקורא להגיה: ת"ר *ק"ש ככתבה דברי רבי וחכמים אומרים *בכל לשון מ"ט דרבי אמר קרא והיו בהוייתן יהו ורבנן מאי טעמייהו אמר קרא שמע בכל לשון שאתה שומע ולרבי נמי הא כתיב שמע ההוא מבעי ליה השמע לאזניך מה שאתה מוציא מפיך *ורבנן סברי להו כמאן דאמר לא השמיע לאזנו יצא ולרבנן נמי הא כתיב והיו ההוא מבעי להו שלא יקרא למפרע ורבי שלא יקרא למפרע מנא ליה נפקא ליה מדברים הדברים ורבנן דברים הדברים לא דרשי למימרא דסבר רבי דכל התורה כלה בכל לשון נאמרה דאי סלקא דעתך בלשון הקדש נאמרה והיו דכתב רחמנא למה לי אצטריך משום דכתיב שמע למימרא דסברי רבנן דכל התורה כלה בלשון הקדש נאמרה דאי סלקא דעתך בכל לשון נאמרה שמע דכתב רחמנא למה לי אצטריך משום דכתיב והיו: ת"ר והיו שלא יקרא למפרע הדברים על לבבך יכול תהא כל הפרשה צריכה כונה ת"ל האלה עד כאן צריכה כונה מכאן ואילך אין צריכה כונה דברי רבי אליעזר א"ל רבי עקיבא הרי הוא

אומר

גמ' לא שיעקר יעקב ממקומו. שהרי מלינו שקראו הקב"ה יעקב אחר זאת ברדתו למצרים שנאמר ויאמר אלהים לישראל ויאמר יעקב יעקב ויאמר הנני (בראשית מו): הנני עושה חדשה. בתר אל תזכרו ראשונות כתיב: בתחלה אב לארם. לאנשי מדינתו שמארץ ארם היה שנאמר בעבר הנהר ישבו אבותיכם (יהושע כד) ואומר אל ארם נהרים אל עיר נחור (בראשית כד): אב לכל העולם. אב המון גוים (שם יז): שרי. לשון יחיד משמע שרתי: מסדר שבחיה. דמעיקרא אשר בחרת בו בהיות שמו אברם ושמת שמו אברהם:

הדרן עלך מאימתי

היה קורא בתורה. פרשת ק"ש: והגיע זמן המקרא. זמן ק"ש: בפרקים. בין הפסקות ולקמן מפרש להו במתני' בין *פרש' ראשונה לשנייה בין שנייה לשמע כו': שואל מפני הכבוד. שואל בשלום אדם נכבד שראוי להקדים לו שלום: ומשיב. שלום אם הקדימו לו ובגמרא פריך כיון דשואל פשיטא דמשיב: באמצע. באמצע הברכה או הפרשה: מפני היראה. אדם שהוא ירא מפניו שלא יהרגהו אבל מפני הכבוד לא: ר"י. בגמרא מפרש פלוגתייהו: בין ויאמר לאמת ויציב לא יפסיק. בגמרא (דף יד.) מפרש טעמייהו: והיה אם שמוע נוהג בין ביום בין בלילה. דמשתעי בתלמוד תורה דכתיב ולמדת' אותם את בניכם (דברים יא): ויאמר אינו נוהג אלא ביום. דמשתעי בציצית שאינה נוהגת אלא ביום דכתיב וראיתם אותו פרט לכסות לילה (שבת ד' כז:): **גמ'** ש"מ מצות צריכות כונה. שיהא מתכוין לשם מצות ותקשה לרבא דאמר במס' ר"ה (ד' כח.) התוקע לשיר יצא: כיון לקרות. אבל לצאת ידי מצוה לא בעינן שיהא מתכוין אלא לקרות בתורה בעלמא: הא קא קרי. הא בקורא קא עסיק תנא ואתי דקתני היה קורא בתורה: בקורא להגיה. את הספר אם יש בו טעות דאפילו לקריאה נמי לא מתכוין: ככתבה. בלה"ק: מדברים הדברים. דהוה ליה למכתב והיו דברים האלה (דברים ו) למדרש שיקרא הדברים כסדרן ולא למפרע כגון ובשעריך ביתך מזוזות: לימא קסבר ר' וכו'. ומדאצטריך ליה קרא לק"ש שתהא ככתבה שבירא ליה בשאר כל התורה בכל לשון נאמר' לקרות: משום דכתיב שמע. דלא תדרוש שמע בכל לשון שאתה שומע כרבנן: עד כאן. עד על לבבך:

איכא

היה קורא. אם כיון לבו יצא. בירושלמי אמרינן ברכות אינן מעכבות דאע"פ שלא אמר שתים לפניה ושתים לאחריה יצא דאם לא כן תקשי מאי מהני אם כיון לבו הרי לא בירך תחלה וא"ת הא בפ"ק (דף יב.) מסקינן סדר ברכות אין מעכבות הא ברכות מעכבות וי"ל דהתם איירי בלבור דיקא כמו דקתני אמר להם הממונה:

ובאמצע שואל מפני וכו'. ופסק רבינו שמעיה דבמקום שאסור לספר אסור לדבר אפילו בלה"ק וכן משמע מתוך מתני' ובירושלמי קאמר אפי' באמצע הפסוק רב הונא בשם ר' יוסף אמר ודברת בם מכאן שיש לך רשות לדבר בם. והיינו כמו דאמרינן בפ"ק דיומא (ד' יט:) ודברת בם ולא בתפלה פי' שאין משיבין בה מפני הכבוד:

בקורא להגיה. פי' בקונטרס שאין מתכוין לקרות תימא אכתי הא קא קרי ע"כ נראה בקורא להגיה שאינו קורא התיבות כהלכתן וכנקודתן אלא ככתיבתן קרי כדי להבין בחסרות וביתירות כמו לטטפת ומזזת ואם כיון לבו לאו דוקא אלא כלומר לקרות כדין כנקודתן וכהלכתן:

וחכ"א בכל לשון. אומר הר"י דהלכה כחכמים דהלכה כרבי מחבירו ולא מחביריו (עירובין ד' מו:) ועוד דרבנן סבירא להו כמאן דאמר לא השמיע לאזנו יצא וכוותיה פסקי' לקמן (דף טו:)

*__בלשון__ הקדש נאמרה. פירש רש"י פרק שני דמגילה (ד' יז:) לקרות בתורה ולא נהירא דהא עזרא תיקן קריאת התורה ומקמי דאתא עזרא והיו למה לי וי"ל דמיירי בפרשיות המחויבין לקרות דאורייתא כמו פרשת זכור [ע"ש במגילה בתוס' ד"ה כל] א"נ מקרא בכורים ווידוי מעשר ופרשת חליצה שמצוה בתורה לקרותן אעפ"כ בכל לשון נאמרה בסיני שכל דבור ודבור שהיה יוצא מפי הקב"ה היה מתחלק לע' לשון (כדאיתא שבת פח:):

עד כאן צריכה כונה. עד בכל מאדך שבשני פסוקים אלו מדברים בייחוד ה' באהבתו וביראתו:

אשר

מסורת הש"ס

[פירוש' גרס בהיסף]

תוספתא פ"א מכילתא פ' בא

[ע' תוס' ע"ז ג: ד"ה ולכו וכו' מגלה שהי' לפניהם גירס' אחרת]

תוספתא פ"א

[ר"ה כח:]

[ע' תוס' לקמן יד:]

[עירובין לה: פסחי' קיד: סוטה לב: מגילה יז.]

עין משפט נר מצוה

א אמיימ' פ"ב מהלכות ק"ש הל' א' סמ"ג עשין יח טוש"ע א"ח סי' ס סעי' ה

ב במייי' שם הלכה טו וסמ"ג שם טוש"ע א"ח סימן ס"ו סעי' א

ג גמיי' שם הלכה יז טוש"ע שם סעי' ה

ד המיי' פ"ג מהל' ציצית הל' ז' סמ"ג עשין כו טוש"ע א"ח סי' י"ח סעיף א

ה ומיי' כ"ב מה' שופר הל' ד' ופ"ב מה' מגלה הל' ה' טור וש"ע א"ח סי' ק' סעיף ד'

ו זמיי' פ"ב מהל' ק"ש הל' י' סמ"ג עשין י"ח טוש"ע א"ח סי' ס"ב סעי' ב'

[נ"ב בכל לשון]

[עיין בן קרחה פי' תוס' בשבת קנ. ועי' תוס' פסחי' קיז: וברכות כח.]

[עי' תוס' סוטה לב: ד"ה ורבנן]

°אשר אנכי מצוך היום על לבבך מכאן אתה למד שכל הפרשה כולה צריכה כונה אמר רבה בר בר חנה א"ר יוחנן הלכה כר' עקיבא איכא דמתני לה אהא דתניא *הקורא את שמע צריך שיכוין את לבו ר' אחא משום ר' יהודה אומר כיון שכיון לבו בפ' ראשון שוב אינו צריך אמר רבה בב"ח א"ר יוחנן הלכה כר' אחא שאמר משום ר' יהודה תניא אידך והיו שלא יקרא למפרע על לבבך ר' זוטרא אומר עד כאן מצות כונה מכאן ואילך מצות קריאה ר' יאשיה אומר עד כאן מצות קריאה מכאן ואילך מצות כונה מ"ש מכאן ואילך מצות קריא' דכתיב לדבר בם הכא נמי הא כתיב ודברת בם ה"ק עד כאן מצות כונה וקריאה מכאן ואילך קריאה בלא כונה ומ"ש עד כאן מצות כונה וקריאה דכתיב על לבבך ודברת בם התם נמי הא כתיב על לבבכם לדבר בם ההוא מבעי ליה לכדר' יצחק *דאמר °ושמתם את דברי אלה צריכה שתהא שימה כנגד הלב: אמר מר רבי יאשיה אומר עד כאן מצות קריאה מכאן ואילך מצות כונה מ"ש מכאן ואילך מצות כונה משום דכתיב על לבבכם הכא נמי הא כתיב על לבבך ה"ק עד כאן מצות קריאה וכונה מכאן ואילך כונה בלא קריאה ומ"ש עד כאן מצות קריאה וכונה דכתיב על לבבך ודברת בם דתם נמי הא כתיב על לבבכם לדבר בם ההוא בדברי תורה כתיב והכי קאמר רחמנא אגמירו בנייכו תורה כי היכי דליגרסו בהו: ת"ר °שמע ישראל ה' אלהינו ה' אחד [א]עד כאן צריכה כונת הלב דברי ר"מ אמר רבא הלכה כר"מ תניא סומכוס אומר [ב]כל המאריך באחד מאריכין לו ימיו ושנותיו אמר רב אחא בר יעקב ובדלי"ת אמר רב אשי [ג]ובלבד שלא יחטוף בחי"ת ר' ירמיה הוה יתיב קמיה דר' [חייא בר אבא] חזייה דהוה מאריך טובא א"ל [ד]כיון דאמליכתיה למעלה ולמטה ולארבע רוחות השמים תו לא צריכת: אמר רב נתן בר מר עוקבא אמר רב יהודה על לבבך בעמידה על לבבך סלקא דעתך אלא אימא [ה]עד על לבבך בעמידה מכאן ואילך לא ורבי יוחנן אמר כל הפרשה כולה בעמידה ואזדא ר' יוחנן לטעמיה דאמר רבה בר בר חנה אמר ר' יוחנן הלכה כר' אחא שאמר משום ר' יהודה:

ת"ר שמע ישראל ה' אלהינו ה' אחד זו קריאת שמע של רבי יהודה הנשיא אמר ליה רב לרבי חייא לא חזינא ליה לרבי דמקבל עליה מלכות שמים א"ל *בר פחתי *[ו]בשעה שמעביר ידיו על פניו מקבל עליו עול מלכות שמים חוזר וגומרה או אינו חוזר וגומרה בר קפרא אומר אינו חוזר וגומרה ר"ש ברבי אומר חוזר וגומרה א"ל בר קפרא לר"ש ברבי בשלמא לדידי דאמינא אינו חוזר וגומרה היינו דמהדר רבי אשמעתא דאית בה יציאת מצרים אלא לדידך דאמרת חוזר וגומרה למה ליה לאהדורי כדי להזכיר יציאת מצרים בזמנה אמר ר' אילא בריה דרב שמואל בר מרתא משמיה דרב אמר שמע ישראל ה' אלהינו ה' אחד ונאנס בשינה יצא א"ל רב נחמן לדרו עבדיה [ז]בפסוק' קמא צערן טפי לא תצערן א"ל רב יוסף לרב יוסף בריה דרבה אבוך היכי הוי עביד א"ל בפסוק' קמא הוה קא מצער נפשיה טפי לא הוה מצער נפשיה אמר *רב יוסף [ח]פרקדן לא יקרא ק"ש מקרא הוא דלא ליקרי הא מיגנא שפיר דמי ודא ר' יהושע ב"ל *לייט אמאן דגני אפרקיד אמרי מיגנא כי מצלי שפיר דמי מקרא אע"ג דמצלי נמי אסיר ודא ר' יוחנן מצלי וקרי שאני ר' יוחנן דבעל בשר הוה: ובפרקים שואל וכו': משיב מחמת מאי אילימא מפני הכבוד השתא משאל שאיל אהדורי מיבעיא אלא שואל מפני הכבוד ומשיב שלום לכל אדם איכא סיפא ובאמצע שואל מפני היראה ומשיב משיב מחמת מאי אילימא מפני היראה השתא משאל שאיל אהדורי מיבעיא אלא מפני הכבוד היינו דר"י דתנן ר' יהודה אומר באמצע שואל מפני היראה ומשיב מפני הכבוד ובפרקים שואל מפני הכבוד ומשיב שלום לכל אדם חסורי מחסרא והכי קתני בפרקים שואל מפני הכבוד ואצ"ל שהוא משיב ובאמצע שואל מפני היראה ואצ"ל שהוא משיב דברי ר"מ ר' יהודה אומר באמצע שואל מפני היראה ומשיב מפני הכבוד ובפרקים

אשר אנכי מלוך. דאי כדקא אמרת הוה ליה למכתב אשר לויתיך דמלוך משמע אפי' מכאן ואילך ומ"מ אצטריך האלה דאי לאו הכי הוה אמינא דאף פרשה שניה בכלל:

אמר רבא הלכה כר' מאיר. והכי הלכתא דקיימא לן כרבא דהוא בתרא:

על לבבך בעמידה. בירושלמי מפרש לאו דאי היה יושב עומד אלא דאם היה מהלך עומד אע"ג דב"ה אמרי כל אדם קורא כדרכו מ"מ מצוה מן המובחר לעמוד כשהוא מהלך לפי שאינו מיושב כל כך ואינו יכול לכוין כשהוא מהלך כאשר היה עומד וכן הלכה דמהלך בדרך מצוה לעמוד בפסוק א' ובעינן כונה בפסוק ראשון לבד וכן איתא בתנחומא רב יהודה בשם שמואל אמר אסור לקבל עליו עול מלכות שמים כשהוא מהלך אלא יעמוד ויקרא וכשיגיע לואהבת ילך לדרכו:

שואל מפני היראה וכו'. רבי מאיר ור' יהודה הלכה כר' יהודה דאמר אפי' באמצע משיב מפני הכבוד אם כן נראה שמותר לענות קדיש וקדושה באמצע ק"ש דאין לך מפני הכבוד גדול מזה אבל באמצע י"ח אסור דמשמע לקמן בפ' אין עומדין (דף לא.) *דבין גאולה לתפלה אין לענות וכ"ש בתפלה עצמה ומי שמתפלל לבדו וש"ץ מגיע למודים ישחה למודים אבל לא יאמר מודים ודוקא שהיה באמצע הברכה אבל בסוף הברכה לא דברא' כורע בשביל הברכה ואמרינן (לקמן ד' לד.) דאין לכרוע בכל הברכות אלא באותן שתקנו חכמים ור"ת היה רגיל שהיה ממתין בעושה פלא כדי לענות קדיש וקדושה עם הצבור והיה קוצר אפי' שהה כדי לגמור את הכל אינו חוזר לראש: ימים

איכא דמתני לה. להא דרבה בב"ח: בפ' ראשון. כל פרשת שמע: ע"כ מצות כונה כו'. כולה מפרש לה ואזיל: א"ר יאשיה ע"כ. פרק ראשון: מצות כונה כו'. קס"ד דכונה בלא קריאה: מכאן ואילך. פרשת והיה אם שמוע: שתהא שימה כנגד הלב. דהא ושמתם דכתיב לאו בקריאה וכונה איירי אלא בשימת תפילין של יד שיהא שם אותה על גובה של יד כנגד הלב על קבורת הזרוע בדו"ן: ה"ג ההיא בדברי תורה כתיב. כדמוכח קרא ולמדתם אותם את בניכם וגו': עד כאן. פסוק ראשון לבדו: ובדלי"ת. ולא בחי"ת דכל כמה דלאמר אח בלא דל"ת לא משתמע מידי ומה בלע בהארכתו אבל בדלי"ת יאריך עד כשיעור שיחשבו בלבו יחיד בשמים ובארץ ולארבע רוחותי' כדמפרש לקמן: ובלבד שלא יחטוף בחי"ת. בשביל אריכות הדל"ת לא ימהר בקריאתה שלא יקראנה בחטף בלא פתח ואין זה כלום: דאמליכתיה למעלה כו'. שהארכת שיעור שתחשוב בלבך ה' אחד בשמים ובארץ וד' רוחותיה: בעמידה. אפי' לב"ה דאמרי [לעיל יא.] עוסקין במלאכתן וקורין ומהלכין וקורין מודים הם שצריך לעמוד במקום אחד עד המקרא זה לפי שעד כאן מצות כונה: לא חזינא דמקבל עליה מלכות שמים. שהיה שונה לתלמידיו מקודם זמן ק"ש וכשהגיע הזמן לא ראיתיו מפסיק: חוזר וגומרה. לאחר שעמדו התלמידי': דקא מהדר. לשנות לתלמידים בכל יום שמעתא דאית בה יציאת מצרים במקום פרשת ציצית ואמת ויציב: בזמנה. בזמן ק"ש: בפסוקא קמא צערן. אם ראיתני מתנמנם לערני עד שאנער יפה בפסוק ראשון: פרקדן: שוכב על גבו ופניו למעלה: לייט מאן דגני אפרקיד. שמא יתקשה אברו בתוך שנתו ונראה לרבים והוא דרך גנאי: מיגנא. לישן: כי מצלי שפיר דמי. כשהוא מוטה על לדו מעט שפיר דמי אבל מקרי ק"ש אפי' מצלי נמי אסור שמקבל עליו מלכות שמים דרך שררה וגאוה: לכל אדם. אפי' אינו נכבד: חסורי מחסרא. דהוה ליה למתני בתרוייהו אין צ"ל ותו ליכא למיקשי מידי: אהי

עין משפט נר מצוה
ז
א מיי' פ"ב מהל' ק"ש הל' א סמג עשין יח טוש"ע א"ח סי' ס סעי' ה ובסי' סג סעי' ד
ח
ב ג ד מיי' שם הל' ט וסמ"ג שם טוש"ע א"ח סי' סא סעי' ו ח
ט
ה מיי' שם הל' ג וסמג שם טוש"ע א"ח סי' סג סעי' ג
י
ו טוש"ע א"ח סי' סא סעי' ה
יא
ז מיי' וסמ"ג שם טוש"ע א"ח סי' סג סעי' ה
*ר"ל ממאי דאמרי' התם א"ח דבר לאחר אמת ויציב וכגי' הרי"ף ורא"ש ע"ש כ"ה בהי' גרסאות. [והוא דחוק ולענ"ד צ"ל דמשמע לעיל י: וע' תוס' לקמן כא: ד"ה עד]
יב
ח מיי' שם הל' ב' טוש"ע שם סעי' א

מסורת הש"ס
תוספתא פ"ב
ספרי פרשת ואתחנן [מנחות לז:]
[שלא יראו עיניו כשהוא מקבלן ומתגנה ערוך בע' בר פחתי וע"ש עוד פי' אחרי']
[פי' בן גדולי ע' שבת ג: כע. נזיר נע. וברש"י שם]
נדה יד. [תיבת לייט לקמן טו.] קידושין לג: [וסם נסמן]

תורה אור
דברים ו
דברים יא
דברים ו

him: Behold it says, [13b] *Which I command thee this day upon thy heart.*[3] From this you learn that the whole section requires to be said with *kawanah*. Rabbah b. Ḥanah said in the name of R. Joḥanan: The *halachah* is as laid down by R. Akiba. Some refer this statement[5] to the following, as it has been taught: One who reads the *Shema'* must pay proper attention[6] to what he says. R. Aḥa said in the name of R. Judah: If he has paid proper attention to the first section, he need not do so for the rest. Rabba b. Bar Ḥanah said in the name of R. Joḥanan: The *halachah* is as stated by R. Aḥa in the name of R. Judah.

Another [Baraitha] taught: *'And they shall be'*: this teaches that they must not be said backwards. *'Upon thy heart'*: R. Zuṭra says: Up to this point extends the command of *kawanah*,[7] from this point only the command of reciting applies. R. Josiah says: Up to this point extends the command of reciting; from this point the command of *kawanah* applies. Why this difference in the application from this point of the command of reciting? [Presumably] because it is written *'to speak of them'*;[8] here too [in the first] also it
a is written, *'and thou shalt speak of them'!*[1] What he means is this: Up to this point applies the command both of *kawanah* and reciting; from this point onwards applies the command of reciting [even] without *kawanah*.[2] And why this difference in the application up to the point of the command both of reciting and *kawanah?* [Presumably] because it is written, *upon thy heart and thou shalt speak of them?*[3] [In the second section] there too it is written, *'upon thy hearts to speak of them.*[4] That text was required for the lesson enunciated by R. Isaac, who said: 'Ye shall put these my words [*upon your hearts*]';[4] it is requisite that the placing [of the *tefillin*] should be opposite the heart.

The Master stated [above]: 'R. Josiah said: Up to this point extends the command of reciting; from this point onwards the command of *kawanah* applies'. Why this difference in the application from this point onward of the command of *kawanah?* [Presumably] because it is written, *'Upon your heart'?* There too [in the first section] also it is written *Upon thy heart?*—What he meant is this: Up to this point applies the command of reciting and *kawanah*, from this point onwards applies that of *kawanah* [even] without reciting.[5] Why this difference in the application up to this point of the command of reciting and *kawanah?* [Presumably] because it is written, *'Upon thy heart and thou shalt speak of them?'* There too [in the second section] also it is written, *'Upon your heart to speak, of them'!* These words have reference to words of Torah, and what the All-Merciful meant is this: Teach your children Torah, so that they may be fluent in them.

Our Rabbis taught: *Hear, O Israel, the Lord our God, the Lord is one.*[6] Up to this point concentration[7] is required. So says R. Meir. Raba said: The *halachah* is as stated by R. Meir.

It has been taught: Symmachus says: Whoever prolongs the word *eḥad* [one], has his days and years prolonged. R. Aḥa b. Jacob said: [He must dwell] on the *daleth*.[8] R. Ashi said: Provided
b he does not slur over the *ḥeth*.[1] R. Jeremiah was once sitting before R. Ḥiyya b. Abba, and the latter saw that he was prolonging [the word *eḥad*] very much. He said to him: Once you have declared Him king[2] over [all that is] above and below and over the four quarters of the heaven, no more is required.

R. Nathan b. Mar 'Ukba said in the name of Rab Judah: *'Upon thy heart'* must be said standing. [Only] 'Upon thy heart'? How can you assume this? Rather say: Up to 'upon thy heart' must be said standing; from there onwards not [necessarily]. R. Joḥanan, however, said: The whole [first] section must be said standing. And R. Joḥanan in this is consistent; for Rabbah b. Bar Ḥanah said in the name of R. Joḥanan: The *halachah* is as stated by R. Aḥa in the name of R. Judah.[3]

Our Rabbis taught: *'Hear, O Israel, the Lord our God, the Lord is one'*: this was R. Judah the Prince's recital of the *Shema'*.[4] Rab said once to R. Ḥiyya: I do not see Rabbi accept upon himself the yoke of the kingdom of heaven.[5] He replied to him: Son of Princes![6] In the moment when he passes his hand over his eyes, he accepts upon himself the yoke of the kingdom of heaven. Does he finish it afterwards or does he not finish it afterwards?[7] Bar Ḳappara said: He does not finish it afterwards; R. Simeon son of Rabbi said, He does finish it afterwards. Said Bar Ḳappara to R. Simeon the son of Rabbi: On my view that he does not finish it afterwards, there is a good reason why Rabbi always is anxious to take a lesson in which there is mention of the exodus from Egypt.[8] But on your view that he does finish it afterwards, why is he anxious to take such a lesson?—So as to mention the going forth from Egypt at the proper time.[9]

R. Ela the son of R. Samuel b. Martha said in the name of Rab: If one said *'Hear, O Israel, the Lord our God, the Lord is one'*, and was then overpowered by sleep, he has performed his obligation.
c R. Naḥman said to his slave Daru: For the first verse prod me,[1] but do not prod me for any more. R. Joseph said to R. Joseph the son of Rabbah: How did your father use to do? He replied: For the first verse he used to take pains [to keep awake], for the rest he did not use to take pains.

R. Joseph said: A man lying on his back should not recite the *Shema'*. [This implies] that he may not read [the *Shema'* lying on his back], but there is no objection to his sleeping in this posture. But did not R. Joshua b. Levi curse anyone who slept lying on his back?[2] In reply it was said: To sleeping thus if he turns over a little on his side there is no objection, but to read the *Shema'* thus is forbidden even if he turns over somewhat. But R. Joḥanan turned over a little and read the Scripture?—R. Joḥanan was an exception, because he was very corpulent.

IN THE BREAKS HE MAY GIVE GREETING etc. For what may he RETURN GREETING? Shall I say, out of respect? But seeing that he may give greeting, is there any question that he may return it? Rather [what I must say is]: He gives greeting out of respect and returns greeting to anyone. [But then] read the next clause: IN THE MIDDLE HE GIVES GREETING OUT OF FEAR AND RETURNS IT. Returns it for what reason? Shall I say, out of fear? But seeing that he may give greeting, is there any question that he may return it? Rather [what we must say is], out of respect. But then this is the view of R. Judah,[3] as we learn, R. JUDAH SAYS: IN THE MIDDLE HE GIVES GREETING OUT OF FEAR AND RETURNS IT OUT OF RESPECT, AND IN THE BREAKS HE GIVES GREETING OUT OF RESPECT AND RETURNS GREETING TO ANYONE?—There is a lacuna, and [our Mishnah] should read as follows: IN THE BREAKS HE GIVES GREETING OUT OF RESPECT, and needless to say he may return it, AND IN THE MIDDLE HE GIVES GREETING OUT OF FEAR and needless to say he may return it. So R. Meir. R. Judah says: IN THE MIDDLE HE GIVES GREETING OUT OF FEAR AND RETURNS IT OUT OF RESPECT,

(5) Of Rabbah b. Bar Ḥanah's statement of the *halachah*. (6) Lit., 'direct his heart'. I.e., have *kawanah*. (7) Presumably *kawanah* here means concentration without reciting, i.e., reading with the eyes. (8) Ibid. VI; XI. This is the command of reciting.

a (1) Deut. VI. (2) I.e., attention is optional. (3) Ibid. 6. (4) Ibid. XI, 18. E.V. *'lay up in your heart'*. (5) I.e., it is permitted to read with the eyes. (6) Ibid. VI, 4. (7) Lit., 'direction of the heart'. (8) Because the word does not mean *'one'* till he comes to this letter.

b (1) Omitting its vowel and so make the word meaningless. (2) I.e., in your thoughts while saying the word. (3) *Supra*, that the first section requires *kawanah*. (4) I.e., he said only this verse and no more. (5) V. *supra*, 13a, n.b7. Rabbi commenced studying with his disciples before daybreak and did not break off when the time came for reciting the *Shema'*. (6) I.e., of great scholars; Rab was a nephew of R. Ḥiyya. (7) After he dismisses his disciples. (8) As a substitute for this, the third section, which deals with the exodus. (9) I.e., when the *Shema'* is to be recited.

c (1) Lit., 'worry me so that I may be wide awake'. (2) V. *infra* 15a. (3) Who is supposed to differ from R. Meir, whose views we have been stating so far.

[14a] AND IN THE BREAKS HE GIVES GREETING OUT OF RESPECT AND RETURNS IT TO ANYONE. It has been taught similarly: If one was reciting the *Shema'* and his teacher or superior meets him in the breaks, he may give greeting out of respect, and needless to say he may return it, and in the middle he may give greeting out of fear and needless to say he may return it. So R. Meir. R. Judah said: In the middle he may give greeting out of fear and return it out of respect, and in the breaks he may give greeting out of respect and return it to anyone.

a Ahi the Tanna[1] of the school of R. Ḥiyya put a question to R. Ḥiyya: What of interrupting [to give greeting] during the recital of *Hallel*[2] and the reading of the *Megillah*?[2] Do we argue *a fortiori* that if he may interrupt during the recital of the *Shema'* which is a Biblical precept, there is no question that he may do so during the recital of *Hallel*, which is a Rabbinical precept, or do we say that the proclaiming of the miracle[3] is more important?—He replied: He may interrupt, and there is no objection. Rabbah said: On the days on which the individual says the complete *Hallel*,[4] he may interrupt between one section and another but not in the middle of a section; on the days on which the individual does not say the complete *Hallel*[5] he may interrupt even in the middle of a section. But that is not so. For surely Rab b. Shaba once happened to visit Rabina on one of the days on which the individual does not say the complete *Hallel* and he [Rabina] did not break off to greet him?—It is different with Rab b. Shaba, because Rabina had no great respect for him.

Ashian the Tanna[1] of the school of R. Ammi enquired of R. Ammi: May one who is keeping a [voluntary][6] fast take a taste?[7] Has he undertaken to abstain from eating and drinking, and this is really not such, or has he undertaken not to have any enjoyment, and this he obtains?—He replied: He may taste, and there is no objection. It has been taught similarly: A mere taste does not require a blessing, and one who is keeping a [voluntary] fast may take a taste, and there is no objection. How much may he taste?—
b R. Ammi and R. Assi used to taste as much as a *rebi'ith*.[1]

Rab said: If one gives greeting to his fellow before he has said his prayers[2] it is as if he made him a high place, as it says, *Cease ye from man in whose nostrils is a breath, for how little is he to be accounted!*[3] Read not *bammeh* [how little], but *bammah* [high place].[4] Samuel interpreted: How come you to esteem this man and not God?[5] R. Shesheth raised an objection: IN THE BREAKS HE GIVES GREETING OUT OF RESPECT AND RETURNS IT![6]—R. Abba explains the dictum to refer to one who rises early to visit another.[7] R. Jonah said in the name of R. Zera: If a man does his own business before he says his prayers, it is as if he had built a high place. He said to him: A high place, do you say? No, he replied; I only mean that it is forbidden.[8] R. Idi b. Abin said in the name of R. Isaac b. Ashian:[9] It is forbidden to a man to do his own business before he says his prayers, as it says, *Righteousness shall go before him and then he shall set his steps on his own way.*[10]

R. Jonah further said in the name of R. Zera: Whoever goes seven days without a dream is called evil, as it says, *And he that hath it shall abide satisfied; he shall not be visited with evil.*[11] Read not *sabea'*, [satisfied] but *sheba'* [seven].[12] R. Aḥa the son of R. Ḥiyya b. Abba said to him: Thus said R. Ḥiyya in the name of R. Joḥanan: Whoever sates himself with words of Torah before he retires will receive no evil tidings, as it says, *And if he abides sated he shall not be visited with evil.*

THE BREAKS ARE AS FOLLOWS etc. R. Abbahu said in the name of R. Joḥanan: The *halachah* follows R. Judah, who says that one should not interrupt between 'your God' and 'True and firm'. R. Abbahu said in the name of R. Joḥanan: What is R. Judah's

a (1) The one who repeated the section of the Mishnah for the teacher to expound. V. Glos. s.v. (*b*). (2) V. Glos. (3) The *Hallel* proclaims the exodus on Passover, and the *Megillah* the miraculous deliverance from Haman. (4) E.g., Tabernacles and Hanukah. V. 'Ar. 10*b*. (5) Viz., New Moon and the last six days of Passover. (6) V. Tosaf s.v. (7) To see if food is cooked properly.

b (1) A fourth of a *log*, i.e., about an egg and a half. (2) I.e., before he recites the *tefillah*. (3) Isa. II, 22. (4) And render, if he is esteemed he becomes a high place. (5) Samuel draws a similar lesson without altering the text. (6) Though the *Shema'* is said before the *tefillah*. (7) After the manner of the Roman *clientes* with their patrons. But if one meets his neighbour he may greet him. (8) But it is not so bad as idolatry. (9) This is the reading of Rashi. Cur. edd. have: This agrees with the dictum of R. Idi b. Abin etc., which is obviously a contradiction. (10) Ps. LXXXV, 14. 'Righteousness' here is taken to mean justification by prayer. E.V., '*Righteousness shall go before Him and shall make His footsteps a way*'. (11) Prov. XIX, 23. (12) And render, 'if he abides seven nights without and is not visited (with a dream, this shows that) he is evil'.

ובפרקים שואל מפני הכבוד ומשיב שלום לכל אדם תניא נמי הכי הקורא את שמע ופגע בו רבו או גדול הימנו בפרקים שואל מפני הכבוד וא"צ לומר שהוא משיב ובאמצע שואל מפני היראה וא"צ לומר שהוא משיב דברי ר' מאיר רבי יהודה אומר באמצע שואל מפני היראה ומשיב מפני הכבוד ובפרקים שואל מפני הכבוד ומשיב שלום לכל אדם בעי מיניה אחי תנא דבי רבי חייא מרבי חייא בהלל ובמגילה מהו שיפסיק מי אמרינן ק"ו ק"ש דאורייתא פוסק הלל דרבנן מבעיא או דילמא *פרסומי ניסא עדיף א"ל פוסק ואין בכך כלום אמר רבה ימים שהיחיד גומר בהן את ההלל בין פרק לפרק פוסק באמצע הפרק אינו פוסק וימים שאין היחיד גומר בהן את ההלל אפילו באמצע הפרק פוסק איני והא רב בר שבא איקלע לגביה דרבינא וימים שאין היחיד גומר את ההלל הוה ולא פסיק ליה שאני רב בר שבא דלא חשיב עליה דרבינא: בעי מיניה אשיאן תנא דבי רבי אמי מרבי אמי השרוי בתענית מהו שיטעום אכילה ושתיה קביל עליה והא ליכא או דילמא הנאה קביל עליה והא איכא א"ל טועם ואין בכך כלום תניא נמי הכי מטעמת אינה טעונה ברכה והשרוי בתענית טועם ואין בכך כלום עד כמה ר' אמי ורבי אסי טעמי עד שיעור רביעתא: אמר רב כל הנותן שלום לחבירו קודם שיתפלל כאלו עשאו במה שנאמר °חדלו לכם מן האדם אשר נשמה באפו כי במה נחשב הוא אל תקרי במה אלא במה ושמואל אמר במה חשבתו לזה ולא לאלוה מתיב רב ששת בפרקים שואל מפני הכבוד ומשיב תרגומה ר' אבא במשכים לפתחו א"ר יונה א"ר זירא כל העושה חפציו קודם שיתפלל כאלו בנה במה א"ל במה אמרת א"ל לא אסור קא אמינא וכדרב אידי בר אבין דאמר רב אידי בר אבין אמר רב יצחק בר אשיאן אסור לו לאדם לעשות חפציו קודם שיתפלל שנאמר °צדק לפניו יהלך וישם לדרך פעמיו ואמר רב אידי בר אבין אמר רב יצחק בר אשיאן כל המתפלל ואח"כ יוצא לדרך הקב"ה עושה לו חפציו שנאמר צדק לפניו יהלך וישם לדרך פעמיו: וא"ר יונה א"ר זירא *כל הלן שבעת ימים בלא חלום נקרא רע שנאמר °ושבע ילין בל יפקד רע אל תקרי שבע אלא שבע א"ל ר' אחא בריה דר' חייא בר אבא הכי א"ר חייא א"ר יוחנן כל המשביע עצמו מדברי תורה ולן אין מבשרין אותו בשורות רעות שנאמר ושבע ילין בל יפקד רע: אלו הן בין הפרקים וכו': א"ר אבהו אמר ר' יוחנן הלכה כר' יהודה דאמר בין אלהיכם לאמת ויציב לא יפסיק *א"ר אבהו א"ר יוחנן מאי טעמיה דרבי יהודה דכתיב וה'

אחי. כך שמו: תנא דבי רבי חייא. שהיה שונה בבית ר' חייא: מהו שיפסיק. לשאלת שלום: ימים שהיחיד גומר בהן את ההלל. שהוא חובה לכל אדם והם כ"א יום בשנה כדאמרינן במסכת ערכין (ד' י.): מהו שיטעום. את התבשיל לדעת אם צריך מלח או תבלין: מטעמת. טעימת תבשיל: רביעתא. רביעית הלוג: חדלו לכם מן האדם. כשים לכם לעסוק בכבוד המקום אל תתעסקו בכבוד אדם דאי לאו הכי למה ליה לחדול: ושמואל. לא דריש לשון במה אלא כמשמעו במה חשבתו לזה שהקדמת כבודו לכבודי: שואל מפני הכבוד. והא ק"ש קודם תפלה הוא וקתני שואל: תרגומה רבי אבא. להא דרב ושמואל דאסרי: במשכים לפתחו. אבל פגעו בדרך שואל: ה"ג אמר רב אידי בר אבין אמר רב יצחק בר אשיאן אסור לאדם לעשות חפציו עד שיתפלל: צדק. תפלה שמצדיקו לבוראו והדר וישם פעמיו לדרכי חפציו: אל תקרי שבע אלא שבע. ילין בל יפקד מן השמים בחלום הרי הוא רע לכך אין משגיחים לפקדו: וה'

ימים שהיחיד גומר בהם את ההלל. לאו דוקא יחיד אלא אפי' צבור קורא יחיד כיון שאין כל ישראל ביחד כמו שהיו בשחיטת פסחים בי"ד בניסן ולאו דוקא גומר דודאי ק"ל דימים שאין יחיד גומר את ההלל אין חובה לאומרו כלל אפילו בדלוג דהכי משמע בערכין (פ"ב י:) דחשיב כ"א יום דיחיד גומר בהן את ההלל ופריך ר"ה וי"כ נמי ליתא משמע דבשאר ימים טובים כמו בראשי חדשים פשיטא ליה דאין לומר מדלא חשיב יותר מכ"א יום וגם מדלא קאמר לגמור בר"ה וביוה"כ דאז הוה משמע דבשאר ימים טובים כמו בר"ח ודאי אין גומרין אבל קורין אבל עתה משמע אפילו קורין לא וכן משמע בפרק בתרא דתענית (ד' כח:) רב איקלע לבבל חזינהו דהוו קא קרו בר"ח סבר לאפסוקינהו פירוש שהיה סובר שהיו גומרים אותו כיון דחזא דקא מדלגי דלוגי אמר ש"מ מנהג אבותיהם בידיהם אלמא דימים דאין גומרין בהן הלל אין חובה לאמרו ומה שאנו אומרין אותו הייינו משום מנהג. וכתוב במחזור ויטרי כיון שאינו אלא מנהג בעלמא לא מברכינן עליה כדאמר פרק לולב וערבה (ד' מד:) אין מברכין על דבר שהוא מנהג ומיהו אומר ר"ת דאינו ראיה דאטלטול ודאי לא מברכינן אבל על מלוה פשיטא דמברכינן דהא חזינן כל יום שני אינו אלא מנהגא ומברכין והכא נמי משמע דמברכין דאי לא מברכין מאי הפסקה שייך בה ועוד ראיה דמברכינן על מנהגא מהא דרב על לבי כנישתא וכו' ואם לא ברכו בתחלה אמאי לא הרגיש רב דהוה מנהגא עד שדלגו אלא בודאי ברכו ומפני שמברכין בטוב על מנהגא ובשביל כן לא הרגיש עד הדלוג ור"ת אמאי לא אסיק אדעתיה אם ברכו לקרות או לגמור וי"ל דבכך אין לחוש שבטוב יכול לברך לגמור אפי' כשהוא מדלג או איפכא ומה שמברכין כך על הדלוג לקרות וכשהן גומרין לגמור כדי שלא יטעו ומשום הכי לא היה יכול להבין מתוך הברכה עד הדלוג ויש שרוצין לומר דיחיד האומר הלל בימים שאין גומרין שאין לו לברך ומיהו השר מקוצי היה אומר דכיון שרצה לחייב עצמו מברך ואין זו ברכה לבטלה מידי דהוה אלולב ואתפילין דהכי מברכות אע"ג שאינן חייבות ובלילי פסחים יש שמברכין פעמים ובתחלה לקרות ואחר הסעודה אחר שפוך מברכין לגמור ומייתי ראיה מירושלמי (דפרק א) מההיא דמייתי עלה דכל הברכות *פותחין בברוך חוץ מן הברכות הסמוכות לחברתה וברכת הפירות והמצות ופריך בירושלמי עלה והא איכא גאולה פי' אשר גאלנו דסמוכה לחברתה ואמאי פותחת בברוך. שכי"א דאם שמעה בבית הכנסת יצא ופריך והרי קופה פי' יהללוך דאינה סמוכה שהסעודה מפסקת ואפילו הכי אינה פותחת בברוך ומשני שתים הנה אחת להבא ואחת לשעבר פי' אחת להבא זו היא אותה ברכה שמברכין אחר אכילה לגמור ולאותה ברכה היא סמוכה אחת לשעבר היינו אותה שבירך קודם אכילה אלמא דמברכין שני פעמים אבל זה הפי' אינו מיושב דהרי קיפא משמע דקאי אברכה דאשר גאלנו דקאי בה מתחלה. אלא ודאי אברכה דאשר גאלנו קאי כאשר אפרש ומיהו משמע בירושלמי כאשר פירשתי תחלה שהיו מברכין ב' פעמים תחלה וסוף אבל אומר ר' יהודה דזו היא תמיהא גדולה ומאחר שבירך קודם אכילה אמאי מפסיק ואוכל בנתים שהרי בימים שאין יחיד גומר בהן את ההלל כיון שבירך תחלה כמו הכא אינו מותר לפסוק אלא מפני הכבוד דאי בשלא בירך אמאי לא יפסיק באמצע אפילו שלא מפני הכבוד הא לא היה מפסיק שום ברכה אלא נראה הא דפריך בירושלמי הרי גאולה דמשמע דמברכים עליה בתחלה איירי באדם שעושה הסדר בבת אחת שאז אינו מפסיק שאינו צריך אבל אנו שמפסיקין לאכול אין לנו לברך כלל לא בתחלה ולא בסוף והא דקאמר בירושלמי והרי קיפא זהו אשר גאלנו דחותמת בברוך ואמאי והא הודאה בעלמא היא כברכת פירות ואמאי חותמת בברוך ומשני שתים הנה *שני גאולות אחת להבא ואחת לשעבר פי' לעתיד כמו יגיענו וגם היא ארוכה קצת וגם יש בה לשעבר כמו אשר גאלנו מגאולת מצרים לפיכך חותמת בברוך ומה שהקשה מיהללוך שאינה סמוכה לפי מה שפרשתי עתה ואפילו הכי אינה פותחת בברוך יש ליתן טעם לפי שהיא הודאה בעלמא ואפילו שהיא ארוכה קצת תקנו בה חתימה ולא פתיחה כמו אלהי נשמה. וכן משמע בירושלמי שהיה דרכן לומר הלל בבית הכנסת ואח"כ שותין כוסות שלהם בביתם בלא שום סדר דבעי בירושלמי (פ' ע"פ) שתאן בבת אחת מהו פירוש זה אחר זה בלא הלל וסדר בנתים מהו שמעינן מן הדא דא"ר יוחנן הלל אם שמע בבית הכנסת יצא וכן משמע בתוספתא דמי שלא היה יודע וכנס בבית הכנסת וכו' והשתא נמי מיושב דבשביל כך פותחת ברכה דאשר גאלנו בברוך דטעמא שאינה סמוכה כי הא דאם קרא הלל בבית הכנסת יצא:

או דלמא הנאה קיבל עליה. הא לישנא משמע דמיירי בתענית יחיד שקבל עליו אבל בתענית הכתוב לא:

טועם ואין בכך כלום. פי' ר"ח שמחזר ופולט דלא חשיב הנאה מן הטעימה אבל בולע לא אפילו בשאר תעניות ומשום הכי הפולט אינו צריך ברכה שאינו נהנה: **במשכים** לפתחו. וכן הלכה אבל פגעו בשוקא מותר: למה

עין משפט נר מצוה

יג א טוש"ע א"ח סי' תכב סעי' ב

יד ב מיי' פ"ג מהל' חנוכה הלכה ד טוש"ע א"ח סי' תכב סעי' ד וסי' תרמד סעיף א

טו ג מיי' פ"א מה' ברכות הל' ב סמג הל' ברכות טוש"ע א"ח סי' רי סעיף ב

טז ד מיי' פ"ק מהל' תענית הלכה יד טוש"ע א"ח סי' תקסז סעי' א [רב אלפס תענית פ"א ד' קעב]

יז ה מיי' פ"ו מהל' תפלה הלכה ד סמג עשין יט טוש"ע א"ח סי' פט סעיף ב

יח ו מיי' שם טוש"ע שם סעיף ג

יט ז מיי' פ"ב מהל' ק"ש הלכה יז סמג עשין יח טוש"ע א"ח סי' סו סעיף ה

מסורת הש"ס · תורה אור

[שבת כג:] · ישעיה ב · תהלים פה · הרוא' כה: [ושם אי' ר' זעירא וכ"ה בשאלתות] · משלי יט · [נ"ל ומאי] · [פותחות וחותמות בברוך כצ"ל רש"א] · [נ"ל שתי]

°וה' אלהים אמת חוזר ואומר אמת או אינו חוזר ואומר אמת א"ר אבהו א"ר יוחנן חוזר ואומר אמת רבה אמר א"אינו חוזר ואומר אמת: ההוא דנחית קמיה דרבה שמעיה רבה דאמר אמת אמת תרי זימני אמר רבה כל אמת אמת תפסיה להאי אמר רב יוסף כמה מעליא הא שמעתתא דכי אתא רב שמואל בר יהודה אמר אמרי במערבא ערבית דבר אל בני ישראל ואמרת אליהם אני ה' אלהיכם אמת א"ל אביי מאי מעליות' והא אמר רב כהנא אמר רב לא יתחיל ואם התחיל גומר וכי תימא ואמרת אליהם לא הוי' התחלה והאמר רב שמואל בר יצחק אמר רב דבר אל בני ישראל לא הוי' התחלה ואמרת אליהם הוי' התחלה אמר רב פפא קסברי במערבא ואמרת אליהם נמי לא הוי' התחלה עד דאמר ועשו להם ציצית אמר אביי הלכך אנן אתחולי מתחלינן דקא מתחלי במערבא וכיון דאתחלינן מגמר נמי גמרינן דהא אמר רב כהנא אמר רב לא יתחיל ואם התחיל גומר חייא בר רב אמר אמר אני ה' אלהיכם צ"ל אמת לא אמר אני ה' אלהיכם אינו צ"ל אמת והא בעי לאדכורי יציאת מצרים דאמר הכי מודים אנחנו לך ה' אלקינו שהוצאתנו מארץ מצרים ופדיתנו מבית עבדים ועשית לנו נסים וגבורות על הים ושרנו לך: א"ר יהושע בן קרחה למה קדמה פרשת שמע וכו': תניא ר"ש בן יוחי אומר בדין הוא שיקדים שמע לוהיה אם שמוע שזה ללמוד וזה ללמד והיה אם שמוע לויאמר שזה *ללמוד וזה לעשות אטו שמע ללמוד אית ביה ללמד ולעשות לית ביה והא כתיב ושננתם וקשרתם וכתבתם ותו והיה אם שמוע ללמד הוא דאית ביה ולעשות לית ביה והא כתיב וקשרתם וכתבתם אלא ה"ק בדין הוא שתקדים שמע לוהיה אם שמוע שזה ללמוד וללמד ולעשות והיה אם שמוע לויאמר שזה יש בה ללמד ולעשות ויאמר אין בה אלא לעשות בלבד ותיפוק ליה מדר' יהושע בן קרחה חדא ועוד קאמר חדא כדי שיקבל עליו עול מלכות שמים תחלה ואח"כ יקבל עליו עול מצות ועוד משום דאית בה הני מילי אחרנייתא רב "משי ידיה וקרא ק"ש ואנח תפילין וצלי והיכי עביד הכי והתניא "החופר כוך למת בקבר פטור מק"ש ומן התפלה ומן התפילין ומכל מצות האמורות בתורה הגיע זמן ק"ש עולה ונוטל ידיו ומניח תפילין וקורא ק"ש ומתפלל הא גופא קשיא רישא אמר פטור וסיפא חייב הא לא קשיא "סיפא בתרי ורישא בחד מ"מ קשיא לרב רב כר' יהושע בן קרחה סבירא ליה דאמר עול מלכות שמים תחלה ואח"כ עול מצות אימר דאמר ר' יהושע בן קרחה להקדים קריאה לקריאה קריאה לעשיה מי שמעת ליה ותו מי סבר ליה כרבי יהושע בן קרחה *והאמר רב חייא בר אשי זימנין סגיאין הוה קאימנא קמיה דרב ומקדים ומשי ידיה ומברך ומתני לן פרקין ומנח תפילין והדר קרי ק"ש וכי תימא בדלא מטא זמן ק"ש א"כ מאי אסהדתיה דרב חייא בר אשי לאפוקי ממאן דאמר למשנה אין צריך לברך קמ"ל דאף למשנה נמי צריך לברך מ"מ קשיא לרב שלוחא הוא דעוית: אמר עולא "כל הקורא ק"ש בלא תפילין כאלו מעיד עדות שקר בעצמו א"ר חייא בר אבא א"ר יוחנן כאלו הקריב עולה בלא מנחה וזבח בלא נסכים: וא"ר יוחנן הרוצה שיקבל עליו עול מלכות שמים שלימה

יפנה

למה קדמה פרשת שמע לוהיה אם שמוע. וא"ת תיפוק ליה דקדמה בתורה וי"ל דהכי קאמר למה קדמה אף לפרשת ציצית דקדמה לכולן אלא ודאי אין אנו חוששין לזה שהיא קודמת בתורה משום דאמרינן אין מוקדם ומאוחר ואם כן היה לנו להקדים והיה שהיא מדברת בלשון רבים:

ויאמר אינה נוהגת אלא ביום. מכאן משמע כר"ש דקאמר בפרק התכלת (ד' מג.) דציצית מ"ע שהזמן גרמא וכן איתא בקדושין (פ"ק ד' לג:) דאמר ציצית מצות עשה שהזמן גרמא. וא"ת א"כ למ"ד (מנחות מ"א.) ציצית חובת טלית הוא ואפילו מונחת בקופסא אפילו הכי חייבת בציצית היכי אשכחן שיהא הזמן גרמא וי"ל דאם היה כסות המיוחד ללילה פטור והכי איתא בירושלמי דקדושין אמר להם ר"ש אי אתם מודים לי דציצית מצות עשה שהזמן גרמא שהרי כסות לילה פטור מן הציצית א"ר אילא טעמא דרבנן שאם היה מיוחד ליום ולילה שחייבת בציצית:

ומנח תפילין ומצלי. ומהתם משמע שמותר להניח תפילין בין גאולה לתפלה וכן בטלית מניח אדם טליתו בין גאולה לתפלה. וכן מצינו שרבי יצחק בר' יהודה שלא אחר טליתו ושהה השליח וכבר קרא ק"ש בברכותי' ונתעטף בטליתו וגמר שמנה עשרה והביא ראיה מהכא מהא דרב. מ"מ יש לחלק בין תפילין לטלית דעיקר ק"ש ותפלה שייכי בתפילין כדאמר בסמוך כאלו מעיד עדות שקר בעצמו. פי' באדון שלוה שהוא קורא והיו לטוטפות ולאות על ידך ואין. ותפלה נמי כדאמרן קרי ק"ש ומתפלל זו היא מלכות שמים אבל ציצית שאינו אלא חובת טלית שאם יש לו טלית חייב ואם אין לו פטור מציצית ויכול לקרות ק"ש בלא ציצית ודאי דהויא הפסקה. והרב ר' משה מקוצי היה אומר דאפילו מכאן אין ראיה דמצי למימר הניח תפילין בלא ברכה ולאחר י"ח ממשמש בהם ומברך עליה' ובהכי סגי שגם מותר להתעטף בטלית בעת שידיו מטונפות ואחר שיטול ידיו ימשמש בטליתו ומברך:

ומכל מצות האמורות בתורה. וא"ת וכי ק"ש לא היה בכלל מצות האמורות בתורה וי"ל דאי לא תני בהדיא קריאת שמע הוה אמינא דדוקא הכי דלית להו קביעות זמן אבל ק"ש דקביע ליה זמן לא הואיל וזמן עובר קמ"ל:

עולה בלא מנחה. ה"ה דמצי למימר בלא נסכים שהרי עולה נמי טעונה נסכים אלא לישנא דקרא נקט עולה ומנחה וגו' (ויקרא כג):

אמאן

וה' אלהים אמת. לכך אין מפסיקין בין אני ה' אלהיכם לאמת: כל אמת אמת תפסיה להאי. ריהטא של אמת תפסתו לזה: הא שמעתת' דרב שמואל בר יהודה אמר אמרי במערבא וכו'. ק"ש של ערבית אין קורין בה פרשת ציצית כולה לפי שאין מצות ציצית בלילה אבל מתחילין אותה ומפסיקין בה ומדלגים ואומרים אני ה' אלהיכ' אמת: לא יתחיל. אין צריך להתחיל ויאמר ערבית: אתחולי מתחלינן. דהא מתחלי במערבא: אמר אני ה' אלהיכם. דהיינו פרשת ציצית: צריך לומר אמת. כדכתיב וה' אלהים אמת: והא בעי אדכורי יציאת מצרים. דתנן (לעיל ד' יב:) מזכירין יציאת מצרים בלילות ואי לא אמר אמת ואמונה ולא אמר פרשת ציצית היכי מדכר יציאת מצרים: ושרנו לך. מי כמוך באלים וגו' מלכותך ראו בניך עד גאל ישראל והשכיבנו: שזה ללמוד. ודברת בם: וזה ללמד. ולמדתם אותם את בניכם ואם לא למד תחלה היאך ילמד את בניו: וזה לעשות. ויאמר אין בה אלא עשייה: וקשרתם. דתפילין: וכתבתם. דמזוזה עשייה היא: רב משי ידיה. פעם אחת ראוהו שעשה כן: והיכי עביד הכי. שהקדים ק"ש לתפילין: כוך. קבר שחופרין בקירות מערה ארכו ארבע ורחבו (ז') [ו'] טפחים: פטור מק"ש. דהעוסק במצוה פטור מן המצוה כדאמרינן בפ"ק (ד' יא.) בשבתך בביתך פרט לעוסק במצוה: וסיפא בתרי. והכי קאמר אם שנים הם מניח את חברו חופר והוא עולה ומקיים מצות ק"ש ותפילין ותפלה וחוזר למלאכה וחברו יעלה ויניח תפילין ויקרא ק"ש ויתפלל: מ"מ. תפילין קודמים לק"ש: עול מצות. דהנחת תפילין עול מצוה הוא: קריאה לקריאה. שמע שהוא קבלת מלכות שמים לוהיה אם שמוע שהוא קבלת עול מצות: ומקדים. משכים: ומברך. על התורה: ומתני פרקין. אלמא מקדים הוא לעסוק בתורה דהיינו עשייה דמצוה מקמי מלכות שמים: שלוחא הוא דעוית. השליח קלקל שאיחר להביא לו תפילין מעיקר' *והגיע זמן ק"ש והוזקק לקרות כדי שלא יעבור הזמן וכי מטי שלוחא דתפילין אנחינהו: כאלו מעיד עדות שקר בעצמו. לישנא מעליא: כאלו הקריב עולה בלא מנחה. שחייבו הכתוב להקריב עמה שנא' (במדבר כח) ועשירית האיפה וגו' אף הקורא ואינו מקיים אינו גומר את המצוה: נסכים. הוא היין המתנסך על גבי המזבח אחר העולה והזבח כדכתיב ונסכיהם חצי ההין וגו' (שם) וה"ה דמצי למימר כאלו הקריב עולה בלא מנחה ונסכים דהא עולה נמי טעונה נסכים אלא לישנא דקרא נקט עולה ומנחה זבח ונסכים:

יפנה

עין משפט נר מצוה

כ
אטוש"ע א"ח סי' סו סעיף ו

כא
בשם סעי' ח

כב
גדמיי' פ"ד מהלכות ק"ש הלכה ג סמג עשין יח טוש"ע א"ח סי' עא סעי' ה ו ובי"ד סימן שסה סעיף א

כג
המיי' פ"ד מהלכות תפילין הלכה כו טוש"ע א"ח סי' כה סעי' ד [רב אלפס כאן ובהלכות תפילין ד' טו. וע"ש הגוספא]

תורה אור

ירמי'

[נ"ל ללמד]

ס"א וחשיב דלא אזיל

לעיל י"א:

מסורת הש"ס

reason? Because we find in Scripture the words, [14*b*] *The Lord* a *God is truth.*[1] Does he repeat the word 'true'[2] or does he not repeat the word 'true'?—R. Abbahu said in the name of R. Joḥanan: He repeats the word 'true'; Rabbah says: He does not repeat the word 'true'. A certain man went down to act as reader before Rabbah, and Rabbah heard him say 'truth, truth', twice; whereupon he remarked: The whole of truth has got hold of this man.[3]

R. Joseph said: How fine was the statement which was brought by R. Samuel b. Judah when he reported that in the West [Palestine] they say [in the evening], *Speak unto the children of Israel and thou shalt say unto them, I am the Lord your God, True.*[4] Said Abaye to him: What is there so fine about it, seeing that R. Kahana has said in the name of Rab: [In the evening] one need not begin [this third section of the *Shema'*] but if he does begin, he should go through with it? And should you say that the words, *'and thou shalt say unto them'* do not constitute a beginning, has not R. Samuel b. Isaac said in the name of Rab, *'Speak unto the children of Israel'* is no beginning, but *'and thou shalt say unto them'* is a beginning?—R. Papa said: In the West they hold that *'and thou shalt say unto them'* also is no beginning, until one says, *'and they shall make unto themselves fringes'*. Abaye said: Therefore we [in Babylon] begin [the section], because they begin it in the West; and since we begin we go through with it, because R. Kahana has said in the name of Rab: One need not begin, but if he begins he should go through with it.

Ḥiyya b. Rab said: If one has said [in the evening] 'I am the Lord your God,' he must say also, 'True [etc.]'; if he has not said 'I am the Lord your God', he need not say 'True'. But one has to men- b tion the going forth from Egypt?[1]—He can say thus: We give thanks to Thee O Lord our God, that Thou hast brought us forth from the land of Egypt and redeemed us from the house of servitude and wrought for us miracles and mighty deeds, by the [Red] Sea, and we did sing unto Thee.[2]

R. JOSHUA B. KORHAH SAID: WHY IS THE SECTION OF 'HEAR' SAID BEFORE etc. It has been taught: R. Simeon b. Yoḥai says: It is right that 'Hear' should come before *'And it shall come to pass'* because the former prescribes learning[3] and the latter teaching,[4] and that *'and it shall come to pass'* should precede *'And the Lord said'* because the former prescribes teaching and the latter performance. But does then *'hear'* speak only of learning and not also of teaching and doing? Is it not written therein, *'And thou shalt teach diligently, and thou shalt bind them and thou shalt write them'?* Also, does *'and it shall come to pass'* speak only of teaching and not also of performance? Is it not written therein, *'and ye shall bind and ye shall write'?*—Rather this is what he means to say: It is right that *'hear'* should precede *'and it shall come to pass'*, because the former mentions both learning, teaching, and doing; and that *'and it shall come to pass'* should precede *'and the Lord said'*, because the former mentions both teaching and doing, whereas the latter mentions doing only. But is not the reason given by R. Joshua b. Korḥah sufficient?—He [R. Simeon b. Yoḥai] gave an additional reason. One is that he should first accept upon himself the yoke of the kingdom of heaven and then accept the yoke of the commandments. A further reason is that it [the first section] has these other features.

Rab once washed his hands and recited the *Shema'* and put on c *tefillin* and said the *tefillah*. But how could he act in this way,[1] seeing that it has been taught: 'One who digs a niche in a grave for a corpse is exempt from reciting *Shema'* and *tefillah* and from *tefillin* and from all the commandments prescribed in the Torah. When the hour for reciting the *Shema'* arrives, he goes up and washes his hands and puts on *tefillin* and recites the *Shema'* and says the *tefillah?'* Now this statement itself contains a contradiction. First it says that he is exempt and then it says that he is under obligation?—This is no difficulty; the latter clause speaks of where there are two,[2] the former of where there is only one. In any case this seems to contradict Rab?—Rab held with R. Joshua b. Korḥah, who said that first he accepts the yoke of the kingdom of heaven and then he accepts the yoke of the commandments.[3] I will grant you that R. Joshua b. Korḥah meant that the recital [of one section] should precede that of the other. But can you understand him to mean that the recital should precede the act [of putting on the *tefillin*]? And further, did Rab really adopt the view of R. Joshua b. Korḥah? Did not R. Ḥiyya b. Ashi say: On many occasions I stood before Rab when he rose early and said a blessing and taught us our section and put on phylacteries and then recited the *Shema'*?[4] And should you say, he did this only when the hour for reciting the *Shema'* had not yet arrived—if that is so what is the value of the testimony of R. Ḥiyya b. Ashi?—To refute the one who says that a blessing need not be said for the study of the Mishnah;[5] he teaches us that for the Mishnah also a blessing must be said. All the same there is a contradiction of Rab?[6]—His messenger was at fault.[7]

'Ulla said: If one recites the *Shema'* without *tefillin* it is as if he d bore false witness against himself.[1] R. Ḥiyya b. Abba said in the name of R. Joḥanan: It is as if he offered a burnt-offering without a meal-offering and a sacrifice without drink-offering.

R. Joḥanan also said: If one desires to accept upon himself the yoke of the kingdom of heaven in the most complete manner [15*a*],

a (1) Jer. X, 10. E.V. *'the true God'*. (2) After concluding the *Shema'* with the word true, does he have to repeat the word which is really the beginning of the next paragraph in the prayers? (3) *Sc.*, he cannot stop saying 'truth'. (4) I.e., the opening and closing words of the third section, omitting the middle part which deals with the fringes, since the law of fringes does not apply at night.

b (1) And if he omits both the third section and 'True and faithful' where does he mention it? (2) And he then continues, 'Who is like unto Thee' and 'Cause us to lie down'. *P.B.*, p. 99. (3) As it says, *and thou shalt speak.* (4) As it says, *and ye shall teach them to your children.*

c (1) Viz., say the *Shema'* before putting on *tefillin.* (2) And one prays while the other goes on digging. (3) By putting on *tefillin.* (4) 'Teaching' is here regarded as equivalent to accepting the yoke of the commandments. (5) V. *supra* 11*b*. (6) The original contradiction has not yet been solved. (7) And brought him his *tefillin* late, so he said the *Shema'* first.

d (1) Rather, he accuses himself of falsehood, i.e., inconsistency.

he should consult nature and wash his hands and put on *tefillin* and recite the *Shema'* and say the *tefillah:* this is the complete acknowledgment of the kingdom of heaven. R. Ḥiyya b. Abba said in the name of R. Joḥanan: If one consults nature and washes his hands and puts on *tefillin* and recites the *Shema'* and says the *tefillah,* Scripture accounts it to him as if he had built an altar and offered a sacrifice upon it, as it is written, *I will wash my hands in innocency and I will compass Thine altar, O Lord.*[2] Said Raba to him: Does not your honour think that it is as if he had bathed himself, since it is written, *I will wash in purity* and it is not written, 'I will wash my hands'.[3]

Rabina said to Raba: Sir, pray look at this student who has come from the West [Palestine] and who says: If one has no water for washing his hands, he can rub[4] his hands with earth or with a pebble or with sawdust. He replied: He is quite correct. Is it written, I will wash in water? It is written: In cleanliness—with anything which cleans. For R. Ḥisda cursed anyone who went looking for water at the time of prayer.[5] This applies to the recital of the *Shema'*, but for the *tefillah* one may go looking. How far?—As far as a *parasang.* This is the case in front of him, but in the rear, he may not go back even a *mil.* [From which is to be deduced], A *mil* he may not go back; but less than a *mil* he may go back.

MISHNAH. IF ONE RECITES THE SHEMA' WITHOUT HEARING WHAT HE SAYS, HE HAS PERFORMED HIS OBLIGATION. R. JOSE SAYS: HE HAS NOT PERFORMED HIS OBLIGATION. IF HE RECITES IT WITHOUT PRONOUNCING THE LETTERS CORRECTLY, R. JOSE SAYS THAT HE HAS PERFORMED HIS OBLIGATION, R. JUDAH SAYS THAT HE HAS NOT PERFORMED
a HIS OBLIGATION. IF HE RECITES IT BACKWARD,[1] HE HAS NOT PERFORMED HIS OBLIGATION. IF HE RECITES IT AND MAKES A MISTAKE HE GOES BACK TO THE PLACE WHERE HE MADE THE MISTAKE.

GEMARA. What is R. Jose's reason?—Because it is written, '*Hear*' which implies, let your ear hear what you utter with your mouth. The first Tanna, however, maintains that '*hear*' means, in any language that you understand. But R. Jose derives both lessons from the word.

We have learnt elsewhere: A deaf person who can speak but not hear should not set aside *terumah;*[2] if, however, he does set aside, his action is valid. Who is it that teaches that the action of a deaf man who can speak but not hear in setting aside *terumah* is valid if done, but should not be done in the first instance?—Said R. Ḥisda: It is R. Jose, as we have learnt: IF ONE RECITES THE SHEMA' WITHOUT HEARING WHAT HE SAYS, HE HAS PERFORMED HIS OBLIGATION. R. JOSE SAYS: HE HAS NOT PERFORMED HIS OBLIGATION. Now R. Jose holds that he has not performed his obligation only in the case of the recital of the *Shema'*, which is Scriptural, but the setting aside of *terumah,* [is forbidden] only on account of the blessing, and blessings are an ordinance of the Rabbis,[3] and the validity of the act does not depend upon the blessing. But why should you say that this[4] is R. Jose's opinion? Perhaps it is R. Judah's opinion, and he holds that in the case of the recital of the *Shema'* also, it is valid only if the act is done, but it should not be done in the first instance, and the proof of this is that he states, IF ONE RECITES, which implies, if done, it is done, but it should not be done in the first instance?—The answer is: The reason why it says, IF ONE RECITES, is to show you how far R. Jose is prepared to go, since he says that even if it is done it is not valid. For as to R. Judah, he holds that even if he does it in the first instance he has performed his obligation. Now what is your conclusion? That it is the opinion of R. Jose. What then of this which we have learnt: A man should not say the grace after meals mentally, but if he does so he has performed his obligation. Whose opinion is this? It is neither R. Jose's nor R. Judah's. For it cannot be R. Judah's, since he said that even if he does so in the first instance he has performed his obligation; nor can it be R. Jose's, since he says that even if done
b it is not valid![1] What must we say then? That it is R. Judah's opinion, and he holds that it is valid only if done but it should not be done in the first instance. But what of this which was taught by R. Judah the son of R. Simeon b. Pazzi: A deaf man who can speak but not hear may set aside *terumah* in the first instance. Whose view does this follow? It can be neither R. Judah's nor R. Jose's. For as for R. Judah, he says that it is valid only if done but it should not be done in the first instance; while R. Jose says that even if done it is not valid! In fact it follows R. Judah's view, and he holds that it may be done even in the first instance, and there is no contradiction [between the two views attributed to him], one being his own and the other that of his teacher, as we have learnt: R. Judah said in the name of R. Eleazar b. Azariah: When one recites the *Shema'*, he must let himself hear what he says,[2] as it says, '*Hear, O Israel, the Lord our God, the Lord is one*'. Said R. Meir to him: Behold it says, '*Which I command thee this day upon thy heart':* on the intention of the heart depends the validity of the words.[3] If you come so far, you may even say that R. Judah agreed with his teacher, and there is no contradiction: one statement[4] gives R. Meir's view, the other R. Judah's.

We have learnt elsewhere:[5] All are qualified to read the *Megillah*[6] except a deaf-mute, an imbecile and a minor; R. Judah declares a minor qualified. Who is it that declares the act of a deaf-mute,
c even if done, to be invalid?[1] R. Mattena says: It is R. Jose, as we have learnt: IF ONE RECITES THE SHEMA' WITHOUT HEARING WHAT HE SAYS, HE HAS PERFORMED HIS OBLIGATION. SO R. JUDAH. R. JOSE SAYS: HE HAS NOT PERFORMED HIS OBLIGATION. But why should we say that the above statement [regarding a deaf-mute] follows R. Jose, and that the act even if done is invalid?

(2) Ps. XXVI, 6. (3) Raba apparently stresses the order of the words in the original, and renders: I will (do the equivalent) of bathing in purity [by washing] my hands. (4) Lit., 'wipe'. (5) And so delayed to say his prayers.

a (1) I.e., with the sections in the wrong order. (2) Because he cannot hear the blessing which he has to say over the action. (3) V. Pes. 7. (4) That a deaf man should not set aside *terumah.*

b (1) Since grace after meals is a Scriptural injunction. (2) I.e., in the first instance, but the act if done is valid. (3) Hence even in the first instance the act is valid. (4) That of R. Judah son of R. Simeon b. Pazzi. (5) Meg. 1*b.* (6) V. Glos.

c (1) The questioner assumes this to be the intention of the statement just quoted.

גמרא

ˣיפנה ויטול ידיו ויניח תפילין ויקרא ק"ש ויתפלל וזו היא מלכות שמים שלימה א"ר חייא בר אבא א"ר יוחנן כל הנפנה ונוטל ידיו ומניח תפילין וקורא ק"ש ומתפלל מעלה עליו הכתוב כאלו בנה מזבח והקריב עליו קרבן דכתיב °ארחץ בנקיון כפי ואסובבה את מזבחך ה' א"ל רבא לא סבר לה מר כאלו טבל דכתיב ארחץ [בנקיון] ולא כתיב ארחיץ [כפי] א"ל רבינא לרבא חזי מר האי צורבא מדרבנן דאתא ממערבא ואמר ˣמי שאין לו מים לרחוץ ידיו מקנח ידיו בעפר ובצרור ובקסמית א"ל שפיר קאמר מי כתיב ארחץ במים בנקיון כתיב כל מידי דמנקי דהא *רב הסדא *לייט אמאן דמהדר אמיא בעידן צלותא והני מילי לק"ש ˣאבל לתפלה מיהדר ועד כמה עד פרסה *והני מילי לקמיה אבל לאחוריה אפילו מיל אינו חוזר [ומינה] מיל הוא דאינו חוזר הא פחות ממיל חוזר: **מתני'** *ˣהקורא את שמע ולא השמיע לאזנו *יצא *ר' יוסי אומר לא יצא ˣקרא ולא דקדק באותיותיה ר' יוסי אמר יצא ר' יהודה אומר לא יצא ˣהקורא למפרע לא יצא קרא וטעה יחזור למקום שטעה: **גמ'** *מאי טעמא דר' יוסי משום דכתיב שמע השמיע לאזנך מה שאתה מוצא מפיך ותנא קמא סבר שמע בכל לשון שאתה שומע ורבי יוסי תרתי שמע מינה: תנן *התם ˣחרש המדבר ואינו שומע לא יתרום ואם תרם תרומתו תרומה מאן תנא חרש המדבר ואינו שומע דיעבד אין לכתחלה לא אמר רב חסדא רבי יוסי היא דתנן הקורא את שמע ולא השמיע לאזנו יצא דברי ר' יהודה ר' יוסי אומר לא יצא עד כאן לא קאמר רבי יוסי לא יצא אלא גבי ק"ש דאורייתא אבל תרומה משום ברכה הוא וברכה דרבנן ולא בברכה תליא מילתא וממאי דר' יוסי היא דילמא ר' יהודה היא ואמר גבי ק"ש נמי דיעבד אין לכתחלה לא תדע דקתני הקורא דיעבד אין לכתחלה לא אמרי האי דקתני הקורא להודיעך כחו דר' יוסי דאמר דיעבד נמי לא *דאי ר' יהודה אפילו לכתחלה נמי יצא במאי אוקימתא כרבי יוסי ואלא הא דתניא *לא יברך אדם ברכת המזון בלבו ואם ברך יצא מני לא ר' יוסי ולא ר' יהודה דאי ר' יהודה הא אמר לכתחלה נמי יצא אי רבי יוסי דיעבד נמי לא אלא מאי ר' יהודה ודיעבד אין לכתחלה לא אלא הא דתני ר' יהודה בריה דר"ש בן פזי חרש המדבר ואינו שומע תורם לכתחלה מני לא ר' יהודה ולא ר' יוסי אי ר' יהודה הא אמר דיעבד אין לכתחלה לא אי רבי יוסי הא אמר דיעבד נמי לא אלא לעולם ר' יהודה ואפילו לכתחלה נמי ולא קשיא הא דידיה הא דרביה *דתנן ר' יהודה אומר משום ר"א בן עזריה הקורא את שמע צריך שישמיע לאזנו שנאמר °שמע ישראל ה' אלהינו ה' אחד א"ל ר' מאיר הרי הוא אומר אשר אנכי מצוך היום על לבבך אחר כונת הלב הן הן הדברים השתא דאתית להכי אפילו תימא ר' יהודה כרביה ס"ל ולא קשיא הא ר"מ הא ר' יהודה: תנן *התם ˣהכל כשרים לקרות את המגילה חוץ מחש"ו ור' יהודה מכשיר בקטן מאן תנא חרש דיעבד נמי לא אמר רב מתנה ר' יוסי היא דתנן הקורא את שמע ולא השמיע לאזנו יצא דברי ר' יהודה רבי יוסי אומר לא יצא ממאי דרבי יוסי היא ודיעבד נמי לא

דילמא

רש"י

יפנה. לנקביו: דכתיב ארחץ בנקיון. משמע לרחוץ כל הגוף ולא כתיב ארחיץ כפי לדרשה אתא לומר שמעלה עליו שכר רחיצת כפים כאלו טבל כל גופו: קיסמית. קיסם: לק"ש. בעידנא דק"ש שזמנו קבוע פן יעבור הזמן: אבל לתפלה. דכל היום זמנה הוא לריך למהדר אמיא:

מתני' ולא דקדק באותיותיה. לפרשן יפה בשפתיו:

גמ' תרתי ש"מ. כי דרשת נמי שמע בכל לשון שאתה שומע ש"מ נמי דלריך להשמיע לאזנו: לא יתרום. לפי שאינו שומע הברכה שהוא מברך עליה: מאן תנא כו'. לא יצא. אפילו בדיעבד הכי מילי כו': ברכה דרבנן היא. דאמור רבנן (פסחים דף ז:) כל המלות כלן מברך עליהן עובר לעשייתן: וממאי דר' יוסי היא. קס"ד האי דמוקמת לה כר' יוסי משום דסבירא לן דר' יהודה לכתחלה נמי מכשיר: דילמא רבי יהודה היא. וק"ש נמי דיעבד אין לכתחלה לא הכי גרסינן ול"ג אפילו: משום ר' יוסי. להודיעך כחו דאפילו דיעבד נמי לא יצא: בלבו. שלא השמיע לאזנו: ואי רבי יוסי דיעבד נמי לא. דהא ברכת המזון דאורייתא היא ואכלת ושבעת וברכת (דברים ח): אלא מאי ר' יהודה. וק"ש דיעבד אין לכתחלה לא והא דתרומה וברכת המזון דר' יהודה: אלא ר"י. לכתחלה קאמר והא דרבי יהודה בריה דר"ש בן פזי ר' יהודה היא ודתרומה ר' יוסי היא ומודה הוא דברכות דרבנן דיעבד שפיר דמי והא דברכת המזון ר' יהודה היא משניה דרביה ר' אלעזר בן עזריה דאומר לריך שישמיע לאזנו וכל לריך לכתחלה משמע הא דיעבד שפיר דמי: אחר כונת הלב כו'. ואפילו לכתחלה נמי אין לריך: השתא דאתית להכי. דאשמעת לן פלוגתא דר' מאיר: אפי' תימא רבי יהודה. דאמר בק"ש נמי יצא דיעבד אין לכתחלה לא והא דברכת המזון ודתרומה ר' יהודה היא ודקא קשיא לך דר' יהודה בריה דר"ש בן פזי מני רבי מאיר היא דמכשיר לכתחלה: מאן תנא חרש דיעבד נמי לא. דקתני גבי שוטה: לא יצא. דיעבד הוא: וממאי. דחוץ מחרש דקאמר דיעבד הוא ור' יוסי היא דפסיל דיעבד: ולכתחלה הוא דלא הא דיעבד שפיר דמי. ובהא איכא למימר דאפילו רבי יהודה מודה דלא שמעי' דפליג בק"ש אלא דיעבד:

מדפיפא

תוספות

אמאן דמהדר אמיא בעידן ק"ש. ויש ספרים דגרסי הכי מילי לק"ש אבל לתפלה לא דקאמר רשב"ל (פסחים ד' מו.) לגבל ולתפלה ד' מילין ונראה דלא גרסינן ליה דהוא הדין לענין צלותא נמי מטעם שלא יעבור זמן תפלה דמ"ש ק"ש מתפלה וגם יש לקמן בפרק מי שמתו (ד' כב.) בטלה נטילותא כדרב חסדא דלייט אמאן דמהדר אמיא בעידן צלותא ומדלא הזכיר שם ק"ש משמע דבכל ענין מותר והיא דרשב"ל דאמר ולתפלה ד' מילין פירש רש"י להתפלל שם במקום:

דילמא ר' יהודה היא. וא"ת והלא לא נזכר רבי יהודה ברישא וי"ל דפשיטא מדסיפא ר' יהודה רישא נמי ר' יהודה ופליגי במילתא דר' יהודה:

להודיעך כחו דרבי יוסי. וא"ת לשמעינן כחו דר' יהודה דכח דהתירא עדיף ויש לומר כיון דר' יהודה לא דרש השמיע לאזנך אין כאן שום חדוש ופשיטא דלכתחלה ומהיכא תיתי לאוסרו אי שרי דיעבד הוא הדין לכתחלה:

אי ר' יוסי דיעבד נמי לא. וא"ת לעולם אימא לך רבי יוסי היא וברכת המזון שאני דלא כתיב ביה שמע דבשלמא תרומה דלעיל ומגילה דלקמן שהן מדרבנן יש לדמותם לק"ש שתקנו שלריך שישמיע לאזנו כמו בק"ש ותקנו נמי שלא יצא כמו בק"ש אבל בברכת המזון שהיא מדאורייתא כיון דלא כתיב ביה שמע למה יש לנו לתקן שלא יצא אם לא השמיע לאזנו כיון דמן התורה יצא וי"ל כיון שתקנו שלריך להשמיע לאזנו כמו בק"ש הואיל ומדרבנן מיהא לריך להשמיע אין לחלק בין ק"ש ובין ברכת המזון דאפילו בדיעבד אית לן למימר שלא יצא:

ור' יהודה מכשיר בקטן. וא"ת באיזה קטן מיירי אי בקטן שלא הגיע לחנוך הא אמרינן בפרק לאוהו ב"ד (דף כט.) שכל שאינו מחוייב בדבר אינו מוציא את הרבים ומאי טעמא דר' יהודה דמכשיר ואי בהגיע לחנוך מאי טעמייהו דרבנן דאסרי הרי קריאת מגילה דרבנן ואמרינן קטן שהגיע לחנוך שמדרבנן כגדול ופוטר דרבנן כדאמר לקמן בפ' מי שמתו (דף כ:) דקטן מוליא אביו שלא אכל אלא כזית דהיינו דרבנן וי"ל שאני ברכת המזון שהיא חומרא יתירא יותר מדאורייתא' ובקל כפטרים מתכה כדאמרינן לקמן (שם) והם החמירו על עלמם או בכזית או בכביצה אי נמי התם ליכא בקטן אלא חד דרבנן דמיירי שהקטן אכל כדי שביעה לכך אתי מדרבנן ומוליא דרבנן אבל הכא דגבי קטן איכא תרתי דרבנן דהמגילה דרבנן והקטן דרבנן אינו יכול להוליא היכא דליכא אלא חד דרבנן:

דילמא

מסורת הש"ס

תורה אור: °ארחץ בנקיון כפי — תהלי' כו

לקמן כב.

פסחים מו. חולין קכג.

ספרי פ' ואתחנן מגילה יט: (בירושלמי גרס ר"מ אומר יצא)

[לעיל יג.]

תרומות פ"א משנה ב

ב"ה במאי אוקימתא כרבי יוסי דאי ר"י [מגילה יט:]

[נ"ל דתניא] דברים ו

מגילה יט:

גי' רש"ל

ק"ל ד"ל יהודה

עין משפט נר מצוה

כד
א טור וש"ע א"ח סי' ג סעיף ו

כה
ב מיי' פ"ב מהל' ק"ש הל' א ופ"ד מהל' תפלה הל' ב סמג עשין יח טוש"ע א"ח סי' ד' סעיף כב וסי' לג סעיף ג ד ה ובסי' קלג סעיף ב [תיבת לייט קידושין לג: ושם נסמן]

כו
ג מיי' פ"ב מהלכות ק"ש הלכה ח סמג עשין יח טוש"ע א"ח סי' סב סעי' ג

כז
ד מיי' שם טוש"ע שם סעיף א

כח
ה מיי' שם הל' יא וסמג שם טוש"ע א"ח סימן סד סעיף א

כט
ו מיי' פ"ד מה' תרומות הלכה ד

ל
ז מיי' פ"א מה' מגילה הל' ב סמג עשין ד' טוש"ע א"ח סי' תרפט סעיף ב

דילמא ר' יהודה היא ולכתחלה הוא דלא הא דיעבד שפיר דמי לא סלקא דעתך דקתני חרש דומיא דשוטה וקטן מה שוטה וקטן דיעבד נמי לא אף חרש דיעבד נמי לא ודילמא הא כדאיתא והא כדאיתא ומי מצית לאוקמה כרבי יהודה והא מדקתני סיפא רבי יהודה מכשיר בקטן מכלל דרישא לאו רבי יהודה היא ודילמא כולה ר' יהודה היא ותרי גווני קטן וחסורי מיחסרא והכי קתני הכל כשרין לקרות את המגילה חוץ מחש"ו בד"א בקטן שלא הגיע לחנוך אבל קטן שהגיע לחינוך אפילו לכתחלה כשר דברי רבי יהודה שרבי יהודה מכשיר בקטן במאי אוקימתא כרבי יהודה ודיעבד אין לכתחלה לא אלא הא דתני רבי יהודה בריה דר"ש בן פזי חרש המדבר ואינו שומע תורם לכתחלה מני לא רבי יהודה ולא רבי יוסי אי ר' יהודה דיעבד אין לכתחלה לא אי ר' יוסי דיעבד נמי לא אלא מאי רבי יהודה ואפילו לכתחלה נמי אלא הא *דתניא לא יברך אדם ברכת המזון בלבו ואם ברך יצא מני לא ר' יהודה ולא ר' יוסי אי ר' יהודה הא אמר אפילו לכתחלה נמי ואי ר' יוסי הא אמר אפילו דיעבד נמי לא לעולם ר' יהודה היא ואפילו לכתחלה נמי ולא קשיא הא דידיה הא דרביה דתניא א"ר יהודה משום ר"א בן עזריה הקורא את שמע צריך שישמיע לאזנו שנאמר שמע ישראל א"ל ר"מ הרי הוא אומר אשר אנכי מצוך היום על לבבך אחר כונת הלב הן הן הדברים השתא דאתית להכי אפילו תימא ר"י כרביה ס"ל ולא קשיא הא ר' יהודה הא ר"מ א"ר חסדא אמר רב שילא [ה]הלכה כרבי יהודה שאמר משום ר"א בן עזריה והלכה כרבי יהודה וצריכא דאי אשמעינן הלכה כרבי יהודה הוה אמינא אפילו לכתחלה קמ"ל הלכה כרבי יהודה שאמר משום ר"א בן עזריה ואי אשמועינן הלכה כרבי יהודה שאמר משום ר"א בן עזריה הוה אמינא *צריך ואין לו תקנה קמ"ל הלכה כרבי יהודה אמר רב יוסף מחלוקת בק"ש אבל בשאר מצות דברי הכל לא יצא דכתיב °הסכת ושמע ישראל מיתיבי לא יברך אדם ברכת המזון בלבו ואם ברך יצא אלא אי אתמר הכי אתמר אמר רב יוסף מחלוקת בק"ש דכתיב שמע ישראל [ב]אבל בשאר מצות דברי הכל יצא והכתיב הסכת ושמע ישראל ההוא בדברי תורה כתיב: קרא ולא דקדק באותיותיה: א"ר טבי א"ר יאשיה הלכה כדברי שניהם להקל וא"ר טבי א"ר יאשיה *מ"ד °שלש הנה לא תשבענה שאול ועוצר רחם וכי מה ענין שאול אצל רחם אלא לומר לך מה רחם מכנים ומוציא אף שאול מכנים ומוציא והלא דברים ק"ו ומה רחם שמכניסין בו בחשאי מוציאין ממנו בקולי קולות שאול שמכניסין בו בקולי קולות אינו דין שמוציאין ממנו בקולי קולות מכאן תשובה לאומרים אין תחיית המתים מן התורה: תני ר' אושעיא קמיה דרבא וכתבתם הכל בכתב אפילו צואות א"ל דאמר לך מני *ר' יהודה היא דאמר גבי סוטה אלות כותב צואות אינו כותב והתם הוא דכתיב °וכתב את האלות האלה אבל הכא דכתיב וכתבתם אפילו צואות נמי אטו טעמיה דר"י משום דכתיב וכתב *טעמיה דר' יהודה משום דכתיב אלות אלות אין צואות לא אצטריך סד"א נילף כתיבה כתיבה מהתם מה התם אלות אין צואות לא אף הכא נמי צואות לא כתב רחמנא וכתבתם אפילו צואות: תני רב עובדיה קמיה דרבא ולמדתם [ג]שיהא למודך תם שיתן ריוח בין הדבקים ענִי רבא בתריה כגון *על לבבך על לבבכם בכל לבבך בכל לבבכם עשב בשדך ואבדתם מהרה הכנף פתיל אתכם מארץ א"ר חמא ברבי חנינא [ד]כל הקורא ק"ש ומדקדק באותיותיה מצננין לו גיהנם שנאמר °בפרש שדי מלכים בה תשלג בצלמון אל תקרי בפרש אלא בפרש אל תקרי בצלמון אלא בצלמות: ואמר רבי חמא בר חנינא למה נסמכו אהלים

תורה אור: דברים כז — משלי ל — במדבר ה — תהלים סח

תוספות

דילמא רבי יהודה וחסורי מחסרא וכו'. תימה דאין זה בשום מקום דקאמר חסורי מחסרא ולאוקמי אליבא דחד תנא ועוד לוקמיה כר' יוסי ובלא חסורי מחסרא וי"ל משום דלקמן פסקינן כרבי יהודה לכך ניחא לאוקמיה אליבא דרבי יהודה:

אבל בשאר מצות יצא. וא"ת הא לעיל אמר דשאר מצות ילפינן מק"ש כגון תרומה ומגילה וברכת המזון וי"ל דרב יוסף פליג אסוגיא דלעיל:

בין הדבקים. *רב אלפס מוסיף כגון וחרה אף דאם לא יתן ריוח אז נראה כמו וחרף וכן מוסיף ולמדתם אותו וזכרתם את ועשיתם את שצריך ליתן ריוח בין מם שבסוף תיבה לאלף שבתחלת תיבה לאחריה וכן צריך להתיז זיי"ן של תזכרו שלא ישמיע שי"ן למען שיהיה לנו שכר מצות ואין לנו לעשות על מנת לקבל פרס:

רש"י

מדסיפא רבי יהודה. דקתני רבי יהודה מכשיר בקטן: ודילמא כולה ר' יהודה היא. וחסורי מחסרא והכי קתני הכל כשרין לקרות את המגילה חוץ מחש"ו. והא כדאיתא והא כדאיתא: בד"א. דקטן לכתחלה לא בקטן שלא הגיע לחנוך אבל הגיע לחנוך אפילו לכתחלה שרי הגיע לחנוך מצות כגון בן תשע ובן עשר כדאמרינן ביומא פרק בתרא (דף פב.): במאי אוקימתא. למתניתין דמגילה: כרבי יהודה. ואשמעת לן דכי אומר רבי יהודה בק"ש יצא דיעבד קאמר ולא לכתחלה: אלא הא דתני כו' תורם. ואע"פ שהוא צריך לברך ואין אזניו שומעות מה: אלא מאי. בעית למימר דר' יהודה היא דק"ש אפילו לכתחלה קאמר כי היכי דתיקו הא דר' יהודה בריה דר' שמעון בן פזי אליביה והאי דאפליגו בדיעבד להודיעך כחו דר' יוסי: אלא הא דתניא כו' מני: לעולם רבי יהודה אפי' לכתחלה מכשיר. ודמגלה ר' יוסי היא ואפילו דיעבד נמי פסול והא דתורם לכתחלה ר' יהודה והא דברכת המזון דרביה הוא דא"ר יהודה משום רבי אלעזר בן עזריה צריך להשמיע לאזנו והאי לישנא לכתחלה משמע אבל דיעבד יצא: השתא דאתי' להכי. דאשמועתן הא פלוגתא דר' מאיר: אפילו תימא ר' יהודה. דאמר בק"ש יצא דיעבד אין לכתחלה לא ומתניתין דמגילה לכתחלה היא דפסלה לחרש ורבי יהודה היא והא דברכת המזון נמי ר' יהודה היא ודקא קשיא לך הא דרבי יהודה בריה דר"ש בן פזי מני ר"מ היא דמכשיר לכתחלה: הלכה כרבי יהודה. דק"ש שלא השמיע לאזנו יצא: הוה אמינא. דר' יהודה לכתחלה נמי אמר והאי דאפלוג דיעבד משום דר' יוסי: ואין לו תקנה. אפילו בדיעבד: בשאר מצות. בכל הברכות: ההוא. הסכת ושמע בדברי תורה כתיב כדאמרינן בפרק הרואה (ד' סג:) כתתו עצמכם על דברי תורה: ולא דקדק. שמגמגם: הלכה כדברי שניהם להקל. הלכה כר' יהודה דלא בעי שמיעה והלכה כר' יוסי דלא בעי דקדוק: שאול ועוצר רחם. פסוק הוא בספר משלי שלש הנה לא תשבענה: רחם מכנים. הזרע ומוציא הולד: שאול. קבר: שמכניסין בו בקולי קולות. של בכי ומספד: וכתבתם. שתהא כתיבה תמה ושלימה: ואפי' הצואות. שבפרשה כגון וקשרתם וכתבתם צריך לכתוב בתפילין ומזוזות: דאמר לך מני. הא דאצטריך ליה קרא לרבות צואות לכתיבה: ר' יהודה היא. דשמעינן גבי כתיבת פרשת סוטה משום דלא כתיב ביה וכתבתם אלא וכתב דאמר אלות אין צואות לא כגון והשביע אותה הכהן ואמר הכהן דתנן (סוטה ד' יז.) רבי יהודה אומר כל עצמו אינו כותב אלא יתן ה' אותך לאלה ולשבועה: משום אלה הוא. דמשמע מעוטא הא לא כתיב מעוטא הוה משמע כולה מלתא מוכתב והכא דליכא מעוטא למה ליה לרבוייהו מוכתבתם: בין הדבקים. תיבות המודבקות זו בזו אם אינו מפרידן כשהתיבה השניה מתחלת באות שהתיבה שלפניה נגמרת הוא קורא אותם שני אותיות באות אחת אם אינו מתעסק ליתן ריוח ביניהם כדמפרש רבא: בפרש שדי. אם תפרש שדי ותבדיל תיבות של מלכות שמים מלכים בה תשלג *בצלמון התורה אשר בה מלכים ימלוכו תשלג ותלבן לך את צל המות: אהלים

עין משפט נר מצוה

לא
א מיי' פ"ב מהל' ק"ש הלכה ח סמג עשין יח טוש"ע א"ח סימן סב סעי' ג [ברב אלפס שלפנינו ליתא אך דזיי"ן של תזכרו בשם הירוש' אמנם ברא"ש ובטור סימן סא אי' כל זה וכתב הב"י שכ"כ ה"ר יונה בספר היראה ע"ש]

לב
ב מיי' פ"א מהל' ברכות הלכה ז סמג עשין כז טוש"ע א"ח סי' קפ"ה סעי' ב ובסי' רו סעי' ג

לג
ג מיי' פ"ב מהלכות ק"ש הלכה ט סמג עשין יח טוש"ע א"ח סי' סב סעי' כ

לד
ד מיי' שם שם סעי' כג

מסורת הש"ס

[מגיל' יט:]

[עירובין מה. יומא סא: יבמות ע. גיטין מ. נזיר מו: הוריו' ח. וע' גיטין עו.]

חלק לב.

[סוטה יז.]

[ע"ש בסוטה היטיב]

[הנך הם שלא כמדקדק ובצלמות כמלאים כמדקדק]

[בערוך ערך פרש ביאר הענין באופן אחר ע"ש]

(5) Deut. XI, 19. (6) *We-limmadetem* (and you shall train them) is read as *we-limmud tam* (and the teaching shall be perfect); cf. n. b10. (7) I.e., not running together two words of which the first ends and the second begins with the same letter. The expression is from I Kings XXII, 34. (8) Ps. LXVIII, 15.

[15b] Perhaps it follows R. Judah, and while the act may not be done [only] in the first instance, yet if done it is valid?—Do not imagine such a thing. For the statement puts a deaf-mute on the same level as an imbecile and a minor, [implying that] just as in the case of an imbecile and a minor the act if done is not valid,[2] so in the case of a deaf-mute the act if done is not valid. But perhaps each case has its own rule?[3]—But [even if so] can you construe this statement as following R. Judah? Since the later clause[4] says that 'R. Judah declares it valid', may we not conclude that the earlier clause does not follow R. Judah?—Perhaps the whole statement follows R. Judah, and two kinds of minor are referred to, and there is a lacuna, and the whole should read thus: All are qualified to read the *Megillah* except a deaf-mute, an imbecile and a minor. This applies only to one who is not old enough to be trained [in the performance of the precepts].[5] But one who is old enough to be trained may perform the act even in the first instance. This is the ruling of R. Judah: for R. Judah declares a minor qualified. How have you construed the statement? As following R. Judah, and that the act is valid only if done but should not be done in the first instance. But then what of that which R. Judah the son of R. Simeon b. Pazzi taught, that a deaf person who can speak but not hear may set aside *terumah* in the first instance—which authority does this follow? It is neither R. Judah nor R. Jose! For if it is R. Judah, he says that the act is valid only if done, but it may not be done in the first instance; and if R. Jose, he says that even if done it is not valid!—What then do you say, that the authority is R. Judah and that the act may be done even in the first instance? What then of this which has been taught: A man should not say the grace after meals mentally, but if he does so he has performed his obligation? Whose opinion is this? It can be neither R. Judah's nor R. Jose's. For as to R. Judah, he has said that it may be done even in the first instance, and as to R. Jose, he has said that even if done it is not valid!—In truth it is the opinion of R. Judah, and the act may be done even in the first instance, and there is no contradiction between his two statements; in one case he is giving his own view, in the other that of his teacher, as it has been taught: R. Judah said in the name of R. Eleazar b. Azariah: One who recites the *Shema'* must let his ear hear what he says, as it says, *'Hear, O Israel'*. Said R. Meir to him: *'Which I command thee this day upon thy heart'*, indicating that the words derive their validity from the attention of the heart. Now that you have come so far, you may even say that R. Judah was of the same opinion as his teacher, and still there is no contradiction: one statement gives the view of R. Judah, the other that of R. Meir.

R. Ḥisda said in the name of R. Shila: The *halachah* is as laid down by R. Judah in the name of R. Eleazar b. Azariah, and the *halachah* is as laid down by R. Judah. Both these statements are necessary. For if we had been told only that the *halachah* is as stated by R. Judah I might have thought that the act may be done even in the first instance. We are therefore informed that the *halachah* is as laid down by R. Judah in the name of R. Eleazar b. Azariah. And if we had been told that the *halachah* is as laid down by R. Judah in the name of R. Eleazar b. Azariah, I might have thought that the act must [be performed thus] and if not
a there is no remedy.[1] We are therefore informed that the *halachah* is as stated by R. Judah.

R. Joseph said: The difference of opinion relates only to the recital of the *Shema'*, but in the case of other religious acts all agree that he has not performed his obligation [if he says the
b formula inaudibly], as it is written, *attend and hear, O Israel.*[1] An objection was raised: A man should not say grace after meals mentally, but if he does he has performed his obligation!—Rather, if this statement was made it was as follows: R. Joseph said: The difference of opinion relates only to the *Shema'*, since it is written, *'Hear O Israel'*; but in regard to all the other religious acts, all are agreed that he performs his obligation. But it is written, *'Attend and hear, O Israel'?*—That [text] applies only to words of Torah.[2]

IF ONE RECITED WITHOUT PRONOUNCING THE LETTERS DISTINCTLY. R. Tabi said in the name of R. Josiah: The *halachah* in both cases follows the more lenient authority.[3]

R. Tabi further said in the name of R. Josiah: What is meant by the text, *There are three things which are never satisfied, ... the grave and the barren womb?*[4] How comes the grave next to the womb? It is to teach you that just as the womb takes in and gives forth again, so the grave takes in and will give forth again. And have we not here a conclusion *a fortiori*: if the womb which takes in silently gives forth with loud noise,[5] does it not stand to reason that the grave which takes in with loud noise[6] will give forth with loud noise? Here is a refutation of those who deny that resurrection is taught in the Torah.[7]

R. Oshaia taught in the presence of Raba: *And thou shalt write them:*[8] the whole section must be written [in the *mezuzah*[9] and *tefillin*], even the commands.[10] He said to him: From whom do you learn this?[11] This is the opinion of R. Judah, who said with
c reference to the *soṭah*:[1] He writes the imprecation but not the commands. [And you argue that] this is the rule in that case, since it is written, *And he shall write these curses,*[2] but here, since it is written, *'and thou shalt write them'*, even the commands are included. But is R. Judah's reason because it is written, *'and he shall write'?* [Surely] R. Judah's reason is because it is written, *'curses'*, which implies, curses he is to write but not commands![3]—It was still necessary.[4] You might have thought that we should draw an analogy between the 'writing' mentioned here and the 'writing' mentioned there, and that just as there he writes curses but not commands, so here he should not write commands. Therefore the All-Merciful wrote *'and thou shalt write them'*, implying, commands also.

R. Obadiah recited in the presence of Raba: *'And ye shall teach them'*:[5] as much as to say thy teaching must be faultless[6] by making a pause 'between the joints'.[7] For instance, said Raba, supplementing his words *'Al lebabeka* [upon thy heart], *'al lebabekem* [upon your heart], *Bekol lebabeka* [with all thy heart], *bekol lebabekem* [with all your heart], *'eseb be-sadeka* [grass in thy field], *wa-'abaddetem meherah* [and ye shall perish speedily], *ha-kanaf pesil* [the corner a thread], *etthkem me-erez* [you from the land]. R. Ḥama b. Ḥanina said: If one in reciting the *Shema'* pronounces the letters distinctly, hell is cooled for him, as it says, *When the Almighty scattereth kings therein, it snoweth in Zalmon.*[8] Read not *be-fares* [when he scattereth] but *be-faresh* [when one pronounces distinctly], and read not *be-ẓalmon* [in Zalmon] but *be-zalmaweth* [in the shadow of death].

R. Ḥama b. Ḥanina further said: Why are 'tents' mentioned

(2) This is deduced in respect of a minor from the fact that he is mentioned in conjunction with an imbecile. (3) I.e., we do not put a deaf-mute on the same footing as an imbecile, although they are mentioned in conjunction. (4) In the passage cited from Meg. (5) I.e., up to nine or ten years old; v. Yoma 82a.

a (1) I.e., even if done, it is not valid.

b (1) Deut. XXVII, 9. E.V. *'Keep silence and hear'*. (2) As explained *infra* 63b. (3) I.e., R. Judah in the matter of audibility, and R. Jose in the matter of pronouncing distinctly. (4) Prov. XXX, 15, 16. (5) The crying of the child. (6) The wailing of the mourners. (7) V. Sanh. 92a. (8) Deut. VI, 9. (9) V. Glos. (10) I.e., the words *'and thou shalt write them, and thou shalt bind them'*. This is derived from וּכְתַבְתָּם being interpreted as וּכְתַבתּם, a complete writing. (11) That a special text is required to include the writing of the commands.

c (1) The woman suspected of adultery, v. Num. V, 11ff. (2) Num. V, 23. (3) And but for that implied limitation the expression 'he shall *write*' by itself would have included commands. (4) To appeal to the exposition based on וכתבתם.

[16*a*] alongside of 'streams' as it says, [*How goodly are thy tents, O*
a *Jacob . . .*][1] *as streams*[2] *stretched out, as gardens by the river side, as aloes planted*[3] etc.? To tell you that, just as streams bring a man up from a state of uncleanness to one of cleanness, so tents[4] bring a man up from the scale of guilt to the scale of merit.

IF ONE RECITES IT BACKWARD, HE HAS NOT PERFORMED HIS OBLIGATION etc. R. Ammi and R. Assi were once decorating the bridal chamber for R. Eleazar. He said to them: In the meantime I will go and pick up something from the House of Study and come back and tell you. He went and found a Tanna reciting before R. Joḥanan: If [reciting the *Shema'*] one [recollects that] he made a mistake but does not know where, if he is in the middle of a section he should go back to the beginning; if he is in doubt which section he has said, he should go back to the first break;[5] if he is in doubt which writing[6] he is on, he goes back to the first one. Said R. Joḥanan to him: This rule applies only where he has not yet got to '*In order that your days may be prolonged*', but if he has got to '*In order that your days may be prolonged*', then [he can assume that] force of habit has kept him right.[7] He came and told them, and they said to him, If we had come only to hear this, it would have been worth our while.

MISHNAH. WORKMEN MAY RECITE [THE SHEMA'] ON THE TOP OF A TREE OR THE TOP OF A SCAFFOLDING, A THING THEY ARE NOT ALLOWED TO DO IN THE CASE OF THE TEFILLAH. A BRIDEGROOM IS EXEMPT FROM THE RECITAL OF THE SHEMA' FROM THE FIRST NIGHT UNTIL THE END OF THE SABBATH, IF HE HAS NOT CONSUMMATED THE MARRIAGE.[8] IT HAPPENED WITH R. GAMALIEL THAT WHEN HE MARRIED HE RECITED THE SHEMA' ON THE FIRST NIGHT: SO HIS DISCIPLES SAID TO HIM: OUR MASTER, YOU HAVE TAUGHT US THAT A BRIDEGROOM IS EXEMPT FROM THE RECITAL OF THE SHEMA'. HE REPLIED TO THEM: I WILL NOT LISTEN TO YOU TO REMOVE FROM MYSELF THE KINGSHIP OF HEAVEN EVEN FOR A MOMENT.

GEMARA. Our Rabbis taught: Workmen may recite [the *Shema'*] on the top of a tree or on the top of a scaffolding, and they may say the *tefillah*, on the top of an olive tree and the top
b of a fig tree,[1] but from all other trees they must come down to the ground before saying the *tefillah*, and the employer must in any case come down before saying the *tefillah*,[2] the reason in all cases being that their mind is not clear.[3] R. Mari the son of the daughter of Samuel[4] pointed out to Rab a contradiction. We have learnt, he said: WORKMEN MAY RECITE [THE SHEMA'] ON THE TOP OF A TREE OR THE TOP OF A SCAFFOLDING which would show that the recital does not require *kawanah*.[5] Contrast with this: When one recites the *Shema'*, it is incumbent that he should concentrate his attention[6] on it, since it says, '*Hear, O Israel*', and in another place it says, *Pay attention and hear, O Israel*,[7] showing that just as in the latter 'hearing' must be accompanied by attention, so here it must be accompanied by attention. He gave no reply. Then he said to him: Have you heard any statement on this point?—He replied: Thus said R. Shesheth: This is the case only if they stop from their work to recite. But it has been taught: Beth Hillel say that they may go on with their work while reciting?—There is no contradiction. The former statement refers to the first section, the latter to the second section [of the *Shema'*].

Our Rabbis taught: Labourers working for an employer recite the *Shema'* and say blessings before it and after it and eat their crust and say blessings before it and after it, and say the *tefillah* of eighteen benedictions, but they do not go down before the
c ark[1] nor do they raise their hands [to give the priestly benediction].[2] But it has been taught: [They say] a *resumé* of the eighteen benedictions?[3]—Said R. Shesheth: There is no contradiction: one statement gives the view of R. Gamaliel, the other of R. Joshua.[4] But if R. Joshua is the authority, why does it say 'labourers'? The same applies to anyone!—In fact, both statements represent the view of R. Gamaliel, and still there is no contradiction: one refers to [labourers] working for a wage, and the other to [those] working for their keep;[5] and so it has been taught: Labourers working for an employer recite the *Shema'* and say the *tefillah* and eat their crust without saying a blessing before it, but they say two blessings after it, namely, [he says] the first blessing[6] right through[7] and the second blessing he begins with the blessing for the land, including 'who buildest Jerusalem' in the blessing[8] for the land. When does this hold good? For those who work for a wage. But those who work for their keep or who eat in the company of the employer say the grace right through.[6]

A BRIDEGROOM IS EXEMPT FROM RECITING THE SHEMA'.[9] Our Rabbis taught: '*When thou sittest in thy house*': this excludes one engaged in the performance of a religious duty. '*And when thou walkest by the way*': this excludes a bridegroom. Hence they deduced the rule that one who marries a virgin is exempt, while one who marries a widow is not exempt. How is this derived?—R. Papa said: [The sitting in the house] is compared to the way: just as the way is optional, so here it must be optional. But are we not dealing [in the words '*walkest by the way*'] with one who goes to perform a religious duty, and even so the All-Merciful said that he should recite?—If that were so, the text should say, 'in going'. What is meant by 'in *thy* going'? This teaches that it is in thy going that thou art under obligation, and in the going

a (1) V. Tosaf., s.v. אהלים. (2) E.V. 'valleys'. (3) Num. XXIV, 5, 6. (4) Where the Torah is studied. (5) I.e., to '*and it shall come to pass*'. (6) I.e., '*and thou shalt write them*' in the first section or '*and ye shall write*' in the second. (7) Lit., 'he has taken his usual course'. (8) Lit., 'performed the act'.

b (1) These trees have thick branches which afford a firm foothold. (2) Seeing that he is not bound to work. (3) To concentrate on their prayers, from anxiety lest they may fall. (4) His mother was carried away captive and he was not born in lawful wedlock, and therefore his father's name is not mentioned. (Rashi). V. Keth. 23*a*. (5) V. Glos. (6) Lit., 'direct his heart'. (7) V. *supra*, 15*b*, n. b1.

c (1) I.e., act as reader to a congregation. (2) Because this would rob their employer of too much of their time. (3) V. *P.B.* p. 55. (4) *Infra*, 28*b*. (5) Those who work for a wage have less time to spare. (6) V. *P.B.* p. 280. (7) Lit., 'as arranged'. (8) The benedictions beginning with 'We thank thee' (ibid.) and 'And rebuild Jerusalem' (p. 282) are condensed into one. (9) For notes on this passage, v. *supra* 11*a*.

תורה אור

אהלים לנחלים דכתיב °כנחלים נטיו כגנות עלי נהר כאהלים נטע וגו' לומר לך מה נחלים מעלין את האדם מטומאה לטהרה אף אהלים מעלין את האדם מכף חובה לכף זכות: הקורא למפרע לא יצא וכו': רבי אמי ורבי אסי הוו קא קטרין ליה גננא לרבי אלעזר אמר להו אדהכי והכי איזיל ואשמע מלתא דבי מדרשא ואיתי ואימא לכו אזל אשכחי' לתנא דקתני קמיה דר' יוחנן *אקרא וטעה *ואינו יודע להיכן טעה באמצע הפרק יחזור *לראש בין פרק לפרק יחזור לפרק ראשון בין כתיבה לכתיבה יחזור לכתיבה ראשונה אמר ליה ר' יוחנן לא שנו אלא שלא פתח בלמען ירבו ימיכם אבל פתח בלמען ירבו ימיכם סרכיה נקט ואתי אתא ואמר להו אמרו ליה *אלו לא באנו אלא לשמוע דבר זה דיינו: **מתני'** בהאומנין קורין בראש האילן ובראש הנדבך מה שאין רשאין לעשות כן בתפלה *גחתן פטור מק"ש לילה *הראשונה ועד מוצאי שבת אם לא עשה מעשה ומעשה בר"ג שנשא אשה וקרא לילה הראשונה אמרו לו תלמידיו *למדתנו רבינו שחתן פטור מק"ש אמר להם איני שומע לכם לבטל הימני מלכות שמים אפילו שעה אחת: **גמ'** *ת"ר האומנין קורין בראש האילן ובראש הנדבך דומתפללין בראש הזית ובראש התאנה ושאר כל האילנות יורדים למטה ומתפללין הובעל הבית בין כך ובין כך יורד למטה ומתפלל לפי שאין דעתו מיושבת עליו רמי ליה רב מרי ברה דבת שמואל לרבא תנן האומנין קורין בראש האילן ובראש הנדבך אלמא לא בעי כונה ורמינהי הקורא את שמע צריך שיכוין את לבו שנאמר שמע ישראל ולהלן הוא אומר °הסכת ושמע ישראל מה להלן בהסכת אף כאן בהסכת אשתיק א"ל מידי שמיע לך בהא א"ל הכי ואמר רב ששת והוא שבטלין ממלאכתן וקורין והתניא ב"ה אומרים עוסקין במלאכתן וקורין לא קשיא הא בפרק ראשון הא בפרק שני *ת"ר הפועלים שהיו עושין מלאכה אצל בעל הבית קורין ק"ש ומברכין לפניה ולאחריה ואוכלין פתן ומברכין לפניה ולאחריה ומתפללין תפלה של שמונה עשרה אבל אין יורדין לפני התיבה ואין נושאין כפיהם והתניא מעין י"ח אמר רב ששת לא קשיא *הא ר"ג הא ר' יהושע אי רבי יהושע מאי איריא פועלים אפילו כל אדם נמי אלא אידי ואידי ר"ג ול"ק כאן °בעושין בשכרן כאן בעושין בסעודתן והתניא הפועלים שהיו עושין מלאכה אצל בעל הבית קורין ק"ש ומתפללין ואוכלין פתן זואין מברכין לפניה אבל מברכין לאחריה שתים כיצד *חברכה ראשונה כתיקונה שניה פותח בברכת הארץ וכוללין בונה ירושלים בברכת הארץ במה דברים אמורים בעושין בשכרן אבל בעושין בסעודתן או שהיה בעל הבית מיסב עמהם מברכין כתיקונה: חתן פטור מק"ש: *ת"ר *בשבתך בביתך פרט לעוסק במצוה ובלכתך בדרך פרט לחתן מכאן אמרו הכונס את הבתולה פטור ואת האלמנה חייב מאי משמע אמר רב פפא כי דרך מה דרך רשות אף הכא נמי רשות מי לא עסקינן דקאזיל לדבר מצוה ואפילו הכי אמר רחמנא ליקרי א"כ לימא קרא בלכת מאי בלכתך שמע מינה בלכת דידך הוא דמחייבת הא דמצוה פטירת אי הכי

רש"י

אהלים לנחלים. כנחלים נטיו כאהלים נטע: אף אהלים. בתי מדרשות. אהלים לשון נטיעה נופלת בהם שנאמר ויטע אהלי אפדנו (דניאל יא): קטרין ליה גננא. קושרין לו חופה להשיאו אשה: יחזור לראש. כגון שהיה יודע שבפרק זה טעה ודלג אבל אינו יודע באיזה מקום בו טעה: בין פרק לפרק. שיודע שגמר הפרש' וצריך להתחיל פרשה אחרת ואינו יודע באיזה מהן: יחזור לפרק ראשון. להפסק ראשון והיה אם שמוע: בין כתיבה לכתיבה. שיודע שצריך לומר וכתבתם ואינו יודע אם של והיה אם שמוע אם שניה: וא"ר יוחנן. לתנא וכו': סרכיה נקט. *אין לטעות מכאן עד אמת ויציב ואין צריך לחזור אלא לאמת שהפרשה שגורה בפיו: **מתני'** האומנין. שהם עסוקים במלאכתן בראש האילן או בראש הנדבך והגיע זמן ק"ש קורין לשם מיד: נדבך. בנין של אבנים כמו נדבכין די אבן גלל (עזרא ו): מה שאין רשאין לעשות כן בתפלה. דצלות' רחמי היא ובעיא כונה הלכך אין מתפללין בראש האילן ובראש הנדבך דמסתפי דלמא נפלי דאין יכולין לעמוד שם אלא ע"י הדחק ומחמת בעתותא לא מצי מכווני: **גמ'** ומתפללין בראש הזית ובראש התאנה. בזמן שעוסקים בהן מפני שענפיה' מרובים ויכולין לעמוד שם שלא בדוחק ואין שם פחד ליפול לפיכך מתפללין בראשם אבל בשאר אילנות אין מתפללין: בין כך ובין כך. כלומר בין מתאנה בין משאר אילנות: יורד ומתפלל. דהא אינו משועבד למלאכה שהוא ברשות עצמו: לפי שאין דעתו מיושבת עליו. מבעתותו ואם הקלו אצל פועלים מפני בטול מלאכה לא הקלו אצל בעל הבית: ברה דבת שמואל. בכונה מקומות קרי ליה בר רחל ובת שמואל היתה ונשבית לבין העובדי כוכבים כדאמר בכתובות (פ"ב דף כג.) ובא עליה אחד ונתעברה הימנו ואחר כך נתגייר ושמי' איסור כדאמרי' בבבא בתרא (פ"ע ד' קמט.) רב מרי בריה הורתו שלא בקדושה הוה לכך לא היה נקרא על שם אביו: תנן האומנין קורין בראש האילן. אפי' בזמן שהן עסוקין אלמא לא בעי כונה: בטלין ממלאכתן וקורין. כדי שיהו קורין בכונה דאין להיבטל ממלאכתן: פרק א'. פרשת שמע בעיא כונה: קורין את שמע ומברכין לפניה ולאחריה. כתקונה וכן בזמן תפלה: אבל אין יורדין לפני התיבה. אין רשאין ליבטל ממלאכתן ולירד לפני התיבה לעשות שליח צבור שיש שם בטול מלאכה יותר מדאי: מעין שמונה עשרה. הביננו לדעת דרכיך כו' שכולל י"ב ברכות בברכה אחת וג' ראשונות וג' אחרונות כהלכתן: הא ר"ג הא ר' יהושע. דתנן בפרק ת"ה (דף כח:) ר"ג אומר בכל יום ויום מתפלל אדם י"ח ברכות ור' יהושע אומר מעין י"ח: עושין בשכרן. שנוטלין שכר פעולתן לבד סעודתן צריכין למהר המלאכה ומתפללין מעין י"ח: אבל עושין בסעודתן. בשביל האכילה לבדה מתפללין י"ח: והתני'. בניחותא דיש חלוק בין עושין בשכרן לעושין בסעודתן: ואין מברכין לפניה. שאינה מן התורה: אבל מברכין לאחריה. שהיא מן התורה דכתיב ואכלת ושבעת וברכת (לקמן דף מח:): וכוללין. *שני ברכות באחת שברכת הארץ ובנין ירושלים דומות: בשבתך פרט לעוסק במצוה. כבר פירשתיה בפרק ראשון [יא.]:

מתני'

תוספות

אהלים לנחלים. פי' הקונטרס דכתיב כנחלים נטיו כאהלים נטע. ולי נראה דאהלים דהאי קרא לאו לשון אהל אלא לשון בשמים אלא נראה מדסמיך מה טובו אהליך לכנחלים נטיו:

הקורא את שמע ואינו יודע להיכן טעה חוזר לראש. פי' מטעם שאינו יודע מהיכן טעה אבל היה יודע מהיכן טעה שדלג תיבה או פסוק אינו צריך לחזור אלא מאותו פסוק ואילך וכן בהלל ומגילה:

מעשה בר"ג שנשא אשה וקרא ק"ש בלילה ראשונה. לאו מעשה לסתור הוא דקמ"ל אם גדול הוא ובוטח בעצמו שיוכל להתכוין והוא רשאי ליטול את השם הרשות בידו:

לפי שאין דעתו מיושבת עליו. וא"ת תיפוק ליה משום דאמרינן לעיל (דף י:) לא יעמוד אדם במקו' גבוה ויתפלל וי"ל דהתם מיירי על גבי כסא או ספסל אבל באילן שעלה שם לעשות מלאכתו הוי כמו עלייה:

הא בפרק ראשון. לאו דוקא נקט פרק א' דהיינו אליבא דרבא ורבא אמר לעיל [יג:] פסוק ראשון לבד והכי הלכתא:

אפי' כל אדם נמי. וא"ת הא שאר כל אדם רשות ופועלים חובה וי"ל דפשיטא ליה כיון שיכול לומר מעין י"ח אין זה שום חדוש אם הפועלים אומרים אפילו לכתחלה:

*וחותם **בברכת** הארץ. אף על גב דמדאורייתא הם יש כח ביד חכמים לעקור דבר מן התור' הואיל ומרודי' במלאכת בעל הבית:

אי הכי

מסורת הש"ס

[ע' ברשב"א]

תוספתא פ"ב (ירוש' גרס יחזור בתחילה למקום הברור לו) למחלת הפרק כצ"ל

[לקמן כד: שבת מח.]

כתובות ו: (בירו' הראשון)

תוספת' פ"ב

תוספת' פ"ב

[לקמן כח:]

לקמן מו.

פ"ק יא. סוכה כה. כתובות ו. שמחות פ"ו

עין משפט נר מצוה

לה
א מיי' פ"ב מהל' ק"ש הל' י"ג יד סמ"ג עשין י"ח טוש"ע א"ח סי' סד סעי' ב ג ד

לו
ב מיי' שם הל' ד' וסמג שם טוש"ע א"ח סי' ס"ג סעי' ח

לז
ג מיי' פ"ד מהלכ' ק"ש הל' א סמ"ג שם טוש"ע א"ח סי' ע סעי' ג

לח
ד מיי' פ"ה מה' תפלה הל' ה' טוש"ע א"ח סי' ל סעי' ב

לט
ה מיי' פ"ב מה' ק"ש הל' ד' סמג שם טוש"ע א"ח סי' ס"ג סעי' ז

מ
ו מיי' פ"ב מה' ברכות הל' ב
* מיי' פ"ה מה' תפלה הל' ח [לכאור' נ"ל פותח אמנם גם הכ"מ פ"ב מה' ברכו' דין ב' העתיק דברי תוס' הללו וחותם וכו' ולכן י"ל דהי' הגי' לפניה' כמ"ש הטו' סי' קל"א שניה פותח וכו' וכולל וכו' וחותם בברכת הארץ]

מא
ח מיי' וסמ"ג שם טוש"ע א"ח סי' קלא סעי' א

[ע' תוס' סוכה כה. ד"ה בלכתך]

דברים כו

במדבר כד

עין משפט נר מצוה

סב
א מיי' פ"ד מהל' תפילין הל' יג ופ"ד מהל' אבל הל' ט' טוש"ע א"ח סי' לח סעי' ה' וי"ד סי' שפח סעי' א
סג
ב מיי' פ"ה מהל' אבילות הל' א ג סמ"ג עשין ב מד"ס טוש"ע י"ד סי' שפ"א סעי' א'
סד
ג מיי' פ"ד מהל' ק"ש הל' ז טוש"ע א"ח סי' ע סעי' ג
סה
ד מיי' פי"ב מהל' אבל הל' יב טוש"ע י"ד סי' שעו סעי' א
סו
[ה] מיי' פ"ד מה' נחלות הל' ה' טוש"ע ח"מ סי' רע"ע סעי' ה'

אי הכי מאי איריא בתולה. אי אמרת בשלמא דטעמא משום טרדא שפיר אלא מאחר שהוא תולה הטעם במצוה אלמנה נמי:

אסטנים אני. ואיכא לער אם לא היה רוחץ דאינו אסור לרחוץ בימי אבלו אלא משום תענוג וגם לחוף ראשו אי אית ליה ערבוביא ברישיה שרי אפילו תוך שבעה וכן התיר רבינו שמואל ליולדת אבלה לרחוץ תוך שבעה ולרחוץ נמי בתשעה באב וכן משמע נמי במסכת יומא (פ"ח ד' עז:) מי שיש לו חטטין בראשו סך כדרכו ביום הכפורים ואינו חושש אף על גב דסיכה כשתיה ביום כפורים וכן משמע בירושלמי אבל אסור ברחילה הדא דתימא ברחילה של תענוג אבל ברחילה שאינה של תענוג מותר כהדא דאתמר מי שיש לו חטטין ברישיה וכו':

אנינות לילה דרבנן. ואם תאמר והרי אונן נמי אינו נוהג אלא במעשר אבל לענין רחילה דאבילות דרבנן הוא ואם כן לעולם אימא לך דאנינות לילה דאורייתא הוי גבי מעשר וי"ל דאי איתא דהוי דאורייתא גבי מעשר גבי שאר דברים דרבנן נמי הוה לן למגזר דכל דתקון רבנן כעין דאורייתא תקון:

אין עומדים עליהם בשורה. דלמא אתי לאסוקי ליוחסין:

תורה אור

אי הכי מאי איריא הכונס את הבתולה אפי' כונס את האלמנה נמי הכא טריד והכא לא טריד אי משום טרדא אפי' טבעה ספינתו בים נמי אלמה *אמר רבי אבא בר זבדא אמר רב אבל חייב בכל מצות האמורות בתורה *חוץ מן התפילין שהרי נאמר בהן פאר שנאמר °פארך חבוש עליך וגו' אמרי התם טרדא (יחזקאל כד) דרשות הכא טרדא דמצוה: **מתני'** *רחץ לילה הראשון שמתה אשתו אמרו לו תלמידיו *למדתנו רבינו *[ב]שאבל אסור לרחוץ אמר להם איני כשאר בני אדם אסטנים אני *וכשמת טבי עבדו קבל עליו תנחומין אמרו לו תלמידיו *למדתנו רבינו שאין מקבלין תנחומין על העבדים אמר להם אין טבי עבדי כשאר כל העבדים כשר היה [ג]חתן *אם רוצה לקרות ק"ש לילה הראשון קורא רשב"ג אומר *לא כל הרוצה ליטול את השם יטול: **גמ'** מ"ט דרשב"ג קסבר *אנינות לילה דרבנן דכתיב °ואחריתה (עמוס ח) כיום מר ובמקום אסטנים לא גזרו ביה רבנן: וכשמת טבי עבדו וכו': ת"ר עבדים ושפחות אין עומדים עליהם בשורה ואין אומרים עליהם ברכת אבלים ותנחומי אבלים *מעשה ומתה שפחתו של ר"א נכנסו תלמידיו לנחמו כיון שראה אותם עלה לעלייה ועלו אחריו נכנס לאנפילון נכנסו אחריו נכנס לטרקלין נכנסו אחריו אמר להם כמדומה אני שאתם נכוים בפושרים עכשיו אי אתם נכוים אפי' בחמי חמין לא כך שניתי לכם [ד]עבדים ושפחות אין עומדין עליהם בשורה ואין אומרים עליהם ברכת אבלים ולא תנחומי אבלים אלא מה אומרים עליהם כשם שאומרים לו לאדם על שורו ועל חמורו שמתו המקום ימלא לך חסרונך כך אומרים לו על עבדו ועל שפחתו המקום ימלא לך חסרונך תניא אידך עבדים ושפחות אין מספידין אותן ר' יוסי אומר אם עבד כשר הוא אומרים עליו הוי איש טוב ונאמן ונהנה מיגיעו אמרו לו אם כן מה הנחת לכשרים: ת"ר *אין קורין אבות אלא לג' ואין קורין אמהות אלא לד' אבות מ"ט אילימא משום דלא ידעינן אי מראובן קא אתינן אי משמעון קא אתינן אי הכי אמהות נמי לא ידעינן אי מרחל קא אתינן אי מלאה קא אתינן אלא עד הכא חשיבי טפי לא חשיבי תניא אידך *[ה] עבדים ושפחות אין קורין אותם אבא פלוני ואמא פלונית ושל ר"ג היו קורים אותם אבא פלוני ואמא פלונית מעשה לסתור משום דחשיבי: א"ר אלעזר מ"ד °כן אברכך בחיי בשמך אשא כפי כן אברכך בחיי (תהלים סג) זו ק"ש בשמך אשא כפי זו תפלה ואם עושה כן עליו הכתוב אומר °כמו חלב (שם) ודשן תשבע נפשי ולא עוד אלא שנוחל שני עולמים העוה"ז והעה"ב שנאמר °ושפתי רננות יהלל פי: (שם) רבי אלעזר בתר דמסיים צלותיה אמר הכי יהי רצון מלפניך ה' אלהינו שתשכן בפורינו אהבה ואחוה ושלום וריעות ותרבה גבולנו בתלמידים ותצליח סופינו אחרית ותקוה ותשים חלקנו בגן עדן ותקננו בחבר טוב ויצר טוב בעולמך ונשכים ונמצא *ייחול לבבינו ליראה את שמך ותבא לפניך קורת נפשנו לטובה ר' יוחנן בתר דמסיים צלותיה אמר הכי יהי רצון מלפניך ה' אלהינו שתציץ בבשתינו ותביט ברעתינו ותתלבש ברחמיך ותתכסה בעזך ותתעטף בחסידותך ותתאזר בחנינותך ותבא לפניך מדת טובך וענותנותך ר' זירא בתר דמסיים צלותיה אמר הכי יהי רצון מלפניך ה' אלהינו שלא נחטא ולא נבוש ולא נכלם *מאבותינו ר' חייא בתר דמצלי אמר הכי יהי רצון מלפניך ה' אלהינו שתהא תורתך אומנותנו ואל ידוה לבנו ואל יחשכו עינינו רב בתר צלותיה אמר הכי יהי רצון מלפניך ה' אלהינו שתתן לנו חיים ארוכים חיים של שלום חיים של טובה חיים של ברכה חיים של פרנסה חיים של חלוץ עצמות חיים שיש בהם יראת חטא חיים שאין בהם בושה וכלימה חיים של עושר וכבוד חיים שתהא בנו אהבת תורה ויראת שמים חיים שתמלא לנו את כל משאלות לבנו לטובה רבי בתר צלותיה אמר הכי *יהי רצון מלפניך ה' אלהינו ואלהי אבותינו שתצילנו מעזי פנים ומעזות פנים מאדם רע (שבת ל.) ומפגע רע מיצר רע מחבר רע משכן רע ומשטן המשחית *ומדין קשה ומבעל דין קשה בין שהוא בן ברית ובין שאינו בן ברית ואע"ג דקיימי קצוצי עליה דרבי רב ספרא בתר צלותיה אמר הכי יהי רצון מלפניך ה' אלהינו שתשים שלום בפמליא

[פי' תלמוד לבבינו בערוך ערך יחל]
[פי' יוסף מאבותינו ערוך בע' הכ"ל]
[מיכלין אנו לדון שלא בקושי בערך הכ"ל]

מתני' רחץ לילה הראשון שמתה אשתו. ונקברה בו ביום ואע"פ שאבל אסור ברחילה הוא רחץ כדאמר טעמא אסטנים אני והוא אדם מעונג ומפונק: **גמ'** קסבר אנינות לילה דרבנן. ואף על פי שהיה ליל יום המיתה וכתיבה אנינות באורייתא דכתיב לא אכלתי באוני ממנו (דברים כו) ופחות מיום אחד איכו אנינות דילפי רבנן מואחריתה כיום מר קסבר ר"ג אין לילה של אחריו עם היום אלא מדרבנן הוא כשאר ימי האבל וגבי אסטנים לא גזור בה רבנן פלוגתייהו דתנאי היא בזבחים (דף לט:) באנינות לילה אי מדאורייתא אי מדרבנן: אין עומדין עליו בשורה. כשחוזרים מבית הקברות היו עושים שורות סביב האבל ומנחמין אותו ואין שורה פחותה מעשרה*: ברכת אבלים. ברכת רחבה שמברכין אותו סעודה ראשונה משל אחרים ומברכין שם ברכת אבלים והיא מפורשת בכתובות פרק ראשון (ד' ח.): לאנפילון. בית קטן שלפני טרקלין הגדול: נכוין בפושרים. כלומר סבור הייתי שתבינו דבר ברמז מועט כשראיתם אותי סר מעליכם ליכנס לאנפילין: הוי. לשון גניחה ולעקה: אין קורין אבות. לישראל: אלא לשלשה. אברהם יצחק ויעקב לאפוקי שבטים: אלא לארבעה. שרה ורבקה רחל ולאה: אבא פלוני אמא פלונית. לא בבניהם קאמר אלא בשאר בני אדם כעין שאנו קורין עכשיו מר פלוני מרת פלונית כך היו רגילין לומר אבא פלוני ואמא פלונית: כן אברכך. וכמו חלב ודשן תרי קראי דסמיכי להדדי: רננות. שתים: בפורינו: בגורלנו: אחרית ותקוה. שתהא אחריתנו טובה ורואה מה שקוינו: ותקננו. לשון תקון: ונשכים ונמצא ייחול לבבינו ליראה את שמך. שלא יתגבר עלינו יצר הרע בהרהור הלילה לסור מאחריך ביום אלא כשנשכים בכל בקר נמצא לבבינו מייחל לך: ותבא לפניך קורת נפשינו. כלומר ספוק צרכנו וקורת רוחנו: ותביט ברעתינו. תדע ותתן לבך ברעה הבאה עלינו: מעזי פנים. שלא יתגברו בי: ומעזות פנים. שלא יוליאו עלי לעז ממזרות: שאינו בן ברית. שאינו מהול: ואע"ג דקיימי קצוצי עליה דרבי. שהיו שוטרים עומדים במלות אנטונינוס להכות ולהכניס בכל העומדים עליו:

מסורת הש"ס
[לעיל י"ח.]
שמחות פ"ו
סנהדרין יט.
מועד קטן טו:
שמחות פ"א
מקוס שנהגו נה.
[ע' פירש"י לקמן יז:]
[פסחי' לג. זבחים לט: ק.]
שמחות פ"א
שמחות פ"א
שמחות פ"א

for a religious duty thou art exempt. [16b] If that is the case, why does it say, One who marries a virgin'? The same would apply to one who marries a widow!—In the former case he is agitated, in the latter case he is not agitated. If his agitation is the ground, then even if his ship has sunk in the sea he should also be exempt? [And if this is so], why then has R. Abba b. Zabda said in the name of Rab: A mourner is under obligation to perform all the precepts laid down in the Torah except that of *tefillin*, because they are called 'headtire', as it says, '*Thy headtire bound upon thy head*' etc.?—The reply is: There the agitation is over an optional matter, here it is over a religious duty.

MISHNAH. [RABBAN GAMALIEL] BATHED ON THE FIRST NIGHT AFTER THE DEATH OF HIS WIFE. HIS DISCIPLES SAID TO HIM: YOU HAVE TAUGHT US, SIR, THAT A MOURNER IS FORBIDDEN TO BATHE. HE REPLIED TO THEM: I AM NOT LIKE OTHER MEN, BEING VERY DELICATE. WHEN ṬABI HIS SLAVE DIED HE ACCEPTED CONDOLENCES FOR HIM. HIS DISCIPLES SAID TO HIM: YOU HAVE TAUGHT US, SIR, THAT CONDOLENCES ARE NOT ACCEPTED FOR SLAVES? HE REPLIED TO THEM: MY SLAVE ṬABI WAS NOT LIKE OTHER SLAVES: HE WAS A GOOD MAN. IF A BRIDEGROOM DESIRES TO RECITE THE SHEMA' ON THE FIRST NIGHT, HE MAY DO SO. RABBAN SIMEON B. GAMALIEL SAYS: NOT EVERYONE WHO DESIRES TO PASS AS
a A SCHOLAR[1] MAY DO SO.

GEMARA. How did Rabban Gamaliel[2] justify his action?[3]—He held that the observance of *aninuth*[4] by night is only an ordinance of the Rabbis, as it is written, [*And I will make it as the*
b *mourning for an only son,*] *and the end thereof as a bitter day,*[1] and where it concerns a delicate person the Rabbis did not mean their ordinance to apply.

WHEN ṬABI HIS SLAVE DIED etc. Our Rabbis taught: For male and female slaves no row [of comforters][2] is formed, nor is the blessing of mourners[3] said, nor is condolence offered. When the bondwoman of R. Eliezer died, his disciples went in to condole with him. When he saw them he went up to an upper chamber, but they went up after him. He then went into an ante-room and they followed him there. He then went into the dining hall and they followed him there. He said to them: I thought that you would be scalded with warm water; I see you are not scalded even with boiling hot water.[4] Have I not taught you that a row of comforters is not made for male and female slaves, and that a blessing of mourners is not said for them, nor is condolence offered for them? What then do they say for them? The same as they say to a man for his ox and his ass: 'May the Almighty replenish your loss'. So for his male and female slave they say to him: 'May the Almighty replenish your loss'. It has been taught elsewhere: For male and female slaves no funeral oration is said. R. Jose said: If he was a good slave, they can say over him, Alas for a good and faithful man, who worked for his living! They said to him: If you do that, what do you leave for free-born?

Our Rabbis taught: The term 'patriarchs' is applied only to three,[5] and the term 'matriarchs' only to four.[6] What is the reason? Shall we say because we do not know if we are descended from Reuben or from Simeon? But neither do we know in the case of the matriarchs whether we are descended from Rachel or from Leah!—[Rather the reason is] because up to this point they were particularly esteemed, from this point they were not so particularly esteemed. It has been taught elsewhere: Male and female slaves are not called 'Father so-and so' or 'Mother so-and so'; those of Rabban Gamaliel, however, were called 'Father so-and-so' and 'Mother so-and-so'. The example [cited] contradicts your rule? It was because they were particularly esteemed.

R. Eleazar said: What is the meaning of the verse, *So will I*
c *bless Thee as long as I live; in Thy name will I lift up my hands?*[1] '*I will bless Thee as long as I live*' refers to the *Shema'*; '*in Thy name I will lift up my hands*' refers to the *tefillah*. And if he does this, Scripture says of him, *My soul is satisfied as with marrow and fatness.*[2] Nay more, he inherits two worlds, this world and the next, as it says, *And my mouth doth praise Thee with joyful lips.*[3]

R. Eleazar on concluding his prayer[4] used to say the following: May it be Thy will, O Lord our God, to cause to dwell in our lot love and brotherhood and peace and friendship, and mayest Thou make our borders rich in disciples and prosper our latter end with good prospect and hope, and set our portion in Paradise, and confirm us[5] with a good companion and a good impulse in Thy world, and may we rise early and obtain the yearning of our heart to fear Thy name,[6] and mayest Thou be pleased to grant the satisfaction of our desires![7]

R. Johanan on concluding his prayer added the following: May it be Thy will, O Lord our God, to look upon our shame, and behold our evil plight, and clothe Thyself in Thy mercies, and cover Thyself in Thy strength, and wrap Thyself in Thy loving-kindness, and gird Thyself with Thy graciousness, and may the attribute of Thy kindness and gentleness come before Thee!

R. Zera on concluding his prayer added the following: May it be Thy will, O Lord our God, that we sin not nor bring upon ourselves shame or disgrace before our fathers![8]

R. Ḥiyya on concluding his prayer added the following: May it be Thy will, O Lord our God, that our Torah may be our occupation, and that our heart may not be sick nor our eyes darkened!

Rab on concluding his prayer added the following: May it be Thy will, O Lord our God, to grant us long life, a life of peace, a life of good, a life of blessing, a life of sustenance, a life of bodily
d vigour,[1] a life in which there is fear of sin, a life free from shame and confusion, a life of riches and honour, a life in which we may be filled with the love of Torah and the fear of heaven, a life in which Thou shalt fulfil all the desires of our heart for good![2]

Rabbi on concluding his prayer added the following: May it be Thy will, O Lord our God, and God of our fathers, to deliver us from the impudent and from impudence, from an evil man, from evil hap, from the evil impulse, from an evil companion, from an evil neighbour, and from the destructive Accuser, from a hard lawsuit and from a hard opponent, whether he is a son of the covenant or not a son of the covenant![3] [Thus did he pray] although guards[4] were appointed[5] to protect Rabbi.

R. Safra on concluding his prayer added the following: May it

a (1) Lit., 'to take the name', viz., of a scholar. (2) Cur. edd.: R. Simeon b. Gamaliel, which can hardly be justified. (3) In bathing while *onan*. (4) The name given to the mourning of the first day, or the whole period before the burial.

b (1) Amos VIII, 10. This shows that according to Scripture mourning is to be observed only by day. (2) It was customary for those returning from a burial to the mourner's house to stand in a row before him to comfort him. (3) Said after the first meal taken by the mourner after the funeral, v. Keth. 8*a*. (4) As much as to say: I thought you would take the first hint, and you do not even take the last! (5) Abraham, Isaac and Jacob. (6) Sarah, Rebeccah, Rachel and Leah.

c (1) Ps. LXIII, 5. (2) Ibid. 6. (3) Ibid. Lit., 'lips of songs', i.e., two songs. (4) I.e., after the last benediction of the *'Amidah*. (5) Or perhaps, cause us to obtain. (6) I.e., may we be filled with pious thoughts on waking. (7) Lit., 'may the coolness of our soul come before Thee for good'. (8) *'Aruch:* more than our fathers.

d (1) Lit,. 'vigour of the bones'. (2) This prayer is now said on the Sabbath on which the New Moon is announced. V. *P.B.* p. 154. (3) I.e., a Jew or non-Jew. This now forms part of the daily prayers. V. *P.B.* p. 7. (4) Lit., 'eunuchs'. (5) By the Roman Government.

be Thy will, O Lord our God, to establish peace [17a] among the celestial family,[6] and among the earthly family,[7] and among the disciples who occupy themselves with Thy Torah whether for its own sake or for other motives; and may it please Thee that all who do so for other motives may come to study it for its own sake!

R. Alexandri on concluding his prayer added the following: May it be Thy will, O Lord our God, to station us in an illumined corner and do not station us in a darkened corner, and let not our heart be sick nor our eyes darkened! According to some this was the prayer of R. Hamnuna, and R. Alexandri on concluding his prayer used to add the following: Sovereign of the Universe, it is known full well to Thee that our will is to perform Thy will,
a and what prevents us? The yeast in the dough[1] and the subjection to the foreign Powers. May it be Thy will to deliver us from their hand, so that we may return to perform the statutes of Thy will with a perfect heart!

Raba on concluding his prayer added the following: My God, before I was formed I was not worthy [to be formed], and now that I have been formed I am as if I had not been formed. I am dust in my lifetime, all the more in my death. Behold I am before Thee like a vessel full of shame and confusion. May it be Thy will, O Lord my God, that I sin no more, and the sins I have committed before Thee wipe out in Thy great mercies, but not through evil chastisements and diseases! This was the confession of R. Hamnuna Zuṭi on the Day of Atonement.[2]

Mar the son of Rabina on concluding his prayer added the following: My God, keep my tongue from evil and my lips from speaking guile. May my soul be silent to them that curse me and may my soul be as the dust to all. Open Thou my heart in Thy law, and may my soul pursue Thy commandments, and deliver me from evil hap, from the evil impulse and from an evil woman and from all evils that threaten to come upon the world. As for all that design evil against me, speedily annul their counsel and frustrate their designs![3] May the words of my mouth and the meditation of my heart be acceptable before Thee, O Lord, my rock and my redeemer![4]

When R. Shesheth kept a fast, on concluding his prayer he added the following: Sovereign of the Universe, Thou knowest full well that in the time when the Temple was standing, if a man sinned he used to bring a sacrifice, and though all that was offered of it was its fat and blood, atonement was made for him therewith. Now I have kept a fast and my fat and blood have diminished. May it be Thy will to account my fat and blood which have been diminished as if I had offered them before Thee on the altar, and
b do Thou favour me.[1]

When R. Joḥanan finished the Book of Job,[2] he used to say the following: The end of man is to die, and the end of a beast is to be slaughtered, and all are doomed to die. Happy he who was brought up in the Torah and whose labour was in the Torah and who has given pleasure to his Creator and who grew up with a good name and departed the world with a good name; and of him Solomon said: *A good name is better than precious oil, and the day of death than the day of one's birth.*[3]

A favourite saying of R. Meir was: Study with all thy heart and with all thy soul to know My ways and to watch at the doors of My law. Keep My law in thy heart and let My fear be before thy eyes. Keep thy mouth from all sin and purify and sanctify thyself from all trespass and iniquity, and I will be with thee in every place.

A favourite saying of the Rabbis of Jabneh was: I am God's creature and my fellow[4] is God's creature. My work is in the town and his work is in the country. I rise early for my work and he rises early for his work. Just as he does not presume to do my work, so I do not presume to do his work. Will you say, I do much[5] and he does little? We have learnt:[6] One may do much or one may do little; it is all one, provided he directs his heart to heaven.

A favourite saying of Abaye was: A man should always be
c subtle in the fear of heaven.[1] *A soft answer turneth away wrath,*[2] and one should always strive to be on the best terms with his brethren and his relatives and with all men and even with the heathen in the street, in order that he may be beloved above and well-liked below and be acceptable to his fellow creatures. It was related of R. Joḥanan b. Zakkai that no man ever gave him greeting first, even a heathen in the street.

A favourite saying of Raba was: The goal of wisdom is repentance and good deeds, so that a man should not study Torah and Mishnah and then despise[3] his father and mother and teacher and his superior in wisdom and rank, as it says, *The fear of the Lord is the beginning of wisdom, a good understanding have all they that do thereafter.*[4] It does not say, 'that do',[5] but '*that do thereafter*', which implies, that do them for their own sake and not for other motives.[6] If one does them for other motives, it were better that he had not been created.

A favourite saying of Rab was: [The future world is not like this world.][7] In the future world there is no eating nor drinking nor propagation nor business nor jealousy nor hatred nor competition, but the righteous sit with their crowns on their heads feasting on the brightness of the divine presence, as it says, *And they beheld God, and did eat and drink.*[8]

[Our Rabbis taught]:[9] Greater is the promise made by the Holy One, blessed be He, to the women than to the men; for it says, *Rise up, ye women that are at ease; ye confident daughters, give ear unto my speech.*[10] Rab said to R. Ḥiyya: Whereby do women earn merit? By making their children go to the synagogue[11] to learn Scripture and their husbands to the Beth Hamidrash to learn Mishnah, and waiting for their husbands till they return
d from the Beth Hamidrash. When the Rabbis[1] took leave from the school of R. Ammi—some say, of R. Ḥanina—they said to him: May you see your requirements provided[2] in your lifetime, and may your latter end be for the future world and your hope for many generations; may your heart meditate understanding, your mouth speak wisdom and your tongue indite song; may your eyelids look straight before you,[3] may your eyes be enlightened by the light of the Torah and your face shine like the brightness of the firmament; may your lips utter knowledge, your reins rejoice in uprightness[4] and your steps run to hear the words of the Ancient of Days. When the Rabbis took leave from the school of R. Ḥisda—others say, of R. Samuel b. Naḥmani—they said to him: *We are instructed, we are well laden*[5] etc. '*We are instructed, we are well laden*'. Rab and Samuel—according to others, R. Joḥanan and R. Eleazar—give different explanations of this. One says: 'We are instructed'—in Torah, 'and well laden'—with precepts. The other says: 'We are instructed'—in Torah and

(6) The Guardian Angels of the various nations. (7) From the context this would seem to refer to the nations of the earth. Rashi, however, takes it to mean the assembly of the wise men.
(1) I.e., the evil impulse, which causes a ferment in the heart. (2) It occupies the same place in the present day liturgy. V. *P.B.* p. 263. (3) MS.M adds: Pay them their recompense upon their heads; destroy them and humble them before me, and deliver me from all calamities which are threatening to issue and break forth upon the world! (4) In the present day liturgy this prayer is also added (in a slightly altered form) at the end of every *'Amidah*. V. *P.B.* p. 54. The last sentence is from Ps. XIX, 15.
b (1) MS.M. adds: A certain disciple after he prayed used to say: 'Close mine eyes from evil, and my ears from hearing idle words, and my heart from reflecting on unchaste thoughts, and my veins from thinking of transgression, and guide my feet to (walk in) Thy commandments and Thy righteous ways, and may Thy mercies be turned upon me to be of those spared and preserved for life in Jerusalem'! (2) M. reads: R. Joḥanan said: When R. Meir finished

מסורת הש"ס

עין משפט נר מצוה

בפמליא של מעלה. בחבורת שרי האומות שכשהשרים של מעלה יש תגר ביניהם תכף יש קטטה בין האומות כדכתיב ועתה אשוב להלחם עם שר פרס (דניאל י): ופמליא של מטה. בחבורת החכמים: בקרן אורה. בזוית אורה: ומי מעכב. שאין אנו עושים רצונך: שאור שבעיסה. יצר הרע שבלבבנו המחמיצנו: איני כדאי. לא הייתי חשוב והגון להיות נוצר: ועכשיו שנוצרתי. מה חשיבותי הרי אני כאלו לא נוצרתי: קל וחומר. שבמיתתי עפר אני: מרק. כלה והתם: כי הוה מסיים ספר איוב. על שם שאיוב נפטר בשם טוב: מרגלא בפומיה. דבר זה רגיל בפיו: אני. העוסק בתורה בריה אני וכן חברי עם הארץ בריה הוא: אני מלאכתי בעיר. כלומר נוחה מלאכתי ממלאכתו: מתגדר. מתגדל לתפוס אומנותי: ושמא תאמר. הדין עמו שאינו מתגדר במלאכתי שאלו היה תופס אומנותי לא היה לו לב פתוח להרבות בתורה כמותי והיה ממעט ואין לו שכר: שנינו. שיש לו שכר לממעיט כמו למרבה: ובלבד שיכוין לבו לשמים. ואגב קרבנות הוא במנחות בסופה*: ערום ביראה. להערים בכל מיני ערמה ליראת בוראו: תכלית חכמה. עיקרה של תורה שיהא עמה תשובה ומעשים טובים: העושה שלא לשמה נוח לו שלא נברא. פירוש שאינו לומד כדי לקיים אלא לקנטר דבפרק מקום שנהגו (ד' כ:) אמרינן רבא רמי כתיב עד השמים חסדך וכתיב מעל השמים כאן בעוסק שלא לשמה כו' והתם איירי במקיים כדי שיכבדוהו וכן משמע בירושלמי דפירקין: ויאכלו וישתו. שבעו מזיו השכינה כאלו אכלו ושתו: גדולה הבטחה. שהרי קראן שאננות ובוטחות: לבי כנישתא. תינוקות של בית רבן היו רגילים להיות לומדין לפני רבן בבית הכנסת: בי רבנן. בית המדרש ששם שונים משנה וגמרא: ונטרין לגברייהו. ממתינות לבעליהם ונותנות להן רשות ללכת וללמוד תורה בעיר אחרת: מפטרי רבנן. זה מזה שהיה נוטל רשות מחבירו לשוב לביתו ולאכלו: עולמך תראה בחייך. כל צרכך תמצא: פיך ידבר חכמות. בלשון ברכה היו אומרים: ייִשירו. לשון יושר שתהא מבין בתורה כהלכה:

[ד' קי.] [יומא פז:] [גי' ע"י א"ר יוחנן כי הוה מסיי' ר"מ ספרא דאיוב]

תורה אור

בפמליא של מעלה ובפמליא של מטה ובין התלמידים העוסקים בתורתך בין עוסקין לשמה בין עוסקין שלא לשמה וכל העוסקין שלא לשמה יהי רצון שיהו עוסקין לשמה ר' אלכסנדרי בתר צלותיה אמר הכי יהי רצון מלפניך ה' אלהינו שתעמידנו בקרן אורה ואל תעמידנו בקרן חשכה ואל ידוה לבנו ואל יחשכו עינינו איכא דאמרי הא רב המנונא מצלי לה ור' אלכסנדרי בתר דמצלי אמר הכי רבון העולמים גלוי וידוע לפניך שרצוננו לעשות רצונך ומי מעכב שאור שבעיסה ושעבוד מלכיות יהי רצון מלפניך שתצילנו מידם ונשוב לעשות חקי רצונך בלבב שלם רבא בתר צלותיה אמר הכי *אלהי עד שלא נוצרתי איני כדאי ועכשיו שנוצרתי כאלו לא נוצרתי עפר אני בחיי קל וחומר במיתתי הרי אני לפניך ככלי מלא בושה וכלימה יהי רצון מלפניך ה' אלהי שלא אחטא עוד ומה שחטאתי לפניך מרק ברחמיך הרבים אבל לא על ידי יסורין וחלאים רעים והיינו וידוי דרב המנונא זוטא ביומא דכפורי מר בריה דרבינא כי הוה מסיים צלותיה אמר הכי [א]אלהי נצור לשוני מרע ושפתותי מדבר מרמה ולמקללי נפשי תדום ונפשי כעפר לכל תהיה פתח לבי בתורתך ובמצותיך תרדוף נפשי ותצילני מפגע רע מיצר הרע ומאשה רעה ומכל רעות המתרגשות לבא בעולם וכל החושבים עלי רעה מהרה הפר עצתם וקלקל מחשבותם יהיו לרצון אמרי פי והגיון לבי לפניך ה' צורי וגואלי רב ששת כי הוה יתיב בתעניתא בתר דמצלי אמר הכי [ב]רבון העולמים גלוי לפניך בזמן שבית המקדש קיים אדם חוטא ומקריב קרבן ואין מקריבין ממנו אלא חלבו ודמו ומתכפר לו ועכשיו ישבתי בתענית ונתמעט חלבי ודמי יהי רצון מלפניך שיהא חלבי ודמי שנתמעט כאלו הקרבתיו לפניך על גבי המזבח ותרצני *רבי יוחנן כי הוה מסיים ספרא דאיוב אמר הכי סוף אדם למות וסוף בהמה לשחיטה והכל למיתה הם עומדים אשרי מי שגדל בתורה ועמלו בתורה ועושה נחת רוח ליוצרו וגדל בשם טוב ונפטר בשם טוב מן העולם ועליו אמר שלמה °טוב שם משמן טוב ויום המות מיום הולדו מרגלא בפומיה דר"מ גמור בכל לבבך ובכל נפשך לדעת את דרכי ולשקוד על דלתי תורתי נצור תורתי בלבך ונגד עיניך תהיה יראתי שמור פיך מכל חטא וטהר וקדש עצמך מכל אשמה ועון ואני אהיה עמך בכל מקום מרגלא בפומייהו דרבנן דיבנה אני בריה וחברי בריה אני מלאכתי בעיר והוא מלאכתו בשדה אני משכים למלאכתי והוא משכים למלאכתו כשם שהוא אינו מתגדר במלאכתי כך אני איני מתגדר במלאכתו ושמא תאמר אני מרבה והוא ממעיט *שנינו אחד המרבה ואחד הממעיט ובלבד שיכוין לבו לשמים מרגלא בפומיה דאביי לעולם יהא אדם ערום ביראה °מענה רך *משיב חמה ומרבה שלום עם אחיו ועם קרוביו ועם כל אדם ואפילו עם נכרי בשוק כדי שיהא אהוב למעלה ונחמד למטה ויהא מקובל על הבריות אמרו עליו על רבן יוחנן בן זכאי שלא הקדימו אדם שלום מעולם ואפי' נכרי בשוק מרגלא בפומיה דרבא תכלית חכמה תשובה ומע"ט שלא יהא אדם קורא ושונה ובועט באביו ובאמו וברבו ובמי שהוא גדול ממנו בחכמה ובמנין שנאמר °ראשית חכמה יראת ה' שכל טוב לכל עושיהם *לעושים לא נאמר אלא לעושיהם לעושים לשמה ולא לעושים שלא לשמה וכל העושה שלא לשמה נוח לו שלא נברא מרגלא בפומיה דרב [לא כהעה"ז העה"ב] [ז]העה"ב אין בו לא אכילה ולא שתיה ולא פריה ורביה ולא משא ומתן ולא קנאה ולא שנאה ולא תחרות אלא צדיקים יושבים ועטרותיהם בראשיהם ונהנים מזיו שכינה שנאמר °ויחזו את האלהים ויאכלו וישתו: גדולה הבטחה שהבטיחן הקב"ה לנשים יותר מן האנשים שנאמר °נשים שאננות קומנה שמענה קולי בנות בוטחות האזנה אמרתי א"ל רב לרבי חייא נשים במאי זכיין *באקרויי בנייהו לבי כנישתא ובאתנויי גברייהו בי רבנן ונטרן לגברייהו עד דאתו מבי רבנן כי הוו מפטרי רבנן מבי ר' אמי ואמרי לה מבי ר' חנינא אמרי ליה הכי עולמך תראה בחייך ואחריתך לחיי העה"ב ותקותך לדור דורים לבך יהגה תבונה פיך ידבר חכמות ולשונך ירחיש רננות עפעפיך יישירו נגדך עיניך יאירו במאור תורה ופניך יזהירו כזוהר הרקיע שפתותיך יביעו דעת וכליותיך תעלוזנה מישרים ופעמיך ירוצו לשמוע דברי עתיק יומין כי הוו מפטרי רבנן מבי רב חסדא ואמרי לה מבי ר' שמואל בר נחמני אמרו ליה הכי °אלופינו מסובלים וגו' אלופינו מסובלים רב ושמואל ואמרי לה ר' יוחנן ור' אלעזר חד אמר אלופינו בתורה ומסובלי' במצות וחד אמר אלופינו בתורה ובמצות ומסובלי' ביסורים

אין

קהלת ז | מנחו' קי. לעיל ה: [וש"נ] משלי טו | [ישיב כל"ג] | תהלים קיא | שמות כד | ישעיה לב | סוטה כא. | תהלים קמד | ס"א ללומדיהם לא נאמר אלא לעושיהם

ונפשי כעפר לכל תהיה. מה עפר אינו מקבל כליה לעולם כן יהי רצון שזרעי לא יכלה לעולם כמו שהוא אומר והיה זרעך כעפר הארץ:

אני בריה וחברי בריה. כלומר יש לו לב כמוני להבחין בין טוב לרע:

העושה שלא לשמה נוח לו שלא נברא. וא"ת האמר רב יהודה אמר רב פרק מקום שנהגו (דף כ:) לעולם יעסוק אדם בתורה ובמצות אפילו שלא לשמה שמתוך שלא לשמה בא לשמה וי"ל דהכא איירי שאינו לומד אלא לקנטר חבריו והתם איירי שלומד על מנת שיכבדוהו*:

פרק

מז [א]טור וש"ע א"ח סימן קכב סעיף א | מח [ב]טור וש"ע א"ח סימן תקסה סעיף ד | מט [ג]מיי' פ"ה מהל' דיעות הלכה ז | נ [ד]מיי' פ"ח מהל' תשובה הלכה ב

[וע"ע תענית ז. תוס' ד"ה וכל העוסק ותו' פסחים כ: ותו' נזיר כג: ד"ה שמתוך ותו' סוטה כב: ד"ה לעולם]

etc. (3) Eccl. VII, 1. R. Joḥanan was prompted to this reflection by the fact that Job departed with a good name. (4) I.e., the *'am ha-arez*, or non-student. (5) In the way of Torah. (6) Men. 110*a*.

c (1) I.e., in finding out new ways of fearing heaven. (2) Prov. XV, 1. (3) Lit., 'kick at'. (4) Ps. CXI, 10. (5) Another reading is, that learn them. (6) I.e., to criticise and quarrel. V. Rashi and Tosaf. ad loc. (7) These words are bracketed in the text. (8) Ex. XXIV, 11. These words are interpreted to mean that the vision of God seen by the young men was like food and drink to them. (9) These words are missing in cur. edd., but occur in MS.M. (10) Isa. XXXII, 9. The women are said to be 'at ease' and 'confident', which is more than is said of the men. (11) Where children were usually taught.

d (1) Who had left home to study with R. Ammi. (2) Lit., 'see your world'. (3) The expression is taken from Prov. IV, 25. The meaning here seems to be, 'may you have a correct insight into the meaning of the Torah'. (4) The reins were supposed to act as counsellors. (5) Ps. CXLIV, 14. E.V. *Our oxen are well laden*.

אין פרץ שלא תהא סיעתינו כסיעתו של דוד שיצא ממנו אחיתופל ואין יוצאת שלא תהא סיעתינו *כסיעתו של שאול שיצא ממנו דואג האדומי ואין צוחה שלא תהא סיעתינו כסיעתו של אלישע שיצא ממנו גחזי ברחובותינו שלא יהא לנו בן או תלמיד שמקדיח תבשילו ברבים: °שמעו אלי אבירי לב הרחוקים מצדקה רב ושמואל ואמרי לה רבי יוחנן ורבי אלעזר חד אמר כל העולם כולו נזונין בצדקה והן נזונין בזרוע וחד אמר כל העולם כולו נזונין בזכותם והם אפילו בזכות עצמן אין נזונין כדרב יהודה אמר רב *דאמר רב יהודה אמר רב בכל יום ויום בת קול יוצאת *מהר חורב ואומרת כל העולם כולו נזונין בשביל חנינא בני וחנינא בני די לו בקב חרובין מערב שבת לע"ש ופליגא דרב יהודה דאמר רב יהודה מאן אבירי לב גובאי טפשאי אמר רב יוסף תדע דהא לא איגייר גיורא מניידהו אמר רב אשי בני מתא מחסיא אבירי לב נינהו דקא חזו יקרא דאורייתא תרי זימני בשתא ולא קמגייר גיורא מניידהו: חתן אם רוצה לקרות וכו': *למימרא דרשב"ג חייש ליוהרא ורבנן לא חיישי ליוהרא והא איפכא שמעינן להו דתנן *מקום שנהגו לעשות מלאכה בט' באב עושין מקום שנהגו שלא לעשות אין עושין וכל מקום תלמידי חכמים בטלים רשב"ג אומר *לעולם יעשה כל אדם את עצמו כתלמיד חכם קשיא דרבנן אדרבנן קשיא דרשב"ג אדרשב"ג א"ר יוחנן מוחלפת השיטה רב שישא בריה דרב אידי אמר לעולם לא תחליף דרבנן אדרבנן לא קשיא ק"ש כיון דכולי עלמא קא קרו ואיהו נמי קרי לא מיחזי כיוהרא *הכא כיון דכולי עלמא עבדי מלאכה ואיהו לא קא עביד מיחזי כיוהרא דרשב"ג אדרשב"ג לא קשיא *התם בכונה תליא מילתא ואנן סהדי דלא מצי לכווני דעתיה אבל *הכא הרואה אומר מלאכה הוא דאין לו *פוק חזי כמה בטלני איכא בשוקא:

הדרן עלך היה קורא

מי *שמתו מוטל לפניו *פטור מקריאת שמע ומן* התפלה ומן התפילין ומכל מצות האמורות בתורה *נושאי המטה וחלופיהן וחלופי חלופיהן את שלפני המטה ואת שלאחר המטה את* שלפני המטה צורך בהם פטורין ואת שלאחר המטה צורך בהן חייבין *ואלו ואלו פטורים מן התפלה קברו את המת וחזרו אם יכולין להתחיל ולגמור עד שלא יגיעו לשורה יתחילו ואם לאו לא יתחילו העומדים בשורה הפנימיים פטורים והחיצונים חייבים (*נשים ועבדים וקטנים פטורים מק"ש ומן התפילין וחייבין בתפלה ובמזוזה ובברכת המזון): **גמ'** מוטל לפניו אין ושאינו מוטל לפניו לא ורמינהי *מי שמתו מוטל לפניו אוכל בבית אחר ואם אין לו בית אחר אוכל בבית חבירו ואם אין לו בית חבירו עושה מחיצה ואוכל ואם אין לו דבר לעשות מחיצה מחזיר פניו ואוכל ואינו מיסב ואוכל ואינו אוכל בשר ואינו שותה יין ואינו מברך ואינו מזמן ואין

פרץ זה אחיתופל. שפרץ פרצה במלכות בית דוד. יוצאת זה דואג שיצא לתרבות רעה כדמפרש בחלק (ד' קו:) גבי ווי יצא זה: **צוחה** זה גחזי. שהיה מצורע וכתיב ביה טמא טמא יקרא והיינו צוחה: **והן** נזונין בזרוע. ולכך יש להגיה *בתקיעות והן בזרוע עדיך באו ולא גרסינן עדיך לא באו: **תרי** זימני בשתא. אבל בעצרת שאינו אלא יום אחד לא היו כל כך מתאספין ושמא כיסא איתרחיש להו ורא"תי בספר העתים שחבר הרב רבי יהודה בר ברזילי ששמע שהיה מנהג של אם יורד מן השמים עליהם בכלה דאלול ובכלה דאדר:

כל העולם כולו נזונין בצדקה. בצדקתו של הקב"ה ולא בזכות שבידן: והם נזונין בזרוע. בזכות שבידם וצדיקים משמעי קרא וקרי להו רחוקים מצדקתו של הקב"ה: אין ניזונין. שאין להם כפי צרכיהם ומתפרנסים בקושי: ופליגא דרב יהודה. דאיהו אמר אבירי לב היינו רשעים: גובאי. שם אומה היא בבבל ובמסכ' קידושין (פ"ד ד' ע:) אמרינן שהיו מן הנתינים: שבחא דאורייתא תרי זימני בשתא. שהיו נאספין שם ישראל באדר לשמוע בהלכות הפסח מדרש דרב אשי ובאלול לשמוע הלכות החג: לא כל הרוצה וכו'. אם לא הוחזק חכם וחסיד לרבים אין זה אלא גאוה שמראה בעצמו שיכול לכוין לבו: אמרי אינשי עבידת' הוא דלית ליה. הרואה אותו שאינו עושה מלאכה אינו מבין שמחמת תשעה באב הוא בטל אלא אין לו מלאכה לעשות: פוק חזי כמה בטלני איכא בשוקא. אף בימי מלאכה:

הדרן עלך היה קורא

מי שמתו כו' פטור מק"ש. לפי שהוא טרוד במחשבת קבורתו והויא דומיא דחתן דפטור משום טירדא דמצוה: וחלופיהן. שכן דרך שמתחלפין לשאת לפי שהכל חפצין לזכות בו: את שלפני המטה. שיתעסקו בו כשתגיע המטה אצלם: ושלאחר המטה. כשאוהו כבר: שלפני המטה צורך בהם פטורים. אם צריכים לשאתו פטורים: ושלאחר המטה. אף אם צורך בהם חייבין הואיל שכבר יצאו ידי חובתן מן המת: ואלו ואלו פטורין מן התפלה. דלאו דאורייתא היא ורבותינו פירשו לפי שיש להם עוד שהות ולא נראה שאין זה לשון פטור: לשורה. שהיו מנחמין את האבל בהקף שורה סביבותיו בשובם מן הקבר: **גמ'** שאינו מוטל לפניו. כגון הוא בבית אחד והמת בבית אחר: אוכל בבית אחר. דנראה כלועג לרש וכו': ואינו מיסב. כדרך המסובים בחשיבות על צדו השמאלית ובמטה: ואינו מברך. ואינו צריך לברך ברכת המוציא: ואינו מזמן. אינו צריך לברך ברכת המזון: ואין

רב ששא בריה דרב אידי אמר לעולם לא תחליף. פר"ח דהלכה כרב *ששת דהוא בתרא והלכה כרשב"ג דאמר לא כל הרוצה ליטול את השם יטול ובכל מקום ששנה רשב"ג במשנתינו הלכה כמותו חוץ מערב וצידן וראיה אחרונה [כתובות עז.] וכן פסק ר"ח ומיהו אנו שבשום פעם אין אנו מכוונים היטב גם חתן יש לקרות דאדרבה נראה כיוהרא אם לא יקרא כלומר אני מכוין בכל שעה אבל לעשות מלאכה בתשעה באב אין לעשות מלאכה:

הדרן עלך היה קורא

מי שמתו מוטל לפניו. רש"י גריס מי שמתו אחר תפלת השחר אבל נראה לר"י שהוא אחר היה קורא דאיירי בסופיה מק"ש וכאן מתחיל נמי מפטור ק"ש ובירושלמי גריס כמו כן: **פטור** מק"ש. בירושלמי מפרש טעמא א"ר בון כתיב למען תזכור כו' עד כל ימי חייך ימים שאתה עוסק בחיים ולא ימים שאתה עוסק במתים: ה"ג פטור מק"ש ומן התפלה ומן התפילין: **הכי** גריס רש"י שלאחר המטה אפילו המטה צריכה להם חייבין לפי שלעולם לא היו רגילים לשאת שכבר נשאו אלקם ותימה קצת הלשון לפרש מאי קאמר אפילו צריכה להם והלא לא היו נושאין כלל את המת לכך נראה כגרסת הספרים שלפני המטה ושלאחר המטה את שהמטה צריכה להם פטורין אין צריכה להם חייבין: **אלו** ואלו פטורין מן התפלה. אבל בק"ש ובתפילין שהן מדאורייתא חייבים וניסא דקאמר מי שמתו מוטל לפניו דפטור מן ק"ש ומן התפילין וכו' כל שכן דפטור מן התפלה אלא לא בעי למיתני בריסא אלא החלוק שבין נושאי המטה למתו מוטל לפניו: **ואינו** מברך. פירש"י ואין זקוק לברך ומשמע מתוך פירושו שאם רצה לברך רשאי מיהו בירושלמי קאמר אם רצה להחמיר אין שומעין לו לברך נראה לומר אינו מברך אינו רשאי לברך ומפרש בירושלמי למה וקאמר מפני כבודו של מת אי נמי מפני שאין לו מי שישא משאו ופריך והתניא פטור מנטילת לולב וקא ס"ד דמיירי ביום טוב וכו והתניא אינו טרוד לישא משאו ומשני תפתר בחול פירוש בחולו של מועד:

עין משפט נר מצוה

[בזכרונו' יום ב' של ר"ה המתחיל אפחד]

נא
א מיי' פ"ה מהלכ' תענית ה"י סמג עשין ג טוש"ע א"ח סי' תקנד סעי' כב

[נ"ל ששא]

[בתעני' דף: כתב רש"י דלא גרסי' מהר חורב ודע דגם בחולין ליתא]

א
ג מיי' פ"ד מהלכו' אבלות ה"ו ופ"ד מהל' ק"ש ה"ג סמג עשין יח ב טוש"ע א"ח סי' עא סעי' א

ב
ד מיי' ה' אבל שם ה"ד טוש"ע שם ובסי' עב סעי' א

ג
ה מיי' פ"ד מה' תפל' ה"י ופ"ד מהלכות ק"ש ה"א סמג עשין יח טוש"ע א"ח סי' קו סעי' א

ד
ז מיי' פ"ד מהל' אבל ה"ז סמג עשין מד"ס ב ג. טוש"ע י"ד סי' שמא סעי' א טוש"ע א"ח סי' קלט סעי' ה

(בירושלמי לא גרים ומן התפלה ומכל מצות)

(ירוש' את שהמטה במקום שלפני המטה ואת שאין המטה במקום ואת שלאחר וכו')

מסורת הש"ס

תורה אור

[ס"יד במסכ'] ישעי' מו

[העירוך מהפך הדברי' למעלה באין פרץ כסיעת' של שאול כו' וע"ש מילתא בטעמא]

חולין פו.

תענית כד:

פסחי' נה.

התם

הכא

התם

[שם כא:]

שמחות פ"י

[מסכ' לקמן ד.]

מועד קטן כג: שמחות פ"י

precepts; 'we are well laden'—with chastisements. [17b] *There is no breach:* [that is], may our company not be like that of David from which issued Ahitophel.[6] *And no going forth:* [that is] may our company not be like that of Saul from which issued Doeg the Edomite.[7] *And no outcry:* may our company not be like that of Elisha, from which issued Gehazi.[8] *In our broad places:* may we produce no son or pupil who disgraces himself[9] in public.[10]

Hearken unto Me, ye stout-hearted, who are far from righteousness.[11] Rab and Samuel—according to others, R. Johanan and R. Eleazar—interpret this differently. One says: The whole world is sustained
a by [God's] charity, and they[1] are sustained by their own force.[2] The other says: All the world is sustained by their merit, and they are not sustained even by their own merit. This accords with the saying of Rab Judah in the name of Rab. For Rab Judah said in the name of Rab: Every day a divine voice goes forth from Mount Horeb and proclaims: The whole world is sustained for the sake of My son Ḥanina, and Ḥanina My son has to subsist on a *kab* of carobs from one week end to the next. This [explanation] conflicts with that of Rab Judah. For Rab Judah said: Who are the 'stout-hearted'? The stupid Gubaeans.[3] R. Joseph said: The proof is that they have never produced a proselyte. R. Ashi said: The people of Mata Meḥasia[4] are 'stout-hearted', for they see the glory of the Torah twice a year,[5] and never has one of them been converted.

A BRIDEGROOM IF HE DESIRES TO RECITE etc. May we conclude from this that Rabban Simeon b. Gamaliel deprecates showing off[6] and the Rabbis do not deprecate it? But do we not understand them to hold the opposite views, as we have learnt: In places where people are accustomed to work in the month of Ab they may work, and in places where it is the custom not to work they may not work; but in all places Rabbinical students abstain from study. R. Simeon b. Gamaliel says: A man should always conduct himself as if he were a scholar.[7] We have here a contradiction between two sayings of the Rabbis, and between two sayings of R. Simeon b. Gamaliel!—R. Johanan said: Reverse the names; R. Shisha the son of R. Idi said: There is no need to reverse. There is no contradiction between the two sayings of the Rabbis. In the case of the recital of the *Shema'*, since everybody else recites, and he also recites, it does not look like showing off on his part; but in the case of the month of Ab, since everybody else does work and he does no work, it looks like showing off. Nor is there a contradiction between the two sayings of R. Simeon b. Gamaliel. In the case of the *Shema'*, the validity of the act depends on the mental concentration and we are witnesses that he is unable to concentrate. Here, however, anyone who sees will say, He has no work; go and see how many unemployed there are in the
b market place.[1]

CHAPTER III

MISHNAH. ONE WHOSE DEAD [RELATIVE] LIES BEFORE
c HIM[1] IS EXEMPT FROM THE RECITAL OF THE SHEMA' AND FROM THE TEFILLAH AND FROM TEFILLIN AND FROM ALL THE PRECEPTS LAID DOWN IN THE TORAH. WITH REGARD TO THE BEARERS OF THE BIER AND THOSE WHO RELIEVE THEM AND THOSE WHO RELIEVE THEM AGAIN,[2] WHETHER IN FRONT OF THE BIER OR BEHIND THE BIER[3]—THOSE IN FRONT OF THE BIER, IF THEY ARE STILL REQUIRED, ARE EXEMPT; BUT THOSE BEHIND THE BIER EVEN IF STILL REQUIRED, ARE NOT EXEMPT.[4] BOTH, HOWEVER, ARE EXEMPT FROM [SAYING] THE TEFILLAH. WHEN THEY HAVE BURIED THE DEAD AND RETURNED [FROM THE GRAVE], IF THEY HAVE TIME TO BEGIN AND FINISH [THE SHEMA'] BEFORE FORMING A ROW,[5] THEY SHOULD BEGIN, BUT IF NOT THEY SHOULD NOT BEGIN. AS FOR THOSE WHO STAND IN THE ROW, THOSE ON THE INSIDE[6] ARE EXEMPT, BUT THOSE ON THE OUTSIDE ARE NOT EXEMPT. [WOMEN, SLAVES AND MINORS ARE EXEMPT FROM RECITING THE SHEMA' AND PUTTING ON TEFILLIN, BUT ARE SUBJECT TO THE OBLIGATIONS OF TEFILLAH, MEZUZAH, AND GRACE AFTER MEALS].[7]

GEMARA. [If the dead] LIES BEFORE HIM, he is exempt,[8] [implying] if it does not lie before him,[9] he is not exempt.[10] This
d statement is contradicted by the following:[1] One whose dead lies before him eats in another room. If he has not another room, he eats in his fellow's room. If he has no fellow to whose room he can go, he makes a partition and eats [behind it]. If he has nothing with which to make a partition, he turns his face away and eats. He may not eat reclining, nor may he eat flesh or drink wine; he does not say a blessing [over food] nor grace after meals[2] [18a],

(6) Who made a 'breach' in the kingdom of David. V. Sanh. 106b. (7) Who went forth to evil ways (ibid.). (8) Who became a leper and had to cry 'unclean, unclean'. (9) Lit., 'spoils his food', by addition of too much salt. A metaphor for the open acceptance of heretical teachings. (10) MS.M. adds: like the Nazarene. (11) Isa. XLVI, 12. Heb. *zedakah*, which is taken by the Rabbis in the sense of 'charity'.
a (1) The 'stout-hearted', i.e., righteous. (2) Lit., 'arm'. I.e., the force of their own good deeds. (3) A tribe in the neighbourhood of Babylon. (4) A suburb of Sura, where one of the great Academies was situated. (5) At the *kallahs* (v. Glos). In Adar and Elul. (6) I.e., show of superior piety or learning. (7) V. Pes. 55a.
b (1) Even on working days.
c (1) I.e., is not yet buried. (2) In carrying the bier to the grave. (3) Those in front of the bier have still to carry; those behind have already carried. (4) Since they have already carried once. (5) To comfort the mourners. V. 16b, n. b2. (6) If they stand two or more deep. (7) Words in brackets belong properly to the next Mishnah, v. *infra* 20a. (8) Lit., 'yes'. (9) This phrase is now understood literally and thus to include the case where he is in a different room. (10) Lit., 'No'.
d (1) M.K. 23b. (2) So Rashi. V. however M.K., Sonc. ed., p. 147, n. 2.

nor do others say a blessing for him nor is he invited to join in the grace. He is exempt from reciting the *Shema'*, from saying the *tefillah*, from putting on *tefillin* and from all the precepts laid down in the Torah. On Sabbath, however, he may recline and eat meat and drink wine, and he says a blessing, and others may say the blessing for him and invite him to join in grace, [and he is subject to the obligation of reading the *Shema'* and *tefillah*],[3] and he is subject to all the precepts laid down in the Torah. R. Simeon b. Gamaliel says: Since he is subject to these, he is subject to all of them; and R. Johanan said: Where do they differ in practice? In regard to marital intercourse.[4] At any rate it states that he is exempt from the recital of the *Shema'* and from saying the *tefillah* and putting on *tefillin* and all the precepts laid down in the Torah?[5]—Said R. Papa: Explain this [Baraitha] as applying only to one who turns his face away and eats.[6] R. Ashi, however, said: Since the obligation of burial devolves on him, it is as if the corpse was before him,[7] as it says: *And Abraham rose up from before his dead,*[8] and it says, *That I may bury my dead out of my sight:*[9] this implies that so long as the obligation to bury devolves upon him, it is as if the corpse were lying before him.[10]

[I infer from our Mishnah] that this is the rule for a dead
a relative but not for one whom he is merely watching.[1] But it has been taught: One who watches a dead [body] even if it is not his dead [relative], is exempt from reciting the *Shema'* and saying the *tefillah* and putting on *tefillin* and all the precepts laid down in the Torah?—[We interpret therefore]: He who watches the dead, even if it is not his dead [relative], [is exempt], and [likewise in the case of] his dead relative, even if he is not watching it, he is [exempt], but if he is walking in the cemetry, he is not. But it has been taught: A man should not walk in a cemetery with *tefillin* on his head or a scroll of the Law in his arm, and recite the *Shema'*,[2] and if he does so, he comes under the heading of *'He that mocketh the poor[3] blasphemeth his Maker'?*[4]—In that case the act is forbidden within four cubits of the dead, but beyond four cubits the obligation [to say *Shema'* etc.] devolves. For a Master has said: A dead body affects four cubits in respect of the recital of the *Shema'*. But in this case he is exempt even beyond four cubits.

[To turn to] the above text: One who watches a dead [body], even though it is not his own dead [relative], is exempt from the recital of the *Shema'* and from saying the *tefillah* and from putting on *tefillin* and from all the precepts laid down in the Torah. If there were two [watching], one goes on watching while the other recites, and then the other watches while this one recites. Ben 'Azzai says: If they were bringing it in a ship, they put it in a corner and both say their prayers in another corner. Why this difference?—Rabina said: They differ on the question whether there is any fear of mice[5] [on board ship]. One held that there is a fear of mice and the other held that there is no fear of mice.

Our Rabbis taught: A man who is carrying bones from place to place should not put them in a saddle-bag and place them on his ass and sit on them, because this is a disrespectful way of treating them. But if he was afraid of heathens and robbers, it is permitted. And the rule which they laid down for bones applies also to a scroll of the Law. To what does this last statement
b refer? Shall I say to the first clause?[1] This is self-evident: Is a scroll of the Law inferior to bones?—Rather; it refers to the second clause.[2]

Rahaba said in the name of Rab Judah: Whoever sees a corpse [on the way to burial] and does not accompany it[3] comes under the head of *'He that mocketh the poor blasphemeth his Maker'*. And if he accompanies it, what is his reward? R. Assi says: To him apply the texts: *He that is gracious unto the poor lendeth unto the Lord,*[4] and *he that is gracious unto the needy honoureth Him.*[5]

R. Ḥiyya and R. Jonathan were once walking about in a cemetery, and the blue fringe of R. Jonathan was trailing on the ground. Said R. Ḥiyya to him: Lift it up, so that they [the dead] should not say: Tomorrow they are coming to join us and now they are insulting us! He said to him: Do they know so much? Is it not written, *But the dead know not anything?*[6] He replied to him: If you have read once, you have not repeated; if you have repeated, you have not gone over a third time; if you have gone over a third time, you have not had it explained to you. *For the living know that they shall die.*[7] these are the righteous who in their death are called living, as it says, *And Benaiah the son of Jehoiada, the son of a living*[8] *man from Kabzeel, who had done mighty deeds, he smote the two altar-hearths of Moab; he went down and also slew a lion in the midst*

(3) Inserted with MS.M. (4) At a time when it is a duty. Rabban Simeon declares the mourner subject to this duty on the Sabbath, though it is otherwise forbidden during the week of mourning. (5) Apparently even if he eats in a neighbour's house, *contra* the implied ruling of our Mishnah. (6) I.e., has no other room and so it does not contradict our Mishnah. (7) And this is the case mentioned in the Baraitha. (8) Gen. XXIII, 3. (9) Ibid. 4. (10) Even if he is in another room. The phrase 'lying before him' is not to be understood literally, and consequently there is no contradiction between the Baraitha and our Mishnah.

a (1) And which he is not under obligation to bury. A dead body, according to Jewish law, must be watched to protect it from mice, v. *infra*. (2) And the same applies even if he is not carrying a scroll. (3) I.e., the dead, who are *'poor'* in precepts. (4) Prov. XVII, 5. (5) The reason why a corpse has to be watched is to protect it from mice.

b (1) That it must not be ridden upon. (2) That in time of danger it is permitted. (3) MS.M. adds, for four cubits. (4) Prov. XIX, 17. (5) Ibid. XIV, 31. (6) Eccl. IX, 5. (7) Ibid. (8) So the *kethib*. E.V., following the keri, *'valiant'*.

תורה אור

ואין מברכין עליו ואין מזמנין עליו ופטור מק"ש ומן התפלה ומן התפילין ומכל מצות האמורות בתורה ובשבת מיסב ואוכל בשר ושותה יין ומברך ומזמן ומברכין עליו ומזמנים עליו וחייב בכל המצות האמורות בתורה *רשב"ג אומר מתוך שנתחייב באלו נתחייב בכולן וא"ר יוחנן מאי בינייהו תשמיש המטה איכא בינייהו קתני מיהת פטור מק"ש ומן התפלה ומן התפילין ומכל מצות האמורות בתורה אמר רב פפא תרגמא אמחזיר פניו ואוכל רב אשי אמר כיון שמוטל עליו לקוברו כמוטל לפניו דמי שנאמר °ויקם אברהם מעל פני מתו ונאמר ואקברה מתי מלפני כל זמן שמוטל עליו לקוברו כמוטל לפניו דמי מתו אין אבל משמרו לא והתניא המשמר את המת אע"פ שאינו מתו פטור מק"ש ומן התפלה ומן התפילין ומכל מצות האמורו' בתור' משמרו אע"פ שאינו מתו מתו אע"פ שאינו משמרו מתו ומשמרו אין אבל מהלך בבי' הקברו' לא והתני' *לא יהלך אדם בבית הקברות ותפילין בראשו וס"ת בזרועו וקורא ואם עושה כן עובר משום °לועג לרש חרף עושהו התם תוך ד' הוא דאסיר חוץ לד' אמות חייב *דאמר מר מת תופס ד' אמות לק"ש הכא חוץ לד' אמות נמי פטור: גופא המשמר את המת אע"פ שאינו מתו פטור מק"ש ומן התפלה ומן התפילין ומכל מצות האמורות בתורה היו ב' זה משמר וזה קורא וזה משמר וזה קורא בן עזאי אומר היו באים בספינה מניחו בזוית זו ומתפללין שניהן בזוית אחרת מאי בינייהו אמר רבינא חוששים לעכברים איכא בינייהו מר סבר חיישינן ומ"ס לא חיישינן: ת"ר *המוליך עצמות ממקום למקום הרי זה לא יתנם בדסקיא ויתנם ע"ג חמור וירכב עליהם מפני שנוהג בהם מנהג בזיון ואם היה מתירא מפני נכרים ומפני לסטים מותר וכדרך שאמרו בעצמות כך אמרו בס"ת אהייא אילימא ארישא פשיטא מי גרע ס"ת מעצמות אלא אסיפא: אמר רחבה *א"ר יהודה כל הרואה המת ואינו מלוהו עובר משום לועג לרש חרף עושהו ואם הלוהו מה שכרו א"ר אסי עליו הכתוב אומר °מלוה ה' חונן דל °ומכבדו חונן אביון: רבי חייא ור' יונתן הוו שקלי ואזלי בבית הקברות הוה קשדיא תכלתיה דרבי יונתן א"ל ר' חייא דליי' כדי שלא יאמרו למחר באין אצלנו ועכשיו מחרפין אותנו אמר ליה ומי ידעי כולי האי והא כתיב °והמתים אינם יודעים מאומה אמר ליה *אם קרית לא שנית אם שלשת לא פירשו לך °כי החיים יודעים שימותו אלו צדיקים שבמיתתן נקראו חיים שנאמר °ובניהו בן יהוידע בן איש חי רב פעלים מקבצאל הוא הכה את שני אריאל מואב והוא ירד והכה את הארי בתוך הבור ביום השלג בן

רש"י

ואין מברכין עליו. אין לריך שיברכו לו אחרים בברכת הלחם: ואין מזמנין עליו. אין מלטרף עם ג' לזימון: תשמיש המטה איכא בינייהו. לר"ש חייב אבל בעונה בשבת: קתני מיהת פטור מק"ש ומכל ברכות. ואפילו כשהוא אוכל בבית חבירו: תרגמא. להא דתני פטור אוני שאין לו בית אחר דקאמר מחזיר פניו ואוכל: רב אשי אמר. לעולם אכולה ומתניתין קאי אפילו בבית אחר כמי פטר ליה דכל שמוטל עליו לקוברו קרי מוטל לפניו: ויקם אברהם וגו' וכתיב ואקברה מתי מלפני. והיא שעתא לאו לפניו הוה: משמרו. אדם אחר שאינו קרובו אלא משמרו: תופס ארבע אמות לק"ש. שאסור לקרות בתוך ארבע אמות שלו משום לועג לרש: פטור מק"ש. משום דעוסק במלוה: חוששין לעכברים. ת"ק חייש לעכברים אפילו בספינה: דסקיא. מרצוף גדול של עור: ואם היה מתירא. ולריך לרכוב על הסוס ולרוץ: אלא אסיפא. אם היה מתירא רוכב: מלוה ה' חונן דל. קרי ביה מלוה את המקום מי שחונן את הדל ואין לך דל מן המת והמלוה אותו כאלו מלוה את המקום: דלייה. הגביהנו: לא שנית. לא חזרת עליו פעם שנית כדי שתתבונן בו: אלו צדיקים. ומאי יודעים שימותו נותנים אל לבם יום המיתה ומושכים ידיהם מן העבירה והרשעים אינם יודעים מאומה שעושים עלמם כאינם יודעים ומוטאים: והוא הכה. השפיל את השנים של דורות משני מקדשים שלא היה בהם כמותו: אריאל. זה בית המקדש שנאמר הוי אריאל אריאל קרית חנה דוד (ישעיה כט): מואב. על שם שבנאו דוד דאתי מבות המואביה: גזיזי

תוספות

והתניא פטור מתקיעת שופר אית לך למימר בחול ולא ביום טוב בתמיה ומשני א"כ חנינא ונכיון שהוא זקוק להכין לו ארון ותכריכין כדתנן (שבת דף קנא.) מחשיכין על התחום להביא לו ארון ותכריכין כמו שהוא נושא ומשאו דמי אלמא משמע דבשבתות וימים טובים אינו רשאי לברך ולהתפלל דעבוד להחשיך לו על התחום להביא ארון ותכריכין וקשיא מסיפא דקתני בשבת מברכין עליו ומזמנין עליו וכן תניא נמי בירושלמי בד"א בחול אבל בשבת מיסב ואוכל ומברך ועונין אחריו אמן ואומר הר"י דפליגי אהדדי רישא וסיפא בירושלמי. ורבי נתנאל היה אומר דאפשר לישבו דודאי אם דעתו להחשיך על התחום אז יש לנו לומר דעבוד להחשיך ואינו רשאי לברך אבל בסיפא איירי בשאין דעתו להחשיך על התחום ומיהו האי טעמא לא שייך לטעמא דמשום כבודו ומן הירושלמי דמשני דפטור מנטילת לולב דאיירי בחול המועד דעבוד ליסא משאו למדנו שבחוה"מ שייך אנינות כשמתו מוטל לפניו וכיון דכשמוטל לפניו שייך אנינות כי מוטל עליו לקוברו כמוטל לפניו דמי וכן איפכא מי שמתו מוטל לפניו ואין עליו לקוברו אינו נוהג אנינות וכן משמע בירושלמי כמסר לרבים אוכל בשר ושותה יין כמסר לכתפים כמסר לרבים ועל כרחך כמסר לרבים ר"ל אפילו לפניו דאי שלא לפניו תיפוק ליה שמיד חל עליו אבילות משילא מפתח ביתו וכיון דלא חל עליה אנינות אם כן אדם שאינו יכול לקבור מתו כגון אדם שמת בבית האסורים ואין המושל מניחו לקברו נראה שאין חייב לנהוג בו אנינות שהרי אין זה מוטל עליו לקוברו מפני שאין יכול לפדותו ולהוציאו ולקברו כדתניא בשמחות (פ"ב הל' י"א) נתיאשו בעליו מלקוברו מתאבלין עליו ופסיק מיניה תורת אנינות מיהו באותו שתפסו מושל גם אבלות אינו חייב דלא דמי לנתיאשו מלקוברו שסם אינו קובר תו *אבל הכא עדיין הוא מלפה אם יוכל לעשות פשרה עם המושל להניחו לקוברו וכן מעשה דרבי אליעזר ב"ר שמעון בבבא מליעא (ד' פד:) דפסק מלות אנינות ומעשה שמתה אחותו של רבינו תם בשבת והודיעו לו במולאי שבת בעיר אחרת ואכל בשר ושתה יין ואמר כיון שיש לה בעל שחייב בקבורתה אינו אסור בבשר ויין ואפשר שגם ר"ת אם היה בעיר עלמו היה מיקל מאותו הטעם:

וספר תורה בזרועו וקורא. והוא הדין דעל פה אסור לקרות:

וירכב עליהן. אבל אם מפשילן לאחוריו על החמור שפיר דמי וכן בס"ת ואפילו אם בדעתך לאסור ס"ת אבל בנביאים ובכתובים שפיר דמי *מדנקט ס"ת ולא מסתבר לומר משום שריותא דעכו"ם ולסטים דהא פשיטא דמותר דלמה יהיה אסור ועוד דבהדיא אמר בירושלמי דקיא מלאה ספרים או שהיו בה עלמות של מת ה"ז מתחילן לאחוריו ורוכב עליו: **אלא** אסיפא. מגמתו לסטים מותר לרכוב עליהם וה"ה לאחוריו מותר אפילו בלא לסטים: **למחר** באים אללנו ועכשיו מלעיגים אותנו. ותימה והא אמרינן פרק התכלת (דף מג.) הציא שעתא ודאי רמינן ליה פי' נותנים ליצית בטליתותיהן משום לועג לרש וי"ל דה"פ הכא דמביישי' אותם במה שהחיים מלווים והמתי' אינם מלווים וגדול המלווה וכו' והציא דהתכלת (היינו) דרמו חוטים למתי' ועכשיו אנו מסלקין אותן *ומאי שנא אומר ר"ת דוקא הם שהיו רגילים כולם בחייהם ללבוש טלית בד' כנפות וללבוש ליצית וגם לכל העוסקים בהם יש להם ליצית והוי לועג לרש אם לא הי' להם ליצית אז משום דכתיב לדורותם לדור תם אבל אנו שגם בחיינו אין מנהגנו ללבוש תמיד ליצית אי הוה רמינן להו הוי כמו לועג לרש וכי תימא נשים לאות' שהיה להם בחייהן אם כן יהיה לועג לרש לאחרי' ועוד אר"ת שמשמע מאכבי לותי"ר דמסירי' הליצית דליצית עולה למנין תרי"ג עם ח' חוטים וחמשה קשרים ואם לובש ליצית נראה כאלו קיים כל התור' ומיחזי כשיקרא וזה לא נהירא דגם חיים עתה למה לובשים הלא לא קיימו כל התורה כולה ומיהו י"ל דאנו קוונכים על מסכת שמחות (פי"ב) שלוה אבא שאול לבניו הטילו תכלת מאפיליוני ולע"פ שהגמרא חולק עליו יש דברים שאנו מניחין הגמרא שלנו ואנו עושין כספרים החיצונים כמו מחזון ישעיהו כפסיקתא וכמו ויחל שיש בגמרא (מגילה דף לא.) דבתענית קורים ברכות וקללות ובמס' סופרים (פרק יז) מפרש ויחל והריצב"א היה רגיל שלא להסירם מן הכנף אלא לקשרם ולהדקם בתוך הכנף לאפוקי נפשיה מפלוגתא אם הם הייבין בליצית יש להם ליצית ואם לאו לאו הרי הם מכוסין *: **שני** אריאל מואב. על שם דוד ושלמה שבנו את הבית ובאו מבות המואביה: בן

מסורת הש"ס

[במ"ק אי' רבן גמליאל וכ"א בשמחו']

בראשי' כג

משלי' יז

סוטה מג:

[שמחות פי"ג בשינוי לשון]

משלי יד שם יד

קהלת ט

שם

שמואל ב כג

[בשאלתו' אי' א"ר יהודה אמר רב]

[מ"ק עז:]

ומיהו נראה דאף בס"ת א"ד מדנקיט בסיפא ס"ת כל"ל

ומאי טעמא כל"ל רש"א

[וע' תוס' פסחי' מ: ד"ה אבל ותוס' ב"ב עד. ד"ה פסקו ותוס' נדה סא. ד"ה אבל ותוס' ע"ז סה: ד"ה אבל]

עין משפט נר מצוה

ה
א מיי' פ"ד מהל' תפילין הכ"ג ופ' יד מהלכ' אבל הי"ג סמ"ג עשין כב טוש"ע א"ח סי' מה סעי' א וסי' עא סעי' ז

ו
ב מיימ' פ"ד מהלכות ק"ש הלכה ג טוש"ע א"ח סי' עא סעי' ג ד ובי"ד סי' שמא סעי' ו

ז
ג מיימ' פ' יד מהלכ' אבל הי"ד סמ"ג עשין ב טוש"ע י"ד סי' תג סעי' י

ח
ד מיימ' וסמג שם טוש"ע י"ד סי' בסא סעי' ג

מסורת הש"ס

גזיזי דברדא. חתיכות של ברד והקרח שקורין גלאצ"ה בלעז והיינו ביום השלג: ונחת וטבל. לקריו כדי לעסוק בתורה: דתנא ספרא דבי רב. תורת כהנים: חלל רשע. על צדקיהו הוא אומר ועדיין בימי יחזקאל חי היה וקוראו חלל: לקריתא. להתעסק בעבודת אחוזתם: אייקר תלמודייהו. נשתכח תלמודם ונגרסם לייקר הוכבד עליהם מחמת שכחה: בצערא דידהו. לצער גופם ממש כגון עקיצת רימה: שתי רוחות. של שתי ילדות מתות: ונשמע. וכדי מה גזרו היום פורענות בעולם שהעולם נדון בראש השנה: הפרגוד. מחיצה המבדלת בין מקום השכינה: ברביעה ראשונה. יורה שלש רביעיות הן בכירה שניה ושלישית לאפילה בי"ז מרחשון שניה בכ"ג שלישית בר"ח כסליו: ברד מלקה אותו. שעתיד ברד ליפול סמוך לרביעה *ראשונ' ומה שנזרע כבר הוקשה והברד שוברו והנזרע בשניה עדיין רך הוא ואינו נשבר בשביל הברד כענין שנאמר והפשתה והשעורה נוכתה והחטה והכוסמת לא נכו (שמות ט): שדפון. נלקה הרך ואינו משדף הקשה: אלמא ידעי. דברים האמורים בין החיים: לחצר מות. לבית הקברות: בצנורא דדשא. בחור ומפתן הבית שהדלת סובב בו: מסרקאי. מסרק שלי: גובתא. קנה ובשביל שמתה ילדה אמרה כן לעגמת נפש: בהדי פלניתא דאתיא למחר. לקבורה: אלמא ידעי. מה שעושים שידעה זו שזו נוקשת וכנויה למות: דלמא דומה. מלאך הוא הממונה על המתים קדים ומכריז להו עכשיו יבא פלוני אבל שאר דברי החיים אינם יודעים: בעינא אבא. מבקש אני את אבא כך היה שמו: אמרו ליה. המתים נגלו לו כאלו הם חוץ מקבריהם ויושבים בעגולה: חזייה. שמואל ללוי *חברו שהיה יושב חוץ לישיבה של שאר מתים: כל כי הנך שני. מספר השנים שלא נכנסתי בישיבתו של ר' אפס במסכת כתובות בפרק הנושא את האשה (דף קג:): חזייה. שמואל לאבוה דקא בכי וחייך: דלעגל אתית. במהרה תקבר: באמתא דרחיא. כל בנין מושב הרחיים קרוי אמת הרחיים: אלמא ידעי. מי חשוב בין החיים: זאת הארץ. במיתת משה כתיב: ואי

[ל"ל שניה]

[ע' תוס' ב"ק פב: ד"ה אתא]

שבת יג: וקנב. סוטה י.

ס"א חבירו

בן איש חי אטו כולי עלמא. בספרים מדוייקים כתיב חי וקרינן חיל ומן הכתוב דייק הכי שלא כתב חיל אלא חי: **ספרא** דבי רב. מהאי דריש שהוא אמור שבספרים: **בתוך** הבור. שהוא באמצע הספרים: **אלמא** ידעי. מדקאמר לעגל קא אתית ולא מצי לשנויי כדלעיל דומה קדים ואמר להו דהיינו דוקא לאלתר אבל כ"כ לא היה מקדים דהוא עצמו אינו יודע: אפילו

תורה אור

בן איש חי אטו כולי עלמא בני מתי נינהו אלא בן איש חי שאפילו במיתתו קרוי חי רב פעלים מקבצאל שריבה וקבץ פועלים לתורה והוא הכה את שני אריאל מואב שלא הניח כמותו לא במקדש ראשון ולא במקדש שני והוא ירד והכה את הארי בתוך הבור ביום השלג איכא דאמרי דתבר גזיזי דברדא ונחת *וטבל איכא דאמרי דתנא ספרא דבי רב ביומא דסיתוא והמתים אינם יודעים מאומה אלו רשעים שבחייהן קרויין מתים שנאמר °ואתה חלל רשע נשיא ישראל ואיבעית אימא מהכא °על פי שנים עדים או (על פי) שלשה עדים יומת המת חי הוא אלא המת מעיקרא: *בני רבי חייא נפוק לקריתא אייקר להו תלמודייהו הוו קא מצערי לאדכוריה אמר ליה חד לחבריה ידע אבון בהאי צערא א"ל אידך מנא ידע והא כתיב °יכבדו בניו ולא ידע א"ל אידך ולא ידע והא כתיב °אך בשרו עליו יכאב ונפשו עליו תאבל ואמר ר' יצחק *קשה רמה למת כמחט בבשר החי אמרי בצערא דידהו ידעי בצערא דאחרינא לא ידעי ולא והתניא *מעשה בחסיד אחד שנתן דינר לעני בערב ר"ה בשני בצורת והקניטתו אשתו והלך ולן בבית הקברות ושמע שתי רוחות שמספרות זו לזו אמרה חדא לחברתה חברתי בואי ונשוט בעולם ונשמע מאחורי הפרגוד מה פורענות בא לעולם אמרה לה חברתה איני יכולה שאני קבורה במחצלת של קנים אלא לכי את ומה שאת שומעת אמרי לי הלכה היא ושטה ובאה ואמרה לה חברתה חברתי מה שמעת מאחורי הפרגוד אמרה לה שמעתי שכל הזורע ברביעה ראשונה ברד מלקה אותו הלך הוא וזרע ברביעה שניה של כל העולם כלו לקה שלו לא לקה לשנה האחרת הלך ולן בבית הקברות ושמע אותן שתי רוחות שמספרות זו עם זו אמרה חדא לחברתה בואי ונשוט בעולם ונשמע מאחורי הפרגוד מה פורענות בא לעולם אמרה לה חברתי לא כך אמרתי לך איני יכולה שאני קבורה במחצלת של קנים אלא לכי את ומה שאת שומעת בואי ואמרי לי הלכה ושטה ובאה ואמרה לה חברתה חברתי מה שמעת מאחורי הפרגוד אמרה לה שמעתי שכל הזורע ברביעה שניה שדפון מלקה אותו הלך וזרע ברביעה ראשונה של כל העולם כלו נשדף ושלו לא נשדף אמרה לו אשתו מפני מה *אשתקד של כל העולם כלו לקה ושלך לא לקה ועכשיו של כל העולם כלו נשדף ושלך לא נשדף סח לה כל הדברים הללו אמרו לא היו ימים מועטים עד שנפלה קטטה בין אשתו של אותו חסיד ובין אמה של אותה ריבה אמרה לה לכי ואראך בתך שהיא קבורה במחצלת של קנים לשנה האחרת הלך ולן בבית הקברות ושמע אותן רוחות שמספרות זו עם זו אמרה לה חברתי בואי ונשוט בעולם ונשמע מאחורי הפרגוד מה פורענות בא לעולם אמרה לה חברתי הניחני דברים שביני לבינך כבר נשמעו בין החיים אלמא ידעי דלמא איניש אחרינא שכיב ואזיל ואמר להו ת"ש דזעירי הוה מפקיד זוזי גבי אושפיזכתי' עד דאתי ואזיל לבי רב שכיבה אזל בתרה לחצר מות אמר לה זוזי היכא אמרה ליה זיל שקלינהו מתותי בצנורא דדשא בדוך פלן ואימא לה לאימא תשדר לי מסרקאי וגובתאי דכוחלא בהדי פלניתא דאתיא למחר אלמא ידעי [דלמא] דומה קדים ומכריז להו ת"ש דאבוה דשמואל הוו קא מפקדי גביה זוזי דיתמי כי נח נפשיה לא הוה שמואל גביה הוו קא קרו ליה בר אכיל זוזי דיתמי אזל אבתריה לחצר מות אמר להו בעינא אבא אמרו ליה אבא טובא איכא הכא בעינא אבא בר אבא אמרו ליה אבא בר אבא נמי טובא איכא הכא אמר להו בעינא אבא בר אבא אבוה דשמואל היכא אמרו ליה סליק למתיבתא דרקיעא אדהכי חזייה ללוי דיתיב אבראי אמר ליה אמאי יתבת אבראי מאי טעמא לא סלקת אמר ליה דאמרי לי כל כי הנך שני דלא סליקת למתיבתא דרבי אפס ואחלישתיה לדעתיה לא מעיילינן לך למתיבתא דרקיעא אדהכי והכי אתא אבוה חזייה דהוה קא בכי ואחיך אמר ליה מאי טעמא קא בכית אמר ליה דלעגל קא אתית מאי טעמא אחיכת דחשיבת בהאי עלמא טובא א"ל אי חשיבנא נעיילוה ללוי ועיילוה ללוי א"ל זוזי דיתמי היכא א"ל זיל שקלינהו באמתא דרחיא עילאי ותתאי דידן ומיצעי דיתמי א"ל מאי טעמא עבדת הכי אמר ליה אי גנבי גנבי מגנבו מדידן אי אכלה ארעא אכלה מדידן אלמא דידעי דלמא שאני שמואל כיון דחשיב קדמי ומכריז *פנו מקום ואף רבי יונתן הדר ביה דאמר רבי שמואל בר נחמני א"ר יונתן מנין למתים שמספרים זה עם זה שנאמר °ויאמר ה' אליו זאת הארץ אשר נשבעתי לאברהם ליצחק וליעקב לאמר מאי לאמר אמר הקדוש ב"ה למשה לך אמור להם לאברהם ליצחק וליעקב שבועה שנשבעתי לכם כבר קיימתיה לבניכם

ואי

יחזקאל כא

דברים יז

איוב יד

כב

[בע"ז מו. כתב רש"י ד"ה בני ר' חייא יהודה וחזקי' שמן]

[סנהד' מז:]

[אד"ר פ"ג]

[כלומר שהם קדמים עליך. וע' תי"ט ב"ב פ"ו מ"ג]

[כתובות עז:]

דברים לד

of a pit in the time of snow.[9] [18*b*] *'The son of a living man'*: are all other people then the sons of dead men? Rather *'the son of a living man'* means that even in his death he was called living. *'From Kabzeel, who had done mighty deeds'*: this indicates that he gathered [*kibbez*] numerous workers for the Torah. *'He smote two altar-hearths of Moab'*; this indicates that he did not leave his like either in the first Temple or in the second Temple.[10] *'He went down and also slew a lion in the midst of a pit in the time of snow'*: some say that this indicates that
a he broke blocks of ice and went down and bathed;[1] others say that he went through the Sifra of the School of Rab[2] on a winter's day. *'But the dead know nothing'*: These are the wicked who in their lifetime are called dead, as it says, *And thou, O wicked one, that art slain, the prince of Israel.*[3] Or if you prefer, I can derive it from here: *At the mouth of two witnesses shall the dead be put to death.*[4] He is still alive! What it means is, he is already counted as dead.

The sons of R. Ḥiyya went out to cultivate their property,[5] and they began to forget their learning.[6] They tried very hard to recall it. Said one to the other: Does our father know of our trouble? How should he know, replied the other, seeing that it is written, *His sons come to honour and he knoweth it not?*[7] Said the other to him: But does he not know? Is it not written: *But his flesh grieveth for him, and his soul mourneth over him?*[8] And R. Isaac said [commenting on this]: The worm is as painful to the dead as a needle in the flesh of the living? [He replied]: It is explained that they know their own pain, they do not know the pain of others. Is that so? Has it not been taught: It is related that a certain pious man gave a *denar* to a poor man on the eve of New Year in a year of drought, and his wife scolded him, and he went and passed the night in the cemetery, and he heard two spirits conversing with one another. Said one to her companion: My dear, come and let us wander about the world and let us hear from behind the curtain[9] what suffering is coming on the world.[10] Said her companion to her: I am not able, because I am buried in a matting of reeds.[11] But do you go, and whatever you hear tell me. So the other went and wandered about and returned. Said her companion to her: My dear, what have you heard from behind the curtain? She replied:
b I heard that whoever sows after the first rainfall[1] will have his crop smitten by hail. So the man went and did not sow till after the second rainfall,[2] with the result that everyone else's crop was smitten and his was not smitten.[3] The next year he again went and passed the night in the cemetery, and heard the two spirits conversing with one another. Said one to her companion: Come and let us wander about the world and hear from behind the curtain what punishment is coming upon the world. Said the other to her: My dear, did I not tell you that I am not able because I am buried in a matting of reeds? But do you go, and whatever you hear, come and tell me. So the other one went and wandered about the world and returned. She said to her: My dear, what have you heard from behind the curtain? She replied: I heard that whoever sows after the later rain will have his crop smitten with blight. So the man went and sowed after the first rain with the result that everyone else's crop was blighted and his was not blighted.[4] Said his wife to him: How is it that last year everyone else's crop was smitten and yours was not smitten, and this year everyone else's crop is blighted and yours is not blighted? So he related to her all his experiences. The story goes that shortly afterwards a quarrel broke out between the wife of that pious man and the mother of the child,[5] and the former said to the latter, Come and I will show you your daughter buried in a matting of reeds. The next year the man again went and spent the night in the cemetery and heard those conversing together. One said: My dear, come and let us wander about the world and hear from behind the curtain what suffering is coming upon the world. Said the other: My dear, leave me alone; our conversation has already been heard among the living. This would prove that they know?—Perhaps some other man after his decease went and told them. Come and hear; for Ze'iri deposited some money with his landlady,
c and while he was away visiting Rab[1] she died. So he went after her to the cemetery[2] and said to her, Where is my money? She replied to him: Go and take it from under the ground, in the hole of the doorpost, in such and such a place, and tell my mother to send me my comb and my tube of eye-paint by the hand of So-and-so who is coming here tomorrow. Does not this[3] show that they know?—Perhaps Dumah[4] announces to them beforehand.[5] Come and hear: The father of Samuel had some money belonging to orphans deposited with him. When he died, Samuel was not with him, and they called him, 'The son who consumes the money of orphans'. So he went after his father to the cemetery, and said to them [the dead], I am looking for Abba.[6] They said to him: There are many Abbas here. I want Abba b. Abba, he said. They replied: There are also several Abbas b. Abba here. He then said to them: I want Abba b. Abba the father of Samuel; where is he? They replied: He has gone up to the Academy of the Sky.[7] Meanwhile he saw Levi sitting outside.[8] He said to him: Why are you sitting outside? Why have you not gone up [to heaven]? He replied: Because they said to me: For as many years as you did not go up to the academy of R. Efes and hurt his feelings,[9] we will not let you go up to the Academy of the Sky. Meanwhile his father came. Samuel observed that he was both weeping and laughing. He said to him: Why are you weeping? He replied: Because you are coming here soon. And why are you laughing? Because you are highly esteemed in this world. He thereupon said to him: If I am esteemed, let them take up Levi; and they did take up Levi. He then said to him: Where is the money of the orphans? He replied: Go and you will find it in the case of the millstones. The money at the top and the bottom is mine, that in the middle is the orphans' He said to him: Why did you do like that? He replied: So that if thieves came, they should take mine, and if the
d earth destroyed any, it should destroy mine. Does not this[1] show that they know?—Perhaps Samuel was exceptional: as he was esteemed, they proclaimed beforehand, Make way [for him]!

R. Jonathan also retracted his opinion. For R. Samuel b. Naḥmani said in the name of R. Jonathan: Whence do we know that the dead converse with one another? Because it says: *And the Lord said unto him. This is the land which I swore unto Abraham, unto Isaac, and unto Jacob, saying.*[2] What is the meaning of *'saying'?*[3] The Holy One, blessed be He, said to Moses: Say to Abraham, Isaac and Jacob: The oath which I swore to you I have already

(9) II Sam XXIII, 20. (10) 'Altar-hearths of Moab' are taken by the Rabbis to refer to the two Temples, on account of David's descent from Ruth the Moabitess.

a (1) To cleanse himself of pollution in order to study the Torah in cleanliness. (2) The *halachic* midrash on Leviticus. Lion-like he mastered in a short time (a winter's day) all the intricacies of this midrash. (3) Ezek. XXI, 30. E.V. *'that art to be slain'*. (4) Deut. XVII, 6. E.V. *'he that is to die'*. (5) Lit., 'to the villages'. (6) Lit., 'their learning grew heavy for them'. (7) Job XIV, 21. (8) Ibid. 22. (9) Screening the Divine Presence. (10) *Sc.*, in the divine judgment pronounced on New Year. (11) And not in a linen shroud.

b (1) The first fall of the former rains, which would be about the seventeenth of Heshvan (Rashi). (2) Which would be about six days after the first. (3) Being not yet sufficiently grown. (4) Being by now strong enough to resist. (5) Whose spirit the pious man had heard conversing.

c (1) Or 'the school house'. (2) Lit., 'court of death'. (3) That she knew someone else was going to die. (4) Lit., 'Silence'. The angel presiding over the dead. (5) That So-and-so will die, but they know nothing else. (6) This was his father's name. (7) Where the souls of the pious learned foregathered. (8) Apart from the other dead. (9) V. Keth. 113*b*.

d (1) His knowing that Samuel would soon die. (2) Deut. XXXIV, 4. (3) Lit., 'to say'.

carried out for your descendants. [19a] Now if you maintain that the dead do not know, what would be the use of his telling them?—You infer then that they do know. In that case, why should he need to tell them?—So that they might be grateful to Moses. R. Isaac said: If one makes remarks about the dead, it is like making remarks about a stone. Some say [the reason is that] they do not know, others that they know but do not care. Can that be so? Has not R. Papa said: A certain man made[4] derogatory remarks about Mar Samuel and a log fell from the roof and broke his skull?[5]—A Rabbinical student is different, because the Holy One, blessed be He, avenges his insult.[6]

R. Joshua b. Levi said: Whoever makes derogatory remarks about scholars after their death[7] is cast into *Gehinnom*, as it says, *But as for such as turn aside*[8] *unto their crooked ways, the Lord will lead them away with the workers of iniquity. Peace be upon Israel:*[9] even at a time when there is peace upon Israel, the Lord will lead them away with the workers of iniquity.[10] It was taught in the school of R. Ishmael: If you see a scholar who has committed an offence by night, do not cavil at him by day, for perhaps he has done penance. 'Perhaps', say you?—Nay, rather, he has certainly done penance. This applies only to bodily [sexual] offences, but if he has misappropriated money, [he may be criticised] until he restores it to its owner.

R. Joshua b. Levi further said: In twenty-four places we find that the Beth din inflicted excommunication for an insult to a
a teacher, and they are all recorded in the Mishnah.[1] R. Eleazar asked him, Where? He replied: See if you can find them. He went and examined and found three cases: one of a scholar who threw contempt on the washing of the hands, another of one who made derogatory remarks about scholars after their death, and a third of one who made himself too familiar towards heaven. What is the case of making derogatory remarks about scholars after their death?—As we have learnt:[2] He[3] used to say: The water [of the *soṭah*][4] is not administered either to a proselyte or to an emancipated woman; the Sages, however say that it is. They said to him: There is the case of Karkemith an emancipated bondwoman in Jerusalem to whom Shemaiah and Abtalyon administered the water? He replied: They administered it to one like themselves.[5] They thereupon excommunicated him, and he died in excommunication, and the Beth din stoned his coffin.[6] What is the case of treating with contempt the washing of the hands?—As we have learnt: R. Judah said: Far be it from us to think that Akabiah b. Mahalalel was excommunicated, for the doors of the Temple hall did not close on any man in Israel[7] the equal of Akabiah b. Mahalalel in wisdom, in purity and in fear of sin. Whom did they in fact excommunicate? It was Eleazar b. Hanoch, who raised doubts about washing the hands, and when he died the Beth din sent and had a large stone placed on his coffin, to teach you that if a man is excommunicated and dies in his excommunication,
b the Beth din stone his coffin.[1]

What is the case of one behaving familiarly with heaven?—As we have learnt: Simeon b. Shetaḥ sent to Ḥoni ha-Me'aggel:[2] You deserve to be excommunicated, and were you not Ḥoni, I would pronounce excommunication against you. But what can I do seeing that you ingratiate yourself[3] with the Omnipresent and He performs your desires, and you are like a son who ingratiates himself with his father and he performs his desires; and to you applies the verse: *Let thy father and thy mother be glad, and let her that bore thee rejoice*.[4]

But are there no more [instances of excommunication]? Is not there the case learnt by R. Joseph: Thaddeus a man of Rome accustomed the Roman [Jews] to eat kids roasted whole[5] on the eve of Passover. Simeon b. Shetaḥ sent to him and said: Were you not Thaddeus, I would pronounce sentence of excommunication on you, because you make Israel [appear to] eat holy things outside the precincts.[6]—We say, in our Mishnah, and this is in a Baraitha. But is there no other in our Mishnah? Is there not this one, as we have learnt: If he cuts it[7] up into rings and puts sand between the rings,[8] R. Eliezar declares that it is [permanently] clean, while the Rabbis declare that it is unclean; and this is the stove of Akna'i. Why Akna'i? Rab Judah said in the name of Samuel: Because they surrounded it with *halachoth* like a serpent [*akna'i*] and declared it unclean. And it has been taught: On that day they brought all the things that R. Eliezer had declared clean[9] and burnt them before him, and in the end they blessed[10] him.[11]—Even so we do not find excommunication stated in our Mishnah.[12] How then do you find the twenty-four places?—R. Joshua b. Levi
c compares one thing to another,[1] R. Eleazar does not compare one thing to another.

THOSE WHO CARRY THE BIER AND THOSE WHO RELIEVE THEM. Our Rabbis taught: A dead body is not taken out shortly before the time for the *Shema'*, but if they began to take it they do not desist. Is that so? Was not the body of R. Joseph taken out shortly before the time for the *Shema'*?—An exception can be made for a distinguished man.

BEFORE THE BIER AND BEHIND THE BIER. Our Rabbis taught: Those who are occupied with the funeral speeches, if the dead body is still before them, slip out one by one and recite the *Shema'*; if the body is not before them, they sit and recite it, and he [the mourner] sits silent; they stand up and say the *tefillah* and he stands up and accepts God's judgement and says: Sovereign of the Universe, I have sinned much before Thee and Thou didst not punish me one thousandth part. May it be Thy will, O Lord our God, to close up our breaches and the breaches of all Thy people the house of Israel in mercy! Abaye said: A man should not speak thus,[2] since R. Simeon b. Lakish said, and so it was taught in the name of R. Jose: A man should never speak in such a way as to give an opening to Satan. And R. Joseph said: What text proves this? Because it says: *We were almost like Sodom*.[3] What did the prophet reply to them? *Hear the word of the Lord, ye rulers of Sodom*.[4]

WHEN THEY HAVE BURIED THE DEAD BODY AND RETURNED, etc. [I understand]: If they are able to begin and go through all of it, yes, but if they have only time for one section or one verse, no. This statement was contradicted by the following: When they have buried the body and returned, if they are able to begin and complete even one section or one verse, [they do so]!—That is just what he says: If they are able to begin and go through even one section or one verse before they form a row, they should begin, but otherwise they should not begin.

(4) MS.M.: Did not R. Papa make etc.; cf. next note. (5) MS.M.: and nearly broke (lit., 'wished to break') his skull. This suits better the reading of MS.M. mentioned in previous note. (6) Lit., 'his honour'. (7) Lit., 'Speaks after the bier of scholars'. (8) Heb. *maṭṭim*, connected by R. Joshua with *miṭṭathan* (their bier) above. (9) Ps. CXXV, 5. (10) To Gehinnom.

a (1) I.e., the Mishnah as a whole. (2) 'Ed. V, 6. (3) Akabiah b. Mahalalel. (4) A woman suspected of infidelity. V. Num. V, 11ff. (5) They were supposed to be descended from Sennacherib and so from a family of proselytes. Others render: they only pretended to administer it. (6) V. 'Ed. V. 6 (Sonc. ed.) notes. (7) When they all assembled there to kill their paschal lambs.

b (1) Pes. 64*b*. (2) The word *Me'aggel* probably means 'circle-drawer'; v. Ta'an. 19*a*. (3) Aliter: 'take liberties with'. (4) Prov. XXIII, 25. V. Ta'an 19*a*. (5) Lit., 'Helmeted goats'—goats roasted whole with their entrails and legs placed on the head, like a helmet. This was how the Passover sacrifice was roasted. (6) V. Pes. (Sonc. ed.) p. 260 notes. (7) An earthenware stove which has been declared unclean, and cannot be used till it has been broken up and remade. (8) To cement them. (9) After contact with such a stove. (10) Euphemism for 'excommunicated'. (11) V. B.M. (Sonc. ed.) 59*b* notes.

תורה אור

ואי ס"ד דלא ידעי כי אמר להו מאי הוי אלא מאי דידעי למה ליה למימר להו לאחזוקי ליה טבותא למשה אמר רבי יצחק כל המספר אחרי המת כאלו מספר אחרי האבן איכא דאמרי דלא ידעי ואיכא דאמרי דידעי ולא איכפת להו איני והא אמר רב פפא חד אישתעי מילתא בתרי' דמר שמואל ונפל קניא מטללא ובזעא לארנקא דמוחי' שאני צורבא מרבנן דקב"ה תבע ביקריה: אריב"ל כל המספר אחר *מטתן של תלמידי חכמים נופל בגיהנם שנא' °והמטים עקלקלותם יוליכם ה' את פועלי האון שלום על ישראל אפילו בשעה ששלום על ישראל יוליכם ה' את פועלי האון תנא דבי ר' ישמעאל אם ראית ת"ח שעבר עבירה בלילה אל תהרהר אחריו ביום שמא עשה תשובה שמא ס"ד אלא ודאי עשה תשובה והני מילי בדברים שבגופו אבל בממונא עד דמהדר למריה: ואמר ריב"ל "בכ"ד מקומות ב"ד מנדין על כבוד הרב וכולן שנינו במשנתינו אמר ליה ר' אלעזר היכא א"ל לכי תשכח נפק דק ואשכח תלת המזלזל בנטילת ידים והמספר אחר מטתן של ת"ח והמגים דעתו כלפי מעלה "המספר אחר מטתן של תלמידי חכמים מאי היא דתנן *הוא היה אומר אין משקין לא את הגיורת ולא את המשוחררת וחכ"א "משקין ואמרו לו מעשה בכרכמית שפחה משוחררת בירושלים והשקוה שמעיה ואבטליון ואמר להם דוגמא השקוה ונדוהו ומת בנדויו וסקלו ב"ד את ארונו "והמזלזל בנטילת ידים מאי היא דתנן *א"ר יהודה חס ושלום שעקביא בן מהללאל נתנדה שאין עזרה ננעלת על כל אדם בישראל בחכמה ובטהרה וביראת חטא כעקביא בן מהללאל אלא את מי נדו את אלעזר בן חנך שפקפק בנטילת ידים וכשמת שלחו ב"ד והניחו אבן גדולה על ארונו *ללמדך "שכל המתנדה ומת בנדויו ב"ד סוקלין את ארונו. המגים דעתו כלפי מעלה מאי היא דתנן *שלח לו שמעון בן שטח לחוני המעגל צריך אתה להתנדות ואלמלא חוני אתה גוזרני עליך נדוי אבל מה אעשה שאתה *מתחטא לפני המקום ועושה לך רצונך כבן שמתחטא לפני אביו ועושה לו רצונו ועליך הכתוב אומר °ישמח אביך ואמך ותגל יולדתך ותו ליכא והא איכא דתני רב יוסף *תודוס איש רומי "הנהיג את בני רומי להאכילן גדיים מקולסין בלילי פסחים שלח לו שמעון בן שטח אלמלא תודוס אתה גוזרני עליך נדוי שאתה מאכיל את ישראל קדשים בחוץ *במשנתינו קאמרי' והא ברייתא היא ובמתניתין ליכא והא איכא הא דתנן *חתכו חוליות ונתן חול בין חוליא לחוליא ר"א מטהר וחכמים "מטמאים וזהו תנורו של עכנאי מאי עכנאי אמר רב יהודה אמר שמואל מלמד שהקיפוהו הלכות כעכנאי זה וטמאוהו *ותניא *אותו היום הביאו כל טהרות שטיהר ר' אליעזר ושרפום לפניו ולבסוף ברכוהו אפילו הכי נדוי במתני' לא תנן אלא בכ"ד מקומות היכי משכחת לה ריב"ל מדמה מילתא למילתא ור"א לא מדמה מילתא למילתא: נושאי המטה וחלופיהן: *ת"ר "אין מוציאין את המת סמוך לק"ש ואם התחילו אין מפסיקין איני והא רב יוסף אפקוהו סמוך לק"ש *אדם חשוב שאני: שלפני המטה ושלאחר המטה: ת"ר "העוסקים בהספד בזמן שהמת מוטל לפניהם נשמטין א' א' וקורין אין המת מוטל לפניהם הן יושבין וקורין והוא יושב ודומם הם עומדים ומתפללים והוא עומד ומצדיק עליו את הדין ואומר רבון העולמים הרבה חטאתי לפניך ולא נפרעת ממני אחד מני אלף יה"ר מלפניך ה' אלהינו שתגדור פרצותינו ופרצות כל עמך בית ישראל ברחמים אמר אביי ['] לא מיבעי ליה לאיניש למימר הכי דאמר *רשב"ל וכן תנא משמיה דר' יוסי לעולם אל יפתח אדם פיו לשטן ואמר רב יוסף מאי קראה שנאמר °כמעט כסדום היינו מאי אהדר להו נביא שמעו דבר ה' קציני סדום: קברו את המת וחזרו וכו': אם יכולים להתחיל ולגמור את כולה אין אבל פרק אחד או פסוק א' לא ורמינהי קברו את המת וחזרו אם יכולין להתחיל ולגמור אפילו פרק אחד או פסוק אחד ה"נ קאמר "אם יכולין להתחיל ולגמור אפי' פרק אחד או אפילו פסוק אחד עד שלא יגיעו לשורה יתחילו ואם לאו לא יתחילו: העומדים

(margin notes beside the Gemara: תלים קכה; משלי כג; [נדה ז:]; ישעיה א)

תוספות

אפילו בשעה שהלום על ישראל. והייכו לאחר מיתתו ולא אתו לאכלויי בהדי המספרים בגנותם מהכא משמע דאיירי לאחר מיתה:

דוגמא השקוה. פרש"י לפי שהיתה גיורת כמו הם שהיו גרים וכן משמע בירושלמי דמ"ק (פ"ג) מהו דוגמא דכוותה. בערוך פירש *דוגמא השקוה מי צבע אבל לא היו מים ממש ולא מחקו התורה עליה אלא ליראה אותה:

מדלגין

רש"י

ואי ס"ד דלא ידעי. אין מזכיר' כלום אלא לערא דגופא: המספר אחר המת. בגנותו של מת אחר מיתתו: קניא מטללא. קנה גדול ובכד נפל מן הגג: טללא. גג: ארנק' דמוחיה. כיס שהמוח מונח בו: והמטים עקלקלותם. לעיל מיניה כתיב הטיבה יי' לטובים וסמיך ליה והמטים עקלקלות' והמכריעים את חובותם יותר על זכיותם להטותם לכף חובה: יוליכם יי את פועלי האון. לגיהנם: בכ"ד מקומות. הפתא משמע מלינו שנדו חכמים בני אדם בכ"ד מקומות לכבוד הרב לפי שלא נהגו כבוד לרבם: הוא היה אומר. עקביא בן מהללאל במס' עדיות: אין משקין. אם קינא לה בעלה ונסתרה: לא את הגיורת. דבני ישראל אמור בפרשה (במדבר ה') פרט לאשת גר ועבד משוחרר: בכרכמית. כך שמה או על שם מקומה: דוגמא השקוה. על שהיו דומים להם הם השקוה שהיו שמעיה ואבטליון מבני בניו של סנחריב כדאמרינן בגיטין בפ' הנזקין (דף נז:): רבי יהודה. פליג אדלעיל דקתני שנדו את עקביא: שאין עזרה ננעלת. בפרק ה' דפסחים (דף סד:) שהיו שערי העזרה ננעלים כששוחטין פסחים של כל כת וכת שהפסח נשחט בשלש כתות: על כל אדם בישראל. כלומר כשהיתה ננעלת עליהם והייכו כשנתמלאה פה לפה לא היה בכולם אדם השוב בחכמה ויראת חטא כעקבי': אלעזר בן חנך שפקפק. זלזל והייכו נמי לכבוד הרב שעבר ע"פ הגוזרים על הידים: אלמלא חוני אתה. שילא שמך בגדולה ובחשיבות: צריך אתה לנדות. לפי שהטריח לפני המקום על עסק גשמים לא כך שאלתי כמה פעמים וכבוד המקום כבוד הרב הוא: מתחטא. לשון מוצא נקל בלבו לחטא לאביו ולהטריחו על תחותו: מקולסין. צלויים כשהן שלמים ותולין כרעיהם וקרבוליהם וקרביהם סביבותן בשפוד ועל שם כך קורהו מקולס שהוא לשון מזויין כדמתרגם וכובע נחושת על ראשו (שמואל א יז) וקולסא דנחשא: בלילי פסחים. זכר לפסח שלולהו שלם שנאמר בו על כרעיו ועל קרבו (שמות יב) כלומר עם כרעיו ועם קרבו: גוזרני עליך נדוי. והייכו נמי לכבוד הרב שאסרו חכמים את הדבר לפי שהוא קרוב להאכיל את ישראל קדשים בחוץ שהרואה סבור שהקדישו לשם פסח: חתכו חוליות. תנור של חרס שהוא עשוי ככלי ומטלטל ותחלת ברייתו מן הטיט ונשרפו בכבשן כשאר קדרות ואם נטמא הצריכו הכתוב נתיצה ואם נתצו בענין זה שחתכו סביב סביב כחוליות עגולות וחזר וחיברו בטיט של חול בין חוליא לחוליא רבי אליעזר מטהר עולמית שאינו עוד ככלי חרס שלא נשרף בכבשן וחכמים מטמאין: כעכנאי. כנחש זה שכורך עצמו בעגולה: כל טהרות. שנעשו בתנור זה או שנגעו באוכלו והיה רבי אליעזר מטהרן והם שרפום: וברכוהו. לפי שהרבה מחד לחלוק בדבר זה כדאמרינן בב"מ בפרק הזהב: נדוי במתני' לא תנן. הא דברכוהו בברייתא הוא דתני לה: מדמי מילתא למילתא'. כל מקום שראה במתניתין שנחלק היחיד על הרבים מחלוקת גדולה או אחד מן החכמים שמדבר קשה כנגד גדול הימנו אומר ראוי היה כאן נדוי: אין מוציאין את המת. לקברו סמוך לק"ש. לפי שמבטלין מן הקריאה: אין המת מוטל לפניהם. שהמת בבית אחר והם מקפידים אותו כאן וי"מ שנתון לצד אחר: והוא יושב ודומם. האבל: למימר הכי. לא נפרעת ממני דמשמע הפרע:

הרואה

מסורת הש"ס

[פי' אחר מעתן לשון הטייה הוא כלומר נטה מדרך הישרה כדקתני דבי רבי ישמעאל אם ראית ת"ח כו' שודאי עשה תשובה לפיכך אסור לספר בזה ערוך ערך אחר בשם ר"ה] עדיות פ"ה מ"ו

שם פסחים סד:

שם מ"ק טו.

תענית יט. (ירו' תענית פ"ג ל"ג ועושה לך רצונך ובמקום לפני אביו גרם על אביו)

פסחים נג. ע"ש. ביצה כג. ע"ש [עירובין נג. מנחות לא: כתובות קע.] ב"מ נט: כלים פ"ה משנה י עדיות פ"ז משנה ז [ב"מ נט:]

שמחות פ"י

[שבת לא. קמג: פסחים קי. מ"ק יא: יג. מגיל' כג: כתובות נג: פו. ב"מ עג. ע"ז ח: דף מח: חולין קלד:] כתובות ח: לקמן ס.

עין משפט נר מצוה

ט אמיי' פ"ו מהל' תלמוד תורה ה' יד טוש"ע י"ד סימן שלד סעיף מג

י במיי' וטוש"ע שם סימן רמג סעיף ז ובסי' שלד סעי' מז

יא גמיי' פ"ב מהל' סוטה הל' ו [בשם רב האי גאון וגרם דוכתא ע"ש ערך דגם]

יב דמיי' פ"ו מהל' ברכות הלכה יט סמג עשין כז טוש"ע א"ח סי' קנח סעיף ט

יג המיי' פ"ז מהלכ' ת"ת הל' ד' טוש"ע י"ד סימן שלד ס"ג

יד ומיי' פ"ח מה' חמץ ומלה הלכה יא טוש"ע א"ח סימן תעו סעיף א

טו זמיי' פט"ז מהל' כלים הל' ה'

טז חמיי' פ"ד מהלכו' ק"ש הלכ' ד סמג עשין יח טוש"ע א"ח סי' עב סעיף ב טוש"ע י"ד סי' שנח סעיף ב [ע' פרש"י דהכא אמנם במסכ' דתעני' לא פי' כלום אלא הנקרא בלע"ז פירפיי"ש אכן במנחות סו: כתב רש"י ד"ה ונתחט' כעייל כמו בן מתחט' לפני אביו ע"כ אבל בבכורו' כז: כתב רש"י סד"ה והכתי' נתחטא לשון ירידה וחבירו במסכ' תענית בן המתחטא לפני אביו ע"כ ודע דהרב מברטנור' מ"ת פ"ג דתענית כת' מתחטא מתגעגע וכתב התי"ע דלשון ארמית היא כמ"ש בערוך כי הילדים רכים ת"י ארום עלייא מתעיין]

יז טמיי' שם הלכה ה סמג שם וש"ע א"ח סימן עב סעיף ג (') [כמ"א בהג"ה ב"ע י"ד סי' שעו סעי' ב] יח 'מיי' שם הלכה ו סמג שם טוש"ע שם סעי' ד:

---

(12) The last statement being from a Baraitha.

c (1) I.e., he takes count of all the cases where the ruling of the Rabbis was disregarded by an individual, and excommunication should have been incurred, even if this is not mentioned. (2) Saying, 'Thou didst not punish me', which is like a hint to punish. (3) Isa. I, 9. E.V. '. . a little. We were like etc.' (4) Ibid. 10.

עין משפט נר מצוה

[חולין עב.]

יט א מיי' פ"ד מהלכו' ק"ש הל' ו וסמג עשין יח טוש"ע א"ח סי' עג סעיף ה

כ ב מיי' פ"י מהל' כלאים הל' כט סמג לאוין רפד טוש"ע י"ד סימן שג ס"א

כא ג מיי' פרק ג מהלכות אבל הל' יד טוש"ע י"ד סימן שעג סעיף א

כב ד מיי' פ"ו מה' קרבן פסח הל' ח

כג ה מיי' פ"ג מה' אבל הל' יד וטור י"ד סימן שעג

כד ו מיי' פרק יא מהלכות אבידה הלכה י"ג יח סמג עשין עד טוש"ע ח"מ סי' רעב סעיף ב ג

[שבת קנב: ד"ה עד שיסתו' כתבו תוספת ביתר ביאור ע"ש ע"ע תוספת כתובות ד: ד"ה עד ותוס' סוכה כג. ד"ה ולא ותו' סנהדרין מז: ד"ה משיסתום]

[וע"ע תוספ' נזי' נג: ותוס' ב"ב ק: ד"ה כרומן] [צ"ל נפש]

העומדים בשורה וכו': *ת"ר "שורה הרואה פנימה פטורה ושאינה רואה פנימה חייבת ר' יהודה אומר הבאים מחמת האבל פטורין מחמת *עצמן חייבין: אמר רב יהודה אמר רב "המוצא כלאים בבגדו פושטן אפילו בשוק מ"ט °אין חכמה ואין תבונה ואין עצה לנגד ה' (משלי כא) *כל מקום שיש חלול השם אין חולקין כבוד לרב מיתיבי "קברו את המת וחזרו ולפניהם שני דרכים אחת טהורה ואחת טמאה בא בטהורה באין עמו בטהורה בא בטמאה באין עמו בטמאה משום כבודו (נזיר נג.) אמאי לימא אין חכמה ואין תבונה לנגד ה' תרגמה ר' אבא בבית הפרס דרבנן *דאמר רב יהודה אמר שמואל "מנפח אדם בית הפרס והולך ואמר רב יהודה בר אשי משמיה דרב "בית הפרס שנדש טהור ת"ש דא"ר אלעזר בר צדוק "מדלגין היינו ע"ג ארונות של מתים לקראת מלכי ישראל ולא לקראת מלכי ישראל בלבד אמרו אלא אפילו לקראת מלכי א"ה שאם יזכה יבחין בין מלכי ישראל למלכי א"ה אמאי לימא אין חכמה ואין תבונה ואין עצה לנגד ה' כדרבא דאמר רבא דבר תורה אהל כל שיש בו חלל טפח חוצץ בפני הטומאה ושאין בו חלל טפח אינו חוצץ בפני הטומאה ורוב ארונות יש בהן חלל טפח וגזרו על שיש בהן משום שאין בהן ומשום כבוד מלכים לא גזרו בהו רבנן ת"ש *גדול כבוד הבריות שדוחה לא תעשה שבתורה ואמאי לימא אין חכמה ואין תבונה ואין עצה לנגד ה' תרגמה רב בר שבא קמיה דרב כהנא בלאו °דלא תסור (דברי' יז) אחיכו עליה לאו דלא תסור דאורייתא היא אמר רב כהנא *גברא רבה אמר מילתא לא תחיכו עליה כל מילי דרבנן אסמכינהו על לאו דלא תסור ומשום כבודו שרו רבנן *ת"ש °והתעלמת (שם כב) מהם פעמים שאתה מתעלם מהם ופעמים שאין אתה מתעלם מהם הא כיצד אם "היה כהן והוא בבית הקברות או היה זקן ואינו לפי כבודו או שהיתה מלאכתו מרובה משל חברו לכך נאמר והתעלמת אמאי לימא אין חכמה ואין תבונה ואין עצה לנגד ה' שאני התם דכתיב והתעלמת מהם ולינגמר מינה *איסורא מממונא לא ילפינן ת"ש *ולאחותו °מה תלמוד לומר (במדבר ו) הרי שהיה הולך לשחוט את פסחו ולמול את בנו ושמע שמת לו מת יכול יחזור ויטמא אמרת לא יטמא יכול כשם שאינו מטמא להם כך אינו מטמא למת מצוה תלמוד לומר ולאחותו לאחותו הוא דאינו מטמא אבל

רש"י

הרואה פנימה. את חלל ההקף אחורי שורה הפנימית והאבל יושב שם: מחמת עצמן. ולא מחמת כבוד שלא באו לנחם אלא לראות את המאורע: אין חכמה. חשובה כנגד יי': אחת טמאה. שיש בה קבר: בא בטהורה. האבל: בבית הפרס. דלא מטמא אלא מדרבנן והוא שדה שנחרש בו קבר וחשו חכמים שמא דלדלו כלי המחרישה את העצמות והדורס עליהם מסיטן ועצם כשעורה מטמא במגע ובמשא ולא באהל וכיון דמדרבנן הוא דאסור רבנן הוא דאחלוה ליקרייהו גבי אבל: מנפח אדם. לפניו שאם היה שם עצם יראנו דאי דאורייתא הוא לא הוינן מזלזלי' ביה כולי האי למיסמך אנפיחה והך בדיקה לעושה פסח איתמרי ולא לאוכלי תרומה כדאמרינן בחומר בקדש (דף כה:): שנדש. ברגלים: לקראת מלכי ישראל. הרי לכבוד הבריות עוברים על לנפש לא יטמא (ויקרא כא) דהא ר' אלעזר בר צדוק כהן הוה כדאמרינן בבכורות (דף לו.): מדלגין. מארון לארון: דבר תורה. הלכה למשה מסיני: אינו חוצץ בפני הטומאה. דנקראת טומאה רצוצה ובוקעת ועולה: את לא תעשה. קס"ד כל לא תעשה קאמר: בלאו דלא תסור וגו' אחיכו עלי'. אחיכו סבור דאפי' אמרו לו דבר תורה והוא עומד בפני הכבוד יעבור עליו והא האי נמי דאורייתא הוא: כל מילי דרבנן וכו'. והכי קאמר להו דבר שהוא מדברי סופרים נדחה מפני כבוד הבריות וקרי ליה לא תעשה משום דכתיב לא תסור ודקא קשיא לכו דאורייתא הוא רבנן אחלוה ליקרייהו לעבור על דבריהם היכא דאיכא כבוד הבריות כגון לטלטל בשבת אבנים של בית הכסא לקנוח (שבת פ"ט דף פא:) או מי שנפסק' ציצית טליתו בכרמלית לא הצריכו להניח טליתו שם וליכנס לביתו ערום (מנחות פ"ד דף ל"ח.): והוא בבית הקברות. האבדה: אינו לפי כבודו. אין האבדה חשובה לפי כבודו להשיבה: או שהיתה מלאכתו מרובה. שדמי בטול מלאכתו לרדוף אחריה יתרים על דמי האבדה ולא ילכו הבעלים להשיב לו יותר ממה שהשיב להם ונמצא הוא מפסיד: ונגמר מינה. לגבי כלאים דאמרן פושטן אפילו בשוק: ממונא. קל מאיסור': ולאחותו מה תלמוד לומר. בנזיר כתיב כל ימי הזירו ליי' על נפש מת לא יבא וסמיך ליה לאביו ולאמו לאחיו ולאחותו לא יטמ' להם דהא כולהו בכלל על נפש מת לא יבא היו ולמה יצאו לאביו פרט למת מצוה לאמו מה תלמוד לומר משום מת מצוה לא אצטריך דמלאביו נפק' ודרשי ליה בסיפרי ללמוד שאם היה נזיר זה כהן דהוו עליה שתי קדושות אף הוא לאמו הוא דלא יטמא אבל מטמא הוא למת מצוה לאחיו מה תלמוד לומר הרי שהיה כ"ג והוא נזיר אף הוא לאחיו לא יטמא אבל יטמא למת מצוה ולאחותו מה ת"ל אם אינו ענין לזה תנהו ענין למי שהולך לשחוט את פסחו ולמול את בנו שמטמא למת מצוה: ושמע שמת לו מת. מקרוביו יכול יטמא להם: אמרת לא יטמא. הואיל ועונת שחיטת הפסח היא וחלה עליו חובת הפסח שהוא בכרת אם יטמא בטל מלעשות פסח ולמול את בנו נמי מצות כרת היא. ואית דאמרי בערבי פסחים נמי קאמר דמילת זכריו מעכב הפסח:

אבל

תוספות

מדלגין היינו ע"ג ארונות. תימה לפ"ה דפי' גולל כיסוי של ארון דתני' *כל אשר יגע על פני השדה לרבות גולל ודופק וא"כ גם הגולל מטמא באהל והיאך היו מדלגין עליו וי"ל דלא קשה דהא תניא בשמחות (פרק ד') כל טומאה שאין הנזיר מגלח עליה אין כהן מוזהר עליה וגולל ודופק אין נזיר מגלח עליהן כדתנן במסכת נזיר פרק כ"ג (דף כד.) והיה אומר ר"ת דליתי' להאי כללי דהא אמר התם רביעית דם אין הנזיר מגלח עליו עד שיהא חצי לוג ואפילו הכי כהן מוזהר עליו כדאמר בפר' בהמה המקשה (דף עב.) דרביעי' דם הבא מב' מתים טמא ומפקי' ליה מעל כל נפשות מת לא יבא וי"ל דהתם מכל מקום הוי שם טומאה שהנזיר מגלח עליה אבל גולל ודופק אינו כלל בנזיר ולכך אין כהן מוזהר עליו א"נ הא ברייתא סברה כזקני' הראשונים* שהיו אומרים רביעית דם גם בתגלחת נזיר ומיהו תימה אמאי אין המת מטמא באהל כיון שהכסוי עמו מקבל טומאה דכל דבר המקבל טומאה אינו חוצץ בפני הטומאה א"כ מטמא באהל וי"ל דאין מטמא אלא צד חיצון שבו אבל צד פנימי טהור כדתנן במסכת אהלו' בפרק ט"ו חבית שהיא מלאה משקין טהורים ומוקפת צמיד פתיל ועשאה גולל לקבר הנוגע בה מטמ' טומאת שבעה והחבית והמשקין טהורין לפי שצד פנימי כולו טהור ומיהו תימ' לפ"ה דפיר' בפ"ק דערובי' (דף טו.) גבי אין עושין מבעלי חיים גולל ודופק לקבר ואי גולל היינו כיסוי הארון וכי עושין מבעלי חיים כיסוי לארון ע"כ פר"ת דגולל היינו מצבה וכן דרך בני אדם ליתן בהמה על הקבר לסימן עד שיתנו עליו מצבה*:

רוב ארונו' יש להם חלל טפח. וא"ל שראש הארון פתוח שאם היה סתום אדרבה כי יש בו פותח טפח מטמא ואפילו בצד הריקן שבו כדאמרינן במסכת אהלות בפ"ז כפש' הטומאה הנוגע בה מן הצדדין טהור פיר' בצד הריקן מפני שטומאה בוקעת ועולה בוקעת ויורדת ואם היה מקום הטומאה טפח על טפח ברוחב טפח הנוגע בה מ"מ טמא מפני שהוא כקבר סתום אלמא בקבר סתום אינו מטמא כל סביביו אלא שיש עליו טפח אבל בטומאה רצוצה אינו מטמא אלא כנגד הטומאה ולא מצד הריקן. ובפ' המוכר פירות (ד' ק' ע"ב) יש להאריך*:

ולאחותו מה ת"ל. גבי נזיר כתיב על (*כל נפשות) מת לא יבא וכתיב בתריה לאביו ולאמו לאחיו ולאחותו לא יטמא וכולהו יתירי נינהו דמכל (*נפשות) מת נפקא ודרשי' לאביו מה ת"ל לגופי' לא איצטריך דהא מכל (*נפשות) מת נפקא כולהו ולא בא אלא להוציא מת מצוה שמותר לטמא בו לאמו מה ת"ל לגופיה לא איצט' ולהתיר מת מצוה מלאביו נפקא אלא להביא שאם היה נזיר וכהן שיש עליו שתי קדושות אין הכתוב מזהירו מלטמא אלא לאמו אבל מטמ' הוא למת מצוה לאחיו מה ת"ל שאם היה כהן גדול ונזיר דקדושתו חמור דגם בלא נזירות אסור לטמא לקרובין אע"פ כן לאחיו הוא דאינו מטמא אבל מטמא הוא למת מצוה ואם אינו ענין לנזיר גרידא ולא לכהן הדיוט נזיר תנהו ענין לכ"ג נזיר ולאחותו מה ת"ל הרי שאם היה כ"ג ונזיר והלך לשחוט פסחו ולמול את בנו דאיכא מצוה עובא אפ"ה לאחותו הוא דאינו מטמא אבל מטמא למת מצוה: אמרת לא יטמא. מפני שקאי על אדם שהוא נזיר וכ"ג ועושה פסח ומשמע דעושה פסח גרידא רשאי לטמא לקרובים ותימה דבזבחים (פי"ב דף ק.) גבי מעשה דיוסף הכהן שמת' אשתו בערב פסח וטמאוהו אחיו בע"כ ופריך מהא ברייתא דהכא דקאמר לא יטמא ומאי פריך דלמא שאני הכא דמיירי דכל קדושות האלו בו כדפרי' אבל עושה פסחו גרידא אימא רשאי לטמא. על כן נראה לפ' אמרת

לא

מסורת הש"ס

תוספתא פ"ב שמחות פ"י (ירוש' גרס משום כבוד)

[ערובין סג. סנהדרין פב. שבועות ל.]

עירובין ל: פסחים לב: מ"ק ה: חגיגה כה: כתובות כח: בכורות כט. נדה נז. [ועיין בכל המקומות ותמצא שינוי נסחאות במאמרים]

מנחות לז: [שב' פא: לד:] מגילה ג: עירובין מא:]

[גיטין כה: נדה כ:]

סנהדרין יח: ב"מ ל.

[כתובות מ: מו: קדושין ב: ב"מ כ:] מגילה ג: נזיר מח: סנהדרין לה. זבחים ק:

[19b] THOSE WHO STAND IN A ROW etc. Our Rabbis taught:
a The row which can see inside[1] is exempt, but one which cannot see inside is not exempt. R. Judah said: Those who come on account of the mourner are exempt, but those who come for their own purposes[2] are not exempt.

R. Judah said in the name of Rab: If one finds mixed kinds[3] in his garment, he takes it off even in the street. What is the reason? [It says]: *There is no wisdom nor understanding nor counsel against the Lord;*[4] wherever a profanation of God's name is involved no respect is paid to a teacher.

An objection was raised: If they have buried the body and are returning, and there are two ways open to them, one clean and the other unclean,[5] if [the mourner] goes by the clean one they go with him by the clean one, and if he goes by the unclean one they go with him by the unclean one, out of respect for him. Why so? Let us say, *There is no wisdom nor understanding against the Lord?*—R. Abba explained the statement to refer to a *beth ha-peras,*[6] which is declared unclean only by the Rabbis;[7] for Rab Judah has said in the name of Samuel: A man may blow in front of him[8] in a *beth ha-peras* and proceed. And Rab Judah b. Ashi also said in the name of Rab: A *beth ha-peras* which has been well trodden is clean.[9]—Come and hear; for R. Eleazar b. Zadok[10] said: We used to leap over coffins containing bodies to see the Israelite kings.[11] Nor did they mean this to apply only to Israelite kings, but also to heathen kings, so that if he should be privileged [to live to the time of the Messiah], he should be able to distinguish between the Israelite and the heathen kings. Why so? Let us say, *'There is no wisdom and no understanding and no counsel before the Lord'?*—[It is in accord
b with the dictum of Raba; for Raba said: It is a rule of the Torah[1] that a 'tent'[2] which has a hollow space of a handbreadth[3] forms a partition against uncleanness, but if it has not a hollow space of a handbreadth it forms no partition against uncleanness.[4] Now most coffins have a space of a handbreadth, and [the Rabbis] decreed that those which had such a space [should form no partition] for fear they should be confused with those which had no space, but where respect to kings was involved they did not enforce the decree.

Come and hear. 'Great is human dignity, since it overrides a negative precept of the Torah'.[5] Why should it? Let us apply the rule, *'There is no wisdom nor understanding nor counsel against the Lord?*—Rab b. Shaba explained the dictum in the presence of R. Kahana to refer to the negative precept of *'thou shalt not turn aside'*.[6] They laughed at him. The negative precept of *'thou shalt not turn aside'* is also from the Torah![7] Said R. Kahana: If a great man makes a statement, you should not laugh at him. All the ordinances of the Rabbis were based by them on the prohibition of *'thou shalt not turn aside'*[8] but where the question of [human] dignity is concerned the Rabbis allowed the act.[9]

Come and hear.[10] *And hide thyself from them.*[11] There are times when thou mayest hide thyself from them and times when thou mayest not hide thyself from them. How so? If the man [who sees the animal] is a priest and it [the animal] is in a graveyard, or if he is an elder and it is not in accordance with his dignity [to raise it], or if his own work was of more importance than that of his
c fellow.[1] Therefore it is said, *And thou shalt hide.* But why so? Let us apply the rule, *'There is no wisdom nor understanding nor counsel against the Lord'?*—The case is different there, because it says expressly, *And thou shalt hide thyself from them.* Let us then derive from this [the rule for mixed kinds]?[2]—We do not derive a ritual ruling from a ruling relating to property.[3] Come and hear:[4] *Or for his sister.*[5] What does this teach us? Suppose he[6] was going to kill his paschal lamb or to circumcise his son, and he heard that a near relative of his had died, am I to say that he should go back and defile himself? You say, he should not defile himself.[7] Shall I say that just as he does not defile himself for them, so he should not defile himself for a *meth mizwah?*[8] It says significantly, *'And*

a (1) I.e., which can see the mourner, if they stand several deep. (2) To see the crowd. (3) Linen and wool. (4) Prov. XXI, 30. (5) Because there is a grave in it. (6) A field in which there was once a grave which has been ploughed up, so that bones may be scatterd about. (7) But not by the Scripture. (8) To blow the small bones away. (9) V. Pes. (Sonc. ed.) p. 492-4 notes. (10) He was a priest. (11) Which proves that showing respect overrides the rules of uncleanness.

b (1) I.e., a 'law of Moses from Sinai'. (2) I.e., anything which overshadows, v. Num. XIX, 14. (3) Between its outside and what it contains. (4) The uncleanness which it overshadows breaks through and extends beyond its confines. (5) Men. 37b. (6) Deut. XVII, 11, and not to negative precepts in general. (7) And the objection still remains. (8) They based on these words their authority to make rules equally binding with those laid down in the Torah, and Rab b. Shaba interprets the words 'negative precept of the Torah' in the passage quoted to mean, 'Rabbinical ordinances deriving their sanction from this negative precept of their Torah'. (9) V. Shab. 81b. (10) For notes V. B.M. (Sonc. ed.) 30a. (11) Deut. XXII, 1, 4.

c (1) I.e., if he stood to lose more from neglecting his own work than the other from the loss of his animal. (2) Of which it was said *supra* that he takes off the garment even in the street. (3) Lit., 'money'. To override a ritual rule is more serious. (4) Nazir 48b. (5) Num. VI, 7. (6) A Nazirite who is also a priest. (7) Because those things must be done at a fixed time, and cannot be postponed. (8) Lit., '(the burial of) a dead, which is a religious obligation'. V. Glos.

for his sister': for his sister he does not defile himself, [20*a*] but he does defile himself for a *meth mizwah*. But why should this be? Let us apply the rule, '*There is no wisdom nor understanding nor counsel against the Lord?*[9]—The case is different there, because it is written, '*And for his sister*'. Let us then derive a ruling from this [for mixed kinds]?—Where it is a case of 'sit still and do nothing', it is different.[10]

Said R. Papa to Abaye: How is it that for the former generations miracles were performed and for us miracles are not performed? It cannot be because of their [superiority in] study, because in the years of Rab Judah the whole of their studies was confined to Nezikin, and we study all six Orders, and when Rab Judah came in [the tractate] '*Ukzin* [to the law], 'If a woman presses vegetables in a pot'[11] (or, according to others, 'olives pressed with their leaves are clean'),[12] he used to say, I see all the difficulties of Rab and
a Samuel here,[1] and we have thirteen versions of *Ukzin*.[2] And yet when Rab Judah drew off one shoe,[3] rain used to come, whereas we torment ourselves and cry loudly, and no notice is taken of us![4] He replied: The former generations used to be ready to sacrifice their lives for the sanctity of [God's] name; we do not sacrifice our lives for the sanctity of [God's] name. There was the case of R. Adda b. Ahaba who saw a heathen woman wearing a red head-dress[5] in the street, and thinking that she was an Israelite woman, he rose and tore it from her. It turned out that she was a heathen woman, and they fined him four hundred *zuz*. He said to her: What is your name. She replied: Mathun. Mathun, he said to her: that makes four hundred *zuz*.[6]

R. Giddal was accustomed to go and sit at the gates of the bathing-place.[7] He used to say to the women [who came to bathe]: Bathe thus, or bathe thus. The Rabbis said to him: Is not the Master afraid lest his passion get the better of him?—He replied: They look to me like so many white geese. R. Johanan was accustomed to go and sit at the gates of the bathing place. He said: When the daughters of Israel come up from bathing they look at me and they have children as handsome as I am.[8] Said the Rabbis to him: Is not the Master afraid of the evil eye?—He replied: I come from the seed of Joseph, over whom the evil eye has no power, as it is written, *Joseph is a fruitful vine, a fruitful vine above the eye*,[9] and R. Abbahu said with regard to this, do not read '*ale 'ayin*, but '*ole 'ayin*'.[10] R. Judah son of R. Ḥanina derived it from this text: *And let them multiply like fishes* [we-yidgu] *in the midst of the earth*.[11] Just as the fishes [*dagim*] in the sea are covered by water and the evil eye has no power over them, so the evil eye has no power over the seed of Joseph. Or, if you prefer I can say: The evil eye has no power over the eye which refused to feed
b itself on what did not belong to it.[1]

(9) For notes V. Sanh. (Sonc. ed.) 35*a*. (10) Wearing mixed kinds is certainly an active breaking of a rule, but it is not clear how attending to a *meth mizwah* comes under the head of 'sit and do nothing'. V. Rashi and Tosaf. ad loc. (11) '*Ukzin*, II, 1. (12) Ibid.

a (1) I.e., this Mishnah itself presents as many difficulties to me as all the rest of the Gemara. (2) I.e., the Mishnah and the various Baraithas and Toseftas. *Aliter*: We have thirteen colleges which are well versed in it. (3) In preparation for fasting. (4) For fuller notes on the passage, v. Sanh. (Sonc. ed.) p. 728. (5) *Aliter*: 'mantle'. (6) The Aramaic for two hundred is *mathan*. Mathun also means 'deliberate'; had he been less rash he would have saved himself 400 *zuz*; there is here a double play on words. (7) Where the women took their ritual bath. (8) R. Johanan was famous for his beauty. V. *supra* 5*b*. (9) Gen. XLIX, 22. (10) Lit., 'rising above the (power of the) eye'. I.e., superior to the evil eye. (11) So lit. E.V. '*grow into a multitude*'. Ibid. XLVIII, 16.

b (1) *Sc*. Potiphar's wife.

תורה אור

*אבל מטמא הוא למת מצוה אמאי לימא אין חכמה ואין תבונה ואין עצה לנגד ה' שאני התם דכתיב לאחותו ולגמר מינה *שב ואל תעשה שאני: א"ל רב פפא לאביי מאי שנ' ראשונים דמתרחיש להו ניסא ומ"ש אנן דלא מתרחיש לן ניסא *אי משום תנוי בשני דרב יהודה כולי תנוי בנזיקין הוה ואנן קא מתנינן שיתא סדרי וכי הוה מטי רב יהודה בעוקצין *האשה שכובשת ירק בקדרה ואמרי לה *זתים שכבשן בטרפיהן טהורים אמר הויות דרב ושמואל קא חזינן הכא ואנן קא מתנינן בעוקצין תליסר מתיבתא ואלו רב יהודה כי הוה שליף חד מסאניה אתי מטרא ואנן קא מצערינן נפשין ומצווח קא צווחינן ולית דמשגח בן אמר ליה קמאי הוו קא מסרי נפשייהו אקדושת השם אנן לא מסרינן נפשין אקדושת השם כי הא דרב אדא בר אהבה חזייה להה' כותית דהויא לביש' *כרבלתא בשוקא סבר דבת ישראל היא קם קרעי' מינה אגלאי מילתא דכותית היא שיימוה בארבע מאה זוזי א"ל מה שמך אמרה ליה מתון אמר לה מתון מתון ד' מאה זוזי שוה: רב גידל הוה רגיל דהוה קא אזיל ויתיב אשערי דטבילה אמר להו הכי טבלה והכי טבלה אמרי ליה רבנן לא קא מסתפי מר מיצר הרע אמר להו דמיין באפאי כי קאקי חיורי *רבי יוחנן הוה רגיל דהוה קא אזיל ויתיב *אשערי דטבילה אמר כי סלקן בנות ישראל ואתיין מטבילה מסתכלן בי ונהוי להו זרעא דשפירי כוותי אמרו ליה רבנן לא קא מסתפי מר מעינא בישא אמר להו אנא *מזרע' דיוסף קא אתינא דלא שלטא ביה עינא בישא דכתיב °בן פורת יוסף בן פורת עלי עין וא"ר אבהו אל תקרי עלי עין אלא עולי עין ר' יוסי בר' חנינא אמר מהכא °וידגו לרוב בקרב הארץ מה דגים שבים מים מכסין עליהם ואין עין הרע שולטת בהם אף זרעו של יוסף אין עין הרע שולטת בהן ואב"א עין שלא רצתה לזון ממה שאינו שלו אין עין הרע שולטת בו:

מתני' ^ג^נשים ועבדים וקטנים פטורין מק"ש ומן

אבל מטמא לטת מצוה. והוא כבוד הבריות ודוחה דבר תורה: שב ואל תעשה שאני. דברים רבים התירו לעקור דבר תורה מפני ס"ג ומפני כבוד הבריות היכא דאיכו עוקר דבר במעש' ידים אלא יושב במקומו ודבר תורה נעקר מאליו כגון תקיעת שופר ולולב בשבת וסדין בציצית ודכותיהו טובא ביבמות (דף צ' ב) אבל מיעקר בידים לא והלובש כלאים עוקרו במעשה ממש שהוא לובשו וטומאת גופים שהותר לכהן ולנזיר ליטמא למ"מ דקא מיעקר בידי' מפני כבוד הבריות דלאו שב ואל תעשה הוא הייכו טעמא דלא גמרי' מיניה דהתם לאו כבוד הבריות הוא דדחי ל"ת דידה דמעיקרא כשכתב ל"ת דטומאה לא על מת מצוה כתב כשם שלא נכתב על הקרובים אבל השבת אבדה ופסח לכל ישראל כאמר ואלא כבוד הבריות נתנו לדחות ע"כ הייכו דדחייתן היכה בידים אלא בישיבתו תדחה המצוה אבל כלאי' דבמעשה ידיו ידחה הזהיר באזהרתו: בנזיקין הוה. לא היו גדולים בכל גמרא של ארבע סדרי' אלא *בתלתא בבי שלכו והאי מלתא כקט הכא משום דמיירי שמוסרין כפשם על קדושת השם ועד השתא איירי כמי בוני שמבזה עצמו על קדושת השם לפשוט כלאים בשוק: האשה שכובשת ירק או זתי' שכבשן בטרפיהן. משנה היא במס' עוקצין *: טהורים. שמוסקים זתים עם העלין כדי לאחוז בהן דהוו להו עלין יד לזתים להביא להם טומאה כדאמרינן בהעור והרוטב (דף קיח.) שהיד מביא טומאה על האוכל ואם כבשן בטרפיהן במוחן בטלה תורת יד מן העלין לפי שהכבישה מרקבתן ומרככתן ואינן ראוין שוב לאחוז בהן: הויות דרב ושמואל קא חזינא הכא. כלומר טעם המשניות הללו קשה עלי ככל הקושיות שהיו שכי רבותי מתקשין בהן בכל הגמרא: בתליסר מתיבת'. בשלש עשרה פנים יש ביכינו משנה וברייתא של ו' סדרים ומסכת עוקצין גם היא בי"ג פנים כגון משנת רבי ור' חייא ומשנת בר קפרא ולוי ותנא דבי שמואל והכי אמרי' במס' נדרים (דף מא.) ר' מתני הלכת' בי"ג פני': כרבלתא. שם לבוש כמו פטשיהון וכרבלתהון (דניאל ג): מתן מתן. לשון מאתן: ד' מאות. שני פעמים שני מאות כלומר השם גרם לי. לשון אחר מתון לשון המתנה אם המתנתי הייתי משתכר ד' מאות זוז: כי קאקי חיורי. אווזים לבני': ר' יוחנן. אדם יפה תואר היה דאמרי' בהשוכר את הפועלים (ד' פד.) שופריה דרבי אבהו מעין שופריה וכו': עולי עין. מסולקין מן העין שאינה שולטת בהן: שלא רצתה לזון. ליהנות מאשת אדוניו:

מתני' נשים ועבדים וקטנים פטורים מק"ש. שהיא מצות עשה שהזמן גרמא וק"ל בקדושין (דף כט.) דנשים פטורות מדאורייתא. ותפילין נמי מצות עשה שהזמן גרמא דשבת לילה ושבת לאו זמן תפילין נינהו: קטני'. אפי' קטן שהגיע לחנוך לא הטילו על אביו לחנכו בק"ש לפי שאינו מצוי תמיד כשמגיע זמן ק"ש:

לא יטמא אפי' עושה פסחו גרידא וא"ת מהיכא פשיטא ליה אמרת לא יטמא וי"ל כדפרש"י דלא אתי עשה שאין בו כרת כטומאת קרובים וידחה עשה שיש בו כרת כגון עושה פסח וגם מילה שייך בה כרת וא"ת התם דפריך על מעשה דיוסף הכהן מכ"ל [לתלמודא] דהכא מיירי בעוש' פסחו לחוד וי"ל מדלא כייל גבי עושה פסחו כמו גבי אחרי' מי שהיה נזיר וכהן הדיוט דמעיקרא נקט נזיר לחוד ואחר כך נזיר וכהן הדיוט וכו'. וא"ת מנא לי' (לתלמודא) דהאי קרא בעוש' פסחו ולמול את בנו הא קרא כתיב בנזיר. וי"ל אם איכו ענין בנזיר דהא כתיבי פסוקים אחרים דמטמא במת מצוה תנהו ענין להולך לשחוט פסחו וכו' והסר מקולי מישב פירוש רש"י דמיירי הכא דיש בו כל הקדושות הללו כו' ומ"מ פריך התם גבי יוסף הכהן דע"כ אף בעושה פסח גרידא איכו רשאי לטמא דאי ק"ד עושה פסח מטמא לקרובים ולאחותו למה לי למימר דמטמא למת מצוה כיון דמטמא לקרובים אלמא עושה פסחו איכו מעלה עליו שום חומרא מפי א"כ פשיטא דמטמא למת מצוה וכי תימא מ"מ צריך קרא דמטמא למת מצוה ומפני שיש בו ג' קדושות נזיר וכהן ועושה פסח ולעולם אימא לך דעוש' פסח גריד' מטמא לקרובים לא היא דהא כבר שמעינן מלאביו ולאמו ולאחיו דנזיר וכהן גדול לא מהכי מידי למת מצוה אם כן ע"כ קראי לא אצטריכו אלא למעלה דפסח ולמה לי פשיטא דאי מטמא לקרובים כ"ש למת מצוה ואף ע"ג דאצטריך קרא דלאמו לכהן הדיוט ונזיר דמטמא למת מצוה אע"ג דכתב קרא דמטמא לקרובים ואצטריך קרא שהן שתי קדושות אע"ג דשמעי' כבר דמעלה דנזיר לא מהכי מידי למת מצוה מלאביו ה"מ כהן דקדושתו קדושת עולם ומ"ה יש לנו לומר כי יש לו שתי קדושות דטפי קדושה ולכך אצטריך קרא אבל עוש' פסח שקדושתו לפי שעה אם אתה מתיר לו לקרובים ה"ה למת מצוה מכ"ש דמאי חזית ליתן לו קדושה טפי גבי מת מצוה יותר מן הקרובים אי נמי יש לפרש בקולר הברייתא מדתני' גריד' על ישראל נזי' ואח"כ נזיר וכהן הדיוט ואח"כ נזיר וכ"ג ואח"כ מסבר' יש לנו לומר כי יש דאיכו מטמא לקרובים כמו נזיר וכלהו איכך ודוק מעלמך:

שב ואל תעשה שאני. וא"ת נזיר וכ"ג קום עשה הוא דיטמא למת ותירץ רש"י דקרא גלי לן דלאו דלא יטמא לא נאמר גבי מת מצוה ולא כהיר' דא"כ כל מקום דאמרינן שעשה דוחה לא תעשה לקרי שב ואל תעשה וכו' והיאך קרי ליה דהייה אימא שאינו דחייה דהתם לא נאמר הלאו ועוד דהא מילה ותמיד ופסח דדחו שבת דאמרינן פרק אלו דברים (דף סט:) אלמא מקרי שפיר דחייה אלא נראה דמנזיר לא גמרינן דמה לנזיר שכן ישנו בשאלה וכן מכהן מה לכהן שכן לאו שאינו שוה בכל:

זתים שכבשן בטרפיהן טהורים. פי' הקונט' כיון דכבשן בקדרה בטלים מתורת יד להביא טומאה ולא כהירא דא"כ מאי האי דקאמר עלה שלא ככבשו אלא למראה מה כתיכת טעם יש דבטליכהו מתורת יד לכך נראה לפ' דטהורי' משום דאותן עלין לא חשיבי אוכל שאיכן ראוין לאכילה אלא ע"י אותה כבישה בקדרה שלא ככבשו אלא למראה כלומר מה שכבש העלין עמהן לא כבשן אלא להראות שהזתים נאים וחדשים ומשום הכי טהורים אבל כבשן להיות ראויין לאכילה משעה שיהו מתוקנין לראיית אכילה טמאים:

תליסר מתיבת'. יש מפרשין תליסר ישיבות יש בנו שבקיאים ותליסר לאו דוקא אלא לשון הרגיל בגמרא כמו *תליסר זוזי פשיטי ורש"י פי' בע"א *:

וקטנים פטורין מק"ש. פי' הקונ' קטן שהגיע לחנוך ולא כהירא דהא בפ' לולב הגזול (דף מב.) אמרינן קטן היודע לשמור תפילין אביו חייב לקנות לו תפילין אלמא כשהגיע לחנוך דמיכי ביה תפילין חייב בתפילין ובק"ש נמי יש לחייבו יותר מסתמא מדאשכחן התם קטן היודע לדבר אביו מלמדו תורה ופסוק ראשון של ק"ש וכראה לר"ת דמיירי בקטן שלא הגיע לחנוך ומיהו סיפא דקתני וחייבין בתפלה היה ר"י ר"ל דמיירי בקטן שהגיע לחנוך דאי לא הגיע לא הוו להו חייבים בתפל' ולא כהירא דא"כ לא הוו להו קטנים דומיא דנשים ועבדים שפטורים בכל ענין וקטנים איכם פטורים אלא בשלא הגיע ואין יודע לשמור תפיליו ופי' ר"ת דודאי איירי הכל בקטן שלא הגיע לחנוך וחייבי' דסיפא קאי אנשים ועבדים לא"ד אבל קטנים פטורים מכל וכל כיון דלא הגיע לחנוך וא"ת אם כן אמאי תנא קטנים בהדי נשים ועבדים כיון דאין שוין כדפרישית וי"ל דכן דרך התנא לשנות יחד נשים ועבדים וקטנים שלא הגיעו לחנוך כמו נשים ועבדים וקטנים פטורים מסוכה (סוכה דף כח.):

בתפלה

תורה אור

[א]ומן התפילין וחייבין [ב]בתפלה [ג]ובמזוזה [ד]ובברכת המזון: **גמ'** ק"ש פשיטא מצות עשה שהזמן גרמא היא *וכל מצות עשה שהזמן גרמא נשים פטורות מהו דתימא הואיל ואית בה מלכות שמים קמ"ל: ומן התפילין: פשיטא מהו דתימ' הואיל ואיתקש למזוזה קמ"ל: וחייבין בתפל': דרחמי נינהו מהו דתימ' הואיל וכתיב בה °ערב ובקר וצהרים כמצות עשה שהזמן גרמ' דמי קמ"ל: ובמזוזה: פשיטא מהו דתימא הואיל ואיתקש לתלמוד תורה קמ"ל: ובברכת המזון: פשיטא מהו דתימ' הואיל וכתיב °בתת ה' לכם בערב בשר לאכול ולחם בבקר לשבוע כמצות עשה שהזמן גרמא דמי קמ"ל: אמר רב *אדא בר אהבה [ה]נשים חייבות בקדוש היום דבר תורה אמאי מצות עשה שהזמן גרמא הוא וכל מצות עשה שהזמן גרמא נשים פטורות אמר אביי מדרבנן א"ל רבא והא דבר תורה קאמר ועוד כל מצות עשה נחייבינהו מדרבנן אלא אמר רבא אמ' קרא °זכור °ושמור כל שישנו בשמיר' ישנו בזכירה והני נשי הואיל ואיתנהו בשמירה איתנהו בזכירה א"ל רבינא לרבא נשים בברכת המזון דאורייתא או דרבנן למאי נפקא מינה לאפוקי רבים ידי חובתן אי אמרת (בשלמא) דאורייתא אתי דאורייתא ומפיק דאורייתא [נ"ל ואי] (אלא *אי) אמרת דרבנן הוי שאינו מחויב בדבר *[ו]וכל שאינו מחויב בדבר אינו מוציא את הרבים ידי חובתן מאי ת"ש *באמת אמרו *[ז]בן מברך לאביו ועבד מברך לרבו ואשה מברכת לבעלה אבל אמרו חכמים תבא מארה לאדם שאשתו ובניו מברכין לו אא"ב דאורייתא אתי דאורייתא ומפיק דאורייתא אלא אי אמרת דרבנן אתי דרבנן ומפיק דאורייתא ולטעמיך קטן בר חיובא הוא אלא הכא במאי עסקי' [ח]כגון דאכל שיעורא דרבנן דאתי דרבנן ומפיק דרבנן: דרש רב עוירא זמנין אמר לה משמיה דרבי אמי וזמנין אמר לה משמיה דר' אסי אמרו מלאכי השרת לפני הקב"ה רבש"ע כתוב בתורתך °אשר לא ישא פנים ולא יקח שחד והלא אתה נושא פנים לישראל דכתיב °ישא ה' פניו אליך אמר להם וכי לא אשא פנים לישראל שכתבתי להם בתורה °ואכלת ושבעת וברכת את ה' אלהיך והם מדקדקים [על] עצמם עד כזית ועד כביצה: **מתני'** בעל קרי מהרהר בלבו ואינו מברך לא לפניה ולא לאחריה ועל המזון מברך לאחריו ואינו מברך לפניו ר' יהודה [ט]אומ' מברך לפניהם ולאחריהם: **גמ'** אמר רבינא זאת אומרת [י]הרהור כדבור דמי דאי סלקא דעתך לאו כדבור דמי למה מהרהר אלא מאי הרהור כדבור דמי יוציא בשפתיו *כדאשכחן בסיני ורב חסדא אמר *הרהור לאו כדבור דאי סלקא דעתך הרהור כדבור דמי יוציא בשפתיו ואלא מאי הרהור לאו כדבור דמי למה מהרהר א"ר אלעזר כדי שלא יהו כל העולם עוסקין בו והוא יושב ובטל ונגרוס בפרקא אחרינא אמר רב אדא בר אהבה בדבר שהצבור עוסקין בו והרי

בתפלה פשיטא כיון דכתיב ערב ובוקר וצהרים אבי"א והתנה כמלות עשה שהזמן גרמא הוי קמ"ל דרחמי נינהו. ורש"י לא גרים לי' שהרי תפלה דרבנן היא ומאי מ"ע שייכי ביה ומכל מקום יש ליישב דהא הלל דרבנן ונשים פטורות מהאי טעמא דמלות עשה שהזמן גרמא הוא כדאמרינן בסוכה (פ"ג דף לח.) מי שהיה עבד ואשה או קטן מקרין אותו עונה אחריהם מה שהם אומרים דאין השומע פטור מקריאתן כיון שהם פטורים:

אית דגרסי בברכת המזון פשיטא. ושפי כיון דכתיב בתת ה' לכם בערב בשר לאכל ולחם בבקר לשבוע כמ"ע שהזמן גרמא הוא קמ"ל:

נשים בברכת המזון דאורייתא או דרבנן. פירש הקונט' דס"ד דלא מיחייבו דאורייתא משום דכתיב על הארץ הטובה ונשים לא נטלו חלק בארץ ומה שנטלו בנות ללפחד חלק אביהם נטלו ותימה כהנים ולוים נמי תבעי שהרי לא נטלו חלק בארץ וא"כ לא יוציאו אחרים ידי חובתן בברכת המזון אלא יש לומר דטעמא משום דכתיב על בריתך שחתמת בבשרנו ועל תורתך שלמדתנו ונשים ליתנהו לא בברית ולא בתורה ואמרינן לקמן (דף מט.) מי שלא אמר ברית ותורה בברכת המזון לא יצא ידי חובתו והשתא קא מבעיא ליה כיון דלא מצו למימר ברית ותורה לא הוו אלא מדרבנן או דלמא כיון דלא שייך בהו הוי שפי' דאורייתא והא דלקמן מיירי באנשים דשייכי בברית ותורה:

בעל קרי מהרהר בלבו ואינו מברך לא לפניה ולא לאחריה. פי' אפי' בהרהור כדמשמע בגמרא והיינו טעמא דשריא טפי בק"ש מברכות משום דק"ש דאוריית' וברכות דרבנן ואפילו למאן דאמר ק"ש דרבנן היינו היכא דהזכיר יציאת מצרים אבל מתניתין שלא הזכיר יציאת מצרים שלא התירו לו לומר אמת ויציב והוי ק"ש דאורייתא ואמת ויציב דרבנן שהרי הזכיר יציאת מצרים בק"ש ואין להקשות כתקן דליתא אמת ויציב ולא ליתא ק"ש דהא עדיף דליתא ק"ש דאית ביה נמי מלכות שמים:

יוציא בשפתיו. כיון דשרית ליה הרהור אעפ"י שהוא כדבור לענין לצאת ידי ק"ש כמו כן מקרי דבור לענין דמקרי עוסק בתורה ומדשרית ליה להרהר אע"פ שהוא בעל קרי תתיר לו גם דבור:

כדאשכחן בסיני. פירוש אע"ג דכדבור דמי לענין שילא מ"מ לאו כדבור דמי לענין שיהא בעל קרי אסור להרהר כדאשכחן בסיני דהי' שם דבור והיו צריכין לטבול ואעפ"י שהיו שותקים שומע כעונה*:

ורב חסדא אמר לאו כדבור דמי. ר"ח פי' דהלכ' כרב חסדא מדתרלי רב אדא ור' אלעזר למלתיה ש"מ כותי' קיימי ולא יצא בק"ש בהרהור:

ומן התפילין. משום דקתני קטן אינו יודע לשמור גופו שלא יפיח בהן: והייבים בתפלה. דתפל' דרחמי היא ומדרבנן היא ותקנוה אף לנשים ולחנוך קטנים: ובמזוזה ובברכת המזון. מזוזה מלות עשה שלא הזמן גרמא ובגמרא פריך פשיטא: ברכת המזון. בגמרא בעי לה דאורייתא או דרבנן: **גמ'** מהו דתימא. נקיש תפילין למזוזה דכתיב וקשרתם וכתבתם מה מזוזה נשים חייבות אף תפילין נשים חייבות קמ"ל: ה"ג תפלה דרחמי נינהו. ולא גר' פשיטא דהא לאו דאורייתא היא: נקיש מזוזה לתלמוד תורה. דכתיב (דברי' יא) ולמדתם אותם את בניכם וסמיך ליה וכתבתם מה תלמוד תורה נשים פטורות ואע"ג דאין הזמן גרמא רחמנ' פטרינהו דכתיב את בניכם ולא בנותיכם אף מזוזה נשים פטורות קמ"ל דנשים חייבות דכתיב למען ירבו ימיכם גברי בעו חיי נשי לא בעו חיי בתמיה: קדוש היום. מ"ע שהזמן גרמא הוא זכור את יום השבת לקדשו (שמות כ) זוכרהו על היין: בשמירה. דלא תעשה מלאכה (שם): והני נשי איתנהו בשמירה. דתנן (קדושין ד' כט:) כל מלות לא תעש' בין שהזמן גרמ' בין שאין הזמן גרמא נשים חייבות. דהשוה הכתוב אשה לאיש לכל עונשים שבתורה: נשים בברכת המזון דאורייתא. דכתיב ואכלת ושבעת (דברים ח) והוה ליה מלות עשה שאין הזמן גרמא: או דרבנן. דכתיב על הארץ הטובה אשר נתן לך (שם) והארץ לא נתנה לנקבות להתחלק ואי משום בנות ללפחד חלק אביהם הם דנטלו שהיה מיוצאי מצרים: בן. קטן מברך ברכת המזון לאביו אם אין אביו יודע לברך: שיעורא דרבנן. כגון כזית לר"מ וכביל' לר' יהודה דמדאורייתא ואכלת ושבעת וברכת כתיב אבל בשיעור כי האי לא מיחייב אלא מדרבנן והלכך אתי קטן דרבנן ומפיק גדול: עד כזית עד כביצה. עד כזית לר"מ עד כביצה לר' יהודה דתנן (לקמן דף מה.) עד כמה מזמנין ר"מ אומר עד כזית רבי יהודה אומר עד כביצ': **מתני'** בעל קרי. מתקנת עזר' ואילך שתקן טבילה לבעלי קריין לעסוק בתור' כדאמרי' בבבא קמא בפרק מרובה (דף פב.): מהרהר. ק"ש בלבו כשמגיע זמן המקרא: ואינו מברך. אפילו בהרהור: לא לפניה ולא לאחריה. כיון דברכות לאו מדאורייתא מחייב לא אצרכוה רבנן: ועל המזון מברך לאחריו. דחיובא דאורייתא הוא: ואינו מברך לפניו. דלאו דאורייתא הוא: רבי יהודה אומר וכו'. בגמרא מפרש לה:

גמ' כדבור דמי. וכל אדם נמי יולא ידי חובתו בהרהור: למה מהרהר. מה מועיל: כדאשכחן בסיני. שהפרישן מאשה דכתיב אל תגשו אל אשה (שמות יט) ועל פרים' זו סמך עזרא לתקן טבילה לבעלי קריין קודם שיעסקו בתורה דכתיב (דברים ד) והודעתם לבניך וסמיך ליה יום אשר עמדת לפני ה' אלהיך בחורב כדאמרינן לקמן בפרקין (דף כב ב): אלא

עין משפט נר מצוה

כז [א]מיי' פ"ד מהל' תפילין הל' יג סמ"ג עשין כב טוש"ע א"ח סי' לח סעי' ג

כח [ב]מיי' פ"א מה' תפלה הל' ב' סמ"ג עשין יט טוש"ע א"ח סי' קו סעי' ב

כט [ג]מיי' פ"ה מה' מזוזה הל' י' סמ"ג עשין כ"ג טוש"ע י"ד סי' רלא סעי' ג

ל [ד]מיי' פ"ה מה' ברכות הל' א' סמ"ג עשין כז טוש"ע א"ח סי' קפו סעי' א ב

לא [ה]מיימ' פ' כט מהל' שבת הל' א' סמ"ג עשין כט טוש"ע א"ח סי' רעא סעי' ב

לב [ו]מיי' פ"א מה' ברכות הל' יא

לג [ז][ח]מיי' פ"ה שם הל' ט"ו וט"ז סמ"ג ע' כ"ז טוש"ע א"ח סי' קפו סעי' ב' [ע' תוס' לעיל טו. ד"ה ור' יהודא]

לד [ט]מיימ' פ"ד מהלכ' ק"ש הל' ח' סמ"ג עשין יט טוש"ע א"ח סי' פח

לה [י]טוש"ע א"ח סי' סב סעי' ג ד

[סוכה לח:]

מסורת הש"ס

קדושין דף כט וש"נ

[שבועת כ': ע"ש]

ר"ה פ"ג דף כט. סוכה פ"ג דף לח. תוספתא פ"ה

ב"ה לג. שבת קכ.

MISHNAH. WOMEN, SLAVES AND MINORS ARE EXEMPT FROM RECITING THE SHEMA' [20b] AND FROM PUTTING ON TEFILLIN, BUT THEY ARE SUBJECT TO THE OBLIGATIONS OF TEFILLAH AND MEZUZAH[2] AND GRACE AFTER MEALS.

GEMARA. That they are exempt from the *Shema'* is self-evident —it is a positive precept for which there is a fixed time?[3] You might say that because it mentions the kingship of heaven it is different. We are therefore told that this is not so.

AND FROM PUTTING ON THE TEFILLIN. This also is self-evident?[4] You might say that because it is put on a level with the *mezuzah*[5] [therefore women should be subject to it]. Therefore we are told that this is not so.

THEY ARE SUBJECT TO THE OBLIGATION OF TEFILLAH. Because this [is supplication for Divine] mercy. You might [however] think that because it is written in connection therewith, *Evening and morning and at noonday,*[6] therefore it is like a positive precept for which there is a fixed time. Therefore we are told [that this is not so].

AND MEZUZAH. This is self-evident?[7] You might say that because it is put on a level with the study of the Torah,[8] [therefore women are exempt]. Therefore it tells us [that this is not so].

AND GRACE AFTER MEALS. This is self-evident?—You might think that because it is written, *When the Lord shall give you in the* a *evening flesh to eat and in the morning bread to the full,*[1] therefore it is like a positive precept for which there is a definite time. Therefore it tells us [that this is not so].

R. Adda b. Ahabah said: Women are under obligation to sanctify the [Sabbath] day[2] by ordinance of the Torah. But why should this be? It is a positive precept for which there is a definite time, and women are exempt from all positive precepts for which there is a definite time?—Abaye said: The obligation is only Rabbinical. Said Raba to him: But it says, 'By an ordinance of the Torah'? And further, on this ground we could subject them to all positive precepts by Rabbinical authority? Rather, said Raba. The text says *Remember* and *Observe*.[3] Whoever has to 'observe' has to 'remember'; and since these women have to 'observe',[4] they also have to 'remember'.[5]

Rabina said to Raba: Is the obligation of women to say grace after meals Rabbinical or Scriptural?—What difference does it make in practice which it is?—For deciding whether they can perform the duty on behalf of others. If you say the obligation is Scriptural, then one who is bound by Scripture can come and perform the duty on behalf of another who is bound by Scripture. But if you say the obligation is only Rabbinical, then [a woman] is not strictly bound to do this, and whoever is not strictly bound to do a thing cannot perform the obligation on behalf of others. What [do we decide]?—Come and hear: 'In truth they did say: A son[6] may say grace on behalf of his father and a slave may say grace on behalf of his master and a woman may say grace on behalf of her husband. But the Sages said: A curse light on the man whose wife or children have to say grace for him.'[7] If now you say that [the obligation of these others] is Scriptural, then there is no difficulty: one who is bound by the Scripture comes and performs the duty on behalf of one who is bound by the Scripture. But if you say that the obligation is Rabbinic, can one who is bound only Rabbinically come and perform the duty on behalf of one who is bound Scripturally?—But even accepting your reasoning, b is a minor subject to obligation [Scripturally]?[1] Nay. With what case are we dealing here? If, for instance, he ate a quantity for which he is only Rabbinically bound [to say grace],[2] in which case one who is Rabbinically bound[3] comes and performs the duty on behalf of one who is only Rabbinically bound.[4]

R. 'Awira discoursed—sometimes in the name of R. Ammi, and sometimes in the name of R. Assi—as follows: The ministering angels said before the Holy One, blessed be He: Sovereign of the Universe, it is written in Thy law, *Who regardeth not persons*[5] *nor taketh reward,*[6] and dost Thou not regard the person of Israel, as it is written, *The Lord lift up His countenance upon thee?*[7] He replied to them: And shall I not lift up My countenance for Israel, seeing that I wrote for them in the Torah, *And thou shalt eat and be satisfied and bless the Lord thy God,*[8] and they are particular [to say the grace] if the quantity is but an olive or an egg.[9]

MISHNAH. A BA'AL ḲERI[10] SAYS THE WORDS [OF THE SHEMA'][11] MENTALLY[12] WITHOUT SAYING A BLESSING EITHER BEFORE OR AFTER. AT MEALS HE SAYS THE GRACE AFTER, BUT NOT THE GRACE BEFORE. R. JUDAH SAYS: HE SAYS THE GRACE BOTH BEFORE AND AFTER.

GEMARA. Said Rabina: This would show that saying mentally is equivalent to actual saying.[13] For if you assume that it is not equivalent to actual saying, why should he say mentally?[14] What then? [You say that] saying mentally is equivalent to actual saying. Then let him utter the words with his lips!—We do as we find c it was done at Sinai.[1] R. Ḥisda said: Saying mentally is not equivalent to actual saying. For if you assume that saying mentally is equivalent to actual saying, then let him utter the words with his lips! What then? [You say that] saying mentally is not equivalent to actual saying? Why then should he say mentally?—R. Eleazar replied: So that he should not have to sit saying nothing while everyone else is engaged saying the *Shema'*. Then let him read some other section?—R. Adda b. Ahaba said: [He must attend

(2) V. Glos. (3) And women are exempt from such precepts. V. *infra*. (4) For the same reason. (5) Since it is written, *and thou shalt bind them, and thou shalt write them.* (6) Ps. LV, 18. (7) For what reason is there for exempting them? (8) As it says, *And ye shall teach them to your sons, and ye shall write them;* and the obligation of teaching applies only to the males.

a (1) Ex. XVI, 8. (2) Over wine. V. *P.B.* p. 124. (3) In the two versions of the Fourth Commandment, viz., Ex. XX, 8 and Deut. V, 12 respectively. (4) I.e., abstain from work. (5) I.e., say sanctification. (*Kiddush*). V. Glos. (6) I.e., a minor. (7) Because he cannot say it himself; v. Suk. 38a.

b (1) As would be presupposed in your argument. (2) Viz., the quantity of an olive according to R. Meir and an egg according to R. Judah. *Infra* 45a. (3) A minor. (4) The father who had less than the minimum quantity. And it is only in such a case that a woman may say grace on behalf of her husband. (5) Lit., 'Who lifteth not up the countenance'. (6) Deut. X, 17. (7) Num. VI, 26. (8) Deut. VIII, 10. (9) Cf. *supra* n. b2. (10) V. Glos. (11) When the hour arrives for reciting it. (12) Lit., 'in his heart'. (13) Lit., 'thinking is like speech'. (14) What religious act does he perform thereby?

c (1) Moses ordered the Israelites to keep away from woman before receiving the Torah, but those who were unclean could still accept mentally.

to that] with which the congregation is engaged. [21*a*] But what of *tefillah* which is a thing with which the congregation is engaged, and yet we have learnt: If he was standing reciting the *tefillah* and he suddenly remembered that he was a *ba'al ḳeri* he should not break off, but he should shorten [each blessing]. Now the reason is that he had commenced; but if he had not yet commenced, he should not do so?—*Tefillah* is different because it does not mention the kingdom of heaven.[2] But what of the grace after meals in which there is no mention of the sovereignty of heaven, and yet we have learnt: AT MEALS HE SAYS GRACE AFTER, BUT NOT THE GRACE BEFORE?—[Rather the answer is that] the recital of the *Shema'* and grace after food are Scriptural ordinances, whereas *tefillah* is only a Rabbinical ordinance.[3]

Rab Judah said: Where do we find that the grace after meals is ordained in the Torah? Because it says: *And thou shalt eat and be satisfied and bless.*[4] Where do we find that a blessing before studying the Torah is ordained in the Torah? Because it says: *When I proclaim the name of the Lord, ascribe ye greatness to our God.*[5] R. Joḥanan said: We learn that a blessing should be said after studying the Torah by an argument *a fortiori* from grace after food; and we learn that grace should be said before food by an argument *a fortiori* from the blessing over the Torah. The blessing after the Torah is learnt *a fortiori* from the grace after food as fol-
a lows: Seeing that food which requires no grace before it[1] requires a grace after it, does it not stand to reason that the study of the Torah which requires a grace before it should require one after it? The blessing before food is learnt *a fortiori* from the blessing over the Torah as follows: Seeing that the Torah which requires no blessing after it[1] requires one before it, does it not stand to reason that food which requires one after it should require one before it? A flaw can be pointed out in both arguments. How can you reason from food [to the Torah], seeing that from the former he derives physical benefit? And how can you reason from the Torah [to food], seeing that from the former he obtains everlasting life? Further, we have learnt: AT MEALS HE SAYS THE GRACE AFTER BUT NOT THE GRACE BEFORE?[2]—This is a refutation.

Rab Judah said: If a man is in doubt whether he has recited the *Shema'*, he need not recite it again. If he is in doubt whether he has said 'True and firm', or not, he should say it again. What is the reason?—The recital of the *Shema'* is ordained only by the Rabbis, the saying of 'True and firm' is a Scriptural ordinance.[3] R. Joseph raised an objection to this,[4] *'And when thou liest down, and when thou risest up'*.—Said Abaye to him: That was written with reference to words of Torah.[5]

We have learnt: A BA'AL ḲERI SAYS MENTALLY, AND SAYS NO BLESSING EITHER BEFORE OR AFTER. AT MEALS HE SAYS THE GRACE AFTER BUT NOT THE GRACE BEFORE. Now if you assume that 'True and firm' is a Scriptural regulation, let him say the blessing after the *Shema'*?—Why should he say [the blessing after]? If it is in order to mention the going forth from Egypt, that is already mentioned in the *Shema'*! But then let him say the former, and he need not say the latter?[6]—The recital of *Shema'*
b is preferable, because it has two points.[1] R. Eleazar says: If one is in doubt whether he has recited the *Shema'* or not, he says the *Shema'* again. If he is in doubt whether he has said the *Tefillah* or not, he does not say it again. R. Joḥanan, however, said: Would that a man would go on praying the whole day!

Rab Judah also said in the name of Samuel: If a man was standing saying the *Tefillah* and he suddenly remembered that he had already said it, he breaks off even in the middle of a benediction. Is that so? Has not R. Naḥman said: When we were with Rabbah b. Abbuha, we asked him with reference to disciples who made a mistake and began the weekday benediction on a Sabbath, whether they should finish it, and he said to us that they should finish that blessing!—Are these cases parallel? In that case one[2] is in reality under obligation,[3] and it is the Rabbis who did not trouble him out of respect for the Sabbath, but in this case he has already said the prayer.

Rab Judah further said in the name of Samuel: If a man had already said the *Tefillah* and went into a synagogue and found the congregation saying the *Tefillah*, if he can add something fresh, he should say the *Tefillah* again, but otherwise he should not say it again. And both these rulings are required.[4] For if I had been told only the first, I should have said, This applies only to [a case where he said the *Tefillah*] alone and [is repeating it] alone [21*b*],

(2) The words 'King of the Universe' are not used in the Eighteen Benedictions. (3) And therefore he need not say it even mentally. (4) Deut. VIII, 10. (5) Ibid. XXXII, 3. E.V. *'for I will proclaim* etc.'. V. Yoma 37*a*.

a (1) I.e., no such grace is distinctly prescribed in the Torah. (2) Which proves that the grace before food is not Biblical. (3) Because it mentions the going forth from Egypt, as prescribed in Deut. XVI, 3. (4) That the *Shema'* is not Scriptural. (5) And it is applied to the *Shema'* only as an allusion. (6) I.e., let him say the blessing openly, and not the *Shema'* mentally.

b (1) It mentions both the Kingdom of Heaven and the going forth from Egypt. (2) Lit., 'the man'. (3) To say the weekday *Tefillah*. (4) This latter ruling and the case where one remembered whilst praying that he had already prayed.

והרי תפלה דדבר שהצבור עסוקין בו ותנן *היה עומד בתפלה ונזכר שהוא בעל קרי לא יפסיק אלא יקצר טעמא דאתחיל הא לא אתחיל לא יתחיל שאני תפלה דלית בה מלכות שמים והרי ברכת המזון לאחריו דלית בה מלכות שמים ותנן על המזון מברך לאחריו ואינו מברך לפניו אלא ק"ש וברכת המזון דאורייתא ותפלה דרבנן: אמר רב יהודה *מנין לברכת המזון לאחריה מן התורה שנאמר °ואכלת ושבעת וברכת מנין לברכת התורה לפניה מן התורה שנאמר °כי שם יי' אקרא הבו גודל לאלהינו אמר ר' יוחנן למדנו ברכת התורה לאחריה מן ברכת המזון מק"ו וברכת המזון לפניה מן ברכת התורה מק"ו ברכת התורה לאחריה, מן ברכת המזון מק"ו ומה מזון שאין טעון לפניו טעון לאחריו תורה שטעונה לפניה אינו דין שטעונה לאחריה וברכת המזון לפניה מן ברכת התורה מק"ו ומה תורה שאין טעונה לאחריה טעונה לפניה, מזון שהוא טעון לאחריו אינו דין שיהא טעון לפניו איכא למפרך מה למזון שכן נהנה ומה לתורה שכן חיי עולם ועוד תנן על המזון מברך לאחריו ואינו מברך לפניו תיובתא: אמר רב *יהודה ספק קרא ק"ש ספק לא קרא אינו חוזר וקורא ספק אמר אמת ויציב ספק לא אמר חוזר ואומר אמת ויציב מאי טעמא ק"ש דרבנן אמת ויציב דאורייתא מתיב רב יוסף °ובשכבך ובקומך אמר לי' אביי ההוא בדברי תורה כתיב תנן בעל קרי מהרהר בלבו ואינו מברך לא לפניה ולא לאחריה ועל המזון מברך לאחריו ואינו מברך לפניו ואי ס"ד אמת ויציב דאורייתא לברך לאחריה מאי טעמא מברך אי משום יציאת מצרים הא אדכר ליה בק"ש ונימא הא ולא לבעי הא ק"ש עדיפא דאית ביה תרתי ורבי אלעזר *אמר ספק קרא ק"ש ספק לא קרא ק"ש חוזר וקורא ק"ש ספק התפלל ספק לא התפלל אינו חוזר ומתפלל ורבי יוחנן *אמר ולואי *שיתפלל אדם כל היום כלו: ואמר רב יהודה אמר שמואל *היה עומד בתפלה ונזכר שהתפלל פוסק ואפי' באמצע ברכה איני והאמר רב נחמן כי הוינן בי רבה בר אבוה בען מיני' הני בני רב דטעו ומדכרי דחול בשבת מהו שיגמרו ואמר לן °גומרין כל אותה ברכה הכי השתא התם גברא בר חיובא הוא ורבנן הוא דלא אטרחוהו משום כבוד שבת אבל הכא הא צלי ליה: ואמר רב יהודה אמר שמואל *התפלל ונכנס לב"ה ומצא צבור שמתפללין אם יכול לחדש בה דבר יחזור ויתפלל ואם לאו אל יחזור ויתפלל וצריכא דאי אשמעינן קמייתא ה"מ יחיד ויחיד

או

תורה אור: דברי' ח | שם לב | שם ו

רש"י

אלא יקצר. כל ברכה וברכה: דלית בה מלכות שמים. אין מלך העולם בברכות של י"ח: ה"ג והרי ברכת המזון לפניה דאית בה מלכות שמים כו'. לישנא אחרינא שאני תפלה דלית בה מלכות שמים קבלת מלכות שמים כדאי' בק"ש שמקבל עליו את השם לאדון ולמלך ומיוחד ולהאי לישנא גר' והרי ברכת המזון לאחריו דלית בה מלכות שמים ולשון זה נראה שהוא עיקר מדמשני ליה אלא ק"ש וברכת המזון דאורייתא והאי בלאחריו עסקינן ואי ללישנא קמא הא לא איירי בברכת המזון לאחריו בדאתקפתיה דלהדרי תלמוד עילויה אלא ק"ש וברכת המזון דאוריית' כו' ואית דגרסי הכא בלשון קושיא ק"ש דרבנן היא אלא ק"ש דאית בה מלכות שמים ברכת המזון דאוריית' לאפוקי תפלה דרבנן ואין בה מלכות שמים למאן דגרס הכי מפרשינן לקמן בשכבך ובקומך בדברי תורה כתיב: כי שם ה' אקרא. כשבא משה לפתוח בדברי שירה אמר להם לישראל אני אברך תחלה ואתם ענו אחרי אמן כי שם ה' אקרא בברכה אתם הבו גודל לאלהינו באמן הכי מפרשי לה במסכת יומא (דף לז.): שאינו טעון לפניו. כלומר שלא מלינו לו מקרא מפורש לברך לפניו: טעון לאחריו. כדכתיב ואכלת ושבעת וברכת: תורה שטעונה לפניה. כדאמרן: איכא למפרך. בתרוייהו כשאתה בא ללמוד תורה מן המזון איכא למפרך מה למזון שכן נהנה וכשאתה בא ללמוד מזון מן התורה איכא למפרך מה לתורה שכן חיי העולם הבא: ק"ש דרבנן. לקמן פריך לה: אמת ויציב דאוריית' היא. שמזכיר בה יציאת מצרים דחובה דאורייתא היא דכתיב למען תזכור את יום צאתך מארץ מצרים (דברים טז): דאית בה תרתי. יציאת מצרים ומלכות שמים: חוזר וקורא ק"ש. קסבר ק"ש דאורייתא היא: ולואי שיתפלל אדם כל היום. בהלכות גדולות פסיק הלכה כרבי יוחנן בספק והלכה כשמואל בודאי התפלל: מהו שיגמרו. את הברכה אם נזכר באמצע הברכה באחת מן הברכות שטעה: יחיד ויחיד. כשהתפלל תחלה היה יחיד וכשחזר שהתפלל והתחיל להתפלל היה ביחיד:

תוספות

והרי תפלה דדבר שהצבור כו'. וא"ת מאי שבק בבא דק"ש דקאי בגווה דדבר שצבור עוסקין בו וקתני אינו מברך לפניהם כו' וי"ל משום רבות' דתפלה פריך מיניה אע"ג דתפלה מעומד וכלאה לכל שאין זה עומד כמותם אפי' הכי אמרינן אם לא התחיל לא יתחיל וא"ת כיון דלא ידע טעמא דבסמוך יקשה גם לרבינא מה לי ק"ש וברכת המזון יותר מתפלה וי"ל דלרבינ' ניחא כיון דהרהור כדבור דמי יש להצריכו בק"ש ובברכת המזון שהם מדאוריית' יותר מתפלה דרבנן אבל לרב חסדא כיון דהרהור אינו כלום רק שלא יהא יושב ובטל מה לי ק"ש מ"ל תפלה:

הא אי לא אתחיל לא יתחיל ואם תאמר אימא דבדבור קאמר הא בהרהור שפיר דמי ויש לומר דמשמע דלא יתחיל אפילו בהרהור מדלא קאמר יקצר בדבור או יהרהר בארוכות:

הכי גרסינן אלא ק"ש וברכת המזון דאורייתא ותפלה דרבנן ולא גרסינן מידי בתר הכי עד אמר רב יהודה אמר רב ופי' הקונ' ק"ש דאוריית' כיון שאינו אומר אמת ויציב כדפי' במתנית' ויש ספרי' גורסי' *ק"ש דרבנן הוא ומשני אלא ק"ש אית ביה מלכות שמים וברכת המזון דאורייתא ותפלה דרבנן וכן הגירסא בפ"ה וקשה דבמתנית' פי' דק"ש דאוריית' לכולי עלמא כיון שלא אמר אמת ויציב דבהכי איירי מתניתי' וגם יש ספרי' גורסי' שאני תפלה דלית בה מלכות שמים והרי ברכת המזון דלית ביה מלכות שמים ותנן על המזון מברך אחריו וכו' אלא הייכו טעמא דק"ש אית ביה מלכות שמים וברכת המזון דאורייתא ותפלה דרבנן וגם על גיר' זו קשה כדפי':

ספק לא אמר אמת ויציב חוזר. ותימה הא ע"כ צריך לומר שהוא מסופק גם מק"ש שאם היה ברור לו מק"ש וספק מאמת ויציב לא יהיה מן התורה כיון שהזכיר יציאת מצרים בק"ש וא"כ הואיל ומסופק משניהם יחזור לק"ש דאית ביה תרתי מלכות שמים ויציאת מצרים דהכי עדיף מלומר אמת ויציב דליכא אלא חדא כדאמר בסמוך גבי מתנית' ואומר ר"י דודאי מתני' גבי בעל קרי שידענו בו שלא אמר ק"ש ולא אמת ויציב כלל ואנו רוצי' להתיר לו הלכך טוב הוא יותר שיאמר ק"ש דאיכא תרתי אבל הכא שהוא ספק אם אמר אמת ויציב ומספקא ליה אם אמר שניהם כדפרי' טוב הוא יותר שיאמר אמת ויציב מלומר ק"ש דכשיאמר אמת ויציב שמא יש לתלות שתקן הכל דאם קרא כבר אמת ויציב גם קרא ק"ש כבר דמסתמא' שתפלל כדרך תפלת ק"ש ואח"כ אמת ויציב ויצא ידי שתיהן וכי כוני תימא דלא אמר כבר שתיהן מ"מ שמא אמר ק"ש ולא אמר אמת ויציב שזה יכול להיות ועתה כשיאמר אמת ויציב נמצא שהשלים הכל וכי תימא שמא לא קרא לא זה ולא זה כיון דספיקא הוא כולי האי לא אטרחוהו רבנן לחזור שניהם אבל אם יאמר ק"ש אין זו תקנ' גמורה כל כך דשמא קרא ק"ש אחרת ולא יצא כלל בזה שעושה עתה ואם ברור שלא אמר כבר ק"ש אם כן לא אמר נמי אמת ויציב שאין רגילות לומר אמת ויציב בלא ק"ש ואם כן כשיאמר מעתה ק"ש לא תקן כלל ולא יצא מידי ספקו עוד אומר הר"ר שמשון דמיירי שפיר שאינו מסופק אלא מאמת ויציב אבל ברור הוא שקרא ק"ש ואפי' הכי הוי אמת ויציב דאורייתא שר"ל ספק לא אמר אמת ויציב עם פרשת ציצית שמסופק אי לא אמר לא פרשת ציצית ולא אמת ויציב ואם כן לא הזכיר כלל יציאת מצרים וכולה מלתא דיציאת מצרים קרי ליה אמת ויציב לפי דטעם אמת ויציב הוי משום יציאת מצרים והלכך הוי פרשת ציצית בכלל אמת ויציב:

ההוא בדברי תורה כתיב. והא דאמרינן לעיל בפרק קמא (דף ב.) בערב משום דכתיב ובשכבך אסמכתא בעלמא הוא*:

ורבי יוחנן אמר ולואי שיתפלל אדם כל היום. אמר ר"י דהלכה כר' יוחנן ודוקא בספק התפלל אבל ודאי התפלל לא *תדע דהא מסתמא לא פליג אהא דאמר רב יהודה אמר שמואל בסמוך ונזכר שהתפלל פוסק וכו' וכן אם יכול לחדש דבר בתפלתו:

עד

מסורת הש"ס

לקמן דף כב ב

נ' כילתא דר"י פ' בא לקמן דף מח ב ע"ש

[נ"ל רב יהודה אמר שמואל וכ"א ברי"ף ורא"ש]

מקום שנהגו דף כד ב

[וכ"ה תוס' לקמן כו. ד"ה טעה]

עין משפט נר מצוה

לו א מיי' פ"ב מהל' ק"ש הל' י"ג סמג עשין יט טוש"ע א"ח סי' סז

לז ב מיי' פ"י מהל' תפלה הל' ו' סמ"ג עשין יט טוש"ע א"ח סי' קז סעי' א

לח ד מיי' שם הל' ז' וסמ"ג שם טוש"ע א"ח סי' רסח סעי' ג'

[ע' תוס' סוט' לג: ד"ה ורבי]

לט ה מיי' פ"א הל' ט ופ"י מה' תפלה הל' ו' סמ"ג שם טוש"ע א"ח סי' קז סעי' א

[וע' תוס' סוטה לג: ד"ה ורבי ותוס' מנחות מג: ד"ה ולאיזהו]

או צבור וצבור אבל יחיד לגבי צבור כמאן דלא צלי דמי קמ"ל ואי אשמועינן הכא משום דלא אתחיל בה אבל התם דאתחיל בה אימא לא צריכא אמר רב הונא הנכנס לב"ה ומצא צבור שמתפללין אם יכול להתחיל ולגמור עד שלא יגיע ש"צ למודים יתפלל ואם לאו אל יתפלל ריב"ל אמר אם יכול להתחיל ולגמור עד שלא יגיע ש"צ לקדושה יתפלל ואם לאו אל יתפלל במאי קא מפלגי מ"ס יחיד אומר קדושה ומ"ס אין יחיד אומר קדושה *וכן אמר רב אדא בר אהבה *מנין שאין היחיד אומר קדושה שנאמר °ונקדשתי בתוך בני ישראל כל דבר שבקדושה לא יהא פחות מעשרה מאי משמע דתני* רבנאי אחו' דרבי חייא בר אבא אתיא תוך תוך כתיב הכא ונקדשתי בתוך בני ישראל וכתיב התם °הבדלו מתוך העדה הזאת *מה להלן עשרה אף כאן עשר' ודכולי עלמא מידת מפסק לא פסיק אבעיא להו מהו להפסיק לידהא שמו הגדול מבורך כי אתא רב דימי אמר ר' יהודה *ור"ש תלמידי דרבי יוחנן אמרי לכל אין מפסיקין חוץ מן יהא שמו הגדול מבורך שאפילו עוסק במעשה מרכבה פוסק ולית הלכתא כותיה: רבי יהודה אומר מברך לפניהם: למימרא דקסבר רבי יהודה בעל קרי מותר בדברי תורה והאמר ריב"ל מנין לבעל קרי שאסור בד"ת *שנאמר °והודעתם לבניך ולבני בניך וסמיך ליה יום אשר עמדת וגומר מה להלן בעלי קריין אסורין אף כאן בעלי קריין אסורין וכי תימא *רבי יהודה *לא דריש סמוכים והאמר *רב יוסף אפילו מאן דלא דריש סמוכים בכל התורה במשנה תורה דריש דהא רבי יהודה לא דריש סמוכים בכל התורה כולה ובמשנה תורה דריש ובכל התורה כולה מנא לן דלא דריש דתניא *בן עזאי אומר נאמר °מכשפה לא תחיה ונאמר כל שוכב עם בהמה מות יומת סמכו ענין לו לומר מה שוכב עם בהמה בסקילה אף מכשפה נמי בסקילה אמר ליה רבי יהודה וכי מפני שסמכו ענין לו נוציא לזה לסקילה אלא אוב וידעוני בכלל כל המכשפים היו ולמה יצאו להקיש להן ולומר לך מה אוב וידעוני בסקילה אף מכשפה בסקילה ובמשנ' תורה מנא לן דדריש דתניא *רבי אליעזר אומר נושא אדם אנוסת אביו ומפותת' אביו אנוסת בנו ומפותת בנו ר' יהודה אוסר באנוסת אביו ובמפות' אביו ואמר רב גידל אמר רב מ"ט דר' יהודה דכתיב °לא יקח איש את אשת אביו ולא יגלה (את) כנף אביו כנף שראה אביו לא יגלה וממאי דבאנוסת אביו כתיב דסמיך ליה ונתן האיש השוכב עמה וגומר אמרי אין במשנה תורה דריש והני סמוכים מבעי ליה לאידך דריב"ל דאמר ריב"ל *כל המלמד לבנו תורה מעלה עליו הכתוב כאלו קבלה מהר חורב שנאמר °והודעתם לבניך ולבני בניך וכתיב בתריה יום אשר עמדת לפני יי' אלהיך בחורב *תנן זב שראה קרי ונדה שפלטה שכבת זרע המשמשת וראתה *דם צריכין טבילה ורבי יהודה פוטר עד כאן לא פטר רבי יהודה אלא בזב שראה קרי דמעיקרא לאו בר טבילה הוא אבל בעל קרי גרידא מיחייב וכי תימא הוא הדין דאפילו בעל קרי גרידא נמי פטר רבי יהודה והאי דקא מפלגי בזב שראה קרי להודיעך כחן דרבנן אימא סיפא משמשת וראתה *דם צריכה טבילה למאן קתני לה אילימא לרבנן פשיטא השתא ומה זב שראה קרי דמעיקרא לאו בר טבילה הוא מחייבי רבנן משמשת וראתה *דם דמעיקרא בת טבילה היא לא כל שכן אלא לאו רבי יהודה הוא ודוקא קתני לה

משמשת

תורה אור: ויקרא כב · במדבר טז · דברים ד · שמות כב · דברים כג

או צבור וצבור. בין בראשונה בין בשניה היה עם הצבור כגון עשרה אחר עשרה וזה עמהם בשתיהן שכבר שהתפלל עם הראשוני': רב הונא. סבר יחיד המתפלל עם הצבור אומר קדוש. הלכך אם לא גמר עד שלא יגיע ש"צ לקדוש לית לן בה אבל מודים אף על פי שיחיד אומר מודים אם אינו אומרו עם הצבור הרואה את כולם כורעים והוא אינו כורע נראה ככופר במי שחבריו משתחוין לו: מפסק לא פסיק. תפלתו לקדושה לענות עם הצבור וכן למודים: במשנה תורה דריש. והאי קרא במשנה תורה הוא כתוב: מכשפה לא תחיה. ולא פירש באיזה מיתה תמות ונאמר אצלו כל שוכב עם בהמה מות יומת: סמכו ענין לו. סמכתו פרשת מכשפה לא תחיה לשוכב עם בהמה: מה שוכב עם בהמה בסקילה. כדאמרינן לה בסנהדרין פרק ד' מיתות (דף כד ב) בגזירה שוה דתהרגו דהכא מכי הרוג תהרגנו דמסית אף מכשף בסקילה: אמר ליה רבי יהודה וכי מפני שסמכו הענין. לשוכב עם בהמה נוציא זה המכשף לסקילה שהיא חמורה מכל מיתות שבתורה אלא מקרא מפורש יש לו במקום אחר שהוא בסקילה: אוב וידעוני בכלל. לא תחיה דכל המכשפים היו ולמה יצאו בפני עצמן כשהפרישן לסקילה כדכתיב באבן ירגמו אותם דמיהם בם (ויקרא כ) להקיש אליהם את כל הכלל שזו מדה בתורה שכל דבר שהיה בכלל ויצא מן הכלל ללמד לא ללמד על עצמו יצא אלא ללמד על הכלל כולו יצא: זב שראה קרי וכו'. לענין טבילה שתקן עזרא לבעלי קריין לעסוק בתורה קאי ולאחר טומאים לא הצריך וקאמר הכא דאם יש לו טומאה אחרת עם הקרי שאינו יכול לצאת מטומאה בטבילה זו כגון זב ונדה שהם טמאים טומאת שבעה אפילו הכי צריך לטבול לקריו קודם שיעסוק בתורה: פולטת שכבת זרע. הרי היא כבעל קרי: ורבי יהודה פוטר. קס"ד דאין טבילה זו מטהרתו מכל וכל: המשמשת למאן קתני לה. להשמיענו כח מי הוצרכו לחלוק בה: אילימא לרבנן. להודיעך כחן דמחייבי בה: השתא זב שראה קרי. שקדמתו טומאת הזיבה מעיקרא: דמעיקרא. בשעה שראה קרי לאו בר טבילה הוא ומחייבי ליה רבנן טבילה לקרי לדברי תורה:

משמשת

עד שלא יגיע שליח צבור למודים. וטעמא לפי שצריך לשוח עם הצבור שלא יראה ככופר במי שהצבור משתחוין לו והוא הדין נמי אם יגיע למודים כששליח צבור יגיע למודים דשפיר דמי כיון שהוא משתחוה עם חביריו אבל אין גמרא פסיק ליה כי האי גונא אבל אין נראה דמשום מודים דרבנן נקט הכי שמלוה לענות שזה לא מצינו לו עיקר בגמרא ור"ת היה רגיל כשהיה מתפלל ביחיד כשהחזן מגיע למודים היה כורע עם הקהל בלא אמירה כלל ודוק' באמצע ברכה אבל בסוף ברכה לא דאמר לקמן (דף לד.) דאסור לשחות בסוף כל ברכה וברכה מיהו לכתחלה אין לעשות כן כדמשמע הכא וכת' רש"י בסוכה פרק לולב הגזול (דף לח ב) דאדם המתפלל ושמע מפי החזן קדיש או קדושה אינו יכול להפסיק ולענות עם הצבו' אלא ישתוק ויכוין מעט דשומע כעונה וי"ל דלכתחלה אין לעשות כן דעכשיו חשיבה טפי הדור מלוה ור"ת ור"י היו אומרים דאדרבה אי שומע כעונ' הוי הפסק' אם שותק ומ"מ נהגו העם לשתוק ולשמוע וגדול המנהג. בירושלמי פ' תפלת השחר קאמר לא התפלל ובא ומלאן מתפללי' מוסף אם היה יודע שיהיה מתפלל וגומר עד שלא יתחיל ש"ל כדי לענות אמן מתפלל אם לאו לא יתפלל באיזה אמן אמרו פליגי ביה תרי אמוראי חד אמר באמן של האל הקדוש וחד אמר באמן של שומע תפלה ולא פליגי כאן בחול כאן בשבת והא דאמרינן באמן של שומע תפלה היינו בחול לכך יש ליזהר לענות אמן בהאל הקדוש וגם לענות אמן בשומע תפלה ומתוך הירושלמי משמע שהיו רגילין לומר י"ח ברכות שלמות במוסף של חול כגון בר"ח ובחול המועד ומיהו אנן סמכינן אהא דאמר פרק תפלת השחר (דף כט.) דקאמר תמני סרי תקון תשסרי לא תקון ומה שאנו אומרים עננו בין גואל לרופא לא קשה שאינו אלא לש"ל אבל יחיד כוללה בש"ת ועוד אומר הר"ר חיים דאיתא בתוספתא (פרק ג) בהדיא כמנהגנו דקא' התם ימים שיש בהם קרבן מוסף כגון ר"ח וח"ה מערבית ושחרית מתפלל י"ח שלמו' ואומר מעין המאורע בעבוד' ואם לא אמר מחזירי' אותו ובמוספי' מתפלל שבע ואומר קדושת היום באמצע ובירושלמי נמי י"ל דטעות סופר הוא ול"ג של מוסף אלא בא ומלאן מתפללי' וכן משמע בירושלמי פר' מי שמתו דגם זו המימר' כתוב' שם ולא הזכיר של מוסף כלל:

אין יחיד מתפלל קדושה. וכן הלכ' אבל המתפלל י"ח עם החזן לכשיגיע ש"ל לקדושה יאמר עם השליח צבור כקדם וכל הקדושה משלם יכול לענות עם הצבור דאין זה קרוי יחיד:

נחזי

עין משפט נר מצוה

מ
א ב מיי' פ"י מהלכ' תפלה הל' ע"ז סמ"ג עשין י"ט טוש"ע א"ח סי' קט סעי' א

מא
ג מיי' פ"ח שם הל' ד' טוש"ע א"ח סי' נה סעי' א

מב
ד מיי' פ"י שם הל' ע"ז טוש"ע א"ח סי' קד סעי' ז

מג
ה מיי' פי"א מה' עכו"ם הל' טו סמ"ג לאוין כה טור י"ד סי' קעט

מד
ו מיי' פ"ב מה' אסורי ביאה הל' יג

[אולי צ"ל ור"ש בן לקיש ועי' כתובו' קיא:]

[ע' תוס' יבמו' ד. ד"ה וכי מפני ותוס' קדושין נג. ד"ה וסמך לי']

מסורת הש"ס

[תיב' וכן ליתא בריף]

מגילה ד' כג ב

[שם: ע"ש סנהדרין עד: ע"ש:]

[נ"ל ואתיא עדה עדה דכתיב עד מתי לעדה הרעה הזאת מה להלן כו' כך איתא במגילה]

[ע' תוס' ב"ק פב: ד"ה אתא]

[פסחים כח. יבמות פ"א דף ד.]

שם ד' מיתות דף סז ב

יבמות פ' יא דף לז. וע"ש במשנה

דברים כג

[קדושין ל. ע"ש]

שם ד

לקמן דף כו.

[נ"ל נדה] [נ"ל נדה] [נ"ל נדה]

or [where he said it] with a congregation and [is repeating it] with a congregation,[5] but when [one who has prayed] alone goes into a congregation, it is as if he had not prayed at all. Hence we are told that this is not so. And if we had been told only the second case, I might think that this ruling applies only because he had not commenced, but where he had commenced I might say that he should not [break off]. Therefore both are necessary.

R. Huna said: If a man goes into a synagogue and finds the congregation saying the *Tefillah*, if he can commence and finish before
a the reader[1] reaches 'We give thanks',[2] he may say the *Tefillah*,[3] but otherwise he should not say it. R. Joshua b. Levi says: If he can commence and finish before the reader reaches the Sanctification,[4] he should say the *Tefillah*, but otherwise he should not say it. What is the ground of their difference? One authority held that a man praying by himself does say the Sanctification, while the other holds that he does not. So, too, R. Adda b. Abahah said: Whence do we know that a man praying by himself does not say the Sanctification? Because it says: *I will be hallowed among the children of Israel;*[5] for any manifestation of sanctification not less than ten are required. How is this derived? Rabinai the brother of R. Ḥiyya b. Abba taught: We draw an analogy between two occurrences of the word 'among'. It is written here, *I will be hallowed* among *the children of Israel*, and it is written elsewhere, *Separate yourselves from* among *this congregation*.[6] Just as in that case ten are implied,[7] so here ten are implied. Both authorities, however, agree that he does not interrupt [the *Tefillah*].[8]

The question was asked: What is the rule about interrupting [the *Tefillah*] to respond, *May His great name be blessed?*[9]—When R. Dimi came from Palestine, he said that R. Judah and R. Simeon[10] the disciples of R. Joḥanan say that one interrupts for nothing except 'May His great name be blessed', for even if he is engaged in studying the section of the work of [the Divine] Chariot,[11] he must interrupt [to make this response]. But the law is not in accordance with their view.[12]

R. JUDAH SAYS: HE SAYS THE GRACE BOTH BEFORE AND AFTER. This would imply that R. Judah was of opinion that a *ba'al keri* is permitted to [occupy himself] with the words of the Torah. But has not R. Joshua b. Levi said: How do we know that a *ba'al keri* is forbidden to study the Torah? Because it says,
b *Make them known unto thy children and thy children's children*,[1] and immediately afterwards, *The day that thou stoodest [before the Lord thy God in Horeb]*,[2] implying that just as on that occasion those who had a seminal issue were forbidden,[3] so here too those who have a seminal issue are forbidden? And should you say that R. Judah does not derive lessons from the juxtaposition of texts, [this does not matter] since R. Joseph has said: Even those who do not derive lessons from the juxtaposition of texts in all the rest of the Torah, do so in Deuteronomy; for R. Judah does not derive such lessons in all the rest of the Torah, and in Deuteronomy he does. And how do we know that in all the rest of the Torah he does not derive such lessons?—As it has been taught; Ben 'Azzai says: *Thou shalt not suffer a sorceress to live*,[4] and it says [immediately afterwards], *Whosoever lieth with a beast shall surely be put to death*.[5] The two statements were juxtaposed to tell you that just as one that lieth with a beast is put to death by stoning, so a sorceress also is put to death by stoning. Said R. Judah to him: Because the two statements are juxtaposed, are we to take this one out to be stoned? Rather [we learn it as follows]: They that divine by a ghost or a familiar spirit come under the head of sorceress. Why then were they mentioned separately?[6] To serve as a basis for comparison: just as they that divine by a ghost or familiar spirit are to be stoned, so a sorceress is to be stoned. And how do we know that he derives lessons from juxtaposition in Deuteronomy?—As it has been taught: R. Eliezer said, A man may marry a woman who has been raped by his father or seduced by his father, one who has been raped by his son, or one who has been seduced by his son. R. Judah prohibits one who has been raped by his father or seduced by his father. And R. Giddal said with reference to this: What is the reason of R. Judah? Because it is written: *A man shall not take his father's wife and shall not uncover*
c *his father's skirt;*[1] which implies, he shall not uncover the skirt which his father saw. And how do we know that the text is speaking of one raped by his father?—Because just before it are the words, *Then the man that lay with her shall give unto the father*, etc.![2]—They replied: Yes, in Deuteronomy he does draw such lessons, but this juxtaposition he requires for the other statement of R. Joshua b. Levi. For R. Joshua b. Levi said: If any man teaches his son Torah, the Scripture accounts it to him as if he had received it from Mount Horeb, as it says, *'And thou shalt make them known unto thy children and thy children's children'*, and immediately afterwards it is written, *'The day that thou stoodest before the Lord thy God in Horeb*.[3]

We have learnt: A sufferer from gonorrhoea who had an emission, a *niddah* from whom semen has escaped and a woman who became *niddah* during sexual intercourse require ritual ablution;[4] R. Judah, however, exempts them.[5] Now R. Judah's exemption extends only to a gonorrhoeic person who had an emission, because ritual ablution in his first condition[6] is useless for him,[7] but an ordinary person who has an emission requires ritual ablution![8] And should you maintain that R. Judah exempts an ordinary *ba'al keri* also, and the reason why he and the Rabbis joined issue over the gonorrhoeic person was to show how far the Rabbis are prepared to go, then look then at the next clause: 'A woman who became *niddah* during sexual intercourse requires a ritual ablution'. Whose opinion is here stated? Shall I say it is the Rabbis? Surely this is self-evident! Seeing that a gonorrhoeic person who has an emission, although a ritual ablution is useless in his first condition, was yet required by the Rabbis to take one, how much more so a woman who becomes *niddah* during sexual intercourse, for whom in her
d first condition a ritual ablution was efficacious![1] We must say therefore that it states the opinion of R. Judah, and he meant

(5) I.e., after having prayed with one congregation, he goes in to another.
a (1) Lit., 'the messenger of the congregation'. (2) The seventeenth benediction, v. *P.B.* p. 51. (3) In order that he may be able to bow at this point with the congregation. (4) Recited in the third benediction. In this also the congregation joins in, v. *P.B.* p. 45. (5) Lev. XXII, 32. (6) Num. XVI, 21. (7) The 'congregation' referred to being the ten spies, Joshua and Caleb being excluded. V. Meg. 23*b*. (8) If he has commenced his *Tefillah* he does not interrupt in order to say the Sanctification with the congregation or to bow down with them. (9) In the *Kaddish*, v. Glos. (10) I.e., Judah b. Pazzi and Simeon b. Abba. (11) V. Ḥag. 11*b*. (12) So MS.M. Cur. edd., 'with him'.
b (1) Deut. IV, 9. (2) Ibid. 10. (3) V. *supra* 20*b*, n. c1. (4) Ex. XXII, 17. (5) Ibid. 18. (6) In Lev. XX, 27. *'A man also .... that divineth by a ghost or a familiar spirit shall surely be put to death; they shall stone them with stones'*.
c (1) Deut. XXIII, 1. (2) Ibid. XXII, 29. This shows that R. Judah derives lessons from juxtaposed texts in Deuteronomy. How then does he permit a *ba'al keri* to occupy himself with Torah in view of Deut. IV, 9 and 10? (3) Ibid. IV, 9 and 10. (4) In order to be able to read *Shema'* or other words of the Torah. (5) V. *infra* 26*a*. (6) I.e., before he experienced the emission. (7) He has to wait seven days before he is clean. (8) *Contra* his own ruling in our Mishnah.
d (1) To cleanse her from the seminal issue that took place before the *niddah*.

exemption to apply only to this case, [22*a*] so that a woman who becomes *niddah* during sexual intercourse does not require a ritual ablution, but an ordinary *ba'al keri* does require ritual ablution!—Read [in the Mishnah] not: [R. JUDAH SAYS,] HE SAYS THE BLESSING, but 'He says mentally'. But does R. Judah [in any case] prescribe saying mentally? Has it not been taught: A *ba'al keri* who has no water for a ritual ablution recites the *Shema'* without saying a blessing either before or after, and he eats bread and says a blessing after it. He does not, however, say a blessing before it, but says it mentally without uttering it with his lips. So R. Meir. R. Judah says: In either case he utters it with his lips?—Said R. Naḥman b. Isaac: R. Judah put it on the same footing as the *halachoth* of *Derek Erez*,[2] as it has been taught: '*And thou shalt make them known to thy children and thy children's children*', and it is written immediately afterwards, '*The day on which thou didst stand before the Lord thy God in Horeb*'. Just as there it was in dread and fear and trembling and quaking, so in this case too[3] it must be in dread and fear and trembling and quaking. On the basis of this they laid down that sufferers from gonorrhoea, lepers, and those who had intercourse with *niddoth* are permitted to read the Torah, the Prophets and the Hagiographa, and to study the Mishnah, [Midrash][4] the Talmud,[5] *halachoth* and *haggadoth*, but a *ba'al keri* is forbidden.[6] R. Jose said: He may repeat those with which he is familiar, so long as he does not expound the Mishnah. R. Jonathan b. Joseph said: He may expound the Mishnah but he must not expound the Talmud.[7] R. Nathan b. Abishalom says: He may expound the Talmud also, provided only he does not mention the divine names that occur[8] in it. R. Joḥanan the sandal-maker, the disciple of R. Akiba, said in the name of R. Akiba: He should not enter upon the Midrash at all. (Some read, he should not enter the Beth Ha-midrash at all.) R. Judah says: He may
a repeat the laws of *Derek Erez*.[1] Once R. Judah after having had a seminal issue was walking along a river bank, and his disciples said to him, Master repeat to us a section from the laws of *Derek Erez*, and he went down and bathed and then repeated to them. They said to him: Have you not taught us, Master, 'He may repeat the laws of *Derek Erez*'? He replied: Although I make concessions to others, I am strict with myself.

It has been taught: R. Judah b. Bathyra used to say: Words of Torah are not susceptible of uncleanness. Once a certain disciple was mumbling over against R. Judah b. Bathyra.[2] He said to him: My son, open thy mouth and let thy words be clear, for words of Torah are not susceptible to uncleanness, as it says, *Is not My word like as fire*.[3] Just as fire is not susceptible of uncleanness, so words of Torah are not susceptible of uncleanness.

The Master said: He may expound the Mishnah, but he must not expound the Talmud. This supports R. Ila'i; for R. Ila'i said in the name of R. Aḥa b. Jacob, who gave it in the name of our Master:[4] The *halachach* is that he may expound the Mishnah but he must not expound the Talmud. The same difference of opinion is found among Tannaim. 'He may expound the Mishnah but he must not expound the Talmud'. So R. Meir. R. Judah b. Gamaliel says in the name of R. Ḥanina b. Gamaliel: Both are forbidden. Others report him as having said: Both are permitted. The one who reports 'Both are forbidden' concurs with R. Joḥanan the sandal-maker; the one who reports, 'both are permitted' concurs with R. Judah b. Bathyra.

R. Naḥman b. Isaac said: It has become the custom[5] to follow these three elders, R. Ila'i in the matter of the first shearing,[6] R. Josiah in the matter of mixed kinds, and R. Judah b. Bathyra in the matter of words of Torah. 'R. Ila'i in the matter of the first shearing', as it has been taught: R. Ila'i says: The rule of the first shearing applies only in Palestine. 'R. Josiah in the matter of mixed kinds', as it is written, *Thou shalt not sow thy vineyard with two kinds*
b *of seeds*.[1] R. Josiah says: The law has not been broken until one sows wheat, barley and grape kernels with one throw.[2] 'R. Judah b. Bathyra in the matter of words of Torah,' as it has been taught: R. Judah b. Bathyra says: Words of Torah are not susceptible of uncleanness. When Ze'iri came [from Palestine], he said: They have abolished the ritual ablution. Some report him to have said: They have abolished the washing of hands. The one who reports 'they have abolished the ritual ablution' concurs with R. Judah b. Bathyra. The one who reports 'they have abolished the washing of hands' is in accord with R. Ḥisda, who cursed anyone who went looking for water at the hour of prayer.[3]

Our Rabbis taught: A *ba'al keri* on whom nine *kabs*[4] of water have been thrown is clean. Naḥum a man of Gimzu[5] whispered it to R. Akiba, and R. Akiba whispered it to Ben 'Azzai, and Ben 'Azzai went forth and repeated it to the disciples in public. Two Amoraim in the West differed in regard to this, R. Jose b. Abin and R. Jose b. Zebida. One stated: He repeated it, and one taught, He whispered it. The one who taught 'he repeated it' held that the reason [for the concession] was to prevent neglect of the Torah and of procreation. The one who taught 'he whispered it' thought that the reason was in order that scholars might not always be with their wives like cocks.[6]

R. Jannai said: I have heard of some who are lenient in this matter,[7] and I have heard of some who are strict in it;[8] and if anyone is strict with himself in regard to it, his days and years are prolonged.

R. Joshua b. Levi said: What is the sense of those who bathe in the morning? [He asks], What is the sense! Why, it was he himself who said that a *ba'al keri* is forbidden [to occupy himself] with the words of the Torah! What he meant is this: What is the
c sense of bathing in forty *se'ahs*[1] when one can make shift with nine *kabs*? What is the sense of going right in when throwing the water over one is sufficient? R. Ḥanina said: They put up a very valuable fence by this,[2] as it has been taught: Once a man enticed a woman to commit an offence and she said to him: Vagabond,[3] have you forty *se'ahs* to bathe in, and he at once desisted. Said R. Huna to the disciples: My masters, why do you make so light of this bathing? Is it because of the cold? You can use the baths! Said R. Ḥisda to him: Can ablution be performed in hot baths?—He replied: R. Adda b. Ahabah is of the same opinion as you. R. Ze'ira used to sit in a tub of water in the baths and say to his servant, Go and fetch nine *kabs* and throw over me. R. Ḥiyya b. Abba said to him: Why, sir, do you take this trouble, seeing that you are sitting in [that quantity of] water?—He replied: The nine *kabs* must be like the forty *se'ahs*: just as the forty *se'ahs* are for immersion and not for throwing, so the nine *kabs* are for throwing and not for immersion. R. Naḥman prepared an ewer holding nine *kabs*.[4] When R. Dimi came, he reported that R. Akiba and R. Judah Glostera[5] had said: The rule,[6] was laid down only for a sick person who has an emission involuntarily, but for a sick person who has a voluntary emission[7] forty *se'ahs* [are required]. Said R. Joseph: R. Naḥman's ewer was broken.[8] When Rabin came, he said: The thing took

(2) Lit., 'Good Behaviour', two small tractates which did not enjoy the same authority as the rest of the Mishnah. (3) Viz., the study of the Torah. (4) Inserted with MS.M. (5) So MS.M.; cur. edd. Gemara, v. *supra* 11*b*, n. a9. (6) Because the seminal issue is a sign of frivolity. (7) Rashi reads 'Midrash'. (8) In the Biblical verses which it expounds (Rashi).
a (1) V. M.K. 15*a*. (2) He had had an issue and was afraid to say the words distinctly. (3) Jer. XXIII, 29. (4) Rab. (5) Lit., 'the world is accustomed'. (6) V. Deut. XVIII, 4.
b (1) Deut. XXII, 9. (2) Wheat and barley being mixed seeds, and grape kernels mixed seeds of the vineyard. (3) V. *supra* 15*a*. (4) A *kab* is four *logs* or twenty-four eggs. (5) V. Ta'an. 21*a*. (6) And therefore he did not want it to be too well known among the scholars. (7) Of using only nine *kabs*,

משמשת וראתה נדה אינה צריכה טבילה אבל בעל קרי גרידא מחייב לא תימא מברך אלא מהרהר ומי אית ליה לר' יהודה הרהור והתני' בעל קרי שאין לו מים לטבול קורא ק"ש ואינו מברך לא לפניה ולא לאחריה ואוכל פתו ומברך לאחריה ואינו מברך לפניה אבל מהרהר בלבו *ואינו מוצי' בשפתיו דברי ר"מ ר' יהודה אומר בין כך ובין כך מוציא בשפתיו אמר רב נחמן בר יצחק עשאן רבי יהודה כהלכות דרך ארץ דתני' *°והודעתם לבניך ולבני בניך וכתיב בתרי' יום אשר עמדת לפני ה' אלהיך בחורב מה להלן באימה וביראה וברתת ובזיע אף כאן באימה וביראה וברתת ובזיע מכאן אמרו **הזבים והמצורעים ובאין על נדות *מותרים לקרות בתורה ובנביאים ובכתובים לשנות במשנה וגמרא ובהלכות ובאגדות אבל בעלי קריין אסורים ר' יוסי אומר שונה הוא ברגיליות ובלבד שלא *יציע את המשנה ר' יונתן בן יוסף אומר מציע הוא את המשנה ואינו מציע את הגמרא ר' נתן בן *אבישלום אומר אף מציע את הגמרא ובלבד שלא יאמר אזכרות שבו רבי יוחנן הסנדלר תלמידו של ר' עקיבא משום ר"ע אומר לא יכנס למדרש כל עיקר ואמרי לה לא יכנס לבית המדרש כל עיקר רבי יהודה אומר שונה הוא בהלכות דרך ארץ מעשה ברבי יהודה שראה קרי והיה מהלך על גב הנהר א"ל תלמידיו רבינו שנה לנו פרק אחד בהלכות דרך ארץ ירד וטבל ושנה להם אמרו לו לא כך למדתנו רבינו שונה הוא בהלכות דרך ארץ אמר להם אע"פי שמיקל אני על אחרים מחמיר אני על עצמי: תניא רבי יהודה בן בתירא היה אומר *אין דברי תורה מקבלין טומאה מעשה בתלמיד אחד שהיה מגמגם למעלה מרבי יהודה בן בתירא א"ל בני פתח פיך ויאירו דבריך שאין דברי תורה מקבלין טומאה שנאמר °הלא כה דברי כאש נאם ה' מה אש אינו מקבל טומאה אף ד"ת אינן מקבלין טומאה אמר מר מציע את המשנה ואינו מציע את הגמרא מסייע ליה לרבי אלעאי דאמר ר' אלעאי אמר רב אחא בר יעקב משום רבינו הלכה מציע את המשנה ואינו מציע את הגמרא כתנאי מציע את המשנה ואינו מציע את הגמרא דברי ר"מ רבי יהודה בן גמליאל אומר משום רבי חנינא בן גמליאל זה וזה אסור ואמרי לה זה וזה מותר מ"ד זה וזה אסור כרבי יוחנן הסנדלר מ"ד זה וזה מותר כרבי יהודה בן בתירא אמר רב נחמן בר יצחק *נהוג עלמא כהני תלת סבי כרבי אלעאי בראשית הגז כרבי יאשיה בכלאים כרבי יהודה בן בתירא בדברי תורה כרבי אלעאי בראשית הגז דתניא *רבי אלעאי אומר [ב]ראשית הגז אינו נוהג אלא בארץ כר' יאשיה בכלאים דכתיב °כרמך לא תזרע כלאים *ר' יאשיה אומר [ג]לעולם *אינו חייב עד שיזרע חטה ושעורה וחרצן במפולת יד כרבי יהודה בן בתירא בדברי תורה דתניא רבי יהודה בן בתירא אומר [ד]אין דברי תורה מקבלין טומאה כי אתא זעירי אמר בטלוה לטבילותא ואמרי לה בטלוה לנטילותא מאן דאמר בטלוה לטבילותא כרבי יהודה בן בתירא מ"ד בטלוה לנטילותא כי הא *דרב חסדא לייט אמאן דמהדר אמיא בעידן צלותא: ת"ר בעל קרי שנתנו עליו תשעה קבין מים טהור נחום איש גם זו לחשה לר' עקיבא ור' עקיבא לחשה לבן עזאי ובן עזאי יצא ושנאה לתלמידיו בשוק פליגי בה תרי אמוראי במערבא רבי יוסי בר אבין ורבי יוסי בר זבידא חד תני שנאה וחד תני לחשה מאן דתני שנאה משום בטול תורה ומשום בטול פריה ורביה ומאן דתני לחשה [ה]שלא יהו ת"ח מצויים אצל נשותיהם כתרנגולים אמר ר' ינאי שמעתי שמקילין בה ושמעתי שמחמירין בה [ו]וכל המחמיר בה על עצמו מאריכין לו ימיו ושנותיו אמר ריב"ל מה טיבן של טובלי שחרין מה טיבן הא איהו דאמר בעל קרי אסור בדברי תורה הכי קאמר מה טיבן בארבעים סאה אפשר בתשעה קבין מה טיבן בטבילה אפשר בנתינה אמר רבי חנינא גדר גדול גדרו בה דתניא מעשה בא' שתבע אשה לדבר עבירה אמרה לו ריקא יש לך ארבעים סאה שאתה טובל בהן מיד פירש אמר להו רב הונא לרבנן רבותי מפני מה אתם מזלזלין בטבילה זו אי משום צינה אפשר במרחצאות אמר ליה רב חסדא [ז]וכי יש טבילה בחמין אמר ליה רב אדא בר אהבה קאי כותך *רבי זירא הוה יתיב באגנא דמיא בי מסותא א"ל לשמעיה זיל ואייתי לי ט' קבין ושדי עלואי א"ל רבי חייא בר אבא למה ליה למר כולי האי והא יתיב בגויידו אמר ליה כארבעים סאה מה ארבעים סאה בטבילה ולא בנתינה אף [ח]ט' קבין בנתינה ולא בטבילה רב נחמן תקן חצבא בת תשעה קבין כי אתא רב דימי אמר רבי עקיבא ורבי יהודה גלוסטרא אמרו לא שנו אלא לחולה לאונסו אבל לחולה המרגיל ארבעים סאה אמר רב יוסף אתבר חצביה דרב נחמן כי אתא רבין אמר *באושא הוה עובדא בקילעא

תורה אור: דברי' ד' — ירמיה כג — דברים כב

*משמשת וראתה נדה. דטומאת קרי קדמה וכשראת' הקרי ראוי' היתה לטבול מיד: לא כל שכן. דלא אתיא טומאת נדה שהיא חמורה ומפקעה לטבילה שנתחייבה בה כבר: אלא לאו רבי יהודה. קתני להודיעך דאפי' היכא דקדם הקרי אתיא טומאת נדה ומפקעה טבילה דאין טבילה אלא המטהרת ואי לרבי יהודה לית ליה תקנת עזרא למה לי' לאשמועינן בהא כל בעלי קריין נמי לא בעו טבילה לדברי תורה הלכך על כרחך דוקא קתני לה: לא תימא. במתני' מברך אלא מהרהר: עשאן ר' יהודה. לברכת המזון: כהלכות דרך ארץ. שמותר לשונה בעל קרי כדבריו: מה להלן באימה. דכתיב וירא העם וינועו וגו' (שמות כ): מכאן אמרו. כל הטמאים מותרים בתורה שאף הם יכולי' להיות באימה וברתת אבל בעל קרי אינו אלא מתוך קלות ראש וזחות הדעת: ובועלי נדות. אם טבלו לקריין לדברי תורה הטבילה *אינו עולה להם לטהרם מטומאת בועל נדה שהיא שבעת ימים אבל לתקנת עזרא עולה להם כדתנן במתניתין זב שראה קרי ונדה כו' צריכין טבילה: ברגיליות. במשניות השגורות בפיו שהוא מוליאן מפיו במרוצה ואין צריך להאריך בהן: שלא יציע. בטעמי פירושיהן: ואינו מציע את המדרש. גרסי' מפני שצריך הוא תמיד להזכיר בו את הפסוקים שהוא דורש: אזכרות. שבמקראות הכדרשים: לא יכנס למדרש כל עיקר. לא להציע ולא לשנות אבל לבית המדרש הוא נכנס ושותק: הלכות דרך ארץ. כגון דרכה של ת"ח שהוא *ברייתא ופרק

בן עזאי הכותן ארבעה דברים אל לבו: מגמגם. וקורא. בעל קרי היה: כראה בעיני דה"ג א"ר אלעאי הלכה כו' ולא גרסינן מסייע ליה: משום רבינו. רב: כי הנך תלת סבי. וכולהו לקולא: אינו נוהג אלא בארץ. בשחיטת חולין יליף טעמא בפרק הזרוע: חטה ושעורה וחרצן. שלשתן במפולת יד דהוו להו כלאי זרעים וכלאי הכרם כאחת: לטבילותם. דבעלי קריין: חד תני. בבן עזאי לחשה לתלמידים: משום בטול פריה ורביה. שהיו נמנעי' מתשמיש מפני טורח הטבילה: שמקילין בה. במרחצאות או בנתינת תשעה קבין: שמחמירין בה. בארבעים סאה: של טובלי שחרין. בעלי קריין הטובלין שחרית: והא איהו אמר כו'. לעיל ברים שמעתין: אפשר בנתינה. תשעה קבין ואע"ג דלא תנא (*לעיל) אלא בחולה קתם תלמידי חכמים חולים הם כדאמר במסכת נדרים (פ"ו דף מט:) כמאן מצלינן אקלירי ואמריעי כרבי יוסי. קלירי חולין מריעי רבנן: גדר גדול גדרו. במה שהצריכו בארבעים סאה: אותה אשה. פנויה היתה וחכמים גזרו על הייחוד אף על הפנויה: אתם מזלזלים. לנהוג כרבי יהודה בן בתירא: אפשר במרחצאות. חמין: קאי כותך. דבעי טבילה זו במקוה כשאר טבילות: באגנא דמיא. גיגית: תקן חצבא. ליתן מים לתלמידים עליהם שחרית קודם קריאת התורה: לא שנו. דסגי בנתינה אלא בחולה שראה קרי לאונסו: המרגיל. וממשיך את הקרי עליו שמשמש מטתו: אתבר חצביה. אינו צריך לנו דחולה לאונסו לא שכיח:

בקילעא

מסורת הש"ס: [כל זה וגם ד"ה לכ"ש וגם ד"ה אלא לאו שייכים לסוף עמוד ב' דלעיל בסמוך] (ירוש' גרס קורא ואינו משמיע לאזנו) [מ"ק טו.] (צ"ל אינה) תוספת' פ"ב (בירוש' מוסיף נדות ויולדות) [בערוך ערך לע פירש שלא ילמד לאחרים ודבר זה אנו לומדין מק"ו מסיני אם ללמוד אסור ללמד לכ"ש] במס' ד"א פ"ג [ע' תוס' ב"ק פב: ד"ה אתא] ירמיה כג חולין פ' יא דף קלו ב' שם דברים כב קדושין דף לט. חולין ד' פב ב בכורו' דף כד. לעי' דף טו. [תענית יג.] [גר' הערוך באישא הוה בקילעא דרבי הושעיא וכו' באישא פי' חולה]

עין משפט נר מצוה: מה [א]מיי' פ"ד מהלכות ק"ש הל' ח' סמ"ג עשין י"ח טוש"ע א"ח סי' פח — מו [ב]מיי' פ"י מה' בכורים הל' א סמ"ג עשין קמ"ג טוש"ע י"ד סי' שלג סעי' א [נ"ל לקמן] — מז [ג]מיי' פ"ה מה' כלאים הל' א סמ"ג לאוין ר"פ טוש"ע י"ד סי' רצ"ו סעי' א — מח [ד]מיי' פ"ד מה' ק"ש הל' ח ופ"ד מה' תפלה הל' ד ופ"א מה' ברכות הל' ט ופ"י מה' ספר תורה הל' ח סמ"ג עשין י"ח טוש"ע א"ח סי' פ"ח וטוש"ע י"ד סי' רפ"ב סעי' ט [ע' תוס' יומא לח: ותוס' כתובות קד: ד"ה שני] — מט [ה]מיי' פ"ה מה' דעות הל' ד' ופ"ד מה' תפלה הל' ד' סמ"ג לאוין פא טוש"ע א"ח סי' ר"מ סעי' א וטוש"ע אה"ע סי' כ"ה סעי' ב — נ [ו]טור א"ח סי' רמא — נא [ז]טוש"ע י"ד סי' לא סעי' עה — נב [ח]טור א"ח בב"י סי' פח [ע' ברש"י קדושין לז. ד"ה לא קי"ל כר' יאשי' וכו' וטעמיה דר' יאשי' לא ידענ' מהיכא נפקא ליה וכו' וע' תוס' בכורות כה. סד"ה דגן ועוד בתוס' חולין פב: ד"ה לאתויי מה שכתבו בשם ר"י]

or not bathing at all. (8) Insisting on forty *se'ahs*.

c (1) The minimum quantity of water required for ritual ablution. (2) Insisting on forty *se'ahs*. (3) *Rekah* (*Raka*) 'empty one', 'good for nothing'. (4) For the use of the disciples. (5) According to some, this word means 'locksmith'. (6) That nine *kabs* are sufficient. (7) Lit., 'a sick person who induces it'. I.e., after marital intercourse. (8) I.e., rendered useless, because in view of his teaching nine *kabs* can rarely be of effect. (9) I.e., the disciples can still make use of it.

תורה אור

בקילעא דרב אושעיא אתו ושאלו לרב אסי אמר להו לא שנו אלא לחולה המרגיל אבל לחולה לאונסו פטור מכלום א"ר יוסף אצטמיד חצביה דרב נחמן מכדי כולהו אמוראי ותנאי בדעזרא קמפלגי ונחזי עזרא היכי תקן אמר אביי עזרא תקן לבריא המרגיל ארבעים סאה ובריא לאונסו ט' קבין ואתו אמוראי ופליגי בחולה מר סבר חולה המרגיל כבריי' המרגיל וחולה לאונסו כבריא לאונסו ומר סבר חולה המרגיל כבריא לאונסו וחולה לאונסו פטור מכלום אמר רבא נהי דתקן עזרא טבילה נתינה מי תקן והאמר מר *עזרא תקן טבילה לבעלי קריין אלא אמר רבא עזרא תקן טבילה לבריא המרגיל מ' סאה ואתו רבנן והתקינו לבריא לאונסו תשעה קבין ואתו אמוראי וקא מפלגי בחולה מר סבר חולה המרגיל כבריא המרגיל וחולה לאונסו כבריא לאונסו ומר סבר לברי' המרגיל מ' סאה וחולה המרגיל כבריא לאונסו ט' קבין אבל לחולה לאונסו פטור מכלום אמר רבא *הלכתא בריא המרגיל וחולה המרגיל ארבעים סאה ובריא לאונסו תשעה קבין אבל לחולה לאונסו פטור מכלום: *ת"ר בעל קרי שנתנו עליו תשעה קבין מים טהור בד"א לעצמו אבל *לאחרים ארבעים סאה רבי יהודה אומר מ' סאה מכל מקום רבי יוחנן וריב"ל ורבי אלעזר ור' יוסי בר' חנינא חד מהאי זוגא וחד מהאי זוגא אריש' ח"א הא דאמרת במה דברים אמורים לעצמו אבל לאחרים ארבעים סאה לא שנו אלא לחולה המרגיל אבל לחולה לאונסו תשעה קבין וחד אמר כל לאחרים אפי' חולה לאונסו עד דאיכא ארבעים סאה וחד מהאי זוגא וחד מהאי זוגא אסיפא חד אמר הא דאמר רבי יהודה ארבעים סאה מכל מקום לא שנו אלא בקרקע אבל בכלים לא וחד אמר אפי' בכלים נמי בשלמא למאן דאמר אפילו בכלים היינו דקתני רבי יהודה אומר ארבעים סאה מכל מקום אלא למאן דאמר בקרקע אין בכלים לא מכל מקום לאתויי מאי לאתויי מים שאובין רב פפא ורב הונא בריה דרב יהושע ורבא (ברבי) בר שמואל כרוכו ריפתא בהדי הדדי אמר להו רב פפא הבו לי לדידי לברוך דנפול עילואי תשעה קבין אמר להו רבא (ברבי) בר שמואל תנינא במה דברים אמורים לעצמו אבל לאחרים ארבעים סאה אלא הבו לי לדידי לברוך דנפול עילואי ארבעים סאה אמר להו רב הונא הבו לי לדידי לברוך דליכא עילואי לא האי ולא האי רב חמא טביל במעלי יומא דפסחא להוציא רבים ידי חובתן ולית הלכתא כותיה: **מתני'** *היה עומד בתפלה ונזכר שהוא בעל קרי לא יפסיק אלא יקצר ירד לטבול אם יכול לעלות ולהתכסות ולקרות עד שלא תהא הנץ החמה יעלה ויתכסה ויקרא ואם לאו יתכסה במים ויקרא ולא יתכסה לא במים הרעים ולא *במי המשרה עד שיטיל לתוכן מים *וכמה ירחיק מהן ומן הצואה ד' אמות: **גמ'** ת"ר היה עומד בתפלה ונזכר שהוא בעל קרי לא יפסיק אלא יקצר היה קורא בתורה ונזכר שהוא בעל קרי אינו מפסיק ועולה אלא מגמגם וקורא רבי מאיר אומר אין בעל קרי רשאי לקרות בתורה יותר משלשה פסוקים תניא אידך היה עומד בתפלה וראה צואה כנגדו מהלך לפניו עד שיזרקנה לאחוריו ד' אמות והתניא לצדדין לא קשיא הא דאפשר הא דלא אפשר היה מתפלל ומצא צואה במקומו אמר רבה אע"פ שחטא תפלתו תפלה מתקיף ליה רבא והא °זבח רשעים תועבה אלא אמר רבא הואיל וחטא *אע"פי שהתפלל תפלתו תועבה*: ת"ר היה עומד בתפלה ומים שותתין על ברכיו פוסק עד שיכלו המים וחוזר ומתפלל להיכן חוזר רב חסדא ורב המנונא חד אמר חוזר לראש וחד אמר למקום שפסק לימא בהא קמפלגי

מר

בקילעא. כניסת הבית חדר שלפני הטרקלין שקורין פורטיג"ו בלע"ז: אצטמיד. נתחזקו שבריו ונלמדו כלומר לורך לנו עוד בו: וקא מפלגי אמוראי. רב דימי ורבין: דאמר מר. גבי עשר תקנות בב"ק בפרק מרובה: אמר רבא הלכתא וכו'. אפלוגתא דאמוראי הוא דפסיק רבא דפליגי אליבא דרבנן ומיהו השתא אין כרבי יהודה בן בתירא נהגינן כדאמר רב נחמן לעיל ורב נחמן בר יצחק בתרא הוא: לעצמו. לעסוק בתורה לעצמו אבל ללמד לאחרים מ' סאה: ור"י אומר מ' סאה מ"מ. מ' סאה שאמרו בכל ענין שהן ולקמן מפרש לה: חד מהאי זוגא וחד מהאי זוגא. פליגי ארישא בפירושא דמילתא דת"ק: אסיפא. דר' יהודה: לא שנו אלא בקרקע. לא תימא מ"מ דר' יהודה לאכשורי בכלי אתא דאין כשר אלא ארבעים סאה בקרקע ולקמן בעי א"כ מאי מ"מ: אבל לאחרים מ' סאה. והכי נמי דלאפוקי אחרי' ידי חובתן כלאחרים דמי: דנפיל עילואי. לאו דוקא אלא טבלתי במ' סאה: לא האי ולא האי. לא הוצרכתי לא לזו ולא לזו שלא ראיתי קרי: טבל. ובירך. רגיל היה לעשות כן דה"ל ללמד אחרים ובשאר ימות השנה לא היה טובל אלא נותן עליו ט' קבין: ולית הלכתא כוותיה. דכי היכי דלעצמו בנתינה לאחרים נמי בנתינה אי נמי דקי"ל כרבי יהודה בן בתירא: **מתני'** לא יפסיק. תפלתו לגמרי אלא יקצר כל ברכה וברכה ואומר כל הברכות בקוצר: במים הרעים. מים סרוחים: עד שיתן לתוכן מים. ובגמרא (דף כה:) מפרש כמה מיא רמי ואזיל ומפרש לה בחסורי מחסרא והכי קתני לא יקרא אבל מי רגלים עד שיתן לתוכן מים: וכמה ירחק מהם. ממי רגלים: **גמ'** מגמגם. במרולה: יותר מג' פסוקים. כגון בבית הכנסת דאי אפשר לפחות כדתנן (מגילה פ"ג דף כג.) הקורא בתורה לא יפחות מג' פסוקים: והתניא לצדדין. א"ל להלך עד שתהא לאחוריו: דאפשר. לילך לפניו ילך לפניו עד שתהא לאחוריו: לא אפשר. כגון יש נהר לפניו מסתלק לצדדים: דמר

ונחזי עזרא היכי תקן. בהרבה מקומות גבי אחר תקנות לא פריך גמרא הכי אלא שאני הכא דדבר הרגיל בכל יום הוא על כן אנו זכורים:

ולית הלכתא כוותיה. דטבילה בכל יום בארבעים סאה אלא אפילו לאחרים נמי סגי בתשעה קבין אי נמי הכי פירושו ולית הלכתא כוותיה אלא כר' יהודה בן בתירא דאמר דברי תורה אין מקבלין טומאה וי"מ דוקא לתורה אבל לתפלה בעי *טבילה ופי' ר"י דלא שנא והטובל ב"ה אין לו לברך והמברך הוא ברכה לבטלה:

*__אלא__ לכולי עלמא חוזר לראש. וה"ה דה"מ לאוקמי דכולי עלמא אין חוזר לראש ומדלא מוקי הכי ש"מ דהלכה דחוזר לראש וכן לקמן בהדיא אמר ר' אבהו חוזר לראש ותימה דבמסכת ר"ה (דף לד:) א"ר יוחנן שמע תשע תקיעות בט' שעות ביום יצא אלמא תקיעות מלטרפות אע"ג דשהה כדי לעשות כולם וכן במגילה (פ"ב דף יח:) נמי דאמרינן אמר רב אין הלכה כרבי מונא דאמר אם שהה חוזר לראש דקאמר נקוט דרב בידך ואומר השר מקוצי דיש לחלק דשאני הכא דאין ראוי לקרות וכן לקמן (דף כד:) דרבי אבהו איל במבואות המטונפות דהתם כ"ע מודו דחוזר לראש אבל היכא דגברא חזי כמו מגילה ושופר כולי עלמא מודו דאינו חוזר לראש אלא למקום שפסק ורבינו יהודה פי' דהכא לא מצי למימר דכולי עלמא דאין חוזר לראש ובדשהה קמיפלגי דהא לכ"ע הוי גברא חזי כיון דאינו חוזר לראש אבל ודאי אי ה"מ למימר הכי הוה אמר ליה:

והא זבח רשעים תועבה. פר"י דדוקא במקום שהיה יכול להסתפק ולהתלות שיש שם לוחה:

אע"פ שהתפלל תפלתו תועבה. והוי מעוות לא יוכל לתקון ור"י פי' דיחזור ויתפלל:

ממתין עד שיכלו המים. במשתין ע"ג קרקע או ע"ג בגדי' ואין שם טופח ע"מ להטפיח כדמשמע לקמן (דף כה.) כגון דעבד טיף טיף שנבלעין מהרה כן פי' הרב רבי יוסף ומיהו נראה אפי' אם יש בהן טופח על מנת להטפיח מותרין כיון דמדאורייתא אינן אסורין אלא כנגד העמוד בלבד ורבנן הוא דגזור וכיון שעומד כבר בתפלתו לא אטרחוהו רבנן לחזור בתפלה:

הגהות הב"ח

עין משפט נר מצוה

נג
א מיי' פ"ד מה' תפלה הלכה ו [ע' תוספות חולין קכב: ד"ה לגבל]

[שייך לדף כג.]

נד
ג מיי' פ"ב מה' ק"ש הלכה ז

נה
ד מיי' פ"ד מהל' תפלה הל' יע סמג עשין יע טוש"ע א"ח סי' פא סעי' ב

נו
ה מיי' וסמג שם טוש"ע א"ח סימן עו סעיף ח

נז
ו מיי' שם הל' יג וסמג שם טוש"ע א"ח סי' עח

(ירושלמי גרס אבל אינו מוציא אחרים י"ח עד שיבוא במ' סאה)

[ע' פי' רש"י לקמן כה: ד"ה מי המשרה]

כ"א מאי מקנתי להדר ולילך

מסורת הש"ס

מכות' ד' פג.

תוספתא פ"ג

[לעיל כא.]

מגילה פ"ד דף כג.

משלי כא

[ע' תוספת עירובין סד. ד"ה שיכול]

place in Usha [22b] in the anteroom of R. Oshaia. They came and asked R. Assi, and he said to them, This rule was laid down only for a sick person whose emission is voluntary, but a sick person whose emission is involuntary requires nothing at all. Said R. Joseph: R. Naḥman's ewer has been repaired again.[9]

Let us see! The dispute between all these Tannaim and Amoraim is as to the ordinance of Ezra. Let us see then what Ezra did ordain! Abaye said: Ezra ordained that a healthy man whose emission is voluntary must immerse in forty *se'ahs*, and a healthy man whose emission is involuntary must use nine *ḳabs*, and the
a Amoraim came and differed over the sick person.[1] One held that a sick person whose emission is voluntary is on the same footing as a healthy person whose emission is voluntary, and a sick person whose emission is involuntary as a healthy person whose emission is involuntary; while the other held that a sick person whose emission is voluntary is on the same footing as a healthy person whose emission is involuntary and a sick person whose emission is involuntary requires nothing at all. Raba said: Granted that Ezra ordained immersion, did he ordain throwing? Has not a master said: Ezra ordained immersion for persons who have had a seminal emission? Rather, said Raba, Ezra ordained for a healthy person whose emission is voluntary forty *se'ahs*, and the Rabbis [after Ezra] came and ordained for a healthy person whose emission is involuntary nine *ḳabs*, and the [Tanaim and][2] Amoraim came and differed with regard to a sick person,[3] one holding that a sick person whose emission is voluntary is on the same footing as a healthy person whose emission is voluntary and a sick person whose emission is involuntary as a healthy person whose emission is involuntary, while the other held that a healthy person whose emission is voluntary requires forty *se'ahs* and a sick person whose emission is voluntary is on the same footing as a healthy person whose emission is involuntary and requires nine *ḳabs*, while a sick person whose emission is involuntary requires nothing at all. Raba said: The law is that a healthy person whose emission is voluntary and a sick person whose emission is voluntary require forty *se'ahs*, a healthy person whose emission is involuntary requires nine *ḳabs*, and a sick person whose emission is involuntary requires nothing at all.[4]

Our Rabbis taught: A *ba'al ḳeri* over whom nine *ḳabs* of water have been thrown is clean. When is this the case? When it is for
b himself;[1] but when it is for others,[2] he requires forty *se'ahs*. R. Judah says: Forty *se'ahs* in all cases. R. Joḥanan and R. Joshua b. Levi and R. Eleazar and R. Jose son of R. Ḥanina [made pronouncements]. One of the first pair and one of the second pair dealt with the first clause of this statement. One said: This statement of yours, 'When is this the case? When it is for himself, but for others he requires forty *se'ahs*', was meant to apply only to a sick person whose emission is voluntary, but for a sick person whose emission is involuntary nine *ḳabs* are enough. The other said: Wherever it is for others, even if he is a sick person whose emission is involuntary, there must be forty *se'ahs*. One of the first pair and one of the second pair differed as to the second clause of the statement. One said: When R. Judah said that 'forty *se'ahs* are required in all cases', he was speaking only of water in the ground,[3] but not in vessels. The other said: Even in vessels. On the view of the one who says 'even in vessels', there is no difficulty, that is why R. Judah taught: 'Forty *se'ahs in all cases*'. But on the view of the one who says 'in the ground, yes, in vessels, no', what is added by the words 'in all cases'?—They add drawn water.[4]

R. Papa and R. Huna the son of R. Joshua and Raba b. Samuel were taking a meal together. Said R. Papa to them: Allow me to say the grace [on your behalf] because nine *ḳabs* of water have been thrown on me. Said Raba b. Samuel to them: We have learnt: When is this the case? When it is for himself; but if it is for others, forty *se'ahs* are required. Rather let me say the grace, since forty *se'ahs* have been thrown on me. Said R. Huna to them: Let me say the grace since I have had neither the one nor the other on me.[5] R. Ḥama bathed on the eve of Passover in order [that he might be qualified] to do duty on behalf of the public,[6] but the law is not as stated by him.[7]

MISHNAH. IF A MAN WAS STANDING SAYING THE TEFILLAH AND HE REMEMBERS THAT HE IS A BA'AL ḲERI, HE SHOULD NOT
c BREAK OFF BUT HE SHOULD SHORTEN [THE BENEDICTIONS].[1] IF HE WENT DOWN TO IMMERSE HIMSELF, IF HE IS ABLE TO COME UP AND COVER HIMSELF AND RECITE THE SHEMA' BEFORE THE RISING OF THE SUN, HE SHOULD GO UP AND COVER HIMSELF AND RECITE, BUT IF NOT HE SHOULD COVER HIMSELF WITH THE WATER AND RECITE. HE SHOULD, HOWEVER, NOT COVER HIMSELF EITHER WITH FOUL WATER[2] OR WITH WATER IN WHICH SOMETHING[3] HAS BEEN STEEPED UNTIL HE POURS FRESH WATER INTO IT. HOW FAR SHOULD HE REMOVE HIMSELF FROM IT[2] AND FROM EXCREMENT? FOUR CUBITS.

GEMARA. Our Rabbis taught: If a man was standing saying the *Tefillah* and he remembered that he was a *ba'al ḳeri*, he should not break off but shorten the benedictions. If a man was reading the Torah and remembered that he was a *ba'al ḳeri*, he should not break off and leave it but should go on reading in a mumbling tone. R. Meir said: A *ba'al ḳeri* is not permitted to read more than three verses in the Torah. Another [Baraitha] taught: If a man was standing saying the *Tefillah* and he saw excrement in front of him, he should go forward until he has it four cubits behind him. But it has been taught: He should move to the side?—There is no contradiction; one statement speaks of where it is possible for him [to go forward], the other of where it is not possible.[4] If he was praying and he discovered some excrement where he was standing, Rabbah says, even though he has sinned,[5] his prayer is a valid one. Raba demurred to this, citing the text, *The sacrifice of the wicked is an abomination?*[6] No, said Raba: Since he has sinned, although he said the *Tefillah*, his prayer is an abomination.

Our Rabbis taught: If a man was standing saying the *Tefillah* and water drips over his knees, he should break off until the water stops and then resume his *Tefillah*. At what point should he resume?—R. Ḥisda and R. Hamnuna gave different replies. One said that he should go back to the beginning, the other said, to the place where he halted. May we say that the ground of their

(9) I.e., the disciples can still make use of it.
a (1) Inserted with *D.S.* (2) Inserted with MS.M. (3) Cf. n. 1. (4) This ruling was previous to, and therefore superseded by, that of R. Naḥman, that the law follows R. Judah b. Bathyra.
b (1) E.g., if he wants to study. (2) E.g., if he has to teach. (3) E.g., in a cistern, river or well. (4) I.e., water not directly from a spring. (5) I.e., I have required neither the one nor the other. (6) Say grace on their behalf. (7) That immersion is required to qualify for acting on behalf of others. Or it may mean that the law follows R. Judah b. Bathyra.
c (1) I.e., say a shorter form of each one. (2) I.e., urine, as explained below. (3) E.g., flax. (4) E.g., if there is a river in the way. (5) I.e., is himself responsible, v. Tosaf. (6) Prov. XXI, 27.

difference is this [23*a*], that one authority holds that if one stops long enough to finish the whole he goes back to the beginning, while the other holds that he goes back [in any event] to the
a place where he stopped?[1] Said R. Ashi: In that case the statement should distinguish between whether he stopped [long enough] or did not stop.[2] We must therefore say that both are agreed that if he stopped long enough to finish the whole of it he goes back to the beginning, and here they differ in regard to the case where he did not stop [so long], one holding that the man was unfit[3] [to have commenced his prayers] and hence his prayer is no prayer, while the other holds that the man was [nevertheless] in a fit state [to pray] and his prayer is a valid one.

Our Rabbis taught: If a man needs to consult nature he should not say the *Tefillah,* and if he does, his prayer is an abomination. R. Zebid—or as some say Rab Judah—said: They meant this to apply only if he is not able to hold himself in, but if he is able to hold himself in, his prayer is a valid one. How much must he be able to hold himself in?—R. Shesheth said: Long enough to go a *parasang*. Some teach this statement as part of the Baraitha [just quoted], thus: When is this the case [that his prayer is an abomination]? When he cannot hold himself in; but if he can hold himself in, his prayer is valid. And how long must he be able to do so?—R. Zebid said: Long enough for him to walk a *parasang*.

R. Samuel b. Naḥmani said in the name of R. Jonathan: One who needs to ease himself should not say the *Tefillah*, as it says, *Prepare to meet thy God, O Israel.*[4] R. Samuel b. Naḥmani also said in the name of R. Jonathan: What is the meaning of the verse, *Guard thy foot when thou goest to the house of God?*[5] Guard thyself so that thou shouldst not sin, and if thou dost sin, bring an offering
b before Me. *And be ready to hearken.*[1] Raba said. Be ready to hearken to the words of the wise who, if they sin, bring an offering and repent. *It is better than when the fools give!*[2] Do not be like the fools who sin and bring an offering and do not repent. *For they know not to do evil,*[3]—if that is the case, they are righteous?—What it means is: Do not be like the fools who sin and bring an offering and do not know whether they bring it for a good action or a bad action. Says the Holy One, blessed be He: They do not distinguish between good and evil, and they bring an offering before Me. R. Ashi,—or, as some say, R. Ḥanina b. Papa—said: Guard thy orifices[4] at the time when thou art standing in prayer before Me.

Our Rabbis taught: One who is about to enter a privy should take off his *tefillin* at a distance of four cubits and then enter. R. Aḥa son of R. Huna said in the name of R. Shesheth: This was meant to apply only to a regular privy,[5] but if it is made for the occasion, he takes them off and eases himself at once, and when he comes out he goes a distance of four cubits and puts them on, because he has now made it a regular privy. The question was asked, What is the rule about a man going in to a regular privy with his *tefillin* to make water? Rabina allowed it; R. Adda b. Mattena forbade it. They went and asked Raba and he said to them: It is forbidden, since we are afraid that he may ease himself in them, or, as some report, lest he may break wind in them. Another [Baraitha] taught: One who enters a regular privy takes off his *tefillin* at a distance of four cubits and puts them in the window on the side of the public way[6] and enters, and when he comes out he goes a distance of four cubits and puts them on So Beth Shammai. Beth Hillel say: He keeps them in his hand and enters. R. Akiba said: He holds them in his garment and enters. 'In his garment', do you say? Sometimes they may slip out[7] and fall!—Say rather, he holds them in his hand and in his garment, and enters, and he puts them in a hole on the side of the privy, but he should not put them in a hole on the side of the public way, lest they should be taken by passers-by, and he should render himself suspect. For a certain student once left his *tefillin* in a hole adjoining the public way, and a harlot passed by and took them, and she came to the Beth ha-Midrash and said: See what So-and-so gave me for my hire, and when the student heard it, he went to the top of a roof and threw himself down and killed himself. Thereupon they ordained that a man should hold them in his garment and in his hand and then go in.

The Rabbis taught: Originally they used to leave *tefillin* in holes on the side of the privy, and mice used to come and take them. They therefore ordained that they should be put in the windows on the side of the public way. Then passers-by came and took them. So they ordained that a man should hold them in his hand and enter. R. Meyasha the son of R. Joshua b. Levi said: The
c *halachah* is that he should roll them up like a scroll[1] and keep them in his right hand, opposite his heart. R. Joseph b. Manyumi said in the name of R. Naḥman: He must see that not a handbreadth of strap hangs loose from his hand. R. Jacob b. Aḥa said in the name of R. Zera: This is the rule only if there is still time left in the day to put them on[2] but if there is no time left in the day, he makes a kind of bag for them of the size of a handbreadth and puts them there.[3] Rabbah b. Bar Ḥanah said in the name of R. Joḥanan: In the daytime [when he enters a privy] he rolls them up like a scroll and keeps them in his hand opposite his heart, and for the night he makes a kind of bag for them of the size of a handbreadth, and puts them there. Abaye said: This rule was meant to apply only to a bag which is meant for them, but if the bag is not meant for them, even less than a handbreadth is sufficient. Mar Zuṭra—or as some say R. Ashi—said: The proof is that
d small vessels[1] protect [the contents from uncleanness] in a tent of the dead.[2]

Rabbah b. Bar Ḥanah further said: When we were following R. Joḥanan [as disciples], when he wanted to enter a privy, if he had a book of *Aggada*, he used to give it to us to hold, but if he was wearing *tefillin* he did not give them to us, saying, since

a (1) V. *infra* 24*b*. (2) I.e., the two Rabbis should have stated their views on this case also. (3) Since he could not contain himself till he finished. Lit., 'rejected'. Cur. edd. add 'and he is unfit', which is omitted in MS.M. (4) Amos. IV, 12. Interpreted to mean, Put thyself in a fit state to meet etc. (5) Eccl. IV, 17.

b (1) Eccl. IV, 17. (2) Ibid. (3) Ibid. This is the literal rendering; E.V. '*for they know not that they do evil*'. (4) This is an alternative rendering of the word *ragleka* (thy foot) which is taken in the same sense as in I Sam. XXIV, 4. (5) Where there is already excrement. (6) The privies in Babylon were out in the fields. (7) V. MS.M.

c (1) I.e., wind the straps round them. (2) It was customary to wear the *tefillin* the whole of the day and take them off at night-time. (3) A bag of this size would protect them from uncleanness.

d (1) With a tight fitting cover. V. Num. XIX, 15. (2) Even if they are less than one handbreadth in size.

מר סבר *אם שהה כדי לגמור את כולה חוזר לראש ומ"ס למקום שפסק אמר רב אשי האי אם שהה אם לא שהה מיבעי ליה *אלא *דכולי עלמא אם שהה כדי לגמור את כולה חוזר לראש *והתם בדלא שהה קמיפלגי דמ"ס גברא דחויא הוא ואין ראוי ואין תפלתו תפלה ומ"ס גברא חזיא הוא ותפלתו תפלה ת"ר ^ב^הנצרך לנקביו אל יתפלל ואם התפלל תפלתו תועבה אמר רב זביד ואיתימא רב יהודה לא שנו אלא שאינו יכול לשהות בעצמו אבל אם יכול לשהות בעצמו תפלתו תפלה ועד כמה אמר רב ששת ^ג^עד פרסה איכא דמתני לה אמתניתא במה דברים אמורים כשאין יכול לעמוד על עצמו אבל אם יכול לעמוד על עצמו תפלתו תפלה ועד כמה אמר רב זביד *עד פרסה אמר ר' שמואל בר נחמני אמר ר' יונתן *^ד^הנצרך לנקביו הרי זה לא יתפלל משום שנאמר °הכון לקראת אלהיך ישראל וא"ר שמואל בר נחמני א"ר יונתן מאי דכתיב °שמר רגלך כאשר תלך אל בית האלהים שמור עצמך שלא תחטא ואם תחטא הבא קרבן לפני וקרוב לשמוע *דברי חכמים אמר רבא הוי קרוב לשמוע דברי חכמים שאם חוטאים מביאים קרבן ועושים תשובה מתת הכסילים אל תהי ככסילים שחוטאים ומביאים קרבן ואין עושים תשובה כי אינם יודעים לעשות רע אי הכי צדיקים נינהו אלא אל תהי ככסילים שחוטאים ומביאים קרבן ואינם יודעים אם על הטובה הם מביאים אם על הרעה הם מביאים אמר הקב"ה בין טוב לרע אין מבחינים והם מביאים קרבן לפני רב אשי ואיתימא רב חנינא בר פפא אמר שמור נקביך בשעה שאתה עומד בתפלה לפני ת"ר *^ה^הנכנס לבית הכסא חולץ תפיליו ברחוק ד' אמות ונכנס אמר רב אחא בר רב הונא אמר רב ששת לא שנו אלא בית הכסא קבוע אבל בית הכסא עראי חולץ ונפנה לאלתר ^ו^וכשהוא יוצא מרחיק ד' אמות ומניחן מפני שעשאו בית הכסא קבוע איבעי' להו מהו שיכנס אדם בתפילין לבית הכסא קבוע להשתין מים רבינא שרי רב אדא בר מתנא ^ז^אסר אתו שיילוה לרבא אמר להו אסור שחיישינן שמא יפנה בהן ואמרי לה שמא יפיח בהן תני' אידך הנכנס לבית הכסא קבוע חולץ תפיליו ברחוק ד' אמות ומניחן בחלון הסמוך לר"הר ונכנס וכשהוא יוצא מרחיק ד' אמות ומניחן דברי ב"ש וב"ה אומרים אוחזן בידו ונכנס ר"ע אומר אוחזן בבגדו ונכנס בבגדו ס"ד זמנין מישתלי להו ונפלי אלא אימא אוחזן בבגדו ובידו ונכנס ומניחם בחורים הסמוכים לבית הכסא ולא יניחם בחורים הסמוכים לרה"ר שמא יטלו אותם עוברי דרכים ויבא לידי חשד ומעשה בתלמיד א' שהניח תפיליו בחורים הסמוכים לרשות הרבים ובאת זונה אחת ונטלתן ובאת לבית המדרש ואמרה ראו מה נתן לי פלוני בשכרי כיון ששמע אותו תלמיד כך עלה לראש הגג ונפל ומת באותה שעה התקינו ^ח^שיהא אוחזן בבגדו ובידו ונכנס תנו רבנן בראשונה היו מניחין תפילין בחורין הסמוכין לבית הכסא ובאין עכברים ונוטלין אותן התקינו שיהו מניחין אותן בחלונות הסמוכות לרשות הרבים ובאין עוברי דרכים ונוטלין אותן התקינו שיהא אוחזן בידו ונכנס א"ר מיאשא *בריה דרבי יהושע בן לוי הלכה ^ט^גוללן כמין ספר ואוחזן בימינו כנגד לבו אמר רב יוסף בר מניומי אמר רב נחמן ובלבד ^י^שלא תהא רצועה יוצאת מתחת ידו טפח אמר רבי יעקב בר אחא אמר ר' זירא ^כ^לא שנו אלא שיש שהות ביום ללבשן אבל אין שהות ביום ללבשן עושה להן כמין כיס טפח ומניחן *אמר רבה בר בר חנה אמר ר' יוחנן ביום גוללן כמין ספר ומניחן בידו כנגד לבו ובלילה עושה להן כמין כיס טפח ומניחן אמר אביי ^ל^לא שנו אלא בכלי שהוא כליין אבל בכלי שאינו כליין אפילו פחות מטפח אמר מר זוטר' ואיתימא רב אשי תדע שהרי פכין קטנים מצילין באהל המת ואמר רבה בר בר חנה כי הוה אזלינן בתרי' דרבי יוחנן כי הוה בעי למיעל לבית הכסא כי הוה נקיט סיפרא דאגדתא הוה יהיב לן כי הוה נקיט תפילין לא הוה יהיב לן אמר הואיל ושרונהו רבנן

ננטרן

תורה אור: עמוס ד — קהלת ד

רש"י

מר סבר. כל המפסיק בתפלתו אם שהה כדי לגמור כולה חוזר לראש כדאמרינן גבי ק"ש לקמן בפרקין (דף כד:) ובשהה קא מיפלגי הכא: האי אם שהה אם לא שהה מיבעי ליה. במילתיה דרב חסדא ורב המנונא מיבעי ליה לאפלוגי בין שהה ללא שהה ומדלא אפליג שמע מינה אפילו בדלא שהה קאמר: גברא דחויא הוא. כשהתחיל להתפלל והיה צריך לנקביו דחוי הוא מלהתפלל הלכך מה שהתפלל אינה תפלה וחוזר לראש: ומר סבר גברא חזיא. אע"פ שאינו יכול להמתין עד שיסיים תפלתו תפלה רצויה היא מה שהתפלל קודם שתייתו: ועד כמה. יכול להעמיד עצמו ונקביו שיהא מותר להתחיל בתפלה: איכא דמתני. להאי במה דברים אמורים במתניתא גופא ולא משמעתא דרב זביד ורב יהודה וכי איירי אינהו בשיעורא הוא דאיירי: שמור עצמך שלא תחטא. ותצטרך רגלך ללכת אל בית האלהים להביא חטאת: הוי קרוב לשמוע. תשובה בהבאת קרבנך מתת אותו ככסילים בלא תשובה: שמור נקביך. מבין רגליך כמו להסך את רגליו (שמואל א כד) שמור נקביך שלא יפיחו: בית הכסא קבוע. שיש בו לואה וכל בתי כסאות שבגמרא על פני השדה הם בלא חפירה: עראי. שזה מתחיל עכשיו לעשותו בית הכסא: חולץ ונפנה לאלתר. ויאחז תפילין בידו כדאמרינן לקמן ובקבוע כמי אוחזן בידו אלא שצריך לחלצן ברחוק ד' אמות שבזמן שהם בראשו הם בגלוי וגנאי הדבר: מהו שיכנס בתפיליו. כשהן בראשו קאמר: שמא יפנה בהן. גדולים: בחורים הסמוכים לבית הכסא. לפנים מן הגדר בשדה שהוא נפנה בה כותבן בחורים שבכותל: בחורים הסמוכים לרשות הרבים. חורי כותלי מחילות השדה שאין עכברים מצויין במקום הילוך בני אדם והוא יכנס לאחורי הגדר לפנות: גוללן. ברצועות שלהן: שלא תצא רצועה. שיש בה קדושה שהרי בהן הוא קושרן ובקשר כראה בעשייתו כמין דל"ת על שם אחת מאותיות של שדי והשי"ן עשויה בכותלי הקציצה החיצונה והיו"ד עשויה בראש רצועת תפילין של יד ורצועה קטנה מאד כפוף ראשה וכראית כמין יו"ד: ואוחזן בימינו. שלא בבגדו כדי שלא יפלו: ביום. כשהוא חולצן בשביל בית הכסא גוללן כמין ספר כדאמרן: ובלילה. כשהוא חולצן בביתו על מנת להצניע עד הבקר: עושה להם כיס טפח. דאלו טפח דחשיב הכלי אהל להפסיק בינם לקרקע: לא שנו. דבעי טפח: אלא בכלי שהוא כליין. כיס העשוי לצרכן דכליין קבוע להיות בעל אהלם הלכך בעינן דבר הניכר שיהא חולץ בפניהם: שהרי פכין קטנים מצילין. בהיקף צמיד פתיל באהל המת ואע"ג דלא הוו טפח חיילי: אמר הואיל ושרונהו רבנן. לאוחזן בידו משום שמירתן:

תוספות

חיישינן שמא יפנה בהן ואסור. ודוקא בבית הכסא קבוע חיישינן שמא יפנה בהן אבל בבית הכסא עראי שאין רגילים לפנות שם מותר להשתין בהן ולא חיישינן שמא יפנה בהן והא *דתנן לקמן לא ישתין בהן אפילו בבית הכסא עראי היינו דוקא כשאוחזן בידו דחיישינן שמא ישפשף בהן הניצוצות אם יפלו מים על רגליו או יגע באמה:

שהרי פכין קטנים מצילין באהל המת. ועל כרחך מטעם אויר הוא דאי לית בהו אויר כלל לא היו מצילין דהוי כמו אוכלין שגבלן בטיט שמקבלין טומאה באוהל המת:

דברים

עין משפט נר מצוה

[דתניא]

נח ^א^מיי' פ"ד מה' תפלה הל' יג סמג עשין יט טוש"ע א"ח סימן קד סעיף ה

נט ^ב^מיי' שם הל' י סמג שם טוש"ע א"ח סימן לב סעיף א

ס ^ד^מיי' וסמג שם טוש"ע שם סעיף א ב

ולאי פיסקא רב אדא עד פרסה כל"ל רש"ל

סא ^ה^מיי' פ"ד מהל' תפילין הלכה יז סמג עשין כב טוש"ע א"ח סימן מג סעיף ה

(רב אלפס כאן ובה' תפילין דף עה:)

סב ^ו^מיי' וסמג שם טוש"ע שם סעיף א

סג ^ח^ט^מיי' וסמג שם טוש"ע שם סעיף ה

סד ^כ^ל^מיי' שם הל' יט וסמג שם טוש"ע שם סעיף ו

[בר בריה דריב"ל כל"ל וכ"ה בשאלתות פ' בא וכן איתא לקמן דף כד:]

מסורת הש"ס

[לקמן כד: ר"ה ל"ד:]

[ע"ש דב: סוס' ד"ה אלא]

ודבא

תוספת' פ"ב

(טעות הדפוס וע' הגוספא בעין יעקב)

שבת פ"ו דף סב

הך דרבה בב"ח ל"ל קודם הא דר' יעקב בר אחא רש"ל

נגטרן אמר רבא כי הוה אזלינן בתריה דרב נחמן כי הוה נקיט סיפרא דאגדת' יהיב לן כי הוה נקיט תפילין לא יהיב לן אמר הואיל ושרונהו רבנן נגטרן תנו רבנן [א]לא יאחז אדם תפילין בידו וספר תורה בזרועו ויתפלל [ב]ולא ישתין בהן מים *[ג]ולא יישן בהן לא שנת קבע ולא שנת עראי אמר שמואל [ד]סכין ומעות וקערה וככר הרי אלו כיוצא בהן אמר רבא אמר רב ששת לית הלכתא כי הא מתניתא דבית שמאי היא דאי ב"ה השתא בית הכסא קבוע שרי בית הכסא עראי מיבעיא מיתיבי דברים שהתרתי לך כאן אסרתי לך כאן מאי לאו תפילין אי אמרת בשלמא בית הלל התרתי לך כאן קבוע אסרתי לך כאן בית הכסא עראי אלא אי אמרת ב"ש הא לא שרו ולא מידי כי תניא ההיא לענין טפח וטפחיים דתני חדא כשהוא נפנה מגלה לאחריו טפח ולפניו טפחיים ותניא אידך לאחריו טפח ולפניו ולא כלום מאי לאו אידי ואידי באיש ולא קשיא כאן לגדולים כאן לקטנים ותסברא אי בקטנים לאחריו טפח למה לי אלא אידי ואידי בגדולים ולא קשיא [ה]הא באיש הא באשה אי הכי הא דקתני עלה זהו *קל וחומר שאין עליו תשובה מאי אין עליו תשובה דרכא דמילתא הכי איתא אלא לאו תפילין ותיובתא דרבא אמר רב ששת תיובתא מכל מקום קשיא השתא בית הכסא קבוע שרי בית הכסא עראי לא כל שכן הכי קאמר בית הכסא קבוע דליכא ניצוצות שרי בית הכסא עראי דאיכא ניצוצות אסרי אי הכי אמאי אין עליו תשובה תשובה מעלייתא היא הכי קאמר הא מילתא תיתי לה בתורת טעמא ולא תיתי לה בקל וחומר דאי אתיא לה בתורת קל וחומר זהו ק"ו שאין עליו תשובה: *תנו רבנן [ו]הרוצה ליכנס לסעודת קבע מהלך עשרה פעמים ארבע אמות או ארבע פעמים עשר אמות ויפנה ואחר כך נכנס אמר רבי יצחק הנכנס לסעודת קבע חולץ תפיליו ואחר כך נכנס ופליגא דרבי חייא דאמר רבי חייא [ז]מניחן על שולחנו וכן הדור לו ועד אימת אמר רב נחמן בר יצחק [ח]עד זמן ברכה תני חדא צורר אדם תפיליו עם מעותיו באפרקסותו ותניא אידך לא יצור לא קשיא הא דאזמניה הא דלא אזמניה דאמר רב חסדא *[ט]האי סודרא דתפילין דאזמניה למיצר ביה תפילין צר ביה תפילין אסור למיצר ביה פשיטי אזמניה ולא צר ביה ולא אזמניה שרי למיצר ביה זוזי ולאביי דאמר *הזמנה מילתא היא אזמניה אע"ג דלא צר ביה צר ביה אי אזמניה אסור אי לא אזמניה לא בעא מיניה רב יוסף בריה דרב נחוניא מרב יהודה מהו שיניח אדם תפיליו תחת מראשותיו [י]תחת מרגלותיו לא קא מיבעיא לי שנוהג בהן מנהג בזיון כי קא מיבעיא לי תחת מראשותיו מאי אמר ליה הכי אמר שמואל [כ]מותר אפילו אשתו עמו מיתיבי לא יניח אדם תפיליו תחת מרגלותיו מפני שנוהג בהן דרך בזיון אבל מניחן תחת מראשותיו ואם היתה אשתו עמו אסור היה מקום שגבוה שלשה טפחים או נמוך ג' טפחים מותר תיובתא דשמואל תיובתא אמר רבא אף ע"ג דתני' תיובתא דשמואל הלכתא כותיה מאי טעמא

כל

נגטרן. ישמרוני אכניסם עמי וישמרוני מן המזיקין: לא יאחוז בידו וכו' ויתפלל. שאין דעתו מיושבת עליו בתפלה שהרי לבו תמיד עליהן שלא יפלו מידו: ולא יישן בהן. שמא יפיח: הרי אלו כיוצא בהן. לענין תפלה שדואג עליהן שלא תפול הסכין ותזיקנו. והקערה תשפך והמעות יאבדו והככר תטנף: לית הלכתא כי הא מתניתא. דקתני לא ישתין בתפילין: דבית שמאי היא. דאמרי לעיל מכיחן בחלון הסמוך לר"ה ולא יכניסם בידו ויכנס: דאי ב"ה. הא אמרי לעיל אוחזן בידו ונכנס: בית הכסא עראי. כגון להשתין שאין אדם הולך בשבילם לבית הכסא והפעם הזאת נעשה המקום הזה בית הכסא תחלה: שהתרתי לך כאן. בבית הכסא קבוע: אסרתי לך כאן. בבית הכסא עראי: מאי לאו תפילין. שאמרו בית הלל אוחזן בידו ונכנס לבית הכסא קבוע ולהשתין בהם אסרו כדמפרש טעמא לקמן: הא לא שרו. בבית הכסא קבוע: כי תניא ההיא. לאו לענין תפילין תניא אלא לענין גלוי טפח וטפחיים דלגדולי' היכו מגלה אלא טפח ולקטנים מגלה טפחיים ועלה קאי גלוי טפחיים שהתרתי לך כאן אסרתי לך כאן: לאחריו טפח. ולא יותר משום לניעות: מלפניו טפחיים. משום קילוח מי רגלים הנתזין למרחוק: מאי לאו כו'. והייכו דקאמר לעיל דברים שהתרתי לך בבית הכסא עראי אסרתי לך בקבוע: אלא אידי ואידי בגדולים. ומתוך שהוא דוחק עצמו לגדולים הוא בא לידי קטנים הלכך באיש מלאחריו טפח ומלפניו טפחיים ובאשה מלפניה ולא כלום והכי קאמר הא דלעיל דברים שאסרתי לך באשה התרתי לך באיש: אי הכי. דלענין טפח וטפחיים קתני דברים שהתרתי לך כאן אסרתי לך כאן: הא דקתני עלה. בסיפא דידה וזה הוא ק"ו שאין עליו תשובה בדבר הזה יש לך להשיבני ק"ו ואין לי עליו תשובה להחזיר לך אי אמרת בשלמא בתפילין קאמר וכדאמרן וב"ה היא הייכו דקתני דיש כאן להקשות קל וחומר השתא בית הכסא קבוע שרו בית הכסא עראי מיבעיא ואין לי תשובה להשיבך עליו אלא אי אמרת לענין טפח וטפחיים מאי ק"ו יש להקשות כאן: אורחא דמילתא הכי הוא. שהאיש לריך לגלות לפניו ולא האשה: תיובתא דרבא אמר רב ששת. דאמר בית שמאי היא ולא בית הלל דאם כן לא משכחת מידי לאוקמה הך ברייתא דקתני מאי שהתרתי לך כאן אסרתי לך כאן: דליכא נצוצות. שיהא לריך לשפשף בימינו מעל רגליו: בית הכסא עראי. לקטנים: דאיכא ניצוצות. הניתזין על גבי רגליו ואמרי' במסכת יומא (דף ל.) מלוה לשפשף שאסור לאדם שילא בניצוצות שעל גבי רגליו שמא יראה ככרות שפכה ומלא מוליא לעז על בניו שהם ממזרים הלכך אי אפשר לאחוז תפילין בידו: הא מילתא. דתפילין דבית הכסא עראי וקבוע: תיתי לה בתורת טעמא. להתיר בבית הכסא קבוע את האסור בבית הכסא עראי משום טעמא דניצוצות: דאי אתיא לה בתורת ק"ו. לומר דין הוא להקל בבית הכסא עראי קל ולהחמיר בבית הכסא חמור ולא תזול בתר טעמא אלא בתר חומרא וקולא ואכן עבדינן איפכא אין לי עליו מה להשיבך שאין לי למצוא שיהא בשום מקום בית הכסא עראי חמור מן הקבוע שאוכל להשיבך אם התרתי בקבוע שהוא קל בדבר פלוני כתיר בשל עראי שהוא חמור בה אבל טעמא איכא למאי דעבדינן דהכא איכא ניצוצות והכא ליכא ודבר זה לאו קל ולא חומר: הנכנס לסעודת קבע. ונגאי הוא שילטרך לנקביו בתוך הסעודה: מהלך עשרה פעמים כו'. ובכל פעם ופעם בודק עצמו ויושב אולי יכול להפנות שהילוך מוריד הגדולים לנקב: חולץ תפיליו. שמא ישתכר בסעודה ויתגנה בתפיליו: וכן הדור לו. שיהו מזומנים לו ויחזור ויניחם בשעת ברכה: באפרקסותיה. סודר של ראשו: עם מעותיו. לא עם המעות ממש אלא שני קשרים זה אצל זה: ה"ג הא דאזמניה הא דלא אזמניה. להיות סודר לתפילין דכיון דאזמניה שוב אסור ללור בו מעות מאחר שהקלו לכך: צר ביה. אי אזמניה אין אי לא אזמניה לא קדיש ושרי למיצר ביה דהכי תניא בהדיא בסנהדרין הניח בו תפיליו יניח בו מעות: ולאביי דאמר הזמנה מילתא היא. גבי אורג בגד למת בסנהדרין בפרק נגמר הדין (דף מח:): מהו שיניח תפיליו תחת מראשותיו. בלילה כשהוא ישן: אם היה מקום גבוה ג' טפחים. למעלה מראשותיו ועליו נותן התפילין או למטה מראשותיו יולא מקום מן המטה:

דברים שהתרתי לך כאן כו'. ולא בעי לשנויי דברים שהתרתי לך בבית הכסא עראי אסרתי לך בקבוע דאסור לפנות בגדולים והתפילין בראשו אבל להשתין מותר משום דלא אשכחן בברייתא אבל הך דטפח וטפחיים אשכחן ליה בברייתא בהדיא הר"ר יוסף: והא

עין משפט נר מצוה

סה [א]מיי' פ"ה מהלכ' תפלה הל' ה' סמ"ג עשין יט טוש"ע א"ח סי' לו סעי' א

סו [ב]מיי' פ"ד מה' תפילין הל' י"ז וסמג עשין כב טוש"ע א"ח סי' מג סעי' א

סז [ג]מיי' שם הל' ט"ו סמ"ג שם טוש"ע א"ח סי' מד

סח [ד]מיי' פ"ה מה' תפלה הל' ה' סמ"ג עשין יט טוש"ע א"ח סי' לו סעי' א

סט [ה]מיי' פ"ה מהל' דיעות הל' ו טוש"ע א"ח סי' ג' סעי' ד

ע [ו]מיי' פ"ד מהלכ' דעו' הל' ב

עא [ז][ח]מיי' פ"ד מהל' תפיל'ן הל' י"ו סמ"ג עשין כב טוש"ע א"ח סי' מ סעי' א

עב [ט]מיי' שם הל' ט וסמ"ג שם טוש"ע א"ח סי' מב סעי' ב

עג [י][כ]מיי' שם הל' כ"ד וסמג שם טוש"ע א"ח סי' מ סעי' ג

מסורת הש"ס

סוכה פ"ג דף מח:

[ב"מ לה.]

שבת פ"ח דף פב.

סנהדרין פ"ו דף מח.

[שם מז: מח מגילה כו: מנחות לד:]

the Rabbis have permitted them[3] [23b] they will protect me.[4] Raba said: When we were following R. Naḥman, if he had a book of *Aggada* he used to give it to us, but if he was wearing *tefillin* he did not give them to us, saying, since the Rabbis have permitted them, they will guard me.

Our Rabbis taught: A man should not hold *tefillin* in his hand or a scroll of the Law in his arm while saying the *Tefillah*,[5] nor should he make water while wearing them, nor sleep in them, whether a regular sleep or a short snatch. Samuel says: A knife, money, a dish and a loaf of bread are on the same footing as *tefillin*.[6] Raba said in the name of R. Shesheth: The law is not in accordance with this Baraitha,[7] since it expresses the view of Beth Shammai. For seeing that Beth Hillel declare it permissible in a regular privy [to hold the *tefillin*] is there any question that they would permit it in an *ad hoc* privy?

An objection was raised: The things which I have permitted to you in the one place I have forbidden to you in the other. Presumably this refers to *tefillin*. Now if you say the Baraitha quoted follows Beth Hillel, there is no difficulty. 'I have permitted it to you in the one place'—the regular privy, 'and I have forbidden it to you in the other'—the *ad hoc* privy. But if you say it is Beth Shammai, they do not permit anything!—That statement[8] refers to the baring of the handbreadth and two handbreadths, as one [Baraitha] taught: When a man eases himself, he may bare a handbreadth behind and two handbreadths in front, and another taught: a handbreadth behind and in front not at all. Is it not the case that both statements refer to a man, and there is no contradiction, the former referring to easing and the latter to making water? But do you think so? If for making water, why a handbreadth behind? Rather both refer to easing, and there is no contradiction, the one referring to a man and the other to a woman. If
a that is the case,[1] what of the succeeding statement, 'This is an *a fortiori* which cannot be rebutted'? What is the point of 'which cannot be rebutted'? This[2] is merely the natural way! We must say therefore that *tefillin* are referred to [in the Baraitha], and it is a refutation of what Raba said in the name of R. Shesheth.—It is a refutation. Still a difficulty remains: If it is permissible in a regular privy, how much more so in an *ad hoc* privy!—What it means is this: In a regular privy where there is no splashing, it is permitted; in an *ad hoc* privy where there is splashing,[3] it is forbidden. If that is the case, how can you say, 'which cannot be rebutted'? There is an excellent refutation?—What it means is this: This[4] rule is based upon a reason[5] and not upon an argument *a fortiori*; for if we were to employ here an argument *a fortiori*,[6] it would be one which could not be rebutted.

Our Rabbis taught: One who wishes to partake [in company] of a regular meal,[7] should walk four cubits ten times or ten cubits four times and ease himself and then go in. R. Isaac said: One who wishes to [partake of] a regular meal should take off his *tefillin*[8] and then go in. He differs from R. Ḥiyya; for R. Ḥiyya said: He places them on his table, and so it is becoming for him. How long does he leave them there? Until the time for grace.[9]

One [Baraitha] taught: A man may tie up his *tefillin* in his head-
b gear[1] along with his money, while another teaches, He should not so tie them!—There is no contradiction; in the one case he sets it aside for this purpose, in the other he does not set it aside. For R. Hisda said: If a man has [mentally] set aside a cloth to tie up *tefillin* in, once he has tied up *tefillin* in it it is forbidden to tie up in it money; if he has set it aside but not tied up the *tefillin* in it, or if he has tied them up in it without setting it aside for the purpose, he may tie up money in it. According to Abaye, however, who says that mere setting aside is operative,[2] once he has set it aside, even though he has not tied up *tefillin* in it, it is forbidden to tie up money, and if he has tied up *tefillin* in it, if he has set it aside it is forbidden to tie up money, but if he has not set it aside it is not forbidden.

R. Joseph the son of R. Neḥunia asked Rab Judah: What is the rule about placing one's *tefillin* under one's pillow? About putting them under the place of his feet I have no need to ask, because that would be treating them contemptuously. What I do want to know is, what is the rule about putting them under his pillow?—He replied: Thus said Samuel: It is permitted, even if his wife is with him. An objection was raised. A man should not put his *tefillin* under the place of his feet, because this is treating them contemptuously, but he may place them under his pillow, but if his wife is with him this is forbidden. If, however, there is a place three handbreadths above his head or three handbreadths below,[3] he may put them there. Is not this a refutation of Samuel?—It is. Raba said: Although it has been taught that this is a refutation of Samuel, the law follows his opinion. What is the reason?

(3) To hold them to one's hand. (4) From evil spirits. Var. lec.: we need not trouble (to take them off). (5) The fear of dropping them will distract his attention. (6) They also will distract his attention if he is holding them. (7) That it is forbidden to make water in *tefillin*. (8) 'The things I have forbidden to you, etc.'.

a (1) If the Baraitha, 'The things which I have permitted to you in the one place' etc. refers to the difference between a man and a woman. (2) Difference between man and woman. (3) Since it is used for urine only. (4) To permit in a regular privy and prohibit in an *ad hoc* one. (5) The risk of soiling the hand. (6) Viz., from a regular one to an *ad hoc* one. (7) And is doubtful if he can contain himself, and to leave the company would be impolite. (Rashi.) (8) As it would not be respectful to eat in them. (9) When he puts them on again.

b (1) *Aparkesuth*, a head-covering which flowed down over the body. *Aliter:* 'underwear', or 'sheet'. (2) In the matter of weaving a sheet for a dead body, Sanh. 47b. (3) Projecting from the bed.

[24a]—Whatever conduces to their safe keeping[4] is of more importance.[5] Where should he put them? R. Jeremiah said: Between the coverlet and the pillow, not opposite to his head. But R. Ḥiyya taught: He puts them in a turban[6] under his pillow?—It
a must be in such a way as to make the top of the turban[1] project outside [the pillow]. Bar Kappara used to tie them in the bed-curtain and make them project outside.[2] R. Shesheth the son of R. Idi used to put them on a stool and spread a cloth over them. R. Hamnuna the son of R. Joseph said: Once when I was standing before Raba he said to me: Go and bring me my *tefillin*, and I found them between the coverlet and the pillow, not just opposite his head, and I knew that it was a day of ablution [for his wife],[3] and I perceived that he had sent me in order to impress upon me a practical lesson.

R. Joseph the son of R. Neḥunia inquired of Rab Judah: If two persons are sleeping in one bed, how would it be for one to turn his face away and recite the *Shema'*, and for the other to turn his face away and recite?—He replied: Thus said Samuel: [It is permitted] even if his wife is with him. R. Joseph demurred to this. [You imply, he said] 'His wife', and needless to say anyone else. On the contrary, [we should argue]: His wife is like himself,[4] another is not like himself! An objection was raised: If two persons are sleeping in one bed, one turns his face away and recites the *Shema'* and the other turns his face away and recites the *Shema'*. And it was taught in another [place]: If a man is in bed and his children and the members of his household[5] are at his side, he must not recite the *Shema'* unless there is a garment separating them, but if his children and the members of his household are minors, he may. Now I grant you that if we accept the ruling of R. Joseph there is no difficulty, as we can explain one [statement] to refer to his wife and the other to another person. But if we accept Samuel's view there is a difficulty?—Samuel can reply: And on R. Joseph's view is there no difficulty, seeing that it has been taught: If a man was in bed, and his sons[6] and the members of his household with him,[7] he should not recite the *Shema'* unless his garments separated them from him? What then must you say? That in R. Joseph's opinion there is a difference of opinion among Tannaim as to his wife. In my opinion also there is a difference
b among Tannaim.[1]

The Master has said: 'One turns his face away and recites the *Shema'*. But there is the contact of the buttocks?—This supports the opinion of R. Huna, who said: Contact of the buttocks is not sexual. May we say that it supports the following opinion of R. Huna: A woman may sit and separate her *ḥallah*[2] naked, because she can cover her nakedness in the ground[3] but not a man!—Said R. Naḥman b. Isaac: It means, if her nakedness was well covered by the ground.[4]

The Master said: 'If his children and the members of his household were minors, it is permitted'. Up to what age?—R. Ḥisda said: A girl up to three years and one day, a boy up to nine years and one day. Some there are who say: A girl up to eleven years and a day, and a boy up to twelve years and a day; with both of them [it is] up to the time when *Thy breasts were fashioned and thy hair was grown.*[5] Said R. Kahana to R. Ashi: In the other case[6] Raba said that, although there was a refutation of Samuel, yet the law followed his ruling. What is the ruling here?[7]—He replied to him: Do we weave them all in the same web?[8] Where it has been stated [that the law follows him] it has been stated, and where it has not been stated it has not been stated.

R. Mari said to R. Papa: If a hair protrudes through a man's garment,[9] what is the rule?—He exclaimed: 'Tis but a hair, a hair![10]

R. Isaac said: A handbreadth [exposed] in a [married] woman constitutes sexual incitement.[11] In which way? Shall I say, if one gazes at it? But has not R. Shesheth [already] said: Why did Scripture enumerate the ornaments worn outside the clothes with
c those worn inside?[1] To tell you that if one gazes at the little finger of a woman, it is as if he gazed at her secret place!—No, it means, in one's own wife, and when he recites the *Shema'*. R. Ḥisda said: A woman's leg is a sexual incitement, as it says, *Uncover the leg, pass through the rivers,*[2] and it says afterwards, *Thy nakedness shall be uncovered, yea, thy shame shall be seen.*[3] Samuel said: A woman's voice is a sexual incitement, as it says, *For sweet is thy voice and thy countenance is comely.*[4] R. Shesheth said: A woman's hair is a sexual incitement, as it says, *Thy hair is as a flock of goats.*[5]

R. Ḥanina said: I saw Rabbi hang up his *tefillin*. An objection was raised: If one hangs up his *tefillin*, his life will be suspended. The *Dorshe ḥamuroth*[6] said: *And thy life shall hang in doubt before thee:*[7] this refers to one who hangs up his *tefillin!*—This is no difficulty: the one statement refers to hanging by the strap, the other to hanging by the box. Or if you like, I can say that in either case, whether by the strap or by the box, it is forbidden, and when Rabbi hung his up it was in a bag. If so, what does this tell us?—You might think that they must be resting on something like a scroll of the Law. Therefore we are told that this is not necessary.

R. Ḥanina also said: I saw Rabbi [while saying the *Tefillah*]

(4) From mice or robbers. (5) Than preserving them from disrespect. (6) Which he uses as a bag.
a (1) I.e., the side where the cases of the *tefillin* can be recognized. (2) I.e., away from the bed. (3) Which showed that he had slept with her. (4) Lit., 'like his body'. (5) I.e., slaves. (6) Baḥ. omits this word. (7) 'Members of the household' must here be understood to include the wife. This is a very unusual use of the expression, and Tosaf. emends, 'If he was in bed and his wife was by his side, etc.'.
b (1) As to his wife or another person. (2) V. Num. XV, 20. A blessing is prescribed for this rite. (3) Although the posteriors are exposed. (4) So that even the posteriors are covered. (5) Ezek. XVI, 7. (6) Of putting the *tefillin* under the pillow, *supra*. (7) In regard to reciting the *Shema'* in bed. (8) I.e., adopt all his rulings indiscriminately. (9) Is it regarded as indecent exposure? (10) I.e., it does not matter. (11) Lit., 'nakedness'.
c (1) Among the ornaments taken by the Israelites from the women of Midian (Num. XXXI, 50) was the *kumaz* (E.V. '*girdles*') which the Rabbis supposed to have been worn inside under the garments, while the others were worn outside. (2) Isa. XLVII, 2. (3) Ibid. 3. (4) Cant. II, 14. (5) Ibid. IV, 1. (6) Lit., 'Expounders of essentials', a school of early homiletical exegetes; v. Pes. (Sonc. ed.) p. 266, n. 9. (7) Deut. XXVIII, 66.

תורה אור

כל לנטורינהו טפי עדיף והיכא מנח להו א"ר ירמיה *בין כר לכסת שלא כנגד ראשו והא תני רבי חייא מניחן בכובע תחת מראשותיו דמפיק ליה למורשא דכובע לבר *בר קפרא צייר להו בכילתא ומפיק למורשהון לבר רב שישא בריה דרב אידי ‎ב‎מנח להו אשרשיפא ופרים סודרא עלוייהו אמר רב המנונא בריה דרב יוסף זימנא חדא הוה קאימנא קמיה דרבא ואמר לי זיל אייתי לי תפילין ואשכחתינהו בין כר לכסת שלא כנגד ראשו והוה ידענא דיום טבילה הוה ולאגמורן *הלכה למעשה הוא דעבד בעי מיניה רב יוסף בריה דרב נחוניא מרב יהודה שנים שישנים במטה אחת מהו שזה יחזיר פניו ויקרא ק"ש וזה יחזיר פניו ויקרא ק"ש א"ל הכי אמר שמואל ואפי' אשתו עמו מתקיף לה רב יוסף אשתו ולא מיבעי' אחר ‎ג‎אדרבה *אשתו כגופו ‎ד‎אחר לאו כגופו מיתיבי שנים שישנים במטה אחת זה מחזיר פניו וקורא וזה מחזיר פניו וקורא ותניא אחריתי הישן במטה ובניו ובני ביתו בצדו הרי זה לא יקרא ק"ש אלא א"כ היתה טלית מפסקת בינידן ואם היו בניו ובני ביתו קטנים מותר בשלמא לרב יוסף לא קשיא הא באשתו הא באחר אלא לשמואל קשיא אמר לך שמואל לרב יוסף מי ניחא והתניא היה ישן במטה ובניו ובני ביתו במטה לא יקרא ק"ש אא"כ היתה טליתו מפסקת בינידן אלא מאי אית לך למימר אשתו לרב יוסף תנאי היא לדידי נמי תנאי היא: אמר מר זה מחזיר פניו וקורא ק"ש והא איכא עגבות מסייע ליה לרב הונא דאמר רב הונא עגבות אין בהם משום ערוה לימא מסייע ליה לרב הונא *‎ה‎האשה יושבת וקוצה לה חלתה ערומה מפני שיכולה לכסות פניה בקרקע אבל לא האיש תרגמא רב נחמן בר יצחק כגון שהיו ‎ו‎פניה טוחות בקרקע: אמר מר ‎ז‎אם היו בניו ובני ביתו קטנים מותר ועד כמה אמר רב חסדא תינוקת בת שלש שנים ויום אחד ותינוק בן ט' שנים ויום אחד איכא דאמרי ‎ח‎תינוקת בת י"א שנה ויום אחד ותינוק בן שתים עשרה שנה ויום אחד *אידי ואידי עד כדי °שדים נכונו ושערך צמח א"ל רב כהנא לרב אשי התם אמר רבא אע"ג דתיובתא דשמואל הלכתא כוותיה דשמואל הכא מאי אמר ליה *אטו כולהו בחדא מחתא מחתינהו אלא היכא דאתמר אתמר והיכא דלא אתמר לא אתמר א"ל רב מרי לרב פפא שער יוצא בבגדו מהו קרא עליה שער שער: אמר רבי יצחק טפח באשה ערוה למאי אילימא לאיסתכולי בה והא *אמר רב ששת למה מנה הכתוב תכשיטין שבחוץ עם תכשיטין שבפנים לומר לך ‎ט‎כל המסתכל באצבע קטנה של אשה כאלו מסתכל במקום התורף אלא ‎י‎באשתו ולק"ש אמר רב חסדא שוק באשה ערוה שנא' °גלי שוק עברי נהרות וכתיב °תגל ערותך וגם תראה חרפתך *אמר שמואל ‎כ‎קול באשה ערוה שנאמר כי °קולך ערב ומראך נאוה אמר רב ששת ‎ל‎שער באשה ערוה שנאמר °שערך כעדר העזים: אמר ר' חנינא אני ראיתי את רבי שתלה תפיליו מתיבי ‎מ‎התולה תפיליו יתלו לו חייו *דורשי חמורות אמרו °והיו חייך תלואים לך מנגד זה התולה תפיליו לא קשיא הא ברצועה הא בקציצה ואיבעית אימא לא שנא רצועה ולא שנא קציצה אסור וכי תלה רבי ‎נ‎בכיסתא תלה אי הכי מאי למימר' מהו דתימא תיבעי הנחה כספר תורה קמ"ל: ואמר ר' חנינא אני ראיתי את רבי °שגיהק ופיהק ונתעטש ורק וממשמש

(יחזקאל טז · ישעיה מז · שם · שיר ב · שם ד · דברים כח)

רש"י

כל לנטורינהו טפי עדיף. להו מבזיוני כמה שהוא מוזהר על שמירתן מן העכברים ומן הגנבים טפי עדיף להו מבזיוני: בכובע. הוא הכים שלהם: למורשא דכובע. שהתפילין יכרין בבליטתן בקלה הכים והוא כמורשא: צייר להו בכילתא. בירעה הפרושה סביבות מטתו קושרן: ומפיק למורשיהון לבר. בליטת הקשר שהתפילין בולטין מן הירעה היה הופך לצד החוץ ולא לצד המטה: אשרשיפא. ספסל: יום טבילה הוה. יום שטבלה אשתו דהוה ליה ליל תשמיש והייכו כשמואל דאמר אפילו אשתו עמו: ולאגמורן הלכה למעשה. מה שאוכי להביאם לו לא עשה אלא ללמדני הלכה לעשות מעשה כשמואל: ואפילו אשתו עמו. שיחזיר פניו דכל זמן שהן פונים פנים כנגד פנים פשיטא ליה דאסור דאיכא הרהור נגיעת ערוה על ידי אברי תשמיש: אשתו כגופו. ורגיל בה וליכא הרהור כולי האי: בשלמא לרב יוסף. דאמר אשתו היא דשריא אבל אחר לא מתרץ להו למתניתא הא באשתו הא באחר והא דקתני בני ביתו היינו אשתו: היה ישן במטה ובני ביתו. ואשתו בכלל ביתו: לדידי נמי. בין אשתו בין אחר פלוגתא דהכי תנאי היא: הא איכא עגבות. דנגעי אהדדי: וקוצה חלתה ערומה. ואע"פ שערום אסור לברך אשה יושבת מותרת שבישיבת' פני' שלמטה מכוסים בקרקע: אבל לא האיש. מפני שהבצים והגיד בולטין ונראין ואע"פ שמגולות עגבותיה והייכו קייעתא: כגון שהיו פניה טוחות. דבוקות ומכוסות בקרקע טוחות משמע לשון שעיעות טיח חלק שאינה בולטות אפלטייר"א בלע"ז: בת שלשה ובן תשעה. שהוא זמן שהן באין לכלל ביאה: בת י"א ובן י"ב. זמן שהן באות לכלל שערות ושדיהן נכונים שמשם ואילך באות לכלל [ביאה] שאדם מתאוה להן: התם אמר רבא. גבי תפילין תחת מראשותיו דקאמר שמואל אפילו אשתו עמו הלכה כשמואל: הכא. גבי שנים שהם ישנים דקא שרי שמואל באשתו עמו מאי: מחתא מחתינהו. באריגה אחת *ארגתם: יצא שערו בבגדו. שנקב בגדו כנגד זקן התחתון ויצא מן השער בנקב מהו מי הוי ערוה לקרות ק"ש כנגדו או לא: שער שער. כלומר מה בכך: לאסתכולי בה. אם אשת איש היא: תכשיטין שבפנים. כומז דפוס של בית הרחם שהיו עושין לבנותיהן ומוקבין כותלי בית הרחם כדרך שנוקבין את האזנים ותוחבין אותו כדי שלא יזדקקו להן זכרים: עם תכשיטין שבחוץ. אצעדה וצמיד הן הביאו אותן על כפרת הרהור עבירה שנסתכלו בבנות מדין: לאשתו ולק"ש. אם טפח מגולה בה לא יקרא ק"ש כנגדה: שוק. *באשת איש: ערוה. להסתכל וכן באשתו לק"ש: גלי שוק. וכתיב בתריה תגל ערותך: קולך ערב. ומדמשבח לה קרא בגוה ש"מ תאוה היא: התולה תפיליו. ביתד יתלו חייו: דורשי רשומות. קשרים וסתומי' הכלולים בתורה דורשי חמורות גרסי' והיא היא: זה התולה תפיליו. שהתורה חייו של אדם ורמז לך הכתוב שיתלו חייו: ברצועה. והקציצה למטה גנאי הוא להם אבל תולה הוא אותם בקציצה ותהא הקציצה מונחת על היתד והרצועה למטה: בכיסתא תלה. בתוך תיקן היו ותלה התיק: שגיהק. ריט"ייר בלעז פעמים שאדם מוליא מגופו לפיו כפיחה מתוך שובעו וריחה כריח המאכל שאכל: פיהק. באליי"ר בלעז איך מלקוחיו פותח להוליא רוח הפה מלא כאדם שרולה לישן או שעמד משינה: מתעטש. סטרכוד"ר בלע"ז ויש שדורשים גיהק מוריקין גו הקיס שטרילי"ר פיהק פיו הקיס: ורק. ע"ג קרקע:

תוספות

והא תני רבי חייא מניחן בכובע תחת מראשותיו. ואם תאמר אימא בכובע שלא כנגד ראשו שהרי בברייתא דלעיל כמי תני תחת מראשותיו ולא פריך מיניה משום דמלינן לפרושי שלא כנגד ראשו ואומר הרב דא"כ מאי איריא בכובע אפילו שלא בכובע כמי אלא שמע מיניה דמיירי אפילו כנגד ראשו ומכל מקום קשיא ליסבי דמיירי באשתו עמו דבעיא כלי בתוך כלי ול"ע:

שנים שהיו ישנים במטה. וא"ת והלא רואה ערות עצמו וי"ל שיוציא ראשו לחוץ וא"ת והרי לבו רואה את הערוה וי"ל דקסבר לבו רואה את הערוה מותר אי כמי חולץ בבגדו כנגד לבו:

והתניא היה ישן במטה ובני ביתו וכו'. פירש רש"י אשתו בכלל ביתו ולא נהירא חדא דלא אשכחן אשתו דמקריא בני ביתו ועוד לפירושו הל"ל והא קתני כאן כיון דאברייתא דלעיל קאי אבל מדקאמר והתניא משמע דברייתא אחרת היא ואומר ה"ר יוסף דגרסינן היה ישן במטה ואשתו ישנה בצדו לא יחזיר פניו ויקרא אא"כ היתה טלית מפסקת בינו לבינה:

וממשמש

עין משפט נר מצוה

עד
‎א‎מיי' וסמג ועוש"ע שם

עה
‎ב‎טוש"ע א"ח סי' כמ סעי' ו

עו
‎ג‎מיימ' פ"ג מה' ק"ש הל' יח סמג עשין יח טוש"ע א"ח סימן עג סעי' ב

עז
‎ד‎שם סעי' א

עח
‎ה‎מיי' פ"א מה' ברכו' הל' ע סמג עשין כז טוש"ע א"ח סי' עד סעי' ד ובסי' רו סעי' ג

עט
‎ז‎מיימ' פ"ג מה' ק"ש הל' יח סמג עשין יח טוש"ע א"ח סי' עג סעיף ב

פ
‎ח‎מיי' שם הל' יט טוש"ע שם סעיף ד

פא
‎ט‎מיי' פכ"א מה' איסו' ביאה הלכה ב סמג לאוין קכו טוש"ע אה"ע סי' כא סעי' א

[שבת קמח. פסחים מג. חולין כח:]

פב
‎י‎מיי' פ"ג מה' ק"ש הל' יו סמג עשין יח טוש"ע א"ח סימן עה סעי' א

פג
‎כ‎שם סעי' ג וטוש"ע אה"ע סי' כא סעי' א

פד
‎ל‎טוש"ע א"ח סי' עה סעי' ב וטוש"ע אה"ע שם

פה
‎מ‎מיי' פ"ד מה' תפילין הלכה ע סמג עשין כב טוש"ע א"ח סי' מ סעיף א

פו
‎נ‎מיי' פ"ד מה' תפלה הל' יא סמג עשין יע טוש"ע א"ח סי' לז סעיף א

מסורת הש"ס

בשאלתות פ' בא איתא' רב פפא

[שבת כד. ביצה כט: ב"ב קל: ע"ז עד. סנהד' יא.]

[כתובו' סו. מנחות לג: בכורו' לה:]

חלה פ"ב משנה ג

[קידושין פא:]

שבת סד: [בחולין כח. פרש"י ביתר ביאור ע"ש]

[קידושין ע.]

[פסחי' כד. חולין קלד:]

[ע' ב"ח בא"ח סי' עה פי' על דברי רש"י הללו]

ומממש בבגדו. פירש"י להעביר הכינה העוקצתו אבל לא מתעטף אם נפלה טליתו דתרי מילי נינהו ור"ח פי' דחדא מילתא היא פירוש מושמש בבגדו תקן שלא יפול מעל ראשו אבל אם נפל מעל ראשו לא היה מתעטף שהרי היא הפסקה אם מתעטף כיון שנפל לגמרי אבל לתקן קצת שלא יפול לא הוי הפסקה:

ואומר רבון העולמים. מיד באמצע תפלתו ואחר כך מתחיל ממקום שפסק:

אמר ליה לדידי לא סבירא לי. פירוש משום תרתי מילי חדא דסבירא' דאיכו אזר לראש דאמר רבי יוחנן (ר"ה לד:) שמע תשע תקיעות בתשע שעות יצא ועוד דסביר' לי מניח ידו על פיו ואם כן הוי ליה ראוי אלא לדידך דסבירא לך דחייב להפסיק וכו':

בחבלי השוא. כלומר בחנם מושכים עליהם עון כי טוב היה שלא היו מקיימין אותו כלל:

*פסק ר"ח כרב חסדא דאסור לקרות ק"ש אפי' לוחה תחת בגדו על בשרו וס"ל כל עצמותי תאמרנה (תהלים לה) דאע"ג דרב חסדא תלמיד דרב הונא היה לאומרא אזלינן ורב אלפס פסק כרב הונא מדאקשי גמרא מיניה ביומא פרק המנוכה (דף ל.): לית

ומשמש בבגדו. להעביר הכינה העוקצתו: אבל לא היה מתעטף. אם נפלה טליתו כשהוא מתפלל לא היה נוטלה ומתעטף שלא להפסיק: על סנטרו. מנטו"ן בלעז שלא תראה פתיחת פיו: הרי זה מקטני אמנה. כאלו אין הקב"ה שומע תפלת לחש ומגביה הרבה: הרי זה מנביאי השקר. דכתיב ויקראו בקול גדול (מלכים א יח): המגהק והמפהק הרי זה מגסי הרוח. וי"א כיכר שהוא מכוער גרסינן: אלא עטוש אעטוש קשיא. דאין עטוש אלא לאוכסו: למטה. מפיח בקול: ותקילא לי כי כולי תלמודאי. שקולה עלי וחביבה לפי שהיה רגיל להתענות: כשם שעושי' לו נחת רוח. שהעטוש נחת רוח לאדם: כך עושים לו נחת רוח מלמעלה. מן השמים למלאת שאלתו: אפשר כדרב יהודה. להבליעו באפרקסותו סודר שברא סו ושני ראשין תלוין בפניו: פתקיה. זרקו: מישתמיט מיניה. לא היה נראה אליו לפי שהיה ר' אבא חפץ לעלות לא"י ורב יהודה אוסר לו לפיכך לא היה נכנס לבית המדרש: ואשמע מיניה מילתא. מבחוץ: מבית ווערא. מבית המדרש: ונתעטש. מלמטה: עד שיכלה הרוח. מגופו שכודף מאותו רוח: וחוזר לתפלה. למקום שפסק: ואומר. בתוך התפלה דהא מופסקת ועומדת כבר על ידי הרוח לפיכך יכול להפסיק נמי ולומר דבר זה באמצע: הוציץ בטליתו על צוארו. מה שיש מן הטלית ולמעלה מן כתפיו מדביק בצוארו וביתן ערום קאמר: לדידי לא סבירא לי. לא הייתי מזקיקו להפסיק: בחבלי השוא. בחבלים שאינם חזקים אלא נוחין להנתק הן מושכין העון על עצמם אף זה על ידי דבור בטלה הוא נענש: ובדבר הזה. בשביל דבור זה שכזהרתם עליו תאריכון ימים: היתה טליתו חגורה על מתניו. לכסותו ממתניו ולמטה אע"פ שממתניו ולמעלה הוא ערום קורא קריאת שמע: אבל

[א]וממשמש בבגדו [ב]אבל לא היה מתעטף [ג]*וכשהוא מפהק היה מניח ידו על סנטרו מיתיבי המשמיע קולו בתפלתו הרי זה מקטני אמנה המגביה קולו בתפלתו הרי זה מנביאי השקר מגהק ומפהק הרי זה מגסי הרוח המתעטש בתפלתו סימן רע לו ויש אומרים ניכר שהוא מכוער הרק בתפלתו כאלו רק בפני המלך בשלמא מגהק ומפהק לא קשיא [ד]כאן לאונסו כאן לרצונו אלא מתעטש אמתעטש קשיא מתעטש אמתעטש נמי לא קשיא [ה]כאן מלמעלה כאן מלמטה דא"ר זירא הא מילתא *אבלעא לי בי רב המנונא *ותקילא לי כי כולי תלמודאי המתעטש בתפלתו סימן יפה לו כשם שעושים לו נחת רוח מלמטה כך עושין לו נחת רוח מלמעלה אלא רק ארק קשיא רק ארק נמי לא קשיא אפשר כדרב יהודה דאמר רב יהודה [ו]היה עומד בתפלה ונזדמן לו רוק מבליעו בטליתו ואם טלית נאה הוא מבליעו באפרקסותו רבינא הוה קאי אחורי דרב אשי נזדמן לו רוק פתקיה לאחוריה אמר ליה לא סבר לה מר להא דרב יהודה מבליעו באפרקסותו אמר ליה אנא [ז]אנינא דעתאי: [ח]המשמיע קולו בתפלתו הרי זה מקטני אמנה אמר רב הונא [ט]לא שנו אלא שיכול לכוין את לבו בלחש אבל אין יכול לכוין את לבו בלחש מותר וה"מ ביחיד אבל בצבור אתי למיטרד צבורא: רבי אבא הוה קא משתמיט מיניה דרב יהודה דהוה קא בעי למיסק לארעא דישראל *דאמר רב יהודה כל העולה מבבל לארץ ישראל עובר בעשה שנאמר °בבלה יובאו ושמה יהיו עד יום פקדי אותם נאם ה' אמר איזיל ואשמע מיניה מילתא *מבית ווערא והדר אפיק אזל אשכחיה לתנא דקתני קמיה דרב יהודה [י]היה עומד בתפלה ונתעטש ממתין עד שיכלה *הרוח וחוזר ומתפלל איכא דאמרי [כ]היה עומד בתפלה ובקש להתעטש מרחיק לאחריו ארבע אמות ומתעטש וממתין עד שיכלה הרוח וחוזר ומתפלל ואומר רבונו של עולם יצרתנו נקבים נקבים חלולים חלולים גלוי וידוע לפניך חרפתינו וכלימתינו בחיינו ובאחריתנו רימה ותולעה ומתחיל ממקום שפסק אמר ליה *אלו לא באתי אלא לשמוע דבר זה דיי: תנו רבנן היה ישן בטליתו ואינו יכול להוציא את ראשו מפני הצנה חוציץ בטליתו על צוארו וקורא קריאת שמע וי"א [ל]על לבו ותנא קמא הרי לבו רואה את הערוה קסבר לבו רואה את הערוה מותר א"ר הונא א"ר יוחנן היה מהלך במבואות המטונפות מניח ידו על פיו וקורא קריאת שמע אמר ליה רב חסדא האלהים אם אמר' לי רבי יוחנן בפומיה לא צייתנא ליה איכא דאמרי אמר רבה בר בר חנה אמר רבי יהושע בן לוי היה מהלך במבואות המטונפות מניח ידו על פיו וקורא קריאת שמע אמר ליה רב חסדא האלהים אם אמרה לי רבי יהושע בן לוי בפומיה לא צייתנא ליה ומי אמר רב הונא הכי והאמר רב הונא [מ]תלמיד חכם אסור לו לעמוד במקום הטנופת לפי שאי אפשר לו לעמוד בלא הרהור תורה לא קשי' כאן בעומד כאן במהלך ומי אמר רבי יוחנן הכי והאמר *רבה בר בר חנה א"ר יוחנן [נ]בכל מקום מותר להרהר בדברי תורה חוץ מבית המרחץ ומבית הכס' וכי תימ' הכא נמי כאן בעומד כאן במהלך איני והא *רבי אבהו הוה קא אזיל בתריה דרבי יוחנן והוה קא קרי קריאת שמע כי מטא במבואות המטונפות אשתיק אמר ליה לרבי יוחנן [ס]להיכן אהדר אמר ליה אם שהית כדי לגמור את כולה חזור לראש הכי קאמר ליה לדידי לא סבירא לי לדידך דסבירא לך אם שהית כדי לגמור את כולה חזור לראש תניא כותיה דרב הונא תניא כותיה דרב חסדא תניא כותיה דרב הונא המהלך במבואות המטונפות מניח ידו על פיו ויקרא ק"ש תניא כותיה דרב חסדא *[ע]היה מהלך במבואות המטונפות לא יקרא קריאת שמע ולא עוד אלא שאם היה קורא ובא פוסק לא פסק מאי אמר רבי מיאשא בר בריה דרבי יהושע בן לוי עליו הכתוב אומר °וגם אני נתתי להם חקים לא טובים ומשפטים בל [לא] יחיו רבי אסי אמר °הוי מושכי העון בחבלי השוא רב אדא בר אהבה אמר מהכא °כי דבר ה' בזה ואם פסק מה שכרו אמר רבי אבהו עליו הכתוב אומר °ובדבר הזה תאריכו ימים: אמר רב הונא היתה טליתו חגורה לו על מתניו מותר לקרות קריאת שמע תניא נמי הכי [פ]היתה טליתו של בגד ושל עור ושל שק חגורה על מתניו מותר לקרות קריאת שמע אבל

עין משפט נר מצוה
פז [א]טוש"ע א"ח סי' לז סעי' ג
פח [ב]שם סעיף ד
פט [ג][ד]שם סעי' א
צ [ה]טוש"ע א"ח סי' קג סעי' ג
צא [ו]מיימ' פ"ד מהלכות תפלה הלכה יא סמג עשין יט טוש"ע א"ח סי' לז סעיף ב
[שייך לקמן כה.]
צב [ח][ט]מיי' פ"ה שם הלכה ט סמג שם טוש"ע א"ח סי' קא סעי' ב
צג [י]מיי' פ"ד שם הלכה יא סמג שם טוש"ע א"ח סי' קג סעיף א
צד [כ]שם סעיף ב מבית ווער ואתי ואזיל כל"ל רש"א
צה [ל]מיי' פ"ג מהלכות ק"ש הל' יז סמג עשין יח טוש"ע א"ח סי' עד סעי' א
צו [מ]טוש"ע י"ד סי' רמו סעיף כו
צז [נ]מיי' שם הל' ד וסמג שם טוש"ע א"ח סי' פה סעי' ב
צח [ס][ע]מיי' שם הל' י"ד ופ"ב הל' י"ב טוש"ע א"ח סי' פה סעי' א וסי' סה סעיף א וסימן עח
צט [פ]מיי' פ"ג שם הלכה יז סמג שם טוש"ע א"ח סי' עד סעי' ו

מסורת הש"ס
תיבות וכשהוא מפהק ליתא מן הגמ' אלא מפי' רש"י העמידוהו בגמ' רש"א
ק"ל לידגני לי
מנחות יז.
ירמיה כז
שבת מא. כתובות קי:
[כ"ה ברא"ש אבל בטוש"ע אי' הריח]
[לעיל טז.]
שבת מ: קנ. קדושין לג. ע"ז מד: זבחים קב: ר"ה לד:
תוספת' פ"ב
יחזקאל כ
ישעיה ה
במדבר טו
דברים לב

belch and yawn and sneeze and spit [24b] and adjust his garment,[8] but he did not pull it over him;[9] and when he belched, he would put his hand to his chin. The following objection was cited: 'One who says the *Tefillah* so that it can be heard is of the small of faith;[10] he who raises his voice in praying is of the false prophets;[11] he who belches and yawns is of the arrogant; if he sneezes during his prayer it is a bad sign for him—some say, it shows that he is a low fellow; one who spits during his prayer is like one who spits before a king'. Now in regard to belching and yawning there is no difficulty; in the one case it was involuntary, in the other case deliberate. But the sneezing in Rabbi's case does seem to contradict the sneezing in the other?— There is no contradiction between sneezing and
a sneezing either; in the one case it is above, in the other below.[1] For R. Zera said: This dictum was casually imparted to me in the school of R. Hamnuna, and it is worth all the rest of my learning: If one sneezes in his prayer it is a good sign for him, that as they give him relief below [on earth] so they give him relief above [in heaven]. But there is surely a contradiction between the spitting in the one case and the other?—There is no contradiction between the two cases of spitting either, since it can be done as suggested by Rab Judah. For Rab Judah said: If a man is standing saying the *Tefillah*, and spittle collects in his mouth, he covers it up in his robe, or, if it is a fine robe, in his scarf.[2] Rabina was once standing behind R. Ashi and he wanted to spit, so he spat out behind him. Said R. Ashi to him: Does not the Master accept the dictum of Rab Judah, that he covers it up in his scarf? He replied: I am rather squeamish.

'One who says the *Tefillah* so that it can be heard is of the small of faith'. R. Huna said: This was meant to apply only if he is able to concentrate his attention when speaking in a whisper, but if he cannot concentrate his attention when speaking in a whisper, it is allowed. And this is the case only when he is praying alone, but if he is with the congregation [he must not do so because] he may disturb the congregation.

R. Abba kept away from Rab Judah because he wanted to go up to Eretz Israel; for Rab Judah said, Whoever goes up from Babylon to Eretz Israel transgresses a positive precept, since it says, *They shall be carried to Babylon and there shall they be, until the day that I remember them, saith the Lord.*[3] He said: I will go and listen
b to what he is saying from outside[1] the Academy.[2] So he went and found the Tanna[3] reciting in the presence of Rab Judah: If a man was standing saying the *Tefillah* and he broke wind, he waits until the odour passes off and begins praying again. Some say: If he was standing saying the *Tefillah* and he wanted to break wind, he steps back four cubits and breaks wind and waits till the wind passes off and resumes his prayer, saying, Sovereign of the Universe, Thou hast formed us with various hollows and various vents. Well dost Thou know our shame and confusion, and that our latter end is worms and maggots! and he begins again from the place where he stopped. He said:[4] Had I come only to hear this, it would have been worth my while.

Our Rabbis taught: If a man is sleeping in his garment and cannot put out his head on account of the cold, he folds his garment round his neck to make a partition[5] and recites the *Shema'*. Some say, round his heart. But how can the first Tanna [say thus]? His heart is surely in sight of the sexual organ!—He was of opinion that if the heart is in sight of the sexual organ, it is still permissible [to say the *Shema'*]:

R. Huna said in the name of R. Joḥanan: If a man is walking in a dirty alley way, he puts his hand over his mouth and recites the *Shema'*. Said R. Ḥisda to him: By God, had R. Joḥanan said this to me with his own mouth, I would not have listened to him.[6] (Some report: Rabbah b. Bar Ḥanah said in the name of R. Joshua b. Levi: If a man is walking in a dirty alley way, he puts his hand over his mouth and recites the *Shema'*. Said R. Ḥisda to him: By God, had R. Joshua b. Levi said this to me with his own mouth, I would not have listened to him.) But could R. Huna have said this, seeing that R. Huna has said: A scholar is forbidden to stand in a place of filth, because he must not stand still without meditating on the Torah?—There is no contradiction: one statement speaks of standing, the other of walking. But could R. Joḥanan have said this, seeing that Rabbah b. Bar Ḥanah has said in the name of R. Joḥanan: In every place it is permitted to meditate on words of Torah except in the bath and in a privy? And should you reply, here also one statement speaks of standing and one of walking, can that be so, seeing that R. Abbahu was once walking behind R. Joḥanan and reciting the *Shema'*, and when he came to a dirty alley way, he stopped; and [when they emerged] he said to R. Joḥanan, Where shall I commence again, and he replied: If you have stopped long enough to finish it, go back to the beginning?—What he meant to say to him was this: I do not hold [that you need have stopped]. But taking your view, that it was necessary, if you have stopped long enough to finish it, go back to the beginning. There is a teaching in accordance with R. Huna, and there is a teaching in accordance with R. Ḥisda. It has been taught in accordance with R. Huna: If one was walking in a dirty alley way, he puts his hand over his mouth and recites the *Shema'*. It has been taught in accordance with R. Ḥisda: If one was walking in a dirty alley way, he should not recite the *Shema'*; and what is more, if he was reciting and came to one, he should stop. Suppose he does not stop, what happens? R. Meyasha the grandson of R. Joshua b. Levi said: Of him Scripture says: *Wherefore I gave them also statutes that were not good and ordinances whereby they should*
c *not live.*[1] R. Assi said: *Woe unto them that draw iniquity with cords of vanity.*[2] R. Adda b. Ahabah said: *Because he hath despised the word of the Lord.*[3] And if he stops, what is his reward?—R. Abbahu said: Of him Scripture says: *Through this word*[4] *ye shall prolong your days.*[5]

R. Huna said: If a man's garment is girded round his waist,[6] he may recite the *Shema'*. It has been taught similarly: If his garment whether of cloth or of leather or of sacking, is girded round hi

(8) *Aliter:* 'feel his garment', to remove insects. (9) If it fell right off, as this would constitute an interruption in the *Tefillah*. So Rashi. R. Hananel, however, renders: He adjusted his robe so that it should not fall off his head, but if it did fall he did not replace it. (10) Because he imagines that otherwise God will not hear him. (11) Cf. I Kings XVIII, 28.

a (1) Euphemism. (2) *Aliter:* underwear. V. *supra* 23b, n. b1. (3) Jer. XXVII, 22; v. Keth. 110b.

b (1) V. Rashi. (2) Lit., 'House of Meeting'. (3) V. Glos. s.v. (b). (4) Omitting 'to him' of cur. edd. V. BaḤ. (5) Between his face and the lower par of his body, if it was bare. (6) I.e., he would not permit it.

c (1) Ezek. XX, 25. (2) Isa. V, 18. (3) Num. XV, 31. (4) E.V. 'thing (5) I.e., through being careful with regard to the utterance of the Torah. Deut XXXII, 47. (6) And hangs down from there, leaving his upper part un covered.

waist, he may recite the *Shema'* [25*a*], but the *Tefillah* he may not say until he covers his chest.[7] R. Huna further said: If a man forgot and entered a privy while wearing his *tefillin*, he places his hand over them till he finishes. 'Till he finishes'? How can this be assumed? Rather it is as R. Naḥman b. Isaac said: Until he finishes the first discharge. But why should he not stop at once and get up?—On account of the dictum of R. Simeon b. Gamaliel, as it has been taught: R. Simeon b. Gamaliel says: Keeping back the faeces brings on dropsy, keeping back urine brings on jaundice.

It has been stated: If there is some excrement on a man's flesh
a or if his hand is inside a privy,[1] R. Huna says that he is permitted to say the *Shema'*, while R. Ḥisda says he is forbidden to say the *Shema'*. Raba said: What is the reason of R. Huna?—Because it is written, *Let everything that hath breath praise the Lord.*[2] R. Ḥisda says that it is forbidden to say the *Shema'*. What is the reason of R. Ḥisda?—Because it is written, *All my bones shall say, Lord, who is like unto Thee.*[3]

It has been stated: [If there is] an evil smell [proceeding] from some tangible source, R. Huna says that one removes [from the source of the smell] four cubits and recites the *Shema'*; R. Ḥisda says: He removes four cubits from the place where the smell ceases, and then recites the *Shema'*. It has been taught in accordance with R. Ḥisda: A man should not recite the *Shema'* either in front of human excrement or of the excrement of dogs or the excrement of pigs or the excrement of fowls or the filth of a dungheap which is giving off an evil smell. If, however, it is in a place ten handbreadths above him or ten handbreadths beneath him, he can sit at the side of it and recite the *Shema'*; otherwise he removes himself out of sight of it; and similarly for the *Tefillah*. [If there is] an evil smell [proceeding] from a tangible object, he removes four cubits from [the source of] the smell and recites the *Shema'*. Raba said: The law is not as stated in this Baraitha,[4] but it has been taught in the following: A man should not recite the *Shema'* in front either of human excrement or excrement of pigs or excrement of dogs when he puts skins in them.[5] They asked R. Shesheth: What of
b an evil smell which has no tangible source?[1] He said to them: Come and see these mats in the school house; some sleep on them[2] while others study. This, however, applies only to study,[3] but not to the *Shema'*. And even as regards study it applies only if the smell is made by another but not if it is made by himself.

It has been stated: If manure is being carried past one, Abaye says it is permitted to recite the *Shema'*,[4] while Raba says it is forbidden to recite the *Shema'*. Said Abaye: Whence do I derive my opinion? Because we have learnt: If an unclean person is standing under a tree and a clean one passes by, he becomes unclean. If a clean person is standing under a tree and an unclean one passes by, he remains clean, but if he [the unclean person] stands still, he becomes unclean. And similarly with a stone smitten with leprosy.[5] To which Raba can reply: In that case the deciding factor is the permanence,[6] as it is written, *He shall dwell alone, without the camp shall his dwelling be.*[7] But in this case, the All-Merciful has said, *Therefore shall thy camp be holy,*[8] and this condition is not fulfilled.

R. Papa said: The snout of a pig is like manure being carried past. This is obvious?[9]—It required to be stated, to show that it applies even if the animal is coming up from the river.

Rab Judah said: If there is a doubt about [the presence of] excrement, it is forbidden; if there is a doubt about urine, it is permitted. Some there are who say: Rab Judah said: If there is a doubt about excrement in the house, it is permitted,[10] in the dungheap it is forbidden. If there is a doubt about urine, it is permitted even in the dungheap. He adopted the view of R. Hamnuna; for R. Hamnuna said: The Torah forbade the recital of the *Shema'* only in face of the stream [of urine]. And this is as taught by R. Jonathan; for R. Jonathan contrasted two texts. It is written: *Thou shalt have a*
c *place also without the camp, whither thou shalt go forth abroad,*[1] and it is also written, *And thou shalt have a paddle . . . thou shalt cover that which cometh from thee.*[2] How are these two statements to be reconciled? The one speaks of easing, the other of urine. This proves that urine was not forbidden by the Torah save in face of the stream only, and once it has fallen to the ground it is permitted, and it is the Rabbis who imposed a further prohibition, and when they did so, it was only in a case of certainty but not in a case of doubt. And in a case of certainty, how long is it forbidden?—Rab Judah said in the name of Samuel: So long as it moistens [the ground]. And so said Rabbah b. Ḥanah in the name of R. Joḥanan: So long as it moistens [the ground]. So too said 'Ulla: So long as it moistens [the ground]. Ganiba said in the name of Rab: So long as the mark is discernible. Said R. Joseph: May Ganiba be forgiven by his Master![3] Seeing that even of excrement Rab Judah has said in the name of Rab that as soon as it has dried on top it is permitted, is there any question about urine! Said Abaye to him: What reason have you for relying on this statement? Rely rather on this one which was made by Rabbah b. Bar Ḥanah in the name of Rab: Even if excrement is as a potsherd, it is forbidden [to recite the *Shema'* near it]. What is the test of its being as dry as a potsherd?—So long as one can throw it [on to the ground] and it does not break, [it is not so dry]. Some say: So long as one can roll it without breaking it.[4] Rabina said: I was once standing before Rab Judah of Difti, and he saw dung and said to me, Look if the top has dried, or not. Some say that what he said to him was this: Look if it has formed cracks. What is the ultimate decision?[5] It has been stated: When dung is like a potsherd, Amemar says it is forbidden and Mar Zuṭra says it is permitted [to say the *Shema'* near it]. Raba said: The law is that if dung is as dry as a potsherd it is forbidden, and in the case of urine as long as it is moistening [the ground]. An objection was raised: As long as urine is moistening [the ground] it is forbidden; if it has been absorbed
d [in the ground] or has dried up,[1] it is permitted. Now are we not to understand that 'absorption' here is compared to 'drying', and that just as after drying there is no mark left, so after absorption there must be no mark left, and that if there is still a mark it is forbidden, even though it no longer moistens?—But adopting your line of argument, let us see the first clause: 'As long [as urine] is moistening [the ground] it is forbidden', which implies that if there is a mark it is permitted.[2]—The fact is from this [Baraitha] we cannot infer [either way].

Shall we say that there is a difference of Tannaim [on this point]? [For it was taught:] If urine has been poured out of a vessel, it is forbidden to recite the *Shema'* in front of that vessel. As for urine itself, if it has been absorbed in the ground it is permitted, if it has not been absorbed it is forbidden. R. Jose says: So long as it moistens the ground. Now what is meant by the 'absorbed' and 'not absorbed' mentioned by the first Tanna? Shall I say that 'absorbed' means that it does not moisten and that 'not absorbed' means that it still moistens, and R. Jose came and said that so long as it moistens it is forbidden, but if only the mark is discernible it is permitted? This is the same as the first Tanna says! We must say then that 'absorbed' means that the mark is not discernible and 'not absorbed' means that the mark is discernible, and R. Jose came and said that so long as it moistens it is forbidden, but if only the mark is discernible it is permitted?—No; both agree that so long as it moistens it is forbidden, and if only the mark is dis-

(7) Because in the *Tefillah* he is like one standing before a king.
a (1) I.e., he was standing outside with his hand inside the window. (2) Ps. CL, 6. As much as to say, only the mouth and other breathing organs are concerned with praise. (3) Ibid. XXXV, 10. (4) With reference to the excrement of dogs etc. (5) The excrement of pigs and dogs was used for tanning.

(1) I.e., from the breaking of wind. (2) And break wind. (3) Rashi: lit., 'words of Torah'. He cannot study if he has to leave the school-house. (4) And one need not break off. (5) V. Kid. 33*b*. Neg. XIII, 7. (6) I.e., the standing still of the unclean object. (7) Lev. XIII, 46. This implies that the leper spreads uncleanness only if he remains in one place. (8) Deut. XXIII, 15,

מסורת הש"ס

אבל לתפלה. לריך הוא להראות את עלמו כעומד לפני המלך ולעמוד באימה אבל ק"ש אינו מדבר לפני המלך: **הדרוקן.** חולי המלבה את הכרס: **סילון.** של מי רגלים: **ירקון.** חולי ששמו גלכי"ה: **ידיו בבית הכסא.** מחילה יש בינו לבין בית הכסא ופשט ידיו לפנים מן המחילה: **כל הנשמה.** הפה והחוטם בכלל ההילול ולא שאר אברים: **שיש לו עיקר.** שהלואה מונחת שם ומסרחת ושאין לו עיקר הפחת רוח: **מרחיק ד' אמות.** מן העיקר ואע"פ שהריח בא אליו וכגון שהיא לאחוריו שאינו רואה אותה: **ממקום שפסק הריח.** שהריח כלה שם: **לא כנגד צואת אדם כו'.** ואע"פ שאין ריח: **לית הלכתא כי הא מתניתא.** דלעיל דאסרה לואת כלבים וחזירים בשאין בהם עורות: **בזמן שיש בהן עורות.** אלואת כלבים וחזירים קאי שדרכן לתתן בעבוד העורות אבל לואת אדם אפי' בלא עורות שהרי אין דרכן לתתם שם הלכך ע"כ בלא עורות קאמר: **שאין לו עיקר.** הפחת רוח: **ציפי.** מאללות של בית המדרש: **דהני גנו והני גרסי.** ואע"פ שדרך הישיני' להפיח: **וה"מ לגרסא.** משום דלא אפשר: **אבל לק"ש.** ילא לחוץ ויקרא: **אבל לדידיה.** הפיח הוא עלמו ממתין עד שיכלה הריח: **צואה עוברת.** אדם שנושאים לפניו גרף של רעי להעבירו: **מותר לקרות.** וא"ל להפסיק: **הטמא עומד תחת האילן.** ולא בנושא את המת קאי דמת לא שנא עומד ול"ש יושב ול"ש הולך אוהל הוא וגבי מלורע קתני לה בת"כ דגלי ביה רחמנ' ישיבה דכתיב בדד ישב מחוץ למחנה מושבו: **טמא.** מכאן אמרו עומד כמי כיושב דמי דקביע אבל מהלך לא קביע: **אבן המנוגעת.** הרי היא כמלורע שהקיש' הכתוב זאת התורה לכל נגע הלרעת ולנתק וללרעת הבגד ולבית (ויקרא יד): **פשיטא.** דפי חזיר אינו בלא לואה: **בבית מותר.** דאין דרך להניח לואה בבית: **לא אסרה תורה.** במי רגלים אלא לקרות כנגד עמוד הקלוח בלבד: **ויצאת שמה חוץ.** ולא הלריכו כסוי וכתיב וכסית: **עד כמה.** ישהו על גבי קרקע ויהא אסור: **שרא ליה מריה.** ימחול לו רבונו דודאי שקר העיד משמיה דרב: היבשה כפרכת היא יותר מן הלחה: **איכא דאמרי.** חומרא היא אע"פ שאם זורק' כפרכת הואיל ואינה כפרכת מגלגול לחה היא: **קרמו.** לשון קרום עי"א כלומר גלד מעט: **אי מפלאי אפלויי.** אם יש בה סדקים סדקים יבשה היא ושרי: **מאי הוי עלה.** דמי רגלים: **נבלעו.** בארץ: **יבשו.** על גבי אבנים בחמה:

טופח

בכורות מד: לקמן סב:
תמיד כ"ז: יומא ל.
ולא כנגד אשפה כל"ל (ס"מ)
[בר"ף וברא"ש ליתא] [תוס' פ"ב]
קידושין לג: נגעים פי"ג משנה ז תוספתא דנגעים פ"ז ת"כ פ' מלורע

לית הלכתא כי הא מתניתא אלא כי הא דתניא כו'. פרש"י לית הלכתא כי הא מתניתא דלעיל דאסרה לואת כלבים וחזירים אפי' בשאין בהם עורות אבל בלואת אדם לא שייך ואסור בכל ענין משמע אבל בלואת תרנגולים לא איירי רבא ובאידך ברייתא לא גרס לואת תרנגולים כלל ולא פליג בהא אמתניתא דלעיל ולפי זה יש לאסור לואת תרנגולין ואומר רבינו יהודה דדוקא כשהן בלול שלהם שיש שם סרחון גדול אבל בתרנגולים ההולכים בבית אין חוששין ובירושלמי יש דאדומים בלבד יש לחוש *ולא ידעינן לפרש ועוד קאמר מרחיקין מגללי בהמה ד' אמות רבי שמואל בר' ילחק אומר ובלבד של חמור:

ריח רע שאין לו עיקר. י"מ דבתי כסאות שלנו בעומק אם יש בהן מחילה מפסקת הויא כמו ריח רע שאין לו עיקר כמו בתי כסאו' דלפרסאי לקמן (ד' כו.):

והרי

עין משפט נר מצוה
ק אשם ובסי' לא סעיף א
קא במיי' פ"ד מהל' תפילין הלכ' כ סמג עשין כב טוש"ע א"ח סימן מג סעיף א [בגדולת מרדכי פי' לפי שבארץ אדום היו השעורים מלויי' כדאי' כתובות סד: והיו מאכילין התרנגולין שעורים ולואתם מסרחת וע' ב"י סימן ע"ט]
קב גמיי' פ"ג מהלכות ק"ש הלכה יא טוש"ע א"ח סימן עו סעיף ד
קג דמיי' פ"ג מה' ק"ש הל' יב סמג עשין יח טוש"ע א"ח סימן עט סעיף א
קד השם סעיף ח
קה ושם סעיף ב
קו זמיי' פ"ד מהלכות תפלה הלכ' ח סמג שם טוש"ע א"ח סימן ל סעיף כו
קז חמיי' פ"ג מה' ק"ש הל' ו סמג שם טוש"ע א"ח סי' עט סעי' ד
קח טיכשם סעי' ט
קט למיי' שם הלכה יג וסמג שם טוש"ע א"ח סי' עו סעי' ג
קי ממיי' פ"י מהל' טומאת לרעת הל' יב
קיא נמיי' פ"ג מהל' ק"ש הל' יב סמג עשין יח טוש"ע א"ח סי' עו סעי' ג
קיב סעשם סעיף ז
קיג פמיי' וסמג שם טוש"ע א"ח סי' עב ס"א

תורה אור

אבל לתפלה עד שיכסה את לבו ואמר רב הונא שכח ונכנס בתפילין לבית הכסא מניח ידו עליהן עד שיגמור ס"ד אלא כדאמר רב נחמן בר יצחק עד שיגמור עמוד ראשון וליפסוק לאלתר וליקום משום דרשב"ג *דתניא רשב"ג אומר עמוד החוזר מביא את האדם לידי הדרוקן סילון החוזר מביא את האדם לידי ירקון: *איתמר צואה על בשרו או ידו מונחת בבית הכסא רב הונא אמר מותר לקרות ק"ש רב חסדא אמר אסור לקרות ק"ש אמר רבא מ"ט דרב הונא דכתיב °כל הנשמה תהלל יה ורב חסדא אמר אסור לקרות ק"ש מ"ט דרב חסדא דכתיב °כל עצמותי תאמרנה יי' מי כמוך: איתמר ריח רע שיש לו עיקר רב הונא אמר מרחיק ארבע אמות וקורא ק"ש ורב חסדא אמר מרחיק ד' אמות ממקום שפסק הריח וקורא ק"ש תניא כותיה דרב חסדא לא יקרא אדם ק"ש לא כנגד צואת אדם ולא כנגד צואת כלבים ולא כנגד צואת חזירים ולא כנגד צואת תרנגולים *ולא כנגד צואת אשפה שריחה רע ואם היה מקום גבוה י' טפחים או נמוך עשרה טפחים יושב בצדו וקורא ק"ש ואם לאו מרחיק מלא עיניו וכן לתפלה ריח רע שיש לו עיקר מרחיק ד' אמות ממקום הריח וקורא ק"ש אמר רבא לית הלכתא כי הא מתניתא (*בכל הני שמעתתא) אלא כי הא *דתניא לא יקרא אדם ק"ש לא כנגד צואת אדם ולא כנגד צואת חזירים ולא כנגד צואת כלבים בזמן שנתן עורות לתוכן בעו מיניה מרב ששת ריח רע שאין לו עיקר מהו אמר להו °אתו חזו הני ציפי דבי רב דהני גנו והני גרסי וה"מ בדברי תורה אבל בק"ש לא ודברי תורה נמי לא אמרן אלא דחבריה אבל דידיה לא: איתמר צואה עוברת אביי אמר מותר לקרות ק"ש רבא אמר אסור לקרות ק"ש אמר אביי מנא אמינא לה *דתנן °הטמא עומד תחת האילן והטהור עובר טמא טהור עומד תחת האילן וטמא עובר טהור ואם עומד טמא וכן באבן המנוגעת ורבא אמר לך התם בקביעתא תליא מילתא דכתיב °בדד ישב מחוץ למחנה מושבו הכא °והיה מחניך קדוש אמר רחמנא והא ליכא: א"ר פפא פי חזיר כצוא' עוברת דמי פשיטא לא צריכא אע"ג דסליק מנהרא אמר רב יהודה ספק צואה אסורה ספק מי רגלים מותרים א"ד אמר רב יהודה °ספק צואה בבית מותרת באשפה אסורה ספק מי רגלים אפי' באשפה נמי מותרין סבר לה כי הא דרב המנונא דאמר רב המנונא לא אסרה תורה אלא כנגד עמוד בלבד וכדר' יונתן דר' יונתן רמי כתיב °ויד תהיה לך מחוץ למחנה ויצאת שמה חוץ וכתיב °ויתד תהיה לך וגו' וכסית את צאתך הא כיצד כאן בגדולים כאן בקטנים אלמא קטנים לא אסרה תורה אלא כנגד עמוד בלבד הא נפול לארעא שרי ורבנן הוא דגזרו בהו וכי גזרו בהו רבנן בודאן אבל בספקן לא גזור ובודאן עד כמה אמר רב יהודה אמר שמואל כל זמן שמטפיחין וכן אמר רבה בב"ח א"ר יוחנן כל זמן שמטפיחין וכן אמר עולא כל זמן שמטפיחין גניבא משמיה דרב אמר כל זמן שרשומן ניכר אמר רב יוסף שרא ליה מריה לגניבא השתא צואה אמר רב יהודה אמר רב כיון שקרמו פניה מותר מי רגלים מיבעיא א"ל אביי מאי חזית דסמכת אהא סמוך אהא דאמר רבה בר רב הונא אמר רב צואה אפי' כחרס אסורה והיכי דמי צואה כחרס אמר רבה בב"ח א"ר יוחנן כל זמן שזורקה ואינה נפרכת וא"ד כל זמן שגוללה ואינה נפרכת אמר רבינא הוה קאימנא קמיה דרב יהודה מדפתי חזא צואה אמר לי עיין אי קרמו פניה אי לא א"ד הכי א"ל עיין אי מפלאי אפלויי מאי הוי עלה איתמר צואה כחרס אמימר אמר אסורה ומר זוטרא אמר מותרת אמר רבא °הלכתא צואה כחרס אסורה ומי רגלים כל זמן שמטפיחין מיתיבי מי רגלים כל זמן שמטפיחין אסורין נבלעו או יבשו מותרין מאי לאו נבלעו דומיא דיבשו מה יבשו דאין רשומן ניכר אף נבלעו דאין רשומן ניכר הא רשומן ניכר אסור אע"ג דאין מטפיחין ולטעמיך אימא רישא כל זמן שמטפיחין הוא דאסור הא רשומן ניכר שרי *אלא מהא ליכא למשמע מינה לימא כתנאי כלי שנשפכו ממנו מי רגלים אסור לקרות ק"ש כנגדו ומי רגלים עצמן שנשפכו נבלעו מותר לא נבלעו אסור רבי יוסי אומר כל זמן שמטפיחין מאי נבלעו ומאי לא נבלעו דקאמר ת"ק אילימא נבלעו דאין מטפיחין לא נבלעו דמטפיחין ואתא רבי יוסי למימר כל זמן שמטפיחין הוא דאסור הא רשומן ניכר שרי היינו ת"ק אלא נבלעו דאין רשומן ניכר לא נבלעו דרשומן ניכר ואתא רבי יוסי למימר כל זמן שמטפיחין הוא דאסור הא רשומן ניכר שרי לא דכ"ע כל זמן שמטפיחין הוא דאסור הא רשומן ניכר שרי

והכא

תהלים קנ
שם לה
ויקרא יג
דברים כג
שם
שם

[שבת קכא. וע"ש ברש"י מגיל' כב. כח. יבמות עו: נדרי' ס: עב. וע"ש ב"מ כו: ל. לד. פא: ב"ב קד. קלג: קסב: ע"ז כב. עב. שבועות לח. זבחים פע: מנחות קה. נדה לג: ועי' היטב קידושין ה:]

(9) That a pig's snout must always contain filth. (10) Because excrement is not usually found in the house.

c (1) Deut. XXIII, 13. (2) Ibid. 14. Here 'covering' is mentioned. (3) For reporting Rab wrongly. (4) This is a more severe test. (5) With regard to urine.

d (1) On stones. (2) Which is apparently in contradiction to the implication of the second clause.

והכא בטופח על מנת להטפיח איכא בינייהו: ירד לטבול אם יכול לעלות כו': לימא תנא סתמא כר' אליעזר דאמר עד הנץ החמה אפי' תימא ר' יהושע ודילמא כותיקין *דא"ר יוחנן ותיקין היו גומרין אותה עם הנץ החמה: ואם לאו יתכסה במים ויקרא: והרי לבו רואה את הערוה א"ר אלעזר ואיתימא ר' אחא בר אבא בר אחא משום רבינו במים עכורין שנו דדמו כארעא סמיכתא שלא יראה לבו ערותו: ת"ר מים צלולין ישב בהן עד צוארו וקור' וי"א עוכרן ברגלו ות"ק והרי לבו רואה את הערוה קסבר לבו רואה את הערוה מותר והרי עקבו רואה את הערוה קסבר עקבו רואה את הערוה מותר אתמר עקבו רואה את הערוה מותר נוגע אביי אמר אסור ורבא אמר מותר רב זביד מתני לה להא שמעתא הכי רב חיננא בריה דרב איקא מתני לה הכי נוגע דברי הכל אסור רואה אביי אמר אסור רבא אמר מותר *לא נתנה תורה למלאכי השרת והלכתא נוגע אסור רואה מותר אמר רבא צואה בעששית מותר לקרות ק"ש כנגדה ערוה בעששית אסור לקרות ק"ש כנגדה צואה בעששית מותר לקרות ק"ש כנגדה דצואה בכיסוי תליא מילתא והא מיכסיא ערוה בעששית אסור לקרות ק"ש כנגדה ולא יראה בך ערות דבר אמר רחמנא והא קמיתחזיא אמר אביי צואה כל שהוא מבטלה ברוק אמר רבא וברוק עבה אמר רבא צואה בגומא מניח סנדלו עליה וקורא ק"ש בעא מר בריה דרבינא צואה דבוקה בסנדלו מאי תיקו *אמר רב יהודה נכרי ערום אסור לקרות ק"ש כנגדו מאי איריא נכרי אפי' ישראל נמי פשיטא ליה דאסור אלא נכרי אצטריכא ליה מהו דתימא הואיל וכתיב בהו אשר בשר חמורים בשרם אימא כחמור בעלמא הוא קמ"ל דאינהו נמי איקרו ערוה דכתיב וערות אביהם לא ראו: ולא יתכסה לא במים הרעים ולא במי המשרה עד שיטיל לתוכן מים: וכמה מיא רמי ואזיל אלא ה"ק לא יתכסה לא במים הרעים ולא במי המשרה כלל ומי רגלים עד שיטיל לתוכן מים ויקרא ת"ר *כמה יטיל לתוכן מים כל שהוא ר' זכאי אומר רביעית אמר רב נחמן מחלוקת לבסוף אבל בתחלה כל שהן ורב יוסף אמר מחלוקת לכתחלה אבל לבסוף דברי הכל רביעית אמר ליה רב יוסף לשמעיה אייתי לי רביעיתא דמיא כר' זכאי: *ת"ר גרף של רעי ועביט של מי רגלים אסור לקרות ק"ש כנגדן ואע"פ שאין בהן כלום ומי רגלים עצמן עד שיטיל לתוכן מים וכמה יטיל לתוכן מים כל שהוא רבי זכאי אומר רביעית בין לפני המטה בין לאחר המטה רבן שמעון בן גמליאל אומר לאחר המטה קורא לפני המטה אינו קורא אבל מרחיק הוא ארבע אמות וקורא רבי שמעון בן אלעזר אומר אפילו *בית מאה אמה לא יקרא עד שיוציאם או שיניחם תחת המטה איבעיא להו היכי קאמר אחר המטה קורא מיד לפני המטה מרחיק ארבע אמות וקורא או דילמא הכי קאמר לאחר המטה מרחיק ארבע אמות וקורא לפני המטה אינו קורא כלל תא שמע דתניא ר' שמעון בן אלעזר אומר אחר המטה קורא מיד לפני המטה מרחיק ד' אמות רבן שמעון ב"ג אומר אפי' בית מאה אמה לא יקרא עד שיוציאם או שיניחם תחת המטה בעיין איפשיטא לן מתנייתא קשי' אהדדי איפוך בתרייתא מה חזית דאפכת בתרייתא איפוך קמייתא מאן שמעת ליה דאמר *כוליה בית כארבע אמות דמי רבי שמעון בן אלעזר היא אמר רב יוסף בעאי מיניה מרב הונא מטה פחות משלשה פשיטא לי דכלבוד דמי שלשה ארבעה חמשה ששה שבעה שמנה תשעה מהו א"ל לא ידענא עשרה ודאי לא מיבעיא לי אמר אביי שפיר עבדת דלא איבעיא לך כל עשרה רשותא אחריתי היא אמר רבא הלכתא פחות משלשה כלבוד דמי עשרה רשותא אחריתי היא משלשה עד עשרה היינו דבעא מיניה רב יוסף מרב הונא ולא פשט ליה אמר רב הלכה כרבי שמעון בן אלעזר וכן אמר באלי אמר רב יעקב *ברה דבת שמואל הלכה כרבי שמעון בן אלעזר ורבא אמר אין הלכה כרבי שמעון בן אלעזר רב אחאי איעסק ליה לבריה בי רב יצחק בר שמואל בר מרתא עייליה לחופה ולא הוה מסתייעא מילתא אזל בתריה לעייוני חזא ספר תורה דמנחא אמר להו איכו השתא לא אתיא סכנתון לברי דתניא בית שיש בו ספר תורה או תפילין אסור לשמש בו את המטה עד שיוציאם או שיניחם כלי בתוך כלי אמר אביי לא שנו אלא בכלי שאינו כליין אבל בכלי שהוא כליין אפילו עשרה מאני כחד מאנא דמי אמר רבא גלימא אקמטרא

תורה אור: דברי' כג · יחזקאל כג · בראשי' ט

רש"י

טופח על מנת להטפיח איכא בינייהו. ת"ק בעי על מנת להטפיח ורבי יוסי מחמיר: לימא תנא סתמא כרבי אליעזר. והלכה כמותו: דלמא לותיקין קאמר מתני' עם הנץ החמה אבל לכ"ע עד ג' שעות: והרי לבו רואה את הערוה. קס"ד כל אבר שאין דרכו לראות את הערוה אותו בשעה שקורא בתורה קרינא ביה ולא יראה בך ערות דבר: לא נתנה תורה למלאכי השרת. שאין להם ערוה על כרחנו יש לנו ערוה ואין אנו יכולי' להשמר מכל זה: כל שהוא. מעט: ברוק. רוקק עליה ומכסה אותה ברוק: בעששית. לנטר"נא בלע"ז כלומר מחיצת זכוכית או קלף דק מפסיק בנתיים והיא נראית: בכסוי תליא מילתא. וכסית את צאתך: מים הרעים. סרוחים: *מי המשרה. ששורים שם הפשתה והקנבוס והם מסריחים: וכמה מיא רמי ואזיל. כמה ישליך לתוכם ויבטלם הלא מרובין הם: ומי רגלים. מועטין והם בכלי והוא בא לקרות ק"ש אצלם: לבסוף. שמי רגלים בכלי וזה נותן לתוכן מים בהא קאמר רבי זכאי רביעית: אבל לכתחלה. שקדמו המים למי רגלים דברי הכל כל שהוא שכשמטיל מי רגלים בכלי לבסוף ראשון ראשון שנופל לתוך המים מתבטל ואע"פ שהם רבים והולכין כבר בטלו: אייתי לי רביעיתא. אפי' בתחלה: גרף ועביט. שניהם כלי חרס הם אלא של רעי קרוי גרף ושל מי רגלים קרוי עביט: אסור לקרות ק"ש כנגדם. הואיל ומיוחדין לכך ואף על פי שאין בתוכן כלום: ומי רגלים עצמן. בכלי שאינו מיוחד להם: בין לפני המטה. שאין המטה מפסקת בינו לבינם: בין לאחר המטה. שהמטה מפסקת ביניהם אסור: או שיניחם תחת המטה גרסינן. ולא גרסינן כלי בתוך כלי: תחת המטה. כאלו היו טמוני' בארץ: היכי קאמר. רשב"ג: בעיי' אפשיטא לן. שאלתנו נתפרשה לנו בחלוק שבין לפני המטה ולאחר המטה: מתנייתא מיה' קשיין. שהוחלפ' שיטתן: מאן שמעת ליה כו'. לא ידעתי היכן היא: פשיטא לי. במניחן תחת המטה ורגלי' קצרים שאין הימנה ולקרקע שלשה טפחים כלבוד דמי והרי הן כטמוני': עשרה ודאי. לא שאלתי ממנו דנראה כאלו אינה תחתיה מאחר שיש הפסק כל כך אין זה כסוי: עיילי' לחופה ולא הוה מסתייעא מילתא. דנישואים. שלא היה יכול לבעול: סכנתון לברי. כמעט שנכנס את בני למות בעונש העון: אפילו עשרה מאני. וכולן כליין כחד מאנא דמו:

אקמטרא

תוספות

והרי לבו רואה את הערוה. פי' ר"י מדפריך גמרא הכי בפשיטות משמע דלבו רואה את הערוה אסור אלא דרבינו שמעיה תלמידו של רש"י פסק כת"ק דלבו רואה את הערוה מותר ומיהו בסמוך משמע דאסור דלא פליגי הכי אמוראי אלא בעקבו רואה את הערוה אבל בלבו רואה את הערוה כולי עלמא מודו דאסור: והלכתא נוגע עקבו אסור. וטעמא דגזרינן נוגע עקבו שמא יגע בידיו: גרף של רעי. פי' רש"י של חרס בלוע משמע לפירושו אבל כלי דלא בלע כגון זכוכית אפשר דשרי: ובלבד שיטיל בהן רביעית מים. אבל בגרף אפשר דלא מהני מים:

ספר

עין משפט נר מצוה

קיד א מיימ' פ"ג מהל' ק"ש הלכה ז ופ"ג הל' יז סמג עשין יח טוש"ע א"ח סימן עד סעיף ב

קטו ב מיי' שם פ"ג הלכה יז טוש"ע שם סעיף ה

קטז ג מיי' פ"ג שם הל' יוד וסמג שם טוש"ע א"ח סימן עו סעיף א

קיז ד מיימ' שם הלכה טז וסמג שם טוש"ע א"ח סימן עה סעיף ה

קיח ה מיי' שם הל' יא וסמג שם טוש"ע א"ח סימן עו סעיף ו

קיט ז ח מיימ' שם הלכה יא טוש"ע שם סעיף ב

קכ ט מיי' שם הל' יו וסמג שם טוש"ע א"ח סימן עה סעיף ד

קכא י מיימ' שם פ"ג הלכה ז טוש"ע א"ח סי' עד סעיף ב וסימן פו

קכב כ ל מיי' שם פ"ג הלכה י טוש"ע א"ח סי' עז סעי' א

קכג מ נ מיימ' שם הל' יב וסמג שם טוש"ע א"ח סימן פז סעיף א

קכד ס ע מיי' פ"ד מהל' תפילין הל' כד ופ"י מה' ס"ת הל' ז סמג עשין כב טוש"ע א"ח סימן מ סעיף ב ובסימן רמ סעיף ו

מסורת הש"ס

לעיל דף ט: לקמן כו.

[דיבור זה שייך לעיל במשנה כב:]

יומא ל. קידושין כד. [מעילה יד:]

[שבת קכ. ע"ש]

[נזיר לח.]

תוספת' פ"ב

[ירוש' גרס טרקלין יוד על יוד וכו' ובמקום שיוציאם גרס שיכסנו]

[עירובין מג:]

[ע' פירש"י לעיל טז: ד"ה ברה]

cernible it is permitted, [25b] and here the difference between them is whether it must be wet enough to moisten something else?[3]

IF HE WENT DOWN [TO IMMERSE HIMSELF], IF HE IS ABLE TO COME UP etc. May we say that the Mishnah teaches anonymously the same as R. Eliezer, who said that [the *Shema'* may be recited] until the rising of the sun?[4] You may even say a that it is the same as R. Joshua,[1] and perhaps [the Mishnah] means this to apply to the *wathikin*, of whom R. Joḥanan said: The *wathikin* used to finish the recital with the rising of the sun.[2]

IF NOT, HE SHOULD COVER HIMSELF WITH WATER AND RECITE. But in this case his heart sees the sexual organs?—R. Eleazar said—or as some also say, R. Aḥa b. Abba b. Aḥa said in the name of our teacher:[3] They meant this to apply to turbid water which is like solid earth, in order that his heart should not see his sexual organ.

Our Rabbis taught: If the water is clear, he may sit in it up to his neck and say the *Shema'*; some say, he should stir it up with his foot. On the ruling of the first Tanna, his heart sees his nakedness?—He held that if his heart sees the sexual organ it is permitted. But his heel sees his nakedness?[4]—He held that if his heel sees his nakedness it is permitted. It has been stated: If his heel sees his nakedness it is permitted [to read the *Shema'*]; if it touches, Abaye says it is forbidden and Raba says it is permitted. This is the way in which R. Zebid taught this passage. R. Ḥinnena the son of R. Iḳa thus: If it touches, all agree that it is forbidden. If it sees, Abaye says it is forbidden and Raba says it is permitted; the Torah was not given to the ministering angels.[5] The law is that if it touches it is forbidden, but if it sees it is permitted.

Raba said: If one sees excrement through a glass,[6] he may recite the *Shema'* in face of it; if he sees nakedness through a glass, he must not recite the *Shema'* in face of it. 'If he sees excrement through a glass he may recite the *Shema'* in face of it', because [the permission or otherwise] in the case of excrement depends on whether it is covered.[7] 'If he sees nakedness through a glass it is forbidden to recite in face of it', because the All-Merciful said, *that He see no unseemly thing in thee*,[8] and here it is seen.

Abaye said: A little excrement may be neutralized with spittle; to which Raba added: It must be thick spittle. Raba said: If the excrement is in a hole, he may put his shoe over it and recite the *Shema'*. Mar the son of Rabina inquired: What is the rule if there is some dung sticking to his shoe?—This was left unanswered.

Rab Judah said: It is forbidden to recite the *Shema'* in face of a naked heathen. Why do you say a heathen? The same applies even to an Israelite!—In the case of an Israelite there is no question to him that it is forbidden, but this had to be stated in the case of a heathen. For you might have thought that since Scripture says of them, *Whose flesh is as the flesh of asses and whose issue is as* b *the issue of horses*,[1] therefore he is just like a mere ass. Hence we are told that their flesh also is called 'nakedness', as it says, *And they saw not their father's nakedness*.[2]

HE SHOULD NOT COVER HIMSELF EITHER WITH FOUL WATER OR WITH WATER IN WHICH SOMETHING HAS BEEN STEEPED UNTIL HE POURS WATER INTO IT. How much water must he go on pouring?[3]—What it means is this: He must not cover himself with foul water or with water used for steeping at all, nor [may he recite in face of] urine until he pours water into it.

Our Rabbis taught: How much water must he pour into it? A few drops [are enough]. R. Zakkai says: A *rebi'ith*.[4] R. Naḥman said: Where they differ is when the water is poured in last, but if the water was there first, a few drops are sufficient.[5] R. Joseph, however, said: Where they differ is if the water was there first; but if the water was poured in afterwards both agree that there must be a *rebi'ith*. R. Joseph once said to his attendant: Bring me a *rebi'ith* of water, as prescribed by R. Zakkai.

Our Rabbis taught: It is forbidden to recite the *Shema'* in face of a chamber pot for excrement or urine even if there is nothing in it, or in face of urine itself [if it is in another vessel] until he pours water into it. How much must he pour? A few drops. R. Zakkai says: A *rebi'ith*, whether it is in front of the bed or behind c the bed.[1] R. Simeon b. Gamaliel says: If it is behind the bed, he may recite the *Shema'*, if it is in front of the bed he may not recite, but he must remove four cubits and then recite. R. Simeon b. Eleazar says: Even if the room is a hundred cubits long he should not say the *Shema'* in it until he takes it away or places it under the bed. The question was asked: How did he [R. Simeon b. Gamaliel] mean? That if it is behind the bed he may recite at once and that if it is in front of the bed he must remove four cubits and then recite? Or did he perhaps mean it this way, that if it is behind the bed he removes to a distance of four cubits, but if it is in front of the bed he does not recite at all?—Come and hear, for it has been taught: R. Simeon b. Eleazar says: If it is behind the bed he may recite at once, if it is in front of the bed he removes four cubits. R. Simeon b. Gamaliel says: Even in a room a hundred cubits long he should not recite until he takes it out or puts it under the bed. Our question has been answered, but there is a contradiction between the Baraithas?—Reverse the [names in] the second one. What reason have you for reversing the second one? Why not reverse the first?—Who is recorded to have said that the whole room is like four cubits? R. Simeon b. Eleazar.[2]

R. Joseph said: I asked R. Huna as follows: There is no question in my mind that a bed with legs less than three handbreadths long is reckoned as being attached to the soil.[3] What of one with legs four, five, six, seven, eight or nine handbreadths long?—He replied: I do not know. About ten I was certain and did not need to ask. Said Abaye: You did well not to ask; ten handbreadths constitutes a different domain.[4] Raba said: The law is that less than three is regarded as attached to the soil, ten constitutes a different domain, from ten to three is what R. Joseph asked R. Huna about and he did not decide it for him. Rab said: The *halachah* follows R. Simeon b. Eleazar. So too said Bali in the name of R. Jacob the son of the d daughter of Samuel:[1] The *halachah* follows R. Simeon b. Eleazar. Raba, however, said: The *halachah* does not follow R. Simeon b. Eleazar.

R. Aḥai contracted a match for his son with the house of R. Isaac b. Samuel b. Marta. He brought him into the bridal chamber but it was not a success.[2] He went in after him to look, and saw a scroll of the Torah lying there. He said to them:[3] Had I not come now, you would have endangered the life of my son, for it has been taught: It is forbidden to have marital intercourse in a room in which there is a scroll of the Law or *tefillin*, until they are taken out or placed in one receptacle inside of another. Abaye said: This rule applies only to a receptacle which is not meant for them, but if the receptacles are specially meant for them, ten are no

(3) Only in this case does the first Tanna forbid, but R. Jose is more stringent. (4) V. *supra* 9b. And so the *halachah* is according to him.

a (1) Who says that the time is up to the third hour, v. *supra* 9b. (2) V. *supra* 9b, n. b4. (3) Rab. (4) Since his knees are bent under him. (5) As much as to say, too much must not be expected of human beings. (6) Lit., 'a lantern' or 'anything transparent'. (7) I.e., there is a partition between. (8) Deut. XXIII, 15.

b (1) Ezek. XXIII, 20. (2) Gen. IX, 23—of the sons of Noah. (3) As much as to say, how can he hope to neutralize such a quantity? (4) A quarter of a *log*. (5) Because each drop of urine becomes neutralized as it falls in.

c (1) I.e., whether the bed is between him and it or not. (2) The source of this dictum is not known (Rashi). (3) *Labud*, v. Glos. And therefore anything placed under it is like being buried in the ground, (e.g., a chamber pot) and the *Shema'* may be recited. (4) And therefore it is no covering.

d (1) V. *supra* 16a, n. b4. (2) Euphemism. (3) To the relatives of his daughter-in-law.

better than one. Raba said: A covering [26a] over a chest is like a receptacle within a receptacle.

R. Joshua b. Levi said: For a scroll of the Law it is necessary to make a partition of ten [handbreadths].[4] Mar Zuṭra was visiting R. Ashi, and he saw that in the place where Mar the son of R. Ashi slept there was a scroll of the Law and a partition of ten [handbreadths] was made for it. He said to him: Which authority are you following? R. Joshua b. Levi, is it not? I presume that R. Joshua b. Levi meant this to apply only where one had not another room, but your honour has another room! He replied: I had not thought of it.

HOW FAR SHOULD HE REMOVE FROM IT AND FROM EXCREMENT? FOUR CUBITS. Raba said in the name of R. Seḥora reporting Rab: This was meant only if he leaves it behind him, but if he keeps it in front of him he must remove completely out of sight. The same rule applies to *Tefillah*. Is that so? Has not Rafram b. Papa said in the name of R. Ḥisda: A man can stand facing a privy [four cubits away] and say the *Tefillah?*—What is referred to here?[5] A privy in which there is no excrement. Is that so? Has not R. Joseph b. Ḥanina said: When they spoke of a privy, they meant, even if there is no excrement in it, and when they spoke of a bath,[1] they meant even if there is no one in it! But in fact what is referred to here?[2] A new one. But surely this is the very thing about which Rabina asked a question: If a place has been set aside for a privy [but not yet used], what is the rule? Does setting aside count or does it not count?[3]—What Rabina wanted to know was whether one might stand in it to pray therein, but as to facing it [he was] not [in doubt].[4] Raba said: These Persian privies, although there is excrement in them, are counted as closed in.[5]

MISHNAH. A GONORRHOEIC PERSON WHO HAS AN EMISSION AND A NIDDAH FROM WHOM SEMEN ESCAPES AND A WOMAN WHO BECOMES NIDDAH DURING INTERCOURSE REQUIRE A RITUAL BATH; R. JUDAH, HOWEVER EXEMPTS THEM.[6]

GEMARA. The question was raised: What is R. Judah's opinion about a *ba'al ḳeri* who has become gonorrhoeic? Are we to say that the case in which R. Judah exempted was that of a gonorrhoeic patient who had a seminal issue, because his first condition precludes him from ablution,[7] but he does not exempt a *ba'al ḳeri* who becomes gonorrhoeic because in his first condition he does require ablution,[8] or are we to say that there is no difference?—Come and hear: A WOMAN WHO BECOMES NIDDAH DURING INTERCOURSE REQUIRES A RITUAL BATH: R. JUDAH, HOWEVER, EXEMPTS HER. Now a woman who becomes *niddah* during intercourse is on the same footing as a *ba'al ḳeri* who becomes gonorrhoeic, and R. Judah exempts her. This proves [that there is no difference]. R. Ḥiyya taught expressly: A *ba'al ḳeri* who has become gonorrhoeic requires ablution; R. Judah, however, exempts him.

CHAPTER IV

MISHNAH. THE MORNING TEFILLAH [CAN BE SAID] UNTIL MIDDAY; R. JUDAH SAYS TILL THE FOURTH HOUR. THE AFTERNOON PRAYER[1] [CAN BE SAID] TILL EVENING; R. JUDAH SAYS, UNTIL THE MIDDLE OF THE AFTERNOON.[2] THE EVENING PRAYER HAS NO FIXED LIMIT.[3] THE TIME FOR THE ADDITIONAL PRAYERS[4] IS THE WHOLE OF THE DAY; R. JUDAH SAYS, TILL THE SEVENTH HOUR.

GEMARA. [TILL MIDDAY]. This was contrasted with the following: The proper time for it [the *Shema'*] is at the rising of the sun, so that *ge'ullah* should be followed immediately by *Tefillah*, with the result that he would say the *Tefillah* in the day time![5]—That was taught in reference only to the *wathikin;* for R. Joḥanan said: The *wathikin* used to conclude it [the *Shema'*] as the sun rose.[6] And may other people delay till midday, but no longer? Has not R. Mari the son of R. Huna the son of R. Jeremiah b. Abba said in the name of R. Joḥanan: If a man erred and did not say the evening *Tefillah*, he says it twice in the morning. [If he erred] in the morning, he says it twice in the afternoon?—He may go on praying the whole day. But up to midday he is given the reward of saying the *Tefillah* in its proper time; thereafter he is given the reward of saying *Tefillah*, but not of saying *Tefillah* in its proper time.

The question was raised: If a man erred and did not say the afternoon *Tefillah*, should he say it twice in the evening? Should you argue from the fact that if he erred in the evening he prays twice in the morning, [I may reply that] this is because it is all one day, as it is written, *And there was evening and there was morning, one day;*[1] but in this case, prayer being in the place of sacrifice,[2] since the day has passed the sacrifice lapses. Or should we rather say that since prayer is supplication for mercy, a man may go on praying as long as he likes?—Come and hear: For R. Huna b. Judah said in the name of R. Isaac reporting R. Joḥanan: If a man erred and did not say the afternoon *Tefillah*, he says it twice in the evening, and we do not apply here the principle that if the day has passed the offering lapses. An objection was raised: *That which is crooked cannot be made straight, and that which is wanting cannot be numbered.*[3] *'That which is crooked cannot be made straight':* this applies to one who omitted the *Shema'* of the evening or the *Shema'* of the morning or the *Tefillah* of the evening or the *Tefillah* of the morning. *'And that which is wanting cannot be numbered':* this applies to one whose comrades formed a group to perform a religious act and he was not included with them.—R. Isaac said in the name of R. Joḥanan: With what case are we dealing here?[4] With one who omitted deliberately. R. Ashi said: The proof of this is that it says 'omitted', and it does not say, 'erred'. This proves it.

(4) To permit intercourse in the same room. (5) In the ruling of R. Ḥisda.

a (1) As being a forbidden place for meditating on words of Torah. (2) In the ruling of R. Ḥisda. (3) Shab. 10a; Ned. 7a. (4) That it was permitted at a distance of four cubits. (5) They were sloping and the excrement rolled into a deep hole out of sight. (6) V. *supra*, 21b, n. c4. (7) A gonorrhoeic patient has to wait seven days. (8) Before being able to study the Torah, according to the ordinance of Ezra, *supra*, 22b.

b (1) *Minḥah*, v. Glos. (2) This is explained in the Gemara. (3) V. *infra* in the Gemara. (4) *Musaf*, v. Glos. (5) I.e., just after day-break. (6) V. *supra* 9b.

c (1) Gen. I, 5. (2) V. *infra* 26b. (3) Eccl. I, 15. (4) In the teaching cited.

תורה אור

אקמטרא *ככלי בתוך כלי דמי אמר רבי יהושע בן לוי ספר תורה צריך לעשות לו מחיצה עשרה מר זוטרא איקלע לבי רב אשי חזייא לדוכתיה דמר בר רב אשי דמנח ביה ספר תורה ועביד ליה מחיצה עשרה א"ל כמאן כריב"ל *אימר דאמר ריב"ל דלית ליה ביתא אחרינא מר הא אית ליה ביתא אחרינא אמר ליה *לאו אדעתאי: כמה ירחיק מהן ומן הצואה ארבע אמות: אמר רבא אמר רב סחורה אמר רב הונא לא שנו אלא לאחוריו אבל לפניו מרחיק מלא עיניו וכן לתפלה איני והא אמר רפרם בר פפא אמר רב חסדא עומד אדם כנגד בית הכסא ומתפלל הכא במאי עסקינן בבית הכסא שאין בו צואה איני והאמר *רב יוסף בר חנינא בית הכסא שאמרו אע"פ שאין בו צואה ובית המרחץ שאמרו אע"פ שאין בו אדם אלא הב"ע בחדתי *והא מיבעיא ליה לרבינא הזמינו לבית הכסא מהו יש זימון או אין זימון כי קא מיבעיא ליה לרבינא למיקם עליה לצלויי בגויה אבל כנגדו לא אמר רבא הני בתי כסאי דפרסאי אף על גב דאית ביה צואה כסתומין דמו:

מתני' *זב שראה קרי ונדה שפלטה שכבת זרע והמשמשת שראתה נדה צריכין טבילה ורבי יהודה פוטר:

גמ' איבעיא להו בעל קרי שראה זיבה לר"י מהו כי פטר רבי יהודה התם בזב שראה קרי דמעיקרא לאו בר טבילה הוא אבל בעל קרי שראה זיבה דמעיקרא בר טבילה הוא מחייב או דילמא לא שנא ת"ש המשמש' וראתה נדה צריכה טבילה ורבי יהודה פוטר והא משמשת וראתה נדה כבעל קרי שראה זיבה דמיא וקא פטר רבי יהודה ש"מ תני רבי חייא בהדיא בעל קרי שראה זיבה צריך טבילה ורבי יהודה פוטר:

הדרן עלך מי שמתו

תפלת השחר עד חצות ר' יהודה אומר עד ד' שעות תפלת *המנחה עד הערב ר' יהודה אומר עד פלג המנחה תפלת הערב אין לה קבע *ושל מוספין כל היום (ר' יהודה אומר עד שבע שעות):

גמ' ורמינהי מצותה עם הנץ החמה כדי שיסמוך גאולה לתפלה ונמצא מתפלל ביום כי תניא ההיא לותיקין *דאמר ר' יוחנן ותיקין היו גומרין אותה עם הנץ החמה וכולי עלמא עד חצות ותו לא והאמר ר' מרי בריה דרב הונא בריה דר' ירמיה בר אבא א"ר יוחנן טעה ולא התפלל ערבית מתפלל בשחרית שתים שחרית מתפלל במנחה שתים כולי יומא מצלי ואזיל עד חצות יהבי ליה שכר תפלה בזמנה מכאן ואילך שכר תפלה יהבי ליה שכר תפלה בזמנה לא יהבי ליה איבעיא להו טעה ולא התפלל מנחה מהו שיתפלל ערבית ב' אם תימצי לומר טעה ולא התפלל ערבית מתפלל שחרית ב' משום דחד יומא הוא דכתיב °ויהי ערב ויהי בקר יום אחד אבל הכא תפלה במקום קרבן היא וכיון דעבר יומו בטל קרבנו או דילמא כיון דצלותא רחמי היא כל אימת דבעי מצלי ואזיל תא שמע דאמר רב הונא בר יהודה א"ר יצחק א"ר יוחנן טעה ולא התפלל מנחה מתפלל בערבית ב' ואין בזה משום דעבר יומו בטל קרבנו מיתיבי °מעות לא יוכל לתקון וחסרון לא יוכל להמנות *מעות לא יוכל לתקן זה שבטל ק"ש של ערבית וק"ש של שחרית או תפלה של ערבית או תפלה של שחרית וחסרון לא יוכל להמנות זה שנמנו חבריו לדבר מצוה ולא נמנה עמהם א"ר יצחק א"ר יוחנן הכא במאי עסקינן שבטל במזיד אמר רב אשי דיקא נמי דקתני בטל ולא קתני טעה שמע מינה:

תנו

רש"י

אקמטרא. ארגז של ספרים ובמגילה (ד' כו:) קמטרי דספרי וכן תרגם יונתן ובגנזי ברומים (יחזקאל כז) אולמין דזהירין מחתין בקמטרין וכן לאשר על המלתחה (מלכי' ב י) לדעל *קמטר': ככלי בתוך כלי דמי. דהא גלימא לאו כליין הוא: מחיצה עשרה. ואם לאו לא ישמש: לדוכתיה. במקום מטתו: לאו אדעתאי. לא נתתי לבי: כנגד בית הכסא. ברחוק ארבע אמות: דלית בה צואה. שפינו אותה: בית המרחץ. אסור להרהר בו: דפרסאי. בחפירה היו ופיהם ברחוק מן הגומא והוא בשיפוע והרעי מתגלגל ונופל לגומא:

מתני' זב שראה קרי. אף ע"פ שטומא טומאת ז' משום זיבה ואין טבילה זו מטהרתו אפ"ה צריך טבילה לדברי תורה כתקנת עזרא משום קרי וכן נדה אם באה להתפלל י"ח: פולטת שכבת זרע. הרי היא כבעל קרי כדאשכחן בסיני שלשת ימים אל תגשו אל אשה וגומר (שמות יט) לפי ששכבת זרע מטמא בפליטתו כל שלשה ולאחר מיכן כבר הסריח בגופה ואין ראוי עוד להזריע להיות עוד ולד נוצר הימנה וה"פ נדה שפלטה עתה התשמיש ששמשה אתמול קודם שראתה: ורבי יהודה פוטר. קסלקא דעתך השתא הואיל וטומאת זיבה קודמת והרי הוא טמא טומאה חמורה ואינה אוסרתו בדברי תורה כדאמרינן בפירקין הזבים והמצורעי' מותרים תו לא אתיא טומאת קרי דקילא ואסרה ליה:

גמ' לאו בר טבילה הוא. לדברי תורה ואע"פ שטומאתו חמור' ותו לא אתי קרי ומצריך ליה:

הדרן עלך מי שמתו

תפלת השחר: עד הערב. עד חשכ': עד פלג המנחה. בגמרא מפרש לה: אין לה קבע. כל הלילה זמנה ובגמרא מפרש מאי לשון אין לה קבע:

גמ' מצותה. של קריאת שמע: לותיקין. המקדימין למצות ומחזרי' לעשות דבר בזמנו ומצותו מקדימין לאחר הנץ החמה להתפלל וכי תנן במתניתין לאחרין שלא יאחר יותר מחצות שמשם ואילך עבר הזמן: וכולי עלמא. שאר המתפללין המאחרין עד חצות יכולין לאחר ותו לא: במנחה. הייתו אחר חצות: אם תימצי לומר. כלומר אם תשיבני בשאלתי מה שאמרנו טעה ולא התפלל ערבית וכו': וכיון דעבר יומו בטל קרבנו. ואינו מקריבו ביום אחר אם זמנו קבוע כגון *מוספים של כל יום ויום:

מבדיל

תוספות

ס"ת עושה לו מחילה. ודוקא ס"ת וגם בחומשים יש להחמיר כמו בס"ת אבל בשאר ספרים דיין בכסוי בעלמא:

הדרן עלך מי שמתו

תפלת השחר עד חצות וכו' תפלת המנחה עד הערב. ואם תאמר אמאי לא קתני גבי תפלת המנחה כל היום כמו גבי תפלת המוספין וי"ל דזמן מוספין הוא כל היום אפילו משחרית שהרי קרבנות יכול להקריב מיד אחר התמיד א"כ גם תפלת מוספין יכול להתפלל מיד מן הבקר מה שאין כן במנחה אלא משש שעות ומחצה והכי נמי בפ"ק דעכו"ם (דף ז:) לא ליצלי איניש תפלה דמוספין בתלת שעי קמייתא בריש שתא ביחיד כו' אלמא בשאר ימות השנה יכול להתפלל ולהכי מקדים תפלת המנחה לתפלת המוספים משום שהיא תדיר' בכל יום אע"פ שתפלת מוספים קודמת:

טעה ולא התפלל ערבית מתפלל בשחרית שתים. וא"ת והאמר רב לקמן (דף כז:) תפלת ערבית רשות וקי"ל כוותיה באיסורי ועוד קשה דאמר לקמן (דף ל:) טעה ולא התפלל יעלה ויבא בלילה אין מחזירין אותו משום דאין מקדשין את החדש בלילה ולמה ליה האי טעמא תיפוק ליה דתפלת ערבי' רשות ויש לומר הא דאמרינן דתפלת ערבית רשות היינו לגבי מצוה אחרת והיא עובר' דאז אמרינן תדחה תפלת ערבית מפניה אבל לחנם אין לו לבטלה *ומיהו אם איחר עד המנחה כראה דעבר זמנו בטל קרבנו כיון ששהה כל כך ולאחר ב' תפלות לא מלינו שתיקנו חכמים לחזור ולהתפלל אם שכח ואפילו תפלה אחת אם בטל במזיד לא יוכל לתקן ובשמוך קרי ליה מעות לא יוכל לתקן:

איבעיא להו טעה ולא התפלל תפלת מנחה כו'. לא בעי אם טעה ולא התפלל תפלת מוסף דהא ודאי אינו מתפלל בערבי' דהיאך יקרא את הקרבנו' וכבר עבר זמן מוסף וגם לא תיקנו שבע ברכות של מוסף אלא משום ונשלמה פרים שפתינו ומזה ודאי עבר זמנו בטל קרבנו אבל שאר תפלות דרחמי נינהו ולואי שיתפלל אדם כל היום כולו ואין כאן עבר זמנו בתפלת אחרת:

טעה

מסורת הש"ס

וכ"ה בל' יון

[שבת לה. ע"ש בפירש"י עירובין כט: ביצה דב. קידושין לג: פא: כתובו' ס: סנהדרין ה: מנחות לה: חולין ו.]

שבת פ"א ד' י. [ושם אי' ר' יוסי]

[נדרים ז. שבת י.]

לעיל ד' כא:

[ע' תו' לקמן כח. ד"ה ושל] פ"ק ד' ע: כה: תמידין

ברכות א

קהלת א

חגיגה ט:

עין משפט נר מצוה

קכה
א ב מיי' פ"י מה' ס"ת הל' ז' טוש"ע פ"ח סי' רמ סעי' ו

קכו
ג מיי' פ"ג מה' ק"ש הל' ח טוש"ע א"ח סי' עט סעי' א

קכז
ד מיי' שם הלכה ב' סמג עשין יח טוש"ע א"ח סי' פג סעי' א

קכח
ה מיי' שם הל' ג טוש"ע שם סעי' ב

קכט
ו שם סעי' ד

קל
ז מיי' פ"ד מהלכות ק"ש הל' ח ופ"ד מהל' תפלה הלכה ה סמג עשין יח טור א"ח סי' פח

[וע"ע תוס' יומא פז: ד"ה והאמ' ותוס' חגיגה ט: ד"ה או]

א
ח ט מיי' פ"ג מהל' תפלה הל' א' סמג עשין יט טוש"ע א"ח סי' פט סעי' א

ב
י מיי' שם הל' ה ט וסמג שם טוש"ע א"ח סי' קח סעי' ב'

ג
כ מיי' שם טוש"ע שם סעי' א

[ע' תוס' פסחים קז. ד"ה סמוך למנחה וכו' שני טעמים שנקרא תפלת המנחה]

ד
ל טוש"ע א"ח סי' פט סעי' א

ה
מ מיי' שם טוש"ע א"ח סי' קח סעי' ב וסי' רלד סעי' ב

ו
נ ס מיי' שם הל' ח טוש"ע שם סי' קח סעי' ז

תנו רבנן טעה ולא התפלל מנחה בערב שבת מתפלל בליל שבת שתים טעה ולא התפלל מנחה בשבת מתפלל במוצאי שבת שתים של חול מבדיל בראשונה ואינו מבדיל בשניה ואם הבדיל בשניה ולא הבדיל בראשונה שניה עלתה לו ראשונה לא עלתה לו למימרא דכיון דלא אבדיל בקמייתא כמאן דלא צלי דמי ומהדרינן ליה ורמינהי *טעה ולא הזכיר גבורות גשמים בתחיית המתים ושאלה בברכת השנים מחזירין אותו הבדלה בחונן הדעת אין מחזירין אותו מפני שיכול לאומרה על הכוס קשיא: אתמר ר' יוסי ב"ר חנינא אמר תפלות אבות תקנום *ר' יהושע בן לוי אמר תפלות כנגד תמידין תקנום תניא כותיה דר' יוסי ב"ר חנינא ותניא כותיה דרבי יהושע בן לוי תניא כותיה דר' יוסי בר' חנינא אברהם תקן תפלת שחרית שנאמר וישכם אברהם בבקר אל המקום אשר עמד שם* ואין עמידה אלא תפלה שנאמר ויעמוד פינחס ויפלל יצחק תקן תפלת מנחה שנאמר ויצא יצחק לשוח בשדה לפנות ערב ואין שיחה אלא תפלה שנאמר תפלה לעני כי יעטוף ולפני ה' ישפוך שיחו יעקב תקן תפלת ערבית שנאמר ויפגע במקום וילן שם *ואין פגיעה אלא תפלה שנאמר ואתה אל תתפלל בעד העם הזה ואל תשא בעדם רנה ותפלה ואל תפגע בי ותניא כותיה דרבי יהושע בן לוי *מפני מה אמרו תפלת השחר עד חצות שהרי תמיד של שחר קרב והולך עד חצות ור' יהודה אומר עד ארבע שעות שהרי תמיד של שחר קרב והולך עד ארבע שעות ומפני מה אמרו תפלת המנחה עד הערב שהרי תמיד של בין הערבים קרב והולך עד הערב רבי יהודה אומר עד פלג המנחה שהרי תמיד של בין הערבים קרב והולך עד פלג המנחה ומפני מה אמרו תפלת הערב אין לה קבע שהרי אברים ופדרים שלא נתעכלו מבערב קרבים והולכים כל הלילה ומפני מה אמרו של מוספין כל היום שהרי קרבן של מוספין קרב כל היום רבי יהודה אומר עד שבע שעות שהרי קרבן מוסף קרב והולך עד שבע שעות ואיזו היא מנחה גדולה משש שעות ומחצה ולמעלה ואיזו היא מנחה קטנה מתשע שעות ומחצה ולמעלה איבעיא להו רבי יהודה פלג מנחה קמא קאמר או פלג מנחה אחרונה קאמר ת"ש דתניא רבי יהודה אומר פלג מנחה אחרונה אמרו והיא אחת עשרה שעות חסר רביע נימא תיהוי תיובתיה דר' יוסי ברבי חנינא אמר לך רבי יוסי ב"ר חנינא לעולם אימא לך תפלות אבות תקנום ואסמכינהו רבנן אקרבנות דאי לא תימא הכי תפלת מוסף לר' יוסי ב"ר חנינא מאן תקנה אלא תפלות אבות תקנום ואסמכינהו רבנן אקרבנות: רבי יהודה אומר עד ארבע שעות: איבעיא להו *עד ועד בכלל או דילמא עד ולא עד בכלל ת"ש רבי יהודה אומר עד פלג המנחה אי אמרת בשלמא עד ולא עד בכלל היינו דאיכא בין רבי יהודה לרבנן אלא אי אמרת עד ועד בכלל רבי יהודה

היינו

מבדיל בראשונה. פעם ראשונה ומתפלל בשביל תפלה של עכשיו לפיכך אומר בה הבדלה בחונן הדעת והשניה היא בשביל תשלומי תפלת שבת אינו מבדיל בה: שניה עלתה לו. בשביל תפלת מוצ"ש וראשונה לא עלתה לו שאינה כלום שאין לו להקדים תפלה שעבר זמנה לתפלה שזמנה עכשיו והשניה נמי לא עלתה לו לשל שבת הואיל והבדיל בה גילה דעתו שאינה של שבת והיא תחשב לשל ערבית: אבות תקנום. כדקתני בברייתא לקמיה: כנגד תמידים תקנום. אנשי כנסת הגדולה: רבי יהודה. ס"ל שאין תמיד של שחר קרב אלא עד ארבע שעות: אברים. של עולות: ופדרים. של שאר קרבנות שנזרק דמן קודם שקיעת החמה קרבין כל הלילה וכנגדן תקנו תפלת ערבית: מנחה גדולה. אם בא להקדים תמיד של בין הערבים אינו יכול להקדימו קודם שש שעות ומחצה דבין הערבים כתיב ביה מכי ינטו צללי ערב משהחמה נוטה למערב דהיינו משש שעות ומחצה ולמעלה דאמר מר חצי שש וחצי שבע חמה עומדת בראש כל אדם באמצע הרקיע (פסחים דף לד.): מנחה קטנה. זמן תמיד של בין הערבים בכל יום מתשע שעות ומחצ' ולמעלה כדתנן בתמיד נשחט (דף כח.) נשחט בשמונה ומחצה וקרב בתשע ומחצה והתם מפרש טעמא: פלג מנחה אחרונה. חלק את ב' שעות ומחצה הנותרים ביום ותמצא פלג אחרון של מנחה מי"א שעות חסר רביע ולמעלה: דאי לא תימא הכי. דמודה רבי יוסי ברבי חנינא דרבנן אסמכינהו אקרבנות: תפלת המוספין מאן תקנה. אלא ע"כ רבנן אסמכינהו אקרבנות וכי עיינו במוספין ולא מצאו תפלה כנגדה עמדו הם ותקנוה: עד ועד בכלל. לרבי יהודה הוא דקא בעי דאלו לרבנן עד ולא עד בכלל:

היינו

טעה ולא התפלל ע"ש וכו' טעה ולא התפלל מנחה בשבת מתפלל ערבית שתים דהיינו של מוצאי שבת ומבדיל בראשונה וכו'. כתב רבינו יהודה אם טעה ולא הזכיר ר"ח במנח' לא יתפלל עוד בלילה דלמה יתפלל עוד הרי כבר התפלל כל תפלת המנחה מבעוד יום לבד ר"ח שלא הזכיר א"כ אין מרויח כלום אם יחזור ויתפלל במוצאי ר"ח הרי לא יזכיר עוד תפלת ר"ח וי"ח כבר התפלל ולא דמי להא דאמר הכא טעה ולא התפלל מנחה בשבת דמתפלל ערבי' בחול שתים פירוש של חול משום שלא התפלל כלל אם כן ירויח תפלת י"ח כשמתפלל במוצאי שבת אף על פי שלא יזכיר של שבת וא"ת והלא הוא מתפלל יותר ממה שהוא חייב להתפלל שלא היה לו להתפלל כי אם שבע ברכות והוא מתפלל י"ח בכך אין לחוש שגם בשבת היה דין שיתפלל כל י"ח רק שלא הצריכוהו מפני הטורח נמצא שמרויח כל תפלתו. אבל כשטעה ולא הזכיר של ר"ח כבר התפלל א"כ לא ירויח כלום אם יתפלל במוצאי ר"ח דהא נמי אם התפלל במנחה בשבת י"ח שלמו' ולא הזכיר של שבת נראה דלמ"ש לא יתפלל שתים דכבר התפלל י"ח ברכות ומיהו ברב אלפס לא משמע כן דאפילו היכא דאינו מרויח כלום מצריך להתפלל פעם אחרת וזה לשונו שכתב הא דקאמר שמבדיל בראשונה ואינו מבדיל בשני' ואם לא הבדיל בראשונה והבדיל בשני' שניה עלת' לו ראשונה לא עלת' לו דאיבעי ליה לאקדומי תפלה שניה ברישא דהכי חובה וכיון דלא אבדיל ברישא ואבדיל בבתרייתא גלי דעתיה דהך בתרייתא היא חובה הלכך בעי למהדר ולצלויי זימנא אחריתי כדי להקדים חובת שעתיה ברישא ואי אבדיל בתרוייהו אף ע"ג דלא מיבעי ליה למעבד הכי לא מחייב לאהדורי ואי לא אבדיל אפילו בחדא מנהון לא מהדרינן ליה דתניא טעה ולא הזכיר הבדלה בחונן הדעת אין מחזירין אותו מפני שיכול לאומר' על הכוס עכ"ל אלמא דמצריך להתפלל זימנא אחריתי אף ע"ג שלא יחזור ויתפלל פעם שניה יותר מבראשונה. כך היה נראה לה"ר משה מא"לאוור' מתוך לשון האלפסי:

קשיא תימה אמאי לא משני דמיירי קודם שהעשירו דאמרי' לקמן בפר' אין עומדין (דף לג.) העשירו קבעוה על הכוס וי"ל דלא אשכחן ברייתא דשנית בין ב' תקנות:

יצחק תקן תפלת המנחה. ואע"ג דאמרי' [יומא כח:] צלו צלות' דאברה' מכי שחרי כתלי ויש לומר היינו אחר שתקנה יצחק: ואין שיחה אלא תפלה שנאמר תפלה לעני כי יעטוף. תימה דבפ"ק דעכו"ס (ד' ז: וע"ש) מוכיח דשיחה [זו] תפלה מויצא יצחק לשוח בשד' י"ל דכיוצא בו מצינו במגילה (פ"ק דף יג.) ויהי אומן את הדסה ואין הדסי' אלא צדיקים דכתיב והוא עומד בין ההדסים ובפרק חלק (ד' לג.) הוא אומר להפך: יעקב תקן תפלת ערבית. תימה דאמר בפרק גיד הנשה (ד' לא:) וילך חרנה כי מטי לחרן בעי למיהדר אמר אפשר שעברתי במקום וכו' אלמא דהתם מוכח דהתפלל ערבית ביום מאחר שהתפלל כבר והוה דעתיה למהדר וקשה למתני' דפ"ק דקאמר שאינו זמן תפלה עד צאת הכוכבי' ולפי מה שפירשנו דקי"ל כרבי יהודה דאמר עד פלג המנחה ניחא ויפה מנהג שלנו *דאדרבה טוב להתפלל מבעוד יום קצת: עד פלג המנח'. תימה מנא ליה הא בשלמא עד ט' שעות ומחצ' דעד אותה זמן הוי תפלת המנחה ניחא דהיינו מנח' קטנה אבל הא מנא ליה וי"ל דר"י ס"ל דתפלה כנגד קטרת תקנוה דכתיב תכון תפלתי קטרת לפניך (תהלים קמא): איבעיא להו עד ועד בכלל וכו'. תימה דאמר בנדה פרק הרואה כתם (ד' נח:) כל שיעורי חכמים להחמיר חוץ מכגרים של כתמים אלמא עד ולא עד בכלל וי"ל אי אמרי' עד ועד בכלל יש בו גם חומרא שיתפלל ולא אמרינן עבר זמנו בטל קרבנו ואפילו במזיד:

ת"ש

עין משפט נר מצוה

ז
א מיי' פ"ג מהלכו' תפלה הל' טו סמג עשין יט טוש"ע א"ח סי' קח סעי' ע

ח
ב שם סעי' י

ט
ג מיי' פרק י שם הלכה ח סמג שם טוש"ע א"ח סי' קיד סעיף ה'

י
ד מיי' שם הל' ט וסמג שם טוש"ע א"ח סי' קיז סעי' ד

יא
ה מיי' שם הלכה יד טוש"ע א"ח סי' רלד סעי' א

יב
ו מיי' פ"א מה' תפלה הלכה ה ו טוש"ע א"ח סי' לא סעי' ד [רב אלפס ברכו' פ"ג דף יד:]

יג
ז ח מיי' פ"ג שם הלכה ד וסמג שם טוש"ע א"ח סי' רלג סעי' א

[עיי' פסקי תוס' פ' הקומץ רבה סקי"ז]

מסורת הש"ס

תוספתא פ"ג לקמן ד' כט. דף לג. תענית כ"ז דף ג:

(גי' ירוש' ריב"ל אמר תפלות מאבות למדום)

[לעיל ו:]

[תענית ז: ס'. סוטה יד. סנה' לה:]

תוספת' פ"ג

[עירובין פב: פסחים קיז: ר"ה ל: סוכה מח: נזיר ו: מנחות סח: חולין מו. כד: עירובין יח. נדה כח:]

תורה אור

בראשית יט
תהלים קו
בראשית כד
תהלים קב
בראשית כח
ירמיה ז

[26b] Our Rabbis taught: If a man erred and did not say the afternoon prayer on the eve of Sabbath, he says the [Sabbath] *Tefillah*[5] twice on the night of the Sabbath. If he erred and did not say the afternoon *Tefillah* on Sabbath, he says the [weekday] *Tefillah* twice on the outgoing of the Sabbath; he says *habdalah*[6] in the first but not in the second;[7] and if he said *habdalah* in the second and not in the first, the second is counted to him, the first is not counted to him. This is equivalent, is it not, to saying that since he did not say *habdalah* in the first, it is as if he had not said the *Tefillah* and we make him say it again. To this was opposed the following: If one forgot and did not mention the miracle of rain[8] in the benediction for the resurrection of the dead[9] and prayed for rain in the benediction of the years,[10] he is turned back; if he
a forgot *habdalah* in 'who graciously grants knowledge',[1] he is not turned back, because he can say it over wine!—This is indeed a difficulty.

It has been stated: R. Jose son of R. Ḥanina said: The *Tefillahs* were instituted by the Patriarchs. R. Joshua b. Levi says: The *Tefillahs* were instituted[2] to replace the daily sacrifices. It has been taught in accordance with R. Jose b. Ḥanina, and it has been taught in accordance with R. Joshua b. Levi. It has been taught in accordance with R. Jose b. Ḥanina: Abraham instituted the morning *Tefillah*, as it says, *And Abraham got up early in the morning to the place where he had stood*,[3] and 'standing' means only prayer, as it says, *Then stood up Phineas and prayed*.[4] Isaac instituted the afternoon *Tefillah*, as it says, *And Isaac went out to meditate in the field at eventide*,[5] and 'meditation' means only prayer, as it says, *A prayer of the afflicted when he fainteth and poureth out his meditation*[6] *before the Lord*.[7] Jacob instituted the evening prayer, as it says, *And he lighted* [wa-yifga'] *upon the place*,[8] and *'pegi'ah'* means only prayer, as it says, *Therefore pray not thou for this people neither lift up prayer nor cry for them, neither make intercession to* [tifga'] *Me*.[9] It has been taught also in accordance with R. Joshua b. Levi: Why did they say that the morning *Tefillah* could be said till midday? Because the regular morning sacrifice could be brought up to midday. R. Judah, however, says that it may be said up to the fourth hour because the regular morning sacrifice may be brought up to the fourth hour. And why did they say that the afternoon *Tefillah* can be said up to the evening? Because the regular afternoon offering can be brought up to the evening. R. Judah, however, says that it can be said only up to the middle[10] of the afternoon, because the evening offering could only be brought up to the middle of the afternoon. And why did they say that for the evening *Tefillah* there is no limit? Because the limbs[11] and the fat[12] which were not consumed [on the altar] by the evening could be brought for the whole of the night. And why did they say that the addi-
b tional *Tefillahs*[1] could be said during the whole of the day? Because the additional offering could be brought during the whole of the day. R. Judah, however, said that it can be said only up to the seventh hour, because the additional offering can be brought up to the seventh hour. Which is the 'greater afternoon'? From six hours and a half onwards.[2] And which is the 'small afternoon'? From nine hours and onwards.[3] The question was raised: Did R. Judah refer to the middle of the former afternoon-tide or the middle of the latter afternoon-tide?[4] Come and hear: for it has been taught: R. Judah said: They referred to the middle of the latter afternoon-tide, which is eleven hours less a quarter.[5] Shall we say that this is a refutation of R. Jose b. Ḥanina?[6] R. Jose b. Ḥanina can answer: I can still maintain that the Patriarchs instituted the *Tefillahs*, but the Rabbis found a basis for them in the offerings. For if you do not assume this,[7] who according to R. Jose b. Ḥanina instituted the additional *Tefillah*? He must hold therefore that the Patriarchs instituted the *Tefillahs* and the Rabbis found a basis for them in the offerings.[8]

R. JUDAH SAYS: TILL THE FOURTH HOUR. It was asked: Is the point mentioned itself included in the UNTIL or is it not included?[9]—Come and hear: R. JUDAH SAYS, UNTIL THE MIDDLE OF THE AFTERNOON. If you say that the point mentioned is included in the UNTIL, then there is no difficulty; this is where the difference lies between R. Judah and the Rabbis.[10] But if you say
c that the point mentioned is not included,[1] then R. Judah says

(5) V. Glosses. Vilna Geron. (6) V. *P.B.* p. 46. (7) Because the one which is said in compensation is always said second. (8) Lit., 'the (divine) power (manifested) in rain'. (9) The second benediction. (10) The ninth benediction.
a (1) The fourth benediction. (2) By the Men of the Great Synagogue. (3) Gen. XIX, 27. (4) Ps. CVI, 30. (5) Gen. XXIV, 63. (6) E.V. *'complaint'*. (7) Ps. CII, 1. (8) Gen. XXVIII, 11. (9) Jer. VII, 16. (10) The precise time meant is discussed *infra*. (11) Of the burnt-offerings. (12) Of the other offerings.
b (1) Said on Sabbaths, New Moons, and holy days. (2) From 12.30 p.m. to 6 p.m. taking the day from 6 a.m. to 6 p.m. (3) From 3.30 onwards. (4) I.e., does he in his statement in the Mishnah mean midway between 12.30 and 6 or between 3.30 and 6? (5) Viz., midway between $9\frac{1}{2}$ hours and 12. (6) According to him it was the Patriarchs who instituted the prayers, and the time of the sacrifice should have no bearing on the time of the recital of the prayers. (7) That R. Jose admits that the Rabbis based the *Tefillah* on the offerings. (8) And accordingly added a *musaf tefillah* to those instituted by the Patriarchs, and for the same reason they made the time of the prayers to be determined by the time of the sacrifices. (9) I.e., does he mean the beginning or the end of the fourth hour? (10) Assuming that R. Judah meant the middle of the latter afternoontide, i.e., eleven hours less a quarter.
c (1) So that 'until' means until the end of the point fixed by him.

the same thing as the [27*a*] Rabbis?—You conclude then that the point mentioned is not included in the UNTIL? Look now at the next clause: THE TIME FOR THE ADDITIONAL PRAYERS IS THE WHOLE DAY; R. JUDAH SAYS, TILL SEVEN HOURS, and it has been taught: If a man had two *Tefillahs* to say, one for *musaf*[2] and one for *minḥah*,[2] he says first the *minḥah* prayer and afterwards the *musaf* one, because the former is daily and the latter is not daily. R. Judah, however, says: He says the *musaf* one and afterwards the *minḥah* one, because the [time for] the former [soon] lapses, while the [time for] the latter does not [so soon] lapse.[3] Now if you say that the point mentioned is included in the UNTIL there is no difficulty: on this supposition you can find a time which is appropriate to both of the *Tefillahs*.[4] But if you say that the point mentioned is not included in the UNTIL where can you find a time which is appropriate to both the *Tefillahs*?[5] As soon as the time for *minḥah* has arrived, the time for *musaf* has passed!—What then? You say that the point mentioned is included in the UNTIL? Then there is the [afore-mentioned] difficulty of the first clause—what difference is there between R. Judah and the Rabbis?—Do you think that this MIDDLE OF THE AFTERNOON mentioned by R. Judah means the second half? It means the first half, and what he meant is this: When does the first half [of the second part of the afternoon] end and the second half begin? At the end of eleven hours less a quarter.

R. Naḥman said: We also have learnt: R. Judah b. Baba testified five things—that they instruct a girl-minor to refuse,[6] that a woman may remarry on the evidence of one witness [that her husband
a is dead],[1] that a cock was stoned in Jerusalem because it killed a human being,[2] that wine forty days old was poured as a drink-offering on the altar,[3] and that the morning daily offering was brought at four hours.[4] This proves, does it not, that the point mentioned is included in the UNTIL? It does. R. Kahana said: The *halachah* follows R. Jose because we have learnt in the Select Tractate[5] as taught by him.

'And concerning the regular daily offering that it was brought at four hours'. Who is the authority for what we have learnt: *And as the sun waxed hot it melted:*[6] this was at four hours. You say at four hours: or is it not so, but at six hours? When it says *'in the heat of the day'*,[7] here we have the expression for six hours. What then am I to make of *'as the sun waxed hot it melted'?* At four hours. Whose opinion does this represent? Apparently neither R. Judah's nor the Rabbis'. For if we go by R. Judah, up to four hours also is still morning;[8] if we go by the Rabbis, up to six hours is also still morning!—If you like I can say it represents the opinion of R. Judah, and if you like of the Rabbis. 'If you like I can say it represents the opinion of the Rabbis': Scripture says, *morning by morning*,[9] thus dividing the morning into two.[10] 'If you like I can say R. Judah': this extra 'morning' indicates that they began [gathering] an hour beforehand.[11] At any rate all agree that *'as the sun waxed hot it melted'* refers to four hours. How does the text imply this? R. Aḥa b. Jacob said: The text says, *As the sun waxed hot it melted*. Which is the hour when the sun is hot and the shade is cool? You must say, at four hours.

THE AFTERNOON TEFILLAH TILL EVENING. R. Ḥisda said to R. Isaac: In the other case [of the morning offering] R. Kahana said that the *halachah* follows R. Judah because we have learnt in the Select Tractate as [taught] by him. What is the decision in this case?—He was silent, and gave him no answer at all. Said R. Ḥisda: Let us see for ourselves. Seeing that Rab says the Sabbath *Tefillah* on the eve of Sabbath while it is still day, we
b conclude that the *halachah* follows R. Judah![1]—On the contrary, from the fact that R. Huna and the Rabbis did not pray till night time, we conclude that the *halachah* does not follow R. Judah! Seeing then that it has not been stated definitely that the law follows either one or the other, if one follows the one he is right and if one follows the other he is right. Rab was once at the house of Genibah and he said the Sabbath *Tefillah* on the eve of Sabbath, and R. Jeremiah b. Abba was praying behind Rab and Rab finished but did not interrupt the prayer of R. Jeremiah.[2] Three things are to be learnt from this. One is that a man may say the Sabbath *Tefillah* on the eve of Sabbath. The second is that a disciple may pray behind his master. The third is that it is forbidden to pass in front of one praying. But is that so? Did not R. Ammi and R. Assi use to pass?—R. Ammi and R. Assi used to pass outside a four cubit limit. But how could R. Jeremiah act thus, seeing that Rab Judah has said in the name of Rab: A man should never

(2) V. Glos. (3) *Musaf* can be said up to seven hours and *minḥah* up to eleven hours less a quarter. (4) Viz., the second half of the seventh hour. (5) Because when R. Judah says that the time for *musaf* is 'till the seventh hour', he must exclude the whole of the seventh hour itself. (6) If a girl-minor who has lost her father is betrothed by her mother, when she becomes mature she can refuse to continue to be bound to her husband, and on some occasions the Beth din instruct her to refuse. V. Glos. s.v. *mi'un;* Yeb. 109*a*.
a (1) V. Yeb. 122*a*. (2) It pierced the skull of a child. (3) Being no longer 'new wine', v. 'Ed. VI, 1. (4) As R. Judah says; which shows that he included the 'four hours' in the 'until'. (5) *Beḥirta* (selected). Eduyyoth is so called because all its statements are accepted as *halachah;* v. Introduction to 'Ed. (Sonc. ed.). (6) Ex. XVI, 21. (7) Gen. XVIII, 1. Here the word 'day' is used, implying that it was hot everywhere, and not only in the sun, v. *infra*. (8) It says that the Israelites gathered the manna every morning; why then had they stopped at this hour if it was still morning? (9) Ex. loc. cit. Lit., 'in the morning, in the morning'. (10) And the Israelites gathered in the first 'morning'. (11) Thus finishing in the third hour of the day.
b (1) That after the middle of the afternoon-tide, the afternoon *Tefillah* can no longer be said, and evening begins. (2) By passing in front of him to resume his seat.

תורה אור

היינו רבנן אלא מאי עד ולא עד בכלל *אימא סיפא ושל מוספין כל היום ר' יהודה אומר עד שבע שעות ותניא *היו לפניו שתי תפלות אחת של מוסף ואחת של מנחה מתפלל של מנחה ואח"כ של מוסף שזו תדירה וזו אינה תדירה רבי יהודה אומר מתפלל של מוסף ואח"כ של מנחה שזו עוברת וזו אינה עובר' אי אמרת בשלמא עד ועד בכלל היינו דמשכחת להו ב' תפלות בהדי הדדי אלא אי אמרת עד ולא עד בכלל היכי משכחת להו שתי תפלות בהדי הדדי כיון דאתיא לה של מנחה אזלא לה של מוספין אלא מאי עד ועד בכלל קשיא רישא מאי איכא בין רבי יהודה לרבנן מי סברת דהאי פלג מנחה פלג אחרונה קאמר פלג ראשונה קאמר והכי קאמר אימת נפיק פלג ראשונה ועייל פלג אחרונה מכי נפקי י"א שעות חסר רביע אמר רב נחמן אף אנן נמי תנינא *רבי יהודה בן בבא העיד ה' דברים [א]שממאנין את הקטנה ושמשיאין [ב]את האשה ע"פ עד אחד ועל [ג]תרנגול שנסקל בירושלים על שהרג את הנפש ועל [ד]יין בן מ' יום שנתנסך ע"ג המזבח *ועל [ה]תמיד של שחר שקרב בארבע שעות ש"מ [ו]עד ועד בכלל ש"מ אמר רב כהנא [ז]הלכה כר' יהודה הואיל ותנן *בבחירתא כוותיה: ועל תמיד של שחר שקרב בד' שעות מאן תנא להא *דתנן °וחם השמש ונמס בארבע שעות אתה אומר בד' שעות או אינו אלא בשש שעות כשהוא אומר °כחום היום הרי שש שעות אמור הא מה אני מקיים וחם השמש ונמס בד' שעות מני לא רבי יהודה ולא רבנן אי ר' יהודה עד ארבע שעות נמי צפרא הוא אי רבנן עד חצות נמי צפרא הוא אי בעית אימא רבי יהודה אי בעית אימא רבנן אי בעית אימא רבנן אמר קרא בבקר בבקר חלקהו לשני בקרים ואי בעית אימא רבי יהודה האי בקר יתירא להקדים לו שעה אחת דכולי עלמא מיהא וחם השמש ונמס בארבע שעות מאי משמע אמר רבי אחא בר יעקב אמר קרא וחם השמש ונמס איזו הוא שעה שהשמש חם והצל צונן הוי אומר בארבע שעות: תפלת המנחה עד הערב וכו': אמר ליה רב חסדא לרב יצחק התם אמר רב כהנא הלכה כר' יהודה הואיל ותנן בבחירתא כוותיה הכא מאי אשתיק ולא אמר ליה ולא מידי אמר רב חסדא נחזי אנן מדרב מצלי של שבת בערב שבת מבעוד יום שמע מינה הלכה כרבי יהודה אדרבה מדרב הונא ורבנן לא הוו מצלו עד אורתא ש"מ אין הלכה כר' יהודה השתא דלא אתמר הלכתא לא כמר ולא כמר [ח]דעבד כמר עבד ודעבד כמר עבד רב איקלע לבי גניב' וצלי של שבת בערב שבת והוה מצלי ר' ירמיה בר אבא לאחוריה דרב וסיים רב ולא פסקיה לצלותיה דרבי ירמיה שמע מינה תלת ש"מ [ט]מתפלל אדם של שבת בערב שבת ושמע מינה מתפלל תלמיד אחורי רבו ושמע מינה [י]אסור לעבור כנגד המתפללין מסייע ליה לריב"ל דאמר ריב"ל אסור לעבור כנגד המתפללין איני והא ר' אמי ור' אסי חלפי ר' אמי ור' אסי חוץ לארבע אמות הוא דחלפי ורבי ירמיה היכי עביד הכי והא אמר רב יהודה אמר רב לעולם אל יתפלל אדם לא

שמות טז / דברים יח (margin references: שמות יו, בראשית יח)

רש"י

היינו רבנן. דקס"ד רבי יהודה פלג אחרון של מנחה אחרונה קאמר: מתפלל של מנחה וכו'. רבנן לטעמייהו דאמרי תפלת המוספים כל היום כמו של מנחה הלכך תדיר קודם ורבי יהודה לטעמיה דאמר מוספין עד שבע שעות ותו לא והויא לה מלוה עוברת ושל מנחה יש לה עוד שהות עד פלג המנחה: שתי תפלות בהדי הדדי. אלי האחרון של שעה שביעית הוא זמן לשתיהן דהא אמר מנחה גדולה משש שעות ומחצה ולמעלה: היכי משכחת לה. הרי עבר זמן המוספין משעברה שעה ששית: פלג ראשונה. של מנחה אחרונה ועד בכלל ואע"ג דתנא יהב סימנא לפלג אחרונה דקתני איזו פלג מנחה מי"א שעות חסר רביע ה"ק כו': אף אנן נמי תנינא. לרבי יהודה עד ועד בכלל: שממאנין את הקטנה. קטנה שהשיאתה אמה לאחר מיתת אביה דמדאורייתא אין קידושיה כלום שהרי קטנה אינה בת דעת ואת אמה לא זכתה תורה להיות לה כח לקדשה אלא לאב שנ' את בתי נתתי לאיש הזה (דברים כב) ומיהו רבנן תקינו לה קידושין להצריכה מיאון כדי שישאוה ולא תלא לזנות לפיכך אם מיאנה לאחר זמן ואמרה אי אפשי בו יוצאת ומותרת לכל אדם ואינה צריכה הימנו גט. והעי"ד רבי יהודה בן בבא שפעמים שמלוה על ב"ד ללמדה שתמאן בו כגון שני אחים נשואין שתי אחיות יתומות אחת גדולה וקידושי' קידושי תורה ואחת קטנה שאין קידושיה אלא מדרבנן ומת בעלה של גדולה בלא בנים ונפלה לפני אחיו ליבום ונמצאת זקוק' לו מן התורה וזיקה זו אוסרת את אשתו עליו משום אחות זקוקה שהיא כאחות אשתו וא"ר אליעזר במסכת יבמות (ד' קט.) מלמדין קטנה זו שתמאן בבעלה ותעקור קידושי' למפרע ותעשה כל בעילותיה כאלו הן של זנות כדי להתיר את בעלה ליבם את אחותה דתנן נושאים על האנוסה ועל המפותה (יבמות דף לז.) והעיד רבי יהודה בן בבא ביום שנשנית עדיות שהלכה כרבי אליעזר: על פי עד אחד. שאמר להמית בעלך במדינות הים (יבמות דף קכב.): שנסקל תרנגול. שנקר קדקדו של תינוק במקום שהמוח רופס ונקב את מוחו וסקלוהו כמשפט שור שנגח את האדם דכתיב (שמות כא) השור יסקל וגמרינן בג"ש שור שור משבת לעשות כל בהמה חיה ועוף כשור (ב"ק דף כד:): ועל יין בן מ' יום. שיצא מכלל יין מגתו ובא לכלל יין גמור וקרינן ביה נסך שכר (במדבר כח): בד' שעות. ותו לא אלמא כרבי יהודה ס"ל וקאמר בד' שעות אלמא לרבי יהודה עד ועד בכלל: הלכה כרבי יהודה. דמתניתין דאין תמיד של שחר קרב לאחר ד' שעות וה"ה לתפלה: בבחירתא. עדיות קרי בחירתא שהלכה כאותן עדיות: כשהוא אומר כחום היום הרי ו' שעות אמור. כלומר מליכו במקום אחר שכינה הכתוב בלשונו ואמר והוא יושב פתח האוהל כחום היום ולא אמר כחום השמש אלא היום משמע כל המקומות חמין בין חמה בין צל הוא ומדבר בשעה ששית הא מה אני מקיים וחם השמש דמשמע השמש חם והצל צונן: בד' שעות. דאלו קודם ד' שעות אף השמש צונן: מני. הא דמשמע דד' לאו בקר הוא דהא כתיב וילקטו אותו בבקר בבקר וחם השמש ונמס הנותר ומדמוקי ונמס בד' שעות מכלל דלאו זמן לקיטה היא ולאו בקר מיקרי: ד' שעות נמי צפרא הוא. דהא אמרת עד ועד בכלל וגבי תמיד כתיב תעשה בבקר: לשני בקרים. שלא היו לוקטים אלא בשלש שעות ראשונות שהוא בקר ראשון: התם אמר רב כהנא. גבי תפלת השחר: של שבת בערב שבת. שקבל עליו שבת מבעוד יום: שמע מינה. כרבי יהודה ס"ל דאמר מפלג המנחה אזל ליה זמן תפלת המנחה ועייל ליה זמן תפלת ערבית: ולא פסקיה לצלותיה. כלומר לא הפסיק בין רבי ירמיה ולכותל לעבור לפניו ולישב במקומו אלא עמד על עמדו:

תוספות

תא שמע ושל מוספין כל היום ורבי יהודה אומר עד שבע שעות ותניא היו לפניו וכו' ולא גרסינן אימא סיפא ושל וכו' שאינו במשנה שדברי ר' יהודה שאמר עד ז' שעות אינו במשנה ויש ספרים שהגיהו אותו במשנה ומיהו בכל הספרים הישנים אינו. וא"ת ורבי למה לא הזכיר אותו במשנה וי"ל משום דלא ס"ל כוותיה בהא דאמר עד ז' שעות אבל בהא דקאמר עד ד' שעות ס"ל כוותיה משום דתנן בבחירת' כוותיה ובההיא דפלג המנחה נמי משום דאמרינן לקמן דעבד כמר עבד ודעבד כמר עבד דהכי פירושו דעבד כר' יהודה (עבד) דאמר מפלג המנחה ליליא הוא עבד ומשום הכי מנחה לא אבל אין לפרש הכל בתפלת המנחה ועבד כרבי יהודה שהתפלל מנחה קודם פלג דפשיטא דרבנן מודו בשיעורו דרבי יהודה:

דרב צלי של שבת בע"ש. תימה דהא אמרינן בפרק במה מדליקין (דף כג:) ובלבד שלא יקדים ושלא יאחר וי"ל דהתם בשאינו מקבל עליו שבת מיד אבל הכא מיירי שמקבל עליו שבת מ"ד הלכך לא הויא הקדמה וטעמא משום דס"ל כרבי יהודה וכן הכך דלקמן שהתפלל של מ"ש בשבת היינו משום דסבירא להו כר' יהודה לענין תפלת הערב שהיא שעה ורביע קודם הלילה אעפ"כ [אין] אסור לעשות מלאכה *במ"ש מיד לאחר פלג המנחה וכן לענין תוספת שבת *(וע' בתב) ויה"כ דק"ל שהוא מן התור' *א"כ לא צריך שיעור גדול כל כך: ולא

מסורת הש"ס

[ע' תוס' חולין כח. ד"ה כל שיעורי] לקמן דף כח:

עדיות פ"ו דף ז: נדה פ"ק דף ח.

[ע' תוס' מנחו' כד: ד"ה ועל]

[קידושין כד: בכורות כו.] מכילתא דר"י פרשת בשלח

עין משפט נר מצוה

יד [א]מיי' פ"ד מה' יבום וחליצה הל' טו טוש"ע אה"ע סי' קנה סעי' יא

טו [ב]מיי' פי"ג מה' גרושין הלכה טו סמג עשין נ טוש"ע אה"ע סי' יז סעי' ג

טז [ג]מיי' פרק י' מה' נזקי ממון הל' ב סמג עשין ז

יז [ד]מיי' פרק ו מה' איסורי מזבח הל' ה

יח [ה]מיי' פ"א מה' תמידין הל' ב סמג עשין קל

יט [ו] [ז] מיי' פרק ג מהלכות תפל' הל' א' סמג ע' יט טוש"ע א"ח סי' פט סעיף א

[בע"ם] [וי"ע] [אפ"ה]

כ [ח]מיי' שם הל' ז וסמג שם טוש"ע א"ח סי' רלג סעיף א

כא [ט]מיי' שם הלכ' ז סמג ע' כט טוש"ע א"ח סי' רסז סעיף ב

כב [י]מיי' פרק ה מהלכו' תפלה הלכה ה סמג עשין יט טוש"ע א"ח סי' קב סעי' ד

כנגד

לא [א]כנגד רבו ולא אחורי רבו ותניא ר' אליעזר אומר [ב]המתפלל אחורי רבו והנותן שלום לרבו והמחזיר שלום לרבו *[ג]והחולק על ישיבתו של רבו והאומר *[ד]דבר שלא שמע מפי רבו גורם לשכינה שתסתלק מישראל שאני רבי ירמיה בר אבא [ה]דתלמי' חבר הוה והיינו *דקאמר ליה רבי ירמיה בר אבא לרב מי בדלת אמר ליה אין בדילנא ולא אמר מי בדיל מר ומי בדיל והאמר רבי אבין פעם אחת התפלל ר' של שבת בע"ש ונכנס למרחץ ויצא ושנה לן פרקין ועדיין לא חשכה *אמר רבא ההוא דנכנס להזיע וקודם גזירה הוה איני והא אביי שרא ליה לרב דימי בר ליואי לכברויי סלי ההוא [ו]טעותא הואי וטעותא מי הדרא והא אמר אבידן פעם אחת נתקשרו שמים בעבים כסבורים העם לומר חשכה הוא ונכנסו לבית הכנסת והתפללו של מוצאי שבת בשבת ונתפזרו העבים וזרחה החמה ובאו ושאלו את רבי ואמר הואיל והתפללו התפללו שאני [ז]צבור דלא מטרחינן להו: אמר ר' חייא בר אבין רב צלי של שבת בערב שבת רבי יאשיה מצלי של מוצאי שבת בשבת רב מצלי של שבת בערב שבת אומר קדושה על הכוס או אינו אומר קדושה על הכוס ת"ש דאמר רב נחמן אמר שמואל [ח]מתפלל אדם של שבת בערב שבת ואומר קדושה על הכוס והלכתא כוותיה רבי יאשיה מצלי של מוצאי שבת בשבת אומר הבדלה על הכוס או אינו אומר הבדלה על הכוס ת"ש דאמר רב יהודה אמר שמואל [ט]מתפלל אדם של מוצאי שבת בשבת ואומר הבדלה על הכוס אמר רבי זירא אמר רבי אסי אמר רבי אלעזר אמר רבי חנינא אמר רב בצד עמוד זה התפלל ר' ישמעאל ברבי יוסי של שבת בערב שבת כי אתא עולא אמר בצד תמרה הוה ולא בצד עמוד הוה ולא רבי ישמעאל ברבי יוסי הוה אלא ר' אלעזר בר' יוסי הוה ולא של שבת בערב שבת הוה אלא של מוצאי שבת בשבת הוה: תפלת הערב אין לה קבע: מאי אין לה קבע אילימא [י]דאי בעי מצלי כוליה ליליא ליתני תפלת הערב כל הלילה אלא מאי אין לה קבע כמאן דאמר *תפלת ערבית רשות דאמר רב יהודה אמר שמואל תפלת ערבית רבן גמליאל אומר חובה ר' יהושע אומר *רשות אמר אביי הלכה כדברי האומר חובה ורבא אמר [כ]הלכה כדברי האומר רשות ת"ר מעשה בתלמיד אחד שבא לפני ר' יהושע א"ל תפלת ערבית רשות או חובה אמר ליה רשות בא לפני רבן גמליאל אמר ליה תפלת ערבית רשות או חובה א"ל חובה א"ל והלא ר' יהושע אמר לי רשות אמר ליה *המתן עד שיכנסו בעלי תריסין לבית המדרש כשנכנסו בעלי תריסין עמד השואל ושאל תפלת ערבית רשות או חובה א"ל ר"ג חובה אמר להם רבן גמליאל לחכמים כלום יש אדם שחולק בדבר זה אמר ליה רבי יהושע לאו אמר ליה והלא משמך אמרו לי רשות אמר ליה יהושע עמוד על רגליך ויעידו בך עמד רבי יהושע על רגליו ואמר אלמלא אני חי והוא מת יכול החי להכחיש את המת ועכשיו שאני חי והוא חי היאך יכול החי להכחיש את החי היה רבן גמליאל יושב ודורש ור' יהושע עומד על רגליו עד שרננו כל העם ואמרו לחוצפית התורגמן עמוד ועמד אמרי עד כמה נצעריה וניזול בר"ה אשתקד צעריה בבכורות במעשה דרבי צדוק צעריה הכא נמי צעריה תא ונעבריה מאן נוקים ליה נוקמיה לרבי יהושע בעל מעשה הוא נוקמיה לר"ע דילמא עניש ליה דלית ליה זכות אבות אלא נוקמיה לרבי אלעזר בן עזריה דהוא חכם והוא עשיר והוא עשירי לעזרא הוא חכם דאי מקשי ליה מפרק ליה והוא עשיר דאי אית ליה לפלוחי לבי קיסר אף הוא אזיל ופלח והוא עשירי לעזרא דאית ליה זכות אבות ולא מצי עניש ליה אתו ואמרו ליה ניחא ליה למר דליהוי ריש מתיבתא אמר להו איזיל ואימליך באינשי ביתי אזל ואמלך בדביתהו אמרה ליה

דילמא

כנגד רבו. אצל רבו ונראה כאלו הם שוים: אחורי רבו. נמי יוהרא הוא: שלום לרבו. כשאר כל אדם שלום עליך ולא אמר לו שלום עליך רבי: והיינו דקאמר ליה. אותו היום שהתפלל רב של שבת בערב שבת אמר ליה רבי ירמיה מי בדלת מן המלאכה הואיל וקבלת עליך שבת בתפלתך: ולא אמר ליה מי בדיל מר. שמע מינה תלמיד חבר הוי ליה: לבית המרחץ. סלקא דעתא לאח' שגזרו על הזיעה ועל הרחיצה בשבת כדאמרינן במסכת שבת בפרק כירה שהסיקוה (דף מ.) אלמא אע"ג דצלי לא בדיל מאיסורי שבת: אמר רבא להזיע. נכנס להזיע מחמת חום בית המרחץ ולא נתן עליו מים: וקודם גזרה. עד שלא גזרו על הזיעה ובכל דוכתא דאמרינן כדאמר רבא להזיע כו' מהכא אמרינן: לכברויי סלי. לעשן אותן בגפרית לאחר שהתפלל של שבת בערב שבת: טעותא הואי. לא קבל עליו תוספת שבת משעת תפלה ומדעת אלא יום המעונן היה וכסבור חשכה ואחר כך זרחה חמה: הואיל והתפללו התפללו. ולא הצריכם להתפלל משתחשך אלמא תפלה היא ואף על פי שלא הותרו במלאכה התם הוא דלא לעבור על דברי תורה אבל לענין תוספת אף ע"ג דבטעות הוה תוספת הוא על ידי תפלה הואיל ואחר תפלה קבלה היא: בעלי תריסין. חכמים המנצחים זה את זה בהלכה: היאך יכול החי להכחיש את החי. על כרחי אני צריך להודות שאמרתי לו רשות: התורגמן. שהיה עומד לפני רבן גמליאל ומשמיע לרבים את הדרשה מפי רבן גמליאל: עמוד. שתוק: אשתקד. שנה שעברה: בראש השנה. במסכת ראש השנה (פ"ב דף כה.) שאמר לו גוזר אני עליך שתבא אצלי במקלך ובמעותיך ביום הכפורים שחל להיות בחשבונך: בבכורות. במסכת בכורות (פרק ה דף לו.): מעשה דרבי צדוק. בבכורו' הוא ר' צדוק הוה ליה בוכרא ואמר ליה רבן גמליאל לר' יהושע עמוד על רגלך כו' כי הכא: תא ונעבריה. בואו ונעביר אותו מן הנשיאו': בעל מעשה הוא. והוה ליה לרבן גמליאל לצערא טפי: לית ליה זכות אבות. ודלמא עניש ליה רבן גמליאל: מעברין לך. יורידוך מן הנשיאות בשביל אחר: ה"ג

ולא אחורי רבו. פי' רש"י משום יוהרא ויש מפרש שנראה כמשתחוה לרבו: והנותן שלום לרבו והמחזיר שלום. פירוש כשאר בני אדם שאינו אומר שלום עליך רבי והיינו דאמרינן (ב"ק דף עג:) כדי שאלת תלמיד לרב אי נמי שהוא לכתחלה קאמר ובתלמיד חבר דשרי ככל הכי דלקמן: הואיל והתפללו וכו'. הכא נמי כיון *לענין חומרא ואמאי שרא ליה ובקונטרס פירש בפנים אחר: שאני צבור. אף על גב דלא מטא זמן אין איסורא איסור בעשיית מלאכה אף על גב *דטעותא הוא: צלי של מוצאי שבת וכו'. יש לומר דהכא איירי שיש לו צורך מצוה לעשות במוצאי שבת כגון ללכת למול תינוק ולא יהיה לו יין להבדלה אם לא יקדים דודאי צריך להוסיף מחול על הקדש דאורייתא אבל בחנם לא ופשיטא שלא היו ממהרים להבדיל ולהתפלל של מוצאי שבת בשבת דגם במלאכה אסור עם חשכה: הלכה כדברי האומר רשות. לאו דוקא רשות אלא כדפרישית לעיל (דף כו.) ולכך נקרא רשות לבטלה עבור מצוה אחרת העוברת: והלכתא כוותיה דרב. ונראה דלכך תקנו פסוקים וקדיש בין גאולה לתפלה דרשות היא: [עי' תוספות לעיל ד: ד"ה אמר ריב"ל]: ושל

עין משפט נר מצוה

כג [א] מיי' פ"ה מה' ת"ת הל' ו סמג ע' יב טוש"ע א"ח סי' ל סעי' כד *לעיל לחומר' כל"ל רש"א

כד [ב] מיי' שם הל' ה סמג ע' יב טוש"ע י"ד סי' רמב סעי' יו *עיין רש"ל ורש"א

כה [ג] מיי' שם הל' ב טוש"ע י"ד שם סעי' ב

כו [ד] מיי' שם הל' ט טוש"ע י"ד שם סעי' כד

כז [ה] מיי' שם טוש"ע א"ח סי' ל סעי' כה

כח [ו ז] ש"ע א"ח סי' רסג סעי' יד

כט [ח] מיי' פרק ג מהלכ' תפלה הל' ז ופרק כט מהלכות שבת הל' יא סמג עשין כט טוש"ע א"ח סי' רסז סעיף ב

ל [ט] מיי' וסמג שם טוש"ע א"ח סי' רצג סעיף ג

לא [י] מיי' פ"ג מהלכות תפלה הל' ו

לב [כ] מיי' פרק א מהל' תפלה הל' ו ופרק ג הל' ו ופרק ט הלכה ט סמג עשין יט טא"ח סי' רלה רלו ורלז

[בכורות לו. וע"ש בתוס']

מסורת הש"ס

חלק דף קי. וע"ש סוכה דף כז: וסוף מס' כלה

[עירובין מ:]

ביצה פ"ד דף לג.

[לעיל ד: שבת ט:]

ס"א רשות והלכתא כדברי האומר חוב' ורבא אמר הלכ' כדברי האומ' רשות עיין יומא דף פז ב

pray [27b] either next to this master[3] or behind his master?[4] And it has been taught: R. Eleazar says: One who prays behind his master, and one who gives [the ordinary] greeting to his master[5] and one who returns a greeting to his master[6] and one who joins issue with [the teaching of] the Academy of his master and one who says something which he has not heard from his master causes the Divine Presence to depart from Israel?—R. Jeremiah b. Abba is different, because he was a disciple-colleague; and that is why R.
a Jeremiah b. Abba said to Rab: Have you laid aside,[1] and he replied: Yes, I have; and he did not say to him, Has the Master laid aside. But had he laid aside? Has not R. Abin related that once Rab said the Sabbath *Tefillah* on the eve of Sabbath and he went into the bath[2] and came out and taught us our section, while it was not yet dark?—Raba said: He went in merely to perspire, and it was before the prohibition had been issued.[3] But still, is this the rule?[4] Did not Abaye allow R. Dimi b. Levai to fumigate some baskets?[5]—In that case there was a mistake.[6] But can [such] a mistake be rectified? Has not Abidan said: Once [on Sabbath] the sky became overcast with clouds and the congregation thought that is was night-time and they went into the synagogue and said the prayers for the termination of Sabbath, and then the clouds scattered and the sun came out and they came and asked Rabbi, and he said to them, Since they prayed, they have prayed?[7]—A congregation is different, since we avoid troubling them [as far as possible].[8]

R. Ḥiyya b. Abin said: Rab used to say the Sabbath *Tefillah* on the eve of Sabbath;[9] R. Josiah said the *Tefillah* of the outgoing of Sabbath on Sabbath. When Rab said the Sabbath *Tefillah* on the eve of Sabbath, did he say sanctification over wine or not?—Come and hear: for R. Naḥman said in the name of Samuel: A man may say the *Tefillah* of Sabbath on the eve of Sabbath, and say sanctification over wine; and the law is as stated by him. R. Josiah used to say the end-of-Sabbath *Tefillah* while it was yet Sabbath. Did he say *habdalah* over wine or did he not say *habdalah* over wine?—Come and hear: for Rab Judah said in the name of Samuel: A man may say the end-of-Sabbath *Tefillah* while it is yet Sabbath and say *habdalah* over wine. R. Zera said in the name of R. Assi reporting R. Eleazar who had it from R. Ḥanina in the name of Rab: At the side of this pillar R. Ishmael son of R. Jose said the Sabbath *Tefillah* on the eve of Sabbath. When 'Ulla came he reported that it was at the side of a palm tree and not at the side of a pillar, and that it was not R. Ishmael son of R. Jose but R. Eleazar son of R. Jose, and that it was not the Sabbath *Tefillah* on the eve of Sabbath but the end-of-Sabbath *Tefillah* on Sabbath.

THE EVENING PRAYER HAS NO FIXED LIMIT. What is the meaning of HAS NO FIXED LIMIT? Shall I say it means that if a man wants he can say the *Tefillah* any time in the night? Then let it state, 'The time for the evening *Tefillah* is the whole night'!—But what in fact is the meaning of HAS NO FIXED LIMIT? It is equivalent to saying, The evening *Tefillah* is optional. For Rab Judah said in the name of Samuel: With regard to the evening *Tefillah*, Rabban Gamaliel says it is compulsory, whereas R. Joshua says it is optional. Abaye says: The *halachah* is as stated by the one who says it is compulsory; Raba says the *halachah* follows the one who says it is optional.

It is related that a certain disciple came before R. Joshua and asked him, Is the evening *Tefillah* compulsory or optional? He replied: It is optional. He then presented himself before Rabban Gamaliel and asked him: Is the evening *Tefillah* compulsory or optional? He replied: It is compulsory. But, he said, did not R.
b Joshua tell me that it is optional? He said: Wait till the champions[1] enter the Beth ha-Midrash. When the champions came in, someone rose and inquired, Is the evening *Tefillah* compulsory or optional? Rabban Gamaliel replied: It is compulsory. Said Rabban Gamaliel to the Sages: Is there anyone who disputes this? R. Joshua replied to him: No. He said to him: Did they not report you to me as saying that it is optional? He then went on: Joshua, stand up and let them testify against you! R. Joshua stood up and said: Were I alive and he [the witness] dead, the living could contradict the dead. But now that he is alive and I am alive, how can the living
c contradict the living?[1] Rabban Gamaliel remained sitting and expounding and R. Joshua remained standing, until all the people there began to shout and say to Huẓpith the *turgeman*,[2] Stop! and he stopped. They then said: How long is he [Rabban Gamaliel] to go on insulting him [R. Joshua]? On New Year last year he insulted him;[3] he insulted him in the matter of the firstborn in the affair of R. Zadok;[4] now he insults him again! Come, let us depose him! Whom shall we appoint instead? We can hardly appoint R. Joshua, because he is one of the parties involved. We can hardly appoint R. Akiba because perhaps Rabban Gamaliel will bring a curse on him because he has no ancestral merit. Let us then appoint R. Eleazar b. Azariah, who is wise and rich and the tenth in descent from Ezra. He is wise, so that if anyone puts a question to him he will be able to answer it. He is rich, so that if occasion arises for paying court[5] to Caesar he will be able to do so. He is tenth in descent from Ezra, so that he has ancestral merit and he [Rabban Gamaliel] cannot bring a curse on him. They went and said to him: Will your honour consent to become head of the Academy? He replied: I will go and consult the members of my family. He went and consulted his wife. She said to him: [28a]

(3) Because he seems to put himself on a level with him. (4) This also is a sign of pride. Or perhaps, because he seems to be bowing down to him (Tosaf.). (5) I.e., he says, 'Peace upon thee' simply instead of 'Peace upon thee, my master'. (6) Omitted by Alfasi and Asheri.

a (1) Have you laid aside all work, since you said the Sabbath *Tefillah* so early? Lit., 'have you made the distinction' (*sc.* between weekdays and Sabbath)? (2) An act forbidden on the Sabbath. (3) Against bathing and perspiring on Sabbath, v. Shab. 40*a*. (4) That work may not be done after saying the Sabbath prayer early on Sabbath eve. (5) After saying the Sabbath prayer. (6) It was a dark afternoon, and he said the Sabbath prayer thinking that Sabbath had already commenced. (7) And since the prayer need not be repeated, work in the case of Sabbath eve ought to be forbidden! (8) To repeat the *Tefillah*. (9) Before evening set in.

b (1) Lit., 'masters of bucklers', 'shield-bearers', i.e., great scholars. The Rabbis often applied warlike terms to *halachic* discussion.

c (1) I.e., how can I deny that I said this? (2) Lit., 'interpreter', the man who expounded the ideas of the teacher to the public. The more usual later name is *Amora*. (3) By telling him to appear before him on the Day of Atonement with his staff and wallet. V. R.H. 25*a*. (4) V. Bek. 36*a*. (5) Lit., 'serve'.

Perhaps they will depose you later on. He replied to her: [There is a proverb:] Let a man use a cup of honour[6] for one day even if it be broken the next. She said to him: You have no white hair. He was eighteen years old that day, and a miracle was wrought for him and eighteen rows of hair [on his beard] turned white. That is why R. Eleazar b. Azariah said: Behold I am *about* seventy years old,[7] and he did not say [simply] seventy years old. A Tanna taught: On that day the doorkeeper was removed and permission was given to the disciples to enter. For Rabban Gamaliel had issued a proclamation [saying], No disciple whose character does
a not correspond to his exterior[1] may enter the Beth ha-Midrash. On that day many stools[2] were added. R. Joḥanan said: There is a difference of opinion on this matter between Abba Joseph b. Dosethai and the Rabbis: one [authority] says that four hundred stools were added, and the other says seven hundred. Rabban Gamaliel became alarmed and said: Perhaps, God forbid, I withheld Torah from Israel![3] He was shown in his dream white casks full of ashes.[4] This, however, really meant nothing; he was only shown this to appease him.[5]

A Tanna taught: Eduyyoth[6] was formulated on that day—and wherever the expression 'on that day' is used, it refers to that day—and there was no *halachah* about which any doubt existed in the Beth ha-Midrash which was not fully elucidated. Rabban Gamaliel also did not absent himself from the Beth ha-Midrash a single hour, as we have learnt: On that day Judah, an Ammonite proselyte, came before them in the Beth ha-Midrash. He said to them: Am I permitted to enter the assembly?[7] R. Joshua said to him: You are permitted to enter the congregation. Said Rabban Gamaliel to him: Is it not already laid down, *An Ammonite or a Moabite shall not enter into the assembly of the Lord?*[8] R. Joshua replied to him: Do Ammon and Moab still reside in their original homes? Sennacherib king of Assyria long ago went up and mixed up all the nations, as it says, *I have removed the bounds of the peoples and have robbed their treasures and have brought down as one mighty their inhabitants;*[9] and whatever strays [from a group] is assumed to belong to the larger section of the group.[10] Said Rabban Gamaliel to him: But has it not been said: *But afterward I will bring back the*
b *captivity of the children of Ammon, saith the Lord,*[1] so that they have already returned? To which R. Joshua replied: And has it not been said, *And I will turn the captivity of My people Israel,*[2] and they have not yet returned? Forthwith they permitted him to enter the congregation. Rabban Gamaliel thereupon said: This being the case,[3] I will go and apologize to R. Joshua. When he reached his house he saw that the walls were black. He said to him: From the walls of your house it is apparent that you are a charcoal-burner.[4] He replied: Alas for the generation of which you are the leader, seeing that you know nothing of the troubles of the scholars, their struggles to support and sustain themselves! He said to him: I apologize,[5] forgive me. He paid no attention to him. Do it, he said, out of respect for my father. He then became reconciled to him. They said: Who will go and tell the Rabbis? A certain fuller said to them: I will go. R. Joshua sent a message to the Beth ha-Midrash saying: Let him who is accustomed to wear the robe wear it;[6] shall he who is not accustomed to wear the robe[7] say to him who is accustomed to wear it, Take off your robe and I will put it on? Said R. Akiba to the Rabbis: Lock the doors so that the servants of Rabban Gamaliel should not come and upset the Rabbis.[8] Said R. Joshua: I had better get up and go to them. He came and knocked at the door. He said to them: Let the sprinkler son of a sprinkler[9] sprinkle; shall he who is neither a sprinkler nor the son of a sprinkler say to a sprinkler son of a sprinkler, Your water is cave water[10] and your ashes are oven ashes?[11] Said R. Akiba to him: R. Joshua, you have received your apology, have we done anything except out of regard for your
c honour? Tomorrow morning you and I will wait on him.[1] They said: How shall we do? Shall we depose him [R. Eleazar b. Azariah]? We have a rule that we may raise an object to a higher grade of sanctity but must not degrade it to a lower.[2] If we let one Master preach on one Sabbath and one on the next, this will cause jealousy. Let therefore Rabban Gamaliel preach three Sabbaths and R. Eleazar b. Azariah one Sabbath. And it is in reference to this that a Master said: 'Whose Sabbath was it? It was the Sabbath of R. Eleazar b. Azariah'.[3] And that disciple[4] was R. Simeon b. Yoḥai.

THE TIME FOR THE ADDITIONAL PRAYER IS THE WHOLE DAY. R. Joḥanan said: And he is [nevertheless] called a transgressor.[5]

Our Rabbis taught: If a man had two *Tefillahs* to say, one for *minḥah* and one for *musaf*, he says the one for *minḥah*, and afterwards he says the one for *musaf*, because the one is daily[6] and the other is not daily. R. Judah says: He says the *musaf* one first and then he says the *minḥah* one; the former is an obligation that will soon lapse[7] while the other is an obligation that will not lapse. R. Joḥanan said: The *halachah* is that he says the *minḥah Tefillah* first and then the *musaf* one. When R. Zera was tired from studying, he used to go and sit by the door of the school of R. Nathan b. Tobi. He said to himself: When the Rabbis pass by, I will rise before them and earn a reward.[8] R. Nathan b. Tobi came out. He said to him: Who enunciated a *halachah* in the Beth ha-Midrash? He replied: Thus said R. Joḥanan: The *halachah* does not follow R. Judah who said that a man first says the *musaf Tefillah* and then the *minḥah* one. He said to him: Did R. Joḥanan say it?—He replied, Yes.[9] He repeated it after him forty times. He said to him: Is this the one [and only] thing you have learnt [from him][10]
d or it is a new thing to you?[1] He replied: It is a new thing to me, because I was not certain [whether it was not the dictum] of R. Joshua b. Levi.

R. Joshua b. Levi said: If one says the *musaf Tefillah* after seven hours, then according to R. Judah the Scripture says of him, *I will gather them that are destroyed* [nuge][2] *because of the appointed season, who are of thee.*[3] How do you know that the word *'nuge'* here implies destruction? It is as rendered by R. Joseph [in his Targum]:[4] Destruction comes upon the enemies of Israel[5] because they put off till late the times of the appointed seasons[6] in Jerusalem.

R. Eleazar said: If one says the morning *Tefillah* after four hours, then according to R. Judah the Scripture says of him, *'I will gather them that sorrow because of the appointed season, who are of thee'*. How do we know that this word *nuge* implies sorrow? Because it is written, *My soul melteth away for heaviness* [tugah].[7] R. Naḥman b. Isaac said: We learn it from here: *Her virgins are afflicted* [nugoth]

(6) I.e., one used on state occasions. *Aliter:* 'a cup of filigree work'. (7) V. *supra* 12*b*, n. c7.
a (1) Lit., 'whose inside is not as his outside'; a common Talmudic expression. (2) Or 'benches'. (3) By keeping out so many disciples. (4) Signifying that those he kept out were in fact not genuine. (5) I.e., they were in fact genuine. (6) Lit., 'testimonies' not necessarily the Tractate Eduyyoth which we now have. (7) I.e., marry a Jewess. (8) Deut. XXIII, 4. (9) Isa. X, 13. (10) E.g., if there are nine shops in a street selling *kasher* meat and one selling *trefa*, and we find a piece of meat in the street, we presume that it came from one of the *kasher* shops, v. Keth. 15*a*. So here, we presume that this man came from one of the other nations.
b (1) Jer. XLIX, 6. (2) Amos IX, 14. (3) Since he is held in such high respect. (4) *Aliter* 'smith'. (5) Lit., 'I am humbled to thee'. (6) I.e., let Rabban Gamaliel be restored to the presidency. (7) I.e., R. Eleazar b. Azariah. (8) The Rabbis did not want Rabban Gamaliel to be restored, being afraid of his autocratic disposition. (9) I.e., a priest, son of a priest, sprinkle the water of purification. The reference is again to Rabban Gamaliel who had an hereditary claim to the presidency. (10) And not living water as required, v. Num. XIX, 17. (11) And not from the Red Heifer.
c (1) I.e., on R. Eleazar b. Azariah. Lit., 'we will rise early to his door'.

תורה אור

דלמא מעברין לך אמר לה [לשתמש אינש] יומא חדא בכסא דמוקרא ולמחר ליתבר אמרה ליה לית לך חיורתא ההוא יומא *בר תמני סרי שני הוה אתרחיש ליה ניסא ואהדרו ליה תמני סרי דרי חיורתא היינו דקאמר ר"א בן עזריה *הרי אני כבן שבעים שנה ולא בן שבעים שנה תנא אותו היום סלקוהו לשומר הפתח ונתנה להם רשות לתלמידים ליכנס שהיה ר"ג מכריז ואומר *כל תלמיד שאין תוכו כברו לא יכנס לבית המדרש ההוא יומא אתוספי כמה ספסלי א"ר יוחנן פליגי בה אבא יוסף בן דוסתאי ורבנן חד אמר אתוספו ד' מאה ספסלי וחד אמר ז' מאה ספסלי הוה קא חלשה דעתיה דר"ג אמר דילמא חס ושלום מנעתי תורה מישראל אחזו ליה בחלמיה חצבי חיורי דמליין קטמא ולא היא ההיא ליתובי דעתיה הוא דאחזו ליה תנא עדיות בו ביום נשנית וכל היכא דאמרינן בו ביום ההוא יומא הוה ולא היתה הלכה שהיתה תלויה בבית המדרש שלא פירשוה ואף ר"ג לא מנע עצמו מבית המדרש אפילו שעה אחת דתנן *בו ביום בא יהודה גר עמוני לפניהם בבית המדרש אמר להם מה אני לבא בקהל אמר ליה ר"ג אסור אתה לבא בקהל אמר ליה ר' יהושע מותר אתה לבא בקהל אמר ליה ר"ג והלא כבר נאמר לא יבא עמוני ומואבי בקהל ה' אמר לו רבי יהושע וכי עמון ומואב במקומן הן יושבין *כבר עלה סנחריב מלך אשור ובלבל את כל האומות שנאמר ואסיר גבולות עמים ועתידותיהם שושתי ואוריד כאביר יושבים *וכל דפריש מרובא פריש אמר לו רבן גמליאל והלא כבר נאמר ואחרי כן אשיב את שבות בני עמון נאם ה' וכבר שבו אמר לו רבי יהושע והלא כבר נאמר ושבתי את שבות עמי ישראל ועדיין לא שבו מיד התירוהו לבא בקהל אמר ר"ג הואיל והכי הוה איזיל ואפייסיה לרבי יהושע כי מטא לביתיה חזנהו לאשיתא דביתיה דמשחרן א"ל מכותלי ביתך אתה ניכר *שפחמי אתה אמר לו אוי לו לדור שאתה פרנסו *שאי אתה יודע בצערן של תלמידי חכמים במה הם מתפרנסים ובמה הם נזונים אמר לו נעניתי לך מחול לי לא אשגח ביה עשה בשביל כבוד אבא פייס אמרו מאן ניזיל ולימא להו לרבנן אמר להו ההוא כובס אנא אזילנא שלח להו ר' יהושע לבי מדרשא מאן דלביש מדא ילבש מדא ומאן דלא לביש מדא יימר ליה למאן דלביש מדא שלח מדך ואנא אלבשיה אמר להו רבי עקיבא לרבנן טרוקו גלי דלא ליתו עבדי דרבן גמליאל ולצערו לרבנן א"ר יהושע מוטב דאקום ואיזיל אנא לגבייהו אתא טרף אבבא אמר ליה מזה בן מזה יזה ושאינו לא מזה ולא בן מזה יאמר למזה בן מזה מימיך מי מערה ואפרך אפר מקלה א"ל ר"ע רבי יהושע נתפייסת כלום עשינו אלא בשביל כבודך למחר אני ואתה נשכים לפתחו אמרי היכי נעביד נעבריה *גמירי מעלין בקדש ואין מורידין נדרוש מר חדא שבתא ומר חדא שבתא אתי לקנאויי אלא לדרוש ר"ג *תלתא שבתי וראב"ע חדא שבתא והיינו דאמר מר שבת של מי היתה של ראב"ע היתה ואותו תלמיד ר"ש בן יוחאי הוה: ושל מוספין כל היום: א"ר יוחנן ונקרא פושע ת"ר *היו לפניו שתי תפלות אחת של מנחה ואחת של מוסף מתפלל של מנחה ואח"כ מתפלל של מוסף שזו תדירה וזו אינה תדירה ר' יהודה אומר מתפלל של מוסף ואחר כך מתפלל של מנחה שזו מצוה עוברת וזו מצוה שאינה עוברת *אמר ר' יוחנן הלכה מתפלל של מנחה ואחר כך מתפלל של מוסף ר' זירא כי הוה חליש מגירסיה הוה אזיל ויתיב אפתחא דבי רבי נתן בר טובי אמר כי חלפי רבנן אז איקום מקמייהו ואקבל אגרא נפק אתא ר' נתן בר טובי א"ל מאן אמר הלכה בי מדרשא א"ל הכי א"ר יוחנן אין הלכה כרבי יהודה דאמר מתפלל אדם של מוסף ואחר כך מתפלל של מנחה אמר ליה רבי יוחנן אמרה אמר ליה אין *תנא מיניה ארבעין זימנין אמר ליה חדא היא לך או חדת היא לך א"ל חדת היא לי משום דמספקא לי בר' יהושע בן לוי: אמר ריב"ל כל המתפלל תפלה של מוספין לאחר שבע שעות לר' יהודה עליו הכתוב אומר נוגי ממועד אספתי ממך היו מאי משמע דהאי נוגי לישנא דתברא הוא כדמתרגם רב יוסף תברא אתי על שנאיהון דבית ישראל על דאחרו זמני מועדיא דבירושלים אמר ר' אלעזר כל המתפלל תפלה של שחרית לאחר ד' שעות לרבי יהודה עליו הכתוב אומר נוגי ממועד אספתי ממך מאי משמע דהאי נוגי לישנא דצערא הוא דכתיב דלפה נפשי מתוגה רב נחמן בר יצחק אמר מהכא בתולותיה נוגות והיא מר לה רב

ה"ג דלמא מעברין לך אמר לה יומא חדא בכסא דמוקרא ולמחר ליתבר. ול"ג מעלין בקדש: כסא דמוקרא. כוס זכוכית יקרה שקורין לה בלשון ישמעאל עקרי"א ואומרים בני אדם במשל הדיוט יום אחד ישתמש בו בעליו ויתכבד בו ואם ישבר ישבר: לית לך חיורתא. אין לך שערות לבנות של זקנה ונאה לדרשן להיות זקן: י"ח דרי חיורתא. י"ח שורות של זקנה: קא חלשא דעתיה דר"ג. כשראה שנוספו היום תלמידים רבים והיה דואג שלא יענש במה שמנעם ביומיו מלבא: דמליין קטמא. כלומר אף אלו אינם ראויים: תלויה. בספק שלא פירשוה מתוך שרבו התלמידים רב החדוד והפלפול: לאשיתא דביתיה דמשחרן. כותלי ביתו של רבי יהושע שהיו שחורות: שפחמי אתה. עושה פחמים וי"א נפח: נעניתי לך. דברתי למולך יותר מן הראוי: דלביש מדא. הרגיל ללבוש המעיל ילבוש כלומר הרגיל בכשיאות יהיה נשיא: מזה בן מזה. כהן בן כהן יזה את מי חטאת: אפר מקלה. אפר הקלוי בתנורים ובכירות כלומר אפר סתם: שבת של מי היתה. במס' חגיגה (ד' ג'.): ואותו תלמיד. שאלה תפלת ערבית רשות או חובה רשב"י הוה: ונקרא פושע. המאחר כ"כ: מתפלל של מנחה. מאחר שהגיע זמנה כדי להקדימה בתחלת זמנה שלא יקרא פושע גם עליה: ואח"כ של מוספין. הואיל ואיחר *זמנה איכו עובר דהא אמרי רבנן ושל מוספים כל היום: שזו מצוה עוברת. ר' יהודה לטעמיה דאמר עד ז' שעות ותו לא: כי חלפי רבנן. תלמידים ההולכין מבית ר' נתן: מאן אמר הלכה בי מדרשא. מי מבני הישיבה אמר בבית המדרש שהלכה כר' יהודה: חדא היא לך או חדת היא לך. אחת היא לך שלא למדת דבר משמו של ר' יוחנן אלא זו בלבד לכך חביבה היא לך או חדשה היא לך שהיית סבור שאחד מן האחרי' אמרה: ה"ג א"ל חדת היא לי. דמספקא לי בריב"ל. סבור הייתי שריב"ל אמרה: אמר ריב"ל. גרסי' ול"ג דאמר: ממועד. מחמת שהעבירו מועדי התפלות וחגים יהיו נוגים ואסופים וכלים: לא

ושל מוספין כל היום. הקשה הרב רבינו שמשון ז"ל דאמר בפרק תמיד נשחט (דף כח.) מוספין בשש בזיכין בשבע וכ"ת ה"מ למצוה אבל דיעבד כל יומא נמי זמניה הוא הרי *בתמור' (פ"ב דף יד.) משמע שהמוספים היו נשחטין עם התמיד וקטרים עמו ותירץ דהתם איירי בשבת:

הלכה מתפלל של מנחה ואח"כ מתפלל של מוסף. מכאן יש ליזהר בי"הכ להתפלל תפלת שחרית קודם שש שעות ומחצה דהיינו קודם שהגיע שעת המנחה דאל"כ היו צריכין להתפלל תפלת המנחה קודם והר"י אומר דאינו צריך דהא דקאמר שיתפלל תפלת המנחה קודם היינו כשיש לו לעשות צרכיו שלא יוכל להתפלל תפלת המנחה בזמנה וצריך להתפלל שניהם מיד כגון שהיה לו לילך לסעודה גדולה כמו לנשואין ומתירא שמא ימשוך בסעודתו או שישתכר אבל אם היה לו שהות להתפלל אחר תפלת מוסף תפלת המנחה בזמנה אין לו להקדים תפלת המנחה אלא יתפלל כסדר מוסף ואח"כ מנחה:

כדמתרגם רב יוסף על דאחרו זמני מועדיא. ואי משתעי ברגלים אין שייך לומר לשון איחור שהרי אין להן תשלומין אלא ע"כ בתפלה משתעי קרא:

כיון

עין משפט נר מצוה

[ביומא ד"ע. כ"כ המג"א סי' רפא] [עיי' רש"ל ורש"א]

לג אמיי' פ"ד מה' ת"ת הל' א טוש"ע י"ד סי' רמו סעי' ז

לד במיי' פי"ב מה' איסורי ביאה הל' כה סמג לאוין קיו טוש"ע אה"ע סי' ד סעיף י

לה גמיי' פ"א מה' ת"ת הל' ע ופ"י מה' מתנות עניי' הל' יח

לו דמיי' פ"א מה' מלכים הל' ז טוש"ע י"ד סי' רמה סעיף כב

לז המיי' פ"ג מהלכ' תפלה הלכה ה סמג עשין יט טוש"ע א"ח סי' רפו סעיף א

לח ושם סעיף ד

לט חשם סעי' א

מסורת הש"ס

[וע' פירש"י לקמן לא. ד"ה כסא]

(בירוש' אמר בן טז שנה היה)

לעיל יב:

[דוגמתו יומא עב:]

מס' ידי' פ"ד משנה ד

[יומא כד. וע' תוס' מגילה יב: ותוס' יבמות עו: ובתוס' ע. ד"ה מכימין]

ס"א ואוי לה לספינה שאתה קברניטה

ל"ל חמנה פע"ל

דברי' כג

ישעי' י

ירמי' מט

עמוס ט

[יומא כד: יבמות עז: כתובות עז. קידושין עב. זבחים עב.] (בירוש' גרס אשכחי' יתיב עביד מחטין)

[יומא יב: עג. מגיל' ט: כא. הוריות יב: שבת כא: מנחות לט. ולט. ושם מציק לה מקפל ול"ע לשון גמירי]

לפניה ג

[יותר נכון לגרוס תרתי וכ"ה בהקדמה מפי' משניות להרמב"ם למס' יבמו'] חגיגה ג' ונגיס לח. [שם יב. לח.] פסחי' עג. מגילה ז: כתובות כב. כ.]

תהלים קיט

איכה א

(2) V. e.g. Yoma 12*b*. (3) Hag. 3*a*. (4) Who asked the question about the evening *Tefillah*. (5) If he delays too much. (6) Lit., 'continual', 'regular'. (7) Its time being limited, in the view of R. Judah, until the seventh hour. (8) In the next world. (9) Var. lec. (v. D.S.): 'Who enunciated a *halachah* etc.'? He replied, R. Joḥanan. He said to him, What was it. He replied, A man may say first etc.'. (10) *Sc.* R. Joḥanan.

d (1) That you set so much store by it. (2) E.V. '*Them that sorrow for*'. (3) Zeph. III, 18. (4) To R. Joseph is ascribed the Targum on the prophets, v. Graetz, *Geschichte*, IV, 326. (5) Euphemism. (6) I.e., the festival prayers. (7) Ps. CXIX, 28.

עין משפט נר מצוה

לא על לפרקא דרב יוסף. שהיה דורש ברבים בשבת קודם תפלת המוספין ולאחר הדרשה היו הולכים לבית הכנסת ומתפללים תפלת המוספין: בצבור שנו. אם הוא בצבור לא יקדים להתפלל: **מתני'** מה מקום. כלומר מה טיבה: **גמ'** ולא אכשל. וישמחו חברי על כשלוני הרי רעות שתים שיבאו ע"י שאגרום להם *שיענשו: מיושבי קרנות. חנונים או עמי הארץ שעוסקים בדבר שיחה: מן ההגיון. לא תרגילום במקרא יותר מדאי משום דמשכא לשון אחר משיחת ילדים: דעו לפני מי וכו'. כדי שתתפללו ביראה ובכונה: עמוד הימיני. שני עמודים העמיד שלמה באולם שם הימיני יכין ושם השמאלי בועז (מלכים א' ז) הימיני לעולם חשוב: פטיש. המפוצץ פי"ק בלעז: אוסרני. חובש אותי: מיתת עולם. לעוה"ב: הייתי בוכה. מאימת משפטו אם לדין מוליכין אותי לפניו: עד כאן. בתמיה כלומר ולא יותר ממורא בשר ודם: ולואי. שיהא כמורא בשר ודם שאם כן תחדלו מעבירות הרבה: עבירה. בסתר ממורא הבריות ויודע שהכל הוא גלוי להקדוש ברוך הוא ואינו מניח בכך: מפני הטומאה. טומאת אהל המת בכל הבית: לחזקיהו שבא. אלי ללוותי: **מתני'** מעין שמנה עשרה. בגמ' מפרש: הושע ה' וכו'. זו תפלה קצרה: בכל פרשת העבור כו'. מפרש בגמרא: אם אינו יכול לירד. שאין לו מי שיאחז את חמורו: יחזיר את פניו. לצד ירושלים: באסדא. כמו ותשם בסד רגלי (איוב יג) בית הסהר שקורין ליי"פש בלעז לשון אחר עלים הקשורים זה עם זה הרבה יחד ובלשון מקרא קורא אותה רפסודות (ד"ה ב' ב) ובלע"ז רד"ייל ובלשון אשכנז ולו"ס ומשימין בנהר להוליכן ממקום למקום ויכולין להלך עליהן כמו בספינה: **גמ'** הבו לי"י בני אלים. שהוא רמז לאבות וגבורות וקדושת השם כדאמרינן בראש השנה (דף לב.) מנין שאומרים אבות תלמוד לומר הבו לי"י בני אלי' כו': שיתפקקו. שיראו הפקקים הם הקשרים כמו שכינו (ב"ב פ':) בקנים ובגפנים מן הפקק שלמעלה והיא הקשר שחלל הקנה פקוק וסתום שם: איסר. שני קמעים אחד מלמטה ואחד מלמעלה וכאיסר רוחב בשר באמצעי: דמצער נפשיה. שהוא ניכר שחפץ לכרוע אלא שהוא מצטער: הפקולי. מוכר פקולי למר גפן שקורין קו"טון: ביבנה תקנוה. לאחר זמן מרובה:

[ע' בפי"ע]

תורה אור

כיון שהגיע זמן תפלת המנחה אסור לטעום כלום וכו'. ולית ליה לרבי יהושע מפסיקין ואפילו מן האכילה ולא היא: ל"יש

רב אויא חלש ולא אתא לפרקא דרב יוסף למחר כי אתא בעא אביי לאנוחי דעתיה דרב יוסף אמר ליה מאי טעמא לא אתא מר לפרקא אמר ליה דהוה חליש לבאי ולא מצינא אמר ליה אמאי לא טעמת מידי ואתית אמר ליה לא סבר לה מר להא דרב הונא דאמר רב הונא אסור לו לאדם שיטעום כלום קודם שיתפלל תפלת המוספין אמר ליה איבעי ליה למר לצלויי צלותא דמוספין ביחיד ולטעום מידי ולמיתי אמר ליה ולא סבר לה מר להא דאמר ר' יוחנן "אסור לו לאדם שיקדים תפלתו לתפלת הצבור אמר ליה לאו אתמר עלה אמר רבי אבא "בצבור שנו ולית הלכתא "לא כרב הונא "ולא כרבי יהושע בן לוי כרב הונא הא דאמרן כרבי יהושע בן לוי דאמר רבי יהושע בן לוי *כיון שהגיע זמן תפלת המנחה אסור לו לאדם שיטעום כלום קודם שיתפלל תפלת המנחה: **מתני'** ר' נחוניא בן הקנה היה מתפלל בכניסתו לבית המדרש וביציאתו תפלה קצרה אמרו לו מה *מקום לתפלה זו אמר להם בכניסתי אני מתפלל שלא יארע דבר תקלה על ידי וביציאתי אני נותן הודאה על חלקי: **גמ'** ת"ר "בכניסתו מהו אומר יהי רצון מלפניך ה' אלהי שלא *יארע דבר תקלה על ידי ולא אכשל בדבר הלכה וישמחו בי חברי ולא אומר על טמא טהור ולא על טהור טמא ולא יכשלו חברי בדבר הלכה ואשמח בהם ביציאתו מהו אומר מודה אני לפניך ה' אלהי ששמת חלקי מיושבי בית המדרש ולא שמת חלקי מיושבי קרנות שאני משכים והם משכימים אני משכים לדברי תורה והם משכימים לדברים בטלים אני עמל והם עמלים אני עמל ומקבל שכר והם עמלים ואינם מקבלים שכר אני רץ והם רצים אני רץ לחיי העה"ב והם רצים לבאר שחת: ת"ר כשחלה רבי אליעזר נכנסו תלמידיו לבקרו אמרו לו ר' למדנו ארחות חיים ונזכה בהן לחיי העולם הבא אמר להם הזהרו בכבוד חבריכם ומנעו בניכם מן ההגיון והושיבום בין ברכי תלמידי חכמים וכשאתם מתפללים דעו לפני מי אתם עומדים ובשביל כך תזכו לחיי העולם הבא וכשחלה רבן יוחנן בן זכאי נכנסו תלמידיו לבקרו כיון שראה אותם התחיל לבכות אמרו לו תלמידיו נר ישראל עמוד הימיני פטיש החזק מפני מה אתה בוכה א"ל אלו לפני מלך בשר ודם היו מוליכין אותי שהיום כאן ומחר בקבר שאם כועס עלי אין כעסו כעס עולם ואם אוסרני אין איסורו איסור עולם ואם ממיתני אין מיתתי מיתת עולם ואני יכול לפייסו בדברים ולשחדו בממון אף על פי כן הייתי בוכה ועכשיו שמוליכים אותי לפני ממ"ה הקב"ה שהוא חי וקים לעולם ולעולמי עולמים שאם כועס עלי כעסו כעס עולם ואם אוסרני איסורו איסור עולם ואם ממיתני מיתתי מיתת עולם ואיני יכול לפייסו בדברים ולא לשחדו בממון ולא עוד אלא שיש לפני שני דרכים אחת של ג"ע ואחת של גיהנם ואיני יודע באיזו מוליכי' אותי ולא אבכה אמרו לו רבינו ברכנו א"ל י"ר "שתהא מורא שמים עליכם כמורא בשר ודם א"ל תלמידיו עד כאן אמר להם ולואי תדעו כשאדם עובר עבירה אומר שלא יראני אדם בשעת פטירתו אמר להם פנו כלים מפני הטומאה והכינו כסא לחזקיהו מלך יהודה שבא: **מתני'** ר"ג אומר בכל יום ויום מתפלל אדם י"ח ר' יהושע אומר מעין י"ח ר"ע אומר "אם שגור' תפלתו בפיו מתפלל י"ח ואם לאו מעין י"ח רבי אליעזר אומר העושה תפלתו קבע אין תפלתו תחנונים רבי יהושע אומר ההולך במקום סכנה מתפלל *תפלה קצרה ואומר הושע יי' את עמך את שארית ישראל בכל פרשת העבור יהיו צרכיהם לפניך ברוך אתה ה' שומע *תפלה היה רוכב על החמור ירד ויתפלל ואם אינו יכול לירד יחזיר את פניו ואם אינו יכול להחזיר את פניו יכוין את לבו כנגד בית קדשי הקדשים היה מהלך בספינה או באסדא יכוין את לבו כנגד בית קדשי הקדשים: **גמ'** הני י"ח כנגד מי א"ר הלל בריה דרבי שמואל בר נחמני *כנגד י"ח אזכרות שאמר דוד °הבו לי"י בני אלים רב יוסף אמר כנגד שמונה עשרה אזכרות שבקריאת שמע אמר רבי תנחום אמר רבי יהושע בן לוי כנגד שמונה עשרה חליות שבשדרה: ואמר רבי תנחום אמר ריב"ל "המתפלל צריך שיכרע עד שיתפקקו כל חליות שבשדרה עולא אמר "עד כדי שיראה איסר כנגד לבו רבי חנינא אמר "כיון שנענע ראשו שוב אינו צריך אמר רבא "והוא דמצער נפשיה ומחזי כמאן דכרע. הני תמני סרי תשסרי הויין א"ר לוי ברכת הצדוקים ביבנה תקנוה כנגד מי תקנוה אמר רבי לוי בריה דרבי שמואל בר נחמני לרבי הלל כנגד °אל הכבוד הרעים לרב יוסף כנגד אחד שבקריאת שמע לרבי תנחום א"ר יהושע בן לוי כנגד חוליא קטנה שבשדרה: *ת"ר שמעון הפקולי הסדיר שמונה עשרה ברכות לפני ר"ג על הסדר ביבנה אמר להם ר"ג לחכמי' כלום יש אדם שיודע לתקן ברכת הצדוקים עמד שמואל הקטן ותקנה לשנה אחרת שכחה

והשקיף

מ א מיי' פ"י מהלכ' תפלה הל' יו סמג עשין יט טוש"ע א"ח סי' ל סעי' י

מא ב מיי' פ"ו שם הל' ד סמג שם טוש"ע א"ח סי' רפו סעי' ג

מב ד מיי' וסמג שם טוש"ע א"ח סי' רלב סעי' ג

מג ה מיי' פ"י מה' ברכות הל' כ"ב כ"ד סמ"ג עשין כז טור וש"ע א"ח סי' קי סעי' ח

מד ו טור וש"ע א"ח סי' א סעי' ל

מה ז מיי' פ"ב מהל' תפל' ה"א סמ"ג עשין יט טוש"ע א"ח סי' ק"י סעי' א

מו ח ט מיי' פ"ה שם הי"ב סמג שם טוש"ע א"ח סי' ק"ג סעי' ד

מז י כ מיי' שם טוש"ע שם סעי' ה

מסורת הש"ס

שבת ט:

(בירושלמי גרס מה טיבה של תפלה זו)

(ירושלמי גרס שלא אקפיד כנגד חבירי ולא יקפידו ועוד הרבה שנוים שם)

(ירושלמי גרס תפלה קצרה מעין י"ח)

(ירוש' מוסיף ותחנונים)

תוספתא פ"ג תהלים כט

שם

מגילה י"ז:

(5) Ps. XXIX.

d (1) A coin, v. Glos. (2) I.e., till the flesh bulges. (3) V. Glos. The reading 'Sadducees' in our edd. is a censor's correction. (4) After the rest. (5) This is a marginal correction of the reading in the text, R. Levi son of R. Samuel b. Naḥmani said: R. Hillel etc. (6) Ps. XXIX, 3. The Hebrew for God here is *El*. (7) Which is also considered a Divine Name. (8) Possibly this word means 'cotton seller'. On this passage, cf. Meg. 17. (9) On a subsequent occasion. (10) V. n. d3.

and she herself is in bitterness.[8] [28*b*] R. 'Awia was once ill and did not go to hear the lecture of R. Joseph.[9] On the next day when he came Abaye tried to appease R. Joseph. He said to him [R. 'Awia]: Why did your honour not come to the lecture yesterday? He replied: I felt weak and was not able. He said to him: Why did you not take some food and come? He replied: Does not your honour hold with the dictum of R. Huna? For R. Huna said: It is forbidden to a man to taste anything until he has said the *musaf Tefillah*. He said to him: Your honour ought to have said the *musaf Tefillah* privately and taken something and come. He replied: Does not your honour hold with what R. Johanan has laid down, that it is forbidden for a man to say his *Tefillah* before the congregation says it? He said to him: Has it not been said in regard to this: This refers to when he is with the congregation? And the law is neither as stated by R. Huna nor by R. Joshua b. Levi. 'It is not as stated by R. Huna', namely in what we have
a just said.[1] 'It is not as stated by R. Joshua b. Levi', namely, in what R. Joshua b. Levi said: When the time for the *minhah Tefillah* arrives it is forbidden to a man to taste anything until he has said the *minhah Tefillah*.

MISHNAH. R. NEHUNIA B. HA-KANEH USED TO SAY A PRAYER AS HE ENTERED THE BETH HA-MIDRASH AND AS HE LEFT IT—A SHORT PRAYER. THEY SAID TO HIM: WHAT SORT OF PRAYER IS THIS? HE REPLIED: WHEN I ENTER I PRAY THAT NO OFFENCE SHOULD OCCUR THROUGH ME,[2] AND WHEN I LEAVE I EXPRESS THANKS FOR MY LOT.

GEMARA. Our Rabbis taught: On entering what does a man[3] say? 'May it be Thy will, O Lord my God, that no offence may occur through me, and that I may not err in a matter of *halachah* and that my colleagues may rejoice in me[4] and that I may not call unclean clean or clean unclean, and that my colleagues may not err in a matter of *halachah* and that I may rejoice in them'. On his leaving what does he say? 'I give thanks to Thee, O Lord my God, that Thou hast set my portion with those who sit in the Beth ha-Midrash and Thou hast not set my portion with those who sit in [street] corners,[5] for I rise early and they rise early, but I rise early for words of Torah and they rise early for frivolous talk; I labour and they labour, but I labour and receive a reward and they labour and do not receive a reward; I run and they run, but I run to the life of the future world and they run to the pit of destruction.

Our Rabbis taught: When R. Eliezer fell ill, his disciples went in to visit him. They said to him: Master, teach us the paths of life so that we may through them win the life of the future world. He said to them: Be solicitous for the honour of your colleagues,
b and keep your children from meditation,[1] and set them between the knees of scholars, and when you pray know before whom you are standing and in this way you will win the future world.

When Rabban Johanan ben Zakkai fell ill, his disciples went in to visit him. When he saw them he began to weep. His disciples said to him: Lamp of Israel, pillar of the right hand,[2] mighty hammer! Wherefore weepest thou? He replied: If I were being taken today before a human king who is here today and tomorrow in the grave, whose anger if he is angry with me does not last for ever, who if he imprisons me does not imprison me for ever and who if he puts me to death does not put me to everlasting death, and whom I can persuade with words and bribe with money, even so I would weep. Now that I am being taken before the supreme King of Kings, the Holy One, blessed be He, who lives and endures for ever and ever, whose anger, if He is angry with me, is an everlasting anger, who if He imprisons me imprisons me for ever, who if He puts me to death puts me to death for ever, and whom I cannot persuade with words or bribe with money—nay more, when there are two ways before me, one leading to Paradise and the other to Gehinnom, and I do not know by which I shall be taken, shall I not weep? They said to him: Master, bless us. He said to them: May it be [God's] will that the fear of heaven shall be upon you like the fear of flesh and blood. His disciples said to him: Is that all?[3] He said to them: If only [you can attain this]! You can see [how important this is], for when a man wants to commit a transgression, he says, I hope no man will see me.[4] At the moment of his departure he said to them: Remove the vessels so that they shall not become unclean, and prepare a throne for Hezekiah the
c king of Judah who is coming.[1]

MISHNAH. RABBAN GAMALIEL SAYS: EVERY DAY A MAN SHOULD SAY THE EIGHTEEN BENEDICTIONS. R. JOSHUA SAYS: AN ABBREVIATED EIGHTEEN.[2] R. AKIBA SAYS: IF HE KNOWS IT FLUENTLY HE SAYS THE ORIGINAL EIGHTEEN, AND IF NOT AN ABBREVIATED EIGHTEEN. R. ELIEZER SAYS: IF A MAN MAKES HIS PRAYERS A FIXED TASK, IT IS NOT A [GENUINE] SUPPLICATION. R. JOSHUA SAYS: IF ONE IS TRAVELLING IN A DANGEROUS PLACE, HE SAYS A SHORT PRAYER, SAYING, SAVE, O LORD, THY PEOPLE THE REMNANT OF ISRAEL; IN EVERY TIME OF CRISIS[3] MAY THEIR REQUIREMENTS NOT BE LOST SIGHT OF BY THEE. BLESSED ART THOU, O LORD, WHO HEARKENEST TO PRAYER. IF HE IS RIDING ON AN ASS HE DISMOUNTS AND PRAYS. IF HE IS UNABLE TO DISMOUNT HE SHOULD TURN HIS FACE [TOWARDS JERUSALEM]; AND IF HE CANNOT TURN HIS FACE HE SHOULD CONCENTRATE HIS THOUGHTS ON THE HOLY OF HOLIES. IF HE IS TRAVELLING IN A SHIP OR ON A RAFT,[4] HE SHOULD CONCENTRATE HIS THOUGHTS ON THE HOLY OF HOLIES.

GEMARA. To what do these eighteen benedictions correspond? R. Hillel the son of Samuel b. Nahmani said: To the eighteen times that David mentioned the Divine Name in the Psalm, *Ascribe unto the Lord, O ye sons of might.*[5] R. Joseph said: To the eighteen times the Divine Name is mentioned in the *Shema'*. R. Tanhum said in the name of R. Joshua b. Levi: To the eighteen vertebrae in the spinal column.

R. Tanhum also said in the name of R. Joshua b. Levi: In saying the *Tefillah* one should bow down [at the appropriate places] until all the vertebrae in the spinal column are loosened. 'Ulla says:
d Until an *issar*[1] of flesh is visible opposite his heart.[2] R. Hanina said: If he simply bows his head, he need do no more. Said Raba: This is only if it hurts him [to stoop] and he shows that he would like to bow down.

These eighteen are really nineteen?—R. Levi said: The benediction relating to the *Minim*[3] was instituted in Jabneh.[4] To what was it meant to correspond?—R. Levi said: On the view of R. Hillel the son of R. Samuel b. Nahmani,[5] to *The God of Glory thundereth;*[6] on the view of R. Joseph, to the word 'One'[7] in the *Shema'*; on the view of R. Tanhum quoting R. Joshua b. Levi, to the little vertebrae in the spinal column.

Our Rabbis taught: Simeon ha-Pakuli[8] arranged the eighteen benedictions in order before Rabban Gamaliel in Jabneh. Said Rabban Gamaliel to the Sages:[9] Can any one among you frame a benediction relating to the *Minim?*[10] Samuel the Lesser arose and

(8) Lam. I, 4. (9) R. Joseph was the head of the school at Pumbeditha and he used to lecture every Sabbath morning before the *musaf* prayer.

a (1) That he must not eat anything before saying *musaf*. (2) E.g., by giving a wrong decision. (3) Lit., 'he say'; referring perhaps to R. Nehunia. (4) Rashi translates: so that my colleagues may rejoice over me, i.e., over my discomfiture, and so bring sin upon themselves; and similarly in the next clause. (5) Rashi explains this to mean shopkeepers or ignorant people. For an alternative rendering v. Sanh., Sonc. ed., p. 6, n. 4.

b (1) Rashi explains this to mean too much reading of Scripture, or alternatively, childish talk. Others explain it as philosophic speculation. (2) The reference is to the two pillars in the Temple. V. I Kings VII, 21. (3) Should not the fear of God be more than that? (4) And therefore if the fear of God is no more than this, it will keep him from many sins.

c (1) *Sc.* to accompany me into the next world. Perhaps because he, like Hezekiah, had acted mightily for the spread of Torah; v. Sanh. 94*b*. (2) Lit., 'like the eighteen'. V. *infra* in the Gemara. (3) Lit., 'section of the crossing', i.e., transition from one condition to another. (4) *Aliter:* in prison.

composed it. The next year[11] he forgot it [29a] and he tried for two or three hours to recall it, and they did not remove him.[12] Why did they not remove him seeing that Rab Judah has said in the name of Rab: If a reader made a mistake in any of the other benedictions, they do not remove him, but if in the benediction of the *Minim*, he is removed, because we suspect him of being a *Min?*—Samuel the Lesser is different, because he composed it. But is there not a fear that he may have recanted?—Abaye said: We have a tradition that a good man does not become bad. But does he not? It is not written, *But when the righteous turneth away from his righteousness and committeth iniquity?*[13]—Such a man was originally wicked, but one who was originally righteous does not do so. But is that so? Have we not learnt: Believe not in thyself until
a the day of thy death?[1] For lo, Johanan the High Priest officiated as High Priest for eighty years and in the end he became a *Min?* Abaye said: Johanan[2] is the same as Jannai.[3] Raba said: Johanan and Jannai are different; Jannai was originally wicked and Johanan was originally righteous. On Abaye's view there is no difficulty, but on Raba's view there is a difficulty?—Raba can reply: For one who was originally righteous it is also possible to become a renegade. If that is the case, why did they not remove him?—Samuel the Lesser is different, because he had already commenced to say it [the benediction]. For Rab Judah said in the name of Rab—or as some say, R. Joshua b. Levi: This applies only if he has not commenced to say it, but if he has commenced, he is allowed to finish.

To what do the seven blessings said on Sabbath[4] correspond?—R. Halefta b. Saul said: To the seven voices mentioned by David [commencing with] *'on the waters'*.[5] To what do the nine said on New Year [*Musaf-Tefillah*] correspond?[6] Isaac from Kartignin[7] said: To the nine times that Hannah mentioned the Divine Name in her prayer.[8] For a Master has said: On New Year Sarah, Rachel and Hannah were visited.[9] To what do the twenty-four said on a fast day correspond?[10] R. Helbo said: To the twenty-four times that Solomon used the expression 'prayer' etc. on the occasion when he brought the ark into the Holy of Holies.[11] If that is so, then let us say them every day?—When did Solomon say them? On a day of supplication;[12] We also say them on a day of supplication.

R. JOSHUA SAYS: AN ABBREVIATED EIGHTEEN. What is meant by 'AN ABBREVIATED EIGHTEEN'? Rab said: An abbreviated form of each blessing; Samuel said: Give us discernment, O Lord, to know Thy ways, and circumcise our heart to fear Thee, and forgive us so that we may be redeemed, and keep us far from our sufferings, and fatten us in the pastures of Thy land, and gather our dispersions from the four corners of the earth, and let them who err from Thy prescriptions be punished,[1] and lift up Thy hand against the wicked, and let the righteous rejoice in the building of Thy city and the establishment of the temple and in the exalting of the horn of David Thy servant and the preparation of a light for the son of Jesse Thy Messiah; before we call mayest Thou answer; blessed art Thou, O Lord, who hearkenest to prayer.[2] Abaye cursed anyone who prayed 'Give us discernment'.[3]

R. Nahman said in the name of Samuel: A man may say 'Give us discernment' any time of the year except on the outgoing of Sabbath and of festivals, because he has to say *habdalah* in 'that graciously giveth knowledge'. Rabbah b. Samuel demurred to this. Let him, [he said] make a fourth blessing[4] of it by itself. Have we not learnt: R. Akiba says: He says it as a fourth blessing by itself; R. Eleazar says: He says it in the thanksgiving?[5]—Do we follow R. Akiba all the year that we should follow him now? Why do we not follow R. Akiba the rest of the year? Because eighteen blessings were instituted, not nineteen. Here too, seven were instituted,[6] not eight. Mar Zutra demurred to this. Let him [he said] include it[7] in 'Give us discernment' [by saying], O Lord, our God, who distinguisheth between holy and profane.—This is indeed a difficulty.

R. Bibi b. Abaye said: A man may say 'Give us discernment' any time in the year except in the rainy season, because he requires
c to make a request in the benediction of the years.[1] Mar Zutra demurred to this. Let him include it [by saying], And fatten us in the pastures of Thy land and give dew and rain?—He might become confused. If so, by saying *habdalah*[2] in 'that grantest discernment' he might equally become confused? They replied: In that case, since it comes near the beginning of the *Tefillah* he will not become confused, here, as it comes in the middle of the *Tefillah* he will become confused. R. Ashi demurred to this. Let him say it in 'that hearkenest to prayer'?[3] For R. Tanhum said in the name of R. Assi: If a man made a mistake and did not mention the miracle of rain[4] in the benediction of he resurrection of the dead, we turn him back;[5] [if he forgot] the request for rain in the benediction of the years,[6] we do not turn him back, because he can say it in 'that hearkenest unto prayer', and [if he forgot] *habdalah* in 'that grantest knowledge' we do not turn him back, because he can say it later over wine?[7]—A mistake is different.[8]

The text above [said]: R. Tanhum said in the name of R. Assi: If one made a mistake and did not mention the miracle of rain in the benediction of the resurrection, he is turned back; [if he forgot] the request in the benediction of the years he is not turned back, because he can say it in 'that hearkenest unto prayer'; [if he forgot] *habdalah* in 'that grantest knowledge' he is not turned back, because he can say it later over wine. An objection was raised: If one made a mistake and did not mention the miracle of rain in the benediction of the resurrection, he is turned back; [if he forgot] the request in the benediction of the years, he is turned back; [if he forgot] *habdalah* in 'that grantest knowledge' he is not turned back because he can say it later over wine!—There is no contradiction; the one case where he is turned back refers to where he is saying it by himself, the other, with the congregation. What is the reason why he is not turned back when he says it with the
d congregation? Because he hears it from the Reader,[1] is it not? If so then instead of 'because he can say it in "who hearkenest unto prayer"', we should have 'because he hears it from the Reader'?—In fact in both cases he is saying it by himself, and still there is no contradiction; the one case refers to where he remembers before

(11) Apparently this benediction was at that time not recited daily as now, but on special annual occasions. (12) From his post as reader. (13) Ezek. XVIII, 24.

(1) Ab. II, 4. (2) The Hasmonean king, John Hyrcanus, is meant. (3) Alexander Jannaeus who was always hostile to the Pharisees, and who massacred Pharisaic Sages. Cf. Kid., Sonc. ed., p. 332, n. 12. (4) In the *Tefillah*, instead of the eighteen on week-days. V. *P.B.* 136-142. (5) Ps. XXIX, 3. (6) V. P.B. p. 239-242. (7) Carthage or Carthagena in Spain. (8) I Sam. II, 1-10. (9) V. R.H. 11*a*. (10) Ta'an. II, 3, where six additional blessings to be said on fast days are mentioned. (11) I Kings VIII, 23-53. (12) Because the gates would not open. V. M.K. 9*a*.

(1) Rashi, following *Halakoth Gedoloth* emends, Let those who err in judgment, judge according to Thy word. (2) Thus Samuel included the contents of the twelve middle benedictions in one. (V. *P.B.* p. 55.) The first and last three must in every case be said in full. (3) Instead of the eighteen benedictions in full. (4) After the first three. (5) *Infra* 33*a*. (6) I.e., the first and last three and 'Give us discernment'. (7) The reference to *habdalah*.

c (1) The twelfth. (2) In the *Tefillah* on the termination of the Sabbath. (3) Which is at the conclusion of the prayer. (4) Lit., 'the (divine) might (manifested) in the rain'. (5) Because this, not being a prayer, cannot be said in 'that hearkenest unto prayer'. (6) V. *P.B.* p. 47. (7) V. ibid. p. 216. (8) From something which can confuse the person praying.

d (1) When he repeats the *'Amidah*. V. Glos.

והשקיף בה שתים ושלש שעות ולא העלוהו אמאי לא העלוהו והאמר רב יהודה אמר רב *טעה בכל הברכות כולן אין מעלין אותו בברכת הצדוקים מעלין אותו חיישינן שמא מין הוא שאני שמואל הקטן דאיהו תקנה וניחוש דלמא הדר ביה אמר אביי גמירי טבא לא הוי בישא ולא והכתיב °ובשוב צדיק מצדקתו ועשה עול ההוא רשע מעיקרו אבל צדיק מעיקרו לא ולא והא תנן *אל תאמן בעצמך עד יום מותך שהרי *יוחנן כהן גדול שמש בכהונה גדולה שמנים שנה ולבסוף נעשה צדוקי *אמר אביי הוא ינאי הוא יוחנן רבא אמר ינאי לחוד ויוחנן לחוד ינאי רשע מעיקרו ויוחנן צדיק מעיקרו הניחא לאביי אלא לרבא קשיא אמר לך רבא צדיק מעיקרו נמי דילמא הדר ביה אי הכי אמאי לא אסקוהו שאני שמואל הקטן דאתחיל בה דאמר רב יהודה אמר רב ואיתימא רבי יהושע בן לוי [ב]לא שנו אלא שלא התחיל בה אבל התחיל בה גומרה: הני שבע דשבתא כנגד מי א"ר חלפתא בן שאול כנגד שבעה קולות שאמר דוד על המים הני תשע דראש השנה כנגד מי א"ר יצחק דמן קרטיגנין כנגד תשעה אזכרות שאמרה חנה בתפלתה דאמר מר *בראש השנה נפקדה שרה רחל וחנה הני עשרים וארבע דתעניתא כנגד מי א"ר חלבו כנגד כ"ד רננות *שאמר שלמה בשעה שהכניס ארון לבית קדשי הקדשים אי הכי כל יומא נמי נמרינהו אימת אמרינהו. שלמה ביומא דרחמי אנן נמי ביומא דרחמי אמרי להו: רבי יהושע אומר מעין שמנה עשרה: מאי מעין י"ח רב אמר מעין כל ברכה וברכה ושמואל אמר [ג]הבינו ה' אלהינו לדעת דרכיך ומול את לבבנו ליראתך ותסלח לנו להיות גאולים ורחקנו ממכאובינו ודשננו בנאות ארצך ונפוצותינו מארבע תקבץ והתועים על דעתך ישפטו ועל הרשעים תניף ידיך וישמחו צדיקים בבנין עירך ובתקון היכלך ובצמיחת קרן לדוד עבדך ובעריכת נר לבן ישי משיחך טרם נקרא אתה תענה ברוך אתה ה' שומע תפלה *לייט עלה אביי אמאן דמצלי הבינו אמר רב נחמן אמר שמואל [ד]כל השנה כולה מתפלל אדם הבינו חוץ ממוצאי שבת וממוצאי ימים טובים מפני שצריך לומר הבדלה בחונן הדעת מתקיף לה רבה בר שמואל ונימרה ברכה רביעית בפני עצמה מי לא תנן *רבי עקיבא אומר אומרה ברכה רביעית בפני עצמה רבי אליעזר אומר בהודאה *אטו כל השנה כולה מי עבדינן כר' עקיבא דהשתא נמי נעבד כל השנה כולה מ"ט לא עבדינן כר' עקיבא תמני סרי תקון תשסרי לא תקון הכא נמי שבע תקון תמני לא תקון מתקיף לה מר זוטרא ונכללה מכלל הבינו ה' אלהינו המבדיל בין קדש לחול קשיא: אמר רב ביבי בר אביי [ה]כל השנה כולה מתפלל אדם הבינו חוץ מימות הגשמים מפני שצריך לומר שאלה בברכת השנים מתקיף לה מר זוטרא ונכללה מכלל ודשננו בנאות ארצך ותן טל ומטר אתי לאטרודי אי הכי הבדלה בחונן הדעת נמי אתי לאטרודי אמרי התם כיון דאתיא בתחלת צלותא לא מטריד הכא כיון דאתיא באמצע צלותא מטריד מתקיף לה רב אשי ונימרה בשומע תפלה דאמר ר' תנחום אמר רב אסי טעה ולא הזכיר גבורות גשמים בתחיית המתים מחזירין אותו שאלה בברכת השנים אין מחזירין אותו מפני שיכול לאומרה בשומע תפלה והבדלה בחונן הדעת אין מחזירין אותו מפני שיכול לאומרה על הכוס טעה שאני: גופא אמר ר' תנחום אמר רב אסי טעה ולא הזכיר גבורות גשמים בתחיית המתים מחזירין אותו שאלה בברכת השנים אין מחזירין אותו מפני שיכול לאומרה בשומע תפלה והבדלה בחונן הדעת אין מחזירין אותו מפני שיכול לאומרה על הכוס מיתיבי *טעה ולא הזכיר גבורות גשמים בתחיית המתים מחזירין אותו [ו]שאלה בברכה השנים מחזירין אותו [ז]והבדלה בחונן הדעת אין מחזירין אותו מפני שיכול לאומרה על הכוס לא קשיא הא ביחיד הא בצבור בצבור מ"ט לא משום דשמעה משליח צבור אי הכי האי מפני שיכול לאומרה בשומע תפלה מפני ששומע משליח צבור מיבעי ליה אלא אידי ואידי ביחיד ולא קשיא °הא דאדכר קודם שומע תפלה

הא

תורה אור: יחזקאל יח

נ"ל ולמאי

רש"י

והשקיף. חשב לזכור אותה לשון סוכה כדמתרגמינן וישקף ואסתכי (בראשית יט): רשע מעיקרו. ושב מרשעתו פעמים שחוזר ונעשה רשע: הוא ינאי. שהרגו בקידושין (פ"ג דף סו.) שהרג חכמי ישראל: ינאי רשע מעיקרו. ונעשה לדיק וחזר לרשעתו: דאתחיל בה. התחיל לאמרה וטעה באמצעיתה: לא שנו. הא דאמר רב יהודה מעלין אותו: שבעה קולות. במזמור קול ה' על המים (תהלים כט): שאמרה חנה. בפרשת עלץ לבי (שמואל א' ב'): כ"ד רננות. בפרשת ויעמוד שלמה (מלכים א' ח') רנה תפלה תחנה כלהון כ"ד איכא: ביומא דרחמי. שהולך לבקש רחמים שדבקו שערים זה בזה ולא היו מניחין להכניס ארון לבית קדשי הקדשים כדאמרינן במועד קטן (ד' ט.): מעין כל ברכה. אומר בקוצר ומברך על כל אחת ואחת: הבינו. ואינו מברך אלא שומע תפלה בכל הברכות שבין שלש ראשונות לשלש אחרונות הבינו כנגד אתה חונן ומול את לבבנו כנגד השיבנו לסלוח לנו כנגד סלח לנו להיות גאולים כנגד גאולה וכן כולם: בנאות ארצך. לשון נוה כמו בנאות דשא ירביצני (תהלים כג) והוא כנגד ברכת השנים: והתועים על דעתך. העוברים על דבריך ישפטו כנגד צדקה ומשפט לשון אחר והתועים במשפט על דעתך ישפטו השיבם ללמדם לשפוט כדבריך וכן עיקר נראה לי וכן בהלכות גדולות: לייט עלה אביי. לפי שמדלג הברכות וכוללן בברכה אחת: כל השנה מי עבדינן כר' עקיבא. כלומר כשאנו מתפללין י"ח שלמות מי עבדינן כר' עקיבא לומר ברכה רביעית בפני עצמה דהשתא כשמתפללין הבינו נעבד כותיה: שבע תקון. שלש ראשונות ושלש אחרונות והבינו: ונכלל. להבדלה: מכלל. בתוך הבינו כדרך שהוא כוללה בחונן הדעת ויאמר הבינו ה' אלהינו המבדיל בין קודש לחול לדעת דרכיך: לאטרודי. לטעות: בתחלת התפלה. יכול אדם לכוין דעתו יותר מן האמצע: גבורות גשמים. הזכרה בעלמא היא לפיכך מחזירין אותו שאינה תפלה שיכול לאומרה בש"ת: ביחיד. מחזירין אותו: בצבור. יחיד המתפלל עם הצבור: דאדכר קודם ש"ת. אין מחזירין אותו שיכול לאומרה בש"ת:

תחנונים

תוספות

לייט עלה אביי אמאן דמצלי הבינו. והכי קי"ל ויש ספרים דמסיק ה"מ במתא אבל בדרך שרי כדמשמע במכילתין גבי ר' יוסי וכו':

ונכלליה בהבינו. והא דאמרינן בפ"ק דנדה (דף ח:) כל השנה כולה מתפלל אדם י"ח חוץ ממוצאי יה"כ מפני טורח צבור מפני התענית וי"א שמתפללים י"ח שלמות מפני שצ"ל הבדלה בחונן הדעת ותימה אמאי לא פריך ונכלליה בהבינו וי"ל דלא דמי דהתם כל השנה כולה מתפלל י"ח ואין לנו להקשות ונכלליה מכלל כדי לשנות המנהג של כל השנה אבל הכא שכל השנה מתפלל הבינו פריך שפיר למה לי לשנות המנהג בשביל אתה חוננתנו ונכלליה בהבינו:

מפני שיכול לאומרה בש"ת. כדאמר (ע"ז דף ח.) שואל אדם לרכיו בש"ת ודוקא לרכיו כגון שיש לו חולה בתוך ביתו או שצריך שדהו מים דהוא מעין תפלה וכן שאלה אבל הזכרה והבדלה ושאר שבחא אסור שאינם מעין ש"ת ונראה שכל האומר ברוך אתה ה' ש"ת אחר שסיי' דברי תחנונים מיושב מגונה כדאמרינן (מגילה דף יח.) מכאן ואילך אסור לספר בשבחו של מקום כלומר להוסיף ברכות על אלו ואפילו אם בא להתפלל שמנה עשרה עוד פעם אחרת אסור שנרא' כמוסיף על הברכות והא דאמר לעיל (דף כא.) הלואי שיתפלל אדם כל היום היינו דוקא ספק התפלל אבל ודאי אוקימנן לעיל שפוסק אפילו באמצע ברכה כשמואל בפרק מי שמתו (שם) ומה שהליח לבור שוהה בהן היינו להוציא רבים ידי חובתן ומה שמתפלל בלחש היינו כדי להסדיר תפלתו כדמוקמינן בפ"ד דר"ה (דף ל"ד:):

הא

עין משפט נר מצוה

מח
א ב מיי' פ"י מהלכות תפלה הלכה ג סמג עשין יט טוש"ע א"ח סי' קכו סעי' א

מט
ג ד מיי' פ"ב שם הל' ג ד סמג שם טוש"ע א"ח סי' קי סעי' א

נ
ה מיי' פ"י שם הל' ח סמג שם טוש"ע א"ח סי' קיד סעי' ה

נא
ו מיי' שם הל' ע וסמג שם טוש"ע א"ח סי' קיז סעי' ד

נב
ז מיי' שם הל' יד וסמג שם טוש"ע א"ח סי' רלד סעי' א

נג
ט מיי' שם הל' ט וסמג שם טוש"ע א"ח סי' קיז סעי' ה

מסורת הש"ס

[אבות פ"ב מ"ד] [יומא ט.]

[ר"ה יא. יבמות סד:]

[שבת ל.]

[קידושין לג: וש"נ]

אין עומדין לג. נדה ח. [לקמן לג.]

תוספתא פ"ג לעיל כו: לקמן לג. תענית ג:

תורה אור

הא דאדכר בתר שומע תפלה: א"ר תנחום א"ר אסי אמר ריב"ל "טעה ולא הזכיר של ראש חדש בעבודה חוזר לעבודה נזכר בהודאה חוזר לעבודה בשים שלום חוזר לעבודה ואם סיים חוזר לראש אמר רב פפא בריה דרב אחא בר אדא הא דאמרן סיים חוזר לראש לא אמרן אלא שעקר רגליו אבל לא עקר רגליו חוזר לעבודה א"ל מנא לך הא א"ל מאבא מרי שמיע לי ואבא מרי מרב אמר רב נחמן בר יצחק הא דאמרן עקר רגליו חוזר לראש לא אמרן אלא שאינו רגיל לומר תחנונים אחר תפלתו אבל רגיל לומר תחנונים אחר תפלתו חוזר לעבודה איכא דאמרי אמר רב נחמן בר יצחק הא דאמר כי לא עקר רגליו חוזר לעבודה לא אמרן אלא שרגיל לומר תחנונים אחר תפלתו אבל אם אינו רגיל לומר תחנונים אחר תפלתו חוזר לראש: רבי אליעזר אומר העושה תפלתו קבע וכו': מאי קבע א"ר יעקב בר אידי א"ר אושעי' "כל שתפלתו דומה עליו כמשוי ורבנן אמרי "כל מי שאינו אומרה בלשון תחנונים רבה ורב יוסף דאמרי תרוייהו כל שאינו יכול לחדש בה דבר א"ר זירא אנא יכילנא לחדושי בה מילתא ומסתפינא דלמא מטרידנא אביי בר אבין ורבי חנינא בר אבין דאמרי תרוייהו כל שאין מתפלל עם דמדומי חמה דאמר רבי חייא בר אבא אמר רבי יוחנן *מצוה "להתפלל עם דמדומי חמה ואמר רבי זירא מאי קראה °ייראוך עם שמש ולפני ירח דור דורים *לייטי עלה במערבא אמאן דמצלי עם דמדומי חמה מאי טעמא דילמא מיטרפא ליה שעתא: ר' יהושע אומר המהלך במקום סכנה מתפלל תפלה קצרה וכו' בכל פרשת העבור: מאי פרשת העבור אמר רב חסדא אמר מר עוקבא אפילו בשעה שאתה מתמלא עליהם עברה כאשה עוברת יהיו כל צרכיהם לפניך איכא דאמרי אמר רב חסדא אמר מר עוקבא אפילו בשעה שהם עוברים על דברי תורה יהיו כל צרכיהם לפניך ת"ר *המהלך במקום גדודי חיה ולסטים מתפלל תפלה קצרה ואיזה היא תפלה קצרה רבי אליעזר אומר עשה רצונך בשמים ממעל ותן נחת רוח ליריאך מתחת והטוב בעיניך עשה ברוך אתה ה' שומע תפלה ר' יהושע אומר שמע שועת עמך ישראל ועשה מהרה בקשתם בא"י ש"ת רבי אליעזר בר' צדוק אומר שמע צעקת עמך ישראל ועשה מהרה בקשתם בא"י ש"ת אחרים אומרים צרכי עמך ישראל מרובין ודעתם קצרה יהי רצון מלפניך ה' אלהינו שתתן לכל אחד ואחד כדי פרנסתו ולכל גויה וגויה די מחסורה בא"י ש"ת אמר רב הונא "הלכה כאחרי' א"ל אליהו לרב יהודה אחוה דרב סלא חסידא "לא תרתח ולא תחטי לא תרוי ולא תחטי וכשאתה יוצא לדרך המלך בקונך וצא מאי המלך בקונך וצא א"ר יעקב אמר רב חסדא זו תפלת הדרך וא"ר יעקב אמר רב חסדא כל היוצא לדרך צריך להתפלל תפלת הדרך מאי ת"ה "יר"מ ה' אלהי שתוליכני לשלום ותצעידני לשלום ותסמכני לשלום ותצילני מכף כל אויב ואורב בדרך ותשלח ברכה במעשה ידי ותתנני לחן לחסד ולרחמים בעיניך ובעיני כל רואי ברוך אתה ה' שומע תפלה אמר אביי "לעולם

לישתף

רש"י

תחנונים. כגון אלהי נצור לשוני מרע שאנו אומרים בעמידה אחר תפלה: אבל אם אינו רגיל. הוה סיום תפלתו כעקירה אפי' לא עקר: כמשוי. והיינו לשון קבע חוק קבוע הוא עלי להתפלל וצריך אני לצאת ידי חובתי: מי שאינו יכול. לכוין לבו לשאול צרכיו: לחדש בה דבר. בבקשתו והיינו לשון קבע כהיום כן אתמול כן מחר: דלמא מטרידנא. שמא אטעה ולא אדע לחזור למקום שהפסקתי: שאינו מתפלל עם דמדומי חמה. והיינו לשון קבע תפלתו עליו חק קבוע לצאת ידי חובתו ואינו מקפיד לחזר אחר שעת מצוה ועת רצון: עם דמדומי חמה. תפלת יוצר עם הנץ החמה ותפלת המנחה עם שקיעת החמה: ייראוך עם שמש. זו תפלת יוצר: ולפני ירח. זו מנחה: לייטי במערבא. על מי שמשהה תפלת המנחה עד דמדומי חמה שמא תטרף לו השעה ע"י אונס ועבר הזמן: בכל פרשת העבור וכו'. כמו פרישת העבור אפי' בשעה שאתה מתמלא עליהם עברה כאשה עוברת. והכי משמע בכל ענייני פרישת העבור כגון עברה *בעברה: יהיו כל צרכיהם. גלוים לפניך לרחם עליהם: אפי' בשעה שהם עוברים. ולשון פרשת העבור שהן פורשין לעבירה: עשה רצונך בשמים. שאין שם חטא ואין רצונך עליהם אלא לטוב ועבור לתחתונים על רצונך: ותן. להם ליראיך: נחת רוח. שלא יתערבב רוחם ע"י הבריות כגון ע"י חיות ולסטים: והטוב בעיניך עשה. אתה להם ודוגמא זו מצינו בספר שופטים (י) ויאמרו בני ישראל חטאנו עשה אתה לנו כטוב בעיניך אך הצילנו וגו': שועת. לשון בכייה יותר מתפלה: ודעתם קצרה. ואינם יודעים לפרש צרכיהם: לא תרתח ולא תחטי. לא תכעוס שמתוך הכעס אתה בא לידי חטא: לא תרוי. לא תשתכר ביין: המלך. טול רשות:

לישתף

תוספות

הא דאדכר אחר שומע תפלה. אז ודאי מחזירין אותו מיהו אם לא עקר רגליו אינו צריך לחזור לראש ולא לברכת השנים אלא חוזר לשומע תפלה וכן משמע בירוש' פרק אין עומדין דקאמר אם לא שאל בברכת השנים מחזירין אותו והיכן חוזר רבי שמעון בשם רבי יוחנן אמר בר"ח אם עקר רגליו חוזר לראש ואם לאו חוזר לעבודה הכא נמי אם עקר רגליו חוזר לראש ואם לאו חוזר לשומע תפלה אלמא משמע בהדיא דאינו חוזר אלא לשומע תפלה כי לא עקר רגליו מיהו הירושלמי פליג אגמרא דידן בגבורות גשמים דהכא קתני לא הזכיר גבורות גשמים מחזירין אותו ולא קאמר לאומרו בשומע תפלה ובירושלמי קאמר אם לא שאל בברכת השנים אומרה בשומע תפלה ודכותה אם לא הזכיר גבורות גשמים בתחיית המתים מזכיר בשומע תפלה ומה אם שאלה שהיא מדוחק אומרה בשומע תפלה אזכרה שהיא מריוח לא כ"ש אלמא דבהדיא איתא התם דחוזר בגבורות גשמים לשומע תפלה ואפשר להיות שהגמרא שלנו לא חשש לפרשו משום הקל וחומר כדאיתא בירושלמי והא דקתני לא הזכיר גבורות גשמים מחזירין אותו איירי שלא הזכיר כלל בשומע תפלה והא ליתא דהא במסקנא מוקי האי מימרא בנזכר קודם שומע תפלה משום פירכא דשאלה ובירושלמי קאמר היה עומד בטל והזכיר של גשם מחזירין אותו פירוש בימות הקיץ ופריך והא תניא בטל וברוחות לא חייבו חכמים להזכיר והכי פריך כי היכי דאם לא הזכיר כלל מטל אינו עיכוב ואם היה רוצה להזכיר מזכיר ה"כ אם עמד בטל והזכיר של גשם אין לחוש דלא גרע מדלא הזכיר טל כלל ומשני דלא דמי ההוא דמקל ומללי להאי דמללי ולא מקל פירוש מקלל כלומר אינו דומה כשעומד בטל והזכיר של גשם שהוא סימן קללה למי שאינו מזכיר כלל לא טל ולא גשם שאינו מקלל וכן הלכה למעשה שאם עומד בשל טל והזכיר של גשם דמחזירין אותו ואם לא הזכיר משניהם כלל אין מחזירין אותו והדר קאמר בירושלמי קאי בגשם והזכיר בשל טל אין מחזירין אותו ופריך מהכא והתניא או שלא הזכיר גבורות גשמים מחזירין אותו ומשני הא, דאדכר הא דלא אדכר הא דלא אדכר לא טל ולא מטר לכך מחזירין אותו הא דהזכי' של טל ומטר ולא כהירא דפשיט' אם הזכיר שניה' דאין מחזירין אותו ואם לא הזכיר כלל פשיטא דמחזירין אותו אלא ודאי יש לפרש הא דאדכר טל הא דלא אדכר כלל לא טל ולא מטר לפיכך מחזירין אותו אבל אם הזכיר טל אף בימות הגשמים אין מחזירין אותו לכך יש בני אדם שאומרים כל שעה טל מתוך שהם רגילים אם כן בימות הגשמים אם שכח מוריד הגשם אין מחזירין אותו:

טעה ולא הזכיר של ראש חדש בעבודה חוזר לעבודה. ובהלכות גדולות פי' דוקא ביחיד אבל בצבור אינו חוזר מפני ששומעה מש"צ מיהו צריך לדקדק מפי החזן כל אות ואות של תפלה אף על פי שהוא בקי דהא אמרינן בראש השנה (פ"ד ד' ל"ה.) כשם שמוציא את שאינו בקי כך מוציא הבקי ואע"ג דאמרינן התם לא פטר רבן גמליאל אלא העם שבשדות משום דאניסי וטרידי אבל *טעה לא ויש לומר היינו שלא התפלל כלל אבל היכא שהתפלל כבר לא חשבינן ליה כאלו לא התפלל כלל והוא הדין לכל דבר שמחזירין אותו אי הדר שמע ליה משלוחא דצבורא מראש ועד סוף נפיק והרב רבי מאיר פסק דוקא שכח להזכיר של ראש חדש אבל שכח ברכה שלימה מחזירין אותו ואינו יוצא בשמיעתו משליח צבור*: **איכא** דאמרי אמר רב נחמן וכו'. רב אלפס פסק כאיכא דאמרי דברגיל לומר תחנונים ולא עקר רגליו אינו חוזר לראש ואם אינו רגיל גם כי לא עקר רגליו חוזר לראש ואם עקר גם כי רגיל לומר תחנונים כמו אלהי נצור לשוני חוזר לראש: **כל** שאינו יכול לומר תחנונים. פירש ר"ח דאם יכול לומר תחנונים אפי' עליו כמשא הוי תפלה מעליא דלא בעינן אלא לשון תחנונים בלבד:

והיכי

עין משפט נר מצוה

נד א מיי' פ"י מהל' תפלה הל' יוד סמג עשין יט טוש"ע א"ח סי' תכב סעי' א

נה ב מיי' פ"ד שם הלכה יו סמג שם טוש"ע א"ח סי' לח סעי' ג

נו ג מיי' פ"ג שם הל' א ד סמג שם טוש"ע א"ח סי' פט סעי' א ובסי' רל"ג סעי' א

נז ד מיי' פ"ד שם הלכה יט סמג שם טוש"ע א"ח סי' קי סעי' ג

נח ה מיי' פ"א מה' דיעות הלכה ד ופ"ג הל' ג

נט ו מיי' פ"י מה' ברכות סמג ע' כז [ע"ש ולא תמצא והב"י סי' קי תמה על הכמב"ס שהשמיט] טוש"ע א"ח סי' קי סעי' ד

מסורת הש"ס

[ועובדה עי' קידושי' לגדו']

שבת קיח:

[קדושין לב: וסס נסמן]

תהלים עב

תוספתא פ"ג.

[בעי' לא כל"ל וכ"ה שם בכה"מ] [ועיין עוד תוספות ר"ה לד: ד"ה כך]

he comes to 'that hearkenest unto prayer' [29b], the other case where he only remembers after 'that hearkenest unto prayer'.

R. Tanhum said in the name of R. Assi quoting R. Joshua b. Levi: If one made a mistake and did not mention the New Moon in the '*Abodah*[2] benediction, he goes back to the '*Abodah*. If he remembered in the 'thanksgiving',[3] he goes back to the '*Abodah*; if he remembers in 'grant peace',[4] he goes back to the '*Abodah*. If he has finished, he goes back to the beginning. R. Papa son of R. Aha b. Ada said: In saying that if he has finished he goes back to the beginning, we mean only, if he has moved his feet; but if he has not yet moved his feet[5] he goes back to the '*Abodah*. He said to him: From where have you that?—He replied: I have heard it from Abba Meri,[6] and Abba Meri had it from Rab. R. Nahman b. Isaac said: When we say that if he has moved his feet he goes back to the beginning, we mean this to apply only to one who is not accustomed to say a supplication after his *Tefillah*,[7] but if he is accustomed to say a supplication after his *Tefillah*, he goes back to the '*Abodah*. Some report: R. Nahman b. Isaac said: When we say that if he has not moved his feet he goes back to the '*Abodah*, we mean this to apply only to one who is accustomed to say a supplication after his *Tefillah*, but if he is not accustomed to say a supplication after his *Tefillah*, he goes back to the beginning.

R. ELIEZER SAYS: HE WHO MAKES HIS PRAYER A FIXED TASK etc. What is meant by a FIXED TASK?—R. Jacob b. Idi said in the name of R. Oshaiah: Anyone whose prayer is like a heavy burden on him. The Rabbis say: Whoever does not say it in the
a manner of supplication.[1] Rabbah and R. Joseph both say: Whoever is not able to insert something fresh in it.[2] R. Zera said: I can insert something fresh, but I am afraid to do so for fear I should become confused.[3] Abaye b. Abin and R. Hanina b. Abin both said: Whoever does not pray at the first and last appearance of the sun.[4] For R. Hiyya b. Abba said in the name of R. Johanan: It is a religious duty to pray with the first and last appearance of the sun. R. Zera further said: What text confirms this?—*They shall fear Thee with the sun, and before the moon throughout all generations.*[5] In the West they curse anyone who prays [*minhah*] with the last appearance of the sun. Why so?—Perhaps he will miss the time.[6]

R. JOSHUA SAYS: HE WHO IS WALKING IN A DANGEROUS PLACE SAYS A SHORT PRAYER . . . IN EVERY TIME OF CRISIS. What is 'TIME OF CRISIS' ['*ibbur*]? R. Hisda said in the name of Mar 'Ukba: Even at the time when Thou art filled with wrath ['*ebrah*] against them like a pregnant woman, may all their need not be overlooked by Thee.[7] Some there are who say that R. Hisda said in the name of Mar 'Ukba: Even at the time when they transgress ['*oberim*] the words of the Torah may all their requirements not be overlooked by Thee.

Our Rabbis taught: One who passes through a place infested with beasts or bands of robbers says a short *Tefillah*. What is a short *Tefillah*?—R. Eliezer says: Do Thy will in heaven above,[8] and grant relief[9] to them that fear Thee below and do that which is good in Thine eyes.[10] Blessed art Thou, O Lord, who hearest prayer. R. Joshua says: Hear the supplication of Thy people Israel and speedily fulfil their request. Blessed art Thou, O Lord, who hearest prayer. R. Eleazar son of R. Zadok says: Hear the cry of thy people Israel and speedily fulfil their request. Blessed art Thou, O Lord, who hearkenest unto prayer. Others say: The
b needs of Thy people Israel are many and their wit is small.[1] May it be Thy will, O Lord our God, to give to each one his sustenance and to each body what it lacks. Blessed art Thou, O Lord, who hearkenest unto prayer. R. Huna said: The *halachah* follows the 'Others'.

Said Elijah to Rab Judah the brother of R. Sala the Pious: Fall not into a passion and thou wilt not sin, drink not to excess and thou wilt not sin; and when thou goest forth on a journey, seek counsel of thy Maker and go forth. What is meant by 'seek counsel of thy Maker and go forth'?—R. Jacob said in the name of R. Hisda: This refers to the prayer before setting forth on a journey. R. Jacob also said in the name of R. Hisda: Whoever sets forth on a journey should say the prayer for a journey. What is it?—'May it be Thy will, O Lord my God, to lead me forth in peace, and direct my steps in peace and uphold me in peace, and deliver me from the hand of every enemy and ambush by the way, and send a blessing on the works of my hands, and cause me to find grace, kindness, and mercy in Thy eyes and in the eyes of all who see me. Blessed art Thou, O Lord, who hearkenest unto prayer'.[2]

(2) Lit., 'Service': the name of the sixteenth benediction. (3) The last benediction but one. (4) The last benediction. (5) On concluding the *Tefillah*, one steps back three paces. (6) Or, my father, my teacher. (7) E.g., My God, keep my tongue from guile etc. V. *P.B.* p. 54. Cf. also *supra* 16b, 17a.

a (1) I.e., as if he were really asking for a favour. (2) So as to to vary it in case of need. (3) And not know where I broke off. (4) I.e., the morning *Tefillah* in the former case and the afternoon one in the latter. Lit., (*a*) 'the reddening of the sun', (*b*) 'the stillness of the sun' i.e., the time in the morning and evening when the sun appears to stand still, v. Jast. (5) Ps. LXXII, 5. E.V. '*They shall fear Thee while the sun endureth, and so long as the moon*'. (6) Through delaying so long. (7) There is a play here on the words '*ibbur* (passage transition), '*ebrah* (wrath) and '*ubereth* (pregnant) which are all from the same root, though with different meanings. (8) Among the angels who never merit punishment. (9) Lit., 'ease of spirit', i.e., a clear mind without fear of danger. (10) Cf. Judg. X, 15.

b (1) I.e., they do not know how to ask for their needs. (2) V. *P. B.* p. 310.

Abaye said: A man should always [30a] associate himself with the congregation. How should he say? 'May it be Thy will, O Lord *our* God, to lead *us* forth in peace etc'. When should he say this prayer?—R. Jacob said in the name of R. Ḥisda: At the moment he starts on his journey. How long [is it still permissible to say it]?[3]—R. Jacob said in the name of R. Ḥisda: Until [he has gone][4] a *parasang*. How is he to say it? R. Ḥisda said: Standing still; R. Shesheth said: [He may] also [say it] while proceeding. Once R. Ḥisda and R. Shesheth were going along together, and R. Ḥisda stood still and prayed. R. Shesheth asked his attendant, What
a is R. Ḥisda doing?[1]—He replied: He is standing and praying. He thereupon said to him: Place me in position also that I may pray; if thou canst be good, do not be called bad.[2]

What is the difference between 'Grant us discernment' and the SHORT PRAYER?—'Grant us discernment' requires to be accompanied by the first and last three blessings [of the '*Amidah*], and when he returns home he need not say the *Tefillah* again. The 'short prayer' does not require to be accompanied either by the first or the last three blessings, and when one returns home he must say the *Tefillah*. The law is that 'Grant us discernment' must be said standing, a 'short prayer' may be said either standing or journeying.

IF ONE WAS RIDING ON AN ASS etc. Our Rabbis taught: If one was riding on an ass and the time arrived for saying *Tefillah*, if he has someone to hold his ass, he dismounts and prays, if not, he sits where he is and prays. Rabbi says: In either case he may sit where he is and pray, because [otherwise] he will be worrying.[3] Raba—or, as some say, R. Joshua b. Levi—said: The *halachah* follows Rabbi.

Our Rabbis taught: A blind man or one who cannot tell the cardinal points should direct his heart towards his Father in Heaven, as it says, *And they pray unto the Lord.*[4] If one is standing outside Palestine, he should turn mentally towards Eretz Israel, as it says, *And pray unto Thee towards their land.*[5] If he stands in Eretz Israel he should turn mentally towards Jerusalem, as it says, *And they pray unto the Lord toward the city which Thou hast chosen.*[6] If he is standing in Jerusalem he should turn mentally towards the Sanctuary, as it says, *If they pray toward this house.*[7] If he is standing in the Sanctuary, he should turn mentally towards the Holy of Holies, as it says, *If they pray toward this place.*[8] If he was standing in the Holy of Holies he should turn mentally towards
b the mercy-seat.[1] If he was standing behind the mercy-seat[2] he should imagine himself to be in front of the mercy-seat. Consequently, if he is in the east he should turn his face to the west; if in the west he should turn his face to the east; if in the south he should turn his face to the north; if in the north he should turn his face to the south. In this way all Israel will be turning their hearts towards one place. R. Abin—or as some say R. Abina—said: What text confirms this?—*Thy neck is like the tower of David builded with turrets* [talpioth],[3] the elevation [*tel*][4] towards which all mouths (*piyyoth*) turn.[5]

When Samuel's father and Levi were about to set out on a journey, they said the *Tefillah* before [dawn],[6] and when the time came to recite the *Shema'*, they said it. Whose authority did they follow?—That of the following Tanna, as it has been taught: If a man got up early to go on a journey, they bring him [before dawn] a *shofar* and he blows,[7] a *lulab*[8] and he shakes it,[9] a *megillah*[8] and he reads it[10] and when the time arrives for reciting the *Shema'*, he recites it. If he rose early in order to take his place in a coach or in a ship,[11] he says the Tefillah,[12] and when the time arrives for reciting the *Shema'*, he recites it. R. Simeon b. Eleazar says: In either case he recites the *Shema'* and then says the *Tefillah*, in order that he may say the *ge'ullah* next to the *Tefillah*. What is the ground of the difference between the two authorities?—One held that it is more important to say the *Tefillah* standing,[13] the other that it is more important to say *ge'ullah* next to *Tefillah*. Meremar and Mar Zuṭra used to collect ten persons on the Sabbath before a festival[14] and say the *Tefillah*, and then they went out and delivered their lectures.[15] R. Ashi used to say the *Tefillah* while still with the
c congregation sitting,[1] and when he returned home he used to say it again standing. The Rabbis said to him: Why does not the Master do as Meremar and Mar Zuṭra did?—He replied: That[2] is a troublesome business. Then let the Master do like the father of Samuel and Levi?—He replied: I have not seen any of the Rabbis who were my seniors doing thus.[3]

MISHNAH. R. ELEAZAR B. AZARIAH SAYS: THE MUSAF PRAYERS ARE TO BE SAID ONLY WITH THE LOCAL CONGREGATION;[4] THE RABBIS, HOWEVER, SAY: WHETHER WITH OR WITHOUT THE CONGREGATION. R. JUDAH SAID IN HIS NAME:[5] WHEREVER THERE IS A CONGREGATION, AN INDIVIDUAL IS EXEMPT FROM SAYING THE MUSAF PRAYER.[6]

GEMARA. R. Judah says the same thing as the first Tanna?—They differ on the case of an individual living in a place where there is no congregation; the first Tanna holds that he is exempt, while R. Judah holds that he is not exempt. R. Huna b. Ḥinena said in the name of R. Ḥiyya b. Rab: The *halachah* follows R. Judah, citing R. Eleazar b. Azariah. Said R. Ḥiyya b. Abin to him: You are quite right; for Samuel said: All my life I have never

(3) Another rendering is: How long must the journey be before this prayer is required to be said. (4) Or, (v. previous note) up to the distance of a *parasang*.
a (1) R. Shesheth was blind. (2) I.e., although I may pray walking, to pray standing is still better. (3) At the delay of his journey. (4) I Kings VIII, 44. (5) Ibid. 48. (6) Ibid. 44. (7) II Chron. VI, 26. (8) I Kings VIII, 35.
b (1) V. Ex. XXV, 17. (2) In the western part of the Forecourt of the Temple. (3) Cant. IV, 4. (4) Taken as an expression for the Temple. (5) Var. lec. omit 'mouths' and read: towards which all turn (*ponim*). (6) So Rashi. Tosaf., however, says, before sunrise. (7) On New Year. (8) V. Glos. (9) On Tabernacles. (10) On Purim. (11) Where he cannot stand. (12) Before leaving. (13) Which is not possible when journeying, hence the *Tefillah* is said at home before setting out. (14) When they preached in public, before daybreak. (15) Apparently the public who had gathered in the schoolhouse from early dawn said the *Shema'* before he came, and after the lecture they would not wait to say the *Tefillah* together, each saying it by himself.
c (1) In the course of his lecture, when the *turgeman* (v. Glos.) was explaining his remarks to the public. He did not stand, as the congregation would have felt it their duty to rise with him. (2) To collect ten persons. (3) Saying *Tefillah* before dawn before the *Shema'*. (4) I.e., in a place where at least ten Jews are living. On the term חבר עיר, a town organization, v. Meg. Sonc. ed., p. 164, n. 1. (5) The name of R. Eleazar b. Azariah. (6) If he says prayers alone.

לישתף איניש נפשיה בהדי צבורא היכא נימא יהי רצון ה' אלהינו שתוליכנו לשלום וכו' אימת מצלי א"ר יעקב אמר רב חסדא משעה שמהלך בדרך עד כמה א"ר יעקב אמר רב חסדא עד פרסה והיכי מצלי לה רב חסדא אמר מעומד רב ששת אמר אפילו מהלך רב חסדא ורב ששת הוו קאזלי באורחא קם רב חסדא וקא מצלי א"ל רב ששת לשמעיה מאי קא עביד רב חסדא א"ל קאי ומצלי א"ל אוקמן נמי לדידי ואצלי מהיות טוב אל תקרי רע: מאי איכא בין הביננו לתפלה קצרה הביננו בעי לצלויי ג' קמייתא וג' בתרייתא וכי מטי לביתיה לא בעי למהדר לצלויי בתפלה קצרה לא בעי לצלויי לא ג' קמייתא ולא ג' בתרייתא וכי מטי לביתיה בעי למהדר לצלויי והלכתא הביננו מעומד תפלה קצרה בין מעומד בין מהלך: היה רוכב על החמור וכו': ת"ר היה רוכב על החמור והגיע זמן תפלה אם יש לו מי שיאחז את חמורו ירד למטה ויתפלל ואם לאו ישב במקומו ויתפלל רבי אומר בין כך ובין כך ישב במקומו ויתפלל לפי שאין דעתו מיושבת עליו אמר רבא ואיתימא ריב"ל הלכה כרבי: ת"ר סומא ומי שאינו יכול לכוין את הרוחות יכוין לבו כנגד אביו שבשמים שנאמר והתפללו אל ה' היה עומד בחוצה לארץ יכוין את לבו כנגד ארץ ישראל שנאמר והתפללו אליך דרך ארצם היה עומד בארץ ישראל יכוין את לבו כנגד ירושלים שנאמר והתפללו אל ה' דרך העיר אשר בחרת היה עומד בירושלים יכוין את לבו כנגד בית המקדש שנאמר והתפללו אל הבית הזה היה עומד בבית המקדש יכוין את לבו כנגד בית קדשי הקדשים שנאמר והתפללו אל המקום הזה היה עומד בבית קדשי הקדשים יכוין את לבו כנגד בית הכפורת היה עומד אחורי בית הכפורת יראה עצמו כאלו לפני הכפורת נמצא עומד במזרח מחזיר פניו למערב במערב מחזיר פניו למזרח בדרום מחזיר פניו לצפון בצפון מחזיר פניו לדרום נמצאו כל ישראל מכוונין את לבם למקום אחד א"ר אבין ואיתימא ר' אבינא מאי קראה כמגדל דוד צוארך בנוי לתלפיות תל שכל פיות פונים בו: אבוה דשמואל ולוי כי הוו בעו למיפק לאורחא הוו מקדמי ומצלו וכי הוה מטי זמן ק"ש קרו כמאן כי האי תנא דתניא השכים לצאת לדרך מביאין לו שופר ותוקע לולב ומנענע מגילה וקורא בה וכשיגיע זמן ק"ש קורא השכים לישב בקרון או בספינה מתפלל ולכשיגיע זמן ק"ש קורא רשב"א אומר בין כך ובין כך קורא ק"ש ומתפלל כדי שיסמוך גאולה לתפלה במאי קמיפלגי מר סבר תפלה מעומד עדיף ומ"ס מסמך גאולה לתפלה עדיף מרימר ומר זוטרא הוו מכנפי בי עשרה בשבתא דרגלא ומצלו והדר נפקי לפרקא רב אשי מצלי בהדי צבורא ביחיד מיושב כי הוה אתי לביתיה הדר ומצלי מעומד אמרו ליה רבנן ולעביד מר כמרימר ומר זוטרא אמר להו טריחא לי מלתא ולעביד מר כאבוה דשמואל ולוי אמר להו לא חזינא להו לרבנן קשישי מינן דעבדי הכי:

מתני' ר' אלעזר בן עזריה אומר אין תפלת המוספין אלא בחבר עיר וחכמים אומרים בחבר עיר ושלא בחבר עיר רבי יהודה אומר משמו כל מקום שיש שם חבר עיר יחיד פטור מתפלת המוספין: **גמ'** ר' יהודה היינו ת"ק איכא בינייהו יחיד שלא בחבר עיר תנא קמא סבר פטור ורבי יהודה סבר חייב אמר רב הונא בר חיננא אמר רב חייא בר רב הלכה כר' יהודה שאמר משום ראב"ע אמר ליה רב חייא בר אבין שפיר קאמרת דאמר שמואל מימי לא מצלינא צלותא דמוספין ביחיד

בנהרדעא

לישתף נפשיה. אל יתפלל תפלה קצרה בלשון יחיד אלא בלשון רבים שמתוך כך תפלתו נשמעת: **עד כמה.** זמנה להתפלל: **עד פרסה.** אבל לא לאחר שהלך פרסה ובה"ג מפרש עד כמה יהא יליך שיהא צריך להתפלל עד פרסה אפילו אין לו ליליך אלא עד פרסה אבל דרך פחות מפרסה אין צריך להתפלל תפלה זו: **רב ששת.** מאור עינים הוה: **מהיות טוב אל תקרי רע.** הואיל ואני יכול להתפלל מעומד שהרי חבורתי עומדת לא אקרא רע להתפלל מהלך ואע"פ שמותר: **וכי מטי לביתיה בעי מהדר לצלויי.** שהרי לא התפלל כלום מתפלת י"ח: **שאין דעתו מיושבת עליו.** שקשה עליו עכוב הדרך: **לכוין את הרוחות.** לצד ארץ ישראל כדבעי למימר תל שהכל פונים בו: **אחורי בית הכפורת.** במערב העזרה היו י"א אמה חלל מכותל בית קדשי הקדשים לכותל מערבי של עזרה והעומד שם מחזיר פניו לבית הכפורת למזרח: **הוו מקדמי.** קודם היום: **בקרון ובספינה.** איכא בעתותא דמילי: **קורא ק"ש.** ימתין עד שיגיע זמן ק"ש ויקראנו ואח"כ יתפלל: **תפלה מעומד עדיף.** שיכול לכוין את לבו לפיכך היו מקדימין להתפלל מעומד בביתם שלא יצטרכו להתפלל בדרך במהלך: **שבתא דרגלא.** שלפני פסח ועצרת וסכות ומרימר בעירו ומר זוטרא בעירו היו הדרשנים ושחרית היו העם הולכים לבית המדרש וכשמגיע זמן ק"ש קורין והדרשן דורש והעם שומעים ומתפללין איש איש לבדו ולכך הם היו מאספין להם י' שחרית קודם שילכו לבית המדרש וקורין ק"ש ומתפללין בסמיכת גאולה לתפלה והדר נפקי לפרקא ודרשי: **ומצלו בהדי צבורא.** ל"ג: **רב אשי.** היה ראש ישיבה במתא מחסיא ודורש והוא לא היה מתפלל קודם בית המדרש אלא כשמגיע זמן ק"ש לוחש הרבה יחד למתורגמן העומד לפניו ובעוד שהמתורגמן משמיע לרבים הוא קורא את שמע וסומך גאולה לתפלה ומתפלל מיושב שלא היה רוצה לצאת שלא להטריח את הצבור לקום מפניו: **בהדי צבור'.** בשעה שהצבור שומעין ומתפללין אי נמי בהדי צבורא כמו שהוא יושב בתוך הצבור כלומר שאינו יוצא וכי הוה אתי לביתיה חוזר ומתפלל מעומד לכוין את לבו: **טריחא לי מילתא.** לאחר בית המדרש עד שאתפלל: **ולעביד מר כאבוה דשמואל ולוי.** שמתפללין קודם היום בביתם מעומד ולא תצטרך לב' תפלות ומשום מסמך גאולה לתפלה כיון דמצלו קודם ק"ש לא קפדי: **לא חזינן להו לרבנן קשישי מינן דעבדי הכי.** שיקדימו תפלה לק"ש הלכך כיון דממתין מתפלה עד זמן ק"ש מצוה לסמוך תפלה אחר גאולה לפיכך מתפלל מיושב במקומו ולפי שאין דעתו מיושבת עליו כ"כ צריך לחזור ולהתפלל בביתו: **מתני' אין תפלת המוספין אלא בחבר עיר.** לא תקנוה אלא בצבור: **חבר עיר.** חבורת העיר אבל לא ליחיד: **משמו.** של ראב"ע: **כל מקום כו'.** ובגמרא פריך היינו ת"ק אליבא דר"א ב"ע: **גמ' יחיד שלא בחבר עיר.** יחיד הדר בעיר שאין שם עשרה לת"ק אליבא דר' אלעזר דאמר לא תקנוה אלא בעשרה יחיד זה פטור ולר' יהודה אין יחיד פטור אלא במקום עשרה שתפלת צבור פוטרו:

והיכי מצלי לה. אתפלת הדרך קאי ורב ששת אמר אפי' מהלך וקי"ל כרב ששת ומיהו בתוספתא פסק הר' יוסף כרב חסדא וכן רב אלפס פי' דרב חסדא עדיפא ליה טפי:

מאי איכא בין הביננו לתפלה קצרה. תימה ליימא דאיכא בינייהו דתפלה קצרה אינו מתפלל אלא במקום סכנה והביננו מתפלל אפי' שלא במקום סכנה וי"ל דהכי קא בעי מאי בינייהו כל א' במקומו תפלה קצרה במקום סכנה והביננו שלא במקום סכנה:

הלכה כרבי. שלא ירד למטה ואפי' שלא במקום סכנה ואפילו במהלך מתפלל ואינו צריך להחזיר פניו כנגד ירושלים:

היה עומד בח"ל יכוין כנגד א"י. ול"ג לבו דאפניו קאי כדקתני סיפא היה עומד במזרח מחזיר פניו למערב:

לתלפיות תל שכל פיות פונים בו. וכהך שמעתא ק"ל וכן מסקינן בלא יחפור (דף כה ב) דקאמר אתון דקיימיתון לצפונא דא"י אדרומו ולא כהני אמוראי דלעיל (שם) דפליגי אי השכינה במזרח או במערב עכשיו אנו במערבה של ארץ ישראל על כן אנו פונין למזרח:

אבוה דשמואל ולוי הוו מקדמי ומצלו. פירש רש"י קודם עמוד השחר ולא נראה דאם כן לא היו יוצאין בו כלל דעדיין אינו יום לכך נראה כפי' ר"ח דמשעלה עמוד השחר קאמר והוו מקדמי קודם הנץ החמה קאמר ועדיין אינו עיקר זמן תפלה:

מסמך גאולה לתפלה עדיף. מלהתפלל מעומד והכי פסקי בה"ג הלכה כר"ש בן אלעזר ומשמע די"ח ברכות מותר להתפלל בדרך במהלך ואין צריך לעמוד וא"ת ומ"ש מהביננו דמסקי' לעיל דמעומד דוקא וי"ל דשאני הביננו שהיא קצרה ואין כאן בטול דרך כ"כ כמו בי"ח ברכות ועוד פירש הר"ס דהכא כי הדר לביתיה מצלי מעומד כדאמרינן בסמוך רב אשי מצלי בהדי צבורא ביחיד מיושב כדי לקרות ק"ש בשעתה וכי הדר לביתיה מצלי מעומד ור"ח פסק כאבוה דשמואל ולוי ומיהו מדקאמר רב אשי לא חזינא לרבנן קשישי דקא עבדי הכי משמע דאין הלכה כמותם: אין

עין משפט נר מצוה

ס
א טור וש"ע א"ח סי' קי סעי' ז

סא
ב שם סעי' ד

סב
ד מיי' פרק ה מהל' תפלה הלכה ג טוש"ע שם סעיף א ג

סג
ה מיי' פרק ה שם הלכה ג סמג עשין יט טוש"ע א"ח סימן צד סעי' ד

סד
ו מיי' שם הל' ג טוש"ע שם סעיף ג

סה
ח מיי' שם הל' ב טוש"ע שם סעיף א

סו
ט טוש"ע א"ח סי' פ"ט סעיף ח

סז
כ טוש"ע א"ח סי' רפו סעי' ב

מסורת הש"ס

תורה אור

[ב"ק פ"א:]

תוספתא פ"ג

תוספתא פ"ג

(נוסח' ירוש' מתפללין כלפי מעלן)

(תחת יכוין את לבו גרס ירוש' הופכין פניהם וכן להלן)

מלכי' א ח

שם

שם

ד"ה ב ו

מלכי' א ח

עיי' בהרא"ש

שיר ד

תוספתא פ"ג

תורה אור

בנהרדעא לבר מההוא יומא דאתא פולמוסא דמלכא למתא ואטרידו רבנן ולא צלו וצלי לי ביחיד והואי יחיד שלא בחבר עיר יתיב רבי חנינא קרא קמיה דר' ינאי ויתיב וקאמר הלכה כר' יהודה שאמר משום ראב"ע א"ל *פוק קרא קראיך לברא דאין הלכה כרבי יהודה שאמר משום ראב"ע א"ר יוחנן אני ראיתי את רבי ינאי דצלי והדר צלי א"ל ר' ירמיה לר' זירא *ודילמא מעיקרא לא כיון דעתיה ולבסוף כיון דעתיה א"ל *חזי מאן גברא רבא דקמסהיד עליה: *ר' אמי ורבי אסי ב אע"ג דהוו להו תליסר בי כנישתא בטבריא לא הוו מצלי אלא ביני עמודי היכא דהוו גרסי אתמר רב יצחק בר אבדימי משום רבינו אמר הלכה כר' יהודה שאמר משום ראב"ע ר' חייא בר אבא צלי והדר צלי א"ל רבי זירא מ"ט עביד מר הכי אילימא משום דלא כיון מר דעתיה והאמר ר"א גלעולם ימוד אדם את עצמו *אם יכול לכוין את לבו יתפלל ואם לאו אל יתפלל אלא דלא אדכר מר דריש ירחא והתניא טעה ולא הזכיר של ר"ח בערבית אין מחזירין אותו מפני שיכול לאומרה בשחרית דבשחרית אין מחזירין אותו מפני שיכול לאומרה במוספין *במוספין אין מחזירין אותו מפני שיכול לאומרה במנחה אמר ליה לאו אתמר עלה אמר ר' יוחנן הבצבור שנו: כמה ישהה בין תפלה לתפלה רב הונא ורב חסדא חד אמר וכדי שתתחונן דעתו עליו וח"א כדי שתתחולל דעתו עליו מ"ד כדי שתתחונן דעתו עליו דכתיב °ואתחנן אל ה' ומאן דאמר כדי שתתחולל דעתו עליו דכתיב °ויחל משה: אמר רב ענן אמר רב זטעה ולא הזכיר של ר"ח ערבית אין מחזירין אותו לפי שאין ב"ד מקדשין את החדש אלא ביום אמר אמימר מסתברא מלתיה דרב בחדש מלא אבל בחדש חסר מחזירין אותו אמר ליה רב אשי לאמימר מכדי רב טעמא קאמר חמה לי חסר מה לי מלא אלא לא שנא:

הדרן עלך תפלת השחר

אין טעומדין להתפלל אלא מתוך כובד ראש חסידים הראשונים היו שוהין שעה אחת ומתפללין כדי שיכוונו לבם *לאביהם שבשמים אפילו המלך שואל בשלומו לא ישיבנו ואפילו נחש כרוך על עקבו לא יפסיק: **גמ'** מנא הני מילי א"ר אלעזר דאמר קרא °והיא מרת נפש ממאי דילמא חנה שאני דהוות מרירא ליבא טובא אלא א"ר יוסי בר חנינא מהכא °ואני ברב חסדך אבא ביתך אשתחוה אל היכל קדשך ביראתך ממאי דילמא דוד שאני דהוה מצער נפשיה ברחמי טובא אלא אמר ריב"ל מהכא °השתחוו לה' בהדרת קדש אל תקרי בהדרת אלא בחרדת ממאי דילמא לעולם אימא לך הדרת ממש כי הא דרב יהודה יהוה מציין נפשיה והדר מצלי אלא א"ר נחמן בר יצחק מהכא °עבדו את יי' ביראה וגילו ברעדה *מאי וגילו ברעדה א"ר אדא בר מתנא אמר *רבה במקום גילה שם תהא רעדה אביי הוה יתיב קמיה דרבה חזייה דהוה קא בדח טובא אמר וגילו ברעדה כתיב א"ל אנא תפילין מנחנא ר' ירמיה הוה יתיב קמיה דר' זירא חזייה דהוה קא בדח טובא א"ל °בכל עצב יהיה מותר כתיב א"ל אנא תפילין מנחנא מר בריה דרבינא עבד הלולא לבריה חזנהו לרבנן דהוו קבדחי טובא

איתי

רש"י

בנהרדעא. לפי שיש שם לגור והשליח פוטרני: **פולמוסא.** חיל*: **דצלי והדר צלי.** ולמה ליה ב' תפלות אלא אחת של שחרית ואחת של מוספין ש"מ לית ליה דראב"ע: **ודילמא מעיקרא לא כיון דעתיה.** ותלוייהו דשחרית: **מאן גברא רבא מסהיד עליה.** כרי יוחנן שמעיד על הדבר יפה דקדק שבשביל תפלת המוספין היתה: **משום רבינו.** רב: **בצבור שנו.** דאין מחזירין משום דשמע ליה מש"צ ואיכא מקלת הזכרה אבל ביחיד צריך לחזור ובה"ג מפרש לה בש"צ משום טרחא דצבורא אבל יחיד הדר: **טעה ולא הזכיר במוספים.** שהתפלל אתה חונן: **כמה ישהה בין תפלה לתפלה.** מי שיש עליו לחזור ולהתפלל או משום דטעה או משום מוספין כמה ישהה בין זו לזו: **שתתחונן.** שתהא דעתו מיושבת לערוך דבריו בלשון תחנה: **שתתחולל.** לשון חילוי והיא היא אלא בלישנא בעלמא פליגי: **בחדש מלא.** כשהחדש שעבר מלא עושין ר"ח ב' ימים הלכך יוכל לאומר' למחר דערבית של מחר ר"ח גמור יותר מן הראשון: **מכדי טעמא קאמר.** שאין מקדשין את החדש בלילה:

הדרן עלך תפלת השחר

כובד ראש. הכנעה: **שוהין שעה אחת.** במקו' שבאו להתפלל: **גמ' אשתחוה אל היכל קדשך ביראתך.** מתוך יראה: **מציין נפשיה.** מקשט עצמו בבגדיו: **עבדו את ה' ביראה.** תפלה שהיא לנו במקום עבודה עשו אותה ביראה: *בכל עצב יהיה מותר. שכשאדם מראה את עצמו עצב יהיה לו שכר: **דהוה קא בדח טובא.** יותר מדאי וכראה כפורק עול: **תפילין מנחנא.** והם עדות שממשלת קוני ומוראתו עלי:

כסא

תוספות

אין הלכה כר' יהודה דאמר משום ראב"ע. אלא הלכה כרבנן וכן פסק ר"ח דלהכי מייתי ר' אמי ור' אסי שהיו מתפללים ביחיד כרבנן ביני עמודי דגרסי לאשמועינן דהלכה כרבנן:

והתניא טעה ולא הזכיר של ר"ח בערבית אין מחזירין אותו. ל"ג ליה דהא אמרי' בסמוך טעה ולא הזכיר של ר"ח אין מחזירין אותו לפי שאין מקדשי' כו' אי כמי אי איתא אגב אחריני' נקט לי':

כמה ישהה בין תפלה לתפלה. כגון אדם שטעה וצולה להתפלל שנית וכן בין תפלת שחרית לתפלת המוספין:

כדי שתתחולל דעתו עליו. ומפרש בירוש' דהיינו כשילך ד' אמות:

לפי שאין מקדשים את החדש כו'. פי' לעיל בריש פרקין (דף כז.) מה שמקשין ותפוק ליה משום לשות משום דהיינו דוקא לעשות מלוה אחרת עוברת וי"מ דוקא בלילה רחשוכה אין מחזירין אותו לפי שאין מקדשין החדש בלילה אבל בלילה שניה מחזירין אותו שכבר מקודש מיום שלפניו ולא נראה לחלק:

מסתברא מלתיה דרב בחדש מלא. כלומר שהיה אותו שלפניו מלא דאז יכול לאומרה בערבית של מחר שהוא עיקר והיה אומר ה"ר יצחק לכל דבר שאמרו חכמים אין מחזירין אותו כגון יעלה ויבא בערבית ועל הנסים לא מבעיא אם עקר רגליו ופתח בברכה שלאחריה דאין מחזירין אותו אלא אפילו לא עקר אלא שסיים אותה ברכה שתקנו בה לאומרה אין מחזירין אותו ולא כהירא לרבינו אלחנן דהא אזיכן בברכת המזון דאותן שאמרו חכמים מחזירין וגם אותן שאין מחזירין שוין היכא דלא עקר רגליו כדאמר לקמן (דף מט.) אם שכח של שבת וסיים הברכה כולה ועדיין לא התחיל בברכת הטוב והמטיב אומר ברוך אשר נתן שבתות למנוחה כו' וקאמר נמי התם אם טעה ולא הזכיר של ר"ח קודם שעקר רגליו דהייכו קודם שיתחיל ברכת הטוב והמטיב דאותה קורא עקר רגליו אומר ברוך אשר כתן ראשי חדשים וכו' אלמא היכא דלא עקר אלו ואלו שוים ואם עקר רגליו שהתחיל בברכת הטוב והמטיב של שבת חוזר לראש ושל ר"ח מעוות לא יוכל לתקון וה"כ יחזור באותה ברכה אם לא התחיל בברכ' שלאחרי' ומיהו אין ראיה מהתם דשאני התם בברכת המזון שכבר בירך ג' ברכות וברכות הטוב והמטיב לאו דאורייתא היא על כן אין מחזירין אותו לגמרי כי אין דומה שם הפסק כל כך ואין להביא ממנו ראיה לשמנה עשרה ברכות דאם יחזירוהו בדבר שאין לו לחזור הוי כמו הפסקה ועוד דאין להביא ראיה לכאן דאם היית אומר היכא שלא עקר רגליו בי"ח ברכות שהיה לו לחזור אם כן היה צריך לחזור לראש ואין זה הגון ומיהו אומר ר"י דלאה את ר"ת דהיכא דלא עקר רגליו חוזר לרלה אפי' בדברים שאין מחזירין כגון על הנסים וכן עולה דבר:

הדרן עלך תפלת השחר

אל תקרי בהדרת אלא בחרדת. תימה אמאי לא מוכח בהדיא מדכתיב בתריה חילו מלפניו כל הארץ. וי"ל היינו קרא דכתיב במזמור הבו לה' בני אלים ומהאי קרא בעי להוכיח במסכת מגילה (דף יז:) שאומרים אבות וגבורות וקדושת השם וי"ח ברכות תקנו כנגד האזכרות ומשום הכי דייק מאותו קרא שכתוב באותה פרשה אבל אותו דחילו וגו' איכו כתוב באותה פרשה:

איתי

עין משפט נר מצוה

סח א מיי' פ"ד מהלכות תפלה הלכה טו ופ"י הל' א

סט ב מיי' פ"ה מהלכות תפלה הלכה ג סמג עשין יט טוש"ע א"ח סימן צ סעיף יח

ע ג מיי' פ"ד שם הלכה טו סמג שם טוש"ע א"ח סימן קא סעיף א

עא ד מיי' פרק י שם הלכה יב סמג שם טוש"ע א"ח סי' קכו סעי' ג

[ע' תוספות לקמן לד: ד"ה יכוין]

[רי"ף ורא"ש ל"ג זה וע' בטור סי' קד"ו וקד"ב]

עב ה מיי' שם הלכ' טו סמג שם טוש"ע א"ח סי' קה

עג ו מיי' וסמ"ג שם טוש"ע א"ח סי' תכב סעיף א

א ז מיי' פרק ד שם הלכה יו סמג שם טוש"ע א"ח סי' לג סעי' ב

ב ח מיי' פרק ה' שם הלכה ה סמג שם טוש"ע א"ח סי' לג סעי' ו

מסורת הש"ס

מלה יונית

[יבמות מ. כתובות כו.]

[חולין ז.]

לעיל ח.

[דיבורי רש"י נתהפכו בזה]

דברים ג

שמות לב

(לאביהם שבשמים ליתא בירוש')

שמואל א' א'

תהלים ה

שם כט

שם ב

יומא ד:

[ע"ש]

משלי יד

said the *musaf* prayer alone [30*b*] in Nehardea except on that day when the king's forces came to the town and they disturbed the Rabbis and they did not say the *Tefillah*, and I prayed by myself, being an individual where there was no congregation. R. Ḥanina the Bible teacher[7] sat before R. Jannai and said: The *halachah* is as stated by R. Judah in the name of R. Eleazar b. Azariah. He said to him: Go and give your bible-reading outside; the *halachah* is not as stated by R. Judah citing R. Eleazar b. Azariah. R. Joḥanan said: I have seen R. Jannai pray [privately], a and then pray again.[1] R. Jeremiah said to R. Zera: Perhaps the first time he was not attending to what he said, and the second time he did attend?—He said to him: See what a great man it is who testifies concerning him.[2]

Although there were thirteen synagogues in Tiberias, R. Ammi and R. Assi prayed only between the pillars, the place where they studied.[3]

It has been stated: R. Isaac b. Abdimi said in the name of our Master:[4] The *halachah* is as stated by R. Judah in the name of R. Eleazar b. Azariah. R. Ḥiyya b. Abba prayed once and then prayed again. Said R. Zera to him: Why does the Master act thus? Shall I say it is because the Master was not attending? Has not R. Eleazar said: A man should aways take stock of himself: if he can concentrate his attention he should say the *Tefillah*, but if not he should not say it? Or is it that the Master did not remember that it is New Moon?[5] But has it not been taught: If a man forgot and did not mention the New Moon in the evening *Tefillah*, he is not made to repeat, because he can say it in the morning prayer; if he forgot in the morning prayer, he is not made to repeat, because he can say it in the *musaf*; if he forgot in *musaf*, he is not made to repeat, because he can say it in *minḥah*?—He said to him: Has not a gloss been added to this: R. Joḥanan says: This applies only to prayer said in a congregation?[6]

What interval should be left between one *Tefillah* and another?[7] —R. Huna and R. Ḥisda gave different answers: one said, long enough for him to fall into a suppliant frame of mind; the other b said, long enough to fall into an interceding frame of mind.[1] The one who says a suppliant frame of mind quotes the text, *And I supplicated* [wa-ethḥanan] *the Lord;*[2] the one who says an interceding frame of mind quotes the text, *And Moses interceded* [wa-yeḥal].[3]

R. 'Anan said in the name of Rab: If one forgot and made no mention of New Moon in the evening prayer, he is not made to repeat, because the Beth din sanctify the New Moon only by day. Amemar said: This rule of Rab seems right in a full month,[4] but in a defective month he is made to repeat. Said R. Ashi to Amemar: Let us see: Rab gave a reason, so what does it matter whether it is full or defective? In fact there is no difference.

CHAPTER V

MISHNAH. ONE SHOULD NOT STAND UP TO SAY TEFILLAH c SAVE IN A REVERENT FRAME OF MIND.[1] THE PIOUS MEN OF OLD[2] USED TO WAIT AN HOUR BEFORE PRAYING IN ORDER THAT THEY MIGHT CONCENTRATE THEIR THOUGHTS UPON THEIR FATHER IN HEAVEN. EVEN IF A KING GREETS HIM [WHILE PRAYING] HE SHOULD NOT ANSWER HIM: EVEN IF A SNAKE IS WOUND ROUND HIS HEEL HE SHOULD NOT BREAK OFF.

GEMARA. What is the [Scriptural] source of this rule?—R. Eleazar said: Scripture says, *And she was in bitterness of soul.*[3] But how can you learn from this? Perhaps Hannah was different because she was exceptionally bitter at heart! Rather, said R. Jose son of R. Ḥanina: We learn it from here: *But as for me, in the abundance of Thy lovingkindness will I come into Thy house, I will bow down toward Thy holy temple in the fear of Thee.*[4] But how can we learn from this? Perhaps David was different, because he was exceptionally self-tormenting in prayer! Rather, said R. Joshua b. Levi, it is from here: *Worship the Lord in the beauty of holiness.*[5] Read not *hadrath* [beauty] but *ḥerdath* [trembling]. But how can you learn from here? Perhaps I can after all say that the word *'hadrath'* is to be taken literally, after the manner of Rab Judah, who used to dress himself up before he prayed! Rather, said R. Naḥman b. Isaac: We learn it from here: *Serve the Lord with fear and rejoice with trembling.*[6] What is meant by *'rejoice with trembling'*?—R. Adda b. Mattena said in the name of Rab: In the place where there is rejoicing there should also be trembling. Abaye was sitting before Rabbah, who observed that he seemed very merry. He said: It is written, *And rejoice with* d *trembling*?—He replied: I am putting on *tefillin*.[1] R. Jeremiah was sitting before R. Zera who saw that he seemed very merry. He said to him: It is written, *In all sorrow there is profit*?[2]—He replied: I am wearing *tefillin*. Mar the son of Rabina made a marriage feast for his son. He saw that the Rabbis were growing very merry

(7) Heb. *ḳara*, a professional reciter of the Hebrew Scriptures.

a (1) I.e., apparently, first the morning prayer and then the *musaf*. (2) Viz., R. Joḥanan, who was not likely to have made a mistake. (3) I.e., they said even the *musaf* there, privately. (4) Rab (Rashi); Hyman (*Toledoth*, p. 785): Rabbi. (5) And omitted the appropriate reference to it in the first prayer. (6) Because then he hears the Reader repeat it, and as R. Ḥiyya b. Abba was praying privately he rightly repeated the *Tefillah*. (7) On any occasion when two are to be said.

b (1) The difference between them is little more than verbal. (2) Deut. III, 23. (3) Ex. XXXII, 11. (4) When the preceding month is thirty days, two new moon days are observed, viz., the concluding day of the old month and the next day which is the first of the next; in this case if he omitted the reference on one evening, he can rectify the error on the next.

c (1) Lit., 'with heaviness of head'. Cf. Latin *gravitas*. (2) Perhaps identical with the *wathikin*. V. *supra* 9*b*, n. b4. (3) I Sam. I, 10. (4) Ps. V, 8. (5) Ibid. XXIX, 2. (6) Ibid. II, 11.

d (1) And this is a guarantee that I am not going too far (2) Prov. XIV, 23. E.V. *'In all labour'*.

[31a], so he brought a precious cup[3] worth four hundred *zuz* and broke it before them, and they became serious. R. Ashi made a marriage feast for his son. He saw that the Rabbis were growing very merry, so he brought a cup of white crystal and broke it before them and they became serious. The Rabbis said to R. Hamnuna Zuṭi at the wedding of Mar the son of Rabina: Please sing us something. He said to them: Alas for us that we are to die! They said to him: What shall we respond after you? He said to them: Where is the Torah and where is the *mizwah* that will shield us![4]

R. Joḥanan said in the name of R. Simeon b. Yoḥai: It is forbidden to a man to fill his mouth with laughter in this world, because it says, *Then will our mouth be filled with laughter and our tongue with singing.*[5] When will that be? At the time when *'they shall say among the nations, The Lord hath done great things with these'.*[6] It was related of Resh Laḳish that he never again filled his mouth with laughter in this world after he heard this saying from R. Joḥanan his teacher.

Our Rabbis taught: A man should not stand up to say *Tefillah* either immediately after trying a case or immediately after a [discussion on a point of] *halachah;*[7] but he may do so after a *halachic* decision which admits of no discussion.[8] What is an example of a *halachic* decision which admits of no discussion?—Abaye said: Such a one as the following of R. Zera; for R. Zera said:[9] The daughters of Israel have undertaken to be so strict with themselves that if they see a drop of blood no bigger than
a a mustard seed they wait seven [clean] days after it.[1] Raba said: A man may resort to a device with his produce and bring it into the house while still in its chaff[2] so that his animal may eat of it without its being liable to tithe.[3] Or, if you like, I can say, such as the following of R. Huna. For R. Huna said in the name of R. Zeiri:[4] If a man lets blood in a consecrated animal, no benefit may be derived from it [the blood] and such benefit constitutes a trespass. The Rabbis followed the rule laid down in the Mishnah,[5] R. Ashi that of the Baraitha.[6]

Our Rabbis taught: One should not stand up to say *Tefillah* while immersed in sorrow, or idleness, or laughter, or chatter, or frivolity, or idle talk, but only while still rejoicing in the performance of some religious act.[7] Similarly a man before taking leave of his fellow should not finish off with ordinary conversation, or joking, or frivolity, or idle talk, but with some matter of *halachah*. For so we find with the early prophets that they concluded their harangues with words of praise and comfort; and so Mari the grandson of R. Huna the son of R. Jeremiah b. Abba learnt: Before taking leave of his fellow a man should always finish with a matter of *halachah*, so that he should remember him thereby. So we find that R. Kahana escorted R. Shimi b. Ashi from Pum Nahara to Be-Zinyatha[8] of Babylon, and when he arrived there he said to him, Sir, do people really say that these palm trees of Babylon are from the time of Adam?—He replied: You have reminded me of the saying of R. Jose son of R. Ḥanina. For R. Jose son of R. Ḥanina said: What is meant by the verse, *Through a land that no man passed through and where no man dwelt?*[9] If no one passed, how could anyone dwell? It is to teach you that any land which Adam decreed should be inhabited is inhabited, and any
b land which Adam decreed should not be inhabited is not inhabited.[1] R. Mordecai escorted R. Shimi b. Abba from Hagronia to Be Kafi, or, as some report, to Be Dura.[2]

Our Rabbis taught: When a man prays, he should direct his heart to heaven. Abba Saul says: A reminder of this is the text, *Thou wilt direct their heart, Thou wilt cause Thine ear to attend.*[3] It has been taught: Such was the custom of R. Akiba; when he prayed with the congregation, he used to cut it short and finish[4] in order not to inconvenience the congregation,[5] but when he prayed by himself, a man would leave him in one corner and find him later in another, on account of his many genuflexions and prostrations.

R. Ḥiyya b. Abba said: A man should always pray in a house with windows, as it says, *Now his windows were open.*[6]

I might say that a man should pray the whole day? It has already been expressly stated by the hand of Daniel, *And three times,* etc.[7] But perhaps [this practice] began only when he went into captivity? It is already said, *As he did aforetime.*[8] I might say that a man may pray turning in any direction he wishes? Therefore the text states, *Toward Jerusalem.*[9] I might say that he may combine all three *Tefillahs* in one? It has already been clearly stated by David, as is written, *Evening and morning and at noonday.*[10] I might say that he should let his voice be heard in praying? It has already been clearly stated by Hannah, as is said, *But her voice could not be heard.*[11] I might say that a man should first ask for his own requirements[12] and then say the *Tefillah?*[13] It has been clearly stated by Solomon, as is said, *To hearken unto the cry and to the prayer:*[14] *'cry'* here means *Tefillah, 'prayer'* means [private] request. A [private] request is not
c made after 'True and firm',[1] but after the *Tefillah*, even the order of confession of the Day of Atonement[2] may be said. It has also been stated: R. Ḥiyya b. Ashi said in the name of Rab: Although it was laid down that a man asks for his requirements in 'that hearkenest unto prayer', if he wants to say something after his prayer, even something like the order of confession on the Day of Atonement, he may do so.

R. Hamnuna said: How many most important laws can be learnt from these verses relating to Hannah![3] *Now Hannah, she spoke in her heart:* from this we learn that one who prays must direct his heart. *Only her lips moved:* from this we learn that he who prays must frame the words distinctly with his lips. *But her voice could not be heard:* from this, it is forbidden to raise one's voice in the *Tefillah*. *Therefore Eli thought she had been drunken:* from this, that a drunken person is forbidden to say the *Tefillah*. *And Eli said unto her, How long wilt thou be drunken,* etc.[4] R. Eleazar said: From this we learn that one who sees in his neighbour [31b]

(3) *Aliter:* crystal cup. (4) From the punishment that is to come. (5) Ps. CXXVI, 2. (6) Ibid. 3. (7) Because through thinking of it he may be unable to concentrate on his prayer. (8) Lit., 'a decided *halachah*'. (9) Nid. 66*a*.

a (1) Though Scripture requires this only if they saw three issues. (2) I.e., before it is winnowed. (3) Whereas if it had been winnowed before being brought into the house, it would have been liable to tithe, v. Pes., Sonc. ed. p. 39, n. 5. (4) Me'il. 12*b*. (5) That one should rise to pray only in a reverent frame of mind. (6) That one should pray only after dealing with an undisputed *halachah*. (7) I.e., he should first say something like Ps. CXLIV. (8) Lit., 'among the palms'. The district of the old city of Babylon which was rich in palms. (9) Jer. II, 6.

b (1) And Adam decreed that this should be inhabited, and so there have always been palm trees here. On the identification of all the places mentioned in this message v. Soṭah, Sonc. ed., p. 243 notes. (2) The text here seems to be defective, as we are not told what either of the Rabbis said. (3) I.e., if the heart is directed to heaven, then God will attend. Ps. X, 17. (4) Lit., 'ascend', 'depart'. (5) By detaining them; the congregation would not resume the service until R. Akiba had finished his *Tefillah*. (6) Dan. VI, 11. (7) Ibid. (8) Ibid. (9) Ibid. (10) Ps. LV, 18. (11) I Sam. I, 13. (12) In the middle benedictions of the *'Amidah*. (13) The first three benedictions. (14) I Kings VIII, 28.

c (1) And before the first three benedictions. (2) V. *P.B.* p. 258. (3) I Sam. I, 10ff. (4) Ibid. 14.

תורה אור

אייתי כסא דמוקרא בת ד' מאה זוזי ותבר קמייהו ואעציבו. רב אשי עבד הלולא לברי' חזנהו לרבנן דהוו קא בדחי טובא אייתי כסא *דזוגיתא חיורתא ותבר קמייהו ואעציבו אמרו ליה רבנן לרב המנונא זוטי בהלולא דמר בריה דרבינא לישרי לן מר אמר להו ווי לן דמיתנן ווי לן דמיתנן אמרי ליה אנן מה נעני בתרך א"ל הי תורה והי מצוה דמגני עלן א"ר יוחנן משום רשב"י [א]אסור לאדם שימלא שחוק פיו בעוה"ז שנאמר °אז ימלא שחוק פינו ולשוננו רנה אימתי בזמן שיאמרו בגוים הגדיל יי' לעשות עם אלה אמרו עליו על ר"ל שמימיו לא מלא שחוק פיו בעה"ז מכי שמעה מרבי יוחנן רביה: ת"ר [ב]אין עומדין להתפלל לא מתוך דין ולא מתוך דבר הלכה אלא מתוך הלכה פסוקה והיכי דמי הלכה פסוקה אמר אביי כי הא דר' זירא *דא"ר זירא [ג]בנות ישראל החמירו על עצמן *שאפילו רואות טיפת דם כחרדל יושבות עליה ז' נקיים רבא אמר כי הא דרב הושעיא דאמר רב הושעיא *[ד]מערים אדם על תבואתו ומכניסה במוץ שלה כדי שתהא בהמתו אוכלת ופטורה מן המעשר ואב"א כי הא דרב הונא דאמר רב הונא *אמר ר' זעירא [ה]המקיז דם בבהמת קדשים אסור בהנאה ומועלין בו רבנן עבדי כמתניתין רב אשי עביד כברייתא: ת"ר *[ו]אין עומדין להתפלל *לא מתוך עצבות ולא מתוך עצלות ולא מתוך שחוק ולא מתוך שיחה ולא מתוך קלות ראש ולא מתוך דברים בטלים אלא *מתוך *שמחה של מצוה וכן לא יפטר אדם מחברו לא מתוך שיחה ולא מתוך שחוק ולא מתוך קלות ראש ולא מתוך דברים בטלים אלא מתוך דבר הלכה שכן מצינו בנביאים הראשונים שסיימו דבריהם בדברי שבח ותנחומי' וכן תנא *מרי בר בריה דרב הונא בריה דרבי ירמיה בר אבא אל יפטר אדם מחברו אלא מתוך דבר הלכה שמתוך כך זוכרהו כי הא *דרב כהנא אלוייה לרב שימי בר אשי מפום נהרא עד בי צניתא דבבל כי מטא להתם אמר ליה מר ודאי דאמרי אינשי הני צניתא דבבל איתנהו מאדם הראשון ועד השתא א"ל אדכרתן מילתא דר' יוסי ב"ר חנינא דאמר רבי יוסי ב"ר חנינא מאי דכתיב °בארץ אשר לא עבר בה איש ולא ישב אדם שם וכי מאחר דלא עבר היאך ישב אלא לומר לך כל ארץ שגזר עליה אדם הראשון לישוב נתישבה וכל ארץ שלא גזר עליה אדם הראשון לישוב לא נתישבה רב מרדכי אלוייה *לרב שימי בר אשי מהגרוניא ועד בי כיפי ואמרי לה עד בי דורא: *ת"ר [ז]המתפלל צריך שיכוין את לבו לשמים אבא שאול אומר סימן לדבר °תכין לבם תקשיב אזניך תניא *א"ר יהודה כך היה מנהגו של ר"ע [ח]כשהיה מתפלל עם הצבור היה מקצר ועולה מפני טורח צבור [ט]וכשהיה מתפלל בינו לבין עצמו אדם מניחו בזוית זו ומוצאו בזוית אחרת וכל כך למה מפני כריעות והשתחויות: א"ר חייא בר אבא *לעולם [י]יתפלל אדם בבית שיש בו חלונות שנאמר °וכוין פתיחן ליה וגו': *יכול יתפלל אדם כל היום כלו כבר מפורש ע"י דניאל °וזמנין תלתא וגו' יכול משבא לגולה הוחלה כבר נאמר °די הוא עבד מן קדמת דנא יכול יתפלל אדם לכל רוח שירצה ת"ל °(לקבל) [נגד] ירושלים יכול יהא כוללן בבת אחת כבר מפורש ע"י דוד דכתיב °ערב ובקר וצהרים וגו' יכול ישמיע קולו בתפלתו כבר מפורש ע"י חנה שנאמר °וקולה לא ישמע יכול *ישאל אדם צרכיו ואח"כ יתפלל כבר מפורש ע"י שלמה שנאמר °לשמוע אל הרנה ואל התפלה רנה זו תפלה תפלה זו בקשה אין אומר דבר *(בקשה) אחר אמת ויציב אבל [כ]אחר התפלה אפי' כסדר וידוי של יה"כ אומר אתמר נמי אמר רב חייא בר אשי אמר רב *אע"פ שאמרו שואל אדם צרכיו בשומע תפלה אם בא לומר אחר תפלתו אפילו כסדר של יה"כ אומר: אמר רב המנונא כמה הלכתא גברוותא איכא למשמע מהני קראי דחנה °וחנה היא מדברת על לבה מכאן [ל]למתפלל צריך שיכוין לבו רק שפתיה נעות [מ]מכאן למתפלל שיחתוך בשפתיו וקולה לא ישמע מכאן [נ]שאסור להגביה קולו בתפלתו ויחשבה עלי לשכורה מכאן *[ס]ששכור אסור להתפלל ויאמר אליה עלי עד מתי תשתכרין וגומר אמר רבי אלעזר מכאן לרואה בחברו

דבר

רש"י

כסא דמוקרא. *כוס של זכוכית לבנה: לישרי לן מר. שירה: הי תורה והי מצוה דמגנו עלן. היכן התורה שעסקנו והיכן המצוה שאנו מקיימין שיגינו עלינו מדינה של גיהנם: הלכה פסוקה. שאינה צריכה עיון שלא יהא מהרהר בה בתפלתו: יושבות עליה ז' נקיים. לבד מאותו יום שפוסקת והתורה לא הצריכה ז' נקיים אלא לזבה שנאמר ואם טהרה מזובה ואין זבה אלא הרואה שלשה ימים רצופים בתוך י"א יום שבין נדה לנדה: ומכניסה. בבית: במוץ שלה. קודם שיזרע אותה שאין מתחייב במעשר מן התורה אלא בראיית פני הבית ומשנמרח בכרי אבל לפני מירוח אין ראיית פני הבית קובעתו דגבי תרומ' ומעשר כתיב דגן ראשית דגנך (דברים יח) והוא המירוח לפיכך כשמכניסה לבית קודם מירוח לא הוקבעה למעשר מן התורה ורבנן הוא דאסרו אכילת קבע בדבר שלא נגמר מלאכתו אבל אכילת עראי לא אסרו ומאכל בהמה עראי הוא דתנן במסכת פאה (פ"א מ"ו) מאכיל לבהמה חיה ועוף עד שימרח הלכך בהמתו אוכלת ופטורה אבל איהו אסור באכילת קבע: אסור בהנאה ומועלין בו. ואע"ג דקי"ל אין מועלין בדמים וילפינן לה מקראי במסכת יומא (דף נט:) ובשחיטת חולין (דף קיז.) ה"מ כשנשחטו בעזרה דאיכא למימר נתתיו לכם על המזבח לכפר (ויקרא יז) לכפר נתתיו לך ולא למעילה אבל בדם הקזה מועלין כלומר אם נהנה מביא קרבן מעילה והנך הויין הלכות פסוקות שאין עליהן קושיות ותירוצים שיהא צריך להרהר בהן: כמתניתין. מתוך כובד ראש: כברייתא. מתוך הלכה פסוקה: שיחה. ליצנות: מתוך קלות ראש. חילוף של כובד ראש ומתוך זחות לב ועתק: אלא מתוך שמחה. כגון דברי תנחומין של תורה כגון סמוך לגאולת מצרים או סמוך לתהלה לדוד שהוא של שבח ותנחומין כגון רצון יראיו יעשה שומר ה' את כל אוהביו וכגון מקראות הסדורות בתפלת ערבית כי לא יטוש ה' את עמו וכיוצא בהן: אלוייה. ליוהו בדרך: צניתא. דקלים: אדכרתן מילתא כו'. וזה שאומרים מימות אדם הראשון הם שהוא גזר על אותו מקום ליטוע דקלים: אם תכין לבם. אז תקשיב אזנך: זמנין תלתא. שחרית מנחה וערבית: יכול משבא לגולה הוחלה. התפלה הזאת הוחלה כמו כתחלה אבל קודם לכן לא היה רגיל בכך: יכול יהא כוללן. לשלש תפלות הללו בשעה אחת: יכול ישאל צרכיו. כגון ברכות דאתה חונן עד ש"ת ואח"כ יתפלל ג' ברכות ראשונות שהן של שבח: רנה זו תפלה. של שבח: בקשה. שאלת צרכיו: אחר אמת ויציב. קודם ג' ראשונות:

שצריך

תוספות

אייתי כסא דזוגיתא חיורתא. מכאן נהגו לשבר זכוכית בנשואין:

*במקום גילה שם תהא רעדה. פשוטו של מקרא עבדו את ה' ביראה וכשיבא יום רעדה תגילו והכי מפורש בירושלמי עבדו את ה' ביראה היינו תפלה דאיקרי עבודה כדתניא *בסיפרי (פ' עקב) ולעבדו בכל לבבכם זו תפלה:

המקיז דם לבהמת קדשים וכו'. וקשה דאמר בפרק כל הצלמים (דף מד.) גבי דמים אירוניי' ודמים פנימיים של קרבנות אלו ואלו נמכרים לגננים לזבל אלמא דאין מועלין בהן *ויש לומר דהתם היינו לאחר זריקת דמים וכבר נתכפרו בעלי' מה שאין כן הכא:

רבנן עבדי כמתני'. וכותייהו ק"ל ולכן אין מתפללין מתוך קלות ראש ושחוק אלא מתוך כובד ראש ושמחה של מצוה כגון שעסק בדברי תורה ולכן נהגו לומר פסוקי דזמרה ואשרי קודם תפלה:

רב אשי עביד כברייתא. ירושלמי לא יעמוד ויתפלל אלא מתוך דבר הלכה אמר רבי ירמיה העוסק בצרכי צבור כעוסק בדברי תורה דמי:

שכן מצינו בנביאים הראשונים שסיימו דבריהם בדברי שבח ותנחומין. ומקשה בירושלמי חוץ מירמיה כו' והא כתיב כי אם מאוס מאסתנו (איכה ה') מיהו *מההוא קרא דסוף תרי עשר וקהלת לא פריך מידי שחושבו בטוב בדברי תנחומי' ולא מיירי בפורענות דישראל:

ומוצאו בזוית אחרת. תימה דאמר לקמן (דף לד.) הבא לשחות בסוף כל ברכה וברכה מלמדין אותו שלא ישחה ותירץ ה"ר יוסף דהכא מיירי בתחנונים שהיה אומר אחר י"ח ברכות ולא נהירא דהא מי"ח קאמר ונראה להר"י דודאי בסוף כל ברכה אסור לשחות אבל באמצע הברכה מיהא מותר לשחות ובהכי מיירי הכא וכשהיה מגיע לסוף הברכה היה זוקף ולכך נהגו העולם בר"ה ובי"ה כשמתפללין זכרנו ובכן תן ותמלוך ששוחים כשמגיעים לפסוקים ובסוף ברכה זוקפין שאין לשחות בסוף ברכות אלא היכא דתקון:

דבר

מסורת הש"ס

[ע"ל כח. פירש"י ד"ה כסא]

[ע' תוס' שבת ד: ד"ה אכן ותוס' ב"מ כט: וחולין פד: ד"ה בזוגית']

נדה סו. מגילה כח: [ע' פירש"י ותוס' במגילה דח:] פסחי' ע. מנחות סז: נדה עז: [ע"ז מא:] מעילה יב:

תוספתא פ"ג (מן לא עד עצלות ליתא בירוש')

שבת ל: פסחי' קיז. (ירוש' גרס דבר של תורה)

עירובין סד.

סוטה מו:

[לרב אשי כ"ה בסוטה וכ"כ רב"י בגיטין כט. ד"ה זילו ע"ש שכך (מוכרח וע"ע ברב"י בילה ו. ד"ה א"כ] לקמן לד: דניאל ו תוספת' שם דניאל שם שם. שם

תהלים נה שמואל א א ע"ז ז: מלכים א ח רי"ף ורא"ש ל"ג ע"ז ח. שמואל א א

ערובין סד.

תהלים קכו

ירמיה ב

תוספ' פ"ד

תלי'

תוספ' שם

עין משפט נר מצוה

[וכ"א להדי' תעני' ג.]

ג [א]טוש"ע א"ח סי' תקס סעיף ה

[וע' תוס' יומא כט: ד"ה הוא ותוס' מעילה יב: ד"ה המקיז]

ד [ב]מיי' פ"ד מהל' תפלה הלכה יח סמג עשין יט טוש"ע א"ח סי' צג סעי' ב

ה [ג]מיי' פרק יא מהלכות אסורי ביאה הל' ד סמג לאוין קיא טוש"ע י"ד קצו

[רב אלפס כא ובשבועו' דף סי' רפט.]

ו [ד]מיי' פרק ג מהל' מעשר הל' ב טוש"ע י"ד סי' שלא סעיף כד

ז [ה]מיי' פרק ב' מה' מעילה הל' יא סמג עשין רי

ח [ו]מיי' פרק ד מהלכות תפלה הל' יח סמג עשין יט טוש"ע א"ח סי' צג סעי' ב

ט [ז]מיי' שם הל' יו וסמג שם טוש"ע א"ח סי' לח סעיף א

י [ח]מיי' פ"ו שם הלכה ב ש"ע א"ח סי' כג סעי' יא

יא [ט]טור א"ח סי' קד

יב [י]מיי' פ"ה מה תפל' הל' ו סמג שם טוש"ע א"ח סי' ל סעיף ד

יג [כ]מיי' פ"ו שם הל' ב טוש"ע א"ח סי' קיט סעיף א

יד [ל]מיי' פ"ד שם הלכה יו סמג שם טוש"ע א"ח סי' לח סעי' א

טו [מ][נ]מיי' פ"ה שם הל' ט סמג שם טוש"ע א"ח סי' קא סעי' ב

טז [ס]מיי' פ"ד שם הלכה יז סמג שם טור ש"ע א"ח סי' לט סעיף א

*דבר שאינו הגון צריך להוכיחו °ותען חנה ותאמר לא אדני אמר עולא ואיתימא ר' יוסי בר' חנינא אמרה ליה לא אדון אתה בדבר זה ולא רוח הקודש שורה עליך שאתה חושדני בדבר זה איכא דאמרי הכי אמרה ליה לא אדון אתה לאו איכא שכינה ורוח הקודש גבך שדנתני לכף חובה ולא דנתני לכף זכות מי לא ידעת דאשה קשת רוח אנכי. °ויין ושכר לא שתיתי א"ר אלעזר מכאן לנחשד בדבר שאין בו שצריך להודיעו. °אל תתן את אמתך לפני בת בליעל אר"א מכאן לשכור שמתפלל כאלו עובד ע"ז כתיב הכא לפני בת בליעל וכתיב התם °יצאו אנשים בני בליעל מקרבך מה להלן ע"ז אף כאן ע"ז. °ויען עלי ויאמר לכי לשלום אר"א מכאן לחושד את חברו בדבר שאין בו שצריך לפייסו ולא עוד אלא שצריך לברכו שנאמר ואלהי ישראל יתן את שלתך. ותדור נדר ותאמר יי צבאות א"ר אלעזר מיום שברא הקב"ה את עולמו לא היה אדם שקראו להקב"ה צבאות עד שבאתה חנה וקראתו צבאות אמרה חנה לפני הקב"ה רבונו של עולם מכל צבאי צבאות שבראת בעולמך קשה בעיניך שתתן לי בן אחד משל למה הדבר דומה למלך בשר ודם שעשה סעודה לעבדיו בא עני אחד ועמד על הפתח אמר להם תנו לי פרוסה אחת ולא השגיחו עליו דחק ונכנס אצל המלך א"ל אדוני המלך מכל הסעודה שעשית קשה בעיניך ליתן לי פרוסה אחת. אם ראה תראה א"ר אלעזר אמרה חנה לפני הקב"ה רבונו של עולם אם ראה מוטב ואם לאו תראה אלך ואסתתר בפני אלקנה בעלי וכיון דמסתתרנא משקו לי מי סוטה ואי אתה עושה תורתך פלסתר שנאמר °ונקתה ונזרעה זרע הניחא למאן דאמר אם היתה עקרה נפקדת שפיר אלא למאן דאמר אם היתה יולדת בצער יולדת בריוח נקבות יולדת זכרים שחורים יולדת לבנים קצרים יולדת ארוכים מאי איכא למימר דתניא *ונקתה ונזרעה זרע מלמד *שאם היתה עקרה נפקדת דברי ר' ישמעאל א"ל רבי עקיבא אם כן ילכו כל העקרות כולן ויסתתרו וזו שלא קלקלה *נפקדת אלא מלמד שאם היתה יולדת בצער יולדת בריוח קצרים יולדת ארוכים שחורים יולדת לבנים אחד יולדת שנים. מאי אם ראה תראה *ד"ת כלשון בני אדם. בעני אמתך אל תשכח את אמתך ונתת לאמתך אמר ר' יוסי בר' חנינא ג' אמתות הללו למה אמרה חנה לפני הקב"ה רבש"ע *ג' בדקי מיתה בראת באשה ואמרי לה שלשה דבקי מיתה ואלו הן נדה וחלה והדלקת הנר כלום עברתי על אחת מהן. ונתת לאמתך זרע אנשים מאי זרע אנשים אמר רב גברא בגוברין ושמואל אמר זרע שמושח שני אנשים ומאן אינון שאול ודוד ורבי יוחנן אמר זרע ששקול כשני אנשים ומאן אינון משה ואהרן שנאמר °משה ואהרן בכהניו ושמואל בקוראי שמו ורבנן אמרי זרע אנשים זרע שמובלע בין אנשים כי אתא רב דימי אמר לא ארוך ולא גוץ ולא קטן ולא אלם ולא צחור ולא גיחור ולא חכם ולא טפש. אני האשה הנצבת עמכה בזה אמר ריב"ל מכאן *שאסור לישב בתוך ארבע אמות של תפלה. אל הנער הזה התפללתי א"ר אלעזר שמואל מורה הלכה לפני רבו היה שנאמ' וישחטו את הפר ויביאו הנער אל עלי משום דוישחטו את הפר הביאו הנער אל עלי אלא אמר להן עלי קראו כהן ליתי ולשחוט חזנהו שמואל דהוו מהדרי בתר כהן למשחט אמר להו למה לכו לאהדורי בתר כהן למישחט *שחיטה בזר כשרה איתיוהו לקמיה דעלי אמר לי' מנא לך הא אמר ליה *מי כתיב ושחט הכהן °והקריבו הכהנים כתיב *מקבלה ואילך מצות כהונה מכאן לשחיטה שכשרה בזר אמר ליה מימר שפיר קא אמרת מיהו מורה הלכה בפני רבך את *וכל *המורה הלכה בפני רבו חייב מיתה אתי' חנה וקא צוחה קמיה אני האשה הנצבת עמכה בזה וגו' אמר לה שבקי לי דאענשיה ובעינא רחמי ויהיב לך רבא מיניה אמרה ליה אל הנער הזה התפללתי. וחנה היא מדברת על לבה א"ר אלעזר משום רבי יוסי בן זמרא על עסקי לבה אמרה לפניו רבש"ע כל מה שבראת באשה לא בראת דבר אחד לבטלה עינים לראות ואזנים לשמוע חוטם להריח פה לדבר ידים לעשות בהם מלאכה רגלים להלך בהן דדים להניק בהן דדים הללו שנתת על לבי למה לא להניק בהן תן לי בן ואניק בהן: וא"ר אלעזר משום ר' יוסי בן זמרא *כל היושב בתענית בשבת קורעין לו גזר דינו של שבעים שנה ואעפ"כ חוזרין ונפרעין ממנו דין עונג שבת *מאי תקנתיה אמר רב נחמן בר יצחק *ליתיב תעניתא לתעניתא וא"ר אלעזר חנה הטיחה דברים כלפי מעלה שנאמר ותתפלל על יי' מלמד שהטיחה דברים כלפי מעלה וא"ר אלעזר אליהו הטיח דברים כלפי מעלה שנאמר *ואתה הסבות את לבם אחורנית א"ר שמואל בר רב יצחק מנין שחזר הקב"ה והודה לו לאליהו דכתיב

שצריך להודיעו. הנחשד צריך לנקות עצמו ולהודיע את חושדו שאין בו אותו דבר מגונה: לפני בת בליעל. אל תחשבני כבת בליעל לחשדני בשכרות: ואסתתר. אתיחד עם אחרים ויחשדני בעלי: פלסתר. שקר: שלש אמתות. דריש להו לשון מיתה: בדקי מיתה. שהאשה נבדקת בהן בשעת הסכנה שאם ימצא בה אחד מהם תמות: נדה וחלה והדלקת נר. של שבת על ג' עבירות הללו נשים מתות וטעמא יליף במסכת שבת (ד' לב:): שמובלע בין אנשים. רב דימי מפרש לה לא ארוך ולא גוץ וכו': אלם. פירוש עב: *צחור. כו"ש בלעז: גיחור. שהוא לבן יותר מדאי: ולא חכם. יותר מדאי שלא יהיה תימה בעיני הבריות ומתוך שמדברין בו שולטת בו עין הרע: הנצבת עמכה. משמע אף הוא עמה בעמידה: אל הנער הזה. על זה ולא לאחר מכאן שהטא לעלי ורצה לענשו ולהתפלל שינתן לה בן אחר: והקריבו הכהנים. אמרי בפרק קמא דחגיגה (דף יא.) והקריבו זה קבלת הדם: של שבעים שנה. כלומר אפילו נגזר עליו מנעוריו לפי שתענית קשה בשבת לפי שהכל מתענגים בו והוא מתענה: תעניתא לתעניתא. יתענה למחר: ותתפלל על יי'. כך כתוב הוא במקרא ולא גרסינן הכא אל תקרי: שחזר והודה לאליהו. לדבריו הודה לאחר זמן בנבואת נביאים אחרים: דכתיב

דבר שאינו הגון. פירוש אע"ג דליכא איסורא דאורייתא דאי איכא איסורא דאורייתא פשיטא הוכח תוכיח כתיב (ויקר' יט):
גברא בגוברין. פי' אדם שיהא חשוב ליימנות בין אנשים:
*מכאן שהשכור אסור להתפלל. ירושלמי במסכת תרומות פרק קמא רבי זירא בעי קמיה דרבי אמי שכור מהו שיברך אמר לי' ואכלת ושבעת וברכת ואפילו מדומדם פירוש ואפי' הוא שתוי ושכור כל כך שאינו יכול לדבר כראוי דהכי משמע ושבעת וברכת:
מכאן שאסור לישב בד' אמות של תפלה. בין מלפניו (בין מלאחריו) ובין מן הצדדין ופירשו תשובות הגאונים דוקא ביושב ובטל אבל אם היה עוסק בק"ש ובברכותיה וכיוצא בהם אפי' יושב שפיר דמי:
עמכה. משמע בתוך ארבע אמות משום דכתיב עמכה מלא בה"א כלומר שלא היה יושב בתוך ארבע אמות שלה כי אם בחמישית:
מורה הלכה בפני רבך את. ואף על פי שלא למד עדיין בפניו מ"מ גדול הדור היה ובא ללמוד בפניו:
כל היושב בתענית בשבת. פירש ר"ח בתענית חלום וכן איתא במדרש תילים וכשיושב בתענית חלום בשבת פירש בה"ג שאומר עננו באלהי נצור ואפילו קובע ברכה לעצמו כיון שאינו בתוך י"ח:
גדולה

עין משפט נר מצוה

[שייך לעמוד א']

יז א מיי' פ"ו מהל' דיעות הל' ז סמג עשין יא

יח ב מיי' פ"ג מהל' סוטה הל' כב

יט ג מיי' פ"ה מהל' תפלה הלכ' ו סמג עשין יט טוש"ע א"ח סי' קב סעי' א

כ ד ה מיי' פ"ט מהלכ' ביאת המקדש הל' ו' ופ"ה מהל' מעשה הקרבנות הל' א ופ"א מהלכ' פסולי המוקדשין הל' א סמג לאוין שט

כא ו מיי' פ"ה מה' ת"ת הל' ב סמג ע' יג טוש"ע י"ד סי' רמב סעיף ד

כב ז ח מיי' פ"ל מה' שבת הל' יב פ"א מהל' תעניות הל' יב סמג עשין ג טוש"ע א"ח סי' רפח סעי' ד

מסורת הש"ס

ערכין יו:

[אמור שהו' לבן כו' גיחור כו"ש בלע"ז כל"ל וכ"ה לקמן נח: וגמ' בכורות מה: וע' פירש"י לקמן נט:]

כ"א נפקדת [יבמות סד. כתובות סז: קידושין יז: גיטין מא: נדרי' ג. ב"מ לא: ל"ד ע"ב כו. זבחים קח: כריתות יא. ערכין ג. נדה לב: מד.]

תורה אור

שמואל א א — שם — שם — דברי' יג — ש"א א

במדבר ה. סוטה כו. [ושם מוחלפ' השיטה וע"ש בתו' ובתוס' מנחות יז: ול"ע קלא]

שבת לב.

תהלים צט

זבחים לב ויקרא א

עירובין סג.

[תעני' יב:]

מלכים א יח

---

(8) So as not to be talked about and so become exposed to the evil eye. (9) I Sam. I, 26. (10) Because the words imply that Eli also was standing.

c (1) I Sam. I, 27. (2) Ibid. 25. (3) Lev. I, 5 (4) V. Zeb. 32*a*. (5) Lit., upon'. (6) I Sam. I, 13. (7) E.g., to avert the omen of a dream. (8) I.e., even though it is high time that it was carried out (Rashi).

d (1) Lit., 'she hurled words'. (2) The Hebrew word is '*al*, lit., 'upon', 'against'. (3) I Sam. I, 10. (4) I Kings XVIII, 37. As much as to say, it was God's fault that they worshipped idols.

something unseemly must reprove him. *And Hannah answered and said, No, my lord.*[5] 'Ulla, or as some say R. Jose b. Ḥanina, said: She said to him: Thou art no lord in this matter, nor does the holy spirit rest on thee, that thou suspectest me of this thing. Some say, She said to him: Thou art no lord, [meaning] the *Shechinah* and the holy spirit is not with you in that you take the harsher and not the more lenient view of my conduct.[6] Dost thou not know that *I am a woman of sorrowful spirit: I have drunk neither wine nor strong drink*. R. Eleazar said: From this we learn that one who is suspected wrongfully must clear himself. *Count not thy handmaid for a daughter of Belial;*[7] a man who says the *Tefillah* when drunk is like one who serves idols. It is written here, *Count not thy handmaid for a daughter of Belial,* and it is written elsewhere, *Certain sons of Belial have gone forth from the midst of thee.*[8] Just as there the term is used in connection with idolatry, so here. *Then Eli answered*
a *and said, Go in peace.*[1] R. Eleazar said: From this we learn that one who suspects his neighbour of a fault which he has not committed must beg his pardon;[2] nay more, he must bless him, as it says, *And the God of Israel grant thy petition.*[1]

And she vowed a vow and said, O Lord of Ẓebaoth [Hosts].[3] R. Eleazar said: From the day that God created His world there was no man called the Holy One, blessed be He, *Ẓeboath* [hosts] until Hannah came and called Him *Ẓebaoth*. Said Hannah before the Holy One, blessed be He: Sovereign of the Universe, of all the hosts and hosts that Thou hast created in Thy world, is it so hard in Thy eyes to give me one son? A parable: To what is this matter like? To a king who made a feast for his servants, and a poor man came and stood by the door and said to them, Give me a bite,[4] and no one took any notice of him, so he forced his way into the presence of the king and said to him, Your Majesty, out of all the feast which thou hast made, is it so hard in thine eyes to give me one bite?

If Thou wilt indeed look.[5] R. Eleazar said: Hannah said before the Holy One, blessed be He: Sovereign of the Universe, if Thou wilt look, it is well, and if Thou wilt not look, I will go and shut myself up with someone else in the knowledge of my husband Elkanah,[6] and as I shall have been alone[7] they will make me drink the water of the suspected wife, and Thou canst not falsify Thy law, which says, *She shall be cleared and shall conceive seed.*[8] Now this would be effective on the view of him who says that if the woman was barren she is visited. But on the view of him who says that if she bore with pain she bears with ease, if she bore females she now bears males, if she bore swarthy children she now bears fair ones, if she bore short ones she now bears tall ones, what can be said? As it has been taught: *'She shall be cleared and shall conceive seed'*: this teaches that if she was barren she is visited. So R. Ishmael. Said R. Akiba to him, If that is so, all barren women will go and shut themselves in with someone and she who has not misconducted herself will be visited! No, it teaches that if she formerly bore with pain she now bears with ease, if she bore short children she now bears tall ones, if she bore swarthy ones she now bears fair ones, if she was destined to bear one she will now bear two. What then is the force of '*If Thou wilt indeed look*'?—The Torah used an ordinary form of expression.

If Thou wilt indeed look on the afflictation of Thy handmaid . . . . *and not forget Thy* handmaid, *but wilt give unto Thy* handmaid etc. R. Jose son of R. Ḥanina said: Why these three 'handmaids'? Hannah said before the Holy One, blessed be He: Sovereign of the Universe, Thou hast created in woman three criteria [*bidke*]
b of death[1] (some say, three armour-joints [*dibke*] of death),[2] namely, *niddah*, *ḥallah* and the kindling of the light [on Sabbath].[3] Have I transgressed in any of them?

But wilt give unto Thy handmaid a man-child. What is meant by '*a man-child*'? Rab said: A man among men;[4] Samuel said: Seed that will anoint two men, namely, Saul and David; R. Joḥanan said: Seed that will be equal to two men, namely, Moses and Aaron, as it says, *Moses and Aaron among His priests and Samuel among them that call upon His name;*[5] the Rabbis say: Seed that will be merged among men.[6] When R. Dimi came [from Palestine] he explained this to mean: Neither too tall nor too short, neither too thin nor too corpulent,[7] neither too pale nor too red, neither over-clever[8] nor stupid.

I am the woman that stood by thee here.[9] R. Joshua b. Levi said: From this we learn that it is forbidden to sit within four cubits of one saying *Tefillah*.[10]

c *For this child I prayed.*[1] R. Eleazar said: Samuel was guilty of giving a decision in the presence of his teacher; for it says, *And when the bullock was slain, the child was brought to Eli.*[2] Because the bullock was slain, did they bring the child to Eli? What it means is this. Eli said to them: Call a priest and let him come and kill [the animal]. When Samuel saw them looking for a priest to kill it, he said to them, Why do you go looking for a priest to kill it? The *shechitah* may be performed by a layman! They brought him to Eli, who asked him, How do you know this? He replied: Is it written, 'The priest shall *kill*'? It is written, *The priests shall present* [*the blood*]:[3] the office of the priest begins with the receiving of the blood, which shows that *shechitah* may be performed by a layman.[4] He said to him: You have spoken very well, but all the same you are guilty of giving a decision in the presence of your teacher, and whoever gives a decision in the presence of his teacher is liable to the death penalty. Thereupon Hannah came and cried before him: '*I am the woman that stood by thee here* etc.'. He said to her: Let me punish him and I will pray to God and He will give thee a better one than this. She then said to him: '*For this child I prayed*'.

Now Hannah, she spoke in[5] *her heart.*[6] R. Eleazar said in the name of R. Jose b. Zimra: She spoke concerning her heart. She said before Him: Sovereign of the Universe, among all the things that Thou hast created in a woman, Thou hast not created one without a purpose, eyes to see, ears to hear, a nose to smell, a mouth to speak, hands to do work, legs to walk with, breasts to give suck. These breasts that Thou hast put on my heart, are they not to give suck? Give me a son, so that I may suckle with them.

R. Eleazar also said in the name of R. Jose b. Zimra: If one keeps a fast on Sabbath,[7] a decree of seventy years standing against him is annulled;[8] yet all the same he is punished for neglecting to make the Sabbath a delight. What is his remedy? R. Naḥman b. Isaac said: Let him keep another fast to atone for this one.

d R. Eleazar also said: Hannah spoke insolently[1] toward heaven, as it says, *And Hannah prayed unto*[2] *the Lord.*[3] This teaches that she spoke insolently toward heaven.

R. Eleazar also said: Elijah spoke insolently toward heaven, as it says, *For Thou didst turn their heart backwards.*[4] R. Samuel b. Isaac said: Whence do we know that the Holy One, blessed be He,

(5) Ibid. 15. (6) Lit., 'You have judged me in the scale of guilt and not of merit'. (7) So lit. E.V. '*wicked woman*'. V. Ḳid. 16. (8) Deut. XIII, 14. E.V. '*certain base fellows*'.

a (1) I Sam. I, 17. (2) Lit., 'appease him'. (3) Ibid. 11. (4) Lit., 'morsel' (*sc.* of bread). (5) Ibid. (6) So that he will become jealous and test me. (7) Lit., 'as I will have been hidden'. (8) Num. V, 28.

b (1) Three things by which she is tested to see whether she deserves death. (2) I.e., three vulnerable points. Hannah plays on the resemblance of the word *amateka* (thy handmaid) to *mithah* (death). (3) V. Shab. 32a: For three transgressions woman die in childbirth; because they are not careful with *niddah*, with *ḥallah* and with the kindling of the light. (4) I.e., conspicuous among men. (5) Ps. XCIX, 6. (6) I.e., average, not conspicuous. (7) So Rashi.

gave Elijah right? [32a] Because it says, *And whom I have wronged.*[5]

R. Ḥama said in the name of R. Ḥanina: But for these three texts,[6] the feet of Israel's enemies[7] would have slipped. One is *Whom I have wronged;* a second, *Behold as the clay in the potter's hand, so are ye in My hand, O house of Israel;*[8] the third, *And I will take away the stony heart out of your flesh, and I will give you a heart of flesh.*[9] R. Papa said: We learn it from here: *And I will put My spirit within you and cause you to walk in My statutes.*[10]

R. Eleazar also said: Moses spoke insolently towards heaven, as it says, *And Moses prayed unto the Lord.*[11] Read not *el* [unto] the Lord, but *'al* [upon] the Lord, for so in the school of R. Eliezer *alefs* were pronounced like *'ayins* and *'ayins* like *alefs.* The school of R. Jannai learnt it from here: *And Di-Zahab.*[12] What is *'And Di-Zahab'?* They said in the school of R. Jannai: Thus spoke Moses before the Holy One, blessed be He: Sovereign of the Universe, the silver and gold [*zahab*] which Thou didst shower on Israel until they said, Enough [*dai*], that it was which led to their making the Calf. They said in the school of R. Jannai: A lion does not roar over a basket of straw but over a basket of flesh. R. Oshaia said: It is like the case of a man who had a lean but large-limbed cow. He gave it lupines to eat and it commenced to kick him. He said to it: What led you to kick me except the lupines that I fed you with? R. Ḥiyya b. Abba said: It is like the case of a man who had a son; he bathed him and anointed him and gave him plenty to eat and drink and hung a purse round his neck and set him down at the door of a bawdy house. How could the boy help sinning? R. Aḥa the son of R. Huna said in the name of R. Shesheth: This bears out the popular saying: A full stomach is a bad sort, as it says, *When they were fed they became full, they were filled and*
a *their heart was exalted; therefore they have forgotten Me.*[1] R. Naḥman learnt it from here: *Then thy heart be lifted up and thou forget the Lord.*[2] The Rabbis from here: *And they shall have eaten their fill and waxen fat, and turned unto other gods.*[3] Or, if you prefer, I can say from here. *But Jeshurun waxed fat and kicked.*[4] R. Samuel b. Naḥmani said in the name of R. Jonathan. Whence do we know that the Holy One, blessed be He, in the end gave Moses right? Because it says, *And multiplied unto her silver and gold, which they used for Baal.*[5]

And the Lord spoke unto Moses, Go, get thee down.[6] What is meant by *'Go, get thee down'?* R. Eleazar said: The Holy One, blessed be He, said to Moses: Moses, descend from thy greatness. Have I at all given to thee greatness save for the sake of Israel? And now Israel have sinned; then why do I want thee? Straightway Moses became powerless and he had no strength to speak. When, however, [God] said, *Let Me alone that I may destroy them,*[7] Moses said to himself: This depends upon me, and straightway he stood up and prayed vigorously and begged for mercy. It was like the case of a king who became angry with his son and began beating him severely. His friend was sitting before him but was afraid to say a word until the king said, Were it not for my friend here who is sitting before me I would kill you. He said to himself, This depends on me, and immediately he stood up and rescued him.

Now therefore let Me alone that My wrath may wax hot against them, and that I may consume them, and I will make of thee a great nation.[8] R. Abbahu said: Were it not explicitly written, it would be impossible to say such a thing: this teaches that Moses took hold of the Holy One, blessed be He, like a man who seizes his fellow by his garment and said before Him: Sovereign of the Universe, I will not let Thee go until Thou forgivest and pardonest them.

And I will make of thee a great nation etc. R. Eleazar said: Moses said before the Holy One, blessed be He: Sovereign of the Uni-
b verse, seeing that a stool with three legs[1] cannot stand before Thee in the hour of Thy wrath, how much less a stool with one leg! And moreover, I am ashamed before my ancestors, who will now say: See what a leader he has set over them! He sought greatness for himself, but he did not seek mercy for them!

And Moses besought [wa-yeḥal] *the Lord his God.*[2] R. Eleazar said: This teaches that Moses stood in prayer before the Holy One, blessed be He, until he [so to speak] wearied Him [*heḥelahu*]. Raba said: Until he remitted His vow for Him. It is written here *wa-yeḥal,* and it is written there [in connection with vows], *he shall not break* [yaḥel] *his word;*[3] and a Master has said: He [himself] cannot break, but others may break for him.[4] Samuel says: It teaches that he risked his life for them,[5] as it says, *And if not, blot me, I pray Thee, out of Thy book which Thou hast written.*[6] Raba said in the name of R. Isaac: It teaches that he caused the Attribute of Mercy to rest [*heḥelah*] on them. The Rabbis say: It teaches that Moses said before the Holy One, blessed be He: Sovereign of the Universe, it is a profanation [*ḥullin*] for Thee to do this thing.

And Moses besought the Lord. It has been taught: R. Eliezer the Great says: This teaches that Moses stood praying before the Holy One, blessed be He, until an *aḥilu* seized him. What is *aḥilu?* R. Eleazar says: A fire in the bones. What is a fire in the bones? Abaye said: A kind of fever.

Remember Abraham, Isaac and Israel Thy servants, to whom Thou didst swear by Thyself.[7] What is the force of *'by Thyself'?* R. Eleazar said: Moses said before the Holy One, blessed be He: Sovereign of the Universe, hadst Thou sworn to them by the heaven and the earth, I would have said, Just as the heaven and earth can pass away, so can Thy oath pass away. Now, however, Thou hast sworn to them by Thy great name: just as Thy great name endures for ever and ever, so Thy oath is established for ever and ever.

And saidst unto them, I will multiply your seed as the stars of heaven
c *and all this land that I have spoken of* etc.[1] *'That I have spoken of'?* It should be, 'That *Thou* hast spoken of'![2]—R. Eleazar said: Up to this point the text records the words of the disciple,[3] from this point the words of the master.[4] R. Samuel b. Naḥmani, however, said: Both are the words of the disciple, only Moses spoke thus before the Holy One, blessed be He: Sovereign of the Universe, the things which Thou didst tell me to go and tell Israel in Thy name I did go and tell them in Thy name; now what am I to say to them?

Because the Lord was not able [yekoleth].[5] It should be *yakol!*[6] R. Eleazar said: Moses said before the Holy One, blessed be He: Sovereign of the Universe, now the nations of the world will say, He has grown feeble like a female and He is not able to deliver. Said the Holy One, blessed be He, to Moses: Have they not already seen the wonders and miracles I performed for them by the Red Sea? He replied: Sovereign of the Universe, they can still say, He could stand up against one king, He cannot stand up against thirty. R. Joḥanan said: How do we know that in the end the Holy One, blessed be He, gave Moses right? Because it says, *And the Lord said, I have pardoned according to thy word.*[7] It was taught in the school of R. Ishmael: *According to thy word:* the nations of the world will one day say, Happy is the disciple to whom the master gives right!

But in very deed, as I live.[8] Raba said in the name of R. Isaac: This teaches that the Holy One, blessed be He, said to Moses: Moses, you have revived Me[9] with your words.

R. Simlai expounded: A man should always first recount the praise of the Holy One, blessed be He, and then pray. Whence do we know this? From Moses; for it is written, *And I besought the*
d *Lord at that time,*[1] and it goes on, *O Lord God, Thou hast begun to show Thy servant Thy greatness and Thy strong hand; for what god is there in heaven and earth who can do according to Thy works and according to Thy mighty acts,* and afterwards is written, *Let me go over, I pray Thee, and see the good land* etc.

[Mnemonic: Deeds, charity, offering, priest, fast, lock, iron].[2]

(5) Micah IV, 6. This is taken to mean that God admits having wronged sinners by creating in them the evil impulse. E.V. *'afflicted'*. (6) Which show that God is responsible for the evil impulse. (7) Euphemism. (8) Jer. XVIII, 6. (9) Ezek. XXXVI, 26. (10) Ibid. 27. (11) Num. XI, 2. (12) Deut. I, 1.

a (1) Hos. XIII, 6. (2) Deut. VIII, 14. (3) Ibid. XXXI, 20. (4) Ibid. XXXII, 15. (5) Hos. II, 10. (6) Ex. XXXII, 7. (7) Deut. IX, 14. (8) Ex. XXXII, 10.

b (1) The three Patriarchs. (2) Ex. XXXII, 11. (3) Num. XXX, 3. (4) I.e., find a ground of absolution. (5) Connecting *wayeḥal* with *ḥalal*, slain. (6) Ex.

עין משפט נר מצוה

כב אמיי' פ"א מה' תפלה הל' ג

מסורת הש"ס

דכתיב ואשר הרעותי. לישנא דקרא אוספה הצולעה והנדחה אקבצה ואשר הרעותי אני גרמתי להם שהרעתי יצר הרע: אלמלא שלש מקראות הללו. שמעידים שיש ביד הקב"ה לתקן יצרנו ולהסיר יצר הרע ממנו: נתמוטטו. רגלינו במשפט אבל עכשיו יש לנו פתחון פה שהוא גרם לנו שברא יצר הרע: דשיח. לשון זריקה כמו כמטחוי קשת (בראשית כא): אין ארי נוהם. שמח ומשתגע וצוחק: מלי כריסיה זני בישי. מילוי הכרס הוא ממיני מעשים הרעים. זני. מתרגמינן למינהו לזנוהי (בראשית א): הרף ממני. הראהו שיש כח בידו למחול ע"י תפלה: הניחה לי. משמע שהיה אוחז בו: שלש רגלים. אברהם יצחק ויעקב: שהחלהו. הפליג בו אמוראי בלעז: נדרו. דבורו שאמר ואכלם: שמסר עצמו למיתה. ויחל לשון חלל: שהחלה עליהם מדת רחמים. כמו יחולו על ראש יואב (ש"ב ג) לשון הניח: שאחזתו אחילו גו': אשתא דגרמי. מול"ייר בלע"ז: אשר נשבעת להם בך. שהאמר בעקדת יצחק בי נשבעתי (בראשית כב): עד כאן. עד ככבי השמים: מכאן ואילך דברי הרב. אמר לו אעשה כדבריך: דברים שאמרת לי. בהנה אמרת לי אעלה אתכם מעני מצרים אל ארץ טובה ורחבה (שמות ג): החייתני. בפני האומות:

עלה

תורה אור

[סוכה נב: ע"ש] [מגילה כד: יומא פו: [פסח' קב.]

דכתיב °ואשר הרעותי: *אמר רב חמא ברבי חנינא אלמלא שלש מקראות הללו נתמוטטו רגליהם של שונאי ישראל חד דכתיב ואשר הרעותי וחד דכתיב °הנה כחומר ביד היוצר כן אתם בידי בית ישראל וחד דכתיב °והסירותי את לב האבן מבשרכם ונתתי לכם לב בשר רב פפא אמר מהכא °ואת רוחי אתן בקרבכם ועשיתי את אשר בחקי תלכו: ואמר רבי אלעזר משה הטיח דברים כלפי מעלה שנאמר °ויתפלל משה אל יי' אל תקרי אל יי' אלא על יי' שכן דבי ר' אליעזר בן יעקב *קורין לאלפין עיינין ולעיינין אלפין דבי ר' ינאי אמרי מהכא °ודי זהב מאי ודי זהב אמרי *דבי רבי ינאי כך אמר משה לפני הקב"ה רבונו של עולם בשביל כסף וזהב שהשפעת להם לישראל עד שאמרו די הוא גרם שעשו את העגל אמרי דבי ר' ינאי אין ארי נוהם מתוך קופה של תבן אלא מתוך קופה של בשר אמר רבי אושעיא משל לאדם שהיתה לו פרה כחושה ובעלת אברים האכילה כרשינין והיתה מבעטת בו אמר לה מי גרם ליך שתהא מבעטת בי אלא כרשינין שהאכלתיך אמר רבי חייא בר אבא אמר רבי יוחנן משל לאדם אחד שהיה לו בן הרחיצו וסכו והאכילו והשקהו ותלה לו כיס על צוארו והושיבו על פתח של זונות מה יעשה אותו הבן שלא יחטא אמר רב אחא בריה דרב הונא אמר רב ששת היינו דאמרי אינשי מלי כריסיה זני בישי שנ' °כמרעיתם וישבעו שבעו וירם לבם על כן שכחוני רב נחמן אמר מהכא °ורם לבבך ושכחת את יי' ורבנן אמרי מהכא °ואכל ושבע ודשן ופנה ואי בעית אימא מהכא °וישמן ישורון ויבעט אמר רבי שמואל בר נחמני אמר רבי יונתן מנין שחזר הקדוש ברוך הוא והודה לו למשה שנאמר °וכסף הרביתי להם וזהב עשו לבעל: °וידבר יי' אל משה לך רד מאי לך רד אמר רבי אלעזר אמר לו הקדוש ברוך הוא למשה משה רד מגדולתך כלום נתתי לך גדולה אלא בשביל ישראל ועכשיו ישראל חטאו אתה למה לי מיד תשש כחו של משה ולא היה לו כח לדבר וכיון שאמר °הרף ממני ואשמידם אמר משה דבר זה תלוי בי מיד עמד ונתחזק בתפלה ובקש רחמים משל למלך שכעס על בנו והיה מכהו מכה גדולה והיה אוהבו יושב לפניו ומתירא לומר לו דבר אמר המלך אלמלא אוהבי זה שיושב לפני הרגתיך אמר דבר זה תלוי בי מיד עמד והצילו: °ועתה הניחה לי ויחר אפי בהם ואכלם ואעשה אותך לגוי גדול וגו' אמר רבי אבהו אלמלא מקרא כתוב אי אפשר לאומרו מלמד שתפסו משה להקדוש ברוך הוא כאדם שהוא תופס את חבירו בבגדו ואמר לפניו רבונו של עולם אין אני מניחך עד שתמחול ותסלח להם: °ואעשה אותך לגוי גדול וגומר אמר רבי אלעזר אמר משה לפני הקדוש ברוך הוא רבונו של עולם ומה כסא של שלש רגלים אינו יכול לעמוד לפניך בשעת כעסך כסא של רגל אחד על אחת כמה וכמה ולא עוד אלא שיש בי בושת פנים מאבותי עכשיו יאמרו ראו פרנס שהעמיד עליהם בקש גדולה לעצמו ולא בקש עליהם רחמים: °ויחל משה את פני יי' אמר ר' אלעזר מלמד שעמד משה בתפלה לפני הקדוש ברוך הוא עד שהחלהו *ורבא אמר עד *שהפר לו נדרו כתיב הכא ויחל וכתיב התם °לא יחל דברו *ואמר מר הוא אינו מיחל אבל אחרים מחלין לו ושמואל אמר מלמד שמסר עצמו למיתה עליהם שנאמר °ואם אין מחני נא מספרך **אמר רבא אמר רב יצחק מלמד שהחלה עליהם מדת רחמים ורבנן אמרי מלמד שאמר משה לפני הקדוש ברוך הוא רבונו של עולם *חולין הוא לך מעשות כדבר הזה: ויחל משה את פני יי' תניא ר' אליעזר הגדול אומר מלמד שעמד משה בתפלה לפני הקב"ה עד שאחזתו אחילו *מאי אחילו אמר רבי אלעזר אש של עצמות מאי אש של עצמות אמר אביי אשתא דגרמי °זכור לאברהם ליצחק ולישראל עבדיך אשר נשבעת להם בך מאי בך אמר רבי אלעזר אמר משה לפני הקדוש ברוך הוא רבונו של עולם אלמלא נשבעת להם בשמים ובארץ הייתי אומר כשם ששמים וארץ בטלים כך שבועתך בטלה ועכשיו נשבעת להם בשמך הגדול מה שמך הגדול חי וקים לעולם ולעולמי עולמים כך שבועתך קיימת לעולם ולעולמי עולמים: °ותדבר אלידם ארבה את זרעכם ככוכבי השמים וכל הארץ הזאת אשר אמרתי האי אשר אמרתי אשר אמרת מיבעי ליה אמר רבי אלעזר עד כאן דברי תלמיד מכאן ואילך דברי הרב ורבי שמואל בר נחמני אמר אלו ואלו דברי תלמיד אלא כך אמר משה לפני הקדוש ברוך הוא רבונו של עולם דברים שאמרת לי לך אמור להם לישראל בשמי הלכתי ואמרתי להם בשמך עכשיו מה אני אומר להם: °מבלתי יכולת יי' יכול יי' מיבעי ליה אמר רבי אלעזר אמר משה לפני הקדוש ברוך הוא רבונו של עולם עכשיו יאמרו אומות העולם תשש כחו כנקבה ואינו יכול להציל אמר הקדוש ברוך הוא למשה והלא כבר ראו נסים וגבורות שעשיתי להם על הים אמר לפניו רבונו של עולם עדיין יש להם לומר למלך אחד יכול לעמוד לשלשים ואחד מלכים אינו יכול לעמוד א"ר יוחנן מנין שחזר הקב"ה והודה לו למשה שנאמר °ויאמר יי' סלחתי כדבריך תנא דבי ר' ישמעאל כדבריך עתידים אומות העולם לומר כן אשרי תלמיד שרבו מודה לו: °ואולם חי אני אמר רבא אמר רב יצחק מלמד שאמר לו הקב"ה למשה משה חחייתני בדבריך: דרש *רבי שמלאי *לעולם יסדר אדם שבחו של הקדוש ברוך הוא ואחר כך יתפלל מנלן ממשה דכתיב °ואתחנן אל ה' בעת ההיא וכתיב יי' אלהים אתה החלות להראות את עבדך את גדלך ואת ידך החזקה אשר מי אל בשמים ובארץ אשר יעשה כמעשיך וכגבורותיך וכתיב בתריה אעבר' נא ואראה את הארץ הטובה וגומר: (סימ"ן מעשי"ם צדק"ה קרב"ן כה"ן תעני"ת מנע"ל ברז"ל)

אמר

מיכה ד; ירמי' יח; יחזקאל לו; שם; במדבר יא; דברים א; הושע יג; דברים ח; שם לב; שם לב; הושע ב; שמות לב; דברים ט; שמות לב; שם; שם; במדבר ל; חגיגה י.; שמות לב; [*ע"ז ד.] גיטין ע.; שם; שם; במדבר יד; שם; שם; ע"ז ז:; דברים ג; [חולי' ל"ל ורב]

[נ"ל שהתיר וכ"ה בילקוט ובע"י והוא נכון כדאיתא נדרי' ע"ז: וב"ב קד: וע' תוס' בכורו' לז. ד"ה מפירין] [*רב יצחק אמר מלמ' כו' כל"ל וכ"ה בילקוט ובע"י]

XXXII, 32. (7) Ibid. 13.

c (1) Ex. XXXII, 13. (2) If Moses were reporting God's promises to the Patriarchs, the words, 'that I have spoken of' are out of place. (3) Moses. (4) God. (5) Num. XIV, 16. (6) The ordinary form, which is masculine, while *yekoleth*, the word used, is feminine. (7) Ibid. 20. (8) Ibid. 21. (9) I.e., preserved My estimation among the nations (Rashi).

d (1) Deut. III, 23ff. (2) This is a mnemonic for the seven dicta of R. Eleazar which follow.

תורה אור

א"ר אלעזר גדולה תפלה יותר ממעשים טובים שאין לך גדול במעשים טובים יותר ממשה רבינו אע"פ כן לא נענה אלא בתפלה שנאמר °אל תוסף דבר אלי וסמיך ליה עלה ראש הפסגה: וא"ר אלעזר גדולה תענית יותר מן הצדקה מאי טעמא זה בגופו וזה בממונו: וא"ר אלעזר גדולה תפלה יותר מן הקרבנות שנאמר °למה לי רוב זבחיכם וכתיב °ובפרשכם כפיכם א"ר יוחנן **כל כהן שהרג את הנפש לא ישא את כפיו שנאמר °ידיכם דמים מלאו: *וא"ר אלעזר מיום שחרב בה"מ ננעלו שערי תפלה שנאמר °גם כי אזעק ואשוע שתם תפלתי ואע"פ ששערי תפלה ננעלו שערי דמעה לא ננעלו שנאמר °שמעה תפלתי יי' ושועתי האזינה אל דמעתי אל תחרש רבא לא גזר תעניתא ביומא דעיבא משום שנאמר °סכותה בענן לך מעבור תפלה: וא"ר אלעזר מיום שחרב בית המקדש נפסקה חומת ברזל בין ישראל לאביהם שבשמים שנאמר °ואתה *קח לך מחבת ברזל ונתת אותה קיר ברזל בינך ובין העיר: א"ר חנין א"ר חנינא כל המאריך בתפלתו אין תפלתו חוזרת ריקם מנא לן ממשה רבינו שנאמר °ואתפלל אל יי' וכתיב בתריה וישמע יי' אלי גם בפעם ההיא איני והא *א"ר חייא בר אבא א"ר יוחנן כל המאריך בתפלתו ומעיין בה סוף בא לידי כאב לב שנאמר °תוחלת ממושכה מחלה לב מאי תקנתיה יעסוק בתורה שנאמר °ועץ חיים תאוה באה ואין עץ חיים אלא תורה שנאמר °עץ חיים היא למחזיקים בה לא קשיא [2]הא דמאריך ומעיין בה הא דמאריך ולא מעיין בה א"ר חמא בר' חנינא אם ראה אדם שהתפלל ולא נענה יחזור ויתפלל שנאמר °קוה אל יי' חזק ויאמץ לבך וקוה אל יי': ת"ר ארבעה צריכין חזוק ואלו הן תורה ומעשים טובים תפלה ודרך ארץ תורה ומעשים טובים מנין שנאמר °רק חזק ואמץ מאד לשמור ולעשות ככל התורה חזק בתורה ואמץ במעשים טובים תפלה מנין שנאמר קוה אל יי' חזק ויאמץ לבך וקוה אל יי' דרך ארץ מנין שנאמר °חזק ונתחזק בעד עמנו וגו': °ותאמר ציון עזבני יי' ויי' שכחני היינו עזובה היינו שכוחה אמר ריש לקיש אמרה כנסת ישראל לפני הקב"ה רבש"ע אדם נושא אשה על אשתו ראשונה זוכר מעשה הראשונה אתה עזבתני ושכחתני אמר לה הקב"ה בתי שנים עשר מזלות בראתי ברקיע ועל כל מזל ומזל בראתי לו שלשים חיל ועל כל חיל וחיל בראתי לו שלשים לגיון ועל כל לגיון ולגיון בראתי לו שלשים רהטון ועל כל רהטון ורהטון בראתי לו שלשים קרטון ועל כל קרטון וקרטון בראתי לו שלשים גסטרא ועל כל גסטרא וגסטרא תליתי בו שלש מאות וששים וחמשה אלפי רבוא כוכבים כנגד ימות החמה וכולן לא בראתי אלא בשבילך ואת אמרת עזבתני ושכחתני °התשכח אשה עולה אמר הקב"ה כלום אשכח עולות אילים ופטרי רחמים שהקרבת לפני במדבר אמרה לפניו רבש"ע הואיל ואין שכחה לפני כסא כבודך שמא לא תשכח לי מעשה העגל אמר לה °גם אלה תשכחנה אמרה לפניו רבש"ע הואיל ויש שכחה לפני כסא כבודך שמא תשכח לי מעשה סיני אמר לה °ואנכי לא אשכחך והיינו דא"ר אלעזר א"ר אושעיא מאי דכתיב גם אלה תשכחנה זה מעשה העגל ואנכי לא אשכחך זה מעשה סיני: חסידים הראשונים היו שוהים שעה אחת: מנא הני מילי א"ר יהושע בן לוי אמר קרא °אשרי יושבי ביתך ואמר ריב"ל המתפלל צריך לשהות שעה אחת אחר תפלתו שנאמר °אך צדיקים יודו לשמך ישבו ישרים את פניך תניא נמי הכי [3]המתפלל צריך שישהא שעה אחת קודם תפלתו ושעה אחת אחר תפלתו קודם תפלתו מנין שנאמר אשרי יושבי ביתך לאחר תפלתו מנין דכתיב אך צדיקים יודו לשמך ישבו ישרים את פניך ת"ר חסידים הראשונים היו שוהין שעה אחת ומתפללים שעה אחת וחוזרין ושוהין שעה אחת וכי מאחר ששוהין תשע שעות ביום בתפלה תורתן היאך משתמרת ומלאכתן היאך נעשית אלא מתוך שחסידים הם תורתן משתמרת ומלאכתן מתברכת: [4]אפי' המלך שואל בשלומו לא ישיבנו: אמר רב יוסף [5]לא שנו אלא למלכי ישראל אבל למלכי אומות העולם פוסק מיתיבי [6]המתפלל וראה אנס בא כנגדו ראה קרון בא כנגדו לא יהא מפסיק אלא מקצר ועולה לא קשיא הא [7]דאפשר לקצר *(יקצר ואם לאו פוסק): ת"ר מעשה בחסיד א' שהיה מתפלל בדרך בא שר אחד ונתן לו שלום ולא החזיר לו שלום המתין לו עד שסיים תפלתו לאחר שסיים תפלתו א"ל ריקא והלא כתוב בתורתכם °רק השמר לך ושמור נפשך וכתיב °ונשמרתם מאד לנפשותיכם כשנתתי לך שלום למה לא החזרת לי שלום אם הייתי חותך ראשך בסייף מי היה תובע את דמך מידי א"ל המתין לי עד שאפייסך בדברים א"ל אלו היית עומד לפני מלך בשר ודם ובא חברך ונתן לך שלום היית מחזיר

גדולה תפלה יותר ממעשים טובים. דהא תפלה שהרי משה רבינו ע"ה אף על פי שהיו בידו מעשים טובים הולך לתפלה:

כל המאריך בתפלתו ומעיין בה. פירש"י *מלפ' [שתעש'] בקשתו לפי שכיון בתפלתו. תימה דהכא משמע דעיון תפלה לאו מעליות' הוא וכן משמע פ' הרואה (דף נה.) ג' דברים מזכירים עונותיו של אדם וקאמר עיון תפלה ולא כן משמע בפרק מפנין (דף קכז.) דקאמר אדם אוכל פירותיהן בעה"ז וקא חשיב עיון תפלה אלמא מעליות' הוא וכן משמע בגט פשוט (דף קסד:) דקאמר משלשה דברים אין אדם ניצול בכל יום וקאמר עיון תפלה פירוש שאין אדם מעיין בה א"כ משמע שהוא טוב וי"ל דתרי עיון תפלה יש עיון תפלה דהכא המלפה שתבא בקשתו ועיון תפלה דהתם שמכוין את לבו לתפלה:

אל דמעתי אל תחרש. פרש"י דדייק מדיוקא מדלא קאמר ודמעתי תראה ש"מ שהיא נראת בכל פעם ואין להתפלל רק שתתקבל:

קודם תפלתו מנין שנאמר אשרי יושבי ביתך. ולפיכך תקנו לומר זה הפסוק קודם תהלה לדוד לאפוקי מהכי דאמרי אשרי הרבה: אבל

עלה ראש הפסגה. בדבר תפלה זו כתרלתי להראותך אותה: ובפרשכם כפיכם. אי לאו דגדולה תפלה כיון דאמר למה לי רוב זבחיכם למה לי תו ובפרישכם הא אפילו זבחיהם לא ניחא ליה: אל תחרש. מדלא כתיב את דמעתי תראה ש"מ נראית היא לפניו ואין צריך להתפלל אלא שתתקבל לפניו: ונתת אותה קיר ברזל. סימן למחילת ברזל המפסקת בינו לבינם: ומעיין בה. מלפה שתעשה בקשתו על ידי הארכתו סוף שאינה נעשית וכמלאת תוחלת ממושכ' חכם והיא כאב לב כשאדם מלפה ואין תאותו באה: תוחלת. לשון אלוי ותאו': ועץ חיים תאוה באה. סופו של מקרא הוא: קוה. והתחזק ואל תמשוך ידך אלא חזור וקוה: צריכין חזוק. שיתחזק אדם בהן תמיד בכל כחו: דרך ארץ. אם אומן הוא לאומנותו אם סוחר הוא לסחורתו אם איש מלחמה הוא למלחמתו: שלשים חיל. כאשי גייסות וחבורות חלוקות: לגיון וקרטון וגסטר'. שמות של שרר' כגון שלטון והגמון ודוכוס ופחה: עולה. כמו עולות וקרבנו': גם אלה. מעשה העגל שאמרו אלה אלהיך ישראל (שמות לב): ואנכי זה מעשה סיני. שנאמר בו אנכי ה' אלהיך (שמות כ): יושבי ביתך. והדר יהללוך: יודו לשמך. והדר ישבו ישרים את פניך: תשע שעות. לשלש תפלות: תורתם משתמרת. בתוך לבם שאין תלמוד' משתכח: אבל למלכי אומות העולם פוסק. שלא יהרגנו: הא דאפשר. בקצור כגון שסמוך לגמור תפלתו: אבל

עין משפט נר מצוה

עיי' תוס' שבת קיז: ד"ה עיון תפלה

כד
[א]מיי' פט"ו מהלכות תפלה הלכה ג סמג עשין כ טוש"ע א"ח סימן קכח סעיף לה

[וע"ע תוס' סנהדרין לה: וכן בתוס' דיבמות ז. ד"ה שנאמר]

כה
[ב]טוש"ע א"ח סימן לח סעי' ה

כו
[ג]מיי' פ"ד מהלכות תפלה הלכה יו סמג עשין יט טוש"ע א"ח סי' לג סעיף א

כז
[ד]מיי' פ"ו שם הלכה ט סמג שם טוש"ע א"ח סי' קד סעי' א

כח
[ה]מיי' שם טוש"ע שם סעיף ב

כט
[ו]שם סעי' א

מסורת הש"ס

[ע' תוס' סנהדרין לה: וכן בתוס' דיבמות ז. ד"ה שנאמר] ב"מ כט.

בן אדם קח לך כצ"ל

לקמן נה.

[ברב אלפס לי' והא דלא אפשר לקצר אפשר לקצר יקצר ואי לא מפסיק]

דברי' ג; ישעי' א; שם; שם; איכ' ג; תהלי' לט; ישעי' ל; איכ' ג; יחזקאל ד; דברי' ט; משלי' יג; שם; שם ג; תהלים כז; יהושע א; שמואל ב י; ישעיה מט; שם; שם; שם; תהלים פד; שם קמ; דברים ד; שם

found in *J.T.* (6) Alfasi reads: In the one case it is possible for him to curtail, in the other it is not possible; where he can curtail he should, otherwise he may break off.

d (1) *Raka;* v. *supra* 22a, n. c3. (2) Deut. IV, 9. (3) Ibid. 15. '*Soul*' in these texts is taken to mean 'life'.

[32b] R. Eleazar said: Prayer is more efficacious even than good deeds, for there was no-one greater in good deeds than Moses our Master, and yet he was answered only after prayer, as it says, *Speak no more unto Me,*[3] and immediately afterwards, *Get thee up into the top of Pisgah.*[4]

R. Eleazar also said: Fasting is more efficacious than charity. What is the reason? One is performed with a man's money, the other with his body.

R. Eleazar also said: Prayer is more efficacious than offerings, as it says, *To what purpose is the multitude of your sacrifices unto Me,*[5] and this is followed by, *And when ye spread forth your hands.*[6] R. Joḥanan said: A priest who has committed manslaughter should not lift up his hands [to say the priestly benediction], since it says [in this context], '*Your hands are full of blood*'.

R. Eleazar also said: From the day on which the Temple was destroyed the gates of prayer have been closed, as it says, *Yea, when I cry and call for help He shutteth out my prayer.*[7] But though the gates of prayer are closed, the gates of weeping are not closed, as it says, *Hear my prayer, O Lord, and give ear unto my cry; keep not silence at my tears.*[8] Raba did not order a fast on a cloudy day because it says, *Thou hast covered Thyself with a cloud so that no prayer* [a] *can pass through.*[1]

R. Eleazar also said: Since the day that the Temple was destroyed, a wall of iron has intervened between Israel and their Father in Heaven, as it says, *And take thou unto thee an iron griddle, and set it for a wall of iron between thee and the city.*[2]

R. Ḥanin said in the name of R. Ḥanina: If one prays long his prayer does not pass unheeded. Whence do we know this? From Moses our Master; for it says, *And I prayed unto the Lord,*[3] and it is written afterwards, *And the Lord hearkened unto me that time also.*[4] But is that so? Has not R. Ḥiyya b. Abba said in the name of R. Joḥanan: If one prays long and looks for the fulfilment of his prayer, in the end he will have vexation of heart, as it says, *Hope deferred maketh the heart sick?*[5] What is his remedy? Let him study the Torah, as it says, *But desire fulfilled is a tree of life;*[6] and the tree of life is nought but the Torah, as it says, *She is a tree of life to them that lay hold on her!*[7]—There is no contradiction: one statement speaks of a man who prays long and looks for the fulfilment of his prayer, the other of one who prays long without looking for the fulfilment of his prayer.[8] R. Ḥama son of R. Ḥanina said: If a man sees that he prays and is not answered, he should pray again, as it says, *Wait for the Lord, be strong and let thy heart take courage; yea, wait thou for the Lord.*[9]

Our Rabbis taught: Four things require to be done with energy,[10] namely, [study of] the Torah, good deeds, praying, and one's worldly occupation. Whence do we know this of Torah and good deeds? Because it says, *Only be strong and very courageous to observe to do according to all the law:*[11] '*be strong*' in Torah, and '*be courageous*' in good deeds. Whence of prayer? Because it says, '*Wait for the Lord, be strong and let thy heart take courage, yea, wait thou for the Lord*'. Whence of worldly occupation? Because it says, *Be of good courage* [b] *and let us prove strong for our people.*[1]

But Zion said, The Lord hath forsaken me, and the Lord hath forgotten me.[2] Is not '*forsaken*' the same as '*forgotten*'? Resh Laḳish said: The community of Israel said before the Holy One, blessed be He: Sovereign of the Universe, when a man takes a second wife after his first, he still remembers the deeds of the first. Thou hast both forsaken me and forgotten me! The Holy One, blessed be He, answered her: My daughter, twelve constellations have I created in the firmament, and for each constellation I have created thirty hosts, and for each host I have created thirty legions, and for each legion I have created thirty cohorts, and for each cohort I have created thirty maniples, and for each maniple I have created thirty camps, and to each camp[3] I have attached three hundred and sixty-five thousands of myriads of stars, corresponding to the days of the solar year, and all of them I have created only for thy sake, and thou sayest, Thou hast forgotten me and forsaken me! *Can a woman forsake her sucking child* ['ullah]?[4] Said the Holy One, blessed be He: Can I possibly forget the burnt-offerings ['*olah*] of rams and the firstborn of animals[5] that thou didst offer to Me in the wilderness? She thereupon said: Sovereign of the Universe, since there is no forgetfulness before the Throne of Thy glory, perhaps Thou wilt not forget the sin of the Calf? He replied: '*Yea, "these"*[6] *will be forgotten*'. She said before Him: Sovereign of the Universe, seeing that there is forgetfulness before the Throne of Thy glory, perhaps Thou wilt forget my conduct at Sinai? He replied to her: '*Yet "the I"*[7] *will not forget thee*'. This agrees with what R. Eleazar said in the name of R. Oshaia: What is referred to by the text, '*yea, "these" will be forgotten*'? This refers to the sin of the Calf. '*And yet "the I" will not forget thee*': this refers to their conduct at Sinai.

THE PIOUS MEN OF OLD USED TO WAIT AN HOUR. On what is this based?—R. Joshua b. Levi said: On the text, *Happy are* [c] *they that dwell in Thy house.*[1] R. Joshua b. Levi also said: One who says the *Tefillah* should also wait an hour after his prayer, as it says, *Surely the righteous shall give thanks unto Thy name, the upright shall sit in Thy presence.*[2] It has been taught similarly: One who says the *Tefillah* should wait an hour before his prayer and an hour after his prayer. Whence do we know [that he should wait] before his prayer? Because it says: '*Happy are they that dwell in Thy house*'. Whence after his prayer? Because it says, '*Surely the righteous shall give thanks unto Thy name, the upright shall dwell in Thy presence*'. Our Rabbis taught: The pious men of old used to wait for an hour and pray for an hour and then wait again for an hour. But seeing that they spend nine hours a day over prayer, how is their knowledge of Torah preserved and how is their work done? [The answer is] that because they are pious, their Torah is preserved[3] and their work is blessed.[4]

EVEN IF A KING GREETS HIM HE SHOULD NOT ANSWER HIM. R. Joseph said: This was meant to apply only to Jewish kings, but for a king of another people he may interrupt. An objection was raised: If one was saying *Tefillah* and he saw a robber[5] coming towards him or a carriage coming towards him, he should not break off but curtail it and clear off!—There is no contradiction: where it is possible for him to curtail [he should curtail, otherwise he should break off].[6]

Our Rabbis taught: It is related that once when a certain pious man was praying by the roadside, an officer came by and greeted him and he did not return his greeting. So he waited for him till he had finished his prayer. When he had finished his prayer he said [d] to him: Fool![1] is it not written in your Law, *Only take heed to thyself and keep thy soul diligently,*[2] and it is also written, *Take ye therefore good heed unto your souls?*[3] When I greeted you why did you not return my greeting? If I had cut off your head with my sword, who would have demanded satisfaction for your blood from me? He replied to him: Be patient and I will explain to you. If, [he went on], you had been standing before an earthly king and your friend had come and given you greeting, would you [33a]

(3) Ibid. 26. The meaning is apparently that his good deeds did not avail to procure him permission to enter the land, but his prayer procured for him the vision of Pisgah. (4) Ibid. 27. (5) Isa. I, 11. (6) Ibid. 15. Since spreading of hands is mentioned after sacrifice, it must be regarded as more efficacious. (7) Lam. III, 8. (8) Ps. XXXIX, 13. This shows that the tears are at any rate observed.

a (1) Lam. III, 44. (2) Ezek. IV, 3. This wall was symbolical of the wall separating Israel from God. (3) Deut. IX, 26. This seems to be quoted in error for, *And I fell down before the Lord forty days and forty nights*, in v. 18; v. MS.M. (4) Ibid. 19. (5) Prov. XIII, 12. (6) Ibid. (7) Ibid. III, 18. (8) V. B.B. (Sonc. ed.) p. 717, n. 8. (9) Ps. XXVII, 14. (10) Lit., 'require vigour'. (11) Joshua I, 7.

b (1) II Sam. X, 12. (2) Isa. XLIX, 14. (3) These terms are obviously taken from Roman military language. There is, however, some difficulty about identifying *rahaton* (cohorts) and *karton* (maniples) in the text. (4) Ibid. 15. (5) Lit., 'opening of the womb'. (6) Referring to the golden calf incident when Israel exclaimed 'These *are thy gods*', Ex. XXXII, 4. (7) Referring to the revelation at Sinai when God declared, 'I *am the Lord Thy God*'. This incident will not be forgotten. R.V. '*Yet will* I *not forget thee*'.

c (1) Ps. LXXXIV, 5. (2) Ibid. CXL, 14. (3) I.e., they do not forget it. (4) I.e., a little goes a long way. (5) The Heb. *annes* usually means 'a man of violence'. Some suppose that it is here equivalent to *ḥamor*, ass, which is actually have returned it? No, he replied. And if you had returned his greeting, what would they have done to you? They would have cut off my head with the sword, he replied. He then said to him: Have we not here then an *a fortiori* argument: If [you would have behaved] in this way when standing before an earthly king who is here today and tomorrow in the grave, how much more so I when standing before the supreme King of kings, the Holy One, blessed be He, who endures for all eternity? Forthwith the officer accepted his explanation, and the pious man returned to his home in peace.

EVEN IF A SNAKE IS WOUND ROUND HIS FOOT HE SHOULD NOT BREAK OFF. R. Shesheth said: This applies only in the case of a serpent, but if it is a scorpion, he breaks off.[4] An objection was raised: If a man fell into a den of lions [and was not seen again] one cannot testify concerning him that he is dead; but if he fell into a trench full of serpents or scorpions, one can testify concerning him that he is dead!—The case there is different, because on account of his crushing them [in falling] they turn and bite him. R. Isaac said: If he sees oxen [coming towards him] he may break off; for R. Oshaia taught: One should remove from a *tam*[5] ox fifty cubits, and from a *mu'ad*[6] ox out of sight. It was taught in the name of R. Meir: If an ox's head is in a [fodder] basket,[7] go up to a roof and kick the ladder away.[8] Samuel said: This applies only to a black ox and in the month of Nisan, because then Satan is dancing
a between his horns.[1]

Our Rabbis taught: In a certain place there was once a lizard[2] which used to injure people. They came and told R. Ḥanina b. Dosa. He said to them: Show me its hole. They showed him its hole, and he put his heel over the hole, and the lizard came out and bit him, and it died. He put it on his shoulder and brought it to the Beth ha-Midrash and said to them: See, my sons, it is not the lizard that kills, it is sin that kills! On that occasion they said: Woe to the man whom a lizard meets, but woe to the lizard which R. Ḥanina b. Dosa meets![3]

MISHNAH. THE MIRACLE OF THE RAINFALL[4] IS MENTIONED IN THE BENEDICTION OF THE RESURRECTION, AND THE PETITION[5] FOR RAIN IN THE BENEDICTION OF THE YEARS, AND HABDALAH[6] IN 'THAT GRACIOUSLY GRANTEST KNOWLEDGE'.[7] R. AKIBA SAYS: HE SAYS IT AS A FOURTH BLESSING[8] BY ITSELF; R. ELIEZER SAYS: IT IS SAID IN THE THANKSGIVING BENEDICTION.[9]

GEMARA. THE MIRACLE OF THE RAINFALL etc. What is the reason?—R. Joseph said: Because it is put on a level with the resurrection of the dead, therefore it was inserted in the benediction of the resurrection.

THE PETITION FOR RAIN IN THE BENEDICTION OF THE YEARS. What is the reason?—R. Joseph said: Because [the petition] refers to sustenance, therefore it was inserted in the benediction of sustenance.

HABDALAH IN 'THAT GRACIOUSLY GRANTEST KNOWLEDGE'. What is the reason?—R. Joseph said: Because it is a kind of wis-
b dom,[1] it was inserted in the benediction of wisdom. The Rabbis, however, say: Because the reference is to a weekday, therefore it was inserted in the weekday blessing. R. Ammi said: Great is knowledge, since it was placed at the beginning of the weekday blessings. R. Ammi also said: Great is knowledge since it was placed between two names,[2] as it says, *For a God of knowledge is the Lord.*[3] And if one has not knowledge, it is forbidden to have mercy on him, as it says, *For it is a people of no understanding, therefore He that made them will have no compassion upon them.*[4] R. Eleazar said: Great is the Sanctuary, since it has been placed between two names, as it says, *Thou hast made, O Lord, the sanctuary, O Lord.*[5] R. Eleazar also said: Whenever there is in a man knowledge, it is as if the Sanctuary had been built in his days; for knowledge is set between two names, and the Sanctuary is set between two names. R. Aḥa Karḥina'ah demurred to this. According to this, he said, great is vengeance since it has been set between two names, as it says, *God of vengeance, O Lord;*[6] He replied: That is so; that is to say, it is great in its proper sphere; and this accords with what 'Ulla said: Why two vengeances here?[7] One for good and one for ill. For good, as it is written, *He shined forth from Mount Paran;*[8] for ill, as it is written, *God of vengeance, O Lord, God of vengeance, shine forth.*[6]

R. AKIBA SAYS: HE SAYS IT AS A FOURTH BLESSING, etc. R. Shaman b. Abba said to R. Joḥanan: Let us see: It was the Men of the Great Synagogue[9] who instituted for Israel blessings and prayers, sanctifications and *habdalahs.*[10] Let us see where they inserted them!—He replied: At first they inserted it [the *habdalah*] in the *Tefillah:* when they [Israel] became richer, they instituted that it should be said over the cup [of wine]; when they became poor again they again inserted it in the *Tefillah;* and they said that one who has said *habdalah* in the *Tefillah* must say it [again] over the cup [of wine]. It has also been stated: R. Ḥiyya b. Abba said in the name of R. Joḥanan: The Men of the Great Synagogue instituted for Israel blessings and prayers, sanctifications and *habdalahs.* At first they inserted the *habdalah* in the *Tefillah.* When they [Israel] became richer, they instituted that it should be said over the cup [of wine]. When they became poor again, they inserted it in the *Tefillah;* and they said that one who says *habdalah* in the *Tefillah* must [also] say it over the cup [of wine]. It has also been stated: Rabbah and R. Joseph both say: One who has said *habdalah* in the *Tefillah* must [also] say it over the cup [of wine]. Said Raba: We can bring an objection against this ruling [from the following]: If a man forgot and did not mention the miracle of the rain in the resurrection blessing, or petition for rain in the blessing of the years, he is made to repeat the *Tefillah.* If, however, he forgot *habdalah* in 'that graciously grantest knowledge', he is
c not made to repeat, because he can say it over the cup [of wine]![1] Do not read, because he *can* say it over the cup [of wine], but read, because he *says* it over the cup [of wine].

It has also been stated: R. Benjamin b. Jephet said: R. Jose asked R. Joḥanan in Sidon—some report, R. Simeon b. Jacob from Tyre asked R. Joḥanan: But I have heard that one who has said *habdalah* in the *Tefillah* says it over the cup [of wine]; or is it not so? He replied to him: He must say it over the cup [of wine].

The question was raised: If one has said *habdalah* over the cup [of wine], need he say it [again] in the *Tefillah?*—R. Naḥman b. Isaac replied: We learn the answer *a fortiori* from the case of *Tefillah.* The essential place of the *habdalah* is in the *Tefillah,* and yet it was laid down that one who has said it in the *Tefillah* must say it also over the cup [of wine]. Does it not then stand to reason that if he has said it over the cup [of wine], which is not its essential
d place, he must say it [again] in the *Tefillah?* R. Aḥa Arika[1] recited in the presence of R. Ḥinena: He who says *habdalah* in the *Tefillah* is more praiseworthy than he who says it over the cup [of wine], and if he says it in both, may blessings rest on his head! This statement contains a contradiction. It says that he who says *habdalah* in the *Tefillah* is more praiseworthy than he who says it over the cup [of wine], which would show that to say it in *Tefillah* alone is sufficient, and again it teaches, 'and if he says it in both, may blessings rest on his head', but since he has said it in one he is quit, the second is a blessing which is not necessary, and Raba, or as some say Resh Laḳish, or again as some say, both Resh Laḳish and R. Joḥanan, have said: Whoever says a blessing which is not necessary transgresses the command of 'thou shalt not take [God's name in vain]'![2] Rather read thus: If he has said *habdalah* in one and not in the other, blessings shall rest upon his head.

R. Ḥisda inquired of R. Shesheth: If he forgot in both,[3] what is he to do?—He replied: If one forgot in both, he says the whole

(4) A scorpion is more certain to sting. (5) One which has not gored before. (6) One which has gored three times. For these terms, v. Glos. (7) I.e., even if it is busy eating. (8) This is a humorous exaggeration.

מסורת הש"ס

אבל עקרב פוסק. וטעמו לפי שהעקרב מסוכן לעקוץ יותר משהנחש מוכן לישוך: ואין מעידין עליו. לומר לאשתו מת בעלך להתירה לינשא שפעמים שאין האריות רעבים ואין אוכלין אותו: נחשים ועקרבים. או זה או זה מעידים עליו שמת אלמא מועד הנחש לישוך: אגב איצצא. כשנפל עליהם ודוחקם הזיקוהו: שור תם. שלא נגח אדם: מועד. שנגח ג' פעמים: בדקולא. סל שתולין בו תבן בראשו ואוכל: ושדי דרגא. לאו דוקא אלא כלומר היזהר ממנו הרבה: ביומי ניסן. מתוך שעברו ימי הסתיו שהארץ יבשה ועכשיו רואה אותה מלאה דשאים זחה דעתו עליו ונכנס בו יצר הרע: ערוד. מן הנחש והצב בא שמזדווגין זה עם זה ויוצא משניהם ערוד*: את חורו. שהוא יוצא משם: ומת הערוד. מצאתי בה"ג אמרי במערב' כשהערוד נושך את האדם אם הערוד קודם למים מת האדם ואם האדם קודם למים מת הערוד ונעשה נס לר' חנינא ונבקע מעין מתחת עקבו: מתני' מזכירין גבורות גשמים. משיב הרוח שאינו לשון בקשה אלא לשון הזכרה ושבח: ושואלין. ותן טל ומטר לשון בקשה: והבדלה בחונן הדעת. במוצאי שבת אתה חוננתנו: גמ' מתוך שהיא חכמה. החכם יודע להבדיל בין קדש לחול ובין טמא לטהור: בין שתי אותיות. בין שתי הזכרות: במילתה מידא גדולה היא. במקום שצריכה נקמה דבר גדול הוא: שתי נקמות הללו למה אחת לרעה. להנקם מן האומות שלא קבלו את התור': ואחת לטובה. כדאמרי' בב"ק (ד' לח.) ומפרקן הופיע והפקיר ממונן לישראל שור של ישראל שנגח שור של נכרי פטור: הופיע. גלה והפקיר כשלא קבלו את התור': *העשירו. לקנות יין: קבועה על הכוס. ולא כשתקנוה תקנת עזרא וכשחזרו והענו קבעוה בתפלה ונחלקו היאך יאמרוה: *בתחלה. כשעלו מן הגולה והיו דחוקים: קדושות. קדוש היום: מפני שיכול. משמע אם ירצה שלא לחזו' ולהתפלל הא אם אמר' בתפל' א"צ לאומר' על הכוס: ואנא שמעית. הכי שמעתי: חוזר לראש. לתפלה ולכוס: הלכתא

[חולין קכז.] [לעיל כח:] יבמות קכא. ע"פ קיב: [תוספ' פ"ג] ירוש' גרס חברבר וכן גר' ערוד כאן דהוא הוא כי מה שנקרא בחולין קכז. ערוד קורהו בב"ר פ' פ"ג חברבר.) תענית ב. לעיל כט. נדה ח. [תעני' ב.] חלק לב. ע"ש

[דבורי רש"י נדפסו בטעותי וצריך להפכם]

תורה אור

מחזיר לו א"ל לאו ואם היית מחזיר לו מה היו עושים לך א"ל היו חותכים את ראשי בסייף א"ל והלא דברים ק"ו ומה אתה שהיית עומד לפני מלך בשר ודם *שהיום כאן ומחר בקבר כך אני שהייתי עומד לפני מלך מלכי המלכים הקב"ה שהוא חי וקים לעד ולעולמי עולמים על אחת כמה וכמה מיד נתפייס אותו השר ונפטר אותו חסיד לביתו לשלום: *אפילו נחש כרוך על עקבו לא יפסיק: אמר רב ששת לא שנו אלא נחש אבל עקרב פוסק מתיבי *נפל לגוב אריות אין מעידין עליו שמת נפל לחפירה מלאה נחשים ועקרבים מעידין עליו שמת שאני התם דאגב איצצא מזקי א"ר יצחק ראה שוורים פוסק דתני רב אושעי' *מרחיקין משור תם חמשים אמה ומשור מועד כמלא עיניו תנא משמיה דר' מאיר ריש תורא בדקולא סליק לאגרא ושדי דרגא מתותך אמר שמואל ה"מ בשור שחור וביומי ניסן מפני שהשטן מרקד לו בין קרניו: ת"ר *מעשה במקום אחד שהיה *ערוד והיה מזיק את הבריות באו והודיעו לו לר' חנינא בן דוסא אמר להן הראו לי את חורו הראוהו את חורו נתן עקבו על פי החור יצא ונשכו ומת אותו ערוד נטלו על כתפו והביאו לבית המדרש אמר להם ראו בני אין ערוד ממית אלא החטא ממית באותה שעה אמרו אוי לו לאדם שפגע בו ערוד ואוי לערוד שפגע בו ר' חנינא בן דוסא: **מתני'** *מזכירין גבורות גשמים בתחיית המתים ושאלה בברכת השנים והבדלה בחונן הדעת *ר' עקיבא אומר אומרה ברכה רביעית בפני עצמה ר' אליעזר אומר בהודאה: **גמ'** מזכירין גבורות גשמים מ"ט אמר רב יוסף *מתוך ששקולה כתחיית המתים לפיכך קבעוה בתחיית המתים ושאלה בברכת השנים מ"ט אמר רב יוסף מתוך שהיא פרנסה לפיכך קבעוה בברכת פרנסה הבדלה בחונן הדעת מ"ט אמר רב יוסף מתוך שהיא חכמה קבעוה בברכת חכמה ורבנן אמרי מתוך שהיא חול לפיכך קבעוה בברכת חול א"ר אמי גדולה דעה שנתנה בתחלת ברכה של חול וא"ר אמי *גדולה דעה שנתנה בין שתי אותיות שנאמר °כי אל דעות יי' וכל מי שאין בו דעה אסור לרחם עליו שנ' °כי לא עם בינות הוא ע"כ לא ירחמנו עשהו א"ר אלעזר גדול מקדש שנתן בין שתי אותיות שנ' °פעלת יי' מקדש יי' וא"ר אלעזר כל אדם שיש בו דעה כאלו נבנה בית המקדש בימיו דעה נתנה בין שתי אותיות מקדש נתן בין שתי אותיות מתקיף לה רב *אחא קרחינאה אלא מעתה גדולה נקמה שנתנה בין שתי אותיות שנא' °אל נקמות יי' א"ל אין במילתה מידא גדולה היא והיינו דאמר עולא שתי נקמות הללו למה אחת לטובה ואחת לרעה לטובה דכתיב °הופיע מהר פארן לרעה דכתיב אל נקמות יי' אל נקמות הופיע: ר' עקיבא אומר אומרה ברכה רביעית כו': א"ל רב שמן בר אבא לר' יוחנן מכדי אנשי כנסת הגדולה תקנו להם לישראל ברכות ותפלות קדושו' והבדלות נחזי היכן תקון א"ל בתחלה קבעוה בתפלה העשירו קבעוה על הכוס העני חזרו וקבעו' בתפל' והם אמרו *המבדיל בתפלה צריך שיבדיל על הכוס אתמר נמי א"ר חייא בר אבא א"ר יוחנן אנשי כנסת הגדולה תקנו להם לישראל ברכות ותפלות קדושות והבדלות בתחל' קבעוה בתפלה העשירו קבעוה על הכוס חזרו והענו קבעוה בתפלה והם אמרו המבדיל בתפלה צריך שיבדיל על הכוס אתמר נמי רבה ורב יוסף דאמרי תרוייהו המבדיל בתפלה צריך שיבדיל על הכוס אמר רבא *ומותבינן אשמעתיה *טעה ולא הזכיר גבורות גשמים בתחיית המתים ושאלה בברכת השנים מחזירין אותו והבדלה בחונן הדעת אין מחזירין אותו מפני שיכול לאומרה על הכוס לא תימא מפני שיכול לאומרה על הכוס אלא אימא מפני שאומרה על הכוס אתמר נמי א"ר בנימין בר יפת שאל רבי יוסי את ר' יוחנן בצידן ואמרי ליה ר' שמעון בן יעקב דמן צור את ר' יוחנן ואנא שמעית המבדיל בתפלה צריך שיבדיל על הכוס או לא וא"ל צריך שיבדיל על הכוס איבעיא להו המבדיל על הכוס מהו שיבדיל בתפלה אמר רב נחמן בר יצחק ק"ו מתפלה ומה תפלה דעיקר תקנתא היא אמרי המבדיל בתפלה צריך שיבדיל על הכוס המבדיל על הכוס דלאו עיקר תקנתא היא לכ"ש תני ר' אחא *אריכא קמיה דרב חיננא המבדיל בתפלה משובח יותר ממי שיבדיל על הכוס ואם הבדיל בזו ובזו *ינוחו לו ברכות על ראשו הא גופא קשיא אמרת המבדיל בתפלה משובח יותר ממי שיבדיל על הכוס אלמא תפלה לחודה סגי והדר תני אם הבדיל בזו ובזו ינוחו לו ברכות על ראשו וכיון דנפק ליה בחדא אפטר והויא *ברכה שאינה צריכה ואמר רב ואי תימא ר"ל ואמרי לה ר' יוחנן ור"ל דאמרי תרוייהו *כל המברך ברכה שאינה צריכה עובר משום °לא תשא אלא אימא הכי אם הבדיל בזו ולא הבדיל בזו ינוחו לו ברכות על ראשו בעא מניה רב חסדא מרב ששת טעה בזו ובזו מהו אמר ליה °טעה בזו ובזו חוזר לראש

אמר

שמואל א ב; ישעיה כז; שמות טו; שם ע"ש; תהלים צד; דברים לג; [שבת קנ: ע"ש פסחים קה: קז.]; תוספת' פ"ג; לעיל כו: ודף כט.; [ע' שבת קיח. קיג.]; [שבת לח. מגילה כה: ע"ז ס:]; [יומא ע. סוטה מח:]; שמות כ

אבל עקרב פוסק. בירושלמי קאמר דאם היה נחש מרתיע לבא כנגדו פוסק לפי שבא כנגדו בכעס מתכוין להזיקו ומיהו לא מליכו אם פסק שיחזור לראש ודלא קאמר ואם פסק חוזר לראש אבל לתחלת ברכה ומיהא יחזור ואם טעה בג' ראשונות או בג' אחרונות חוזר לתחלת הג' באבות בראשונות ובעבודה באחרונות כדאמרינן לקמן בפרקין (דף לד.): אמר

עין משפט נר מצוה

ל אב מיי' פ"ו מהלכות תפלה שם סמג עשין יט טוש"ע א"ח סי' קד סעי' ג

לא ג מיי' פי"ג מהל' גירושין הל' יז סמג עשין נ טוש"ע אה"ע סי' יז סעי' כט

לב ד מיי' פ"ו מהל' תפלה הל' ט סמג עשין יט טוש"ע א"ח סי' קד סעי' ד

לג ו מיי' פ"ב שם הלכ' טו סמג שם טוש"ע א"ח סי' קיד סעיף א

לד ז מיי' שם הל' יו וסמ"ג שם טוש"ע א"ח סי קי"ז סעיף א

לה חט מיי' שם הל' ד יב וסמג שם טוש"ע א"ח סימן רצ"ד סעיף א

לו י מיי' פ"י שם הלכה ח סמג שם טוש"ע א"ח סי' קיד סעיף ה

לז כ מיי' שם הל' ט וסמג שם טוש"ע א"ח סי' קיז סעיף ד

לח ל מיי' שם הל' יד וסמג שם טוש"ע א"ח סי רלד סעי' א

לט מ טור א"ח שם [קידושין ל. וש"כ]

מ נ מיי' פ"א מהלכ' ברכות הלכה טו סמג עשין כז טוש"ע א"ח סי' כו סעי' ו ובסי' רטו סעיף ד

מא ס טוש"ע א"ח סי' רלד סעיף ו

a (1) I.e., it is high spirited and full of mischief in the spring. (2) Heb. *yarod*, apparently a cross-breed of a snake and a lizard. (3) According to *J.T.* a spring of water had miraculously opened at the feet of R. Ḥanina, and that sealed the fate of the lizard, for (it is asserted) when a lizard bites a man, if the man reaches water first, the lizard dies, but if the lizard reaches water first the man dies. (4) The formula 'that causest the wind to blow' etc., *P.B.* p. 44. (5) The words 'and grant dew and rain for a blessing', ibid. p. 47. (6) V. Glos. (7) Ibid. p. 46. (8) After the first three. (9) Ibid. p. 51.

b (1) Viz., discerning between holy and profane and between clean and unclean etc. (2) I.e., two mentions of the Deity. Lit., 'letters'; var. lec. 'words'. (3) I Sam. II, 3. (4) Isa. XXVII, 11. (5) Ex. XV, 17. (lit. trans.). (6) Ps. XCIV, 1. (7) The word 'vengeance' is written twice in the verse cited from Psalms. (8) Deut. XXXIII, 2. It is difficult to see what this has to do with vengeance. It seems that in fact the text does not explain the statement of 'Ulla, and instead shows how there are two kinds of 'shining forth'. V. Sanh. 92*a*. (9) V. Aboth I, 1. (10) The various divisions mentioned in the *habdalah* benediction.

c (1) V. *infra* 26*b*. Which seems to show that it is optional.

d (1) The Tall. (2) Ex. XX, 7. (3) In the case of *habdalah* over the cup, he failed to say the last benediction which contains the enumeration of the various divisions. V. *D.S.* a.l.

עין משפט
נר מצוה

[נ"ל פירוש']

מב
א מיי' פ"ה מהלכ' בית הבחירה הל' א

מג
ב מיי' פ"ב מהלכת תפלה הלכה יב סמג עשין יט טוש"ע א"ח סימן תלא סעיף ב

מד
ג מיי' פ"ט מהלכות תפלה הל' ז סמג שם

מה
ד מיי' שם הלכ' ד וסמ"ג שם טוש"ע א"ח סי' קכא סעיף ב

מו
ה מיי' פ"י מה' ברכות הלכה ג סמג עשין כז טוש"ע א"ח סי' רכב סעי' ג

מז
ו מיי' פ"ט מהל' תפלה הלכה ז טוש"ע א"ח סימן קיג סעיף ט

מח
ז מיי' פ"ה מהל' תשובה הל' ד עיי' במגדול עח

מט
ח מיי' פ"ב מהלכות ק"ש הלכה יא סמג עשין יח טוש"ע א"ח סימן סא סעיף ט

[ברב אלפס וברא"ש סדר המשנ' דהכא בזה"ל האומ' יברכוך טובי' הרי זה דרך המינות האומר על קן צפור וכו' וע"ש פרש"י ורבינו יונה וכן במה שפי' הרא"ש ודע שבסדר הזה כשנית ג"כ במשנה דמגילה כה. מכוון ממש]
[ע' תוספות מגילה ותוס' כה:]

תוספות

הלכתא מאי. המבדיל בתפלה צריך שיבדיל על הכוס או לא: ביום טוב שחל להיות אחר השבת. שאין מתפללין אתה חוננו: ה"נ הלכה מכלל דפליגי ולא פליגי והא פליגי רבנן איזמר דפליגי רבנן בשאר ימות השנה ביום טוב שחל להיות אחר השבת מי פליגי והא פליג רבי עקיבא אטו כל השנה מי עבדינן כר' עקיבא דהשתא נעביד וכו'. והכי *פריך א"ל רבי זירא הלכה מכלל דפליגי במתני' ופריך הגמ' ולא פליגי והא פליגי רבנן וכו': והא פליג רבי עקיבא. לומר ברכה רביעית לעצמה ואצטריך למימר הלכה כרבי אליעזר לאפוקי מדרבי עקיבא: אטו כל השנה כולה מי עבדינן כרבי עקיבא דהשתא נעביד כוותיה. דאצטריך למימר הלכה כר"א: הלכה. מ"ד הלכה דרשינן לה בפרקין ומ"ד מטין מדרש לא דרשינן ברבים אבל אורויי מורינן ליחיד לעשות כרבי אליעזר בי"ט שחל להיות באחד בשבת ומ"ד נראין אורויי נמי לא מורינן ואי עביד לא מהדרינן עובדא: מודים. חכמים לרבי אליעזר ביום טוב שחל להיות אחר השבת: נקוט דר' חייא בר אבא בידך. שהוא מדקדק בלשון רבו וקובע בו סימנים שלא יתחלף לו מטין במודים או בנראין: כרחבא. שהיה מדקדק בלשון רבו ואומר סטיו כפול היה ואף על פי שבלשון משנה קורהו אצטבא בפסחים ובסוכה על גב האצטבא הוא דקדק בלשון רבו ולא אמר אצטבא כפולה היתה. יש פותרין הא דרחבא ודאמר רבי יהודה דדייק ספיקי דרבוותיה אי מדרבי יהודה אי מדרב יהודה וקשיא לי בגוה טובא חדא דרחבא לא ראה רבי יהודה מימיו לא רבי יהודה בר' אלעאי ולא רבי יהודה *נשיאה ועוד כולהו אמוראי נמי דייקי לומר דבר בשם אומרו ועוד ליכא למימר מהא דדייק ליכא דמשמעתא אלא ספיקי דרבוותא: סטיו כפול. אצטבאות זו לפנים מזו בהיקף

רש"י

עגול לישב שם: לא האי ידענא כו'. לא נראין ולא מודי' ולא מטין: ותודיענו. לומר במקום ותתן לנו ולכשיגיע לבין קדושת שבת לקדושת י"ט וכו' הבדלת וקדשת את עמך ישראל בקדושתך יאמר ותתן לנו יי' אלהינו מועדים לשמחה וכו' ומסיים מקדש ישראל והזמני':

מתני' האומר. בתפלתו על קן צפור יגיעו רחמיך אנשים שהיו מראים עצמם כמתכוונים להעמיק בלשון תחנונים ואומרים רחום וחנון אתה ועל קן צפור יגיעו רחמיך שאמרת לשלח את האם או שאומר על טוב שאתה עושה לנו יזכר שמך או שאומר מודים מודים משתקין אותו: גמ' שמטיל קנאה. לומר על אלה חס ולא על שאר בריותיו: מדותיו. מצותיו והוא לא לרחמים עשה אלא להטיל על ישראל חקי גזרותיו להודיע שהם עבדיו ושומרי מצותיו וגזרות חקותיו אף בדברים שיש לשטן ולאו"ה להשיב עליהם ולומר מה צורך במצוה זו: ורבה נמי לחדודי לאביי הוא דבעי. שישיב לו מה שהשיב: אי לאו דאמרינהו משה. האל הגדול הגבור והנורא אשר לא ישא פנים ולא יקח שוחד (דברים י): ותקנינהו בתפלה. כשהתפלל עזרא על מעל הגולה בספר עזרא (נחמיה ט): הכל בידי שמים. כל הבא על האדם ביד הקב"ה הוא כגון ארוך קצר עני עשיר חכם שוטה לבן שחור הכל בידי שמים הוא אבל צדיק ורשע אינו בא על ידי שמים את זו מסר בידו של אדם ונתן לפניו שני דרכים והוא יבחר לו יראת שמים: מילתא מילתא ותני לה. כל תיבה ותיבה חוזר ושונה מגונה הוי שתוקי לא משתקינן ליה שאין זה דומה למקבל עליו שתי מלכיות אלא למתלוצץ. אמר פסוק שלם ותני ליה משתקינן ליה דמחזי כשתי רשויות:

חברותא

מסורת הש"ס

[שבת קו: ושם נסמן]
[לעיל כט.]
עירובין מו:
[לקמן לח: פסחים נג:]
סוכה מה:
פסחים יג:
כב:
מגילה כה.
לקמן כד:
[עירובין יג:
מגילה שם
נזיר נט:
זבחים יב.
חולין מג:
נדה ז: מה.]
נדה יז:
מגילה כה.
דברים י
ישעיה לג
מגילה שם
[סוכה נג:]

תורה אור

אמר ליה רבינא לרבא הלכתא מאי א"ל כי קדוש מה קדוש אף על גב דמקדש בצלות' מקדש אכסא אף הבדלה נמי אע"ג דמבדיל בצלותא מבדיל אכסא: ר' אליעזר אומר בהודאה: ר' זירא הוה רכיב חמרא הוה קא שקיל ואזיל ר' חייא בר אבין בתריה אמר ליה ודאי דאמריתו משמיה דר' יוחנן הלכה כר' אליעזר בי"ט שחל להיות אחר השבת א"ל *אין הלכה מכלל דפליגי ולא פליגי והא פליגי רבנן אימר דפליגי רבנן בשאר ימות השנה בי"ט שחל להיות אחר השבת מי פליגי והא פליג ר' עקיבא *אטו כל השנה כולה מי עבדינן כר' עקיבא דהשתא ניקום ונעביד כותיה כל השנה כולה מ"ט לא עבדינן כר' עקיבא דתמני סרי תקון תשסרי לא תקון הכא נמי שבע תקון תמני לא תקון א"ל לאו הלכה אתמר אלא מטין אתמר *דאתמר רב יצחק בר אבדימי אמר משום רבינו הלכה ואמרי לה מטין ר' יוחנן אמר מודים ור' חייא בר אבא אמר נראין א"ר זירא נקוט דר' חייא בר אבא בידך *דדייק וגמר שמעת' מפומא דמרא שפיר כרחבא דפומבדית' דאמר רחבא *א"ר יהודה הר הבית סטיו כפול היה והיה סטיו לפני' מסטיו אמר רב יוסף אנא לא האי ידענא ולא האי ידענא אלא מדרב ושמואל ידענא דתקינו לן מרגניתא בבבל ותודיענו יי' אלהינו את משפטי צדקך ותלמדנו לעשות חקי רצונך ותנחילנו זמני ששון וחגי נדבה ותורישנו קדושת שבת וכבוד מועד וחגיגת הרגל בין קדושת שבת לקדושת י"ט הבדלת ואת יום השביעי מששת ימי המעשה קדשת הבדלת וקדשת את עמך ישראל בקדושתך ותתן לנו וכו': **מתני'** *האומר *על קן צפור יגיעו רחמיך ועל טוב יזכר שמך מודים מודים משתקין אותו: **גמ'** בשלמא מודים מודים משתקין אותו משום דמחזי כשתי רשויות ועל טוב יזכר שמך נמי משמע על הטובה ולא על הרעה *ותנן חייב אדם לברך על הרעה כשם שמברך על הטובה אלא על קן צפור יגיעו רחמיך מ"ט פליגי בה תרי אמוראי במערבא ר' יוסי בר אבין ור' יוסי בר זבידא חד אמר מפני שמטיל קנאה במעשה בראשית וחד אמר מפני שעושה מדותיו של הקב"ה רחמים ואינן אלא גזרות ההוא דנחית קמיה דרבה ואמר אתה חסת על קן צפור אתה חוס ורחם עלינו אמר רבה כמה ידע האי צורבא מרבנן לרצויי למריה א"ל אביי והא משתקין אותו תנן *ורבה נמי לחדודי לאביי הוא דבעי ההוא דנחית קמיה דר' חנינא אמר האל הגדול הגבור והנורא והאדיר והעזוז והיראוי החזק והאמיץ והודאי והנכבד המתין לו עד דסיים כי סיים א"ל סיימתינהו לכולהו שבחי דמרך למה לי כולי האי אנן הני תלת דאמרי' אי לאו דאמרינהו משה רבינו באורייתא ואתו אנשי כנסת הגדולה ותקנינהו בתפלה לא הוינן יכולין למימר להו ואת אמרת כולי האי ואזלת משל למלך בשר ודם שהיו לו אלף אלפי דינרי זהב והיו מקלסין אותו בשל כסף והלא גנאי הוא לו: ואמר *ר' חנינא *הכל בידי שמים חוץ מיראת שמים שנאמר °ועתה ישראל מה יי' אלהיך שואל מעמך כי אם ליראה אטו יראת שמים מלתא זוטרתא היא והא"ר חנינא משום ר' שמעון בן יוחי אין לו להקב"ה בבית גנזיו אלא אוצר של יראת שמים שנאמר °יראת ה' היא אוצרו אין לגבי משה מילתא זוטרתא היא דא"ר חנינא משל לאדם שמבקשים ממנו כלי גדול ויש לו דומה עליו ככלי קטן קטן ואין לו דומה עליו ככלי גדול: מודים מודים משתקין אותו: *אמר רבי זירא כל האומר שמע שמע כאומר מודים מודים דמי מיתיבי הקורא את שמע וכופלה הרי זה מגונה מגונה הוא דהוי שתוקי לא משתקינן ליה לא קשיא הא דאמר מילתא מילתא ותני לה והא דאמר פסוקה פסוקה ותני ליה א"ל רב פפא לאביי ודילמא מעיקרא לא כיון דעתיה ולבסוף כיון דעתיה

הגה"ה

אמר ליה

חברותא

again.[4] [33b] Rabina said to Raba: What is the law?[5] He replied to him: The same as in the case of sanctification. Just as the sanctification, although it has been said in the *Tefillah*, is also said over the cup [of wine], so *habdalah*, although it has been said in the *Tefillah*, is also to be said over the cup [of wine].

R. ELIEZER SAYS: IN THE THANKSGIVING BENEDICTION. R. Zera was once riding on an ass, with R. Ḥiyya b. Abin following on foot.[6] He said to him: Did you really say in the name of R. Joḥanan that the *halachah* is as stated by R. Eliezer on a festival that falls after Sabbath?[7] He replied: Yes, that is the *halachah*. Am I to assume [he replied] that they [the Rabbis] differ from
a him?[1]—And do they not differ? Surely the Rabbis differ!—I would say that the Rabbis differ in regard to the other days of the year, but do they differ in regard to a festival which falls after a Sabbath?—But surely R. Akiba differs?[2]—Do we follow R. Akiba the rest of the year that we should now[3] commence to follow him? Why do we not follow R. Akiba all the rest of the year? Because eighteen blessings were instituted, not nineteen. Here too [on the festival] seven were instituted, not eight![4] [R. Zera then] said to him: It was not stated that such is the *halachah*,[5] but that we incline to this view.[6] It has been stated: R. Isaac b. Abdimi said in the name of our teacher [Rab]: Such is the *halachah*, but some say, we [merely] incline to this view. R. Joḥanan said: [The Rabbis] agree [with R. Eliezer].[7] R. Ḥiyya b. Abba said: This appears correct.[8] R. Zera said: Choose the statement of R. Ḥiyya b Abba, for he is very accurate in repeating the statements of his teacher, like Raḥaba of Pumbeditha. For Raḥaba said in the name of Rabbi Judah: The Temple Mount was a double stoa—a stoa within a stoa.[9] R. Joseph said: I know neither one nor the other,[10] but I only know that Rab and Samuel instituted for us a precious pearl in Babylon:[11] 'And Thou didst make known unto us, O Lord our God, Thy righteous judgments and didst teach us to do the statutes that Thou hast willed, and hast made us inherit seasons of gladness and festivals of freewill-offering, and didst transmit to us the holiness of Sabbath and the glory of the appointed season and the celebration of the festival. Thou hast divided between the holiness of Sabbath and the holiness of the festival, and hast sanctified the seventh day above the six working days: Thou hast separated and sanctified Thy people Israel with Thy holiness. And
b Thou hast given us' etc.[1]

MISHNAH. IF ONE [IN PRAYING] SAYS 'MAY THY MERCIES EXTEND TO A BIRD'S NEST',[2] 'BE THY NAME MENTIONED FOR WELL-DOING', OR 'WE GIVE THANKS, WE GIVE THANKS', HE IS SILENCED.[3]

GEMARA. We understand why he is silenced if he says 'WE GIVE THANKS, WE GIVE THANKS', because he seems to be acknowledging two Powers;[4] also if he says, 'BE THY NAME MENTIONED FOR WELL-DOING', because this implies, for the good only and not for the bad, and we have learnt, A man must bless God for the evil as he blesses Him for the good.[5] But what is the reason for silencing him if he says 'THY MERCIES EXTEND TO THE BIRD'S NEST'?—Two Amoraim in the West, R. Jose b. Abin and R. Jose b. Zebida, give different answers; one says it is because he creates jealousy among God's creatures,[6] the other, because he presents the measures taken by the Holy One, blessed be He, as springing from compassion, whereas they are but decrees.[7] A certain [reader] went down [before the Ark] in the presence of Rabbah and said, 'Thou hast shown mercy to the bird's nest, show Thou pity and mercy to us'. Said Rabbah: How well this student knows how to placate his Master! Said Abaye to him: But we have learnt, HE IS SILENCED?—Rabbah too acted thus only to test[8] Abaye.

A certain [reader] went down in the presence of R. Ḥanina and said, O God, the great, mighty, terrible, majestic, powerful, awful, strong, fearless, sure and honoured. He waited till he had finished, and when he had finished he said to him, Have you concluded all the praise of your Master? Why do we want all
c this? Even with these three that we do say,[1] had not Moses our Master mentioned them in the Law[2] and had not the Men of the Great Synagogue come and inserted them in the *Tefillah*, we should not have been able to mention them, and you say all these and still go on! It is as if an earthly king had a million *denarii* of gold, and someone praised him as possessing silver ones. Would it not be an insult to him?

R. Ḥanina further said: Everything is in the hand of heaven except the fear of heaven,[3] as it says, *And now, Israel, what doth the Lord thy God require of thee but to fear.*[4] Is the fear of heaven such a little thing? Has not R. Ḥanina said in the name R. Simeon b. Yoḥai: The Holy One, blessed be He, has in His treasury nought except a store of the fear of heaven, as it says, *The fear of the Lord is His treasure?*[5]—Yes; for Moses it was a small thing; as R. Ḥanina said: To illustrate by a parable, if a man is asked for a big article and he has it, it seems like a small article to him; if he is asked for a small article and he does not possess it, it seems like a big article to him.

WE GIVE THANKS, WE GIVE THANKS, HE IS SILENCED. R. Zera said: To say 'Hear, hear', [in the *Shema'*] is like saying 'We give thanks, we give thanks'. An objection was raised: He who recites the *Shema'* and repeats it is reprehensible. He is reprehensible, but we do not silence him?—There is no contradiction; in the one case he repeats each word as he says it,[6] in the other each sentence.[7] Said R. Papa to Abaye: But perhaps [he does this because] at first he was not attending to what he said and the second time he

(4) He recites anew the *Tefillah* and the benediction over the cup of wine. (5) About saying *habdalah* over wine, after having mentioned it in the *Tefillah*. (6) Lit., 'betaking himself and going'. (7) I.e., on Saturday night, when the fourth benediction 'that graciously grantest knowledge' is not said.

a (1) Because otherwise there would be no need to say that the *halachah* follows him. (2) R. Akiba provides for *habdalah* a benediction by itself. Consequently is was necessary to declare the *halachah* follows R. Eliezer on a festival which follows Sabbath, to exclude the view of R. Akiba. (3) On a festival following Sabbath. (4) Why then is it necessary to say that the *halachah* is as R. Eliezer, not as stated by R. Akiba? (5) And is to be taught as such in public. (6) And we advise individuals to act thus if they inquire. (7) When a festival falls on Saturday night. (8) We do not recommend this, but if one does so, we do not interfere. (9) Though the word used in the Mishnah of Pes. (13a) is not *stoa* (colonnade) but the more familiar *iẓṭaba* which has the same meaning. V. Pes. (Sonc. ed.) p. 59. nn. 10—11 and Beẓ. (Sonc. ed.) p. 54 n. 9. (10) That we incline towards the view of R. Eliezer or that we regard it as probable. (11) To be inserted in the fourth benediction of the festival *'Amidah*.

b (1) This form of *habdalah* prayer is used with slight variants on a festival that follows Sabbath, v. *P.B.* p. 227. (2) V. Deut. XXII, 6. (3) For the reasons, v. the Gemara. This Mishnah is found in Meg. 26a with a somewhat different reading. (4) The dualism of the Persians—the God of darkness and the God of light. (5) *Infra* 54a. (6) By implying that this one is favoured above others. (7) V. Meg. (Sonc. ed.) p. 149 notes. (8) Lit., 'sharpen'. He wanted to see if he knew the law.

c (1) Great, mighty, and terrible, in the first benediction. (2) Deut. X, 17. (3) I.e. all a man's qualities are fixed by nature, but his moral character depends on his own choice. (4) Deut. X, 12. (5) Isa. XXXIII, 6. (6) This is merely reprehensible. (7) In this case he is silenced since this is as if he were addressing two Powers.

does attend?—He replied: [34a] Can one behave familiarly with Heaven? If he did not recite with attention at first, we hit him with a smith's hammer until he does attend.

MISHNAH. [IF ONE SAYS, LET THE GOOD BLESS THEE,
a THIS IS A PATH OF HERESY].[1] IF ONE WAS PASSING BEFORE THE ARK AND MADE A MISTAKE, ANOTHER SHOULD PASS IN HIS PLACE, AND AT SUCH A MOMENT ONE MAY NOT REFUSE. WHERE SHOULD HE COMMENCE? AT THE BEGINNING OF THE BENEDICTION IN WHICH THE OTHER WENT WRONG. THE READER[2] SHOULD NOT RESPOND AMEN AFTER [THE BENEDICTIONS OF] THE PRIESTS[3] BECAUSE THIS MIGHT CONFUSE HIM. IF THERE IS NO PRIEST THERE EXCEPT HIMSELF, HE SHOULD NOT RAISE HIS HANDS [IN PRIESTLY BENEDICTION], BUT IF HE IS CONFIDENT THAT HE CAN RAISE HIS HANDS AND GO BACK TO HIS PLACE IN HIS PRAYER,[4] HE IS PERMITTED TO DO SO.

GEMARA. Our Rabbis taught: If one is asked to pass before the Ark, he ought to refuse,[5] and if he does not refuse he resembles a dish without salt; but if he persists too much in refusing he resembles a dish which is over-salted. How should he act? The first time he should refuse; the second time he should hesitate; the third time he should stretch out his legs and go down.

Our Rabbis taught: There are three things of which one may easily have too much[6] while a little is good, namely, yeast, salt, and refusal.

R. Huna said: If one made a mistake in the first three [of the *Tefillah*] blessings, he goes back to the beginning; if in the middle
b blessings, he goes back to 'Thou graciously grantest knowledge;[1] if in the last blessings, he goes back to the *'Abodah*.[2] R. Assi, however, says that in the middle ones the order need not be observed.[3] R. Shesheth cited in objection: 'Where should he commence? At the beginning of the benediction in which the other went wrong'.[4] This is a refutation of R. Huna, is it not?[5]—R. Huna can reply: The middle blessings are all one.[6]

Rab Judah said: A man should never petition for his requirements either in the first three benedictions or in the last three, but in the middle ones. For R. Ḥanina said: In the first ones he resembles a servant who is addressing a eulogy to his master; in the middle ones he resembles a servant who is requesting a largess from his master, in the last ones he resembles a servant who has received a largess from his master and takes his leave.

Our Rabbis taught: Once a certain disciple went down[7] before the Ark in the presence of R. Eliezer, and he span out the prayer to a great length. His disciples said to him: Master, how long-winded this fellow is! He replied to them: Is he drawing it out any more than our Master Moses, of whom it is written: *The forty days and the forty nights* [that I fell down]?[8] Another time it happened that a certain disciple went down before the Ark in the presence of R. Eliezer, and he cut the prayer very short. His disciples said to him: How concise this fellow is! He replied to them: Is he any more concise than our Master Moses, who prayed, as it is written: *Heal her now, O God, I beseech Thee?*[9] R. Jacob said in the name of R. Ḥisda: If one prays on behalf of his fellow, he need not mention his name, since it says: *'Heal her now, O God, I beseech Thee'*, and he did not mention the name of Miriam.

Our Rabbis taught: These are the benedictions in saying which
c one bows [in the *Tefillah*]: The benediction of the Patriarchs,[1] beginning and end, and the thanksgiving, beginning and end.[2] If one wants to bow down at the end of each benediction and at the beginning of each benediction, he is instructed not to do so. R. Simeon b. Pazzi said in the name of R. Joshua b. Levi, reporting Bar Ḳappara: An ordinary person bows as we have mentioned;

a (1) *Minuth*, (v. Glos. s.v. *Min*) implying that only the good are invited to bless God. This passage is wanting in the separate editions of the Mishnah, but occurs in Meg. 25*a*. (2) Lit., 'he who passes before the Ark'. (3) V. *P.B.* 283*a* (15th ed.). (4) Without making a mistake in the prayers. (5) As feeling himself unworthy for the sacred duty. (6) Lit., 'a large quantity is hard'.

b (1) The fourth benediction in the *Tefillah*, v. *P.B.* p. 46. (2) Lit., 'service'. The seventeenth blessing, v. *P.B.* p. 50. (3) And if one was accidentally omitted it can be inserted anywhere. So Rashi. Tosaf., however, say that he goes back to that blessing and continues from there. (4) So M.S. M. cur. edd. read: 'To where does he go back'. (5) Because it shows that he need not go back to 'Thou graciously grantest'. (6) And if one errs in any of them he has to go back to 'Thou graciously grantest'. (7) The reading desk was at a lower level than the floor of the Synagogue. (v. *supra* 10*b*); hence the expression 'went down'. (8) Deut. IX, 25. (9) Num. XII, 13.

c (1) The first benediction. (2) V. *P.B.* 51 and 53.

חברותא כלפי שמיא. מנהג שנוהג אדם בחבירו ינהג אצל המקום ולא יזהר בתפלתו: **מחינן ליה.** כלומר מלמדין אותו שיכוין ומכין אותו אם ינהיג בכך: **מרזפתא.** קורנס ותפש את המקבת בידה מתרגמי' מרזפתא (שופטים ד): **מתני' ולא יהא סרבן באותה שעה.** לפי שאר יורדין לפני התיבה כשאומרים לו לך רד צריך לסרב פעם אחת כלומר איני כדאי לכך כדאמרינן לקמן בשמעתין אבל זה לא יסרב מפני שגנאי הוא שתהא התפלה מופסקת כל כך: **מתחלת הברכה שטעה זה.** אם דלג אחת מן הברכות ואמר אחר' ואינו יודע לשוב ולאחוז סדרו יתחיל העובר תחתיו אותה ברכה שדלג זה ואומר משם ולהלן: **לא יענה אמן אחר הכהנים.** הש"ץ בסוף כל ברכה וברכה: **מפני הטירוף.** שלא תטרף דעתו ויטעה לפי שש"צ הוא צריך להתחיל ברכה שניה ולומר לפני הכהני' כל תיבה ותיב' כדאמרי' במס' סוט' (פ"ז דף לט:) ובעניתו אמן לא יוכל לכוין מהר ולהתחיל בברכה שלאחריו: **אם אין שם כהן אלא הוא.** החזן: **לא ישא את כפיו.** שמא לא יוכל לחזור לתפלתו לדעת לכוין להתחיל בשים שלום שדעתו מטורפת מאימת הצבור: **ואם הבטחתו.** כלומר אם בטוח הוא שאין דעתו מטורפ' מאימת הצבור: **גמ' יסרב.** כשאומרים לו לך יעשה עצמו כלא רוצה כלומר איני כדאי: **שהקדיחתו.** לשון שרפה כמו כי אש קדחה באפי (דברים לב): **מהבהב.** כלומר מזמין עצמו כמו כנער לעמוד: **אין להן סדר.** ואם דלג ברכה אחת ואח"כ נזכר בה אומרה אף שלא במקומה: **מתחלת הברכה שטעה זה.** ומילא משמע דגומר מנכה והלאה אלמא על סדרה צריך לחזור ולומרה: **חדא ברכתא נינהו.** ודקתני מתני' מתחלת ברכה שטעה זה היינו אתה חונן: **ונפטר.** נוטל רשות: **א"צ להזכיר שמו.** של חולה: **תחלה וסוף.** במודים ולך נאה להודות:

מגילה כה. | שם [ועמ"ש לעיל לג: גירסת הרי"ף והרא"ש] | [סוטה לח:] | גיטין ע. ע"ש [בירוש' רובן ומיעוטן רע ובינונן יפה] | [נ"ל תיובת' דרב ...] | [מכילת' דר"י פ' בשלח] | במדבר יב | [תוספת' פ"א]

תורה אור

*חברותא כלפי שמיא מי איכא אי לא כוין דעתיה מעיקרא מחינן ליה במרזפתא דנפחא עד דמכוין דעתיה: **מתני'** (*האומר יברכוך טובים הרי זה דרכי טעות) *העובר לפני התיבה וטעה יעבור אחר תחתיו ולא יהא סרבן באותה שעה מהיכן הוא מתחיל מתחלת הברכה שטעה *זה העובר לפני התיבה לא יענה אמן אחר הכהנים מפני הטרוף ואם אין שם כהן אלא הוא לא ישא את כפיו *ואם הבטחתו שהוא נושא את כפיו וחוזר לתפלתו רשאי: **גמ'** ת"ר העובר לפני התיבה צריך לסרב ואם אינו מסרב דומה לתבשיל שאין בו מלח ואם מסרב יותר מדאי דומה לתבשיל שהקדיחתו מלח כיצד הוא עושה פעם ראשונה יסרב ב' *מהבהב ג' פושט את רגליו ויורד *ת"ר ג' *רובן קשה ומיעוטן יפה ואלו הן שאור ומלח וסרבנות [זה] אמר רב הונא טעה בג' ראשונות חוזר לראש באמצעיות חוזר לאתה חונן באחרונות חוזר לעבודה ורב אסי אמר אמצעיות אין להן סדר מתיב רב ששת מהיכן הוא חוזר מתחלת ברכה שטעה זה *תיובתא דרב הונא אמר לך רב הונא אמצעיות כלהו חדא ברכתא נינהו אמר רב יהודה לעולם אל ישאל אדם צרכיו לא בג' ראשונות ולא בג' אחרונות אלא באמצעיות דא"ר חנינא ראשונות דומה לעבד שמסדר שבח לפני רבו אמצעיות דומה לעבד שמבקש פרס מרבו אחרונות דומה לעבד שקבל פרס מרבו ונפטר והולך לו *ת"ר מעשה בתלמיד אחד *שירד לפני התיבה בפני ר"א והיה מאריך יותר מדאי א"ל תלמידיו רבינו כמה ארכן הוא זה אמר להם כלום מאריך יותר ממשה רבינו דכתיב ביה °את (דברים ט) ארבעים היום ואת ארבעים הלילה וגו' שוב מעשה בתלמיד אחד שירד לפני התיבה בפני ר"א והיה מקצר יותר מדאי א"ל תלמידיו כמה קצרן הוא זה א"ל כלום מקצר יותר ממשה רבינו דכתיב °אל נא רפא נא לה (במדבר יב) א"ר יעקב אמר רב חסדא כל המבקש רחמים על חבירו א"צ להזכיר שמו שנאמר אל נא רפא נא לה ולא קמדכר שמה דמרים: ת"ר *אלו ברכות שאדם שוחה בהן באבות תחלה וסוף [תוספתא פ"א] בהודאה תחלה וסוף ואם בא לשוח בסוף כל ברכה וברכה ובתחלת כל ברכה וברכה מלמדין אותו שלא ישחה אר"ש בן פזי אריב"ל משום בר קפרא הדיוט כמו שאמרנו כהן

אמר מודים מודים משתקין אותו. ירושל' הדא דתימא בצבור אבל ביחיד תחנונים הם: [שייך לד' לג:]

אמר פסוקא פסוקא וכפלי'. פי' בקונ' משתקין אותו דמחזי כעושה שתי רשוי' ובה"ג ובפר"ח מפרש איפכא פסוקא ופסוקא אין משתקין אותו מיהו מגונה הוי אך לשון הגמ' לא משמע כפי' ואותן בני אדם שאומרים ב' או שלשה פעמים שמע ישראל בי"ה משתקין אותן לפרש"י ולפר"ח מגונה מיהא הוי או שמא אין לחוש רק כשקורא ק"ש בעונתה ומקבל עליו עול מלכות שמים ומ"מ טוב שלא לומר אך מה שאומרים ה' הוא האלהים ז' פעמים בי"ה ויום ערבה כנגד ז' רקיעים משבחים לבורא שהוא דר למעלה מז' מנהג כשר הוא וגם מליהו בקרא שתי פעמים ה' הוא האלהים גבי אליהו (מלכים א יח): [ג"ז שייך שם]

מהיכן הוא מתחיל מתחלת הברכה שטעה בה. ירוש' בעיני' אשתתק באופניא אתון שיילון לרבי בון אמר להו בשם ריב"ל זה שעבר תחתיו יתחיל ממקום שפסק ופריך והתנן מתחיל מתחלת הברכה שטעה *בה אמר להו מכיון דעניתון קדושת השם כמי שהוא תחלת הברכה דמי:

לא יענה אמן אחר הכהנים מפני הטרוף. תימה תיפוק ליה דמפסיק תפלה אם עונה אמן וי"ל מאחר שלא אמר האי טעמא ש"מ דעניית אמן לא חשיב ליה הפסקה מאחר שצורך תפלה הוא אבל לקרו' כהנים לדוכן אומר ר"ת שאין ש"צ יכול לקראם דחשיב הפסקה לתפלה אם קוראם אלא אחד מבני הקהל קוראם והא דאמרינן בסוטה פ' אלו נאמרים (ד' לח.) לשנים קורא כהנים וכו' לאו אשליח צבור קאי אלא אחזן כדתניא בספרי (פרשת נשא) אמור להם מלמד שהחזן אומר להם אמרו וחזן לאו היינו שליח צבור דחזן היינו המתעסק בצרכי צבור וכן משמע נמי בסוטה (דף לט:) דלאו אשליח צבור קאי דמעיקרא קאמר אין הכהנים רשאין להתחיל בברכ' עד שיכלה הדבור מפי הקורא פי' הקורא כהנים ואח"כ אומר אין שליח צבור רשאי וכו' משמע דשנים הם ויש שהיו רוצים לומר דכמו כן אין ש"צ רשאי להקרות יברכך לכהנים דכמו כן הוי הפסקה אמנם רבינו יהודה פירש דבהדיא יש במדרש טעמי יתרות וחסרות אומר להם מלמד ששליח צבור אומר להם על כל דבור ודבור וכן יש שרוצים להתיר לשליח צבור עצמו לקרות כהנים אפילו לפר"ת דמה דפי' דהויא הפסקה היינו דוקא בימיהם מיד כשסיימו ברכ' הודאה לא היו אומרים או"א ברכנו בברכה כדמשמע בסוטה (ד' לט:) דקאמר אין הקורא רשאי לקרות כהנים עד שיכלה אמן מפי הצבור פי' אמן שעונין בסיום ברכת הודאה אלמא משמע שלא היו אומרים אלא כהנים מיד אבל עכשיו שהורגלו לומר אלהינו בלשון ברכה ותפלה אין זו הפסקה דלא גרע מעניי' אמן דהכא דלא חשיבא הפסק כדפרי'*:

אמצעיות אין להם סדר. פי' בקונ' ואם דלג ברכה אחת ואח"כ נזכר בה שלא במקומה אומרה במקום שנזכר ולא נהיר' דהא תנן במגילה (פ"ב ד' יז.) הקורא את המגילה למפרע לא יצא ותני' (שם) וכן בהלל וכן בק"ש וכן בתפלה לכך נראה כפירוש רשב"ם ורב אלפס דאין להן סדר דקאמר היינו שיתחיל במקום שדלג הברכה ומשם ואילך יאמר הכל על הסדר אבל ודאי לא יתחיל באתה חונן כמו בג' ראשונות וג' אחרונות שחוזר לראש ולא' מדתני' בתוספת' דמכילתין הקורא את שמע והשמיט בה פסוק א' לא יקרא אותו פסוק בפני עצמו אלא מתחיל מאותו פסוק ואילך וגומר עד סופה ותני' נמי בפ"ב דמגל' (ד' יח:) שאם השמיט פסוק א' במגילה שקורא על הסדר מאותו פסוק ואילך והתם משוי תפלה למגילה לענין הך מילתא כדפרישית ובה"ג פסק כרב אסי דאמר אמצעיות אין להן סדר הלא דרב הונ' כתלמיד לגבי רב אסי כדאמרינן בכמה מקומות אמר רב הונא אמר רב אסי ועוד דלרב הונא צריך לדחוק ולשנויי מתני' דכולהו חדא ברכת' נינהו ואשנויי דחיקי לא ניקום ונסמוך ועוד דרב אסי ורב ששת קיימי בחד שיטתא ועוד דבעל סופרי' הלך אחר המיקל וא"כ אדם שטעה ודלג ברכה אחת באמצעיות או שלא אמר המלך המשפט בין ר"ה ליה"כ דקי"ל בפ"ק (ד' יב:) דמחזירין אותו לא יחזו' לאתה חונן אלא לאותה ברכה שדלג ומשם ואילך יאמר על הסדר כדפי' רשב"ם והיכא שטעה בג' ראשונות כגון שטעה בחתימתן או לא הזכיר בין ר"ה ליה"כ בברכת אבות זכרנו או בתחיי' המתים מי כמוך או שלא אמר המלך הקדוש חוזר לראשונה והיכא שטעה בג' אחרונו' כגון שטעה כמו כן בחתימתן או שלא הזכיר בין ר"ה ליה"כ בשים שלום בספר חיים טובי' או וכתוב לחיי' טובים בהודא' חוזר לעבודה וטעמ' דכיון שכול' שבח הוי כברכה א' ותעני' צבור דש"צ קובע ברכה לעצמו שאומר עננו בין גואל לרופא אם שכחה ונזכר בה קודם סיום תפלה אין מחזירין אותו כיון שהיה צריך לחזו' ולומר על הסדר כפי' רשב"ם א"כ הויא ברכה לבטלה אם מחזירין אותו אבל לפירוש הקונ' היה אומרה במקום שנזכר ואין כאן ברכה לבטל': **אל** ישאל אדם צרכיו לא בג' ראשונות ולא בג' אחרונו'. פי' ר"ח ורבינו האיי דוק' ליחיד אבל לצרכי צבור שואלין ולכך אנו אומרים זכרנו וקרובץ ויעלה ויבא בהם ותדע דדוקא יחיד קאמר שהרי עיקר ברכות אחרונות לצרכי צבור הם*: **מלמדין** אותו שלא ישחה. וא"ת וישחה ומה בכך וי"ל שלא יבא לעקור דברי חכמים שלא יאמרו כל אחד ומחמיר כמו שהוא רוצה ואין כאן תקנת חכמים וחיישינן ליוהרא:

קידה

נ א מיי' פ"י מהל' תפלה ה"ג סמג עשין יט טוש"ע א"ח סי' קכו סעי' ב
נא ב מיי' שם טוש"ע שם ובסי' נג סעי' יז
נב ג מיי' שם ה"ד וסמ"ג שם טוש"ע שם ובסי' קיט סעי' ג ובסי' קכו ס"ב
נג ד מיי' פ' י"ד מהל' נשיאות כפים ה"ה סמ"ג עשין כ' טוש"ע א"ח סי' קכח סעי' יט
נד ה מיי' שם פט"ו הל' יד טוש"ע שם סעי' כ
נה ו טוש"ע א"ח סי' נג סעי' יז
נו ז מיי' פ"י מה' תפלה ה"א סמ"ג ע' י טוש"ע א"ח סי' קכו סעי' ב
[לפי שמלוה להתפלל במקר' כמוך כדאית' ברכות יוד: הלכך קתני ירד ע' רש"י ד"ה לב. ד"ה ירד]
נז ח מיי' שם פ"א ה"ד ופ"ו שם ה"ג סמ"ג שם טוש"ע א"ח סי' קיב סעי' א
נח ט מיי' פ"ה שם הל' יא, טוש"ע קכ"ג ס"א
נט י מיי' פ"ה שם ה"י סמ"ג שם טוש"ע א"ח סי' קיג סעי' א'
[וע"ע תוס' מנחות מד. ד"ה כל כהן]
[וע"ע תוס' ע"ז ח. ד"ה אם בא]

קידה על אפים. ומייתי קרא אע"ג דאשכחן כמי בענין אחר י"ל דקים ליה מקבלה דקידה על אפים ומייתי קרא דמסייעו: חזינא לאביי ורבא דמצלו אצלויי. פירו' שהיו מטין על צדיהן: יכוין לבו באחת מהן. והא דאמרי' בסוף פ' תפלת השחר (דף ל:) לעולם ימוד אדם דעתו אם יכול לכוין יתפלל ואם לאו לא יתפלל יש לפרש התם כמי באחת מהן:

חציף עלי מאן דמצלי בבקתא. וא"ת הכתיב ויצא יצחק לשוח בשד' (בראשית כד) וי"ל דהתם מיירי בהר המוריה כדאמרינן בפסחים פרק האשה (דף פח.) לא כיצחק שקראו שדה וכו' א"נ בקתא דהכא מיירי בבקעה במקו' שרגילין שם בני אדם לעבור והולכי דרכים:

כסוי חטאה. וטעמ' לפי שאז מתביים על חטאו אבל אם מפרש חטאיו דומה שאינו מתבייש עליו ואמרינן לעיל פ"ק (דף יב:) כל העושה דבר ומתבייש מוחלים לו מיד:

הדרן עלך אין עומדין

כהן גדול בסוף כל ברכה. כל מה שהוא גדול ביותר צריך להכניע ולהשפיל עצמו: אינו זוקף. עד שיגמור: קם מלפני מזבח יי' מכרוע. רישיה דקרא ויהי ככלות שלמה להתפל' והדר קם מכרוע: ארצה. לשון משתטח משמע: דמצלו אצלויי. כשנופלין על פניהם אין פושטין ידיהם ורגליהם אלא מטין על צדיהן: בתחלה. כורע: חזינא לרב נחמן דכרע. תחלה וסוף: בהודאה דהלל. הודו לה' כי טוב: מתני' אם שגורה. אם סדורה תפלתי בפי במרוצה ואיני נכשל ותמכתי כובעת מלבי אל פי כל מה שאני חפץ להאריך בתחנונים: שהוא מטורף. החולה. לשון אחר טורפין לו תפלתו בפניו כלומר התפלה שהתפלל עליו מטורפת וערודה ממנו ואינה מקובלת: גמ' אהייא. בהיכא ובאיזו מן הברכות הוי טעות בסימן רע: באבות. שהוא תחלת התפלה רמז הוא שאין חפץ בה: בורא ניב שפתים. כשהכיב בריא באדם אז מובטח על השלום: לא נתנבאו. הטובות והנחמות: עין לא ראתה. לא נראית ולא נגלית לשום נביא: רחוק. שהיה רחוק כל ימיו מן העבירה דהיינו צדיק מעיקרו: הלצתו חמה. שלפתו כינלה ומגופו החמה הוא החולי הקודחו. הלצתו לשון חלץ מהם: לא הסרת'. כעה: כעבד. בן בית נכנס ויוצא שלא ברשות: כשר לפני המלך. שאינו רגיל לבא לפניו: חלונות. שגורמין לו שיכוין לבו שהוא מסתכל כלפי שמים ולבו נכנע: דמצלי בבקתא. בבקע' שכשהוא במקו' צניעות אלה עליו אימת מלך ולבו נשבר:

הדרן עלך אין עומדין

כהן גדול בסוף כל ברכה וברכה והמלך תחלת כל ברכה וברכה וסוף כל ברכה וברכה א"ר יצחק בר נחמני לדידי מפרשא לי מיניה דריב"ל *הדיוט כמו שאמרנו כהן גדול תחלת כל ברכה וברכה המלך כיון שכרע שוב אינו זוקף שנאמר °ויהי ככלות שלמה להתפלל וגו' קם מלפני מזבח יי' מכרוע על ברכיו: ת"ר *קידה על אפים שנאמר °ותקד בת שבע אפים ארץ כריעה על ברכים שנאמר מכרוע על ברכיו השתחואה זו פשוט ידים ורגלים שנ' °הבא נבא אני ואמך ואחיך להשתחות לך ארצה *אמר רב חייא בריה דרב הונא חזינא להו לאביי ורבא דמצלו אצלויי תני חדא הכורע בהודאה הרי זה משובח ותניא אידך הרי זה מגונה לא קשיא הא בתחלה הא לבסוף רבא כרע בהודאה תחלה וסוף אמרי ליה רבנן אמאי קא עביד מר הכי אמר להו חזינא לרב נחמן דכרע וחזינא ליה לרב ששת דקא עבד הכי והתני' הכורע בהודאה ה"ז מגונה ההיא בהודאה שבהלל והתני' הכורע בהודאה ובהודאה של הלל הרי זה מגונה כי תני' ההיא בהודאה דברכת המזון: **מתני'** המתפלל וטעה סימן רע לו ואם שליח צבור הוא סימן רע לשולחיו מפני *ששלוחו של אדם כמותו אמרו עליו על ר' חנינא בן דוסא שהיה מתפלל על החולים ואומר זה חי וזה מת אמרו לו מנין אתה יודע אמר להם אם שגורה תפלתי בפי יודע אני שהוא מקובל ואם לאו יודע אני שהוא מטורף: **גמ'** אהייא א"ר חייא אמר רב ספרא משום חד דבי רבי באבות איכא דמתני לה אברייתא המתפלל צריך שיכוין את לבו בכולן ואם אינו יכול לכוין בכולן יכוין את לבו באחת א"ר חייא אמר רב ספרא משום חד דבי רבי באבות: אמרו עליו על רבי חנינא וכו': מנא הני מילי א"ר יהושע בן לוי דאמר קרא °בורא ניב שפתים שלום שלום לרחוק ולקרוב אמר יי' ורפאתיו א"ר חייא בר אבא *א"ר יוחנן כל הנביאים כולן לא נתנבאו אלא למשיא בתו לתלמיד חכם ולעושה פרקמטיא לת"ח ולמהנה ת"ח מנכסיו אבל תלמידי חכמים עצמן °עין לא ראתה אלהים זולתך יעשה למחכה לו ואמר רבי חייא בר אבא אמר רבי יוחנן כל הנביאים כולן לא נתנבאו אלא לימות המשיח אבל לעולם הבא עין לא ראתה אלהים זולתך ופליגא דשמואל *דאמר שמואל אין בין העוה"ז לימות המשיח אלא שעבוד מלכיות בלבד שנאמר °כי לא יחדל אביון מקרב הארץ וא"ר חייא בר אבא א"ר יוחנן כל הנביאים כולן לא נתנבאו אלא לבעלי תשובה אבל צדיקים גמורים עין לא ראתה אלהים זולתך ופליגא דר' אבהו דא"ר אבהו מקום שבעלי תשובה עומדין צדיקים גמורים אינם עומדין שנאמר °שלום שלום לרחוק ולקרוב לרחוק ברישא והדר לקרוב ורבי יוחנן אמר לך מאי רחוק שהיה רחוק מדבר עבירה מעיקרו ומאי קרוב שהיה קרוב לדבר עבירה ונתרחק ממנו השתא. *מאי עין לא ראתה אמר ריב"ל זה יין המשומר בענביו מששת ימי בראשית רבי *שמואל בר נחמני אמר זה עדן שלא שלטה בו עין כל בריה שמא תאמר אדם הראשון היכן היה בגן ושמא תאמר הוא גן הוא עדן תלמוד לומר °ונהר יוצא מעדן להשקות את הגן גן לחוד ועדן לחוד: ת"ר מעשה שחלה בנו של ר"ג שגר שני ת"ח אצל רבי חנינא בן דוסא לבקש עליו רחמים כיון שראה אותם עלה לעלייה ובקש עליו רחמים בירידתו אמר להם לכו שחלצתו חמה אמרו לו וכי נביא אתה אמר להם לא נביא אנכי ולא בן נביא אנכי אלא כך מקובלני אם שגורה תפלתי בפי יודע אני שהוא מקובל ואם לאו יודע אני שהוא מטורף ישבו וכתבו וכיונו אותה שעה וכשבאו אצל ר"ג אמר להן העבודה לא חסרתם ולא הותרתם אלא כך היה מעשה באותה שעה חלצתו חמה ושאל לנו מים לשתות ושוב מעשה ברבי חנינא בן דוסא שהלך ללמוד תורה אצל ר' יוחנן בן זכאי וחלה בנו של ריב"ז אמר לו חנינא בני בקש עליו רחמים ויחיה הניח ראשו בין ברכיו ובקש עליו רחמים וחיה אמר רבן יוחנן בן זכאי אלמלא הטיח בן זכאי את ראשו בין ברכיו כל היום כלו לא היו משגיחין עליו אמרה לו אשתו וכי חנינא גדול ממך אמר לה לאו אלא הוא דומה כעבד לפני המלך ואני דומה כשר לפני המלך. *ואמר רבי חייא בר אבא אמר רבי יוחנן °אל יתפלל אדם אלא בבית שיש שם חלונות שנאמר °וכוין פתיחן ליה בעיליתי' (לקבל) [נגד] ירושלים אמר רב כהנא חציף עלי מאן דמצלי בבקתא ואמר רב כהנא *חציף עלי מאן דמפרש חטאיה שנאמר °אשרי נשוי פשע כסוי חטאה:

הדרן עלך אין עומדין

עין משפט נר מצוה: ס א מיי' פ"ה מה' תפלה הל' י. סא ב מיי' שם הל' יג סמג עשין יט [*כונה תוס' מכאן דאמרינן לעיל כו: אין שיחה אלא תפלה]. סב ג מיי' שם הי"ג ופ"ט שם ה"ה טוש"ע א"ח סי' קלא סעי' א. סג ד מיי' פ"ה מה' תפלה הל' א סמג שם טוש"ע א"ח סי' קא סעי' א. סד ה מיי' פ"ז מה' דעות הל' ג. סה ו מיי' פ"ז מה' תשובה הל' ז. סו ז מיי' פ"ח מה' תשובה הל' ב ופ"ז מה' מלכים הל' ב. סז ח מיי' פ"ז מה' תשובה הל' ד. סח ט מיי' פ"ה מה' תפל' הל' ו סמג עשין יט טוש"ע א"ח סימן צ סעי' ד. סט י טוש"ע שם סעי' ה. ע כ מיי' פ"ב מה' תשובה הל' ה וטוש"ע א"ח סי' תרז סעי' ב.

מסורת הש"ס: מגילה כב: שבועות יז: [מגילה כב: ע"ש] [הושע ה'] [חגיגה יד: קדושין מג. נדרים עב: נזיר יב: ב"מ לו: מנחות לג:] ישעיה כז סנהדרין צט. ישעיה סד שבת סג. וקכא: דברים טו ישעיה כז פסחים קיט. סנהדרין צט: [*שם איתא ר"ל] בראשית ב [לעיל לא. ע"ש] דניאל ו סוטה ז: ע"ש תהלים לב

תורה אור: מלכים א' ח. שם א. בראשית לז.

[34b] a high priest at the end of each benediction; a king at the beginning of each benediction and at the end of each benediction.[3] R. Isaac b. Naḥmani said: It was explained to me by R. Joshua b. Levi that an ordinary person does as we have mentioned; a high priest bows at the beginning of each blessing; and a king, once he has knelt down, does not rise again [until the end of the *Tefillah*], as it says: *And it was so that when Solomon had made an end of praying, . . . he arose from before the Altar of the Lord, from kneeling on his knees.*[4]

Ḳidah [bowing] is upon the face, as it says: *Then Bath-Sheba bowed with her face to the ground.*[5] *Keri'ah* [kneeling] is upon the knees, as it says: *From kneeling on his knees.* Prostration is spreading out of hands and feet, as it says: *Shall I and thy mother and thy brethren come to prostrate ourselves before thee on the ground.*[6]

R. Ḥiyya the son of R. Huna said: I have observed Abaye and Raba bending to one side.[7] One [Baraitha] taught: To kneel in the thanksgiving benediction is praiseworthy, while another taught: It is reprehensible?—There is no contradiction: one speaks of the beginning,[8] the other of the end. Raba knelt in the thanksgiving at the beginning and at the end. The Rabbis said to him: Why does your honour act thus? He replied to them: I have seen R. Naḥman kneeling, and I have seen R. Shesheth doing thus. But it has been taught: To kneel in the thanksgiving is reprehensible?—That refers to the thanksgiving in *Hallel*.[9] But it has been taught: To kneel in the thanksgiving and in the thanksgiving of *Hallel* is reprehensible?—The former statement refers to the
a thanksgiving in the Grace after Meals.[1]

MISHNAH. IF ONE MAKES A MISTAKE IN HIS TEFILLAH IT IS A BAD SIGN FOR HIM, AND IF HE IS A READER OF THE CONGREGATION[2] IT IS A BAD SIGN FOR THOSE WHO HAVE COMMISSIONED HIM, BECAUSE A MAN'S AGENT IS EQUIVALENT TO HIMSELF. IT WAS RELATED OF R. ḤANINA BEN DOSA THAT HE USED TO PRAY FOR THE SICK AND SAY, THIS ONE WILL DIE, THIS ONE WILL LIVE. THEY SAID TO HIM: HOW DO YOU KNOW? HE REPLIED: IF MY PRAYER COMES OUT FLUENTLY,[3] I KNOW THAT HE IS ACCEPTED, BUT IF NOT, THEN I KNOW THAT HE IS REJECTED.[4]

GEMARA. In which blessing [is a mistake a bad sign]?—R. Ḥiyya said in the name of R. Safra who had it from a member of the School of Rabbi: In the blessing of the Patriarchs.[5] Some attach this statement to the following: 'When one says the *Tefillah* he must say all the blessings attentively, and if he cannot say all attentively he should say one attentively'. R. Ḥiyya said in the name of R. Safra who had it from a member of the School of Rabbi: This one should be the blessing of the Patriarchs.

IT WAS RELATED OF RABBI ḤANINA etc. What is the [Scriptural] basis for this?—R. Joshua b. Levi said: Because Scripture says: *Peace to him that is far off and to him that is near, saith the Lord that createth the fruit of the lips, and I will heal him.*[6]

R. Ḥiyya b. Abba said in the name of R. Joḥanan: All the prophets prophesied only on behalf of[7] one who gives his daughter in marriage to a scholar and who conducts business on behalf of a scholar and who allows a scholar the use of his possessions. But as for the scholars themselves, *Eye hath not seen, oh God, beside*
b *Thee what He will do for him that waiteth for Him.*[1]

R. Ḥiyya b. Abba also said in the name of R. Joḥanan: All the prophets prophesied only for the days of the Messiah, but as for the world to come, '*Eye hath not seen, oh God, beside Thee*'. These Rabbis differ from Samuel; for Samuel said: There is no difference between this world and the days of the Messiah except [that in the latter there will be no] bondage of foreign Powers, as it says: *For the poor shall never cease out of the land.*[2]

R. Ḥiyya b. Abba also said in the name of R. Joḥanan: All the prophets prophesied only on behalf of penitents; but as for the wholly righteous, '*Eye hath not seen, oh God, beside Thee*'. He differs in this from R. Abbahu. For R. Abbahu said: In the place where penitents stand even the wholly righteous cannot stand, as it says: *Peace, peace to him that was far and to him that is near*[3]—to him that was far first, and then to him that is near. R. Joḥanan, however, said: What is meant by '*far*'? One who from the beginning was far from transgression. And what is meant by '*near*'? That he was once near to transgression and now has gone far from it.[4] What is the meaning of '*Eye hath not seen*'? R. Joshua b. Levi said: This is the wine which has been preserved in its grapes from the six days of Creation.[5] R. Samuel b. Naḥmani said: This is Eden,[6] which has never been seen by the eye of any creature. Perhaps you will say, Where then was Adam? He was in the garden. Perhaps you will say, the garden and Eden are the same? Not so! For the text says: *And a river went out of Eden to water the garden*[7]—the garden is one thing and Eden is another.

Our Rabbis taught: Once the son of R. Gamaliel fell ill. He sent two scholars to R. Ḥanina b. Dosa to ask him to pray for him. When he saw them he went up to an upper chamber and prayed for him. When he came down he said to them: Go, the fever has left him; They said to him: Are you a prophet? He replied: I am neither a prophet nor the son of a prophet, but I learnt this from experience. If my prayer is fluent in my mouth, I know that he
c is accepted: but if not, I know that he is rejected.[1] They sat down and made a note of the exact moment. When they came to R. Gamaliel, he said to them: By the temple service! You have not been a moment too soon or too late, but so it happened: at that very moment the fever left him and he asked for water to drink.

On another occasion it happened that R. Ḥanina b. Dosa went to study Torah with R. Joḥanan ben Zakkai. The son of R. Joḥanan ben Zakkai fell ill. He said to him: Ḥanina my son, pray for him that he may live. He put his head between his knees and prayed for him and he lived. Said R. Joḥanan ben Zakkai: If Ben Zakkai had stuck his head between his knees for the whole day, no notice would have been taken of him. Said his wife to him: Is Ḥanina greater than you are? He replied to her: No; but he is like a servant before the king,[2] and I am like a nobleman before a king.[3]

R. Ḥiyya b. Abba said in the name of R. Joḥanan: A man should not pray save in a room which has windows,[4] since it says, *Now his windows were open in his upper chamber towards Jerusalem.*[5]

R. Kahana said: I consider a man impertinent who prays in a valley.[6] R. Kahana also said: I consider a man impertinent who openly[7] recounts his sins, since it is said, *Happy is he whose transgression is forgiven, whose sin is covered.*[8]

(3) I.e., the greater the individual, the more he humbles himself. (4) I Kings VIII, 54. (5) Ibid. I, 31. (6) Gen. XXXVII, 10. (7) And not completely prostrating themselves. (8) This is praiseworthy. (9) The verse, *Give thanks unto the Lord, for he is good*, etc., v. *P.B.* p. 222.

a (1) *P.B.* p. 281. (2) Lit., 'An agent of the congregation'. (3) Lit., 'is fluent in my mouth'. (4) Lit., 'he is torn'. The word, however, may refer to the prayer, meaning that it is rejected. (5) The first blessing in the *Tefillah*. (6) Isa. LVII, 19. *Bore* translated '*created*' has also the meaning 'strong', hence the verse is rendered to mean: if the fruit of the lips (prayer) is strong (fluent) then I will heal him. (7) I.e., their promises and consolations had reference to.

b (1) Isa. LXIV, 3. (2) Deut. XV, 11. '*Never*' i.e., not even in the Messianic era. (3) Isa. LVII, 19. (4) I.e., the penitent. (5) To feast the righteous in the future world. (6) Paradise. (7) Gen. II, 10.

c (1) V. *supra*, 34b, n. a4. (2) Who has permission to go in to him at anytime. (3) Who appears before him only at fixed times. (4) So that he should have a view of the heavens. (5) Dan. VI, 11. (6) A level stretch of ground where people constantly pass; one should pray in an enclosed and secluded spot. (7) As though unashamed. (8) Lit. trans. E.V. '*whose sin is pardoned*' Ps. XXXII, 1.

CHAPTER VI

MISHNAH. [35a] WHAT BLESSINGS ARE SAID OVER FRUIT? OVER FRUIT OF THE TREE ONE SAYS, WHO CREATEST THE FRUIT OF THE TREE, EXCEPT FOR WINE, OVER WHICH ONE SAYS, WHO CREATEST THE FRUIT OF THE VINE. OVER THAT WHICH GROWS FROM THE GROUND ONE SAYS: WHO CREATEST THE FRUIT OF THE GROUND, EXCEPT OVER BREAD, FOR WHICH ONE SAYS, WHO BRINGEST FORTH BREAD FROM THE EARTH. OVER VEGETABLES ONE SAYS, WHO CREATEST THE FRUIT OF THE GROUND; R. JUDAH, HOWEVER, SAYS: WHO CREATEST DIVERS KINDS OF HERBS.

a *GEMARA.* Whence is this derived?[1]—As our Rabbis have taught: *The fruit therof shall be holy, for giving praise unto the Lord.*[2] This[3] teaches that they require a blessing both before and after partaking of them. On the strength of this R. Akiba said: A man is forbidden to taste anything before saying a blessing over it.

But is this the lesson to be learnt from these words *'Holy for giving praise'?* Surely they are required for these two lessons: first, to teach that the All-Merciful has declared: Redeem it[4] and then eat it, and secondly, that a thing which requires a song of praise requires redemption,[5] but one that does not require a song of praise does not require redemption,[6] as has been taught by R. Samuel b. Naḥmani in the name of R. Jonathan. For R. Samuel b. Naḥmani said in the name of R. Jonathan: Whence do we know b that a song of praise is sung only over wine?[1] Because it says, *And the vine said unto them: Should I leave my wine which cheereth God and man?*[2] If it cheers man, how does it cheer God? From this we learn that a song of praise is sung only over wine.

Now this reasoning[3] is valid for him who teaches 'The *planting* of the fourth year'.[4] But for him who teaches 'The *vineyard* of the fourth year', what can be said? For it has been stated: R. Ḥiyya and R. Simeon the son of Rabbi [taught differently]. One taught, 'Vineyard of the fourth year', the other taught, 'Planting of the fourth year'.—For him who teaches 'Vineyard of the fourth year' also there is no difficulty if he avails himself of a *gezerah shawah.*[5] For it has been taught: Rabbi says: It says there, *that it may yield unto you more richly the* increase *thereof,*[6] and it says in another place, *the* increase *of the vineyard.*[7] Just as in the latter passage *'increase'* refers to the vineyard, so here it refers to the vineyard. Thus one *hillul* is left over to indicate that a blessing is required. But if he does not avail himself of a *gezerah shawah,* how can he derive this lesson? And even if he does avail himself of a *gezerah shawah,* while we are satisfied that a blessing is required after it,[8] whence do we learn that it is required [before partaking]?—This is no difficulty. We derive it by argument *a fortiori:* If he says a blessing when he is full, how much more so ought he to do so when he is hungry?[9]

We have found a proof for the case of [the produce of the vineyard]: whence do we find [that a benediction is required] for other species?[10] It can be learnt from the vineyard. Just as the vineyard being something that is enjoyed requires a blessing, so everything that is enjoyed requires a blessing. But this may be refuted: How can we learn from a vineyard, seeing that it is c subject to the obligation of the gleanings?[1]—We may cite the instance of corn.[2] How can you cite the instance of corn, seeing that it is subject to the obligation of *ḥallah?*[3]—We may then cite the instance of the vineyard, and the argument goes round in a circle: The distinguishing feature of the first instance is not like that of the second, and *vice versa.* The feature common to both is that being things which are enjoyed they require a blessing; similarly everything which is enjoyed requires a blessing. But this [argument from a] common feature [is not conclusive], because there is with them[4] the common feature that they are offered on the altar![5] We may then adduce also the olive from the fact that it is offered on the altar. But is [the blessing over] the olive derived from the fact that it is offered on the altar? It is explicitly designated *kerem,*[6] as it is written, *And he burnt up the shocks and the standing corn and also the olive yards* [kerem]?[7]—R. Papa replied: It is called an olive *kerem* but not *kerem* simply. Still the difficulty remains: How can you learn [other products] from the argument of a common factor, seeing that [wine and corn] have the common feature of being offered on the altar?—Rather it is learnt from the seven species.[8] Just as the seven species are something which being enjoyed requires a blessing,[9] so everything which is enjoyed requires a blessing. How can you argue from the seven species, seeing that they are subject to the obligation of first-fruits? And besides, granted that we learn from them that a blessing is to be said after partaking, how do we know it is to be said before?—This is no difficulty, being learnt *a fortiori:* If he says a blessing when he is full, how much more should he do so when he is hungry? Now as for the one who reads 'planting of the fourth year', we may grant he has proved his point with regard to anything planted. But whence does he derive it in regard to things that are not planted, such as meat, eggs and fish?—The fact is that it is a reasonable supposition that it is forbidden to a man to enjoy anything d of this world without saying a blessing.[1]

Our Rabbis have taught: It is forbidden to a man to enjoy anything of this world without a benediction, and if anyone enjoys anything of this world without a benediction, he commits sacrilege.[2] What is his remedy? He should consult a wise man. What will the wise man do for him? He has already committed the offence!—Said Raba: What it means is that he should consult a wise man beforehand, so that he should teach him blessings and he should not commit sacrilege. Rab Judah said in the name of Samuel: To enjoy anything of this world without a benediction is like making personal use of things consecrated to heaven, since it says, *The earth is the Lord's and the fulness thereof.*[3] R. Levi contrasted two texts. It is written, *'The earth is the Lord's and the fulness thereof',* and it is also written, *The heavens are the heavens of the Lord, but the earth hath He given to the children of men!*[4] There is no contradiction: in the one case it is before a blessing has been

(1) That a benediction is necessary before partaking of any food. (2) Lev. XIX, 24, with reference to the fruit of the fourth year. (3) The fact that the word *hillulim* (praise) is in the plural, indicating that there must be two praises. (4) The fruit of the fourth year, if it is to be eaten outside Jerusalem. (5) This is learnt from a play on the word *hillulim,* which is read also as *ḥillulim* (profaned, i.e., redeemed). (6) Thus limiting the law relating to the fruit of the fourth year only to the vine, as *infra.*

b (1) By the Levites at the offering of the sacrifices. (2) Judg. IX, 13. (3) That we learn the requirement of saying a blessing from the word *hillulim.* (4) I.e., that the verse quoted from Leviticus refers to all fruit of the fourth year and not to the vine only. In this case the word *hillulim* can not be used to prove that only the vine requires redemption, and is available for teaching that a blessing must be said over fruit. (5) V. Glos. (6) Lev. XIX, 25. (7) Deut. XXII, 9. (8) On the analogy of grace after meals as prescribed in Deut. VIII, 10. (9) And is about to satisfy his hunger. (10) On the view that Lev. XIX, 24 refers only to a vineyard.

c (1) Cf. Lev. XIX, 10. And this may be the reason why it requires a blessing. (2) Which is not subject to the obligation of gleanings, and yet requires a blessing, as laid down in Deut. VIII, 10. (3) The heave-offering of the dough. (4) I.e., wine and corn. (5) In the form of drink-offering and meal-offering. (6) Lit. 'vineyard', and therefore it is on the same footing as wine. (7) Judg. XV, 5. (8) Mentioned in Deut. VIII, 8. (9) As distinctly prescribed in Deut. VIII, 8.

d (1) Whether we take the law of the fourth year to apply to the vine or to all fruit trees, we cannot derive from it the law for saying a blessing over all things—in the former case because of the difficulty about the altar, in the

תורה אור

כיצד מברכין על הפירות *על פירות האילן הוא אומר בורא פרי העץ חוץ מן היין שעל היין הוא אומר ב״פ הגפן *ועל פירות הארץ הוא אומר ב״פ האדמה חוץ מן הפת שעל הפת הוא אומר המוציא לחם מן הארץ *ועל הירקות הוא אומר בורא פרי האדמה רבי יהודה אומר בורא מיני דשאים:

גמ׳ מנא ה״מ *דתנו רבנן °קדש הלולים ליי׳ מלמד שטעונים ברכה לפניהם ולאחריהם מכאן אמר ר׳ עקיבא אסור לאדם שיטעום כלום קודם שיברך והאי קדש הלולים להכי הוא דאתא האי מבעי ליה חד דאמר רחמנא אחליה והדר אכליה ואידך דבר הטעון שירה טעון חלול ושאינו טעון שירה אין טעון חלול וכדרבי שמואל בר נחמני א״ר יונתן *דא״ר שמואל בר נחמני א״ר יונתן מנין [א] שאין אומרים שירה אלא על היין שנאמר °ותאמר להם הגפן החדלתי את תירושי המשמח אלהים ואנשים אם אנשים משמח אלהים במה משמח מכאן שאין אומרים שירה אלא על היין הניחא למאן דתני [ב] נטע רבעי אלא למאן דתני כרם רבעי מאי איכא למימר דאתמר רבי חייא ורבי שמעון ברבי חד תני כרם רבעי וחד תני נטע רבעי ולמאן דתני כרם רבעי הניחא אי יליף ג״ש דתניא רבי אומר נאמר כאן °להוסיף לכם תבואתו ונאמר להלן °ותבואת הכרם מה להלן כרם אף כאן כרם אייתר ליה חד הלול לברכה ואי לא יליף גזירה שוה ברכה מנא ליה ואי נמי יליף גזירה שוה אשכחן לאחריו לפניו מנין הא ל״ק דאתיא בק״ו *כשהוא שבע מברך כשהוא רעב לא כ״ש אשכחן כרם שאר מינין מנין דיליף מכרם מה כרם דבר שנהנה וטעון ברכה אף כל דבר שנהנה וטעון ברכה איכא למפרך מה לכרם שכן חייב בעוללות קמה תוכיח מה לקמה שכן חייבת בחלה כרם יוכיח *וחזר הדין לא ראי זה כראי זה ולא ראי זה כראי זה הצד השוה שבהן דבר שנהנה וטעון ברכה אף כל דבר שנהנה טעון ברכה מה להצד השוה שבהן שכן יש בו צד מזבח ואתי נמי זית דאית ביה צד מזבח וזית מצד מזבח אתי והא בהדיא כתיב ביה כרם דכתיב °ויבער מגדיש ועד קמה ועד כרם זית *אמר רב פפא כרם זית אקרי כרם סתמא לא אקרי מ״מ קשיא מה להצד השוה שבהן שכן יש בהן צד מזבח אלא דיליף לה משבעת המינין מה שבעת המינין דבר שנהנה וטעון ברכה אף כל דבר שנהנה טעון ברכה מה לשבעת המינין שכן חייבין בבכורים ועוד התינח לאחריו לפניו מנין הא ל״ק דאתי׳ בק״ו כשהוא שבע מברך כשהוא רעב לכ״ש ולמאן דתני נטע רבעי הא תינח כל דבר נטיעה דלאו בר נטיעה כגון בשר ביצים ודגים מנ״ל אלא סברא הוא אסור לו לאדם שיהנה מן העה״ז בלא ברכה ת״ר *אסור לו לאדם שיהנה מן העה״ז בלא ברכה *וכל הנהנה מן העה״ז בלא ברכה מעל מאי תקנתיה ילך אצל *חכם ילך אצל חכם מאי עביד ליה הא עבד ליה איסורא אלא אמר רבא ילך אצל חכם מעיקרא וילמדנו ברכות כדי שלא יבא לידי מעילה א״ר יהודה אמר שמואל כל הנהנה מן העה״ז בלא ברכה כאלו נהנה מקדשי שמים שנאמר °ליי׳ הארץ ומלואה ר׳ לוי רמי כתיב ליי׳ הארץ ומלואה וכתיב °השמים שמים ליי׳ והארץ נתן לבני אדם ל״ק כאן קודם ברכה כאן

ויקרא יט | שופטי׳ ט | ויקרא יט | דברי׳ כב | שופטי׳ טו | תהלים כד | שם קטו

כיצד מברכין וכו׳ חוץ מן היין. שמתוך חשיבותו קבעו לו ברכה לעצמו וכן הפת: בורא מיני דשאי׳. לפי שיש בכלל פרי האדמ׳ דשאים הרבה כגון קטניות ור׳ יהודה בעי היכר ברכה לכל מין ומין: **גמ׳** קדש הלולים. בנטע רבעי כתיב ומשמע שני הלולים טעון באכילתו כשאוכלנו בשנה הד׳ שהוא מותר באכיל׳: האי מבעי ליה. הלולי׳ לשון חלולים חד מנייהו אתא לאורויי אחליה והדר אכליה הוציאו לחולין ע״י פדיון אם בא לאכלו חוץ לירושלים וחד ללמדך שלא נאמרה תורת רבעי אלא בכרם שנאמר קדש הלולים דבר שמהללין בו טעון חלול והיינו יין: שאין אומרים. הלוים שיר של קרבן במקדש אלא על היין כשמנסכין נסכי מזבח: הניחא למאן דאמר כו׳. כולה שמעתא דפרכא הוא וה״ק הניחא הא דילפת ברכה מהכא למאן דתני נטע רבעי דאית ליה כל פירות האילן בתורת רבעי ולא דריש מהכ׳ דבר דטעון הלול טעון חלול אייתר ליה חד הלול לברכה: מאי איכא למימר. הא מבעי׳ ליה למדרש שאין חלול אלא במקום הלול: חד תני כרם רבעי. בכל מקום שיש במשנה נטע רבעי תני איהו כרם: הניחא אי יליף בג״ש. דריש למלתיה בג״ש ואייתר ליה חד הלול לברכה: אשכחן לאחריו. כדאשכחן בברכת המזון דכתי׳ ואכלת ושבע׳ וברכת (דברי׳ ח): חייב בעוללות. וכרמך לא תעולל (ויקרא יט) איזהו עולל׳ כל שאין לה פסיגין לא כתף ולא נוטף אלא שורה יחידית של ענבים: קמה תוכיח. דאשכחן דאצרכ׳ רחמנא ברכה דכתיב תאכל בה לחם וגומר (דברים ח) וסמוך ליה ואכלת ושבעת וברכת: צד מזבח. יין לנסכי׳ וסלת למנחות: שבע׳ מינין. האמורים בארץ חטה ושעורה וגו׳ (שם ח) ובתרייהו כתיב ואכלת ושבעת וברכת: שכן טעונים בכורים. דהכי אמרי׳ במנחו׳ (פ״ע דף פד:) נאמ׳ כאן ארץ *כי באתי אל הארץ (דברים כו) ונאמר להלן ארץ חטה ושעור׳ מה להלן שבח הארץ אף כאן שבח הארץ: אלא סברא הוא. דלתרוייהו אית להו פירכא למאן דתני כרם ויליף ברכה מז׳ המינים איכא פירכא שכן טעונים בכורים ולמאן דתני נטע רבעי איכא למפרך התינח מידי דבר נטיע׳ דלאו בר נטיע׳ מנלן אלא סברא הוא דכיון דנהנה צריך להודות למי שבראם: מעל. כנהנה מן ההקדש דכתיב לה׳ הארץ ומלואה כדאמרי׳ לקמן: לאחר ברכה. הרי היא לבני אדם:

מסורת הש״ס
[לקמן לז.]
ת״כ פרשת קדושים פ״ג פ״ו
ערכין יא. יב.
[לקמן מח: ע״ש פי׳ רש״י ד״ה כשהוא שבע וכו׳ ת״ה כשהוא רעב וכו׳]
[קדושין ה: כא. וש״נ]
ב״מ פז:
תוספתא פ״ד (בירוש׳ איתא עד שיתירו לו כל המצות)
גזל

כיצד מברכין. לא שייך להקשו׳ תנא היכ׳ קאי דקתני כיצד כדפריך בריש מכילתין (ד׳ ב.) משו׳ דהכא סבר׳ הוא לברך כדמסיק בגמרא דאסור ליהנות מן העולם הזה בלא ברכה אי נמי י״ל דקאי אמתני׳ דמי שמתו (ד׳ כ:) דקתני בעל קרי מברך לאחריו ואינו מברך לפניו והכי נמי שייך הכא לברך על כל דבר ודבר ע״כ קאמר הכא כיצד מברכין:

אחליה והדר אכליה. תימה למה לי קרא הא בפ״ב דקדושין (דף כד:) גמרינן קדש קדש ממעשר שני א״כ נילף ממעשר שני וי״ל אי לאו קרא דהלולים הוה אמינא דאדרב׳ נילף לחומר׳ קדש קדש משביעית ואין לו פדיון. עוד פירש רבינו חיים כהן אי מהת׳ הוה אמינא כי מעשר שני ממש ודוק׳ בזמן שמעש׳ שני נוהג כמו בשנה ראשונה ושניה ורביעית וחמישית לשמט׳ נוהג חלול אבל שלישי׳ וששית שמעשר עני דוקא אימא לא קמ״ל חלולים*:

שאין אומרי׳ שירה אלא על היין. פירוש אין אומרים שירה על שום אכילת מזבח כגון זריקת דמים ונסוך המים כי אם על היין אבל ודאי מצינו שירה בלא יין כגון הלל שבשחיטת פסחים (תמיד נשחט ד׳ סד.) [ע״ש בתו׳]:

ולמאן דתני כרם רבעי וכו׳. ועתה קיימא לן דרבעי נוהג אף בח״ל ומיהו בכרם נוהג ולא בשאר אילנו׳ דכל המיקל בארץ הלכ׳ כמותו בח״ל *וכרם רבעי בזמן הזה מחללין על שוה פרוטה ושוחקו ומטילו לנהר וכן מפורש בשאלתות דרב אחאי (פ׳ קדושים)*:

ואתי נמי זית. במה הצד וא״ת איכא למפרך מה להצד השוה שכן חייבי׳ בלקט דפרט בכרם היינו לקט משא״כ בזית דאין בו לקט וי״ל דניחא ליה למפרך פירכא אפילו יהא הצד השוה חשוב למיתי זית מניה מ״מ קאמר דשאר מינים לא ידע מניה:

תינח לאחריו. דעיקר ברכה לאחריו כדכתיב ואכלת ושבעת וברכת:

לפנין לכ״ש. לאו ק״ו הוא דאם כן תהא ברכה דלפניו מדאורייתא ולעיל פ׳ מי שמתו (ד׳ כא.) משמע גבי בעל קרי דלאו דאורייתא הוא ואפי׳ ר׳ יהודה לא פליג אלא משום דעשאן כהלכות דרך ארץ (שם ד׳ כב*.):

דבר שאין גדולו מן הקרקע כגון בשר וחלב. וא״ת מאי אריא בשר אפילו ירקות נמי לא אתי ליה וי״ל דאיכא למימר קמה תוכיח ולפירוש רש״י ניחא דגרים דלאו בר נטיע׳ מנין וליכא למימר דאתא משאר אילנות דאיכא למפרך מה להנך שכן חייבי׳ בפאה:

אלא סברא הוא דאסור לאדם שיהנה וכו׳. וקרא דכתיב לעיל אסמכתא בעלמא והגמרא היה סבור מתחל׳ דלמוד גמור הוא:

כאן

עין משפט נר מצוה
א אמיי׳ פ״ח מהל׳ ברכות הל׳ א סמ״ג עשין כז טוש״ע א״ח סי׳ רב סעי׳ א
ב במיי׳ וסמ״ג שם טוש״ע א״ח סי׳ ר״ג סעיף א
ג גמיי׳ פ״ג שם ה״ב סמ״ג שם טוש״ע א״ח סי׳ קס״ז סעי׳ ב
[*ע׳ תוס׳ ב״ק סט: ד״ה קדש וכו׳ ביתר ביאור ותוס׳ קדושין כד: ד״ה גמר]
ד דמיי׳ פ״א שם סמ״ג שם הל׳ א טוש״ע א״ח סי׳ רה סעי׳ א
(*[ד] מיי׳ פ״ג מה׳ כלי המקדש הל׳ ג) ועי׳ היטיב תוס׳ קדושין ב: ד״ה אתרוג
[סי׳ ק׳]
(*[ה] מיי׳ פ״ט מה׳ מעשר שני הל׳ א טוש״ע י״ד סי׳ רלד סעי׳ ז ובהגה שם)
ה המיי׳ פ״א שם ה״ב סמג שם טוש״ע א״ח סי׳ רי סעי׳ א
[וע״ע תוס׳ יומא עט. ותוס׳ סוכ׳ כו: ותוס׳ חולין קז. ד״ה ולא]

---

latter because of the difficulty about things other than plants. Nor can we derive the law from the 'seven kinds', because of the difficulty about first-fruits. Hence we are driven back upon 'reasonable supposition'. (2) Heb. *ma'al*, the technical term for the personal use of consecrated things by a layman. (3) Ps. XXIV, 1. (4) Ibid. CXV, 16.

עין משפט נר מצוה

מסורת הש"ס

תורה אור

כאן לאחר ברכה א"ר חנינא בר פפא כל הנהנה מן העולם הזה בלא ברכה כאלו גוזל להקב"ה וכנסת ישראל שנאמר °גוזל אביו ואמו ואומר אין פשע חבר הוא לאיש משחית ואין אביו אלא הקב"ה שנאמר °הלא הוא אביך קנך ואין אמו אלא כנסת ישראל שנאמר °שמע בני מוסר אביך ואל תטוש תורת אמך מאי חבר הוא לאיש משחית א"ר חנינא בר פפא חבר הוא לירבעם בן נבט שהשחית את ישראל לאביהם שבשמים: ר' חנינא בר פפא רמי כתיב °ולקחתי דגני בעתו וגו' וכתיב °ואספת דגנך וגו' ל"ק כאן בזמן שישראל עושים רצונו של מקום כאן בזמן שאין ישראל עושים רצונו של מקום: ת"ר [א]ואספת דגנך מה ת"ל לפי שנאמר °לא ימוש ספר התורה הזה מפיך יכול דברים ככתבן ת"ל ואספת דגנך הנהג בהן מנהג דרך ארץ דברי ר' ישמעאל ר"ש בן יוחי אומר אפשר אדם חורש בשעת חרישה וזורע בשעת זריעה וקוצר בשעת קצירה ודש בשעת דישה וזורה בשעת הרוח תורה מה תהא עליה אלא בזמן שישראל עושים רצונו של מקום מלאכתן נעשית ע"י אחרים שנאמר °ועמדו זרים ורעו צאנכם וגו' ובזמן שאין ישראל עושים רצונו של מקום מלאכתן נעשית ע"י עצמן שנאמר °ואספת דגנך ולא עוד אלא שמלאכת אחרים נעשית על ידן שנאמר °ועבדת את אויביך וגו' אמר אביי הרבה עשו כר' ישמעאל ועלתה בידן כרשב"י ולא עלתה בידן א"ל רבא לרבנן במטותא מנייכו ביומי ניסן וביומי תשרי לא תתחזו קמאי כי היכי דלא תטרדו במזונייכו כולא שתא: אמר רבה בר בר חנה א"ר יוחנן משום ר"י בר' אלעאי בא וראה שלא כדורות הראשונים דורות האחרונים דורות הראשונים עשו תורתן קבע ומלאכתן עראי זו וזו נתקיימו בידן דורות האחרונים שעשו מלאכתן קבע ותורתן עראי זו וזו לא נתקיימו בידן ואמר רבה בר בר חנה אר"י משום ר"י בר' אלעאי *בא וראה שלא כדורות הראשונים דורות האחרונים דורות הראשונים היו מכניסין פירותיהן דרך *טרקסמון כדי לחייבן במעשר דורות האחרונים מכניסין פירותיהן דרך גגות דרך חצרות דרך קרפיפות כדי [ב]לפטרן מן המעשר *דא"ר ינאי אין הטבל מתחייב במעשר עד שיראה פני הבית שנאמר °בערתי הקדש מן הבית ור' יוחנן אמר אפילו חצר קובעת שנאמר °ואכלו בשעריך ושבעו: חוץ מן היין וכו': מ"ש יין אילימא משום דאשתני לעלויא אשתני לברכה והרי שמן דאשתני לעלויא ולא אשתני לברכה, דאמר *רב יהודה אמר שמואל וכן א"ר יצחק א"ר יוחנן שמן זית מברכין עליו בפה"ע אמרי התם משום דלא אפשר היכי נבריך נבריך בורא פרי הזית פירא גופיה זית אקרי ונבריך עלידהם בורא פרי עץ זית אלא אמר מר זוטרא חמרא זיין משחא לא זיין ומשחא לא זיין והתנן *[ג]הנודר מן המזון מותר במים ובמלח והוינן בה מים ומלח הוא דלא אקרי מזון הא כל מילי אקרי מזון נימא תהוי תיובתיה דרב ושמואל דאמרי אין מברכין בורא מיני מזונות אלא בה' המינין בלבד וא"ר הונא באומר כל הזן עלי אלמא משחא זיין אלא חמרא סעיד ומשחא לא סעיד *וחמרא מי סעיד *והא רבא הוה [ד]שתי חמרא כל מעלי יומא דפסחא כי היכי דנגרריה ללביה וניכול מצה טפי טובא גריר פורתא סעיד ומי סעיד כלל והכתיב °ויין ישמח לבב אנוש (ולחם לבב אנוש יסעד וגו') נהמא הוא דסעיד חמרא לא סעיד אלא חמרא אית ביה תרתי סעיד ומשמח נהמא מסעד סעיד שמוחי לא משמח א"ה נבריך עליה ג' ברכות לא קבעי אינשי סעודתייהו עלויה א"ל רב נחמן בר יצחק לרבא אי קבע עלויה סעודתיה מאי א"ל לכשיבא אליהו ויאמר אי הויא קביעותא השתא מיהא *בטלה דעתו אצל כל אדם: גופא אמר רב יהודה אמר שמואל וכן א"ר יצחק א"ר יוחנן [ה]שמן זית מברכין עליו ב"פ העץ היכי דמי אילימא [ו]דקא שתי ליה (משתה) אזוקי מזיק ליה *דתניא [ז]השותה שמן של תרומה משלם את הקרן ואינו משלם את החומש [ח]הסך שמן של תרומה משלם את הקרן ומשלם את החומש אלא דקא אכיל ליה ע"י פת א"ה הויא ליה פת עיקר והוא טפל ותנן *זה הכלל [ט]כל שהוא עיקר ועמו טפלה מברך על העיקר ופוטר את הטפלה אלא דקא שתי ליה ע"י אניגרון דאמר רבה בר שמואל *אניגרון מיא דסלקא *אנסיגרון מיא דכולהו

משלי כח | דברי' לב | משלי א | הושע ב | דברים יא | יהושע א | ישעיה סא | דברים יא | דברים כח | שם כו | שם | תלים קד

רש"י

גוזל להקב"ה. את ברכתו: ולכנסת ישראל. שכשחטאו הפירות לוקין: אין פשע. ולפי שהוא מיקל רואים האחרים ולמדין ממנו לעשות כן ליהנות מן העול' בלא ברכה ולכך נקרא זה המיקל חבר לאיש משחי': לירבעם בן נבט. שחטא והחטיא את ישראל כך הוא חוטא ומחטיא: בזמן שעושין רצונו. הדגן שלהם וכשאין עושים רצונו נוטלו ומראה להם שהוא שלו: דברי' ככתבן. שלא יעסוק בדרך ארץ: הנהג בהם. עם דברי תורה: מנהג דרך ארץ. שאם תבא לידי צורך הבריות סופך ליבטל מדברי תורה: אפשר. בתמיה אפשר כדבריך: ביומי ניסן. ימי הקציר: ביומי תשרי. דריכת הגתות והבדים: דרך טרקסמון. דרך שערי החצר והבית: פני הבית. פתח כניסה ויציאה: אין הטבל מתחייב במעשר. מן התורה אבל אכילת קבע אסור לאכול מדרבנן: זית אקרי. והוה ליה בורא פרי הפרי שהפרי קרוי זית ואין זו בריא' שמי' כי בידי אדם היא בריא' זו אבל גבי גפן הגפן היא העץ והענבים הם פרי הגפן: חמרא זיין. להכי חשיב לקבוע לו ברכה לעצמו: ואמר רב הונא. הא דקתני מותר במים ובמלח ואסור בשאר אוכלין ומשקין לאו באומ' קונם מזון עלי דאין מזון אלא מה' מיני דגן חטין ושעורין וכוסמין ושבול' שועל ושיפון אלא באומר כל הזן עלי קונם וכל מילי כהי דלא אקרו מזון מיהו מיזן זייני בר ממים ומלח אלמא משח' זיין: סעיד. חשיב טפי ממזון: והכתיב ויין ישמח לבב אנוש. וסיפא דקרא ולחם לבב אנוש יסעד משמע אבל יין אינו אלא משמח ומשני לאו כדקאמרת אלא לחם יסעד ולא ישמח אבל יין סועד ומשמח: אי הכי. דזיין וסעיד מזון הוא ולבריך עליה ג' ברכות לאחריו ואנן אמרינן לקמן בפרקין (דף לז.) כל שהוא משבעת המינין ולא מין דגן חכמים אומרים ברכה אחת: אזוקי מזיק. לגופיה ואין זו אכילה שטעונה ברכה דגבי ברכה ואכלת כתיב: דתניא. דלאו בר אכילה היא: השותה שמן של תרומה. בשוגג: משלם את הקרן. כשאר מזיק את חבירו בממונו: ואין משלם חומש. דגבי חומש אכילה כתיב ואיש כי יאכל קדש בשגגה (ויקרא כב) פרט למזיק: ע"י הפת. משום לפתן: ע"י אניגרון. מין מאכל הוא ונותנים לתוכו שמן ושכיח במשנה בכמה מקומות: דאמר' רבה בר שמואל. לא אתא הכא אלא לפרושי לן מאי ניהו: מיא דסלקא. מים ששלקו בהן תרדין: דכולהו

תוספות

כאן לאחר ברכה. וכן בפ' כל כתבי (ד' קיט.) אמרי' כשהיו מכינים השלחן היו אומרים לה' הארץ ומלואה וכשהיו מסלקין השלחן היו אומרים השמים שמים לה' והארץ נתן לבני אדם:

כאן בזמן שישראל עושין רצונו של מקום כאמר ואספת דגנך. וא"ת והא לקמן בזמן שאין ישראל עושים רצונו של מקום מוקמינן ליה וי"ל דמיירי ודאי שעושין רצונו אבל אין עושים רצונו כל כך דאינם צדיקים גמורים ועוד י"ל דפליג ליה אהא דלקמן שבא לפרש מה בין עושי' ואין עושין *והכא בעושי' ואין עושים כי הדדי ניינהו:

דרך טרקסמון. פרש"י היינו דאוריית' אבל מדרבנן גם חצר קובע' כדמשמע בפ' יוצא דופן (ד' מז:) איזהו חצר שחייב במעשר וכו' וכן מוכח בפ' המצי' (ביצה ד' לה.):

טובא גריר. מכאן משמע שאסו' לשתות יין בערב פסח מן המנחה ולמעלה ואם רוצה לשתות צריך לשתות הרבה דטובא מגרר גריר:

גיטין פא. | [ע' פרש"י ומוס' בגיטין פא.] | שם | ב"מ פז: | [לקמן לו.] | עירובין כו: | פסחים קז: | [פסחים מב. סוכה ז.] | תוספ' פז דתרומות | לקמן מא. מד. | שבועות כג.

ח גטוש"ע י"ד סי' רי"ז סעי' י"ט [צ"ל אכסיגרון כך איתא ביומא עו. ובשבועות וכן איתא בערוך] ט דטוש"ע א"ח סי' תעא סעי' א י המיי' פ"ח מהל' ברכות ה"ב סמ"ג עשין כז טוש"ע א"ח סי' כ"ב סעי' ד יא זמיי' פ"י מה' תרומה הל' י"א יב חשם הל' ב יג טמיי' פ"ג מהל' ברכות ה"ה סמג עשין כז טוש"ע א"ח סי' כב סעי' ד ובסי' כד סעי' יב ובסי' ריב סעי' א

CIV, 15. (7) As after bread, v. *infra* 37a. (8) *Aliter* 'His opinion is rejected by all men'.

(1) V. Glos. (2) Because the fifth is added only for what can be called food, since it says, *And if a man eat of the holy thing through error* (Lev. XXII, 14). (3) V. *infra* 41a.

said [35b] in the other case after. R. Ḥanina b. Papa said: To enjoy this world without a benediction is like robbing the Holy One, blessed be He, and the community of Israel, as it says, *Whoso robbeth his father or his mother and saith, It is no transgression, the same is the companion of a destroyer;*[5] and *'father'* is none other but the Holy One, blessed be He, as it says, *Is not He thy father that hath*
a *gotten thee;*[1] and *'mother'* is none other than the community of Israel, as it says, *Hear, my son, the instruction of thy father, and forsake not the teaching of thy mother.*[2] What is the meaning of *'he is the companion of a destroyer'?*—R. Ḥanina b. Papa answered: He is the companion of Jeroboam son of Nebat who destroyed Israel's [faith in] their Father in heaven.[3]

R. Ḥanina b. Papa pointed out a contradiction. It is written, *Therefore will I take back My corn in the time thereof,* etc.,[4] and it is elsewhere written, *And thou shalt gather in thy corn,* etc.![5] There is no difficulty: the one text speaks of where Israel do the will of the Omnipresent, the other of where they do not perform the will of the Omnipresent.[6]

Our Rabbis taught: *And thou shalt gather in thy corn.*[5] What is to be learnt from these words? Since it says, *This book of the law shall not depart out of thy mouth,*[7] I might think that this injunction is to be taken literally. Therefore it says, *'And thou shalt gather in thy corn'*, which implies that you are to combine the study of them[8] with a worldly occupation. This is the view of R. Ishmael. R. Simeon b. Yoḥai says: Is that possible? If a man ploughs in the ploughing season, and sows in the sowing season, and reaps in the reaping season, and threshes in the threshing season, and winnows in the season of wind, what is to become of the Torah? No; but when Israel perform the will of the Omnipresent, their work is performed by others, as it says, *And strangers shall stand and feed your flocks,* etc.,[9] and when Israel do not perform the will of the Omnipresent their work is carried out by themselves, as it says, *And* thou *shalt gather in thy corn.*[10] Nor is this all, but the work of others also is done by them, as it says, *And thou shalt serve thine enemy* etc.[11] Said Abaye: Many have followed the advice of Ishmael, and it has worked well; others have followed R. Simeon b. Yoḥai and it has not been successful. Raba said to the Rabbis: I would
b ask you not to appear before me during Nisan and Tishri[1] so that you may not be anxious about your food supply during the rest of the year.

Rabbah b. Bar Ḥanah said in the name of R. Joḥanan, reporting R. Judah b. Ila'i: See what a difference there is between the earlier and the later generations. The earlier generations made the study of the Torah their main concern and their ordinary work subsidiary to it, and both prospered in their hands. The later generations made their ordinary work their main concern and their study of the Torah subsidiary, and neither prospered in their hands.

Rabbah b. Bar Ḥanah further said in the name of R. Joḥanan reporting R. Judah b. Ila'i: Observe the difference between the earlier and the later generations. The earlier generations used to bring in their produce by way of the kitchen-garden[2] purposely in order to make it liable to tithe, whereas the later generations bring in their produce by way of roofs or courtyards or enclosures in order to make it exempt from tithe. For R. Jannai has said: Untithed produce is not subject to tithing[3] until it has come within sight of the house, since it says, *I have put away the hallowed things out of my house.*[4] R. Joḥanan, however, says that even [sight of] a courtyard imposes the obligation, as it says, *That they may eat within thy gates and be satisfied.*[5]

EXCEPT OVER WINE. Why is a difference made for wine? Shall I say that because [the raw material of] it is improved[6] therefore the blessing is different? But in the case of oil also [the raw material of] it is improved, yet the blessing is not different, as Rab Judah has laid down in the name of Samuel, and so R. Isaac stated in the name of R. Joḥanan, that the blessing said over olive oil is 'that createst the fruit of the tree'?[7]—The answer given is that in the case of oil it is not possible to change the blessing. For what shall we say? Shall we say, 'That createst the fruit of the olive'? The
c fruit itself is called olive![1] But we can say over it, 'That createst the fruit of the olive tree'?—Rather [the real reason is], said Mar Zutra, that wine has food value but oil has no food value. But has oil no food value? Have we not learnt: One who takes a vow to abstain from food is allowed to partake of water and salt,[2] and we argued from this as follows: 'Water and salt alone are not called food, but all other stuffs are called food? May we not say that this is a refutation of Rab and Samuel, who say that the blessing "who createst various kinds of food" is said only over the five species [of cereals]?'[3] and R. Huna solved the problem by saying that [the Mishnah] refers to one who says, 'I vow to abstain from anything that feeds'; which shows that oil has food value?[4]—Rather [say the reason is that] wine sustains[5] and oil does not sustain. But does wine sustain? Did not Raba use to drink wine on the eve of the Passover in order that he might get an appetite and eat much unleavened bread?—A large quantity gives an appetite, a small quantity sustains. But does it in fact give any sustenance? Is it not written, *And wine that maketh glad the heart of man ... and bread that stayeth man's heart,*[6] which shows that it is bread which sustains, not wine?—The fact is that wine does both, it sustains and makes glad, whereas bread sustains but does not cheer. If that is the case, let us say three blessings after it?[7]—People do not make it the basis of the meal. R. Naḥman b. Isaac asked Raba: Suppose a man makes it the basis of his meal, what then?—He replied: When Elijah comes he will tell us whether it can really serve as a basis; at present, at any rate, no man thinks of such a thing.[8]

The text [above] stated: 'Rab Judah said in the name of Samuel, and so too said R. Isaac in the name of R. Joḥanan, that the blessing said over olive oil is "that createst the fruit of the tree"'. How are we to understand this? Are we to say that it is drunk? If so, it is injurious, as it has been taught: If one drinks oil of
d *terumah,*[1] he repays the bare value, but does not add a fifth.[2] If one anoints himself with oil of *terumah,* he repays the value and also a fifth in addition. Do we suppose then that he consumes it with bread? In that case, the bread would be the main ingredient and the oil subsidiary, and we have learnt: This is the general rule: If with one article of food another is taken as accessory, a blessing is said over the main article, and this suffices also for the accessory![3] Do we suppose then that he drinks it with *elaiogaron?* (Rabbah b. Samuel has stated: *Elaiogaron* is juice of beetroots; *oxygaron* is juice

(5) Prov. XXVIII, 24. To rob God can only mean to enjoy something without saying a blessing, in recognition that it comes from Him.

a (1) Deut. XXXII, 6. (2) Prov. I, 8. (3) Likewise he who enjoys things without a blessing sets a bad example to others. (4) Hos. II, 11. (5) Deut. XI, 14. (6) Who accordingly takes back the corn and shows that it is His. (7) Joshua I, 8. (8) *Sc.* the words of the Torah. (9) Isa. LXI, 5. (10) Tosaf. point out that this homily conflicts with that given above on the same verse by R. Ḥanina b. Papa. (11) Deut. XXVIII, 48.

b (1) Nisan being the time of the ripening of the corn and Tishri of the vintage and olive pressing. (2) I.e., direct to the house, by the front way. V. *infra.* (3) I.e., according to the Torah. The Rabbis, however, forbade a fixed meal to be made of any untithed produce. (4) Deut. XXVI, 13. (5) Ibid. 12; v. Git. 81a. (6) Lit., 'it has been changed for the better'. (7) As over the olive itself.

c (1) There is no special name in Hebrew for the olive tree as there is for the vine. (2) 'Er. 26b. (3) Wheat, barley, oats, spelt, and rye. (4) Even according to Rab and Samuel. (5) And has more than merely food value. (6) Ps.

of [36a] all other boiled vegetables.) In that case the *elaiogaron* would be the main thing and the oil subsidiary, and we have learnt: This is the general rule: If with one article of food another is taken as accessory, a blessing is said over the main article, and this suffices for the accessory!—What case have we here in mind?[4] The case of a man with a sore throat, since it has been taught: If one has a sore throat, he should not ease it directly with oil on Sabbath,[5] but he should put plenty of oil into *elaiogaron* and swallow it.[6] This is obvious![7]—You might think that since he intends it as a medicine he should not say any blessing over it. Therefore we are told that since he has some enjoyment from it he has to say a blessing.

Over wheaten flour[8] Rab Judah says that the blessing is 'who createst the fruit of the ground',[9] while R. Naḥman says it is, 'By whose word all things exist'. Said Raba to R. Naḥman: Do not join issue with Rab Judah, since R. Joḥanan and Samuel would concur with him. For Rab Judah said in the name of Samuel, and likewise R. Isaac said in the name of R. Joḥanan: Over olive oil the blessing said is 'that createst the fruit of the tree', which shows that although it has been transformed it is fundamentally the same. Here too, although it has been transformed, it is fundamentally the same. But are the two cases alike? In that case [of olive oil] the article does not admit of further improvement, in this case it does admit of further improvement, by being made into bread; and when it is still capable of further improvement we do not say over it the blessing 'that createst the fruit of the ground', but 'by whose word all things exist'!—But has not R. Zera said in the name of R. Mattena reporting Samuel: Over raw cabbage and barley-flour we say the blessing 'by whose word all things exist', and may we not infer from this that over *wheat*-flour we say 'who createst the fruit of the ground'?—No; over wheat-flour also we say 'by whose word all things exist'. Then let him state the rule for wheat-flour, and it will apply to barley-flour as a
a matter of course?[1]—If he had stated the rule as applying to wheat-flour, I might have said: That is the rule for wheat-flour, but over barley-flour we need say no blessing at all. Therefore we are told that this is not so. But is barley-flour of less account than salt or brine, of which we have learnt[2]: Over salt and brine one says 'by whose word all things exist'?—It was necessary [to lay down the rule for barley-flour]. You might argue that a man often puts a dash of salt or brine into his mouth [without harm], but barley-flour is harmful in creating tapeworms, and therefore we need say no blessing over it. We are therefore told that since one has some enjoyment from it he must say a blessing over it.

Over the palm-heart,[3] Rab Judah says that the blessing is 'that createst the fruit of the ground', while Samuel says that it is 'by whose word all things exist'. Rab Judah says it is 'that createst the fruit of the ground', regarding it as fruit, whereas Samuel says that it is 'by whose word all things exist', since subsequently it grows hard. Said Samuel to Rab Judah: *Shinnena!*[1] Your opinion is the more probable, since radish eventually hardens and over it we say 'who createst the fruit of the ground'. This, however, is no proof; radishes are planted for the sake of the tuber,[2] but palms are not planted for the sake of the heart. But [is it the case that] wherever one thing is not planted for the sake of another [which it later becomes], we do not say the blessing [for that other]?[3] What of the caper-bush which is planted for the sake of the caper-blossom, and we have learnt: In regard to the various edible products of the caper-bush, over the leaves and the young shoots, 'that createst the fruit of the ground' is said, and over the berries and buds,[4] 'that createst the fruit of the tree'!—R. Naḥman b. Isaac replied: Caper-bushes are planted for the sake of the shoots, but palms are not planted for the sake of the heart. And although Samuel commended Rab Judah, the *halachah* is as laid down by Samuel.

Rab Judah said in the name of Rab: In the case of an 'uncircumcised'[5] caper-bush outside of Palestine,[6] one throws away the berries and may eat the buds. This is to say that the berries are fruit but the buds are not fruit. A contradiction was pointed out [between this and the following]: In regard to the various edible articles produced by the caper-bush, over the leaves and the young shoots 'that createst the fruit of the ground' is said; over the buds and the berries 'that createst the fruit of the tree' is said!—[Rab Judah] followed R. Akiba, as we have learnt: R. Eliezer says: From the caper-bush tithe is given from the berries and buds. R. Akiba, however, says that the berries alone are tithed, because they are fruit.[7] Let him then say that the *halachah* is as laid down by R. Akiba?—Had he said that the *halachah* is as laid down by R. Akiba, I should have thought that this was so even in the Holy Land. He therefore informs us that if there is an authority who is more lenient in regard to [uncircumcised products in] the Holy Land, the *halachah* follows him in respect of [such products] outside of the Holy Land, but not in the Land itself. But let him then say that the *halachah* is as laid down by R. Akiba for outside the Holy Land, because if an authority is more lenient with regard to the Land, the *halachah* follows him in the case of outside the Land?—Had he said so, I should have argued that this applies to tithe of fruit which in the Holy Land itself was ordained
c only by the Rabbis,[1] but that in the case of *'orlah*, the law for which is stated in the Torah, we should extend it to outside the Land. Therefore he tells us that we do not do so.

Rabina once found Mar b. R. Ashi throwing away [uncircumcised] caper-berries and eating the buds. He said to him: What is your view? Do you agree with R. Akiba who is more lenient?[2] Then follow Beth Shammai, who are more lenient still, as we have learnt: With regard to the caper-bush, Beth Shammai say that it constitutes *kil'ayim*[3] in the vineyard, whereas Beth Hillel hold that it does not constitute *kil'ayim* in the vineyard, while both agree that it is subject to the law of *'orlah*. Now this statement itself contains a contradiction. You first say that Beth Shammai hold that a caper-bush constitutes *kil'ayim* in a vineyard, which shows that it is a kind of vegetable,[4] and then you say that both agree that it is subject to the law of *'orlah*, which shows that it is a kind of tree![5]—This is no difficulty; Beth Shammai were in doubt [whether it was a fruit or a vegetable], and accepted the stringencies of both. In any case,[6] Beth Shammai regard it [the caper-bush] as a doubtful case of *'orlah*, and we have learnt: Where there is a doubt if a thing is subject to *'orlah*, in the Land of Israel, it is prohibited, but in Syria it is allowed; and outside of Palestine one may go down

(4) When it is stated that oil requires a benediction. (5) Medicine being forbidden on Sabbath, for fear one might come to pound drugs. (6) For in this case it is not obvious that he is taking it as a medicine. (7) That in this case one should make a blessing over the oil, because the oil is here the principal item. (8) When eaten raw. (9) Which is the blessing over crushed wheat, v. *infra* 37a.

(1) Since it is inferior to wheat-flour. (2) More correctly, 'as it has been taught', v. *infra* 40b. (3) An edible part of the young palm, which afterwards hardens and becomes part of the tree.

(1) An affectionate designation given by Samuel to his disciple Rab Judah. Apparently it means 'sharp-witted'. V. B.Ḳ. (Sonc. ed.) p. 60, n. 2. (2) To be eaten before it becomes hard and woody. (3) But 'by whose word all things exist'. (4) *Aliter:* 'caper-flowers', or 'husks'. (5) I.e., in its first three years. V. Lev. XIX, 23 (A.V.). (6) To which the Rabbis extended the obligation of *'orlah*, (v. Glos.). (7) But the buds are not fruit.

c (1) Since according to the written Torah, tithe was to be given only on corn, oil and wine. (2) In not exacting tithe for the buds. (3) Diverse seeds, v. Glos. (4) Otherwise it would not constitute *kil'ayim* in a vineyard. (5) Vegetables are not subject to the law of *'orlah*. (6) Rabina resumes here his argument against Mar b. R. Ashi.

דכולהו שלקי א"כ הוה ליה אניגרון עיקר ושמן טפל ותנן זה הכלל כל שהוא עיקר ועמו טפלה מברך על העיקר ופוטר את הטפלה הכא במאי עסקינן בהושש בגרונו דתניא *החושש בגרונו לא יערענו בשמן תחלה בשבת אבל נותן שמן הרבה לתוך אניגרון ובולע פשיטא *מהו דתימא כיון דלרפואה קא מכוין לא לברך עליה כלל קמ"ל כיון דאית ליה הנאה מיניה בעי ברוכי: קמחא דחטי רב יהודה אמר בפ"הא ורב נחמן אמר שהכל נהיה בדברו א"ל רבא לרב נחמן לא תפלוג עליה דרב יהודה דר' יוחנן ושמואל קיימי כוותי' *דא"ר יהודה אמר שמואל וכן א"ר יצחק א"ר יוחנן שמן זית מברכין עליו בפ"הע אלמא אע"ג דאשתני במלתיה קאי הכא נמי אע"ג דאשתני במלתיה קאי מי דמי התם לית ליה עלויא אחרינא הכא אית ליה עלויא אחרינא בפת וכי אית ליה עלויא אחרינא לא מברכינן עליה בפ"הא אלא שהכל והא"ר זירא אמר רב מתנה אמר שמואל אקרא חייא וקמחא דשערי מברכינן עלייהו שהכל נהיה בדברו מאי לאו דחטי בפ"הא לא דחטי נמי שהכל נהיה בדברו ולישמעינן דחטי וכ"ש דשערי אי אשמעינן דחטי הוה אמינא הנ"מ דחטי אבל דשערי לא נברוך עליה כלל קמ"ל ומי גרע ממלח וזמית *דתנן *על המלח ועל *הזמית אומר שהנ"ב אצטריך סלקא דעתך אמינא מלח וזמית עביד איניש דשדי לפומיה אבל קמחא דשערי הואיל וקשה לקוקיאני לא לבריך עליה כלל קמ"ל כיון דאית ליה הנאה מיניה בעי ברוכי: *קורא רב יהודה אמר בפה"א ושמואל אמר שהכל נהיה בדברו רב יהודה אמר ב"פ האדמה פירא הוא ושמואל אמר שהכל נהיה בדברו הואיל וסופו להקשות א"ל שמואל לרב יהודה *שיננא כוותך מסתברא דהא צנון סופו להקשות ומברכינן עליה בפ"הא ולא היא צנון נטעי אינשי אדעתא דפוגלא דיקלא לא נטעי אינשי אדעתא דקורא וכל היכא דלא נטעי אינשי אדעתא דהכי לא מברכינן עליה והרי צלף דנטעי אינשי אדעתא דפרחא ותנן על מיני נצפה על העלין ועל התמרות אומר בפ"הא ועל האביונות ועל הקפריסין אומר בפ"הע א"ר נחמן בר יצחק צלף נטעי אינשי אדעתא דשותא דקלא לא נטעי אינשי אדעתא דקורא ואע"ג דקלסיה שמואל לרב יהודה הלכתא כותיה דשמואל: אמר רב יהודה אמר רב צלף של ערלה בחוצה לארץ זורק את האביונות ואוכל את הקפריסין למימרא דאביונות פירי וקפריסין לאו פירי ורמינהי על מיני נצפה על העלים ועל התמרות אומר בפ"הא ועל האביונות ועל הקפריסין אומר בפ"הע הוא דאמר כר"ע דתנן *ר"א אומר צלף מתעשר תמרות ואביונות וקפריסין ר"ע אומר אין מתעשר אלא אביונות בלבד מפני שהוא פירא ונימא הלכה כר"ע אי אמר הלכה כר"ע הוה אמינא אפילו בארץ קמ"ל *כל המיקל בארץ הלכה כמותו בחוצה לארץ אבל בארץ לא ונימא הלכה כר"ע בח"ל דכל המיקל בארץ הלכה כמותו בח"ל אי אמר הכי הוה אמינא הנ"מ גבי מעשר אילן דבארץ גופא מדרבנן אבל גבי ערלה דבארץ מדאורייתא אימא בח"ל נמי נגזור קמ"ל רבינא אשכחיה למר בר רב אשי דקא זריק אביונות וקאכיל קפריסין א"ל מאי דעתך כר"ע דמיקל ולעביד מר כב"ש דמיקלי טפי דתנן צלף ב"ש אומרים כלאים בכרם וב"ה אומרים אין כלאים בכרם אלו ואלו מודים שחייב בערלה הא גופא קשיא אמרת צלף ב"ש אומרים כלאים בכרם אלמא מין ירק הוא והדר תני אלו ואלו מודים שחייב בערלה אלמא מין אילן הוא הא לא קשיא ב"ש ספוקי מספקא להו ועבדי הכא לחומרא והכא לחומרא מ"מ לב"ש הוה ליה ספק ערלה ותנן *ספק ערלה בא"י אסור ובסוריא מותר ובח"ל יורד ולוקח

רש"י

דכולהו שלקי. כל מיני ירק שלוק: החושש בגרונו. וצריך לתת בו שמן הרבה דהוה ליה שמן עיקר ואניגרון טפל: לא יערענו בשמן בשבת. דמשהי ליה בתוך גרונו ואינו בולעו וכיון דלא בלע ליה מוכחא מלתא דלרפואה הוא וחכמים גזרו על כל רפואות הנכרות משום שחיקת סמנים שהיא מלאכה: תחלה. כלומר לכתחלה לא יתן השמן בפיו לשם ערעור כי אם לשם בליעה ואם בא להשהותו ישהנו: דאית ליה הנאה מיניה. לבד הרפואה יש לו הנאת אכילה: והלכתא וכו' עד פטר להו לא גרסינן ומה"ג הוא: קמחא דחטי. אוכל קמח חטים כמו שהוא: ב"פ האדמה. כשאר כוסס חטין דתני' לקמן בפרקין (דף לז.) שמברך ב"פ האדמה: דאשתני. וגרע הואיל ולא אשתני לעלוי' מעליותא: במלתיה קאי. והוה ליה ככוסס חטין: הכא אית ליה עלויא אחרינא. הלכך יצא מכלל פרי ולכלל דרך אכילתו לא בא אבל השמן מיד בא בשנויו לכלל דרך אכילתו ועיקר הפרי לכך נטעוהו הלכך פרי הוא: מאי לאו. מדאמר שערי מכלל דסבירא ליה בחטי בפ"הא דחשיב: ומי גרע ממלח וזמית. והיכי תיסק אדעתין דלא תבעי ברכה: זמית. שלמי"לא: קוקיאני. תולעים שבמעים: דאית ליה הנאה. באכילה: קורא. רך של דקל כשענפיו גדלים בכל שנה ושנה כדרך כל האילנות הנוסף בשנה זו רך ובשנה שניה מתקשה ונעשה עץ: צנון סופו להקשות. שאם אינו תולשו בעתו הוא מתקשה כעץ: אדעתא דפוגלא. לאכלו כשהוא רך ושמו פוגלא: צלף. מין עץ: אדעתא דפרחא. שם פריו: מיני נצפה. הוא צלף לפי שגדלים בו כמה מיני אכילה קרי ליה מיני: תמרות. בתוך העלים גדלים כמין תמרות ובולטין בעלה כמו בעלין של ערבה: אביונות. הוא הפרי: קפריסין. הוא קליפה גדולה שסביבות הפרי כעין קליפה הגדלה סביב אגוזים דקים: צלף נטעי אינשי אדעתא דשותא. לאכול את העלים ואת התמרות שאינן ממעטין את האילן בכך: דקלא לא נטעי אינשי אדעתא. לאכול את הקור' שהאוכלו ממעט ענפי האילן: ערלה בחוצה לארץ. מדברי סופרים היא: דכל המיקל בארץ. בערלה הלכה כמותו בחוצה לארץ דכיון דאיכא מן התורה הלך אחר המיקל: גבי מעשר. דהא דר"ע לגבי מעשר אתמר דמעשר פירות האילן דבארץ גופה דרבנן שהתורה לא חייבה לעשר אלא דגן תירוש ויצהר: כלאים בכרם. קסבר מין ירק הוא: מ"מ לב"ש הוה ליה ספק ערלה וכו'. הא מ"מ מסקנא דפירכא דרבינא הוא ולמימר שאף הפרי עצמו מותר בחוצה לארץ דהא בארץ ספק הוא ותנן ספ' ערלה כו': בסוריא. ארם צוב' שכבש דוד והוסיפ' על גבול ארץ ישראל: ובחוצה לארץ. הלוקח מן החשוד על הערלה ויודע הוא שיש בפרדסו זקנות ונטיעות: יורד ולוקח. היינו אע"פ שספק הוא אם יביא מן הנטיעות:

ובלבד

תוספות

לא יערענו. פירש רש"י להשהותו וא"ת א"כ לפלוג וליתני בדידה ומאי איריא ע"י אניגרון אפילו בעיני' שרי לבלעו לאלתר דהא אינו אסור אלא לערער דהיינו להשהותו ע"כ פירש הר"י לא יערענו אפילו בבליעה בלא שהיה שכל שתיה שאינה אלא לרפואה קרי ליה ערעור ואפילו כשבולעו והיינו טעמא דמתסר משו' דקא מוכחא מלתא דלרפואה קא מכוין א"כ יש ליישב פירוש רש"י לא יערענו להשהותו אבל נותן הוא לתוך אניגרון ואפי' להשהותו או בולעו בעיני' בלא שהייה:

כיון דאית ליה הנאה מיניה בעי ברוכי. וכראין הדברים דאם אדם שותה *משקין אם המשקין רעים לשתו' דלית ליה הנאה מיניה לא בעי ברוכי ואי אית ליה הנא' מיניה בלא הרפואה בעי ברוכי:

והלכתא שכתוב בספרים לא גרסי' דלשון ה"ג הוא עד קמחא וכו':

קמחא דחטי. נראה דלא איירי בקמחא ממש דאם כן לא שייכא ביה ברכה דב"פ האדמה אלא איירי בקמחא שקורין אישקלא"טיר או בקמח שעושין משבולת שועל שמייבשין בתנור:

לא נטעי איניש אדעתא דקור'. וסבר גמרא כותיה דשמואל וא"כ אותן לולבי גפנים דלא נטעי איניש אדעתא דהכי מברכינן עליהו שהכל נהיה בדברו ואותן שקדים כשהם רכים אוכלים קליפתם החצונה ולא נטעי להו אדעתא דהכי למיכל להו כשהן רכים כי אם לאכול הגרעינין שלהן כשיתבשלו מברך עליהו נמי שהכל:

קליפי

מסורת הש"ס

תוספתא פ"ט דתרומ' [תוספ' שבת פי"ג]

לקמן לח.

[לעיל לה:]

לקמן מ: נדרים נה:

ערובין כח:

[שבת נה. קנג. עירובין כד: חגיגה טו: ר"ה כד: כתובות יב: יד. כג. קידושין לב. ב"ק לו: יד. טו. גיטין עח: ב"ב קלג: ע"ז מג: סנהדרין פ: כריתות יט: נדה יג. יז. כה:]

מעשרות פ"ד מ"ו

שבת קלט.

ערלה פ"ג מ"ט קידושין לט.

עין משפט נר מצוה

יד
א ב מיי' פ"ח מהל' ברכות ה"ב סמג עשין כז טוש"ע א"ח סי' רב סעי' ד

טו
ג מיי' פר' כא מהלכות שבת הל' כד טוש"ע א"ח סי' שכח סעיף לב [רב אלפס שבת פ"ע י"ד ד' מד:]

טז
ד טוש"ע א"ח סי' רד סעי' א

יז
ה מיי' פרק ג מהלכות ברכות הלכה ב סמג עשין כז טוש"ע א"ח סי' רח סעי' ה

יח
ו ז מיי' פ"ח שם הלכה ג ו וסמג שם טוש"ע א"ח סי' רד סעי' א

יט
ט טוש"ע א"ח סי' רג סעי' א

כ
י מיי' פרק ח מהל' ברכות הל' ו' וסמג שם טוש"ע א"ח סי' רב סעי' ו [פי' בערוך מרק והטור בא"ח סי' רד פי' מי מלח ורבינו האי פי' זומית שהוא הקלף]

כא
כ מיי' פרק י מהלכות מ"ע ונטע רבעי הלכה ג סמג עשין קלו טוש"ע י"ד סי' רלד סעי' ג

כב
ל מיי' פרק ב מהל' תרומות הלכה ד

כג
מ מיי' פרק ה מהל' כלאים הל' כ טוש"ע י"ד סי' רצו סעיף טו

כד
נ מיי' פרק י מהל' מאכלות אסורות הל' יא סמג לאוין קמד טוש"ע י"ד סי' רצד סעיף ט י

תורה אור

ולוקח ובלבד שלא יראנו לוקט ר' עקיבא במקום ר"א עבדינן כותיה *וב"ש במקום ב"ה אינה משנה ותיפוק ליה דנעשה שומר לפרי ורחמנא אמר °וערלתם ערלתו את פריו *את הטפל לפריו ומאי נידהו שומר לפרי אמר רבא היכא אמרינן דנעשה שומר לפרי היכא דאיתיה בין בתלוש בין במחובר הכא במחובר איתיה בתלוש ליתיה איתיביה אביי *פיטמא של רמון מצטרפת והנץ שלו אין מצטרף מדקאמר הנץ שלו אין מצטרף אלמא דלאו אוכל הוא ותנא גבי ערלה *קליפי רמון והנץ שלו קליפי אגוזים והגרעינין חייבין בערלה אלא אמר רבא היכא אמרינן דנעשו לדהו שומר לפירי היכא דאיתיה בשעת גמר פירא האי קפרס ליתיה בשעת גמר פירא איני והאמר רב נחמן אמר רבה בר אבוה *הני מתחלי דערלה אסירי הואיל ונעשו שומר לפירי ושומר לפירי אימת הוי בכופרא וקא קרי ליה שומר לפירי רב נחמן סבר לה כרבי יוסי דתנן *ר' יוסי אומר סמדר אסור מפני שהוא פרי ופליגי רבנן עליה מתקיף ליה רב שימי מנהרדעא ובשאר אילני מי פליגי רבנן עליה והתנן *מאימתי אין קוצצין את האילנות בשביעית ב"ש אומרים כל האילנות משיוציאו וב"ה אומרים החרובין משישרשרו והגפנים משיגרעו והזתים משינצו ושאר כל האילנות משיוציאו ואמר רב אסי הוא בוסר הוא גרוע הוא פול הלבן פול הלבן ס"ד אלא אימא שיעורו כפול הלבן מאן שמעת ליה דאמר בוסר אין סמדר לא רבנן וקתני שאר כל האילנות משיוציאו אלא אמר רבא היכא אמרת דהוי שומר לפירי היכא דכי שקלת ליה לשומר מיית פירא הכא כי שקלת ליה לא מיית פירא הוה עובדא ושקלוה לנץ דרמונא ויביש רמונא ושקלוה לפרחא דביטיתא ואיקיים ביטיתא (והלכתא כמר בר רב אשי דזריק את האביונות ואכיל את הקפריסין ומדלגבי ערלה לאו פירי נינהו לגבי ברכות נמי לאו פירי נינהו ולא מברכינן עליה ב"פ העץ אלא ב"פ האדמה): פלפלי רב ששת אמר שהכל רבא אמר ולא כלום ואזדא רבא לטעמיה דאמר רבא *כס פלפלי ביומא דכפורי פטור כס זנגבילא ביומא דכפורי פטור מיתיבי *היה ר"מ אומר ממשמע שנאמר וערלתם ערלתו את פריו איני יודע שעץ מאכל הוא אלא מה ת"ל עץ מאכל להביא עץ שטעם עצו ופריו שוה ואיזהו זה הפלפלין ללמדך שהפלפלין חייבין בערלה וללמדך שאין א"י חסרה כלום שנאמר °ארץ אשר לא במסכנות תאכל בה לחם לא תחסר כל בה ל"ק הא ברטיבתא הא ביבשתא *אמרי ליה רבנן למרימר כס זנגבילא ביומא דכפורי פטור והא אמר *רבא °האי המלתא דאתיא מבי הנדואי שריא ומברכין עליה בפ"הא ל"ק הא ברטיבתא הא ביבשתא: חביץ קדרה וכן דיסא רב יהודה אמר שהכל נהיה בדברו רב כהנא אמר במ"מ בדיסא גרידא כ"ע ל"פ דבמ"מ כי פליגי בדיסא כעין חביץ קדרה רב יהודה אמר שהכל סבר דובשא עיקר רב כהנא אמר במ"מ סבר סמידא עיקר א"ר יוסף כותיה דרב כהנא מסתברא דרב ושמואל דאמרי תרוייהו כל שיש בו מחמשת המינין מברכין עליו בורא מיני מזונות: גופא רב ושמואל דאמרי תרוייהו °כל שיש בו מחמשת המינין מברכין עליו בורא מיני מזונות ואתמר נמי רב ושמואל דאמרי תרוייהו כל שהוא מחמשת המינין מברכין עליו במ"מ וצריכא דאי אשמועינן כל שהוא הוה אמינא משום דאיתיה בעיניה אבל ע"י תערובות לא קמ"ל

ויקרא יט · דברים ח

רש"י

ובלבד שלא יראנו. החבר כשהוא לוקט מן הנטיעות: אינה משנה. ואין זה ספק אלא ודאי: ותיפוק ליה. דאי נמי רבי עקיבא דאמר לענין מעשר דלאו פירא נינהו לענין ערלה אסירי קפריסין דהוה ליה שומר: בתלוש ליתיה. שסופו שנופל הימנו כשמגיע להתבשל: פיטמא של רמון. הפרח שבראשו כעין שיש לתפוחים ולאפרגלין: מצטרפת. לכביצה לטומאת אוכלין: והנץ שלו. כן ברמון כקפרס באביונות: אין מצטרף. אע"ג דקי"ל בהעור והרוטב (דף קיז:) שומרי' מצטרפין לטומאה קלה דהיינו טומאת אוכלין הני מילי קליפת האגוז והרמון אבל הנץ שומר על גבי שומר הוא ואין מצטרף והכי אמרי' בהעור והרוטב' (דף קיח:): חייבי' בערלה. דרחמנא רביניהו מאת פריו הטפל לפריו והא כן ליתי' שומר בתלוש שכשמתבשל נופל מעל הקליפה: קפרס ליתיה בגמר פיר'. כשמגיע סמוך לבשולו הוא נופל ממנו: מתחלי. בתמרי כקפרס בצלף: בכופרא. כשהתמרי' קטנים קודם בשולם: סבר לה כר' יוסי. דכופר' הוי פרי ואע"פ שלא נגמר לפיכך שומר שלו חשוב שומר: סמדר אסור. ענבים כיון שנפל הפרח וכל גרגיר נראה לעצמו קרוי סמדר וקאמר רבי יוסי כיון שבא לכלל סמדר קרוי פרי ואסור משום ערלה: ופליגי רבנן עליה. והלכה כרבים הלכך אביונות בעוד שהקפריסין בהן לאו פירי נינהו ולא מיקרו קפריסין שומר לפרי: בשאר אילנות. חוץ מן הענבים: אין קוצצין בשביעי'. דרחמנא אמר לאכלה ולא להפסד: משיוציאו. את הפרי: משישרשרו. משיראו בהן כמין שרשרות של חרובין: משיגרעו. שהענבים גסים כגריע ולקמן מפרש לה: משינצו. משיגדל הנץ סביב: הוא בוסר הוא גרוע. כל מקום שהזכירו בוסר הוא גרוע: פול הלבן ס"ד. הא בענבים קיימינן: מאן שמע' ליה דאמר. גבי ענבים בוסר הוא דהוי פרי אבל סמדר לא: רבנן. הוא דפליגי עליה דר' יוסי במסכ' ערלה. וקאמרי בשאר אילנות דמשיוציאו הוי פרי סראוי: ביטיתא. אביונות: כס פלפלי. כל דבר שאדם אוכל שלא כדרכו מקרי כוסס': פטור. מכרת: המלתא. ליטוארי"ו בלעז: שריא. אין בה לא משום בשול נכרי' ולא משום געול נכרים: הנדואי. כושיים: חביץ קדרה. מין מאכל קפוי כמו חלב שחבלוהו בקיב' כך עושין מאכל קפוי בקדירה ולקמן מפרש לה קמחא ודובשא ומשחא וקרו ליה אברוש"די: דיסא. של חטים כתושו' במכתשת: דיסא כעין חביץ קדר'. לקמן מפרש לה חיטי דמתברי בחסית' ויהבו בהו דובש' ועביד להו בקדירה: סמידא. סלת:

תוספות

קליפי אגוזים והגרעינים חייבין בערלה. דפירי נינהו ומכאן יש לברך על הגרעינין של גודגדניות וגרעיני אפרסקין ושל תפוחים וכל מיני גרעינים של פירות בורא פרי העץ:

אין קוצצין אילנות בשביעית. וא"ת בלא שביעי' נמי תיפוק ליה דאסור משום לא תשחית את עצה (דברים כ) וי"ל דלא טעין קרא דלא שייך ביה בל תשחית כדאיתא פר' לא יחפור (דף כו.) אי נמי איירי דמעולי' בדמים לעשות מהנה קורות דאז *לא שייך לא תשחית ומיהו משום איסורא דשביעי' איכא לאכלה ולא לסחורה ולא להפסד:

שיעורו כפול הלבן. ופחות מכאן לא הוי פירא מכאן יש ללמוד דעל בוסר פחות מפול לא מברכינן עליה ב"פ העץ אלא ב"פ האדמה:

לשון ה"ג

והלכתא כמר בר רב אשי מדלגבי ערלה לאו פירא הוא וכו'. והיה אומר הר"מ דלגבי ערלה לאו פירא הוא היינו משום דכל המיקל בארץ הלכה כמותו בח"ל אבל בארץ ודאי הוי פירא ומברכין עליו ב"פ העץ ובברכות ליכא חלוק בין בארץ לח"ל:

ברטיבא כגון ליטואר"יו בלע"ז מברכין עליה ב"פ האדמה אבל יבישתא לא מברכינן עליה וכן הלכה בזנגבילא שקורין זינזי"ברו בלע"ז וכן קל"ו של גרו"פלי שאין רגילי' לאכול [אלא] ברטיבא כגון בליטואר"יו אין מברכין עליהם כלל ביבשת' אבל עץ של קנמון שקורין קניל"א מברכין עליו ב"פ האדמה מפני שרגילין לאכלו ביובש וגם הוא גדל על הארץ כמו קנים ועל לוקר"ו מברכין ב"פ העץ כי יערי עם דבשי (שיר ה) זה לוקר"ו והאגוז שקורין מושקד"א מברכין ב"פ העץ שגם נוהגין לאכול אותו ביובש:

כל שיש בו מחמשת המינין מברכין עליהם בורא מיני מזונות. וכן קליירי"ש בלע"ז שעושי' מקמח ומים או מחלב מברכין עליהן בורא מיני מזונות וכן כשנותנים קמח לתוך פולין או לתוך עדשים או כרישי' וכן לתוך שקדים שעושין לחולה אם עושין אותו כדי שיסעוד הלב אז צריך לברך בורא מיני מזונו' ואם לדבק בעלמא אינו צריך לברך בורא מיני מזונות וטוב להחמיר ולגמעו בתוך הסעודה לאחר ברכת המוציא ופטור מתה כפסך: בורא

עין משפט נר מצוה

כה א טוש"ע י"ד סי' רצד סעי' א [כדאיתא ב"ק לא:]
כו ב מיי' פרק ה מהל' טומאת אוכלין הל' א
כז ג מיי' פרק ט מהלכות מ"ש ונטע רבעי הל' יג טוש"ע י"ד סי' רצד סעיף א
כח ד מיי' שם טוש"ע א"ח סי' רב סעיף ג
כט ה מיי' שם הל' יג
ל ו מיי' פ"ה מהלכות שמטה ויובל הל' יח טוש"ע א"ח סי' רב סעי' ב
לא ז מיי' פ"ח מהל' ברכות הל' ו סמג עשין כז טוש"ע א"ח סי' רב סעי' ו
לב ט י כ מיי' שם הלכה ז וסמג שם ומיי' פרק ג מה' שביתת עשור הל"ה סמג לאוין סה טוש"ע א"ח סי' רב סעי' יז ובסי' תריב סעיף ח
לג ל טוש"ע א"ח סי' רג סעי' ו
לד מ נ מיי' פ"ג מהל' ברכות הלכה ד סמג עשין כז טוש"ע א"ח סי' רח סעי' ב וסעי' ט

מסורת הש"ס

[ביצה יא. יבמות עו.]
עוקצין פ"ב מ"ב [חולין קיח:]
ערלה פ"א משנה ח
מקום שנהגו נג:
ערלה פ"א משנה ז
שביעית פ"ד משנה יו"ד
מקום שנהגו נב
יומא פא:
סוכה לה.
[ביומא פא: א"ל רבינא] יומא שם

[36*b*] and buy it, provided he does not see the man plucking
a it![1]—When R. Akiba conflicts with R. Eliezer, we follow him, and the opinion of Beth Shammai when it conflicts with that of Beth Hillel is no Mishnah.[2] But then let us be guided by the fact that it [the bud] is a protection for the fruit, and the All-Merciful said, *Ye shall observe its uncircumcision along with its fruit;*[3] *'with'* refers to that which is attached to its fruit, namely, that which protects its fruit?[4]—Raba replied: When do we say a thing is a protection for the fruit? When it does so both when [the fruit is] still attached [to the tree] and after it is plucked. In this case it protects while [the fruit is] attached, but not after it is plucked.

Abaye raised an objection: The top-piece of the pomegranate is counted in with it,[5] but its blossom is not counted in.[6] Now since it says that its blossom is not counted in with it, this implies that it is not food: and it was taught in connection with *'orlah:* The skin of a pomegranate and its blossom, the shells of nuts and their kernels are subject to the law of *'orlah!*[7]—We must say, then, said Raba, that we regard something as a protection to the fruit only where it is so at the time when the fruit becomes fully ripe; but this caper-bud falls off when the fruit ripens. But is that so? Has not R. Naḥman said in the name of Rabbah b. Abbuha: The calyces surrounding dates in the state of *'orlah* are forbidden, since they are the protection to the fruit. Now when do they protect the fruit? In the early stages of its growth [only]. Yet he calls them 'a protection to the fruit'?—R. Naḥman took the same view as R. Jose, as we have learnt: R. Jose says, The grape-bud is forbidden because it is fruit; but the Rabbis differ from him.[8] R. Shimi from Nehardea demurred: Do the Rabbis differ from him in respect
b of other trees?[1] Have we not learnt: At what stage must we refrain from cutting trees in the seventh year?[2] Beth Shammai say: In the case of all trees, from the time they produce fruit; Beth Hillel say: In the case of carob-trees, from the time when they form chains [of carobs]; in the case of vines, from the time when they form globules; in the case of olive-trees, from the time when they blossom; in the case of all other trees, from the time when they produce fruit; and R. Assi said: *Boser* and *garua'*[3] and the white bean are all one. ('White bean', do you say?[4]—Read instead: the size [of them] is that of the white bean.) Now which authority did you hear declaring that the *boser* is fruit but the grape-bud is not? It is the Rabbis;[5] and it is they who state that we must refrain from cutting down all other trees from the time when they produce fruit![6]—No, said Raba. Where do you say that something is the protection to the fruit? Where if you take it away the fruit dies. Here[7] you can take it away and the fruit does not die. In an actual case, they once took away the blossom from a pomegranate and it withered; they took away the flower from a caper and it survived.[8] (The law is as [indicated by] Mar b. R. Ashi when he threw away the caper-berries and ate the buds. And since for purposes of *'orlah* they [the buds] are not fruit, for the purposes of benedictions also they are not fruit, and we do not say over them, 'who createst the fruit of the tree', but, 'who createst the fruit of the ground'.)[9]

With regard to pepper, R. Shesheth says that the blessing is 'by whose word all things exist'; Raba says: It requires no blessing at all.[10] Raba in this is consistent; for Raba said: If a man chews pepper-corns on the Day of Atonement he is not liable [to *kareth*];[11] if he chews ginger on the Day of Atonement he is not liable. An objection was raised: R. Meir says: Since the text says, *Ye shall*
c *count the fruit thereof as forbidden,*[1] do I not know that it is speaking of a tree for food? Why then does it say [in the same context], ['and shall have planted all manner of] trees for food'? To include a tree of which the wood has the same taste as the fruit. And which is this? The pepper tree. This teaches you that pepper is subject to the law of *'orlah,* and it also teaches you that the land of Israel lacks nothing, as it says, *A land wherein thou shalt eat bread without scarceness, thou shalt not lack anything in it!*[2]—There is no contradiction; one statement refers to moist pepper,[3] the other to dried. The Rabbis[4] said to Meremar: One who chews ginger on the Day of Atonement is not liable [to *kareth*]. But has not Raba said: The preserved ginger which comes from India is permitted,[5] and we say over it the benediction 'Who createst the fruit of the ground'?[6]—There is no contradiction: one statement refers to moist ginger, the other to dried.

With regard to *ḥabiẓ*[7] boiled in a pot, and also pounded grain, Rab Judah says the blessing is 'by whose word all things exist', while R. Kahana says that it is 'who createst various kinds of foods'. In the case of simple pounded grain all agree that the correct blessing is 'who createst various kinds of foods'. Where they differ is in respect of pounded grain made like boiled *ḥabiẓ*.[8] Rab Judah says that the blessing for this is 'by whose word etc.', considering that the honey is the main ingredient; R. Kahana holds that the blessing is 'who createst all kinds of food', considering the flour the main ingredient. R. Joseph said: The view of R. Kahana is the more probable, because Rab and Samuel have both laid down that over anything containing an ingredient from the five species [of cereals] the blessing is 'who createst all kinds of foods'.

The [above] text [states]: 'Rab and Samuel both lay down that over anything containing an ingredient from the five species [of cereals] the blessing is 'who createst all kinds of foods'. It has also been stated: Rab and Samuel both lay down that over anything made of the five species the blessing is 'who createst all kinds of foods'. Now both statements are necessary. For if I had only the statement 'anything made of etc.', I might say, this is because the cereal is still distinguishable, but if it is mixed with something else,

a (1) Consequently Mar b. R. Ashi should have eaten also the berries. (2) Consequently the caper-bud is certainly subject to the law of *'orlah.* (3) Lit. trans. E.V. *'Then ye shall count the fruit thereof as forbidden'.* Lev. XIX, 23. (4) How then did he eat the buds? (5) To bring it to the size of an egg and so render it susceptible to uncleanness. (6) The blossom bears the same relationship to the pomegranate that the caper-bud bears to the berry. (7) Although the blossom of the pomegranate does not protect it after it is plucked. The same should apply to the caper-bud. (8) And the *halachah* follows the Rabbis, who are the majority. And similarly the caper-bud is not subject to *'orlah.*

b (1) And can we say therefore that the *halachah* does not follow R. Naḥman following R. Jose? (2) Cf. Ex. XXIII, 11; Lev. XXV, 4. (3) *Boser* is the sour grape; *garua'* the grape when the stone is formed inside. (4) Lit., 'can you imagine'. (5) Who differ from R. Jose. (6) Which shows that in other cases the *halachah* is according to R. Jose. (7) In the case of the caper-bud. (8) And therefore you cannot argue from one to the other. (9) The passage in brackets reads like a marginal gloss. (10) Not being regarded as food. (11) V. Glos.

c (1) Lev. XIX, 23. (2) Deut. VIII, 9. This contradicts Raba. (3) I.e., preserved only in this condition does it become an article of food. (4) MS.M. Rabina. (5) In spite of the fact that it has been prepared by heathens. (6) Which shows that it is food. How then does the chewing thereof on the Day of Atonement not carry with it the guilt of *kareth.* (7) This is described later as a kind of pulp made of flour, honey, and oil. (8) I.e., to which honey has been added.

this is not [the blessing]. [37a] We are told therefore, 'anything containing an ingredient etc.'. If again I had only the statement, 'anything containing an ingredient etc.', I might think that this applies to the five species [of cereals], but not to rice and millet when they are mixed with other things; but when they are distinguishable the blessing even over rice and millet is 'who createst various kinds of foods'. So we are told that over anything which is made of the five species we say 'who createst various kinds of foods', excluding rice and millet, over which we do not say 'who createst various kinds of foods' even when they are distinguishable.

And over rice and millet do we not say, 'who createst various kinds of foods'? Has it not been taught: If one is served with rice bread or millet bread, he says blessings before and after it as for a cooked dish [of the five species]; and with regard to cooked dishes, it has been taught: He says before partaking, 'Who createst various kinds of foods', and after it, he says one blessing which
a includes three?[1]—It is on a par with cooked dishes in one way and not in another. It resembles cooked dishes in requiring a benediction before and after, and it differs from cooked dishes, because the blessing before these is 'who createst various kinds of foods' and the blessing after is the one which includes three, whereas in this case the blessing before is 'by whose word all things exist', and the blessing after, 'Who createst many living beings with their wants, for all which He has created etc.'[2]

But is not rice a 'cooked dish'?[3] Has it not been taught: The following count as cooked dishes: spelt groats, wheat groats, fine
b flour, split grain, barley groats, and rice?—Whose opinion is this?[1] That of R. Johanan b. Nuri; for it has been taught: R. Johanan b. Nuri says: Rice is a kind of corn, and when leavened it can entail the penalty of *kareth*,[2] and it can be used to fulfil the obligation of [eating unleavened bread on] Passover.[3] The Rabbis, however, do not admit this.[1] But do not the Rabbis admit this? Has it not been taught: If one chews wheat, he says over it the benediction, 'who createst the fruit of the ground'. If he grinds and bakes it and then soaks it [in liquid], so long as the pieces are still whole[4] he says before [partaking the blessing], 'who bringest forth bread from the earth', and after, the grace of three blessings;[5] if the pieces are no longer whole, he says before partaking 'that createst various kinds of foods', and after it one blessing that includes three.[5] If one chews rice, he says before partaking 'who createst the fruit of the ground'. If he grinds and bakes it and then soaks it, even if the pieces are still whole, he says before partaking 'who createst various kinds of foods', and after it the one blessing which includes three? Now whose opinion is this? Shall I say it is R. Johanan b. Nuri's? But he said that rice is a kind of corn, and therefore [according to him] the blessing should be 'who bringest forth food from the earth' and the grace the one of three blessings! It must therefore be the Rabbis'; and this is a refutation of Rab and Samuel, is it not?—It is a refutation.

The Master said [above]: 'If one chews wheat, he says over it the blessing, "who createst the fruit of the ground"'. But it has been taught: 'Who createst various kinds of seeds'?—There is no contradiction: one statement represents the view of R. Judah,[6] the other that of the Rabbis, as we have learnt: Over vegetables one says, 'who createst the fruit of the ground'; R. Judah, however, says: 'Who createst various kinds of herbs'.

The Master said [above]: 'If one chews rice he says over it "Who createst the fruit of the ground". If he grinds and bakes it and then soaks it, even if the pieces are still whole, he says before it, "Who createst the various kinds of foods", and after it one blessing which includes three'. But it has been taught: After it he need
c not say any blessing at all?[1]—R. Shesheth replied: There is no contradiction: the one statement expresses the view of R. Gamaliel, the other that of the Rabbis, as it has been taught: This is the general rule: after partaking of anything that belongs to the seven species,[2] R. Gamaliel says that three blessings should be said, while the Rabbis say, one that includes three. Once R. Gamaliel and the elders were reclining in an upper chamber in Jericho, and dates[3] were brought in and they ate, and R. Gamaliel gave permission to R. Akiba to say grace, and R. Akiba said quickly the one blessing which includes three. Said R. Gamaliel to him: Akiba, how long will you poke your head into quarrels?[4] He replied: Master, although you say this way and your colleagues say the other way, you have taught us, master, that where an individual joins issue with the majority, the *halachah* is determined by the majority. R. Judah said in his [R. Gamaliel's] name:[5] [After partaking of]

(1) The benediction, 'for the nourishment and the sustenance etc.', V. *infra* 44a; v. *P.B.* p. 287ff. (2) Ibid. p. 290. (3) For the purpose of a blessing.
(1) That rice counts as a cooked dish. (2) If eaten on Passover. V. Glos. (3) V. Ex. XII, 19. (4) I.e., have not been softened into a pulp. (5) The grace after meals which originally consisted of three blessings. V. *infra* 46a. (6) Who requires (*infra* 40a) a separate blessing for each kind of fruit or vegetable.

c (1) Rashi explains this to mean, not one of the blessings said after the seven species of food, but simply 'who createst many living creatures etc.', (v. *infra*, and *P.B.* p. 287ff.). (2) Enumerated in Deut. VIII, 8. (3) One of the 'seven species', being included in the term '*honey*' in Deut. VIII, 8. (4) I.e., go against me. (5) So Rashi. We should rather, however, expect it to be R. Akiba's, as R. Gamaliel is mentioned in the statement, and R. Judah can hardly have been a disciple of R. Gamaliel.

קמ"ל כל שיש בו ואי אשמעינן כל שיש בו הוה אמינא כל שיש בו ה' המינים אין *אבל אורז ודוחן לא משום דעל ידי תערובות אבל איתיה בעיניה נימ' אפילו אורז ודוחן נמי מברכין עליו בורא מיני מזונות קמ"ל כל שהוא מה' המינים הוא דמברכים עליו במ"מ לאפוקי אורז ודוחן דאפילו איתיה בעיני' לא מברכינן במ"מ ואורז [ודוחן] לא מברכינן במ"מ והתניא הביאו לפניו פת אורז ופת דוחן מברך עליו תחלה וסוף כמעשה קדרה וגבי מעשה קדרה תניא בתחלה מברך עליו בורא מיני מזונות ולבסוף מברך עליו ברכה אחת מעין שלש כמעשה קדרה ולא כמעשה קדרה כמעשה קדרה דמברכין עליו תחלה וסוף ולא כמעשה קדרה דאלו במעשה קדרה בתחלה במ"מ ולבסוף ברכה אחת מעין שלש ואלו הכא בתחלה מברך עליו שהכל נהיה בדברו ולבסוף בורא נפשות רבות וחסרונן על כל מה שברא ואורז לאו מעשה קדרה הוא והתניא אלו הן מעשה קדרה חילקא טרגים סלת זריז וערסן ואורז הא מני ר' יוחנן בן נורי היא דתניא *ר' יוחנן בן נורי אומר אורז מין דגן הוא וחייבין על המוצו כרת ואדם יוצא בו ידי חובתו בפסח אבל רבנן לא ורבנן לא והתניא *הכוסס את החטה מברך עליה בורא פרי ד אדמה טחנה אפאה ובשלה בזמן שהפרוסות קיימות בתחלה מברך עליה המוציא לחם מן הארץ ולבסוף מברך עליה ג' ברכות אם אין הפרוסות קיימות בתחלה מברך עליה במ"מ ולבסוף מברך עליה ברכה אחת מעין שלש הכוסס את האורז מברך עליו בפ"הא טחנו אפאו ובשלו אע"פ שהפרוסות קיימות בתחלה מברך עליו במ"מ ולבסוף מברך עליו ברכה אחת מעין שלש מני אילימא ר' יוחנן בן נורי היא דאמר אורז מין דגן הוא המוציא לחם מן הארץ ושלש ברכות בעי ברוכי אלא לאו רבנן היא ותיובתא דרב ושמואל תיובתא: אמר מר הכוסס את החטה מברך עליה פ"ב האדמה והתניא בורא מיני זרעים לא קשיא הא ר' יהודה והא רבנן דתנן *ועל הירקות אומר ב"פ האדמה ר' יהודה אומר בורא מיני דשאים: אמר מר הכוסס את האורז מברך עליו ב"פ האדמה טחנו אפאו ובשלו אע"פ שהפרוסות קיימות בתחלה מברך עליו בורא מ"מ ולבסוף ברכה אחת מעין שלש והתניא לבסוף ולא כלום אמר רב ששת לא קשיא הא ר"ג והא רבנן דתניא *זה הכלל כל שהוא משבעת המינים רבן גמליאל אומר שלש ברכות וחכ"א ברכה אחת מעין שלש ומעשה ברבן גמליאל והזקנים שהיו מסובין בעלייה ביריחו והביאו לפניהם כותבות ואכלו ונתן רבן גמליאל רשות לר"ע לברך קפץ ובירך ר"ע ברכה אחת מעין שלש א"ל רבן גמליאל עקיבא עד מתי אתה מכניס ראשך בין המחלוקת א"ל רבינו אע"פ שאתה אומר כן וחביריך אומרים כן למדתנו רבינו *יחיד ורבים הלכה כרבים ר' יהודה אומר משמו כל שהוא משבעת המינים ולא

קמ"ל כל שהוא. דאע"ג דכולהו מחד מינא בעינן דליהוי מחמשת המינין והאי לא מברכינן עליה בורא מיני מזונות: אורז. מי"ל: דוחן. פנ"ץ: כמעשה קדירה. ברכה שמברכין על מעשה קדירה של ה' מינין: ברכה אחת מעין ג'. בשלהי פרקין (דף מד.) מפרש לה על המחיה כו': ואורז לאו מעשה קדירה. דקא מפקת ליה מכלל מעשה קדירה לברכה אחרת: אלו הן מעשה קדירה. לענין ברכה: חילקא טרגים זריז וערסן. מפרש להו במועד קטן (פ"ב דף יג:). חילקא. חיטי דמתברי באסיתא חדא לתרתי. טרגים. חדא לתלת. זריז. חדא לארבע. ערסן. חדא לחמש: הא מני. הך מתניתא דקתני אורז כמעשה קדרה ר' יוחנן בן נורי: ה"ג אבל רבנן לא ורבנן לא והתניא כו' ול"ג והלכתא ומהלכות גדולות הוא: הכוסס. כמות שהיא: אפאה ובשלה. לאחר שאפאה בתנור ועשא' לחם חזר ובשלה במים: שהפרוסות קיימות. שלא נמוחו בבשולן: ברכה אחת מעין שלש. על המחיה ועל הכלכלה ובשלהי פרקין (דף מד.) מפרש לה: אלא לאו רבנן היא. וקתני בורא מיני מזונות ותיובתא דרב ושמואל: הא רבי יהודה כו'. הא דקתני בורא מיני זרעים ר' יהודה היא דקתני לכל מין ומין מעין ברכתו כדמפרש לקמן (דף מ.) בפרקין אליביה הלכך לירקות בורא מיני דשאים לחטים דזרעים נינהו בורא מיני זרעים ולרבנן בין זרעים בין ירקות ב"פ האדמה ולא בעינן לכל מין ומין מעין ברכתו: ולא כלום. כלומר אין טעון מברכות פירות ארץ ישראל ולא כלום אלא בורא נפשות רבות ככל מידי דליתיה משבעת המינין: כותבות. הם תמרים והם דבש האמור בשבעת המינין שהדבש זב מן התמרים: קפץ ובירך. לאחריהן: משמו. של ר"ג: ולא

בורא נפשות רבות וחסרונם. כמו לחם ומים שאי אפשר בלא הם *ועל כל מה שברא להחיות בהם נפש כל חי כלומר על כל מה שבעולם שגם אם לא בראם יכולין העולם להחיות בלא הם שלא בראם כי אם להתענג בעלמא כמו תפוחים וכיוצא בהן ומסיים ברוך חי העולמים ובירושלמי ברוך אתה ה' חי העולמים:

אם הפרוסות קיימות. יש מפרשים דהיינו כשהלחם אינו שרוי במי' כ"כ שאם יקח הפרוס' בלא ישבר:

רש"י פי' אורז מי"ל. ויש מפרשים רי"ז ולהאי פירו' יש לפרש דדוחן היינו מי"ל:

תיובתא דרב ושמואל. באורז אבל אדוחן לא הוי תיובתא ואפשר דהוי' הלכת' כותייהו ולא מברכינן עליה בור' מיני מזונות:

הכוסס חטה צריך לברך עליה ב"פ האדמה. שהרי אפילו בקמחא דחיטי אמרינן לעיל ומברכי' עליה ב"פ האדמה ולרב נחמן לא ס"ל הכי משום דאשתנו ומיהו בלאחריו יש לספק מאי מברכין אם מברכין על המחי' ועל הכלכלה ומסיי' על האדמה ועל פרי האדמה דלא אשכחן ברכת על המחי' ועל הכלכלה אלא היכא דצריך עלייהו ברישא קודם אכילה בורא מיני מזונות ור"ת הגיה במחזור שלו על האדמה ועל פרי האדמה כו' וחזר בו דלא אשכחן בשום מקום הך ברכה דלקמן (דף מד.) מפרש ברכה אחת מעין ג' וקאמר בחמשת המינים על הארץ ועל המחיה ועל ז' המינים על הארץ ועל הפירו' ועל האדמה ועל פרי האדמ' לא הזכיר ועוד ודקאמר הכא על הכוסס את החטה מברך ב"פ האדמה וקאמר בהדיה טחנו ואפאו פת עד אם אין הפרוסות קיימות בתחלה מברך בורא מ"מ ולבסוף ברכה אחת מעין שלש ומדלא קתני הכא גבי כוסס החטה מברך לאחריו ברכה אחת מעין שלש ש"מ דבכוסס ליכא ברכה לאחריו מעין ג' והא דקאמר כל שהוא מין דגן ולא עשאו פת וכו' וחכ"א ברכה אחת מעין ג' מיירי דעבדינהו כעין דייסא דחשיבא אז אכילתו אבל הכוסס את החטה חי דלא חשיבא אכילתו כ"כ אע"ג דהיא מן ה' המינין אינו מברך אחריו ברכה מעין שלש אלא בורא נפשות רבות וכו' ומיהו אומר הר"י שיש לספק שמא חכמים קיילי ליה בההוא מין דגן ולא עשאו פת וכו' וחכמים אומרים ברכה אחת מעין ג' ונכון להחמיר שאין לאכול קליות או חטים שלוקות אלא בתוך הסעודה שאז ברכת המזון פוטרתן אם לא נתמעכו יפה דהוו כמו דייסא ובירושלמי יש שגם האמוראים היו מסופקים דקאמר הדין דאכיל סלת פירוש קליות מאי מברך בסופה רבי ירמיה אמר לא אכלית סלת מן יומא וכו':

נתן ר"ג רשות לרבי עקיבא לברך. סבור היה שיברך ג' ברכות כמו שהוא סובר וא"ת לר"ג הא קי"ל *דאין מזמנים על הפירות וי"ל דר"ג היה סבור שהיה מברך על כל ז' מינין ג' ברכות שלמות וכי בירך ר' עקיבא מעין ג' לעצמו דוקא דקי"ל אין מזמנין על הפירות והאחרים המסובים ברכו כל אחד לעצמו וא"ת לר"ג דאמר ג' ברכות שלמות וס"ל דמזמנים על ז' המינים א"כ ס"ל דברכה טעונה כוס א"כ יזמנו ואח"כ יזמנו לעולם וי"ל דיכול להיות שלא ישתו כלל מן כוס של ברכה וא"ת מ"מ לאותו המברך שהוא טועם צריך לברך פעם אחרת ואם כן אין לדבר סוף וי"ל היכא דאינו שותה בקביעות רק מלא לוגמיו מודה ר"ג דאם לא כן וכי לית ליה לר"ג ברכה אחת מעין שלש בשום מקום: [וע"ע תוספות פסחים קה: ד"ה ש"מ]:

חביצא

עין משפט נר מצוה

[ע' ב"ח סי' רז ובעט"ז שם]

לה א מיי' פ"ג מהלכ' ברכות הל' יוד סמג עשין כז טוש"ע א"ח סי' רח סעי' ז

לו ב מיי' וסמג שם טוש"ע שם סעיף ב

לז ג מיי' פ"ה ה"א ופ"ו ה"ד מהלכ' חמץ ומצה סמג לאוין עה טוש"ע א"ח סי' תנג סעיף א

לח ד מיי' פ"ג מהלכ' ברכות הלכה ב טוש"ע א"ח סי' רח סעי' ד

לט ה מיי' שם הלכה א סמג עשין כז טוש"ע א"ח סי' קסח סעי' י

מ ו מיי' שם הל' יוד וסמג שם טוש"ע א"ח סי' רח סעיף ז

מסורת הש"ס

פסחים לה. וקיד:

תוספת' פ"ד

לעיל לה.

תוספת' פ"ד

[לעיל ע. וש"נ]

[חולין קו.]

ולא מין דגן הוא או מין דגן ולא עשאו פת ר"ג אומר ג' ברכות וחכמים אומרים ברכה אחת כל שאינו לא משבעת המינים ולא מין דגן כגון פת אורז ודוחן רבן גמליאל אומר *ברכה אחת מעין שלש וחכ"א ולא כלום במאי אוקימתא כר"ג אימא סיפא דרישא אם אין הפרוסות קיימו' בתחלה מברך עליה בורא מיני מזונות ולבסוף מברך עליה ברכה אחת מעין שלש מני אי ר"ג השתא אכותבות ואדייסא אמר ר"ג ג' ברכות אם אין הפרוסות קיימות מבעיא אלא פשיטא רבנן אי הכי קשי' דרבנן אדרבנן אלא לעולם רבנן ותני גבי אורז ולבסוף אינו מברך עליו ולא כלום: אמר רבא האי ריהטא דחקלאי דמפשי ביה קמחא מברך במ"מ מ"ט דסמידא עיקר דמחוזא דלא מפשי ביה קמחא מברך עליו שהכל נהיה בדברו מ"ט דובשא עיקר *והדר אמר רבא [לקמן] אידי ואידי במ"מ דרב ושמואל דאמרי תרוייהו כל שיש בו מה' המינים מברכין עליו במ"מ אמר רב יוסף *האי חביצא דאית ביה פרורין כזית בתחלה מברך עליו המוציא לחם מן הארץ ולבסוף מברך עליו ג' ברכות דלית ביה פרורין כזית בתחלה מברך עליו בורא מיני מזונות ולבסוף ברכה אחת מעין שלש אמר רב יוסף מנא אמינא לה *דתניא היה עומד ומקריב מנחות בירושלים אומר ברוך שהחיינו וקיימנו והגיענו לזמן הזה נטלן לאכלן מברך המוציא למ"ה ותני עלה וכולן פותתן כזית א"ל אביי אלא מעתה לתנא *דבי ר' ישמעאל דאמר פורכן עד שמחזירן לסלתן ה"נ דלא בעי ברוכי המוציא לחם מן הארץ וכי תימא ה"נ והתניא לקט מכולן כזית ואכלן אם חמץ הוא ענוש כרת ואם מצה היא אדם יוצא בו ידי חובתו בפסח הכא במאי עסקינן בשערסן אי הכי אימא סיפא והוא שאכלן בכדי אכילת פרס ואי בשערסן האי בשאכלן שאכלו מבעי ליה הכא במאי עסקינן בבא מלחם גדול מאי הוה עלה אמר רב ששת האי חביצא אע"ג דלית ביה פרורין כזית מברך עליו המוציא לחם מן הארץ אמר רבא והוא דאיכא עליה תוריתא דנהמא טרוקנין חייבין בחלה וכי אתא רבין א"ר יוחנן טרוקנין פטורין מן החלה מאי טרוקנין אמר אביי כובא דארעא ואמר אביי טריתא פטור מן החלה מאי טריתא איכא דאמרי גביל מרתח ואיכא דאמרי נהמא דהנדקא ואיכא דאמרי לחם העשוי לכותח תני ר' חייא לחם העשוי לכותח פטור מן החלה והא תניא חייב בחלה התם כדקתני טעמא ר' יהודה אומר מעשיה מוכיחין עליה עשאן כעבין

ולא מין דגן. שבמין דגן יש חילוק שאם עשאו פת הכל מודים שצריך לאחריו ג' ברכות: או. אף אם מין דגן הוא אלא שלא עשאו פת בשתים אלו נחלקו ר"ג וחכמים: במאי אוקימתא. להאי דלעיל דקתני ולבסוף ברכה אחת מעין שלש: כר"ג אימא סיפא דרישא. דהיא מתני' דמתני גבי הכוסס את החטה דהיא רישא דידה וקתני סיפא אין הפרוסות קיימות כו': השתא. אפילו אדייסא אמר ר"ג במתני' בתרייתא או מין דגן ולא עשאו פת מברך אחריו ג' ברכות: אין הפרוסות קיימות. שבתחלתו פת ממש היה: מבעיא. ובשכמות מי גרע מדייסא: אלא לאו רבנן היא. דאמרי גבי דייסא ברכה אחת והאי כמי משכמות לאו פת הוא והוי כדייסא: והלכתא לא גרסינן: רידטא. הוא חבין קדרה דחקלאי. בני כפר: דמפשי ביה קמחא. שמרבים בו קמח: דמחוזא. בני כרך: חביצא. כעין שלביי"קוק שמפררין בתוך האלפס לחם: מנא אמינא לה. דאפרורין כזית מברכין המוציא: היה. ישראל עומד ומקריב מנחות. ונתנה לכהן להקריבה: אומר ברוך שהחיינו. אם לא הביא מנחות זה ימים רבים: נטלן לאכלן. הכהן: ותני עלה. כלומר ותנן על המנחות מנחת מחבת ומנחת מרחשת הקרבות כשהן אפויות: וכלן פותתן. כלו' בולען קודם קמיצה ועושה אותן פתיתין כזתים כדכתיב פתות אותה פתים (ויקרא ב) אלמא פתיתין כזתים מברך עליהן המוציא: מפרכן. למנחות האפויות על המחבת ועל המרחשת קודם קמיצה עד שמחזירן לסלתן: הכי נמי. דפליג אהא דקתני מברך המוציא: והתניא לקט מכולן. פתיתי המנחות: כזית כו'. ומדקאמר יוצא בו ידי חובתו בפסח משום אכילת מצה דמצות עשה היא דכתיב בערב תאכלו מצות והתם לחם בעינן דכתיב בה לחם עוני אלמ' לחם הוי ומברך המוציא והא מתניתין על כרחך רבי ישמעאל היא דהא קתני לקט מכולן כזית אלמא בפתיתין פחותין מכזית קאי: בשערסן. כשחזר וגבלן יחד וחזר ואפאן. ערסן לשון עריסותיכם: והוא שאכלן בכדי אכילת פרס. שלא ישהה משהתחיל לאכול שיעור כזית עד שגמר אכילת השיעור יותר מכדי אכילת חצי ככר של שמונה ביצים דהוי חציו ד' ביצים שזהו צירוף שיעור אכילה ואם שהה יותר אין האכילה מצטרפת והוה ליה כאוכל חצי זית היום וחצי זית למחר ואין בו חיוב כרת אם חמץ הוא: ואי בשערסן והוא שאכלו. לשון יחיד מבעי ליה: הכא במאי עסקינן. ובשלא ערסן היא וכדקאמרת והא דקתני דחשיב למהוי לחם בבא מלחם גדול ונשאר מן הלחם שלא נפרס כולו אבל אם נפרס כולו לא חשיבי פתיתין הפחותים מכזית ולא מברכין המוציא ואין יוצא בהן ידי חובת מצה בפסח: תוריתא דנהמא. תואר מראית הלחם: כובא דארעא. עושה מקום חלל בכירה ונותן בתוכו מים וקמח כמו שעושין באלפס: גביל מרתח. נותנים קמח ומים בכלי וטורחין בכף ושופכים על הכירה כשהיא נסקת: נהמא דהנדקא. בלק שאופין בספוד ומושחים אותו תמיד בשמן או במי ביצים ושמן: לחם העשוי לכותח. אין אופין אותו בתנור אלא בחמה:

כעבין

חביצא דאית ביה פרורין פירש"י כמו שלביי"קוק וא"ת והתניא לעיל בזמן שהפרוסות וכו' אין הפרוסות קיימות לא יברך עליהן המוציא אע"ג דאית ביה כזית וי"ל דרב יוסף מפרש ליה הפרוסות קיימות היינו בכזית ואין הפרוסות קיימות בשאין בהן כזית וכן מפרש נמי בירושלמי וא"ת ואיך מדמה רב יוסף פרורי מנחות לפרורי חביצא וי"ל כיון שנטגנין בשמן כנתבשלו דמי ומיהו קשה דלקט מכולן כזית דקאי אמחבת המיכין ולא אמנחות כמו שאפרש והתם נמי לא מיירי בשנתבשלו ואולי מדמה לחביצא שהוא מבושל לכך נ"ל חביצא היינו פרורין הנדבקים יחד על ידי מרק או על ידי חלב כמו חביצא דתמרי שהן נדבקין:

היה עומד ומקריב מנחות. פירש"י בעל הבית המתנדב מנחה ודוחק גדול הוא דהיה עומד ומקריב משמע דכהן המקריב וכן לישנא נטלן לאכלן משמע דאכהן קאי ונראה בכהן העומד להקריב ראשון במשמרתו וכ"ד משמרות היו וכל שבת מתחדשת משמרה אחרת א"כ כל משמרה איכה משמרת אלא ב' פעמים בשנה וכיון שיש *להם [לקמן] זמן קבוע מברכין שהחיינו ולא כפירש"י דמנחות דמיירי בכהן שלא הקריב מעולם:

לקט מכולן. פירש"י דקאי אמנחו' ולא נראה דאם כן היכי קאמר דאם חמץ הוא וכו' והא אמרי' (במנחות דף נב:) כל המנחות באות מצה ונראה דקאי אחמש' מינין וה"ק לקט מכל מיני לחמים כזית כו':

אמר רבא והוא דאיכא עלייהו תוריתא דנהמא. וכן קיימ' לן דרבא בתרא' הוא ולא בעינן שיהו בפרורין כזית כיון דאיכא תורית' דנהמ' לענין המוציא ואפילו נתבשלו לפירוש רש"י והא דמשמע בירושלמי דפרוסות קיימות הן בכזית היינו לפי שכן דרך להיות תוריתא דנהמא בכזית אבל פעמים דאפילו בפחות מכזית איכא תוריתא דנהמא: תוריתא דנהמא. נראה דהיינו כשמתני' הפרורין במים ואם המים מתלבנים מחמת הפרורין אז ליה תוריתא דנהמא וכן היה רגיל רבינו דוד ממיץ ללבן פרורין במים הלילה כדי לאכלן בשחר בלא ברכת המוציא ובלא ברכת המזון שלא לאחר כדי שיתחזק לאשו ויוכל להגיד ההלכה:

לחם העשוי לכותח פטור מן החלה. והיינו כשעשאו כלמודים ופירש רש"י עיסה שמייבשים בחמה וקשה דהא אמרינן במסכת חלה (פ"א משנ' ה) כל שתחלתו עיסה וסופו סופגנין חייבין בחלה וכל שתחלתו סופגנין וסופו עיסה חייבין נמי בחלה ושתחלתו סופגנין וסופו נמי סופגנין פטור מן החלה ופסק ר"ת אם כן בביצ"לים וריי"סולש דתחלתן עיסה מברכין עליהן המוציא וחייבין בחלה אף על פי דסופן סופגנין ומתחלה היה ר"ל ר"ת דדוקא חייבין בחלה דמצות חלה בעודן עיסה דכתיב עריסותיכם והואיל שהיו מתחלה עיסה חייבין בחלה אבל מן המוציא פטורים דעכשיו הם סופגנין ול"כ דהא לעיל קתני נטלן לאכלן מברך עליהן המוציא גבי מנחה אף על פי דעכשיו הם סופגנין שהמנחות מטוגנו' בשמן: ויר"מ"שיש אע"ג דחייבין בחלה שהיו עיסה מתחל' פטורין מהמוציא ואין מברכין עליהם אלא במ"מ דליתא להו תוריתא דנהמא ואח"כ ברכה מעין ג' על המחיה ועל הכלכלה ורבינו יחיאל ז"ל היה מסופק

עין משפט נר מצוה

מא אמיי' פ"ג מהל' ברכות הל' ג סמג עשין כז טוש"ע א"ח סי' רח סעי' ב

מב במיי' פ"ז מהל' המידין ומוספין הל' יח

מג גמיי' פי"ג מהלכו' מעשה הקרבנות הל' י

מד דהמיי' פ"ג מהל' ברכות הל' ח סמג עשין כז טוש"ע א"ח סי' קסח סעיף י

מה ומיי' פ"ו מהל' בכורים הל' יב סמג עשין קמא טוש"ע י"ד סי' שכט סעיף ה וטוש"ע א"ח סי' קסח סעיף טו

מו חטוש"ע א"ח שם סעיף יז

מז טמיי' פ"ו מהל' בכורים הל' יד סמג עשין קמא טוש"ע י"ד סי' שכט סעיף ז

מסורת הש"ס

(בירוש' גרס מברך לפניו ולאחריו ולא נזכר מעין ג')

[מעין זה שבת פ:: ושם נסמן]

מנחות עה:

שם

(בירוש' תני ר"י אפי' מהזירה לסולתה)

any food from the seven species [37b], not being a kind of corn or which belongs to one of the kinds of corn but has not been made into bread, R. Gamaliel says that three blessings are to be said, while the Sages say, only one blessing [which includes three]. [After] anything which belongs neither to the seven species nor to any kind of corn, for instance bread of rice or millet, R. Gamaliel says that one blessing which includes three is to be said, while the Sages say, no grace at all. To which authority do you then assign this statement?[6] To R. Gamaliel. Look now at the latter
a half of the first statement[1] viz., 'if the pieces are no longer whole, he says before partaking "who createst various kinds of foods", and after partaking one blessing which includes three'. Whose view does this express? Shall I say that of R. Gamaliel? Seeing that R. Gamaliel requires a grace of three blessings after dates and pounded grain,[2] is there any question that he should require it if the pieces are no longer whole?[3] Hence, obviously, it must be the view of the Rabbis.[4] If that is the case, there is a contradiction between two statements of the Rabbis?[5]—No; I still say, it is the view of the Rabbis; and in connection with rice you should read, 'after partaking he does not say any blessing'.

Raba said: Over the *rihata*[6] of the field workers, in which there is a large quantity of flour, the blessing said is 'who createst various kinds of foods'. What is the reason? The flour is the main ingredient. Over the *rihata* of the townspeople in which there is not so much flour, the blessing said is 'by whose word all things exist'. What is the reason? The main ingredient is the honey. Raba, however, corrected himself and said: Over both the blessing is 'who createst various kinds of foods'. For Rab and Samuel both laid down that over anything containing one of the five species as an ingredient, the blessing to be said is 'who createst various kinds of foods'.

R. Joseph said: If in a *ḥabiẓ* there are pieces of bread[7] as big as an olive, the blessing said before it is 'who bringest forth bread from the earth', and after it a grace of three blessings is said. If there are no pieces as big as an olive in it, the blessing said before it is 'who createst various kinds of foods', and after it one blessing which includes three. Said R. Joseph: Whence do I derive this?
b Because it has been taught: If one[1] is in the act of offering meal-offerings in Jerusalem, he says, 'Blessed be He that hath kept us alive and preserved us and brought us to this season'. When he[2] takes them up in order to eat them, he says the blessing, 'Who bringest forth bread from the earth', and it was taught in this connection, They are all[3] broken into fragments of the size of an olive.[4] Said Abaye to him: If that is so, then similarly according to the Tanna of the school of R. Ishmael who says that he crushes them until he reduces them to flour, he should not require to say 'who bringest forth bread from the earth'? And should you reply that that is indeed the case, has it not been taught: If he scraped together as much as an olive from all of them[5] and ate [all of] it, if it is leaven he is punished with *kareth*,[6] and if it is unleaven a man may perform his obligation with it on Passover?[7]—With what case are we dealing here?[8] If he re-kneaded the crumbs.[9] If so, look at the next clause: This is only if he ate them within the time which it takes to eat half [a roll].[10] Now if they are re-kneaded, instead of saying 'to eat *them*', it should say, 'to eat *it*'? [Rather] with what case are we here dealing? When it comes from a large loaf.[11] Now what do we decide upon this matter? R. Shesheth said: If the crumbs of bread in a *ḥabiẓ* are even less than an olive, the benediction 'who bringest forth bread from the earth' is said over it. Raba added: This is only if they still have the appearance of bread.

c *Troknin*[1] is subject to the law of *ḥallah*. When Rabin came, he said in the name of R. Joḥanan: *Troknin* is not subject to the law of *ḥallah*. What is *Troknin*?—Abaye said: [Dough baked] in a cavity made in the ground.

Abaye also said: *Ṭarita* is exempt from the obligation of *ḥallah*. What is *ṭarita*?—Some say, dough just lightly baked;[2] others say, bread baked on a spit;[3] others again, bread used for *kuttaḥ*.[4] R. Ḥiyya said: Bread used for *kuttaḥ* is not liable to *ḥallah*. But it has been taught that it is liable for *ḥallah*?—There the reason is stated: Rab Judah says that the way it is made shows what it is; if it is

(6) That after rice one has to say the one blessing including three.
a (1) In the above-cited Baraitha, 'if one chews wheat etc.', *supra* 37a.
(2) Which is the same as 'corn which has not been made into bread', mentioned in the Baraitha quoted above. (3) Since they were originally bread. (4) Who hold that after pounded grain (v. n. 2) only the one blessing which includes three is said, and where the pieces are no longer whole the cooked wheat is treated like pounded grain. (5) There the Rabbis declare that after bread made of rice no benediction is necessary, while in the previously cited Baraitha they are said to require one benediction which includes three. (6) A dish resembling the *ḥabiẓ*, and containing the same ingredients. (7) I.e., if bread is broken up into it.
b (1) According to Rashi, this is the layman who gives it to the priest to offer; according to Tosaf., the priest himself. (2) The priest. (3) I.e., all the various kinds of meal-offerings mentioned in Lev. II. (4) V. Lev. II, 6. This proves that crumbs must be at least the size of an olive for the benediction 'Who bringest forth bread' to be said. (5) The various kinds of meal-offerings. Tosaf., however, refers it to ordinary crumbs of different species of cereals, since the continuation, 'if it is leaven etc.', could not apply to meal-offerings which had to be unleavened. (6) If he eats it on Passover. (7) And of course the prescribed blessing 'who bringest forth etc.', must be said over it also. (8) In the teaching last cited. (9) Making them into a compact mass. (10) A piece of bread the size of four eggs. If he does not eat the size of an olive within this time, it does not count for any purpose. (11) Some of which still remains unbroken, even though he did not reknead the bread crumbs.
c (1) Bread baked in a hole in the ground. (2) By being poured on the hot hearth and formed into fritters. (3) And covered with oil, or eggs and oil. *Aliter*: 'Indian bread'. (4) A dish made of bread mixed with sour milk and baked in the sun.

made [38*a*] like cakes, it is liable for *ḥallah*, if like boards,[5] it is not liable.

Abaye said to R. Joseph: What blessing is said over dough baked in a cavity in the ground?—He replied: Do you think it is bread? It is merely a thick mass, and the blessing said over it is 'who createst various kinds of foods'. Mar Zuṭra made it the basis of his meal and said over it the blessing, 'who bringest forth bread from the earth' and three blessings after it. Mar son of R. Ashi said: The obligation of Passover can be fulfilled with it. What is the reason? We apply to it the term, 'bread of affliction'.

Mar son of R. Ashi also said: Over honey of the date-palm we say, 'by whose word all things exist'.[6] What is the reason?—Because it is merely moisture [of the tree]. With whose teaching does this accord?—With that of the following Tanna, as we have learnt: With regard to the honey of the date-palm and cider and vinegar from stunted grapes[7] and other fruit juices of *terumah*, R. Eliezer requires [in case of sacrilege] payment of the value
a and an additional fifth,[1] but R. Joshua exempts [from the additional fifth].[2]

One of the Rabbis asked Raba: What is the law with regard to *trimma?*[3] Raba did not quite grasp what he said. Rabina was sitting before Raba and said to the man: Do you mean of sesame[4] or of saffron[5] or of grape-kernels?[6] Raba thereupon bethought himself[7] and said: You certainly mean *ḥashilta*;[8] and you have reminded me of something which R. Assi said: It is permissible to make *trimma*[9] of dates of *terumah*, but forbidden to make mead of them.[10] The law is that over dates which have been used to make into *trimma* we say the blessing 'who createst the fruit of the tree'. What is the reason? They are still in their natural state.

With regard to *shatitha*,[11] Rab said that the blessing is 'by whose word all things were made', while Samuel said that it is 'who createst various kinds of foods'. Said R. Ḥisda: They do not really differ: the latter is said over the thick variety, the former over the thin. The thick is made for eating, the thin for a medicine. R. Joseph raised an objection to this: Both alike[12] say that we may stir up a *shatitha* on Sabbath and drink Egyptian beer. Now if you think that he intends it as a remedy, is a medicine permitted on Sabbath?—Abaye replied: And do you hold that it is not? Have we not learnt: All foods may be eaten on Sabbath for medical purposes and all drinks may be drunk?[13] But what you must say is: in these cases the man intends it for food;[14] here too, the man intends it for food. (Another version of this is: But what you can say is that the man intends it for food and the healing effect comes of itself. So here too, the man intends it for food, and the healing effect comes of itself.) And it was necessary to have this statement
b of Rab and Samuel.[1] For if I had only the other statement[2] I might think that [he says a blessing because] he intends it for food and the healing effect comes of itself; but in this case, since his first intention is to use it for healing, I might think that he should not say any blessing at all over it. We are therefore told that since he derives some enjoyment from it, he has to say a blessing.

FOR OVER BREAD IS SAID, WHO BRINGEST FORTH etc. Our Rabbis taught: What does he say? 'Who bringest forth [*ha-moẓi*] bread from the earth'. R. Nehemiah says: 'Bringing [*moẓi*][3] forth bread from the earth'. Both agree that the word *moẓi* means 'who has brought forth',[4] since it is written, *God who brought them forth* [moẓiam] *from Egypt*.[5] Where they disagree is as to the meaning of *ha-moẓi*. The Rabbis held that *ha-moẓi* means 'who has brought forth', as it is written, *Who brought thee forth* [ha-moẓi] *water out of the rock of flint*,[6] whereas R. Nehemiah held that *ha-moẓi* means 'who is bringing forth', as it says, *Who bringeth you out* [ha-moẓi] *from under the burden of the Egyptians*.[7] The Rabbis, however, say that those words spoken by the Holy One, blessed be He, to Israel were meant as follows: When I shall bring you out, I will do for you something which will show you that it is I who *brought you forth* from Egypt, as it is written, *And ye shall know that I am the Lord your God who* brought you out.[7]

The Rabbis used to speak highly to R. Zera of the son of R. Zebid[8] the brother of R. Simeon son of R. Zebid as being a great man and well versed in the benedictions. He said to them: When you get hold of him bring him to me. Once he came to his house and they brought him a loaf, over which he pronounced the blessing *moẓi*. Said R. Zebid: Is this the man of whom they say that he is a great man and well versed in benedictions? Had he said

(5) I.e., in flat thick pieces not resembling bread. (6) Not 'who createst the fruit of the tree'. (7) I.e., which never come to maturity. So Rashi; v.l. 'winter grapes'.

a (1) V. Lev. V, 15ff. (2) Because he does not regard these things as fruit. (3) τρίμμα, something pounded, but not out of recognition; here, a brew made of pounded fruit. (4) Pounded sesame over which wine is poured. (5) Saffron pounded to extract its oil. (6) Over which water is poured to make mead. (7) Rabina's question suggested to Raba the meaning of the question put to him. (8) A brew made with rounded date-stones. (9) I.e., a mere brew, not so strong as mead. (10) Because then they completely lose their identity. (11) Flour of dried barleycorns mixed with honey. (12) R. Judah and R. Jose b. Judah; v. Shab. 156*a*. (13) Shab. 109*b*. (14) And the healing effect is produced incidentally.

b (1) That *shatitha* though used for medicinal purpose is treated as food and requires a benediction, in addition to the teaching that it is regarded as food and may be partaken of on Sabbath. (2) That all foods may be consumed on Sabbath for medical purposes. (3) *Moẓi* is the present participle; *ha-moẓi* is the same with the definite article. (4) Which is the meaning required. (5) Num. XXIII, 22. (6) Deut. VIII, 15. (7) Ex. VI, 7. (8) So the text. There seems to be some corruption, and Goldschmidt reads: The Rabbis praised the father of R. Simeon b. Zebid to R. Zera b. Rab; cf. *D.S.*

בעבין חייבין בלמודים פטורים א"ל אביי לרב יוסף האי כובא דארעא מאי מברכין עליה א"ל מי סברת נהמא הוא [א]גובלא בעלמא הוא ומברכין עליה בפה"מ מר זוטרא [ב]קבע סעודתיה עליה וברך עליה המוציא לחם מן הארץ וג' ברכות אמר מר בר רב אשי [ג]ואדם יוצא בהן ידי חובתו בפסח מ"ט °לחם עוני קרינן ביה ואמר מר בר רב אשי [ד]האי דובשא דתמרי מברכין עליה שהכל נהיה בדברו מ"ט זיעה בעלמא הוא כמאן כי האי תנא דתנן *דבש תמרים ויין תפוחים וחומץ ספוניות ושאר מי פירות של תרומה ר"א מחייב קרן וחומש ור' יהושע [ה]פוטר א"ל ההוא מרבנן לרבא טרימא מהו לא הוה אדעתיה דרבא מאי קאמר ליה יתיב רבינא קמיה דרבא א"ל דשומשמי קא אמרת או דקורטמי קא אמרת או דפורצני קא אמרת אדהכי והכי אסקיה רבא לדעתיה א"ל חשילתא ודאי קא אמרת ואדכרתן מלתא הא דאמר רב אסי [ו]האי תמרי של תרומה מותר לעשות מהן טרימא ואסור לעשות מהן שכר והלכתא [ז]תמרי ועבדינהו טרימא מברכין עלויהו בורא פרי העץ מ"ט במלתייהו קיימי כדמעיקרא שתיתא רב אמר שהכל נהיה בדברו ושמואל אמר בפה"מ א"ר חסדא ולא פליגי [ח]הא בעבה הא ברכה עבה לאכילה עבדי לה רכה לרפואה קא עבדי לה מתיב רב יוסף *ושוין שבוחשין את השתות בשבת ושותין זיתום המצרי ואי ס"ד לרפואה קמכוין רפואה בשבת מי שרי א"ל אביי ואת לא תסברא והא *תנן [ט]כל האוכלין אוכל אדם לרפואה בשבת וכל המשקין שותה אלא מאי אית לך למימר גברא לאכילה קא מכוין ה"נ גברא לאכילה קא מכוין לישנא אחרינא אלא מאי אית לך למימר גברא לאכילה קא מכוין ורפואה ממילא קא הויא ה"נ לאכילה קא מכוין ורפואה ממילא קא הויא וצריכה דרב (ושמואל) דאי מהאי הוה אמינא לאכילה קא מכוין ורפואה ממילא קא הוי' אבל הכא *כיון דלכתחלה לרפואה קא מכוין לא לברך עליה כלל קמ"ל כיון דאית ליה הנאה מיני' בעי ברוכי: שעל הפת הוא אומר המוציא וכו': תנו רבנן מה הוא אומר המוציא לחם מן הארץ ר' *נחמיה אומר מוציא לחם מן הארץ אמר רבא במוציא כ"ע לא פליגי דאפיק משמע דכתיב °אל מוציאם ממצרים כי פליגי בהמוציא רבנן סברי המוציא דאפיק משמע דכתיב °המוציא לך מים מצור החלמיש ור' נחמיה סבר המוציא דמפיק משמע שנאמר °המוציא אתכם מתחת סבלות מצרים ורבנן ההוא הכי קאמר להו קב"ה לישראל כד מפיקנא לכו עבידנ' לכו מלתא כי היכי דידעיתו דאנא הוא דאפיקית יתכון ממצרים דכתיב °וידעתם כי אני ה' אלהיכם המוציא משתבחין ליה רבנן לר' זירא [את] בר רב זביד אחוה דר"ש בר רב זביד דאדם גדול הוא ובקי בברכות הוא אמר להם לכשיבא לידכם הביאוהו לידי זמנא חדא אקלע לגביה אפיקו ליה רפתא פתח ואמר מוציא אמר זה הוא שאומרים עליו דאדם גדול הוא ובקי בברכות הוא בשלמא אי אמר המוציא אשמעינן

תורה אור
דברים יו · במדבר כג · דברים ח · שמות ו · שם

רש"י

בעבין. עבה ומקושפת כגלוסקאות נאות גלי דעתי' דללחם עשאה: בלמודין. כנסרים בעלמא שלא הקפיד על עריסתם ודוגמתו שנינו במועד קטן (פ"ב דף יב.) עושה לו למודין לחין לבור של יין לכסותו: זיעה בעלמא הוא. ואינו פרי לברך עליו בורא פרי העץ: וחומץ ספוניות. סופי ענבי' שאין מתבשלים עולמית ועושי' מהן חומץ: מחייב קרן וחומש. לשות' ממנו בשוגג: ור' יהושע פוטר. דזיעה בעלמא הוא ואין שם תרומ' חל עליו ואין לך פרי הניתן למשקה אלא זתים וענבים בלבד והיינו כמר בר רב אשי: טרימ' מהו. מה מברכין עליו ושם טריטא כל דבר הכתוש קלת ואינו מרוסק: *לאו אדעתא דרבא. לא היה מבין מהו שואל: א"ל. רבינא להה' מרבנן איזו טרימ' אתה שואל: דקורטמי. כרכום שכותשין אותו ונותנין בו יין ושותין: או דשומשמי. להוליא שמנן: או דפורצני. כתישת ענבים לתת לתוך הקדרות מים לעשות תמד: א"ל רבא חשילתא קא אמרת. מתוך דברי רבינ' הבין רבא את השאלה א"ל דבר מעוך שאלתני כמו ביעי חשילתא דשחיטת חולין (דף מג.): מותר לעשות מהן טרימא. שאינו מפסידה אלא דבמלת' קאי וכיון דהכי הוא מברכין עליה בורא פרי העץ: שתיתא. קמח העשוי מקמח קליות שמתייבשו בתנור בעוד שהשבלים לחים*: עבה לאכילה עבידא. ובמלת' קיימא: שבוחשין. מגיסין בכף לערבו יפה במימיו: זיתום המצרי. מפרש במסכת פסחי' (דף מב:*): וכל המשקים שות'. אלמא לאכילה מכוין ורפואה ממילא הויא הכא נמי לאכיל' מכוין כו': וצריכא דרב ושמואל. ואף ע"ג דתני' לענין שבת דאוכל הוא ומות' לאכלו בשבת אצטריך למימר דטעון ברכה: ה"נ דסד"א כיון דלרפואה קא מכוין לא לבעי ברכה קמשמע לן כיון דמתהני מיניה שהרי מאכל הוא בעי ברוכי. והלכתא ל"ג ובהלכות גדולו' הוא: דאפיק משמע. שהוציא כבר והא ודאי ברכה הגונה דלשעבר בעינן שהרי כבר הוציא הלחם הזה מן הארץ שהוא בא ליהנות הימנו: דכתיב אל מוציאם ממצרים. וכשנאמר' פרשת בלעם כבר יצאו: המוציא לך מים. וכבר הוציא: ור' נחמי' סבר דמפיק משמע. שעתיד להוציא דכתיב המוציא אתכם וכשנאמר פסוק זה למשה עדיין לא יצאו והמוציא לך מים עדיין היה מוציא כל ימי היותם במדבר: דאפיקית יתכון. שאני הוא שהוצאתי אתכם:

לא הוה · סוטה מט. · חולין קכ: · זבחים לח: · פסחים מב · שבת קיא. · פסחים קט: · יומא מט. · לעיל לז. · גירסת הגר"א במקום הכמים

תוספות

מספק אם וירמ"ש חייבין בחלה משום עושה עיסתו כבלק כדי לחלקה פטורין מן החלה דלית בהו שיעורא הכא גבי וירמ"ש כמי פעמים מחלקן שאין משימין שיעור חלה בקדירה אחת אך היה מלכיך ליקח חלה בלא ברכה בשביל הספק וכל דבר שתחלתו סופגנין וסופו עיסה חייבין בחלה ובהמוליא דק"ל כר' יוחנן פרק כל שעה (דף לז.) דפליגי רבי יוחנן ור"ל במעשה אלפס ופליגי בבלילתו רכה דהיינו תחלתו סופגנין וסופו עיסה אם נאפה בתנור או בכיר' או באלפס בלא מים ושמן דר"ל ס"ל דלא הוי חייב אלא כשנאפה בתנור והא קאי מתני' תחלתו סופגנין וסופו עיסה דחייב בחלה אבל באלפ' פטור ורבי יוחנן מחייב דמעשה אלפס סופו עיסה קרינן ביה רק שלא יהיו משקין באלפס דהכי איתא בירושלמי כל שהאור תחתיו חייב בחלה ומברכין עליו המוליא אבל אכי"לים אין מברכין עליו המוליא דלא הוי אלא גובלא בעלמא ומיהו אם קבע סעודתי' עליהו כמו בפורי' מברך המוליא וכל דבר שתחלתו סופגנין וגם סופו כגון הני סופגנין שמטגנין אותן בשמן שקורין בוכ"יש *פטורין מן החלה:

מר זוטר' קבע סעודתי' עליה. וכן כי"לש אי קבע סעודתי' עלי' מברכין עליה המוליא וכן לוה הר"מ בפורים שקובעין סעודתן עליהן לברך המוליא בפת תחלה כדי לפטרן מברכה שהיה מסופק אי הוה קביעותיהו קביעות או לא:

האי דובשא דתמרי מברכין עליו שהכל. וכן משקין מכל מיני פירות בר מתירוש ויצהר כדאמרי' גבי ערל' *ולאפוקי מה"ג שפירש דמיירי שנתן לתוכן מים ושכר דידן אף ע"ג דשמא יש בהן כזית בכדי אכילת פרס לא מברכין עליו בורא מיני מזונות אלא שהכל ואפי' לרב ושמואל דאמרי כל שיש בו מחמשת המינין מברכין עליו בורא מיני מזונות הכא לא הוי בהו ממש שעורי' ואין שכר אלא טעמא בעלמא ועוד משום שיש בו עלויא אחריני' בפת ועוד בשתיה אומר שהכל:

ושוין שבוחשין. רבי ור' יוסי פליגי גבי כותן מים לתוך המורסן ובקליסה מיירי מדקתני ובוחשין ולא קתני לשון גבול והכי דייקינן התם:

ואי ס"ד לרפואה עבדי ליה רפואה בשבת מי שרי. דסובר דכיון דכל שעיקרו לרפואה ואין רגילו' לעשותו לצורך לאכילה אסור בשבת וכו':

והא תנן כל האוכלי' כו'. דמשמע מדנקט כל האוכלין דאפי' כל שעיקרו לרפואה כיון שראוי לאכיל' שפיר דמי מדנקט כל ומסיק הגמרא ולריכא דרב ושמואל דפשיטא למתכי' דשרי' אע"פ שעומד לרפואה אבל דרב ושמואל אשמעינן דלא כימ' כיון דעיקרו לרפואה לא לברך עלי' כלל קמ"ל כיון דמתהני מיני' בעי ברוכי ומ"מ לא יברך אלא שהכל כיון שאינו עשוי לסעוד כ"א לשתות ואם כן כל דבר שיש בו מחמשת המינין ואינו עשוי לסעוד כי אם לבתו' כגון שכר וכיולא בו מברך שהכל וכהאי גווני פסק בה"ג והלכתא שתיתא עבה מברך בורא מיני מזונות קלישתא מברך שהכל ואף ע"פ שלרפואה כעבית היכא דאית ליה הנאה מיניה מברך:

והלכתא

עין משפט נר מצוה

מח [א] מיי' פ"ג מה' ברכו' הל' ט טוש"ע א"ח סי' קס"ח סעי' טו
מט [ב] מיי' פ"ו מה' חמץ ומלה ה"ו טוש"ע א"ח סי' תס"א סעי' ד
נ [ד] מיי' פ"ח מהל' ברכו' ה"ד סמ"ג עשין כז טוש"ע א"ח סי' רב סעי' ח
נא [ה] מיי' פי"א מה' תרומות הל' ב
נב [ז] מיי' פ"ח מה' ברכו' ה"ד סמ"ג ע' כז טוש"ע א"ח סי' רב סעי' ז
[וע' תוס' פסחים לז: ד"ה דכ"ע]
נג [ח] טוש"ע א"ח סי' רח סעי' ו
נד [ט] מיי' פכ"א מהל' שבת הל' כב סמ"ג לאוין סה טוש"ע א"ח סי' שכח סעי' לז
[תרומות פ"א מ"ג]

אשמעינן טעמא ואשמעינן דהלכתא כרבנן אלא דאמר מוציא מאי קמ"ל ואיהו דעבד לאפוקי נפשיה מפלוגתא והלכתא ‏"המוציא לחם מן הארץ דקי"ל כרבנן דאמרי דאפיק משמע: ועל הירקות אומר וכו': קתני ירקות דומיא דפת מה פת שנשתנה ע"י האור אף ירקות נמי שנשתנו ע"י האור אמר רבנאי משמיה דאביי ‏"זאת אומרת שלקות מברכין עליהן בפ"הא (*ממאי מדקתני ירקות דומיא דפת) דרש רב חסדא משום רבינו ומנו רב שלקות מברכין עליהם ב"פ האדמה ורבותינו היורדין מארץ ישראל ומנו עולא משמיה דר' יוחנן אמר שלקות מברכין עליהן שהכל נהיה בדברו ואני אומר ‏"כל שתחלתו בפ"הא שלקו שהכל נהיה בדברו וכל שתחלתו שהכל נהיה בדברו שלקו בפ"הא בשלמא כל שתחלתו שהנ"ב שלקו בפ"הא משכחת לה בכרבא וסלקא וקרא אלא כל שתחלתו בפ"הא שלקו שהכל היכא משכחת לה א"ר נחמן בר יצחק משכחת לה ‏"בתומי וכרתי דרש רב נחמן משום רבינו ומנו שמואל שלקות מברכין עלידם בפ"הא וחבירנו היורדים מארץ ישראל ומנו עולא משמיה דר' יוחנן אמר שלקות מברכין עליהן שהנ"ב ואני אומר במחלוקת שנויה *דתניא יוצאין ברקיק השרוי ובמבושל שלא נמוח דברי ר"מ ור' יוסי אומר ‏"יוצאים ברקיק השרוי אבל לא במבושל אע"פ שלא נמוח ולא היא דכ"ע שלקות מברכין עליהן בפ"הא ועד כאן לא קאמר ר' יוסי התם אלא משום דבעינן טעם מצה וליכא אבל הכא אפילו רבי יוסי מודה א"ר חייא בר אבא א"ר יוחנן שלקות מברכין עליהם בפ"הא ור' בנימין בר יפת א"ר יוחנן שלקות מברכין עליהם שהנ"ב א"ר נחמן בר יצחק קבע עולא *לשבשתיה כרבי בנימין בר יפת *תהי בה ר' זירא וכי מה ענין ר' בנימין בר יפת אצל ר' חייא בר אבא ר' חייא בר אבא *דייק וגמיר שמעתא מרבי יוחנן רביה ורבי בנימין בר יפת לא דייק ועוד רבי חייא בר אבא כל *תלתין יומין מהדר תלמודיה קמי' דר' יוחנן רביה ור' בנימין בר יפת לא מהדר ועוד בר מן דין ובר מן דין דההוא תורמסא *דשלקי ליה שבע זמנין בקדירה ואכלי ליה בקנוח סעודה אתו ושאלו לר' יוחנן ואמר להו מברכינן עליה ב"פ האדמה ועוד א"ר חייא בר אבא אני ראיתי את ר' יוחנן שאכל זית מליח ובריך עליו תחלה וסוף אי אמרת בשלמא שלקות במלתידהו קיימי בתחלה מברך עליו ב"פ העץ ולבסוף מברך עליו ברכה אחת מעין שלש אלא אי אמרת שלקות לאו במלתייהו קיימי בשלמא בתחלה מברך עליו שהכל נהיה בדברו אלא לבסוף מאי מברך דילמא בורא נפשות רבות וחסרונן על כל מה שברא מתיב רב יצחק בר שמואל ‏"ירקות שאדם יוצא בהן ידי חובתו בפסח יוצא בהן ובקלח שלהן אבל לא כבושין ולא שלוקין ולא מבושלין ואי ס"ד במלתייהו קאי שלוקין אמאי לא שאני התם דבעינן טעם מרור וליכא א"ל ר' ירמיה לר' זירא ר' יוחנן היכי מברך על זית מליח ‏"כיון דשקילא לגרעיניה

בצר

אשמעינן טעמא. פירושא דקרא כמו שפירשנוהו ולמדנו פירושו: ואשמעינן הלכה כרבנן. דהמוציא דאפיק הוא: מאי קמשמע לן. הכל מודים בזו: אף ירקות שנשתנו כו'. ואפילו הכי במלתייהו קיימי ומברכים עלייהו בורא פרי האדמה: שלקות. כל ירק שלוק: דרש רב חסד'. כך משום רבינו רב שלקות אומר בורא פרי האדמה ורבותינו כו' ומאן ניניהו עולא אמר ר' יוחנן שהכל הרי הדבר במחלוק': ואני אומר. ליישב דבריהם שאינן חלוקים יש מהן פרי האדמה ויש מהן שהכל: כל. ירק הנאכל חי שתחלתו ב"פ האדמה שלקו אפקי' ממעליה לגריעות' ומברך שהכל ולקמן מוקי לה בתומי וכרתי: וכל. ירק שאין דרכו ליאכל חי שמתחלתו אם אכלו חי שהכל הוא מברך: שלקו. והביאו לדרך אכילתו הוא עיקר פריו ומברך בורא פרי האדמה: דרש רב נחמן. כך: משום רבינו. שמואל. שלקות מברך בורא פרי האדמה וחבירנו כו'. רב נחמן חשוב ולא קרי לעולא רבותינו: אמרו שלקות שהכל ואני אומר. שהם חלוקין בפלוגתא דרבי מאיר ור' יוסי ודברי שמואל ודברי רבי יוחנן בכל מילי ירקות הן חלוקין זה על זה שמואל כר' מאיר דאמר מבושל קאי במלתי' ורבי יוחנן קאי כרבי יוסי: יוצאין ברקיק השרוי במים. ידי אכילת מצה של מצוה וקרינן ביה לחם עוני: אבל לא במבושל. דתו לאו לחם אקרי: אפילו ר' יוסי מודה. דלענין ברכה במלתיה קאי: אמר רב נחמן קבע עולא לשבשתי' כר' בנימין. עולא שאמ' משו' ר' יוחנן לעיל שהכל למד וקבע שבושו כרבי בנימין עד שנתקעה בלבו ועכשיו אומר בבית המדרש בשם ר' יוחנן: תהי בה רבי זירא. במחלוקת זו שהוזכרה בבית המדרש וכי מה ענין להזכיר דברי ר' בנימין אצל דברי רבי חייא בר אבא במחלוקת בית המדרש הרי אינו כדי לחלוק עליו: בר מן דין ובר מן דין. לבד משתי ראיו' הללו שאמרתי שאין ר' בנימין כלום אצל רבי חייא יש לנו עוד ראיה שלא אמר רבי יוחנן מימיו שלקות שהכל אלא בפ"הא אלמא אע"ג דשלקיה קאי במלתיה: שאכל זית מליח. שהי' מלוח זה כמה ימים וקי"ל [פסחים עו.] מליח כרותח: אבל לא כבושין. בירקות של מרור היא שנויה בפ' כל שעה (ד' לט.) לומר שאין יוצאין בהן שלוקין משום מרור אלמא לאו במלתייהו קיימי שלוק הוי כמוח טפי ממבושל: בעינן טעם מרור וליכ'. אבל לענין ברכה שם פרי עליו:

בצר

והלכתא המוציא וכו'. ואע"פ דבמוציא כ"ע לא פליגי דאפיק משמע *וירושלמי מפרש טעמא כדי שלא לערב האותיות כגון העולם מוציא ואע"ג דבלאו הכי איכא עירוב שאני התם דקרא כתיב (תהלים קד) מצמיח חציר לבהמה ועשב לעבודת האדם להוציא לחם מן הארץ ועל כן יש לבצוע בשתי ידיו בעשר אצבעות כנגד י' תיבות שבמקרא זה:

מדקתני ירקו' דומי' דפת. לא הוי ירקו' דומי' דפת שהרי פת אישתני לעלויא ויש ירקות שאין משתנות לעלויא אלא כלומר מה הפת אין בשול מגרע את הברכה אף הירקות כמי במלתייהו קיימי ולא מגרע להו הבשול:

משכחת לה בתומי וכרתי. וא"ת והרי כראה לעינים דהבשול משביחן וי"ל דהיינו בשביל הבשר והמלח שבתוכן וכראי' הדברים שכל דבר שהוא כל כך טוב מבושל כמו חי וחי כמו מבושל כמו מיני קטניות וכן תפוחי' יש להן ברכה ראשונה שכל כך שוין מבושלין כמו חיין ומטעם זה מברכינן נמי על היין מבושל בורא פרי הגפן שכל כך הוא טוב אחר הבשול כמו קודם לכן וקרא וסלקא וכרוב וכיוצא בהן שטובין יות' מבושלין מחיין כשהן חיין מברכין עליהם שהכל ומבושלין ב"פ האדמה וכן אותן ערמוניות ושבושים שאינן ראוין לאכלן חיין כמו מבושלין בתחל' מברכין עליהם שהכל ומבושלין בורא פרי העץ אך אותן ערמוניות שקורין לומיברד"ש מברך עליהן בורא פרי העץ אפי' בתחלה וכל דבר המתקלקל בבשולו כגון תומי וכרתי וכיוצא בהן כשהן חיין מברך עליהן בורא פרי האדמה ומבושלים שהכל כך נראה לרבי' יהודה ומיהו הרב אלפס פסק בשלקות דאשתנו לגריעותא על ידי בשולן אומר בורא פרי האדמה כרב נחמן דאמר שלקות מברכין עליהן בורא פרי האדמה דרבי חייא בר אבא קאי כמי כותיה ובכל שלקות מיירי ר' חייא בר אבא אף באותן דמשתנין לגריעותא מדפליג להו גמרא אהדדי ר' חייא בר אבא ור' בנימין בר יפת ואגח מטוגן בדבש מברך עליו ב"פ העץ דאגוז עיקר:

כל תלתין יומין מהדר תלמודיה. לאו דוק' כל תלמודו אלא כל מה שהיה לומד בל' יום היה חוזר הכל לפניו ביום שלשים ואחד:

זית מליח. ומליח כרותח:

בצר

עין משפט נר מצוה

בירושלמי כל"ל

נה
אמיי' פ"ג מהל' ברכות ה"ב סמ"ג עשין כז טוש"ע א"ח סי' קסז סעי' ב

נו
בגדמיי' פ"ח מה' ברכות ה"ג סמ"ג שם טוש"ע א"ח סי' ר"ה סעי' א ובסי' רב סעי' יב

נז
המיי' פ"ו מה' חמץ ומצה ה"ו סמג ע' מ טוש"ע א"ח סי' תסא סעי' ד

נח
ומיי' פ"ז מהלכות חמץ ה' י"ג סמ"ג ע' מא טוש"ע א"ח סי' תע"ג סעי' ה

נט
זמיי' פ"א מה' ברכות ה"ב ופ"ג הי"ב סמ"ג עשין כז טוש"ע א"ח סי' ר"ו סעי' א

[ע' פירש"י בעירובין סו. ד"ה תהי]

[חולין פו: כריתות כז. וע"ש]

מסורת הש"ס

[ברי"ף ורא"ש ליתא לכל זה]

פסחים מא.

פי' שכשיך לימודו

[לעי' לג. וש"נ]

[נדה כה:]

פסחים לט.

ha-mozi, [38b] he would have taught us the meaning of a text and he would have taught us that the *halachah* is as stated by the
a Rabbis. But when he says *mozi,* what does he teach us?[1] In fact he acted thus so as to keep clear of controversy. And the law is that we say, '*ha-mozi* bread from the earth', since we hold with the Rabbis who say that it means 'who has brought forth'.

OVER VEGETABLES ONE SAYS etc. Vegetables are placed [by the Mishnah] on a par with bread: just as over bread which has been transformed by fire [the same blessing is said], so [the same blessing is said over] vegetables when they have been changed by fire. Rabinnai said in the name of Abaye: This means to say that over boiled vegetables we say 'who createst the fruit of the ground'. [How? —Because the Mishnah puts vegetables on a par with bread].[2]

R. Ḥisda expounded in the name of our Teacher, and who is this? Rab: Over boiled vegetables the blessing to be said is 'who createst the fruit of the ground'. But teachers who came down from the land of Israel, and who are these? 'Ulla in the name of R. Joḥanan, said: Over boiled vegetables the blessing to be said is 'by whose word all things exist'. I say, however,[3] that wherever we say over a thing in its raw state 'who createst the fruit of the ground', if it is boiled we say 'by whose word all things exist'; and wherever we say over it in the raw state 'by whose word all things exist', if it is boiled we say 'who createst the fruit of the ground'. We quite understand that where the blessing over a thing in its raw state is 'by whose word all things were created', if it is boiled we say, 'who createst the fruit of the ground';[4] you have examples in cabbage, beet, and pumpkin. But where can you find that a thing which in its raw state requires 'who createst the fruit of the ground' should, when boiled, require 'by whose word all things exist'?[5]—R. Naḥman b. Isaac replied: You have an instance in garlic and leek.

R. Naḥman expounded in the name of our teacher, and who is this? Samuel: Over boiled vegetables the blessing to be said is 'who createst the fruit of the ground'; but our colleagues who came down from the Land of Israel, and who are these? 'Ulla in the name of R. Joḥanan, say: Over boiled vegetables the blessing to be said is 'by whose word all things exist'. I personally say that
b authorities[1] differ on the matter, as it has been taught: One may satisfy the requirement [of eating unleavened bread on Passover] with a wafer which has been soaked, or which has been boiled, provided it has not been dissolved. So R. Meir. R. Jose, however, says: One fulfils the requirements with a wafer which has been soaked, but not with one which has been boiled, even though it has not been dissolved. But this is not the case.[2] All [in fact] would agree that over boiled vegetables the blessing is 'who createst the fruit of the ground'; and R. Jose was more particular in the case of the wafer only because we require the taste of unleavened bread and it is not there. In this case, however, even R. Jose would admit [that boiling does not alter its character].

R. Ḥiyya b. Abba said in the name of R. Joḥanan: Over boiled vegetables the blessing to be said is 'who createst the fruit of the ground'. R. Benjamin b. Jefet, however, said in the name of R. Joḥanan: Over boiled vegetables the blessing to be said is 'by whose word all things exist'. R. Naḥman b. Isaac said: 'Ulla[3] became confirmed in his error by accepting the word of R. Benjamin b. Jefet. R. Zera expressed his astonishment.[4] How [he said], can you mention R. Benjamin b. Jefet along with R. Ḥiyya b. Abba? R. Ḥiyya b. Abba was very particular to get the exact teaching of R. Joḥanan his master, whereas R. Benjamin b. Jefet was not particular. Further, R. Ḥiyya b. Abba used to go over what he had learnt every thirty days with his teacher R. Joḥanan, while R. Benjamin b. Jefet did not do so. Besides, apart from these two reasons[5] there is the case of the lupines which were cooked
c seven times in the pot, and eaten as dessert,[1] and when they came and asked R. Joḥanan about them, he told them that the blessing to be said was 'who createst the fruit of the ground'. Moreover R. Ḥiyya b. Abba said: I have seen R. Joḥanan eat salted olives and say a blessing both before and after. Now if you hold that boiled vegetables are still regarded as the same, we can understand this: before eating he said 'who createst the fruit of the tree', and after it a grace of one blessing which includes three.[2] But if you hold that vegetables after being boiled are not regarded as the same, no doubt he could say before eating 'by whose word all things are created', but what could he say after?—Perhaps he said, 'who createst many living things and their requirements for all that he has created'.

R. Isaac b. Samuel raised an objection: With regard to the herbs with which one may fulfil the requirement [of eating bitter herbs on] Passover,[3] both they and their stalks may serve this purpose, but not if they are pickled or cooked or boiled.[4] Now if you maintain that after boiling they are still regarded as the same, why may they not be used boiled?—The case is different there, because we require the taste of bitter herbs, and this we do not find.

R. Jeremiah asked R. Zera: How could R. Joḥanan make a blessing over a salted olive? Since the stone had been removed,

a (1) Seeing that all are agreed as to its meaning. (2) These words seem to be a needless repetition, and are bracketed in the text. (3) In order to reconcile the two opinions. (4) Because usually it is improved by boiling. (5) I.e., should deteriorate through being boiled.

b (1) I.e., Tannaim. (2) That the authorities differ with regard to vegetables and that R. Jose supports R. Joḥanan. (3) Who reported *supra* in the name of R. Joḥanan that the blessing is 'by whose word etc.'. (4) That this difference of opinion should have been recorded. (5) Showing that R. Joḥanan did not make the statement attributed to him by R. Benjamin b. Jefet.

c (1) And therefore required a separate blessing. (2) Because in spite of the salting, it was still regarded as an olive. (3) V. Ex. XII, 8. (4) I.e., reduced to a pulp. V. Pes. 39*a*.

[39a] it was less than the minimum size!—He replied: Do you think the size we require is that of a large olive? We require only that of a medium sized olive, and that was there, for the one they set before R. Joḥanan was a large one, so that even when its stone had been removed it was still of the requisite size. For so we have learnt: The 'olive' spoken of[5] means neither a small nor a large one, but a medium one. This is the kind which is called *aguri*. R. Abbahu, however, said: Its name is not *aguri* but *abruti*, or, according to others, *samrusi*. And why is it called *aguri*? Because its oil is collected [*agur*] within it.[6]

May we say that this controversy [about the blessing to be said over boiled vegetables] is found between Tannaim? For once two disciples were sitting before Bar Ḳappara, and cabbage, Damascene plums and poultry were set before him. Bar Ḳappara gave permission to one of them to say a blessing, and he at once said the
a blessing over the poultry.[1] The other laughed at him, and Bar Ḳappara was angry. He said: I am not angry with the one who said the blessing, but with the one who laughed. If your companion acts like one who has never tasted meat in his life, is that any reason for you to laugh? Then he corrected himself and said: I am not angry with the one who laughed, but with the one who said the blessing. If there is no wisdom here, is there not old age here?[2] A Tanna taught: Neither of them saw the year out.[3] Now did not their difference lie in this, that the one who said the blessing held that the benediction over both boiled vegetables and poultry is 'by whose word all things exist', and therefore the dish he liked best had the preference,[4] while the one who laughed held that the blessing over boiled vegetables is 'who createst the fruit of the ground', and that over poultry is 'by whose word all things were created', and therefore the vegetables should have had the preference?[5]—Not so. All agree that for both boiled vegetables and poultry the blessing is 'by whose word all things exist', and their difference lies in this, that one held that what is best liked should have the preference, and the other held that the cabbage should have the preference, because it is nourishing.[6]

R. Zera said: When we were with R. Huna, he told us that with regard to the tops of turnips, if they are cut into large pieces, the blessing is 'who createst the fruit of the ground', but if they are cut into small pieces, 'by whose word all things exist'.[7] But when we came to Rab Judah, he told us that for both the blessing is 'who createst the fruit of the ground', since the reason for their being cut into small pieces is to make them taste sweeter.

R. Ashi said: When we were with R. Kahana, he told us that over a broth of beet, in which not much flour is put, the blessing is 'who createst the fruit of the ground', but for a broth of turnip, in which much flour is put, the blessing is 'who createst all kinds of foods'. Subsequently, however, he said that the blessing for both is 'who createst the fruit of the ground', since the reason why much flour is put in it is only to make it cohere better.

R. Ḥisda said: A broth of beet is beneficial for the heart and good for the eyes, and needless to say for the bowels. Said Abaye:
b This is only if it is left on the stove till it goes *tuk, tuk*.[1]

R. Papa said: It is quite clear to me that beet-water is on the same footing as beet,[2] and turnip-water on the same footing as turnips, and the water of all vegetables on the same footing as the vegetables themselves. R. Papa, however, inquired: What about aniseed water? Is its main purpose to sweeten the taste[3] [to the dish] or to remove the evil smell?[4]—Come and hear: Once the aniseed has given a taste to the dish, the law of *terumah* no longer applies to it,[5] and it is not liable to the uncleanness of foods.[6] This proves that its main purpose is to sweeten the dish, does it not?—It does.

R. Ḥiyya b. Ashi said: Over a dry crust which has been put in a pot [to soak], the blessing is 'who bringeth forth bread etc.'. This view conflicts with that of R. Ḥiyya; for R. Ḥiyya said: The bread should be broken with the conclusion of the blessing.[7] Raba demurred to this. What [he said], is the reason [why *ha-moẓi* should not be said] in the case of dry crust? Because, you say, when the blessing is concluded, it is concluded over a broken piece. But when it is said over a loaf, it finishes over a broken piece!

(5) As a standard of quantity. (6) I.e., can be squeezed out immediately. Probably all these names refer to the place of origin of different kinds of olive.

a (1) As being the principal dish. (2) And why did you not consult me? (3) As a punishment for the disrespect shown to Bar Ḳappara. (4) I.e., he said the blessing over that one first and commenced to eat it. (5) Even though he liked the poultry better, because the blessing over vegetables is more dignified. (6) I.e., more than poultry, v. *infra* 44b. (7) Because they have been more or less spoilt.

b (1) I.e., has been brought to the boil. (2) And the blessing to be said over it is 'who createst the fruit of the earth'. (3) And is the blessing to be said over it 'who createst the fruit of the ground'. (4) And the blessing will be 'by whose word etc.'. (5) It is regarded as merely wood, not liable to *terumah*. (6) 'Uk. III, 4. (7) But this has already been broken off, and therefore the blessing is 'by whose word'.

בצר ליה שיעורא א"ל מי סברת כזית גדול בעינן כזית בינוני בעינן והא איכא וההוא דאייתו לקמיה דר' יוחנן זית גדול הוה דאע"ג דשקלוה לגרעינותיה פש ליה שיעורא *דתנן [א]זית שאמרו לא קטן ולא גדול אלא בינוני וזהו אגורי וא"ר אבהו לא אגורי שמו אלא אברוטי שמו ואמרי לה סמרוסי שמו ולמה נקרא שמו אגורי ששמנו אגור בתוכו נימא כתנאי דהנהו תרי תלמידי דהוו יתבי קמיה דבר קפרא הביאו לפניו כרוב ודורמסקין ופרגיות נתן בר קפרא רשות לאחד מהן לברך קפץ וברך על הפרגיות לגלג עליו חבירו כעס בר קפרא אמר לא על המברך אני כועס אלא על המלגלג אני כועס אם חבירך דומה כמי שלא טעם טעם בשר מעולם אתה על מה לגלגת עליו חזר ואמר לא על המלגלג אני כועס אלא על המברך אני כועס ואמר אם חכמה אין כאן זקנה אין כאן תנא ושניהם לא הוציאו שנתן מאי לאו בהא קא מיפלגי דמברך סבר שלקות ופרגיות שהכל נהיה בדברו הלכך חביב עדיף ומלגלג סבר שלקות בפ"הא פרגיות שהנ"ב [ב]הלכך פירא עדיף לא דכ"ע שלקות ופרגיות שהנ"ב והכא בהאי סברא קמיפלגי מ"ס חביב עדיף ומ"ס כרוב עדיף דזיין א"ר זירא כי הוינא בי רב הונא אמר לן הני גרגלידי דלפתא פרמינהו פרימא רבא ב"פ האדמה פרימא זוטא שנ"ב וכי אתאן לבי רב יהודה אמר לן [ג]אידי ואידי בפ"הא והאי דפרמינהו טפי כי היכי דנמתיק טעמיה אמר רב אשי כי הוינן בי רב כהנא אמר לן תבשיל' דסלקא דלא מפשו בה קמחא ב"פ האדמה דלפת דמפשו בה קמחא טפי במ"מ והדר אמר [ד]אידי ואידי בפ"הא והא דשדי בה קמחא טפי לדבוקי בעלמא עבדו לה אמר רב חסדא *תבשיל של תרדין יפה ללב וטוב לעינים וכ"ש לבני מעים אמר אביי והוא דיתיב אבי תפי ועביד *תוך תוך א"ר פפא פשיטא לי [ה]מיא דסלקא כסלק' ומיא דלפת' כלפת' ומיא דכולהו שלקי כשלקי בעי רב פפא מיא דשיבתא מאי למתוקי טעמא עבדי או לעבורי זוהמא עבדי לה ת"ש *[ו]השבת משנתנה טעם בקדירה אין בה משום תרומה ואינה מטמאה טומאת אוכלים ש"מ למתוקי טעמא עבדי לה ש"מ אמר רב חייא בר אשי פת צנומה בקערה מברכים עליה המוציא ופליגא דרב חייא דאמר רב חייא צריך שתכלה ברכה עם הפת מתקיף לה רבא מ"ש צנומה דלא משום דכי כליא ברכה אפרוסה קא כליא על הפת נמי כי קא גמרה אפרוסה גמרה

אלא

רש"י

בצר ליה שיעורא. וגבי ברכת פירות הארץ אכילה כתיבא ואכילה בכזית: כזית שאמרו. לענין שיעור כל אכילו': אגור בתוכו. מזומן לצאת ממנו שאינו נבלע בפרי כמשקה תפוחים ותותים אלא אגור כמשקה ענבים: דורמסקין. אף הן שלקות מעשב שקורין אקדלש"ע בלעז כך ראיתי בפי' בבא קמא של רבי' יצחק בר' יהודה אבל כאן פיר' פרו"כש וכן שמעתי אני כאן ובבבא קמ' (פ"י דף קיז:) פר"וכש ואי אפשר להעמידה דא"כ הרי ברכתו ב"פ העץ והיאך קדם וברך על הפרגיו' שברכתן שהכל ואינם כדברים חשובים כדמפרש ואזיל: שלא טעם טעם בשר. וכעס' הבשר חביב עליו: פרגיות. בשר עוף שקורי' פרד"רי': זקנה אין כאן. הלא זקן אני והי' לו לשאלני על איזה מהן יברך לפטור את שאר המינין ודברים הללו אינן באין ללפת את הפת אלא שלא מחמת הסעודה הן באין ואמרי' לקמן (דף מא:) דטעונין ברכה לפניהם ואין הפת פוטרתן: דמברך סבר שלקות. דכרוב ודורמסקין שהכל ברכתן כפרגיות דעל דבר שאין גדולו מן הארץ כגון בשר ביצים ודגים תנא במתני' (לקמן מ:) שהכל וכיון דברכותיהם שוות חביב עדיף: ומלגלג סבר שלקות בורא פרי האדמה. שהיא ברכה חשובה לעצמה לדברי חשובי' והיה לו להקדימו: כרוב עדיף דזיין. דתניא לקמן (דף מד:) כרוב למזון ותרדין לרפואה: גרגלידי דלפתא. ראשי לפתו': פרמינהו. מנו"שייר בלעז לשון קיצת ירק: פרמי זוטרי. גריעות' היא ובשאכלו חי קאי: אבי תפי. על מקו' שפיתת הקדירה: ועביד תוך תוך. כלומר ששלוק וכמהה מאד וקול רתיחתו כשמעת כקול תוך תוך: מיא דסלקא. תבשיל של תרדין: כסלק'. לענין ברכה: דשיבתא. ירק שנותנין מעט בקדירה למתק בעלמא ולא לאכלו אנ"יט בלעז: למתוקי טעמא עביד. ומברכין על מימי תבשילו ב"פ האדמה: השבת אין בה. בבד שלה משנתנוה בקדירה והוציאוה אין בה שוב משו' איסור תרומ' דהוה ליה כעץ בעלמא מדקתני משנתנה טעם ש"מ לטעמא עבידא: פת צנומ'. יבשה שנתנה בקערה לשרות וכן °לכוותא דקות: צריך שתכלה. ברכ' המוציא עם פרוסת הפרוסה מן הפת והאי פרוס ועומד הוא: אפרוס' (*כליא). כיון דאמרת עם פריסת הפרוס' תכל' מאי חשיבות' ומאי אהניתא:

אלא

תוספות

בצר ליה שיעורא. הייתו דוקא בברכה שלאחריו דבעינן שיעור אבל בברכ' שלפניו אפי' פחות מכשיעור דאסור ליהנות בעה"ז בלא ברכה בין לענין אכילה בין לענין שתיה אבל בברכה שלאחריו בעינן שיעור מלא לוגמיו על כן יש ליזהר לשתות מכוס של ברכה מלא לוגמיו כדי שיברך לאחריו מעין ג' ברכות והר"י היה אומר בורא נפשות כיון דלאו ברכ' חשובה היא אפי' בבציר משיעור' מברכינן בורא נפשות רבות ולא נראה דכיון דבורא נפשות תקנו' כנגד על הגפן כי היכי דעל הגפן בעי שיעורא בבורא נפשות רבות נמי בעי שיעורא ובירושלמי ר' יוחנן היכי בריך אזית הא לא הוי שיעור' וקאמר משום בריה דאפי' לא אכל אלא פרידה אחת של ענב או פרידה אחת של רמון בעי ברוכי משום דבבריה מברכין אפי' פחות מכזית וחולק על גמרא דידן כדמשמע הכא א"כ אין הלכה כמותו של ירושלמי וה"ר יוסי היה מפרש שהירושלמי אינו חולק על הגמרא שלנו דהכא מיירי שהוסרו הגרעיני' ונמצא אם כן לא היה כברייתו אבל אם אכלו שלם אפי' אם היה פריד' אחת של רמון מברך עליו תחל' וסוף וגמר' ירושלמי היה סבור שהזית היה שלם ולכך הוצרך לתרץ באותו ענין דאכל פרידה *דבריה ואינן חולקי' יחד ועוד יש בירושלמי היכא דצריך אתורמוסא למכליה ונפל מידיה ושקל אחרינ' בעי ברוכי זמנ' אחריתי ופריך מאי שנא מאנת המי' פירוש דמברך לשתו' והכי אזלי והכי אחריני נינהו וא"צ לברך פעם אחרת ומשני הכא הוה דעתו מתחלה לזה שהיה יודע שילכו להן אבל מתורמוס' לא ידע שיפלו מידו ויאמר ברוך שם כ"מ לעולם ועד משום דהוה ברכה לבטלה וכן נכון לומר על כל ברכה לבטלה בשכמל"ו:

דורמסקין פרש"י פרו"כש ולא נראה דבסמוך משמע דמברכין עליהן בורא פרי האדמה וא"כ ב"פ העץ בעי ברוכי ונראה שהוא מין כרוב:

נתן בר קפרא רשו' לאחד מהן לברך. ונראה דמיירי בברכה שלפניו דאי בשל אחריו הא אמרינן * אין מזמנין על הפירו' ומיירי בהסבו ואנו אין לנו שום הסב' אלא על הפת ולכך צריך לברך כל אחד על כל דבר הן בפירות הן ביין:

חביב עדיף. וכן הלכה אם יש לו שני מיני פירות לפניו חביב עדיף וב"פ האדמה עדיפ' משהכל נהיה בדברו דמבוררת טפי וחשובה לעצמה מקרית ויברך על אותו המין ששייך בו ב"פ האדמה אף ע"פ שאותו המין שיש לברך עליו שהכל חביב עליו ואם לפניו פירות שהברכות שוות ואחד מהן הוא מז' המינין יברך תחלה על אותו של ז' המינין דעדיפי:

מיא דסלקא כסלקא. מברכים עלי' ב"פ האדמה אעפ"י שאין בה אלא מים וטעם הירקות מברך עליהן כאשר יברך על הירקות אע"ג דאמרי' לעיל דמי פירו' זיעה בעלמא הוא יש לחלק: פת צנומה בקערה מברכין עליהן המוציא לחם מן הארץ ופליגא דר' חייא. וא"ת היכי מיירי אם יש שלימה לפניו הא אמרינן בסמוך דכ"ע שלימה עדיף ואי ליכא אלא צנומה היכי פליג עלה ר' חייא הא מסקינן לעיל (ד' לז:) פרורין אעפ"י שאין בהן כזית מברכין עליהן המוציא הואיל ואית בהו תורית' דנהמא וי"ל כגון דאיכא שלימה לפניו ובלע מן הצנומה רב חייא בר אשי סבר דהוי כמו שלימה מאחר שהיא חביבה [מברך עלי'] ור' חייא ס"ל צריך שתכלה ברכה עם הפת וא"כ בעינן שתכלה הברכה עם בליעת הפת וכיון שבלועה קודם לכן שלימה עדיף אבל אי ליכא שלימה מודה שיברך על הפירורי' *המוציא לחם מן הארץ:

והלכתא

עין משפט נר מצוה

ס א מיי' פ"ד מה' מאכלות אסורות הלכ' א טוש"ע א"ח סי' תפו
סא ב טוש"ע א"ח סי' ריא סעי' ג
סב ג טוש"ע א"ח סי' רה סעי' ד
סג ד מיי' פ"ב מהל' ברכות ה"ו טוש"ע א"ח סי' ר"ח סעי' ב
סד ה מיי' פ"ח מהל' ברכות הל' ד סמג שם טוש"ע א"ח סי' רה סעי' ב
סה ו מיי' פט"ו מהל' תרומות הל' יב ופ"א מהל' טומאת אוכלין הל' ז

[דבריה היה ואינן כל"ג]
[חולין קל.]
[וע"ע תוס' מנחות עה: ד"ה אבילו]

מסורת הש"ס

כלים פי"ז מ"ח
עירובין כט.
[פסחים עד.]
[ברכות' מא]
גמרה
עוקלין פ"ג מ"ד נדה כח:

אלא אמר רבא מברך ואח"כ בוצע נהרדעי עבדי כר' חייא ורבנן עבדי כרבא אמר רבינא אמרה לי אם אבוך עביד כר' חייא דא"ר חייא צריך שתכלה ברכה עם הפת ורבנן עבדי כרבא והלכתא כרבא דאמר א מברך ואח"כ בוצע: אתמר הביאו לפניהם פתיתין ושלימין אמר רב הונא מברך על הפתיתין ופוטר את השלימין ור' יוחנן אמר ב שלימין מצוה מן המובחר אבל פרוסה של חטין ושלימה מן השעורים דברי הכל מברך על הפרוסה של חטין ופוטר את השלימה של שעורין א"ר ירמיה בר אבא כתנאי *ג תורמין בצל קטן שלם אבל לא חצי בצל גדול ר' יהודה אומר לא כי אלא חצי בצל גדול מאי לאו בהא קמיפלגי דמ"ס חשוב עדיף ומ"ס שלם עדיף היכא דאיכא כהן כולי עלמא לא פליגי דחשוב עדיף כי פליגי דליכא כהן *דתנן ד כל מקום שיש כהן תורם מן היפה וכל מקום שאין כהן תורם מן המתקיים ר' יהודה אומר אין תורם אלא מן היפה אמר רב נחמן בר יצחק *וירא שמים יוצא ידי שניהן ומנו מר בריה דרבינא דמר בריה דרבינא ה מניח פרוסה בתוך השלימה ובוצע תני תנא קמיה דרב נחמן בר יצחק מניח הפרוסה בתוך השלימה ובוצע ומברך א"ל מה שמך א"ל שלמן א"ל שלום אתה ושלימה משנתך ששמת שלום בין התלמידים אמר רב פפא הכל מודים ו בפסח שמניח פרוסה בתוך שלימה ובוצע מ"ט °לחם עוני כתיב *א"ר אבא ז ובשבת חייב אדם לבצוע על שתי ככרות מ"ט °לחם משנה כתיב אמר רב אשי חזינא לרב כהנא ח דנקיט תרתי ובוצע חדא ר' זירא ט הוה בצע אכולא שירותא א"ל רבינא לרב אשי *והא קא מתחזי כרעבתנותא אמר [ליה] כיון דכל יומא לא קעביד הכי והאידנא קא עביד לא מתחזי כרעבתנותא *רב אמי ורב אסי כי הוה מתרמי להו ריפתא דערובא מברכין עליה המוציא לחם מן הארץ אמרי הואיל ואתעביד ביה מצוה חדא נעביד ביה מצוה אחריתי

אמר

מסורת הש"ס

אלא אמר רבא מברך ואח"כ בוצע. וגומר כל הברכה ואח"כ מפריס הפרוס' דכליא ברכה אפת שלם: פתיתין ושלימין אמר רב הונא. אם רצה מברך על הפתיתין ואם הפתיתין גדולים מן השלימין צריך לברך עליהן: כתנאי. הא דאמרת פרוס' של חטין ושלימה של שעורין כו' תנאי היא: אבל לא חצי בצל גדול. ואע"פ שיש בו יותר מקטן שלם: במקום שיש כהן. ונותנו לו מיד: במקום שאין כהן. צריך לישראל שיצניענו עד שיבא כהן ליתנו לו וחצי בצל אין מתקיים: יוצא ידי שניהם. ידי מחלוקת של רב הונא ור' יוחנן: מניח פרוסה תחת השלימה. ונמצאו שתיהן בידיו ובוצע או משתיהן או מן השלימה: לחם עוני כתיב. ודרכו של עני בפרוסה לפיכך צריך שיראה כבוצע מן הפרוס': אכולה שירותא. פרוסה גדולה שהיה די לו לכל הסעוד' בשבת: ריפתא דערובא. שערבו בו אתמול עירובי חצרות:

תורה אור

טול

והלכתא כרבא דמברך ואח"כ בוצע. פי' שלא יפריס הפרוסה מן הפת עד אחר הברכה ויש שנוהגין לברך ברכת המוציא קוד' שיחתוך כדי שתהא הפת שלימה בשעת ברכה ואין המנהג נכון לעשות דהוי היסח הדעת בין הברכה לאכילה ומיהו בשבת נכון להחמיר ולברך קודם שיחתוך שלא תשמט ידו לבצוע קודם שתכלה הברכ' שאז לא יהיה לו לחם משנה ובפר' שלשה שאכלו (דף מז.) מסקינן דבעינן עד שתכל' אמן מפי העונין שלא יבצע קודם ויש שמביאים ראיה שצריך לסיים הברכה קודם שיבצע מדקתני רבי חייא בירושלמי אין מברכין על הפת אלא בשעה שהוא פורס והיינו משום שאם יפרוס קודם הברכה שמא תפול הפרוס' מידו ולא יוכל לאכול פרוסה אחר' שיבצע בלא ברכה אלא יצטרך לחזור ולברך ויש כאן ברכה לבטלה אבל אם (*לא) היה צרי' לברך על כל הפת ולא יוכל לפרוס קודם הברכה אז אם תפול הפרוסה אינו מברך על פרוסה אחרת ויפטר בברכה ראשונה:

מברך על הפתיתין ופוטר את השלימין. פי' רש"י אם הפתיתי' והשלימים שוין יברך על איזה שירצה ואם הפתיתין גדולים צריך לברך על הפתיתין לפטור את השלימין ור' יוחנן אומר על השלמין מצו' מן המובחר אפי' אם הפתיתין גדולי' טפי ותימה א"כ סברא הפוכ' דלרב הונ' פתיתין שהן גדולי' עדיפי ולר' יוחנן שלימה עדיפא ואין סברא לומר דפליגי בהפוך סברות ועוד תימה מאי שנא בסמוך לשונו דנקט לשון פרוס' של חטין על כן פי' ר"ת דמיירי בפתיתין גדולים ושלימים קטני' וה"פ אמר רב הונא מברך על הפתיתין כלומר אם ירצ' והו' הדין על השלימין אם ירצה ור' יוחנן אמר שלימין עיקר וכן הלכה כר' יוחנן דהא רב ור' יוחנן הלכה כר' יוחנן וכ"ש לגבי רב הונא שהלכה כמותו שהיה תלמידו של רב דדוקא באמוראי בתראי אמרי' הלכה כבתראי: אבל פרוסה של חטין ושלימ' של שעורים דברי הכל מברך על הפרוסה של חטין. דחיטי עדיפי משום דאקדמי' קרא אבל פתיתי' ושלימין ממין א' אפילו יהיו הפתיתין מפת נקיה והשלימין מפת קיבר מברך על השלימין כדאית' בתוספתא [פרק ד'] שלימין דגלוסקאות ושלימין דבעל הבית מברך על השלימין דגלוסקאות. פרוסה דגלוסקאות ושלימין דבעה"ב מברך על השלימין דבעל הבית. פת כשר ופת של נכרי מברך על הכשר תחל' וכן אמרינן בירושלמי. פת טהור ופת טמאה מברך על הטהור אבל אם פת של נכרי חביב ונקי ופת של ישראל אינו חביב מברך לאיזה שירצה כדאיתא בירושלמי פת טמאה ופת קיבר טהורה מברך לאיזה שירצה אבל רבינו שמשון צוה לסלק הפת לבן של נכרי' מעל השלחן עד לאחר ברכת המוציא. שני שלימין ממין אחד אם האחד יותר נקי מברך על הנקי דחביב ליה טפי: כתנאי כו'. פי' רש"י חצי בצל גדול קרי חשוב לפי שיש בו יותר מבצל קטן שלם ולא נראה דהא לכאורה משמע דלהכי נקט חצי בצל גדול משום דיש בחצי בצל גדול כמו בקטן שלם ולא יותר ועוד דאם כן לא הויא דומיא דחשוב דגבי פרוסה של חטין דקאי עלה דהתם שוין ויש לפרש דכהדדי שוין הם אבל דגדול טוב יותר לאכילה מן הקטן ועוד פרש"י דמייתי תנאי אסיפא דמברך על הפרוסה של חטין ופוטר את השלימי' של שעורי' ומ"ס חשוב עדיף ומ"ס חטין דמקדמי בקרא עדיפי אבל א"א לפרש דחטין עדיפי משו' שפת של חטין חשוב מפת של שעורי' דהא פי' דמין אחד פת נקיה ופת קיבר השלם עדיף: ומר סבר שלם עדיף. וא"ת מנא ליה הא איכא דחטין דחשיבי טפי משום דאקדמי' קרא וי"ל דהכי מדמ' דהתם אע"ג דמסברא חשוב לכהן עדיף דכתיב בהרימכם את חלבו ממנו (במדבר יח) ואפ"ה קאמר דשלם עדיף ה"נ ניחא שלם עדיף מפתיתי' של חטי' אע"ג דאקדמי' קרא והדין עם רש"י שלא רצה לפרש כתנאי אפלוגתייהו דר' יוחנן ורב הונא שהרי למאי דמפרש לרב הונא כשהן שוין מברך על איזו שירצה א"כ לא קפיד אחשיבות ולא אשלימות וא"כ מאי כתנאי איכא ולפי' ר"ת נמי דפי' דמברך על הפתיתין גדולים אם ירצה ואי בעי בריך על השלימים קטנים אלמא לא חשיב ליה עדיף אלא כי הדדי ניהו לרב הונא וא"כ לא מצי קאי כתנאי אפלוגתא דפתיתים: כל היכא דאיכא כהן כ"ע לא פליגי דחשיב עדיף. והא דלעיל קאמר פתיתין גדולים ושלימים קטנים דמברך על השלימים היינו דוקא לברכה דלא איכפת ליה שיברך בגדול דלמה הואיל ואינו נקי מזה אבל גבי נתינה לכהן איכא נפקותא דיתן לו הגדול החשוב טפי דניחא ליה: מניח פרוסה בתוך השלימה ובוצע. פי' רש"י ובוצע משתיהן או בוצע משלימה בלבד והיינו ע"י שניהן דכיון שהניח הפרוסה תחת השלימה נראה כמו שבוצע נמי אפרוס' ודוקא בוצע משלימ' אבל לא רצה לפרש ובוצע לאיזה מהן שירצה או לפרוסה או לשלימה דמדקאמר לתוך השלימה משמע דהשלימה עיקר ולפי' רש"י ה"פ ירא שמים יוצא ידי שניהם כדרב הונא וכדרבי יוחנן בפתיתי' ושלימה ולפי' ר"ת לא מצינו לפרש הכי דקאי אפתיתין שהרי אינו צריך לעשות כן אלא יברך על השלימה ודי בכך לכולי עלמא דאפי' רב הונא לא קאמר אלא על הפרוסה אם ירצה אבל פשיטא אם בירך על השלימה יצא ונראה *לפי' ר"ת שניהם קאי אשני לחמים אפרוסה של חטים ושלימה של שעורים: הכל מודים בפסח שמניח הפרוסה בתוך השלימה ובוצע מאי טעמא לחם עוני כתיב. משום דכתיב לחם עוני מניח הפרוסה תחת השלימה ויראה כבוצע על הפרוסה ומ"מ אין לבצוע כי אם על השלימה ועל הפרוסה יברך על אכילת מצה ובוצעי' ואוכלים משתיהן יחד כדי שיהא נראה כבוצע על הפרוסה וכן המנהג אבל אין לעשות המוציא וגם על אכילת מצה מן הפרוסה דהוי כעוש' מצות חבילות חבילו' ונראה לי דהא הוי ברכה של נהנין ואינן נקראי' חבילות חבילות דהא אקדוש מברכים קדוש וברכת היין ורבינו מנחם מווי"ינא הי' רגיל לעשות הכל על הפרוסה ואין השלימה באה כ"א בשביל לחם משנה והר"י היה רגיל לברך תחלה ברכת המוציא על שתיהן קודם שיבצע ואח"כ מברך על אכילת מצה ובוצע משתיהן אחר כך ואין זה חבילות מאחר שהיה עושה על שתיהן ופעמים מפיק הר"י נפשי' מפלוגתא ולא היה רוצה לשנות המנהג והיה מברך על השלימה תחלה המוציא והיה בוצע קצת ולא היה מפרידה עד שיברך על הפרוסה על אכילת מצה ובוצע משתיהן יחד:

[ונראה דגרס לר"ת שתיהן וקאי לשני כל"נ]

הביאו

עין משפט נר מצוה

סו
א מיי' פ"ז מהל' ברכות ה"ב סמג עשין כז טוש"ע א"ח סי' קסז סעי' א

סז
ב מיי' וסמג שם טוש"ע א"ח סי' קסח סעיף א

סח
ג מיי' פ"ה מה' תרומות הלכה ב

סט
ד שם הל' א עיין מהרש"א ומהרש"ל

ע
ה מיי' פ"ז מהל' ברכות ה' ד סמג עשין כו טוש"ע א"ח סי' קסח סעי' א

עא
ו מיי' פ"ח מהלכות חמץ ה"ו טוש"ע א"ח סי' תעה סעי' א [רב אלפס כאן ובפ' ע"פ קכט:]

עב
ז ח מיי' פ"ז מהל' ברכות ה' ד ופ"ל מה' שבת ה"ט סמג עשין כט טוש"ע א"ח סי' רעד סעי' א [רב אלפס כאן ובשבת פט"ו ובע"פ קכט:]

עג
ט מיי' פ"ז מהל' ברכות ה"ג טוש"ע שם סעיף ב וש"ע שם סי' שכ"ד ס"ב

תרומות פ"ב מ"ה

שם [מנחות כה.]

[שבת סא.]

דברים טז

שבת קיז:

שמות טז

כתובות לו:

שבת שם

[39b] The fact is, said Raba, that the benediction is said first and a then the loaf is broken.[1] The Nehardeans acted as prescribed by R. Ḥiyya, while the Rabbis acted as prescribed by Raba. Rabina said: Mother told me: Your father acted as prescribed by R. Ḥiyya; for R. Ḥiyya said: The bread should be broken with the conclusion of the blessing, whereas the Rabbis acted as prescribed by Raba. The law is as laid down by Raba, that one says the blessing first and afterwards breaks the loaf.

It has been stated: If pieces and whole loaves are set before one, R. Huna says that the benediction can be said over the pieces,[2] and this serves also for the whole loaves, whereas R. Joḥanan says that the religious duty is better performed if the blessing is said over the whole one. If, however, a broken piece of wheat bread and a whole loaf of barley bread are set before one, all agree that the benediction is said over the piece of wheaten bread, and this serves also for the whole loaf of barley bread. R. Jeremiah b. Abba said: There is the same difference of opinion between Tannaim:[3] *Terumah* is given from a small whole onion, but not from the half of a large onion. R. Judah says: Not so, but also from the half of a large onion.[4] Are we to say that the point in which they differ is this: one authority holds that the fact of being worth more is more important, while the other holds that the fact of being whole is more important?—Where a priest is on the spot,[5] all agree that the fact of being worth more is more important. Where they differ is when there is no priest on the spot, since we have learnt: Wherever a priest is on the spot, *terumah* is given from the best of the produce; where the priest is not on the spot,[6] *terumah* is set aside from that which will keep best. R. Judah said: *Terumah* is in all cases given from the best.[7] R. Naḥman b. Isaac said: A God-b fearing man will seek to satisfy both.[1] Who is such a one? Mar the son of Rabina. For Mar the son of Rabina used to put the broken piece under[2] the whole loaf and then break the bread.[3] A Tanna recited in the presence of R. Naḥman b. Isaac: One should place the broken piece under the whole loaf and then break and say the benediction. He said to him: What is your name? Shalman, he replied. He said to him: Thou art peace [*shalom*] and thy Mishnah is faultless [*shelemah*], for thou hast made peace between the scholars.

R. Papa said: All admit that on Passover one puts the broken cake under the whole one and breaks [them together]. What is the reason? Scripture speaks of '*Bread of poverty*'.[4] R. Abba said: On Sabbath one should break bread from two loaves. What is the reason? Scripture speaks of '*double bread*'.[5] R. Ashi said: I have observed R. Kahana take two and break one. R. Zera used to break off [a piece of bread] sufficient for the whole meal [on Sabbath]. Said Rabina to R. Ashi: Does not this look like greediness? He replied: Since every other day he does not act thus and today he acts thus, it does not look like greediness. When R. Ammi and R. Assi happened to get hold of a loaf which had been used for an '*erub*,[6] they used to say over it the blessing, 'who bringest forth bread from the earth', saying, Since one religious duty has been performed with it, let us perform with it still another.

a (1) So that when the blessing is concluded the bread is still whole. (2) Especially if they are larger than the whole loaf, in which case preference must be given to the broken one (Rashi). (3) In the case where the broken one is of wheat and the whole one of barley. (4) Ter. II, 5. (5) And the *terumah* can be given to him immediately. (6) And the produce has to be kept till he turns up. (7) Ibid. 4.

b (1) I.e., both points of view, *sc.* of R. Huna and R. Joḥanan. (2) V. Rashi. (3) From both, v. Rashi. (4) Deut. XVI, 3. (E.V. '*affliction*'). A poor man has usually only a piece. (5) Ex. XVI, 22, of the manna on Friday. (E.V. '*twice as much bread*'). (6) For allowing transport through the courts on Sabbath. V. Glos.

[40*a*] Rab said: [If the host says to his guests,][7] Take, the benediction has been said,[8] take, the benediction has been said, he [the host] need not say the benediction [again].[9] If he said [between the benediction and the eating], Bring salt, bring relish, he must say the benediction [again]. R. Johanan, however, said that even if he said, Bring salt, bring relish, the benediction need not be repeated. If he said, Mix fodder for the oxen, mix fodder for the oxen, he must repeat the blessing; R. Shesheth, however, said that even if he said, Mix fodder for the oxen, he need not repeat; for Rab Judah said in the name of Rab: A man is forbidden to eat before he gives food to his beast, since it says, *And I will give grass in thy fields for thy cattle,* and then, *thou*
a *shalt eat and be satisfied.*[1]

Raba b. Samuel said in the name of R. Ḥiyya: The one who is about to break the bread is not permitted to do so before salt or relish is placed before each one at table. Raba b. Samuel was once at the house of the Exilarch, and they brought him bread and he broke it at once. They said to him: Has the Master retraced his own teaching?—He replied: This requires no condiment.[2]

Raba b. Samuel also said in the name of R. Ḥiyya: Urine is never completely discharged except when sitting.[3] R. Kahana said: If over loose earth, even when standing. If there is no loose earth, one should stand on a raised spot and discharge down a declivity.

Raba b. Samuel also said in the name of R. Ḥiyya: After every food eat salt, and after every beverage drink water, and you will come to no harm. It has been taught similarly: After every food eat salt, and after every beverage drink water, and you will come to no harm. It has been taught elsewhere: If one ate any kind of food without taking salt after it, or drank any kind of liquor without taking water after it, by day he is liable to be troubled with an evil-smelling mouth, and by night with croup. The Rabbis taught: One who swills down his food with plenty of water will not suffer with his bowels. How much should he drink? R. Ḥisda says: A cupful to a loaf.

R. Mari said in the name of R. Johanan: If one takes lentils regularly once in thirty days, he will keep croup away from his house.[4] He should not, however, take them every day. Why so? Because they cause a bad smell in the mouth. R. Mari also said in the name of R. Johanan: If one takes mustard regularly once in thirty days, he keeps sickness away from his house. He should not, however, take it every day. Why so? Because it is weakening for the heart. R. Ḥiyya b. Ashi said in the name of Rab: One who eats regularly small fish will not suffer with his bowels. Moreover, small fish stimulate propagation and strengthen a man's whole body. R. Ḥama b. Ḥanina said: One who takes regularly black cumin will not suffer from heartburn.[1] The following was cited in objection to this: R. Simeon b. Gamaliel says: Black cumin is one of the sixty poisons, and if one sleeps on the east side of the place where it is stored, his blood will be on his own head?[2]—There is no contradiction: The latter statement speaks of its smell, the former of its taste. The mother of R. Jeremiah used to bake bread for him and stick [black cumin] on it[3] and then scrape it off.[4]

R. JUDAH SAYS, WHO CREATEST DIVERS KINDS OF HERBS. R. Zera, or as some say R. Ḥinnena b. Papa, said: The *halachah* is not as stated by R. Judah. R. Zera, or as some say, R. Ḥinnena b. Papa, further said: What is R. Judah's reason? Scripture says, *Blessed be the Lord day by day.*[5] Are we then to bless Him by day and not bless Him by night? What it means to tell us is that every day we should give Him the blessing appropriate to the day.[6] So here, for every species we should give Him the appropriate blessing.

R. Zera, or as some say, R. Ḥinnena b. Papa, further said: Observe how the character of the Holy One, blessed be He, differs from that of flesh and blood. A mortal can put something into an empty vessel[7] but not into a full one. But the Holy One, blessed be He, is not so; He puts more into a full vessel[8] but not into an empty one; for it says, *If hearkening thou wilt hearken,*[9] implying, if thou hearkenest [once] thou wilt go on hearkening, and if not, thou wilt not hearken. Another explanation is: If thou hearkenest to the old,[1] thou wilt hearken to the new, but if thy heart turns away, thou wilt not hear any more.

MISHNAH. IF ONE SAYS OVER FRUIT OF THE TREE THE BENEDICTION, 'WHO CREATEST THE FRUIT OF THE GROUND', HE HAS PERFORMED HIS OBLIGATION. BUT IF HE SAID OVER PRODUCE OF THE GROUND, 'WHO CREATEST THE FRUIT OF THE TREE', HE HAS NOT PERFORMED HIS OBLIGATION. IF HE SAYS 'BY WHOSE WORD ALL THINGS EXIST' OVER ANY OF THEM, HE HAS PERFORMED HIS OBLIGATION.

GEMARA. What authority maintains that the essence of the tree is the ground?—R. Naḥman b. Isaac replied: It is R. Judah, as we have learnt: If the spring has dried up or the tree has been cut down,[2] he brings the first-fruits but does not make the declaration.[3] R. Judah, however, says that he both brings them and makes the declaration.[4]

OVER FRUIT OF THE GROUND etc. This is obvious, is it not?—R. Naḥman b. Isaac said: It required to be stated in view of the opinion of R. Judah, who maintains that wheat is a kind of tree. For it has been taught: R. Meir holds that the tree of which Adam ate was the vine, since the thing that most causes wailing to a man is wine, as it says, *And he drank of the wine and was drunken.*[5] R. Nehemiah says it was the fig tree, so that they repaired their misdeed with the instrument of it, as it says, *And they sewed fig leaves together.*[6] R. Judah says it was wheat, since a child does not know how to call 'father' and 'mother' until it has had a taste of
d corn.[1] Now you might think that because R. Judah says that wheat is a kind of tree, therefore we should say over it the benediction 'who createst the fruit of the tree'. Therefore we are told that we say 'who createst the fruit of the tree' only in those cases where if you take away the fruit the stem still remains to produce fruit

(7) After saying the blessing on behalf of all. (8) Lit., '(the bread) has been blessed'. (9) In spite of the fact that there has been an interruption between the saying and the eating, because the words spoken have reference to the benediction.

(1) Deut. XI, 15. (2) So Jast. Rashi translates: no delay (in waiting for the salt). (3) Because one who discharges standing is afraid of the drops falling on his clothes (Rashi). (4) Rashi explains that they keep away indigestion which is the cause of croup.

(1) Lit., 'pain of the heart'. (2) Because the west wind will carry the odour to him and poison him. (3) So that it should absorb the taste. (4) To remove the smell. (5) Ps. LXVIII, 20. (6) E.g., on Sabbath the Sabbath blessing, on festivals the festival blessing, etc. (7) Lit., 'in the case of a mortal man, an empty vessel can be made to hold, etc.'. (8) I.e., He gives more wisdom to the wise. (9) Ex. XV, 26, lit. trans. E.V. *'If thou wilt diligently hearken'*.

c (1) I.e., constantly revise what you have learnt. (2) If one has gathered first-fruits, and before he takes them to Jerusalem the spring which fed the tree dries up, or the tree is cut down. (3) V. Deut. XXVI, 5—10, because it contains the words *'of the land which Thou, O Lord, hast given me'*, and the land is valueless without the tree or the spring. (4) Because the land is the essence, not the tree; v. Bik. I, 6. (5) Gen. IX, 21. The reference is to Noah. (6) Ibid. III, 7.

d (1) Hence the Tree of Knowledge must have been some kind of corn.

אמר רב *טול ברוך טול ברוך אינו צריך לברך הבא מלח הבא לפתן צריך לברך ורבי יוחנן אמר אפי' הביאו מלח הביאו לפתן נמי אין צריך לברך גביל לתורי גביל לתורי צריך לברך ורב ששת אמר אפילו גביל לתורי נמי אינו צריך לברך דאמר *רב יהודה אמר *רב [כב] אסור לאדם *שיאכל קודם שיתן מאכל לבהמתו שנאמ' °ונתתי עשב בשדך לבהמתך והדר ואכלת ושבעת: אמר רבא בר שמואל משום ר' חייא אין הבוצע רשאי לבצוע עד שיביאו מלח או לפתן לפני כל אחד ואחד רבא בר שמואל אקלע לבי ריש גלותא אפיקו ליה ריפתא ובצע להדיא אמרו ליה הדר מר משמעתיה אמר להו לית דין צריך בשש: ואמר רבא בר שמואל משום ר' חייא *אין מי רגלים כלים אלא בישיבה אמר רב כהנא ובעפר תיחוח אפי' בעמידה ואי ליכא עפר תיחוח יעמוד במקום גבוה וישתין למקום מדרון: ואמר רבא בר שמואל משמיה דר' חייא אחר כל אכילתך אכול מלח ואחר כל שתייתך שתה מים ואי אתה נזוק תניא נמי הכי אחר כל אכילתך אכול מלח ואחר כל שתייתך שתה מים ואי אתה נזוק תניא אידך אכל כל מאכל ולא אכל מלח שתה כל משקין ולא שתה מים ביום ידאג מן ריח הפה ובלילה ידאג מפני אסכרה ת"ר המקפה אכילתו במים אינו בא לידי חולי מעים וכמה א"ר חסדא קיתון לפת אמר רב מרי א"ר יוחנן הרגיל בעדשים אחת לשלשים יום מונע אסכרה מתוך ביתו אבל כל יומא לא מ"ט משום דקשה לריח הפה ואמר רב מרי א"ר יוחנן הרגיל בחרדל אחת לשלשים יום מונע חלאים מתוך ביתו אבל כל יומא לא מ"ט משום דקשה לחולשא דלבא אמר רב חייא בר אשי אמר רב הרגיל בדגים קטנים אינו בא לידי חולי מעים ולא עוד *אלא שדגים קטנים מפרין ומרבין ומברין כל גופו של אדם אמר ר' חמא ב"ר חנינא *הרגיל בקצח אינו בא לידי כאב לב מיתיבי רשב"ג אומר קצח אחד מששים סמני המות הוא והישן למזרח גרנו דמו בראשו ל"ק הא בריחו הא בטעמו אימיה דר' ירמיה אפיא ליה ריפתא ומדבקא ליה ומקלפא ליה: רבי יהודה אומר בורא מיני דשאים: אמר רבי זירא ואיתימא רבי חיננא בר פפא אין הלכה כר' יהודה *וא"ר זירא ואיתימא ר' חיננא בר פפא מ"ט דר' יהודה אמר קרא °ברוך יי' יום יום וכי ביום מברכין אותו ובלילה אין מברכין אותו אלא לומר כל יום ויום תן לו מעין ברכותיו הכא נמי כל מין ומין תן לו מעין ברכותיו: *וא"ר זירא ואיתימא ר' חיננא בר פפא בא וראה שלא כמדת הקב"ה מדת בשר ודם מדת בשר ודם כלי ריקן מחזיק מלא אינו מחזיק אבל הקב"ה אינו כן מלא מחזיק ריקן אינו מחזיק שנאמר °ויאמר אם שמוע תשמע אם שמוע תשמע ואם לאו לא תשמע ד"א אם שמוע בישן תשמע בחדש ואם יפנה לבבך שוב לא תשמע: **מתני'** בירך על פירות האילן בפה"א יצא ועל פירות הארץ בפה"ע לא יצא ועל כולם *אם אמר שהכל נהיה בדברו יצא: **גמ'** מאן תנא דעיקר אילן ארעא היא אמר רב נחמן בר יצחק ר' יהודה היא דתנן *יבש המעיין ונקצץ האילן מביא ואינו קורא ר' יהודה אומר מביא וקורא: על פירות הארץ וכו': פשיטא אמר רב נחמן בר יצחק לא נצרכה אלא לר' יהודה דאמר חטה מין אילן היא דתניא *אילן שאכל ממנו אדם הראשון ר"מ אומר גפן היה שאין לך דבר שמביא יללה על האדם אלא יין שנאמר °וישת מן היין וישכר ר' נחמיה אומר תאנה היתה שבדבר *שנתקלקלו בו נתקנו שנאמר °ויתפרו עלה תאנה ר' יהודה אומר חטה היתה שאין התינוק יודע לקרות אבא ואמא עד שיטעום טעם דגן ס"ד אמינא הואיל ואמר ר' יהודה חטה מין אילן הוא ליברך עליה בפה"ע קמ"ל היכא מברכינן ב"פ העץ היכא דכי שקלת ליה לפירי איתיה לגווזא והדר מפיק

אבל

תורה אור

רש"י

טול ברוך. הבוצע וקודם שטעם מן הפרוסה בלע מנכה והושיט למי שאללו וא"ל טול ומפרוסת הברכה אע"פ שסח ביניהם אין צריך לחזור לברך ואע"ג דשיחה הויא הפסקה כדאמרינן במנחות (ד' לו.) סח בין תפילין לתפילין צריך לברך וכן בכסוי הדם הך שיחה צורך ברכה ולא מפסקא: הביאו מלח. נמי אין צריך לברך שאף זו צורך ברכה שתהא פרוס' של ברכה כאכלת בטעם: גביל לתורי. גביל את המורסן במים לצורך השוורים: ובצע לה להדי'. כלומ' מיד ולא המתין למלח ולפתן: בשש. עכוב כמו בשש רכבו (שופטים ה) כלומר פת נקיה היא זו ואין צריכה לפתן: אין מי רגלים כלים. מן הגוף: אלא בישיבה. לפי ששהקלוח קרוב לפיסוק הוא דואג שלא יפלו כלוכות על רגליו ומפסיק: עפר תיחוח. ליכא כלוכות: אסכרה. בו"ן מלא"כנו: המקפה אכילתו במים. שותה מים הרבה אחר אכילתו עד שאכילתו לפה במים ויצף הברזל מתרגמינן וקפא ברזלא (מלכים ב ו): מונע אסכר'. שהחולי בא מחמ' עלור בני מעי' והעדשי' משלשלים: קצח. רבותינו מפרשים ניי"לא בלע"ז אבל אני שמעתי מין זרעים שזורעין אותו בארץ ישמעאל: למזרח גורנו. של קלא שרוח מערבית רוח לחה ומתוכת' היא ומכנסת הריח בתוך הגוף: הא בריחו הא בטעמו. הריח קשה והטעם טוב: מדבקא ליה. ברפתא עד שקלט הטעם: ומקלפא ליה. בשביל הריח: כל יום ויום. בשבת מעין שבת ביום טוב מעין יום טוב: כלי מלא. אדם חכם: אם שמוע. פעם אחת שופך שתעה אזן פעם אחרת: אם תשמע בישן. ששנית ושלשת מה ששמעת אשתקד: דעיקר אילן ארעא היא. דעיקר כל הפירות היא הארץ והכל גדל הימנה: יבש המעיין ונקצץ האילן. היה לו בית השלחין ובו מעיין שהוא משקהו ממנו וקצר בכורים ממנו ואח"כ יבש המעיין וכן שדה האילן וקצץ בכורי' ממנו ואח"כ נקצץ האילן: מביא ואינו קורא. שאינו יכול לומר מן האדמה אשר נתת לי דכיון דיבש המעיין ונקצץ האילן ממנה בטלה לה ארעא: מביא וקורא. שהארץ היא עיקר: שהוא הביא יללה. וזה הביא מיתה: שאין התינוק יודע לקרות אבא ואמא. וזה נקרא עץ הדעת: גווזא. הענף של עץ: מפיק. פירי אחריני:

חוץ

תוספות

הביאו מלח וכו' צריך לברך. דהוי היסח הדעת והכי אמרי' בפ"ג דמנחות (ד' לו.) סח בין תפילין לתפילין צריך לברך וכן הלכה אם סח בין ברכת המוציא לאכיל' ובין ברכת קידוש לשתייה צריך לחזור ולברך אי לאו מלתא דשייכא לסעוד' כמו טול ברוך וכן בשחיטה צריך לחזור ולברך אי לאו ממלתא דשחיטה כמו העוף יותר בהמות ותרנגולים לשחוט או שיאמר אחוז היטב שלא ישמט לך שלא תפסל השחיטה אין זו הפסקה ואנו אין אנו רגילין להבי' על השולחן לא מלח ולא לפתן משו' דפת שלנו חשוב והרי הוא כי הא דאמ' בסמוך לית דין צריך בשש מיהו ר' מנחם היה מדקדק מאד להבי' מלח על השולחן כדאית' במדרש כשישראל יושבין על השולחן וממתינין זה את זה עד שיטלו ידיהם והן בלא מצוה השטן מקטרג עליהם וברית מלח מגין עליהם:

ר' יהודה היא דתנן יבש המעיין וכו'. ונראה דהלכ' כר' יהודה דסת' לן תנא כוותי' ואם בירך על פירות האילן בפ"הא יצא:

יבש המעיין כו'. יש מפרשים לכך מביא ואינו קורא מפני שאינו נראה כמשבח להקב"ה אלא כקובל על מה שנתן לו אדמה שאינה ראויה לפירות:

איתיה לגווזא והדר אתי. משמע כראה דתותים ופרי"זיי"ש ובוכטוכ"ש וכיוצא בהן צריכין לברך עליהם בורא פרי העץ שהרי דרך העץ להתקיים ימים רבים וכי שקיל הפרי בשנה זו הדר את' פרי באותו העץ עצמו *ומיהו הרב ר' מנחם הביא ראיה מירושלמי דמסכת כלאי' ספ"ה דמברכין על כל מיני דאטד בורא פרי האדמ' דקאמ' התם הסגין ואטדין מין אילן הם ואינן כלאים בכרם ופריך והתניא אלו הן מיני דשאים הקורדם והאטד ומשני תמן לברכה והכא לכלאים אלמא לענין ברכה מיני דשאין ומיהו לדברי הכל פריז"יי"ש צריך לברך עליהם בורא פרי העץ דאינו גדל על אטדין ועלו מתקיים משנה לשנה:

ורבי

עין משפט נר מצוה

עד א מיי' פ"א מהלכ' ברכות ה"ח סמג עשין כז טוש"ע א"ח סי' קסז סעי' ו וסי' כו סעיף ב

עה ג מיי' פ"ז מהלכ' ברכות ה"ג סמג עשין כז טוש"ע א"ח סי' קסז סעי' ה *[בגיטין אית' שיטעו' כלום עד שיתן וכו' וכן אית' בר"ף והרא"ש]

[כב] מיי' פ"ע מה' עבדים ה' ח' סמג עשין פז ח"ל ומקדימין מזון הבהמו' ועבדי' לסעודו' עצמן הרי הוא אומר כעיני עבדים אל יד אדוניה' וכעיני שפחה אל יד גברתה ולע"ק]

עו ד מיי' פ"ד מה' תפילין הי"ח טוש"ע א"ח סי' ג סעי' יג

[וע' תוס' בכורות ח. ד"ה באילן וכו']

עז ו טוש"ע א"ח סי' קע סעי' כב ובסי' קעט סעי' ו

עח ח מיי' פ"ד מה' דעות הל' ב

עט ט מיי' שם הל' ע

פ כ מיי' פ"ח מה' ברכו' ה"א סמג עשין כז טוש"ע א"ח סי' ר"ה סעי' א

פא ל מיי' שם ה"י וסמג שם טוש"ע א"ח סי' כו סעי' א

פב מ מיי' פ"ד מה' בכורים הל' יב

פג נ טוש"ע א"ח סי' רג סעי' ב

[סנהדרין ע. ע"ש]

[וע' פרש"י סנהדרין ע: ד"ה בדבר וכו' ומ"ש תוס' שם בהשגה ופירשו בענין אחר]

מסורת הש"ס

גטין סב. [ברב אלפס אי' שמואל וברא"ש אית' אמר רב הונא אמר רב]

[ע' תוס' יומא ל. ד"ה מלוה]

דברים יא

[לקמן מז:]

[מס' כלה]

סוכה מו.

תהלים סח

סוכה שם

שמות ע

[לעיל יב.]

בכורים פ"א מ"ו

ברא©ית ע

שם ג

תורה אור

אבל היכא דכי שקלת ליה לפירי ליתא
לגווזא דהדר מפיק לא מברכינן עליה ב"פ
העץ אלא בפ"הא: ועל כולן אם אמר שהכל
וכו': אתמר רב הונא אמר חוץ מן הפת ומן
היין ורבי יוחנן אמר *אפילו פת ויין נימא
כתנאי *ראה פת ואמר כמה נאה פת זו *ברוך
המקום שבראה יצא ראה תאנה ואמר כמה
נאה תאנה זו ברוך המקום שבראה יצא
דברי ר"מ ר' יוסי אומר בכל המשנה ממטבע
שטבעו חכמים בברכות לא יצא ידי חובתו
נימא רב הונא דאמר כר' יוסי ור' יוחנן דאמר
כר"מ אמר לך רב הונא אנא דאמרי אפילו
לר"מ ע"כ לא קאמר ר"מ התם אלא היכא
דקא מדכר שמיה דפת אבל היכא דלא קא
מדכר שמיה דפת אפי' ר"מ מודה ור' יוחנן
אמר לך אנא דאמרי אפילו לר' יוסי ע"כ לא
קאמר ר' יוסי התם אלא משום דקאמר ברכה
דלא תקינו רבנן אבל אמר שהכל נהיה בדברו
דתקינו רבנן אפי' רבי יוסי מודה בנימין רעיא
כרך ריפתא ואמר גבריך מריה דהאי פיתא
אמר רב יצא והאמר רב כל ברכה שאין בה
הזכרת השם אינה ברכה דאמר בריך רחמנא
מריה דהאי פיתא והא בעינן שלש ברכות מאי
יצא דקאמר רב נמי דיצא ידי ברכה ראשונה
מאי קמ"ל אע"ג דאמרה בלשון חול תנינא *ואלו נאמרים בכל לשון פרש' סוטה ודוי מעשר וקריאת שמע
ותפלה וברכת המזון אצטריך סד"א הני מילי דאמרה בלשון חול כי היכי דתקינו רבנן בלשון קדש אבל לא
אמרה בלשון חול כי היכי דתקינו רבנן בלשון קדש אימא לא הקמ"ל: גופא *אמר רב כל ברכה שאין בה
הזכרת השם אינה ברכה *ור' יוחנן אמר וכל ברכה שאין בה מלכות אינה ברכה אמר אביי כותיה דרב
מסתברא *דתניא °לא עברתי ממצותיך ולא שכחתי לא עברתי מלברכך ולא שכחתי מלהזכיר שמך עליו ואלו
מלכות לא קתני *ור' יוחנן תני ולא שכחתי מלהזכיר שמך ומלכותך עליו: **מתני'** *ועל דבר שאין גדולו מן
הארץ אומר שהכל נהיה בדברו *על החומץ *ועל הנובלות ועל הגובאי אומר שהכל נהיה בדברו ר' יהודה
אומר כל שהוא מין קללה אין מברכין עליו היו לפניו הרבה מינין ר' יהודה אומר אם יש ביניהן מין שבעה
עליו הוא מברך וחכ"א מברך על איזה מהן שירצה: **גמ'** ת"ר טעל דבר שאין גדולו מן הארץ כגון בשר בהמות
חיות ועופות ודגים אומר שהכל נהיה בדברו על החלב ועל הבצים ועל הגבינה אומר שהכל *על הפת שעפשה ועל
היין שהקרים ועל התבשיל שעבר צורתו אומר שהכל על המלח ועל הזמית ועל כמהין ופטריות אומר שהכל למימרא
דכמהין ופטריות לאו גדולי קרקע נינהו *והתני' הנודר מפירות הארץ אסור בפירות הארץ ומותר בכמהין
ופטריות ואם אמר כל גדולי קרקע עלי אסור אף בכמהין ופטריות אמר אביי מירבא רבו מארעא מינקי לא
ינקי מארעא והא על דבר שאין גדולו מן הארץ קתני תני על דבר שאין יונק מן הארץ: ועל הנובלות: מאי
נובלות ר' זירא ור' אילעא חד אמר בושלי כמרא וחד אמר תמרא דזיקא תנן ר' יהודה אומר כל שהוא מין
קללה אין מברכין עליו בשלמא למ"ד בושלי כמרא היינו דקרי ליה מין קללה אלא למאן דאמר תמרי דזיקא
מאי מין קללה אשארא איכא דאמרי בשלמא למאן דאמר בושלי כמרא היינו דמברכינן עלייהו שהכל אלא
למ"ד תמרי דזיקא שהכל ב"פ העץ מבעי לברוכי אלא בנובלות סתמא כולי עלמ' לא פליגי דבושלי כמרא
נינהו כי פליגי בנובלות תמרה *דתנן והקלין שבדמאי השיתין והרימין והעוזרדין בנות שוח ובנות שקמה
וגופנין ונצפה ונובלות תמרה שיתין אמר רבה בר בר חנה א"ר יוחנן מין תאנים רימין *כנדי העוזרדין טולשי
*בנות שוח אמר רבה בר בר חנה א"ר יוחנן תאיני חוורתא בנות שקמה אמר רבה בר בר חנה א"ר יוחנן דובלי
גופני שילהי גופני נצפה פרחה נובלות תמרה רבי אילעא ור' זירא חד אמר בושלי כמרא וחד אמר תמרי זיקא
בשלמא למ"ד בושלי כמרא היינו דקתני הקלין שבדמאי ספיקן הוא דפטור הא ודאן חייב אלא למ"ד תמרי זיקא
ודאן חייב הפקרא נינהו הכא במאי עסקינן שעשאן גורן *דא"ר יצחק א"ר יוחנן משום ר"א בן יעקב מהלקט
והשכחה והפאה שעשאן גורן הוקבעו למעשר איכא דאמרי בשלמא

חוץ מן הפת ומן היין. כדאמרינן לקמן (דף מג.) שגורס ברכות הרבה לעלמו בקידוש ובהבדל' ובברכת חתנים: ידי ברכה ראשונה. ברכת הזן: פרשת סוטה. כשהכהן משביעה: ודוי מעשר. בערתי הקדש מן הבית (דברים כו): מלברכך. ברוך אשר קדשנו במלותיו ולונו להפריש תרומה ומעשר: **מתני'** הנובלות. מפרש בגמ': גובאי. חגבים טהורים: מין קללה. חומץ ונובלות וגובאי ע"י קללה הן באין: **גמ'** שהקרים בועי"ר בלע"ז: מירבא רבו מארעא. מלחלוחי' הארץ הם גדלים על העלים ועל הכלים: בישולי כמרא. כמו שרופי חמה שבשלם ושרפם החום ויבשו ותמרי' הם. כמרא חום כמו מכמר בשרא (פסחים דף כח.): תמרי דזיקא. שהרוח משיקן: אשארא. אחומץ וגובאי פליג ר' יהודה: פרי העץ בעי ברוכי. שהרי לא נשתנו לקלקול: הקלי' שבדמאי. פי' שהקלו חכמי' בדמאי שלהן שהלוקחן מעם הארץ אין לריך לעשרן אלו הן: השיתין כו'. שאינן חשובים ואין ע"ה חס עליהם מלעשרן: טולשי. קולמס"י: שילהי גופני. ענבים סתווניות: הא ודאן. אם ידוע שלא הופרש מהן מעשר: שעשאן גורן. העני או מי שלקטן העמיד מהן עריימת כרי: הלקט והשכחה והפאה. אף על פי שפטורי' מן המעשר לקטן עני ועשאן גורן הוקבעו למעש' מדרבנן דמאן דחזי סבר שתבואת קרקעו היא:

בשלמא

ורבי יוחנן אמר אפילו פת ויין. וכן הלכה דרב ורבי יוחנן הלכה כרבי יוחנן וכ"ש לגבי רב הונא שהיה תלמידו של רב:
נימא רב הונא כר' יוסי. וא"ת היכי מלי סובר רב הונא כר' יוסי הא רב הונא מודה בשאר דברים חוץ מפת ויין שאם אמר שהכל יצא ואלו ר' יוסי סבר דלא יצא דכל המשנה ממטבע כו' וי"מ דמלי למימר דאפילו ר' יוסי לא קאמר לא יצא אלא בברוך המקום שאינה ברכה כלל אבל בשהכל מודה:
אמר אביי כוותיה דרב מסתברא כו'. וי"מ דמסתבר' ברייתא כותיה ומיהו רב אלפס פסק כר' יוחנן וכן פסק ר' יהודה דכל ברכה שאין בה מלכות שמים אינה ברכה ולכך היה אומר ר"י שאם היה מדלג מלכו' של ברכת המוליא שלריך לחזור ולברך ואפילו דלג תיבת העולם בלבד דמלך לבד אינו מלכות וברכות *של שמונה עשרה אין בהן מלכות דאינן באין בפתיחה ובחתימ' אין שייך מלכות אבל אלהי אברהם הוי כמו מלכות דאברהם אבינו המליך הקדוש ב"ה על כל העולם שהודיע מלכותו. ומעין שבע דמללי בשבת' הואיל ויש בה האל הקדוש שאין כמוהו הייני כמו מלכות כמו שמע ישראל ה' אלקינו ה' אחד דהוי במקום מלכות ולפי מה דפרישית כל היכא דכתיב אלהי אברהם הוי כמו מלכות כיחא ולרבי יוחנן לא קשיא דלא כתיב מלכותך דאטו כי רוכלא כל האי ליתני וליזיל:

אבל

עין משפט נר מצוה

פד
אמיי' פ"ח מה' ברכות ה"י סמ"ג עשין כז טוש"ע א"ח סי' קפז סעי' י' וסי' רו סעי' א

פה
במיי' פ"א מהל' ברכות הל' ה סמ"ג שם

פו
גד טוש"ע א"ח סי' קפז סעי' י' וסי' קפז כעיף א [עמ"ב תוס' לקמן מט. ד"ה ברוך]

פז
הזמיי' פ"א מה' ברכות הל' ו

פח
ומיי' וסמג שם טוש"ע א"ח סי' ריד

פט
זמיי' שם פ"ח ה"ח טוש"ע א"ח סי' רד סעי' א ב

צ
חט מיי' וסמ"ג שם טוש"ע א"ח שם סעי' א

צא
ימיי' פ"ע מהל' בכו"י הי"א סמ"ג לאוין רמ"ב טוש"ע י"ד סי' ריז סעי' כג [לקמן מט.] וכ"ה הגי' גם ברא"ש ובהגה' הרש"ל אמנם מתוס' ד"ה אמ' אביי משמע דלא גרסינן]

צב
כמיי' פ"ח מה' ברכו' ה"ח סמג שם טוש"ע א"ח סי' רב סעי' ט וסי' רד סעי' א

צג
למיי' פי"ג מה' מעשר הל' א

צד
ממיי' פ"ב מה' תרומות הל' ע

גי' ערוך ע' ככר כנרי רימין

מסורת הש"ס

[תוספ' פ"ד (ניסח ירוש' ברוך שברא וכו' מה נאה הוא זה)]

סוטה לב. שבועות לט.

לעיל יב.

ספרי פ' כי תבא דברים כו נדרים נה.

כ"א על החס- ועל הגבינה ועל הבלים אומר שהכל ב"ב לה:

נדרים שם

דמאי פ"א מ"א

ע"ז יד.

סוטה מג:

(2) Bread because it is the mainstay of the meal, wine because many special benedictions are said over it. (3) Lit., 'doubled (wrapped) a loaf', which seems to mean that he made a sandwich of bread and some relish.

(1) He said it in Aramaic. (2) It was assumed that he said this formula after eating. (3) Num. V, 21ff. (4) Deut. XXVI, 13—15. (5) V. Sot. 32a. (6) Deut. XXVI, 13 in reference to the tithe. (7) The benediction, 'Blessed be He . . . who commanded us to set aside *terumah* and tithe'.

(1) Lit., 'withering products'. This is explained in the Gemara. (2) And the things just mentioned come under this heading. (3) Enumerated in Deut. VIII, 8. (4) V. Ned. 55*b*. (5) Lit., 'they do not suck'. (6) While still on the tree.

c (1) Viz., vinegar and locusts. (2) Since they are still dates. (3) Demai I, 1. (4) I.e., which a *haber* (v. Glos.) need not tithe if he buys them from an *'am ha-arez* (v. Glos.). These things being of little value, the presumption is that they have been tithed. (5) That they have not been tithed. (6) I.e., ownerless (v. Glos.) and not subject to tithe.

d (1) Which he had gathered and which are ordinarily not titheable.

again [40b], but in cases where if you take the fruit the stem does not remain to produce again, the benediction is not 'who createst the fruit of the tree' but 'who createst the fruit of the ground'.

IF HE SAYS, 'BY WHOSE WORD ALL THINGS EXIST' etc. It has been stated: R. Huna said: Except over bread and wine.[2] R. Johanan, however, said: Even over bread and wine. May we say that the same difference of opinion is found between Tannaim? [For it was taught:] 'If a man sees a loaf of bread and says, What a fine loaf this is! Blessed be the Omnipresent that has created it! he has performed his obligation. If he sees a fig and says, What a fine fig this is! Blessed be the Omnipresent that has created it! he has performed his obligation. So R. Meir. R. Jose says: If one alters the formula laid down by the Sages in benedictions, he has not performed his obligation'. May we say that R. Huna concurs with R. Jose and R. Johanan with R. Meir?—R. Huna can reply to you: I can claim even R. Meir as a supporter of my view. For R. Meir went as far as he did in that case only because the bread is actually mentioned, but where the bread is not actually mentioned even R. Meir would admit [that the obligation is not fulfilled]. And R. Johanan can reply to you: I may claim R. Jose also as a supporter of my view. For R. Jose only went as far as he did in that case because he made a benediction which was not instituted by the Sages, but if he says, 'by whose word all things exist', which has been instituted by the Sages, even R. Jose would admit [that he has performed his obligation].

Benjamin the shepherd made a sandwich[3] and said, Blessed be
a the Master of this bread,[1] and Rab said that he had performed his obligation. But Rab has laid down that any benediction in which God's name is not mentioned is no benediction?—We must suppose he said, Blessed be the All-Merciful, the Master of this bread. But we require three blessings?[2]—What did Rab mean by saying that he had performed his obligation? He had performed the obligation of the first blessing. What does this tell us [that we did not already know]? That [he has performed his obligation] even if he says it in a secular language. But we have already learnt this: 'The following may be said in any language: the section of the unfaithful wife,[3] the confession over tithe,[4] the recital of the *Shema'*, and the *Tefillah* and grace after food?[5]—It required to be stated. For you might have thought that this is the case only if one says the grace in a secular language in the same form as was instituted by the Rabbis in the holy tongue, but if one does not say it in the secular language in the same form as was instituted by the Rabbis in the holy tongue, he has not performed his obligation. We are therefore told [that this is not so].

It was stated above: Rab said that any benediction in which the Divine Name is not mentioned is no benediction. R. Johanan, however, said: Any benediction in which [God's] Kingship is not mentioned is no benediction. Abaye said: The opinion of Rab is the more probable. For it has been taught: *I have not transgressed any of Thy commandments, neither have I forgotten.*[6] This means: *'I have not transgressed'* so as not to bless Thee,[7] *'neither have I forgotten'* to mention Thy name therein. Of sovereignty, however, there is no mention here. R. Johanan, however, reads: *'Neither have I forgotten'* to mention Thy name and Thy sovereignty therein.

MISHNAH. OVER ANYTHING WHICH DOES NOT GROW FROM THE EARTH ONE SAYS: 'BY WHOSE WORD ALL THINGS
b EXIST'. OVER VINEGAR, NOBELOTH[1] AND LOCUSTS ONE SAYS, 'BY WHOSE WORD ALL THINGS EXIST'. R. JUDAH SAYS: OVER ANYTHING TO WHICH A KIND OF CURSE ATTACHES NO BENEDICTION IS SAID.[2] IF ONE HAS SEVERAL VARIETIES BEFORE HIM, R. JUDAH SAYS THAT IF THERE IS AMONG THEM SOMETHING OF THE SEVEN KINDS,[3] HE MAKES THE BLESSING OVER THAT, BUT THE SAGES SAY THAT HE MAY MAKE THE BLESSING OVER ANY KIND THAT HE PLEASES.

GEMARA. Our Rabbis taught: Over anything which does not grow from the ground, such as the flesh of cattle, beasts and birds and fishes, one says 'by whose word all things were created'. Over milk, eggs and cheese one says, 'by whose word, etc.'. Over bread which has become mouldy and over wine on which a film has formed and cooked food which has become spoilt one says, 'by whose word'. Over salt and brine and morils and truffles one says, 'by whose word'. This would imply that morils and truffles do not grow from the ground. But has it not been taught: If one vows to abstain from fruit of the ground, he is forbidden to eat of fruit of the ground but is allowed to eat morils and truffles? If he said, I vow abstention from all that grows from the ground, he is forbidden to eat morils and truffles also?[4]—Abaye said: They do indeed spring up from the earth, but their sustenance is not derived[5] from the earth. But it says, 'over anything which grows from the earth'?—Read: Over anything which draws sustenance from the earth.

OVER NOBELOTH. What are NOBELOTH?—R. Zera and R. El'a [gave different answers]. One said: fruit parched by the sun;[6] the other said: dates blown down by the wind. We have learnt: R. JUDAH SAYS: OVER ANYTHING TO WHICH A KIND OF CURSE ATTACHES NO BLESSING IS SAID. This accords with the view of the one who says that *nobeloth* are fruit parched by the sun, which can rightly be called something to which a curse attaches. But if we say they are dates blown down by the wind, what has 'a kind of curse' to do with them?—This expression relates to the
c other things [mentioned].[1]

Some report as follows: On the view of him who says that they are fruit parched by the sun, it is quite right that we should say 'by whose word, etc.'; but according to the one who says that they are dates blown down by the wind, we should say, 'who createst the fruit of the tree'?[2]—The fact is that all are agreed that *nobeloth* in general are fruit parched by the sun. The difference arises over *nobeloth* of the date-palm, since we have learnt:[3] Things in regard to which the law of *demai* is not so strict[4] are *shittin, rimin, 'uzradin, benoth shuah, benoth shikmah, gofnin, nizpah* and the *nobeloth* of the date-palm. *Shittin,* according to Rabbah b. Bar Hanah reporting R. Johanan, are a kind of figs. *Rimin* are lote. *'Uzradin* are crab-apples. *Benoth shuah,* according to Rabbah b. Bar Hanah reporting R. Johanan, are white figs. *Benoth shikmah,* according to Rabbah b. Bar Hanah reporting R. Johanan, are sycamore figs. *Gofnin* are winter grapes. *Nizpah* is the caper-fruit. *Nobeloth* of the date-palm are explained differently by R. Zera and R. El'a. One says that they are fruit parched by the sun, the other that they are dates blown down by the wind. Now the view of him who says that they are fruit parched by the sun accords well with what it teaches [concerning them], 'things about which the law of *demai* is not so strict', and if there is a doubt about them, they are free from the obligation of tithe, which shows that if there is no doubt[5] they are subject to it. But on the view of him who says that they are dates blown down by the wind, must, in case of certainty, tithe be given from them? They are *hefker!*[6]—With what case are we dealing here? Where one made a store of them. For R. Isaac said in the name of R. Johanan reporting R. Eliezer b. Jacob: If [a poor man] has made a store of gleanings, forgotten sheaves and produce
d of the corner,[1] they are liable for tithe.

Some report as follows: [41a] The view of him who says that [they[2] are] dates blown down by the wind accords well with the fact that in one place[3] *nobeloth* simply[4] are spoken of and in the other[5] *nobeloth* of the date-palm. But on the view of him who says they[2] are fruit parched by the sun, in both places we should have *nobeloth* of the date-palm,[6] or in both places *nobeloth* simply, should we not?[7]—This is indeed a difficulty.

IF ONE HAD SEVERAL VARIETIES BEFORE HIM etc. 'Ulla said: Opinions differ only in the case where the blessings [over the several varieties] are the same; in such a case R. Judah holds that belonging to the seven kinds is of more importance, while the Rabbis held that being better liked is of more importance. But where they have not all the same benediction, all agree that a blessing is to be said first on one variety[8] and then on another. An objection was raised: If radishes and olives are set before a person, he says a benediction over the radish, and this serves for the olive also!—With what case are we dealing here? When the radish is the main item.[9] If so, look at the next clause: R. Judah says that the benediction is said over the olive, because the olive is one of the seven species.[10] Now would not R. Judah accept the teaching which we have learnt: Whenever with one article of food another is taken as subsidiary to it, a blessing is said over the main article and this serves for the subsidiary one also?[11] And should you be disposed to maintain that in fact he does not accept it, has it not been taught: R. Judah said, If the olive is taken on account of the radish, a blessing is said for the radish and this serves for the olive?—In fact we are dealing with a case where the radish *is* the main item,[1] and the difference of opinion between R. Judah and the Rabbis is really over a different matter, and there is a lacuna in the text and it should read as follows: If radish and olives are set before a person, he says a benediction over the radish and this serves for the olive also. When is this the case? When the radish is the main item; but if the radish is not the main item, all agree that he says a blessing over one and then a blessing over the other. If there are two varieties of food[2] which have the same blessing, he says it over whichever he prefers. R. Judah, however, says that he says the blessing over the olive, since it is of the seven species.

R. Ammi and R. Isaac Nappaḥa understood this differently. One said that the difference between R. Judah and the Rabbis arises when the blessings over the two kinds of food are the same, R. Judah holding that the fact of belonging to the seven kinds is more important, while the Rabbis held that the fact of being better liked was more important; but where the blessings are not the same, both agreed that a blessing is first said over one kind and then over the other. The other said that R. Judah and the Rabbis differ even when the blessings are not the same. Now accepting the view of him who says that the difference arises when the blessings are the same, we find no difficulty. But accepting the view that they differ also when the blessings are not the same, [we have to ask] on what ground do they differ?[3]—R. Jeremiah replied: They differ on the question of precedence. For R. Joseph, or as some say, R. Isaac, said: Whatever comes earlier in this verse has precedence in the matter of benediction, viz., *A land of wheat and barley, and vine and fig-trees and pomegranates, a land of olive trees and honey.*[4]

[In the exposition of this verse, R. Isaac] differs from R. Ḥanan. For R. Ḥanan said: The whole purpose of the verse was to mention things which serve as standards of measurements. '*Wheat*', as we have learnt: If one enters a house stricken with leprosy with his garments on his shoulder and his sandals and his rings in his hands, both he and they become unclean immediately. If he is wearing his garments and his sandals and has his rings on his fingers, he is immediately unclean but they remain clean until he stays in the
b house long enough to eat a piece of wheat bread,[1] but not of barley bread, reclining and taking with it a relish.[2] '*Barley*', as we have learnt: A bone as large as a barleycorn renders unclean by touch and carrying, but it does not render a tent unclean.[3] '*Vine*', the measurement for a Nazirite[4] is a fourth [of a *log*] of wine.[5] '*Fig-tree*', a dried fig is the measurement of what may be taken out of the house on Sabbath. '*Pomegranates*', as we have learnt: For

(2) The *nobeloth* mentioned in Demai. (3) In our Mishnah. (4) Denoting fruit parched by the sun. (5) In the passage from Demai. (6) Because it is necessary to distinguish the two kinds of *nobeloth*. (7) Because both passages are speaking about the same thing. (8) Which he likes best. (9) And the olive was only eaten to counteract the sharp taste. (10) This shows that we are not dealing with the case where one of the two articles is more important. (11) V. *supra* 35b.

(1) And we cannot say that in all cases a blessing is said first over one variety and then over the other. (2) One of which is of the seven species, e.g., olives. (3) Surely in this case the benediction for the one does not serve the other! (4) Deut. VIII, 8. R. Judah agrees with R. Isaac, and therefore *a fortiori* holds that any of these species should have precedence over other species, whereas the Rabbis agree with the view of R. Ḥanan which follows.

b (1) Which is eaten more quickly than barley bread. (2) Neg. XIII, 9. (3) Oh. II, 3. (4) The quantity of grapes which he may eat without spoiling his Naziriteship. (5) Which is somewhat larger than a *log* (v. Glos.) of water.

בשלמא למ"ד תמרי זיקא היינו דהכא קרי לה נובלות סתמא והתם קרי לה תמרא אלא למ"ד בושלי כמרא ניתני אידי ואידי נובלות תמרה או אידי ואידי נובלות סתמא קשיא: היו לפניו מינין הרבה וכו': אמר עולא מחלוקת בשברכותיהן שוות דרבי יהודה סבר [א]מין שבעה עדיף ורבנן סברי מין חביב עדיף אבל [ב]בשאין ברכותיהן שוות דברי הכל מברך על זה וחוזר ומברך על זה מיתיבי היו לפניו צנון וזית מברך על הצנון ופוטר את הזית הב"ע כשהצנון עיקר א"ה אימא סיפא ר' יהודה אומר מברך על הזית שהזית ממין שבעה לית ליה לר' יהודה הא דתנן *כל שהוא עיקר ועמו טפלה מברך על העיקר ופוטר את הטפלה וכ"ת ה"נ דלית ליה והתניא ר' יהודה אומר אם מחמת צנון בא הזית מברך על הצנון ופוטר את הזית לעולם בצנון עיקר עסקינן וכי פליגי ר' יהודה ורבנן במלתא אחריתי פליגי וחסורי מיחסרא והכי קתני היו לפניו צנון וזית מברך על הצנון ופוטר את הזית בד"א כשהצנון עיקר אבל אין הצנון עיקר ד"ה מברך על זה וחוזר ומברך על זה ושני מינין בעלמא שברכותיהן שוות מברך על איזה מהן שירצה ר' יהודה אומר מברך על הזית שהזית ממין שבעה פליגי בה רבי אמי ורבי יצחק נפחא חד אמר מחלוקת בשברכותיהן שוות דר' יהודה סבר מין שבעה עדיף ורבנן סברי מין חביב עדיף אבל בשאין ברכותיהן שוות ד"ה מברך על זה וחוזר ומברך על זה וחד אמר אף בשאין ברכותיהן שוות נמי מחלוקת בשלמא למ"ד בשברכותיהן שוות מחלוקת שפיר אלא למ"ד בשאין ברכותיהן שוות פליגי במאי פליגי א"ר ירמיה להקדים דא"ר יוסף ואיתימא ר' יצחק כל [ג]המוקדם בפסוק זה מוקדם לברכה שנאמר °ארץ חטה ושעורה וגפן ותאנה ורמון ארץ זית שמן ודבש ופליגא דרב חנן דא"ר חנן *כל הפסוק כולו לשיעורין נאמר חטה דתנן *[ד]הנכנס לבית המנוגע וכליו על כתפיו וסנדליו וטבעותיו בידיו הוא והן טמאין מיד [ה]היה לבוש כליו וסנדליו ברגליו וטבעותיו באצבע הוא טמא מיד והן טהורין *עד שישהא בכדי אכילת פרס פת חטין ולא פת שעורין מיסב ואוכלן בלפתן שעורה דתנן *[ו]עצם כשעורה מטמא במגע ובמשא ואינו מטמא באהל [ז]גפן כדי רביעית יין לנזיר תאנה [ח]כגרוגרות להוצאת שבת רמון כדתנן *כל [ט]כלי בעלי בתים

שיעורן

רש"י

בשלמא למ"ד. כותבת דדומי תמרי דזיקא וכותבות דמתני' אוקימנא בבושלי כמרא היינו דהכא קרי להו כותבו' תמרה ובמתני' תנן (דף מ:) כותבות סתמא: בשברכותיהן שוות. כגון זתים ותפוחים דתרוייהו בורא פרי העץ ובא לפטור את שתיהן בברכה אחת: חביב עדיף. איזה שירצה דמתני' את החביב עליו משמע: אבל בשאין ברכותיהן שוות דברי הכל. אין ברכה אחת פוטרתן ושוב אין כאן מחלוקת ואף ע"ג דתנן (לעיל דף מ.) בירך על פירות האילן בפה"א יצא הני מילי בחד מינא וטעה ובירך עליה בורא פרי האדמה אבל לנון וזית ובירך על הלנון לא פטור זית: פשיט' לא גרסי' עד מתיבי הדא שאין זו שיטת הגמרא מעיקרא קשיא ליה פשיטא דלא אצטריך למימרא והדר קשיא היכי מצי למימרא ועוד דלא פשיטא היא אי לאו דאשמעינן עולא הוה אמינא לנון פוטר את הזית דהתנן בירך על פירות האילן בורא פרי האדמה יצא: שהיה צנון עיקר. שבשבילו התחיל האכילה ולא אכל זית אלא להפיג חורפו של לנון דהוה ליה זית טפל ותנן (דף מד.) כל שהוא עיקר ועמו טפלה מברך על העיקר ופוטר את הטפל': מברך על זה כו'. וכאן לא נחלקו: ושני מיני' בעלמא. כגון זית ותפוח שברכותיהן שוות והאחד ממין שבעה בזה נחלקו: חד אמר מחלוקת בשברכותי' שוות. וכדאמר': ה"ג. וחד אמר אף בשאין ברכותיהן שוות נמי מחלוק' ומפר' לה ואזיל: במאי פליגי. הא ודאי לא מפטרי בחדא ברכה: א"ר ירמיה בלהקדים. פליגי ולא גרסינן אבל בשברכותיהן שוות מברך על איז' מהן שירצה דהשתא בשאינן שוות מקפיד רבי יהודה על הקדמתן והא' מין שבע' עדיף כשבא לפטור זו בזו לא כל שכן: דאמר ר' יצחק כו'. אלמא קפדינן אהקדמה ור' יהודה אית לי' דר' יצחק הלכך כ"ש היכא דחד מהו ממין שבע' דמין שבעה עדיף ורבנן לית להו דר' יצחק במקו' חביב דחביב עדיף: ופליגא דר' חנן. הא דר' יצחק דאמר המוקדם קודם לברכה אלמא קרא לשבח א"י בא שיש בה פירות החשובי' הללו ומכאן כסדר חשיבותם ופליג אדר' חנן דאמר לא בא הכתוב להודיע שבח חשיבות הפירו' בטעם שלהם אלא שבחה של א"י שיש בה פירות ששיעורי תורה נתלין בהן וכיון דהכי הוא לא הקפיד הכתוב על סדרן שהרי בזו כולן שוין: בבית המנוגע. כתיב והבא אל הבית יטמא עד הערב (ויקרא יד) ולא כתיב כבוס בגדים והאוכל בבית יכבס את בגדיו (שם) בשוהא שיעור אכילה ואפי' לא יאכל מדכתיב בסיפיה והשוכב בבית יכבס בגדיו הלכך הנכנס בו ונושא את בגדיו עמו שלא כדרך מלבושו אין אלו בגדיו וטמאים מיד שאף בהן אני קורא והבא אל הבית וכשהוא לבוש מהן בעי שהייה: אכילת פרס. חצי ככר ששיערו בו חכמים את העירוב שהוא כולו מזון שתי סעודו' וחציו מזון סעודה אחת: פת חטין. כאכלת מהר: מסב. דרך הסבה שהיא כאכלת מהר שאינו פונה אנה ואנה: ואינו מטמא באהל. הלכה למשה מסיני היא: כדי רביעית יין לנזיר. אכל חרצנים וזגים ולולבין כשיעור רביעי' יין חייב ואין שיעור רביעי' יין ורביעית מים שוין לפי שהיין עב והמים קלושין ויש ברביעית יין יותר ממה שיש ברביעי' מים כדאמרי' במנחו' (דף קד.) גבי רביעי' דם שיכול לקרוש ולעמוד על כזית משום דסמיך אבל מידי דקליש לא הוה רביעי' דידי' כזית: להוצאת שבת. דתנן המוציא אוכלי' כגרוגרת (שבת דף עה:) והיא תאנה יבשה:

תוספות

אבל בשאין ברכותיהן שוות. פרש"י כגון לנון וזית ושוב אין כאן מחלוקת כיון שאין האחד פוטר את חבירו אפילו ר' יהודה מודה דאין עדיפות בשבעת המיני' אלא יברך על איזה שירצ' תחלה החביב לו ואח"כ יברך על השני וכן יש לפרש דרבי יהוד' מודה לחכמים הואיל ולא פירש הגמרא מועט שכאמר שיחיד מודה לרבים ולא רבים מודי' ליחיד והק' רש"י ולבריך על הלנון ולפטור את הזית דהא תנן לעיל בירך על פירו' האילן בפה"א יצא ותירץ דשאני התם שאין שם אלא חד מינא וטעה ובירך בורא פרי האדמה אבל הכא כשבירך בפה"א על הלנון לא פטר את חבירו שהיה בורא פרי העץ אפילו בדיעבד ואם תאמ' הא אמרינן לעיל (ד' לט.) גבי עובד' דבר קפר' דברכת בפה"א חשיב טפי משהכל לפי שמבוררת טפי אם כן גם בורא פרי העץ חשיב' טפי מברכת בפה"א וי"ל דלא חשיב בפה"ע כ"כ מבפה"א כמו שחשוב בפה"א משהכל ומה שכתב בהלכות גדולו' דבורא פרי העץ תקדום לבפה"א דמבוררת טפי היינו לפי המסקנא דלקמן דפליגי בשאין ברכותיהן שוות וק"ל כר' יהודה אבל להאי לישנ' דאמרי' דלא פליגי בשאין ברכותיהן שוות לא מתוקם פסק דהלכו' גדולו' כדפירשנו לעיל:

מתיבי היו לפניו לנון וזית מברך על הלנון וכו'. ופריך אלמא דמברך בורא פרי האדמ' אפי' לפטור בורא פרי העץ אפי' לגבי זית שהוא משבעת המינים וכ"ש קליות שהן כמו כן משבעת המינין דמברך עליהן בורא פרי האדמה לפטור את *התפוחים לכן צריך להנהיג הכי *כדפרישי' לעיל באין ברכותיהן שוות כמו תפוחי' וקליו':

אמר ר' ירמיה להקדי' דאמר רב יוסף וכו'. פרש"י והר"י לפי גירסא זו אתיא הא דאמר רב יוסף כל המוקדם כר' יהוד' דוקא אבל ר' שמעיה גרים אמר רב יוסף וכו' ואתי' אליבא דרבנן ומיירי שאין חביבין זה מזה דהא אזלי' בתר מוקדם דאי בחביבין פשיטא דחביב קודם דהא אפי' בשאר מינין לגבי שבעת המינין אמרי רבנן דמברך על איזה שירצה ומלתא דרב יוסף מלתא באפי נפשה ולא נהירא דבסמוך משמע דגר' דאמר רב יוסף ואתיא כר' יהודה דוקא דקאמר רב חסדא ורב המנונא הוו יתבי בסעודתא וכו' א"ל לא סבר לה מר להא דרב יוסף דאמ' כל המוקד' וכו':

במאי פליגי. כלומ' מאי טעמ' דר' יהוד' דאמר שבעת המינין עדיף ומאי עדיפות שייכא בהו אחר שאינן יכולין לפטור שאר מיני' ומשני דהעדיפות הוי מן ההקדמה:

גפן כדי רביעית יין וכו'. פירוש אם אכל עלין או לולבין כדי רביעי' יין חייב אבל אם אכל מהן כדי רביעי' מים לא מחייב דקליש' והולכין בכל חוץ מן הכלי אבל כי משערי' יין לריך שיעורא טפי שהיין הוא עב ומחזיק גודש קלת קודם שיפול מן הכוס רביעית יין ואם היה מים היה יולא יותר מרביעית*:

כלי בעלי בתים. גבי כלי עץ מתכוה:

אייתו

עין משפט נר מצוה

צה א ב מיי' פ"ח מה' ברכות הי"ג סמג עשין כז טוש"ע א"ח סי' ריא סעי' א

צו ג מיי' וסמג שם טוש"ע א"ח שם סעי' ד

צז ד מיי' פי"ו מה' טומא' צרע' הל' ז

צח ה שם הל' ו

צט ו מיי' פ"ג מה' טומאת מת הל' ב

ק ז מיי' פ"ה מה' נזירו' הל' ב סמג לאוין קן

קא ח מיי' פי"ח מה' שבת הל' א

קב ט מיי' פ"ו מה' כלים הל' ב

[נראה דהך כדפריסים הוא סיום דיבור התוס' ומתחיל דיבור חדש מן באין ברכותיהן שוות שליין על הגמ' דלעיל ופי' כמו תפוחי' וכו' ותיב' לעיל הוא כמו שליינו הרבה פעמי' כשמהפכו דיבורי תוס' להורות מקום בזה שייך לעי' והמעתיקי' שגו והדפיסו הכל לדיבור אחד וכן הגיה הגאון מהר"א מווילנא]

[וע"ע תוס' עירובין ד. ותוס' סוכה ו.]

מסורת הש"ס

תורה אור

לעיל לה: ולקמן מד.

ע"י' רש"א ורש"ל

דברי' ח

עירובין ד. סוכה ה: *חולין עח: נגעים פי"ג מ"ט

ת"כ פ' מלורע פ"ד פ"ה

אהלות פ"ב מ"ג

עוקצין פ"ו מ"ה

סוכה ו. שבת קיב: עירובין ד.

שיעורן

שיעורן כרמונים ארץ זית שמן א"ר יוסי בר' חנינא ארץ שכל שיעוריה כזתים כל שיעוריה ס"ד והא איכא הנך דאמרן אלא ארץ שרוב שיעוריה כזתים דבש *ככותבת הגסה ביה"כ *ואידך הני שיעורין בהדיא מי כתיבי *אלא מדרבנן וקרא אסמכתא בעלמא רב חסדא ורב המנונא הוו יתבי בסעודתא אייתו לקמיידו תמרי ורמוני שקל רב המנונא בריך אתמרי ברישא א"ל רב חסדא לא סבירא ליה מר להא דאמר רב יוסף ואיתימא ר' יצחק כל המוקדם בפסוק זה קודם לברכה א"ל זה שני לארץ וזה חמישי לארץ א"ל מאן יהיב לן נגרא דפרזלא ונשמעינך: אתמר הביאו לפנידם תאנים וענבים בתוך הסעודה אמר רב הונא טעונים ברכה לפנידם ואין טעונים ברכה לאחרידם וכן אמר רב נחמן טעונים ברכה לפנידם ואין טעונין ברכה לאחרידן ורב ששת אמר טעונין ברכה בין לפנידן בין לאחרידן שאין לך דבר שטעון ברכה לפניו ואין טעון ברכה לאחריו אלא פת הבאה בכסנין בלבד ופליגא דר' חייא *דא"ר חייא פת פוטרת כל מיני מאכל ויין פוטר כל מיני משקים א"ר פפא הלכתא דברים הבאים מחמת הסעודה בתוך הסעודה אין טעונים ברכה לא לפנידם ולא לאחרידם ושלא מחמת הסעודה בתוך הסעודה טעונים ברכה לפנידם ואין טעונים ברכה לאחרידם לאחר הסעודה טעונים ברכה בין לפנידם בין לאחרידם שאלו את בן זומא מפני מה אמרו דברים הבאים מחמת הסעודה בתוך הסעודה אינם טעוני' ברכה לא לפנידם ולא לאחרידם א"ל הואיל ופת פוטרתן א"ה יין נמי נפטריה פת שאני יין דגורם

רש"י

שיעורן כרמוני'. ניקב כמוליא רמון טהור בעלי בתים חסים על כליהם הלכך ניקב כמוליא קטניות מלניעו לזתים ניקב כמוליא זית משתמשין לאגוזים ניקב כמוליא אגוז משתמשין בו רמונים אבל של אומן העומד לימכר לא הוי שיעוריה בהכי: שרוב שיעוריה. אכילת חלב דם נותר ופיגול: דבש. האמור בתורה הוא דבש תמרים וכותבת היא תמרה: זה שני לארץ. ארץ זית שמן ודבש דכתי' בסיפי' דקרא הפסיק ארץ את הסדר וחזר לעשות זתים ותמרי' חשובים מתאני' ורמוני' שהרמון חמישי לארץ הכתובה בראש המקרא ודבש שני לארץ הכתוב' בסופו: מאן יהיב לן נגרי דפרזלא. רגלים של ברזל: ונשמעינך. נשמשך ונלך אחריך תמיד: הביאו לפנידם תאנים וענבים בתוך הסעודה. ולא ללפת את הפת דא"כ הוו להו טפלה ואין חולק בדבר שאין טעון ברכה לא לפניו ולא לאחריו אלא פעמים שבא למתק את פיו בתוך הסעוד' בפירות: מברך לפנידם. דלאו טפלה נינהו: ולא לאחרידם. דברכת המזון פוטרתן: בין לפנידם בין לאחרידם. דלא פטר אלא מידי דזיין והני לא זייני: פת הבאה בכסנין. לאחר אכיל' וברכת המזון היו רגילין להביא כסנין והן קליו' לפי שיפין ללב כדאמרי' בעלמ' (עירובין ד' כט:) הכי כסכי דמעלו לליבא ומביאין עמהם פת שכלוס' עם תבלין כעין אובלי"אש שלנו ויש שעושין אותן כמין לפורים ואילנו' ואוכלין מהן דבר מועט ומתוך שנותנים בה תבלין הרבה ואגוזים ושקדים ומאכלה מועט לא הטעינוה ברכה מעין ג' מידי דהוה אפת אורז ודוחן דאמרינן בפרקין (דף לז:) בתחלה במ"מ ולבסוף ולא כלום: פת פוטרת. בין לפניהן בין לאחריהן: דברים הבאים מחמת הסעודה. ללפ' בהן את הפת: אין טעונין ברכה. דהוו להו טפלה הלכך כל מידי בין מזון בין פירות שהביאו ללפתן אין בו ברכה לא לפניו ולא לאחריו: שלא מחמת הסעודה בתוך הסעודה. כגון דייסא וכן כרוב ותרדין שאינן לפתן ובאין למזון ולשובע: טעונין ברכה לפנידן. דלאו טפלה נינהו ואינן בכלל לחם דנפטר בברכת המוציא: ולא לאחרידן. דמיני מזון נינהו ובה"מ פוטרתן: דברים הרגילין לבא לאחר סעודה. כגון פירות אפי' הביאן בתוך הסעודה שלא מחמת לפתן: טעונין ברכה בין לפנידן. דלאו טפלה נינהו: בין לאחרידן. דאין בה"מ פוטרתן דלאו מזוני נינהו:

דגורם

תוספות

אייתו לקמייהו תמרי ורמוני. ולא ללפת בהן את הפת דא"כ הוו להו פת עיקר והן טפל' ותנן (לק' מד.) מברך על העיקר ופוטר את הטפלה:

זה שני לארץ. מ"מ היכא דאיכא חטה וזית או שעורי' ותמרי אע"ג דשוין לארץ מ"מ מוקדם בפסוק דהיינו לארץ ראשון יקדים לברכה:

הביאו לפניו תאני' וענבי' בתוך הסעודה. וכגון שאין באין ללפת את הפת אלא לקנוח סעודה:

אלא פת הבאה בכיסנין. דטעון ברכה לפניו ואין טעון ברכ' לאחריו רק בכ"כ מידי דהוה אאורז ודוחן דאמרי' לעיל (דף לז:) בתחלה מברך במ"מ ולבסוף ולא כלום הואיל וכתבו בהן שקדים הרבה ופי' רש"י אפי' אם אכל מהן אחר בה"מ קאמר ולא נהירא חדא דאמרי' לעיל כל שיש בו מחמשת המינין צריך ברכה מעין שלש ועוד מאי קאמר כסנין ליתא כמי אורז ודוחן על כן צריך לפרש דמיירי בתוך הסעוד' קודם בה"מ דמיירי בה והכי קאמר חוץ מן הפת הבא' בכיסנין בתוך הסעודה קודם בה"מ דאין טעון ברכה לאחריו דפטר ליה בה"מ אפי' לרב ששת משום דהוי דבר מועט אבל בלא סעודה אף לאחריו צריך מעין ג' ברכות ולהכי לא נקט פת אורז ודוחן שהרי אפילו בלא סעודה כמי אין צריכין ברכה מעין ג' לאחריו: לא קי"ל כרב ששת אלא כרב הונ' ור"נ דאין הלכה כיחיד במקום רבים ה"ג:

ויין פוטר כל מיני משקין. ולכאור' מיירי ביין בלא סעוד' דאי בהדי פת תיפוק ליה דפטר ליה פת דאפי' יין כמי רלה לומר הספר בסמוך דפטור אי לאו טעמא דקובע ברכה לעצמו אלא מיירי בלא סעודה ואפ"ה יין פוטר ולית הלכתא כותיה שהרי מפת פוטרת אין הלכ' כמותו אלא כפסק רב פפא א"כ גם מהא דקאמר יין פוטר וכו' לית הלכתא כותיה:

הלכתא דברים הבאים בתוך הסעודה מחמת הסעודה. פי' הקונט' ללפת בהן את הפת אין טעונין ברכה דהוו להו טפל' ולא נהירא דא"כ מתניתין היא (דף מד.) דמברך על העיקר ופוטר את הטפלה ומאי קמ"ל ועוד קשה דפריך בסמוך יין כמי נפטריה פת ומאי קשה והלא כשותין היין אינו טפלה לפת ואנן במידי דטפל לפת מיירינן ואין לפרש לפירוש הקונט' יין נפטריה פת כששורה פתו ביינו קאמר דהוה ליה יין טפל דהא לא אשכחן שיברך עליו בענין זה אלא ודאי מיירי בשתיה ועוד קשה מה שפי' רש"י דברים הבאים שלא מחמת הסעודה בתוך הסעודה כגון דייסא ותרדין וכרוב שאינן של לפתן ובאין לזון ולשבוע טעונין ברכה לפניהם דלאו טפלה נינהו ומיהו פטורין מבה"מ דמיני מזון נינהו ולא נהירא דאמרי' במתני' ברך על הפת פטר את הפרפרת ובגמר' מפרש דהוא הדין כל מעשה קדרה. ודברים הרגילים לבא לאחר הסעודה פי' רש"י כמו פירות ואפי' הביא אותן בתוך הסעודה שלא מחמת לפתן טעונים ברכה בין לפניהם דלאו טפלה נינהו ובין לאחריהם דאין בה"מ פוטרתן דלאו מזון נינהו דהיינו כרב ששת דאמר לעיל הביאו לפניו תאני' ורמונים בתוך הסעודה דטעונים ברכה בין לפניהם בין לאחריהם והוי דלא כהלכתא דקיימא לן כר"נ וכרב הונא כדפרישית לעיל על כן פירש ר"י דברי' הבאים מחמת הסעודה בתוך הסעודה כלומר הרגילי' לבא מחמת הסעודה בפת שרגילים לאכלן עם הפת כגון בשר ודגים וכל מיני קדרה והביאן בתוך הסעודה אין טעונין ברכה לפניהם ולאחריהם אפי' אכלן בתוך הסעודה בפני עצמן בלא פת דכיון דמשום פת הם באין הפת פוטרתן אבל דברים שאין דרכם לבא בתוך הסעודה כגון תמרים ורמונים ושאר כל פירות שאין רגילים ללפת בהן את הפת טעונין ברכה לפניהן דכיון דלאו משום לפתן אתו אין הפת פוטרתן והיינו כר"נ וכרב הונא דלעיל דאמרי דטעונין ברכה לפניהן ולא לאחריהן:

ולאחר הסעודה גרסי' ותו לא. ולא גרסינן דברים הבאים בהך סיפא. והכי פירושו אם הביאו דברים שהזכרנו אחר הסעודה פירוש לאחר שמשכו ידיהם מן הפת שוב אין הפת פוטרתן כלל והוי כמו שאכלן בלא שום סעודה ובין דברים הרגילים לבא מחמת הסעודה ובין דברים שאין רגילים לבא מחמת הסעודה טעונים ברכה לפניהם ולאחריהם דאכל דברים דלעיל קאי ועכשיו אין לנו דין זה דאין מנהג שלנו למשוך ידינו מן הפת כלל עד לאחר בה"מ אלא כל שעה שאנו אוכלין פירות או שום דבר קודם בה"מ דעתינו לאכול פת כל שעה וקיימא לן כפסק דרב פפא:

א"ה יין כמי נפטריה פת. דודאי יין מחמת סעודה אתי שהוא שותה כמה פעמים דאי לאו הסעודה לא ישתה ולפטריה פת ומשני שאני יין דגורם ברכה לעצמו פירש"י דבהרבה מקומות הוא בא ומברכין עליו אע"פ שאין צריכין לשתות כגון בקידוש ובברכת ארוסין ורשב"א פי' משום דצריך לברך על היין בפה"ג ובתחלה כשהוא ענבים בפה"ע ועל שאר משקין שהכל ומיהו אומר ר"ת דבשאר משקין כמו מים ושכר הבאים מחמת סעודה פת פוטרתן דאפילו יין הוה פוטר אי לאו דקובע ברכה לעצמו ולא כמחזור ויטרי שכתב שמברכין למים ברכה בכל פעם ופעם ואפילו בתוך הסעודה דהוי כמלך והא דלא פריך הכא מהן משום דיין זיין אבל מים לא זייני כדאמרי' (לעיל דף לה:) הכודר מן המזון וכו' ופשיטא דלא פטר להו פת דאינה בכלל

ברכת הפת ומיהו

עין משפט נר מצוה

קג
אמיי' פ"ב מה' שביתת עשור ה"א סמג לאוין סנ טוש"ע א"ח סי' תרי"ב סעי' א
[ע' תוס' סוכה ו. ד"ה אלא]

קד
במיי' פ"ח מה' ברכו' הי"ג סמג עשין כז טוש"ע א"ח סי' ריא סעי' ד

קה
גטוש"ע א"ח סי' קעד סעי' ב

קו
דמיי' פ"ד מהל' ברכו' הי"א סמג שם טוש"ע א"ח סי' קע"ז סעי' א ב

קז
הטוש"ע א"ח סי' קעד סעי' א ז

מסורת הש"ס

ובעירובין ובסוכה מסיק הש"ס אלא הלכת' נינהו

חולין קיא ב

utensils of a private person[6] [41b] the measurement[7] is a pomegranate.[8] *'A land of olive trees'*, R. Jose son of R. Ḥanina said: A land in which the olive is the standard for all measurements. All measurements, do you say? What of those we have just mentioned?—Say rather, in which the olive is the standard for most measurements. *'Honey'*,[9] as much as a large date [is the quantity which renders one liable for eating] on the Day of Atonement. What says the other to this?—Are these standards laid down explicitly? They were instituted by the Rabbis, and the text is only an *asmekta*.[10]

R. Ḥisda and R. Hamnuna were seated at a meal, and dates and pomegranates were set before them. R. Hamnuna took some dates and said a blessing over them. Said R. Ḥisda to him: Does not the Master agree with what R. Joseph, or as some say R. Isaac, said: Whatever is mentioned earlier in this verse has precedence in the matter of benediction?—He replied: This [the date] comes second after the word 'land', and this [the pomegranate]
a comes fifth.[1] He replied: Would that we had feet of iron so that we could always [run and] listen to you!

It has been stated: If figs and grapes were set before them in the course of the meal, R. Huna says that they require a benediction before but they do not require a blessing after;[2] and so said R. Naḥman: They require a blessing before but they do not require a blessing after. R. Shesheth, however, said: They require a blessing both before and after, since there is nothing requiring a blessing before which does not also require a blessing after, save bread taken with the sweets.[3] This is at variance with R. Ḥiyya; for R. Ḥiyya said: [A blessing said over] bread suffices for all kinds of food [taken in the meal], and a blessing said over wine for all kinds of drink. R. Papa said: The law is that things which form an integral part of the meal when taken in the course of the meal require no blessing either before or after; things which do not form an integral part of the meal when taken in the course of the meal require a blessing before but not after, and when taken after the meal require a blessing both before and after.

Ben Zoma was asked: Why was it laid down that things which form an integral part of the meal when taken in the course of a meal require no blessing either before or after?—He replied: Because the [blessing over] bread suffices for them. If so, [they said] let the blessing over bread suffice for wine also?—Wine is

(6) As opposed to an artificer who makes them. (7) The size of a breakage which renders the utensil incapable of becoming unclean. (8) V. Kel. XVI, 1. (9) According to the Rabbis, the honey of dates is meant. (10) Lit., 'support'; here, a kind of mnemonic. For further notes on this passage v. Suk. (Sonc. ed.) pp. 19ff.

a (1) The verse referred to is Deut. VIII, 8, where two lists are given of the products of the Land of Israel, each introduced with the word *'land'*, and in the first pomegranates are mentioned fifth, while in the second honey (i.e., date honey) is mentioned second. (2) The grace after meals serves for them too. (3) More exactly, 'nibblings'—things like nuts or dates brought in to nibble after the grace after meals.

different, he replied, [42*a*] because it is itself a motive for benediction.[4]

a R. Huna ate thirteen rolls[1] of three to a *kab* without saying a blessing after them. Said R. Naḥman to him: This is what [you call] hunger.[2] [R. Naḥman is consistent with his own view, for R. Nahman said:][3] Anything which others make the mainstay of a meal requires a grace to be said after it.

Rab Judah gave a wedding feast for his son in the house of R. Judah b. Ḥabiba.[4] They set before the guests bread such as is taken with dessert. He came in and heard them saying the benediction *ḥa-Moẓi.*[5] He said to them: What is this *ẓiẓi* that I hear? Are you perhaps saying the blessing 'who bringest forth bread from the earth'?—They replied: We are, since it has been taught: R. Muna said in the name of R. Judah: Over bread which is taken with dessert the benediction 'who bringest forth bread' is said; and Samuel said that the *halachah* is as stated by R. Muna. He said to them: It has been stated that the *halachah* is not as stated by R. Muna. They said to him: Is it not the Master himself who has said in the name of Samuel that bread wafers may be used for an *'erub,*[6] and the blessing said over them is 'who bringest forth bread'?—[He replied]: There [we speak] of a different case, namely, where they are made the basis of the meal; but if they are not the basis of the meal, this does not apply.

R. Papa was once at the house of R. Huna the son of R. Nathan. After they had finished the meal, eatables were set before them and R. Papa took some and commenced to eat. They said to him: Does not the Master hold that after the meal is finished it is forbidden to eat?[7] He replied: 'Removed'[8] is the proper term.[9]

Raba and R. Zera once visited the Exilarch. After they had removed the tray from before them, a gift [of fruit] was sent them from the Exilarch. Raba partook, but R. Zera did not partake. Said the latter to him: Does not the Master hold that if the food has been removed it is forbidden to eat? He replied: We can rely
b on the tray of the Exilarch.[1]

Rab said: If one is accustomed to [rub his hands with] oil [after a meal], he can wait for the oil.[2] R. Ashi said: When we were with R. Kahana he said to us: I, for instance, who am accustomed to use oil, can wait for the oil. But the law is not as stated in all those dicta reported above, but as thus stated by R. Ḥiyya b. Ashi in the name of Rab: Three things should follow immediately one on the other. The killing [of the sacrifice] should follow immediately on the laying on of hands. *Tefillah* should follow immediately on *ge'ullah.*[3] Grace should follow immediately on the washing of hands.[4] Abaye said: We will add another case. A blessing follows immediately on [the entertaining of] scholars, since it says, *The Lord hath blessed me for thy sake.*[5] If you prefer, I can learn it from here: *The Lord blessed the Egyptian's house for Joseph's sake.*[6]

MISHNAH. A BLESSING SAID OVER THE WINE TAKEN BEFORE THE MEAL[7] SERVES ALSO FOR THE WINE TAKEN AFTER THE MEAL.[8] A BLESSING OVER THE HORS D'OEUVRES[9] TAKEN BEFORE THE MEAL SERVES FOR THE SWEETS[9] TAKEN AFTER THE MEAL. A BLESSING OVER BREAD SERVES FOR THE SWEETS BUT A BLESSING OVER THE HORS D'OEUVRES DOES NOT SERVE FOR THE BREAD. BETH SHAMMAI SAY: NEITHER [DOES IT SERVE] FOR A COOKED DISH. IF [THOSE AT THE TABLE] ARE SITTING UPRIGHT,[10] EACH ONE SAYS GRACE FOR HIMSELF; IF THEY HAVE RECLINED, ONE SAYS GRACE FOR

(4) When used for such purposes as sanctification, and not merely as a beverage.

a (1) With the 'nibblings'. (2) I.e., such is enough to satisfy any hunger, and therefore should necessitate grace after it. The original is obscure and the meaning doubtful. (3) Inserted with MS.M. and deleting 'but' of cur. edd. (4) Var. lec., R. Ḥabiba. (5) The ordinary blessing over bread. (6) I.e., they are reckoned as substantial food. (7) Until grace after meals had first been said, after which a fresh benediction has to be said. (8) I.e., it is permissible (if grace has not yet been said) to eat as long as the table has not actually been cleared away. (9) Lit., 'it has been stated'.

b (1) I.e., we can be sure that more food will come. (2) I.e., he can go on eating till the oil is brought, even if the table has been cleared. Lit., 'the oil impedes him'. (3) V. *supra*, 4*b*, 9*b*. (4) The second washing, at the end of the meal, the 'latter water' (v. *infra* 53*b*), and this washing is the signal that the meal is finished, whether or not the table has been cleared. (5) Gen. XXX, 27. (6) Ibid. XXXIX, 5. (7) As an appetizer. (8) Before grace is said. (9) Lit., 'dainty'. (10) I.e., do not form a party.

מסורת הש"ס

[ע' תוס' ב"ב קלג: ד"ה כיליאה וע' רש"י ותוס' שבת קיט. ד"ה תליסר]

(בירוש' מוסיף שאמר משום ר"י הגלילי)

[רבה]

פי' אלק [לקמן ד' כ: פי' דיספקא]

מנחות לג. [ביצה ד:]

[יושבין לאכול כ"ה הגי' במשנה שבמשניות אבל בירוש' ובר"ף ורא"ש וכן בשאלתו' לית' וכ"מ בתוס' לקמן ד"ה הסבו אין]

[פסחי' קג:]

[וע"ע תוס' סוטה לט. ד"ה כל כהן]

תורה אור

ויברכני ה' בגללך — בראשית ל

ויברך ה' את בית המצרי בגלל יוסף — שם לט

גמרא

דגורם ברכה לעצמו רב הונא אכל *תליסר ריפתי בני תלתא תלתא בקבא ולא בריך א"ל רב נחמן עדי כפנא אלא "כל שאחרים קובעין עליו סעודה צריך לברך רב יהודה הוה עסיק ליה לבריה בי רב יהודה בר חביבא אייתו לקמייהו פת הבאה בכיסנין כי אתא שמעינהו דקא מברכי המוציא אמר להו מאי ציצי דקא שמענא דילמא המוציא לחם מן הארץ קא מברכיתו אמרי ליה אין דתניא ר' מונא אמר משום ר' יהודה *פת הבאה בכיסנין מברכין עליה המוציא ואמר שמואל הלכה כר' מונא אמר להו "אין הלכה כר' מונא אתמר אמרי ליה והא מר הוא דאמר משמיה דשמואל "לחמניות מערבין בהן ומברכין עליהן המוציא שאני התם "דקבע סעודתיה עלייהו אבל היכא דלא קבע סעודתיה עלייהו לא רב פפא איקלע לבי רב הונא בריה דרב נתן בתר דגמרי סעודתייהו אייתו לקמייהו מידי למיכל שקל רב פפא וקא אכיל אמרי ליה לא סבר לה מר גמר אסור מלאכול אמר להו סלק אתמר *רבא ור' זירא איקלעו לבי ריש גלותא לבתר דסליקו תכא מקמייהו שדרו להו *ריסתנא מבי ריש גלותא רבא אכיל ור' זירא לא אכיל א"ל לא סבר לה מר סלק אסור מלאכול א"ל "אנן אתכא דריש גלותא סמכינן: אמר רב הרגיל בשמן שמן מעכבו אמר רב אשי כי הוינן בי רב כהנא אמר לן כגון אנן דרגילינן במשחא משחא מעכבא לן ולית הלכתא ככל הני שמעתת' אלא כי הא דא"ר חייא בר אשי אמר רב שלש תכיפות הן *"תכף לסמיכה שחיטה "תכף לגאולה תפלה "תכף לנטילת ידים ברכה אמר אביי אף אנו נאמר תכף לתלמידי חכמים ברכה שנאמר °ויברכני ה' בגללך איבעית אימא מהכא שנאמר °ויברך ה' את בית המצרי בגלל יוסף:

מתני' "ברך על היין שלפני המזון פטר את היין שלאחר המזון "ברך על הפרפרת שלפני המזון פטר את הפרפרת שלאחר המזון ברך על הפת פטר את הפרפרת על הפרפרת לא פטר את הפת ב"ש אומרים אף לא מעשה קדרה "היו *יושבין כל אחד מברך לעצמו הסבו א' מברך לכולן בא

רש"י

דגורם ברכה לעצמו. בכמה מקומות הוא בא ומברכין עליו ואע"פ שלא היו צריכים לשתייתו: **רב הונא אכל תליסר ריפתי.** מפת הבאה בכיסנין ולא בירך אחריו: **אמר רב נחמן עדי כפנא** גרסינן. עדי. אלו כלומר אלו לרעבון כאכלו ואכילה מרובה כזו לא כפטרת מברכה אלא כל שאחרים קובעין אכילתן בכך טעון ברכת המזון כך פי' רב האיי ורבותינו פירשו תליסר ריפתי מפת שלנו ולא בירך אחריו משום דלא שבע וקרא כתיב (דברי' ח) ואכלת ושבעת וברכת וכך פי' רב יהודאי בה"ג ואינו כ"ל דלית לי' לרב הונא והם החמירו על עצמן עד כזית ועד כביצה (לעיל כ:) ודלא כר' מאיר ודלא כרבי יהודה (לקמן מט:): **לחמניות.** אובליא"ש בלע"ז: **אסור מלאכול.** עד שיברך ברכת המזון ויחזור ויברך על הבא לפניו דכיון דגמר אסח דעתיה מברכה ראשונה ומסעודתיה: **סלק אתמר.** אם סלק הלחם וכל האוכל מעל השלחן ועדיין לא ברכו אסו' לאכול: **ריסתנא.** אמכי"שטרשיון: **אתכא דריש גלותא סמכינן.** ואין סילוקתנו סלוק שדעתינו אם ישא משאות מאת פניו אלינו כאכל: **הרגיל בשמן.** למשוח ידיו אחר אכיל': **שמן מעכבו.** לענין ברכה שאפי' גמר וסלק ולא משח ידיו עדיין סעוד' קיימת ואוכל בלא ברכה: **ולית הלכתא ככל הני שמעתתא.** אין סיום סעודה תלוי לא בגמר ולא בסלוק ולא בשמן אלא במי' אחרונים כל זמן שלא נטל מים אחרונים הוא מותר לאכול ומשנטל אסור לאכול: **לנטילת ידים.** דמים אחרונים. **ברכת המזון** ולא יאכל כלום עד שיברך על מזונו: **תכף לת"ח.** המקריבו אליו ומאכילו בביתו: **ברכה.** בביתו:

מתני' ברך על היין כו'. נוהגין היו להביא קודם אכילה כוס יין לשתות כדתניא לקמן (דף מג.) כיצד סדר הסב' כו' ומביאין לפניהם פרפראו' להמשיך אכיל' כגון פרגיות ודגים ואח"כ מביאין השלחן ולאחר גמר סעודה יושבים ושותים ואוכלים ומה הן אוכלים פרפראות כגון כיסני דמעלו לליבא ולאמכיות והוא יין ופרפרת שלאחר המזון שכיהם קודם ברכת המזון: **מעשה קדרה.** חלק' טרגים ועיסכי: **היו יושבים.** בלא הסבת מטות שמוטין על לדיהן שמאלי' על המטה ואוכלין ושותין בהסבה: **כל אחד ואחד מברך לעצמו.** דאין קבע סעודה בלא הסבה: בא

תוספות

מיהו ר"י ור"ת היו אומרים שלא לברך כלל אשאר משקין הבאין בתוך הסעודה וטעמא דפת פוטר כל הדברים הבאים בשבילו והשתא יין פוטר כל מיני משקין לפי שעיקר משקה הוא והוא ראש לכל מיני משקין ולכך הוא העיקר והן טפילין לו לענין ברכה והלכך משקין הבאין מחמת הסעוד' שבאין בשביל הפת לשרות המאכל וגם אי אפשר לאכילה בלא שתיה והלכך פת פוטרתן חוץ מן היין כדקאמר גמרא טעמא ולהאי טעמא ניחא מה שאנו מברכים בפסח על החזרת על אכיל' מרור לבד שהטבול' מקמין אמאי אין מברכין נמי בורא פרי האדמה ובורא פרי האדמה דשאר ירקות אינו פוטרה כדקאמר התם כיון דאיכא הגדה והלל אסח דעתיה אלא ולאי טעמא הוי כיון דראשונה קבעיה חובה דכתיב על מצות ומרורים יאכלוהו הוי כמו דברים הרגילין לבא מחמת הסעודה דפת פוטרתן:

לחמניות פרש"י אובלי"אש. ולא נהירא דא"כ אפילו לא קבע נמי ליברך המוציא שהרי הוא לחם גמור שהרי סופו עיסה ונראה לפרש דהיינו כילי"ש מיהו כי קבע סעודתיה עליה מברך עליו המוציא כמו בפורים מיהו רבינו שמשון פי' דאין לברך עליו המוציא דהוי כמו דייסא:

סלק אתמר. משמע שדרכן היה לסלק השלחן קודם ברכת המזון ולכאורה קשה למנהג שלנו שאנו מקפידים שלא לסלק הלחם קודם ושמא בימיהם נמי לא היו מסלקין השלחן מקמי המברך כי אם מלפני שאר המסובין לפי שהיו להן שלחנות קטנים וכל אחד לפני עצמו אוכל על שלחנו אבל אנו שרגילי' לאכול כולנו על שלחן אחד אין נאה לסלק השלחן עד לאחר ברכת המזון:

רבי זירא לא אכל. תימה לפי מה שמפרשים העולם הב לן ונבריך אסור למשתי בלא ברכה שלפניו אמאי לא אכל ליבריך עליה וליכול ושמא היה תבשיל שהיה בו פת והיה צריך ברכת המוציא ונט"י וטורח היה לעשות כל כך:

אתכא דריש גלות' סמכינן. מי ששכח לאכול אפיקומן ואמר הב לן ונבריך אינו היסח הדעת דאכן אתכא דרחמנא סמכינן ואם שכח ובירך ולא אכל אפיקומן א"ל לחזור דכל מלות לאו מלות עשויות והא דאמרי *כי אמר הב לן ונבריך אסור למשתי וכן אסורים כולן היינו דוקא כי אמר בעל הבית אבל לא אורח וכי אסורים כולן היינו כי אמר בעל הבית אבל בשביל אורח אין נאסרין ואף איהו גופי' יכול לחזור ולאכול עם בעל הבית:

אתכא דריש גלותא סמכינן. וכשרגיל לאכול מיני פירות ומביאין להם בזה אחר זה יש אומר שצריך לברך אכל חד וחד לפי שאינן יודעים אם יתן להם בעל הבית יותר וכו' שא"ל לברך לפי שסומכין על שלחן בע"ה והיינו דבי ריש גלותא:

תכף לנטילת ידים ברכה. והלכך כיון שנטל ידיו באחרונה לאחר סעודה אסור לאכול עד שיברך והוא הדין אם אמר הב לן ונבריך אפילו בלא נטילה*:

ברך על הפת פטר את הפרפרת. כו' דמיירי בפרפרת שבתוך הסעודה דאי בפרפרת שלאחר הסעודה הא פסק רב פפא דברים הבאים לאחר סעודה טעונין ברכה לפניהם ולאחריהם ורש"י פי' פרפרת מיני דגים ופרגיות וק"ק א"כ מאי קמ"ל דברך על הפרפרת דלא פטר את הפת ונראה כפי' ר"ח דפי' דפרפרת פת לנומה בקערה דלית בה תוריתא דלחמא דמברכין עליה בורא מיני מזונות והשתא ניחא דאצטריך לאשמעינן ברך על הפרפרת לא פטר את הפת אף על גב דהוא מין פת וכן משמע בגמרא דחשיב פרפרת מעשה קדרה ומעשה קדרה היינו חלקא טרגים וטיסני כדאמרינן לעיל:

הסבו אחד מברך לכלן. ואנו אין לנו הסבה אלא בפת בלבד ופת מהני אפי' בלא הסבה דדוקא לדידהו שהיו אוכלים בהסבה היו צריכים הסבה אלא ישיבה שלנו הוי קביעות לנו כהסבה דידהו שהם היו רגילים כל אחד להסב על מטתו ועל שלחנו אבל עכשיו כולנו אוכלים על שלחן אחד וכשאנו אוכלים יחד היינו קביעותינו והכא דקאמר היו יושבים וכו' בגמרא משמע דמיירי בין בברכת המוציא בין בברכת המזון בברכת המזון כעובדא דתלמידי דרב בברכת המוציא מהסיא דפליגי ביין אי בעי הסבה ומיהו בבני אדם האוכלים בדרך והולכים ולא ישבו כל אחד מברך לעצמו וא"ת מאי שנא דמוגמר אפילו לא הסבו אחד מברך לכולם בירושלמי פריך ומשני משום דמוגמר כולם נהנים ביחד אבל אכילה ושתיה אינה באה אלא לזה אחר זה: אע"פ

עין משפט נר מצוה

קח א מיי' פ"ג מהל' ברכות ה"ט סמג עשין כז טוש"ע א"ח סי' קסח סעיף ו ז

קט ב שם סעי' ו וסעיף ח

קי ג מיי' פ"ד מהל' ברכו' ה"ז סמג שם טוש"ע א"ח סימן קעט סעיף ב

קיא ד מיי' פ"ג מהלכ' מעשה קרבנות הל' יב

קיב ה מיי' פ"ז מה' תפלה הי"ז טוש"ע א"ח סי' קיא סעי' א

קיג ו מיי' פ"ו מה' ברכו' ה"כ סמג עשין כז טוש"ע א"ח סי' קעט סעי' א ובסי' קפו

קיד ז מיי' פ"ד מהלכות ברכות הל' יב סמג שם טור א"ח סימן קעד

קטו ח טור א"ח סימן קעז

קטז ט מיי' פ"ד מהל' ברכות סמג שם טוש"ע א"ח סי' קסז סעי' יא וסי' ריג סעיף א

בא להם יין בתוך המזון כל אחד ואחד מברך לעצמו אחר המזון אחד מברך לכולם והוא אומר על המוגמר ואף ע"פ שאין מביאין את המוגמר אלא לאחר סעודה: **גמ'** אמר רבה בר בר חנה א"ר יוחנן לא שנו אלא בשבתות וימים טובים הואיל ואדם קובע סעודתו על היין אבל בשאר ימות השנה מברך על כל כוס וכוס אתמר נמי אמר רבה בר מרי א"ר יהושע בן לוי לא שנו אלא בשבתות וימים טובים ובשעה שאדם יוצא מבית המרחץ ובשעת הקזת דם הואיל ואדם קובע סעודתו על היין אבל בשאר ימות השנה מברך על כל כוס וכוס רבה בר מרי איקלע לבי רבא בחול חזייה דבריך לפני המזון והדר בריך לאחר המזון א"ל *יישר וכן אמר ריב"ל רב יצחק בר יוסף איקלע לבי אביי בי"ט חזייה דבריך אכל כסא וכסא א"ל לא סבר לה מר להא דריב"ל א"ל נמלך אנא איבעי' להו בא להם יין בתוך המזון מהו שיפטור את היין שלאחר המזון אם תימצי לומר ברך על היין שלפני המזון פוטר את היין שלאחר המזון משום דזה לשתות וזה לשתות אבל הכא דזה לשתות וזה לשרות לא או דילמא לא שנא רב אמר פוטר ורב כהנא אמר אינו פוטר רב נחמן אמר פוטר ורב ששת אמר אינו פוטר רב הונא ורב יהודה וכל תלמידי דרב אמרי אינו פוטר איתיביה רבא לרב נחמן בא להם יין בתוך המזון כל אחד ואחד מברך לעצמו לאחר המזון אחד מברך לכולם א"ל הכי קאמר אם לא בא להם יין בתוך המזון אלא לאחר המזון אחד מברך לכולם: ברך על הפת פטר את הפרפרת על הפרפרת לא פטר את הפת וב"ש אומרים אף לא מעשה קדרה: איבעיא להו ב"ש ארישא פליגי או דילמא אסיפא פליגי דקאמר תנא קמא ברך על הפת פטר את הפרפרת וכ"ש מעשה קדרה ואתו ב"ש למימר לא מבעיא פרפרת דלא פטרה להו פת אלא אפי' מעשה קדרה נמי לא פטרה או דילמא אסיפא פליגי דקתני ברך על הפרפרת לא פטר את הפת הוא דלא פטר אבל מעשה קדרה פטר ואתו ב"ש למימר ואפי' מעשה קדרה נמי לא פטר תיקו: היו יושבין כל אחד ואחד וכו': הסבו אין לא הסבו לא ורמינהי *עשרה שהיו הולכים בדרך אע"פ שכולם אוכלין מככר אחד כל אחד ואחד מברך לעצמו ישבו לאכול אע"פ שכל אחד ואחד אוכל מככרו אחד מברך לכולם קתני ישבו אע"פ שלא הסבו אמר רב נחמן בר יצחק כגון דאמרי ניזיל וניכול לחמא בדוך פלן: כי נח נפשיה דרב אזלו תלמידיו בתריה כי הדרי אמרי ניזיל וניכול לחמא אנהר דנק בתר דכרכי יתבי וקא מבעיא להו הסבו דוקא תנן אבל ישבו לא או דילמא כיון דאמרי ניזיל וניכול ריפתא בדוכתא פלניתא כי הסבו דמי לא הוה בידייהו קם רב אדא בר אהבה

אהדר

בא להם יין בתוך המזון כו'. בגמ' (ד' מג.) מפרש טעמא: והוא אומר על המוגמר. אותו שברך על היין הוא מברך על המוגמר שהיו רגילים להביא לפניהם אחר אכילה אבקת רוכלין על האש במחתות לריח טוב ומברכים עליו בורא עצי בשמים: לאחר סעודה. לאחר ברכת המזון שאינו מצרכי סעודה אפילו הכי מי שברך על היין שהתחיל בברכות אחרונות גומרן: **גמ'** לא שנו. דיין שלפני המזון פוטר את שלאחר המזון: אלא בשבתות כו'. דדעתו לישב אחר המזון ולשתות וכי בריך ברישא אדעתא דהכי בריך: על כל כוס וכוס. דהוה כנמלך ומתחיל בשתיה בכל חד וחד: יישר. יפה עשית: וכן אמר ריב"ל. לעשות: לא סבר לה מר כו'. דבי"ט לא נמלך הוא: נמלך אנא. איני רגיל לקבוע סעודה על היין: בא להם יין בתוך המזון. וקודם המזון לא בא להם: אם תימצי לומר. להביא ראיה ממשנתינו דקתני דיין שלפני המזון פוטר את שלאחר המזון איכא ראיה דהתם זה לשתות וזה לשתות אבל שבתוך המזון לשרות אכילה שבמעיו הוא בא ולא היו רגילין לשתות בתוך הסעודה אלא מעט לשרות: לאחר המזון אחד מברך לכולן. קס"ד דהכי קאמר דכשיביאו יין שני אחר המזון אחד מברך לכלן והא תנא ליה דכל אחד ואחד יברך על שבתוך המזון לעצמו וקא מצריך תו ברכה על שלאחר המזון: פטר את הפרפרת. אע"פ שאין צורך סעודה למלוי הכרס אלא לגומר אכילה: וכל שכן מעשה קדרה. שהוא לאכול לזון ממש: בדוך פלן. במקום פלוני דקבעו להם מתחלה מקום בדבור. ועלה והזמנה הוי קביעות אבל ישבו מאליהן במקום אחד יחד אינה קביעות: אזלו תלמידיו בתריה. דקברוהו בעיר אחרת: נהר דנק. כך שמו: *רישא דוקא. דקתני היו יושבים בלא הזמנת מקום הוא דלא הוי קביעות אבל הנו שהזמינהו לכך הוי קביעות ואחד מברך לכולן:

אהדר

אעפ"י שאין מביאין המוגמר אלא לאחר סעודה. וכבר ברכו ברכת המזון ויש הפסק בין יין למוגמר: **ורב** ששת אמר אינו פוטר ורב נחמן אמר פוטר וכל תלמידי דרב וכו'. ונראה דהלכה כתלמידי דרב דרב ששת קאי כוותייהו והלכתא כותיה דרב נחמן בדיני *וכרב ששת באיסורי ואע"ג דקי"ל *דרב ושמואל הלכה כרב באיסורי שאני הכא דכל תלמידי דרב פליגי עליה מסתמא כך שמעו מרב מיהו אין אנו צריכין לאותו פסק דאין אנו מושכים ידינו מן הפת כלל ונראה דיין שלפני סעודה פוטר את היין שבתוך הסעודה אע"ג דפסקינן הכא דיין שבתוך הסעודה אינו פוטר יין דלאחר הסעודה שאני הכא דזה לשרות וזה לשתות אבל זה לשתות וזה לשתות פוטר שפיר כגון יין שלפני הסעודה פוטר שבתוך הסעודה ומה דנקט שבתות וי"ט לאו דוקא דה"ה אם קבעו סעודה על היין בשאר ימות החול ואם הביא אדם יין לפני הסעודה לשתות בתוך הסעודה פשיטא דיין דלפני סעודה פוטרתו כיון דדעתיה למשתי וכן יין של קדוש פוטר יין שבתוך הסעוד' וכן הבדלה אם הביא על שלחנו להבדיל דפוטר יין שלאחרי כן שבתוך הסעודה ושבתות וי"ט לאו דוקא ולא אתא למעוטי אלא נמלך ואפילו את"ל דדוקא נקט שבתות וי"ט מ"מ יש לומר ה"מ לענין שבת לפטור יין שלאחר המזון שהוא אחר שמשכו ידיהם מן הפת שאין רגילות לקבוע לשתות יין לאחר המזון בקביעות אלא בשבתות וימים טובים ולא בשאר ימים אבל לענין לפטור יין שבתוך המזון שרגילות לשתות ודאי אפילו בשאר ימים פטר ליה יין שלפני המזון אע"פ דזה לשתות וזה לשרות דעד כאן לא איבעיא לן אלא אי לשרות דלא חשיב מפיק לשתות אבל לשתות דחשיב טפי דהיינו יין שלפני המזון פשיטא דפוטר יין דלשרות וכן משמע נמי בערבי פסחים (ד' קא.) גבי שקדשו בב"ה דר' יוחנן אמר אף ידי יין נמי יצאו וא"ל לחזור ולברך על היין שבתוך הסעודה אע"ג דקדשו שלא במקום סעודה ס"ל לר' יוחנן מדיצאו ידי קדוש מידי יין נמי יצאו ואף ע"ג דאתותב ר' יוחנן הייני דוקא בשנוי מקום א"כ נראה משם דה"ה להבדלה דאין לחלק בין הבדלה לקדוש ולאפוקי מהכי דחולקין ואמרי דוקא קדוש פוטר משום דאין קדוש אלא במקום סעודה אבל יין של הבדלה לא פטר אפילו הבדיל לאחר נטילה דהכי מיירי הא דפסקינן דיין שלפני המזון פוטר היין שבתוך המזון דכבר נטל ידיו והכי משמע בסמוך מתוך הברייתא כיצד סדר הסבה וכו' מיהו נראה כיון דנטל ידיו ודעתו לאכול ולשתות שם פוטר אפילו דהבדלה כדפרים' מההיא דערבי פסחים ועוד דלא גרע יין דהבדלה מיין שלפני הסעודה דפטר ומיהו יש שמחמירים להבדיל קודם נטילת ידים לאפוקי נפשייהו מפלוגתא דאז ודאי צריך לברך אחריו ברכה מעין ג' ולא פטר יין שבתוך המזון: **יין** שבתוך המזון מהו שיפטור יין שלאחר המזון. ומיירי דלא הוה להו יין לפני המזון:

הסבו אין לא הסבו לא. תימה אמאי מקשה מדיוקא *תקשי ליה מרישא בהדיא דקתני היו יושבים מברך כל אחד לעצמו ויש לומר דאי מרישא הוה אמינא שישבו בשביל עסק אחר שלא היה דעתם מתחלה לאכול אבל אם ישבו אדעתא לאכול אפילו בלא הסבה נמי מהניא: **עשרה** בני אדם שהיו מהלכין כו' ניזיל וניכול לחמא כו' כישבו והסבו דמיא. והשתא ניחא הא דפריך במתני' דמיירי בין בברכת המוציא בין בברכת המזון כדמשמע הכא מתוך הברייתא דעשרה בני אדם וכו'. ואם תאמר אמאי המתינו למיבעי עד ברכת המזון והיאך ברכו על הפת מתחלה וי"ל שמא מיירי דישבו לאכול זה אחר זה ובירך כל אחד לעצמו המוציא:

כל

עין משפט נר מצוה

קיז אמיי' פ"ז מהלכות ברכות הלכה יג סמג עשין כז טור א"ח סי' קעד

קיח במיי' פ"ד מהלכות ברכות הלכה יב סמג וטור שם

קיט גטוש"ע שם סעיף ז

קכ דמיי' פ"ד מהלכות ברכות הלכה יב סמג וטור שם

קכא המיי' פ"ד מהל' ברכו' ה"ו סמג שם טוש"ע א"ח סי' קע"ו

קכב ווחמיי' פ"א מהלכות ברכות ה"יב סמג שם טוש"ע א"ח סי' קסז סעיף יא

[ע' תוס' עירובין לב. ד"ה ר"ש] [בכורות מט:]

מסורת הש"ס

[שבת נג. קב: עירובין לב: פסחים כב: ב"מ נא. קנה' ק'. שבועות מ. מה: חולין יז: עה: עו:]

[גי' אחרת ה"ל לרש"י בנוסח' הגמ']

[תוספתא פ"ה ע"ם]

[וע' תוס' שבת לט: ד"ה אלא]

ALL. [42b] IF WINE IS BROUGHT TO THEM IN THE COURSE OF THE MEAL, EACH ONE SAYS A BENEDICTION FOR HIMSELF; IF AFTER THE MEAL, ONE SAYS IT FOR ALL. THE SAME ONE a SAYS [THE BENEDICTION] OVER THE PERFUME,[1] ALTHOUGH THE PERFUME IS NOT BROUGHT IN TILL AFTER THE MEAL.[2]

GEMARA. Rabbah b. Bar Ḥanah said in the name of R. Joḥanan: This[3] was meant to apply only to Sabbaths and festivals, because then a man makes wine an essential part of his meal.[4] On others days of the year, however, a blessing is said over each cup.[5] It has also been reported: Rabbah b. Mari said in the name of R. Joshua b. Levi: This was meant to apply only to Sabbaths and festivals, and to meals taken when a man leaves the bath or after bloodletting, because on such occasions a man makes wine an essential part of the meal. On other days of the year, however, a blessing is said over each cup. Rabbah b. Mari was once at the house of Raba on a weekday. He saw him say a blessing [over the wine taken] before the meal and again after the meal. He said to him: 'Well done; and so said R. Joshua b. Levi!'

R. Isaac b. Joseph visited Abaye on a festival, and saw him say a blessing over each cup. He said to him: Does your honour not hold with the rule laid down by R. Joshua b. Levi?—He replied: I have just changed my mind.[6]

A question was asked: If wine was brought round in the course of the meal [but not before], can a blessing over it serve for the wine taken after the meal as well? Should you cite the ruling that A BLESSING SAID OVER THE WINE TAKEN BEFORE THE MEAL SERVES FOR WINE TAKEN AFTER THE MEAL, this may be because both are [drunk] for the sake of drinking. Here, however, where one cup is for steeping [the food in] and the other for drinking, shall I say that this is not the rule, or perhaps it makes no difference? —Rab replied that it does serve; R. Kahana that it does not; R. Naḥman held that it does serve; R. Shesheth that it does not serve. R. Huna and Rab Judah and all the disciples of Rab held that it does not serve. Raba raised an objection to R. Naḥman: IF WINE IS BROUGHT TO THEM IN THE COURSE OF THE MEAL, EACH ONE SAYS A BLESSING FOR HIMSELF; IF AFTER THE b MEAL, ONE SAYS IT FOR ALL.[1]—He replied: The meaning is this: If no wine was brought in during the course of the meal but only after the meal, one says the blessing on behalf of all.

A BLESSING OVER BREAD SERVES FOR THE SWEETS, BUT A BLESSING OVER THE HORS D'OEUVRES DOES NOT SERVE FOR THE BREAD. BETH SHAMMAI SAY: NEITHER [DOES IT SERVE] FOR A COOKED DISH. The question was asked: Do Beth Shammai differ with regard to the first part of the statement or the second part? [Do we understand] that the First Tanna said that A BLESSING OVER BREAD SERVES FOR THE SWEETS and *a fortiori* for cooked dishes, and Beth Shammai on the contrary maintained that not merely does the blessing over bread not suffice for the sweets but it does not serve even for the cooked dishes; or are we perhaps to understand that they differ as to the second half of the statement, that A BLESSING OVER THE HORS D'OEUVRES DOES NOT SERVE FOR THE BREAD, which implies that it does not indeed serve for bread but it does serve for cooked dishes, and Beth Shammai on the contrary maintain that it does not serve even for cooked dishes?—This is left undecided.

IF [THEY] ARE SITTING UPRIGHT, EACH ONE etc. If they are reclining he may, if not he may not. With this was contrasted the following: If ten persons were travelling on the road, even though all eat of one loaf, each one says grace for himself; but if they sat down to eat, even though each one eats of his own loaf, one may say grace on behalf of all. It says here, 'sat', which implies, although they did not recline?—R. Naḥman b. Isaac replied: This is the case if for instance, they say: Let us go and eat bread in such c and such a place.[1]

When Rab died, his disciples followed his bier. When they returned[2] they said, Let us go and eat a meal by the river Danaḳ.[3] After they had eaten, they sat and discussed the question: When we learnt 'reclining', is it to be taken strictly, as excluding sitting, or perhaps, when they say, Let us go and eat bread in such and such a place, it is as good as reclining? They could not find the

a (1) I.e., spices put on coals and brought in after grace is said. (2) And grace has intervened between it and the wine. (3) That a blessing said over wine before the meal serves for wine after the meal. The reason is that from the beginning there is an intention to drink later. (4) Rashi: he intends to linger at the table after the meal and drink wine. (5) Because each cup requires a separate intention. (6) To drink an additional cup, as I did not intend at first to take more wine after the meal.

b (1) Assuming that the grace after the meal refers to a second serving of wine, this seems to show that wine taken in the course of the meal does not serve for wine taken after.

c (1) Which is equivalent to making a party. (2) Rab was buried in another town from that in which his Academy was situated. (3) Perhaps a mistake for Anaḳ, a river near Sura; v. MS.M.

answer. R. Adda b. Ahabah rose [43a] and turned the rent in his garment[4] from front to back and made another rent, saying, Rab is dead, and we have not learnt the rules about grace after meals! At length an old man came and pointed out the contradiction between the Mishnah and the Baraitha, and solved it by saying, Once they have said, Let us go and eat bread in such and such a place, it is as if they were reclining.

IF THEY HAVE RECLINED, ONE SAYS GRACE: Rab said: The rule is that only bread requires reclining, but wine does not require reclining.[5] R. Johanan, however, says that wine also requires reclining. Some report thus: Rab said, This applies only to bread, for which reclining is of effect,[6] but for wine reclining is not of effect. R. Johanan, however, says that for wine also reclining is of effect.

The following was cited in objection [to Rab]: 'What is the procedure for reclining? The guests[7] enter and sit on stools and chairs till they are all assembled. When water is brought, each one washes one hand.[8] When wine is brought, each one says a blessing for himself. When they go up [on to the couches] and recline, and water is brought to them, although each one of them has already washed one hand, he now again washes both hands. When wine is brought to them, although each one has said a blessing for
a himself, one now says a blessing on behalf of all.[1] Now according to the version which makes Rab say that 'this applies only to bread which requires reclining, but wine does not require reclining', there is a contradiction between his view and the first part of this statement?[2]—Guests are different, since they intend to shift their place.[3] According to the version which makes Rab say that this applies only to bread for which reclining is of effect, but for wine reclining is of no effect, there is a contradiction with the second part?[4]—The case is different there because, since reclining is of effect for bread, it is also of effect for wine.[5]

Ben Zoma was asked: Why was it laid down that if wine is brought in the course of the meal, each one says a blessing for himself, but if after the meal, one may say a blessing for all? He replied: Because [during meals] the gullet is not empty.[6]

THE SAME ONE SAYS [THE BENEDICTION] OVER THE PERFUME. Since it says, THE SAME ONE SAYS [THE BENEDICTION] OVER THE PERFUME, we may infer that there is present someone superior to him. Why then does he say it?—Because he washed his hands first [after the meal]. This supports Rab; for R. Ḥiyya b. Ashi said in the name of Rab: The one who first washes his hands [after the meal] can claim the right[7] to say grace. Rab and R. Ḥiyya were once sitting before Rabbi at dinner. Rabbi said to Rab: Get up and wash your hands. He [R. Ḥiyya] saw him trembling.[8] Said R. Ḥiyya to him: Son of princes![9] He is telling you to think over the grace after meals.[10]

R. Zera said in the name of Raba b. Jeremiah: When do they say the blessing over the perfume? As soon as the smoke column ascends. Said R. Zera to Raba b. Jeremiah: But he has not yet smelt it! He replied: According to your reasoning, when one says 'Who brings forth bread from the earth', he has not yet eaten! But [he says it because] it is his intention to eat. So here, it is his intention to smell.

R. Ḥiyya the son of Abba b. Naḥmani said in the name of R. Ḥisda reporting Rab—according to others, R. Ḥisda said in the name of Ze'iri: Over all incense-perfumes the blessing is 'who createst fragrant woods', except over musk, which comes from a living creature and the blessing is, 'who createst various kinds of spices'. An objection was raised: The benediction 'who createst fragrant woods' is said only over the balsam-trees of the household of Rabbi and the balsam-trees of Caesar's household and over
b myrtle everywhere![1]—This is a refutation.

R. Ḥisda said to R. Isaac: What blessing is said over this balsam-oil?—He replied: Thus said Rab Judah: 'Who createst the oil of our land'.[2] He then said to him: Leaving out Rab Judah, who dotes on the Land of Israel, what do ordinary people say?—He replied: Thus said R. Joḥanan: 'Who createst pleasant oil'. R. Adda b. Ahabah said: Over costum the blessing is, 'Who createst fragrant woods', but not over oil in which it is steeped. R. Kahana, however, says: Even over oil in which it is steeped, but not over oil in which it has been ground. The Nehardeans say: Even over oil in which it has been ground.

(4) Which he had made on hearing of the death of Rab. (5) To constitute a party, and even without it one may say the blessing on behalf of all. (6) For the purpose of constituting a party. (7) Probably a party of *Ḥaberim* (v. Glos.) is referred to. (8) To take the wine which is to be offered before the meal.

a (1) Since they now form a party. (2) Which says that, till they have reclined, each one says a blessing for himself over wine. (3) I.e., to go up from the stools on to the couches. (4) Which says that having reclined one says a blessing on behalf of all also for wine. (5) Since the guests on this occasion have been invited to partake of bread, the reclining is of effect also for the wine. (6) The guests might be eating at the moment when the blessing was pronounced and would not be able to answer Amen (Tosaf). (7) Lit., 'he is prepared'. (8) He thought Rab had told him to do this because his hands were dirty or something of the sort. (9) V. *supra* 13b, n. b6. (10) So as to be able to say it fluently.

b (1) I.e., over plants of which the wood itself is fragrant. (2) Balsam-trees grew near Jericho.

אהדר קרעיה לאחוריה וקרע קריעה אחרינא אמר נח נפשיה דרב וברכת מזונא לא גמרינן עד דאתא ההוא סבא רמא להו מתניתין אברייתא ושני להו כיון דאמרו ניזיל וניכול לחמא בדוך פלן כהסבו דמי: הסבו אחד מברך: אמר רב לא שנו אלא פת דבעי הסבה אבל יין לא בעי הסבה ור' יוחנן אמר *אפילו יין נמי בעי הסבה איכא דאמרי אמר רב לא שנו אלא פת דמהניא ליה הסבה אבל יין לא מהניא ליה הסבה ור' יוחנן אמר אפי' יין נמי מהניא ליה הסבה מיתיבי *כיצד סדר הסבה אורחין נכנסין ויושבין על גבי ספסלין ועל גבי קתדראות עד שיכנסו כולם הביאו להם מים כל אחד ואחד נוטל ידו אחת בא להם יין כל אחד ואחד מברך לעצמו עלו והסבו ובא להם מים אע"פ שכל אחד ואחד נטל ידו אחת חוזר ונוטל שתי ידיו בא להם יין אע"פ שכל אחד ואחד ברך לעצמו אחד מברך לכולם להאיך לישנא דאמר רב לא שנו אלא פת דבעיא הסבה אבל יין לא בעי הסבה קשיא רישא שאני אורחין דדעתייהו למיעקר ולהאיך לישנא דאמר רב לא שנו אלא פת דמהניא ליה הסבה אבל יין לא מהניא ליה הסבה קשיא סיפא שאני התם דמגו דקא מהניא ליה הסבה לפת מהניא ליה הסבה ליין: בא להם יין בתוך המזון: *שאלו את בן זומא מפני מה אמרו *בא להם יין בתוך המזון כל אחד ואחד מברך לעצמו לאחר המזון א' מברך לכולם אמר להם הואיל ואין בית הבליעה פנוי: והוא אומר על המוגמר כו': מדקתני והוא אומר על המוגמר מכלל דאיכא עדיף מיניה *ואמאי הואיל והוא נטל ידיו תחלה באחרונה מסייע ליה לרב דאמר רב חייא בר אשי *אמר רב *הנוטל ידיו תחלה באחרונה הוא מזומן לברכה *רב ור' חייא הוו יתבי קמיה דר' בסעודתא א"ל ר' לרב קום משי ידך חזייה דהוה מרתת א"ל רבי חייא *בר פחתי עיין בברכת מזונא קאמר לך: א"ר זירא אמר רבא בר ירמיה *מאימתי מברכין על הריח משתעלה תמרתו א"ל רבי זירא לרבא בר ירמיה והא לא קא ארח א"ל ולטעמיך המוציא לחם מן הארץ דמברך והא לא אכל אלא דעתיה למיכל הכא נמי דעתיה לארוחי אמר ר' חייא בריה דאבא בר נחמני אמר רב חסדא אמר רב ואמרי לה אמר רב חסדא אמר זעירי *כל המוגמרות מברכין עליהן בורא עצי בשמים חוץ *ממושק שמן חיה הוא שמברכין עליו בורא מיני בשמים מיתיבי אין מברכין בורא עצי בשמים אלא על אפרסמון של בית ר' ועל אפרסמון של בית קיסר ועל ההדס שבכל מקום תיובתא א"ל רב חסדא לרב יצחק האי משחא דאפרסמא מאי מברכין עלויה א"ל הכי אמר רב יהודה בורא שמן ארצנו א"ל בר מיניה דרב יהודה דחביב' ליה ארץ ישראל לכולי עלמא מאי א"ל הכי א"ר יוחנן *בורא שמן ערב א"ר אדא בר אהבה האי כשרתא מברכין עלויה בורא עצי בשמים אבל משחא כבישא לא ורב כהנא אמר אפילו משחא כבישא אבל משחא טחינא לא נהרדעי אמרי *אפי' משחא טחינא

אמר

רש"י

אהדר קרעיה לאחוריה. קרע שקרע בהספד רבו החזיר החלוק לאחוריו ומה שלאחוריו לפניו כדי לקרוע קרע אחר להראות אבל עכשיו כיום המיתה על שהיו לריכים להוראה ואין יודעים להורות: רמי להו כו'. כדרמינן לעיל וע"כ מבעי ליה לאוקמי ברייתא בהכי וקתני א' מברך לכולם דקביעות הוא: הביאו להם מים. כך היו רגילים: נוטל ידו אחת. לקבל בה כוס ששותה לפני המזון: עלו. על המטות והסבו: חוזר ונוטל שתי ידיו. שלריך לאכול בשתיהן: אף על פי שכל אחד ואחד ברך לעצמו. לריכין עוד ברכה שאין ברכה ראשונה פוטרתו שאין הראשון קרוי שלפני המזון שאינו במקום סעודה והאי בתרא הוא יין שלפני המזון: אחד מברך לכולן. דכיון דהסבו הוקבעו: קשיא רישא. דקתני כל אחד ואחד מברך לעצמו: שאני אורחין דדעתייהו למיעקר. סופן למיעקר ולעלות ולהסב במקום אחר שאין זה מקום המסיבה אלא כאן ישבו עד שיתכנסו כל הקרואים ודרך בעלי בתים עשירים היה לזמן לסעודתם אורחים עניים להכי קרי להו אורחים והא דאמר רב יין לא בעי הסבה אלא ישיב' בעלמא שלא בשעת סעודה קאמר או בשעת סעודה ובמקום סעודה: הואיל ואין בית הבליעה פנוי. ואין מסובין אל המברך אלא לבלוע: מכלל דאיכא עדיף מיניה. ואפ"ה כיון דאתחיל בהדא עביד לאידך: הנוטל ידיו תחלה. במים אחרונים הוא מזומן לברכת המזון: חזייה. רבי חייא לרב: דהוה מרתת. שמא ראה ידי מלוכלכות או שמא האכלתי באכילה יותר מדאי: עיין בברכת מזונא קאמר לך. כאן נתן לך רשות לברך ברכת המזון שהנוטל ידיו תחלה הוא מברך: על הריח. של מוגמר: תמרתו. קיטור העשן שמתמר ועולה: הא לא ארח. לא הריח בו עדיין ולא נהנה: מברכין עליהן בור' עצי בשמים. ואע"פ שנשרף ואינו בעין אלא שהתימור עולה: חוץ ממושק. מוסג"א בלע"ז*: שהוא מן חיה. מן הרעי של חיה: מיתיבי אין מברכין בורא עצי בשמים אלא על אפרסמון. שהעץ עצמו בא לפנינו: של בית רבי ושל בית קיסר. נקט הכי משום שאינו מצוי אלא בבית מלכים ובעלי גדולה: ועל ההדס שבכל מקום. וה"ה לכל הדומה להם שהעץ עצמו מריח בלא שרפה אלא דהדס שכיח ודברו חכמים בהווה בכל מקום ומוגמר לא מברכינן אלא בורא מיני בשמים: משחא דאפרסמא מאי מברכין. על ריחו: שמן ארצנו. שהיה גדל ביריחו ועל שם הריח היתה נקרא' יריחו והוא פנג האמור בספר יחזקאל (כז) יהודה וארץ ישראל המה רוכליך בחיטי מנית ופנג כך ראיתי בספר יוסף בן גוריון: בר מיני' דרב יהודה. לא תביא לי ראיה מדבריו בזו: כשרתא. קושט: משחא כבישא. שמן שבו טמון הקושט והשמן מריח מן הבושם שבתוכו: לא. הואיל ואין נראה לעינינו אלא השמן: משחא טחינא. שטחנו בו כשרתא:

סמלק

תוספות

כל אחד נוטל ידו אחת. מפני *כבוד הברכה ולא דמי לנוטל ידיו לפירות דהוי מנגבי הגוף כיון שאינו נוטל שתי ידיו:

בא להם יין וכו'. אף על גב דיין שלפני המזון פוטר יין שלאחר המזון כ"ש זה שלפניו הוא שאני הכא כיון שעלו להסב הוי שינוי מקום ולריך לברך:

הואיל ואין בית הבליעה פנוי. ויש מפרש' כשאומר סברי מורי והם מכוונים לאכול כדי לשמוע הברכה ולענות אמן שיהיו פטורים וכן משמע בירושלמי גבי הך ברייתא הכי מילי באורחין אבל בבעל הבית פטור מפני שהכל פונים אלא בעל הבית תני רבי חייא אף בעל הבית בתוך ביתו ואין נראה לרבינו אלחנן דכיון שתקנו חכמים שיברך כל אחד לעצמו אינו יוצא כלל בברכת חבירו וגם שלא תחלוק בין פנוי לשאינו פנוי דלאתי למטעי. והטוב והמטיב יש מפרש שפוטר לאחרים לכולי עלמא דהכי משמע הטוב לעצמו והמטיב לאחריני שהם שותים עמו ורבינו יחיאל היה אומר דלא היא דשייך נמי אין בית הבליעה פנוי ולא פליג בין הטוב ובין ברכת היין דמשום האי טעמא הטוב לדידיה ומטיב לאחריני אינו פוטר אחרים דהא המטיב שייך אפילו שלא בפני המטיבין לו כדאמרינן לקמן בפרק הרואה (דף נט:) אמרו לו ילדה אשתך זכר אומר ברוך הטוב והמטי' הטוב לדידיה והמטיב לאשתו אע"ג דאין אשתו אללו אבל לריך עיון קלת מהבדלה שאנו מבדילים ועומדים היאך אנו פוטרין זה את זה מיין ומהבדלה אחרי שאין אנו לא יושבים ולא מסובין ושמא יש לומר מתוך שקובעין עלמן כדי ללאת ידי הבדלה קבעי כמי אכולה מלתא ולכך נראה וטוב למבדיל וגם לשומעים שישבו בשעת הבדלה שאז יהיה נראה כקבע ופוטר אותם:

כל המוגמרות מברכין עליהן בורא עצי בשמים. אע"פ שנשרפו ואין עצי בשמים בעין:

ועל ההדס שבכל מקום. בעל הלכות גדולות לא גרים תיובתא ומשני תנא הדס וכל דדמי ליה כלומר שעיקרו לריח לאפוקי תפוחים ואתרוגים שאין עיקרו להריח אלא לאכול ומי שהולך בבית שיש שם בשמים ויש שם מיני בשמים שמריח בהן ומספקא ליה אי ממין עץ אי ממין אדמה הוא יש מפרשים שמברך שהכל כהיה בדברו דעל כולן אם ברך שהכל יצא והרב רבינו משה מקולי היה אומר שיברך בורא מיני בשמים:

משחא כבישא. פר"ח שמענו מרבותינו שכובשין שומשמין וורד ועצי בשמים זמן מרובה וקולטין השומשמין ריח של בשמים וטוחנים ועושים אותם משחא ויש בו ריח של בשמים ומשחא טחינה קרוב לטחינתו נותנים עליהם עצי בשמים ואינו קולט כל כך הריח:

שמן

מסורת הש"ס

תוספתא פ"ד

שם

כס"ל מ"ג עד באחרונה לק' מו

[שם]

פי' בר גדולים [שבת ג: ושם פרש"י בן גדולים ע' מה שכתבנו לעיל יג:]

עין משפט נר מצוה

[וע' מ"ס תוס' פסחים קטו. ד"ה כל שטיבולו כו' ותוס' חגיגה יח: ד"ה הנוטל]

קכג א מיי' פ"א מהלכות ברכות ה"יב סמג עשין כז טוש"ע א"ח סי' קע"ד סעיף א

קכד ב מיי' פ"ד שם ה"יב סמג שם טוש"ע א"ח סי' קע"ד סעיף ח

קכה ג מיי' פ"ז שם ה"יב סמג שם טוש"ע א"ח סי' קצ"א סעיף ו

קכו ד מיי' פ"ט שם ה"יב סמג שם טוש"ע א"ח סי' רי"ו סעיף יב

קכז ה מיי' שם טוש"ע שם סעיף יב

קכח ו מיי' שם שם סעיף ג

קכט ז מיי' שם שם סעיף ד

קל ח מיי' שם שם סעיף ה

אמר רב גדל אמר רב האי ^א^סמלק מברכין עלויה בורא עצי בשמים אמר רב חננאל אמר רב הני ^ב^חלפי דימא מברכין עלייהו בורא עצי בשמים אמר מר זוטרא מאי קראה °והיא העלתם הגגה ותטמנם בפשתי העץ (*רב משרשיא אמר) האי ^ג^נרקום דגגוניתא מברכין עלויה בורא עצי בשמים דדברא בורא עשבי בשמים אמר רב ששת הני ^ד^סיגלי מברכין עלייהו בורא עשבי בשמים אמר מר זוטרא ^ה^האי מאן דמורח באתרוגא או בחבושא אומר ברוך שנתן ריח טוב בפירות אמר רב יהודה *^ו^האי מאן דנפיק ביומא ניסן וחזי אילני דקא מלבלבי אומר ברוך שלא חיסר בעולמו כלום וברא בו בריות טובות ואילנות טובות להתנאות בהן בני אדם אמר רב זוטרא בר טוביה אמר רב ^ז^מנין שמברכין על הריח שנאמר °כל הנשמה תהלל יה איזהו דבר שהנשמה נהנת ממנו ואין הגוף נהנה ממנו הוי אומר זה הריח ואמר רב זוטרא בר טוביה אמר רב עתידים *בחורי ישראל שיתנו ריח טוב כלבנון שנאמר °ילכו יונקותיו ויהי כזית הודו וריח לו כלבנון: ואמר רב זוטרא בר טוביה אמר רב מ"ד °את הכל עשה יפה בעתו מלמד שכל אחד ואחד יפה לו הקב"ה אומנותו בפניו א"ר פפא היינו דאמרי אינשי תלה ליה קורא לדבר אחר *ואידו דידיה עביד ואמר רב זוטרא בר טוביה אמר רב אבוקה כשנים וירח כשלשה איבעיא להו אבוקה כשנים בהדי דידיה או דילמא אבוקה כשנים לבר מדידיה ת"ש וירח כשלשה אי אמרת בשלמא בהדי דידיה שפיר אלא אי אמרת לבר מדידיה ארבעה למה לי והאמר מר לאחד נראה ומזיק לשנים נראה ואינו מזיק לשלשה אינו נראה כל עיקר אלא לאו ש"מ אבוקה כשנים בהדי דידיה ש"מ: *ואמר רב זוטרא בר טוביה אמר רב ואמרי לה אמר רב חנא בר ביזנא א"ר שמעון חסידא ואמרי לה א"ר יוחנן משום ר' שמעון בן יוחי נוח לו לאדם שיפיל עצמו לתוך כבשן האש ^ה^ואל ילבין פני חבירו ברבים מנלן מתמר שנאמר °היא מוצאת וגו': ת"ר הביאו לפניו שמן והדס ב"ש אומרים מברך על השמן ואח"כ מברך על ההדס וב"ה אומרים ^ט^מברך על ההדס ואח"כ מברך על השמן אמר ר"ג אני אכריע שמן זכינו לריחו וזכינו לסיכתו הדס לריחו זכינו לסיכתו לא זכינו *א"ר יוחנן הלכה כדברי המכריע רב פפא איקלע לבי רב הונא בריה דרב איקא אייתו לקמייהו שמן והדס שקל רב פפא בריך אהדס ברישא והדר בריך אשמן א"ל לא סבר לה מר הלכה כדברי המכריע אמר ליה הכי אמר רבא הלכה כב"ה ולא היא *לאשתמוטי נפשיה הוא דעבד ת"ר *הביאו לפניהם שמן ויין ב"ש אומרים ^י^אוחז השמן בימינו ואת היין בשמאלו מברך על השמן וחוזר ומברך על היין ב"ה אומרים אוחז את היין בימינו ואת השמן בשמאלו מברך על היין וחוזר ומברך על השמן וטחו בראש השמש ואם שמש תלמיד חכם הוא טחו בכותל מפני שגנאי לת"ח לצאת לשוק כשהוא מבושם ת"ר ששה דברים גנאי לו לתלמיד חכם אל יצא כשהוא מבושם *לשוק *ואל יצא יחידי בלילה ואל יצא במנעלים המטולאים ואל יספר עם אשה בשוק ואל יסב בחבורה של עמי הארץ ואל יכנס באחרונה לבית המדרש ויש אומרים אף לא יפסיע פסיעה גסה ואל יהלך בקומה זקופה ^כ^אל יצא כשהוא מבושם לשוק א"ר אבא בריה דרבי חייא בר אבא א"ר יוחנן במקום שחשודים על משכב זכור אמר רב ששת לא אמרן אלא בבגדו אבל בגופו זיעה מעברא ליה אמר רב פפא *^ל^ושערו כבגדו דמי ואמרי לה כגופו דמי ^מ^ואל יצא יחידי בלילה משום חשדא ולא אמרן אלא דלא קביע ליה עידנא אבל קביע ליה עידנא מידע ידיע דלעידניה קא אזיל ^נ^ואל יצא במנעלים המטולאים מסייע ליה לרב חייא בר אבא *דאמר רב חייא בר אבא גנאי הוא לת"ח שיצא במנעלים המטולאים איני והא ר' חייא בר אבא נפיק אמר מר זוטרא בריה דרב נחמן בטלאי על גבי טלאי ולא אמרן אלא בפנתא אבל בגילדא לית לן בה ובפנתא לא אמרן אלא באורחא אבל בביתא לית לן *בה ולא אמרן אלא בימות החמה אבל בימות הגשמים לית לן בה ^ס^ואל יספר עם אשה בשוק אמר רב חסדא ואפילו היא אשתו תנ"ה אפילו היא אשתו ואפילו היא בתו ואפילו היא אחותו לפי שאין הכל בקיאין בקרובותיו ^ע^ואל יסב בחבורה של עמי הארץ מ"ט דילמא אתי לאמשוכי בתריידו ואל יכנס אחרונה לבית המדרש משום דקרו ליה *פושע וי"א ^פ^אף לא יפסיע פסיעה גסה דאמר מר *פסיעה גסה נוטלת אחד מת"ק ממאור עיניו של אדם מאי תקנתיה להדריה בקדושא דבי שמשי ^צ^ואל יהלך בקומה זקופה דאמר מר המהלך בקומה זקופה אפילו ד' אמות כאלו דוחק רגלי שכינה דכתיב °מלא כל הארץ כבודו:

מתני'

תורה אור: יהושע ב · הושע יד · קהלת ג · תהלים קנ · בראשית לח · ישעיה ו

רש"י: סמלק. ישמי"ן קורין לו בלשון ישמעאל והוא מין עשב שיש בו שלש שורות של עלין זו למעלה מזו ושלשה עלין לכל שורה: חלפי דימא. בושם שקורין אספיג והוא שבולת נרד ועשוי כעין גבעולי פשתן דאשכחן גבעולין דאיקרו עץ: נרקום. חבצלת השרון בה"ג: דגנוניתא. הגדל בגינה: סיגלי. ויול"ש בלע"ז: חבושין. קודוניי"ש בלע"ז: להתנאות. ליהנות: כלבנון. שמריחין עליו ופרחיו: יפה לו אומנותו. ואפילו בורסי נאה אצלו אומנותו בעיניו ועשה הקדוש ברוך הוא כן שלא יחסור העולם אומנות: קורא. לב הגדל בדקל תלה אותו לחזיר והיא יגלגלנו באשפה שזו היא אומנותו: אבוקה. כשני בני אדם לענין היולא בלילה דאמר מר אל יצא אדם יחידי בלילה: וירח כשלשה. ויש חלוק בין שנים לשלשה כדלקמן: לאחד נראה. השד ומזיקו: היא מוצאת והיא שלחה וגו'. ואלו בהדיא לא אמרה אלו הסימנים של יהודה הם ולו אכי הרה אלא לאיש אשר אלה לו אנכי הרה אם יודה יודה ואם לאו אשרף ולא אלבין פניו: שמן והדס. בסוף הסעודה שמן לסוך ידיו להעביר זוהמת האוכלין והדס להריח כמו שאמרנו: אני אכריע. לצד בית שמאי: זכינו לריחו ולסיכתו. כגון משחא כבישא הלכך שמן עדיף: ולא היא. לא אמר רבא הלכתא כב"ה אלא רב פפא אכסיף לפי שטעה והשמיט עצמו בכך: שמן ויין. זהו יין שלאחר המזון ואין זה כוס של ברכה: חוזר ומברך על היין. כגון בחול שאין היין קבע ואין היין שלפני המזון פוטרו: שמן בימינו. לפי שעליו מברך תחלה: מברך על השמן. בורא שמן ערב: וטחו בראש השמש. כדי שלא ילא בידיו מבושמות בשוק שגנאי הוא לתלמיד חכם: שחשודים על משכב זכור. ומבשמין עצמם כדי שיתאוו להם: ושערו כבגדו דמי. דלא שכיח ביה זיעה: ואמרי לה כגופו. דשכיח ביה זיעה: משום חשדא. של זנות: דלא קביע ליה עידנא. שלא קבע לו רבו קביעות ללמדו בלילה: בפנתא. אנפיל"א בלע"ז שעל גבי הרגל: גילדא. עקב שקורין סול"א: בימות הגשמים. הטיט מכסהו: אפילו היא אשתו. שאין הכל מכירין בה וחושדין אותו: דקרו ליה פושע. מתעצל: בקידושא דבי שמשי. שטותה כוס של קידוש בשבת בלילה:

תוספות: שמן והדס. הא שמן להריח הוא דאי להעביר הזוהמא הא אמרינן בפרק אלו דברים (דף נג.) דאין מברכים עליו: הכי אמר רבא הלכתא כבית הלל ולא היא לאשתמוטי נפשיה הוא דקא עבד. כך כתוב בספרים שלנו ובפירוש רש"י אבל רב אלפס פסק כרבא משמע שלא היה גורס בספרו ולא היא וכו': *האי מאן דמורח אתרוג' וחבושא מברך וכו'. ודוקא כשמריח בהם אבל אם בא לאכול מהם אין לברך ברכת ריח כי אם ברכת אכילה:

עין משפט נר מצוה:

קלא ^א^^ב^ מיי' פ"ט מה' ברכו' הל' ו סמג עשין כז טוש"ע א"ח סי' ריו סעי' ז [סייך לעיל קודם ד"ה שמן]

קלב ^ג^ מיי' שם טוש"ע שם סעיף ט

קלג ^ד^ שם סעי' ח

קלד ^ה^ מיי' שם הל' א טוש"ע שם סעיף ב

קלה ^ו^ מיי' פ"י מה' ברכו' הל' יג סמג שם טוש"ע א"ח סימן רכו

קלו ^ז^ מיי' פ"ט מהל' ברכות ה"א סמג שם טוש"ע א"ח סי' ריו סעי' א

קלז ^ח^ מיי' פ"ו מהלכ' דעות הלכה ח

קלח ^ט^ מיי' פ"ט מה' ברכו' הל' ג סמג עשין כז טוש"ע א"ח סי' ריו סעיף יא

קלט ^י^ מיי' פ"ז מה' ברכו' הל' יד ופ"ט הל' ד סמג שם טור א"ח סי' ריב וסימן רו סעיף ד

[ז"ל רמ"ע מפאנו ס"ס ה' רב פפא מסבר' דנפשי' פליג על ר' יוחנן ולא מחמת כסוף' הוא דבעי לאשתמוטי אלא ממדת חסידו' ותלה הגדולה ברבו ואי לאו דקים ליה דהכי הלכתא לא עבד עובדא בנפשיה והכי קי"ל בכל דוכתא מעשה רב]

[הרמב"ם לא הזכיר אלא החלוק בין ימות החמה לאסור וימות הגשמי' דמותר אבל ההפרש בין פנתא לגילדאי וכן בין באורחא לבביתא השמיט]

מסורת הש"ס:

[נ"ל בחורי ישראל שלא טעמו טעם חטא שיהנו כו' ע"י]

[גיר' הערוך והוא לדידיה אזיל ע"ש ערך קר]

ב"מ נט. כתובות סז: סוטה י:

[ע' תוס' פסחים כא. ד"ה אין תוס' ב"ק קנז. ד"ה הכרעה]

[תוספ' פ"ה]

מס' ד"א זוטא פ"ו

[ע' חולין לא. פסחי' יב:]

זבחים יט.

שבת קיד. ע"ש

גי' רב"ל עלל שם יג:

[ע' תוס' תענית יוד: ד"ה פסיעה]

א מנס הרי"ף בברכו' וביותר ביאור בשבת פ' אלו קשרים הביא כל דרכים אלו וע' בלחם משנה הלכות דעות פ"ה דין ט

קמ כלמ^נ^ מיי' פ"ה מהלכות דעות הלכה ט קמא ^ס^שם הל' ז קמב ^ע^שם הלכה ג קמג ^פצ^שם הל' ח

[43*b*]. R. Giddal said in the name of Rab: Over jasmine[3] the blessing is 'who createst fragrant woods'. R. Hananel said in the name of Rab: Over sea-rush[4] the blessing is 'who createst fragrant woods'. Said Mar Zuṭra: What Scriptural verse confirms this? *She had brought them up to the roof and hid them with the stalks of flax.*[5] R. Mesharsheya said: Over garden narcissus the blessing is 'who createst fragrant woods'; over wild narcissus, 'who createst fragrant herbs'. R. Shesheth said: Over violets the blessing is, 'who createst fragrant herbs'. Mar Zuṭra said: He who smells a citron or a quince should say, 'Blessed be He who has given a sweet odour to fruits'. Rab Judah says: If one goes abroad in the days of Nisan [spring time] and sees the trees sprouting, he should say, 'Blessed be He who hath not left His world lacking in anything and has created in it goodly creatures and goodly trees for the enjoyment of mankind'. R. Zuṭra b. Tobiah said in the name of Rab: Whence do we learn that a blessing should be said over
a sweet odours? Because it says, *Let every soul*[1] *praise the Lord.*[2] What is that which gives enjoyment to the soul and not to the body?—You must say that this is fragrant smell.

Mar Zuṭra b. Tobiah further said in the name of Rab: The young men of Israel[3] are destined to emit a sweet fragrance like Lebanon,[4] as it says *His branches shall spread, and his beauty shall be as the olive tree, and his fragrance as Lebanon.*[5]

R. Zuṭra b. Tobiah further said in the name of Rab: What is the meaning of the verse, *He hath made everything beautiful in its time?*[6] It teaches that the Holy One, blessed be He, made every man's trade seem fine in his own eyes. R. Papa said: This agrees with the popular saying:[7] Hang the heart of a palm tree on a pig, and it will do the usual thing with it.[8]

R. Zuṭra b. Tobiah further said in the name of Rab: A torch is as good as two [persons][9] and moonlight as good as three. The question was asked: Is the torch as good as two counting the carrier, or as good as two besides the carrier?—Come and hear: 'Moonlight is as good as three'. If now you say, 'including the carrier', there is no difficulty. But if you say, 'besides the carrier', why do I want four, seeing that a Master has said: To one [person] an evil spirit may show itself and harm him; to two it may show itself, but without harming them; to three it will not even show itself? We must therefore say that a torch is equivalent to two including the carrier; and this may be taken as proved.

R. Zuṭra b. Tobiah further said in the name of Rab—according to others, R. Ḥanah b. Bizna said it in the name of R. Simeon the Pious, and according to others again, R. Joḥanan said it in the name of R. Simeon b. Yohai: It is better for a man that he should cast himself into a fiery furnace rather than that he should put his
b fellow to shame in public.[1] Whence do we know this? From Tamar, of whom it says, *When she was brought forth* etc.[2]

Our Rabbis taught: If oil and myrtle are brought before one,[3] Beth Shammai say that he first says a benediction over the oil and then over the myrtle, while Beth Hillel say that he first says a benediction over the myrtle and then over the oil. Said Rabban Gamaliel: I will turn the scale.[4] Of oil we have the benefit both for smelling and for anointing; of myrtle we have the benefit for smelling but not for anointing. R. Joḥanan said: The *halachah* follows the one who turned the scale. R. Papa was once visiting R. Huna the son of R. Iḳa. Oil and myrtle were brought before him and he took up the myrtle and said the blessing over it first, and then he said the blessing over the oil. Said the other to him: Does not your honour hold that the *halachah* follows the one who turned the scale? He replied: Thus said Raba: The *halachah* follows Beth Hillel. This was not correct,[5] however; he said so only to excuse himself.

Our Rabbis taught: If oil and wine are brought before one,[6] Beth Shammai say that he first takes the oil in his right hand and the wine in his left hand and says a blessing over the oil[7] and then a blessing over the wine. Beth Hillel, however, say that he takes the wine in his right hand and the oil in his left, and says the blessing over the wine and then over the oil. [Before going out] he smears it on the head of the attendant; and if the attendant is a man of learning, he smears it on the wall, since it is unbecoming for a scholar to go abroad scented.

Our Rabbis taught: Six things are unbecoming for a scholar. He should not go abroad scented; he should not go out by night alone; he should not go abroad in patched sandals; he should not
c converse with a woman in the street; he should not take a set meal[1] in the company of ignorant persons; and he should not be the last to enter the Beth ha-Midrash. Some add that he should not take long strides nor carry himself stiffly.[2]

'He should not go abroad scented'. R. Abba the son of R. Ḥiyya b. Abba said in the name of R. Joḥanan: This applies only to a place where people are suspected of pederasty. R. Shesheth said: This applies only to [the scenting of] one's clothes; but [perfuming] the body removes the perspiration. R. Papa said: The hair is on the same footing as clothes; others, however, say: as the body.

'He should not go out at night alone', so as not to arouse suspicion.[3] This is the case only if he has no appointment [with his teacher]; but if he has an appointment, people know that he is going to his appointment.

'He should not go abroad in patched sandals'. This supports R. Ḥiyya b. Abba; for R. Ḥiyya b. Abba said: It is unseemly for a scholar to go abroad in patched sandals. Is that so? Did not R. Ḥiyya b. Abba go out in such?—Mar Zuṭra the son of R. Naḥman said: He was speaking of one patch on top of another. And this applies only to the upper, but if it is on the sole, there is no objection. On the upper too this applies only to the public way; but in the house there is no objection. Further, this is the case only in summer; but in the rainy season there is no objection.[4]

'He should not converse with a woman in the street'. R. Ḥisda said: Even with his wife. It has been taught similarly: Even with his wife, even with his daughter, even with his sister, because not everyone knows who are his female relatives.

'He should not take a set meal with ignorant persons'. What is the reason?—Perhaps he will be drawn into their ways.

'He should not be last to enter the Beth ha-Midrash', because
d he will be called a transgressor.[1]

'Some add that he should not take long strides'; because a Master has said: Long strides diminish a man's eyesight by a five-hundredth part. What is the remedy? He can restore it with [drinking] the sanctification wine of Sabbath eve.[2]

'Nor should he carry himself stiffly'; since a Master has said: If one walks with a stiff bearing even for four cubits, it is as if he pushed against the heels of the Divine Presence,[3] since it is written, *The whole earth is full of His glory.*[4]

(3) According to Krauss, it should be 'elder-tree'. (4) Which has stalks like flax. (5) Lit., 'flax of the tree'. Josh. II, 6.

a (1) Heb. *neshamah*, lit., 'breath'. (2) Ps. CL, 6. (3) MS.M. adds here: 'who have not tasted sin', and this seems to be the proper reading. (4) From its trees and blossoms. (5) Hos. XIV, 7. (6) Eccl. III, 11. (7) Lit., 'this is what people say'. (8) *Sc.* takes it to the dungheap. (9) In respect of the injunction that a man should not go abroad at night unaccompanied, for fear of evil spirits.

b (1) Lit., 'cause his face to blanch'. (2) Gen. XXXVIII, 25. Even to save herself from the stake, Tamar did not mention Judah's name. (3) After a meal, oil for removing dirt from the hands, myrtle for scent. (4) In favour of Beth Shammai. (5) That Raba ever said so. (6) After a meal on a weekday, the perfumed oil being for scent. (7) 'Blessed is He that created pleasant oil'.

c (1) Lit., 'recline'. (2) Lit., 'with erect stature'. (3) Of immoral practices. (4) Because the mud will hide it.

d (1) Var. lec.: 'idler', which in any case is the meaning. (2) V. Shab. 113*b*. (3) I.e., acted haughtily against God. (4) Isa. VI, 3.

MISHNAH. [44a] IF SALTED FOOD IS SET BEFORE HIM AND BREAD WITH IT, HE SAYS A BLESSING OVER THE SALTED FOOD AND THIS SERVES FOR THE BREAD, SINCE THE BREAD IS ONLY SUBSIDIARY TO IT. THIS IS THE GENERAL PRINCIPLE: WHENEVER WITH ONE KIND OF FOOD ANOTHER IS TAKEN AS SUBSIDIARY, A BENEDICTION IS SAID OVER THE PRINCIPAL KIND AND THIS SERVES FOR THE SUBSIDIARY.

GEMARA. But is it ever possible for salted food to be the principal item and bread subsidiary to it?—R. Aḥa the son of R. 'Awira replied, citing R. Ashi: This rule applies to [one who eats] the fruit of Genessareth.[5] Rabbah b. Bar Ḥannah said: When we went after R. Joḥanan to eat the fruit of Genessareth, when there were a hundred of us we used each to take him ten, and when we were ten we used each to take him a hundred, and a hundred could not be got into a basket holding three *se'ahs*, and he used to eat them all and swear that he had not tasted food. Not tasted food, do you say?—Say rather: that he had not had a meal. R. Abbahu used to eat of them [so freely] that a fly slipped
a off his forehead.[1] R. Ammi and R. Assi used to eat of them till their hair fell out. R. Simeon b. Lakish ate until his mind began to wander, and R. Joḥanan told the household of the Nasi, and R. Judah the Prince send a band of men[2] for him and they brought him to his house.

When R. Dimi came [from Palestine], he stated that King Jannaeus[3] had a city in the King's Mountain[4] where they used to take out sixty myriads of dishes of salted fish for the men cutting down fig-trees from one week-end to the next.[5] When Rabin came, he stated that King Jannaeus used to have a tree on the King's Mountain from which they used to take down forty *se'ahs* of young pigeons from three broods every month. When R. Isaac came, he said: There was a town in the Land of Israel named Gofnith[6] in which there were eighty pairs of brothers, all priests, who were married to eighty pairs of sisters, also all of priestly family. The Rabbis searched from Sura to Nehardea and could not find [a similar case] save the daughters of R. Ḥisda who were married to Rami b. Ḥama and to Mar 'Ukba b. Ḥama; and while they were priestesses, their husbands were not priests.

Rab said: A meal without salt is no meal. R. Ḥiyya b. Abba said in the name of R. Joḥanan: A meal without gravy[7] is no meal.

MISHNAH. IF ONE HAS EATEN GRAPES, FIGS OR POMEGRANATES HE SAYS A GRACE OF THREE BLESSINGS AFTER THEM. SO R. GAMALIEL. THE SAGES, HOWEVER, SAY: ONE BLESSING WHICH INCLUDES THREE. R. AKIBA SAYS: IF ONE ATE ONLY BOILED VEGETABLES, AND THAT IS HIS MEAL, HE SAYS AFTER IT THE GRACE OF THREE BLESSINGS. IF ONE DRINKS WATER TO QUENCH HIS THIRST, HE SAYS THE BENEDICTION 'BY WHOSE WORD ALL THINGS EXIST'. R. TARFON SAYS: 'WHO CREATEST MANY LIVING THINGS AND THEIR REQUIREMENTS'.

GEMARA. What is the reason of R. Gamaliel?—Because it is
b written, *A land of wheat and barley*, etc.,[1] and it is also written, *A land wherein thou shalt eat bread without scarceness*,[2] and it is written, *And thou shalt eat and be satisfied and bless the Lord thy God*.[3] The Rabbis, however, hold that the word 'land'[4] makes a break in the context. R. Gamaliel also must admit that 'land' makes a break in the context?—He requires that for excluding one who chews wheat [from the necessity of saying grace].[5]

R. Jacob b. Idi said in the name of R. Ḥanina: Over anything belonging to the five species [of cereals],[6] before partaking the blessing 'who createst all kinds of food' is said, and after partaking one blessing which includes three. Rabbah b. Mari said in the name of R. Joshua b. Levi: Over anything belonging to the seven kinds,[7] before partaking the blessing 'who createst the fruit of the tree' is said, and after it the grace of one blessing which includes three.

Abaye asked R. Dimi: What is the one blessing which includes three?—He replied: Over fruit of the tree he says: 'For the tree and for the fruit of the tree and for the produce of the field and for a desirable, goodly, and extensive land which Thou didst give our ancestors to inherit to eat of its fruit and to be satisfied with its goodness. Have mercy, O Lord our God, on Israel Thy people and on Jerusalem Thy city and on Thy Sanctuary and on Thy altar, and build Jerusalem Thy holy city speedily in our days and bring
c us up into the midst thereof and rejoice us therein,[1] for Thou art good and doest good to all'.[2] Over the five species [of cereals] one says: 'For the provision and the sustenance and the produce of the field etc.', and he concludes, 'For the land and for the sustenance'.

How does one conclude [in the case of fruits]? When R. Dimi came, he said in the name of Rab: On New Moon one concludes, Blessed is He who sanctifies Israel and New Moons.[3]

What do we say in this case [over fruit]?—R. Ḥisda said: 'For the land and for its fruits'; R. Joḥanan said: 'For the land and for the fruits'. R. Amram said: They are not at variance: the one blessing[4] is for us [in Babylon], and the other for them [in Palestine].[5] R. Naḥman b. Isaac demurred to this: Shall they eat and we bless?[6] You must therefore reverse the names, thus: R. Ḥisda said: For the land and for the fruits; R. Joḥanan said, For the land and for its fruits.

(5) Which is highly prized. Tosaf. explains that the rule applies to salted food taken after the fruit of Genessareth to correct the excessive sweetness.

a (1) They made his skin so smooth that it could not obtain a footing. (2) Lit., 'searchers', 'officials'. (3) Of the Hasmonean House. (4) Probably some district in Judea was known by this name. (5) So many workers were required for the task. (6) Supposed to be the Biblical Ophni, modern Jifna. (7) So Rashi. *Aliter*: 'vegetable juices'; *aliter*: 'something sharp'. In all cases the idea is to aid digestion.

b (1) Deut. VIII, 8. (2) Ibid. 9. (3) Ibid. 10. The first two verses show that grapes etc. are on the same footing as bread, while the third verse contains a hint of three blessings, as explained *infra* 48b. (4) In the second half of v. 9 so that '*and thou shalt bless*' in v. 10 refers only to 'bread' mentioned in v. 9. (5) The break is necessary to indicate that '*wheat*' mentioned must first be made into '*bread*' before the three benedictions are necessary. (6) Viz., wheat, barley, oats, rye and spelt. (7) Mentioned in v. 8, other than corn.

c (1) Var. lec. (Similarly *P.B.*): Rejoice us in its rebuilding. MS.M. add (similarly *P.B.*): May we eat of the fruits of the land and be satisfied with its goodness and bless Thee for it in holiness and purity. (2) Cf. *P.B.* p. 287. (3) This paragraph seems to be out of place here and is deleted by Wilna Gaon. MS.M.: On New Moon one concludes etc. What do we say in this case? (4) R. Ḥisda's. (5) R. Ḥisda was from Babylon and R. Joḥanan from Palestine. (6) They eat the fruit of Palestine, and we say *its* fruits!

מתני' "הביאו לפניו מליח תחלה ופת עמו מברך על המליח ופוטר את הפת שהפת טפלה לו *זה הכלל כל שהוא עיקר ועמו טפלה מברך על העיקר ופוטר את הטפלה: גמ' ומי איכא מידי דהוה מליח עיקר ופת טפלה אמר רב אחא בריה דרב עוירא אמר רב אשי באוכל פירות גנוסר שנו *אמר רבה ב"ב חנה כי הוה אזלינן בתריה דרבי יוחנן למיכל פירות גנוסר כי הוינן בי מאה מנקטינן ליה לכל חד וחד עשרה וכי הוינן בי עשר' מנקטינן לי' כל חד וחד מאה וכל מאה מינייהו *הוה מחזיק להו צנא בר תלתא סאוי *ואכיל להו ומשתבע דלא טעם זיונא ס"ד אלא אימא מזונא ר' אבהו אכיל עד דהוה שריק ליה דודבא מאפותיה ורב אמי ורב אסי הוו אכלי עד דנתור מזייהו רשב"ל הוה אכיל עד דמריד ואמר להו רבי יוחנן לדבי נשיאה והוה משדר ליה ר' יהודה נשיאה באלושי אבתריה ומייתי ליה לביתיה כי אתא רב דימי אמר עיר אחת היתה לו לינאי המלך בהר המלך שהיו מוציאים ממנה ששים רבוא ספלי טרית לקוצצי תאנים מערב שבת לע"ש כי אתא רבין אמר אילן אחד היה לו לינאי המלך בהר המלך שהיו מורידין ממנו ארבעים סאה גוזלות משלש בריכות בחדש כי אתא ר' יצחק אמר עיר אחת היתה בא"י וגופנית שמה שהיו בה שמנים זוגות אחים כהנים נשואים לשמנים זוגות אחיות כהנות ובדקו רבנן מסורא ועד נהרדעא ולא אשכחו בר מבנתיה דרב חסדא דהוו נסיבין לרמי בר חמא ולמר עוקבא בר חמא ואע"ג דאינהו הוו כהנתא אינהו לא הוו כהני אמר רב כל סעודה שאין בה מלח אינה סעודה א"ר חייא בר אבא א"ר יוחנן כל סעודה שאין בה *שריף אינה סעודה: מתני' אכל ענבים ותאנים ורמונים מברך אחריהם שלש ברכות דברי ר"ג וחכ"א ברכה אחת (מעין שלש) ר"ע אומ' אפי' אכל שלק והוא מזונו מברך עליו שלש ברכות *השותה מים לצמאו מברך שנ"ב *ר' טרפון אומר *בורא נפשות רבות וחסרונן: גמ' מ"ט דר"ג דכתיב °ארץ חטה ושעורה וגו' וכתיב ארץ אשר לא במסכנות תאכל בה לחם וכתיב °ואכלת ושבעת וברכת את ה' אלהיך ורבנן ארץ הפסיק הענין ור"ג נמי ארץ הפסיק הענין ההוא מיבעי ליה למעוטי הכוסס את החטה א"ר יעקב בר אידי א"ר חנינא "כל שהוא מחמשת המינין בתחלה מברך עליו במ"מ ולבסוף ברכה אחת מעין שלש אמר רבה בר מרי אמר ריב"ל כל שהוא משבעת המינין בתחלה מברך ב"פ העץ ולבסוף ברכה אחת מעין שלש א"ל אביי לרב דימי מאי ניהי ברכה אחת מעין שלש א"ל 'אפירי דעץ על העץ ועל פרי העץ ועל תנובת השדה ועל ארץ חמדה טובה ורחבה שהנחלת לאבותינו לאכול מפריה ולשבוע מטובה רחם יי אלהינו על ישראל עמך ועל ירושלים עירך ועל מקדשך ועל מזבחך ותבנה ירושלים עיר קדשך במהרה בימינו והעלינו לתוכה *ושמחנו בה כי אתה טוב ומטיב לכל. דחמשת המינין על המחיה ועל הכלכלה ועל תנובת השדה כו' וחותם על הארץ ועל המחיה מיחתם במאי חתים כי אתא רב דימי אמר רב חתים בר"ח ברוך מקדש ישראל וראשי חדשים הכא מאי רב חסדא אמר על הארץ ועל פירותיה ור' יוחנן אמר על הארץ ועל הפירות א"ר עמרם *ולא פליגי הא לן והא להו מתקיף לה רב נחמן בר יצחק אינהו אכלי ואנן מברכין "אלא איפוך רב חסדא אמר על הארץ ועל הפירות ור' יוחנן אמר על הארץ ועל פירותיה

אמר

תורה אור: [דף לז.] · קידוש' כט: · דברים ח · שם

מתני' מליח. כל דבר מלוח: גמ' פירות גנוסר. פירות ארץ ישראל ככרת חשובי' מן הפת: זיונא. משמע מידי דבר אכילה: מזונא. דבר הסועד: דשריק דודבא מאפותי'. שהזבוב נחליק ונופלו מתוך לאלת פניו בשרו מחליק: עד דמריד. דעתו מטרפת: באלושי. אוכלוסי בני אדם: ספלי' טרית. ספלי' מלא' חתיכות דג חתוך שקורי' טוני"נא: לקוצצי תאנים. למאכל פועלים שקוצצים תאנים והיו מרובי' עד שכל אלו צריכין להם למאכל: בריכות. קובי"אש בלע"ז: משלש בריכות בחדש. שלש פעמים בחדש מורידי' ממנו כך: שמני' זוגי' אחים. שנים שנים אחים היו כולם וכן נשותיהם: שריף. תבשיל או שיש בו מרק כמו שורפ' היה:

מתני' מברך אחרי' שלש ברכות. ר"ג לטעמי' דאמר לעיל בפירקין (דף לז.) כל שהוא מז' המינים מברך אחריו ג' ברכות: אפי' אכל שלק. של ירק והוא מזונו שסמך עליו למזון: וחסרונן. לצרכי ספוקן: גמ' וברכת. אכולהו קאי ובההוא קרא ג' ברכות רמיזי כדאמרינן בפר' שלש' שאכלו (דף מח:): ארץ הפסיק הענין. ולא קאי וברכת אלא אלחם דסמיך ליה: ור"ג ההיא. הפסקה לפרושי חטה דכתי' בקרא קמא אתא ולמעוטי שאם כססה כמות שהיא אין זו בכלל ברכ' אלא א"כ עשאה לחם: חמשת המיני'. כולם מין דגן חטין ושעורין וכוסמין ושבולת שועל ושיפון כוסמין מין חטה שבולת שועל ושיפון מין שעורה: מברך עליו ב"מ מזונות. אם עשאו תבשיל: כל שהוא משבעת המיני'. משאר שבעת המיני' האמורי' בפסוק ואינו מין דגן: אפירי דעץ. על העץ ועל פרי העץ ועל א"ץ חמדה טובה ורחבה. אתרווייהו קאי כולה עד סופה: רב חתים בראש חדש כו'. אף ע"ג דדמיא לתרתי: הכא מאי. מי חתמינן בתרתי כה"ג כגון על הארץ ועל הפירו' ולא הויא חתימ' בשתים משום כדמפרש לה בפ' ג' שאכלו (דף מט.): הא לן והא להו. רב חסדא מבבל ובבבל חתמי על הארץ ועל פירותיה ורבי יוחנן מארץ ישראל והתם חתמי על הפירות: ואנן מברכינ'. על פירותיה דארץ ישראל לאודה קאי ואנן לא אכלינן מנייהו ומברכי' עלייהו:

קופרא

באוכלי פירות גנוסר שנו. שהמליח עיקר שהוא בא להשיב הלב שנחלש מפני מתיקות הפירות והפת שלאחריו טפל ואינו בא אלא בשביל המליח וא"ת פירות הוי עיקר ומליח טפל ולבריך על הפירו' ולפטר כולהו וי"ל דמיירי שלא אכל הפירו' באותו מעמד אי נמי בשעה שאכל פירות גנוסר לא היה שם עדיין מליח ופת דלא היה יודע שיחלש לבו מחמת המתיקות:

מברך על המליח. ואע"ג דאשמעי' דפת פוטר את הפרפרת איצטריך לאשמועינן דפעמים דפת טפל:

רבי עקיבא אומר אפילו אכל שלק והוא מזונו כו'. ולא דמי להאיה דלעיל *דר"ג נתן רשות לרבי עקיבא לברך וכו' דשאני הכא דאיקבע מזוניה עליה:

על העץ ועל פרי העץ. אבל על היין מברכי' על הגפן ועל פרי הגפן דכיון דיין קובע ברכ' לעצמו משום חשיבותיה הוא הדין לאחריו ובחתימה יש שחותמי' על הארץ ועל הפירו' ויש שחותמין על הגפן ועל פרי הגפן מיהו לכאורה משמע דא"ל לשנות החתימה שהרי אין אנו משנין רק לומר פרי הגפן במקום פרי העץ אבל בעלמא היכי דלא מברכינן על העץ אלא בחתמ' על הארץ ועל הפירות ביין נמי אין לשנות ובספר המיימוני מצריך להזכי' בה מעין המאורע בשבת וביו"ט וכן משמע בירושלמי ומיהו לא נהגו העולם כן ויכול להיו' שמזכירין מעין המאורע היינו דוקא בימיהם שהיו רגילין לקבוע איין ואמיני פירות אבל האידנא לא קבעי ופר"ת היכא דאכל מיני מזונו' כגון דייסא ותאנים ושתי חמרא מברך ברוך א"י אמ"ה על המחי' ועל הכלכלה על הגפן ועל פרי הגפן ועל העץ ועל פרי העץ ועל תנובת השדה וכו' וחות' ברוך א"י אמ"ה על הארץ ועל המחיה ועל הפירו' ולא הוי חתימה בשתי' דהארץ היא המוציאה המחיה והפירות:

אינהו מיכל אכלי ואנן מברכי'. משמע שאין כלא' למקשן שידברו האמוראי' דבבל בשביל בני ארץ ישראל כי כך פר"ת גבי *לעולם ישא אשה ואח"כ ילמוד תורה ותנא אחריני' ילמוד תור' ואח"כ ישא אשה ומסיק הא לן והא להו ופי' ר"ת דרבי יוחנן היה מדבר בשביל תלמידיו שהיו מבבל דשמא הכי קים ליה למקשן דאותה שעה שאמר רב חסדא הא מילתא לא הי' לפניו שום תלמיד מא"י וכן לא שום תלמיד מבבל לפני רבי יוחנן וא"כ לא היה מזכיר רב חסדא שהיה מבבל כי אם לבני בבל ולהכי פריך היאך יברכו בני בבל על הארץ ועל פירותיה משמע דקאי דוקא על פירות של א"י והם אינם אוכלים אותן:

עבידנא

עין משפט נר מצוה

קמד א מיי' פ"ג מה' ברכו' ה"ה סמג עשין כח טוש"ע א"ח סי' ריב סעי' א

קמה ב מיי' פ"ג ה"ג פ"ח שם הי"ד סמג שם טוש"ע א"ח סי' רח סעי' א

קמו ג מיי' פ"ג שם הל' יג ופ"ח הל' יד סמג שם טוא"ח סי' רח

קמז ד מיי' וסמג שם טוש"ע א"ח סי' רח סעי' י

[עי' תוס' לעיל לז. ד"ה בורא ותוס' לקמן מה. ד"ה ר' טרפון]

[ושמחנו בבנינה כי אתה ה' טוב וכו']

מסורת הש"ס

לעיל לה: מא.

עירובין ל.

נ"ל לא הוה רש"ל

ואכיל להו לכולהו כל"ל רש"ל

[נ"ל שרף פי' שמשיג את המאכל שבמעים ערוך]

עירובין יד:

(בירוש' גרס ר' יהודה)

שבת ע:

יומא כח:

מגילה ה.

תענית ד:

קדושין כט:

סוכה מה.

עין משפט נר מצוה

קמח א ב ג מיי' פ"ח מהל' ברכו' ה"א סמג עשין כז טוש"ע א"ח סי' רד סעי' א ז ובסי' רז [מנחות לו:]

קמט ד מיי' פ"ה מהלכו' ברכות ה"א הלכה ח

קנ ה טוש"ע א"ח סי' ריו סעי' א

קנא ו ז מיי' פ"ה מהלכ' ברכות ה"א סמג שם טוש"ע א"ח סי' רד סעי' ז

רש"ל מ"ז

[בתוס' סוכה לט. ד"ה אבל לפניו וכו' ובתו' נדה נא: ד"ה ולבני מערבא יבוא על זה ודע דבתו' נדה שם מבואר הדברי' יפה וע"ע תו' מנחו' לו: ד"ה ושמרת]

[נ"ל יבשי' וכן הוא לקמן נז: וכן איתא בע"ז כט. ע"ש פרש"י]

[בערוך פי' סודני ירא שמים כדכתיב סוד ה' ליראיו וע' פרש"י מנחו' עא. ונדה יב:]

אמר רב יצחק בר אבדימי משום רבינו *על הביעא ועל מיני קופרא בתחלה מברך שהכל ולבסוף בורא נפשות רבות וכו' אבל ירקא לא ורבי יצחק אמר אפילו ירקא אבל מיא לא ורב פפא אמר אפילו מיא מר זוטרא עביד כרב יצחק בר אבדימי ורב שימי בר אשי עביד כר' יצחק וסימניך חד כתרי ותרי כחד אמר רב אשי אנא זמנא דכי מדכרנא עבידנא ככולהו *תנן כל שטעון ברכה לאחריו טעון ברכה לפניו ויש שטעון ברכה לפניו ואין טעון ברכה לאחריו בשלמא לרב יצחק בר אבדימי לאפוקי ירקא לר' יצחק לאפוקי מיא אלא לרב פפא לאפוקי מאי לאפוקי מצות ולבני מערבא דבתר דמסלקי תפילייהו מברכי אקב"ו לשמור חקיו לאפוקי מאי לאפוקי ריחני א"ר ינאי א"ר כל שהוא כביצה ביצה טובה ממנו כי אתא רבין אמר טבא ביעתא מגולגלתא משיתא קייסי סולתא כי אתא רב דימי אמר טבא ביעתא מגולגלתא משיתא מטויתא מארבע מבושלתא כל שהוא כביצה ביצה טובה הימנו לבר מבשרא: ר"ע אומר אפילו אכל שלק כו': ומי איכא מידי דהוה שלק מזוני אמר רב אשי בקלח של כרוב שנו ת"ר *טחול יפה לשינים וקשה לבני מעים כרישין קשין לשינים ויפין לבני מעים כל ירק חי מוריק וכל קטן מקטין וכל נפש משיב את הנפש וכל קרוב לנפש משיב את הנפש כרוב למזון ותרדין לרפואה אוי לו לבית שהלפת עוברת בתוכו: אמר מר טחול יפה לשינים וקשה לבני מעים מאי תקנתיה נלעסיה ונשדייה כרישין קשין לשינים ויפין לבני מעים מאי תקנתיה לשלקינהו ונבלעינהו כל ירק חי מוריק א"ר יצחק בסעודה ראשונה של אחר הקזה א"ר יצחק כל האוכל ירק קודם ארבע שעות אסור לספר הימנו מאי טעמא משום ריחא וא"ר יצחק אסור לאדם שיאכל ירק חי קודם ארבע שעות אמימר ומר זוטרא ורב אשי הוו יתבי אייתו קמייהו ירק חי קודם ארבע שעות אמימר ורב אשי אכול ומר זוטרא לא אכל אמרו ליה מאי דעתך דאמר ר' יצחק כל האוכל ירק קודם ארבע שעות אסור לספר הימנו משום ריחא והא אנן דקא אכלינן וקא משתעית בהדן אמר להו אנא כאידך דרבי יצחק סבירא לי דאמר ר' יצחק אסור לאדם שיאכל ירק חי קודם ארבע שעות כל קטן מקטין אמר רב חסדא אפילו גדיא בר זוזא ולא אמרן אלא דלית ביה רבעא אבל אית ביה רבעא לית לן בה כל נפש משיב נפש אמר רב פפא אפילו גילדני דבי גילי כל הקרוב לנפש משיב את הנפש אמר רב אחא בר יעקב עונקא אמר ליה רבא לשמעיה כי מייתית לי אומצא דבישרא טרח ואייתי לי מהיכא דמקרב לבי ברוך כרוב למזון ותרדין לרפואה כרוב למזון אין ולרפואה לא והא תניא *ששה דברים מרפאין את החולה מחליו ורפואתן רפואה ואלו הן כרוב ותרדין ומי סיסין *דבש וקיבה והרת ויותרת הכבד אלא אימא כרוב אף למזון אוי לו לבית שהלפת עוברת בתוכו איני והא אמר ליה רבא לשמעיה כי חזית לפתא בשוקא לא תימא לי במאי כרכת ריפתא אמר אביי מבלי בשר ורבא אמר מבלי יין אתמר רב אמר מבלי בשר ושמואל אמר מבלי עצים ורבי יוחנן אמר מבלי יין אמר ליה רבא לרב פפא *סודני אנן תברינן לה בבשרא וחמרא אתון דלא נפיש לכו חמרא במאי תבריתו לה אמר ליה בציבי כי הא דביתהו דרב פפא בתר דמבשלא לה תברא לה בתמנן אופי פרסייתא תנו רבנן דג קטן מליח פעמים שהוא ממית בשבעה בשבעה עשר ובעשרים ושבעה ואמרי לה בעשרים ושלשה ולא אמרן אלא במטוי ולא מטוי אבל מטוי שפיר לית לן בה ודלא מטוי שפיר לא אמרן אלא דלא שתה בתריה שכרא אבל שתה בתריה שכרא לית לן בה: השותה מים לצמאו וכו': לאפוקי מאי אמר רב אידי בר אבין לאפוקי

למאן דחנקתיה

עבידנא ככולהו. וכן אנו נוהגין כרב אשי דמברכי' בתר מיא ובתר ירקא בורא נפשות רבות:

ולבני מערבא דמברכי' הכי בתר וכו'. ואנן לא עבדינן כבני מערבא דדוקא לדידהו שהיה דרכם לסלקם בליל' שייכא ברכה דלשמור חקיו כדכתי' ושמרת את החקה הזאת למועדה מימים וגו' אבל אנו שמסלקין אותם בחצי היום או אפי' כשלקן בלילה לא שייך חקה ודוקא לדידהו דקסברי לילה לאו זמן תפילין הוא ומימים ימימה אתא למעוטי לילות שייכא ברכה דחקה אבל אנן דקי"ל *דלילה זמן תפילין הוא ואנן משיימין הפסוק ושמרת החקה וגו' בפסח ומה שאין אנו מניחים אותן בלילה מפני שמא יפיח בהן ואפי' כשתין לסלקן עד הלילה לא מברכינן אף על גב דאנן קיימא לן דשבת וי"ט לאו זמן תפילין אפ"ה לא מברכינן דדוקא לדידהו דסבירא להו חקה קאי אתפילין מברכי' ותדע שהרי איכהו נמי לא הוו מברכין אלא אתפילין לחודייהו משום דכתיב בהו חקה אבל אשאר מצות כגון ציצית ולולב וסוכה לא היו מברכין (וה"ה הכא) וקשה דהוי מצי לשנויי הכי לאפוקי שאר מצות אפי' לבני מערבא*:

דחנקתיה

קופרא. כל מיני בשר: אבל ירקא. לא צריך לברוכי אחריה: חד כתרי. מר זוטר' שהוא כאן יחיד בלא שם אביו עביד כרב יצחק בר אבדימי שהוא בשמו ושם אביו: ותרי כחד. מר בר רב אשי שהוא בשמו ובשם אביו עביד כרבי יצחק שהוא יחיד: ככולהו. אף כרב פפא: כל שטעון ברכה. משנה היא במסכת נדה: למעוטי ירקא. וכ"ש מיא: למעוטי מצות. אין מברכין כשמסלקין תפילין וציצית ואחר תקיעת שופר ולולב: כל שהוא כביצה. אין לך מין מאכל שיעור כביצה שלא תהא ביצה טובה לגוף ממנו: מגולגלת'. צלוי' לחה ורכה ששולפין אותה: קייסי. מדות מחזיקות לוג: מגולגלת' משיתא. טובה משיתא קייסי: מטוית'. צלויה קשה טוב' מארבע קייסי: מבשלתא. במי' עלה א"ר ינאי כל שהוא כביצה ביצה טובה ממנו: בקלח של כרוב שנו. שהוא מזון דתניא לקמן כרוב למזון: כרישין. כרתי: כל ירק חי מוריק. נוטל תואר הפנים: כל קטן. שלא גדל כל צרכו ולקמן מפר' כמה כל צרכו: כל נפש. דבר חי הנאכל שלם כגון דגים קטנים שגדלו כל צרכן: הקרוב לנפש. האוכל מן הבהמה במקום חיות שלה ולקמן מפרש לה: אוי לבית. לכרס האוכל לפת: נלעסי'. כוססו ומשליכו: לשלקינהו. בקדרה הרב' שלא יצטרך לכוססו בשיניו: קוד' ארבע שעות. שאינו זמן סעוד' והריח קש' לבני אדם המספרים עמו קוד' אכילה שהגוף ריקן: כאידך דר' יצחק סבירא לי. אבל אסור לספר לא סבירא לי: בר זוזא. כלו' שמן וטוב ששוה זוז: דלית בה רבעא. שלא גדל עד רביעית שלו כגון טלה רביעית של איל גדי כדי רביעית של שעיר גדול וכן כל דבר: גילדני דבי גילי. דגים קטנים מאד ומצויין בין הקני' באגם ואין דרכן לגדל יותר אבל דג קטן ממין דג גדול ולא גדל רובע זה הוא קטן מקטין: עונקא. צואר מקום בית השחיטה וסמוך ללב ולמעים: לבי ברוך. למקום שברכו שם על השחיטה: ומי סיסין. תבשיל של פולי"אול: והרת. ולדי"רא שהולד נולד בו: ויותרת הכבד. טרפשא דכבדא שקורין איבר"ש: מבלי בשר. הוא קשה אבל כשמבשל' עם בשר שמן מתים כחה: מבלי יין. כשאין שותה אחריה יין: מבלי עצים. שאינו שולקה הרבה: סודני. בעל שכר תמרי' ורב פפא מוכר שכר היה כדאמר באיזהו נשך (דף סה.) עתירא דרב פפא שכרא לא פסיד ואמר רב פפא אי לאו דמזאי שכרא לא איעתרי (פסחים קיג.) והוא נקרא סודני כדאמרי' תמרי בחלוזק לבי סודנא רהוט (שם): דלא נפיש לכו חמרא. שותה שכר אתה: במאי תבריתו לה. לכחו של לפת: אופי פרסייתא. בקעיו' של עצים גדולות היתה שורפת תחת קדרות הלפת: פעמים שהוא ממית. ואלו הן ביום שבעה ימים למליחתו או ביום שבעה עשר או ביום שבעה ועשרים:

מאי

מסורת הש"ס

נדה נא:

[שבת קי.]

[לקמן נז:]

[44*b*] R. Isaac b. Abdimi said in the name of our Master:[7] Over eggs and over all kinds of meat the blessing said before partaking is 'by whose word etc.', and after partaking 'who createst many living creatures etc.'. Vegetables, however, require no blessing [after]. R. Isaac, however, says that even vegetables also require a blessing [after], but not water. R. Papa says: Water also. Mar Zuṭra acted as prescribed by R. Isaac b. Abdimi and R. Shimi b. Ashi as prescribed by R. Isaac. (To remember which is which think of one[8] acting as two and two as one.)[9] R. Ashi
a said: When I think of it, I do as prescribed by all of them.[1]

We have learnt: Whatever requires a blessing to be said after it requires a blessing before it, but some things require a blessing before but not after.[2] Now this is right on the view of R. Isaac b. Abdimi, since it is to exclude vegetables, and on the view of R. Isaac to exclude water; but on the view of R. Papa, what does it exclude?— It is to exclude the performance of religious duties.[3] And according to the Palestinians[4] who after removing their *tefillin* say 'Blessed be Thou . . . who hast sanctified us with Thy commandments and commanded us to observe Thy statutes'—what does it exclude?—It excludes scents.

R. Jannai said in the name of Rabbi: An egg is superior [in food value] to the same quantity of any other kind of food. When Rabin came [from Palestine] he said: A lightly roasted egg is superior to six *kaysi*[5] of fine flour. When R. Dimi came, he said: A lightly roasted egg is better than six [*kaysi*]; a hard baked egg than four;[6] and a [boiled] egg is better than the same quantity of any other kind of boiled food except meat.

R. AKIBA SAYS: EVEN IF ONE ATE BOILED VEGETABLES etc. Is there any kind of boiled vegetable of which one can make a meal?—R. Ashi replied: The rule applies to the stalk of cabbage.

Our Rabbis taught: Milt is good for the teeth but bad for the bowels; horse-beans are bad for the teeth but good for the bowels. All raw vegetables make the complexion pale and all things not fully grown retard growth. Living beings[7] restore vitality[8] and that which is near the vital organs[9] restores vitality. Cabbage for sustenance and beet for healing. Woe to the house[10] through which vegetables are always passing!

The Master has said, 'Milt is good for the teeth and bad for the bowels.' What is the remedy?—To chew it well and then spit it out. 'Horse-beans are bad for the teeth but good for the bowels'. What is the remedy?—To boil them well and swallow them. 'All raw vegetables make the complexion pale'. R. Isaac said: That is, in the first meal taken after blood-letting. R. Isaac also said: If one
b eats vegetables before the fourth hour [of the day],[1] it is forbidden to talk with him. What is the reason? Because his breath smells. R. Isaac also said: It is forbidden to a man to eat raw vegetables before the fourth hour. Amemar and Mar Zuṭra and R. Ashi were once sitting together when raw vegetables were set before them before the fourth hour. Amemar and R. Ashi ate, but Mar Zuṭra would not eat. They said to him: What is your reason? Because R. Isaac said that if one eats vegetables before the fourth hour it is forbidden to converse with him because his breath smells? See, we have been eating, and you have been conversing with us? He replied: I hold with that other saying of R. Isaac, where he said that it is forbidden to a man to eat raw vegetables before the fourth hour.[2] 'Things not fully grown retard growth'. R. Ḥisda said: Even a kid worth a *zuz*.[3] This, however, is the case only with that which has not attained a fourth of its full size; but if it has attained a fourth, there is no objection. 'Living being restore vitality'. R. Papa said: Even tiny fishes from the pools. 'That which is near the vital organs restores vitality'. R. Aḥa b. Jacob said: Such as the neck.[4] Raba said to his attendant: When you buy a piece of meat for me, see that you get it from a place near where the benediction is said.[5] 'Cabbage for sustenance and beet for healing'. Is cabbage then good only for sustenance and not for healing? Has it not been taught: Six things heal a sick person of his disease with a permanent cure, namely, cabbage, beet, a decoction of dry[6] poley, the maw, the womb, and the large lobe of the liver'?—What you must say is that the cabbage is good for sustenance also. 'Woe to the house through which vegetables are always passing'. Is that so? Did not Raba say to his attendant: If you see vegetables in the market, do not stop to ask me, What
c will you put round your bread.[1]—Abaye said: [It means, when they are cooked] without meat;[2] Raba said: [It means, when they are taken] without wine. It has been stated: Rab says, without meat, Samuel says, without wood,[3] and R. Joḥanan says, without wine. Said Raba to R. Papa the brewer:[4] We neutralize[5] it with meat and wine; you who have not much wine, how do you neutralize it?—He replied: With chips [of wood]. R. Papa's wife when she cooked vegetables neutralized their evil effects by using eighty Persian twigs.[6]

Our Rabbis taught: A small salted fish is sometimes deadly, namely on the seventh, the seventeenth and the twenty-seventh day of its salting. Some say, on the twenty-third. This is the case only if it is imperfectly roasted; but if it is well roasted, there is no harm in it. And even if it is not well roasted there is no harm in it unless one neglects to drink beer after it; but if one drinks beer after it, there is no harm.

IF ONE QUENCHES HIS THIRST WITH WATER etc. What does

(7) V. *supra* 30*b*, n. a4. (8) Lit., 'and thy sign is'. (9) I.e., the authority who was mentioned alone without his father (Mar Zuṭra), acted as prescribed by the authority who is mentioned with his father (R. Isaac b. Abdimi) and *vice versa*.

a (1) Saying even after water. (2) Nid. 51*b*. (3) Which require a blessing before the performance of them but not after, such as taking off the *tefillin*, laying aside of the *lulab*, etc. (4) Lit., 'the sons of the West'. (5) A measure equal to a *log*. (6) Var. lec.: a lightly baked egg is better than four hard-baked and a hard-baked than four boiled. (7) Taken whole, like small fish. (8) Lit., 'soul'. (9) Of a slaughtered animal. (10) I.e., stomach.

b (1) When the first meal was taken. (2) But it is not forbidden to converse with him. (3) I.e., a good fat one. (4) Which is near the heart. (5) I.e. the neck, on cutting which a benediction is said. (6) Reading יבשין for בש' in the text, as *infra* 57*b*.

c (1) To eat with it as a kind of sandwich. (2) The juices of which neutralize the evil effects of the vegetables. (3) I.e., a good fire to cook it. (4) *Aliter* (*a*) the landowner (v. Obermeyer p. 309); (*b*) 'Man of Mystery!', i.e., acquainted with the divine mysteries (v. 'Aruch). (5) Lit., 'break (the evil effects)' (6) Twigs from Persian trees.

this exlude?—R. Idi b. Abin said: It excludes one [45a] who is choked by a piece of meat.[7]

R. TARFON SAYS: WHO CREATEST MANY LIVING THINGS AND THEIR REQUIREMENTS. Raba son of R. Ḥanan said to Abaye, according to others to R. Joseph: What is the law? He replied: Go forth and see how the public are accustomed to act.[8]

CHAPTER VII

MISHNAH. IF THREE PERSONS HAVE EATEN TOGETHER, IT IS THEIR DUTY TO INVITE [ONE ANOTHER TO SAY GRACE].[1] ONE WHO HAS EATEN DEMAI,[2] OR FIRST TITHE[3] FROM WHICH TERUMAH HAS BEEN REMOVED,[4] OR SECOND TITHE OR FOOD BELONGING TO THE SANCTUARY THAT HAS BEEN REDEEMED,[5] OR AN ATTENDANT WHO HAS EATEN AS MUCH AS AN OLIVE OR A CUTHEAN MAY BE INCLUDED [IN THE THREE]. ONE WHO HAS EATEN ṬEBEL[6] OR FIRST TITHE FROM WHICH THE TERUMAH HAS NOT BEEN REMOVED, OR SECOND TITHE OR SANCTIFIED FOOD WHICH HAS NOT BEEN REDEEMED,[7] OR AN ATTENDANT WHO HAS EATEN LESS THAN THE QUANTITY OF AN OLIVE OR A GENTILE MAY NOT BE COUNTED. WOMEN, CHILDREN AND SLAVES MAY NOT BE COUNTED IN THE THREE. HOW MUCH [MUST ONE HAVE EATEN] TO COUNT? AS MUCH AS AN OLIVE; R. JUDAH SAYS, AS MUCH AS AN EGG.

GEMARA. Whence is this derived?[8]—R. Assi says: Because Scripture says, *O magnify ye the Lord with me, and let us exalt His name together.*[9] R. Abbahu derives it from here: *When I [one] proclaim the name of the Lord, ascribe ye [two] greatness unto our God.*[10]

R. Ḥanan b. Abba said: Whence do we learn that he who answers Amen should not raise his voice above the one who says the blessing? Because it says, *O magnify ye the Lord with me and*
b *let us exalt His name together.*[1] R. Simeon b. Pazzi said: Whence do we learn that the one who translates[2] is not permitted to raise his voice above that of the reader? Because it says, *Moses spoke and God answered him by a voice.*[3] The words *'by a voice'* need not have been inserted. What then does *'by a voice'* mean? [It means], by the voice of Moses.[4] It has been taught similarly: The translator is not permitted to raise his voice above that of the reader. If the translator is unable to speak as loud as the reader, the reader should moderate his voice and read.

It has been stated: If two have eaten together, Rab and R. Joḥanan differ [as to the rule to be followed]. One says that if they wish to invite one another [to say grace] they may do so, the other says that even if they desire to invite one another they may not do so. We have learnt: IF THREE PERSONS HAVE EATEN TOGETHER IT IS THEIR DUTY TO INVITE ONE ANOTHER. That means to say, three but not two?—No; there [in the case of three] it is a duty, here [in the case of two] it is optional.

Come and hear: If three persons have eaten together, it is their duty to invite one another [to say grace], and they are not permitted to separate. This means to say, three but not two, does it not?[5]—No; there is a special reason there [why they may not separate], because from the outset of the meal they laid upon themselves the duty to invite one another.[6]

Come and hear: If an attendant is waiting on two persons he may eat with them even without their giving him permission;[7] if he was waiting on three, he may not eat with them unless they

(7) And drinks simply to wash it down.
(8) And the general practice is to say 'by whose word' before and 'that createst many living beings' after.

(1) By means of the responses given in *P.B.* p. 279. This invitation is technically known as *zimmun* (inviting). (2) Produce from which it is doubtful whether the tithe has been given. (3) Due to the Levite, v. Num. XVIII, 21. (4) The *terumah* (v. Glos) mentioned here is apparently the tithe, v. ibid. 26. (5) And so has been made available for being eaten out of Jerusalem (cf. Deut. XIV, 22ff) or by a layman. All these are kinds of food which may be legitimately partaken of. (6) Food from which it is known that tithe has not been separated. (7) These are foods of which it is not legitimate to partake. (8) That three who eat together should invite one another to say grace. (9) Ps. XXXIV, 4. *'Ye'* implies two, besides the speaker. (10) Deut. XXXII, 3. E.V. *'For I will proclaim* etc.'.

b (1) I.e., one not louder than the other. (2) The public reading of the Pentateuch in Hebrew was followed by a translation in Aramaic. (3) Ex. XIX, 19. Moses is here compared to a reader and God to a translator, v. however Tosaf. s.v. בקולו. (4) I.e., a voice not raised above that of Moses. (5) Because if two are sufficient, why may not one of the three separate? (6) And though two may invite one another, yet to perform an obligation is more meritorious. (7) And we assume that they approve of it so that they may be able to invite one another, and this is not presumptuous on his part.

דחנקתיה אומצא: רבי טרפון אומר בורא נפשות רבות וחסרונן: *אמר ליה רבא בר רב חנן לאביי ואמרי לה לרב יוסף הלכתא מאי אמר ליה **פוק חזי מאי עמא דבר:

הדרן עלך כיצד מברכין

*שלשה שאכלו כאחת חייבין לזמן אכל דמאי ומעשר ראשון שנטלה תרומתו מעשר שני והקדש שנפדו והשמש שאכל כזית והכותי מזמנין עליו אכל טבל ומעשר ראשון שלא נטלה תרומתו ומעשר שני והקדש שלא נפדו והשמש שאכל פחות מכזית והנכרי אין מזמנין עליו נשים ועבדים וקטנים אין מזמנין עליהן *עד כמה מזמנין עד כזית ר' יהודה אומר עד כביצה: **גמ'** מה"מ אמר רב אסי דאמר קרא (תהלים לד) גדלו לה' אתי ונרוממה שמו יחדיו ר' אבהו אמר מהכא (דברים לב) כי שם ה' אקרא הבו גדל לאלהינו: אמר רב חנן בר *אבא מנין לעונה אמן שלא יגביה קולו יותר מן המברך שנאמר גדלו לה' אתי ונרוממה שמו יחדיו א"ר שמעון בן פזי מנין שאין המתרגם רשאי להגביה קולו יותר מן הקורא שנאמר (שמות יט) משה ידבר והאלהים יעננו בקול שאין ת"ל בקול ומה ת"ל בקול בקולו של משה תנ"ה אין המתרגם רשאי להגביה קולו יותר מן הקורא ואם אי אפשר למתרגם להגביה קולו כנגד הקורא ימעך הקורא קולו ויקרא: אתמר שנים שאכלו כאחת פליגי רב ור' יוחנן חד אמר אם רצו לזמן מזמנין וח"א אם רצו לזמן אין מזמנין תנן ג' שאכלו כאחת חייבין לזמן ג' אין שנים לא התם חובה הכא רשות ת"ש *שלשה שאכלו כאחת חייבין לזמן ואין רשאין ליחלק שלשה אין שנים לא שאני התם דקבעו להו בחובה מעיקרא ת"ש השמש שהיה משמש על השנים ה"ז אוכל עמהם אע"פ שלא נתנו לו רשות היה משמש על השלשה הרי זה אינו אוכל עמהם אלא אם כן נתנו לו רשות שאני התם

דניחא

רש"י

מאי עמא דבר. היאך נוהגים וכבר נהגו לברך בתחלה שהכל ולבסוף בורא נפשות רבות וחסרונן על כל מה שברא:

הדרן עלך כיצד מברכין

שלשה שאכלו וכו' לזמן. להזדמן יחד לצירוף ברכה בלשון רבים כגון נברך: שנטלה תרומתו. קס"ד תרומת מעשר שלו שעל הלוי להפריש: מעשר שני שנפדה. להתירו באכילה חוץ לירושלים ואת פדיונו יעלה לירושלים ויאכל: והשמש. ששמש בסעודה ואכל עמהם כזית כדי להצטרף עמהם לזמון ובכל הכי אצטריך לאשמועינן אע"ג דדמו לאיסור אין כאן ברכה בעבירה כדמפרש ואזיל בגמרא: עד כמה מזמנין. כמה יאכל עמהם ויתחייב עמהם בזמון ונפקא מינה להוציאם ידי חובתן אם יתנו לו הכוס לברך: **גמ'** מה"מ. דשלשה ראוים לברכת צירוף: גדלו לה' אתי. הרי שלשה וכן אקרא הבו גודל היחיד אומר לשנים: אינן רשאין ליחלק. ולברך כל אחד לעצמו דמפקעי לה לתורת זמון: שלשה אין שנים לא. ה"פ דמדקתני אין רשאין ליחלק ש"מ דשלשה מזמנין שנים אין מזמנין ואפי' רצו דאי אמרת ב' נמי אם רצו מזמנין אמאי אין הא' רשאי ליחלק ליזיל הוא ולא מפקעת ברכת זמון בהכי ויזמנו השנים: שאני התם דהוקבעו בחובה מעיקרא. ואי אזיל הוא מפקעת להו חובה וקמו להו ברשו' וגדול המצוה ועושה ממי שאינו מצווה ועושה: אוכל עמהם. אין כאן גאוה דניחא להו דמייתי להו לידי זמון ואי ב' מזמנין אמאי ניחא להו בלאו דידיה נמי אי בעו מזמני:

דניחא

תוספות

דחנקתיה אומצא. ודוקא מים שאין לו הנאה כי אם לשתות מים לצמאו והנאה דחנקתיה אומצא אין זה נחשב הנאה אבל שאר משקים שלעולם הגוף נהנה מהן בכל ענין מברך ואפילו חנקתיה אומצא כדאמרינן לעיל (דף לו.) ואף על גב דלרפואה אתי בעי ברוכי ורב עמרם פירש דדוקא לפניו לא בעי ברוכי אבל לאחריו חייב ורבינו משה פירש דלא שיא דהואיל ואין הנאה אפילו לאחריו לא בעי ברכה:

רבי טרפון אומר בורא נפשות רבות וכו'. פירוש לפניו ופוק חזי מאי עמא דבר והנה נהגו העולם לברך לאחריו אבל לא מלינו לפרש דפליגי בלאחריו דתנא קמא סבר דמברך לפניו ולא לאחריו ור' טרפון סבר אף לאחריו יברך בורא נפשות רבות דאם כן כי פריך לעיל מרב פפא דמברך ליקשי מתלתיה דרבי טרפון שהוא תנא*:

הדרן עלך כיצד מברכין

שלשה שאכלו כאחת. בירושלמי פריך הכא את אמרת אין רשאין ליחלק והכא את אמרת חייבין לזמן. ועתה לכאורה אין זה קשה וכן לק' (דף נ:) פריך תניכ' חדא זימנ' שאין רשאין ליחלק היינו משום דחייבים לזמן ול"נ דהכי פריך הכא את אמרת דאין רשאין ליחלק דמשמע אם גמרו אכילתן יחד אינן רשאין ליחלק אבל האחד רשאי לגמור סעודתו ולברך קודם חברו וחייבין לזמן משמע דחובת זימון עליהם ואינן רשאין לגמור סעודתן זה בלא זה ומשני שהואיל כאן בתחלה כאן בסוף איזהו בתחל' ואיזהו בסוף פליגי בה תרי אמוראי חד אמר נתנו דעתם לאכול זהו בתחלה אכלו כזית זהו בסוף וחד אומר אכלו כזית זהו בתחל' נתנו דעתם לאכול זהו בסוף ורב אלפס תופס דבר* ראשון עיקר וה"פ נתנו דעתם לאכול כלומר שהתחילו מתחלה לאכול ביחד זהו בתחלה אז ודאי חובת זימון עליהם אכלו כזית זהו בסוף כלומר אם האחד התחיל קודם חברו בכזית אז ודאי אם גמרו סעודתם יחד חייבים לזמן אבל רשאין לגמור זה בלא זה ולברך:

אכל טבל אין מזמנין עליו. תימה דאמר בערכין (דף ד.) הכל מצטרפין לזמון כהנים לוים וישראלים ופריך פשיטא ומשני לא צריכ' אע"ג דכהן אכיל תרומה וישראל חולין אלמא אע"ג דתרומה אסורה לישראל אחרי שהכהן יכול לצרף עם ישראל לאכול בחולי' מצטרפי לזמון וה"נ כיון דחד מנייהו אכל טבל דאין ראוי לאחרים אמאי אין מזמנין ויש לומר דאכילת טבל לאו שמה אכילה דלא חזיא אף לכהן אבל תרומה לכל הפחות ראויה לכהן האוכלה* וה"ה אם אכלו שלשתן טבל דאין חייבים לזמן כדאמרי' (ב"ק פ"ט דף לד.) הרי שגזל סאה חטין וטחנן ואפאן ואכלן ומברך עליהן אינו מברך אלא מנאץ מכאן היה אומר רבינו יהודה דג' שאכלו והאחד היה מודר הנאה מן השנים והוא אוכל משלו יכול להצטרף עמהן לזימון דהכי דאינו ראוי לאכול עמהם הם ראוי' לאכול עמו וכן לענין השאר מפת של נכרים אבל אם שלשתן מודרין הנאה זה מזה אין מצטרפין אע"פ שיכולים לשאול על נדרם דהשתא מיהא לא אתשילו:

בקולו של משה. וא"ת היכי מייתי ראיה ממשה והא צריך לאיתויי דמשה היה מתרגם ולא היה מרים קולו יותר מהקב"ה שהיה קורא והוא מביא שהקב"ה היה [קורא ומשה היה] מתרגם ופירש רב אלפס בקולו של משה מסתמא משה היה בכל כחו עונה כדי להשמיע קולו לכל העם אבל הקב"ה לא היה צריך להרים קולו שהרי לא היה מדבר אלא למשה לבד ואפילו הכי היה מגביה קולו כדי שלא יהא קולו של משה המתרגם רם יותר מקולו של הקב"ה שהיה קורא:

אם רצו לזמן אין מזמנין. פרש"י וכן לענין המוציא ושאר ברכות אין האחד מברך להוציא חברו לגבי הא דאמר אביי נקיטינן שנים שאכלו כאחת מצוה ליחלק ולברך כל אחד לעצמו בין בה"מ בין ברכת המוציא לשון רש"י לקמן ולא נהירא דלעיל פרק כילד מברכין (דף מג.) בעובדא דבר קפרא נתן בר קפרא רשות לאחד לברך ושנים הוו התם ועוד אי הוו שלשה התם לא היו שם אלא פירות וכן נמי אמרינן לקמן (דף נג.) דעל המאור אחד מברך לכולן ע"כ נ"ל דבברכה ראשונה מוציאין זה את זה שנים לכ"ע והטעם הואיל ויושבין לאכול יחד דעתן לצרף ואחד מברך להוציא חברו אבל בברכה של סוף סעודה שמסתלקים זה מזה צריך לברך כל אחד לעצמו ויש מחלקי' דיש חלוק בין ברכת המוצי' דלא הויא כי אם דרבנן ע"כ מוציאים זה את זה אבל בבהמ"ז שהיא מדאורייתא לשם החמירו*:

שלשה שאכלו כאחד אין רשאין ליחלק. ופירש"י אמאי אין רשאין ליחלק האחד מפני הב' כיון דשנים נמי מזמנין ליזיל הוא והא לא מיפקע' ברכת זמון. תימה דילמא טעמא דאין רשאין ליחלק משום דיפטרו לשלישי מברכת הזמון וגם הוא אין לו להפקיע ממנו ברכת הזמון ויש לומר דעיקר פרכתו סמיך אסיפא דקתני ד' אין רשאין ליחלק אע"ג דאיכא שנים מכאן וב' מכאן והוי כמו וכו' וכה"ג תנאה בהרבה מקומות ותימה א"כ אמאי לא מקשי מן הסיפא בהדיא ע"כ פירש רבינו יהוד' דודאי פריך מרישא וה"ק דליכא למימר דמשום היחיד קאמר דא"כ הוה ליה למימר אין היחיד רשאי ליחלק אי נמי אין אחד מהם רשאי ליחלק אבל מדקתני אין רשאין ליחלק משמע מכלהו פקע זמון אם נסתלק אחד מהם:

והא

מסורת הש"ס

עירובין יד: | [עירובין שם פסחים כד מכות לה:] | [לקמן נ.] | פסחי' מט: | יומא עט: | [וע' תוס' לקמן מט: ד"ה עד כמ'] | [נ"ל רבא כ"ה בשאלתו' פרשת יתרו] | [לקמן נ.] | [מן וה"ה כו' עד אלא מכאן כו' נ"ב וכ"ז אין כאן מקומו]

תורה אור

תהלים לד | דברים לב | שמות יט | נ"ב מסכת רס"א

עין משפט נר מצוה

קנב

א אמיי' פ"ה מה' ברכות ה"א טוש"ע א"ח סי' רד סעי' ו

ב במיי' פ"ה מהלכו' ברכות הלכה ב סמג עשין כז טוש"ע א"ח סי' קלב סעי' א

ג גמיי' פ"א מה' ברכו' הל' כ סמג שם

ד דטוש"ע א"ח סימן קל"ע סעיף א [וע' רש"י עירובין יד: ד"ה כ"ע]

ה השם סעי' ב

ו ומיי' שם הל' יע וסמג שם טוש"ע א"ח סי' קל סעי' א

ז זמיי' ג"ה מה' ברכו' הל' ז סמג שם טוש"ע א"ח סימן קל"ע סעיף ד

ח חמיי' שם הל' ז טוש"ע שם סעיף ו

ט טמיי' שם הל' ח וסמג שם טוש"ע א"ח סי' קפד סעי' ו וסי' קלו סעי' ד

י ימיי' פ"א מהלכ' ברכות הלכה יד סמג שם טוש"ע א"ח סי' קכד סעיף יב

יא כמיי' פ"ד מה' ת"ת הל' ג וצי"ע מהל' תפלה הל' יא וטוש"ע א"ח סי' קמה סעי' א וטור י"ד סימן רמז

יב למיי' פ"ה מהלכו' ברכות הלכה י סמג עשין כז טוש"ע א"ח סי' קלג סעי' א

יג ממיי' שם הל' יב טוש"ע שם ובסי' קצ סעיף לא [וע' מ"ש תו' באריכות בביאור הדברי' בפולין כו. ד"ה וש"מ שנים שאכלו]

דניחא להו דמקבע להו בחובה מעיקרא ת"ש *"נשים מזמנות לעצמן ועבדים מזמנין לעצמן נשים ועבדים וקטנים אם רצו לזמן אין מזמנין (*והא נשים אפילו מאה) והא מאה נשי כתרי גברי דמיין וקתני נשים מזמנות לעצמן ועבדים מזמנין לעצמן שאני התם דאיכא דעות א"ה אימא סיפא נשים ועבדים אם רצו לזמן אין מזמנין אמאי לא והא איכא דעות שאני התם משום פריצותא תסתיים דרב דאמר אם רצו לזמן אין מזמנין דאמר רב דימי בר יוסף אמר רב שלשה שאכלו כאחת ויצא אחד מהם לשוק קוראין לו ומזמנין עליו טעמא דקוראין לו הא לא קוראין לו לא שאני התם דאקבעו להו בחובה מעיקרא אלא תסתיים דר' יוחנן הוא דאמר אם רצו לזמן אין מזמנין דאמר רבה בר בר חנה א"ר יוחנן שנים שאכלו כאחת אחד מהן יוצא בברכת חבירו והוינן בה מאי קא משמע לן תנינא *"שמע ולא ענה יצא ואמר ר' זירא לומר שאין ברכת הזמון בינידהם תסתיים א"ל רבא בר רב הונא לרב הונא והא רבנן דאתו ממערבא אמרי אם רצו לזמן מזמנין מאי לאו דשמיע להו מר' יוחנן לא דשמיע להו מרב מקמיה דנחית לבבל: גופא אמר רב דימי בר יוסף אמר רב ג' שאכלו כאחת ויצא א' מהם לשוק קוראין לו ומזמנין עליו אמר אביי והוא דקרו ליה ועני אמר מר זוטרא ולא אמרן אלא בשלשה אבל בעשרה עד דנייתי מתקיף לה רב אשי אדרבה איפכא מסתברא תשעה נראין כעשרה שנים אין נראין כשלשה "והלכתא כמר זוטרא מ"ט *כיון דבעי לאדכורי שם שמים בציר מעשרה לאו אורח ארעא אמר אביי נקיטינן שנים שאכלו כאחת מצוה ליחלק *תניא נמי הכי "שנים שאכלו כאחת מצוה ליחלק במה דברים אמורים כששניהם סופרים אבל אחד סופר ואחד בור סופר מברך ובור יוצא: אמר רבא *הא מלתא אמריתה אנא ואיתמרה משמיה דרבי זירא כוותי "שלשה שאכלו כאחת אחד מפסיק לשנים ואין שנים מפסיקין לאחד ולא והא רב פפא אפסיק ליה לאבא מר בריה איהו וחד שאני רב פפא *דלפנים משורת הדין הוא דעביד יהודה בר מרימר ומר בר רב אשי ורב אחא מדפתי כרכי ריפתא בהדי הדדי לא הוה בהו חד דהוה מופלג מחבריה לברוכי להו (*יתבי וקא מבעיא להו הא דתנן) *ג' שאכלו כאחת חייבין לזמן הני מילי היכא דאיכא אדם גדול אבל היכא דכי הדדי נינהו חלוק ברכות עדיף בריך איניש לנפשיה אתו לקמיה דמרימר אמר להו ידי ברכה יצאתם "ידי זימון לא יצאתם וכי תימרו ניהדר ונזמן *אין זימון למפרע: בא ומצאן כשהן מברכים מהו אומר אחריהם רב זביד אמר ברוך ומבורך רב פפא אמר עונה אמן ולא פליגי "הא דאשכחינהו דקא אמרי נברך והא דאשכחינהו דקא אמרי ברוך אשכחינהו דקא אמרי נברך אומר ברוך ומבורך אשכחינהו דקא אמרי ברוך עונה אמן תני חדא העונה אמן אחר ברכותיו הרי זה משובח ותניא אידך הרי זה מגונה לא קשיא "הא בבונה ירושלים הא בשאר ברכות אביי עני ליה בקלא כי היכי דלשמעו פועלים וליקומו דהטוב והמטיב לאו דאורייתא רב אשי "עני ליה בלחישה כי היכי דלא נזלזלו בהטוב והמטיב

רבי

דניחא להו דמקבע להו בחוב'. דגדול המלוה ועושה: אם רצו אין מזמנים. כדמפרש טעמא לקמן שאין קביעותן נאה משום פריצותא בין דנשים בין דמשכב זכור דעבדים בקטני': דאפי' מאה כתרי דמיין. לענין חובה דאין חייבות לזמן ואם רצו מזמנין והוא הדין לשנים: דאיכא דעות. דאע"ג דלענין חובה אינן חייבות לענין השות דעות שלש' חשיבי להודות טפי משני אנשים דאיכא משום גדלו לי"י אתי: קוראין לו. להודיעו שהם רוצים לזמן ויפנה אליהם במקום מעמדו ודי להם בכך: ומזמנין עליו. ואע"פ שאינו בא אצלם: ואמר רבי זירא לומר שאין ברכת זימון בינידהן. לא בא ללמדנו אלא שאין צריכין זימון דכיון דאחד יוצא בברכת חברו אשמעינן דאין זימון דאי יש זימון ברכת שניהם היא שהרי אומ' נברך והוא עונה ברוך הוא: לאו דשמיע להו מרבי יוחנן. דבר מערבא הוא דאלו רב בבבל היה ובני מערבא היכא שמיע להו: והוא דקרו ליה ועני. שסמוך הוא אצלם ועונה ברוך הוא: לא אמרן. דלא צריך למיתי גבייהו אלא שלשה אבל עשרה שילטרפו משום הזכרת השם עד דאתי גבייהו: נראין כעשרה. דאין אדם מוהר להבחין בין עשרה לתשעה: מצוה ליחלק. ולברך כל אחד בפני עצמו בין ברכ' המוציא בין ברכת המזון: אחד מפסיק לשנים. אם גמרו השנים סעודת' ורוצין לזמן דבך ארץ הוא שיהא האחד מפסיק את סעודתו עד שיזמנו עליו עד ברכת הזן דהיינו ברכת זימון וחוזר וגומר סעודתו אבל שנים אין עליהם להפסיק בשביל היחיד ויומתין עד שיגמרו: לפנים משור' הדין. לאחשוביה: לא הוה בהו. מופלג בחכמה ובזקנה מן השנים: דאיכא אדם גדול. שהגדול מברך כדפסקי' לק' הלכת' (דף מז.): בא ומצאן. אחד מן השוק בא ומצא ג' שהיו מזמנין: ברוך ומבורך. דלא מצי למימר שאכלנו משלו: הא. דקאמר ברוך ומבורך כדאשכחינהו דקאמר המזמן נברך אבל אשכחינהו דענו ברוך הוא עונה בתרייהו אמן: הא בבונה ירושלים. שהיא סוף הברכות הרי זה משובח וכן בסוף ברכות דקרית שמע שחרית וערבית ואחר כל ברכותיו דקתני בברייתא הרי זה משובח אחר גמר כל ברכותיו קאמר ואח' כל ברכותיו דקתני הרי זה מגונ' בסוף כל ברכה וברכה קאמר: כי היכי דלשמעו פועלי'. וידעו שנגמרה כל הברכ' שהרי אין המברך עונה אמן אלא לבסוף: וליקומו. לעבידתייהו ואי משום דקמפקע להו מהטוב והמטיב לא אכפת ליה דקסבר דלאו דאורייתא היא אלא ביבנה תקנוה על הרוגי ביתר שנתנו לקבור': רב אשי עני. להאי אמן בלחישה כי היכי דלא לשמעו וידעו שהם גמר הברכות ויזלזלו בהטוב והמטיב ומיהו משום דסוף כל ברכותיו היה ותני' בברייתא הרי זה משובח לא סגי דלא עני ליה:

קטינא

והא ק' נשי כתרי גברי דמיין. לענין קבוץ תפל' ולענין כל דבר שבעשרה ואפילו הכי חשבינן להו כשלשה וה"ה לשנים אבל לא מצי למימר כחד דמיין דאינן יכולות לזמן דהא קתני נשים מזמנות לעצמן ונש"י פירש כתרי לענין חובה דאין חייבו' לזמן ואם רצו מזמנות והוא הדין לשנים:

שאני התם דאיכא דעות. מכאן משמע דנשים יכולות לזמן לעצמן וכן עשו בנות רבינו אברה' חמיו של רבינו יהודה ע"פ אביהן ומיהו לא נהגו העולם כן וקשה אמאי לא נהגו מדקתני מזמנות משמ' דקאמר חייבות לזמן וי"ל דנשים מזמנות לעצמן היינו אם רצו לזמן מזמנות וכן משמע קצת הלשון מדקתני בסמוך נשים ועבדים אם רצו לזמן אין מזמנין ועוד דמדמה ליה הגמרא לשני' משמע דחובה ליכא והא דקאמר בריש ערכין (ד' ג. ושם) הכל מחויבין בזימון לאתויי נשים לענין רשות קאמר ולא לענין חובה ונשים צריך עיון אם יוצאות בברכות הזימון של אנשים מאחר שאין מבינות ויש מביאין ראיה שיוצאות מדאמר לקמן סופר מברך ובור יוצא מכאן משמע שאף הנשים יוצאו' בברכת המזון שלנו מיהו יש לדחות אותה ראי' דשאני בור שמבין בלשון הקדש ויודע קצת מאי קאמר אבל אינו יודע לברך אבל נשים שאינן מבינו' כלל מצי למימר דלא נפקי והא דאמר במגילה (פ"ב דף יז.) לועז ששמע אשורי' יצא פרסומי ניסא בעלמא שאני כדאמרינן התם (דף יח.) האחשתרני' בני הרמכי' מי ידעינן מאי ניהו:

אי הכי אימא סיפא. לא גרסי' אי הכי דהא אפילו מעיקרא נמי הוה מצי למפרך דסיפ' אין מזמנין:

רב זביד אמר ברוך הוא ומבורך. ובה"ג פסק ברוך הוא ומבורך שמו תמיד לעולם ועד ואי הוי עשר' עני בתרייהו ברוך הוא אלהינו ומבורך שמו תמיד לעולם ועד:

הא בבונה ירושלים הא בשאר ברכות. פר"ח וה"ג די"מ בכל ברכ' וברכ' כגון אחר ישתבח ויהללוך ומיהו פוק חזי מאי עמא דבר שלא נהגו לענות אמן אלא אחר בונה ירושלים דב"ה:

רב אשי עני ליה בלחישה. וכן פסק בה"ג ועוד לדידן דליכ' פועלי' אפילו אביי מודה:

לא

עין משפט נר מצוה

יג
[א] מיי' פ"ה מה' ברכות ה"ז סמג עשין כז טוש"ע א"ח סי' קלט סעי' ו

יד
[ב] מיי' פ"א שם הל' יא סמג שם טוש"ע א"ח סי' רי"ג סעי' ב

טו
[ג][ד] מיי' פ"ה שם הל' יג וסמג שם טוש"ע א"ח סי' קלד סעי' ב

טז
[ה] מיי' שם הע"ו וסמג שם טוש"ע א"ח סי' קלג סעי' א

יז
[ו] מיי פ"ז שם ה"ו סמג שם טוש"ע א"ח סי' ר סעי' א

יח
[ז] מיי' פ"ה שם ה"יד טוש"ע א"ח סי' קלד סעיף א

יט
[ח] מיי' פ"ה שם ה"ין סמג שם טוש"ע א"ח סי' קלם סעיף א

כ
[ט] מיי' פ"א שם הל' טז סמג שם טוש"ע א"ח סי' קפח סעי' א ובסי' רעו סעי' א

כא
[י] טוש"ע א"ח סי' קפח סעי' ב

מסורת הש"ס

[ערכין ג.]

[ד' חיבום הללו לריכין מוכן ומלבכי רש"י כלאם דגרם הא אפי' מאה נשי כתרי גברי דמיין]

סוכה לח: [ע"ש היטיב]

מגילה כג:

חולין קו.

[מנחות מ:]

[לעיל ז: ושם נסמן]

[לקמן כ.]

[נ"ל אמרו הא דתנן שלשה שאכלו כאחת וכו' וכ"כ בר"ף והרא"ש]

give him permission!—There is a special reason there [45b], because
a [we assume that] it is with their approval[1] since he [thereby] makes [the *zimmun*] obligatory on them.[2]

Come and hear: Women by themselves invite one another, and slaves by themselves invite one another, but women, slaves and children together even if they desire to invite one another may not do so. Now[3] a hundred women are no better then two men,[4] and yet it says, Women by themselves invite one another and slaves by themselves invite one another?—There is a special reason there, because each has a mind of her own.[5] If that is so, look at the next clause: Women and slaves together, even though they desire to invite one another may not do so. Why not? Each has a mind!—There is a special reason in that case, because it might lead to immorality.

We may conclude that it was Rab who said, 'Even though they [two] desire to invite one another they may not do so', because R. Dimi b. Joseph said in the name of Rab: If three persons ate together and one of them went out, the others call to him and count him for *zimmun*.[6] The reason is, is it not, that they call him, but if they did not call him they could not [invite one another]?—There is a special reason there, that the obligation to invite one another devolved upon them from the outset. Rather you may conclude that it is R. Joḥanan who said that even though they desire to invite one another they may not do so. For Rabbah b. Bar Ḥanah said in the name of R. Joḥanan: If two persons eat together, one of them is exempted by the benediction of his fellow; and we were perplexed to know what it was that he tells us; for we have learnt: If he heard without responding [Amen], he has performed his obligation, and R. Zera explained that he
b tells us that they do not invite one another to say grace.[1] We may therefore draw this conclusion.

Raba b. R. Huna said to R. Huna: But the Rabbis who came from the West[2] say that if they desire to invite one another they may do so; and must they not have heard this from R. Joḥanan?[3]—No; they heard it from Rab before he went down to Babylon.[4]

The [above] text [stated]: 'R. Dimi b. Joseph said in the name of Rab: If three persons ate together and one of them went out into the street, they can call to him and count him for *zimmun*'. Abaye says: This is only when they call to him and he responds.[5] Mar Zuṭra said: This applies only to three; but if it is for [the purpose of completing] ten,[6] they must wait till he comes. R. Ashi demurred to this. We should rather [he said], suppose the contrary; for nine look like ten, but two do not look like three. The law, however, is as laid down by Mar Zuṭra. What is the reason?—Since they [ten] have to mention God's name,[7] it is not proper that there should be less than ten.

Abaye said: We have a tradition that if two persons have eaten together, it is their duty to separate.[8] It has been taught similarly: If two persons have eaten together, it is their duty to separate. When is this case? When they are both educated men. But if one is educated and the other illiterate, the educated one says the benedictions and this exempts the illiterate one.

Raba said: The following statement was made by me independently and a similar statement has been made in the name of R. Zera: If three persons have been eating together, one breaks off to oblige two,[9] but two do not break off to oblige one. But do they not? Did not R. Papa break off for Abba Mar his son, he and another with him?—R. Papa was different because he went
c out of his way[1] to do so.[2] Judah b. Meremar and Mar son of R. Ashi and R. Aḥa from Difti took a meal with one another. No one of them was superior to the other[3] that he should have the privilege of saying grace.[4] They said: Where the Mishnah learnt[5] that IF THREE PERSONS HAVE EATEN TOGETHER IT IS THEIR DUTY TO INVITE [ONE ANOTHER TO SAY GRACE], this is only where one of them is superior [to the others], but where they are all on a level, perhaps it is better that the blessings should be separate. They thus said [the grace] each one for himself. Thereupon they came before Meremar and he said to them: You have performed the obligation of grace, but you have not performed the obligation of *zimmun*. Should you say, Let us start again with *zimmun*, *zimmun* cannot be said out of its place.[6]

If one came and found three persons saying grace,[7] what does he say after them?—R. Zebid says: Blessed and to be blessed [be His Name]. R. Papa said: He answers, Amen. They are not really at variance; the one speaks of the case where he found them saying 'Let us say grace', and the other where he found them saying 'Blessed'. If he found them saying 'Let us say grace', he answers 'Blessed and to be blessed'; if he found them saying 'Blessed', he answers 'Amen'.

One [Baraitha] taught: One who answers 'Amen' after his own blessings is to be commended, while another taught that this is reprehensible!—There is no contradiction: the one speaks of the benediction 'who buildest Jerusalem',[8] the other of the other benedictions. Abaye used to give the response[9] in a loud voice so that the workmen should hear and rise,[10] since the benediction 'Who is good and does good'[11] is not prescribed by the Torah.[12] R. Ashi gave the response in a low voice, so that they should not come to think lightly of the benediction 'Who is good and does good'.

a (1) That the attendant joins them. (2) Cur. edd. add in brackets 'from the outset', which is best omitted. (3) Cur. edd. read here in brackets, 'and surely as for women even a hundred' which is best omitted. (4) In respect of the obligation of *zimmun*. This proves that two by themselves are not sufficient to form a *zimmun*. (5) Lit., 'there are minds' and therefore thanksgiving from three women is more valuable than from two men. (6) Even while he remains outside, provided he joins in the response v. *infra*.

b (1) But one may be exempted by the other. (2) Palestine. (3) Who lived in Palestine. (4) From Palestine to settle there, v. Giṭ. (Sonc. ed.) p. 17, n. 3. (5) I.e., he joins in the responses. (6) V. *infra* 49b. (7) In the response, 'Blessed is our God of whose food we have eaten'. V. *P.B.* p. 279. (8) For the purpose of saying grace. (9) If one has not yet finished, he interrupts his meal to join with the two who have finished for the purpose of *zimmun*.

c (1) Lit., acted within the limits of strict justice'. (2) To show respect to his son. (3) In years or learning. (4) So MS.M. Cur. edd. add: 'for them'. (5) Emended reading, v. Marginal Gloss. The text has, They sat and discussed the question, When the Mishnah says, etc. (6) Lit., 'retrospectively'. I.e., it must come before the actual grace. (7) Sc. the *zimmun* responses. (8) The last of the three Scriptural benedictions in the Grace, v. *P.B.* p. 282. (9) To this third benediction. (10) To go to their work. (11) Which follows 'Who buildest Jerusalem'; v. *P.B.* p. 283. (12) Which prescribes only the first three.

[46a] R. Zera once was ill. R. Abbahu went to visit him, and a made a vow, saying, If the little one with scorched legs[1] recovers, I will make a feast for the Rabbis. He did recover, and he made a feast for all the Rabbis. When the time came to begin the meal,[2] he said to R. Zera: Will your honour please commence for us.[3] He said to him: Does not your honour accept the dictum of R. Johanan that the host should break bread? So he [R. Abbahu] broke the bread for them. When the time came for saying grace he said to him [R. Zera], Will your honour please say grace for us. He replied: Does your honour not accept the ruling of R. Huna from Babylon,[4] who said that the one who breaks bread says grace? Whose view then did R. Abbahu accept?—That expressed by R. Johanan in the name of R. Simeon b. Yohai: The host breaks bread and the guest says grace. The host breaks bread so that he should do so generously,[5] and the guest says grace so that he should bless the host. How does he bless him? 'May it be God's will that our host should never be ashamed in this world nor disgraced in the next world'. Rabbi added some further items: 'May he be very prosperous with all his estates, and may his possessions and ours be prosperous and near a town,[6] and may the Accuser have no influence either over the works of his hands or of ours, and may neither our host nor we be confronted with[7] any evil thought or sin or transgression or iniquity from now and for all time'.

To what point does the benediction of *zimmun* extend?[8]—R. b Nahman says: Up to [the conclusion of] 'Let us bless';[1] R. Shesheth says: Up to [the conclusion of] 'Who sustains'.[2] May we say that there is the same difference between Tannaim? For one [authority] taught: The grace after meals is either two or three benedictions,[3] while another has taught: Either three or four. Now we assume that all agree that 'Who is good and does good' is not Scriptural. Is not then the difference [between the two authorithies cited] this, that the one who says two or three holds that [the benediction of *zimmun*] extends up to 'Who sustaineth',[4] while the one who says three or four holds that it extends up to 'Let us bless'?[5]—No; R. Nahman explains according to his view and R. Shesheth explains according to his view. R. Nahman explains according to his view: All agree that it extends to 'Let us bless'. On the view of him who says, 'three or four', this creates no difficulty.[6] The one who says 'two or three' can say that here we are dealing with a grace said by work-people, regarding which a Master has said, He commences with 'Who sustaineth' and includes 'Who builds Jerusalem' in the benediction of the land.[7] R. Shesheth can also explain according to his view: All agree that the blessing of *zimmun* extends up to 'Who sustaineth'. On the view of him who says 'two or three', this creates no difficulty; while the one who says 'three or four' holds that the benediction 'Who is good and does good' is Scriptural.

R. Joseph said: You may know that the benediction 'who is good and does good' is not Scriptural from the fact that work-people omit it. R. Isaac b. Samuel b. Martha said in the name of Rab: You may know that the benediction 'who is good and does good' is not Scriptural from the fact that it commences with 'Blessed' but does not conclude with 'Blessed', for so it has been taught: All benedictions commence with 'Blessed' and close with 'Blessed', except the blessing over fruits, the blessings said over the performance of precepts, one blessing which joins on to c another, and the last blessing after the recital of the *Shema'*.[1] Some of these commence with 'Blessed' but do not close with 'Blessed'[2]

a (1) A nickname of R. Zera, explained in B.M. 85a. (2) By breaking bread. (3) I.e., break the bread. (4) R. Huna's place of origin is mentioned here because the meal was taking place in Palestine. (5) Lit., 'with a pleasant eye'. (6) So that he can visit them without difficulty. (7) Lit., 'may there not leap before him or us'. (8) The point of this query is not clear. Rashi takes it to mean, How much is said by three which is not said by two or one; but in this case the answer of R. Shesheth is unintelligible, since all agree that one says the blessing 'Who sustaineth'. Tosaf. therefore explain that it refers to the statement above that one person may interrupt his meal to join two others in *zimmun*, and the question is now asked, How long must he wait before resuming.

b (1) The *zimmun* responses proper. (2) The first benediction. (3) Emended reading, the numeral being in the feminine, v. Marginal Gloss. In the text the numeral is in the masculine, and we must translate (with Tosaf.), 'with either two or three men'. Tosaf. *ad loc.* accept this reading and explain it to mean that the recital of the blessings can be shared out between a number of people if no-one knows the whole of it, by assigning to each one benedictions which he happens to know. (4) So that if *zimmun* is said there are three blessings, the *zimmun* formula together with the first blessing constituting on this view one benediction, otherwise two. (5) So that without *zimmun* there are three and with the *zimmun* there is an extra one. (6) If grace is said with *zimmun*, there are four blessings, if without, three. (7) They combine the second and third benedictions into one, and thus when two labourers eat together there are two benedictions, when three, they form *zimmun* and say three.

c (1) Which is separated by the *Shema'* from the two blessings before it, though it is really a continuation of these. (2) E.g., the benediction to be said before the putting on of *tefillin*.

רבי זירא חלש על לגביה ר' אבהו *קביל עליה אי *מתפח קטינא חריך שקי עבידנא יומא טבא לרבנן אתפח עבד סעודתא לכולהו רבנן כי מטא למשרי אמר לי' לרבי זירא לישרי לן מר א"ל לא סבר לה מר להא דרבי יוחנן דאמר [א]בעל הבית בוצע שרא להו כי מטא לברוכי אמר ליה נבריך לן מר אמר ליה לא סבר לה מר להא דר' הונא דמן בבל דאמר בוצע מברך ואיהו כמאן סביר' ליה כי הא דא"ר יוחנן משום רבי שמעון בן יוחי בעל הבית בוצע [ב]ואורח מברך בעל הבית בוצע כדי שיבצע בעין יפה ואורח מברך כדי שיברך בעל הבית מאי מברך יהי רצון שלא יבוש בעל הבית בעולם הזה ולא יכלם לעולם הבא ור' מוסיף בה דברים ויצלח מאד בכל נכסיו ויהיו נכסיו ונכסינו מוצלחים וקרובים לעיר ואל ישלוט שטן לא במעשי ידיו ולא במעשי ידינו ואל *יזדקר לא לפניו ולא לפנינו שום דבר הרהור חטא ועבירה ועון מעתה ועד עולם: [ג]עד היכן ברכת הזמון רב נחמן אמר עד נברך ורב ששת אמר עד הזן נימא כתנאי דתניא חדא [ד]ברכת המזון שנים ושלשה ותניא אידך שלשה וארבעה סברוה דכולי עלמא הטוב והמטיב לאו דאורייתא היא מאי לאו בהא קמפלגי מאן דאמר שתים ושלש קסבר עד הזן ומאן דאמר שלש וארבע קסבר עד נברך לא רב נחמן מתריץ לטעמיה ורב ששת מתריץ לטעמיה רב נחמן מתריץ לטעמיה דכולי עלמא עד נברך מאן דאמר שלש וארבע שפיר ומאן דאמר שתים ושלש אמר לך הכא בברכת פועלים עסקינן דאמר *מר פותח בהזן וכולל בונה ירושלים בברכת הארץ רב ששת מתריץ לטעמיה דכולי עלמא עד הזן מאן דאמר שתים ושלש שפיר ומאן דאמר שלש וארבע קסבר *הטוב והמטיב דאורייתא היא אמר רב יוסף תדע דהטוב והמטיב לאו דאורייתא שדרי פועלים עוקרים אותה אמר רב יצחק בר שמואל בר מרתא משמיה דרב תדע דהטוב והמטיב לאו דאורייתא שהרי פותח בה בברוך ואין חותם בה בברוך כדתניא *[ה]כל הברכות כולן פותח בהן בברוך וחותם בהן בברוך חוץ מברכת הפירות וברכת המצות וברכה הסמוכה לחברתה וברכה אחרונה שבקריאת שמע יש מהן שפותח בהן בברוך ואין חותם בברוך ויש

רש"י

קטינא חריך שקי. כך היו קורין לרבי זירא וטעמא מפרש בבבא מליעא בהשוכר את הפועלים (דף פה.): כי מטי למשרי. ליטול רשות כלומר לפרוס ברכת המוליא ולאכול: רב הונא דמבבל. היינו רב הונא סתמא ולפי שעכשיו היה רבי זירא בארץ ישראל במקום רבי אבהו והיה עלה מבבל קאמר הכי: קרובים לעיר. שיכול לראותן בעל הבית תמיד ולדעת מה הן לריכין: נכסיו. קרקעות: עד היכן ברכת הזמון. שלריכין להיות שלשה וכשהן שנים לא יאמרוה: ברכת המזון שתים ושלש. כעונים שהם שתי ברכות פעמים שהם שלש כיצד כשהם שלשה הן ג' ברכות וכשהם שנים הן שתי ברכות כדמפרש ואזיל: דקסבר. ברכת זימון עד הזן וכשהם שנים אין אומרים אלא ברכת הארץ ובונה ירושלים: ומאן דאמר שלש וארבע. כשהן שנים הרי שלש הזן וברכת הארץ ובונה ירושלים וכשהם שלשה הם מוסיפים נברך עד ובטובו חיינו: מוקי' לה לא גרסינן והכי גרסינן והא דתניא שתים ושלש בברכת פועלים. דאמרי ברכת הארץ ובונה ירושלים בחדא ברכה אין כאן אלא ברכת הזן וברכת הארץ וכשהם שלשה מוסיפים נברך הרי שלש: דאמר מר. לעיל בפרק שני (דף יו.): שהרי פותח בה בברוך. ואי דאורייתא היא הויא סמוכה לחברת' ואין פותחים בה בברוך: כדתניא כו' יש מהן כו'. כגון ברכת פירות ומלות פותח ואינו חות' וטעמא מפרש' בערבי פסחים (דף קד.) משום דכולה חדא הודאה ואין הפסק דבר תחנה או דבר אחר בתוכה כמו שיש בקדוש כי הוא יום תחלה למקראי קדש והכחילנו: ויש

תוספות

לא סבר לה מר להא דאמר רב הונא דמן בבל כו'. מיהו יש ליישב הכי תרי לישני דרבי יוחנן כשבעל הבית מסב עמהם ודאי הוא בולע ואורח מברך וכו' אבל כשאין בעל הבית מסב עמהן הגדול שבהן יעשה המוליא וגם הוא יברך ברכת המזון:

עד היכן ברכת זימון וכו'. פי' רש"י ממתין עד הזן והזן בכלל שנים אינם מברכין הזן ולא נהירא דברכת הזן דאורייתא ואיך יחיד פטור מינה ועוד הכי קיימא לן כרב ששת באיסורי ולדידיה יחיד אומר שנים ובכל דוכתא נקט שלש ברכות ודוחק לומר דלא מיירי אלא בים זימון לרב ששת ועוד דמעשים בכל יום דיחיד מברך שלשה ברכות ועוד דמדתניא לקמן בפרקין (דף מח:*) וברכת זו ברכת הזימון את יי' אלהיך זו ברכת הזן וקשה לרב ששת יאמר הזן זו ברכת הזימון לכן יש לפרש דקאי אדלעיל דקאמר אחד מפסיק לשנים ובעי כמי [עד] היכא לריך להמתין עד שיברכו השנים עד נברך ורב ששת אמר עד שיגמרו הזן ומשם ואילך יכול היחיד לאכול ולא משום דחשיב ברכת הזן מזימון דודאי יחיד נמי מתחייב בהזן אלא משום דכיון דנברך אינה ברכה אינו חוורה לבדה אלא יגמור עמה גם ברכת הזן שהיא ברכה והשתא כיחא דקיימא לן שפיר כרב ששת וכפירוש זה אתמר בירושלמי:

ולמאן דאמר שנים ושלשה קסבר עד הזן. ופרש"י שנים ליחיד ושלשה לזימון ולאי שינתו פירש כן ודוחק גדול הוא כדפירש' וכי יחיד פטור מברכת הזן שהיא דאורייתא ועוד הואיל וקאי אברכת' אמאי נקט לשון זכר שנים ושלשה הוה ליה למנקט לשון נקבה שתים ושלש לכך נראה פירוש של רב אלפס דקאי אבני אדם והכי קאמר ברכת זמון בשנים ושלשה בני אדם היכא שכל אחד אינו יודע כי אם ברכה אחת למאן דאמר שנים ושלשה קא סבר עד הזן כלומר ברכות הזמון עד הזן שמברך עד סוף הזן דכולה כברכה אחת של זמון היא ולהכי קאמר שנים או שלשה כלומר לפעמים נשלמה בשני' והוא הדין באחד אבל נקט שנים לרבותא ופעמים בשלשה בני אדם שאחד יברך מנברך עד הזן והשני נודה לך והשלישי עד בונה ירושלים אבל לאלאין אין לברך אם האחד אינו יודע כי אם חלי הברכה אבל רביעי לא דנברך לבד לא חשיב ברכה ולכך אי אפשר לחלק לשנים נברך והזן ומאן דאמר בד' קסבר עד נברך דנברך חשיב ברכה אחת בפני עלמה והזן ברכה אחרת והיינו בד' שארבעה בני אדם מברכין אותן שאחד יאמר נברך והשני הזן והשלישי נודה לך והרביעי עד בונה ירושלים:

כל הברכות כולן פותחות בברוך וחותמות בברוך חוץ מברכת הפירות וברכת המלות וברכה הסמוכה לחברתה וברכה אחרונה שבק"ש. והא לך הסדר ברכת אשר יצר אינה סמוכה לנטילת ידים דנטילה שייכא בלא אשר יצר והרבה פעמים אומרה לבדה. אלהי נשמה אמאי אינה פותחת בברוך דאינה סמוכה לאשר יצר וכו' כגון אם לא בא מן הנקביים דידיו טהורות אין לריך לברכת אשר יצר ולריך לומר הואיל ואין בה אלא הודאה בעלמא אינה פותחת בברוך ומכל מקום חותמת בברוך הואיל וארוכה קצת וכן נמי לריך לומר גבי אתה הוא עד שלא נברא העולם וכו' וכל הכי ברכות קטנות כל אחת ברכה לעלמה כדאמרינן בעלמא *כד הוה מהלך הוה מברך מלעדי גבל וכן כולן ועוד דהוו קלרות והויין כברכות הפירות. יהי רלון למי היא סמוכה ואומר ר"ת שהיא מן הברכה ברוך אתה יי' המעביר שינה מעיני וכו' ולריך לומר ויהי רלון וא"ת והלא כל הברכות כולן לריך לומר בחתימתן מעין פתיחתן והא ליכא וי"ל דשפיר הוי מעין פתיחה סמוך לחתימה והמעביר דסמוך לחתימה איכא ותגמלני חסדים טובים והיינו גמילות חסדים שהקב"ה מעביר שינה מן האדם ומחדש כמו כדאמרינן במדרש חדשים לבקרים וגומר שהוא מחזיר הנשמה שלוה ושקטה בגוף כאשר היתה בתחלה אע"פ שהיתה עיפה והיינו כעין פתיחתה. ולעסוק בדברי תורה והערב נא הכל ברכה אחת היא ולריך לומר והערב נא. וישתבח סמוכה לברוך שאמר ולכך יש ליזהר שלא לספר ביניהם אע"פ שיש הפסק טובא פסוקי דזמרה מכל מקום לא מפסקי ובזה ניחא ברכה אחרונה שבקרית שמע אמת כו' אמת היא סמוכה אל אהבה וכו' ופסקי לא מפסקי וא"ת ברכה אחרונה למי שהוא קורא בתורה אמאי לריכה לפתוח בברוך הא סמוכה לחברתה לברכה ראשונה וי"ל לפי שהיו רגילים *שלא היו מברכים רק הראשון ברכה ראשונה והאחרון ברכה אחרונה ואיכא הפסק גדול בין ראשון לאחרון ובתר כן שתקנו שתיהן לכל אחד ואחד משום הנכנסין ומשום היוצאים שוב לא זזה ממקומה: והטוב

מסורת הש"ס

[נ"ל קיבל]

[גי' הערוך מעפה ענד וכו' בערך אטפח]

[ברי"ף ובר"ש וכן בטוש"ע ליתא יזדקק]

לעיל יו.

[לקמן מט.]

פסחים קד:

[לקמן מ.]

[מגילה כא.]

עין משפט נר מצוה

כב
[א] מיי' פ"ז מה' ברכות הל' ב סמג עשין כז טוש"ע א"ח סי' קסז סעי' יד

כג
[ב] מיי' וסמג שם טוש"ע א"ח סי' רא סעיף א

[שם אית' וברכ' זו ברכת הזן את ה' אלהיך זו ברכ' הזימון אמנם לכאור' נראה עיקר כגירס' תוס' מפני שיהי' כסדר]

כד
[ג] מיי' פ"ה שם הל' ב סמג שם טוש"ע א"ח סי' ר סעי' ב

כה
[ד] טוש"ע א"ח סי' קלד סעי' ג

כו
[ה] מיי' פ"א מהל' ברכות הל' ה ופי"א הל' א סמג שם

ויש מהן שחותם בהן בברוך ואין פותח בברוך והטוב והמטיב פותח בברוך ואין חותם בברוך מכלל דברכה בפני עצמה היא ואמר רב נחמן בר יצחק תדע דהטוב והמטיב לאו דאורייתא שהרי עוקרין אותה בבית האבל כדתניא *מה הם אומרים בבית האבל ברוך הטוב והמטיב ר"ע אומר ברוך דיין האמת הטוב והמטיב אין דיין אמת לא אלא אימא אף הטוב והמטיב מר זוטרא איקלע לבי רב אשי איתרע ביה מלתא פתח ובריך הטוב והמטיב אל אמת דיין אמת *שופט בצדק לוקח במשפט ושליט בעולמו לעשות בו כרצונו כי כל דרכיו משפט שהכל שלו ואנחנו עמו ועבדיו ובכל אנחנו חייבים להודות לו ולברכו גודר פרצות בישראל הוא יגדור את הפרצה הזאת בישראל לחיים להיכן הוא חוזר רב זביד משמיה דאביי אמר חוזר לראש ורבנן אמרי למקום שפסק והלכתא למקום שפסק: א"ל ריש גלותא לרב ששת אף על גב דרבנן קשישי אתון פרסאי בצרכי סעודה בקיאי מינייכו בזמן שהן שתי מטות גדול מסב בראש ושני לו למעלה הימנו ובזמן שהם שלש גדול מסב באמצע שני לו למעלה הימנו שלישי לו למטה הימנו אמר ליה וכי בעי אשתעויי בהדיה *מתריץ תרוצי ויתיב ומשתעי בהדיה אמר ליה שאני פרסאי דמחוי ליה במחוג מים ראשונים מהיכן מתחילין א"ל מן הגדול ישב גדול וישמור ידיו עד שנוטלין כולן א"ל לאלתר מייתו תכא קמיה מים אחרונים מהיכן מתחילין אמר ליה מן הקטן וגדול יתיב וידיו מזוהמות עד שנוטלין כולן א"ל לא מסלקי תכא מקמיה עד דנמטי מיא לגבי' אמר רב ששת אנא מתניתא ידענא דתניא *כיצד סדר היסב' בזמן שהן שתי מטות גדול מסב בראש ושני לו למטה הימנו בזמן שהן שלש מטות גדול מסב בראש שני לו למעלה הימנו שלישי לו למטה הימנו מים הראשונים מתחילין מן הגדול מים אחרונים בזמן שהם ה' מתחילין מן הגדול ובזמן שהם מאה מתחילין מן הקטן עד שמגיעים אצל ה' וחוזרין ומתחילין מן הגדול ולמקום שמים אחרונים חוזרין לשם ברכה חוזרת מסייע ליה לרב דאמר רב חייא בר אשי אמר רב *כל הנוטל ידיו באחרונה תחלה הוא מזומן לברכה רב ורבי חייא הוו יתבי בסעודתא קמיה דרבי א"ל רבי לרב קום משי ידך חזייה דקא מרתת א"ל בר פחתי עיין בברכת מזונא קאמר לך: ת"ר אין מכבדין לא בדרכים ולא בגשרים ולא

רש"י

ויש מהן חותם ולא פותח. כגון ברכה הסמוכה לחברתה שהרי כבר פתח בברכה ראשונה וברכה אחרונה שבקריאת שמע אמת ויציב אמת ואמונה שאע"פ שק"ש מפסיק בינתי' לברכות דלפניה סמוכה והויא לה סמוכה לחברתה: והטוב והמטיב וכו'. דלאו סמוכה לחברתה היא שאינה מברכ' המזון אלא על קבורת הרוגי ביתר תקנוה: שהרי עוקרים אותה בבית האבל. אליבא דר"ע: להיכן הוא חוזר. מי שנצטרף לזמון ואמרן לעיל אליבא דרב ששת ברכת זמון עד הזן והולך זה להיות מפסיק אכילתו עד שגומר המברך ברכת הזן וחוזר זה שהפסיק לשניים וגומר סעודתו להיכן הוא חוזר לברך לאח' שיגמור סעודתו: חוזר לראש. לתחלת הזן שהרי נתחייב בזמון שבתחלה הוקבע בג': למקום שפסק. לברכת הארץ כשאר יחיד: ה"ג. אע"ג דרבנן אתון פרסאי בצרכי סעודה בקיאי מינייכו: בזמן שהן שתי מטות. רגילין היו לאכול בהסבה על צדו השמאלית מוטה ורגליו לארץ איש איש על מטה אחת: בזמן שהן שנים גדול מסב בראש. כלומר מסב תחלה על מטתו: ושני לו למעלה הימנו. מטת השני לצד מראשותיו של גדול: ובזמן שהן שלשה גדול מסב באמצע שני לו למעלה הימנו שלישי לו למטה הימנו. לצד מרגלותיו: א"ל. רב ששת לריש גלותא: וכי בעי אשתעויי מתריץ תרוצי ויתיב. ואם רצה הגדול לדבר עם שני לו צריך הוא לזקוף עצמו ממסיבתו לישב זקוף דכל זמן שהוא מוטה אינו יכול לדבר עמו לפי שהשני לו אחורי ראשו של גדול הוא ופני הגדול מסובין לצד אחר וטוב לו שישב שני לו למטה הימנו וישמע דבריו כשהוא מוטה: במחוג. מראים בידיהם ובאצבעותיה' ברמיז': מים ראשונים מהיכן מתחילי'. רב ששת קא"ל לריש גלות' מהיכן מתחילים פרסיים מים ראשונים: לאלתר מייתו תבא קמיה. שלחן שלו מביאין מיד לפניו ואוכל ולפני כל אחד ואחד היו מביאין שלחן קטן: לא מסלקי תבא. מקמי גדול עד דמטו כולהו ובעוד שהוא אוכל האחרים נוטלין מים אחרונים: שני לו למטה הימנו. שאם הולך גדול לספר עמו לא יהא צריך לזקוף: ובזמן שהם ג' שני לו למעלה הימנו. ואם בא לספר מספר עם השלישי לו ואם בא לספר עם השני לו טוב הוא שיזקוף ואל ישפיל את השני לו לפני קטן ממנו שיהא הוא למטה וקטן ממנו למעלה ממנו: מתחילין מן הגדול. ולאלתר מייתי תכא קמיה: ובזמן שהם מאה. לאו דוקא דה"ה עשרה ולכל יותר מה' שנראה הוא שיסלקו השלחן מלפני הגדול שיטול ידיו וימתין שם יושב ובטל עד שיטלו כלם לפיכך כשהם יותר מה' מתחילין מן הקטן שיושב בסוף ואין מסלקין שלחן מלפני הגדול עד שיגיעו המים לחמש' שאללו: וחוזרים ומתחילים מן הגדול. ונוטלין שלחן מלפניו: למקום שמים אחרונים חוזרים. כשמגיעין לחמשה אם נטל הגדול הוא מברך ואם רוצה לאחר ליטול קודם לו הוא מברך: הנוטל ידיו באחרונה תחלה. אותו שנוטל בתחלת החמשה אחרוני' קורא תחלה באחרונה: אין מכבדים. לומר היה אתה קודם: לא בדרכים. הולכי דרכים לומר לגדול הימנו לך לפני: ולא

תוספות

והטוב והמטיב. וא"ת ואמאי פותחת בברוך והלא סמוכה לחברתה היא וי"ל דנתקנה בפני עצמה היא בשביל הרוגי ביתר* וא"ת אמאי אינה חותמת בברוך וי"ל משום דקצרה היא רק שתקנו לאחר כך שלש מלכיות ושלש גמולות ושלש טובות. וכאמן אתה של ברכת ההפטרה הוא מן ברכה העליונה *ולכך הוא ככתב גדול שבימים הראשונים היו רגילין לעמוד כל הקהל ולומר בקול רם נאמן אתה וכו' כשהיה התינוק מגיע שם:

להיכן הוא חוזר. פירש רש"י דקאי לאחד דפסיק לשני' ומומתין לאחרים עד הזן והיכן חוזר לאחר סעודתו רבנן אמרי למקום שפסק והלכת' למקום שפסק ותימה דא"כ היכי הלכתא למקום שפסק אחרי שאכל אחר כך פשיטא דיחזור אפי' להזן דהא זן דאורייתא ע"כ צריך לומר דקאי אהא דאמרינן לעיל דהמברך אומר נברך שאכלנו משלו והמסובין עונים ברוך שאכלנו משלו ובטובו חיינו להיכן הוא חוזר המברך לאחר שענו המסובין חוזר לראש שהמברך חוזר ואומר נברך שאכלנו משלו ובטובו חיינו ורבנן אמרי למקום שפסק שאומרי' ברוך שאכלנו משלו וכן הלכתא והר"מ מאייב"רא פיר' דקאי אשלשה שאכלו ויצא אחד מהם לשוק קוראים לו ומזמנים עליו ולעיל נמי הכי פירש עד היכן מקום זמון שצריך להו לאותו אחד דקרו ליה ועני עד נברך ומכאן ואילך ילך לדרכו ואיכ' צריכים האחרים עוד לצרופו והכא בעי לאותו מן השוק להיכן הו' חוזר למקום שפסק דהיינו למר מהזן ואילך ולמר נברך והשתא ניחא דלא קשה מהזן שהרי לא *ספר בינתיים:

מר זוטרא איקלע לבי רב אשי איתרע ביה מלתא. וכוותיה קיימא לן והכי מברכין בא"י אמ"ה האל הטוב והמטיב אל אמת דיין אמת שופט בצדק ולוקח במשפט ושליט במעשיו ואנחנו עבדיו ועמו ובכל אנחנו חייבין להודות לו לברכו גודר פרצות בישראל הוא יגדור פרצה זאת מעלינו ומעל האבל שבתוכנו לחיים ולשלום הרחמן הוא ימלוך עלינו לעולם ועד וגו' ופירש בה"ג דאין לומר במשפט דקיימא לן בפר' במה בהמה יוצאה (דף נה:) דיש מיתה בלא חטא ויש יסורין בלא עון ומיהו בכך אין למחקו:

בזמן שהן שתי מטות גדול מסב בראש שני לו למעלה הימנו. דהיינו כלפי ראשו שמסב על המטה דרך שמאל ולמטה מקרי דרך מרגלותיו דהיינו מימינו ובזה מדקדק רב ששת דאם כן בעי גדול לתרוצי כפשוטיה כשמדבר עם השני כיון שהשני למעל' הימנו ולקמן במתניתא גר' גדול מסב בראש השני למטה הימנו אחו כלפי מרגלותיו והוא מימינו ואז לא מתריץ ויתיב כי בעי לאשתעויי בהדי שני:

אין מכבדין וכו'. וא"ת הא אמרינן בשבת בפרק במה בהמה (דף נא:) לוי ורב הונא בר חייא הוו קא אזלי באורח' קדמיה חמריה דרב הונא לחמרא דלוי בעא רב הונא לאפוקי מדעתיה דלוי כו' אלמא מכבדים בדרכים וי"ל כשילכו לדרך כאחד מכבדין בדרכים אבל אם כל אחד הלך לדרכו ופגעו זה בזה ואירע להם דרך למקום אחד אין מכבדים: אין

עין משפט נר מצוה

[כדאי' לקמן מח:]

[ויתר ביאור תמצא בתוס' פסחים קד: ד"ה חתן]

כז א מיי' פ"ב מה' ברכות הלכה ח סמג עשין כז טוש"ע א"ח סי' קפט סעי' ב טוש"ע י"ד סי' שעט סעי' א

כח ב מיי' שם פ"ה ה"ב טוש"ע א"ח סי' ר סעי' ב

כט ג מיי' פ"ז מה' ברכות הל' א סמג שם

ל ד מיי' וסמג שם טוש"ע א"ח סי' קסה סעיף ב

לא ה מיי' שם הל' יב וסמג שם טוש"ע א"ח סי' קפא סעיף ו

לב ו מיי' שם הל' יב

[ע' רש"א וע' מג"א סי' קפג ס"ק י"א דל"ל סעד]

מסורת הש"ס

[מס' שמחות סוף פי"ד ע"ש]

[שם]

[תרגום של בשלום ובמישור' בשלמא ובתרולא וע' בערוך ערך תירן]

תוספתא פ"ה

לעיל מג. ע"ש

[46*b*], while some close with 'Blessed' but do not open with 'Blessed';[3] and 'who is good and does good' opens with 'Blessed' but does not close with 'Blessed'. This shows that it is a separate blessing. R. Naḥman b. Isaac said: You may know that 'who is good and does good' is not Scriptural from the fact that it is omitted in the house of a mourner,[4] as it has been taught: What blessing is said in the house of a mourner? 'Blessed is He that is good and does good'. R. Akiba says: 'Blessed be the true Judge'. And does one [according to the first authority] say, 'Blessed be He that is good and does good', and not 'Blessed be the true Judge'?—Read: He says also, 'Blessed be He that is good and does good'. Mar Zuṭra visited R. Ashi when the latter had suffered a bereavement, and in the grace after meals he began and uttered the benediction: 'Who is good and does good, God of truth, true Judge, who judges in righteousness and takes away in righteousness, who is Sovereign in His universe to do as pleaseth Him in it, for all His ways are judgment; for all is His, and we are His people and His servants, and for everything it is incumbent upon us to give thanks to Him and to bless Him. He who closes up the breaches of Israel will close up this breach in Israel, granting life'.

Where does he[5] commence again?—R. Zebid says in the name of Abaye: At the beginning; the Rabbis say, at the place where
a he left off.[1] The law is, at the place where he left off.

Said the Exilarch to R. Shesheth: Although you are venerable Rabbis, yet the Persians are better versed than you in the etiquette[2] of a meal. When there are two couches [in the set],[3] the senior guest takes his place first and then the junior one above him.[4] When there are three couches, the senior occupies the middle one, the next to him in rank takes the place above him, and the third one below him.[5] R. Shesheth said to him: So when he wants to talk to him,[6] he has to stretch himself and sit upright to do so![7] He replied: This does not matter to the Persians, because they speak with gesticulation. [R. Shesheth asked the Exilarch:] With whom do they commence the washing of the hands before the meal?—He replied: With the senior one. Is then the senior one to sit still [he exclaimed] and watch his hands[8] until they have all washed?—He replied: They bring a table before him immediately.[9] With whom do they begin the washing after the meal [he asked him]?—He replied: With the junior one present. And is the senior one to sit with greasy hands until all have washed?—He replied: They do not remove the table from before him till
b water is brought to him.[1] R. Shesheth then said: I only know a Baraitha, in which it is taught: 'What is the order of reclining? When there are two couches in a set, the senior one reclines first, and then the junior takes his place below him. When there are three couches, the senior takes his place first, the second next above him, and then the third one below him. Washing before the meal commences with the senior one, washing after the meal, if there are five, commences with the senior, and if there are a hundred[2] it commences with the junior until five are left, and then they start[3] from the senior one. The saying of grace is assigned to the one to whom the washing thus reverts'.[4] This supports Rab; for R. Ḥiyya b. Ashi said in the name of Rab: Whoever washes his hands first at the end of the meal has the right to say grace. Rab and R. Ḥiyya were once dining with Rabbi. Rabbi said to Rab: Get up and wash your hands. R. Ḥiyya saw him trembling and said to him: Son of princes, he is telling you to think over the grace.[5]

Our Rabbis taught: We do not give precedence [to others][6]

(3) E.g., the benedictions in the *Tefillah*. (4) According to R. Akiba. (5) Rashi explains this to mean the one who has interrupted his meal to join with two others in *zimmun*, (cf. *supra* 45*b*) and the question is, on the view of R. Shesheth, (cf. *supra*) where should he resume his grace.

a (1) Viz., (on the view of R. Shesheth) at the second blessing. Tosaf. remark on this that it is very difficult to suppose that he is excused saying the first blessing after having eaten again. They accordingly refer it to the man who leads in the grace, and the question is, after the others have responded 'Blessed be He of whose bounty we have partaken and through whose goodness we live', where does he go on, and the reply is, on Abaye's view, that he repeats his own formula with the addition 'Blessed be He of whose bounty etc.', whereas according to the Rabbis he merely says 'Blessed be He of whose bounty etc.', v. *P.B.* p. 280. (2) Lit., 'requirements'. (3) It was usual for guests at a set meal to recline on couches arranged in sets of two or three (the latter being the Roman *triclinium*). (4) I.e., head to head. (5) I.e., with his head to the other's feet. (6) When the senior wishes to speak to the one who is above him. (7) If he wants to face him. (8) I.e., do nothing. *Aliter:* 'guard them against impurity'. (9) It was usual to place a small table before each guest.

b (1) And meanwhile he can go on eating. (2) *Sc.*, any number more than five. (3) I.e., removing the table (Rashi). (4) I.e., either the senior one, or the one to whom he delegates the honour. (5) V. *supra* 43*a*, nn. a9 and 10. (6) Lit., 'honour', i.e., ask another to go first, out of politeness.

either on the road or on a bridge [47a] or in the washing of the greasy hands [at the end of a meal]. Once Rabin and Abaye were on the road and the ass of Rabin got in front of Abaye, and he [Rabin] did not say to him, Will your honour proceed. Said Abaye: Since this student has come up from the West,[7] he has grown proud. When he arrived at the door of the synagogue, he said, Will your honour please enter. He said to him: Was I not 'Your honour', up to now?—He replied: Thus said R. Johanan: One gives precedence only in a doorway in which there is a *mezuzah*.[8] [You say] only where there is a *mezuzah*, but not where there is no *mezuzah*. If that is so, then in the case of a synagogue and *Beth ha-Midrash* also where there is no *mezuzah* we do not give precedence? What you must say is, in a doorway which is suitable for a *mezuzah*.[9]

R. Judah the son of R. Samuel b. Shilath said in the name of Rab: The guests may not eat anything until the one who breaks bread has tasted. R. Safra sat and stated: The statement was, a 'May not taste'.[1] What difference does it make [in practice]?—[It teaches that] one must repeat the exact words of his teacher.

Our Rabbis taught: Two wait for one another[2] before commencing on the dish,[3] but three need not wait.[4] The one who has broken bread stretches out his hand first, but if he wishes to show respect to his teacher or to anyone senior to himself, he may do so. Rabbah b. Bar Hanah made a marriage feast for his son in the house of R. Samuel son of R. Kattina, and he first sat down and taught his son: The one who acts as host[5] may not break the bread until the guests have finished responding, Amen. R. Hisda said: The bulk of the guests. Rama b. Hama said to him: Why should this be the case only with the majority? Presumably it is because the benediction had not yet been completed.[6] The same should apply also to a minority, for the benediction has not yet been completed?—He replied: What I say is that whoever [draws out] the response of Amen longer than necessary is in error.[7]

Our Rabbis taught: The Amen uttered in response should be neither hurried[8] nor curtailed[9] nor orphaned,[10] nor should one hurl the blessing, as it were, out of his mouth.[11] Ben 'Azzai says: If a man says an 'orphaned' Amen in response, his sons will be orphans; if a hurried Amen, his days will be snatched away; if a curtailed Amen, his days will be curtailed. But if one draws out the Amen, his days and years will be prolonged. Once Rab and Samuel were sitting at a meal and R. Shimi b. Hiyya joined them b and ate very hurriedly.[1] Said Rab to him: What do you want? To join us? We have already finished. Said Samuel to him: If they were to bring me mushrooms, and pigeon to Abba,[2] would we not go on eating?[3] The disciples of Rab were once dining together when R. Aha entered. They said: A great man has come who can say grace for us. He said to them: Do you think that the greatest present says the grace? One who was there from the beginning must say grace! The law, however, is that the greatest says grace even though he comes in at the end.

ONE WHO HAD EATEN DEMAI etc. But this is not a proper food for him?[4]—If he likes he can declare his possessions *hefker*[5] in which case he becomes a poor man, and it is suitable for him. For we have learnt: *Demai* may be given to the poor to eat and also to billeted soldiers.[6] And R. Huna said: A Tanna taught: Beth Shammai say that *demai* is not given to the poor and to billeted soldiers to eat.[7]

OR FIRST TITHE FROM WHICH TERUMAH HAS BEEN REMOVED. This is obvious!—This had to be stated, for the case in which the Levite came beforehand [and thus obtained the first tithe] in the ear and he separated the *terumah* of the tithe,[8] but not the great *terumah*.[9] And the rule stated follows R. Abbahu; for R. Abbahu said in the name of Resh Lakish: First tithe for which [the Levite] has come beforehand [and obtained] in the ear is not liable to great *terumah*, since it says, *ye shall offer up an heave offering of it for the Lord, even a tenth part of the tithe*.[10] I bid you offer a tithe from the tithe, not the great *terumah* plus the *terumah* of the tithe from the tithe. Said R. Papa to Abaye: If that is so, the same c should be the case even if he anticipates it at the heap?[1]—He replied: It was in anticipation of your question that the text says,

(7) Palestine. (8) V. Glos. (9) Excluding open roads and bridges.

a (1) And not 'may not eat'. (2) When one interrupts his eating, the other must wait till he resumes. This was according to the old custom when all diners ate from the same dish. (3) After breaking bread, it was the custom for each of the guests to take something out of the dish. (4) If one interrupts his eating. (5) Who in this case would be the bridegroom. Lit., 'he who breaks (the bread)'. (6) As long as the Amen response had not been finished. (7) And the minority who unduly prolong the Amen response need not be taken into consideration. (8) I.e., the A should not be slurred over. (9) The N should be clearly pronounced. (10) Said by one who has not heard the blessing itself but only the others responding Amen. (11) He should not gabble it.

b (1) So as to be able to join them in the grace. (2) A name of endearment given by Samuel to Rab. (3) As dessert, these being our favourite dishes. Therefore it is as though we had not finished and he may join us. (4) *Sc.* and it is as though he ate stolen property, over which it is forbidden to make a blessing. (5) V. Glos. (6) Dem. III, 1. (7) I.e., it is only Beth Shammai who provided *demai* to the poor but Beth Hillel, with whom the law agrees, differ from them. (8) The tithe given by the Levite to the priest. (9) The ordinary *terumah*, (v. Glos. s.v. *terumah*). (10) Num. XVIII, 26.

c (1) The grain after winnowing, but before being ground.

*ולא בידים מזוהמות רבין ואביי הוו קא אזלי באורחא קדמיה חמריה דרבין לדאביי ולא אמר ליה ניזיל מר אמר מדסליק האי מרבנן ממערב' גס ליה דעתיה כי מטא לפתחא דבי כנישתא אמר ליה ניעל מר אמר ליה ועד השתא לאו מר אנא אמר ליה הכי א"ר יוחנן אין מכבדין אלא בפתח שיש בה מזוזה *דאית בה מזוזה אין דלית בה מזוזה לא אלא מעתה בית הכנסת ובית המדרש דלית בהו מזוזה הכי נמי דאין מכבדין אלא אימא בפתח הראוי למזוזה: אמר רב יהודה בריה דרב שמואל בר שילת משמיה דרב אין המסובין רשאין לאכול כלום עד שיטעום הבוצע יתיב רב ספרא וקאמר לטעום אתמר למאי נפקא מינה *שחייב אדם לומר בלשון רבו ת"ר *שנים ממתינין זה לזה בקערה שלשה אין ממתינין דבוצע הוא פושט ידו תחלה ואם בא לחלוק כבוד לרבו או למי שגדול הימנו הרשות בידו רבה בב"ח הוה עסיק ליה לבריה בי רב שמואל בר רב קטינא קדים ויתיב וקמתני ליה לבריה אין הבוצע רשאי לבצוע עד שיכלה אמן מפי העונים רב חסדא אמר מפי רוב העונים א"ל רמי בר חמא מאי שנא רובא דאכתי לא כלי' ברכה מיעוט' נמי לא כלי' ברכה א"ל שאני אומר כל העונה אמן יותר מדאי אינו אלא טועה ת"ר *אין עונין לא אמן חטופה ולא אמן קטופה ולא אמן יתומה ולא יזרוק ברכה מפיו בן עזאי אומר כל העונה אמן יתומה יהיו בניו יתומים חטופה יתחטפו ימיו קטופה *תקטפו ימיו וכל המאריך באמן מאריכין לו ימיו ושנותיו: רב ושמואל הוו יתבי בסעודתא אתא רב שימי בר חייא הוה קמסרהב ואכיל א"ל רב מה דעתך לאיצטרופי בהדן אנן אכילנא לן א"ל שמואל אלו מייתי לי *ארדילי ונוזלי לאבא מי לא אכילנא: תלמידי דרב הוו יתבי בסעודתא על רב אחא אמרי אתא גברא רבא דמברך לן אמר להו מי סבריתו דגדול מברך עיקר שבסעודה מברך והלכתא *גדול מברך אע"ג דאתא לבסוף: אכל דמאי וכו': הא לא חזי ליה *כיון דאי בעי מפקר להו לנכסי' והוי עני וחזי לי' דתנן *מאכילין את העניים דמאי ואת האכסניא דמאי ואמר רב הונא תנא ב"ש אומרים אין מאכילים את העניים ואת האכסנאי דמאי: מעשר ראשון שנטלה תרומתו: *פשיטא לא צריכא אלא שהקדימו בשבלים והפריש ממנו תרומת מעשר ולא הפריש ממנו תרומה גדולה וכדרבי אבהו דאמר ר' אבהו אמר ריש לקיש *מעשר ראשון שהקדימו בשבלים פטור מתרומה גדולה שנאמר °והרמותם ממנו תרומת ה' מעשר מן המעשר מעשר מן המעשר אמרתי לך ולא תרומה גדולה ותרומת מעשר מן המעשר א"ל *רב פפא לאביי אי הכי אפילו הקדימו בכרי נמי א"ל עליך אמר קרא

מכל

תורה אור

רש"י

ולא בידי' מזוהמות. בטנופת מים אחרונים: ממערבא. לפי שהיה רבין רגיל לעלות מבבל לא"י ולומר הוא דבריו משמו של ר' יוחנן: בפתח הראוי למזוזה. כלומר בבתים כל פתחי' למעוטי דרכים ופרצות: לטעום אתמר. אין חלוק בדבר אלא שחייב לומר בלשון רבו: קדים. רבה בר בר חנה ליישב על השלחן ולשנות לבנו הלכות סעודה לפי שהחתן רגיל לבצוע והיה מלמדו היאך יעשה: לבצוע. לפרוס הפרוס' מן הפת: עד שיכלה אמן מפי העונים. אמן אחר ברכת המוציא דאף עניי' אמן מן הברכה היא ואמרינן בפרק כיצד מברכין (דף לט.) צריך שתכלה ברכה קודם בליעה: חטופה. שקורין את האלף בחטף ולא בפתח ואומר אמן והוא צריך לומר אמן: קטופה. שמחסר קריאת הנו"ן שאינו מוציאה בפה שתהא נכרת: יתומה. שלא שמע הברכה אלא ששמע שעונין אמן והא דאמר בהחליל (דף נא:) שבאלכסנדריא של מצרים היו מניפי' בסודרי' כשהגיע עת לענות אמן אלמא לא שמעי וקא ענו הכהו מידע ידעי שהם עונים אחר ברכה ועל איזו ברכה הם עונים אלא שלא היו שומעי' את הקול: ולא יזרוק ברכה מפיו. במהירות שדומה עליו כמשא אלא שחוק קבוע הוא לו: וקא מסרהב ואכיל. וממהר לאכול כדי להצטרף לזימון ויזמנו עליו: אכילנא לן. גמרה לן סעודתן קודם שבאת ולאי אתה מחייבנו עוד בזימון: אלו מייתי לי ארדילי' ונוזליא לאבא. שמואל חביבין עליו ארדילי' בקנוח הסעוד' והן כמהין ופטריו' ולרב היו חביבי' גוזלות ושמואל היה קורא לרב אבא לכבודו: מי לא אכילנא. הלכך לא גמרה סעודתן ומצטרף: עיקר שבסעודה. אחד מאותן שהיו בתחל' הסבה: הא לא חזי ליה. והויא לה ברכת זמון הבאה בעבירה וכתיב (תהלי' י) בוצע ברך נאץ ה' ואמר מר (ב"ק פ"ט ד' צ"ד.) הרי שגזל סאה של חטים וטחנה ואפאה' וברך עליה אין זה מברך אלא מנאץ: דמאי. חטין הלקוחי' מע"ה ספק עשרן ספק לא עשרן: אכסניא. חיל של מלך שמטיל על בני העיר לזונם בשובם ממלחמתו והרי הם כעניים לפי שהם שלא במקומם: מאכילי' את העניי' דמאי. דרוב עמי הארץ מעשרי' הם וחומרא דרבנן בעלמא היא: שהקדימו בשבלי'. לוי קדם את הכהן ונטל מעשר בשבלי' קודם שנטל כהן תרומה גדולה והכהן היה לו ליטול תרומה גדולה תחלה א' מנ' דרחמנא קרייה ראשית וכתיב (שמות כב) מלאתך ודמעך לא תאחר כמלאת תרומה גדולה של כהן בתוך המעשר הזה א' מחמשים שבו לבד מתרומת מעשר שעל הלוי להפריש תרומה ממעשרו: וכדר' אבהו. אשמעי' מתניתין דהכי הוא כדר' אבהו דפטר ליה ללוי מתרומה גדולה שבו:

מכל

תוספות

אין המסובין רשאי' לטעום עד שיטעו' המבצע. ותימה מההיא סבא דערבי פסחי' (דף קו.) דגחין ושתי אלמא דשתי קודם המברך שמא יש חילוק בין אכילה לשתיה. אי נמי י"ל דלא שת' אלא להראות לו מעשה שלא היה צריך לומר יותר ובירושלמי יש כשיש לכל אחד ככרו או כוסו בידו יכולי' לשתות אפי' קודם המברך וגבי ההו' סבא היה לו כוסו בידו והכי איתא בירוש' אמר ר' בון בשם רב אין המסובין רשאין לטעום עד שיטעום המברך ריב"ל אמר שותין אע"פ שלא שתה המברך ולא פליגי רבי בון בשם רב שזקוק לכוס אחד דריב"ל דהיה לכל אח' כוסו בידו וכן עשה רבינו שמשון בחופ' א' שבלע החתן המוציא והיה בולע רבינו שמשון הפת שהיה לפניו ואוכל והשר מקוצי' היה אומר אם בלע המברך ונתן לכל א' חלקו אין צריך להמתין כל א' עד שיטעום המברך והא דאמרי' הכא אין המסובין רשאין לטעום כו' היינו להקדי' ולבלוע מן הפת שבלע המברך אבל אחר שנתן לכל א' חלקו אין קפידה וכן צריך לומר בסמוך הבוצע הוא פושט ידיו תחלה לטבול פתו ואם בא לחלוק כבוד לרבו רשאי ואמאי והא אין המסובין רשאין לטעו' וכו' ואין לומר דמן הטיבול לחודיה קאמר אך המברך אכיל קודם דאם כן מה כבוד היה זה אבל לפי דפירשתי ניחא ויש מפרש פושט ידיו תחלה בקערה להתחיל באכילה ומכאן משמע שאין צריך למזוג מכוס ברכה לשאר כוסות היכא שיש בפני האורחים כוסות שאינן פגומות אבל אם אותן כוסות פגומות יש קפידא*: אמן יתומה. שאין שומעי' הברכ' מפי המברך ועונה אחר האחרים ששמעו אמן. תימה דהא אמרינן בסוכה (פ"ה נא:) באלכסנדריא של מצרים שהיה שם קהל גדול ולא היו יכולים כלם לשמוע מפי המברך והיו מניפי' בסודרי' כדי שידעו חתימת הברכות ויענו אמן וי"ל שהיו יודעי' באיזו ברכה החזן עומד אמנם לא היו שומעים אותו אבל הכא מיירי שאינם יודעי' כלל היכא החזן עומד ומתפלל ובאיזו ברכה הוא עומד אלא עונה אחר האחרים בלא שמיעה ולא ידיעה*: כל המאריך באמן מאריכין לו ימיו ושנותיו. ובלבד שלא יאריך יותר מדאי וטעמא לפי שאין קריאת התיבה כמשמע' כשהוא מאריך יותר מדאי ומסקנא דמלתא דאין הבוצע רשאי לבצוע עד שיכלה אמן מפי רוב העונים: אלו מייתי לי ארדילי' וכו'. משמ' דכן הלכה דרב נמי לא פליג אבל אי אמר הב לן ונבריך שהסיחו דעתם מלאכול אין שלישי מצטרף עמהם: והלכתא גדול מברך. ומיהו אם הגדול נותן רשו' לקטן לברך שפיר כדאשכחן *דאמר ליה לרב תשי ידך וכו': ומאכילין את האכסני' דמאי. מיירי באכסניא ישראל ומוטלין עליהם לזונם והם כעניים ודוקא דמאי אבל טבל לא דקספו להו איסור מיתה ואי נמי באכסניא של נכרי' שהטיל עליהם המלך ומ"מ דוקא דמאי אבל טבל לא דאם כן פורע חובו מממונו של כהן*: ואמר רב הונא תנא בש"א אין מאכילין. וא"ת רב הונא טעמא דב"ש אתא לאשמועינן דהכי פריך בכמה דוכתי וי"ל דקמ"ל דאי משכחת תנא דאמר אין מאכילין ב"ש היא ולא תיחוש לאותה משנה או ברייתא:

אמר

מסורת הש"ס

[וע' תוס' יומא יא: ד"ה שאין ותוס' מנחות לג. ד"ה והא]
[עדיות פ"א מ"ג שבת טו. בכורות ה. תוספת' פ"ו גיטין כט:]
[תוס' מגילה פ"ג]
(בי"רוש' ספ"ה ופ"א ה"ט דמגילה הגי' תקטף נשמתו)
[פסחים קיט:]
[ב"מ ע. כריתות פד: גיטין יב.] שבת קכז: עירובין יז: לא: פסחי' לה. דמאי פ"ג מ"א [סוכה לה:] עירובין יז:
שבת עירובין פסחים שם ביצה יג: במדבר יח
תמורה ה:

עין משפט נר מצוה

לג א מיי' פ"ז מה' ברכות הל' יב סמג עשין כז טוש"ע א"ח סי' קסז סעיף ו
לד ב מיי' שם הלכה ה וסמג שם טוש"ע א"ח סימן קסז סעיף טו
לה ג מיי' שם הלכה ו וסמג שם טוש"ע א"ח סימן קע סעיף ג
לו ד מיי' שם הלכה ה וסמג שם טוש"ע א"ח סימן קסז סעיף יז
לז ה מיי' שם שם סעי' יז
לח ו מיי' פ"א מה' שם הל' יד סמג שם טוש"ע א"ח סי' קכד סעיף ח
לט ז מיי' פ"א שם הלכה ט טוש"ע א"ח סי' קכד סעי' ח
מ ח מיי' שם ופ"ז ה"ב וסמג שם טוש"ע א"ח סי' רא סעיף א
מא ט מיי' פ"י מה' מעשר הלכה יא
מב י מיי' פ"ה מה' ברכות הלכה כ
מג כ מיי' פ"ב מה' תרומות הל' יג טור י"ד סי' שלא

[וע' תוס' פסחים קו. ד"ה דהוה]
[וע' תוס' סוכה נא: ד"ה וכיון]
[לעיל מג. ומה:]
[וע' היטיב תוס' עירובין י"ז: ד"ה ולא אכסניא]

עין משפט נר מצוה

[וע"ע תוס' חגיגה כב. ד"ה כמאן]

[ע' תוס' שבת קכז: ד"ה הא קמ"ל]

מד אמיי' פ"ה מהלכ' ברכות הלכה כ

מה בטוש"ע א"ח סי' קלט סעיף ג

מו גשם סעי' ד

מז דמיי' פי"ג מהל' אסורי ביאה הל' ו סמג לאוין קיו טוש"ע י"ד סי' רסח סעי' ג

מח המיי' פ"ט מהל' עבדים הלכה ו סמג עשין פז טוש"ע י"ד סי' רסז סעי' עט

מט ומיי' פ"ח מהל' תפלה ה"א סמג עשין יט טוש"ע א"ח סי' נ סעיף יד

אמר רב הונא הלכה כאחרים. והאידנא אין אנו מדקדקים ורגילים אנו לזמן בע"ה כדאמר בחגיגה (פ"ג דף כב.) כמאן מקבלינן האידנא סהדות' מע"ה כמאן כר' יוסי כדי שלא יהא כל אחד הולך ובונה במה לעצמו*:

מצוה דרבי' שאני. ומכאן קשה לה"ג דפירש דמי שמת לו מת בי"ב חדש האחרון דאבילות נוהג ולא אתי י"ב האחרון דרבנן ודחי אבילות דאורייתא דכתיב (עמוס ח) ואחריתה כיום מר דהכא חזינן דאתיא תפלה דרבנן ודחיא קרא דלעולם בהם תעבודו וכן משמע נמי בריש כתובות (ד' ד.) גבי חתן נוהג ז' ימי המשתה ואח"כ נוהג ז' ימי אבילות ומדשבעת ימי המשתה מבטלין אבלו' דאורייתא' כ"ש י"ב שכי:

קטן פורח מזמנין עליו. פרש"י שהביא שתי שערות ועדיין לא הגיע לי"ג שנה ויום אחד ולא נהיר' דא"כ מאי אמר בסמוך לאתויי קטן פורח היינו שהביא שתי שערות דקתני בברייתא בהדיא ע"כ פר"ת קטן פורח בתוך י"ג שנה ועדיין לא הביא שתי שערות ידועות שאינן גדולות כדי לכוף ראשן לעיקרן שכן הוא שיעורם ולהכי קרי ליה פורח שפרח ולמחו בו שערות אבל אינן גדולות כל השיעור והשתא ה"פ אמרת הביא דמשמע הביא דוקא והדר קתני אין מדקדקין בקטן דמשמע אפילו לא הביא אלא ש"מ לאתויי קטן פורח ואתי סיפא לגלויי רישא דמה שהוא אומר ברישא הביא שתי שערות היינו פורחות שאינן שערות ממש וכדפירש שנכנס בתוך י"ג שנה וא"ת והא אמרינן לעיל קטן המוטל בעריסה עושין אותו סניף וי"ל דהתם איירי בעשרה והכא מיירי בשלשה או שמא פליגי אהדדי:

תורה אור

מכל *מעשרותיכם תרימו ומאי ראיה האי אידגן והאי לא אידגן: מעשר שני והקדש שנפדו: פשיטא הב"ע *כגון שנתן את הקרן ולא נתן את החומש *והא קמ"ל דאין חומש מעכב: השמש שאכל כזית: פשיטא מהו דתימא שמש לא קבע קמ"ל: והכותי מזמנין עליו: אמאי לא יהא אלא עם הארץ ותניא *אין מזמנין על ע"ה אביי אמר בכותי חבר רבא אמר אפי' תימא בכותי ע"ה והכא בע"ה דרבנן דפליגי עליה דר' מאיר עסקי' דתני' *איזהו ע"ה כל שאינו אוכל חוליו בטהרה דברי ר"מ וחכמים אומרים כל שאינו מעשר פירותיו כראוי והני כותאי עשורי מעשרי כדחזי דבמאי דכתיב באורייתא מזהר זהירי *דאמר מר כל מצוה שהחזיקו בה כותיי' הרבה מדקדקין בה יותר מישראל ת"ר *איזהו ע"ה כל שאינו קורא ק"ש ערבית ושחרית דברי רבי אליעזר רבי יהושע אומר כל שאינו מניח תפילין בן עזאי אומר כל שאין לו ציצית בבגדו ר' נתן אומר כל שאין מזוזה על פתחו רבי נתן בר יוסף אומר כל שיש לו בנים ואינו מגדלם לת"ת *אחרים אומרים אפי' קרא ושנה ולא שמש ת"ח הרי זה ע"ה א"ר הונא הלכה כאחרים רמי בר חמא לא אזמין עליה דרב מנשיא בר תחליפא דתני ספרא וספרי והלכתא כי נח נפשיה דרמי בר חמא אמר רבא לא נח נפשיה דרמי בר חמא אלא דלא אזמין ארב מנשיא בר תחליפא והתניא אחרים אומרים אפי' קרא ושנה ולא שמש ת"ח הרי זה ע"ה שאני רב מנשיא בר תחליפא דמשמע להו לרבנן ורמי בר חמא הוא דלא דק אבתריה ל"א דשמע שמעתתא מפומייהו דרבנן וגרים להו כצורבא מרבנן דמי: אכל טבל ומעשר וכו': טבל פשיטא לא צריכא בטבל טבול מדרבנן ה"ד בעציץ שאינו נקוב: מעשר ראשון וכו': פשיטא לא צריכא כגון שהקדימו בכרי מהו דתימא כדאמר ליה רב פפא לאביי קמ"ל כדשני ליה: מעשר שני וכו': פשיטא לא צריכא שנפדו ולא נפדו כהלכתן מעשר שני כגון שפדאו על גבי אסימון ורחמנא אמר °וצרת הכסף בידך *כסף שיש לו עליו צורה הקדש שחללו על גבי קרקע ולא פדאו בכסף ורחמנא אמר *°ונתן הכסף וקם לו: והשמש שאכל פחות מכזית: פשיטא איידי דתני רישא כזית תנא סיפא פחות מכזית: והנכרי אין מזמנין עליו: פשיטא הכא במאי עסקינן *בגר שמל ולא טבל *דאמר רבי זירא א"ר יוחנן *לעולם אינו גר עד שימול ויטבול וכמה דלא טבל נכרי הוא: נשים ועבדים וקטנים אין מזמנין עליהן: אמר רבי *יוסי קטן המוטל בעריסה מזמנין עליו והא תנן נשים ועבדים וקטנים אין מזמנין עליהם הוא דאמר כרבי יהושע בן לוי דאמר ריב"ל אע"פ שאמרו קטן המוטל בעריסה אין מזמנין עליו אבל עושין אותו סניף לעשרה ואמר ריב"ל תשעה ועבד מצטרפין מיתיבי *מעשה ברבי אליעזר שנכנס לבית הכנסת ולא מצא עשרה ושחרר עבדו והשלימו לעשרה שחרר אין לא שחרר לא תרי אצטריכו שחרר חד ונפיק בחד והיכי עביד הכי והאמר רב יהודה *כל המשחרר עבדו עובר בעשה שנאמר °לעולם בהם תעבודו לדבר מצוה שאני *מצוה הבאה בעבירה היא מצוה דרבים שאני ואמר ריב"ל *לעולם ישכים אדם לבית הכנסת כדי שיזכה וימנה עם עשרה הראשונים שאפי' מאה באים אחריו קבל עליו שכר כולם *שכר כולם סלקא דעתך אלא אימא נותנין לו שכר כנגד כולם אמר רב הונא תשעה וארון מצטרפין א"ל רב נחמן וארון גברא הוא אלא אמר רב הונא תשעה נראין כעשרה מצטרפין אמרי לה כי מכנפי ואמרי לה כי מבדרי אמר ר' אמי שנים ושבת מצטרפין אמר ליה רב נחמן ושבת גבר' הוא אלא אמר ר' אמי שני ת"ח המחדדין זה את זה בהלכה מצטרפין מחוי רב חסדא כגון אנא ורב ששת מחוי רב ששת כגון אנא ורב חסדא א"ר יוחנן קטן פורח מזמנין עליו תנ"ה קטן שהביא שתי שערות מזמנין עליו ושלא הביא שתי שערות אין מזמנין עליו ואין מדקדקין בקטן הא גופא קשיא אמרת הביא אין לא הביא לא והדר תני אין מדקדקין בקטן לאתויי מאי לאו לאתויי

במדבר יח | דברים יד | ויקרא כז

מכל מעשרותיכם. בפרשת לוים כתיב ואל הלוים תדבר וכתיב בההיא קרא את כל תרומת ה' כל לך תרומה שבו חייבים להפריש ממנו: האי אידגן. משעה שנתמרח בכרי נעשה דגן וכיון דאיקרי דגן חלה עליו רשות כהן תחל' דכתיב ראשית דגנך תתן לו אבל בשבלי' לא אידגן ולא חלה עליו רשו' כהן: מעשר שני והקדש. אם הבעלים פודין אותו מוסיפין חומש: לא קבע. אין לו קביעות לפי שהולך ובא: והכא בע"ה דרבנן. ברייתא דקתני אין מזמנין על ע"ה בע"ה דרבנן: דפליגי עליה דר"מ. וקאמרי כשאינו מעשר פירותיו הלכך כותי מזמנין עליו דעשורי מעשר: איזהו ע"ה. שדברו חכמים בכל מקום: שלא שמש ת"ח. הוא הגמר' התלויה בסברא שהיו נותנים לדברי משנה טעם והיו מתאספים יחד ועוסקים בכך והיא דוגמת הגמרא שסדרו האמוראים: רמי בר חמא לא אזמין עליה. לא רצה לצרפו לשלשה לזמון: דמישמע. משמש: ורמי בר חמא הוא דלא דק. לא בדק לשאול מדת רב מנשיא: שלא נטלה תרומתו. קס"ד תרומת מעשר קאמר: פשיטא. דאין מזמנין דהיינו טבל: שהקדימו בכרי. לאחר שנתמרח והוקבע לתרומה מן התורה קדם לוי את הכהן ונטל מעשר ראשון תחלה ואחד מכ' שבו היה ראוי לתרומה גדולה לכהן ושלא ניטלה תרומתו דקתני לאו תרומת מעשר קאמר אלא תרומה גדולה: מהו דתימא כדאמ' ליה רב פפא לאביי. לעיל אי הכי אפילו הקדימו בכרי נמי קמ"ל: אסימון. כסף שלא נקבע בו צורה וקורין לו פלזו"ן בלע"ז: עד שימול ויטבול. ביבמות (דף מו:) נפקא לן מויקח משה את הדם ויזרוק על העם ואין הזאה בלא טבילה: סניף. חבור לזימון עשרה וכי אמר רב אסי נמי לעשרה קאמר: מצוה דרבים. להוציא רבים ידי חובתם לקדושה: תשעה נראין כעשרה. מפרש ואזיל לה: אמרי לה כי מכנפי. הוו כלאי' כעשרה שאין אדם מבחין בהן כל כך מתוך שהן יחד: ואמרי לה כי מבדרי. כלאין עפי מרובין: שני תלמידי חכמים המחדדין זה את זה בהלכה מצטרפין. להיות שלשה: קטן פורח. שהביא סימנים ולא בא לכלל שניו: לאתויי

מסורת הש"ס

[מתנותיכם כל"ל ע' תוס' עירובין לא: סוף ד"ה ומה וכן איתא על נכון בשב' קכ: וכן ברש"י במדבר י"ח פך"ה]

[גיטין סא. תוספתא ע"ז פ"ג]

[קדושין עו.] חולין ד. [גיטין י.] סוט' כב. ע"ש

שם [ע' תוס' לעיל ע: ד"ה אחרים]

[ב"מ נז. וע' תוס' שב' קכח. ד"ה וכתן]

יבמות מו:

[נ"ל רב אסי וכ"מ מפרש"י ד"ה סניף] גיטין לח:

גיטין שם ויקרא כה [סוכה ל. ב"ק צד.] [מגילה כג.]

(1) I.e., silver not turned into current coin. (2) Deut. XIV, 25. (3) Lev. XXVII, 19. The exact words of the text are: *He shall add the fifth part of the money of thy valuation unto it, and it shall be assured to him*; v. B.M. (Sonc. ed.) p. 321, n. 1. (4) For a congregational service which requires a minimum quorum of ten males over the age of thirteen.

(1) Lev. XXV, 46. V. Giṭ. 38*b*. (2) As in the case of R. Eliezer. (3) In which case the absence of one is not so noticeable. The Ark is probably mentioned as being a focal point which enables us to determine whether the worshippers are close together or scattered. (4) שבת is accordingly explained as an abbreviation for שונים בדברי תורה (two) who study the Law; v. Goldschmidt. (5) R. Shesheth and R. Ḥisda represented each a different type of scholar, the former's forte being an extensive knowledge of traditions, the latter's keen dialectical powers; v. 'Er. 67*a*. (6) I.e., before reaching the age of thirteen years and one day.

[47b] *Out of all your tithes ye shall offer.*[2] But still what reason have you [for including corn in the ear and not grain]?—One has been turned into corn the other has not.[3]

SECOND TITHE OR FOOD BELONGING TO THE SANCTUARY THAT HAS BEEN REDEEMED. This is obvious!—We are dealing here with a case where, for instance, he has given the principal but not the additional fifth;[4] and he teaches us here that the fact that the fifth has not been given is no obstacle.[5]

OR IF AN ATTENDANT WHO HAS EATEN AS MUCH AS AN OLIVE etc. This is obvious!—You might object that the attendant does not sit through the meal.[6] This teaches, therefore, [that this is no objection].

A CUTHEAN MAY BE INCLUDED [IN THE THREE]. Why so? Wherein is he better than an *'am ha-areẓ*, and it has been taught: An *'am ha-areẓ* is not reckoned in for *zimmun?*—Abaye replied: It refers to a Cuthean who is a *ḥaber*. Raba said: You may even take it to refer to a Cuthean who is an *'am ha-areẓ*, the passage cited referring to an *'am ha-areẓ* as defined by the Rabbis who join issue in this matter with R. Meir. For it has been taught: Who is an *'am ha-areẓ?* Anyone who does not eat non-sacred food in ritual cleanness. So R. Meir. The Rabbis, however, say: Anyone who does not tithe his produce in the proper way. Now these Cutheans do tithe their produce in the proper way, since they are very scrupulous about any injunction written in the Torah; for a Master has said: Whenever the Cutheans have adopted a *miẓwah*, they are much more particular with it than the Jews.[7]

Our Rabbis taught: Who is an *'am ha-areẓ?* Anyone who does not recite the *Shema'* evening and morning. This is the view of R. Eliezer. R. Joshua says: Anyone who does not put on *tefillin*. Ben 'Azzai says: Anyone who has not a fringe on his garment. R. Nathan says: Anyone who has not a *mezuzah* on his door. R. Nathan b. Joseph says: Anyone who has sons and does not bring them up to the study of the Torah. Others say: Even if one has learnt Scripture and Mishnah, if he has not ministered
a to the disciples of the wise,[1] he is an *'am ha-areẓ*. R. Huna said: The *halachah* is as laid down by 'Others'.

Rami b. Ḥama refused to count to *zimmun* R. Menashiah b. Taḥalifa who could repeat Sifra,[2] Sifre,[3] and *halachah*. When Rami b. Ḥama died, Raba said: Rami b. Ḥama died only because he would not count R. Menashiah b. Taḥalifa for *zimmun*. But it has been taught: Others say that even if one has learnt Scripture and Mishnah but has not ministered to the disciples of the wise, he is an *'am ha-areẓ?*—R. Menashiah b. Taḥalifa was different because he used to minister to the Rabbis, and it was Rami b. Ḥama who did not make proper inquiries about him. According to another version, he used to hear discussions from the mouth of the Rabbis and commit them to memory, and he was therefore like a Rabbinical scholar.

ONE WHO HAS EATEN ṬEBEL AND FIRST TITHE etc. In the case of *ṭebel* this is obvious!—It required to be stated for the case of that which is *ṭebel* only by the ordinance of the Rabbis. What for instance? Food grown in a pot without a hole in the bottom.[4]

FIRST TITHE etc. This is obvious!—It required to be stated for the case where [the Levite] anticipated [the priest] at the heap. You might think that the law is as indicated by R. Papa's question to Abaye;[5] this teaches that it is as indicated by the latter's answer.

SECOND TITHE etc. This is obvious!—It is required for the case in which the tithe etc., has been redeemed, but not properly redeemed. Second tithe, for instance, if it has been redeemed for
b bar silver,[1] since the All-Merciful said; *Thou shalt bind up* [*we-ẓarta*] *the silver in thy hands,*[2] implying, silver on which a form [*ẓurah*] is stamped. As to FOOD BELONGING TO THE SANCTUARY, if for instance it has been rendered profane for its equivalent in land but has not been redeemed for money, whereas the All-Merciful laid down, *He shall give the money and it shall be assured unto him.*[3]

OR THE ATTENDANT WHO HAS EATEN LESS THAN AN OLIVE. This is obvious!—Since the first clause states the rule for the quantity of an olive, the second clause states it for less than an olive.

A GENTILE MAY NOT BE COUNTED. This is obvious!—We are dealing here with the case of a proselyte who has been circumcised but has not yet made ablution. For R. Zera said in the name of R. Joḥanan: One does not become a proselyte until he has been circumcised and has performed ablution; and so long as he has not performed ablution he is a gentile.

WOMEN SLAVES AND CHILDREN ARE NOT COUNTED [IN THE THREE]. R. Jose said: An infant in the cradle may be counted for *zimmun*. But we have learnt: WOMEN SLAVES AND CHILDREN MAY NOT BE COUNTED?—He adopts the view of R. Joshua b. Levi. For R. Joshua b. Levi said: Although it was laid down that an infant in a cradle cannot be counted for *zimmun*, yet he can be counted to make up ten. R. Joshua b. Levi also said: Nine and a slave may be joined [to make up ten].[4]

The following was cited in objection: Once R. Eliezer entered a synagogue and not finding there ten he liberated his slave and used him to complete the ten. This was because he liberated him, otherwise he could not have done so?—He really required two, and he liberated one and one he used to make up the ten. But how could he act so seeing that Rab Judah has said: If one liberates his slave he transgresses a positive precept, since it says, *they shall*
c *be your bondmen for ever?*[1]—If it is for a religious purpose, it is different. But this is a religious act which is carried out by means of a transgression?—A religious act which affects a whole company[2] is different.

R. Joshua b. Levi also said: A man should always rise early to go to synagogue so that he may have the merit of being counted in the first ten; since if even a hundred come after him he receives the reward of all of them. 'The reward of all of them', say you?—Say rather: He is given a reward equal to that of all of them.

R. Huna said: Nine and the Ark join together [to be counted as ten]. Said R. Naḥman to him: Is the Ark a man? I mean, said R. Huna, that when nine look like ten, they may be joined together. Some say [this means] when they are all close together,[3] others say when they are scattered. R. Ammi said: Two and the Sabbath may be joined together. Said R. Naḥman to him: Is the Sabbath a man? What R. Ammi really said was that two scholars who sharpen one another in the knowledge of the *halachah* may count as three [for *zimmun*].[4] R. Ḥisda gave an example: For instance, I and R. Shesheth. R. Shesheth gave an example: For instance, I and R. Ḥisda.[5]

R. Joḥanan said: A boy [who has reached puberty] before his years[6] may be counted for *zimmun*. It has been taught similarly: A boy who has grown two hairs may be counted for *zimmun*, but if he has not grown two hairs he may not be counted; and we are not particular about a boy. Now this seems to contain a contradiction. You first say that if he has grown two hairs he may count and if not he may not, and then you say, We are not particular

(2) Num, XVIII, 29. The actual word in the text is *'gifts'*. (3) And it is only from what can be called 'corn' that *terumah* has to be given. (4) Required for the redemption of second tithe or anything belonging to the Sanctuary. (5) To render the redemption valid. (6) He has always to be getting up to wait on the guests.

(7) Hence a Cuthean may be reckoned in.

a (1) Rashi explains this to mean that he has not learnt Gemara, which explains the Mishnah. (2) The Midrash on Leviticus. (3) The Midrash on Deuteronomy. (4) So that the earth in it is not in contact with the soil. (5) V. *supra 46b ad fin.*

with a boy. What case does this include? Is it not [48*a*] to include a boy who shows signs of puberty before his years? The law, however, is not as laid down in all these statements, but as in this statement of R. Naḥman: A boy who knows to whom the benediction is addressed may be counted for *zimmun*. Abaye and Raba [when boys] were once sitting in the presence of Rabbah. Said Rabbah to them: To whom do we address the benedictions? They replied: To the All-Merciful. And where does the All-Merciful abide? Raba pointed to the roof; Abaye went outside and pointed to the sky. Said Rabbah to them: Both of you will become Rabbis. This accords with the popular saying: Every pumpkin can be told a from its stalk.[1]

Rab Judah the son of R. Samuel b. Shilath said in the name of Rab: If nine persons have eaten corn and one vegetables, they may combine.[2] R. Zera said: I asked Rab Judah, What of eight, what of seven,[3] and he replied: It makes no difference. Certainly if six [were eating corn][4] I did not need to ask. Said R. Jeremiah to him: You were quite right not to ask. What was the reason there [in the first case]? Because there is a majority [eating corn]; here too there is a majority. He, however, thought that perhaps an easily recognizable majority is required.[5]

King Jannai and his queen were taking a meal together. Now after he had put the Rabbis to death,[6] there was no-one to say grace for them. He said to his spouse: I wish we had someone to say grace for us. She said to him: Swear to me that if I bring you one you will not harm him. He swore to her, and she brought Simeon b. Shetah, her brother.[7] She placed him between her husband and herself, saying, See what honour I pay you. He replied: It is not you who honour me but it is the Torah which b honours me, as it is written, *Exalt her and she shall promote thee,*[1] [*she shall bring thee to honour when thou dost embrace her*].[2] He [Jannai] said to her: You see that he[3] does not acknowledge any authority![4] They gave him a cup of wine to say grace over.[5] He said: How shall I say the grace? [Shall I say] Blessed is He of whose sustenance Jannai and his companions have eaten? So he drank that cup, and they gave him another and he said grace over it. R. Abba the son of R. Ḥiyya b. Abba said: Simeon b. Shetah in acting thus[6] followed his own view. For thus said R. Ḥiyya b. Abba in the name of Johanan: A man cannot say grace on behalf of others until he has eaten at least the size of an olive of corn food with them. Even as it was taught:[7] R. Simeon b. Gamaliel says: If one went up [on the couch] and reclined with them, even though he only dipped [a little bit] with them in brine and ate only one fig with them, he can be combined with them [for *zimmun*]. Now he can be combined with them, but he cannot say grace on behalf of others until he eats the quantity of an olive of corn food. It has also been stated: R. Hanah b. Judah said in the name of Raba: [48*b*]

a (1) Var. lec. from its sap; i.e., as soon as it begins to emerge from the stalk. (2) To say the *zimmun* formula for ten, v. next Mishnah. (3) Who ate corn while two or three ate vegetables. (4) *Aliter:* If six were eating corn and four vegetables (omitting 'certainly'). Rashi's reading (which is found also in Ber. Rab. XCI) is: I am sorry I did not ask what is the rule if six eat (corn). This accords better with what follows. (5) And even if he were to permit in the first case, he would not permit in the case of six. (6) V. Ḳid. (Sonc. ed.) pp. 332ff. notes. (7) Who was a Pharisaic leader and had been in hiding.

b (1) Prov. IV, 8. (2) Cf. Ecclus. XI, 1. (3) Simeon b. Shetah. (4) So according to some edd. Cur. edd.: He said to him, See how they (i.e., the Pharisees) do not accept my authority! His reply to the king was regarded by Jannai as an affront and evidence of the Pharisees' hostility to the throne. (5) Though he had not joined in the meal. (6) In saying grace without having eaten anything. (7) So BaḤ. Cur. edd.: An objection was raised.

לאתויי קטן פורח ולית הלכתא ככל הני שמעתתא אלא כי הא *דאמר רב נחמן ^א^קטן היודע למי מברכין מזמנין עליו אביי ורבא הוו יתבי קמיה דרבה אמר להו רבה למי מברכין אמרי ליה לרחמנא ורחמנא היכא יתיב רבא אחוי לשמי טללא אביי נפק לברא אחוי כלפי שמיא אמר להו רבה תרוייכו רבנן הויתו היינו דאמרי אינשי *בוצין בוצין מקטפיה ידיע א"ר יהודה בריה דרב שמואל בר שילת משמיה דרב ^ב^תשעה אכלו דגן ואחד אכל ירק מצטרפין א"ר זירא בעאי מיניה מרב יהודה שמונה מהו שבעה מהו ^ג^א"ל לא שנא ששה *ודאי לא מבעיא לי א"ל ר' ירמיה שפיר עבדת דלא אבעית לך התם טעמא מאי משום דאיכא רובא הכא נמי איכא רובא ואיהו סבר *רובא דמינכר בעינן ינאי מלכא ומלכתא כריכו ריפתא בהדי הדדי ומדקטל להו לרבנן לא הוה ליה איניש לברוכי להו אמר לה לדביתהו מאן יהיב לן גברא *דמברך לן אמרה ליה אשתבע לי דאי מייתינא לך גברא דלא מצערת ליה אשתבע לה אייתיתיה לשמעון בן שטח אחוה אותביה בין דידיה לדידה א"ל חזית כמה יקרא עבדינא לך א"ל לאו את קא מוקרת לי אלא אורייתא היא דמיקרא לי *דכתיב °סלסלה ותרוממך *תכבדך כי תחבקנה א"ל קא חזית דלא מקבלי מרות יהבו ליה כסא לברוכי אמר היכי אבריך ברוך שאכל ינאי וחביריו משלו שתיי' להדוא כסא יהבו ליה כסא אחרינא ובריך א"ר אבא בריה דרבי חייא בר אבא (*א"ר יוחנן) שמעון בן שטח *דעבד לגרמיה הוא דעבד דהכי א"ר חייא בר אבא א"ר יוחנן לעולם אינו מוציא את הרבים ידי חובתן עד שיאכל כזית דגן מיתיבי רבן שמעון בן גמליאל אומר עלה והיסב עמהם ^ה^אפילו לא טבל עמהם אלא בציר ולא אכל עמהם אלא גרוגרת אחת מצטרף אצטרופי מצטרף אבל ^ו^להוציא את הרבים ידי חובתן עד שיאכל כזית דגן אתמר נמי א"ר חנא בר יהודה משמיה דרבא אפילו לא טבל

רש"י

לאתויי קטן פורח. שאין מדקדקין בו אם בא לכלל שנים או לאו ומה הן שנים י"ג שנים ויום א': **טללא.** גג: **בוצין.** דלעת: **מקטפיה.** מקטנותו: ואית דגרסי מקטפיה וקטף הוא שרף האילן כלומר משעה שהוא חונט ויוצא מתוך השרף ניכר אם יהיה טוב: **ואידהו סבר.** ר' זירא שהי' קובל ומתרעם על שלא שאל על השתא סבר דלמ' רובא דמינכר שפיר בעינן דליכול דגן ואי בעי מיניה השתא לא היה מתיר: **ינאי מלכא.** ממלכי בית חשמונאי היה והרג חכמי ישראל שבאו לפסלו מן הכהונה במסכ' קידושין (דף סו.): **סלסלה ותרוממך.** סיפיה דקרא תכבדך כי תחבקנה: **היכי אבריך.** ולא כהכתי אומר כברך שאכל ינאי וחבריו משלו בתמי': **שמעון בן שטח דעבד.** שבירך להוציאם ידי חובתם בשביל כוס אחד ששת': **לגרמיה הוא דעבד.** אין אדם מודה לו: **עד שיאכל כזית דגן.** ומכי אכל כזית דגן מיהא מפיק אע"ג דכזית דגן שיעורא דרבנן הוא כדאמר בפרק מי שמתו (דף כ:) מיהו כיון דמחייב מדרבנן מחוייב בדבר קרינן ביה ומוצי' רבים ידי חובתן וא"ת בקטן שהגיע לחינוך הא לא אמר הכי ההוא אפי' מדרבנן לא מחייב עליה דאבוה הוא דרמי לחנוכי' ובעל ה"ג פסק דוקא דאכלו איכהו כזית או כביצה דכותיה אבל אכלו ושבעו לא מפיק ואי אפשר להעמידה דהא ינאי וחבריו אכלו ושבעו ואפקינהו שמעון בן שטח ואף על גב דלגרמיה הוא דעבד טעמא משום דלא אכל כזית דגן הא אכל כזית דגן הכי נמי: ובשבת

תוספות

ולית הלכתא ככל הני שמעתתא אלא כי הא קטן היודע. משמע דקאי נמי אר' יוחנן ולא נהירא שהרי אין דרך הגמרא שסותר דברי אמוראים והברייתא שהביא ראיה לדברי ר' יוחנן בלא שום טעם וי"ל דקאי אקטן פורח כלומר קטן פורח מזמנין עליו היינו דוקא היודע למי מברכין ותרוייהו בעינן. ולפירושינו נ"ל דלא מייתי עובדא דאביי ורבא לענין אזמוני עלייהו אלא לפרש מהו קטן היודע למי מברכין דמסתמ' לא פורחים הוו דאם כן מהו רבותייהו אם יודעים למי מברכין ורבה נמי דעבד היינו להראו' שיש בהם בינה והם קטני' ולא מזמנין עלייהו ואו' ר"ת אע"פ דלית הלכתא ככל הני שמעתתא מיהו הלכה כריב"ל דאמ' קטן ממש עושין אותו סניף לעשרה והכא דבעי פורח ויודע היינו דוקא בשלש' ולית הלכת' ככל הני שמעתת' לא קאי אריב"ל ודיקא נמי שהרי מפסיק הגמר' בינתיים באותו מעש' [דר"א] ודלעול' ישכים אדם ותני' כותיה אלא קאי אהני שמעתת' דבתר תני' כותיה דישנים כגון ט' וארון ושבת ושני' ותשע' כראין כעשר' ושני' מחדדין וקטן פורח אע"ג דתני' ברייתא הכי לאתויי פורח יעמידנ' רב נחמן באינו יודע למי מברכי' והיינו נמי כריב"ל דאמר לעיל קטן אין מזמנין עליו פירוש מוטל בעריסה עד שידע למי מברכין אבל עושין אותו סניף לעשר' פי' לברכת המזון וה"ה לתפל' דבהא לא פליג רב נחמן דכי בעי יודע או פורח כדפי' ה"מ לזימון שלש' אבל לסניף מודה לריב"ל דסניף ליו"ד והוא הדין לתפלה דקטן מצטרף ודיק' נמי דפריך עלה ממעשה דר"א שהיה לתפל' לריב"ל דמיירי בב"ה ומיהו תימה דבב"ר (פר' לח) קאמר עלה דריב"ל הדא הוא דתימא לב"ה אבל לתפלה לא והיה אומר ר"ת דאין הלכה כן לפי שחולק על הגמר' שלנו דודאי ריב"ל לענין תפלה נמי קאמר ומדפריך ממעובד' דרבי אליעזר דמיירי בתפלה ויש מכלפין קטן לתפלה רק שיהא חומש בידו ואומר ר"ת דמנהג שטות הוא דכי היכי דאמר אטו אכן גברא הוא הכי נמי אטו חומש גבר' הוא ועוד הא דקאמר קטן מצטרף היינו אפי' בלא חומש ועוד דלא חזינן בשום דוכת' דמהני אלא בעובדא דעבור השנה כשעולין בעליה בפירקין דר' אליעזר (פרק ח) דקאמר בג' מעברין את השנה רבי אליעזר אומר בעשרה ואם נתמעטו מביאין ס"ת ועושין עגולה וכו' ואין מזכיר שם שיהא הקטן אוחז הס"ת והתם נמי לא קאמר אלא ספר תורה העשוי בגליון אבל חומשין שלנו לא ומיהו קאמר בירושלמי אמר ר' יוסי זמנין אכלית עם ר' חלפתא אבא ועם ר' חנינא בר סיסי חבירי ולא מזמנין עלוי עד שהבאתי שתי שערות ומשם משמע דלהצטרף לזימון לא עבדינן עובדא עד שיביא שתי שערו' הא לתפלה עבדי ומתוך ירושלמי זה פר"י דאין עושין קטן סניף לעשרה לא לתפלה ולא לברכת המזון וגם היה אומר ר"י שגם ר"ת עצמו לא היה נוהג לעשות כן לעשות קטן סניף לעשרה וכן עשה מעשה והלכך אפילו חומש בידו לא מהני כדפירשנו כאן דלא אתהני קטן לבדו גם חומש בידו לא אתהני ומיהו *קטן פורח ויודע למי שמברכין משמע שמברכין עליו גם בשלשה כברייתא וליכא מאן דפליג וזה לשון רבינו שפוסק מסקנא דמלתא אין עושין קטן סניף לעשרה לזמון ולתפלה ולשלשה עד שיביא שתי שערות כעובדא דרבי יוסי ברבי חלפתא בירושלמי והא דאמרינן בירושלמי קטן וספר תורה עושין אותו סניף אומר ר"י דגרס התם קטן לספר תורה כלומר סניף לקריאת התורה קאמר ודוקא התם במגילה (פ"ג דף כג.) דקטן עולה למנין שבעה דקאמר הכל עולין למנין שבעה אפילו קטן ואפילו אשה אי לא הוה משום כבוד צבור אבל לשאר דברי' לא ואפילו אם אשכחינן בשום דוכתא דקטן ואפילו לתפלה היינו דוקא העשוי בגליון אבל חומשין שלנו לא לפירוש ר"ת חומש אינו מועיל כלל ביד קטן אבל קטן לחוד הוי סניף אבל תרי לא כדקאמר גבי עובדא דר' אליעזר ור"ת פירש דהסיא דירושלמי דר' יוסי ברבי חלפתא דוקא בשלשה מיירי: **אביי** ורבא הוו יתבי וכו'. וא"ת היכי דמי אי הוו קטנים פורחים מאי רבותא הוה בהו שהבינו כלפי מעלה אלא צריך לומר דהאי לאו לאזמוני עלייהו קא מכוין להו כי היו קטנים טובא אלא לנסותינהו קא עביד שהיה בהם בינה:

תשעה שאכלו דגן ואחד ירק מצטרפין. והכי הלכתא שאם אכל ירק או שתה כוס יין מצטרף ואפי' כברך שאכלנו יכולין לומ' שהרי שתי' בכלל אכיל' ויש שרוצי' לומר דהיינו דוקא לזמון עשרה אבל לשלשה לא מצטרפי דהרי לעיל נמי מחמרינן טפי בצירוף שלשה מעשרה ומיהו בירושלמי תני שנים שאכלו פת ואחד ירק מזמנין וכן פסק ר"י בתוספת' והשר מקוצי מפרש דאין הלכ' כאות' ברייתא דירושלמי חדא שהרי מסיק עלה התם מתני' כרשב"ג כלומ' ורבנן פליגי דלא מצטרפי ואין הלכה כיחיד ועוד דא"כ קשה דר' יוחנן אדר' יוחנן דהכא א"ר יוחנן לעולם אינו מוציא עד שיאכל כזית דגן הא מצטרף שפיר אפי' לא טעם אלא שתיה כעובדא דר"ש בן שטח ובירושלמי קא"ר יוחנן לעולם אין מזמנין עד שיאכל כזית ומשמ' אפי' מצטרף אלא שמע מינה כאן לעשרה ובירושלמי איירי בזמון שלשה ולהשלים לעשרה אפי' איכא שנים ושלשה ששתו מצטרפין ושתיה בכלל אכילה ולא קפדינן אלא ארוב' דמנכר: **עד** שיאכל כזית דגן. משמע שאם אכל כזית דגן שיכול להוציא אף אחרי' שאכלו כל השובע ותימ' והרי כזית אינו חייב אלא מדרבנן והיכי אתי מדרבנן ופטר דאורייתא דהא אמרי' בפרק מי שמתו (דף כ ע"ב) תבא מארה למי שאשתו ובניו מברכי' לו ולא מלי לאוקומי [הא] דשרו לקטן שיכול להוצי' אביו אלא בדאכל אביו כזי' דאתי קטן דרבנן שהגיע לחינוך ופטר אביו שאינו חייב אלא מדרבנן הא אם אכל אביו כדי שביע' אינו יכול לפטרו ופרש"י דמחוייב דרבנן מחוייב קרינן ביה אבל קטן

מסורת הש"ס

[ערכין ג.]

[גי' הערוך בלין מקריה ידיעי ע"ש ומלאתי בתו' דסוכה כו: ד"ה בולינא דגרס' בולינא מקטפי' ידיע]

[ע"ז לז:]

[ע' תוס' פסחים קג: ד"ה כיון]

(בירו' אי' א"ל בס' בן סירא כתי' תסלסלה וגו' ובין נגידים תושיבך)

[ג' היינו הללו ככא' דטעות הדפוס הוא]

[שבת לח: מ"ק כד: סנהדרין יד:]

[קטן כפי' ר"ת ויודע כל"נ]

תורה אור

משלי ד

עין משפט נר מצוה

נ א מיי' פרק ה מהל' ברכות הלכה ז סמג עשין כז טוש"ע א"ח סי' קצט סעיף י

נא ב מיי' שם הלכה ח וסמג שם טוש"ע א"ח סימן קצז סעיף ב

נב ג מיי' שם הל' טו טז טוש"ע א"ח שם סעיף ד

*תיב' ודאי הוא כ"ת וד' אוכלין ירק (כ"מ) ויש גורסי' וי דא וכ"ה בילקוט ובזה א"ש דברי רש"י ד"ה ואיהו

[לפמ"ש מהרש"א בח"א אין זה בכוונת הגמ' אלא רש"י מפרש ע"פ סיפא דקרא ע"ש וע' תוס' ערובין סה. ד"ה בלר וכו' מ"ש בשם הירושלמי וע"ע תו' ב"ק לב: ד"ה משולם]

תורה אור

טבל עמהם אלא בציר ולא אכל עמהם אלא גרוגרת אחת מצטרף ולהוציא את הרבים ידי חובתם אינו מוציא עד שיאכל כזית דגן אמר רב חנא בר יהודה משמיה דרבא הלכתא אכל עלה ירק ושתה כוס של יין מצטרף להוציא אינו מוציא עד שיאכל כזית דגן אמר רב נחמן "משה תקן לישראל ברכת הזן בשעה שירד להם מן יהושע תקן להם ברכת הארץ כיון שנכנסו לארץ דוד ושלמה תקנו בונה ירושלים דוד תקן על ישראל עמך ועל ירושלים עירך ושלמה תקן על הבית הגדול והקדוש הטוב והמטיב ביבנה תקנוה כנגד הרוגי ביתר דאמר רב מתנא *אותו היום שניתנו הרוגי ביתר לקבורה תקנו ביבנה הטוב והמטיב הטוב שלא הסריחו והמטיב שניתנו לקבורה: ת"ר "סדר ברכת המזון כך היא ברכה ראשונה ברכת הזן שניה ברכת הארץ שלישית בונה ירושלים רביעית הטוב והמטיב "ובשבת מתחיל בנחמה ומסיים בנחמה ואומר קדושת היום באמצע ר"א אומר רצה לאומרה בנחמה אומרה בברכת הארץ אומרה בברכה שתקנו חכמים ביבנה אומרה וחכמים אומרים אינו אומרה אלא בנחמה בלבד חכמים היינו תנא קמא איכא בינייהו דיעבד: *תנו רבנן מנין לברכת המזון מן התורה שנאמר °ואכלת ושבעת וברכת *זו "ברכת הזן את יי' אלהיך זו ברכת הזימון על הארץ זו ברכת הארץ הטובה זו בונה ירושלים וכן הוא אומר °ההר הטוב הזה והלבנון אשר נתן לך זו הטוב והמטיב אין לי אלא לאחריו לפניו מנין אמרת קל וחומר *כשהוא שבע מברך כשהוא רעב לא כל שכן *רבי אומר [אינו צריך] ואכלת ושבעת וברכת זו ברכת הזן אבל ברכת הזימון °מגדלו ליי' אתי נפקא על הארץ זו ברכת הארץ הטובה זו בונה ירושלים וכן הוא אומר ההר הטוב הזה והלבנון הטוב והמטיב ביבנה תקנוה אין לי אלא לאחריו לפניו מנין תלמוד לומר אשר נתן לך משנתן לך ר' *יצחק אומר אינו צריך הרי הוא אומר °וברך את לחמך ואת מימיך אל תקרי ובירך אלא וברך ואימתי קרוי לחם קודם שיאכלנו ר' נתן אומר אינו צריך הרי הוא אומר °כבואכם העיר כן תמצאון אותו בטרם יעלה הבמתה לאכול כי לא יאכל העם עד בואו כי הוא יברך הזבח אחרי כן יאכלו הקרואים וכל כך למה לפי שהנשים דברניות הן ושמואל אמר כדי להסתכל ביפיו של שאול דכתיב °משכמו ומעלה גבוה מכל העם ור' יוחנן אמר לפי שאין מלכות נוגעת בחברתה אפילו כמלא *נימא ואין לי אלא ברכת המזון ברכת התורה מנין *א"ר ישמעאל קל וחומר על חיי שעה מברך על חיי עולם הבא לא כל שכן רבי חייא בר נחמני תלמידו של רבי ישמעאל אומר משום רבי ישמעאל אינו צריך הרי הוא אומר °על הארץ הטובה אשר נתן לך ולהלן הוא אומר °ואתנה לך את לוחות האבן והתורה והמצוה וגומר רבי מאיר אומר *מנין שכשם שמברך על הטובה כך מברך על הרעה תלמוד לומר אשר נתן לך יי' אלהיך דיינך בכל דין שדנך בין מדה טובה ובין מדה פורענות ר' יהודה בן בתירה אומר אינו צריך הרי הוא אומר טובה הטובה *טובה זו תורה וכן הוא אומר °כי לקח טוב נתתי לכם הטובה זו בנין ירושלים וכן הוא אומר ההר הטוב הזה והלבנון תניא רבי אליעזר אומר "כל שלא אמר ארץ חמדה טובה ורחבה בברכת הארץ ומלכות בית דוד בבונה ירושלים לא יצא ידי חובתו נחום הזקן אומר צריך שיזכור בה ברית רבי יוסי אומר צריך שיזכור בה תורה פלימו אומר "צריך שיקדים ברית לתורה שזו נתנה בשלש בריתות

רזו

ובשבת מתחיל בנחמה. כלומר אינו צריך לא לסיים ולא להתחיל בשל שבת אלא מתחיל ומסיים בנחמה. דבנין ירושלים קרי נחמה כל היכי דמתחיל בין רחם בין נחמנו: בברכה שתקנו חכמי'. בהטוב והמטיב: איכא בינייהו דיעבד. לרבנן בתראי מהדרי' ליה: בדתני' קמא גרסינן אשר נתן לך זו הטוב והמטיב ולא גרסינן ביבנה תקנוה אלא בדרבי: כשהוא שבע. מלוה לברך ולהודות על שבעו: כשהוא רעב. והוא בא להפיק את רעבו על ידי ברייתו של הקדוש ברוך הוא לא כל שכן שזה צריך לברך להקדוש ברוך הוא יותר: אינו צריך. לקל וחומ' זה ולא גרסינן בדרבי אשר נתן לך זה הטוב והמטיב: אלא וברך את לחמך. ברך על לחמך: כי הוא יברך הזבח אחרי כן יאכלו הקרואים. למדך שטעון לברך לפני אכילה על הזבח הוא אומר ברוך אשר קדשנו במצותיו וצונו לאכול את הזבח והיכן צונו והבשר תאכל (דברים יב): כל כך למה. היו מאריכות בדבריהן: שאין מלכות נוגע' בחברתה. לפי ששמואל היה מנהיג את ישראל ושאול היה נוטל את השררה ומדב' שמואל אליו ואורך דברי' עכב לפי שעה: בין מדה טובה. והתפיל' מדה טוב' היא: ומלכו' בית דוד בבונה ירושלים. שעל ידו נתקדשה ירושלי': וצריך שיזכור ברית. בברכת הארץ שעל ידי ברית נתנה לאברהם בפרשת מילה (בראשית יז) ונתתי לך ולזרעך אחריך את ארץ מגוריך: וצריך שיזכור בה תור'. שאף בזכות התור' והמצות ירשו את הארץ שנאמר למען תחיון ורביתם ובאתם וירשתם את הארץ (דברי' ח): וצריך שיקדים ברית לתורה. כגון על בריתך שחתמת בבשרנו ועל תורתך שלמדתנו ועל חיים שחוננתנו: תורה נתנה בשלש בריתות. בשלשה מקומות ניתנה התורה לישראל בסיני באהל מועד ובהר גריזים ובערבות מואב ובכל אחד נכרתה ברית כדתניא במסכ' סוטה (פ"ז דף לז.) ארור בכלל וארור בפרט וכו' וכן באהל מועד שנאמר (דברים כח) אלה דברי הברית אשר צוה ה' את משה לכרות את בני ישראל בארץ מואב מלבד הברית אשר כרת את' בחורב וכתי' (שם כט) ושמרתם את דברי הברית וגומר: מילה

קטן שהגיע לחינוך לא מיקרי מחוייב דרבנן דאביו חייב לחנכו אבל עליו אין שום חיוב וקשה לפירושו מכל מקום כיון שאינו מן התורה אינו מוציא אחרי' שמחוייבים ועוד דוחק לומר בקטן שהגיע לחינוך קרי אינו מחוייב מדרבנן דאם אינו מחוייב אפי' מדרבנן אם כן אינו פוטר את אביו ובה"ג פירש דאחד שאכל כזית אינו יכול להוציא אחרי' שאכלו כדי שביעה דלא אתי דרבנן ופטר דאורייתא' אבל כשלא אכלו גם האחרים רק כזית פוטר אותם ולא היא דהא שמעי' אעובד' דינאי וחבריו והם אכלו כדי שביעה ואפילו הכי קא חזינן דקא פטר להו שמעון בן שטח אלא נראה לחלק דקטן שאינו בר חיוב כלל דאורייתא' אפי' אכל כדי שביעה הלכך אינו מחוייב בדבר קרינן ביה ולכך לא מפיק ליה אי אכל שיעור' דאורייתא' אבל גדול שהו' בר חיובא מן התורה כי אכיל כדי שביע' מחוייב בדבר קרינן ביה אפי' לא אכל כלל כדאמרינן בראש השנה (פ"ג דף כט.) כל הברכות אף על גב שיצא מוציא חוץ מברכת הלחם וברכת היין והיינו טעמ' דכל ישראל ערבין זה בזה והוא הדין בברכת המזון אף ע"פ שיצא מוציא כדפרי' וכזית דגן אינו צריך אלא שיכול לומר שאכלנו משלו:

מתחיל בנחמה. פירש הקונ' לאו דוק' מתחיל בנחמ' ומסיי' אלא כלומר דאין צריך להזכיר של שבת לא בפתיחה ולא בנחמ' אלא באמצע אבל מתחיל ומסיים בנחמת ירושלים כמו בחול שאומר רחם וחותם בבונה ירושלי' ויש שמתחילין בנחמנו וחותמים בנחמת ציון עירו ובבנין ירושלי' ונותני' טעם לדבריהם דרחם הוי לשון תחנה ואין אומר תחנונים בשבת אבל נחם אינו לשון תחנוני' אלא כמו והנחם על הרעה לעמך (שמות לב) ולא נהירא דהכל משמע לשון תחנונים ואין להקפיד אפילו אי הוי לשון בקשה כדאמר בירושלמי דשבת בפרק אלו קשרים מהו לומר רוענו זוננו פרנסנו בשבת אמ' ליה טופס ברכות כך הוא ומנהג שטות הוא המשנה ברכה של חול:

ברית ותורה. אין צריך להזכי' ברית ותורה וחיים ומזון דדי להזכיר על בריתך שחתמת בבשרנו ועל תורתך שלמדתנו וכו' דהיינו ברית ותור' והגמר' לסימנא בעלמא נקטיה: מאן

עין משפט נר מצוה

נג א מיי' פ"ב מה' ברכות הל' א סמג עשין כז טוש"ע א"ח סי' קפז קפח

נד ב מיי' שם הל' ה וסמג שם טוש"ע א"ח סי' קפח סעיף ד ה

נה ד מיי' שם הל' ג סמג שם טור א"ח סי' קפז

[יתכן להיות זו ברכ' הזימון את ד' אלקיך זו ברכת הזן וכן העתיקו תו' לעיל מו. ד"ה עד היכן]

[שבת ל. מ"ק כח. יומ' לח:]

מסורת הש"ס

תעניות לא. ב"ב קכא:

מכילתא פ' בא [תוספת' פ"ו ע"ש לעיל דף.] (בירוש' גרס זו ברכת הזימון)

דברי' ח

שם ג

[לעיל לה.] (בירוש' גרס ר"ע ע"ש במפרש)

תלים לד

(ירוש' גרס ר' נחמי' במקום ר"י ור' יהודה במקום ר' נתן)

שמות כג

שמואל א ט

שם

[תעני' ה:]

דברים ח

שמות כד

לקמן כד.

[לעיל ה. וש"נ] משלי ד

Even though he only dipped [a little bit] with them in brine or ate with them only one fig, he can be combined with them; but for saying grace on behalf of others he is not qualified until he eats the quantity of an olive of corn food with them. R. Ḥanah b. Judah said in the name of Raba: The law is that if he ate with them a vegetable-leaf and drank a cup of wine, he can be combined; but he cannot say grace on behalf of others until he eats with them the quantity of an olive of corn food.

R. Naḥman said: Moses instituted for Israel the benediction 'Who feeds'[8] at the time when manna descended for them. Joshua
a instituted for them the benediction of the land[1] when they entered the land. David and Solomon instituted the benediction which closes 'Who buildest Jerusalem'.[2] David instituted the words, 'For Israel Thy people and for Jerusalem Thy city',[3] and Solomon instituted the words 'For the great and holy House'.[3] The benediction 'Who is good and bestows good'[4] was instituted in Jabneh with reference to those who were slain in Bethar. For R. Mattena said: On the day on which permission was given to bury those slain in Bethar,[5] they ordained in Jabneh that 'Who is good and bestows good' should be said: 'Who is good', because they did not putrefy, and 'Who bestows good', because they were allowed to be buried.

Our Rabbis taught: The order of grace after meals is as follows. The first benediction is that of 'Who feeds'. The second is the benediction of the land. The third is 'Who buildest Jerusalem'. The fourth is 'Who is good and bestows good'. On Sabbath [the third blessing] commences with consolation and closes with consolation,[6] and the holiness of the day is mentioned in the middle [of this blessing]. R. Eliezer says: If he likes he can mention it in the consolation, or he can mention it in the blessing of the land,[7] or he can mention it in the benediction which the Rabbis instituted in Jabneh.[8] The Sages, however, say that it must be said in the consolation blessing. The Sages say the same thing as the First Tanna?—They differ in the case where he actually did say it [in some other place].[9]

Our Rabbis taught: Where is the saying of grace intimated in the Torah? In the verse, *And thou shalt eat and be satisfied and bless:*[10] this signifies the benediction of 'Who feeds'.[11] *'The Lord Thy God':*
b this signifies the benediction of *zimmun*.[1] *'For the land':* this signifies the blessing for the land. *'The good':* this signifies 'Who buildest Jerusalem'; and similarly it says *This good mountain and Lebanon.*[2] *'Which he has given thee':* this signifies the blessing of 'Who is good and bestows good'. This accounts for the grace after [meals]; how can we prove that there should be a blessing before [food]?—You have an argument *a fortiori;* if when one is full he says a grace, how much more so should he do so, when he is hungry! Rabbi says: This argument is not necessary. *'And thou shalt eat and be satisfied and bless'* signifies the benediction of 'Who feeds'. The responses of *zimmun* are derived from *O magnify the Lord with me.*[3] *'For the land':* this signifies the blessing of the land. *'The good':* this signifies, 'Who buildest Jerusalem'; and so it says, *'This goodly mountain and Lebanon'*. 'Who is good and bestows good' was instituted in Jabneh. This accounts for the grace after [meals]; whence do I learn that a blessing must be said before [food]?—Because it says, *'Which He has given thee'*, implying, as soon as He has given thee.[4] R. Isaac says: This is not necessary. For see, it says, *And He shall bless thy bread and thy water.*[5] Read not *u-berak* [and he shall bless] but *u-barek* [and say a blessing]. And when is it called *'bread'?* Before it is eaten. R. Nathan says: This is not necessary. For see, it says, *As soon as ye be come into the city ye shall straightway find him, before he go up to the high place to eat; for the people will not eat until he come, because he doth bless the sacrifice, and afterwards they eat that be bidden.*[6] Why did they[7] make such a long story of it? Because[8] women are fond of talking. Samuel, however, says that it was so that they might feast their eyes on Saul's good looks, since it is written, *From his shoulders and upward he was higher than any of the people;*[9] while R. Joḥanan says it was because one kingdom cannot overlap another by a hair's breadth.[10]

We have found warrant for blessing over food; whence do we derive it for the blessing over the Torah? R. Ishmael says: It is learnt *a fortiori:* If a blessing is said for temporal life, how much more should it be said for eternal life! R. Ḥiyya b. Naḥmani, the disciple of R. Ishmael, said in the name of R. Ishmael: This is not necessary. For see, it says, *'For the good land which He has given thee'*, and in another place it says, *And I will give thee the tables of*
c *stone and a law and commandments,* etc.[1] (R. Meir says: Whence do we learn that just as one says a blessing for good hap, so he should say one for evil hap?—Because it says, *Which the Lord thy God hath given thee,* [as much as to say,] which He hath judged thee[2]—for every judgment which He has passed on thee, whether it is a doom of happiness or a doom of suffering.) R. Judah b. Bathyrah says: This is not necessary. For see, it says *'the good'* where it need only have said *'good'*. *'Good'* signifies the Torah; and so it says, *For I give you a good doctrine.*[3] *'The good'* signifies the building of Jerusalem; and so it says, *This good mount and Lebanon.*[4]

It has been taught: If one does not say the words 'a desirable, good and extensive land' in the blessing of the land and does not mention the kingdom of the house of David in the blessing 'Who buildest Jerusalem', he has not performed his obligation. Nahum the Elder says: He must mention in it [the second blessing] the covenant. R. Jose says: He must mention in it the Torah. Pelimo says: He must mention the covenant before the Torah, since

(8) The first benediction of the grace.

a (1) The second benediction. (2) The third benediction. (3) In the third benediction. (4) The fourth benediction. (5) The scene of the last stand of the Bar Kocheba Wars, in 135 C.E. (6) I.e., no change is made. The third blessing commences with 'Have mercy', and ends with a prayer for the rebuilding of Jerusalem, which is also a prayer for 'consolation'. (7) I.e., the second. (8) The fourth. (9) In which case the First Tanna insists that it must be said again in the proper place. (10) Deut. VIII, 10. (11) This appears to be a mistake for *'zimmun'*. V. Wilna Gaon Glosses.

b (1) This appears to be a mistake for 'Who feeds'. V. Wilna Gaon Glosses. (2) Deut. III, 25. (3) Ps. XXXIV, 4. (4) Even before partaking thereof. (5) Ex. XXIII, 25. (6) 1 Sam. IX, 13. (7) The women who were talking to Saul. (8) MS.M. inserts, Rab said: Hence (is proved) that women etc. (9) Ibid. 2. (10) Samuel's regime was destined to cease as soon as Saul's commenced.

c (1) Ex. XXIV, 12; the derivation here is based on the principle of *Gezera Shawah*. (2) So BaḤ. Cur. edd.: 'Thy Judge', explaining the term *'thy God Elohim'*, which in Rabbinic thought represents God as Judge. (3) Prov. IV, 2. (4) The text is in disorder, v. *D.S.* a. l.

the latter was given with only three covenants[5] [49a] but the former with thirteen.[6] R. Abba[7] says: He must express thanksgiving at the beginning and end of it, or at the very least once; and one who omits to do so at least once is blameworthy. And whoever concludes the blessing of the land with 'Who givest lands in inheritance' and 'Who buildest Jerusalem' with the words 'Sa-
a viour of Israel' is a boor.[1] And whoever does not mention the covenant and the Torah in the blessing of the land and the kingdom of the house of David in 'Who buildest Jerusalem' has not performed his obligation. This supports R. Ela· for R. Ela said in the name of R. Jacob b. Aḥa in the name of our Teacher:[2] 'Whoever omits to mention covenant and Torah in the blessing of the land and the kingdom of the house of David in 'Who buildest Jerusalem' has not performed his obligation. There is a difference of opinion between Abba Jose b. Dosethai and the Rabbis. One authority says that [God's] kingship must be mentioned in the blessing 'Who is good and bestows good', the other says it need not be mentioned. The one who says it must be mentioned holds that this blessing has only Rabbinic sanction,[3] the one who says it need not be mentioned holds that it has Scriptural sanction.

Our Rabbis taught: How does one conclude the blessing of the building of Jerusalem?—R. Jose son of R. Judah says: Saviour of Israel. 'Saviour of Israel' and not 'Builder of Jerusalem'? Say rather, 'Saviour of Israel' also. Rabbah b. Bar Ḥanah was once at the house of the Exilarch. He mentioned one[4] at the beginning of [the third blessing] and both at the end.[5] R. Ḥisda said: Is it a superior way to conclude with two? And has it not been taught: Rabbi says that we do not conclude with two?

The [above] text [stated]: Rabbi says that we do not conclude with two. In objection to this Levi pointed out to Rabbi that we say 'for the land and for the food'?[6] It means, [he replied] a land that produces food. [But we say,] 'for the land and for the fruits'?[7] —[It means,] a land that produces fruits. [But we say], 'Who sanctifiest Israel and the appointed seasons'?[8]—[It means,] Israel who sanctify the seasons. [But we say,] Who sanctifiest Israel and New Moons?—[It means,] Israel who sanctify New Moons. [But we say,] Who sanctifies the Sabbath, Israel and the seasons?[1] —This is the exception.[2] Why then should it be different?—In this case it[3] is one act, in the other two, each distinct and separate.[4] And what is the reason for not concluding with two?—Because we do not make religious ceremonies into bundles.[5] How do we decide the matter?—R. Shesheth says: If one opens with 'Have mercy on Thy people Israel' he concludes with 'Saviour of Israel'; if he opens with 'Have mercy on Jerusalem', he concludes with 'Who buildest Jerusalem'. R. Naḥman, however, said: Even if one opens with 'Have mercy on Israel', he concludes with 'Who buildest Jerusalem', because it says, *The Lord doth build up Jerusalem, He gathereth together the dispersed of Israel*,[6] as if to say: When does God build Jerusalem?—When He gathereth the dispersed of Israel.

R. Zera said to R. Ḥisda: Let the Master come and teach us [grace]. He replied: The grace after meals I do not know myself, and shall I teach it to others?—He said to him: What do you mean?—Once, he replied, I was at the house of the Exilarch, and I said grace after the meal, and R. Shesheth stretched out his neck at me like a serpent,[7] and why?—Because I had made no mention either of covenant or of Torah[8] or of kingship.[9] And why did you not mention them [asked R. Zera]? Because, he replied, I followed R. Ḥananel citing Rab; for R. Ḥananel said in the name of Rab: If one has omitted to mention covenant, Torah and kingship he has still performed his obligation: 'covenant', because it does not apply to women; 'Torah and kingship' because they apply neither to women nor to slaves. And you [he exclaimed] abandoned all those other Tannaim and Amoraim and followed Rab!

Rabbah b. Bar Ḥanah said in the name of R. Joḥanan: The blessing 'Who is good and bestows good' must contain mention of [God's] kingship. What does he tell us? That any benediction which does not contain mention of [God's] kingship is no proper
c blessing? R. Joḥanan has already said this once![1]—R. Zera said: He tells us that it requires kingship to be mentioned twice,[2] once for itself and once for the benediction 'Who buildest Jerusalem'.[3] If that is so, we should require three times, once for itself, once for 'Who buildest Jerusalem', and once for the blessing of the land?[4] Hence what you must say is: Why do we not require one for the blessing of the land?—Because it is a benediction closely connected with the one which precedes it. Then 'Who buildest Jerusalem' should also not require it, being a benediction closely connected with the one which precedes it?—The fact is that, strictly speaking, the blessing 'Who buildest Jerusalem' also does not require it, but since the kingdom of the house of David is mentioned,[5] it is not seemly that the kingship of heaven also should not be mentioned.[6] R. Papa said: What he [R. Joḥanan] meant is this: It requires two mentions of the kingship [of heaven] besides its own.[7]

R. Zera was once sitting behind R. Giddal, and R. Giddal was sitting facing R. Huna, and as he [R. Giddal] sat, he said: If one forgot and did not mention in the grace Sabbath, he says, 'Blessed be He who gave Sabbaths for rest to His people Israel in love for a sign and a covenant, blessed is He who sanctifies the Sabbath!' He [R. Huna] said to him: Who made this statement?—He replied, Rab. He then continued: If one forgot and did not mention the festival, he says, 'Blessed is He who gave holy days to His people Israel for joy and for remembrance, blessed is He who sanctifies Israel and the festivals'. He again asked him who made the statement, and he answered, Rab. He then continued: If one forgot and did not mention the New Moon, he says, 'Blessed is He who gave New Moons to His people Israel for a remembrance'. But, said R. Zera: I do not know whether he also said that he must add 'for joy', or not, whether he concluded with a benediction or not, or whether he said it on his own authority or was repeating
d the words of his teacher.[1]

Once when R. Giddal b. Manyumi was in the presence of R.

(5) At Mount Sinai (or the ent of Meeting), at Mount Gerizim and in the plains of Moab. (6) The ord of 'covenant' occurring thirteen times in the section of the circumcision f Abraham, Gen. XVII, 1–14. (7) Rab is here intended, v. Marginal Gloss.
) Probably because he leaves out the reference to Palestine and Jerusalem; *infra*. (2) This must refer to Rabbi, Rab, who is usually so designated, eing excluded here, since Rab has already stated his view. (V. 49a, n. 7.)
) Hence it is not a continuation of the preceding blessings, which are Scripral; and therefore kingship must be mentioned afresh in it. (4) Either Israel Jerusalem. The third blessing begins 'Have mercy . . . upon Israel Thy eople and upon Jerusalem Thy city'. (5) Of the third blessing. (6) In ncluding the second blessing. (7) V. *P.B.* p. 289. (8) Ibid. p. 229.
V. *P.B.* p. 229. (2) Israel do not sanctify the Sabbath by means of a rmal proclamation, hence we cannot here apply the same explanation as in the case of festivals and New Moons. (3) God's sanctifying of the Sabbath and Israel. (4) Saving Israel and building Jerusalem. (5) Cf. Pes. 102b. (6) Ps. CXLVII, 2. (7) In astonishment. (8) In the second benediction. (9) The kingship of the house of David in the third benediction.

c (1) V. *supra* 40b. (2) As in fact we find in the benediction of 'Who is good etc.', which begins with the formula, 'Blessed art Thou . . . King of the Universe . . .' and goes on, 'Our father, our King . . .'. (3) Which does not conclude with the formula, 'Blessed art Thou . . . King of the universe'. (4) Which also concludes without the kingship formula. (5) In the third blessing. (6) And therefore we repair the omission in the next benediction. (7) And in fact the benediction proceeds, 'Our father our King . . . the king who is good etc.'.

d (1) Rab.

וזו נתנה בי"ג בריתות ר' *אבא אומר [א]צריך שיאמר בה הודאה תחלה וסוף והפוחת לא יפחות מא' וכל הפוחת מא' הרי זה מגונה וכל החותם מנחיל ארצות בברכת הארץ ומושיע את ישראל בבונה ירושלים הרי זה בור [ב]וכל שאינו אומר ברית ותורה בברכת הארץ ומלכות בית דוד בבונה ירושלים לא יצא ידי חובתו מסייע ליה לר' אילעא דא"ר אילעא א"ר יעקב בר אחא משום רבינו כל שלא אמר ברית ותורה בברכת הארץ ומלכות בית דוד בבונה ירושלים לא יצא ידי חובתו פליגי בה אבא יוסי בן דוסתאי ורבנן חד אמר הטוב והמטיב צריכה מלכות וחד אמר אינה צריכה מלכות מ"ד צריכה מלכות קסבר דרבנן ומ"ד אינה צריכה מלכות *קסבר דאורייתא ת"ר מהו חותם בבנין ירושלים ר' יוסי בר' יהודה אומר מושיע ישראל מושיע ישראל אין בנין ירושלים לא אלא אימא אף מושיע ישראל רבה בר רב הונא איקלע לבי ריש גלותא פתח בחדא וסיים בתרתי א"ר חסדא גבורתא למחתם בתרתי והתניא ר' אומר אין חותמין בשתים: גופא ר' אומר אין חותמין בשתים איתיביה לוי לר' [ג]על הארץ ועל המזון ארץ דמפקא מזון על הארץ ועל הפירות ארץ דמפקא פירות מקדש ישראל והזמנים ישראל דקדשינהו לזמנים מקדש ישראל וראשי חדשים ישראל דקדשינהו לראשי חדשים מקדש *השבת ישראל והזמנים חוץ מזו ומאי שנא הכא חדא היא התם תרתי כל חדא וחדא באפי נפשה וטעמא מאי אין חותמין בשתי' לפי *שאין עושין מצות חבילות חבילות מאי הוי עלה אמר רב ששת פתח ברחם על עמך ישראל חותם במושיע ישראל פתח ברחם על ירושלים חותם בבונה ירושלים ורב נחמן אמר [ד]אפילו פתח ברחם על ישראל חותם בבונה ירושלים משום שנאמר °בונה ירושלים יי' נדחי ישראל יכנס אימתי בונה ירושלים יי' בזמן שנדחי ישראל יכנס א"ל רבי זירא לרב חסדא ניתי מר ונתני א"ל ברכת מזונא לא גמרינן ותנויי מתנינן א"ל מאי האי א"ל דאקלעי לבי ריש גלותא ובריכי ברכת מזונא וזקפיה רב ששת לקועיה עלי כחויא ואמאי דלא אמרי לא ברית ולא תורה ולא מלכות ואמאי לא אמרת כדרב חננאל אמר רב דאמר רב חננאל אמר רב לא אמר ברית ותורה ומלכות יצא ברית לפי שאינה בנשים תורה ומלכות לפי שאינן לא בנשים ולא בעבדים ואת שבקת כל הני תנאי ואמוראי ועבדת כרב. אמר רבה בב"ח א"ר יוחנן הטוב והמטיב צריכה מלכות מאי קמ"ל *כל ברכה שאין בה מלכות לא שמה ברכה והא א"ר יוחנן חדא זימנא א"ר זירא לומר שצריכה שתי מלכיות חדא דידה וחדא דבונה ירושלים אי הכי נבעו תלת חדא דידה וחדא דבונה ירושלים וחדא דברכת הארץ אלא ברכת הארץ מ"ט לא משום דהויא לה ברכה הסמוכה לחברתה בונה ירושלים נמי לא תבעי דהויא לה ברכה הסמוכה לחברתה ה"ה דאפילו בונה ירושלים נמי לא בעיא אלא אידי דאמר מלכות בית דוד לאו אורח ארעא דלא אמר מלכות שמים רב פפא אמר ה"ק [ה]צריכה שתי מלכיות לבר מדידה יתיב ר' זירא אחורי דרב גדל ויתיב רב גדל קמיה דרב הונא ויתיב וקאמר [ו]טעה ולא הזכיר של שבת אומר ברוך שנתן שבתות למנוחה לעמו ישראל באהבה לאות ולברית ברוך מקדש השבת א"ל מאן אמרה רב הדר יתיב וקאמר [ז]טעה ולא הזכיר של י"ט אומר ברוך שנתן ימים טובים לעמו ישראל לשמחה ולזכרון ברוך מקדש ישראל והזמנים א"ל מאן אמרה רב הדר יתיב וקאמר [ח]טעה ולא הזכיר של ראש חדש אומר ברוך שנתן ראשי חדשים לעמו ישראל לזכרון ולא ידענא אי אמר בה שמחה אי לא אמר בה שמחה אי חתים בה אי לא חתים בה אי דידיה אי דרביה.

גדל בר מניומי הוה קאי קמיה דרב נחמן טעה רב נחמן והדר

רש"י

מילה ניתנה בי"ג בריתות. *בפרשת מילה שניתנה לאברהם אבינו הם כתובים: תחלה וסוף. נודה ה' אלהינו ועל כולם ה' אלהינו אנו מודים לך: מאן דאמר צריכה מלכו' קסבר דרבנן. הלכך לאו ברכה הסמוכה לחברתה היא שאינה מברכת הארץ: ומ"ד אינה צריכה מלכות קסבר דאורייתא. היא ומברכת הארץ היא כדאמר לעיל (דף מח:) אשר נתן לך זה הטוב והמטיב והויא לה ברכה הסמוכה לחברתה ומיהו פות' בה בברוך לפי שפתיחתה היא חתימתה שכולה הודאה אחת היא ואין הפסקה ודומה לברכת הפירות והמצות: בונה ירושלים לא. בתמיה אם חתם ב"י לאו חתימה היא הלא עיקר ברכה דירושלים היא: אלא אימא אף מושיע. אם בא לחתום מושיע ישראל ולא חתם ב"י ילא שתשוע' ישראל היא בנין ירושלי': פתח בחדא. כשהתחיל בברכה לא אמר רחם ה' על ישראל עמך ועל ירושלי' עירך אלא אחת מהן וכשחתם חתם בשתים מושיע ישראל וב"י: אין חותמין בשתים. שדומין לעושין מצות חבילות כי היכי דאמר (פסחים קב:) אין אומר שני קדושות על כוס א': מקדש השבת ישראל והזמנים. והכא ליכא למימר ישראל מקדשי לשבת וזמנים דאלו זמנים תלויין בב"ד לקדש חדשים על פי הראייה אבל שבת קדישא וקיימא: חוץ מזו ומ"ש דהכא חדא היא. אין כאן אלא ברכת מקדש שמברך להקב"ה שמקדש השבת והזמנים אבל מושיע ישראל ובונה ירושלים תרתי מילי נינהו ואין כוללים שני דברים בברכה אחת ולא גר' הא בהא תליא ובה"ג גרסינן הכי חוץ מזו ומ"ש הכי תרתי קדושי נינהו ומודה רבי דחתמינן בהו בשתים אבל כאותה חדא מילתא היא ובחדא בעי למחת' ואינו כ"ל דא"כ אית ליה לר' חותמין בשתי' והכא היינו טעמא דהא בהא תליא ולא היה לו לכלול ולומר אין חותמין בשתים ועוד ר' כי אמרה לאו אכאותה אמרה: פותח בעל ישראל עמך כו'. דבעינן חתימה מעין פתיחה: ורב נחמן כו'. ב"י תשועת ישראל היא דכתיב (תהלים קמז) בונה ירושלים ה' ואז נדחי ישראל יכנס: לאו אורח ארעא דלא אמר מלכות שמים. בבונה ירושלים הלכך מהדר לה בהטוב והמטיב (ואומר מלך העול' הטוב והמטיב): שתי מלכיות. כגון אבינו מלכנו אדירנו בוראנו גואלנו קדושנו קדוש יעקב רוענו רועה ישראל המלך הטוב והמטיב לכל וכו': לבר מדידה. שפותחת ברוך אתה יי' אלהינו מלך העולם וכו': ויתיב רב גדל וקאמר טעה כו' אמר ליה. רב הונא לרב גדל מאן אמרה: ולא ידענא. ר' זירא קאמר ליה לא ידענ' אי אמר רב לזכרון ולשמחה אי לא אמר ואי אמרה משמיה דרב אי לא אמרה: אי חתם בה. מקדש ישראל וראשי חדשים אי לא חתים:

והדר

תוספות

מאן דאמר אינה צריכה מלכו' קסבר דאורייתא. הקשה רש"י הואיל והיא דאורייתא אמאי פותחת בברוך הא סמוכה היא ותירץ דקצר' היא והויא הודאה בעלמא כברכת פירות וכברכ' מצות ותימ' אמאי שינו אותה יותר משאר ברכו' הסמוכות שחותמות ולא פותחות הואיל ודאורייתא היא היה לנו להאריך בה ולחתום בברוך ולא לשנות משאר סמוכות וי"ל דאין ה"נ ולמאן דאית ליה שהיא דאורייתא היה חותם ולא פותח וכן איתא בתוספתא בהדיא רבי יוסי הגלילי היה מאריך בה וחות' ומיהו אנן קי"ל שהיא מדרבנן ולכך צריכה מלכות כדאמ' צריכ' שתי מלכיות בר מדיד': לומר שצריכה שתי מלכיות בר מדידה. אחא דב"י דלאו אורח וכו' וגם בה אין יכולין לומר מלכות דהא סמוכ' היא ע"כ אומר' בהטוב והמטיב הואיל ואמר בה מלכות דב"י דלאו אורח ארעא וכו' אמר נמי דברכ' הארץ אע"פ שהיא סמוכה לחברתה הואיל ולא נתקנו בזה אחר זה דיהושע תקן ברכת הארץ ומשה תקן ברכת הזן ומשום הכי נקט מלכות דלא הוי סמוכות ומיהו אנן הואיל ונתקנו על הסדר אין אנו פותחין בברוך ויש שנוהגין לומר בב"י מלכות: ברוך שנתן שבתות למנוחה וכו'. וא"ת והא סמוכה היא וי"ל הואיל ולא נתקנה שם אלא לאומרה לפרקים כששכח רצה והחליצנו אין זה קרוי סמוכ' וצריך פתיחה בברוך ובברכות של י"ח ברכות כולם סמוכות לברכת אל חי וקיים אי נמי אלהי אברהם היינו מלכות *כדאמרינן (לעיל דף ז:) משנברא העולם לא היה אדם שקראו להקב"ה אדון עד שבא אברהם וקראו אדון שנא' ה' אלהים מה תתן לי (בראשית טו) ואם הוא יום טוב כולל ואומר ברוך שנתן שבתות למנוחה וי"ט לעמו ישראל לששון וכן כי מקלע שבת וראש חדש:

אי בעי

עין משפט נר מצוה

נו [א]מיי' פ"ב מה' ברכות הל' ג סמג עשין כז טור א"ח סי' קפז

נז [ב]מיי' וסמג שם טוש"ע שם סעי' ג ד ובסימן קפח סעי' ג

נח [ג]מיי' וסמג שם טור א"ח סימן קפז

נט [ד]מיי' שם הל' ד וסמג שם טוש"ע א"ח סימן קפח סעיף ד

ס [ה]מיי' שם הל' ז וסמג שם טוש"ע א"ח סי' קפט סעי' א

סא [ו]מיי' שם הל' יב וסמג שם טוש"ע א"ח סי' קפח סעי' ו

סב [ז]מיי' שם הל' יג טוש"ע א"ח שם סעיף ז

[וע' תו' לעיל מ: ד"ה אמר אביי]

[טעמא דבעינן שיהא לבו פנוי למלוה אחת ולא יפנה גלמו הימנה כ"כ תו' מ"ק ס: ד"ה לפי וכו']

מסורת הש"ס

[ע' תי"ט נדרים פ"ג מי"א ד"ה שנכרת]

[רב אבא הוא רב ונקרא שמו רב אבא ע' ערוך ערך רב]

[לעיל מו.]

[ביצה יז.]

[פסחים קב: סוטה ח.]

תלים קמז

והדר לרישא א"ל מאי טעמא עביד מר הכי א"ל דאמר רבי שילא אמר רב טעה חוזר לראש והא אמר רב הונא אמר רב טעה אומר ברוך שנתן א"ל לאו אתמר עלה אמר רב מנשיא בר תחליפא א"ר לא שנו אלא שלא פתח בהטוב והמטיב אבל פתח בהטוב והמטיב חוזר לראש א"ר אידי בר אבין אמר רב עמרם אמר רב נחמן אמר שמואל טעה ולא הזכיר של ראש חדש בתפלה מחזירין אותו בברכת המזון אין מחזירין אותו אמר ליה רב אבין לרב עמרם מאי שנא תפלה ומאי שנא ברכת המזון א"ל אף לדידי קשיא לי ושאילתיה לרב נחמן ואמר לי מיניה דמר שמואל לא שמיע לי אלא נחזי אנן תפלה דחובה היא מחזירין אותו ברכת מזונא דאי בעי אכיל אי בעי לא אכיל אין מחזירין אותו אלא מעתה שבתות וימים טובים דלא סגי דלא אכיל הכי נמי דאי טעי הדר א"ל אין דאמר ר' שילא אמר רב טעה חוזר לראש והא אמר רב הונא אמר רב טעה אומר ברוך שנתן לאו אתמר עלה לא שנו אלא שלא פתח בהטוב והמטיב אבל פתח בהטוב והמטיב חוזר לראש: עד כמה מזמנין וכו': למימרא דר"מ חשיב ליה כזית ור' יהודה כביצה והא איפכא שמעינן להו *דתנן וכן מי שיצא מירושלים ונזכר שהיה בידו בשר קודש אם עבר צופים שורפו במקומו ואם לאו חוזר ושורפו לפני הבירה מעצי המערכה עד כמה הם חוזרים רבי מאיר אומר זה וזה בכביצה ורבי יהודה אומר זה וזה בכזית *א"ר יוחנן מוחלפת השטה אביי אמר לעולם לא תיפוך הכא בקראי פליגי רבי מאיר סבר *ואכלת זו אכילה ושבעת זו שתיה ואכילה *בכזית ורבי יהודה סבר ואכלת ושבעת אכילה שיש בה שביעה ואיזו זו כביצה התם בסברא פליגי ר' מאיר סבר חזרתו *כטומאתו מה טומאתו בכביצה אף חזרתו בכביצה ור' יהודה סבר חזרתו כאיסורו מה איסורו בכזית אף חזרתו בכזית: **מתני'** כיצד מזמנין בשלשה אומר נברך בשלשה והוא אומר ברכו בעשרה אומר נברך אלהינו בעשרה והוא אומר ברכו אחד עשרה ואחד עשרה רבוא במאה הוא אומר נברך ה' אלהינו במאה והוא אומר ברכו באלף הוא אומר נברך לי"י אלהינו אלהי ישראל באלף והוא אומר ברכו ברבוא אומר נברך לי"י אלהינו אלהי ישראל אלהי צבאות יושב הכרובים על המזון שאכלנו ברבוא והוא אומר ברכו כענין שהוא מברך כך עונים אחריו ברוך יי' אלהינו אלהי ישראל אלהי צבאות יושב הכרובים על המזון שאכלנו ר' יוסי הגלילי אומר לפי רוב הקהל הם מברכים שנאמר °במקהלות ברכו אלהים יי' ממקור ישראל אמר ר"ע מה מצינו בבית הכנסת אחד מרובים ואחד מועטים אומר ברכו את יי' ר' ישמעאל אומר ברכו את יי' המבורך: **גמ'** אמר שמואל לעולם אל יוציא אדם את עצמו מן הכלל תנן בג' והוא אומר ברכו אימא אף

תורה אור

והדר לרישא. לתחלת ברכת המזון כדאמר' (לעיל דף כט:) גבי תפלה עקר את רגליו חוזר לראש התם הוא דאיכא עקירת רגלים אבל הכא סיום הברכה הוא עקירת הרגלים: מי שיצא מירושלים. לעיל מיניה מיירי בהולך לשחוט את פסחו ונזכר שיש לו חמץ בתוך ביתו אם יכול לחזור ולבער ולחזור למצותו יחזור ויבער ואם לאו יבטל בלבו וכן מי שיצא מירושלים ונזכר שיש בידו בשר קדש ונפסל ביציאתו חוץ לחומה: אם עבר צופים. מקום שיכול לראות בית המקדש: לפני הבירה. מקום בהר הבית שיש שם בית הדשן גדול ששורפין פסולי קדשים קלים כדאמרינן בזבחי' בפרק טבול יום (ד' קד:): זה וזה. חמץ ובשר קדש: חזרתו כטומאתו גרסי'. שיעור חזרתו כשיעור טומאתו מידי דחשיב לענין טומאה חשיב נמי לענין חזרה: **מתני'** בשלשה והוא אומר ברכו. דהא בלאו דידיה איכא זימון וכן כולם: א' עשרה וא' עשרה רבוא. כלומר הכל שוה משראוים להזכיר את השם אין צריכין לשנות ובגמרא פריך הא קתני סיפא במאה והוא אומר כו': לפי רוב הקהל הם מברכים. כמו שאמר שיש חלוק בין מאה לעשרה ובין מאה לאלף ובין אלף לרבוא והא דקתני אחד עשרה ואחד עשרה רבוא ר"ע היא דאמר מה מצינו בבית הכנסת משהגיעו לעשרה אין חילוק בין רבים בין מועטים אף כאן אין חילוק הכי מוקי לה בגמרא: **גמ'** אל יוציא עצמו. אף על פי שבארבעה הוא קשה לומר לשלשה ברכו טוב לו שיאמר נברך ואל יוציא עצמו מכלל המברכים: תנן בג' והוא אומר ברכו. אלמא הכי עדיף כלומר רבים אתם ואפי' איני עמכם: אף

אי בעי אכיל ואי בעי לא אכיל. וא"ת והא הוי ר"ח מיומ' דלא להתענות בהון במגלת תעני' וי"ל דה"פ אי בעי אכיל ואי בעי לא אכיל פת שיתחייבנו בברכת המזון אבל ביום טוב צריך לאכול פת ותימה דאמרינן בסוכה (פ"ב דף כז.) אי בעי אכיל ואי לא בעי לא אכיל חוץ מלילה הראשונה דיליף חמשה עשר מחג המצות וי"ל דה"פ שאינו צריך לאכול בסוכה אם לא ירצה אבל בשביל י"ט צריך לאכול וא"ת מכ"מ אם צריך לאכול בשביל י"ט או בשביל סוכות *ומיהו אומר רבינו יהוד' דנפקא מינה כגון שירדו גשמים ואכל חוץ לסוכה דהשתא אם לכבוד י"ט שפיר אבל אם בשביל סוכה בי"ט ראשון צריך לחזור ולאכול בסוכה לאחר שיפסקו הגשמים דילפינן חמשה עשר מחג המצות אבל בשאר ימים אינו צריך והא דאמרינן בפרק אלו דברים (פסחים סח:) מר בריה דרבינא הוה יתיב בתעניתא כולה שתא משמע שהיה מתענה בי"ט מפרש ר"י דבתענית חלום קאמר אבל בשאר תעניות אסור וסעודה שלישית של שבת היה מסופק ר"י דשמא אי בעי לא אכיל אלא מיכי תרגימא כדפירש ר"ת כדאמרינן בסעודת סוכה מיהו בכתובות פרק אע"פ (דף סד:) חשיב גבי משרה אשתו על ידי שליש שלש סעודות ג' משל שבת אם כן משמע דכולן שוות ועוד כיון דילפינן *ממן אלמא דשוות הן ומיהו אם אכל סעודה רביעית ושכח של שבת לא הדר לרישא דודאי אי לא בעי לא אכיל הך סעודה רביעית כלל:

*__עד__ כמה מזמנים וכו'. ה"ה ברכת המזון בלא זימון אלא רבותא אשמעינן דאפילו על כזית מזמנין:

אם עבר צופים. פרש"י בפסחים (פ"ג דף מט.) מקום ששמו צופים ול"נ דא"כ ה"ל למימר וכמדתו לכל רוח כדקאמר התם גבי מודיעים ולפנים אלא י"ל שאינו מקום וצופים הויא לשון ראיה וה"פ אם הרחיק מירושלים כ"כ שאינו יכול לראות ירושלים שורפו במקומו:

רבי מאיר סבר ואכלת זו אכילה ואכילה בכזית. ואומר הר"י דהני קראי אסמכתא בעלמא נינהו דמדאורייתא בעינן שביעה גמורה כדאמר פרק מי שמתו (דף כ.) ואני לא אשא פנים לישראל וכו' וכן אמרי' התם בן מברך לאביו ומוקי לה במאן דאכיל שיעורא דרבנן ופי' רש"י היינו כזית או כביצה ועוד אי כזית או כביצה הוי דאורייתא איזה שיעור דרבנן. וקי"ל כבי' דלפי מה שמחליף ר' יוחנן קאמר ר' יהודה בכזית ור"מ ורבי יהודה הלכה כרבי יהודה וגם לאביי דלא מחליף ור"מ אית ליה עד כזית נראה דהלכה כר"מ בכזית אע"ג דבעלמא *ר"מ ור' יהודה הלכה כר' יהודה בהא הלכה כר' מאיר דהא קים ליה ר' יוחנן בשיטתו לעיל *דאינו מוציא רבים ידי חובתן עד שיאכל כזית וכן לעיל *גבי שאכל כזית מליח וכן פסק בה"ג ור"ח ושאלתות *ולענין שתיה אור"י דיש להחמיר ולברך עליו אפילו בפחות ממלא לוגמיו אע"ג דלענין יום הכפורים ליתא לא ילפינן מינה לענין ברכה תדע דלענין בכזית לברכת המזון ולענין יה"כ עד דהוי דוקא *ככותבת: **נברך** אלהינו גרסינן ולא גרסינן נברך לאלהינו בלמ"ד דדוקא גבי שיר והודאה כתיב למ"ד כמו שירו לי"י הודו לי"י גדלו לי"י אבל גבי ברכה לא מצינו זה הלשון וכן מפרש בסדר רב עמרם: **אמר** ר"ע מה מצינו בבית הכנסת אחד לעשרה וכו'. משמע דרבי יוסי הגלילי מודה בבית הכנסת מדקאמר מה מצינו וכו' כלומר שאתה מודה לי ומאי שנא דפליגי בברכת המזון ומודו בבית הכנסת ויש לומר דודאי לא חלקו בין עשרה למאה בתפלה דאלו נכנסים ואלו יוצאים ולאו אדעתיה דש"ץ אבל בברכת המזון שהן קבועין ומעורבין שם יחד אין לטעות בזה שאין יוצאין עד לאחר ברכת המזון: **לעולם** אל יוציא אדם עצמו מן הכלל. ופריך בירושלמי מן הקורא בתורה ומן החזן שאומר ברכו ומפרש כיון שאומר המבורך אין זה מוציא עצמו מן הכלל: **תנן** בג' והוא אומר ברכו. ק"ד השתא דברכו עדיף משום דברכו היינו לווי לברך את השם אבל נברך אינו אלא כנטילת רשות: אלא

עין משפט נר מצוה

כג
א מיי' פרק ב מה' ברכות הל' יב סמג עשין כז טוש"ע א"ח סי' קפח סעיף ז [וע' היטב תו' סוכה דז. ד"ה אי בעי]

כד
ב מיי' שם הל' יב טוש"ע א"ח שם סעי' ו

כה
ד מיי' פרק יט מה' פסולי המוקדשין הל' ח

כו
ו מיי' פרק ה מהל' ברכות הלכה ב ד סמג עשין כז טוש"ע א"ח סי' קלב סעי' א (ו) טוש"ע א"ח סימן כז סעיף א [שבת קיז:]

שייך למשנה לעיל מה.

מסורת הש"ס

פסחים מט. פא:

לעיל יז:

[יומא עט.]
[שם פא.]
[פסחים מט.]
פה. וקדא.]

תהלים סח

[ערכין מו:]
[מח.]

[לח:]
פ' יחכו קדש סימן כג

[וע"ע תו' יומ' עט. ד"ה ולא בעיך באריכות]

Naḥman, R. Naḥman made a mistake [in the grace],[2] [49b] and he went back to the beginning. He said to him: What is the reason why your honour does this?—He replied: Because R. Shila said in the name of Rab: If one makes a mistake, he goes back to the beginning. But R. Huna has said in the name of Rab: If he goes wrong, he says, 'Blessed be He who gave [etc.]'?—He replied: Has it not been stated in reference to this that R. Menashia b. Taḥalifa said in the name of Rab: This is the case only where he has not commenced, 'Who is good and bestows good'; but if he has commenced 'Who is good and bestows good', he goes back to the beginning.

R. Idi b. Abin said in the name of R. Amram quoting R. Naḥman who had it from Samuel: If one by mistake omitted to mention New Moon in the *Tefillah*, he is made to begin again; if in the grace after meals, he is not made to begin again. Said R. Idi b. Abin to R. Amram: Why this difference between *Tefillah* and grace?—He replied: I also had the same difficulty, and I asked R. Naḥman, and he said to me: From Mar Samuel personally I have not heard anything on the subject, but let us see for ourselves. [I should say that] in the case of *Tefillah*, which is obligatory, he is made to begin again, but in the case of a meal, which he can eat or not eat as he pleases, he is not made to begin again. But if that is so [said the other], in the case of Sabbaths and festivals, on which it is not possible for him to abstain from eating, I should also say that if he makes a mistake he must go back to the beginning?—He replied: That is so; for R. Shila said in the name of Rab: If one goes wrong, he goes back to the beginning. But has not R. Huna said in the name of Rab that if one goes wrong he says 'Blessed is He who gave [etc.]'?—Has it not been stated in reference to this that this is the case only if he has not commenced 'Who is good and bestows good', but if he has commenced, 'Who is good and bestows good', he goes back to the beginning?

HOW MUCH [MUST ONE HAVE EATEN] TO COUNT etc. This would seem to show that R. Meir's standard is an olive and R. Judah's an egg. But we understand the opposite, since we have learnt: Similarly, if one has left Jerusalem and remembers that he
a has in his possession holy flesh, if he has gone beyond Zofim[1] he burns it on the spot, and if not he goes back and burns it in front of the Temple with some of the wood piled on the altar. For what minimum quantity do they turn back? R. Meir says: In either case,[2] the size of an egg; R. Judah says: In either case the size of an olive.[3] R. Joḥanan said: The names must be reversed. Abaye said: There is no need to reverse. In this case [of *zimmun*] they differ in the interpretation of a Scriptural text. R. Meir holds that '*thou shalt eat*' refers to eating and '*thou shalt be satisfied*' to drinking, and the standard of eating is an olive. R. Judah holds that '*And thou shalt eat and be satisfied*' signifies an eating which gives satisfaction, and this must be as much as an egg. In the other case, they differ in their reasoning. R. Meir considers that the return for a thing should be analogous to its defilement; just as its defilement is conditioned by the quantity of an egg, so is the return for it conditioned by the quantity of an egg.[4] R. Judah held that the return for it should be analogous to its prohibition. Just as the prohibition thereof comes into force for the quantity of an olive, so is the return for it conditioned by the quantity of an olive.

MISHNAH. WHAT IS THE FORMULA FOR ZIMMUN? IF THERE ARE THREE, HE [THE ONE SAYING GRACE] SAYS, 'LET US BLESS [HIM OF WHOSE BOUNTY WE HAVE EATEN]'. IF THERE ARE THREE BESIDE HIMSELF HE SAYS, 'BLESS'. IF THERE ARE TEN, HE SAYS, 'LET US BLESS OUR GOD'; IF THERE ARE TEN BESIDE HIMSELF HE SAYS, 'BLESS'. IT IS THE SAME
b WHETHER THERE ARE TEN OR TEN MYRIADS.[1] IF THERE ARE A HUNDRED HE SAYS, 'LET US BLESS THE LORD OUR GOD'; IF THERE ARE A HUNDRED BESIDE HIMSELF HE SAYS, 'BLESS'. IF THERE ARE A THOUSAND HE SAYS 'LET US BLESS THE LORD OUR GOD, THE GOD OF ISRAEL'; IF THERE ARE A THOUSAND BESIDE HIMSELF HE SAYS 'BLESS'. IF THERE ARE TEN THOUSAND HE SAYS, 'LET US BLESS THE LORD OUR GOD, THE GOD OF ISRAEL, THE GOD OF HOSTS, WHO DWELLS AMONG THE CHERUBIM, FOR THE FOOD WHICH WE HAVE EATEN'. IF THERE ARE TEN THOUSAND BESIDE HIMSELF HE SAYS, 'BLESS'. CORRESPONDING TO HIS INVOCATION THE OTHERS RESPOND, 'BLESSED BE THE LORD OUR GOD THE GOD OF ISRAEL, THE GOD OF HOSTS, WHO DWELLS AMONG THE CHERUBIM, FOR THE FOOD WHICH WE HAVE EATEN'. R. JOSE THE GALILEAN SAYS: THE FORMULA OF INVOCATION CORRESPONDS TO THE NUMBER ASSEMBLED, AS IT SAYS: BLESS YE GOD IN FULL ASSEMBLIES, EVEN THE LORD, YE THAT ARE FROM THE FOUNTAIN OF ISRAEL.[2] SAID R. AKIBA: WHAT DO WE FIND IN THE SYNAGOGUE? WHETHER THERE ARE MANY OR FEW[3] THE READER SAYS, 'BLESS YE THE LORD'.[4] R. ISHMAEL SAYS: BLESS YE THE LORD WHO IS BLESSED.

GEMARA. Samuel said: A man should never exclude himself from the general body.[5] We have learnt: IF THERE ARE THREE

(2) I.e., forgot to mention Sabbath or New Moon.
a (1) Mt. Scopus, the furthest point from which the Temple was still visible. (2) The case of holy flesh just mentioned, and the case of leaven which one who is bringing the Paschal lamb remembers that he has not cleared out of his house. (3) V. Pes. (Sonc. ed.) p. 23 notes. (4) Less than the quantity of an egg does not communicate defilement in case of food.
b (1) This is the opinion of R. Akiba, as appears *infra*. (2) Ps. LXVIII, 27. (3) Provided there are ten. (4) V. *P.B.* p. 37 and p. 68. (5) He should always say 'Let us bless'.

BESIDE HIMSELF HE SAYS 'BLESS'?[6]—[50a] Read: he may also say 'Bless'; but all the same to say 'Let us bless' is preferable. For R. Adda b. Ahabah said: The school of Rab say: We have
a learnt that [a company consisting of from] six to ten may divide.[1] Now if you say that 'Let us bless' is preferable, we can see a reason why they should divide. But if you say that 'Bless' is preferable, why should they divide?[2] You must therefore conclude that 'Let us bless' is preferable; and so we do conclude.

It has been taught to the same effect: Whether he says 'Bless' or 'Let us bless', no fault is to be found with him for this. But those who are punctilious do find fault with him for this.[3] And from the way a man says the benedictions it may be recognized whether he is a scholar or not. For example, Rabbi says: If he says 'and by his goodness', he is a scholar; if he says 'and *from* his goodness', he shows himself an ignoramus.[4] Said Abaye to R. Dimi: But it is written, *And from thy blessing let the house of thy servant be blessed for ever?*[5]—In a petition it is different.[6] But of a petition also it is written, *Open thy mouth wide and I will fill it?*[7]—That was written with reference to words of Torah. It has been taught: Rabbi says: If one says, 'And by his goodness we live', he shows himself a scholar; if he says 'they live', he shows himself an ignoramus.[8] The scholars of Neharbel[9] state the opposite,[10] but the law is not as stated by the scholars of Neharbel. R. Johanan says: If one says 'let us bless Him of whose bounty we have partaken' he shows himself a scholar; if he says 'Let us bless the one of whose bounty we have partaken', he shows himself an ignoramus.[11] Said R. Aha the son of Raba to R. Ashi: But do we not say 'We will bless the one who wrought for our ancestors and for us all these miracles'?[12]—He replied: There the meaning is obvious, for who performs miracles? The Holy One, blessed be He. R. Johanan said: If one says 'Blessed is He of whose bounty we have eaten', he shows
b himself a scholar. If he says, 'For the food which we have eaten',[1] he shows himself an ignoramus. R. Huna the son of R. Joshua said: This is the case only where there are three, since the name of heaven is not mentioned [in the *zimmun*],[2] but if there are ten, since the name of heaven is mentioned, it is clear what is meant, as we have learnt: CORRESPONDING TO HIS INVOCATION THE OTHERS RESPOND, 'BLESSED BE THE LORD OUR GOD, THE GOD OF ISRAEL, THE GOD OF HOSTS, WHO DWELLS AMONG THE CHERUBIM, FOR THE FOOD WHICH WE HAVE EATEN'.

IT IS THE SAME WHETHER THERE ARE TEN OR TEN MYRIADS. There seems here to be a contradiction. You say, IT IS THE SAME WHETHER THERE ARE TEN OR TEN MYRIADS, which would show that they are all alike. Then it states: IF THERE ARE A HUNDRED HE SAYS SO and SO, IF THERE ARE A THOUSAND HE SAYS, IF THERE ARE TEN THOUSAND HE SAYS?—R. Joseph said: There is no contradiction; the one statement expresses the view of R. Akiba, the other of R. Jose the Galilean, since we have learnt: R. JOSE THE GALILEAN SAYS: THE FORMULA OF INVOCATION CORRESPONDS TO THE NUMBER ASSEMBLED, AS IT SAYS: BLESS YE GOD IN ALL ASSEMBLIES, EVEN THE LORD, YE THAT ARE FROM THE FOUNTAIN OF ISRAEL.

SAID R. AKIBA: WHAT DO WE FIND IN THE SYNAGOGUE etc. And what does R. Akiba make of the verse cited by R. Jose the Galilean?—He wants it for the following lesson, as it has been taught: R. Meir used to say: Whence do we learn that even children [yet unborn] in their mothers' womb chanted a song by the Red Sea?—Because it says, *Bless ye the Lord in full assemblies, even the Lord, ye that are from the fountain of Israel.*[3] What says the other [R. Jose] to this?—He derives the lesson from the word *'fountain'*.

Raba said: The *halachah* is as laid down by R. Akiba. Rabina and R. Hama b. Buzi once dined at the house of the Exilarch, and R. Hama got up and commenced to look about for a hundred. Said Rabina to him: There is no need for this. For thus said Raba: The *halachah* is as stated by R. Akiba.

Raba said: When we take a meal at the house of the Exilarch,
c we say grace in groups of three.[1] Why not in groups of ten?[2]—Because the Exilarch might hear them and be angry.[3] But could not the grace of the Exilarch suffice for them?—Since everybody would respond loudly, they would not hear the one who says grace.

Raba Tosfa'ah said: If three persons had a meal together and one said grace for himself before the others, his *zimmun* is effective for them but theirs is not effective for him,[4] since *zimmun* cannot be said out of its place.[5]

R. ISHMAEL SAYS. Rafram b. Papa once attended the synagogue of Abi Gobar.[6] He was called up to read in the Scroll and he said, 'Bless ye the Lord' and stopped, without adding 'who is to be blessed'. The whole congregation cried out, 'Bless ye the Lord who is to be blessed'. Raba said to him: You black pot![7] Why do you want to enter into controversy?[8] And besides, the general custom is to use the formula of R. Ishmael.

MISHNAH. IF THREE PERSONS HAVE EATEN TOGETHER THEY MAY NOT SEPARATE [FOR GRACE].[9] SIMILARLY WITH FOUR AND SIMILARLY WITH FIVE.[10] SIX MAY DIVIDE,[11] [AND HIGHER NUMBERS] UP TO TEN; BETWEEN TEN AND TWENTY THEY MAY NOT DIVIDE. IF TWO GROUPS EAT IN THE SAME ROOM, AS LONG AS SOME OF THE ONE CAN SEE SOME OF THE OTHER THEY COMBINE [FOR ZIMMUN], BUT OTHERWISE EACH GROUP MAKES ZIMMUN FOR ITSELF. A BLESSING IS NOT SAID OVER THE WINE UNTIL WATER IS PUT IN IT.[12] SO R. ELIEZER. THE SAGES, HOWEVER, SAY THAT THE BLESSING MAY BE SAID.

GEMARA. What does this tell us? We have already learnt
d it once: Three persons who have eaten together must say *zimmun?*[1]—This teaches us the same thing as was stated by R. Abba in the name of Samuel: If three persons have sat down to eat, even though they have not yet commenced, they are not at liberty to separate. Another version: R. Abba said in the name of Samuel: What is meant is this: if three persons sit down to eat together, even though each eats of his own loaf, they are not at liberty to separate. Or [it may teach us] the same as R. Huna; for R. Huna said: If three persons from these groups come together,[2] they are not at liberty to separate.[3] R. Hisda said: This is only if they come from three groups of three men each.[4] Raba said: [50b]

(6) Thus excluding himself from their company.

a (1) I.e., form groups of three or four. But ten may not divide, since they will not then be able to say 'Our God'. (2) Rashi reads: 'Why should six divide?' If they form two groups of three, neither can say 'bless'. (3) For excluding himself from the group. (4) Because he belittles the goodness of the Almighty. (5) II Sam. VII, 29. (6) The petitioner likes to be modest in his request. (7) Ps. LXXXI, 11. (8) Because he excludes himself from their company. (9) Nehar Bel, east of Bagdad. (10) Taking 'they live' to refer to the whole of mankind. (11) Because this form may be taken to refer to the host. (12) In the Haggadah on Passover eve.

b (1) Without assigning its ownership to God. (2) In the responses 'Let us bless our God'. (3) The lesson being derived from the word 'assemblies'.

c (1) Before the Exilarch finishes and says grace. (2) So as to add the word 'Our God'. (3) At their not waiting for him. (4) I.e., he does not perform the *mizwah* of *zimmun*. (5) V. *supra*. 45b, n. c6. (6) Be Gobar, in the vicinity of Mahuzah. (7) Probably he was of swarthy complexion. (8) I.e., follow a minority view. (9) But must say *zimmun* together. (10) One or two may not say grace for themselves. (11) Into two groups of three. (12) To dilute it, otherwise it is too strong to be drunk.

d (1) V. *supra* 45b. (2) Each having left his group for one reason or another. (3) But they must say grace together even though they have not eaten together. (4) So that each of them was under the obligation of *zimmun*.

מסורת הש"ס

[תוספ' פ"ה]

תוספתא ברכו' פ"א

[סנהד' יז:]

[פסחים קטז:]

[דמסתמא כמאן דמברך לי' למזון כי"ק וכא"ש]

כתובות ז: [סוטה ל:]

[לעיל מה:]

[לעיל מה:]

לעיל מה.

תורה אור

אף ברכו ומ"מ נברך עדיף דאמר רב אדא בר אהבה אמרי בי רב תנינא ו' נחלקין עד י' אא"ב נברך עדיף משום הכי נחלקין אלא א"א ברכו עדיף אמאי נחלקין אלא לאו ש"מ נברך עדיף ש"מ תניא נמי הכי *בין שאמר ברכו בין שאמר נברך אין תופסין אותו על כך *והנקדנין תופסין אותו על כך ומברכותיו של אדם ניכר אם תלמיד חכם הוא אם לאו כיצד רבי אומר ובטובו הרי זה ת"ח ומטובו הרי זה בור א"ל אביי לרב דימי והכתיב ומברכתך יברך (את) בית עבדך לעולם (שמואל ב ז) בשאלה שאני בשאלה נמי הכתיב הרחב פיך ואמלאהו (תילים פא) ההוא בדברי תורה כתיב תניא רבי אומר בטובו חיינו הרי זה ת"ח חיים הרי זה בור *נהרבלאי מתני איפכא ולית הלכתא כנהרבלאי א"ר יוחנן נברך שאכלנו משלו הרי זה ת"ח למי שאכלנו משלו הרי זה בור א"ל רב אחא בריה דרבא לרב אשי והא אמרינן *למי שעשה לאבותינו ולנו את כל הנסים האלו א"ל התם מוכחא מלתא מאן עביד ניסי קודשא ב"ה א"ר יוחנן ברוך שאכלנו משלו הרי זה ת"ח על המזון שאכלנו הרי זה *בור אמר רב הונא בריה דרב יהושע לא אמרן אלא בשלשה דליכא שם שמים אבל בעשרה דאיכא שם שמים מוכחא מלתא כדתנן כענין שהוא מברך כך עונין אחריו ברוך יי' אלהי ישראל אלהי הצבאות יושב הכרובים על המזון שאכלנו: אחד עשרה ואחד עשרה רבוא: הא גופא קשיא אמרת אחד עשרה ואחד עשרה רבוא אלמא כי הדדי נינהו והדר קתני במאה אומר באלף אומר ברבוא אומר אמר רב יוסף לא קשיא הא ר' יוסי הגלילי הא ר"ע דתנן ר' יוסי הגלילי אומר לפי רוב הקהל הם מברכין שנאמר במקהלות ברכו אלהים (תילים סח): אמר רבי עקיבא מה מצינו בבית הכנסת וכו': ור"ע האי קרא דרבי יוסי הגלילי מאי עביד ליה מיבעי ליה לכדתניא *היה ר"מ אומר מניין שאפילו עוברין שבמעי אמן אמרו שירה על הים שנאמר במקהלות ברכו אלהים יי' ממקור ישראל ואידך ממקור נפקא אמר רבא הלכה כר"ע רבינא ורב חמא בר בוזי אקלעו לבי ריש גלותא קם רב חמא וקא מהדר אבי מאה א"ל רבינא לא צריכת הכי אמר רבא הלכה כר"ע אמר רבא כי אכלינן רפתא בי ריש גלותא מברכינן ג' ג' וליברכו י' י' שמע ריש גלותא ואיקפד וניפקו בברכתא דריש גלותא איידי דאוושו כ"ע לא שמעי אמר רבה תוספאה הני ג' דכרכי רפתא בהדי הדדי וקדים חד מניידהו ובריך לדעתיה אינון נפקין בזימון דידיה איהו לא נפיק בזימון דידהו *לפי שאין זימון למפרע: ר' ישמעאל אומר: רפרם בר פפא איקלע לבי כנישתא דאבי גיבר קם קרא בספרא ואמר ברכו את יי' ואשתיק ולא אמר המבורך אוושו כ"ע ברכו את ה' המבורך אמר רבא פתיא *אוכמא בהדי פלוגתא למה לך ועוד הא נהוג עלמא כר' ישמעאל:

מתני' *ג' שאכלו כאחת אינן רשאין ליחלק וכן ארבעה וכן חמשה ששה נחלקין עד עשרה ועשרה אין נחלקין עד עשרים שתי חבורות שהיו אוכלות בבית אחד בזמן שמקצתן רואין אלו את אלו הרי אלו מצטרפין לזימון ואם לאו אלו מזמנין לעצמן ואלו מזמנין לעצמן אין מברכין על היין עד שיתן לתוכו מים דברי ר' אליעזר וחכמים אומרים מברכין:

גמ' מאי קמ"ל תנינא חדא זימנא *ג' שאכלו כאחת חייבין לזמן הא קמ"ל כי הא דא"ר אבא אמר שמואל ג' שישבו לאכול כא' ועדיין לא אכלו אינן רשאין ליחלק ל"א א"ר אבא אמר שמואל הכי קתני ג' שישבו לאכול כאחת אע"פ שכל אחד ואחד אוכל מככרו אינן רשאין ליחלק א"נ כי הא דרב הונא דאמר רב הונא ג' שבאו מג' חבורות אינן רשאין ליחלק א"ר חסדא והוא שבאו מג' חבורות של ג' בני אדם אמר רבא ולא

רש"י

אף ברכו. שפיר דמי ומיהו טוב לו להיות בכלל המברכים: תנינא. סייעתא לשמואל: ששה נחלקין. אם רצו ליחלק לשתי חבורות ולזמן אלו לעצמן ואלו לעצמן רשאין הן שהרי יש זימון כאן וכאן: עד עשרה. כלומר וכן ז' וכן ח' לשתי חבורות וכן ט' לשתי חבורות או לשלשה עד עשרה אבל אם היו עשרה חלה עליהן הזכרת השם ואם יחלקו לא יהיה שם הזכרה אין נחלקין עד שיהיו שם עשרים: ה"ג אי אמרת ברכו עדיף אמאי ששה נחלקין. אם ירצו הא מעיקרא יכולין לומר ברכו והשתא תו לא אמרי: אלא לאו ש"מ. אף ברכו קאמר מתני' וכיון דמתני' אף ברכו קאמר מסברא היא שטוב לו לאדם להיות מן המברכים וסייעתא דשמואל וגירסא הכי איתא ששה עד עשרה ואי אמרת ברכו דוקא אמאי ששה נחלקים אלא לאו ש"מ אף ברכו ש"מ: תנ"ה. דמתני' אף ברכו קאמר: והנקדנין. דווקנין תופסין אותו על שהוציא עצמו מן הכלל: ומטובו הרי זה בור. שמשמע בתגמוליו של מקום דמשמע דבר מועט כדי חיים: בשאלה שאני. שהשואל שואל כעני על פתח שאינו מרים ראש לשאול שאלה גדולה: הרחב פיך. לשאול כל תאותך: חיים הרי זה בור. דהוציא עצמו מן הכלל: מתני איפכא. חיים עדיף שכולל את כל באי עולם: נברך שאכלנו משלו. משמע שהוא יחידי שהכל אוכלים משלו: למי שאכלנו משלו. משמע מרובים הן זה זן את זה וזה זן את זה ולפי דבריו מברך את בעל הבית: התם מוכחא מילתא. דבמעשה נסים ליכא למימר מרובין: כדתנן על המזון שאכלנו. ולא קתני משלו: ואידך. עוברים ממקור כפקא ואכן ממקהלות דרשינן: הלכה כר"ע. בברכת המזון דאחד עשרה ואחד עשרה רבוא: הוה מברכינן בתלת' תלתא. ריש גלותא מאריך בסעודתו ואנן כל ג' וג' שגמרו סעודתן מזמנין בקול נמוך ויושבין אחר הברכה עד שגמר ריש גלותא וזימנו הוא והיושבין אצלו בקול רם ולקמן פריך וניפקו בברכה דריש גלותא: שמע ריש גלותא. אם היו מזמנין י' י' היה צריך המברך להגביה קולו וישמע ריש גלותא ויחרה לו שאנו עושין חבורה לעצמנו בפרהסיא אף על גב דמפקי נפשייהו מידי זימון של הזכרת השם וכי הדר ומזמן ריש גלותא בהזכרת השם לאו איכהו נפקי ביה כדאמר רבה תוספאה דאין זימון למפרע אפ"ה ניחא להו בהכי משום דאוושי כולי עלמא שהיו שם מסובין רבים ואין קול המברך נשמע: ובריך לדעתיה. לעצמו בלא זימון: למפרע. משבירך וידי זימון לא יצא: פתיא. כלי חרס כדאמר (בע"ז דף לג:) הכי פתיותא דבי מכסי: בהדי פלוגתא למה לך. טוב לך לאחוז דברי רבי ישמעאל שאף רבי עקיבא מודה דכי אמר המבורך טפי עדיף אלא שאין צריך:

מתני' אינן רשאין ליחלק. דאחייבו להו בזימון: וכן ד'. אין הג' מזמנין והיחיד יחלק מהם דאיהו כמי איקבע בחובת זימון: ששה נחלקים. כדי זימון לכאן וכדי זימון לכאן: עד י'. אבל י' אין נחלקים דאחייבו להו בזימון הזכרת השם עד שיהו כ' אז יחלקו אם רצו לב' חבורות:

גמ' ג' שבאו מג' חבורות. וכדמסיים רב חסדא שבאו מג' חבורות של ג' בני אדם בכל חבורה ונתחייבו אלו בזימון ועמד אחד מכל חבורה ונצטרפו ג' לחבורה אחת חייבין לזמן ואין רשאין ליחלק שכבר הוקבעו ואפילו לא אכלו אלו הג' משנצטרפו יחד שכבר גמרו סעודתן עם הראשונים:

תוספות

אלא ש"מ נברך עדיף. לאו דוקא עדיף אלא כי הדדי נינהו ועדיף היינו חשוב *כמו הקישא עדיף וג"ש עדיף פרק איזהו מקומן (דף מח.) ר"ל דהקיש חשיב ואין לבטלו מפני הג"ש וה"נ קאמר נברך חשיב כמו ברכו ולפיכך לא יוציא עצמו מן הכלל והקונטרס מוחק עדיף ומיהו אתי שפיר עדיף כדפי':

על המזון הרי זה בור. דמשמע דמברך לבעל הבית המאכילו דאי לרחמנא למה הוא מזכיר מזון בלא מזון יש הרבה לברכו:

אמר רבא הלכה כרבי עקיבא. פירש ר"ח דהכי קי"ל והלכך בין בעשרה בין במאה בין ברבוא אומר נברך אלהינו על המזון שאכלנו אבל בג' לא יזכיר על המזון כדאמר לעיל וגם בעשרה אם אינו רוצה להזכיר על המזון הרשות בידו ואומר ובטובו חיינו:

שלשה שישבו לאכול כאחת. אע"פ שהיו חלוקין בככר שכל אחד ואחד אוכל מככרו אין רשאין ליחלק כלומר אע"פ שהן חלוקין בככרות וס"ד אין זה צרוף ולא חל עליהם חובת זימון אפ"ה אינן רשאין ליחלק: *אבל אי אקדימו ואזמינו עליהן בדוכתייהו פירוש שאכל כל אחד והשלשה והפסיק לשתים שהיו מסובין עמו עד הזן כדאיתא לעיל (דף מה:) פרח חובת זימון מעליהם כלומר פטורין מן הזימון ורשאין עתה ליחלק ורש"י לא פירש כן: חלקוה

עין משפט נר מצוה

[עיין חולין ד' ל"ו ריש ע"א]

סז
אבגדה מיי' פ"ה מה' ברכות ה"ד טוש"ע א"ח סימן קלב סעיף א

סח
ו טוש"ע א"ח סימן קלג סעיף א

[והנקדנין פי' המדקדק שלא בדבר לורך ובלשון ערבי קורין אותו תרגגול' המנקר באשפה ערוך ע' נקד].

סט
ז מיי' פרק ה מה' ברכות הל' יד סמג עשין כז טוש"ע א"ח סימן קלד סעיף א [סייך לע"ב והוא דיבור בפני עצמו]

ע
ח מיי' פרק ט מהלכת תפלה הלכה א ופי"ב הלכה ה סמג עשין יט טוש"ע א"ח סימן כז סעיף א

עא
ט מיי' פרק ה מהלכת ברכות הלכה יוד סמג עשין כז טוש"ע א"ח סי' קלג סעיף א

עב
י מיי' שם הלכה יב סמג שם טוש"ע א"ח סימן קלה סעיף א

עג
כל מיי' שם הלכה י יא וסמג שם טוש"ע א"ח סי' קלג סעיף ד

עד
מנ מיי' שם טוש"ע א"ח שם סעיף ה

[פסחים פח. מגילה יד: ע"ז עז: ע"ש פירש"י לשבח]

ולא אמרן אלא דלא אקדימו הנך ואזמון עלידהו בדוכתיידהו אבל אזמון עלידהו בדוכתיידהו פרח זימון מנייהו אמר רבא מנא אמינא לה *דתנן [א]מטה שנגנבה חציה או שאבדה חצי' או שחלקוה אחין או שותפין טהורה החזירוה מקבלת טומאה מכאן ולהבא מכאן ולהבא אין למפרע לא אלמא כיון דפלגוה פרח לה טומאה מינה ה"נ כיון דאזמון עלידהו פרח זמון מנייהו: ב' חבורות וכו': תנא [ב]אם יש שמש בינידם שמש מצרפן: אין מברכין על היין: ת"ר יין *עד שלא נתן לתוכו מים אין מברכין עליו ב"פ הגפן אלא ב"פ העץ ונוטלין ממנו לידים משנתן לתוכו מים מברכין עליו ב"פ הגפן ואין נוטלין ממנו לידים דברי רבי אליעזר וחכמים אומרים בין כך ובין כך מברכים עליו ב"פ הגפן [ג]ואין נוטלין הימנו לידים כמאן אזלא הא *דאמר שמואל [ד]עושה אדם כל צרכיו בפת כמאן כרבי אליעזר א"ר יוסי בר' חנינא *מודים חכמים לרבי אליעזר בכוס של ברכה שאין מברכין עליו עד שיתן לתוכו מים מאי טעמא אמר רב אושעיא בעינן מצוה מן המובחר ורבנן למאי חזי א"ר זירא *חזי לקורייטי *ת"ר [ה]ארבעה דברים נאמרו בפת אין מניחין בשר חי על הפת ואין מעבירין כוס מלא על הפת ואין זורקין את הפת ואין סומכין את הקערה בפת אמימר ומר זוטרא ורב אשי כרכו רפתא בהדי הדדי איתו לקמייהו תמרי ורמוני שקל מר זוטרא פתק לקמיה דרב אשי דסתנא א"ל לא סבר לה מר להא דתניא אין זורקין את האוכלין ההיא בפת תניא והתניא כשם שאין זורקין את הפת כך *אין זורקין את האוכלין א"ל והתניא אע"פ שאין זורקין את הפת אבל זורקין את האוכלין אלא לא קשיא הא [ו]במידי דממאיס הא במידי דלא ממאיס ת"ר *[ז]ממשיכין יין בצנורות לפני חתן ולפני כלה וזורקין לפניהם קליות ואגוזים בימות החמה אבל לא בימות הגשמים אבל לא גלוסקאות לא בימות החמה ולא בימות הגשמים: אמר רב יהודה שכח והכניס אוכלין לתוך פיו בלא ברכה מסלקן לצד אחד ומברך תניא חדא בולען ותניא אידך פולטן ותניא אידך מסלקן ל"ק הא דתניא [ח]בולען במשקין והא דתניא [ט]פולטן במידי דלא ממאיס והא דתניא מסלקן במידי דממאיס במידי

ולא אמרן אלא דלא אקדימו הנך. חבורות שפרשו אלו מהן ולזמון עלייהו דהכי כגון אם היו ארבעה בכל חבורה ונשאר בכל אחת כדי זימון והפורשים הללו היו צריכים לצאת לשוק קודם שגמרו החבורות את סעודתם: אבל אזמון עלידהו. דהכי כגון שנצטרפו אלו עמהם לזימון כדאמר לעיל קורין לו ומזמנים עליו וברכו החבורו' ואלו לא היו שם אלא כדי כברך וברוך הוא ועכשיו הם באים לברך לא מזמני דפרח מנייהו חובת זימון ותו לא הדר עלייהו: מטה. טמאה: שנגנבה חציה. אלמא כיון דפלגוה פקע שם מטה מינה ושם טומאה אף על גב דהדר הדרוה והרי היא מטה לא הדרה טומאתה הכי נמי כיון דפקע שם שלשה מנייהו בהפרדם ושם זימון על ידי שזמנו הראשונים עליהם אף על גב דהדרי לכלל שם שלשה לא הדרי לכלל זימון אבל כי לא אזמון לא פקע חובת זימון מהן אף לפי פרידתם: אם יש שמש בינידן. שמשמש לשתיהם: שמש מצרפן. אף על פי שאין אלו רואין את אלו כגון יריעה פרוסה ביניהם: אין מברכין עליו בורא פרי הגפן. לפי שהיה יינם חזק מאד ואין ראוי לשתיה בלא מים הלכך אכתי לא אשתני למעליותא ולא זז מברכתו הראשונה והרי הוא כענבים וברכתו בורא פרי העץ: ונוטלין ממנו לידים. דשם מים עליו דמי פירות בעלמא מקרי: ומשנתן לתוכו מים. שם יין עליו ואין נוטלין אלא במים. לשון אחר הכי גרסינן יין עד שלא נתן לתוכו מים מברכין עליו בורא פרי העץ ואין נוטלין הימנו לידים משנתן לתוכו מים מברכין עליו בורא פרי הגפן ונוטלין הימנו לידים דברי רבי אליעזר וחכמים אומרים בין כך ובין כך מברכים עליו בורא פרי הגפן ואין נוטלים ממנו לידים וטעמייהו דרבנן משום הפסד אוכלין כך מצאתי בהלכות גדולות אצל קידוש והבדלה ובדקתי בתוספתא ולא גרסי' בה הכי אלא כמו שהוא בספרים: כרבי אליעזר. דאמר נוטלין הימנו לידים ולא חייש להפסד אוכלים: למאי חזי. לשתיה דמברכין עליו ברכת היין: לקורייטי. פייסו"ן בלע"ז ובלשון חכמים אכומלית ואלונתית: אין מעבירין כוס מלא על הפת. שלא ישפך על הפת ותהא הפת בזויה: פתק. זרק: דסתנא. אמיכטריסו"ן בלע"ז מכה של בשר מבושל: מידי דממאיס. שמתמעך בזריקתו כגון תאנים שבשלו כל צרכם ותותים: דלא ממאיס. רמון ואגוז וכל דבר קשה: ממשיכין יין בצנורות. משום סימן טוב ואין כאן משום בזיון והפסד לפי שמקבלים אותו בראש פי הצנור בכלי: בימות החמה. שאין טיט בדרכים: אבל לא גלוסקאות. שהרי אף בימות החמה הן נמאסין בזריקתן: בולען. בלא ברכה: פולטן. ומברך וחוזר ואוכלן: משקין. בולען שאי אפשר לסלקן לאחד מלוגמיו ולברך ולא לפולטם שמפסידן: פולטן במידי דלא ממאיס. במה שנתנו בפיו ויכול לחזור ולאוכלו:

במידי

חלקוה האחים או השותפין טהורה. תימה דאמר בסוכה (פ"ק דף יו.) מטה מטמאה אברים כגון ארוכה ושתי כרעים ולי נראה דהתם מיירי להחזירה כאשר בתחלה ולתקנה שהכרעים בעין והדיוט יכול להחזירה וא"ת אמאי לא פריך הכא מכל כלי שנשבר וטהור אלמא כיון דפלגוה פרח לה טומאה ול"נ דשאני התם שאינו ראוי עוד להצטרף הכלי יחד ולקבל טומאה אפי' מכאן ולהבא ולא הוי דומיא דשלשה בני אדם דהוו ראוים עוד להצטרף לזימון: שמש מצרפן לזימון. וה"ה בשני בתים ובני אדם עומדים ומשמשין מזו לזו מצטרפין וכן איתא בירושלמי ובלבד שישמעו ברכת המזון מפי המברך והא דקתני במתני' בית [אחד] משום חדוש דסיפא דאפילו בבית אחד אם לאו אין מזמנין וכן בבית חתנים כשאוכלים בחופה בב' בתים ובני אדם משמשין מזו לזו מצטרפין ובלבד שישמעו ברכת המזון מפי המברך: בורא פרי העץ ונוטלין ממנו לידים. פי' רש"י כי לא נתן לתוכו מים לא הוי אלא כמי פירות ומכאן משמע דמי פירות כשרין לנטילת ידים ויש לחלק בין הכי דאמרינן בפרק כל הבשר (דף קז.) דלאחזותא קפידיתו ומיהו יש מפרשים לנטילת ידים בעינן מים דכתיב וידיו לא שטף במים: כמאן אזלא הא דאמר שמואל וכו' כרבי אליעזר לכאורה משמע מתוך דאמר ר"א נוטלין וכו' ותימה דאמרינן בפרק במה טומנין (דף כ:) אימר דאמר שמואל במידי דלא ממאיס במידי דממאיס מי אמר ואם כן היכי מוקים לה הא דשמואל כרבי אליעזר דהא יין מידי דממאיס בנטילת ידים ובמידי דממאיס מודה שמואל ועוד קשה דהכא משמע דאין הלכה כשמואל מדמוקי לה כרבי אליעזר ובפרק שני דביצה (דף כח:) קאמר סתמא דגמרא דסופלי לאיותא בי"ט דמטלטלינן להו אגב רפתא כשמואל משמע דקי"ל כותיה וי"ל דהכא לא קאמר אלא לדברי ר"א סבר לה כשמואל ועדיפא מיניה קאמר שמתיר אפילו היכא דממאיס ולא נחת כאן אלא לפרש טעמא דרבי אליעזר כדפירשנו ובה"ג אמר דהלכה כרבנן דהכא והלכה נמי כשמואל דכי קאמר שמואל הכי מילי מידי דלא ממאיס אבל מידי דממאיס לא ודלא כפי' ר"ת שפסק דלא כשמואל מדמוקי לה כר"א אלא ודאי קיימא לן כשמואל כדפירשנו ואם כן מותר לסמוך הקערה בפת היכא דלא ממאיס ויש אומרים דצריך לאכלו אחר כך ויש נוהגים לאכול דייסא בפת הואיל ואוכלין הפת אחר כך אבל במסכת סופרים אוסרו דאמרינן במסכת סופרים (פ"ג) אין אוכלין אוכלין באוכלין אלא אם כן אוכלן בבת אחת ושמא ההוא דלא כשמואל:

מודים חכמים לר"א בכוס של ברכה דאין מברכין עליו עד שיתן לתוכו מים. תימה דאמרינן לקמן ד' דברים נאמרו בכוס של ברכה חי ומלא וי"ל דבעינן שיתנו חי לתוך הכוס ואח"כ ימזגנו אי נמי בעינן חי מן החבית אי נמי קאי אכוס עצמו ומאי חי שלם כדאיתא במכות (דף טז:) ריסק ע' כזיתים ואחד חי וכו' אלמא דאותו חי היינו שלם ה"נ בעינן שיהא הכוס שלם בלא *שבירה: למאי חזי. פירוש ולמאי אשתני לעלויא ומשני לקורייטי וכן הלכה כרבנן דיין חי מברכין עליו בורא פרי הגפן דאמרינן שתאו חי יצא: אין זורקין את האוכלין. בהני שלשה מודה שמואל אין מעבירין כוס מלא על הפת וגם אין סומכין עליו בשר חי ואין זורקין את הפת אפילו לא ממאיס וכן שאר אוכלין אסור לזרוק במידי דממאיס: ולא בימות הגשמים. אע"פ שבאגוזים אין האוכל נמאס בתוכו מ"מ כשהן נופלים בטיט נמאסים ומיהו עכשיו שדרכן לזרוק חטים בבית חתנים צריכים ליזהר שלא יזרקום אלא במקום נקי:

מעיקרא

עין משפט נר מצוה

עה [א]מיי' פכ"ו מהלכות כלים הלכה יב

עו [ב]מיי' פרק ה מהל' ברכות הלכה יב סמג עשין כז טוש"ע א"ח סי' קצה סעיף א

עז [ג][ד][ה][ו]מיי' פ"ז שם הלכה ט סמג שם טוש"ע א"ח סי' קפ סעיף יב וסימן קעא סעיף א

עח [ז]מיי' וסמג שם טוש"ע א"ח סי' קעא סעיף ד

עט [ח]מיי' פרק א שם הלכה י"ב סמג שם טוש"ע א"ח סימן קעב סעיף א

פ [ט]מיי' שם טוש"ע א"ח שם סעיף ב

מסורת הש"ס

כלים פי"ח מ"ט

[תוספתא פ"ד]

שבת כ: וקמג. ביצה כח:

ב"ב לז:

[ע"ז ד: ע"ש מס' דרך ארץ פ"ט [ושם קחשיב חמשה דברים ואין יושבין על האוכלין]

[מס' סופרים פ"ג]

[תוספת' פ"ח דשבת]

[וע"ע תו' שבת עו: ד"ה כדי ובערובין כט: ופסחים קח: ד"ה שתאן וב"ב לז: ד"ה עד]

This applies only if the groups had not already counted them for *zimmun;* but if they had reckoned upon them where they were,[5] the obligation of *zimmun* has departed from them. Said Raba: Whence do I derive this rule? Because we have learnt: If the half of a bed has been stolen or lost, or if a bed has been divided by brothers or partners, it cannot receive uncleanness. If it is restored [to its original state] it can receive uncleanness thenceforward. Thenceforward it can, but not retrospectively.[6] This shows that from the time it was divided, uncleanness no longer attached to it.[7] So here, once they had used them for *zimmun*, the obligation of *zimmun* no longer attached to them.[8]

TWO GROUPS etc. A Tanna taught: If there is an attendant waiting on both, the attendant combines them.[9]

A BLESSING IS NOT SAID OVER WINE. Our Rabbis taught: If wine has not yet been mixed with water, we do not say over
a it the blessing 'Who createst the fruit of the vine',[1] but 'Who createst the fruit of the tree', and it can be used for washing the hands.[2] Once water has been mixed with it, we say over it the blessing 'Who createst the fruit of the vine', and it may not be used for washing the hands. So R. Eliezer. The Sages, however, say: In either case we say over it the blessing 'Who createst the fruit of the vine', and we do not use it for washing the hands. Whose view is followed in this statement of Samuel: A man may use bread for any purpose he likes?[3]—Whose view? That of R. Eliezer. R. Jose son of R. Ḥanina said: The Sages agree with R. Eliezer in the matter of the cup of wine used for grace, that a blessing should not be said over it until water has been added. What is the reason?—R. Oshaiah said: For a religious ceremony we require the best. And according to the Rabbis—for what kind of drink is undiluted wine suitable?—It is suitable for [mixing with] *karyotis*.[4]

Our Rabbis taught: Four things have been said with reference to bread. Raw meat should not be placed on bread; a full cup should not be passed along over bread;[5] bread should not be thrown; and a dish should not be propped up on bread. Amemar and Mar Zuṭra and R. Ashi were once taking a meal together. Dates and pomegranates were served to them, and Mar Zuṭra took some and threw them in front of R. Ashi as his portion. He said to him: Does not your honour agree with what has been taught, that eatables should not be thrown?—[He replied]: That was laid down with reference to bread. But it has been taught that just as bread is not to be thrown, so eatables should not be thrown? But, he replied, it has also been taught that although bread is not to be thrown, eatables may be thrown? But in fact there is no contradiction; one statement refers to things which are spoilt
b by throwing,[1] the other to things which are not spoilt.

Our Rabbis taught: Wine can be run through pipes[2] before the bridegroom and the bride, and roasted ears of corn and nuts may be thrown in front of them in the summer season but not in the rainy season;[3] while cakes may not be thrown in front of them either in the summer or the rainy season.[4]

Rab Judah said: If one forgot and put food into his mouth without saying a blessing, he shifts it to the side of his mouth and says the blessing. One [Baraitha] taught that he swallows it, and another taught that he spits it out, and yet another taught that he shifts it to one side. There is no contradiction. Where it says that he swallows it, the reference is to liquids; where it says that he spits it out, the reference is to something which is not spoilt thereby; and when it says that he shifts it, the reference is to

(5) I.e., if the party to which they belonged consisted of four persons each and they had left only after their respective parties has said the *zimmun* formula introducing the grace. (6) Kelim XVIII, 9. (7) An incomplete article does not contract defilement. (8) Lit., 'flew away from them'. (9) Even though they do not see one another.

a (1) Because as yet it shows no improvement over its original condition. This, of course, refers to the very strong wine of the ancients. (2) Like fruit juice. (3) I.e., wiping his hands after a meal, in spite of the general rule that food must not be wasted. (4) A kind of date with the shape of a nut, used for medicinal purpose. (5) For fear some should spill on the bread.

b (1) I.e., ripe, juicy figs. (2) This was done either as a symbol of prosperity, or for the purpose of diffusing a pleasant odour; it could be caught up in cups and so not wasted. (3) Because they may be spoilt by the muddy roads. (4) Because in either case they may be spoilt.

something which would be spoilt [by being spat out]. [51a] But why should he not also shift to one side anything which would not be spoilt and say the blessing?—R. Isaac Kaskasa'ah[5] gave the reason in the presence of R. Jose son of R. Abin, quoting R. Joḥanan: Because it says, *My mouth shall be filled with Thy praise.*[6]

R. Ḥisda was asked: If one has eaten and drunk without saying a blessing, should he say the blessing afterwards?—He replied: If one has eaten garlic so that his breath smells, should he eat more garlic so that his breath should go on smelling?[7] Rabina said: Therefore[8] even if he has finished his meal he should say the blessing retrospectively, since it has been taught: If a man has taken a ritual immersion and come out of the water, he should say on his emerging, 'Blessed be He who has sanctified us with His commandments and commanded us concerning immersion'. This, however, is not correct. In that case [of immersion] the
a man at the outset was not in a fit state to say a blessing;[1] in this case the man at the outset was in a fit state, and once it has been omitted it must remain omitted.

Our Rabbis taught: *Asparagus* brew[2] is good for the heart and good for the eyes, and, needless to say, for the bowels. If one uses it regularly it is good for the whole body, but if one gets drunk on it it is bad for the whole body. Since it is stated that it is good for the heart, we infer that we are dealing with a brew of wine. Yet it states that it is, needless to say, good for the bowels; but surely it has been taught: For *La'AT*[3] it is good, for *RaMaT*[4] it is bad?—Our statement[5] was made with reference to a brew of old wine,[6] as we have learnt: If one takes a vow to abstain from wine because it is bad for the bowels and they say to him, Is not the old wine good for the bowels, and he says nothing, he is forbidden to drink new wine but permitted to drink old wine.[7] This proves [that we are dealing with old wine].

Our Rabbis taught: Six things were said with reference to *asparagus*. It is only taken when the wine is undiluted and from a [full] cup; it is received in the right hand and held in the left hand when drunk; one should not talk after drinking it, nor stop in the middle of drinking it, and it should be returned only to the person who served it; one should spit after drinking it, and he should take immediately after it[8] only something of the same kind. But it has been taught: He should take immediately after it only bread?—There is no contradiction: the one statement applies to a brew of wine, the other to a brew of beer.[9]

One [authority] teaches: It is good for *La'AT* and bad for *RaMaT*, while another teaches that it is good for *RaMaT* and bad for *La'AT!* There is no contradiction: one statement speaks of a brew of wine, the other of a brew of beer. One [authority] teaches that if he spits after it he will suffer, another that if he does not spit after it he will suffer! There is no contradiction: the one statement speaks of a brew of wine, the other of a brew of beer. R. Ashi said: Now that you say that if he does not spit after it he will suffer, he should eject the liquid even in the presence of a king.

R. Ishmael b. Elisha said: Three things were told me by Suriel
b the Officer of the [Divine] Presence.[1] Do not take your shirt from the hand of your attendant when dressing in the morning,[2] and do not let water be poured over your hands by one who has not already washed his own hands, and do not return a cup of *asparagus* brew to anyone save the one who has handed it to you, because a company of demons (according to others, a band of destroying angels) lie in wait for a man and say, When will the man do one of these things so that we can catch him.

R. Joshua b. Levi says: Three things were told me by the Angel of Death. Do not take your shirt from your attendant when dressing in the morning, and do not let water be poured on your hands by one who has not washed his own hands,[3] and do not stand in front of women when they are returning from the presence of a dead person, because I go leaping in front of them with my sword in my hand, and I have permission to harm. If one should happen to meet them what is his remedy?—Let him turn aside four cubits; if there is a river, let him cross it, and if there is another road let him take it, and if there is a wall, let him stand behind it;[4] and if he cannot do any of these things, let him turn his face away and say, *And the Lord said unto Satan, The Lord rebuke thee, O Satan*
c etc.,[1] until they have passed by.

R. Zera said in the name of R. Abbahu—according to others, it was taught in a Baraitha: Ten things have been said in connection with the cup used for grace after meals. It requires to be rinsed and washed, it must be undiluted and full, it requires crowning and wrapping,[2] it must be taken up with both hands and placed in the right hand, it must be raised a handbreadth from the ground, and he who says the blessing must fix his eyes on it. Some add that he must send it round to the members of his household. R. Joḥanan said: We only know of four: rinsing, washing, undiluted and full. A Tanna taught: Rinsing refers to the inside, washing to the outside. R. Joḥanan said: Whoever says the blessing over a full cup is given an inheritance without bounds, as it says, *And full with the blessing of the Lord; possess thou the sea and the south.*[3] R. Jose son of R. Ḥanina says: He is privileged to inherit two worlds, this world and the next. 'Crowning': Rab Judah crowned it with disciples;[4] R. Ḥisda surrounded it with cups. 'And undiluted': R. Shesheth said: Up to the blessing of the land.[5] 'Wrapping': R. Papa used to wrap himself in his robe and sit down [to say grace over a cup]; R. Assi spread a kerchief over his head. 'It is taken in both hands': R. Ḥinena b. Papa said: What is the Scriptural warrant for this?—*Lift up your hands in holiness and bless ye the Lord.*[6] 'And placed in the right hand'. R. Ḥiyya b. Abba said in the name of R. Joḥanan: The earlier [students] asked: Should the left hand support the right?—R. Ashi said: Since the earlier [students] inquired and the question

(5) The reading is not certain. (6) Ps. LXXI, 8. There should be no room for anything besides the benediction. (7) I.e., having made one mistake, should he make another by not saying a blessing over the part he has still to eat (Maharsha). (8) Since he stops in the middle to say the blessing which he did not say at the beginning.

a (1) Having been unclean. (2) A beverage made by soaking certain roots in wine or beer. (3) L = *leb* (heart); 'A = *'ayin* (eyes); Ṭ = *ṭeḥol* (milt). (4) R = *rosh* (head); M = *me'ayim* (bowels); Ṭ = *ṭaḥtonioth* (piles). (5) Lit., 'that'. (6) At least three years old (Rashi). (7) Ned. 66a. (8) Lit., 'he must only support it with'. (9) According to Rashi, bread should be taken after wine; according to the Aruch, after beer.

b (1) I.e., an angel of high rank. (2) But get it yourself. (3) MS.M. inserts: and do not return the cup of *asparagus* brew to anyone save the one who has handed it to you. Do not enter alone a synagogue in which children are not being taught, because I hide there my weapons; and when there is a pestilence raging in the city do not walk in the middle of the road but on the side, and when there is peace in the city, do not walk on the side but in the middle of the road. (4) MS.M. inserts: and turn his face to the wall.

c (1) Zech. III, 2. (2) This is explained *infra*. (3) Deut. XXXIII, 23. (4) I.e., made them sit around him. (5) I.e., up to this point he leaves it undiluted, then he adds water. This is the reading of Alfasi; the reading of our text which has the words 'R. Ḥanan said' before 'and undiluted' is not intelligible. (6) Ps. CXXXIV, 2.

במידי דלא ממאים נמי ליסלקינהו לצד אחד וליברך תרגמה רב יצחק קסקסאה קמיה דר' יוסי ברבי אבין משמיה דר' יוחנן משום שנא' °ימלא פי תהלתך בעו מיניה מרב חסדא מי שאכל ושתה ולא ברך מהו שיחזור ויברך אמר להו מי שאכל שום וריחו נודף יחזור ויאכל שום אחר כדי שיהא ריחו נודף אמר רבינא הלכך אפי' גמר סעודתו יחזור ויברך *דתניא א טבל ועלה אומר בעלייתו ברוך אשר קדשנו במצותיו וצונו על הטבילה ולא היא התם מעיקרא גברא לא חזי הכא ב מעיקרא גבר' חזי והואיל ואידחי אידחי: ת"ר אספרגוס יפה ללב וטוב לעינים וכ"ש לבני מעים והרגיל בו יפה לכל גופו והמשתכר הימנו קשה לכל גופו מדקתני יפה ללב מכלל דבחמרא עסקי' וקתני וכל שכן לבני מעים והתניא ללע"ט יפה לרמ"ת קשה כי תניא ההיא במיושן *כדתנן קונם יין שאני טועם שהיין קשה לבני מעים אמרו לו והלא מיושן יפה הוא לבני מעים ושתק אסור בחדש ומותר במיושן שמע מינה ת"ר ששה דברים נאמרו באספרגוס אין שותין אותו אלא כשהוא חי ומלא מקבלו בימין ושותהו בשמאל ואין משיחין אחריו ואין מפסיקין בו ואין מחזירין אותו אלא למי שנתנו לו ורק אחריו ואין סומכין אותו אלא במינו והתניא אין סומכין אותו אלא בפת לא קשיא הא בדחמרא הא בדשכרא תני חדא ללע"ט יפה לרמ"ת קשה ותניא אידך לרמ"ת יפה ללע"ט קשה ל"ק הא בדחמרא הא בדשכרא תני חדא רק אחריו לוקה ותניא אידך לא רק אחריו לוקה ל"ק הא בדחמרא הא בדשכרא אמר רב אשי השתא דאמרת לא רק אחריו לוקה מימיו נזרקין אפי' בפני המלך: א"ר ישמעאל בן אלישע ג' דברים סח לי סוריאל שר הפנים אל תטול חלוקך בשחרית מיד השמש ותלבש ג ואל תטול ידיך ממי שלא נטל ידיו ואל תחזיר כוס אספרגוס אלא למי שנתנו לך מפני שתכספית ואמרי לה איסתלגנית של מלאכי חבלה מצפין לו לאדם ואומרים אימתי יבא אדם לידי אחד מדברים הללו וילכד אמר ריב"ל ג' דברים סח לי מלאך המות אל תטול חלוקך שחרית מיד השמש ותלבש ואל תטול ידיך ממי שלא נטל ידיו ד ואל תעמוד לפני הנשים בשעה שחוזרות מן המת מפני שאני מרקד ובא לפניהן וחרבי בידי ויש לי רשות לחבל ואי פגע מאי תקנתיה לינשוף מדוכתי' ד' אמות אי איכא נהרא ליעבריה ואי איכא דרכא אחרינא ליזיל בה ואי איכא גודא ליקו אחורא ואי לא ליהדר אפיה ולימא °ויאמר יי' אל השטן יגער יי' בך וגו' עד דחלפי מיניה: א"ר זירא א"ר אבהו ואמרי לה במתניתא תנא עשרה דברים נאמרו בכוס של ברכה טעון הדחה ושטיפה חי ומלא עיטור ועיטוף נוטלו בשתי ידיו ונתנו בימין ומגביהו מן הקרקע טפח ונותן עיניו בו וי"א אף משגרו במתנה לאנשי ביתו א"ר יוחנן אנו אין לנו אלא ארבעה בלבד *ה הדחה שטיפה *חי ומלא תנא הדחה מבפנים ושטיפה מבחוץ א"ר יוחנן כל המברך על כוס מלא נותנין לו נחלה בלא מצרים שנא' °ומלא ברכת יי' ים ודרום ירשה ר' יוסי ברבי חנינא אומר זוכה ונוחל שני עולמים העולם הזה והעולם הבא עיטור רב יהודה מעטרה בתלמידים רב חסדא מעטר לי' בנטלי א"ר *חנן *ובחי *אמר *רב *ששת *ובברכת *הארץ עיטוף רב פפא מעטף ויתיב רב אסי פרס סודרא על רישי' ו נוטלו בשתי ידיו א"ר חיננא בר פפא מאי קראה °שאו ידיכם קדש וברכו את ה' ונותנו לימין א"ר חייא בר אבא א"ר יוחנן ראשונים שאלו שמאל מהו שתסייע לימין אמר רב אשי הואיל וראשונים איבעיא להו ולא איפשט להו אנן

תורה אור: תהלי' עא | זכרי' ג | דברים לג | תהלים קלד

רש"י

במידי דלא ממאים נמי. למה לי פולטן לסלקינהו לצד אחד: יחזור ויאכל שום אחר. כדי שיסריח יותר כלומר יוסיף על סרחונו *ויעשה ברכה לבטלה: *מי שאכל ושתה ולא ברך. לפניהם קאי אברכת המוציא וברכת היין: מהו שיחזור וכו'. לאחר אכילה ושתיה: הלכך. כיון דאם נזכר באמצע יכול לברך אפילו גמר סעודתו נמי יכול לברך: על הטבילה. אלמא אע"ג דעבר הויא ברכה: התם מעיקרא לא חזי. דרוב טבילות משום קרי הם ובעלי קריין אסורים בברכות שהם דברי תורה כדאמרינן בפרק מי שמתו (דף כ:) ודחוי מעיקרא לאו דחוי הוא ולכי מתקן הדר מברך אבל האי מעיקרא איחזי וכיון דגמר אידחי והואיל ואידחי אידחי: אספרגוס. כוס שהיו שותים בכל בקר אליבא ריקנא לרפואה: דבחמרא עסקינן. דאמרינן לקמן בשמעתין אספרגוס ללע"ט יפה ואוקמינן בשל יין וסימן לע"ט לב עין טחול: וכ"ש לבני מעים. קושיא היא כלומר בדאורא קתני וכל שכן לבני מעים: והתניא. לקמן לרמ"ת קשה אספרגוס של יין וסימן רמ"ת ראש מעים תחתוניות: כי תניא ההיא. דקתני וכל שכן לבני מעים: ביין מיושן. של שלש שנים כדתנן בבבא בתרא (ד' לח.) ישן מבל אשתקד מיושן של שלש שנים: קונם יין שאני טועם. כהקדש יהא עלי יין שאני טועם: אלא חי. יין חי שאינו מזוג: אין מפסיקין בו. אלא שותהו בבת אחת: ואין סומכין אותו. לאכול אחריו מיד: בדחמרא. סמיכתו בפת: בדשכרא. סמיכתו במינו אם שכר תאנים סומכו בתאני' ואם של תמרים הוא סומכו בתמרים: לוקה. בחולי: בדחמרא. לא ירוק: בדשכרא. אם לא רק מים הבאים בפיו אחריו לוקה: ואפילו בפני המלך. ירוק ואל יסתכן: סוריאל. מלאך חשוב לבא לפני המלך: אל תטול הלוקך שחרית מיד השמש. אלא אתה בעצמך טלהו ממקום שהוא שם ותלבשנו: תכספית. שם חבורת שדים: איסתלגנית. שם חבורת מלאכי חבלה: אימתי יבא אדם לידי אחד מן הדברים הללו וילכד. ר' ישמעאל עלה לרקיע ע"י שם בברייתא דמעשה מרכבה: גודא. כותל: כוס של ברכה. ברכת המזון: הדחה ושטיפה וכו'. כולהו מפרש להו ואזיל: מן הקרקע. אם על גב קרקע הסב ואם ע"ג שלחן מגביהו מן השלחן: במתנה. דרך דורן וחשיבות: לאנשי ביתו. לאשתו: חי. שמוזגו במים לאחר שנתנו בכוס חי אבל לברך עליו חי הא אמרן במתניתין אין מברכין אי נמי חי בלע"ז פרים"ק להביאו מן החבית לשמו: מעטרהו בתלמידים. תלמידיו סובבין אותו כשהוא מברך: בנטלי. כוסות: ובברכת הארץ. כשמגיע לברכת הארץ מוסיף עליה: מעטף. בטליתו:

תוספות

מעיקרא גברא לא חזי. תימה והלא טמא אינו אסור לברך ובקונטרס פירש דבעלי קריין אסורים בדברי תורה וי"ל דמיירי בטבילת גרים ומפני אותה טבילה הצריכו לכל שאר טבילות לברך לאחר טבילה וכן בנטילת ידים שפעמים אדם בא מבית הכסא ואין אדם ראוי לברך עד לאחר הנטילה נהגו העם לברך כל שאר ברכות ידים לאחר *נטילה:

אין לנו אלא ארבעה דברים. ומיהו לא משמע כן דפליג ר' יוחנן אההיא דנותנו לימינו כדאמרי' לקמן א"ר יוחנן ראשונים שאלו מהו שתסייע שמאל לימין משמע שכן היו נוהגים ומיהו מדהאמוראים היו עושים עיטור ועיטוף משמע שהיו מחמירים על עצמן והיו נזהרים בכולן ולפיכך יש להחמיר בכוס של ברכה:

שטיפה חי ומלא. ירוש' דסוף פירקין אמר ר' אחא ג' דברים נאמרו בכוס של ברכה מלא עיטור ומודח ושלשתן מקרא נפתלי שבע רצון ומלא ברכת יי' שבע עיטור רצון מודח מלא כמשמעו:

שטיפה מבחוץ והדחה מבפנים ופירש ר"י דוקא שאין הכוס יפה שיש בו שיורי כוסות אבל אם הוא יפה בלאו הכי שפיר דמי דלא בעינן אלא שיהא כוס של ברכה יפה:

זוכה לשני עולמים. פי' הרב ר' יוסף מורשילי"א מדהוה ליה למכתב ים ודרום רש וכתב ירשה הרי יו"ד ה' יתירה וביו"ד ה"א נבראו שני עולמים כדאמרינן במנחות (דף כט:) כי ביה ה' צור עולמים *אל *תקרי *צור *אלא *צר וכו':

שמאל מהו שתסייע לימין. בכוסות גדולות מיירי או בר"ח טבת שחל להיות בשבת שהוא בחנוכה או בנישואין וצריך להאריך בברכת המזון: אין

עין משפט נר מצוה

פא א מיי' פרק י"א מהלכות ברכות הלכה ז סמג עשין כז טוש"ע י"ד סימן רסח סעיף ב

פב ב מיי' פ"ד שם הלכה ב טוש"ע א"ח סימן קסז סעיף ח

פג ג ש"ע א"ח סימן ד סעיף יח

פד ד ש"ע י"ד סימן שכט סעיף ב

פה ה מיי' פרק ז שם הלכה טו סמג שם טור וש"ע א"ח סי' קפ"ג סעיף א ב ג

פו ו שם סעיף ד

[וע"ע תו' פסחים ז: ד"ה על]

[כל זה לית' לפנינו שם]

[ע' תוס' לעיל כ: ד"ה מודים וע"ע תוספו' סנהדרין ע. ד"ה כ"ת]

בהרא"ש ליתא לכל זה גם בהרי"ף כדפס בפנים בין שני חלאי עיגולים וכן מוסק ד"ת

מסורת הש"ס

[ע' רש"א]

[דיבור זה וד"ה מהו שיחזור כו' לכאורה צ"ל קודם ד"ה יחזור ויאכל]

פסחים ז:

נדרים סו. ע"ש

וסימן המשים

[שם על הגליון ועיקר הגיר' שהיתה לפני רב אלפס כך אי' חי אמר רב ששת עד ברכת הארץ וכ"כ ר' יונה וכ"כ הב"י סי' קפ"ג ע"ש וע"ע תו' שבת עו: ד"ה כדי ותו' עירובין כ"ט: ותו' פסחים קח: ותו' ב"ב לז: ד"ה עד וכו' מה שפי' ר"ת על מה דאמרינן בברכת הארץ נגד פירוש רש"י דהכא]

עין משפט
נר מצוה

פז
א ב ג ד מיי' פ"ז מהלכות ברכות הלכה יד ופ"ט הלכה ד סמג עשין כז טוש"ע א"ח סי' קפ"ג סעיף ד

פח
ה שם סעי' ו

פט
ו מיי' פרק ד שם ה"א סמג שם טוש"ע א"ח סי' קפג סעיף ט

א
ז מיי' פכ"ט מהלכות שבת הלכה ו סמג עשין כט טוש"ע א"ח סימן רעא סעי' י

ב
ח מיי' פרק ט מהלכות ברכות הלכה ח ופכ"ט מהלכות שבת הלכה כה סמג עשין כז כט טוש"ע א"ח סי' ריז סעיף ב ה ו וסימן רלז סעיף ב וסי' רלח סעיף יב

ג
ט טוש"ע א"ח סי' קעד סעיף ג

ד
י מיי' פרק א מהלכות ברכות הלכה יג סמג עשין כז טוש"ע א"ח סימן רטו סעיף ב

(ירוש' לא גרס מלת לא ובמקו' של ע"א גרס שלפני ע"א)

אין מסיחין בכוס של ברכה. פרש"י שלא יסיח דעת המברך משנתנו לו כוס של ברכה וה"ה המסובין שאין רשאין להסיח דבעינן שיתכוין שומע ומשמיע וגם אין להפסיק השומעים בשיחת חולין כמו שאין המברך רשאי להסיח ואע"פ שאמר התם (פ' בתרא דר"ה דף לד:) שמע תשע תקיעות בתשע שעות ביום יצא משמע שהשומע שח בינתים ואפילו הכי יצא אך לכתחלה אין לעשות כן ומיהו נראה דהיינו דוקא בשעה שהמברך שותק מעט בין ברכה לברכה אבל בשעה שהוא מברך אם היה מדבר אפילו בדעבד לא יצא:

והלכתא בכולהו יושב ומברך. לפי שברכת המזון דאורייתא החמירו בה להיות יושב ומברך שהרי עשרה דברים נאמרו בו מה שאין כן בשאר ברכות והוא נוטריקון ואכלת ושבעת שב עת וברכת לברכת המזון ומפי רבי משה אלברט:

הדרן עלך שלשה שאכלו

תורה אור

אאנן נעבד לחומרא בומגבידהו מן הקרקע טפח א"ר אחא בר' חנינא מאי קראה °כוס ישועות אשא ובשם יי' אקרא גונותן עיניו בו כי היכי דלא ניסח דעתיה מיניה דומשגרו לאנשי ביתו במתנה כי היכי דתתברך דביתהו עולא אקלע לבי רב נחמן כרוך ריפתא בריך ברכת מזונא יהב ליה כסא דברכתא לרב נחמן א"ל רב נחמן לישדר מר כסא דברכתא לילתא א"ל הכי אמר ר' יוחנן אין פרי בטנה של אשה מתברך אלא מפרי בטנו של איש שנאמר °וברך פרי בטנך פרי בטנה לא נאמר אלא פרי בטנך תנ"ה רבי נתן אומר מנין שאין פרי בטנה של אשה מתברך אלא מפרי בטנו של איש שנאמר וברך פרי בטנך פרי בטנה לא נאמר אלא פרי בטנך אדהכי שמעה ילתא קמה בזיהרא ועלתה לבי חמרא ותברא ד' מאה דני דחמרא א"ל רב נחמן נשדר לה מר כסא אחרינא שלח לה כל האי נבגא דברכתא היא שלחה ליה ממהדורי מילי ומסמרטוטי כלמי אמר רב אסי האין מסיחין על כוס של ברכה ואמר רב אסי אין מברכין על כוס של פורענות מאי כוס של פורענות אמר רב נחמן בר יצחק כוס שני תנ"ה השותה כפלים לא יברך משום שנאמר °הכון לקראת אלהיך ישראל והאי לא מתקן א"ר אבהו ואמרי לה במתניתא תנא האוכל ומהלך מברך מעומד וכשהוא אוכל מעומד מברך מיושב וכשהוא מיסב ואוכל יושב ומברך והלכתא בכולהו יושב ומברך:

תלים קיו | דברי' ז | עמוס ד

הדרן עלך שלשה שאכלו

אלו *דברים שבין בית שמאי ובין בית הלל בסעודה ב"ש אומרים מברך על היום ואח"כ מברך על היין זוב"ה אומרים מברך על היין ואח"כ מברך על היום ב"ש אומרים נוטלין לידים ואח"כ מוזגין את הכוס וב"ה אומרים מוזגין את הכוס ואח"כ נוטלין לידים ב"ש אומרים מקנח ידיו במפה ומניחה על השלחן וב"ה אומרים על הכסת ב"ש אומרים מכבדין את הבית ואח"כ נוטלין לידים וב"ה אומרים נוטלין לידים ואח"כ מכבדין את הבית *ב"ש אומרי' נר ומזון בשמים והבדלה וב"ה אומרים נר ובשמים מזון והבדלה ב"ש אומרי' שברא מאור האש וב"ה אומרים בורא מאורי האש האין מברכין *לא על הנר ולא על הבשמים של כושיים ולא על הנר ולא על הבשמים של מתים ולא על הנר ולא על הבשמים של ע"א ואין מברכין על הנר עד שיאותו לאורו מי שאכל ושכח ולא ברך ב"ש אומרים יחזור למקומו ויברך וב"ה אומרים יברך במקום שנזכר ועד מתי מברך עד כדי שיתעכל המזון שבמעיו *בא להן יין אחר המזון אם אין שם אלא אותו כוס ב"ש אומרים מברך על היין ואח"כ מברך על המזון טוב"ה אומרים מברך על המזון ואח"כ מברך על היין יועונין אמן אחר ישראל המברך ואין עונין אמן אחר כותי המברך עד שישמע כל הברכה כולה: **גמ'** *ת"ר דברים שבין ב"ש וב"ה בסעודה ב"ש אומרים מברך על היום ואח"כ מברך על היין שהיום גורם ליין שיבא וכבר קדש היום ועדיין יין לא בא וב"ה אומרים מברך על היין ואח"כ מברך על היום שהיין גורם לקדושה שתאמר *דבר אחר ברכת היין תדירה וברכת היום אינה תדירה תדיר ושאינה תדיר תדיר קודם והלכה כדברי ב"ה מאי ד"א וכי תימא התם תרתי והכא חדא ה"נ תרתי נינהו ברכת היין תדירה וברכת היום אינה תדירה תדיר ושאינו תדיר תדיר קודם והלכה כדברי ב"ה פשיטא דהא נפקא *בת קול איבעית אימא קודם בת קול ואיבעית אימא לאחר בת קול

ורבי

א:ן נעבד לחומרא. שלא תסייע שמאל לימין בשעת ברכה: שמעה ילתא. שלא ישגר לה כוס של ברכה: קמה בזיהרא. עמדה בכעס: כל האי נבגא דברכתא הוי. כל יין שבחבית ככוס של ברכה הוא שתי ממנו. נבגא כוס כמו כשתי מן *אנבגא: ממהדורי מילי. ממחזרי בעיירות ירבו תמיד דברים: ומסמרטוטי כלמי. וממשחקי בגדים בלויים וממלוטים ירבו כנים. כנים מתרגמינן כלמתא: אין מסיחין. משאחזו עד שיברך: כוס שני. שהוא של זוגות והעומד על שלחנו ושתי זוגות ניזוק ע"י שדים: כפלים. זוגות: הכון לקראת. בדברים נאים ולא בדברי פורענות: מסב. במטה דרך הסבה: והלכתא בכולהו יושב ומברך:

הדרן עלך שלשה שאכלו

אלו דברים וכו' בסעודה. שנחלקו בהלכות סעודה: מברך על היום. בקדוש שבתות וימים טובים: ואחר כך מוזגין את הכוס. יין שבא לפני המזון כדאמרינן בפרק כיצד מברכין (דף מג.) הסבו אע"פ שנטל כו' הביאו להם יין וכו' וקאמרי ב"ש נוטלין לידים ואחר כך שותים את הכוס ואוכלים סעודתם בהסיבה נטילה וב"ה אומרים מוזגין את הכוס ושותין אותו ואחר כך נוטלין לידים וטעמא דתרוייהו מפרש בגמרא: מקנח ידיו במפה. מנטילת מים לאשונים: ומניחה. על השלחן: ומקנח בה ידיו. תמיד מזוהמת התבשיל: וב"ה אומרים. על הכר או על הכסת יניחנה אחרי כן ושם יקנח בה ידיו תמיד וטעמא מפרש בגמרא: מכבדין את הבית. מקום שאכלו שם אם הסבו על גבי קרקע מכבדי' את הקרקע או אם הסבו על השלחן מכבדין את השלחן משיורי אוכלין שנתפזרו עליו: ואחר כך נוטלין לידים. מים אחרונים: נר ומזון. מי שאין לו אלא כוס אחד במוצאי שבת מניחו עד לאחר המזון וסודר עליו נר ומזון ובשמים והבדלה כו': אין מברכים על הנר ועל הבשמי' של נכרים ושל מתים. טעם דכולהו מפרש בגמרא: שיאותו. שיהנו כהנים ממנו: עד כדי שיתעכל המזון. מפרש שיעורא בגמרא: מברך על היין. בגמרא מפרש פלוגתייהו: עונין אמן אחר ישראל המברך. אפילו לא שמע אלא סוף ברכה אבל לא לאחר כותי שמא ברך להר גריזים:

גמ' שהיום גורם ליין שיבא. כוס זה לא בא אלא בשביל שבת לקדוש: וכבר קדש היום. משקבלו עליו או מלאת הכוכבים: ועדיין יין לא בא. לשלחן וכשם שקודם לכניס' כך קודם לברכה: שהיין גורם לקדושה שתאמר. שאם אין יין לא מקדשין והמקדש על הפת גם הוא במקום יין וברכת הפת קודמת: תדיר קודם. כדפקא לן במסכת זבחים מהאי קרא דכתיב במוספין מלבד עולת הבוקר אשר לעולת התמיד תעשו את אלה מלבד משמע לאחר שהקרבתם התמיד הקריבו המוספין וקא דרשי' אשר לעולת התמיד קרא יתירא למילף דבשביל שהיא תמיד הקדימו הכתוב ומכאן אתה למד לכל התמידין:

ורבי

מסורת הש"ס
[קידושין ע.]
ע"ב קיד. סוכה כו.
ע"פ קג.
[לקמן נג.]
תוספתא פ"ה [פסחים קיד.]
ע"פ שם זבחים לא.
עירובין יג:

was not decided [51*b*] we will follow the more stringent view.[7] 'He raises it a handbreadth from the ground': R. Aḥa b. Ḥanina said: What Scriptural text have we for this?—*I will lift up the cup of salvation and call upon the name of the Lord.*[8] 'He fixes his eyes on it': so that his attention should not wander from it. 'He sends it round to the members of his household': so that his wife may be blessed.

'Ulla was once at the house of R. Naḥman. They had a meal and he said grace, and he handed the cup of benediction to R. Naḥman. R. Naḥman said to him: Please send the cup of bene-
a diction to Yaltha.[1] He said to him: Thus said R. Joḥanan: The fruit of a woman's body is blessed only from the fruit of a man's body, since it says, *He will also bless the fruit of thy body.*[2] It does not say the fruit of *her* body, but the fruit of *thy* body. It has been taught similarly: Whence do we know that the fruit of a woman's body is only blessed from the fruit of a man's body? Because it says: *He will also bless the fruit of thy body.* It does not say the fruit of *her* body, but the fruit of *thy* body. Meanwhile Yaltha heard,[3] and she got up in a passion and went to the wine store and broke four hundred jars of wine. R. Naḥman said to him: Let the Master send her another cup. He sent it to her with a message: All that wine[4] can be counted as a benediction. She returned answer: Gossip comes from pedlars and vermin from rags.[5]

R. Assi said: One should not speak over the cup of benediction.[6] R. Assi also said: One should not speak over the cup of punishment. What is the cup of punishment?—R. Naḥman b. Isaac said: a second cup.[7] It has been taught similarly: He who drinks an even number[8] should not say grace,[9] because it says, *Prepare to meet thy God, O Israel,*[10] and this one is not fitly prepared.

R. Abbahu said (according to others, it was taught in a Baraitha): One who eats as he walks says grace standing; if he eats standing up, he says grace sitting; if he eats reclining he sits up to say grace. The law is that in all cases he says grace sitting.

CHAPTER VIII

MISHNAH. THESE ARE THE POINTS [OF DIFFERENCE] BETWEEN BETH SHAMMAI AND BETH HILLEL IN RELATION TO A MEAL. BETH SHAMMAI SAY THAT THE BENEDICTION IS
b FIRST SAID OVER THE DAY[1] AND THEN OVER THE WINE, WHILE BETH HILLEL SAY THAT THE BENEDICTION IS FIRST SAID OVER THE WINE AND THEN OVER THE DAY. BETH SHAMMAI SAY THAT WASHING THE HANDS PRECEDES THE FILLING OF THE CUP,[2] WHILE BETH HILLEL SAY THAT THE FILLING OF THE CUP PRECEDES THE WASHING OF THE HANDS. BETH SHAMMAI SAY THAT AFTER WIPING HIS HANDS WITH A NAPKIN THE DINER PLACES IT ON THE TABLE, WHILE BETH HILLEL SAY THAT HE PLACES IT ON THE CUSHION.[3] BETH SHAMMAI SAY THAT [AFTER THE MEAL] THE FLOOR IS SWEPT BEFORE THE WASHING OF THE HANDS,[4] WHILE BETH HILLEL SAY THAT [THE DINERS] WASH THEIR HANDS AND THEN THE FLOOR IS SWEPT. BETH SHAMMAI SAY THAT [THE PROPER ORDER[5] IS] LIGHT, GRACE, SPICES, AND HABDALAH, WHILE BETH HILLEL SAY: LIGHT, SPICES, GRACE, AND HABDALAH.[6] BETH SHAMMAI SAY [THAT THE BLESSING OVER LIGHT CONCLUDES WITH THE WORDS], WHO CREATED THE LIGHT OF THE FIRE, WHILE BETH HILLEL SAY [THAT THE WORDS ARE], WHO IS CREATING THE LIGHTS OF THE FIRE.

A BENEDICTION MAY NOT BE SAID OVER THE LIGHTS OR THE SPICES OF IDOLATERS OR OVER THE LIGHTS OR THE SPICES OF DEAD,[7] OR OVER THE LIGHTS OR THE SPICES OF IDOLATRY, AND A BLESSING IS NOT SAID OVER THE LIGHT UNTIL IT HAS BEEN UTILIZED.

IF ONE HAS EATEN AND FORGOTTEN TO SAY GRACE, BETH SHAMMAI SAY THAT HE MUST RETURN TO THE PLACE WHERE HE ATE AND SAY THE GRACE, WHILE BETH HILLEL SAY THAT HE SHOULD SAY IT IN THE PLACE WHERE HE REMEMBERED. UNTIL WHEN CAN HE SAY THE GRACE? UNTIL SUFFICIENT TIME HAS PASSED FOR THE FOOD IN HIS STOMACH TO BE DIGESTED. IF WINE IS SERVED TO THEM AFTER THE FOOD, AND THAT IS THE ONLY CUP THERE, BETH SHAMMAI SAY THAT A BLESSING IS FIRST SAID OVER THE WINE AND THEN [THE GRACE] OVER THE FOOD, WHILE BETH HILLEL SAY THAT A BLESSING IS FIRST SAID OVER THE FOOD AND THEN OVER THE WINE. ONE SAYS AMEN AFTER A BLESSING SAID BY AN ISRAELITE BUT NOT AFTER A BLESSING SAID BY A
c CUTHEAN, UNLESS THE WHOLE OF IT HAS BEEN HEARD.[1]

GEMARA. Our Rabbis taught: The points of difference between Beth Shammai and Beth Hillel in relation to a meal are as follows: Beth Shammai say that the blessing is first said over the [sanctity of] the day and then over the wine, because it is on account of the day that the wine is used, and [moreover] the day has already become holy[2] before the wine has been brought. Beth Hillel say that a blessing is said over the wine first and then over the day, because the wine provides the occasion for saying a benediction.[3] Another explanation is that the blessing over wine is said regularly[4] while the blessing of the day is said only at infrequent intervals, and that which comes regularly always has precedence over that which comes infrequently. The *halachah* is as laid down by Beth Hillel. What is the point of the 'other explanation'?—Should you say that there [in explanation of Beth Shammai's view] two reasons are given and here [in explanation of Beth Hillel's] only one, we reply, there are two here also, [the second one being that] the blessing over wine is regular and the blessing of the day infrequent, and that which is regular has precedence over that which is infrequent, 'And the *halachah* is as
d stated by Beth Hillel'. This is self-evident, for the *Bath Kol*[1] went forth [and proclaimed so]![2] If you like I can reply that this statement was made before the *Bath Kol* [had issued forth], and if you

(7) And do not support with the left. (8) Ibid. CXVI, 13.
a (1) R. Naḥman's wife. (2) Deut. VII, 13. (3) That 'Ulla had refused to send her the cup. (4) I.e., all the wine of the flask from which the cup of benediction was poured. (5) As much as to say, what could be expected from a man like 'Ulla. (6) Once it is taken up for grace, it is not permitted to speak. (7) Even numbers were supposed to be unlucky. (8) Lit., 'Doubles'. (9) Probably it means, lead in the grace. (10) Amos IV, 12.
b (1) E.g., Sabbath or festival. (2) The cup of benediction drunk before meals, v. *supra* 43*a*. (3) The reason is given in the Gemara. (4) The 'latter water' before grace. (5) After a meal on the conclusion of the Sabbath or festival when *habdalah* (v. Glos.) has to be said. (6) I.e., the principal benediction in the *habdalah*, v. Glos. (7) Used at a funeral, cf. Roman *turibula* and *fasces*.
c (1) For fear he may have made an allusion to Mount Gerizim. (2) At sunset or before by the formal acceptance of the sanctity of the day in prayers or otherwise. (3) If there is no wine or its equivalent, no benediction is said. (4) I.e., practically every day.
d (1) Lit., 'daughter of a voice', 'A heavenly voice'. (2) V. 'Er. 13*b*.

like I can say that it was made after the *Bath Kol* [52a] and that it represents the view of R. Joshua, who said that we pay no attention to a *Bath Kol*.[3]

But do Beth Shammai hold that the blessing over the day is more important, seeing that it has been taught: 'When one goes into his house on the outgoing of Sabbath, he says blessings over wine and light and spices and then he says the *habdalah* [benediction].[4] If he has only one cup, he keeps it for after the meal and then says the other blessings in order after it?—But how do you know that this represents the view of Beth Shammai? Perhaps it represents the view of Beth Hillel?—Do not imagine such a thing. For it mentions first light and then spices; and who is it that we understand to hold this view? Beth Shammai, as it has been taught: R. Judah says: Beth Shammai and Beth Hillel concurred in holding that the grace after food comes first and the *habdalah* [benediction] last. In regard to what did they differ? In regard to the light and the spices, Beth Shammai holding that light should come first and then spices, and Beth Hillel that spices should come first and then light. And how do you know that this represents the view of Beth Shammai as reported by R. Judah? Perhaps it represents the view of Beth Hillel as reported by R. Meir![5]—Do not imagine such a thing. For it states here, BETH SHAMMAI SAY, LIGHT, GRACE AND SPICES, AND HABDALAH; WHILE BETH HILLEL SAY LIGHT, SPICES, GRACE, AND HABDALAH, and there in the Baraitha it says, 'If he has only one cup he keeps it for grace and says the others in order after it'. This shows that it represents the view of Beth Shammai as reported by R.
a Judah. In any case there is a difficulty?[1]—Beth Shammai hold that the entrance of a [holy] day is different from its outgoing. At its entrance, the earlier we can make it the better, but at its exit, the longer we can defer it the better, so that it should not seem to be a burden on us.

But do Beth Shammai hold that grace requires a cup [of wine] seeing that we have learnt: IF WINE IS SERVED TO THEM AFTER THE FOOD,[2] AND THAT IS THE ONLY CUP THERE, BETH SHAMMAI SAY THAT A BLESSING IS FIRST SAID OVER THE WINE AND THEN [THE GRACE] OVER THE FOOD. Does not this mean that he says a blessing over it and drinks it?[3]—No; he says a blessing over it and puts it aside.[4] But a Master has said: [After saying the blessing] one must taste it?—He does taste it. But a Master has said: If he tastes it he spoils it?[5]—He tastes it with his finger. But a Master has said: The cup of benediction must have a certain quantity, and he diminishes it?—We must suppose that he has more than the prescribed quantity. But it says, 'If there is only that cup'?—There is not enough for two but more than enough for one. But R. Ḥiyya taught: Beth Shammai say that he says a blessing over wine and drinks it and then says grace?—Two Tannaim report Beth Shammai differently.[6]

BETH SHAMMAI SAY etc. Our Rabbis taught: Beth Shammai say that washing of the hands precedes the filling of the cup. For should you say that the filling of the cup comes first, there is a danger lest liquid on the back of the cup will be rendered unclean through one's hands and it in turn will render the cup unclean. But would not the hands make the cup itself unclean?—Hands receive uncleanness in second degree,[7] and that which has received uncleanness in the second degree cannot pass on the uncleanness to a third degree in the case of non-sacred things,
b save through liquids.[1] Beth Hillel, however, say that the cup is first filled and then the hands are washed. For if you say that the hands are washed first, there is a danger lest the liquid on the hands should become unclean through the cup[2] and should then in turn make the hands unclean. But would not the cup make the hands themselves unclean?—A vessel does not make a man unclean. But would not [the cup] render unclean the liquid inside it?—We are here dealing with a vessel the outside of which has been rendered unclean by liquid, in which case its inside is clean and its outside unclean, as we have learnt: If the outside of a vessel has been rendered unclean by liquids, its outside is unclean [52b]

(3) 'Er. 7a. (4) Which is the blessing of the day. (5) *Infra*.

a (1) That Beth Shammai seem to give precedence to the blessing over wine over that of the day. (2) But before grace has been said. (3) That is if he wishes, he can drink the wine before the grace. (4) To serve as the cup of benediction. (5) For other ceremonial purposes. (6) R. Ḥiyya reporting them as saying that the grace after meals does not require a cup of benediction. (7) They are rendered unclean by something which has become unclean through touching something by its nature unclean.

b (1) This is a Rabbinic rule enunciated in Ṭoh. II, 3. (2) Supposing that this happens to be unclean.

*ורבי יהושע היא דאמר אין משגיחין בבת קול וסררי ב"ש דברכת היום עדיפא והתני' *הנכנס לביתו במוצאי שבת מברך על היין ועל המאור ועל הבשמים ואח"כ אומר הבדלה ואם אין לו אלא כוס אחד מניחו לאחר המזון ומשלשלן כולן לאחריו והא ממאי דב"ש היא דילמא ב"ה היא לא ס"ד דקתני מאור ואח"כ בשמים ומאן שמעת ליה דאית ליה האי סברא ב"ש *דתניא א"ר יהודה לא נחלקו ב"ש וב"ה על המזון שבתחלה ועל הבדלה שהיא בסוף על מה נחלקו על המאור ועל הבשמים *ב"ש אומרים מאור ואח"כ בשמים וב"ה אומרים בשמים ואחר כך מאור וממאי דב"ש היא ואליבא דר' יהודה דילמא ב"ה היא ואליבא דר"מ לא ס"ד דקתני הכא במתניתין ב"ש אומרים נר ומזון בשמים והבדלה וב"ה אומרים נר ובשמים ומזון והבדלה והתם בברייתא קתני אם אין לו אלא כוס אחד מניחו לאחר המזון ומשלשלן כולן לאחריו שמע מינה דבית שמאי היא ואליבא דרבי יהודה ומ"מ קשיא קא סברי ב"ש *שאני עיולי יומא מאפוקי יומא עיולי יומא כמה דמקדמינן ליה עדיף אפוקי יומא כמה דמאחרינן ליה עדיף כי היכי דלא להוי עלן כמשוי וסברי ב"ש ברכת המזון טעונה כוס והא תנן בא להם יין לאחר המזון אם אין שם אלא אותו כוס ב"ש אומרים מברך על היין ואחר כך מברך על המזון מאי לאו דמברך עילוי' ושתי ליה לא דמברך עילוי' ומנח ליה והאמר מר *המברך צריך שיטעום דטעים ליה והאמר מר *[א]טעמו פגמו דטעים ליה בידיה והא אמר מר *כוס של ברכה צריך שיעור והא קא פחית ליה משיעוריה דנפיש ליה טפי משיעוריה והא אם אין שם אלא אותו כוס קתני תרי לא הוי ומחד נפיש והא תני ר' חייא ב"ש אומרים מברך על היין ושותהו ואחר כך מברך ברכת המזון אלא תרי תנאי ואליבא דב"ש: ב"ש אומרים וכו': ת"ר ב"ש אומרים נוטלין לידים ואח"כ מוזגין את הכוס שאם אתה אומר מוזגין את הכוס תחלה גזרה *שמא יטמאו משקין שאחורי הכוס מחמת ידיו ויחזרו ויטמאו את הכוס וליטמו ידים לכוס ידים שניות הן *[ב]ואין שני עושה שלישי בחולין [ג]אלא על ידי משקין וב"ה אומרים מוזגין את הכוס ואח"כ נוטלין לידים שאם אתה אומר נוטלין לידים תחלה גזרה שמא יטמאו משקין שבידים מחמת הכוס ויחזרו ויטמאו את הידים וניטמו כוס לידים [ד]אין כלי מטמא אדם וניטמו למשקין שבתוכו הכא בכלי שנטמא אחוריו במשקין עסקינן דתוכו טהור וגבו טמא *דתנן [ה]כלי שנטמאו אחוריו במשקין אחוריו טמאין תוכו

רש"י

ור' יהושע היא. בבבא מציעא בתנורו של עכנאי בפ' הזהב (דף נט:): ומשלשלן. לשון שלשלת כלומר סודרן לאחר המזון: וממאי דבית שמאי היא כו'. אלמא לב"ש מאור ואחר כך בשמים וכן ברייתא נמי מאור ואחר כך בשמים קאמר אלמא בית שמאי היא וקתני יין ברישא מקמי הבדלה: ודלמא ב"ה היא ואליבא דרבי מאיר. דתנן במתניתין בית הלל אומרים נר ובשמים ואמר בגמרא כרבי מאיר היא: לא סלקא דעתך. לאוקומי ברייתא כמתניתין דמתניתין קתני מזון באמצע וברייתא קתני משלשלן כולן לאחריו כר' יהודה דאמר על המזון שבתחלה ומדקתני לר' יהודה מאור ואח"כ בשמים בית שמאי היא: ומ"מ קשיא. דברכת היין קודמת להבדלה: עיולי יומא. קדוש עיולי הוא והבדלה אפוקי היא: ברכה טעונה כוס. ברכת המזון דקתני מניחו לאחר המזון: והתנן. מתני' בפרקין: בא להן. כל ימות השנה קאמר: אחר המזון. ובתוך המזון לא בא להם וכשגמרו סעודתם בא להם לפני ברכת המזון מאי לאו דשתי ליה וה"ק ב"ש אם רצה מברך על היין ושותהו ואין צריך להניחו לברכת המזון: טעמו פגמו. לברכת המזון ולקדוש ולהבדלה בפר' ערבי פסחים (דף קה:): הכי גרסי' אלא תרי תנאי אליבא דב"ש. תנא דמתני' ותנא דר' חייא תנא דרבי חייא אליבא דב"ש אמר אין ברכה טעונה כוס ותנא דמתניתין דלעיל דר' יהודה אליבא דבית שמאי סבר ברכה טעונה כוס: גזרה שמא יטמאו משקין. שנפלו באחורי הכוס מחמת ידים דתנן (פרה פ"ח מ"ז) כל הפוסל את התרומה מטמא משקין להיות תחלה ויחזרו ויטמאו את הכוס וב"ש סברי אסור להשתמש בכוס שאחוריו טמאו' כדלקמן: וליטמו ידים לכוס. למה ליה דקאמר משקין שאחורי הכוס בלא משקין נמי ניטמו ידים לכוס: אלא ע"י משקין. שהמשקין נעשין ראשונים מדרבנן וא"ת כלי אינו מקבל טומאה אלא מאב הטומאה הני מילי מדאורייתא וחכמים גזרו שיהו משקין ראשונים מטמאים כלי גזרה משום משקין זב וזבה שהן אבות הטומאה כגון רוקו ומימי רגליו: ובית הלל אומרים כו'. בתוספתא הכי גרסינן לה ובית הלל אומרים אחורי הכוס לעולם טמאים דבר אחר תכף לנטילת ידים סעודה ומאי דחיישיתו שלא יטמאו הידים את אחורי הכוס לאו חששא היא שאפילו לכתחלה מותר להשתמש בכלי שאחוריו טמאים ותוכו טהור כגון זה שנטמא אחוריו מחמת משקין דאמרינן ביה במשנתין תוכו טהור הלכך מוזגין ושותין את הכוס תחלה קודם נטילה שאם אתה אומר נוטלין לידים תחלה שמא לא יהו הידים נגובות יפה ממי הנטילה ויטמאו המשקין שבידים מחמת כוס והן נעשים תחלה ויחזרו ויטמאו את הידים ונמצא אוכל בידים מסואבות: וניטמי כוס לידים. למה לי משקין בידים אפילו ידים נגובות נמי יטמא כוס לידים וכיון דהכי הוא הכי נמי דבכוס שלפני המזון עבוד ב"ה תקנתא דשותהו קודם נטילה כוסות הבאין בתוך המזון מה תהא עליהן הלא מטמאין את הידים: אין כלי מטמא אדם. כלומר כלי כזה שנטמא בולד הטומאה אינו מטמא את הידים דקיימא לן כרבנן דפליגי עליה דר' יהושע במסכת ידים (פ"ג) בכלים שנטמאו במשקין ואומר את שנטמא באב הטומאה מטמא את הידים ושנטמא בולד הטומאה אינו מטמא את הידים שאין שני עושה שני ואע"פ שהספר מטמא את הידים אין למדים הימנו הלכך כוסות שבתוך המזון שהידים נגובות אינן מטמאין את הידים וא"ת פעמים שיש משקה תבשיל טופח על הידים אין תורת משקין עליו אלא תורת אוכל: כלי שנטמאו אחוריו במשקין. בכלי שטף קאמר דאלו כלי חרס אין מטמאין מגבן אפילו בטומאה דאורייתא: שנטמאו אחוריו במשקין. אין לך משקה שאינו ראשון לטומאה שאף אם נגע בשני עשאוהו חכמים תחלה: אחוריו טמאין. אע"פ שאין אדם וכלים מקבלין טומאה מן התורה אלא מאב הטומאה גזרו חכמים שיהו משקין מטמאין כלים מפני שאלינו משקה שהוא אב הטומאה לטמא אדם וכלים מן התורה כגון זובו של זב ורוקו ומימי רגליו גזרו על כל המשקין טמאין שיטמאו כלים: תוכו

תוספות

ורבי יהושע היא דאמר אין משגיחין בבת קול. וא"ת א"כ קשה הלכתא אהלכתא דהא קי"ל דר' יהושע דתנור של עכנאי קי"ל כר' יהושע וקי"ל כב"ה וי"ל דדוקא התם קאמר דאין משגיחין בבת קול דהבת קול היה כנגד הרוב וכבר אמרה תורה אחרי רבים להטות (שמות כג) אבל ב"ה היו רבים אע"פ שמייתי ר' יהושע הכא אע"ג דלא דמי דשאני התם דהבת קול היה כנגד הרוב האי תנא סבר טפי מרבי יהושע דאמר אין משגיחין בבת קול אע"פ שרוב מסייע לבת קול הואיל וב"ש מחדדי טפי וא"ת מ"ש דבקדוש והבדלה מברכין קודם על היין ובברכת המזון אין מברכין עד לאחר שלש ברכות וי"ל דהיכי נעביד אם נברך קודם ברכת המזון א"כ יהא ברכת המזון היסח הדעת דבשלמא בשאר ברכות לא עקר נפשיה משתיה דבקדוש היה רוצה לאכול ובהבדלה היה רוצה לשתות אבל בברכת המזון עקר נפשיה משתיה:

ומניחו עד לאחר המזון. הכא משמע שמותר לטעום קודם הבדלה תימה הא אמימר בת טוות פי' לן מעונה (ע"פ ד' קז.) לפי שלא היה לו יין להבדיל עליו וי"ל דשאני אמימר שהיה סבור שיהיה לו כוס למחר או נחמיר על עצמו היה והכא שאני דקסבר ברכת המזון טעונה כוס ולכך מניחו לברכת המזון:

טעמו פגמו. פרשב"ם דוקא לקדוש ולהבדלה צריך שלא יהא פגום אבל לשתות צריך לברך עליו אע"פ שהוא פגום דאסור ליהנות מן העולם הזה בלא ברכה וקדוש והבדלה נמי לא אמרן אלא במקום דאפשר אבל אי אפשר מברך אפילו אפגום ונותן לתוכו מים כדאיתא בירושלמי ר' יונה טעים אכסא ומתקן ליה פי' לאחר ששתה ממנו הוסיף עליו כל שהוא מים או יין והיה מברך עליו:

גזרה שמא יטמאו משקין שבידים. אבל בתוך הסעודה ליכא למיחש שהרי אדם מנגב ידיו יפה קודם אכילה כדאמרינן *האוכל בלא ניגוב ידים וכו' אבל בשתיה אין אדם מדקדק לנגב ידיו כל כך:

תכף

עין משפט נר מצוה

ה אמיי' פכ"ט מה' שבת הל"ז טוש"ע א"ח סי' קפב סעיף ב

ו במיי' פ"א מהל' אבות הטומאות הלכה ג

ז גמיי' פ"ז שם הלכה ה

ח דמיי' פ"ח שם הלכה א

ט המיי' פ"ז שם הלכה ג ופי"ג מהלכו' כלים הלכה ד

[סוטה ד:]

[עיין תוס' עירובין לג. ד"ה היו ובחולין פז: ד"ה כל ובבכורות יב: ד"ה וכלב]

מסורת הש"ס

[עירובין ז.] ב"מ נט: חולין מד. תוספתא פ"ה יבמות יד. ע"פ קיד. תוספתא פ"ה [פסחים קג:] קה: ירוש' שונה ב"ש במקום ב"ה [פסחים קה:] [עירובין ס: פסחים קה:] שם שם תוספתא פ"ה פרה פ"ח משנה ה טהרות פ"ב משנה ג [חולין לג.] חגיגה כב: בכורות לח. נליט ע"ו מ"ו נדה ז:

תוכו ואוגנו ואזנו וידיו טהורין נטמא תוכו נטמא כולו במאי קא מפלגי ב"ש סברי אסו' להשתמש בכלי שנטמאו אחוריו במשקין גזרה משום נצוצות וליכא למגזר שמא יטמאו המשקין שבידים בכוס וב"ה סברי שמותר להשתמש בכלי שנטמאו אחוריו במשקין אמרי נצוצות לא שכיחי ואיכא למיחש שמא יטמאו משקין שבידים מחמת הכוס ד"א *תכף לנ"י סעודה מאי ד"א ה"ק להו ב"ה לב"ש לדידכו דאמריתו אסור להשתמש בכלי שאחוריו טמאין דגזרינן משום נצוצות אפ"ה הא עדיפא *דתכף לנ"י סעודה: ב"ש אומרים מקנח וכו': ת"ר *ב"ש אומרים מקנח ידיו במפה ומניחה על השלחן שאם אתה אומר על הכסת גזירה שמא יטמאו משקין שבמפה מחמת הכסת ויחזרו ויטמאו את הידים ונטמיי' כסת למפה אין *כלי מטמא כלי ונטמיי' כסת לגברא גופיה אין כלי מטמא אדם וב"ה אומרים על הכסת שאם אתה אומר על השלחן גזרה שמא יטמאו משקים שבמפה מחמת השלחן ויחזרו ויטמאו את האוכלין ולטמא שלחן לאוכלין שבתוכו הכא בשלחן שני עסקי' ואין *שני עושה שלישי בחולין אלא ע"י משקין במאי קמפלגי ב"ש סברי אסור להשתמש בשלחן שני גזרה משום אוכלי תרומה וב"ה סברי מותר להשתמש בשלחן שני אוכלי תרומה זריזין הם ד"א אין נ"י לחולין מן התורה מאי ד"א הכי קאמרי להו ב"ה לב"ש וכי תימרו מ"ש גבי אוכלין דחיישינן ומ"ש גבי ידים דלא חיישינן אפילו הכי הא עדיפא דאין נטילת ידים לחולין מן התורה מוטב שיטמאו ידים דלית להו עיקר מדאורייתא ואל יטמאו אוכלים דאית להו עיקר מדאורייתא: בש"א מכבדין וכו': *ת"ר בש"א מכבדין את הבית ואחר כך נוטלין לידים שאם אתה אומר נוטלין לידים תחלה נמצא אתה מפסיד את האוכלין אבל נ"י לב"ש תחלה לא סבירא להו מ"ט משום פרורין ובה"א אם שמש תלמיד חכם הוא נוטל פירורין שיש בהן כזית ומניח פרורין שאין בהן כזית מסייע ליה לר' יוחנן *דא"ר יוחנן פירורין שאין בהן כזית מותר לאבדן ביד במאי קמפלגי ב"ה סברי אסור להשתמש בשמש ע"ה וב"ש סברי מותר להשתמש בשמש ע"ה א"ר יוסי בר חנינא אמר רב הונא בכוליה פרקין הלכה כב"ה בר מהא דהלכה כב"ש ור' אושעיא מתני אפכא ובהא נמי הלכה כב"ה: בש"א נר ומזון וכו': *רב הונא בר יהודה איקלע לבי רבא חזייה לרבא דבריך אבשמים ברישא א"ל מכדי ב"ש וב"ה אמאור לא פליגי *דתניא בש"א נר ומזון בשמים והבדלה ובה"א נר ובשמים מזון והבדלה עני רבא בתריה זו דר"מ אבל ר' יהודה אומר לא נחלקו ב"ש וב"ה על המזון שהוא בתחלה ועל הבדלה שהיא בסוף על מה נחלקו על המאור ועל הבשמים שבש"א על המאור ואחר כך בשמים ובה"א בשמים ואח"כ מאור וא"ר יוחנן נהגו העם כב"ה אליבא דרבי יהודה: בש"א שברא כו': אמר *רבא בברא כ"ע לא פליגי דברא משמע כי פליגי בבורא ב"ש סברי בורא דעתיד למברא וב"ה סברי בורא נמי דברא משמע מתיב רב יוסף °יוצר אור ובורא חשך °יוצר הרים ובורא רוח °בורא השמים ונוטיהם אלא אמר רב יוסף בברא ובורא כ"ע לא פליגי דברא משמע כי פליגי במאור ומאורי דב"ש סברי חדא נהורא איכא בנורא וב"ה סברי טובא נהורי איכא בנורא תנ"ה אמרו להם ב"ה לב"ש הרבה מאורות יש באור: אין מברכין כו': בשלמא נר משום דלא שבת אלא בשמים מ"ט לא אמר רב יהודה אמר רב הכא במסבת כושיים עסקינן מפני שסתם מסבת כושיים לע"א היא הא מדקתני סיפא אין מברכין לא על הנר ולא על הבשמים של כושיים מכלל דרישא לאו בכושיים עסקינן א"ר חנינא מסורא מה טעם קאמר מה טעם אין מברכין לא על הנר ולא על הבשמים של כושיים מפני שסתם מסבת כושיים לע"א ת"ר אור ששבת מברכין עליו ושלא שבת אין מברכין עליו *(מאי שבת) ומאי לא שבת

אי נימא

תורה אור

תוכו ואוגנו ואזנו וידיו טהורין. דכיון דטומאה זו דרבנן היא עבדו בה היכרא דכדעו דמדרבנן היא כי היכי דלא לשרוף עלה תרומ' וקדשים והקלו בה וכן מפורש [בבכורות*]. אוגנו שפתו הכפולה לצד חוץ הראוי לתשמיש. אזנו כמו אזן הקבית שקורין אנ"שא בלע"ז וידיו כלי שיש לו יד כגון מחבת: גזרה משום נצוצות. שמא יתזו כלולות מתוכו על אחוריו ויטמאו משקין שאחריו מחמת אחורים ויטמאו את הידים הלכך נוטלים לידים תחלה שלא יטמאו את אחורי הכוס ולמאי דחיישי ב"ה מחמת אחוריו לאו משמא הוא דהא אסור לאשתמושי ביה: וב"ה סברי מותר להשתמש בו. הלכך לחששא דידן איכא למיחש אבל לחששא דידכו ליכא למיחש דלא איכפת לן אם יטמאו אחוריו: הא עדיפא. למזוג הכוס תחלה ואחר כך נטילת ידים תכף לסעודה ולא אתיא חששא דכלולות ומפקעא הלכתא וזו מהלכות סעודה היא: משקין שבמפה. שמא יהא משקה טופח עליה מחמת נגוב הידי' ויחזרו ויטמאו את הידים כשיקנח בה תמיד בתוך הסעודה: ונטמייה כסת למפה. בלא משקים: אין כלי. שאינו אב הטומאה מטמא כלים ולא אדם והוא יזהר שלא יגעו ידיו בכסת אם ראשונה היא לטומאה: מחמת שלחן. כדמפרש לקמיה דסברי ב"ה מותר להשתמש בשלחן שני: משום אוכלי תרומה. שהשני פוסל את התרומה: אפילו הכי הא עדיפא. לחוש שמא יארע מקרה שישתמשו בשלחן שני ולא יניחנה על גבי השלחן שלא תטמא את האוכלין מחמת משקין שבה מלחוש שלא תטמא מחמת כסת ותחזור ותטמא את הידים: מפסיד את האוכלין. שמים אחרונים נתזין עליהם ונמאסים: ה"ג בתוספתא ובה"א אם שמש ת"ח הוא נוטל פרורים שיש בהן כזית ומניח פרורין שאין בהן כזית: מתני אפכא. ומפיך בהך סיפא דב"ש לב"ה ודב"ה לב"ש וקבע בהא נמי הלכה כב"ה: וא"ר יוחנן גרסינן: דברא משמע. לשעבר ויפה לאומרו שעל בריית האור שברא בששת ימי בראשית משבחין אותו לפי שבמ"ש נברא כדאמרינן בפסחים (דף נד.): בורא. דבר שהוא בורא תמיד והא לא שייכא הכא שהרי כבר נברא: הרבה מאורות. שלהבת אדומה לבנה וירקרקת: משום דלא שבת. ממלאכת עבודה שהכותי עושה מלאכה לאורו ותניא לקמן אור שלא שבת אין מברכין עליו הואיל ונעבדה בו עבירה: במסבת כושיים. לאכילה לסעודה:

אי

תכף לנטילת ידים סעודה. והאי דלא חשיב ליה לעיל בפ' כ"מ (דף מב.) בהדי אידך תכיפות משום דשניה *במשנה לא קא מתכוי':

דבר אחר אין נטילת ידים לחולין מן התורה וכו'. יש ספרים שכתוב בהן הכי קאמרי להו ב"ש לבית הלל אפילו לדידכו דאמריתו אסור להשתמש בשלחן שני משום אוכלי תרומה הא עדיפא דאין נטילת ידים לחולין מן התורה מוטב וכו' ואל יטמא וכו' ול"כ דהא קאמרי ב"ש דאסור להשתמש בשלחן שני ודוחק לומר כמו שפירש רש"י שמא במקרה בעלמא ישתמש אלא נראה כספרים שכתוב בהן מאי דבר אחר הכי קאמרי להו ב"ה לב"ש וכ"ת מ"ש גבי אוכלין דחיישינן ומ"ש גבי ידים דלא חיישינן וכו' והשתא לא הוי האי דבר אחר כי ההיא דלעיל שאינו צריך לטעם ראשון אבל הכא האי ד"א לא בא אלא לפרש טעמא דב"ה קאמר וליישב דבריהם:

פרורין דלית בהו כזית מותר לאבדן ביד. מיהו קשה לעניותא כדאמרינן בפרק כל הבשר (דף קה:):

בכוליה פירקין הלכה כב"ה לבר מהא. וא"ת והא בההוא דיחזור למקומו ויברך משמע דהלכה כב"ש לקמן (דף נג.) בשמעתין ומדעבדי אמוראי בתרייהו י"ל דלא חשיב לה משום דהתם אפילו ב"ה מודו לבית שמאי אלא שלא הטריחוהו *לכך:

נהגו העם כב"ה אליבא דרבי יהודה. תימה דאכן אפילו לכתחלה נוהגים כן ובפרק *הדר (ד' סג:) אומר נהגו אורויי לא מורינן ואי עבד הכי לא מהדרינן ליה וי"ל דהתם איכא אמוראי דפליגי חד אמר הלכה והוה פי' הלכה לכתחלה ומורינן הכי א"כ נהגו דקאמר אידך הוי דיעבד אבל הכא יכול להיות דאין כאן אלא נהגו *גרידא:

בברא כ"ע ל"פ. וא"ת הואיל ול"פ בלשון ברא אמאי אמר בורא וי"ל דלשון קרא עדיף:

וכי

עין משפט נר מצוה [בברייתא]

י א טוש"ע א"ח סימן קנו

יא ב מיי' פ"ז מהלכות ברכות הלכה יא סמג עשין כז טוש"ע א"ח סימן קפ סעיף ג

יב ד מיי' פכ"ט מהלכות שבת הלכה כד סמג עשין כט טוש"ע א"ח סימן רצו סעיף א ג

יג ה מיי' וסמג שם טוש"ע א"ח סימן רצח סעיף א

יד ו מיי' שם הלכה כה ופ"ע מה' ברכות הל' ע סמג עשין כז כט טוש"ע א"ח סי' ריז סעיף ו וסי' רצז סעיף ב

[ועיין תוס' סוכה ג. ד"ה דאמר לך]

[לפנינו שם ליתא רק במס' תענית כו: איתא כך]

[וע"ע תו' פסחים קג. ד"ה ואמר כ"ה כו: ד"ה וכי]

[דתנן]

[אולי צ"ל רבה]

[ע' בהרי"ף והרא"ש גרסה כך נוסחתם מאי לא שבת שלא שבת ממלאכת עבירה אבל אור של חיה ושל חולה מברכין עליו תניא נמי הכי עששית שהיתה וכו']

מסורת הש"ס

[דף לח.]

[תוספתא פ"ה]

שם

[פסחי' יט: חגיגה כ.]

[חולין לג.]

תוספתא שם

שבת קמג. [ע"ש תוס' וע"ע תוספו' במנחות כח: דזה מסוגית הפוכות]

ע"פ קג.

ישעיה מה

עמוס ד

ישעיה מב

while its inside, its rim, its handle and its haft are clean. If its inside has been rendered unclean, it is all unclean. What is the point at issue between them?—Beth Shammai hold that it is forbidden to use a vessel the outside of which has been rendered unclean by liquids for fear of drippings,[3] and consequently there is no need to fear that the liquid on the hands will be rendered unclean by the cup.[4] Beth Hillel on the other hand hold that it is permitted to use a vessel the outside of which has been rendered unclean by liquids, considering that drippings are unusual, and consequently there is a danger lest the liquid on the [undried] hands should be rendered unclean through the cup.[5] Another explanation is, so that the meal should follow immediately the washing of the hands. What is the point of this 'other explanation'?—Beth Hillel argued thus with Beth Shammai: Even from your standpoint, that it is forbidden to use a vessel the outside of which has been rendered unclean by liquids, for fear of drippings, even so our ruling is superior, because the washing of the hands is immediately followed by the meal.

BETH SHAMMAI SAY THAT AFTER WIPING HIS HAND WITH THE NAPKIN etc. Our Rabbis taught: Beth Shammai say that [the diner] after wiping his hands with the napkin places it on the table. For if you say that he places it on the cushion, there is a danger lest liquid on the napkin may be rendered unclean through the cushion and then in turn render the hands unclean. But will not the cushion make the napkin itself unclean?—One vessel does not render another unclean. But will not the cushion make the man himself unclean?—A vessel does not render a man unclean. Beth Hillel, however, say that he puts it on the cushion. For if you say that he puts it on the table there is a fear lest the liquid on the napkin should be rendered unclean through the table and should in turn render the food unclean. But will not the table render the food on it unclean?—We are dealing here with a table which is unclean in the second degree, and that which is unclean in the second degree does not pass on uncleanness to a third degree in the case of non-sacred things, save through the medium of liquids. What is the point at issue between them?—Beth Shammai hold that it is forbidden to use a table which is unclean in the second degree for fear lest it may be used by persons
a eating *terumah*,[1] while Beth Hillel hold that it is permissible to use a table which is unclean in the second degree since persons who eat *terumah* are careful [to avoid such]. Another explanation is that washing of hands for non-sacred food is not prescribed by the Torah. What is the point of the 'other explanation'?—Beth Hillel argued thus with Beth Shammai: Should you ask what reason is there for being particular in the case of food[2] and not being particular in the case of hands, even granting this, our rule is better, since washing of hands for non-sacred food is not prescribed by the Torah. It is better that hands, the rule for which has no basis in the Torah, should become unclean, rather than food, the rule for which has a basis in the Torah.

BETH SHAMMAI SAY THAT THE FLOOR IS SWEPT etc. Our Rabbis taught: Beth Shammai say: The floor is swept and then they wash their hands. For should you say that the hands are washed first, the result might be to spoil the food. (Beth Shammai
b do not hold that the washing of the hands comes first.)[1] What is the reason?—On account of the crumbs [of bread]. Beth Hillel, however, say that if he the attendant is a scholar, he removes the crumbs which are as large as an olive and leaves those which are smaller than an olive. This supports the dictum of R. Johanan; for R. Johanan said: It is permissible to destroy wilfully crumbs [of bread] smaller than an olive.[2] What is the ground of their difference?—Beth Hillel hold that it is not permissible to employ an attendant who is an *'am ha-arez*,[3] while Beth Shammai hold that is is permissible to employ an attendant who is an *'am ha-arez*. R. Jose b. Ḥanina said in the name of R. Huna: In all this chapter the *halachah* is as stated by Beth Hillel, save in this point where it is as stated by Beth Shammai. R. Oshaia, however, reverses the teaching[4] and in this point also the *halachah* follows Beth Hillel.

BETH SHAMMAI SAY, LIGHT, GRACE, etc. R. Huna b. Judah was once at the house of Raba, and he saw Raba say the blessing over spices first.[5] He said to him: Let us see. Beth Shammai and Beth Hillel do not differ with respect to the light [that it should come first], as we learnt: BETH SHAMMAI SAY, [THE ORDER IS] LIGHT, GRACE, SPICES, AND HABDALAH, WHILE BETH HILLEL SAY THAT IT IS LIGHT, SPICES, GRACE AND HABDALAH!—Raba answered after[6] him: These are the words of R. Meir, but R. Judah said: Beth Shammai and Beth Hillel agreed that grace comes first and *habdalah* last. Where they differed was in respect of light and spices, Beth Shammai maintaining that light comes first and then spices, while Beth Hillel held that spices comes first and then light; and R. Johanan has stated: The public have adopted the custom of following Beth Hillel as reported by R. Judah.

BETH SHAMMAI SAY, WHO CREATED etc. Raba said: All are
c agreed that the word *bara*[1] refers to the past. Where they differ is with respect to the word *bore*.[2] Beth Shammai maintain that *bore* means 'who will create in the future', while Beth Hillel hold that *bore* can also refer to the past. R. Joseph cited in objection [to Beth Shammai] the verses, *I form the light and create* [bore] *darkness*,[3] *He formeth the mountains and createth* [bore] *the wind*,[4] *He that created* [bore] *the heavens and stretched them forth*.[5] Rather, said R. Joseph: Both sides are agreed that both *bara* and *bore* can refer to the past. Where they differ is as to whether *ma'or* [light] or *me'ore* [lights] should be said. Beth Shammai are of the opinion that there is only one light in the fire, while Beth Hillel are of the opinion that there are several.[6] It has been taught to the same effect: Said Beth Hillel to Beth Shammai: There are several illuminations in the light.

A BLESSING IS NOT SAID etc. There is a good reason in the case of the light [of idolaters], because it has not 'rested'.[7] But what reason is there in the case of the spices?—Rab Judah said in the name of Rab: We are dealing here with [spices used at] a banquet of idolaters,[8] because ordinarily a banquet of idolaters is held in honour of idolatry. But since it is stated further on, OR OVER THE LIGHT OR THE SPICES OF IDOLATRY, we may infer that the earlier statement does not refer to idolaters?—R. Ḥanina of Sura replied: The latter statement is explanatory. What is the reason why a blessing is not said over the light and the spices of idolaters? Because ordinarily a banquet of idolaters is in honour of idolatry.

Our Rabbis taught: A blessing may be said over a light which has 'rested', but not over one which has not 'rested'. What is

(3) Drops from the inside may spill on to the outside, and in virtue of the uncleanness of the cup the drops would render the hands unclean. (4) Since *ex hypothesi* the cup may not be used. Hence it is quite safe to wash the hands before filling the cup. (5) Hence it is safer to wash the hands after the cup has been filled.

a (1) And *terumah* would be rendered unclean by a table unclean in the second degree. (2) To protect it from uncleanness.

b (1) This sentence seems to be an interpolation. (2) In spite of the prohibition against wasting food. (3) Who would not know the difference between crumbs of the size of an olive and those of smaller size. Probably a meal of *ḥaberim* (v. Glos.) is referred to. (4) I.e., ascribes to Beth Hillel the teaching that an *'am ha-arez* may be employed, and consequently the floor is swept first. (5) I.e., before the light. (6) I.e., supplemented the reading in our Mishnah as follows.

c (1) Past tense, 'he created'. (2) Participle, 'creating', or 'who creates'. (3) Isa. XLV, 7. (4) Amos. IV, 13. (5) Isa. XLII, 5. (6) I.e., several colours in the light—red, white, green etc. (7) I.e., forbidden work has been done by its light. (8) Lit., 'Cutheans' which throughout this passage is probably a censor's correction for 'Gentiles'.

meant by 'which has not rested'? [53a]. Shall we say that it has not rested on account of work [done by it], even permissible
a work?[1] But it has been taught: A blessing may be said over a light used for a woman in confinement or for the sake of a sick person?—R. Naḥman b. Isaac replied: What is meant by 'rested'? That it rested from work which is a transgression on Sabbath. It has been taught to the same effect: A blessing may be said over a lamp which has been burning throughout the day[2] to the conclusion of Sabbath.[3]

Our Rabbis taught: We may say the blessing over a light kindled by a Gentile[4] from an Israelite or by an Israelite from a Gentile, but not by a Gentile from a Gentile. What is the reason for barring a light kindled by a Gentile from a Gentile? Because it may not have rested.[5] But a light kindled by an Israelite from a Gentile also may not have rested? Perhaps you will say that the prohibited [flame] has vanished and the light is now a different one and is reborn in the hand of the Israelite.[6] What then of this which has been taught: If one carries out a flame to the public way [on Sabbath],[7] he is liable to a penalty.[8] Why is he liable? That which he took up he did not set down and that which he set down he did not take up?[9]—We must say therefore that [in our present case] the prohibited flame is still present, only the blessing which he says is said over the additional permitted part. If that is the case [a blessing over] a light kindled by a Gentile from a Gentile should also be permitted?—That is so; but [the prohibition is] a precaution on account of the first Gentile[1] and the first flame.[2]

Our Rabbis taught: If one was walking [at the termination of Sabbath] outside the town and saw a light, if the majority [of the inhabitants] are Gentiles he should not say a benediction, but if the majority are Israelites he may say the benediction. This statement is self-contradictory. You first say, 'if the majority are Gentiles, he may not say the blessing', which implies that if they are half and half he may say it, and then it states, 'if the majority are Israelites, he may say it', which implies that if they are half and half he may not say it!—Strictly speaking, even if they are half and half he may say it, but since in the first clause it says 'the majority are Gentiles', in the second clause it says 'the majority are Israelites'.

Our Rabbis taught: If a man was walking outside the town and saw a child with a torch in its hands, he makes inquiries about it; if it is an Israelite child, he may say the benediction, but if it is a Gentile he may not. Why does it speak of a child? The same applies even to a grown-up!—Rab Judah said in the name of Rab: We suppose this to happen immediately after sunset. In the case of a grown-up it is obvious that he must be a Gentile.[3] In the case of a child, I can suppose that it is an Israelite child who happened to take hold [of the light].

Our Rabbis taught: If one was walking outside the town at the termination of Sabbath and saw a light, if it is thick like the opening of a furnace he may say the benediction over it,[4] otherwise not. One [authority] states: A benediction may be said over the light of a furnace, while another says that it may not!—There is no contradiction: one speaks of the beginning of the fire, the other of the end.[5] One [authority] teaches: A benediction may be said over the light of an oven or a stove, while another says that it may not, and there is no contradiction: one speaks of the beginning of the fire, the other of the end.[1] One [authority] teaches: The benediction may be said over the light of the synagogue or the Beth ha-Midrash, while another says it may not, and there is no contradiction: one speaks of a case where an eminent man is present,[2] the other of a case where no eminent man is present. Or if you like, I can say that both speak of where an eminent man is present, and there is no contradiction: one speaks of where there is a beadle,[3] and the other of where there is no beadle. Or if you like, I can say that both speak of where there is a beadle, and there is no contradiction; one speaks of where there is moonlight,[4] the other of where there is no moonlight.

Our Rabbis taught: If people were sitting in the Beth ha-Midrash and light was brought in [at the termination of the Sabbath], Beth Shammai say that each one says a blessing over it for himself, while Beth Hillel say that one says a blessing on behalf of all, because it says, *In the multitude of people is the King's glory.*[5] Beth Hillel at any rate explain their reason; but what is the reason of Beth Shammai?—It is probably to avoid an interruption of study.[6] It has been taught similarly: The members of the household of Rabban Gamaliel did not use to say 'Good health'[7] in the Beth ha-Midrash so as not to interrupt their study.

A BENEDICTION MAY NOT BE SAID OVER THE LIGHTS OR THE SPICES OF THE DEAD. What is the reason?—The light is kindled only in honour of the dead, the spices are to remove the bad smell. Rab Judah said in the name of Rab: Wherever [the person buried is of such consequence that] a light would be carried before him either by day or by night, we do not say a blessing over the light [if he is buried on the termination of
d Sabbath];[1] but if he is one before whom a light would be carried only at night, we may say the blessing.[2]

R. Huna said: A blessing is not said over spices used in a privy[3] or oil used for removing grease [from the hands].[4] This implies that wherever [spice] is not used for scent no blessing is said over it. An objection was raised [to this]: If one enters a spice-dealer's shop and smells the fragrance, even though he sits there the whole day he makes only one blessing, but if he is constantly going in and out he makes a blessing each time he enters. Now here is a case where it is not used for smell,[5] and yet one makes a blessing?—In fact it is used for smell, the object being that people should smell and come and make purchases thereof.

Our Rabbis taught: If one was walking outside the town and smelt an odour [of spices], if the majority of the inhabitants are idolaters he does not say a blessing, but if the majority are Israelites he does say a blessing. R. Jose says: Even if the majority are Israelites he does not say a blessing, because the daughters of Israel use incense for witchcraft. Do all of them use incense for witchcraft?—The fact is that a small part is used for witchcraft and a small part for scenting garments, with the result that the greater part of it is not used for smell, and wherever the greater part is not used for smell a blessing is not said over it. R. Ḥiyya b. Abba said in the name of R. Joḥanan: If one was walking on the eve of Sabbath in Tiberias, or at the conclusion of Sabbath in Sepphoris, and smelt an odour [of spices], he does not say a blessing, because the probability is that they are being used only to perfume garments. Our Rabbis taught: If one was walking in a street of idolaters and smelt the spices willingly, he is a sinner.

a (1) E.g., a light lit for the sake of a sick person. (2) I.e., which was lit before Sabbath came in. (3) Because no Sabbath transgression had been performed with it. (4) On the termination of Sabbath. (5) I.e., some forbidden work has been done by its light. (6) The light being regarded as not having a continuous existence but as consisting of a series of flashes. (7) E.g., if burning wick is placed in oil in a potsherd so small that the prohibition of carrying on Sabbath does not apply to it. (8) For transferring from one domain to another on Sabbath, v. Beẓah 39a. (9) Such transference renders liable only when the same object is taken up from its place in one domain and set down in its place in the other. Here the flame which is taken from its place in the house is not the same as is set down outside. The reason therefore why he is liable must be because the flame is in fact considered throughout to be one and the same.

b (1) I.e., against the light kindled by a Gentile on Sabbath. (2) Lit., 'pillar'. The first flame of the light kindled on Sabbath, by the Gentile. (3) Since a grown-up Israelite would not use a light immediately on the termination of the Sabbath, before saying *habdalah*. (4) Because this is a genuine light. (5) A furnace (of lime burners) is first lit to burn the lime, but afterwards it is kept alight for the purpose of lighting.

c (1) The fire is lit for cooking, but afterwards chips are thrown in to give light.

מסורת הש"ס

תורה אור

אי נימא לא שבת מחמת מלאכה אפילו ממלאכה דהיתרא והתניא אור של חיה ושל חולה מברכין עליו אמר רב נחמן בר יצחק מאי שבת ששבתה מחמת מלאכת עבירה תנ"ה עששית שהיתה דולקת והולכת כל היום כולו למ"ש מברכין עליה: ת"ר כותי שהדליק מישראל וישראל שהדליק מכותי מברכים עליו כותי מכותי אין מברכין עליו מ"ש כותי מכותי דלא משום דלא שבת אי הכי ישראל מכותי נמי הא לא שבת וכי תימא הך איסורא אזל ליה והא אחרינא הוא ובידא דישראל קא מתילדא אלא הא *דתניא המוציא שלהבת לר"ה חייב אמאי חייב מה שעקר לא הניח ומה שהניח לא עקר אלא לעולם דאיסורא נמי איתיה וכי קא מברך אתוספתא דהיתרא קא מברך אי הכי כותי מכותי נמי אין ה"נ גזרה משום כותי ראשון ועמוד ראשון: ת"ר היה מהלך חוץ לכרך וראה אור אם רוב כותים אינו מברך אם רוב ישראל מברך הא גופא קשיא אמרת אם רוב כותים אינו מברך הא מחצה על מחצה מברך והדר תני אם רוב ישראל מברך הא מחצה על מחצה אינו מברך בדין הוא דאפילו מחצה על מחצה נמי מברך ואיידי (דתנן) רישא רוב כותים תנא סיפא רוב ישראל: ת"ר היה מהלך חוץ לכרך וראה תינוק ואבוקה בידו בודק אחריו אם ישראל הוא מברך אם כותי הוא אינו מברך מאי אריא תינוק אפילו גדול נמי אמר רב יהודה אמר רב הכא בסמוך לשקיעת החמה עסקינן גדול מוכחא מילתא דודאי כותי הוא תינוק אימר ישראל הוא אקרי ונקיט: ת"ר היה מהלך חוץ לכרך וראה אור אם עבה כפי הכבשן מברך עליו ואם לאו אינו מברך עליו תני חדא אור של כבשן מברכין עליו ותניא אידך אין מברכין עליו ל"ק הא בתחלה הא לבסוף תני חדא אור של תנור ושל כירים מברכין עליו ותניא אידך אין מברכין עליו לא קשיא הא בתחלה הא לבסוף תני חדא אור של בית הכנסת ושל בית המדרש מברכין עליו ותניא אידך אין מברכין עליו ל"ק הא דאיכא אדם חשוב הא דליכא אדם חשוב ואב"א הא והא דאיכא אדם חשוב ולא קשיא הא דאיכא חזנא הא דליכא חזנא ואב"א הא והא דאיכא חזנא ולא קשיא הא דאיכא סהרא והא דליכא סהרא: ת"ר היו יושבין בבית המדרש והביאו אור לפניהם ב"ש אומרים כל אחד ואחד מברך לעצמו ובית הלל אומרים אחד מברך לכולן משום שנאמר (משלי יד) ברוב עם הדרת מלך בשלמא ב"ה מפרשי טעמא אלא ב"ש מאי טעמא קסברי מפני בטול בית המדרש *תנ"ה של בית רבן גמליאל לא היו אומרים מרפא בבית המדרש מפני בטול בית המדרש: אין מברכין לא על הנר ולא על הבשמים של מתים: מ"ט נר לכבוד הוא דעבידא בשמים לעבורי ריחא הוא דעבידי אמר רב יהודה אמר רב כל שמוציאין לפניו ביום ובלילה אין מברכין עליו וכל שאין מוציאין לפניו אלא בלילה מברכין עליו אמר רב הונא בשמים של בית הכסא ושמן העשוי להעביר את הזוהמא אין מברכין עליו למימרא דכל היכא דלאו לריחא עבידא לא מברכין עליה מתיבי *הנכנס לחנותו של בשם והריח ריח אפילו ישב שם כל היום כלו אינו מברך אלא פעם אחד נכנס ויצא נכנס ויצא מברך על כל פעם ופעם והא הכא דלאו לריחא הוא דעבידא וקמברך אין לריחא נמי הוא דעביד כי היכי דנירחו אינשי וניתו ונזבון מניה: ת"ר היה מהלך חוץ לכרך והריח ריח אם רוב ע"א אינו מברך אם רוב ישראל מברך ר' יוסי אומר אפילו רוב ישראל נמי אינו מברך מפני שבנות ישראל מקטרות לכשפים אטו כולהו לכשפים מקטרן ה"ל מיעוטא לכשפים ומיעוטא נמי לגמר את הכלים אשתכח רובא דלאו לריחא עביד וכל רובא דלאו לריחא עביד לא מברך א"ר חייא בר אבא א"ר יוחנן המהלך בערבי שבתות בטבריא ובמוצאי שבתות בצפורי והריח ריח אינו מברך מפני שחזקתו אינו עשוי אלא לגמר בו את הכלים ת"ר היה מהלך בשוק של ע"א ונתרצה להריח הרי זה חוטא: ואין

לא

רש"י

אי נימא לא שבת מחמת מלאכה ואפי' היא מלאכה של היתר. כגון של חולה ושל חיה קאמר דאין מברכין: עששית שהיתה דולקת והולכת. מע"ש ובבית ישראל: למ"ש מברכין. לפי שלא נעשה בה עבירה שלא הודלקה בשבת: כותי שהדליק מישראל. משחשכה מ"ש: הך איסורא אזלא. מתוך שלהבת דולקת והולכת קמא פרח ליה: המוציא שלהבת בר"ה. בשבת חייב ומוקמינן לה במסכת ביצה כגון דשייפא לחרס משחא ותלי בה נורא דגחלת ליכא אלא שלהבת ומשום חרס לא מחייב דלית בה שיעורא: מה שעקר לא הניח. והוצאת שבת לא מחייבא עד דאיכא עקירה מרשות זו והנחה ברשות זו: גזרה משום כותי ראשון ועמוד ראשון. אי שרית בכותי שהדליק מכותי משחשכה אתי לברוכי בכותי שהדליקו מבעוד יום ובאותו אור עצמו שלא נתוסף משחשכה כגון שמברך עליו סמוך לחשכה: גדול מוכחא מלתא דכותי הוא. ואין צריך לבדוק אחריו דאי איתא דישראל הוא לא היה מהלך סמוך לחשכה מיד לאחוז האור בידו: כפי דכבשן. שורפים בו אבנים לסיד אם עבה כאור היוצא מפי הכבשן כהורא בריא היא ולהשתמש לאורה היא נעשית: ואם לאו. לאו לאורה נעשית אלא לבשל ואין מברכין אלא על שנעשה להאיר: בתחלה. בתחלת שרפת אבנים אין האור להאיר: בסוף. לאחר שנשרפו האבנים רובן מדליקין אור גדול מלמעלה למרק שרפת האבנים ומשתמשין נמי לאורה: של תנור. בסוף מברכין עליו לאחר שהוסק התנור והפת בתוכו מדליקין קסמין דקין בפיו להאיר ולקלוט חומו לתוכו וכיון דמשתמש לאורו מברכים עליו: אור של בית הכנסת. בדאיכא אדם חשוב לכבודו הדליקוה ולא שצריך לאור אלא לכבוד בעלמא ואין מברכין עליו: ליכא אדם חשוב. להאיר להם הדליקוה ומברכין: הא והא דאיכא אדם חשוב. ואי איכא חזנא שמש שאוכל בבית הכנסת אף לאורה עשויה שיאכל החזן לאורה ומברכין: הא והא דאיכא חזנא ואיכא סהרא. שהחזן יכול לאכול לאורה אין מברכין על הנר שלא להאיר הדליקוה אלא לכבוד אדם חשוב: מפני בטול בית המדרש. שבזמן שא' מברך לכולם הם צריכים לשתוק מגרסתם כדי שיתכוונו כולם וישמעו אליו ויענו אמן: מרפא. לאדם המתעטש שרגילים לומר אסותא: נר לכבוד. המת עביד': בשמים עבידי לעבורי ריחא. דסרחונו של מת עבידי ולא להריח: כל. מת שהוא חשוב להוליא לפניו נר ביום אם הוליאוהו בלילה במוצאי שבת לקבורה אין מברכין על אותו נר דלכבוד עבידא ולא להאיר: וכל. מת שאינו חשוב להוליא נר לפניו ביום אלא בלילה מברכין עליו אם הוליאוהו במוצאי שבת לקבורה: מברכין עליו. דלהאיר עבידא: בשמים. שמוליך אדם אסטניס לבית הכסא להעביר מאוס ריח רע של בית הכסא אין מברכין עליו: ושמן העשוי להעביר את הזוהמא. שמוציאים בסוף הסעודה לסוך ידים מזוהמות והוא מבוסם בבשמים: אין מברכין עליו. בורא עצי בשמים אלא בורא שמן ערב ומברכין אם שמן אפרסמון הוא והא דאמר בכילד מברכין (דף מג.) האי משחא כבישא ועתיקא מברכין עליו בע"ב לא בבא בתוך הסעודה קאמר אלא בבא להריח: לגמר את הכלים. לבשם בעשנו את הבגדים: בטבריא. היו רגילים לגמר ערבי שבתות ובצפורי במוצאי שבתות:

תוספות

וכי תימא הא דאיסורא אזיל ליה. ה"מ לאקשויי אי הכי כותי מכותי נמי אלא עדיפא מיניה פריך דה"מ לשנויי כדמשני בסמוך:

גזרה משום כותי ראשון וכותי ראשון משום עמוד ראשון וכו'. אלא גזרה היא דגזרו חכמים כל אש כותי שביד הכותי דאי לא הא לא קיימא הא אבל כותי שהדליק מישראל וישראל מכותי מברכין עליו והכי קיימא לן:

הא דאיכא אדם חשוב. אם כן משום כבודו של חשוב ולא לאורה כך פרש"י ור"ח פירש איפכא באדם חשוב לאורה ובדליכא אדם חשוב עשוי לכבוד בית הכנסת:

אין מברכין עליו. פרש"י מיהו מברכין בורא שברא שמן ערב והא דאמר לעיל בכילד מברכין (דף מג.) האי משחא כבישא מברכין עליו היינו בבא להריח ולא מיירי בתוך הסעודה:

עין משפט נר מצוה

טו א טוש"ע א"ח סי' רצח סעיף ה

ב' הערוך לא"ש מכבה ומדליקה ע' בערך עששית וברב אלפס כך אי' ת"נה עששית שהית' דולקת והולכת כל היום כולו מביאין ממנה אור להבדלה וע' בהרא"ש

טז ג מיי' פ' כט מהלכות שבת הלכה כו טוש"ע א"ח שם סעיף ו

יז ד מיי' פי"ח מה' שבת הל' ה סמג עשין כט

יח ה ו מיי' כ"ט מהלכ' ברכות הלכה ט ופכ"ט מהל' שבת הלכה כו סמג עשין כז כט טוש"ע א"ח סי' ריז סעיף ז וסי' רצח ס"ז

יט ז מיי' פ' כט מהל' שבת שם סמג עשין כט טוש"ע א"ח סימן רצח סעיף י

כ ח ט מיי' שם טוש"ע א"ח שם סעיף יא

כא י שם סעי' יד

כב ל מיי' פ"ד מה' ת"ת הל' ט טוש"ע י"ד סימן רמו סעיף יז

כג מ טור א"ח סימן רצח

כד נ מיי' פ"ט מהלכ' ברכות הל' ח ופ' כט מהלכו' שבת סמג עשין כז וכט טוש"ע א"ח סימן ריז סעיף ב וסי' רצז סעיף ב

כה ס מיי' פ"ט מהלכו' ברכו' הלכ' ה סמג עשין כז טוש"ע א"ח סימן ריז סעיף א

כו ע מיי' שם ה"ח שם סעי' ג

מסורת הש"ס (גליון)

ביצה לט. תוספתא דשבת פ"י

[דתניא]

תוספת' ספ"ב דשבת וע"ש היטב ותרצה פליאה

שם פ"ה

(2) In whose honour the light has been kindled. (3) Who has his meals in the synagogue. (4) Which suffices for the beadle, and the light must have been kindled out of respect for an eminent man. (5) Prov. XIV, 28. (6) One may be in the middle of a difficult part just at the moment for saying Amen. (7) To someone who sneezed.

d (1) Because the light is carried for his honour. (2) Because the light is really to give light. (3) To counteract the bad smell. (4) This oil contained spices, and the blessing said over it was that for oil and not for spices. (5) But for sale.

תורה אור

ואין מברכין על הנר עד שיאותו: אמר רב יהודה אמר רב לא יאותו יאותו ממש אלא כל שאלו עומד בקרוב ומשתמש לאורה ואפי' ברחוק מקום וכן אמר רב אשי ברחוק מקום שנינו מתיבי **היתה לו נר טמונה בחיקו או בפנס או שראה שלהבת *ולא נשתמש לאורה או נשתמש לאורה ולא ראה שלהבת אינו מברך עד שיראה שלהבת וישתמש לאורה בשלמא משתמש לאורה ולא ראה שלהבת משכחת לה דקיימא בקרן זוית אלא ראה שלהבת ולא נשתמש לאורה היכי משכחת לה לאו דמרחקה לא כגון דעמיא ואזלא: ת"ר גנחלים לוחשות מברכין עליהן אוממות אין מברכין עליהן ה"ד לוחשות אמר רב חסדא כל שאלו מכנים לתוכן קיסם ודולקת מאליה *איבעיא להו אוממות או עוממות ת"ש דאמר רב חסדא בר אבדימי °ארזים לא עממוהו בגן אלהים (יחזקאל לא) ורבא אמר יאותו ממש וכמה אמר עולא כדי שיכיר בין איסר לפונדיון חזקיה אמר דכדי שיכיר בין *מלוזמא של טבריא למלוזמא של צפורי רב יהודה מברך אדבי אדא דיילא רבא מברך אדבי גוריא בר חמא אביי מברך אדבי בר אבוה אמר רב יהודה אמר רב האין מחזרין על האור כדרך שמחזרין על המצות א"ר זירא מריש הוה מהדרנא כיון דשמענא להא דרב יהודה אמר רב אנא נמי לא מהדרנא אלא אי מקלע לי ממילא מבריכנא: ומי שאכל וכו': אמר רב זביד ואיתימא רב דימי בר אבא מחלוקת בשכח ואבל במזיד ד"ה יחזור למקומו ויברך פשיטא ושכח תנן מהו דתימא ה"ה אפילו במזיד והאי דקתני ושכח להודיעך כחן דב"ש קמ"ל תניא אמרו להם ב"ה לב"ש לדבריכם מי שאכל בראש הבירה ושכח וירד ולא ברך יחזור לראש הבירה ויברך אמרו להן ב"ש לב"ה לדבריכם מי ששכח ארנקי בראש הבירה לא יעלה ויטלנה לכבוד עצמו הוא עולה לכבוד שמים לא כל שכן הנהו תרי תלמידי חד עביד בשוגג כב"ש ואשכח ארנקא דדהבא וחד עביד במזיד כב"ה ואכליה אריא רבה בב"ח הוה קאזיל בשיירתא אכל ואשתלי ולא בריך אמר היכי אעביד אי אמינא להו אנשאי לברך אמרי לי בריך כל היכא דמברכת לרחמנא מברכת מוטב דאמינא להו אנשאי יונה דדהבא אמר להו אנטרו לי דאנשאי יונה דדהבא אזיל ובריך ואשכח יונה דדהבא מאי שנא *יונה דמתלי' כנסת ישראל ליונה דכתיב °כנפי יונה נחפה בכסף ואברותיה בירקרק חרוץ (תלים סח) מה יונה אינה נצולת אלא בכנפיה אף ישראל אינן נצולין אלא במצות: עד אימתי הוא וכו': כמה שיעור עכול א"ר יוחנן יכל זמן שאינו רעב וריש לקיש אמר כל זמן שיצמא מחמת אכילתו אמר ליה רב יימר בר שלמיא למר זוטרא ואמרי לה רב יימר בר שזבי למר זוטרא מי אמר ריש לקיש הכי והאמר רב אמי אמר ריש לקיש כמה שיעור עכול כדי להלך ארבע מילין ל"ק כאן באכילה מרובה כאן באכילה מועטת: בא להם יין וכו': למימרא דישראל אע"ג דלא שמע כולה ברכה עונה °וכי לא שמע היכי נפיק אמר חייא בר רב טבשלא אכל עמהן וכן אמר רב נחמן אמר רבה בר אבוה בשלא אכל עמהן *א"ל רב לחייא בריה ברי יחטוף ובריך וכן אמר רב הונא לרבה בריה חטוף ובריך למימרא דמברך עדיף ממאן דעני אמן והתניא ר' יוסי אומר גדול העונה אמן יותר מן המברך א"ל ר' נהוראי השמים כן הוא תדע שהרי *גולייריו יורדין ומתגרין (במלחמה) וגבורים יורדין ומנצחין תנאי היא דתניא אחד המברך ואחד העונה אמן במשמע אלא שממהרין למברך יותר מן העונה אמן בעא מיניה שמואל מרב מהו לענות אמן אחר תינוקות של בית רבן א"ל כאחר הכל עונין אמן חוץ מתינוקות של בית רבן הואיל ולהתלמד עשויין וה"מ בדלא עידן מפטרייהו אבל בעידן מפטרייהו עונין: ת"ר שמן מעכב את הברכה דברי רבי זילאי רבי זיואי אומר אינו מעכב רבי אחא אומר שמן טוב מעכב רבי זוהמאי אומר כשם שמזוהם פסול לעבודה כך ידים מזוהמות פסולות לברכה אמר רב נחמן בר יצחק אנא לא זילאי ולא זיואי ולא זוהמאי ידענא אלא מתניתא ידענא דאמר רב יהודה אמר רב ואמרי לה במתניתא תנא °והתקדשתם אלו מים ראשונים והייתם קדושים לאלו מים אחרונים כי קדוש זה שמן אני יי' אלהיכם זו ברכה: (ויקרא יא)

הדרן עלך אלו דברים

באכילה מרובה. ד' מילין כך פרש"י ולי נראה דזה מועט יותר מאכילה מועטת אלא נראה לפרש איפכא אכילה מרובה כל זמן שהוא צמא דאין שם קצבה אבל מועט ד' מילין: **והייתם** קדושים אלו מים אחרונים. דוקא להם שהיו רגילין ליטול ידיהם אחר הסעודה מפני מלח סדומית אבל אנו שאין מלח סדומית מצוייה בינינו ואין אנו רגילין ליטול אחר הסעודה אין הנטילה מעכבת עלינו לברך ומיהו אנשים מעונגים הרגילין ליטול ידיהן אחר הסעודה ודאי להם מעכבת הנטילה לברך ברכת המזון וצריכים ליטול את ידיהם קודם ב"ה*:

הדרן עלך אלו דברים

לא יאותו ממש. שאפילו לא נהנה ממנו מברכים עליו ומאי עד שיאותו עד שיהא ראוי לאותו ליהנות ממנו לעומדים סמוך לו ואז מברכים עליו אפילו הרחוקים ממנו ובלבד שיראוהו: בפנס. בעששית: יאותו ממש. עומד בסמוך: וכמה. הוא צריך להיות בסמוך: מלוזמא. משקל: רב יהודה. היה מברך על אור שבבית אדא דיילא ורחוק מביתו היה רב יהודה לטעמיה דלא בעי סמוך: רבא מבר' אדבי גוריא בר חמא. סמוך לביתו היה רבא לטעמיה דאמ' סמוך בעינן: אין מחזרין על האור. אם אין לו אור א"צ לחזר אחריו: חד עבד בשוגג כב"ש. אף על פי ששגג ונעקר מן המקום על ידי ששכח החמיר על עצמו כב"ש וחזר למקום שאכל ובירך: חד עבד במזיד. נעקר ממקום שאכל במזיד כדי לברך במקום אחר שהולך לילך: אנשאי יונה דדהבא. שכחתי יונה של זהב: יונה אינה נצולת אלא בכנפיה. או בורחת או נלחמת בראשי אגפיה: אכילה מרובה. ד' מילין: בא להם יין אחר המזון. הא פרים לה בגמרא בריש פרקין לבית שמאי אין ברכת המזון טעונה כוס ולב"ה טעונה כוס: היכי נפיק. קס"ד באחד מן המסובים עסקינ' במתניתין: חטוף ובריך. כשמושיטין כוס של ברכה הוי מחזר שיתנהו לך ותברך: במשמע. העונה והמברך במשמע קומו ברכו את יי' אלהיכם בספר עזרא (נחמי' ט) ואומר ויברכו את שם כבודך והיא עניית אמן שבמקדש במס' תענית (פ"ב דף טז: ולקמן דף סג.) מפרש קומו ברכו בתחלת ברכה ויברכו את שם כבודך (שם) במקום עניית אמן שבמקדש אומר בשכמל"ו: שממהרין למברך. ליתן שכר: אח' תינוקות. כשלומדים ברכות מפי רבן: הואיל ולהתלמד עשויין. שאין מתכוונים לברך אלא ללמוד: אבל בעידן מפטרייהו. כשאומרים ההפטרה ומברכין בתורה ובנביא עונים אחריהן אמן: שמן מעכב את הברכה. שמן שהיו רגילין להביא בסוף הסעודה לסוך אחר הסעודה את הידים אחר מים אחרונים להעביר את זוהמתן: מעכב את הברכה. שאסור לזמן עד שיובא וכן לענין שמעכב ברכות כל דבר הבא בתוך סעודה שמותר לאוכלו בלא ברכה עד שיסכוהו: שמן טוב. שיש בו בשמים מעכב את הברכה למי שרגיל בו:

הדרן עלך אלו דברים

עין משפט נר מצוה

כז א ש"ע א"ח סימן רלא סעיף טו

כח ב מיי' פכ"ט מה' שבת הל' כו סמג עשין כט טוש"ע א"ח שם סעיף ט [וע"ע תוס' חולין קה. ד"ה מים]

כט ג מיי' שם הכ"ה שם סעי' ד

ל ד מיי' שם הכ"ו שם סעי' א

לא ה מיי' פ"ד מהלכ' ברכות ה"א סמג עשין כז טוש"ע א"ח סימן קפד סעיף א

לב ו מיי' פ"ב מהלכו' ברכו' הלכה יד) [הרמב"ם לא הביא לכל זה וע' בכ"מ טעם רחוק] סמג שם טוש"ע א"ח שם סעיף ה

לג ח מיי' פ"א מהלכו' ברכו' הלכה יא ש"ע א"ח סי' ריג סעיף ג

לד ט מיי' שם הי"ג סמג עשין כז טוש"ע א"ח סימן רטו סעיף ב ג

לה י מיי' שם הי"א טוש"ע א"ח סי' רא סעיף ד

לו כ מיי' שם הל' יב טו וסמג שם טוש"ע א"ח סי' רטו סעיף ב ג

לז ל מיי' פ"ז מהל' ברכות הלכה יא יב יג סמג טוש"ע א"ח סימן קפא סעיף א י [בערך גליור כתב הרב המוסיף הערוך פי' בלשון יוני משרתים של אנשי המלחמ' ע"ש]

מסורת הש"ס

[תוספ' פ"ה]

(ירוש' מוסיף עששית אע"פ שלא כבתה ולא כרש"י דפנס היינו עששית וע' רשב"א וב"י ס"ס רצה)

פסחים עה: ע"ש שבת עו: ע"ש

[בערוך פי' מטבע]

[שבת מא. וע"ש גיטין מה. סנה' לה.]

נזיר סו:

[53*b*]. A BLESSING IS NOT SAID OVER THE LIGHT TILL IT HAS BEEN UTILIZED. Rab Judah said in the name of Rab: This does not mean literally till it has been utilized, but it means a light which can be serviceable if one stands near enough to it, and then even those at a distance [may say the blessing]. So too said R. Ashi: We have learnt that it serves for those at a distance.

An objection was raised: If one had a light hidden in the folds of his dress or in a lamp, or if he could see a flame but could not use its light, or if he could do something by the light but saw no flame, he should not say the blessing; he must both see a flame and be able to use the light. We understand the statement 'he can use its light but sees no flame'; this can happen when the light is in a corner. But how can it happen that he sees the flame and cannot make use of the light? Is it not when he is at a distance?—No; it is when, for instance, the flame keeps on flickering.

Our Rabbis taught: We may say the blessing over glowing coals but not over dying coals. How do you define 'glowing'?—R. Ḥisda replied: This means coals from which a chip, if inserted between them, will catch of itself. The question was asked: Is the
a proper form *omemoth* or *'omemoth*?[1]—Come and hear: for R. Ḥisda b. Abdimi quoted the verse, *The cedars in the garden of God could not darken* ['amamuhu] *it*.[2]

Rab, however,[3] said that [the Mishnah means literally] 'utilize it'. How near must one be?—'Ulla said: Near enough to distinguish between an *as* and a *dupondium*.[4] Hezekiah said: Near enough to distinguish between a *meluzma*[5] of Tiberias and one of Sepphoris. Rab Judah used to say the blessing over the light in the house of Adda the waiter.[6] Raba said the blessing over the light in the house of Guria b. Ḥama.[7] Abaye said it over the light in the house of Bar Abbuha. Rab Judah said in the name of Rab: We do not go looking for a light[8] in the same way as we do in the case of other commandments. R. Zera said: At first I used to go looking for a light. But since hearing this statement of Rab Judah reporting Rab, I also do not look for one, but if one comes my way I say the blessing over it.

IF ONE HAS EATEN etc. R. Zebid, or as some say R. Dimi b. Abba, said: Opinions differ only in the case where one forgot, but if he omitted wilfully he must return to his place and say grace. This is obvious! The Mishnah says 'HAS FORGOTTEN'?—You might think that the rule is the same even if he did it purposely, and the reason why it says 'HAS FORGOTTEN' is to show you how far Beth Shammai are prepared to go. Therefore we are told [that this is not so]. It has been taught: Beth Hillel said to Beth Shammai: According to you, if one ate at the top of the Temple Mount and forgot and descended without having said grace, he should return to the top of the Temple Mount and say grace? Beth Shammai replied to Beth Hillel: According to you, if one forgot a purse at the top of the Temple Mount, is he not to go up and get it? And if he will ascend for his own sake, surely he should do so all the more for the honour of Heaven!

There were once two disciples who omitted to say grace. One
b who did it accidentally followed the rule of Beth Shammai[1] and found a purse of gold, while the other who did it purposely[2] followed the rule of Beth Hillel,[3] and he was eaten by a lion. Rabbah b. Bar Ḥanah was once travelling with a caravan, and he took a meal and forgot to say grace. He said to himself: What shall I do? If I say to the others, I have forgotten to say grace, they will say to me, Say it [here]: wherever you say the benediction you are saying it to the All-Merciful. I had better tell them that I have forgotten a golden dove. So he said to them: Wait for me, because I have forgotten a golden dove. He went back and said grace and found a golden dove. Why should it have been just a dove?—Because the community of Israel are compared to a dove, as it is written, *The wings of the dove are covered with silver, and her pinions with the shimmer of gold*.[4] Just as the dove is saved only by her wings, so Israel are saved only by the precepts.

UNTIL WHEN CAN HE SAY THE GRACE. How long does it take to digest a meal?—R. Joḥanan said: Until he becomes hungry again; Resh Laḳish said: As long as one is thirsty on account of the meal. Said R. Yemar b. Shelemia to Mar Zuṭra, or, according to others R. Yemar b. Shezbi to Mar Zuṭra: Can Resh Laḳish have said this? Has not R. Ammi said in the name of Resh Laḳish: How long does it take to digest a meal? Long enough for one to walk four *mil*?—There is no contradiction: one statement refers
c to a light meal, the other to a heavy one.[1]

IF WINE IS SERVED etc. This implies, [if] an Israelite [says the grace],[2] even though one has not heard the whole of it he responds [Amen]. But if he has not heard how can he have performed his duty by doing so?[3]—Ḥiyya b. Rab replied: This applies to one who has not joined in the meal. Similarly said R. Naḥman in the name of Rabbah b. Abbuha: It refers to one who has not joined in the meal. Said Rab to his son Ḥiyya: My son, snatch [the cup of wine] and say grace.[4] And so said R. Huna to his son Rabbah: My son, snatch and say grace. This implies that he who says the grace is superior to one who answers, Amen. But it has been taught: 'R. Jose says: Greater is he who answers, Amen than he who says the blessing?—Said R. Nehorai to him: I swear to you by heaven that it is so. The proof is that while the common soldiers advance and open the battle, it is the seasoned warriors who go down to win the victory!'—On this point there is a difference between Tannaim, as it has been taught: Both he who says the blessing and he who answers, Amen are equally implied,[5] only he who says the blessing is more quickly [rewarded] than he who answers, Amen.

Samuel inquired of Rab: Should one respond Amen after [a blessing said by] schoolchildren?—He replied: We respond Amen after everyone except children in school, because they are merely learning. This is the case only when it is not the time for them
d to say the *haftarah*;[1] but when it is the time for them to say the *haftarah*, we respond Amen after them.

Our Rabbis taught: The absence of oil[2] is a bar to the saying of grace. So said R. Zilai. R. Ziwai said: It is no bar. R. Aḥa said: Good oil is indispensable. R. Zuhamai said: Just as a dirty person is unfit for the Temple service, so dirty hands unfit one for saying grace. R. Naḥman b. Isaac said: I know nothing either of Zilai or Ziwai or Zuhamai, but I do know the following teaching, viz.: Rab Judah said in the name of Rab: some say it was taught in a Baraitha, *Sanctify yourselves*:[3] this refers to washing of the hands before the meal;[4] *And be ye holy*: this refers to washing of the hands after the meal;[5] *'For holy'*: this refers to the oil; *'Am I the Lord your God'*: this refers to the grace.

a (1) I.e., does the word translated 'dying' commence with an *alef* or an *'ayin*. (2) Ezek. XXXI, 8. (3) This goes back to the statement of Rab Judah in the name of Rab above. (4) A *dupondium* was twice the size of an *as*. (5) According to Rashi, a weight; according to Jastrow, a stamp of a coin. (6) Which was some distance away. (7) Which was quite near. (8) To say the blessing.

b (1) And returned to the place where he forgot, thus following the stricter rule. (2) Being in a hurry to go somewhere else. (3) Which applies only to accidental omission. (4) Ps. LXVIII, 14.

c (1) According to Rashi, it takes the time for walking four *mil* to digest a heavy meal; according to Tosaf., to digest a light one. (2) V. *supra* 51*b*, n. c1. (3) He assumes that he is one of the diners, who too must hear the grace. (4) I.e., seize every opportunity of saying it on behalf of the company. (5) In the text of Neh. IX, 5, which speaks of those who *'stand up and bless'*, and those who respond *'Blessed be Thy glorious name'*, which is equivalent to Amen, v. *infra* 63*a*.

d (1) The prophetical reading following the public reading of the Pentateuch on Sabbath and festivals and public fasts. (2) For cleansing the hands after the meal. (3) Lev. XI, 44. (4) Lit., 'the first water'. (5) Lit., 'the latter water'.

CHAPTER IX

MISHNAH. [54a] IF ONE SEES A PLACE WHERE MIRACLES HAVE BEEN WROUGHT FOR ISRAEL, HE SHOULD SAY, BLESSED BE HE WHO WROUGHT MIRACLES FOR OUR ANCESTORS IN THIS PLACE. ON SEEING A PLACE FROM WHICH IDOLATRY HAS BEEN EXTIRPATED, HE SHOULD SAY, BLESSED BE HE WHO EXTIRPATED IDOLATRY FROM OUR LAND. [ON WITNESSING] SHOOTING STARS, EARTHQUAKES, THUNDERCLAPS, STORMS AND LIGHTNINGS ONE SHOULD SAY, BLESSED BE HE WHOSE STRENGTH AND MIGHT FILL THE WORLD. ON SEEING MOUNTAINS, HILLS, SEAS, RIVERS AND DESERTS HE SHOULD
a SAY, BLESSED BE HE WHO WROUGHT CREATION.[1] R. JUDAH SAYS: IF ONE SEES THE GREAT SEA[2] ONE SHOULD SAY, BLESSED BE HE WHO MADE THE GREAT SEA, [THAT IS] IF HE SEES IT AT [CONSIDERABLE] INTERVALS. FOR RAIN AND FOR GOOD TIDINGS ONE SAYS, BLESSED BE HE THAT IS GOOD AND BESTOWS GOOD. FOR EVIL TIDINGS ONE SAYS, BLESSED BE THE TRUE JUDGE. ONE WHO HAS BUILT A NEW HOUSE OR BOUGHT NEW VESSELS SAYS, BLESSED BE HE WHO HAS KEPT US ALIVE AND PRESERVED US AND BROUGHT US TO THIS SEASON. OVER EVIL A BLESSING IS SAID SIMILAR TO THAT OVER GOOD AND OVER GOOD A BLESSING IS SAID SIMILAR TO THAT OVER EVIL,[3] BUT TO CRY OVER THE PAST IS TO UTTER A VAIN PRAYER. IF A MAN'S WIFE IS PREGNANT AND HE SAYS, [GOD] GRANT THAT MY WIFE BEAR A MALE CHILD, THIS A VAIN PRAYER. IF HE IS COMING HOME FROM A JOURNEY AND HE HEARS CRIES OF DISTRESS IN THE TOWN AND SAYS, [GOD] GRANT THAT THIS IS NOT IN MY HOUSE, THIS IS A VAIN PRAYER. ONE WHO [IN THE COURSE OF A JOURNEY] GOES
b THROUGH A CAPITAL CITY[1] SHOULD SAY TWO PRAYERS, ONE ON ENTERING AND ONE ON LEAVING. BEN AZZAI SAYS, FOUR,[2] TWO ON ENTERING AND TWO ON LEAVING—HE GIVES THANKS FOR PAST MERCIES AND SUPPLICATES FOR THE FUTURE. IT IS INCUMBENT ON A MAN TO BLESS [GOD] FOR THE EVIL IN THE SAME WAY AS FOR THE GOOD, AS IT SAYS, AND THOU SHALT LOVE THE LORD THY GOD WITH ALL THY HEART ETC.[3] 'WITH ALL THY HEART' MEANS, WITH THY TWO IMPULSES, THE EVIL IMPULSE AS WELL AS THE GOOD IMPULSE; 'WITH ALL THY SOUL' MEANS, EVEN THOUGH HE TAKES THY SOUL [LIFE]; 'WITH ALL THY MIGHT' MEANS, WITH ALL THY MONEY. ANOTHER EXPLANATION OF 'WITH ALL THY MIGHT [ME'ODEKA]' IS, WHATEVER TREATMENT[4] HE METES OUT TO THEE.

ONE SHOULD AVOID SHOWING DISRESPECT TO THE EASTERN GATE[5] BECAUSE IT IS IN A DIRECT LINE WITH THE HOLY OF HOLIES.[6] A MAN SHOULD NOT ENTER THE TEMPLE MOUNT WITH HIS STAFF OR WITH HIS SHOES ON OR WITH HIS WALLET OR WITH HIS FEET DUST-STAINED; NOR SHOULD HE MAKE IT A SHORT CUT [ḲAPPANDARIA], AND SPITTING [ON IT IS FORBIDDEN] A FORTIORI.

AT THE CONCLUSION OF THE BENEDICTIONS SAID IN THE TEMPLE THEY USED AT FIRST TO SAY SIMPLY, 'FOR EVER'.[7] WHEN THE SADDUCEES PERVERTED THEIR WAYS AND ASSERTED THAT THERE WAS ONLY ONE WORLD, IT WAS ORDAINED THAT THE RESPONSE SHOULD BE, FROM EVERLASTING TO EVERLASTING.[8] IT WAS ALSO LAID DOWN THAT GREETING SHOULD BE GIVEN IN [GOD'S] NAME,[9] IN THE SAME WAY AS IT SAYS, AND BEHOLD BOAZ CAME FROM BETHLEHEM AND SAID UNTO THE REAPERS, THE LORD BE WITH YOU; AND THEY
c ANSWERED HIM, THE LORD BLESS THEE;[1] AND IT ALSO SAYS, THE LORD IS WITH THEE, THOU MIGHTY MAN OF VALOUR;[2] AND IT ALSO SAYS, AND DESPISE NOT THY MOTHER WHEN SHE IS OLD;[3] AND IT ALSO SAYS, IT IS TIME TO WORK FOR THE LORD; THEY HAVE MADE VOID THY LAW.[4] R. NATHAN SAYS: [THIS MEANS] THEY HAVE MADE VOID THY LAW BECAUSE IT IS A TIME TO WORK FOR THE LORD.

GEMARA. Whence is this rule[5] derived?—R. Joḥanan said: Because Scripture says, *And Jethro said, Blessed be the Lord who hath delivered you*, etc.[6] And is a blessing said only for a miracle wrought for a large body, but not for one wrought for an individual? What of the case of the man who was once travelling through Eber Yemina[7] when a lion attacked him, but he was miraculously saved, and when he came before Raba he said to him, Whenever you pass that place say, Blessed be He who wrought for me a miracle in this place? There was the case, too, of Mar the son of Rabina who was once going through the valley of 'Araboth[8] and was suffering from thirst and a well of water was miraculously created for him and he drank, and another time he was going through the manor of Maḥoza[9] when a wild camel attacked him and at that moment the wall of a house just by fell in and he escaped inside; and whenever thereafter he came to 'Araboth he used to say, Blessed be He who wrought for me miracles in 'Araboth and with the camel, and when he passed through the manor of Maḥoza he used to say, Blessed be He who wrought for me miracles with the camel and in 'Araboth?—The answer [is that] for a miracle done to a large body it is the duty of everyone to say a blessing, for a miracle
d done to an individual he alone[1] is required to say a blessing.

Our Rabbis taught: If one sees the place of the crossing of the Red Sea, or the fords of the Jordan, or the fords of the streams of Arnon, or hail stones [*abne elgabish*] in the descent of Beth Horon, or the stone which Og king of Bashan wanted to throw at Israel, or the stone on which Moses sat when Joshua fought with Amalek, or [the pillar of salt of] Lot's wife,[2] or the wall of Jericho which sank into the ground,[3] for all of these he should give thanksgiving and praise to the Almighty. I grant you the passage of the Red Sea, because it is written, *And the children of Israel went into the midst of the sea upon the dry ground;*[4] also the fords of the Jordan, because it is written, *And the priests that bore the ark of the covenant of the Lord stood firm on dry ground in the midst of the Jordan, while all Israel passed over on dry ground, until all the nation were passed clean over the Jordan*.[5] But whence is the rule derived for the fords of the streams of Arnon?—Because it is written: *Wherefore it is said in the book of the Wars of the Lord, Eth and Heb in the rear;*[6] [in explanation of which] a Tanna taught: '*Eth and Heb in the rear*' were two lepers who followed in the rear of the camp of Israel, and when the Israelites were about to pass through

a (1) Var. lec.: who fashions the work of creation. (2) Generally taken to refer to the Mediterranean Sea. (3) This is explained in the Gemara.

b (1) The residence of a governor or ruler. (2) As explained in the Gemara. (3) Deut. VI, 5. (4) Heb. Lit., 'measure'; Heb. *middah*, a play on *me'odeka*. (5) Of the Temple Mount. (6) I.e., a direct line led from it through the other gates up to the inner shrine. (7) Heb. *le'olam*, which can also mean, 'for the world'. (8) Or 'from world to world', i.e., two worlds. (9) I.e., the Tetragrammaton, although this might appear to be breaking the third commandment. The reason of this ordinance is not certain. Marmorstein, *The Old Testament Conception of God, etc.* I, pp. 24ff conjectures this to have been designed to counteract the Hellenistic teaching that God had no name.

c (1) Ruth II, 4. (2) Judg. VI, 12. (3) Prov. XXIII, 22. (4) In time of emergency the law of God may be set aside. Ps. CXIX, 126. E.V. '*for the Lord to work*'. The relevance of these citations is explained in the Gemara. (5) Of saying a blessing over a miracle. (6) Ex. XVIII, 10. (7) Lit., 'the south side'. The southern suburb of Maḥoza, v. Obermeyer, p. 181. (8) Between the river Chabor and the canal of Is. (9) Rostaḳa di Maḥoza, v. Obermeyer, p. 172.

d (1) Alfasi adds, His son and his son's son. (2) V. Gen. XIX, 26. (3) Lit., 'was swallowed in its place'. (4) Ex. XIV, 22. (5) Josh. III, 17. (6) Num. XXI, 14. E.V. '*Vahab in Suphah*'.

מסורת הש"ס

הרואה מקום שנעשו בו נסים לישראל אומר ברוך שעשה נסים לאבותינו במקום הזה מקום שנעקרה ממנו ע"ז אומר ברוך שעקר ע"ז מארצנו על הזיקין ועל הזועות ועל הרעמים ועל הרוחות ועל הברקים אומר ברוך שכחו וגבורתו מלא עולם על ההרים ועל הגבעות ועל הימים ועל הנהרות ועל המדברות אומר ברוך עושה בראשית רבי יהודה אומר הרואה את הים הגדול אומר ברוך שעשה את הים הגדול בזמן שרואהו לפרקים על הגשמים ועל בשורות טובות אומר ברוך הטוב והמטיב על בשורות רעות אומר ברוך דיין האמת בנה בית חדש וקנה כלים חדשים אומר ברוך שהחיינו וקימנו והגיענו לזמן הזה מברך על הרעה מעין על הטובה ועל הטובה מעין על הרעה והצועק לשעבר הרי זה תפלת שוא היתה אשתו מעוברת ואומר יהי רצון שתלד אשתי זכר הרי זו תפלת שוא היה בא בדרך ושמע קול צוחה בעיר ואומר יהי רצון שלא תהא בתוך ביתי הרי זו תפלת שוא הנכנס לכרך מתפלל שתי' אחת בכניסתו ואחת ביציאתו בן עזאי אומר ארבע שתים בכניסתו ושתים ביציאתו נותן הודאה על שעבר וצועק על העתיד חייב אדם לברך על הרעה כשם שמברך על הטובה שנא' ואהבת את יי' אלהיך בכל לבבך וגו' בכל לבבך בשני יצריך ביצר טוב וביצר הרע בכל נפשך אפי' הוא נוטל את נפשך בכל מאדך בכל ממונך ד"א בכל מאדך בכל מדה ומדה שהוא מודד לך הוי מודה לו במאד מאד לא יקל אדם את ראשו כנגד שער המזרח שהוא מכוון כנגד בית קדשי הקדשים ולא יכנס להר הבית במקלו ובמנעלו ובפונדתו ובאבק שעל רגליו ולא יעשנו קפנדריא ורקיקה מקל וחומר כל חותמי ברכות שבמקדש היו אומרים עד העולם משקלקלו הצדוקי' ואמרו אין עולם אלא אחד התקינו שיהו אומרים מן העולם ועד העולם והתקינו שיהא אדם שואל את שלום חברו בשם שנ' והנה בעז בא מבית לחם ויאמר לקוצרים יי' עמכם ויאמרו לו יברכך יי' ואומר יי' עמך גבור החיל ואומר אל תבוז כי זקנה אמך ואו' עת לעשות ליי' הפרו תורתך רבי נתן אומר הפרו תורתך משום עת לעשות ליי': **גמ'** מנא ה"מ א"ר יוחנן דאמר קרא ויאמר יתרו ברוך ה' אשר הציל וגו' אניסא דרבים מברכינן אניסא דיחיד לא מברכינן והא ההוא גברא דהוה קא אזיל בעבר ימינא נפל עליה אריא איתעביד ליה ניסא ואיתצל מניה אתא לקמיה דרבא וא"ל כל אימת דמטית להתם בריך ברוך שעשה לי נס במקום הזה ומר בריה דרבינא הוה קאזיל בפקתא דערבות וצחא למיא אתעביד ליה ניסא איברי ליה עינא דמיא ואשתי ותו זמנא חדא הוה קא אזיל ברסתקא דמחוזא ונפל עליה גמלא פריצא אתפרקא ליה אשיתא על לגוה כי מטא לערבות בריך ברוך שעשה לי נס בערבות ובגמל כי מטא לרסתקא דמחוזא בריך ברוך שעשה לי נס בגמל ובערבות אמרי אניסא דרבים כולי עלמא מחייבי לברוכי אניסא דיחיד איהו חייב לברוכי: ת"ר הרואה מעברות הים ומעברות הירדן מעברות נחלי ארנון אבני אלגביש במורד בית חורון ואבן שבקש לזרוק עוג מלך הבשן על ישראל ואבן שישב עליה משה בשעה שעשה יהושע מלחמה בעמלק ואשתו של לוט וחומת יריחו שנבלעה במקומה על כולן צריך שיתן הודאה ושבח לפני המקום בשלמא מעברות הים דכתיב ויבאו בני ישראל בתוך הים ביבשה מעברות הירדן דכתיב ויעמדו הכהנים נשאי ארון יי' בחרב' בתוך הירדן הכן וכל ישראל עוברים בחרב' עד תום כל העם לעבור את הירדן אלא מעברות נחלי ארנון מנלן דכתיב על כן יאמר בספר מלחמות יי' את והב בסופה וגו' תנא את והב בסופה שני מצורעים היו דהוו מהלכין בסוף מחנה ישראל כי הוו קא חלפי ישראל אתו אמוראי

עבדי

תורה אור: דברי' ו; רות ב; שופטי' ו; משלי כג; תהלי' קיט; שמו' יח; שם יד; יהושע ג; במדבר כא

רש"י

הרואה מקום שנעשו בו נסים לישראל. כגון הנך דקתני לקמן מעברות הים והירדן ונחלי ארנון כו': זיקין וזועות ורעמים. מפרש בגמרא: מלא עולם. לפי שאלו נראין או נשמעין למרחוק: ברוך עושה בראשית. ובגמרא (ד' נט.) פריך אטו הנך דלעיל לאו מעשה בראשית נינהו: לפרקים. מפרש בגמרא (שם ע"ב) ולפי שהוא חשוב וגדול מכולן קבע ליה ר' יהודה ברכה לעצמו: מברך על הרעה מעין על הטובה. דיין האמת: ועל הטובה מעין על הרעה. הטוב והמטיב ובגמרא מפרש היכי דמי: הנכנס לכרך. המהלך בדרך וצריך לעבור כרך ושם מלויים מושלים רעים ומחפשים עלילות: אחת בכניסתו. מתפלל שיכנס לשלום: ביציאתו. מתפלל שיצא לשלום: ארבע. כדמפרש נותן הודאה על שעבר וצועק על העתיד כמלא ד' כדמפרש בגמ': חייב אדם לברך על הרעה כו'. מפרש בגמרא: ד"א בכל מאדך. מדות מדודות לך בין מדה טובה בין מדת פורענות: לא יקל ראשו. לא ינהג קלות ראש: כנגד שער המזרח. חוץ להר הבית אשר בחומה הנמוכה אשר לרגלי הבית במזרח לפי שכל השערים מכוונים זה כנגד זה שער מזרח שער עזרת נשים ושער עזרת ישראל ופתח האולם וההיכל ובית קדשי הקדשים ביומי מקדש ראשון כשהיה אמה טרקסין: בפונדתו. חגור חלול ונותנים בו מעות: מק"ו. בגמרא מפרש ליה: כל חותמי ברכות שבמקדש היו אומרים עד העולם. במסכת תענית (טז:) אמרינן אין עונין אמן במקדש המברך אומר בסוף כל ברכה בא"י אלהי ישראל מן העולם ועד העולם ברוך חונן הדעת וכן בכולם והעונים אומרים בשכמל"ו וילפינן לה מקרא דתפלת עזרא וסיעתו ואשמעינן הכא דבמקדש ראשון לא היו אומרים אלא ברוך ה' אלהי ישראל עד מן העולם: משקלקלו הצדוקים. ואמרו אין עולם אלא זה: התקינו. עזרא וסיעתו שיהו אומרים מן העולם ועד העולם לומר ששני עולמות יש להוציא מלב הכופרים בתחיית המתים: שיהא אדם שואל את שלום חברו בשם. בשמו של הקב"ה ולא אמרינן מזלזל הוא בכבודו של מקום בשביל כבוד הבריות להוציא שם שמים עליו ולמדו מבעז שאמר יי' עמכם ומן המלאך שאמר לגדעון יי' עמך גבור החיל: ואומר אל תבוז כי זקנה אמך. למוד מדברי זקני אומתך לעשות מה שראית שעשו הם ובגמ' מפרש מאי ואומר: ואומר עת לעשות ליי' הפרו תורתך. פעמים שמבטלים ד"ת כדי לעשות ליי' אף זה המתכוי' לשאול לשלום חברו זהו רצונו של מקום שנאמר בקש שלום ורדפהו ומותר להפר תורה ולעשות דבר הנראה אסור:

גמ'. ה"ג מנלן דמברכים אניסא אמר ר' יוחנן דאמר קרא ויאמר יתרו ברוך ה' אשר הציל אתכם וגו': בעבר ימינא. שם מדינה בדרומו של פרת: בפקתא. בקעה: ערבות. שם מקום: וצחא למיא. וצמא למים: ברסתקא. בשוק: גמלא פריצא. גמל משוגע שעקציו רעים: אתפרק' ליה אשיתא. נפלה חומת בית שהיה סמוך לו ונכנס לתוך הבית מפני הגמל: מעברות הים. מקום שעברו ישראל ים סוף: ומעברות הירדן. בימי יהושע: מעברות נחלי ארנון. לקמן מפ' מאי היא: במורד בית חורון. בימי יהושע היה בספר יהושע (י): ואבן שזרק עוג. לקמן מפ':

תוספות

הרואה וכו' אומר ברוך שעשה נסים לאבותינו וכו'. פירש רבי' שמעיה דכל הני ברכות צריכות להזכרת שם ומלכות ברוך א"י אמ"ה וכן כתב רבינו שמשון מקולי כי הר"י היה רגיל לברך על הברקים בא"י אלהינו מלך העולם שכחו וגבורתו מלא עולם וכן פר"י ומייתי ירושלמי דפירקין ר' זעירא וכו' כל ברכה שאין בה וכו' ונראה לרבינו דדוקא לרואה משלשים יום לשלשים יום דומיא דרואה ים הגדול לפרקים דאמר בירושלמי דפרקים היינו שלשים יום:

שעקר ע"א מארצנו. בירושל' מתני כשנעקרה ע"א מכל ארץ ישראל:

על הנהרות. לאו על כל נהרות איירי אלא ד' נהרות דכתיבי בקרא כמו חדקל ופרת:

אבני

עין משפט נר מצוה

א
א מיי' פ"י מהל' ברכות ה"ט סמ"ג ע' כז טוש"ע א"ח סי' ריח סעיף א [ע' תו' לקמן נט. ד"ה על] תיבת מכל ע"פ וגם ברא"ש ליתא

ב
ב ג מיי' שם ה' טו וסמ"ג שם טוש"ע א"ח סי' רכח סעי' א

[ע' תו' סוכה מו. ד"ה העושה וכו' מ"ש בשם רב שרירא גאון]

ג
ד מיי' שם טוש"ע א"ח סי' ריח סעיף ג וסי' רכד סעי' יג

ד
ה מיי' וסמ"ג שם ה"ג טוש"ע א"ח סי' רכב סעי' ג

ה
ו מיי' שם ה' כב כה כו וסמ"ג שם טוש"ע א"ח סי' רל סעיף א

[מכות כג:]

ו
ז מיי' פ"ז מה' בית הבחירה הל' יב סמ"ג עשין קסד

ז
ח טוש"ע א"ח סי' ריח סעיף ה

ח
ט מיי' פ"י מה' ברכו' ה"ט סמ"ג עשין כז טוש"ע שם סעיף ג

ט
כ מיי' שם טוש"ע א"ח שם סעיף ד

י
ל מיי' שם שם סעיף א

מסורת הש"ס (גליון)

ירושלמי גרס מלא עולמים

[פסחים כ.]

נוסחת ירוש' בזמן שרואה לפרקים ברוך עושה מ"ב

לעיל לג: מח: מגילה כה.

[ג"י ירוש' הוי מודה לו מאד מאד]

יבמות ו.

[מן העולם כ"א במשנה שבמשניות כן פי' הר"ב מברטנורה ע"ש]

עבדי להון נקירתא וטשו בהן אמרי כי חלפי ישראל הכא נקטלינון ולא הוו ידעי דארון הוה מסגי קמיידהו דישראל והוה ממיך להו טורי מקמיידהו כיון דאתא ארון אדבקו טורי בהדי הדדי וקטלינון ונחת דמיידהו לנחלי ארנון כי אתו את והב חזו דמא דקא נפיק מביני טורי אתו ואמרי להו לישראל ואמרו שירה היינו דכתיב °ואשד הנחלים אשר נטה לשבת ער ונשען לגבול מואב. אבני אלגביש מאי אבני אלגביש תנא אבנים שעמדו על גב איש וירדו ע"ג איש עמדו על גב איש זה משה דכתיב °והאיש משה עניו מאד וכתיב °ויחדלו הקולות והברד ומטר לא נתך ארצה ירדו על גב איש זה יהושע דכתיב °קח לך את יהושע בן נון איש אשר רוח בו וכתיב °ויהי בנוסם מפני (בני) ישראל הם במורד בית חורון וי"י השליך עליהם אבנים גדולות. אבן שבקש עוג מלך הבשן לזרוק על ישראל גמרא גמירי לה אמר מחנה ישראל כמה הוי תלתא פרסי איזיל ואיעקר טורא בר תלתא פרסי ואישדי עלייהו ואיקטלינהו אזל עקר טורא בר תלתא פרסי ואייתי על רישיה ואייתי קודשא בריך הוא עליה קמצי ונקבוה ונחית בצואריה הוה בעי למשלפה משכי שיניה להאי גיסא ולהאי גיסא ולא מצי למשלפה והיינו דכתיב °שני רשעים שברת וכדרבי שמעון בן לקיש *דאמר ר' שמעון בן לקיש מאי דכתיב שיני רשעים שברת אל תקרי שברת אלא שרבבת *משה כמה הוי עשר אמות שקל נרגא בר עשר אמין שוור עשר אמין ומחייה בקרסוליה וקטליה. ואבן שישב עליה משה דכתיב °וידי משה כבדים ויקחו אבן וישימו תחתיו וישב עליה. ואשתו של לוט שנאמר °ותבט אשתו מאחריו ותהי נציב מלח. וחומת יריחו שנבלעה דכתיב °ותפול החומה תחתיה. בשלמא כולהו ניסא אלא אשתו של לוט פורענותא הוא דאמר ברוך דיין האמת והא הודאה ושבח קתני תני *על לוט ועל אשתו מברכים שתים על אשתו אומר ברוך דיין האמת ועל לוט אומר ברוך זוכר הצדיקים *א"ר יוחנן אפילו בשעת כעסו של הקב"ה זוכר את הצדיקים שנא' °ויהי בשחת אלהים את ערי הככר ויזכור אלהים את אברהם וישלח את לוט מתוך ההפכה וגו' וחומת יריחו שנבלעה והא נפלה שנא' °ויהי כשמוע העם את קול השופר ויריעו העם תרועה גדולה ותפול החומה תחתיה כיון דפותיה ורומה כי הדדי נינהו משום הכי אבלעה בלועי. אמר רב יהודה אמר רב *ארבעה צריכין להודות יורדי הים הולכי מדברות ומי שהיה חולה ונתרפא ומי שהיה חבוש בבית האסורים ויצא. יורדי הים מנלן דכתיב °יורדי הים באניות וגו' המה ראו מעשה י"י ואומר ויעמד רוח סערה יעלו שמים ירדו תהומות ואומר יחוגו וינועו כשכור ואומר ויצעקו אל י"י בצר להם וממצוקותיהם יוציאם ואומר יקם סערה לדממה ואומר וישמחו כי ישתוקו ואומר יודו לי"י חסדו ונפלאותיו לבני אדם. הולכי מדברות מנלן דכתיב תעו במדבר בישימון דרך עיר מושב לא מצאו ויצעקו אל י"י וידריכם בדרך ישרה יודו לי"י חסדו. מי שחלה ונתרפא דכתיב אוילים מדרך פשעם ומעונותיהם יתענו כל אוכל תתעב נפשם ויצעקו אל י"י בצר להם וגו' ישלח דברו וירפאם וגו' יודו לי"י חסדו. מי שהיה חבוש בבית האסורין מנלן דכתיב יושבי חשך וצלמות כי המרו אמרי אל וגו' ואומר ויכנע בעמל לבם וגו' ואומר ויצעקו אל י"י בצר להם ואומר יוציאם מחשך וצלמות וגו' ואומר יודו לי"י חסדו. מאי מברך אמר רב יהודה ברוך גומל חסדים טובים אביי אמר וצריך לאודויי קמי עשרה דכתיב וירוממוהו בקהל עם וגו' מר זוטרא אמר ותרין מנייהו רבנן שנאמר ובמושב זקנים יהללוהו מתקיף לה רב אשי ואימא כולהו רבנן מי כתיב בקהל זקנים בקהל עם כתיב ואימא בי עשרה שאר עמא ותרי רבנן קשיא. רב יהודה חלש ואתפח על לגביה רב חנא בגדתאה ורבנן אמרי ליה בריך רחמנא דיהבך ניהלן ולא יהבך לעפרא אמר להו פטרתון יתי מלאודויי והא אמר אביי בעי אודויי באפי עשרה דהוו בי עשרה והא איהו לא קא מודה לא צריך דעני בתריידהו אמן: אמר רב יהודה שלשה צריכין שימור ואלו הן חולה חתן וכלה במתניתא תנא חולה חיה חתן וכלה וי"א אף אבל וי"א אף תלמידי חכמים בלילה. ואמר רב יהודה שלשה דברים [המאריך בהן] מאריכין ימיו ושנותיו של אדם המאריך בתפלתו והמאריך על שלחנו והמאריך בבית הכסא והמאריך בתפלתו מעליותא היא והאמר רבי חייא בר אבא א"ר יוחנן

כל

עבדי להון נקירתא. מערות מעברות כחלי ארכון עמק עמוק בין ב' הרים גבוהים והיו ישראל צריכים לעבור בתוכו עמק עשו אמוריים מערות בצדי ההרים ונחבאו שם: וטשו. נחבאו: מסגי. עובר: ממיך טורי. משפיל הרים ומתפשטין זה לצד זה עד שהעמק שוה: חזו דמא. כשחזרו ההרים למקומן: ואשד. ושפך: אשר נטה לשבת ער. ההר שבעבר העמק נטה והתפשט לצד חברו ההר אשר לצד עבר מואב והם ארץ מואב ער: שעמדו. באויר: לא נתך ארצה. לא הגיע לארץ אלא עמדו באויר: מחנה ישראל כמה הוי תלתא פרסי. עוג חשב כן בלבו מחנה ישראל תלתא פרסי דכתיב (במדבר לג) ויחנו מבית הישימון עד אבל השטים ואמר רבה בר בר חנה לדידי חזי לי ההוא דוכתא והוה תלתא פרסי אורכא ותלתא פרסי פותיא (עירובין פ"ה ד' נה:): קמצי. נמלים: שרבבת. לשון *אשתרבובי אשתרבוב ילדו וגדלו למטה: משה כמה הוי עשר אמין. שהרי הוא הקים את המשכן ולהשכן הקים את עצמו לקומת המשכן וכתיב בית עשר אמות אורך הקרש (שמות כו): שוור. קפץ למעלה: בקרסוליה. קבי"ליא בלע"ז: וידי משה כבדים. ואינו יכול לפושטן כל היום אלא א"כ תומכים בזרועותיו ויקחו אבן וישימו תחתיו: תחתיה. משמע במקומה ואי אפשר זו אלא על ידי בליעה: דאמר ברוך דיין האמת. תיהוא הוא: זוכר את הצדיקים. שזכר את אברהם: כיון דפותיה ורומה כי הדדי הוו. ואין נפילה ניכרת בה אם לא נבלעה משום הכי אבלעה והוה דרך נפילה לחומה כזו: צריכין להודות. כשיוצאין מן הסכנה: וירוממוהו בקהל עם. בסוף פרשת המזמור: ואתפח. נתרפא: בגדתאה. שם עירו בגדד ה' עיר החשובה שבבבל משהרב *בבל: שימור. מן המזיקין: חולה. שהורע מזלו לפיכך השד מתגרה בו וכן חיה אשה שילדה וכן אבל: חתן וכלה ותלמידי חכמים. מקנאתו מתגרה בהם: המאריך על שלחנו. שמתוך כך עניים באין ומתפרנסים: המאריך בבית הכסא. רפואה היא לו:

ומעיין

---

*אבני אלגביש במורד בית חורון. וה"ה מקום שנפל שם מחנה סנחריב דלא גרע חזקיה מאלה *המסויים אלא לא חש לפרש לפי שידוע מקום שבית ירושלים. ושוב היה נראה לרבינו יהודה כיון שאין הכל ידוע ע"פ המקום כי הכך אין מברכין עליו אלא אותם שנעשה להם הנס. וכן כל אדם מברך על ניסו אע"פ שאינו ניכר מתוך המקום:

ארבעה צריכים להודות יורדי הים וכו'. ובתהלים לא חשיב כזה הסדר אלא חשיב הולכי המדבר ראשון דקרא נקט סדר המסוכנין יותר תחלה וגמרא נקט המצויים תחלה:

ואימא בי עשרה ותרי רבנן. *ועבדי לחומרא ואפילו ליכא תרי רבנן ונהגו העולם לברך אחר שקורא בתורה ודוקא בחולה שנפל למטה אבל אם בראשו או במעיו ואינו מוטל למטה לא. ה"ר יוסף:

פטרתון יתי מלאודויי. וא"ת והאמרינן *ברכה שאין בה מלכות אינה ברכה וי"ל דרב יהודה היה מתלמידי דרב ורב סבר לעיל בפרק כילד מברכין (דף מ:) דלא בעינן אלא הזכרת השם (או מלכות ורחמנא הייכו מלכות):

לך

תורה אור

ואשד הנחלים אשר נטה לשבת ער — במדבר כא
ויחדלו הקולות — שמות ט
קח לך את יהושע — במדבר כז
ויהי בנוסם מפני — יהוש' י
שני רשעים שברת — תהלי' ג
וידי משה — שמות יז
ותבט אשתו — בראשי' יט
ותפול החומה — יהוש' ו
ויהי בשחת — בראשי' יט
ויהי כשמוע — יהוש' ו
יורדי הים — תהלים קז

מסורת הש"ס

[קדושין עג:]
[מגילה טו: סוטה יב:]
[וע' פירש"י יבמות סז. וכתובות ז: יוד:]
[לעיל מ:]

עין משפט נר מצוה

סייך לע"א [הכזכר בירושלמי הביאו הרא"ש סי' א]

יא א טוש"ע א"ח סי' ריח סעי' א

יב ב מיי' פ"י מה' ברכות הלכה ח סמג עשין כז טוש"ע א"ח סי' ריט סעי' א [הטור בא"ח סי' ר"ט העתיק דברי תוס' הללו בז"הל וכיון דלא איפסיק' עבדינן לחומרא ובעינן תרוייהו]

[כל זה מוחק המעי"ע]

יג ג מיי' שם טוש"ע שם סעיף ב

יד ד מיי' שם ועוש"ע שם סעי' ג [בכורו' מד.]

טו ה שם סעי' ד

[בשאלתות פ' וישלח סי' כו איתא דאמר ר"י]

[תשובת רב האי גאון על דלא קחשיב הכך ד' דצריכין להודות כסדר הנאמר בפסוק עיין בערוך ערך ארבע תמלא נחת וכלל דבריו דבקרא סידרן מה שהכיח עפי ובגמ' מסדר לפוס הקרובין לסכנה ול"ע בתו' ד"ה ארבע' וכו' שכתבו להיפך וע"ע בתו' דשבת ב. ד"ה יציאות וכן מפרש רב האי בד' צריכין להודו' ע"ש היטב]

[the valley of Arnon] the Amorites came [54b] and made cavities [in the rocks] and hid in them, saying, When Israel pass by here we will kill them. They did not know, however, that the Ark was advancing in front of Israel and levelling the hills before them. When the Ark arrived there, the mountains closed together and killed them, and their blood flowed down to the streams of Arnon. When Eth and Heb came they saw the blood issuing from between the rocks[7] and they went and told the Israelites, who thereupon broke out into song. And so it is written, *And he poured forth the streams*[8] [from the mountain] which *inclined toward the seat of Ar*[9] *and leaned upon the border of Moab.*[10]

'Hailstones [*abne elgabish*]'. What are '*abne elgabish*'? A Tanna taught: Stones [*abanim*] which remained suspended for the sake of a man ['*al gab ish*] and came down for the sake of a man. 'They remained suspended for the sake of a man': this was Moses, of
a whom it is written, *Now* the man *Moses was very meek,*[1] and it is also written, *And the thunders and hail ceased, and the rain poured not upon the earth.*[2] 'They came down for the sake of a man': this was Joshua, of whom it is written, *Take thee Joshua the son of Nun,* a man *in whom there is spirit,*[3] and it is written, *And it came to pass as they fled from before Israel, while they were at the descent of Beth-Horon, that the Lord cast down great stones.*[4]

'The stone which Og, king of Bashan wanted to throw at Israel'. This has been handed down by tradition. He said: How large is the camp of Israel? Three parasangs. I will go and uproot a mountain of the size of three parasangs and cast it upon them and kill them. He went and uprooted a mountain of the size of three parasangs and carried it on his head. But the Holy One, blessed be He, sent ants which bored a hole in it, so that it sank around his neck. He tried to pull it off, but his teeth projected on each side, and he could not pull it off. This is referred to in the text, *Thou hast broken the teeth of the wicked,*[5] as explained by R. Simeon b. Lakish. For R. Simeon b. Lakish said: What is the meaning of the text, *Thou hast broken the teeth of the wicked?* Do not read, *shibbarta* [Thou hast broken], but *shirbabta* [Thou hast lengthened]. The height of Moses was ten cubits.[6] He took an axe ten cubits long, leapt ten cubits into the air, and struck him on his ankle and killed him.

'The stone on which Moses sat'. As it is written, *But Moses' hands were heavy; and they took a stone and put it under him and he sat thereon.*[7]

'Lot's wife'. As it says, *But his wife looked back from behind him and she became a pillar of salt.*[8]

'And the wall of Jericho which sank into the ground'. As it is
b written, *And the wall fell down flat.*[1]

We understand [why this blessing should be said over] all the others, because they are miracles, but the transformation of Lot's wife was a punishment. One should say on seeing it, Blessed be the true Judge,[2] yet [the Baraitha] says: 'Thanksgiving and praise'? —Read: 'For Lot and his wife two blessings are said. For his wife we say, "Blessed be the true Judge", and for Lot we say, "Blessed be He who remembereth the righteous"'. R. Johanan said: Even in the hour of His anger the Holy One, blessed be He, remembers the righteous, as it says, *And it came to pass when God destroyed the cities of the Plain, that God remembered Abraham and sent Lot out of the midst of the overthrow.*[3]

'And the wall of Jericho which sank [into the ground]'. But did the wall of Jericho sink [into the ground]? Surely it fell, as it says, *And it came to pass when the people heard the sound of the horn, that the people shouted with a great shout and the wall fell down flat?*[4]— Since its breadth and its height were equal, it must have sunk [into the ground].[5]

Rab Judah said in the name of Rab: There are four [classes of people] who have to offer thanksgiving: those who have crossed the sea, those who have traversed the wilderness, one who has recovered from an illness, and a prisoner who has been set free. Whence do we know this of those who cross the sea?—Because it is written, *They that go down to the sea in ships .... these saw the works of the Lord .... He raised the stormy wind .... they mounted up to the heaven, they went down to the deeps .... they reeled to and fro and staggered like a drunken man .... they cried unto the Lord in their trouble, and He brought them out of their distresses. He made the storm a calm .... then were they glad because they were quiet .... Let them give thanks unto the Lord for His mercy, and for His wonderful works*
c *to the children of men.*[1] Whence for those who traverse the desert?— Because it is written: *They wandered in the wilderness in a desert way; they found no city of habitation .... Then they cried unto the Lord .... and He led them by a straight way .... Let them give thanks unto the Lord for His mercy.*[2] Whence for one who recovers from an illness?—Because it is written: *Crazed because of the way of their transgression, and afflicted because of their iniquities, their soul abhorred all manner of food .... They cried unto the Lord in their trouble. He sent His word unto them .... Let them give thanks unto the Lord for His mercy.*[3] Whence for a prisoner who was set free?— Because it is written: *Such as sat in darkness and in the shadow of death .... Because they rebelled against the words of God .... Therefore He humbled their heart with travail .... They cried unto the Lord in their trouble .... He brought them out of darkness and the shadow of death .... Let them give thanks unto the Lord for His mercy.*[4] What blessing should he say? Rab Judah said: 'Blessed is He who bestows lovingkindnesses'. Abaye said: And he must utter his thanksgiving in the presence of ten, as it is written: *Let them exalt Him in the assembly of the people.*[5] Mar Zutra said: And two of them must be rabbis, as it says, *And praise Him in the seat of the elders.*[6] R. Ashi demurred to this: You might as well say [he remarked], that all should be rabbis!—Is it written, 'In the assembly of elders'? It is written, 'In the assembly of the people'!—Let us say then, in the presence of ten ordinary people and two rabbis [in addition]?—This is a difficulty.

Rab Judah was ill and recovered. R. Hanna of Bagdad and other rabbis went to visit him. They said to him: 'Blessed be the All-Merciful who has given you back to us and has not given you to the dust'. He said to them: 'You have absolved me from the obligation of giving thanks'. But has not Abaye said that he must utter his thanksgiving in the presence of ten!—There were ten present. But he did not utter the thanksgiving?—There was no need, as he answered after them, Amen.

d Rab Judah said: Three persons require guarding,[1] namely, a sick person, a bridegroom, and a bride. In a Baraitha it was taught: A sick person, a midwife, a bridegroom and a bride; some add, a mourner, and some add further, scholars at night-time.

Rab Judah said further: There are three things the drawing out of which prolongs a man's days and years; the drawing out of prayer, the drawing out of a meal, and the drawing out of [easing in] a privy. But is the drawing out of prayer a merit? Has not

(7) Lit., 'mountains'. After they had opened out again. (8) E.V. '*and the slope of the valleys*'. (9) I.e., Moab. (10) Ibid. 15.
a (1) Num. XII, 3. (2) Ex. IX, 33. (3) Num. XXVII, 18. (4) Josh. X, 11. (5) Ps. III, 8. (6) About fifteen feet. (7) Ex. XVII, 12. MS.M. adds: 'Had not Moses a cushion or bolster to sit upon? Moses said to himself: Since Israel are suffering, I will suffer with them'; v. Ta'an. 11a. (8) Gen. XIX, 26.
b (1) Josh. VI, 20. This sentence is obviously out of place and should be transferred to the next paragraph. (2) The formula recited on hearing bad news. (3) Gen. XIX, 29. (4) Josh. VI, 20. (5) To enable the people to enter the city. According to Rashi this is also signified by the word translated 'flat', which means literally 'under it' or 'in its place'.
c (1) Ps. CVII, 23—31. (2) Ibid. 4—8. (3) Ibid. 17—21. (4) Ibid. 10—15. (5) Ibid. 32. (6) Ibid.
d (1) Against evil spirits (Rashi).

R. Ḥiyya b. Abba said in the name of R. Joḥanan: [55*a*] If one draws out his prayer and expects therefor its fulfilment, he will in the end suffer vexation of heart, as it says, *Hope deferred maketh the heart sick;*[2] and R. Isaac also said: Three things cause a man's sins to be remembered [on high], namely, [passing under] a shaky wall,[3] expectation of [the fulfilment of] prayer, and calling on heaven to punish his neighbour?[4]—There is no contradiction; one statement speaks of a man who expects the fulfilment of his prayer, the other of one who does not count upon it. What then does he do?—He simply utters many supplications. 'He who draws out his meal', because perhaps a poor man will come and he will give him something, as it is written, *The altar of wood three cubits high .... and he said to me, This is the table that is before the Lord.*[5] [Now the verse] opens with *'altar'* and finishes with *'table'?* R. Joḥanan and R. Eleazar both explain that as long as the Temple stood, the altar atoned for Israel, but now a man's table atones for him. 'To draw out one's stay in a privy', is this a good thing? Has it not been taught: Ten things bring on piles; eating the leaves of reeds, and the leaves of vines, and the sprouts of vines, and the rough parts of the flesh of an animal,[6] and the backbone of a fish, and salted fish not sufficiently cooked, and drinking wine lees, and wiping oneself with lime, potters' clay or pebbles which have been used by another. Some add, to strain oneself unduly in a privy!—There is no contradiction: one statement refers to one who stays long and strains himself, the other to one who stays long without straining himself. This may be illustrated by what a certain matron said to R. Kudah b. R. Ila'i: Your face is [red]
a like that of pig-breeders and usurers,[1] to which he replied: On my faith, both [occupations] are forbidden me, but there are twenty-four privies between my lodging and the Beth ha-Midrash, and when I go there I test myself in all of them.[2]

Rab Judah also said:[3] Three things shorten a man's days and years: To be given a scroll of the Law to read from and to refuse, to be given a cup of benediction to say grace over and to refuse, and to assume airs of authority. 'To be given a scroll of the Law to read from and to refuse', as it is written: *For that is thy life and the length of thy days.*[4] 'To be given a cup of benediction to say grace over and to refuse', as it is written: *I will bless them that bless thee.*[5] 'To assume airs of authority', as R. Ḥama b. Ḥanina said: Why did Joseph die before his brethren?[6] Because he assumed airs of authority.

Rab Judah also said in the name of Rab: There are three things for which one should supplicate: a good king, a good year, and a good dream.[7] 'A good king', as it is written: *A king's heart is in the hands of the Lord as the water-courses.*[8] 'A good year', as it is written: *The eyes of the Lord thy God are always upon it, from the beginning of the year even unto the end of the year.*[9] 'A good dream', as it is written; *Wherefore cause Thou me to dream*[10] *and make me to live.*[11]

R. Joḥanan said: There are three things which the Holy One, blessed be He, Himself proclaims, namely, famine, plenty, and a good leader. 'Famine', as it is written: *The Lord hath called for a famine.*[12] 'Plenty', as it is written: *I will call for the corn and will increase*
b *it.*[1] 'A good leader', as it is written: *And the Lord spoke unto Moses, saying, See I have called by name Bezalel, the son of Uri.*[2]

R. Isaac said: We must not appoint a leader over a Community without first consulting it, as it says: *See, the Lord hath called by name Bezalel, the son of Uri.*[3] The Holy One, blessed be He, said to Moses: Do you consider Bezalel suitable? He replied: Sovereign of the Universe, if Thou thinkest him suitable, surely I must also! Said [God] to him: All the same, go and consult them. He went and asked Israel: Do you consider Bezalel suitable? They replied: If the Holy One, blessed be He, and you consider him suitable, surely we must!

R. Samuel b. Naḥmani said in the name of R. Joḥanan: Bezalel was so called on account of his wisdom. At the time when the Holy One, blessed be He, said to Moses; Go and tell Bezalel to make me a tabernacle, an ark and vessels,[4] Moses went and reversed the order, saying, Make an ark and vessels and a tabernacle. Bezalel said to him: Moses, our Teacher, as a rule a man first builds a house and then brings vessels into it; but you say, Make me an ark and vessels and a tabernacle. Where shall I put the vessels that I am to make? Can it be that the Holy One, blessed be He, said to you, Make a tabernacle, an ark and vessels? Moses replied: Perhaps you were in the shadow of God[5] and knew!

Rab Judah said in the name of Rab: Bezalel knew how to combine the letters by which the heavens and earth were created.[6] It is written here, *And He hath filled him with the spirit of God, in* wisdom *and in* understanding, *and in* knowledge,[7] and it is written elsewhere, *The Lord by* wisdom *founded the earth; by* understanding *He established the heavens,*[8] and it is also written, *By His* knowledge *the depths were broken up.*[9]

R. Joḥanan said: The Holy One, blessed be He, gives wisdom only to one who already has wisdom, as it says, *He giveth wisdom unto the wise, and knowledge to them that know understanding.*[10] R.
c Taḥlifa from the West[1] heard and repeated it before R. Abbahu. He said to him: You learn it from there, but we learn it from this text, namely, *In the hearts of all that are wise-hearted I have put wisdom.*[2]

R. Ḥisda said: Any dream rather than one of a fast.[3] R. Ḥisda also said: A dream which is not interpreted is like a letter which is not read.[4] R. Ḥisda also said: Neither a good dream nor a bad dream is ever wholly fulfilled. R. Ḥisda also said: A bad dream is better than a good dream.[5] R. Ḥisda also said: The sadness caused by a bad dream is sufficient for it and the joy which a good dream gives is sufficient for it.[6] R. Joseph said: Even for me[7] the joy caused by a good dream nullifies it. R. Ḥisda also said: A bad dream is worse than scourging, since it says, *God hath so made it that men should fear before Him,*[8] and Rabbah b. Bar Ḥanah said in the name of R. Joḥanan: This refers to a bad dream.

A prophet that hath a dream let him tell a dream: and he that hath My word let him speak My word faithfully. What hath the straw to do with the wheat, saith the Lord.[9] What is the connection of straw and wheat with a dream? The truth is, said R. Joḥanan in the name of R. Simeon b. Yoḥai, that just as wheat cannot be without straw, so there cannot be a dream without some nonsense. R. Berekiah said: While a part of a dream may be fulfilled, the whole of it is never fulfilled. Whence do we know this? From Joseph, as it is written, *And behold the sun and the moon [and eleven stars bowed down to me,]*[10]

(2) Prov. XIII, 12. Cf. 32*b*. (3) Which is, as it were, tempting Providence. (4) Which is a mark of selfrighteousness. Lit., 'surrendering the case against his fellow to heaven'. (5) Ezek. XLI, 22. (6) E.g., the palate. Lit., 'threshing-sledge'.

a (1) Who were notoriously good livers. (2) Cf. Ned. 49*b*. (3) We should probably add, 'In the name of Rab'. (4) Deut. XXX, 20. (5) Gen. XII, 3. The one who says grace blesses his host. (6) As we learn from Ex. I, 6: '*And Joseph died and* (then) *all his brethren*'. (7) These things depending directly upon the will of God. (8) Prov. XXI, 1. (9) Deut. XI, 12. (10) E.V. '*Recover Thou me*'. The Talmud, however, connects the word in the text *taḥalimeni* with *ḥalom*, a dream. (11) Isa. XXXVIII, 16. (12) II Kings VIII, 1.

b (1) Ezek. XXXVI, 29. (2) Ex. XXXI, 1. (3) Ibid. XXXV, 30. (4) This is the order in Ex. XXXI, 7. (5) Heb. *bezel el*. (6) The Kabbalah assigns mystic powers to the letters of the Hebrew alphabet. (7) Ibid. XXXV, 31. (8) Prov. III, 19. (9) Ibid. 20. (10) Dan. II, 21.

c (1) I.e., Palestine. (2) Ex. XXXI, 6. It was preferable to learn it from a text of the Pentateuch. (3) I.e., to dream oneself fasting. So Rashi. The Aruch, however, explains: There is reality in every dream save one that comes in a fast. (4) Compare the dictum *infra*, 'A dream follows its interpretation'. (5) Because it incites one to repentance. (6) I.e., there is no need for them to be fulfilled. (7) R. Joseph was blind, and consequently could not derive so much pleasure from a dream. (8) Eccl. III, 14. (9) Jer. XXIII, 28. (10) Gen. XXXVII, 9.

ומעיין בה. אומר בלבו שתיעשה בקשתו לפי שהתפלל בכונה: כאב לב. שאין בקשתו נעשה: תוחלת. לשון תפלה כמו ויחל משה (שמות לב): מזכירין עונותיו. שעל ידיהן מפשפשים למעלה במעשיו לומר בוטח זה בזכיותיו נראה מה הם: קיר נטוי. מקום סכנה: מוסר דין. בוטח הוא בזכיותיו שחברו יהיה נענש על ידו: ה"ג הא דמעיין הא דלא מעיין: לולבי גפנים. וידי"ש בלע"ז: מוריגי בהמה. כל בשר שבבהמה שאינו חלק אלא דומה למורג חרוץ שאינו חלק כמו החיך והלשון והכרס הפנימי ובית הכוסות: התולה. שאינו יושב אלא על ברכיו שמתוך כך נקביו נפתחין יותר מדאי: ה"ג הא דמאריך ותלי הא דמאריך ולא תלי: למגדלי חזירים ומלוי ברבית. שכן מרובה בלא טורח ושמחים בחלקם לכך פניהם להוטים: הימנותא. לשון שבועה כלומר באמונה שיהן אסורות לי: ואברכה מברכיך. והמברך ברכת המזון מברך לבעל הבית: יוסף מת קודם לאחיו. דכתיב וימת יוסף וכל אחיו (שמות א): צריכים רחמים. צריכים לבקש רחמים שיבואו לפי שהם בידו של הקב"ה ואין להם רשות לבא אלא ברשותו: ראה קראתי בשם. ראה משמע היה בלבך תן עיניך בדבר: לך אמור לו לבצלאל עשה משכן ארון וכלים. שכן הם סדורים בפרשת כי תשא ראה קראתי בשם וגו' את אהל מועד ואת הארון לעדות וכל הפרשה ומשה אמר לו עשה ארון וכלים כגון שלחן ומנורה ואחר כך משכן דס"ל לר' יוחנן שכסדר שהם סדורים בויקחו לי תרומה אמר לו: אותיות שנבראו בהן שמים וארץ. ע"י צרופן ובספר יצירה תני להו: כל חלום ולא טוות. כל חלומות יראה אדם ולא יראה אחד מאותן שהוא שרוי בתענית שאינו טוב. טוות לשון תענית כמו ובת טוות האמור בדריוש (דניאל ו): דלא מפשר. שלא פתרוהו: כאגרתא דלא מקריא. ולא טוב ולא רע הוא שכל החלומות הולכין אחר הפתרון: עדיף מחלמא טבא. שמביא את האדם לידי תשובה: עציבותיה מסתייה. דיו עלבונו מה שאדם מתעצב עליו מבטל את החלום: אפילו לדידי. שאני מאור עינים: בדיחותיה מפכחא ליה. מבטלה: מנגדא. ממלקות קשה לגוף האדם יותר ממלקות לפי שדואג ממנו: זה חלום רע. מיראתו ישוב ויכנע:

והדיא

תורה אור

*כל המאריך בתפלתו ומעיין בה סוף בא לידי כאב לב שנאמר °תוחלת ממושכה מחלה לב *וא"ר יצחק שלשה דברים מזכירים עונותיו של אדם ואלו הן קיר נטוי ועיון תפלה ומוסר דין על חברו לשמים הא לא קשיא *הא דמעיין בה הא דלא מעיין בה והיכי עביד דמפיש ברחמי והמאריך על שלחנו דילמא אתי עניא ויהיב ליה דכתיב °המזבח עץ שלש אמות גבוה וכתיב °וידבר אלי זה השלחן אשר לפני יי' *פתח במזבח וסיים בשלחן ר' יוחנן ור' אלעזר דאמרי תרוייהו כל זמן שבה"מ קיים מזבח מכפר על ישראל ועכשיו שלחנו של אדם מכפר עליו והמאריך בבית הכסא מעליותא הוא *והתניא עשרה דברים מביאין את האדם לידי תחתוניות האוכל עלי קנים ועלי גפנים ולולבי גפנים ומוריגי בהמה ושדרו של דג ודג מליח שאינו מבושל כל צרכו והשותה שמרי יין והמקנח בסיד ובחרסית והמקנח בצרור שקנח בו חבירו ויש אומרים אף התולה עצמו בבית הכסא יותר מדאי ל"ק הא דמאריך ותלי הא דמאריך ולא תלי כי הא דאמר' ליה ההיא מטרוניתא לרבי יהודה ברבי אלעאי *פניך דומים למגדלי חזירים ולמלוי ברבית אמר לה הימנותא לדידי תרוייהו אסירין אלא עשרים וארבעה בית הכסא איכא מאושפיזאי לבי מדרשא דכי אזילנא בדיקנא נפשאי בכולהו: ואמר רב יהודה שלשה דברים מקצרים ימיו ושנותיו של אדם מי שנותנין לו ספר תורה לקרות ואינו קורא °כוס של ברכה לברך ואינו מברך והמנהיג עצמו ברבנות ס"ת לקרות ואינו קורא דכתיב °כי הוא חייך ואורך ימיך כוס של ברכה לברך ואינו מברך דכתיב °ואברכה מברכיך והמנהיג עצמו ברבנות *דא"ר חמא בר' חנינא מפני מה מת יוסף קודם לאחיו מפני שהנהיג עצמו ברבנות ואמר רב יהודה אמר רב שלשה צריכים רחמים מלך טוב שנה טובה וחלום טוב מלך טוב דכתיב °פלגי מים לב מלך ביד יי' שנה טובה דכתיב °תמיד עיני ה' אלהיך בה מראשית השנה ועד אחרית שנה חלום טוב דכתיב °ותחלימני (*ותחייני): א"ר יוחנן שלשה דברים מכריז עליהם הקדוש ברוך הוא בעצמו ואלו הן רעב ושובע ופרנס טוב רעב דכתיב °כי קרא יי' לרעב וגו' שובע דכתיב °וקראתי אל הדגן והרבתי אותו פרנס טוב דכתיב (°*ויאמר) יי' אל משה לאמר ראה קראתי בשם בצלאל וגו' א"ר יצחק אין מעמידין פרנס על הצבור אלא אם כן נמלכים בצבור שנאמר °ראו קרא יי' בשם בצלאל אמר לו הקדוש ברוך הוא למשה הגון עליך בצלאל אמר לו רבונו של עולם אם לפניך הגון לפני לא כל שכן אמר לו אף על פי כן לך אמור להם הלך ואמר להם לישראל הגון עליכם בצלאל אמרו לו אם לפני הקדוש ברוך הוא ולפניך הוא הגון לפנינו לא כל שכן א"ר שמואל בר נחמני אמר רבי יונתן בצלאל על שם חכמתו נקרא בשעה שאמר לו הקדוש ברוך הוא למשה לך אמור לו לבצלאל עשה לי משכן ארון וכלים הלך משה והפך ואמר לו עשה ארון וכלים ומשכן אמר לו משה רבינו מנהגו של עולם אדם בונה בית ואחר כך מכנים לתוכו כלים ואתה אומר עשה לי ארון וכלים ומשכן כלים שאני עושה להיכן אכניסם שמא כך אמר לך הקב"ה עשה משכן ארון וכלים אמר לו שמא בצל אל היית וידעת אמר רב יהודה אמר רב יודע היה בצלאל לצרף אותיות שנבראו בהן שמים וארץ כתיב הכא °וימלא אותו רוח אלהים בחכמה *ובתבונה ובדעת וכתיב התם °יי' בחכמה יסד ארץ כונן שמים בתבונה וכתיב °בדעתו תהומות נבקעו א"ר יוחנן אין הקב"ה נותן חכמה אלא למי שיש בו חכמה שנאמר °יהב חכמתא לחכימין ומנדעא לידעי בינה שמע רב תחליפא בר מערבא ואמרה קמיה דר' אבהו אמר ליה אתון מהתם מתניתו לה אנן מהכא מתנינן לה דכתיב °ובלב כל חכם לב נתתי חכמה: אמר רב חסדא *כל חלום ולא טוות ואמר רב חסדא חלמא דלא מפשר כאגרתא דלא מקריא ואמר רב חסדא לא חלמא טבא מקיים כוליה ולא חלמא בישא מקיים כוליה ואמר רב חסדא חלמא בישא עדיף מחלמא טבא ואמר רב חסדא חלמא בישא עציבותיה מסתייה חלמא טבא חדויה מסתייה אמר רב יוסף חלמא טבא אפילו לדידי בדיחותיה מפכחא ליה ואמר רב חסדא חלמא בישא קשה מנגדא שנאמר °והאלהים עשה שייראו מלפניו ואמר רבה בר בר חנה א"ר יוחנן זה חלום רע °הנביא אשר אתו חלום יספר חלום ואשר דברי אתו ידבר דברי באמת מה לתבן את הבר נאם יי' וכי מה ענין בר ותבן אצל חלום אלא א"ר יוחנן משום ר"ש בן יוחי *כשם שאי אפשר לבר בלא תבן כך אי אפשר לחלום בלא דברים בטלים אמר רבי ברכיה חלום אף על פי שמקצתו מתקיים כולו אינו מתקיים מנא לן מיוסף דכתיב °והנה השמש והירח וגו'

והדיא

לך אמור לבצלאל עשה לי משכן ארון וכלים. וא"ת היכא אשכחן שלוה הקדוש ברוך הוא לעשות משכן תחלה הרי בפרשת תרומה כתיב ארון תחלה. וי"ל דבפרשת כי תשא כתיב את אהל מועד ואת ארון העדות:

שבע

עין משפט
נר מצוה

טז
א טוש"ע א"ח סי' לא סעי' ה
יז
ב טוש"ע א"ח סי' רא סעיף ג

[סב' פא. ע"ש]

והחייני

וידבר

[בפר' ויקהל פל"א כתיב בתבונה בלא וי"ו אכן דע בפ' כי תשא ל"א פ"ג כתיב ואמלא אותו רוח אלהים בחכמה ובתבונה ובדעת ובכן יתכן להיות כתוב הכא ואמלא אותו וכו' והוא קרא מוקדם]

מסורת הש"ס
לעיל לב:
[ר"ה טז:]
חגיגה כו.
מנחות לז. ע"ש
נדרים מט: ע"ש
סוטה יג: ע"ש
שם
משלי ג
שם
דניאל ב
שמות לא
[פי' כל חלום יש בו שום גנגשות אבל מה שהוא רואה כשהוא לא אין בו ממשות עכוך בערך טוות]
קהלת ג
ירמיה כג
נדרים ח.
ברכות לג

משלי יג
יחזק' מא
שם
דברי' ל
ברא' יב
משלי כא
דברי' יא
ישעי' לח
מ"ב ח
יחזק' לו
שמות לא
שם לה

עין משפט נר מצוה

יח
א טוש"ע א"ח סי' רך סעיף א

יט
ב טוש"ע א"ח סי' קל

והדיא שעתא. דהכא אמיה לא הות: יצפה. שיתקיים: מיוסף. שלא נתקיימו השתחוואות הללו עד עשרים ושתים שנה כשירד יעקב למצרים שכבר היה הרעב שתי שנים דכתיב כי זה שנתים הרעב (בראשית מה): לאדם טוב מראים לו חלום רע. כדי שידאג ולא יחטא ושיכפר לו עלבונו: לאדם רע מראין לו חלום טוב. כדי לשמחו שיאכל עולמו: ודוד לא ראה חלום טוב והא כתיב וכו' לא גרסינן הכי אלא גרסי' והא כתיב לא תאנה אליך רעה וגו'. קשיא לרב הונא דאמר לאדם טוב מראין לו חלום רע ומשני איהו לא חזי אחריני חזו ליה חלום רע: וכי לא חזי איהו מעליותא הוא. כיון דלא חזי חלום רע כדקאמר שלא יבהילוהו וחלום טוב לא כל שכן דלא חזי דהא קתני כל ימיו של דוד לא ראה חלום טוב א"כ לא חזי חלום כלל: אלא שבע. שבע לילות ילין ולא יפקד בשום חלום הרי הוא רע ושוכאים אותו ואין מראין לו כלום: ומשני דחזי ולא ידע מאי חזי. אדם טוב מראין לו חלום טוב ועד שלא יקיץ משכחא ממנו כדי שלא ישמח: זקפא. גודל: עלי עין עולי עין. שליטין על העין ולא העין עולה בהן: אטרפא דנחיריה דשמאליה. דופן השמאלי של חוטמו: האי מאן דחלש. מי שחלה: דסני לי לחדי לי. ומתוך כך ישוב חרון אף מעלי: הרהורי לבו. מה שהוא מהרהר ביום: רעיונך. מחשבותיך וכן כל ל' רעיון שבמקרא איננו לשון רצון אלא לשון מחשבה וזה יוכיח ורעיונים יבהלוניה (דניאל ז) וכי רצונו של אדם מבהלו אלא מחשבותיו מבהלין אותו: דיקלא דדהבא. דבר שלא הורגל לראות ולא הרהר בו מעולם: קופא דמחטא. נקב המחט: קיסר

תורה אור

והדיא שעתא אמיה לא הות א"ר לוי לעולם יצפה אדם לחלום טוב עד כ"ב שנה מנלן מיוסף דכתיב °אלה תולדות יעקב יוסף בן שבע עשרה שנה וגו' וכתיב °ויוסף בן שלשים שנה בעמדו לפני פרעה וגו' מן שבסרי עד תלתין כמה הוי תלת סרי ושב דשבעא ותרתי דכפנא הא כ"ב אמר רב הונא לאדם *טוב אין מראין לו חלום טוב ולאדם רע אין מראין לו חלום רע תנ"ה כל שנותיו של דוד לא ראה חלום טוב וכל שנותיו של אחיתופל לא ראה חלום רע והכתיב °לא תאנה אליך רעה *ואמר רב חסדא אמר רב ירמיה בר אבא שלא יבהילוך לא חלומות רעים ולא הרהורים רעים ונגע לא יקרב באהלך שלא תמצא אשתך ספק נדה בשעה שאתה בא מן הדרך אלא איהו לא חזי ליה אחריני חזי ליה וכי לא חזא איהו מעליות' הוא והאמר ר' זעירא *כל הלן שבעה ימים בלא חלום נקרא רע שנאמר °ושבע ילין בל יפקד רע אל תקרא שבע אלא שבע אלא הכי קאמר דחזא ולא ידע מאי חזא אמר רב הונא בר אמי אמר רבי פדת א"ר יוחנן הרואה חלום ונפשו עגומה ילך ויפתרנו בפני שלשה יפתרנו והאמר רב חסדא חלמא דלא מפשר כאגרתא דלא מקריא אלא אימא *יטיבנו בפני שלשה לייתי תלתא ולימא להו חלמא טבא חזאי ולימרו ליה הנך טבא הוא וטבא לידוי רחמנא לשוייה לטב שבע זמנין לגזרו עלך מן שמיא דלהוי טבא ויהוי טבא ולימרו ג' הפכות וג' פדויות ושלש שלומות שלש הפכות °הפכת מספדי למחול לי פתחת שקי ותאזרני שמחה °אז תשמח בתולה במחול בחורים וזקנים יחדיו והפכתי אבלם לששון וגו' °ולא אבה יי' אלהיך לשמוע אל בלעם ויהפוך וגו' שלש פדויות דכתיב °פדה בשלום נפשי מקרב לי וגו' °ופדויי יי' ישובון וגו' °ויאמר העם אל שאול °היונתן ימות אשר עשה הישועה וגו' שלש שלומות דכתיב °בורא ניב שפתים שלום שלום לרחוק ולקרוב אמר יי' ורפאתיו °ורוח לבשה את עמשי וגו' °ואמרתם כה לחי אתה שלום וביתך שלום וגו' אמימר ומר זוטרא ורב אשי הוו יתבי בהדי הדדי אמרי כל חד וחד מינן לימא מלתא דלא שמיע ליה לחבריה פתח חד מניהו ואמר °האי מאן דחזא חלמא ולא ידע מאי חזא ליקום קמי כהני בעידנא דפרסי ידייהו ולימא הכי *רבש"ע אני שלך וחלומותי שלך חלום חלמתי ואיני יודע מה הוא בין שחלמתי אני לעצמי ובין שחלמו לי חברי ובין שחלמתי על אחרים אם טובים הם חזקם ואמצם כחלומותיו של יוסף ואם צריכים רפואה רפאם כמי מרה על ידי משה רבינו וכמרים מצרעתה וכחזקיהו מחליו וכמי יריחו על ידי אלישע וכשם שהפכת קללת בלעם הרשע לברכה כן הפוך כל חלומותי עלי לטובה ומסיים בהדי כהני דעני צבור' אמן ואי לא לימא הכי אדיר במרום שוכן בגבורה אתה שלום ושמך שלום יהי ר"מ שתשים עלינו שלום פתח אידך ואמר האי מאן דעייל למתא ודחיל מעינא בישא לנקוט זקפא דידא דימיניה בידא דשמאליה וזקפא דידא דשמאליה בידא דימיניה ולימא הכי אנא פלוני בר פלוני *מזרעא דיוסף קאתינא דלא שלטא ביה עינא ביש' שנאמר °בן פורת יוסף בן פורת עלי עין וגו' אל תקרי עלי עין אלא עולי עין ר' יוסי בר' חנינא אמר מהכא °וידגו לרוב בקרב הארץ מה דגים שבים מים מכסים עליהם ואין עין רעה שולטת בהם אף זרעו של יוסף אין עין רעה שולטת בהם ואי דחיל מעינא בישא דיליה לחזי אטרפה דנחיריה דשמאליה פתח אידך ואמר האי מאן דחליש יומא קמא לא לגלי כי היכי דלא לתרע מזליה מכאן ואילך לגלי *כי הא דרבא כי הוה חליש יומא קמא לא מגלי מכאן ואילך אמר ליה לשמעיה פוק אכריז רבא חליש מאן דרחים לי לבעי עלי רחמי ומאן דסני ליה לחדי לי וכתיב °בנפול אויבך אל תשמח ובכשלו אל יגל לבך פן יראה יי' ורע בעיניו והשיב מעליו אפו שמואל כי הוה חזי חלמא בישא אמר °וחלומות השוא ידברו וכי הוה חזי חלמא טבא אמר וכי החלומות השוא ידברו והכתיב °בחלום אדבר בו רבא רמי כתיב בחלום אדבר בו וכתיב וחלומות השוא ידברו לא קשיא כאן על ידי מלאך כאן על ידי שד א"ר ביזנא בר זבדא א"ר עקיבא א"ר פנדא אמר ר' נחום אמר רבי בירים משום זקן אחד ומנו ר' בנאה עשרים וארבעה פותרי חלומות היו בירושלים פעם אחת חלמתי חלום והלכתי אצל כולם ומה שפתר לי זה לא פתר לי זה וכולם נתקיימו בי לקיים מה שנאמר *כל החלומות הולכים אחר הפה אטו כל החלומות הולכים אחר הפה קרא הוא אין וכדרבי אלעזר דא"ר אלעזר מנין *שכל החלומות הולכין אחר *הפה שנאמר °ויהי כאשר פתר לנו כן היה אמר רבא והוא דמפשר ליה מעין חלמיה שנאמר °איש כחלומו פתר °וירא שר האופים מנא ידע א"ר אלעזר מלמד שכל אחד ואחד הראוהו חלומו ופתרון חלומו של חברו *א"ר יוחנן השכים ונפל לו פסוק לתוך פיו הרי זו נבואה קטנה וא"ר יוחנן ג' חלומות מתקיימין חלום של שחרית וחלום שחלם לו חברו וחלום שנפתר בתוך חלום וי"א אף חלום שנשנה שנאמר °ועל השנות החלום וגו' א"ר שמואל בר נחמני א"ר יונתן אין מראין לו לאדם אלא מהרהורי לבו שנאמר °אנת מלכא רעיונך על משכבך סליקו ואיבעית אימא מהכא °ורעיוני לבבך תנדע אמר רבא תדע דלא מחוו ליה לאינש לא דקלא דדהבא ולא *פילא דעייל בקופא דמחטא:

אמר

שבע זמנין ליגזרו עלך. כך הוא הלחש שבע זימנין ליגזרו עלך ויש מפרש דשבע זמנין צריך לומר הלמא טבא חזאי וכן לעניות אחריו. אבל ר"י לא היה רגיל לאומרו אלא שלשה פעמים:

פותרי חלומות. פי' ר"י דמזל שעת הלידה גורם ואין הדבר תלוי בחכמה:

הרואה

[ע' פירש"י דהכא ונרסתו וכן הגירס' בע"י לאדם טוב מראין לו חלום רע ולאדם רע מראין לו חלום טוב תכי' כ"ה וכו']

(בירו' נוסח תפלה זו משונה מאוד ומוסיף פסוקי ג' הפכות האמורים למעלה)

לעיל כ. ב"מ פד. ב"ב קיח: סוטה לו:

[ע' תו' שבת קכט. ד"ה וכמן]

(בירוש' ספ"ד ממ"ש איתא אחר פתרוניהן שנא' ויהי וגו')

[שם כז: וקל"ע]

מסורת הש"ס

[סנה' קב. ע"ש היטב]

לעיל יד. ע"ש

[נדרים מ.]

[לקמן נו.]

[ב"מ לח:]

בראשית לז
שם מא
תהלים נה
משלי יט
תהלים ל
ירמיה לא
דברים כג
תהלים נה
ישעיה לה
שמואל א יד
ישעיה נז
ד"ה א יב
שמואל א כה
בראשית מט
שם מח
משלי כד
זכריה י
במדבר יב
בראשית מא
שם שם מ
שם מא
דניאל ב
שם

the bad man his reward in this world. (4) Ps. XCI, 10. (5) Prov. XIX, 23. (6) And translate: If he abides seven nights without being visited, it is evil. (7) And therefore what harm can it do?

b (1) Ps. XXX, 12. (2) Jer. XXXI, 13. (3) Deut. XXIII, 6. (4) Ps. LV, 19. (5) Isa. XXXV, 10. (6) I Samuel XIV, 45. (7) Isa. LVII, 19. (8) I Chron. XII, 19. (9) I Sam. XXV, 6. (10) To say the priestly benediction. (11) Var. lec. adds here the words: And may they be fulfilled.

c (1) This prayer is included in the prayer books and recited in some congregations between each of the three blessings constituting the priestly benediction, whether they have dreamt or not. (2) I.e., he is unable to finish it together with the priests. Var. lec.: when the priests (at the conclusion of the benediction) turn their faces (to the ark). (3) I.e., his own sensual passions. (4) Gen. XLIX, 22. (5) Ibid. XLVIII, 16. (6) V. *supra* 20a, nn. a9 and 10. (7) Prov. XXIV, 17.

d (1) Zech. X, 2. (2) Num. XII, 6. (3) 'Mouth' here seems to have the sense of interpretation. (4) As the formula 'thus confirming' etc., would seem to imply. (5) Gen. XLI, 13. (6) Ibid. 12. (7) Ibid. XL, 16. (8) R. Eleazar stresses the word 'saw'. (9) I.e., either he spontaneously utters it, or he hears a child repeating it. (10) Ibid. XLI, 32.

e (1) Dan. II, 29. (2) Ibid. 30. (3) Because he never thinks of such things.

and [55b] at that time his mother was not living. R. Levi said: A man should await the fulfilment of a good dream for as much as twenty-two years. Whence do we know this? From Joseph. For it is written: *These are the generations of Jacob. Joseph being seventeen years old, etc.*;[11] and it is further written, *And Joseph was thirty years* a *old when he stood before Pharaoh.*[1] How many years is it from seven teen to thirty? Thirteen. Add the seven years of plenty and two of famine,[2] and you have twenty-two.

R. Huna said: A good man is not shown a good dream, and a bad man is not shown a bad dream.[3] It has been taught similarly; David, during the whole of his lifetime, never saw a good dream and Ahitophel, during the whole of his lifetime, never saw a bad dream. But it is written, *There shall no evil befall thee,*[4] and R. Ḥisda said, in the name of R. Jeremiah: this means that you will not be disturbed either by bad dreams or by evil thoughts, *neither shall any plague come nigh thy tent*[4] . . . . i.e., thou shalt not find thy wife doubtfully menstruous when thou returnest from a journey?—Though he does not see an evil dream, others see one about him. But if he does not see one, is this considered an advantage? Has not R. Ze'ira said: If a man goes seven days without a dream he is called evil, since it says, *He shall abide satisfied, he shall not be visited by evil?*[5]—Read not *sabe'a* [satisfied] but [seven] *sheba'.*[6] What he means is this: He sees, but he does not remember what he has seen.

R. Huna b. Ammi said in the name of R. Pedath who had it from R. Joḥanan: If one has a dream which makes him sad he should go and have it interpreted in the presence of three. He should have it interpreted! Has not R. Ḥisda said: A dream which is not interpreted is like a letter which is not read?[7]—Say rather then, he should have a good turn given to it in the presence of three. Let him bring three and say to them: I have seen a good dream; and they should say to him, Good it is and good may it be. May the All-Merciful turn it to good; seven times may it be decreed from heaven that it should be good and may it be good. They should say three verses with the word *hapak* [turn], and three with the word *padah* [redeem] and three with the word *shalom* [peace]. Three with the word 'turn', namely (i) *Thou didst* turn *for me my mourning into dancing, Thou didst loose my sackcloth and gird me with* b *gladness;*[1] (ii) *Then shall the virgin rejoice in the dance, and the young men and the old together; for I will* turn *their mourning into joy and will comfort them and make them rejoice from their sorrow;*[2] (iii) *Nevertheless the Lord thy God would not hearken unto Balaam; but the Lord thy God* turned *the curse into a blessing unto thee.*[3] Three verses with the word 'redeem', namely, (i) *He hath* redeemed *my soul in peace, so that none came nigh me;*[4] (ii) *And the* redeemed *of the Lord shall return and come with singing unto Zion . . . . and sorrow and sighing shall flee away;*[5] (iii) *And the people said unto Saul, Shall Jonathan die who hath wrought this great salvation in Israel? . . . . So the people* redeemed *Jonathan that he died not.*[6] Three verses with the word 'peace', namely, (i) Peace, peace, *to him that is far off and to him that is near, saith the Lord that createth the fruit of the lips; and I will heal him;*[7] (ii) *Then the spirit clothed Amasai who was chief of the captains: Thine are we, David, and on thy side, thou son of Jesse:* Peace, peace, *be unto thee and* peace *be to thy helpers, for thy God helpeth thee,*[8] (iii) *Thus ye shall say: All hail! and* peace *be both unto thee, and* peace *be to thy house, and* peace *be unto all that thou hast.*[9]

Amemar, Mar Zuṭra and R. Ashi were once sitting together. They said: Let each of us say something which the others have not heard. One of them began: If one has seen a dream and does not remember what he saw, let him stand before the priests at the time when they spread out their hands,[10] and say as follows: 'Sovereign of the Universe, I am Thine and my dreams are Thine. I have dreamt a dream and I do not know what it is. Whether I have dreamt about myself or my companions have dreamt about me, or I have dreamt about others, if they are good dreams, confirm them and reinforce them[11] like the dreams of Joseph, and if they require a remedy, heal them, as the waters of Marah were healed by Moses, our teacher, and as Miriam was healed of her leprosy and Hezekiah of his sickness, and the waters of Jericho by Elisha. As thou didst turn the curse of the wicked Balaam into c a blessing, so turn all my dreams into something good for me'.[1] He should conclude his prayer along with the priests, so that the congregation may answer, Amen! If he cannot manage this,[2] he should say: Thou who art majestic on high, who abidest in might, Thou art peace and Thy name is peace. May it be Thy will to bestow peace on us.

The second commenced and said: If a man on going into a town is afraid of the Evil Eye,[3] let him take the thumb of his right hand in his left hand and the thumb of his left hand in his right hand, and say: I, so-and-so, am of the seed of Joseph over which the evil eye has no power, as it says: *Joseph is a fruitful vine, a fruitful vine by a fountain.*[4] Do not read *'ale 'ayin* [by a fountain] but *'ole 'ayin* [overcoming the evil eye]. R. Jose b. R. Ḥanina derived it from here: *And let them grow into a multitude* [weyidgu] *in the midst of the earth;*[5] just as the fishes [*dagim*] in the sea are covered by the waters and the evil eye has no power over them, so the evil eye has no power over the seed of Joseph.[6] If he is afraid of his own evil eye, he should look at the side of his left nostril.

The third commenced and said: If a man falls ill, the first day he should not tell anyone, so that he should not have bad luck; but after that he may tell. So when Raba fell ill, on the first day he did not tell anyone, but after that he said to his attendant: Go and announce that Raba is ill. Whoever loves him, let him pray for him, and whoever hates him, let him rejoice over him; for it is written: *Rejoice not when thine enemy falleth, and let not thy heart be glad when he stumbleth, lest the Lord see it and it displease Him and He turn away His wrath from him.*[7]

When Samuel had a bad dream, he used to say, *The dreams speak* d *falsely.*[1] When he had a good dream, he used to say, Do the dreams speak falsely, seeing that it is written, *I* [*God*] *do speak with him in a dream?*[2] Raba pointed out a contradiction. It is written, *'I do speak with him in a dream'*, and it is written, *'the dreams speak falsely'.*—There is no contradiction; in the one case it is through an angel, in the other through a demon.

R. Bizna b. Zabda said in the name of R. Akiba who had it from R. Panda who had it from R. Nahum, who had it from R. Biryam reporting a certain elder—and who was this? R. Bana'ah: There were twenty-four interpreters of dreams in Jerusalem. Once I dreamt a dream and I went round to all of them and they all gave different interpretations, and all were fulfilled, thus confirming that which is said: All dreams follow the mouth.[3] Is the statement that all dreams follow the mouth Scriptural?[4] Yes, as stated by R. Eleazar. For R. Eleazar said: Whence do we know that all dreams follow the mouth? Because it says, *and it came to pass, as he interpreted to us, so it was.*[5] Raba said: This is only if the interpretation corresponds to the content of the dream: for it says, *to each man according to his dream he did interpret.*[6] *When the chief baker saw that the interpretation was good.*[7] How did he know this? R. Eleazar says: This tells us that each of them was shown his own dream and the interpretation of the other one's dream.[8]

R. Joḥanan said: If one rises early and a Scriptural verse comes to his mouth,[9] this is a kind of minor prophecy. R. Joḥanan also said: Three kinds of dream are fulfilled: an early morning dream, a dream which a friend has about one, and a dream which is interpreted in the midst of a dream. Some add also, a dream which is repeated, as it says, *and for that the dream was doubled unto Pharoah twice*, etc.[10]

R. Samuel b. Naḥmani said in the name of R. Jonathan: A man is shown in a dream only what is suggested by his own thoughts, as it says, *As for thee, Oh King, thy thoughts came into thy mind upon* e *thy bed.*[1] Or if you like, I can derive it from here: *That thou mayest know the thoughts of thy heart.*[2] Raba said: This is proved by the fact that a man is never shown in a dream a date palm of gold, or an elephant going through the eye of a needle.[3]

(11) Ibid. 2.

a (1) Gen. XLI, 46. (2) After which Joseph saw his brothers. (3) Rashi reads: A good man is shown a bad dream and a bad man is shown a good dream. The purpose is to turn the good man to repentance and to give

[56*a*] The Emperor [of Rome][4] said to R. Joshua b. R. Hananyah: You [Jews] profess to be very clever. Tell me what I shall see in my dream. He said to him: You will see the Persians[5] making you do forced labour, and despoiling you and making you feed unclean animals with a golden crook. He thought about it all day, and in the night he saw it in his dream.[6] King Shapor [I] once said to Samuel: You [Jews] profess to be very clever. Tell me what I shall see in my dream. He said to him: You will see the Romans coming and taking you captive and making you grind date-stones in a golden mill. He thought about it the whole day and in the night saw it in a dream.

Bar Hedya was an interpreter of dreams. To one who paid him he used to give a favourable interpretation and to one who did not pay him he gave an unfavourable interpretation. Abaye and Raba each had a dream. Abaye gave him a *zuz*, and Rab did not give him anything, They said to him: In our dream we had to read the verse, *Thine ox shall be slain before thine eyes*,[7] etc. To Raba he said: Your business will be a failure, and you will be so grieved that you will have no appetite to eat. To Abaye he said: Your business will prosper, and you will not be able to eat from sheer joy. They then said to him: We had to read in our dream the verse, *Thou shalt beget sons and daughters but they shall not be thine*,[8] etc. To Raba he interpreted it in its [literal] unfavourable sense. To Abaye he said: You have numerous sons and daughters, and your daughters will be married and go away, and it will seem to you as if they have gone into captivity. [They said to him:] We were made to read the verse: *Thy sons and thy daughters shall be*
a *given unto another people*.[1] To Abaye he said: You have numerous sons and daughters; you will want your daughters to marry your relatives, and your wife will want them to marry her relatives, and she will force you to marry them to her relatives, which will be like giving them to another people. To Raba he said: Your wife will die, and her sons and daughters will come under the sway of another wife. (For Raba said in the name of R. Jeremiah b. Abba, reporting Rab: What is the meaning of the verse: '*Thy sons and thy daughters shall be given to another people*'? This refers to a step-mother.) [They further said]: We were made to read in our dream the verse, *Go thy way, eat thy bread with joy*, etc.[2] To Abaye he said: Your business will prosper, and you will eat and drink, and recite this verse out of the joy of your heart. To Raba he said: Your business will fail, you will slaughter [cattle] and not eat or drink and you will read Scripture to allay your anxiety. [They said to him]: We were made to read the verse, *Thou shalt carry much seed out into the field, [and shalt gather little in, for the locusts will consume it]*.[3] To Abaye he interpreted from the first half of the verse; to Raba from the second half. [They said to him:] We were made to read the verse, *Thou shalt have olive trees throughout all thy borders, [but thou shalt not anoint thyself*, etc.][4] To Abaye he interpreted from the first half of the verse; to Raba from the second half. [They said to him:] We were made to read the verse: *And all the peoples of the earth shall see that the name of the Lord is called upon thee*, etc.[5] To Abaye he said: Your name will become famous as head of the college, and you will be generally feared. To Raba he said: The King's treasury[6] will be broken into, and you will be arrested as a thief, and everyone will draw an inference from you.[7] The next day the King's treasury was broken into and they came and arrested Raba: They said to him: We saw a lettuce on the mouth of a jar. To Abaye he said: Your business will be doubled like a lettuce. To Raba he said: Your business will be bitter like a lettuce. They said to him: We saw some meat on the mouth of a jar. To Abaye he said: Your wine will be sweet, and everyone will come to buy meat and wine from you. To Raba he said: Your wine will turn
b sour, and everyone will come to buy meat to eat with it.[1] They said: We saw a cask hanging on a palm tree. To Abaye he said: Your business will spring up like a palm tree. To Raba he said: Your goods will be sweet like dates.[2] They said to him: We saw a pomegranate sprouting on the mouth of a jar. To Abaye he said: Your goods will be high-priced like a pomegranate. To Raba he said: Your goods will be stale like a [dry] pomegranate. They said to him: We saw a cask fall into a pit. To Abaye he said: Your goods will be in demand according to the saying: The *pu'ah*[3] has fallen into a well and cannot be found.[4] To Raba he said: Your goods will be spoilt and they will be thrown into a pit. They said to him: We saw a young ass standing by our pillow and braying. To Abaye he said: You will become a king,[5] and an *Amora*[6] will stand by you. To Raba he said: The words 'The first-born of an ass'[7] have been erased from your *tefillin*. Raba said to him: I have looked at them and they are there. He replied to him: Certainly the *waw* of the word *ḥamor* [ass] has been erased from your *tefillin*.[8]

Subsequently Raba went to him by himself and said to him: I dreamt that the outer door fell. He said to him: Your wife will die. He said to him: I dreamt that my front and back teeth fell out. He said to him: Your sons and your daughters will die. He said: I saw two pigeons flying. He replied: You will divorce two wives.[9] He said to him: I saw two turnip-tops.[10] He replied: You will receive two blows with a cudgel. On that day Raba went and sat all day in the Beth ha-Midrash. He found two blind men quarrelling with one another. Raba went to separate them and they gave him two blows. They wanted to give him another blow but he said, Enough! I saw in my dream only two.

Finally Raba went and gave him a fee. He said to him: I saw a wall fall down. He replied: You will acquire wealth without end. He said: I dreamt that Abaye's villa fell in and the dust of it covered me. He replied to him: Abaye will die and [the presidency of] his College will be offered to you. He said to him: I saw my own villa fall in, and everyone came and took a brick. He said to him: Your teachings will be disseminated throughout the world. He said to him: I dreamt that my head was split open and my brains fell out. He replied: The stuffing will fall out of your pillow. He said to him: In my dream I was made to read the *Hallel* of
c Egypt.[1] He replied: Miracles will happen to you.

Bar Hedya was once travelling with Raba in a boat. He said to himself: Why should I accompany a man to whom a miracle will happen?[2] As he was disembarking, he let fall a book. Raba found it, and saw written in it: All dreams follow the mouth. He exclaimed: Wretch! It all depended on you and you gave me all this pain! I forgive you everything except [what you said about] the daughter of R. Ḥisda.[3] May it be God's will that this fellow be delivered up to the Government, and that they have no mercy on him! Bar Hedya said to himself: What am I to do? We have been taught that a curse uttered by a sage, even when undeserved, comes to pass; how much more this of Raba, which was deserved! He said: I will rise up and go into exile. For a Master has said: Exile makes atonement for iniquity. He rose and fled to the Romans. He went and sat at the door of the keeper of the King's wardrobe. The keeper of the wardrobe had a dream, and said to him: I dreamt that a needle pierced my finger. He said to him: Give me a *zuz!* He refused to give him one, and he would not say a word to him. He again said to him: I dreamt that a worm[4] fell between two of my fingers. He said to him: Give me a *zuz*. He refused to give him one, and he would not say a word to him. I dreamt that a worm filled the whole of my hand. He said to him: Worms have been spoiling all the silk garments. This became known in the palace, and they brought the keeper of the wardrobe in order to put him to death. He said to them: Why execute me? Bring the man who knew and would not tell. So they brought Bar Hedya, and they said to him: Because of your *zuz*, the king's silken garments have

(4) Probably Trajan, when he passed through Palestine during his expedition to Persia. (5) I.e., the Parthians. (6) Trajan was defeated by the Parthians in 116 C.E. (7) Deut. XXVIII, 31. (8) Ibid. 41.
a (1) Deut. XXVIII, 32. (2) Eccl. IX, 7. (3) Deut. XXVIII, 38. (4) Ibid. 40. (5) Ibid. 10. (6) Where the tax payments were received. (7) Saying: If Raba is suspect, how much more so are we.
b (1) I.e., to dip in it. (2) Rashi explains this to mean: Sweet to the customer because of its cheapness. (3) A vegetable dyer's madder, a prophylactic. (4) I.e., it is a useless remedy, v. Shab. 66*b*. MS.M. reads: Your goods will be in demand like something which has fallen into a pit. (5) I.e., president

אמר ליה קיסר לרבי יהושע בר׳ (°חנינא)
אמריתו דחכמיתו טובא אימא לי מאי חזינא
בחלמאי א״ל חזית דמשחרי לך פרסאי וגרבי
בך ורעיי בך שקצי בחוטרא דדהבא הרהר
כוליה יומא ולאורתא חזא א״ל שבור מלכא
לשמואל אמריתו דחכמיתו טובא אימא לי
מאי חזינא בחלמאי אמר ליה חזית דאתו
רומאי ושבו לך וטחני בך קשייתא ברחייא
דדהבא הרהר כוליה יומא ולאורתא חזא. בר
הדיא מפשר חלמי הוה מאן דיהיב ליה אגרא
מפשר ליה למעליותא ולמאן דלא יהיב ליה
אגרא מפשר ליה לגריעותא אביי ורבא חזו
חלמא אביי יהב ליה זוזא ורבא לא יהב ליה
אמרי ליה אקרינן בחלמין °שורך טבוח לעיניך
וגו׳ לרבא אמר לי׳ פסיד עסקך ולא אהני לך
למיכל מעוצבא דלבך לאביי א״ל מרווח
עסקך ולא אהני לך למיכל מחדוא דלבך
אמרי לי׳ אקרינן °בנים ובנות תוליד וגו׳ לרבא
א״ל כבישותיה לאביי א״ל בנך ובנתך נפישי
ומינסבן בנתך לעלמא ומדמיין באפך כדקא
אזלן בשביה אקרינן °בניך ובנותיך נתונים
לעם אחר לאביי א״ל בנך ובנתך נפישין *את
אמרת לקריבך והיא אמרה לקריבה ואכפה
לך ויהבת להון לקריבה דהוי כעם אחר לרבא א״ל דביתהו שכיבא ואתו בניה
ובנתיה לידי אתתא אחריתי *דאמר רבא א״ר ירמיה בר אבא אמר רב מאי
דכתיב בניך ובנותיך נתונים לעם אחר זו אשת האב אקרינן בחלמין °לך אכול בשמחה לחמך לאביי א״ל
מרווח עסקך ואכלת ושתית וקרית פסוקא מחדוא דלבך לרבא אמר ליה פסיד עסקך טבחת ולא אכלת
ושתית וקרית לפכוחי פחדך אקרינן °זרע רב תוציא השדה לאביי א״ל מרישיה לרבא א״ל מסיפיה אקרינן
°זתים יהיו לך בכל גבולך וגו׳ לאביי א״ל מרישיה לרבא א״ל מסיפיה אקרינן °וראו כל עמי הארץ וגו׳ לאביי
א״ל נפק לך שמא דריש מתיבתא הוית אימתך נפלת בעלמא לרבא א״ל בדייני דמלכא אתבר ומתפסת
כגנבי ודייני כולי עלמא ק״ו מינך למחר אתבר בדייני דמלכא ואתו ותפשי ליה לרבא אמרי ליה חזן חסא על
פום דני לאביי א״ל עיף עסקך כחסא לרבא א״ל מריר עסקך כי חסא אמרי ליה חזן בשרא על פום דני
לאביי א״ל בסים חמרך ואתו כולי עלמא למזבן בשרא וחמרא מינך לרבא א״ל תקיף חמרך ואתו כולי עלמא
למזבן בשרא למיכל ביה אמרי ליה חזן חביתא דתלי בדיקלא לאביי א״ל מדלי עסקך כדיקלא לרבא א״ל
חלי עסקך כתמרי אמרי ליה חזן רומנא דקדחא אפום דני לאביי א״ל עשיק עסקך כרומנא לרבא א״ל קאוי
עסקך כרומנא אמרי ליה חזן חביתא דנפל לבירא לאביי א״ל מתבעי עסקך *כדאמר נפל פתא בבירא ולא
אשתכח לרבא א״ל פסיד עסקך ושדיא ליה לבירא אמרי ליה חזינן בר חמרא דקאי אאיסדן ונוער לאביי א״ל
מלכא הוית וקאי אמורא עלך לרבא א״ל פטר חמור גהיט מתפילך א״ל לדידי חזי לי ואיתיה א״ל וא״ו דפטר
חמור ודאי גהיט מתפילך לסוף אזל רבא לחודיה לגביה א״ל חזאי דשא ברייתא דנפל א״ל אשתך שכבא
א״ל חזאי *ככי ושיני דנתור א״ל בנך ובנתך שכבן א״ל חזאי תרתי יוני דפרחן א״ל תרי נשי מגרשת א״ל
חזאי תרי גרגלידי דלפתא א״ל תרין קולפי בלעת אזל רבא ההוא יומא ויתיב בי מדרשא כוליה יומא אשכח
הנהו תרי סגי נהורי דהוי קמנצו בהדי הדדי אזל רבא לפרוקינהו ומחוהו לרבא תרי דלו למחוייה אחריתי
אמר מסתיי תרין חזאי לסוף אתא רבא ויהיב ליה אגרא א״ל חזאי *אשיתא דנפל א״ל נכסים בלא מצרים
קנית א״ל חזאי אפדנא דאביי דנפל וכסיין אבקיה א״ל אביי שכיב ומתיבתיה אתיא לגבך א״ל חזאי אפדנא
דידי דנפיל ואתו כולי עלמא שקיל לבינתא לבינתא א״ל שמעתתך מבדרן בעלמא א״ל חזאי דאבקע רישי
ונתר מוקרי א״ל *אודרא מבי סדיא נפיק א״ל אקריון הללא מצראה בחלמא אמר לו ניסי מתרחשין לך הוה
קא אזיל בהדיה בארבא אמר בהדי גברא דמתרחיש ליה ניסא למה לי בהדי דקא סליק נפל סיפרא מניה
אשכחיה רבא וחזא דהוה כתיב ביה *כל החלומות הולכין אחר הפה אמר רשע בדידך קיימא וצערתן כולי
האי כולהו מחילנא לך בר מברתיה דרב חסדא יהא רעוא דלמסר ההוא גברא לידי דמלכותא דלא מרחמו
עליה אמר מאי אעביד גמירי *דקללת חכם אפילו בחנם היא באה וכ״ש רבא דבדינא קא לייט אמר איקום
ואגלי *דאמר מר גלות מכפרת עון קם גלא לבי רומאי אזל יתיב אפתחא דריש *טורזינא דמלכא ריש טורזיא
חזא חלמא א״ל חזאי חלמא דעייל מחטא באצבעתי א״ל הב לי זוזא ולא יהיב ליה לא א״ל ולא מידי א״ל
חזאי דנפל תכלא בתרתין אצבעתי א״ל הב לי זוזא ולא יהב ליה ולא א״ל אמר ליה חזאי דנפל תכלא בכולה
ידא א״ל נפל תכלא בכולהו שיראי שמעי בי מלכא ואתיוה לריש טורזיא קא קטלי ליה א״ל אנא אמאי
אתיוה להאי דהוה ידע ולא אמר אתיוה לבר הדיא א״ל אמטו זוזא דידך חרבו
שיראי

רש״י

קיסר. מלך רומי והיה לו תגר עם פרסיים: מאי חזינא. מאי אראה בלילה בחלום: משחרי לך פרסאי. עושים בך עבודת המלך כמו לא חמרא דחד מנהון שחרית (תרגום במדבר טז) ולשון חכמים (ספרי פ׳ דברים) הדבק לשחור ויסתחוו לך: ושבו לך. ישללוך בשבי: וטחני בך קשייתא. יכופו אותך לטחון גרעיני תמרים: שבור. מלך פרס: פסיד עסקך. תתקלקל פרקמטיא שלך: ולא אהני לך למיכל. מתוך צערך לא יטעם לך שום מאכל: מרווח עסקך. ומתוך שמחתך לא תאוה לאכול שתהיה שבע בשמחתך: והיא. אשתך: לפכוחי פחדך. להפיג דאגתך: מרישיה. זרע רב תוציא השדה: בדייני דמלכא. אומר שתכשיטי המלך שם ישבר על ידי גנבים ויעלילו עליך לומר שאתה גנבתם: ק״ו ממך. אם רבא נחשד כל שכן שיחשדוהו חסו ויראו ממך: חסא. חזרת: עיף עסקך. כפול בריוח כחזרת שהיא רחבה וכפולה: מריר עסקך. שכאוי לכל ומר יהיה סחורה שלך: חביתא. הם היו משתכרים ביין: חלי עסקך. מתוק כלומר שתתן סחורתך בזול: דקדחא. גדלה: עשיק עסקך. ביוקר תמכרנו כמו עשיק לגבך (ב״מ דף כב.): לרבא א״ל קאוי עסקך. לשון קהוי הכל ישכחוהו: מתבעי עסקך. יתבקש עסקך ויחזרו אחריו לקנות: דקאי אאיסדן. מראשותיו כדמתרגמינן מראשותיו אסדוהי (בראשית כח): מלכא הוית. ראש ישיבה הדורש דרשות והמתורגמן עומד עליו באמורא להשמיע בקול רם לרבים כקול חמור הנוער: וי״ו דפטר חמור גהיט מתפילך. בפרשת והיה כי יביאך וכל פטר חמור תפדה בשה והוא חסר וי״ו ובתפילין של רבא כתבו הכותב מלא ואח״כ מחקו והיינו גהיט מחוק: דשא ברייתא. דלת חיצון שבבית: אתתך מתה. השומרת את הבית: ככי. שיניים הפנימיות שקורין מסי״לארי: תרתי נשי מגרשת. שאשתו של אדם קרויה יונה דכתיב יונתי תמתי: תרי קולפי בלעת. מכת מקל עד שראשו כראשי לפתות: בלא מצרים. נחלה בלא מצרים. כלו׳ קרקעות רחבים ורבים: וכסיין אבקיה. כסכי עפר הפורח ממפולת החומה: ונתר מוקרי. נשר מוחו: אודרא מבי סדיא. המוכין יוצאין מן הכר שבמראשותיו: הללא מצראה. הלל שאנו קורין בפסח לפי שיש הלל אחר הקרוי הלל הגדול קורין לזה הלל המצרי: ניסי מתרחשי לך. שע״י נסים נקרא כיון על כל צרה הבאה לישראל אומרים אותו על גאולתן: הוה קא אזיל. בר הדיא בהדיה דרבא: בארבא. בספינה: אמר בהדי גברא דמתרחיש לי׳ ניסא למה לי. שמא כאן יארע לו הנס שתטבע הספינה והוא ינצל: בדידך קיימא. בך הוא תלוי הפתרון אם לטובה אם לרעה והפכת לי לרעה: בר מברתי׳ דר״ח. אשתו של רבא בת רב חסדא היתה: טורזינא דמלכא. שומר אוצר המלך: נפל תכלא. תולע:

חגיגה

תורה אור

דברים כח
שם
שם

מסורת הש״ס

נדרים כג. קידושין מה: יבמות סג: ע״ש ושם אי׳ רב חנן בר רבא קהלת ט דברים כח שם שם [שבת סו:] [ע׳ היטב בע״ז כח. בפרש״י ותו׳ שם ד״ה ככי] [יסוד לחומות ביתו כך פירש״י ב״ק כ. ד״ה לאושין וכו׳ ע״ש ובערוך פי׳ כותל] [לעיל נה:] מכו׳ יח. *סנהדרין לז:

[גי׳ הערוך סודרא פי׳ כולה]
[גי׳ הערוך וורא״יא פי׳ שומר המעילי׳]

c (1) I.e., the *Hallel* as said on Passover Eve to celebrate the going forth from Egypt, v. Glos. s.v. *Hallel.* (2) As much as to say, he will be saved but I will not. (3) Raba's wife, whose death Bar Hedya had foretold. (4) *Aliter*: 'decay'.

of a college. (6) An interpreter. (7) Ex. XIII, 13. This passage is one of the four contained in the *tefillin*. (8) BaḤ adds: 'Raba examined and found that the *waw* of *ḥamor* had been erased etc.'. (9) A wife is compared to a dove in Cant. V, 2. (10) Looking like sticks.

תורה אור

שיראי דמלכא כפיתו תרין ארזי בחבלא אסור חד
כרעיה לחד ארזא וחד כרעיה לחד ארזא ושרו לחבלא
עד דאצטליק רישיה *אזל כל חד וחד וקם אדוכתיה [ע' בע"י]
ואצטליק ונפל בתרין שאל בן דמא בן אחותו של ר'
ישמעאל את ר' ישמעאל ראיתי שני לחיי שנשרו
אמר שני גדודי רומי יעצו עליך רעה ומתו א"ל בר
קפרא לר' ראיתי חוטמי שנשר א"ל חרון אף נסתלק
ממך א"ל ראיתי ב' ידי שנחתכו א"ל לא תצטרך
למעשה ידיך א"ל ראיתי ב' רגלי שנקטעו א"ל על
סוס אתה רוכב חזאי דאמרי לי באדר מיתת וניסן
לא חזית א"ל באדרותא מיתת ולא אתית לידי נסיון
וא"ל ההוא צדוקי לר' ישמעאל ראיתי שאני משקה
שמן לזיתים א"ל בא על אמו א"ל חזאי דקטיף לי
כוכבא א"ל בר ישראל גנבת' א"ל חזאי דבלעתיה לכוכבא א"ל בר ישראל זבנתיה ואכלת לדמי א"ל חזאי
עיני דנשקן אהדדי א"ל בא על אחותו א"ל חזאי דנשקי סיהרא א"ל בא על אשת ישראל א"ל חזאי דדריכנא
בטונא דאסא א"ל בא על נערה המאורסה א"ל חזאי טונא מעילאי והוא מתתאי א"ל משכבא הפוך א"ל חזאי
עורבי דהדרי לפורייה א"ל אשתך זנתה מאנשים הרבה א"ל חזאי יוני דהדרי לפורייה א"ל נשים הרבה טמאת
א"ל חזאי דנקיט תרי יוני ופרחן א"ל תרתי נשי נסבת ופטרתינהו בלא גט א"ל חזאי דקליפנא ביעי אמר ליה
שכבי קא משלחת אמר ליה כולהו איתנהו בי בר מהא דליתיה אדהכי והכי אתיא האי איתתא ואמרה ליה
האי גלימא דמכסה דגברא פלוני הוא דמית ואשלחתיה אמר ליה חזאי דאמרי לי שבק לך אבוך נכסי
בקפודקיא אמר ליה אית לך נכסי בקפודקיא אמר ליה לאו אזל אבוך לקפודקיא אמר ליה לאו אם כן קפא
כשורא דיקא עשרה זיל חזי קפא דריש עשרה שהיא מלאה זוזי אזיל אשכח שהיא מלאה זוזי א"ר חנינא
בראשית כו הרואה באר בחלום רואה שלום שנאמר °ויחפרו עבדי יצחק בנחל וימצאו שם באר מים חיים ר' נתן אומר
משלי ח מצא תורה שנאמר °כי מוצאי מצא חיים וכתיב הכא באר מים חיים רבא אמר חיים ממש אמר רבי חנן
ישעיה סו שלש שלומות הן נהר צפור וקדרה נהר דכתיב °הנני נוטה אליה כנהר שלום צפור דכתיב °כצפרים עפות כן
שם לא שם כו יגן (עליהם) ה' צבאות וגומר קדרה דכתיב °ה' תשפות שלום לנו אמר ר' חנינא ובקדרה שאין בה בשר
מיכה ג *שנינו °ופרשו כאשר בסיר וכבשר בתוך הקלחת א"ר יהושע בן לוי הרואה נהר בחלום ישכים ויאמר הנני
ישעיה נט נוטה אליה כנהר שלום קודם שיקדמנו פסוק אחר °כי יבא כנהר צר הרואה צפור בחלום ישכים ויאמר [מכא' כל"ל זכ"א בילקוט ישעי' סוף רמז כלו]
משלי כז כצפרים עפות כן יגן וגו' קודם שיקדמנו פסוק אחר °כצפור נודדת מקינה וגומר הרואה קדירה בחלום ישכים
יחזקאל כד ויאמר ה' תשפות שלום לנו קודם שיקדמנו פסוק אחר °שפות הסיר שפות הרואה ענבים בחלום ישכים
הושע ט ויאמר °כענבים במדבר קודם שיקדמנו פסוק אחר °ענבימו ענבי רוש הרואה הר בחלום ישכים ויאמר °מה
דברים לב נאוו על ההרים רגלי מבשר קודם שיקדמנו פסוק אחר °על ההרים אשא בכי ונהי הרואה שופר בחלום
ישעיה נב ישכים ויאמר °והיה ביום ההוא יתקע בשופר גדול קודם שיקדמנו פסוק אחר °תקעו שופר בגבעה הרואה
ירמיה ט כלב בחלום ישכים ויאמר °ולכל בני ישראל לא יחרץ כלב לשונו קודם שיקדמנו פסוק אחר °והכלבים עזי
ישעיה כז הושע ה נפש הרואה ארי בחלום ישכים ויאמר °אריה שאג מי לא יירא קודם שיקדמנו פסוק אחר °עלה אריה מסבכו
שמות יא ישעיה נו הרואה תגלחת בחלום ישכים ויאמר °ויגלח ויחלף שמלותיו קודם שיקדמנו פסוק אחר (כי) °אם גולחתי וסר
עמוס ג ירמיה ד ממני כחי הרואה באר בחלום ישכים ויאמר °באר מים חיים קודם שיקדמנו פסוק אחר °כהקיר בור מימיה
בראשית מא שופטים טז הרואה קנה בחלום ישכים ויאמר °קנה רצוץ לא ישבר קודם שיקדמנו פסוק אחר °הנה בטחת על משענת
שה"ש ד ירמיה ו קנה הרצוץ ת"ר הרואה קנה בחלום יצפה לחכמה שנאמר °קנה חכמה קנים יצפה לבינה שנאמר °ובכל
ישעיה מב קנינך קנה בינה אמר ר' זירא קרא קורא קירא קניא כולהו מעלו לחלמא תניא אין מראין דלועין אלא למי
מלכים ב יח שהוא ירא שמים בכל כחו הרואה שור בחלום ישכים ויאמר °בכור שורו הדר לו קודם שיקדמנו פסוק אחר
משלי ד שם דברים לג °כי יגח שור את איש ת"ר חמשה דברים נאמרו בשור האוכל מבשרו מתעשר נגחו הויין ליה בנים שמנגחים
שמות כא בתורה נשכו יסורים באים עליו בעטו דרך רחוקה נזדמנה לו רכבו עולה לגדולה והתניא רכבו מת לא קשיא
זכריה ט הא דרכיב הוא לתורא הא דרכיב תורא לדידיה הרואה חמור בחלום יצפה לישועה שנאמר °הנה מלכך יבא
לך צדיק ונושע הוא עני ורוכב על חמור הרואה חתול בחלום באתרא דקרו ליה שונרא נעשית לו שירה נאה
שינרא נעשה לו שינוי רע הרואה ענבים בחלום לבנות בין בזמנן בין שלא בזמנן יפות שחורות בזמנן יפות
ע' סנה' לג. שלא בזמנן רעות הרואה סוס *לבן בחלום בין בנחת בין ברדוף יפה לו אדום בנחת יפה ברדוף קשה הרואה
ישמעאל בחלום תפלתו נשמעת ודוקא ישמעאל בן אברהם אבל טייעא בעלמא לא הרואה גמל בחלום
בראשית מו מיתה נקנסה לו מן השמים והצילוהו ממנה א"ר חמא ברבי חנינא מאי קראה °אנכי ארד עמך מצרימה
שמואל ב יב ואנכי אעלך גם עלה רב נחמן בר יצחק אמר מהכא °גם ה' העביר חטאתך לא תמות הרואה פינחס בחלום
[לקמן נז:] פלא נעשה לו *הרואה פיל בחלום פלאות נעשו לו פילים פלאי פלאות נעשו לו והתניא כל מיני חיות יפין
לחלום חוץ מן הפיל ומן הקוף לא קשיא
הא

שיראי דמלכא. מעילים של מלך: דאצטליק. נחלק לב' ודוגמתו בהעור והרוטב (דף קכ"ד.) דללקי מללקת: יעצו עליך רעה. והם
הלחיים פה שיעץ עליך רעה: חרון אף. כיכל בחוטם שמתחמם ומוליא הבל על כן הוא קרוי חרון אף: לא תצטרך למעשה ידיך.
שתתעשר: באדרותא מיתת. בכבוד ובהדר תמות: אמו בעל. דומיא דשמן שהוא בתוך הזית השקה את אמו: קטיף לי כוכבא. עקרתי
כוכב בחלום: גנבת. שנמשלו לכוכבים: נערה המאורסה. היו רגילין לעשות לה חופה של הדס בכניסתה לחופה וקורין לה הינומא
כדאמרינן בכתובות (דף טו.) שילתה בהינומא ולאשה פרוע:
טונא דאסא. עולא דאסא: שכבי משלחת. מתים הפשטת:
אם כן. דלית לך התם נכסי ואבוך לא שכיב התם: קפא. דאמרי
לך היא כשורה שבלשון פרס ויון קורים לכשורא קפא: דיקא. הוא
עשרה דבלשון יוני קורין לעשרה דיקא והכי אמרי לך יש לך
ממון בקורה עשירית: דריש עשרה. קורה שבראש עשרה: שלש
שלומות הם. שלש אלומות המבשרים שלום: ופרשו כאשר בסיר.
אלמא פורענותא היא: ובכל קנינך. לשון מרובה הוא אף קנים
הרבה קנה של בינה הוא: קרא קורא קירא קניא. קרא דלעת
כדאמרינן לקמן הרואה דלועין בחלום ירא שמים הוא לשון דלו
עיני למרום (ישעיה לח): קורא. לב הגדל בענפי הדקל בכל
שנה כדרך שאר אילנות ולשנה שניה הוא מתקשה ונעשה עץ:
קירה. שעוה: קניא. קנה: האוכל מבשרו. בחלום: בין ברדוף.
כשהוא רץ: גם עלה. קרוב לנוטריקון של גמל: פלא נעשה לו.
כמו שנעשה לפינחס כדאמרינן בסנהדרין (ד' פב.):
דמסרג

for placing a pot on a fire. (4) Ibid. XXVI, 12. (5) V. Marginal Gloss. (6) Micah III, 3. (7) Isa. LIX, 19. (8) Prov. XXVII, 8. (9) Ezek. XXIV, 3. (10) Hos. IX, 10. (11) Deut. XXXII, 12. Isa. LII, 7. (13) Jer. IX, 9. (14) Isa. XXVII, 13. (15) Hos. V, 8. This introduces a denunciation. (16) Ex. XI, 7. (17) Isa. LVI, 11. (18) Amos III, 8. (19) Jer. IV, 7.

d (1) Gen. XLI, 14. (2) Judg. XVI, 17. Spoken by Samson. (3) Cant. IV, 15. (4) Jer. VI, 7. (5) Isa. XLII, 3. (6) Ibid. XXXVI, 6. (7) Prov. IV, 5. (8) Ibid. 7. (9) They all resemble in sound the word 'reed' and hence have a favourable significance. (10) Despite their large size they do not grow high above the ground, and are plants symbolic of the Godfearing man who, despite his worth, remains lowly and humble. (R. Nissim, Gaon.) (11) Deut. XXXIII, 17. (12) Ex. XXI, 28. (13) Lit., 'gore' (one another). (14) The original can equally mean 'it rides upon him'.

e (1) Zech. IX, 9. (2) MS.M. reads: If in a place . . . *shunara* he will undergo a change for the worse; if *shunara* a beautiful song, etc. (3) MS.M. adds: He should offer supplication. If (he dreamt) that he had eaten these, he can be assured that he is a son of the world to come. (4) Cf. Gen. XXI, 17. (5) Who is also called Ismael. (6) Gen. XLVI, 4. The last words in the Hebrew are *gam 'aloh*, which resemble *gamal*, 'a camel'. (7) II Sam. XII, 13. The derivation in this case is not clear; perhaps it is from the word *gam* 'also' which resembles *gamal*.

been ruined [56b]. They tied two cedars together with a rope, tied one leg to one cedar and the other to the other, and released
a the rope, so that even his head was split.[1] Each tree rebounded to its place and he was decapitated and his body fell in two.

Ben Dama, the son of R. Ishmael's sister, asked R. Ishmael: I dreamt that both my jaws fell out; [what does it mean]?—He replied to him: Two Roman counsellors[2] have made a plot against you, but they have died.

Bar Ḳappara said to Rabbi: I dreamt that my nose fell off. He replied to him: Fierce anger[3] has been removed from you. He said to him: I dreamt that both my hands were cut off. He replied: You will not require the labour of your hands. He said to him: I dreamt that both my legs were cut off. He replied: You will ride on horseback. I dreamt that they said to me: You will die in Adar and not see Nisan. He replied: You will die in all honour [*adrutha*], and not be brought into temptation [*nisayon*].

A certain *Min* said to R. Ishmael: I saw myself [in a dream] pouring oil on olives. He replied: [This man][4] has outraged his mother. He said to him: I dreamt I plucked a star. He replied: You have stolen an Israelite.[5] He said to him: I dreamt that I swallowed the star. He replied: You have sold an Israelite and consumed the proceeds. He said to him: I dreamt that my eyes were kissing one another. He replied: [This man] has outraged his sister. He said to him: I dreamt that I kissed the moon. He replied: He has outraged the wife of an Israelite. He said to him: I dreamt that I was walking in the shade of a myrtle. He replied: He has outraged
b a betrothed damsel.[1] He said to him: I dreamt that there was a shade above me, and yet it was beneath me. He replied: It means unnatural intercourse. He said to him: I saw ravens keep on coming to my bed. He replied: Your wife has misconducted herself with many men. He said to him: I saw pigeons keep on coming to my bed. He replied: You have defiled many women. He said to him: I dreamt that I took two doves and they flew away. He replied: You have married two wives and dismissed them without a bill of divorce. He said to him: I dreamt that I was shelling eggs. He replied: You have been stripping the dead. He then said to him: You are right in all of these, except the last, of which I am not guilty. Just then a woman came and said to him: This cloak which you are wearing belonged to So-and-so who is dead, and you have stripped it from him. He said to him: I dreamt that people told me: Your father has left you money in Cappadocia. He said to him: Have you money in Cappadocia? No, he replied. Did your father ever go to Cappadocia? No. In that case, he said, *kappa* means a beam and *dika* means ten.[2] Go and examine the beam which is at the head of ten, for it is full of coins. He went, and found it full of coins.

R. Ḥanina said: If one sees a well in a dream, he will behold peace, since it says: *And Isaac's servants digged in the valley, and found there a well of living water.*[3] R. Nathan said: He will find Torah, since it says, *Whoso findeth me findeth life*[4] and it is written here, *a well of living water.*[5] Raba said: It means life literally.

Rab Ḥanan said: There are three [kinds of dreams which signify] peace, namely, about a river, a bird, and a pot. 'A river', for it is
c written: *Behold I will extend peace to her like a river.*[1] 'A bird', for it is written: *As birds hovering, so will the Lord of Hosts protect Jerusalem.*[2] 'A pot' for it is written, *Lord, thou wilt establish*[3] *peace for us.*[4] Said R. Ḥanina: But this has been said of a pot in which there is no meat, [for it says]:[5] *They chop them in pieces, as that which is in the pot and as flesh within the cauldron.*[6]

R. Joshua b. Levi said: If one sees a river in his dreams, he should rise early and say: *Behold I will extend peace to her like a river,*[1] before another verse occurs to him, viz., *for distress will come in like a river.*[7] If one dreams of a bird he should rise early and say: *As birds hovering, so will the Lord of Hosts protect,*[2] before another verse occurs to him, viz., *As a bird that wandereth from her nest, so is a man that wandereth from his place.*[8] If one sees a pot in his dreams, he should rise early and say, *Lord thou will establish* [tishpoth] *peace for us,*[4] before another verse occurs to him, viz., *Set* [shefoth] *on the pot, set it on.*[9] If one sees grapes in his dream, he should rise early and say: *I found Israel like grapes in the wilderness,*[10] before another verse occurs to him, viz., *their grapes are grapes of gall.*[11] If one dreams of a mountain, he should rise early and say: *How beautiful upon the mountains are the feet of the messenger of good tidings,*[12] before another verse occurs to him, viz., *for the mountains will I take up a weeping and wailing.*[13] If one dreams of a horn he should rise early and say: *And it shall come to pass in that day that a great horn shall be blown,*[14] before another verse occurs to him, viz., *Blow ye the horn of Gibeah.*[15] If one sees a dog in his dream, he should rise early and say: *But against any of the children of Israel shall not a dog whet his tongue,*[16] before another verse occurs to him, viz., *Yea, the dogs are greedy.*[17] If one sees a lion in his dream he should rise early and say: *The lion hath roared, who will not fear?*[18] before another verse occurs to him, viz., *A lion is gone up from his thicket.*[19] If one dreams of shaving, he should rise early and say: *And Joseph*
d *shaved himself and changed his raiment,*[1] before another verse occurs to him, viz., *If I be shaven, then my strength will go from me.*[2] If one sees a well in his dream, he should rise early and say: *A well of living waters,*[3] before another verse occurs to him, viz., *As a cistern welleth with her waters, so she welleth with her wickedness.*[4] If one sees a reed, he should rise early and say, *A bruised reed shall he not break,*[5] before another verse occurs to him, viz., *Behold thou trusteth upon the staff of this bruised reed.*[6]

Our Rabbis taught: If one sees a reed [*ḳaneh*] in a dream, he may hope for wisdom, for it says: *Get* [ḳeneh] *wisdom.*[7] If he sees several reeds, he may hope for understanding, since it says: *With all thy getting* [ḳinyaneka] *get understanding.*[8] R. Zera said: A pumpkin [*ḳara*], a palm-heart [*ḳora*], wax [*ḳira*], and a reed [*ḳanya*] are all auspicious in a dream.[9] It has been taught: Pumpkins are shown in a dream only to one who fears heaven with all his might.[10] If one sees an ox in a dream, he should rise early and say: *His firstling bullock, majesty is his,*[11] before another verse occurs to him, viz., *If an ox gore a man.*[12]

Our Rabbis taught: There are five sayings in connexion with an ox in a dream. If one [dreams that he] eats of its flesh, he will become rich; if that an ox has gored him, he will have sons who will contend together[13] in the study of the Torah; if that an ox bit him, sufferings will come upon him; if that it kicked him, he will have to go on a long journey; if that he rode upon one, he will rise to greatness. But it has been taught: If he dreamt that he rode upon one,[14] he will die?—There is no contradiction. In the one case the dream is that he rides on the ox, in the other that the ox rode upon him.

If one sees an ass in a dream, he may hope for salvation, as it says, *Behold thy king cometh unto thee; he is triumphant and victorious,*
e *lowly and riding upon an ass.*[1] If one sees a cat in a dream, if in a place where they call it *shunara*, a beautiful song [*shirah na'ah*] will be composed for him; if in a place where they call it *shinra*, he will undergo a change for the worse [*shinnui ra'*].[2] If one sees grapes in a dream, if they are white, whether in their season or not in their season, they are a good sign; if black, in their season they are a good sign, not in their season a bad sign.[3] If one sees a white horse in a dream, whether walking gently or galloping, it is a good sign, if a red horse, if walking gently it is a good sign, if galloping it is a bad sign. If one sees Ishmael in a dream, his prayer will be heard.[4] And it must be Ishmael, the son of Abraham, but not an ordinary Arab.[5] If one sees a camel in a dream, death has been decreed for him from heaven and he has been delivered from it. R. Ḥama b. Ḥanina said: What is the Scriptural text for this?—*I will go down with thee into Egypt, and I will also surely bring thee up again.*[6] R. Naḥman b. Isaac derives it from here: *The Lord also hath put away thy sin, thou shalt not die.*[7] If one sees Phineas in a dream, a miracle will be wrought for him. If one sees an elephant [*pil*] in a dream, wonders [*pela'oth*] will be wrought for him; if several elephants, wonders of wonders will be wrought for him. But it has been taught: All kinds of beasts are of good omen in a dream except the elephant and the ape?—There is no contradiction.

a (1) Another reading is: 'released the rope till he was split in two. Said Raba: I will not forgive him till his head is split. Each tree, etc.'. (2) Signified by 'jaws' because of their powers of speech. (3) The word for 'nose' (*af*) means also 'anger'. (4) In attributing to him such a crime he would not address him in the second person. (5) The Israelites being compared to stars. Gen. XV, 5.

b (1) For whom it is usual to make a canopy of myrtle. (2) *Kappa* in the sense of 'beam' is an Aramaic word (*Kofa*), while *dika* in the sense of ten is the Greek δέκα. The *Jer.* more plausibly explains *kappa* as the Greek letter equivalent to twenty, and *dokia* as representing the Greek δοκή, a beam. (3) Gen. XXVI, 19. (4) Prov. VIII, 35. (5) Lit. 'water of life'.

c (1) Isa. LXVI, 12. (2) Ibid. XXXI, 5. (3) Heb. *tishpoth*, which is also used

[57a] The elephants are of good omen[8] if saddled, of bad omen if not saddled. If one sees the name Huna in a dream, a miracle will be wrought for him.[9] If one sees the name Ḥanina, Ḥananiah
a or Jonathan, miracles will be wrought for him.[1] If one dreams of a funeral oration [*hesped*] mercy will be vouchsafed to him from heaven and he will be redeemed.[2] This is only if he sees the word in writing.[3] If one [in a dream] answers, 'May His great name be blessed', he may be assured that he has a share in the future world. If one dreams that he is reciting the *Shema'*, he is worthy that the Divine presence should rest upon him, only his generation is not deserving enough. If one dreams he is putting on *tefillin*, he may look forward to greatness, for it says: *And all the peoples of the earth shall see that the name of the Lord is called upon thee, and they shall fear thee;*[4] and it has been taught: R. Eliezer the Great says: This refers to the *tefillin* of the head.[5] If one dreams he is praying, it is a good sign for him, provided he does not complete the prayer.[6]

If one dreams that he has intercourse with his mother, he may expect to obtain understanding, since it says, *Yea, thou wilt call understanding 'mother'*.[7] If one dreams he has intercourse with a betrothed maiden, he may expect to obtain knowledge of Torah, since it says, *Moses commanded us a law* [Torah], *an inheritance of the congregation of Jacob*.[8] Read not *morashah* [inheritance], but *me'orasah* [betrothed]. If one dreams he has had intercourse with his sister, he may expect to obtain wisdom, since it says, *Say to wisdom, thou art my sister.*[9] If one dreams he has intercourse with a married woman, he can be confident that he is destined for the future world,[10] provided, that is, that he does not know her and did not think of her in the evening.

R. Ḥiyya b. Abba said: If one sees wheat in a dream, he will see peace, as it says: *He maketh thy borders peace; He giveth thee in plenty the fat of wheat.*[11] If one sees barley[12] in a dream, his iniquities
b will depart, as it says: *Thine iniquity is taken away, and thy sin expiated.*[1] R. Zera said: I did not go up from Babylon to the Land of Israel until I saw barley in a dream.[2] If one sees in a dream a vine laden with fruit, his wife will not have a miscarriage, since it says, *thy wife shall be as a fruitful vine.*[3] If one sees a choice vine, he may look forward to seeing the Messiah, since it says, *Binding his foal unto the vine and his ass's colt unto the choice vine.*[4] If one sees a fig tree in a dream, his learning will be preserved within him, as it says: *Whoso keepeth the fig tree shall eat the fruit thereof.*[5] If one sees pomegranates in a dream, if they are little ones, his business will be fruitful like a pomegranate; if big ones, his business will increase like a pomegranate. If they are split open, if he is a scholar, he may hope to learn more Torah, as it says: *I would cause thee to drink of spiced wine, of the juice of my pomegranate;*[6] if he is unlearned, he may hope to perform precepts, as it says: *Thy temples are like a pomegranate split open.*[7] What is meant by '*Thy temples*' [*raḳothek*]?—Even the illiterate [*reḳanim*][8] among thee are full of precepts like a pomegranate. If one sees olives in a dream, if they are little ones his business will go on fructifying and increasing like an olive. This is if he sees the fruit; but if he sees the tree he will have many sons, as it says: *Thy children like olive plants, round about thy table.*[3] Some say that if one sees an olive in his dream he will acquire a good name, as it says, *The Lord called thy name a leafy olive-tree, fair and goodly fruit.*[9] If one sees olive oil in a dream, he may hope for the light of the Torah, as it says, *That they bring unto thee pure olive oil beaten for the light.*[10] If one sees palm-trees in a dream his iniquities will come to an end, as it says, *The punishment of thine iniquity is accomplished, O daughter of Zion.*[11]

R. Joseph said: If one sees a goat in a dream, he will have a blessed year; if several goats, several blessed years, as it says:
c *And there will be goat's milk enough for thy food.*[1] If one sees myrtle in his dream, he will have good luck with his property,[2] and if he has no property he will inherit some from elsewhere. 'Ulla said—according to others, it was taught in a Baraitha: this is only if he sees myrtle on its stem.[3] If one sees citron [*hadar*] in his dream, he is honoured [*hadur*] in the sight of his Maker, since it says: *The fruit of citrons,*[4] *branches of palm-trees.*[5] If one sees a palm branch in a dream, he is single-hearted in devotion to his Father in Heaven.[6] If one sees a goose in a dream, he may hope for wisdom, since it says: *Wisdom crieth aloud in the street;*[7] and he who dreams of being with one will become head of an academy. R. Ashi said: I saw one and was with one, and I was elevated to a high position.[8] If one sees a cock in a dream he may expect a male child; if several cocks, several sons; if a hen, a fine garden and rejoicing.[9] If one sees eggs in a dream, his petition remains in suspense;[10] if they are broken his petition will be granted. The same with nuts and cucumbers and all vessels of glass and all breakable things like these.

If one dreams that he enters a large town, his desire will be fulfilled, as it says, *And He led them unto their desired haven.*[11] If one dreams that he is shaving his head, it is a good sign for him; if his head and his beard, for him and for all his family. If one dreams that he is sitting in a small boat, he will acquire a good name; if in a large boat, both he and all his family will acquire one; but this is only if it is on the high sea. If one dreams that he is easing himself, it is a good omen for him, as it is said, *He that is bent down shall speedily be loosed,*[12] but this is only if he did not wipe himself [in his dream]. If one dreams that he goes up to a roof, he will attain a high position; if that he goes down, he will be degraded. Abaye and Raba, however, both say that once he has attained a high position he will remain there. If one dreams he is tearing
d his garments, his evil decree[1] will be rent. If one dreams that he is standing naked, if in Babylon he will remain sinless,[2] if in the Land of Israel he will be bare of pious deeds.[3] If one dreams that he has been arrested by the police, protection will be offered him; if that he has been placed in neckchains,[4] additional protection will be afforded him. This is only [if he dreams] of neck-chains, not a mere rope. If one dreams that he walks into a marsh, he will become the head of an academy;[5] if into a forest he will become the head of the collegiates.[6]

R. Papa and R. Huna the son of Joshua both had dreams. R. Papa dreamt that he went into a marsh and he became head of an academy.[7] R. Huna the son of R. Joshua dreamt that he went into a forest and he became head of the collegiates. Some say that both dreamt they went into a marsh, but R. Papa who was carrying a drum[8] became head of the academy, while R. Huna the son of R. Joshua who did not carry a drum became only the head of the collegiates. R. Ashi said: I dreamt that I went into a marsh and carried a drum and made a loud noise with it.

A Tanna recited in the presence of R. Naḥman b. Isaac: If one dreams that he is undergoing blood-letting, his iniquities are forgiven.[9] But it has been taught: His iniquities are recounted?—What is meant by recounted? Recounted so as to be forgiven.

A Tanna recited in the presence of R. Shesheth: If one sees a
e serpent in a dream, it means that his living is assured;[1] if it bites him it will be doubled; if he kills it he will lose his living. R. Shesheth said to him: [In this case] all the more will his living be doubled! This is not so, however; R. Shesheth [explained thus] because he saw a serpent in his dream and killed it.[2]

A Tanna recited in the presence of R. Joḥanan: All kinds of drinks are a good sign in a dream except wine; sometimes one may drink it and it turns out well and sometimes one may drink it and it turns out ill. 'Sometimes one may drink it and it turns out well', as it says: *Wine that maketh glad the heart of man'.*[3] 'Sometimes one may drink it and it turns out ill', as it says: *Give strong drink unto him that is ready to perish, and wine unto the bitter in soul.'*[4] Said R. Joḥanan unto the Tanna: Teach that for a scholar it is always good, as it says: *Come eat of my bread and drink of the wine which I have mingled.*[5]

(8) Lit., 'this is . . . that is'. (9) The Hebrew for miracle, *nes*, also contains the letter *nun*.

a (1) These names contain more than one *nun*. (2) *Hesped* is here connected with *ḥus* 'to have pity' and *padah* 'to redeem'. (3) And similarly the proper names Huna, etc. enumerated above. (4) Deut. XXVIII, 10. (5) V. *supra 6a*. (6) I.e., wakes up before it is finished. (7) Prov. II, 3 with a slight change of reading. E.V. *Yea, if thou wilt call for understanding*. (8) Deut. XXXIII, 4. (9) Prov. VII, 4. (10) The signification being that he obtains his own share and that of his neighbour (Rashi). (11) Ps. CXLVII, 14. (12) *Se'orim* (barley) equals *sar 'awon*, 'iniquity has departed'.

b (1) Isa VI, 7. (2) A visit to the Holy Land was held to bring with it an expiation for sin. (3) Ps. CXXVIII, 3. (4) Gen. XLIX, 11. This verse is supposed to refer to the Messiah. (5) Prov. XXVII, 18. (6) Cant. VIII, 2. (7) Ibid. IV, 3. (8) Lit., 'the empty ones'. (9) Jer. XI, 16. (10) Ex. XXVII, 20. (11) Lam. IV, 22. *Temarin* (palm-trees) suggest *tammu morin*, 'finished are rebels (sins)'.

c (1) Prov. XXVII, 27. (2) Like a myrtle which has numerous leaves. (3) I.e., attached to the soil. (4) E.V. '*Goodly trees*'. (5) Lev. XXIII, 40. (6) The palm branch having no twigs. (7) Prov. I, 20. (8) He became the head of the Academy of Matha Mehasia (a suburb of Sura). (9) The Hebrew word

הא דמסרג הא דלא מסרג הרואה הונא
בחלום נס נעשה לו חנינא חנניא יוחנן נסי
נסים נעשו לו *הרואה הספד בחלום מן השמים
חסו עליו ופדאוהו וה"מ בכתבא העונה יהא
שמיה רבא מברך מובטח לו שהוא בן העולם
הבא הקורא ק"ש *ראוי שתשרה עליו שכינה
אלא שאין דורו זכאי לכך המניח תפילין
בחלום יצפה לגדולה שנאמר °וראו כל עמי
הארץ כי שם יי' נקרא עליך וגו' *ותניא ר'
אליעזר הגדול אומר אלו תפילין שבראש
המתפלל בחלום סימן יפה לו והני מילי דלא
סיים הבא על אמו בחלום יצפה לבינה
שנאמר °כי אם לבינה תקרא הבא על נערה
מאורסה יצפה לתורה שנאמר °תורה צוה
לנו משה מורשה קהלת יעקב *אל תקרי
מורשה אלא *מאורשה הבא על אחותו בחלום
יצפה לחכמה שנאמר °אמור לחכמה אחותי
את הבא על אשת איש בחלום מובטח לו
שהוא בן העולם הבא וה"מ דלא ידע לה
ולא הרהר בה מאורתא א"ר חייא בר אבא
הרואה חטים בחלום רואה שלום שנאמר
°השם גבולך שלום חלב חטים ישביעך הרואה
שעורים בחלום סרו עונותיו שנאמר °וסר עונך וחטאתך תכפר א"ר זירא אנא לא סלקי מבבל לא"י עד
דחזאי שערי בחלמא הרואה גפן טעונה בחלום אין אשתו מפלת נפלים שנאמר °אשתך כגפן פוריה שורקה
יצפה למשיח שנאמר °אוסרי לגפן עירה ולשרקה בני אתנו הרואה תאנה בחלום תורתו משתמרת בקרבו
שנאמר °נוצר תאנה יאכל פריה הרואה רמונים בחלום זוטרי פרי עסקיה כרמונא רברבי רבי עסקי' כרמונא
פלגי אם ת"ח הוא יצפה לתורה שנאמר °אשקך מיין הרקח מעסיס רמוני ואם עם הארץ הוא יצפה למצות
שנאמר °כפלח הרמון רקתך מאי רקתך *אפילו ריקנים שבך מלאים מצות כרמון הרואה זיתים בחלום זוטרי
פרי ורבי וקאי עסקי' כזתים וה"מ פרי אבל אילני הויין ליה בנים מרובים שנאמר °בניך כשתילי זתים וגו' א"ד
הרואה זית בחלום שם טוב יוצא לו שנאמר °זית רענן יפה פרי תאר קרא יי' שמך הרואה שמן זית בחלום
יצפה למאור תורה שנאמר °ויקחו אליך שמן זית זך הרואה תמרים בחלום תמו עונותיו שנאמר °תם עונך
בת ציון אמר רב יוסף הרואה עז בחלום שנה מתברכת לו עזים שנים מתברכות לו שנאמר °ודי חלב עזים
ללחמך הרואה הדס בחלום נכסיו מצליחין לו ואם אין לו נכסים ירושה נופלת לו ממקום אחר אמר עולא
ואמרי לה במתניתא תנא והוא דחזא בכניידו הרואה אתרוג בחלום הדור הוא לפני קונו שנאמר °פרי עץ
הדר כפת תמרים הרואה לולב בחלום אין לו אלא לב אחד לאביו שבשמים הרואה אווז בחלום יצפה לחכמה
שנאמר °חכמות בחוץ תרנה והבא עליה הוי ראש ישיבה אמר רב אשי אני ראיתיה ובאתי עליה וסלקית
לגדולה הרואה תרנגול בחלום יצפה לבן זכר תרנגולים יצפה לבנים זכרים תרנגולת יצפה לתרביצא נאה
וגילה הרואה ביצים בחלום תלויה בקשתו נשתברו נעשית בקשתו וכן אגוזים וכן קשואים וכן כל כלי זכוכית
וכן כל הנשברים כאלו הנכנס לכרך נעשו לו חפציו שנאמר °וינחם אל מחוז חפצם המגלח ראשו בחלום
סימן יפה לו ראשו וזקנו לו ולכל משפחתו היושב בעריבה קטנה שם טוב יוצא לו בעריבה גדולה לו ולכל
משפחתו וה"מ דמדליה דלויי הנפנה בחלום סימן יפה לו שנאמר °מהר צעה להפתח וה"מ דלא קנח העולה
לגג בחלום עולה לגדולה ירד יורד מגדולתו אביי ורבא דאמרי תרוייהו כיון שעלה עלה הקורע בגדיו בחלום
קורעים לו גזר דינו העומד ערום בחלום בבבל עומד בלא חטא בא"י ערום בלא מצות הנתפש לסרדיוט
שמירה נעשה לו נתנוהו בקולר הוסיפו לו שמירה על שמירתו וה"מ בקולר אבל חבלא בעלמא לא הנכנס
לאגם בחלום נעשה ראש ישיבה ליער נעשה ראש לבני כלה רב פפא ורב הונא בריה דרב יהושע חזו חלמא
רב פפא דעייל לאגמא נעשה ראש ישיבה רב הונא בריה דרב יהושע דעייל ליער נעשה ראש לבני כלה
א"ד תרוייהו לאגמא עיילי אלא רב פפא דתלי טבלא נעשה ראש ישיבה רב הונא בריה דרב יהושע דלא
תלי טבלא נעשה ראש לבני כלה אמר רב אשי אנא עיילית לאגמא ותלאי טבלא ונבחי בה נבוחי תני תנא
קמיה דרב נחמן בר יצחק המקיז דם בחלום עונותיו מחולין לו והתניא עונותיו סדורין לו *מאי סדורין סדורין
לימחל תני תנא קמיה דרב ששת הרואה נחש בחלום פרנסתו מזומנת לו נשכו נכפלה לו הרגו אבדה
פרנסתו א"ל רב ששת כל שכן שנכפלה פרנסתו ולא היא רב ששת הוא דחזא חויא בחלמיה וקטליה תני
תנא קמיה דרבי יוחנן כל מיני משקין יפין לחלום חוץ מן היין יש שותהו וטוב לו ויש שותהו ורע לו יש
שותהו וטוב לו שנאמר °ויין ישמח לבב אנוש ויש שותהו ורע לו שנאמר °תנו שכר לאובד ויין למרי נפש
א"ל ר' יוחנן לתנא תני תלמיד חכם לעולם טוב לו שנאמר °לכו לחמו בלחמי ושתו ביין מסכתי
א"ר

דמסרג. שיש לו אוכף על גביו *יפה: נס נעשה לו. נו"ן כנגד נו"ן וכגון שראה השם כתוב: חנינא. נוני"ן הרבה נסים רבים: והני מילי בכתבא. אכולהו קאי שראה הונא או חנינא או תיבה זו של הספד כתובה דמשמע חסו עליו ופדאוהו: דלא סיים. שנעור משנתו קודם שנסתלק סימן הוא שסמוך אצל הקב"ה: מובטח לו שהוא בן העולם הבא. ונוטל חלקו וחלק חברו בגן עדן דדמי לאשת איש: פלגי. רמונים שנחלקו: יצפה לתורה. שנאמר אשקך מיין הרקח היינו תורה: מעסיס רמוני. שנאמר מן הרמונים: נכסיו מצליחין. כהדס זה שעליו משולשים זה על זה כמין קליעה: בכניידו. על כנם במקומם במחובר: הוי ראש ישיבה. שמכריז ומלוה לרבים: אני ראיתיה וכו'. ועל כן נעשתי ראש ישיבה במתא מחסיא: תרביצא. גינה אי נמי בית המדרש תרבילא נאה וגילה נוטריקון של תרנגול: תלויה בקשתו. בספק כבלים הללו שהאוכל סתום בם: נשתברו. נתגלה האוכל: וינחם אל מחוז. היינו כרך: חפצם. סימן הוא להיות חפציו נעשים: המגלח. סימן גדולה ותפארת היא לו כמו ויגלח ויחלף וגו' (בראשית מא): בעריבה. בספינה: דמדליה. שהולכת בגובה של ים: הנפנה. סימן הוא שסרחונו וגנותו נפרש וילך מעליו: והוא דלא קנח. שלא המאיס ידיו: בבבל עומד בלא חטא. לפי שח"ל אין לה זכות אלא עון יש בישיבתה והוא עומד ערום בלא אותן עונות: בא"י. שהרבה מצות תלויות בה והוא העומד ערום סימן שהוא ערום ממצותיה: הנתפש לסרדיוט. שומרין אותו שלא יברח אלמא סימן שמירה הוא שמשמרים אותו מידי היזק: אגם. שיש בו קנים גדולים וקטנים וסמוכים זה לזה סימן לראש ישיבה שהגדולי' והקטני' מתקבלים יחד קבוץ גדול ובאים לשמוע דרשה מפיו: יער. אילנות גדולים ואינן סמוכין זה לזה אף זה סימן לראש לתלמידי הרב והוא ראש לבני כלה שמפרש לתלמידים שמועה אחר שעמד הרב והם מחזרין על שמועתם ויש תלמידים שלא יבינו בדברי הרב ככל הצורך והוא מבינה להם: תלי טבלא. נראה לו שהיה זוג ועינבול תלוי בצוארו ומשמיע קול והוא סימן לראש ישיבה שמשמיע קול לרבים: ונבחי בה נבוחי. קשקשתי בה בקול: עונותיו מחולין לו. לפי שהעונות קרויין אדומים שנאמר אם יאדימו כתולע (ישעיה א) ואומר נכתם עונך (ירמי' ב) וסימן הוא שפורשין ממנו: פרנסתו מזומנת. כנחש שהעפר לחמו ומצוי לו בכל מקום: הרגו לנחש. כל שכן שנכפלה לו. שהרי נתגבר עליו: ולא היא. אלא רב ששת דורש להנאתו לפתור חלומו לטובה: יש שותהו כו'. לפיכך אין לעמוד על פתרונו:

השכים

תורה אור: דברים כח; משלי ב; דברים לג; משלי ז; תהלים קמז; ישעי' ו; תהלים קכח; בראשית מט; משלי כז; שיר ח; שם ד; תהלים קכח; ירמיה יא; שמות כז; איכה ד; משלי כז; ויקרא כג; משלי א; תהלים קז; ישעיה נא; תהלים קד; משלי לא; שם ט

מסורת הש"ס: [וע' בפרש"י בעמוד ב' ד"ה דמסרג] ב"ק נה. [סנהד' יח.] לעיל ו. מנחות ד' לה: [מגילה טז: סוטה יז. חולין פט:] [פסחים מט:] [סנהד' כט.] [עירובין יט. חגיגה כז. מגילה ו. סנה' לז.] [יומא פז.]

for cock (*tarnegol*) suggests these interpretations. (10) Like the contents of the egg, of which one is doubtful as long as the shell is unbroken (Rashi). (11) Ps. CVII, 30. (12) Isa. LI, 14.

d (1) The evil decreed against him from heaven. (2) V. Keth. 110b. He who dwells outside the Land of Israel is as though he worshipped idols. To stand naked in a dream in Babylon hence means to be sinless. (3) V. Keth. 111a. He who dwells in the Land abides sinless. To stand naked in a dream in Palestine hence means to be bare of pious deeds. (4) With which criminals were strung together to be led to execution. (5) Short and long reeds in a marsh are figurative of the students of different ages and standards attending the Academy. (6) The full-grown trees in a forest represent the mature students who meet often for discussion and study. V., however, Rashi. (7) He became the head of the school in Naresh, near Sura. (8) Such as was used for announcing the approach of a man of distinction. (9) Sins are described as crimson, cf. Isa. I, 18.

e (1) Because the serpent eats dust of which there is always abundance. (2) And he wished to give his dream a favourable interpretation. (3) Ps. CIV, 15. (4) Prov. XXXI, 6. (5) Ibid. IX, 5.

עין משפט נר מצוה

כ
א מיי' פרק י' מהל' ברכות הלכה ט סמג עשין כז טוש"ע א"ח סימן רכד סעיף א
[בא"ר"ב פ"מ לים' ובזה אתי שפיר ג' נביאים]
כא
ב מיי' שם וטוש"ע א"ח שם סעיף ב
כב
ד שם סעיף ג
כג
ה מיי' שם טוש"ע א"ח שם ובסימן ריח סעיף ז
כד
ו טוש"ע א"ח סימן רכד סעי' ד

[ג' הערוך קריא כוס וינשוף הכנוס קריא וקיפא]

ע"ז יא. וכע.
[בכל הספרים ופיקונים כתיב גיים והקרי גוים ומלוה להסכיל]

(בירוש' איתא ר' ישמעאל בן גמליאל)

הרואה מרקולים. בתוספתא תנן במקום מרקולים דהכא ע"א ואם כן לאו דוקא מרקולים אלא לפי שבמקומו של תכא היו עובדים לה ועתה אין אנו רגילים לברך לפי שאנו רואים אותה בכל יום וכל הכך הרואים אומר לעיל דהוי משלשים יום לשלשים יום:

הרואה מרקולים. פירש ר"י לא ידענ' אמאי נקט מרקולים יותר משאר ע"א ונראה לי דאין צריך לברך רק במקום שבונים ע"א או שהועמדה שם מחדש ולכך נקט מרקולים שרוגמין בה אבנים בכל יום והוי כמגדל ע"א אבל לא על ע"א קבועה שם מקודם ובירושלמי יש נעקרה ע"א ממקום אחד וניתנה למקום אחר במקום שניתנה אומר ברוך שנתן ארך אפים לעוברי רצונו ובמקום שנעקרה אומר ברוך שעקר ע"א מן המקום הזה: הרואה

תורה אור

*א"ר יוחנן השכים ונפל פסוק לתוך פיו הרי זה נבואה קטנה ת"ר *שלשה מלכים הם הרואה דוד בחלום יצפה לחסידות שלמה יצפה לחכמה אחאב ידאג מן הפורענות ג' נביאים הם הרואה ספר מלכים יצפה לגדולה *יחזקאל *יצפה *לחכמה ישעיה יצפה לנחמה ירמיה ידאג מן הפורענות שלשה כתובים גדולים הם הרואה ספר תהלים יצפה לחסידות משלי יצפה לחכמה איוב ידאג מן הפורענות ג' כתובים קטנים הם הרואה שיר השירים בחלום יצפה לחסידות קהלת יצפה לחכמה קינות ידאג מן הפורענות והרואה מגלת אסתר נס נעשה לו ג' חכמים הם הרואה רבי בחלום יצפה לחכמה ראב"ע יצפה לעשירות רבי ישמעאל בן אלישע ידאג מן הפורענות ג' תלמידי חכמים הם הרואה בן עזאי בחלום יצפה לחסידות בן זומא יצפה לחכמה אחר ידאג מן הפורענות כל מיני חיות יפות לחלום חוץ מן הפיל והקוף והקפוד והאמר מר הרואה *פיל בחלום פלא נעשה לו ל"ק הא דמסרג הא דלא מסרג כל מיני מתכות יפין לחלום חוץ ממר פסל וקרדום והני מילי דחזנהו בקתייהו כל מיני פירות יפין לחלום חוץ מפגי תמרה כל מיני ירקות יפין לחלום חוץ מראשי לפתות והאמר רב לא איעתרי עד דחזאי ראשי לפתות כי חזא בכניידהו חזא כל מיני צבעונין יפין לחלום חוץ מן התכלת כל מיני עופות יפין לחלום חוץ מן *קריא וקפופא וקורפראי: [הגו"ף הגו"ף מע"ן משיב"ן ומרחיב"ן סימן]: שלשה נכנסין לגוף ואין הגוף נהנה מהן גודגדניות וכפניות ופגי תמרה ג' אין נכנסין לגוף והגוף נהנה מהן אלו הן רחיצה וסיכה ותשמיש ג' מעין העולם הבא אלו הן שבת שמש ותשמיש תשמיש דמאי אילימא תשמיש המטה הא מכחש כחיש אלא תשמיש נקבים ג' משיבין דעתו של אדם אלו הן קול ומראה וריח ג' מרחיבין דעתו של אדם אלו הן דירה נאה ואשה נאה וכלים נאים: [חמש"ה ושש"ה ועשר"ה סימן]: חמשה אחד מששים אלו הן אש דבש ושבת ושינה וחלום אש אחד מששים לגיהנם דבש אחד מששים למן שבת אחד מששים לעולם הבא שינה אחד מששים למיתה חלום אחד מששים לנבואה ששה דברים סימן יפה לחולה אלו הן עטוש זיעה שלשול קרי ושינה וחלום עטוש דכתיב °עטישותיו תהל אור זיעה דכתיב °בזעת אפך תאכל לחם שלשול דכתיב °מהר צועה להפתח לא ימות לשחת קרי דכתיב °יראה זרע יאריך ימים שינה דכתיב °ישנתי אז ינוח לי חלום דכתיב °ותחלימני [והחייני] *ששה דברים מרפאין את החולה מחליו ורפואתו רפואה אלו הן כרוב ותרדין וסיסין יבשין וקיבה והרת ויותרת הכבד וי"א אף דגים קטנים ולא *עוד אלא שדגים קטנים מפרין ומברין כל גופו של אדם עשרה דברים מחזירין את החולה לחליו וחליו קשה אלו הן האוכל בשר שור בשר שמן בשר צלי בשר צפרים וביצה צלויה ותגלחת ושחלים והחלב והגבינה והמרחץ וי"א אף אגוזים וי"א אף קשואין תנא דבי רבי ישמעאל *למה נקרא שמן קשואין מפני שהן קשים לגוף כחרבות איני והכתיב °ויאמר יי' לה שני גוים בבטנך *אל תקרי גוים אלא גיים ואמר רב יהודה אמר רב אלו אנטונינוס *ור' שלא פסק משלחנם לא צנון ולא חזרת ולא קשואין לא בימות החמה ולא בימות הגשמים ל"ק הא ברברבי הא בזוטרי ת"ר מת בבית שלום בבית אכל ושתה בבית סימן יפה לבית נטל כלי מן הבית סימן רע לבית תרגמה רב פפא במסאנא וסנדלא כל דשקיל שכבא מעלי בר ממסאנא וסנדלא וכל דיהיב שכבא מעלי בר מעפרא וחרדלא: מקום שנעקרה ממנו ע"א: ת"ר *ᵃהרואה מרקולים אומר ברוך שנתן ארך אפים לעוברי רצונו ᵇמקום שנעקרה ממנו ע"א אומר ברוך שעקר ע"א מארצנו וכשם שנעקרה ממקום זה כן תעקר מכל מקומות ישראל והשב לב עובדיהם לעבדך ובח"ל א"צ"ל והשב לב עובדיהם לעבדך מפני שרובה כותיים *רשב"א אומר ᶜאף בח"ל צ"ל כן מפני שעתידים להתגייר שנאמר °אז אהפוך אל עמים שפה ברורה דרש רב המנונא ᵈהרואה בבל הרשעה צריך לברך חמש ברכות ראה בבל אומר ברוך שהחריב בבל הרשעה ראה ביתו של נבוכדנצר אומר ברוך שהחריב ביתו של נבוכדנצר הרשע ᵉראה גוב של אריות או כבשן האש אומר ברוך שעשה נסים לאבותינו במקום הזה ראה מרקולים אומר ברוך שנתן ארך אפים לעוברי רצונו ᶠראה מקום שנטלו ממנו עפר אומר ברוך אומר ועושה גוזר ומקיים רבא כי הוה חזי חמרי דשקלי עפרא טריף להו ידא על גבייהו ואמר רהוטו צדיקי למעבד רעותא דמרייכו מר בריה דרבינא כי הוה מטו לבבל הוה שקיל עפרא בסודריה ושדי לברא לקיים מה שנאמר °וטאטאתי' במטאטא השמד אמר רב אשי אנא הא דרב המנונא לא שמיע לי אלא מדעתאי בריכתינהו לכולהו

[Verse references in the margin between the Gemara and Rashi: איוב מא; בראשית ג; ישעיה נא; שם כג (?); איוב ג; ישעיה לח; בראשית כה; צפניה ג; ישעיה יד]

השכים. העומד ממטתו ונפל לו פסוק בפיו: שיר השירים. כולו ילאת שמים ואבת המקום בלב כל ישראל: ר' ישמעאל בן אלישע. מהרוגי מלכות היה והפשיטו עור קרקפתו בחייו: חוץ מן הפיל והקוף והקפוד. שמשונין במראיהן. קפוד היה שדומה לקוף ויש לה זכב ארוך ושמה מרטיכא: דמסרג. אוכף על גביו וי"א כתון באפסר: חוץ ממר. פסו"ל בלע"ז: פסל. דולו"ל: דחזנהו בקתייהו. שראוין למלאכתן לחבל ולהשחית: פגי תמרה. שלא בשלו כל לרכן: בכניידהו. במחובר אבל בתלוש סימן הוא למכות כדפשר ליה *בר הדיא לרבא קולפי בלעת: תכלת. ירוק הוא ומי שפניו ירוקים חולה הוא: קריא. ייב"ץ: קפופא. לואיט"א בלע"ז ויש לה לסתות כל חיי אדם לפיכך הן מגונים: קורפראי. טלפ"א: נורגדניות. לירת"ים: כפניות. מין תמרים רעים: שמש. חמה זורחת: קול. של מיני זמר או קול ערב של אשה: עטוש. אשטר"נודר: מהר צועה. מי שלריך להריק מעיו. הרקת כלי נקראת לעיה שנאמר (ירמיה מח) ושלחתי לו לועים ולעוהו וכליו יריקו במואב כתיב: ותחלימני והחייני. בחזקיה כתיב: תרדין. בלי"ץ: מי סיסין. בסול פולי"אול: והרת. וידל"ייר שהשליל בתוכה: יותרת הכבד. איבר"ש של בהמה: ומבריא. לשון בריאות: ותגלחת. אם מגלח: זוטרי. יפין: מסאנא וסנדלא. סימן יולאי חוץ הוא שמוליא אחרים מן הבית: עפרא. סימן הוא שרוצה להם קבורה: לב עובדיהם. על פושעי ישראל מתפלל: כבשן של אש. חפירה שהוסק בה כבשנס של חנניה מישאל ועזריה: מקום שנוטלין ממנו עפר. מקום יש בבבל שאין בהמה יולאה משם אם אין נותנין עליה עפר מעפר המקום והוא סימן השמד ומקללותיה של בבל היא וביסוד מהר"ר ילחק לאיתי שנוטלים משם עפר לטיט לבנינו המקום וסוף סוף אותו מקום אין בו ישוב ולא זרע ולא נטיעה: גוזר ומקיים. שגזר להשמידה וקיים: נתקללה

מסורת הש"ס

[לעיל נה:] [וקל"ע]
[אדר"כ פ"מ וע"ש]
[לעיל נו.]
[לעיל נו:]
לעיל מד: ע"א כט.
[לעיל מ.]
בראשית כה
[ע' תוס' ע"ז יא. ד"ה לגון]
[תוספ' פ"ו]
לפניה ג

good sign in a dream except the mole. All kinds'. (10) A kind of clover (11) Lit., 'service'. (12) I.e., sexual intercourse.
(1) Lit., 'enlarge his spirit'. (2) Job XLI, 10. (3) Gen. III, 19. (4) Isa. LI, 14. E.V. '*He that is bent down shall speedily*, etc.'. (5) Ibid. LIII, 10. (6) Job. III, 13. (7) Isa. XXXVIII, 16. V. 55*a*, n. a10. (8) Gen. XXV, 23.

c (1) V. A.Z. (Sonc. ed.) p. 50, n. 3. (2) Heb. *Markolis*, the Latin Mercurius. This was the commonest of the heathen images. (3) I.e., of renegade Israelites. (4) Zeph. III, 9. (5) Daniel and Hananiah, Mishael and Azariah.
d (1) The ruins of the city of Babylon from which earth was taken for building elsewhere, v. Obermeyer, p. 303. (2) Isa. XIV, 23.

[57b] R. Johanan said: If at the moment of rising a text occurs to one, this is a minor kind of prophecy.

Our Rabbis taught there are three kings [who are important for dreams]. If one sees David in a dream, he may hope for piety; if Solomon, he may hope for wisdom; if Ahab, let him fear for punishment. There are three prophets [of significance for dreams]. If one sees the Book of Kings, he may look forward to greatness; if Ezekiel, he may look forward to wisdom; if Isaiah he may look forward to consolation; if Jeremiah, let him fear for punishment. There are three larger books of the Hagiographa [which are significant for dreams]. If one sees the Book of Psalms, he may hope for piety; if the Book of Proverbs, he may hope for wisdom; if the Book of Job, let him fear for punishment. There are three smaller books of the Hagiographa [significant for dreams]. If one sees the Songs of Songs in a dream, he may hope for piety;[6] if Ecclesiastes, he may hope for wisdom; if Lamentations, let him fear for punishment; and one who sees the Scroll of Esther will have a miracle wrought for him. There are three Sages [significant for dreams]. If one sees Rabbi in a dream, he may hope for wisdom;
a if Eleazar b. Azariah, he may hope for riches;[1] if R. Ishmael b. Elisha, let him fear for punishment.[2] There are three disciples[3] [significant for dreams]. If one sees Ben 'Azzai in a dream, he may hope for piety; if Ben Zoma, he may hope for wisdom; if Aher,[4] let him fear for punishment.

All kinds of beasts are a good sign in a dream, except the elephant, the monkey and the long-tailed ape. But a Master has said: If one sees an elephant in a dream, a miracle will be wrought for him?[5]—There is no contradiction; in the latter case it is saddled, in the former case it is not saddled. All kinds of metal implements are a good sign in a dream, except a hoe, a mattock, and a hatchet; but this is only if they are seen in their hafts.[6] All kinds of fruit are a good sign in a dream, except unripe dates. All kinds of vegetables are a good sign in a dream, except turnip-tops. But did not Rab say: I did not become rich until I dreamt of turnip-tops?—When he saw them, it was on their stems.[7] All kinds of colours are a good sign in a dream, except blue.[8] All kinds[9] of birds are a good sign in a dream, except the owl, the horned owl and the bat.

(Mnemonic: The body, The body, Reflex, Restore, Self-esteem.) Three things enter the body without benefiting it: *melilot*,[10] date-berries, and unripe dates. Three things benefit the body without being absorbed by it: washing, anointing, and regular motion. Three things are a reflex of the world to come: Sabbath, sunshine, and *tashmish*.[11] *Tashmish* of what? Shall I say of the bed?[12] This weakens. It must be then *tashmish* of the orifices. Three things restore a man's good spirits: [beautiful] sounds, sights, and smells.
b Three things increase a man's self-esteem:[1] a beautiful dwelling, a beautiful wife, and beautiful clothes.

(Mnemonic: Five, Six, Ten). Five things are a sixtieth part of something else: namely, fire, honey, Sabbath, sleep and a dream. Fire is one-sixtieth part of Gehinnom. Honey is one-sixtieth part of manna. Sabbath is one-sixtieth part of the world to come. Sleep is one-sixtieth part of death. A dream is one-sixtieth part of prophecy.

Six things are a good sign for a sick person, namely, sneezing, perspiration, open bowels, seminal emission, sleep and a dream. Sneezing, as it is written: *His sneezings flash forth light*.[2] Perspiration, as it is written, *In the sweat of thy face shalt thou eat bread*.[3] Open bowels, as it is written: *If he that is bent down hasteneth to be loosed, he shall not go down dying to the pit*.[4] Seminal emission, as it is written: *Seeing seed, he will prolong his days*.[5] Sleep, as it is written: *I should have slept, then should I have been at rest*.[6] A dream, as it is written: *Thou didst cause me to dream and make me to live*.[7]

Six things heal a man of his sickness with a complete cure, namely, cabbage, beet, a decoction of dried poley, the maw [of an animal], the womb, and the large lobe of the liver. Some add small fishes, which [not only have this advantage] but also make fruitful and invigorate a man's whole body.

Ten things bring a man's sickness on again in a severe form, namely, to eat beef, fat meat, roast meat, poultry and roasted egg, shaving, and eating cress, milk or cheese, and bathing. Some add, also nuts; and some add further, also cucumbers. It was taught in the school of R. Ishmael: Why are they called *kishshu'im* [cucumbers]? Because they are painful [*kashim*] for the body like swords. Is that so? See, it is written: *And the Lord said unto her, Two nations are in thy womb*.[8] Read not *goyim* [nations] but *ge'im* [lords], and Rab Judah said in the name of Rab: These are Antoninus and Rabbi, whose table never lacked either radish, lettuce
c or cucumbers either in summer or winter![1]—There is no contradiction; the former statement speaks of large ones, the latter of small ones.

Our Rabbis taught: [If one dreams of] a corpse in the house, it is a sign of peace in the house; if that he was eating and drinking in the house, it is a good sign for the house; if that he took articles from the house, it is a bad sign for the house. R. Papa explained it to refer to a shoe or sandal. Anything that the dead person [is seen in the dream] to take away is a good sign except a shoe and a sandal; anything that it puts down is a good sign except dust and mustard.

A PLACE FROM WHICH IDOLATRY HAS BEEN UPROOTED. Our Rabbis taught: If one sees a statue of Hermes,[2] he says, Blessed be He who shows long suffering to those who transgress His will. If he sees a place from which idolatry has been uprooted, he says, Blessed be He who uprooted idolatry from our land; and as it has been uprooted from this place, so may it be uprooted from all places belonging to Israel; and do Thou turn the heart of those that serve them[3] to serve Thee. Outside Palestine it is not necessary to say: Turn the heart of those that serve them to serve Thee, because most of them are idolaters. R. Simeon b. Eleazar says: Outside Palestine also one should say this, because they will one day become proselytes, as it says, *For then will I turn to the peoples a pure language*.[4]

R. Hamnuna said in a discourse: If one sees the wicked Babylon, he should say five benedictions: On seeing [the city] Babylon itself he says, Blessed be He who has destroyed the wicked Babylon. On seeing the palace of Nebuchadnezzar, he says, Blessed be He who destroyed the palace of the wicked Nebuchadnezzar. On seeing the lions' den, or the fiery furnace, he says, Blessed be He who wrought miracles for our ancestors[5] in this place. On seeing the statue of Hermes, he says, Blessed be He who shows long suffering to those that transgress His will. On seeing the place
d from which dust is carried away,[1] he says, Blessed be He who says and does, who decrees and carries out. Rab, when he saw asses carrying dust, used to give them a slap on the back and say, Run, ye righteous ones, to perform the will of your Master. When Mar the son of Rabina came to [the city of] Babylon, he used to put some dust in his kerchief and throw it out, to fulfil the text, *I will sweep it with the besom of destruction*.[2] R. Ashi said: I had never heard this saying of R. Hamnuna, but of my own sense I made all these blessings.

(6) The Song of Songs being calculated to implant in the reader the love of God

a (1) R. Eleazar was very wealthy. (2) R. Ishmael suffered martyrdom under the Romans, v. Halevi, *Doroth* I, p. 309. (3) Who became authorities though they were never ordained as Rabbis. (4) Elisha b. Abuya, called Aher (lit., 'Another') when he came a renegade, v. Hag. 15a. (5) V. *supra* 56b. (6) Otherwise they portend blows, as stated above. (7) I.e., attached to the soil. (8) The colour of sickness. (9) MS.M. inserts: 'of reptiles are a

[58*a*] R. Jeremiah b. Eleazar said: When Babylon was cursed, her neighbours were also cursed; but when Samaria was cursed, her neighbours were blessed. 'When Babylon was cursed her neighbours were cursed', as it is written: *I will also make it a possession for the bittern and pools of water.*[3] 'When Samaria was cursed her neighbours were blessed', as it is written: *Therefore I will make Samaria a heap in the field, a place for the planting of vineyards.*[4]

R. Hamnuna further said: If one sees a crowd of Israelites, he should say: Blessed is He who discerneth secrets.[5] If he sees a crowd of heathens, he should say: *Your mother shall be ashamed,* etc.[6]

Our Rabbis taught: If one sees a crowd of Israelites, he says, Blessed is He who discerneth secrets, for the mind of each is different from that of the other, just as the face of each is different from that of the other. Ben Zoma once saw a crowd on one of the steps of the Temple Mount. He said, Blessed is He that discerneth secrets, and blessed is He who has created all these to serve me. [For] he used to say: What labours Adam had to carry out before he obtained bread to eat! He ploughed, he sowed, he reaped, he bound [the sheaves], he threshed and winnowed and selected the ears, he ground [them], and sifted [the flour], he kneaded and baked, and then at last he ate; whereas I get up, and find all these things done for me. And how many labours Adam had to carry out before he obtained a garment to wear! He had to shear, wash [the wool], comb it, spin it and weave it, and then at last he obtained a garment to wear; whereas I get up and find all these things
a done for me. All kinds of craftsmen[1] come early to the door of my house, and I rise in the morning and find all these before me.

He used to say: What does a good guest say? 'How much trouble my host has taken for me! How much meat he has set before me! How much wine he has set before me! How many cakes he has set before me! And all the trouble he has taken was only for my sake!' But what does a bad guest say? 'How much after all has mine host put himself out? I have eaten one piece of bread, I have eaten one slice of meat, I have drunk one cup of wine! All the trouble which my host has taken was only for the sake of his wife and his children!' What does Scripture say of a good guest? *Remember that thou magnify his works, whereof men have sung.*[2] But of a bad guest it is written: *Men do therefore fear him; [he regardeth not any that are wise of heart].*[3]

And the man was an old man in the days of Saul, stricken in years among men.[4] Raba (or, as some say, R. Zebid; or again, as some say, R. Oshaia) said: This is Jesse, the father of David, who went out with a crowd and came in with a crowd, and expounded [the Torah] to a crowd. 'Ulla said: We have a tradition that there is no crowd[5] in Babylon. It was taught: A multitude is not less than sixty myriads.

Our Rabbis taught: On seeing the Sages of Israel one should say: Blessed be He who hath imparted of His wisdom to them that fear Him. On seeing the Sages of other nations, one says, Blessed be He who hath imparted of His wisdom to His creatures. On seeing kings of Israel, one says: Blessed be He who hath imparted of His glory to them that fear Him. On seeing non-Jewish kings, one says: Blessed be He who hath imparted of His glory to His creatures. R. Johanan said: A man should always exert himself and run to meet an Israelitish king; and not only a king of Israel but also a king of any other nation, so that if he is deemed
b worthy,[1] he will be able to distinguish between the kings of Israel and the kings of other nations.

R. Shesheth was blind. Once all the people went out to see the king, and R. Shesheth arose and went with them. A certain Sadducean[2] came across him and said to him: The whole pitchers go to the river, but where do the broken ones go to?[3] He replied: I will show you that I know more than you. The first troop passed by and a shout arose. Said the Sadducean: The king is coming. He is not coming, replied R. Shesheth. A second troop passed by and when a shout arose, the Sadducean said: Now the king is coming. R. Shesheth replied: The king is not coming. A third troop passed by and there was silence. Said R. Shesheth: Now indeed the king is coming. The Sadducean said to him: How did you know this?—He replied: Because the earthly royalty is like the heavenly. For it is written: *Go forth and stand upon the mount before the Lord. And behold, the Lord passed by and a great and strong wind rent the mountains, and broke in pieces the rocks before the Lord; but the Lord was not in the wind; and after the wind an earthquake; but the Lord was not in the earthquake; and after the earthquake a fire; but the Lord was not in the fire; and after the fire a still small voice.*[4] When the king came, R. Shesheth said the blessing over him. The Sadducean said to him: You, you say a blessing for one whom you do not see? What happened to that Sadducean? Some say that his companions put his eyes out; others say that R. Shesheth cast his eyes upon him and he became a heap of bones.

R. Shila administered lashes to a man who had intercourse with an Egyptian[5] woman. The man went and informed against him to the Government, saying: There is a man among the Jews who passes judgment without the permission of the Government. An official was sent to [summon] him. When he came he was asked: Why did you flog that man? He replied: Because he had intercourse with a she-ass. They said to him: Have you witnesses? He replied: I have. Elijah thereupon came in the form of a man and gave evidence. They said to him: If that is the case he ought to be put to death! He replied: Since we have been exiled from our land, we have no authority to put to death; do you do with him what you please. While they were considering his case, R. Shila
c exclaimed, *Thine, Oh Lord, is the greatness and the power.*[1] What are you saying? they asked him. He replied: What I am saying is this: Blessed is the All-Merciful who has made the earthly royalty on the model of the heavenly, and has invested you with dominion, and made you lovers of justice. They said to him: Are you so solicitous for the honour of the Government? They handed him a staff[2] and said to him: You may act as judge. When he went out that man said to him: Does the All-Merciful perform miracles for liars? He replied: Wretch! Are they not called asses? For it is written: *Whose flesh is as the flesh of asses.*[3] He noticed that the man was about to inform them that he had called them asses. He said: This man is a persecutor, and the Torah has said: If a man comes to kill you, rise early and kill him first.[4] So he struck him with the staff and killed him. He then said: Since a miracle has been wrought for me through this verse, I will expound it. '*Thine, Oh Lord, is the greatness*': this refers to the work of creation; and so it says: *Who doeth great things past finding out.*[5] '*And the power*': this refers to the Exodus from Egypt, as it says: *And Israel saw the great work,* etc.[6] '*And the glory*': this refers to the sun and moon which stood still for Joshua, as it says: *And the sun stood still and the moon stayed.*[7] '*And the victory* [nezah]': this refers to the fall of Rome,[8] as it says: *And their life-blood* [nizham] *is dashed against my garments.*[9] '*And the majesty*': this refers to the battle of the valleys of Arnon, as it says, *Wherefore it is said in the book of the Wars of the Lord: Vaheb in Supah, and the valleys of Arnon.*[10] '*For all that is in heaven and earth*': this refers to the war of Sisera, as it says: *They fought from heaven, the stars in their courses fought against Sisera.*[11] '*Thine is the kingdom, O Lord*': this refers to the war against Amalek. For so it says: *The hand upon the throne of the Lord, the Lord will*
d *have war with Amalek from generation to generation.*[1] '*And Thou art exalted*': this refers to the war of Gog and Magog; and so it says: *Behold I am against thee, Oh Gog, chief prince of Meshech and Tubal.*[2] '*As head above all*': R. Hanan b. Raba said in the name of R. Johanan: Even a waterman[3] is appointed from heaven. It was taught in a Baraitha in the name of R. Akiba: '*Thine, oh Lord, is the greatness*': this refers to the cleaving of the Red Sea. '*And the power*': this refers to the smiting of the first-born. '*And the glory*': this refers to the giving of the Torah. '*And the victory*': this refers to Jerusalem. '*And the majesty*': this refers to the Temple.

תורה אור

*אמר רבי ירמיה בן אלעזר נתקללה בבל נתקללו שכניה נתקללה שומרון נתברכו שכניה נתקללה בבל נתקללו שכניה דכתיב °ושמתי' למורש קפוד ואגמי מים נתקללה שומרון נתברכו שכניה דכתיב °ושמתי שומרון לעי השדה למטעי כרם וגו': אמר רב המנונא *הרואה אוכלוסי ישראל אומר ברוך חכם הרזים אוכלוסי עכו"ם אומר °בושה אמכם וגו' ת"ר *הרואה אוכלוסי ישראל אומר ברוך חכם הרזים שאין דעתם דומה זה לזה ואין פרצופיהם דומים זה לזה בן זומא ראה אוכלוסא על גב מעלה בהר הבית אמר ברוך חכם הרזים *וברוך שברא כל אלו לשמשני הוא היה אומר כמה יגיעות יגע אדם הראשון עד שמצא פת לאכול חרש וזרע וקצר ועמר ודש וזרה וברר וטחן והרקיד ולש ואפה ואח"כ אכל ואני משכים ומוצא כל אלו מתוקנים לפני וכמה יגיעות יגע אדם הראשון עד שמצא בגד ללבוש גזז ולבן ונפץ וטוה וארג ואחר כך מצא בגד ללבוש ואני משכים ומוצא כל אלו מתוקנים לפני כל *אומות שוקדות ובאות לפתח ביתי ואני משכים ומוצא כל אלו לפני הוא היה אומר אורח טוב *מהו אומר כמה טרחות טרח בעל הבית בשבילי כמה בשר הביא לפני כמה יין הביא לפני כמה גלוסקאות הביא לפני וכל מה שטרח לא טרח אלא בשבילי אבל אורח רע מהו אומר מה טורח טרח בעל הבית זה פת אחת אכלתי חתיכה אחת אכלתי כוס אחד שתיתי כל טורח שטרח בעל הבית זה לא טרח אלא בשביל אשתו ובניו על אורח טוב מהו אומר °זכור כי תשגיא פעלו אשר שוררו אנשים על אורח רע כתיב °לכן יראוהו אנשים וגו': °והאיש בימי שאול זקן בא באנשים אמר *רבא ואיתימא רב זביד ואיתימא רב אושעיא זה ישי אבי דוד שיצא באוכלוסא ונכנס באוכלוסא ודרש באוכלוסא אמר עולא נקיטינן אין אוכלוסא בבבל תנא אין אוכלוסא פחותה משישים רבוא: ת"ר [a]הרואה חכמי ישראל אומר ברוך שחלק מחכמתו ליראיו [b]חכמי אומות העולם אומר ברוך שנתן מחכמתו לבריותיו [c]הרואה מלכי ישראל אומר ברוך שחלק מכבודו ליראיו מלכי א"ה אומר ברוך שנתן מכבודו לבריותיו א"ר יוחנן *[d]לעולם ישתדל אדם לרוץ לקראת מלכי ישראל ולא לקראת מלכי ישראל בלבד אלא אפילו לקראת מלכי א"ה שאם יזכה יבחין בין מלכי ישראל למלכי א"ה רב ששת סגי נהור הוה הוו קאזלי כולי עלמא לקבולי אפי מלכא וקם אזל בהדייהו רב ששת אשכחיה ההוא צדוקי א"ל חצבי לנהרא כגני לייא א"ל תא חזי דידענא טפי מינך חלף גונדא קמייתא כי קא אוושא א"ל ההוא צדוקי אתא מלכא א"ל רב ששת לא קאתי חלף גונדא תנינא כי קא אוושא א"ל ההוא צדוקי השתא קא אתי מלכא א"ל רב ששת לא קא אתי מלכא חלף תליתאי כי קא שתקא א"ל רב ששת ודאי השתא אתי מלכא א"ל ההוא צדוקי מנא לך הא א"ל דמלכותא דארעא כעין מלכותא דרקיעא דכתיב °צא ועמדת בהר לפני יי' והנה יי' עובר ורוח גדולה [וחזק] מפרק הרים ומשבר סלעים לפני יי' לא ברוח יי' ואחר הרוח רעש לא ברעש יי' ואחר הרעש אש לא באש יי' ואחר האש קול דממה דקה כי אתא מלכא פתח רב ששת וקא מברך ליה א"ל ההוא צדוקי למאן דלא חזית ליה קא מברכת ומאי הוי עליה דההוא צדוקי א"ד חברוהי כחלינהו לעיניה ואיכא דאמרי רב *ששת *נתן עיניו בו ונעשה גל של עצמות ר' שילא [3]נגדיה להדוא גברא דבעל מצרית אזל אכל ביה קורצי בי מלכא אמר איכא חד גברא ביהודאי דקא דיין דינא בלא הרמנא דמלכא שדר עליה פריסתקא כי אתא א"ל מ"ט נגדתיה להאי אמר להו דבא על חמרתא אמרי ליה אית לך סהדי אמר להו אין אתא אליהו אדמי ליה כאינש ואסהיד אמרי ליה אי הכי בר קטלא הוא אמר להו אנן מיומא דגלינן מארעין לית לן רשותא למקטל אתון מאי דבעיתון עבידו ביה עד דמעייני ביה בדינא פתח רבי שילא ואמר °לך יי' הגדולה והגבורה וגו' אמרי ליה מאי קאמרת אמר להו הכי קאמינא בריך רחמנא דיהב מלכותא בארעא כעין מלכותא דרקיעא ויהב לכו שולטנא ורחמי דינא אמרו חביבא עליה יקרא דמלכותא כולי האי יהבי ליה קולפא אמרו ליה דון דינא כי הוה נפיק א"ל ההוא גברא עביד רחמנא ניסא לשקרי הכי א"ל רשע לאו חמרי איקרו דכתיב °אשר בשר חמורי' בשרם חזייה דקאזיל למימר' להו דקרינהו חמרי אמ' האי רודף הוא *והתורה אמרה אם בא להרגך השכ' להרגו מחייה בקולפא וקטלי' אמר הואיל ואתעביד לי ניסא בהאי קרא דרשינא ליה לך יי' הגדולה זו מעשה בראשית וכן הוא אומר °עושה גדולות עד אין חקר והגבורה זו יציאת מצרים שנאמר °וירא ישראל את היד הגדולה וגו' והתפארת זו חמה ולבנה שעמדו לו ליהושע שנאמר °וידום השמש וירח עמד וגו' והנצח זו מפלתה של בבל וכן הוא אומר °ויז נצחם על בגדי וגו' וההוד זו מלחמת נחלי ארנון שנאמר °על כן יאמר בספר מלחמות יי' את והב בסופה וגו' כי כל בשמים ובארץ זו מלחמת סיסרא שנאמר °מן שמים נלחמו הככבים ממסילותם וגו' לך יי' הממלכה זו מלחמת עמלק וכן הוא אומר °כי יד על כס יה והמתנשא זו מלחמת גוג ומגוג וכן הוא אומר °הנני אליך גוג נשיא ראש משך ותובל לכל לראש אמר *רב חנן בר רבא א"ר יוחנן אפילו ריש גרגיתא מן שמיא מנו ליה במתניתא תנא משמיה דרבי עקיבא לך יי' הגדולה זו קריעת ים סוף והגבורה זו מכת בכורות והתפארת זו מתן תורה והנצח זו ירושלים וההוד זו בית המקדש:

תנו

נתקללה בבל נתקללו שכניה. כלומר אוי לרשע אוי לשכינו: קאת וקפוד. חיות ועופות רעים ומזיקין את השכנים אבל ע' השדה ומטעי כרם שנתקללו בה ערי ישראל הנאה היא לשכנים: אוכלסי. חיל גדול של ששים רבוא: חכם הרזים. היודע מה שבלב כל אלו: לשמשני. שהם חורשים וזורעים ואני מוצא מוכן: כל אומו' שוקדות ובאות לפתחי. עשיר היה והכל באין אצלו לסחורה: שאם יזכה. לעולם הבא ויראה בכבוד מלך המשיח: יבחין. כמה יתר כבוד מלכי ישראל יותר ממה שהיה כבוד האומות בעולם הזה: הצבי לנהרא. הכדים השלמים הולכים לנהר לשאוב מים: כגני לייא. השבורי' להיכן כלו' למה הולכים ואף אתה שאתה סומא ולא תראהו להיכן תלך: גונדא. כת: ורחמי דינא. אוהבי' משפט: *כחלינהו לעיניה. נקרו לעיניו: קולפא. מקל לרדות: התורה אמרה אם בא להרגך השכם להרגו. אם במחתרת וגו' (שמות כב) לפי שבא על עסקי נפשות שיודע הוא שאם ימצא ותעמדנו חותר לא תעמיד עצמך מלהציל ממונך והוא בא לדעת כן שיקום עליך ויהרגך אמרה תורה השכם אתה והרגהו: הממלכה זו מלחמת עמלק. דכתיב בה כסא מלכות כי יד על כס יה (שמות יז) כלומר על ידי מלחמה ליי' בעמלק יתעלה כסאו: המתנשא. מדכתיב לשון נשיאות משמע על נשיא ראש משך ותובל: לכל לראש. לכל הקם להיות לראש הוא מתנשא כלומר שהוא גוזר ומעמידו: ריש גרגיתא. גזר הממונה על החופרין חפירות למלאותן מים כדי להשקות בהן שדותיהן:

ברוך

[עיין לעיל קודס ד"ה ורחמי דינא]

כה א מיי' פ"י מהלכות ברכות הלכה יא סמג עשין כז טוש"ע א"ח סימן רכד סעיף ה

כו ב מיי' שם טוש"ע א"ח שם סעי' ו

כז ג מיי' שם טוש"ע א"ח שם סעי' ז

כח ד מיי' שם טוש"ע א"ח שם סעי' ח

כט ה מיי' פ"ג מהל' אבל הל' יד טוש"ע א"ח שם סעי' ט

ל ו מיי' פ"ג מה' אסורי ביאה הלכה א סמג לאוין קיב טוש"ע א"ה סימן כא סעיף א

[גי' הערוך א"ד מלתא א' רב ששת ונפקו בזעיא דנורא וכבינהו לעיני' ערך בזע]

[ב"ב לה: ושם אי' א"ר חנן ב"ר אמ' ר' וכו' והת' מייתי ליה בהדי' אחר מימרות שאמר בשם רב ע"ש]

מסורת הש"ס

עירובין יח: ישעי' יד מיכה א ירמי' נ [תוספתא פ"ו] [בירוש' ליתא בדברי ב"ז רק ברוך שברא וכו'] נ"ל אומניות [ע' תו' ב"מ כב: ד"ה באושפיזא] איוב לו שם לג שמואל א יז [יבמות עו: ע"ש] [לעיל ט: יט:] מלכים א יט שבת לד. [ב"ב עה. סנה' ק.] ד"ה א כט יחזקאל כג [לקמן סב: סנהדרין עב.] איוב ט שמות יד יהושע י ישעיה סג במדבר כא שופטים ה שמות יז יחזקאל לח

(3) Ibid. The whole neighbourhood of Babylon became desolate. (4) Micah I, 6. (5) Lit., 'wise in secrets'. Viz., the secrets of each one's heart. (6) Jer. L, 12.

a (1) So Marginal Gloss. Cur. edd. 'peoples'. (2) Job XXXVI, 24. (3) Ibid. XXXVII, 24. (4) I Sam. XVII, 12. (5) Of Israelites assembled to hear the Torah.

b (1) Of the Messianic age. (2) MS.M. *min* (v. Glos.). (3) As much as to say: What is the use of a blind man going to see the king. (4) I Kings XIX, 11f. (5) Var. lec. Gentile.

c (1) I Chron. XXIX, 11. (2) Or perhaps, 'strap' (*J.T.*). (3) Ezek. XXIII, 20. (4) This lesson is derived by the Rabbis from Ex. XXII, 1 which declares it legitimate to kill a burglar who is prepared to commit murder. (5) Job. IX, 10. (6) Ex. XIV, 31. (7) Josh. X, 13. (8) MS.M.: The wicked kingdom. (9) Isa. LXIII, 3. (10) Num. XXI, 14. (11) Judg. V, 20.

d (1) Ex. XVII, 16. (2) Ezek. XXXVIII, 3. (3) A man who looked after the well from which fields were irrigated—quite a menial office.

ת"ר *הרואה בתי ישראל בישובן אומר ברוך מציב גבול אלמנה בחורבנן אומר ברוך דיין האמת ²בתי עכו"ם בישובן אומר °בית גאים יסח ה' בחורבנן אומר °אל נקמות ה' אל נקמות הופיע: עולא ורב חסדא הוו קא אזלי באורחא כי מטו אפתחא דבי רב חנא בר חנילאי נגד רב חסדא ואתנח אמר ליה עולא אמאי קא מתנחת *והאמר רב אנחה שוברת חצי גופו של אדם שנאמר °ואתה בן אדם האנח בשברון מתנים וגו' ור' יוחנן אמר אף כל גופו של אדם שנאמר °והיה כי יאמרו אליך על מה אתה נאנח ואמרת אל שמועה [כי באה] ונמס כל לב וגו' א"ל היכי לא אתנח ביתא דהוו בה שיתין אפיתא ביממא ושיתין אפייתא בליליא ואפיין לכל מאן דצריך ולא שקל ידא מן כיסא דסבר דילמא אתי עני בר טובים ואדמטו ליה לכיסא קא מכסיף ותו הוו פתיחין ליה ארבע בבי לארבע רוחתא דעלמא וכל דהוה עייל כפין נפיק כי שבע והוו שדו ליה חטי ושערי בשני בצורת אבראי דכל מאן דכסיפא מלתא למשקל ביממא אתי ושקיל בליליא השתא נפל בתלא ולא אתנח אמר ליה הכי א"ר יוחנן מיום שחרב ב"ה נגזרה גזירה על בתיהן של צדיקים שיחרבו שנאמר °באזני יי' צבאות אם לא בתים רבים לשמה יהיו גדולים וטובים מאין יושב ואמר רבי יוחנן עתיד הקב"ה להחזירן לישובן שנא' °שיר המעלות לדוד הבוטחים ביי' כהר ציון מה הר ציון עתיד הקב"ה להחזירו לישובו אף בתיהן של צדיקים עתיד הקב"ה להחזירן לישובן חזייה דלא מיישב' דעתי' א"ל דיו לעבד שיהא כרבו: ת"ר ⁷הרואה קברי ישראל אומר ברוך אשר יצר אתכם בדין וזן אתכם בדין וכלכל אתכם בדין ואסף אתכם בדין ועתיד להקימכם בדין מר ברי' דרבינא מסיים בה משמיה דרב נחמן ויודע מספר כולכם והוא עתיד להחיותכם ולקיים אתכם ברוך מחיה המתים: קברי עכו"ם אומר °בושה אמכם וגו': אמר ריב"ל ⁷הרואה את חבירו לאחר שלשים יום אומר ברוך שהחיינו וקיימנו והגיענו לזמן הזה לאחר י"ב חדש אומר ברוך מחיה המתים אמר רב *אין המת משתכח מן הלב אלא לאחר שנים עשר חדש שנא' °נשכחתי כמת מלב הייתי ככלי אובד רב פפא ורב הונא בריה דרב יהושע הוי קאזלי באורחא פגעו בי' ברב חנינא בריה דרב איקא אמרו ליה בהדי דחזינך בריכינן עלך תרתי ברוך אשר חלק מחכמתו ליריאיו ושהחיינו אמר להו אנא נמי כיון דחזיתינכו חשבתינכו עלואי כשיתין רבוון בית ישראל וברכינא עלייכו תלתא הנך תרתי וברוך חכם הרזים אמרו ליה חכימת כולי האי *יהבי ביה עיניהו ושכיב אמר ריב"ל הרואה את הבהקני' אומר ברוך משנה הבריות מיתיבי *ᵃראה את הכושי ואת הגיחור ואת הלווקן ואת הקפח ואת הננס *ואת הדרניקום אומר ברוך משנה את הבריות ᵇאת הקטע ואת הסומא ואת פתויי *הראש ואת החגר ואת המוכה שחין ואת הבהקנים אומר ברוך דיין אמת ל"ק הא ממעי אמו הא בתר דאתיליד דיקא נמי דקתני דומיא דקטע שמע מינה: ת"ר ᶜהרואה פיל קוף וקפוף אומר ברוך משנה את הבריות ראה *ᵈבריות טובות ואילנות טובות אומר *ברוך שככה לו בעולמו: על הזיקין: ᵉמאי זיקין אמר שמואל *כוכבא דשביט ואמר שמואל נהירין לי שבילי דשמיא כשבילי דנהרדעא לבר מכוכבא דשביט דלא ידענא מאי ניהו וגמירי דלא עבר כסלא ואי עבר כסלא חרב עלמא והא קא חזינן דעבר זויה הוא דעבר ומתחזי כדעבר איהו רב הונא בריה דרב יהושע אמר וילון הוא דמקרע *דמגלגל ומחזי נהורא דרקיעא רב אשי אמר כוכבא הוא דעקר מהאי גיסא דכסלא וחזי ליה חברי' מהך גיסא ומבעית ומחזי כמאן דעבר שמואל רמי כתיב °עושה עש כסיל וכימה וכתיב °עושה כימה וכסיל הא כיצד אלמלא חמה של כסיל לא נתקיים עולם מפני צנה של כימה ואלמלא צנה של כימה לא נתקיים עולם מפני חמה של כסיל וגמירי אי לאו עוקצא דעקרבא דמנח בנהר דינור כל מאן דהוה טריקא ליה עקרבא לא הוה חיי והיינו דקאמר ליה רחמנא לאיוב °התקשר מעדנות כימה ומושכות כסיל תפתח מאי כימה אמר שמואל כמאה כוכבי אמרי לה דמכנפי ואמרי לה *דמבדרן מאי עש אמר רב יהודה יותא מאי יותא אמרי לה זנב טלה ואמרי לה רישא דעגלא ומסתברא כמאן דאמר זנב טלה דכתיב °ועיש על בניה תנחם אלמא חסרה ומתחזיא

כטרפא

תוספות

הרואה חברו אחר שלשים יום אומר שהחיינו. אומר ר"י דוקא חברו החביב עליו אבל בענין אחר לא:

וילון הוא דמקרע ומחזי כהורא ברקיעא. לפי הענין משמע דגם רב הונא לתרץ דלא עבר כסלא ולא קאי אמתניתין לפרושי מאי זיקין דהא רב אשי דבתריה קאי אשמואל דלא עבר כסלא ודלא כפירוש רש"י:

רש"י

ברוך מציב גבול אלמנה. כגון בישוב בית שני: אמאי. קא מתנחת: נפל ליה בתלא. שנפל לו ונעשה תל: דיו לעבד שיהא כרבו. שהרי בית המקדש חרב שהוא ביתו של הקב"ה: ככלי אובד. והתם כלי לאחר י"ב חדש משתכח מן הלב דיאוש בעלים לאחר י"ב חדש בפרק אלו מציאות (דף כח.) מי שמצא כלי או שום מציאה חייב להכריז שלש רגלים ואם מצאה אחר הסכות צריך להמתין ולהכריז בפסח ובעצרת ובחג דהיינו י"ב חדש ושוב אין צריך להכריז: אשר חלק ושהחיינו. דלאחר שלשים יום הוה: מחכמתו ליראיו. ברב חנינא דחכים טפי: בהקנים. ליכטיי"ליום בעדשים: כושי. שחור הרבה: *גיחור. אדום הרבה רו"ש בלע"ז: לווקן. לבן יותר מדאי: קפח. בטן גדול מתוך עוביו נראית קומתו מקופחת לשון אחר קפח ארוך הרבה ופרצופו משונה ובולטו דמכוער *הוי: דרניקום. רוד"אם לשון אחר פיו עקום: פתויי ראש. ששערו כנמלא כל שערו דבוק זה בזה פלטר"דיר בלע"ז: אומר ברוך משנה את הבריות. דממעי אמן הוו: קטע. שנקטעו ידיו הכא הוא דקטע משמע דידים הוא משום דקתני תרתי קטע וחגר אבל היכא דקתני קטע לחוד משמע דרגלים כדתנן (שבת פ"ו דף סה:) הקטע יוצא בקב שלו: היכא דאיתרע ליה בתר דאיתיליד. לאחר שנולד נולדו בו: אומר ברוך דיין האמת. דומיא דקטע וקטע בתר דאתיליד הוא: קפוף. עוף שקורין ולטי"ר ויש לו לסתות ולחיים כאדם: כוכבא דשביט. כוכב היורה כחץ ברקים ממקום למקום ואורך כשבט שהוא' יורה ונראה כמי שפותח רקיע: וגמירי דלא עבר כסלא. שאינו מעביר מזל כסיל כשהוא שביט: כסלא. כסיל: רב הונא אמר. מאי זיקין וילון הוא דמקרע ומתחזי רקיע דרך הקריעה כרומח: כתיב עושה עש כסיל וכימה. דקדמיה ליה כסיל לכימה: הא כיצד. מלמד ששניהם שוין: שאלמלא חמה של כסיל וכו'. כסיל שולט בימות החמה להכי אקדמיה קרא כימה שולט בימות הגשמים ולהכי אקדמיה קרא: מעדנות כימה. קשרים של כימה: עקרב היינו כימה ומזל טלה הוא: עוקצא דעקרבא. זנב העקרב: נהר דינור. מתשת כחו של עקרב: כמאה כוכבי. יש בין הככבים של כימה שהן כחה של כימה: אמרי לה דמכנפי. אותן שהן כחה של כימה ואמרי לה דמבדרן: יותא אמרי לה. דקיימא בזנב טלה ואמרי לה דקיימ' בריש עגלה: רישא דעגל'. ראשו של עגל והיינו מזל שור והוא כמשך אחר מזל טלה ראש השו' סמוך לזנב טלה שכן הסדר טלה שור תאומים: ומסתברא כמאן דאמר זנב. היינו ככבים העשוין כזנב ומדכתיב ועיש על בניה תנחם: אלמא חסרא. והאי זנב מחזי כטרפא דטריף:

כטרפא

עין משפט נר מצוה

לא
ᵃמיי' פ"י מהלכות ברכות הלכה יח סמג עשין כז טוש"ע א"ח סימן רכד סעי' יח

לב
ᵇמיי' שם הל' יט טוש"ע א"ח שם סעיף יא [כתובו' סב.]

לג
ᶜמיי' שם טוש"ע א"ח שם סעי' יב

לד
ᵈמיי' פרק י מהלכות ברכות הלכה ג סמג עשין כז טוש"ע א"ח סימן רכה סעיף א

לה
ᵉמיי' שם הל' יב טוש"ע א"ח שם סעיף ח

לו
ᶠמיי' שם טוש"ע א"ח שם סעי' ט

לז
ᶻמיי' שם טוש"ע א"ח שם סעיף ח

לח
ʰמיי' שם הל' יג טוש"ע א"ח שם סעיף י

לט
ᵗמיי' שם הל' יד וסמג שם טוש"ע א"ח סי' רכו סעי' א

[ב"ב יד.]

[גי' הערוך בדרניקוס פירש גמון שהוא איש שקומתו ארוכה יותר משאר בני אדם]

[ע' ערוך ערך ככב וע' זק מה שפי' בשם רב האי גאון]

[מלת דמגלגל ליתא ברש"י ולא בתוס' וכן בע"י ליתא ולכן בערוך ערך ויל גרס וילון הוא דמתגלגל ומתחזי כהורא דרקיע]

תורה אור

משלי טו; תהלי' צד; יחזקאל כא; שם; ישעי' ה; תהלי' קכה; ירמי' נ; תהלי' לא; איוב ט; עמוס ה; איוב לח; שם

מסורת הש"ס

[ע' רש"י לעיל לא: ד"ה גיחור]

[וע' בכורו' מה: קפח וכו' והיינו להדי' כלשון אחר ול"ע על הפי' הראשון וכן תמה המג"א בסי' קכ"ה והניח בצ"ע אכן לגירס' הערוך בבכורו' כיפח' בכ"ף כים']

[מ"ק ח: ע"ש]

[תוספת' פ"ו]

[פי' מי שאין ראשו סגולגל' אלא רחבה ערוך ערך פתי]

[ע"ז ד. ע"ש]

[נוסחת ירוש' ברוך שכך ברא בריות נאות בעולמו וכדומה בע"ז (כ.)]

[58b] Our Rabbis taught: On seeing the houses of Israel, when inhabited one says: Blessed be He who sets the boundary of the widow;[4] when uninhabited, Blessed be the judge of truth. On seeing the houses of heathens, when inhabited, one says: *The Lord will pluck up the house of the proud;*[5] when uninhabited he says: *O Lord, thou God, to whom vengeance belongeth, thou God, to whom vengeance belongeth, shine forth.*[6]

Once when 'Ulla and R. Ḥisda were walking along the road, they came to the door of the house of R. Ḥana b. Ḥanilai. R. Ḥisda broke down and sighed. Said 'Ulla to him: Why are you sighing, seeing that Rab has said that a sigh breaks half a man's body, since it says, *Sigh therefore thou son of man, with the breaking of thy loins,*[7] etc.; and R. Joḥanan said that it breaks even the whole of a man's body, as it says: *And it shall be, when they say unto thee, wherefore sighest thou? Thou shalt say: Because of the tidings for it cometh; and every heart shall melt,* etc.?[8]—He replied: How shall I refrain from sighing on seeing the house in which there used to be sixty[9] cooks by day and sixty cooks by night, who cooked for every one who was in need. Nor did he [R. Ḥana] ever take his hand away from his purse, thinking that perhaps a respectable poor man might come, and while he was getting his purse he would be put to shame. Moreover it had four doors, opening on different sides, and whoever went in hungry went out full. They used also to throw wheat and barley outside in years of scarcity, so that anyone who was ashamed to take by day used to come and take by night. Now it has fallen in ruins, and shall I not sigh?—He replied to him: Thus said R. Joḥanan: Since the day when the Temple was destroyed, a decree has been issued against the houses of the righteous that they should become desolate, as it says: *In mine ears, said the Lord of hosts: Of a truth many houses shall be*
a *desolate, even great and fair, without inhabitants.*[1] R. Joḥanan further said: The Holy One, blessed be He, will one day restore them to their inhabited state, as it says: *A Song of Ascents. They that trust in the Lord are as Mount Zion.*[2] Just as the Holy One, blessed be He, will restore Mount Zion to its inhabited state, so will He restore the houses of the righteous to their inhabited state. Observing that he was still not satisfied, he said to him: Enough for the servant that he should be like his master.[3]

Our Rabbis taught: On seeing Israelitish graves, one should say: Blessed is He who fashioned you in judgment, who fed you in judgment and maintained you in judgment, and in judgment gathered you in, and who will one day raise you up again in judgment. Mar, the son of Rabina, concluded thus in the name of R. Naḥman: And who knows the number of all of you; and He will one day revive you and establish you. Blessed is He who revives the dead.[4] On seeing the graves of heathens one says: *Your mother shall be sore ashamed,* etc.

R. Joshua b. Levi said: One who sees a friend after a lapse of thirty days says: Blessed is He who has kept us alive and preserved us and brought us to this season. If after a lapse of twelve months he says: Blessed is He who revives the dead. Rab said: The dead is not forgotten till after twelve months, as it says: *I am forgotten as a dead man out of mind; I am like a lost vessel.*[5] R. Papa and R. Huna the son of R. Joshua were once going along the road when they met R. Ḥanina, the son of R. Iḳa. They said to him: Now that we see you we make two blessings over you: 'Blessed be He who has imparted of His wisdom to them that fear Him', and 'That has kept us alive etc.'. He said to them: I, also, on seeing you counted it as equal to seeing sixty myriads of Israel, and I made three blessings over you, those two, and 'Blessed is He that discerneth secrets'. They said to him: Are you so clever as all
b that? They cast their eyes on him and he died.[1]

R. Joshua b. Levi said: On seeing pock-marked persons one says: Blessed be He who makes strange creatures. An objection was raised: If one sees a negro, a very red or very white person, a hunchback, a dwarf or a dropsical person, he says: Blessed be He who makes strange creatures. If he sees one with an amputated limb, or blind, or flatheaded, or lame, or smitten with boils, or pock-marked, he says: Blessed be the true Judge!—There is no contradiction; one blessing is said if he is so from birth, the other if he became so afterwards. A proof of this is that he is placed in the same category as one with an amputated limb; this proves it.

Our Rabbis taught: On seeing an elephant, an ape, or a long-tailed ape, one says: Blessed is He who makes strange creatures. If one sees beautiful creatures and beautiful trees, he says: Blessed is He who has such in His world.

OVER SHOOTING-STARS [ZIḲIN]. What are ZIḲIN? Samuel said: A comet.[2] Samuel also said: I am as familiar with the paths of heaven as with the streets of Nehardea, with the exception of the comet, about which I am ignorant. There is a tradition that it never passes through the constellation of Orion, for if it did, the world would be destroyed. But we have seen it pass through?—Its brightness passed through, which made it appear as if it passed through itself. R. Huna the son of R. Joshua said: Wilon[3] was
c torn asunder and rolled up,[1] showing the brightness of Rakia.[2] R. Ashi said: A star was removed from one side of Orion and a companion star appeared on the other side, and people were bewildered and thought the star had crossed over.[3]

Samuel contrasted two texts. It is written, *Who maketh the Bear, Orion, and the Pleiades.*[4] And it is written elsewhere, *That maketh Pleiades and Orion.*[5] How do we reconcile these? Were it not for the heat of Orion the world could not endure the cold of Pleiades; and were it not for the cold of Pleiades the world could not endure the heat of Orion. There is a tradition that were it not that the tail of the Scorpion has been placed in the Stream of Fire,[6] no one who has ever been stung by a scorpion could live. This is what is referred to in the words of the All-Merciful to Job: *Canst thou bind the chains of Pleiades or loose the bands of Orion?*[7]

What is meant by *Kimah* [Pleiades]?[4] Samuel said: About a hundred [*ke'me-ah*] stars. Some say they are close together; others say that they are scattered. What is meant by "*Ash* [the Bear]'?[4]—Rab Judah said: *Jutha*. What is *Jutha?*—Some say it is the tail of the Ram; others say it is the hand of the Calf.[8] The one who says it is the tail of the Ram is more probably right, since it says: '*Ayish will be comforted for her children.*[9] This shows that it lacks

(4) *Sc.*, Jerusalem. (5) Prov. XV, 25. (6) Ps. XCIV, 1. (7) Ezek. XXI, 11. (8) Ibid. 12. (9) I.e., a great many.

a (1) Isa. V, 9. (2) Ps. CXXV, 1. (3) I.e., that R. Ḥana's house should be like the house of God. (4) V. *P.B.* p. 319. (5) Ps. XXXI, 13. A thing is not given up as lost till after twelve months.

b (1) Apparently they thought he was sarcastic. (2) *Kokeba di-Shabi* Lit., 'Star that draws'. What exactly is meant is a matter of dispute. Rashi explains as 'shooting-stars'. (3) The lowest of the seven firmaments, which is a kind of 'Veil' to the others.

c (1) Rashi and Tosaf. omit 'and rolled up'. (2) Lit., 'firmament'. The next of the seven firmaments. (3) I.e., mere error of perspective, v. on the passage Brodetsky, *Jewish Review* July, 1909, p. 167 ff. (4) Job IX, 9. (5) Amos V, 8. The order is here reversed. (6) Mentioned in Dan. VII, 10, denoting probably the Milky Way. (7) Job. XXXVIII, 31. (8) This constellation follows that of the Ram. (9) Ibid. 32. E.V. *'or canst thou guide the Bear with her sons'*.

something, [59a] and in fact it looks like a piece torn off;[10] and the reason why she follows her is because she is saying to her: Give me my children. For at the time when the Holy One, blessed be He, wanted to bring a flood upon the world, He took two stars from *Kimah* and brought a flood upon the world. And when He wanted to stop it, He took two stars from *'Ayish* and stopped it. But why did He not put the other two back?—A pit cannot be filled with its own clods;[11] or another reason is, the accuser cannot become advocate. Then He should have created two other stars
a for it?—*There is nothing new under the sun.*[1] R. Naḥman said: The Holy one, blessed be He, will one day restore them to her, as it says: *and 'Ayish will be comforted for her children.*[2]

AND OVER EARTHQUAKES [ZEWA'OTH]. What are ZEWA'OTH? R. Kaṭṭina said: A rumbling of the earth. R. Kaṭṭina was once going along the road, and when he came to the door of the house of a certain necromancer, there was a rumbling of the earth. He said: Does the necromancer know what this rumbling is? He called after him, Kaṭṭina, Kaṭṭina, why should I not know? When the Holy One, blessed be He, calls to mind His children, who are plunged in suffering among the nations of the world, He lets fall two tears into the ocean, and the sound is heard from one end of the world to the other, and that is the rumbling. Said R. Kaṭṭina: The necromancer is a liar and his words are false. If it was as he says, there should be one rumbling after another! He did not really mean this, however. There really was one rumbling after another, and the reason why he did not admit it was so that people should not go astray after him. R. Kaṭṭina, for his own part, said: [God] clasps His hands, as it says: *I will also smite my hands together, and I will satisfy my fury.*[3] R. Nathan said: [God] emits a sigh, as it is said: *I will satisfy my fury upon them and I will be eased.*[4] And the Rabbis said: He treads upon the firmament, as it says: *He giveth a noise as they that tread grapes against all the inhabitants of the earth.*[5] R. Aḥa b. Jacob says: He presses his feet together beneath the throne of glory, as it says: *Thus saith the Lord, the heaven is my throne and the earth is my foot-stool.*[6]

AND OVER THUNDERS [RE'AMIM]. What are RE'AMIM?—Clouds in a whirl, as it says: *The voice of Thy thunder was in the whirlwind; the lightning lighted up the world, the earth trembled and shook.*[7] The Rabbis, however, say: The clouds pouring water into one another, as it says: *At the sound of His giving a multitude of waters in the heavens.*[8] R. Aḥa b. Jacob said: A powerful lightning flash that strikes the clouds and breaks off hailstones. R. Ashi said: The clouds are puffed out and a blast of wind comes and blows across the mouth of them and it makes a sound like wind blowing across the mouth of a jar. The most probable view is that of R. Aḥa b. Jacob; for the lightning flashes and the clouds rumble and then rain falls.

AND OVER STORMS [RUḤOTH]. What are RUḤOTH?—Abaye said: A hurricane. Abaye further said: We have a tradition that a hurricane never comes at night. But we see that it does come?—It must have commenced by day. Abaye further said: We have a tradition that a hurricane does not last two hours, to fulfil the words of Scripture, *Troubles shall not rise up the second*
b *time.*[1] But we have seen it lasting as long?—There was an interval in the middle.

OVER LIGHTNINGS [BERAḲIM] ONE SAYS, BLESSED IS HE WHOSE STRENGTH AND MIGHT FILL THE WORLD. What are BERAḲIM? Raba said: Lightning. Rab also said: A single flash, white lightning, blue lightning, clouds that rise in the west and come from the south, and two clouds that rise facing one another are all [signs of] trouble. What is the practical bearing of this remark? That prayer is needed [to avert the omen]. This is only the case by night; but in the daytime there is no significance in them. R. Samuel b. Isaac said: Those morning clouds have no significance,[2] as it is said: *Your goodness is as a morning cloud.*[3] Said R. Papa to Abaye: But there is a popular saying: When on opening the door you find rain, ass-driver, put down your sack and go to sleep [on it]?[4]—There is no contradiction; in the one case the sky is covered with thick clouds, in the other with light clouds.

R. Alexandri said in the name of R. Joshua b. Levi: Thunder was created only to straighten out the crookedness of the heart, as it says: *God hath so made it that men should fear before him.*[5] R. Alexandri also said in the name of R. Joshua b. Levi: One who sees the rainbow in the clouds should fall on his face, as it says, *As the appearance of the bow that is in the cloud, and when I saw it I fell*
c *upon my face.*[1] In the West [Palestine] they cursed anyone who did this, because it looks as if he was bowing down to the rainbow; but he certainly makes a blessing. What blessing does he say?—'Blessed is He who remembers the Covenant'. In a Baraitha it was taught: R. Ishmael the son of R. Joḥanan b. Beroḳa says: He says: Who is faithful with his Covenant and fulfils his word.

FOR MOUNTAINS AND HILLS, etc. Do all the things we have mentioned hitherto not belong to the work of creation? Is it not written, *He maketh lightnings for the rain?*[2]—Abaye said: Combine the two statements.[3] Raba said: In the former cases he says two blessings, 'Blessed be He whose strength fills the world and who has wrought the work of creation'; in this case there is ground for saying 'Who has wrought creation' but not for 'Whose strength fills the world'.[4]

R. Joshua b. Levi said: If one sees the sky in all its purity, he says: Blessed is He who has wrought the work of creation. When does he say so?—Abaye said: When there has been rain all the night, and in the morning the north wind comes and clears the heavens. And they differ from Rafram b. Papa quoting R. Ḥisda. For Rafram b. Papa said in the name of R. Ḥisda: Since the day when the Temple was destroyed there has never been a perfectly

(10) And then stuck on artificially. (11) V. *supra*, 3b, n. c1.
(1) Eccl. I, 9. (2) Job. XXXVIII, 32. E.V. *'or canst thou guide the Bear with her sons'*. (3) Ezek. XXI, 22. (4) Ibid. V, 13. (5) Jer. XXV, 30. (6) Isa. LXVI, 1. (7) Ps. LXXVII, 19. (8) Jer. X, 13.

b (1) Nahum I, 9. (2) I.e., do not portend a good fall of rain. (3) Hosea VI, 4. (4) Because corn will be cheap on account of the abundant rain. (5) Eccl. III, 14.
c (1) Ezek. I, 28. (2) Ps. CXXXV, 7. (3) I.e., say in all cases the double blessing. (4) Because the mountains are not all in one place.

כטרפא דטריף והאי דאזלא בתרה דאמרה
לה הב לי בני שבשעה שהקב"ה בקש להביא
מבול לעולם נטל שני כוכבים מכימה והביא
מבול לעולם וכשבקש לסתמה נטל שני
כוכבים מעיש וסתמה ולידהדר לה *אין הבור
מתמלא מחוליתו א"נ *אין קטיגור נעשה
סניגור וליברי לה תרי ככבי אחריני °אין כל
חדש תחת השמש אמר רב נחמן עתיד
הקב"ה להחזירן לה שנ' °ועיש על בניה תנחם:
ועל הזועות: [א]מאי זועות אמר רב קטינא גוהא רב קטינא הוה קאזיל באורחא
כי מטא אפתחא דבי אובא טמיא גנח גוהא אמר מי ידע אובא טמיא האי
גוהא מהו רמא ליה קלא קטינא קטינא אמאי לא ידענא בשעה שהקב"ה
זוכר את בניו ששרויים בצער בין אומות העולם מוריד שתי דמעות לים הגדול
וקולם נשמע מסוף העולם ועד סופו והיינו גוהא אמר רב קטינא אובא טמיא
כדיב הוא ומיליה כדיבין אי הכי גוהא גוהא מיבעי ליה ולא היא גוהא גוהא
עביד והאי דלא אודי ליה כי היכי דלא ליטעו כולי עלמא אבתריה ורב
קטינא דידיה אמר סופק כפיו שנאמר °גם אני אכה כפי אל כפי והניחותי
חמתי רבי נתן אומר אנחה מתאנח שנאמר °והניחותי חמתי בם והנחמתי
ורבנן אמרי בועט ברקיע שנאמר °הידד כדרכים יענה אל כל יושבי הארץ
רב אחא בר יעקב אמר דוחק את רגליו תחת כסא הכבוד שנאמר °כה אמר
ה' השמים כסאי והארץ הדום רגלי: ועל הרעמים: [ב]מאי רעמים אמר שמואל
ענני בגלגלא שנאמר °קול רעמך בגלגל האירו ברקים תבל רגזה ותרעש
הארץ ורבנן אמרי ענני דשפכי מיא להדדי שנאמר °לקול תתו המון מים
בשמים רב אחא בר יעקב אמר ברקא תקיפא דבריק בעננא ומתבר גזיזי
דברזא רב אשי אמר ענני *חלחולי מחלחלי ואתי זיקא ומנשב אפומייהו
ודמי כזיקא על פום דני ומסתברא כרב אחא בר יעקב דבריק ברקא ומנהמי
ענני ואתי מטרא: ועל הרוחות: [ג]מאי רוחות אמר אביי זעפא ואמר אביי גמירי
דזעפא בליליא לא הוי והא קא חזינן דהוי ההוא דאתחולי בימָמא ואמר
אביי גמירי דזעפא תרתי שעי לא קאי לקיים מה שנאמר °לא תקום פעמים
צרה והא קא חזינן דקאי דמפסיק ביני ביני: ועל הברקים אומר ברוך שכחו
וגבורתו מלא עולם: [ד]מאי ברקים אמר רבא ברקא ואמר רבא ברקא יחידאה
וברקא חיורא וברקא ירוקתא וענני דסלקן בקרן מערבית ואתיין מקרן דרומית
ותרתי ענני דסלקן חדא לאפי חברתה כולהו קשיין למאי נפקא מינה למבעי
רחמי והני מילי בליליא אבל בצפרא לית בהו מששא *אמר רב שמואל בר
יצחק הני ענני דצפרא לית בהו מששא דכתיב °וחסדכם כענן בקר וגומר
א"ל רב פפא לאביי הא אמרי אינשי כד מפתח בבי מטרא בר חמרא מוך
שקיך וגני ל"ק הא דקטר בעיבא הא דקטר בעננא א"ר אלכסנדרי אמר ריב"ל
לא נבראו רעמים אלא לפשוט עקמומית שבלב שנ' °והאלהים עשה שייראו
מלפניו וא"ר אלכסנדרי אמר ריב"ל הרואה את הקשת בענן צריך שיפול על
פניו שנ' °כמראה הקשת אשר יהיה בענן וגו' ואראה ואפול על פני *לייטי
עלה במערבא משום דמחזי כמאן דסגיד לקשת' אבל ברוכי ודאי מברך מאי
מברך ברוך זוכר הברית במתניתא תנא ר' ישמעאל בנו של רבי יוחנן בן
ברוקא אומר נאמן בבריתו וקיים במאמרו *אמר רב פפא הלכך נימרינהו
לתרוייהו [ה]ברוך זוכר הברית ונאמן בבריתו וקיים במאמרו: על ההרים ועל
הגבעות: אטו כל הני דאמרן עד השתא לאו מעשה בראשית נינהו והכתיב
°ברקים למטר עשה אמר אביי כרוך ותני רבא אמר [ו]התם מברך תרתי ברוך
שכחו מלא עולם ועושה מעשה בראשית הכא עושה מעשה בראשית איכא
שכחו מלא עולם ליכא אריב"ל הרואה רקיע בטהרתה אומר ברוך עושה
*בראשית אימתי אמר אביי כי אתא מטרא כולי ליליא ובצפרא אתא אסתנא
ומגלי' להו לשמים ופליגי דרפרם בר פפא אמר רב חסדא דאמר רפרם בר
פפא אמר רב חסדא מיום שחרב ב"ה לא נראית רקיע בטהרתה שנאמר
°אלביש שמים קדרות ושק אשים כסותם: ת"ר

בתקופתה

רש"י

כטרפא דטריף. דבר שהוא חסר וסתמוהו מגופו שעשאוהו כנוס
ומתחזי כמכה בקורקס טרפא דטריף מוכה בהכאות כמו בילה
*טרופה ל"א דמתחזיא כדטרפא מטרף כדבק יחד ועשאו קניפין
כמין חיבור: והאי דאזלא. עיש אחר כימה: דאמרה לה הב לי
בני. שני ככבים שלי: ולידהדר. לכימה אותן ככבים עצמן שנטל
הימנה: זוהא. בלשונם קורין רעידת
הארץ גוהא: אובא טמיא. בעל
אוב של עצמות שעושה כשוף בעצמו'
המת. טמיא עצמות. ודומה לו
במסכת כלים בית מלא טמיא ופי'
רב האי מלא טמיא בית שהוא
מלא עצמות והביא ראיה מברייתא'
רבה דקתני אדיכום שחיק טמיא
דהיינו שחיק עצמות ואין לפרש
אוב טמא שאין זה הלשון: גנח גוהא.
ותגעש ותרעש כלו' נזדעזעה הארץ
מאד מאד. גנח גוהא הדא מלתא
היא וכן הלשון: גוהא גוהא מיבעי
ליה. שני פעמים היה לו להזדעזע
כנגד שתי דמעות: סופק כפיו.
ומאותו קול מזדעזעת הארץ שמליכו
שכפיו סופק שנ' גם אני אכה כפי
אל כפי (יחזקאל כא): אנחה
מתאנח. ומאותה אנחה מרעיד
הקרקע ומליכו שמתאנח שנאמר
והניחותי חמתי בם (יחזקאל ה)
כביכול כאדם שיש לו חמה ומתאנח
ומתנחם דעתו ועושה לו נחת רוח:
והנחמתי. אנחם על הרעה שעשיתי
להם: הידד כדורכים יענה. שדורך
ובועט ברקיע: והארץ הדום רגלי.
כגון שדחה תחת כסא הכבוד ומגיע
בעוטו עד לארץ שהיא הדום רגליו:
ענני בגלגלא. עננים מתחופפים
ומתחככין ונשמע הקול לשון אחר
העננים פוגעים בגלגל ומתגלגלות
עם הגלגל בעל כרחם ואותו הקול
היינו רעמים: ברקא. ברקים של
אש: ומתבר גזיזי דברזא. ואותו
הקול היינו רעמים. גזיזי גלליי"ש
חתיכות של ברד: חלחולי מחלחלי.
ענני ומנשב זיקא עלייהו והיינו
רעמים: מנהמי ענני. הומות העננים:
זעפא. סופטו"רבי"ל: ברקא.
אישלוחי"רא ל' מבריק להר: ברקא
יחידאה. שלא הבריק אלא פעם
א': וברקא חיורא וברקא ירוקתא
כולהו קשיין. שאינם של ברכה:
דסלקן חדא לאפי חברתה. שהני
עננים פוגעים זה את זה: ענן בקר.
לא קבוע: כד מפתח בבי מטרא
בר חמרא מוך שקיך וגני. אם
כשתפתח דלתיך בבקר ירד לך
מטר לך אני אומר חמר ההולך
ממקום למקום להביא תבואה מוך
שקיך וגני כפול שקך תחתיך ותישן
עליו ולא תלך אנה ואנה להביא
תבואה לפי שיהיו החטים בזול
בשביל הגשם: ה"ג הא דקטר בעיבא.
כתקשרו השמים בעב עבה אז טוב
כי ירד גשם רב: הא דקטר בעננא.
ענן קליש הוא ענן בקר שאין בו
ממש: צריך שיפול על פניו. לפי
שהוא מראה כבוד ה': כרוך ותני.
בכולהו ברוך עושה בראשית וברוך
שכחו מלא עולם. כרוך ותני לכולהו
בחדא בבא ועל כולם שתי ברכות
הללו: על ההרים. לא מלי לברוכי
מלא עולם שאינן במקום אחד אלא כל אחד ואחד במקומו: אומר ברוך עושה בראשית. שכך היתה ברייתו אח"כ כסוהו עננים:
אסתנא. רוח לפונית:

תוספות

*על הרוחות אומר שכחו וגבורתו מלא עולם. ירושלמי מתני'
כשבאים בזעם אבל כשבאים בנחת אומר ברוך עושה בראשי':
הלכך נימרינהו לתרוייהו. אומר ר"י דאין חותמין בברוך בברכה
זו והיכי מברך בא"י אלהינו מ"ה נאמן בבריתו וקיים
בשבועתו וזוכר הברית:
רבא אמר התם מברך שכחו
וגבורתו מלא עולם ועושה
מעשה בראשית. פירוש אומר או
האי או האי איזה שירצה וכן פירש
רב אלפס:
*הלכך נימרינהו לתרוייהו רוב
ההודאות ואל ההודאות.
ולפיכך תקנו בישתבח אחר סיום
הברכה בא"י אל מלך גדול בתשבחו'
אל ההודאות: הטוב

עין משפט נר מצוה

ם
אבנד[א]מיי' פ"י מהלכות ברכות הל' יד סמג עשין כז טוש"ע א"ח סימן רכז סעי' א
מא
[ב]מיי' שם הל' יו וסמג שם טוש"ע א"ח סי' רכט סעיף א
מב
[ג]מיי' וסמג שם טוש"ע א"ח סי' רכז סעיף א

מסורת הש"ס

[סייך לעיל במשנה נד.]
[שבת פ:]
לעיל ג: סנהדרין יו.
פי' חלולין קלת
תענית ו: ע"ש
קידושין לג: וש"כ
[לקמן עמוד ב תענית ז. מגילה כח: לקמן ס:]
[חגיגה יג: ר"ה כו. קידושין ה.]
(עיין רש"י)

תורה אור

קהלת א; איוב לח; יחזקאל כא; שם ה; ירמיה כה; ישעיה סו; תלים עז; ירמי' י; במדבר [?] ; הושע ו; קהלת ג; יחזקאל א; תלים קלה; ישעי' נ

תורה אור

ת"ר

ת"ר [א]הרואה חמה בתקופתה לבנה *בגבורת' וככבים במסילותם ומזלות כסדרן אומר ברוך עושה בראשית ואימת הוי אמר אביי כל כ"ח שנין והדר מחזור ונפלה תקופת ניסן בשבתאי באורתא דתלת נגהי ארבע: ר' יהודה אומר הרואה הים וכו': לפרקים עד כמה אמר רמי בר אבא א"ר יצחק [ב]עד שלשים יום ואמר רמי בר אבא א"ר יצחק הרואה פרת אגשרא דבבל אומר ברוך עושה בראשית [ג]והאידנא דשניוה פרסאי מבי שבור ולעיל רב יוסף אמר מאיהי דקירא ולעיל ואמר רמי בר אבא הרואה דגלת אגשרא דשביסתנא אומר ב"ע בראשית מאי °*חדקל א"ר אשי מימיו חדין וקלין מאי פרת שמימיו פרין ורבין ואמר רבא האי דחריפי בני מחוזא משום דשתו מיא דדגלת האי דגיהורי משום דמשמשי בימָמא והאי דנידי עינייהו משום דדיירו בבית אפל: על הגשמים כו': ועל הגשמים הטוב והמטיב מברך *והא"ר אבהו ואמרי לה במתניתא תנא [ד]מאימתי מברכין על הגשמים משיצא חתן לקראת כלה מאי מברכין אמר רב יהודה [ה]מודים אנחנו לך על כל טפה וטפה שהורדת לנו ורבי יוחנן מסיים בה הכי אלו פינו מלא שירה כים וכו' אין אנו מספיקין להודות לך ה' אלהינו עד תשתחוה בא"י רוב ההודאות רוב ההודאות ולא כל ההודאות אמר רבא אימא האל ההודאות א"ר פפא הלכך [ו]נימרינהו לתרוייהו רוב ההודאות והאל ההודאות ואלא קשיא ל"ק הא דשמע משמע הא דחזא מחזי דשמע משמע היינו בשורות טובות ותנן על בשורות טובות אומר ברוך הטוב והמטיב אלא אידי ואידי דחזי מחזי ולא קשיא הא דאתא פורתא הא דאתא טובא ואב"א הא והא דאתא טובא ולא קשיא [ז]הא דאית ליה ארעא הא דלית ליה ארעא אית ליה ארעא הטוב והמטיב מברך והא (*תנן) בנה בית חדש וקנה כלים חדשים אומר ברוך שהחיינו וקיימנו והגיענו לזמן הזה שלו ושל אחרי' אומר הטוב והמטיב ל"ק [ח]הא דאית ליה שותפות הא דלית ליה שותפות והתניא [ט]קצרו של דבר על שלו הוא אומר ברוך שהחיינו וקיימנו על שלו ועל של חבירו אומר ברוך הטוב והמטיב וכל היכא דלית לאחרינא בהדיה לא מברך הטוב והמטיב והתניא א"ל [י]ילדה אשתו זכר אומר ברוך הטוב והמטיב התם נמי דאיכא אשתו בהדיה דניחא לה בזכר ת"ש [כ]מת אביו והוא יורשו בתחלה אומר ברוך דיין האמת ולבסוף הוא אומר ברוך הטוב והמטיב התם נמי דאיכא אחי דקא ירתי בהדיה ת"ש *שינוי יין א"צ לברך [ל]שינוי מקום צריך לברך ואמר רב יוסף בר אבא א"ר יוחנן [מ]אע"פ שאמרו שינוי יין א"צ לברך אבל אומר ברוך הטוב והמטיב התם נמי [נ]דאיכא בני חבורה דשתו בהדיה: [ס]בנה בית חדש וקנה כלים חדשים וכו': א"ר הונא לא שנו אלא שאין לו כיוצא בהן אבל יש לו כיוצא בהן א"צ לברך ור' יוחנן אמר אפילו יש לו כיוצא בהן צריך לברך

מכלל

בתקופתה. מקום שהיא חוזרת שם לתחלת הקיפה הוא שעת תליית המאורות ומאז התחילה להקיף ולשמש: אימת הוי. אחמה בתקופתה קאי: כל כ"ח שנים. של תקופת ניסן *שבסוף כ"ח כשחוזר מחזור גדול של חמה להיות תקופה נופלת בשעת תליית המאורות בשבתאי היא שעה תחלת ליל ד': באורתא דתלת נגהי ארבע. שהעריב שמשו של ג' בשבת ויתחיל ליל ד': נגהי. ליל כדאמר בפסחי' בשמעתא קמייתא (דף ג.) דאיכא דוכתא דקרו ללילי' נגהי. שבתאי. שם שעה ראשונה של ליל רביעי שבאותה שעה נתלו מאורות ושבע שעות הן ומחזרות חלילה של"ס חנכ"ל תמלא בהקף סדרן של עולם סימני שעות תחלת הלילות כלכ"ש חל"ס מולאי שבת ככב תחלת ליל ב' לדק תחלת ליל ג' נוגה תחלת ליל רביעי שבתאי תחלת ליל ה' חמה תחלת ליל ששי לבנה תחלת ליל שב' מאדים וסדר תחלת היומים כעלות השחר חל"ס כלכ"ש ותקופה מושכת מחברתה ז' שעות ומחלה כלומר מתאחרת אחר היום והשעה שנפלה בה חברתה ז' שעות ומחלה הרי שלשים שעות לד' תקופות הרי יום ורביע לשנה לד' שנים ה' ימים למדת שאין תקופה נופלת בתחלת הלילה אלא לסוף ד' שנים שהוא מחזור קטן וז' מחזורים קטנים למחזור גדול וסימניך דב"ז הג"או הרי שהיא באה לתחלת ליל ד' אלא מכ"ח שנים לכ"ח שנים בראש כל מחזור קטן באה לתחלת הלילה ובראש מחזור הגדול באה לתקופה הראשונה שהיא תחלת ליל ד': אגשרא דבבל אומר ברוך עושה בראשית. קים להו שלא נשתנה פרת מהלוכו ע"י אדם משם ולמעלה אבל משם ולמטה השבוהו בני אדם דרך אחרת: והאידנא דשניוה פרסאי. מלמעלה לגשר אין מברך עליו עושה בראשית אלא מאיהי דקיר' ולעיל. איהי דקירא שם מחוז שהוא על הפרת: חדין. חריפין מיא וקלין לשקול במאזנים וטובים לשתות שאין מכבידין את הגוף: ה"ג והאי דגיהורי משום דמשמשי בימָמא. לפיכך בניהם אדומים כאדמונית היום רו"ש בלעז: דנידי עינייהו. [סניא] עיניהם כדים ונעים: משיצא חתן לקראת כלה. שהמים קבולין על הארץ וכשהטפה נופלת עליהן טפה התחתונה בולטת לקראתה: דשמע משמע. ששמעוהו לאמר ירדו גשמים בלילה אומר הטוב והמטיב: אתא פורתא. מודים אנחנו לך: אתא טובא. הטוב והמטיב: אית ליה ארעא. הטוב והמטיב שהטיב לו: בנה בית חדש. שכולו שלו אומר שהחיינו: שלו ושל אחרים. הטוב והמטיב: ה"ג (והתנן) [והתניא] בנה בית חדש וכו' לא קשיא הא דאית ליה שותפות הא דלית ליה שותפות. ול"ג אלא הא והא דלית ליה ארעא וה"פ תירוצא דשינן קאי בדוכתיה מודים אנחנו לך בדלית ליה ארעא הטוב והמטיב בדאית ליה ודקא קשיא לך בנה בית חדש אומר שהחיינו לא קשיא ההוא דבנה בית חדש שאין לו שותפות בה ועליה מברך שהחיינו אבל גשמים בדאית ליה ארעא טובה שיש לו שותפות בה היא שהרי כל מי שיש לו קרקע שותף עמו בטובה זו: והתניא. בניחותא: קצרו של דבר. כלומר כללו של דבר: ולבסוף הוא אומר הטוב והמטיב. על בשורת הירושה שכשהרה לו ירושה מאביו שכן בשרוהו מת אביו ויורשו כלומר הניח נכסים: שינוי יין. שתה יין בסעודה והביאו לו יין אחר טוב מן הראשון אין צריך לברך בורא פרי הגפן: שינוי מקום. יצא מכאן והלך לבית אחר והביאו לו יין: רבי יוחנן אמר אפילו יש לו כיוצא בהן. מירושה הואיל ולעניין קניה חדש הוא אללו צריך לברך:

דקנה

הטוב והמטיב. אבל אשינוי לחם ואשינוי בשר אין מברכין הטוב והמטיב דדוקא איין דאית ביה תרתי דסעיד ומשמח מברכים הטוב והמטיב אבל בשר ולחם לא ופרשב"ם בערבי פסחים (דף קא. ושם) דדוקא כשהאחרון משובח מברכים הטוב והמטיב אבל בגרוע בו לא *אך בירוש' דגרסי' מברכין א"ר אבא בר רב הונא צריך לברך על יין חדש וישן שינוי יין א"צ לברך שינוי מקום צריך לברך היאך הדעת כשינוי מקום משמע דוקא כשהאחרון ישן דעדיף טפי ור"ת פי' דאפילו אין האחרון חשוב רק שלא ישתנה לגריעותא יותר מדאי ומסייע בה רבי על כל חבית וחבית שהיה פותח היה מברך הטוב והמטיב ומשמע דלא קפיד אם האחרון משובח אם לאו אף על גב דישן אידכר בסוף מכל מקום כיוצא דרבי פליג עליה ולפרשב"ם יעמידנה להך דרבי במסופק אם האחרון טוב ומספק היה מברך על כל אחד שמא משובח הוא אך ר"ת מפרש דעובדא דרבי בא לחלק כדפי' וי"מ דההוא דחדש וישן מיירי בברכת ב"פ הגפן דומיא דשינוי מקום דבתר הכי אבל לא מליכו כן *בגמרא שלנו:

התם דאיכא בני חבורה דשתו בהדיה. וה"ה אם אשתו ובניו עמו אבל יחיד לא ואפי' שהחייהו אין מברך יחיד על שינוי יין דלא אשכחן יחיד שמברך שהחייהו רק אחדתא וכן כל פרי חדש כשאוכלו מברך שהחייהו כדאמרינן בסוף בכל מערבין (דף מ:):

ורבי יוחנן אמר אפילו קנה כיוצא בהם. והלכתא כר' יוחנן אליבא דלישנא בתרא אפילו קנה וחזר קנה שהיו לו כלים חדשים כיוצא באלו צריך לברך דק"ל כרבי יוחנן לגבי דרב מכל שכן דלגבי רב *הלכת' כותיה ואור"י דוקא בבגדי' חשובים דומיא דבית חדש נקט כלים חדשים אבל שאינם חשובים כ"כ כמו מנעלים ואנפליאות וחלוק וכיוצא בהן א"ל לברך. בירושלמי א"ר חייא בר אבא לא סוף דברים חדשים אלא אפילו שחקים כאלו חדשים הן ר' יעקב בשם ר' חייא בר אבא אמר קנה אומר שהחייהו ניתן לו אומר הטוב והמטיב לבש בגדי' אומר מלביש ערומים ול"ע בגמרא שלנו דלא אשכחן הטוב והמטיב אלא בדאיכא אחרינא בהדיה:

אשר

עין משפט נר מצוה

[וכן משמע כל"ב]

מג
[א]מיי' פ"י מהלכות ברכות הלכה יח סמג עשין כז טוש"ע א"ח סי' רכט סעי' ב

מד
[ב]מיי' שם הל' טו וסמג שם טוש"ע א"ח סימן ריח סעי' ג וסימן רכד סעיף יג

מה
[ג]ש"ע א"ח סי' רכח סעיף ב

[וע' היטב תו' פסחים קא. ד"ה שינוי יין]

מו
[ד]מיי' שם הל' ו וסמג שם טוש"ע א"ח סי' רכא סעיף א

מז
[ה]מיי' שם הלכה ה טוש"ע א"ח שם סעיף ב

[רב הונא]

מח
[ט]מיי' שם הל' ז וסמ"ג שם טוש"ע א"ח סימן רכב סעיף א

מט
[י]מיי' שם טוש"ע א"ח סי' רכג סעיף א

נ
[כ]מיי' וסמג שם טוש"ע שם סעי' ב

נא
[ל]מיי' פרק ז מהלכות ברכות הלכה ג סמג שם טוש"ע א"ח סימן קעה סעיף א

נב
[מ]מיי' וסמג שם טוש"ע א"ח סי' קעה סעיף ה

נג
[נ]מיי' שם טוש"ע שם סעיף ד

נד
[ס]מיי' פרק י' מהלכות ברכות ה"א סמג שם טוש"ע א"ח סימן רכג סעיף ג

מסורת הש"ס

שבתחלת

(ירוש' גרס בתקופתה מן וככבים עד כסדרן ל"ג ומוסיף את הרקיע בטהרת')

[בכורות נה:]

תענית ו: ע"ש

ברכות' ב

[סניא]

[והתניא] ע"פ קא:

clear sky, since it says: *I clothe the heavens with blackness* [59b] *and I make a sackcloth their covering.*[5]

Our Rabbis taught:* He who sees the sun at its turning point,[6]
a the moon in its power,[1] the planets in their orbits,[2] and the signs of the zodiac in their orderly progress,[3] should say: Blessed be He who has wrought the work of creation. And when [does this happen]?[4]—Abaye said: Every twenty-eight years when the cycle[5] begins again and the Nisan [Spring] equinox falls in Saturn on the evening of Tuesday,[6] going into Wednesday.

R. JUDAH SAYS: IF ONE SEES THE GREAT SEA etc. How long must the intervals be? Rami b. Abba said in the name of R. Isaac: From thirty days. Rami b. Abba also said in the name of R. Isaac: If one sees the River Euphrates by the Bridge of Babylon, he says:
b Blessed is He who has wrought the work of creation.[1] Now, however, that the Persians have changed it,[2] only if he sees it from Be Shapor[3] and upwards. R. Joseph says: From Ihi Dekira[4] and upwards. Rami b. Abba also said: If one sees the Tigris by the Bridge of Shabistana,[5] he says: Blessed is He who wrought the work of creation. Why is it [the Tigris] called *Ḥiddekel?*[6]—R. Ashi said: Because its waters are sharp [*had*] and swift [*kal*]. Why is it [the Euphrates] called *Perath?*—Because its waters are fruitful [*parim*] and multiply. Raba also said: The reason why people of Maḥoza are so sharp is because they drink the waters of the Tigris; the reason why they have red spots is because they indulge in sexual intercourse in the daytime; the reason why their eyes blink is because they live in dark houses.[7]

FOR THE RAIN etc. Is the benediction for rain 'Who is good and does good'? Has not R. Abbahu said—some say it has been taught in a Baraitha: From when do they say the blessing over rain? From the time when the bridegroom goes out to meet his bride.[8] What blessing do they say? R. Judah said: We give thanks to Thee for every drop which Thou hast caused to fall for us; and R. Joḥanan concluded thus: 'If our mouths were full of song like the sea . . . . we could not sufficiently give thanks unto Thee, O Lord our God, etc.' up to 'shall prostrate itself before Thee. Blessed
c art Thou, O Lord, to whom abundant thanksgivings are due'.[1] (Is it abundant thanksgivings and not all thanksgivings?—Raba said: Say, 'the God to whom thanksgivings are due'. R. Papa said: Therefore let us say both 'to whom abundant thanksgivings are due' and 'God of thanksgivings'.) But after all there is a contradiction?—There is no contradiction; the one blessing[2] is said by one who has heard [that it has been raining]; the other by one who has seen it. But one who hears of it hears good tidings, and we have learnt: For good tidings one says: Blessed is He who is good and does good?[3]—In fact both are said by one who sees it, and still there is no contradiction: the one is said if only a little falls, the other, if much falls. Or if you like, I can say that both are said for a heavy fall, and still there is no contradiction: the one is said by a man who has land, the other by one who has no land. Does one who has land say the blessing, 'Who is good and does good'? Has it not been taught: One who has built a new house or bought new clothes says: Blessed is He who has kept us alive and brought us to this season; [if it is] for himself along with others, he says: 'Who is good and does good'?[4]—This is no contradiction. The one blessing[2] is said if he has a partnership, the other[5] if he has no partnership. And thus it has been taught: In a word, for his own things he says: Blessed is He who has kept us alive and preserved us; for things which belong to him in conjunction with this neighbour, he says: Blessed is He who is good and does good.[6] And if no-one is associated with him in the ownership, does he never say the blessing, Who is good and does good? Has it not been taught: If a man is told that his wife has borne a son, he says: Blessed is He that is good and does good?—In that case, too, his wife is associated with him, because she is glad to have a son. Come and hear: If a man's father dies and he is his heir, first he says: Blessed is the true Judge, and afterwards he says: Blessed is He who is good and does good?—There, too, it is a case where there are brothers who inherit with him. Come and
d hear: Over a new kind of wine[1] there is no need to make a blessing; but if one goes to another place,[2] he must say a blessing again; and R. Joseph b. Abba said in the name of R. Joḥanan: Although they said that over a fresh kind of wine there is no need to make a blessing, still he says: Blessed is He who is good and does good?—There, too, it is a case where there are other members of the company who drink with him.

ONE WHO HAS BUILT A NEW HOUSE OR BOUGHT NEW VESSELS etc. R. Huna said: This is the rule only if he does not possess similar things; but if he has similar ones, he need not say the blessing. R. Joḥanan, however, says: Even if he has similar

(5) Isa. L. 3.
(6) In its apparent motion in the ecliptic, the sun has four 'turning points' which mark the beginnings of the four respective seasons. These points are generically referred to as the *teḳufoth* (sing. *teḳufah*). They are: the two equinoctial points when the sun crosses the equator at the beginning of spring and autumn respectively, and 'turns' from one side of the equator to the other; and the two solstices, when the sun is at its maximum distance, or declination, from the equator, at one or other side of it, at the beginning of summer and winter respectively, and instead of progressively increasing its declination it 'turns' to decrease it progressively. (It may be mentioned that the term '*teḳufah*' is also used not only for the beginning of a season but for the whole of the season itself.)

a (1) As the sun and moon were created to rule the day and night respectively (Gen. I, 16), they are necessarily endowed with the attribute of power (cf. Sabbath Liturgy כח וגבורה נתן בהם). In this passage, however, 'the moon in its power' may have a special significance, because at the Nisan, or spring equinox, the spring tides are greatest, owing to the combined action of the sun and the moon in conjunction, or new moon. The moon in its power to cause tides (a fact known to Pliny and Aristotle, and referred to by Maimonides (Guide II, 10), although never directly mentioned in the Talmud), is therefore best seen at this time. (2) The orbits of the planets which are now known to be ellipses, were, on the Ptolemaic system, which prevailed at that time, assumed to be traced out by a most ingenious combination of eccentric circles and epicycles, (v. for instance, the epicyclic theory of the moon in Feldman W.M., *Rabbinical Mathematics and Astronomy*, London, 1931, pp. 132ff). Hence the contemplation of the planets in their orbits was an adequate reason for pronouncing the blessing. (3) The vernal or autumnal equinox is not a fixed point in relation to the signs of the zodiac, but keeps on changing its position to the extent of 50.1″. (50.1 seconds of arc) per year. This movement which is called 'precession of the equinoxes' is due to the continual shifting of the point of intersection of the ecliptic with the equator, but was believed by the ancients to be due to the progressive movement of the signs of the zodiac. As the result of precession, the equinoctial point which 2,000 years ago was the beginning of the sign Ram (first point of Aries) has since shifted 30° to the sign Pisces, although it is still spoken of as the first point of Aries. (4) The reference is to the sun at its turning point (Rashi). (5) This means here the Big or Solar Cycle. Taking a Samuel, or Julian, year to consist of $365\frac{1}{4}$ days or 52 weeks $1\frac{1}{4}$ days, every *teḳufah* occurs $1\frac{1}{4}$ days later in the week every consecutive year, so that after 4 years it occurs at the same time of the day but ($1\frac{1}{4} \times 4 =$) 5 days later in the week. After 28, or 4×7 years, the *teḳufah* will recur not only at the same time of the day, but also on the same day of the week. V. Feldman, op. cit. p. 199. (6) As the sun and moon were created on the 4th day, the beginning of the 28 years cycle is always on a Wednesday which begins at the vernal equinox at 6 p.m. on Tuesday. This, according to computation coincides with the rise of Saturn, v. Rashi.

b (1) Because it was supposed that the River Euphrates from that point upwards had never changed its course since the days of Adam (Rashi). (2) By making canals. (3) Piruz Shabur on the eastern side of the Euphrates at the part where the Nahr Isa Canal branches off from the Euphrates connecting it at Bagdad with the Tigris (Obermeyer p. 57). (4) The modern Hit. (5) The bridge on the southern Tigris forming part of the great trading route between Khurzistan and Babylon during the Persian period (Obermeyer pp. 62ff.). For a full discussion and explanation of this whole passage v. Obermeyer pp. 52ff. (6) Gen. II, 14. (7) I.e., well-shaded from the sun. (8) I.e., when the drops commence to rebound from the earth.

c (1) V. *P.B.* p. 125. (2) I.e., 'Who is good and does good'. (3) And why should we be taught this again in the case of rain? (4) And a landowner presumably does not share his land with others. (5) The blessing, 'Who has kept us alive, etc.'. (6) And the landowner shares the rain with all other landowners. (V. Rashi and Asheri).

d (1) I.e., if one drinks a new (and better) kind of wine in the course of a meal. (2) To finish his meal, and wine is brought to him there. (3) E.g., from an inheritance.

(*) Note 6 and the notes on the following page are based on material supplied by the late Dr. W. M. Feldman, M.D., B.S., F.R.C.P., F.R.A.S., F.R.S. (Edin.), shortly before his death on July 1st, 1939.

ones[3] he must make the blessing.[4] [60a] We infer from this that if one bought things, and then bought some more, all agree that he need not say a blessing.[5] Some say: R. Huna said, This rule applies only where he does not buy again after already buying; but if he buys again after already buying, he need not say the blessing. R. Joḥanan, however, says: Even if he buys again after already buying, he must make a blessing. We infer from this that if he buys a kind of thing which he has already,[6] all agree that he has to say a blessing. An objection was raised: If one builds a new house, not having one like it already, he must say a blessing. If he already has any like them, he need not say a blessing. So R. Meir. R. Judah says: In either case he must make a blessing. Now this accords well with the first version, R. Huna following R. Meir and R. Joḥanan following R. Judah. But if we take the second version, it is true that R. Huna follows R. Judah, but whom does R. Joḥanan follow? It is neither R. Meir nor R. Judah![7]—R. Joḥanan can reply: The truth is that according to R. Judah also if one buys again after already buying, he must make a blessing, and the reason why they join issue over the case of his buying something of a kind which he has already is to show you how far R. Meir is prepared to go, since he says that even if he buys something of a kind which he already has, he need not make a blessing, and all the more so if he buys again after already buying, he need not make a blessing. But should they rather not join issue over the case of buying again after already buying, where
a there is no need to say a blessing,[1] to show how far he [R. Judah] is prepared to go?[2]—He prefers that the stronger instance should be a case of permission.[3]

OVER EVIL A BLESSING IS SAID etc. How is this to be understood?—For instance, if a freshet flooded his land. Although it is [eventually] a good thing for him, because his land is covered with alluvium and becomes more fertile, nevertheless for the time being it is evil.[4]

AND OVER GOOD etc. How can we understand this?—If for instance he found something valuable. Although this may [eventually] be bad for him, because if the king hears of it he will take it from him, nevertheless for the time being it is good.

IF A MAN'S WIFE IS PREGNANT AND HE SAYS, MAY [GOD] GRANT THAT MY WIFE BEAR etc. THIS IS A VAIN PRAYER. Are prayers then [in such circumstances] of no avail? R. Joseph cited the following in objection: *And afterwards she bore a daughter and called her name Dinah.*[5] What is meant by 'afterwards'? Rab said: After Leah had passed judgment on herself, saying, 'Twelve tribes are destined to issue from Jacob. Six have issued from me and four from the handmaids, making ten. If this child will be a male, my sister Rachel will not be equal to one of the handmaids'. Forthwith the child was turned to a girl, as it says, *And she called her name Dinah!*[6]—We cannot cite a miraculous event [in refutation of the Mishnah]. Alternatively I may reply that the incident of Leah occurred within forty days [after conception], according to what has been taught: Within the first three days a man should pray that the seed should not putrefy; from the third to the fortieth day he should pray that the child should be a male; from the fortieth day to three months he should pray that it should not
b be a *sandal;*[1] from three months to six months he should pray that it should not be still-born; from six months to nine months he should pray for a safe delivery. But does such a prayer[2] avail? Has not R. Isaac the son of R. Ammi said: If the man first emits seed, the child will be a girl; if the woman first emits seed, the child will be a boy?[3]—With what case are we dealing here? If, for instance, they both emitted seed at the same time.

IF HE WAS COMING FROM A JOURNEY. Our Rabbis taught: It once happened with Hillel the elder that he was coming from a journey, and he heard a great cry in the city, and he said: I am confident that this does not come from my house. Of him Scripture says: *He shall not be afraid of evil tidings; his heart is steadfast, trusting in the Lord.*[4] Raba said: Whenever you expound this verse you may make the second clause explain the first, or the first clause explain the second. 'You may make the second clause explain the first', thus: *'He will not fear evil tidings'*. Why? Because *'his heart is steadfast, trusting in the Lord'*. 'You may explain the second clause by the first', thus: *'His heart is steadfast trusting in the Lord'*; therefore, *'he shall not be afraid of evil tidings'*. A certain disciple was once following R. Ishmael son of R. Jose in the market place of Zion. The latter noticed that he looked afraid, and said to him: You are a sinner, because it is written: *The sinners in Zion are afraid.*[5] He replied: But it is written: *Happy is the man that feareth alway?*[6]—He replied: That verse refers to words of Torah.[7] R. Judah b. Nathan used to follow R. Hamnuna. Once he sighed, and the other said to him: This man wants to bring suffering on himself, since it is written; *For the thing which I did fear is come upon*
c *me, and that which I was afraid of hath overtaken me.*[1] But [he replied] it is written: *'Happy is the man who feareth alway'?*—He replied: That is written in connection with words of Torah.

ONE WHO GOES THROUGH A CAPITAL CITY. Our Rabbis taught: What does he say on entering? 'May it be Thy will O Lord, my God, to bring me into this city in peace'. When he is inside he says: 'I give thanks to Thee, O Lord, my God, that Thou hast brought me into this city in peace'. When he is about to leave he says: 'May it be Thy will, O Lord, my God, and God of my fathers, to bring me out of this city in peace'. When he is outside he says: 'I give thanks to Thee, O Lord, my God, that Thou hast brought me out of this city in peace, and as Thou hast brought me out in peace, so mayest Thou guide me in peace and support me in peace and make me proceed in peace and deliver me from the hands of all enemies and liers-in-wait by the way'. R. Mattena said: This applies only to a city where criminals are not tried and sentenced:[2] but in a city where criminals are tried and sentenced, this is unnecessary. Some report: R. Mattena said: Even in a city where criminals are tried and sentenced, for sometimes he may happen not to find a man who can plead in his defence.

Our Rabbis taught: On entering a bath-house one should say: 'May it be Thy will O Lord, my God, to deliver me from this and from the like of this, and let no humiliation or iniquity befall me; and if I do fall into any perversity or iniquity, may my death be an atonement for all my iniquities'. Abaye said: A man should not speak thus, so as not to open his mouth for the Satan.[3] For Resh Laḳish said—and so it was taught in the name of R. Jose: A man should never open his mouth for the Satan. R. Joseph said: What text proves this?—Because it is written, *We should have been as Sodom, we should have been like unto Gomorrah.*[4] What did the prophet answer them? *Hear the word of the Lord, ye rulers of Sodom,* etc.[5] On leaving the bath-house what does he say? R. Aḥa said: 'I give thanks unto Thee, O Lord, my God, that Thou hast delivered me from the fire'. R. Abbahu once went into the bath-house and the floor of the bath-house gave way beneath him, and a miracle was wrought for him, and he stood on a pillar and rescued a hundred and one men with one arm. He said: This is what R.
d Aḥa meant.[1]

On[2] going in to be cupped one should say: 'May it be Thy will, O Lord, my God, that this operation may be a cure for me, and mayest Thou heal me, for Thou art a faithful healing God, and Thy healing is sure, since men have no power to heal, but this is a habit with them'.[3] Abaye said: A man should not speak thus, since it was taught in the school of R. Ishmael: [It is written], *He shall cause him to be thoroughly healed.*[4] From this we learn that permission has been given to the physician to heal. When he gets up [after cupping] what does he say?—R. Aḥa said: Blessed be He who heals without payment.

מכלל דרבי קנה וחזר וקנה דברי הכל אין צריך לברך ואיכא דאמרי אמר רב הונא לא שנו אלא שלא קנה וחזר וקנה אבל קנה וחזר וקנה אין צריך לברך ור' יוחנן אמר *אפילו קנה וחזר וקנה צריך לברך מכלל דרבי יש לו וקנה דברי הכל צריך לברך מתיבי בנה בית חדש ואין לו כיוצא בו קנה כלים חדשים ואין לו כיוצא בהם צריך לברך יש לו כיוצא בהם אין צריך לברך דברי ר' מאיר ר' יהודה אומר בין כך ובין כך צריך לברך בשלמא ללישנא קמא רב הונא כרבי מאיר ורבי יוחנן כרבי יהודה אלא ללישנא בתרא בשלמא רב הונא כרבי יהודה אלא ר' יוחנן דאמר כמאן לא כרבי מאיר ולא כרבי יהודה אמר לך ר' יוחנן הוא הדין דלרבי יהודה קנה וחזר וקנה נמי צריך לברך והא דקא מפלגי ביש לו וקנה להודיעך כחו דרבי מאיר דאפילו קנה ויש לו אין צריך לברך וכל שכן קנה וחזר וקנה דאין צריך לברך וליפלגו בקנה וחזר וקנה דאין צריך לברך להודיעך כחו דרבי יהודה *כח דהיתרא עדיף ליה: °מברך על הרעה כו': היכי דמי כגון דשקל בדקא בארעיה אע"ג דטבא היא לדידיה דמסקא ארעא שירטון ושבחא השתא מיהא רעה היא: °ועל הטובה כו': ה"ד כגון דאשכח מציאה אע"ג דרעה היא לדידיה דאי שמע בה מלכא שקיל לה מניה השתא מיהא טובה היא: °היתה אשתו מעוברת ואמר יהי רצון שתלד כו' הרי זו תפלת שוא: ולא מהני רחמי מתיב רב יוסף °ואחר ילדה בת ותקרא את שמה דינה מאי ואחר אמר רב לאחר שדנה לאה דין בעצמה ואמרה י"ב שבטים עתידין לצאת מיעקב ששה יצאו ממני וארבעה מן השפחות הרי עשרה אם זה זכר לא תהא אחותי רחל כאחת השפחות מיד נהפכה לבת שנאמר ותקרא את שמה דינה *אין מזכירין מעשה נסים ואיבעית אימא מעשה דלאה בתוך ארבעים יום הוה כדתניא שלשה ימים הראשונים יבקש אדם רחמים שלא יסריח משלשה *עד ארבעים יבקש רחמים שיהא זכר מארבעים יום ועד שלשה חדשים יבקש רחמים שלא יהא סנדל משלשה חדשים ועד ששה יבקש רחמים שלא יהא נפל משששה ועד תשעה יבקש רחמים שיצא בשלום ומי מהני רחמי והא"ר יצחק בריה דרב אמי *איש מזריע תחלה יולדת נקבה אשה מזרעת תחלה יולדת זכר שנאמר °אשה כי תזריע וילדה זכר הכא במאי עסקינן כגון שהזריעו שניהם בבת אחת: היה בא בדרך: ת"ר מעשה בהלל הזקן שהיה בא בדרך ושמע קול צוחה בעיר אמר מובטח אני שאין זה בתוך ביתי ועליו הכתוב אומר °משמועה רעה לא יירא נכון לבו בטוח בה' אמר רבא כל היכי דדרשת להאי קרא *מרישיה לסיפיה מדריש מסיפיה לרישיה מדריש מרישיה לסיפיה מדריש משמועה רעה לא יירא מה טעם נכון לבו בטוח בה' מסיפיה לרישיה מדריש נכון לבו בטוח בה' משמועה רעה לא יירא ההוא תלמידא דהוה קא אזיל בתריה דרבי ישמעאל ברבי יוסי בשוקא דציון חזייה דקא מפחיד אמר ליה חטאה את דכתיב °פחדו בציון חטאים א"ל *והכתיב °אשרי אדם מפחד תמיד אמר ליה ההוא בדברי תורה כתיב יהודה בר נתן הוה שקיל ואזיל בתריה דרב המנונא אתנח א"ל יסורים בעי ההוא גברא לאתויי אנפשיה דכתיב °כי פחד פחדתי ויאתיני ואשר יגרתי יבוא לי והא כתיב אשרי אדם מפחד תמיד ההוא בדברי תורה כתיב: הנכנס לכרך: תנו רבנן °בכניסתו מהו אומר יהי רצון מלפניך ה' אלהי שתכניסני לכרך זה לשלום נכנס אומר מודה אני לפניך ה' אלהי שהכנסתני לכרך זה לשלום בקש לצאת אומר יהי רצון מלפניך ה' אלהי ואלהי אבותי שתוציאני מכרך זה לשלום יצא אומר מודה אני לפניך ה' אלהי שהוצאתני מכרך זה לשלום וכשם שהוצאתני לשלום כך תוליכני לשלום ותסמכני לשלום ותצעידני לשלום ותצילני מכף כל אויב ואורב בדרך אמר רב מתנא ל"ש אלא בכרך שאין דנין והורגין בו אבל בכרך שדנין והורגין בו לית לן בה א"ד אמר רב מתנא אפילו בכרך שדנין והורגין בו זימנין דלא מתרמי ליה איניש דיליף ליה זכותא ת"ר °הנכנס לבית המרחץ אומר יהי רצון מלפניך ה' אלהי שתצילני מזה ומכיוצא בו ואל יארע בי דבר קלקלה ועון ואם יארע בי דבר קלקלה ועון תהא מיתתי כפרה לכל עונותי אמר אביי לא לימא איניש הכי דלא לפתח פומיה לשטן *דאמר ר"ל וכן תנא משמיה דר' יוסי לעולם אל יפתח אדם פיו לשטן אמר רב יוסף מאי קראה דכתיב °כמעט כסדום היינו לעמורה דמינו מאי אהדר להו נביא שמעו דבר ה' קציני סדום וגו' כי נפיק מאי אומר א"ר אחא מודה אני לפניך ה' אלהי שהצלתני מן האור ר' אבהו על לבי בני אפחית בי בני מתותיה אתרחיש ליה ניסא קם על עמודא שזיב מאה וחד גברי בחד אבריה אמר היינו דר' אחא [*דא"ר אחא] °הנכנס להקיז דם אומר יהי רצון מלפניך ה' אלהי שיהא עסק זה לי לרפואה ותרפאני כי אל רופא נאמן אתה ורפואתך אמת לפי שאין דרכן של בני אדם לרפאות אלא שנהגו אמר אביי לא לימא איניש הכי *דתניא דבי ר' ישמעאל °ורפא ירפא °מכאן שניתנה רשות לרופא לרפאות כי קאי מאי אומר א"ר אחא ברוך רופא חנם:

מסורת הש"ס

דקנה וחזר וקנה דברי הכל אין צריך לברך. דהא רבי יוחנן לא אמר צריך לברך אלא משום דלענין קנייה חדש הוא: ואיכא דאמרי כו' מכלל דרבי יש לו וקנה דברי הכל צריך לברך. דהא רב הונא לא אמר אין צריך לברך אלא דקנה וחזר וקנה דליכא חידוש כלל אבל יש לו וקנה דאיכא חידוש מודה הוא דצריך: בין כך ובין כך. בין שיש לו בין שאין לו הואיל ולא קנה הראשונים ועכשיו קנה צריך לברך: לא כרבי מאיר ולא כרבי יהודה. דאפילו רבי יהודה לא פליג אלא ביש לו וקנה אבל בקנה וחזר וקנה לא: דמסקא ארעא שרטון. לשון מחמת המים והוה ליה לזבל: השתא מידא רעה היא. שמקלקלת תבואה של שנה זו ומברך ברוך דיין האמת: ועל הטובה שהיא מעין הרעה. יברך הטוב והמטיב: מאי היא. כגון דאשכח מציאה: שלא יסריח. הזרע אלא יקלוט ויהיה ולד ולאחר שלשה ימים אם לא קלט כבר הסריח ואין תפלה מועלת: שלא יהא סנדל. שלא תתעבר אשתו ולד אחר ויהיה פוחת צורתו של ראשון ודומה לדג של ים ששמו סנדל הכי אמרינן במס' נדה (דף כה:) סנדל דומה לסנדל של ים ותחלתו ולד היה אלא שנראה משל לאדם שסטר את חבירו והחזיר צוארו לאחוריו: ומי מהני. תפלה לזכר אפילו בתוך ארבעים יום והלא הדבר תלוי בהזרעה תחלה: הכי גרסינן משכחת לה דמהני כגון שהזריעו שניהם בב"א: כל היכי דדרשת ליה להאי קרא. מדרים לאחד משמעות מסיפיה לרישיה מדרים מי שנכון לבו בטוח בה' משמועה רעה לא יירא: בדברי תורה כתיב אשרי אדם מפחד תמיד שמא תשתכח ממנו שמתוך כך הוא מחזיר לשנותם תמיד: תנו רבנן. בן עזאי אמרה דאמר שתים בכניסתו שתים ביציאתו: לית לן בה. יזהר בעצמו שלא יפשע או אם פשע כבר אל יכנס במקום סכנה: בי בני. בית המרחץ: מתותיה. חפירה שהמים נופלים לתוכה ובני אדם רוחצים על גבי תקרה שעל גבה: בחד אבריה. בזרועו החזיק אחד או שנים וזה בזה החזיקו עד מאה ואחד: היינו דרבי אחא. דבעי אודויי שהוצאתני לשלום: שאין דרכן של בני אדם וכו'. כלומר לא היה להם לעסוק ברפואות אלא לבקש רחמים: התכבדו

תורה אור

[עירובין עג: ביצה ג: קדושין ס: גיטין מה: עד: חולין כח. נדה כט:] בראשית ל [יבמות קכח. חולין מג.] ויקרא יב תהלים קיב ישעיה לג משלי כח איוב ג [לעיל יט. כתובות ח:] ישעיה א ב"ק פה. שמות כא

עין משפט נר מצוה

נה א מיי' פרק י מהלכות ברכות ה"א סמג עשין כו טוש"ע א"ח סי' רכג סעיף ג

נו ב מיי' שם הלכ' ד וסמג שם טוש"ע א"ח סימן רכב סעי' ד

נז ד מיי' שם הלכה כה כו וסמג שם טוש"ע א"ח סי' רל סעי' א

נח ו מיי' שם הלכה כ טוש"ע א"ח שם סעי' ג

נט ז מיי' שם הלכה כא טוש"ע א"ח שם סעי' ד

[בי' על זה כתב רש"י ביצה ג: ד"ה התירא וע' בכ"מ פ"י מה' ברכות ה"א]

ס ח טוש"ע י"ד סי' שלו סעיף א

[וע' תוס' סנה' דז. ד"ה ארבעים] נדה כה: ודף לא. ע"ש

[לקמן סג. סנהד' ע.] גיטין כח.

ב' תיבות אלו צריכי' למחוק וענין הנכנס להקיז דם הוא ענין בפ"ע וע' ברי"ף ורא"ש

הנכנס

(4) Because the buying at any rate is fresh. (5) Because in this case it is not a fresh buying. (6) By inheritance or presentation. (7) Because even R. Judah holds that if he buys again after already buying, he need not make a blessing.

a (1) For the second purchase according to R. Meir. (2) In demanding a blessing for the second purchase. (3) I.e., a case in which a blessing need not be made. (4) Because it spoils the produce of this year, and he has to say the blessing, 'Blessed is the true Judge'. (5) Gen. XXX, 21. (6) Lit., 'judgment'.

b (1) A kind of abortion resembling a flat-shaped fish called *sandal*. (2) That the child should be a male. (3) Which shows that it is all fixed beforehand. (4) Ps. CXII, 7. (5) Isa. XXXIII, 14. (6) Prov. XXVIII, 14. (7) A man should always be afraid lest he may forget them.

c (1) Job III, 25. (2) I.e., where the protection of the law can not be relied on (3) Cf. *supra* 19a. (4) Isa. I, 9. (5) Ibid., 10.

d (1) In saying that one should give thanks on emerging. (2) Cur. edd. introduce this with the words 'for R. Aḥa said': but this is best left out. (3) To be cupped. (4) Ex. XXI, 19.

*הנכנס לבית הכסא אומר התכבדו מכובדים קדושים משרתי עליון תנו כבוד לאלהי ישראל הרפו ממני עד שאכנס ואעשה רצוני ואבא אליכם אמר אביי לא לימא איניש הכי דילמא שבקי ליה ואזלי אלא לימא שמרוני שמרוני עזרוני עזרוני סמכוני סמכוני המתינו לי המתינו לי עד שאכנס ואצא שכן דרכן של בני אדם כי נפיק אומר ברוך אשר יצר את האדם בחכמה וברא בו נקבים נקבים *חללים חללים גלוי וידוע לפני כסא כבודך שאם יפתח אחד מהם או אם יסתם אחד מהם אי אפשר לעמוד לפניך מאי חתים אמר רב רופא חולים אמר שמואל קא שוינהו *אבא לכולי עלמא קצירי אלא רופא כל בשר רב ששת אמר מפליא לעשות אמר רב פפא הלכך נמרינהו לתרווייהו רופא כל בשר ומפליא לעשות הנכנס לישן על מטתו אומר משמע ישראל עד והיה אם שמוע ואומר ברוך המפיל חבלי שינה על עיני ותנומה על עפעפי ומאיר לאישון בת עין יר"מ יי' אלהי שתשכיבני לשלום ותן חלקי בתורתך ותרגילני לידי מצוה ואל תרגילני לידי עבירה ואל תביאני לידי חטא ולא לידי עון ולא לידי נסיון ולא לידי בזיון וישלוט בי יצר טוב ואל ישלוט בי יצר הרע ותצילני מפגע רע ומחלאים רעים ואל יבהלוני חלומות רעים והרהורים רעים ותהא מטתי שלמה לפניך והאר עיני פן אישן המות בא"י המאיר לעולם כולו בכבודו כי מתער אומר אלהי נשמה שנתת בי טהורה אתה יצרתה בי אתה נפחתה בי ואתה משמרה בקרבי ואתה עתיד ליטלה ממני ולהחזירה בי לעתיד לבא כל זמן שהנשמה בקרבי מודה אני לפניך יי' אלהי ואלהי אבותי רבון כל העולמים אדון כל הנשמות ברוך אתה יי' המחזיר נשמות לפגרים מתים כי שמע קול תרנגולא לימא ברוך אשר *נתן לשכוי בינה להבחין בין יום ובין לילה כי פתח עיניה לימא ברוך פוקח עורים כי *תריץ ויתיב לימא ברוך מתיר אסורים כי לביש לימא ברוך מלביש ערומים כי זקיף לימא ברוך זוקף כפופים כי נחית לארעא לימא ברוך רוקע הארץ על המים כי מסגי לימא ברוך המכין מצעדי גבר כי סיים מסאניה לימא ברוך שעשה לי כל צרכי כי אסר המייניה לימא ברוך אוזר ישראל בגבורה כי פרים סודרא על רישיה לימא ברוך עוטר ישראל בתפארה כי מעטף בציצית לימא ברוך אשר קדשנו במצותיו וצונו להתעטף בציצית כי מנח *תפילין אדרעיה לימא ברוך אשר קדשנו במצותיו וצונו להניח תפילין ארישיה לימא ברוך אשר קדשנו במצותיו וצונו על מצות תפילין כי משי ידיה לימא ברוך אשר קדשנו במצותיו וצונו על נטילת ידים כי משי אפיה לימא ברוך המעביר חבלי שינה מעיני ותנומה מעפעפי ויהי רצון מלפניך יי' אלהי שתרגילני בתורתך ודבקני במצותיך ואל תביאני לא לידי חטא ולא לידי עון ולא לידי נסיון ולא לידי בזיון וכוף את יצרי להשתעבד לך ורחקני מאדם רע ומחבר רע ודבקני ביצר טוב ובחבר טוב בעולמך ותנני היום ובכל יום לחן ולחסד ולרחמים בעיניך ובעיני כל רואי ותגמלני חסדים טובים ברוך אתה יי' גומל חסדים טובים לעמו ישראל: חייב אדם לברך כו': מאי חייב לברך על הרעה כשם שמברך על הטובה אילימא כשם שמברך על הטובה הטוב והמטיב כך מברך על הרעה הטוב והמטיב והתנן על בשורות טובות אומר הטוב והמטיב על בשורות רעות אומר ברוך דיין האמת אמר רבא לא נצרכה אלא לקבולינהו בשמחה אמר רב אחא משום ר' לוי מאי קראה חסד ומשפט אשירה לך יי' אזמרה אם חסד אשירה ואם משפט אשירה ר' שמואל בר נחמני אמר מהכא *ביי' אהלל דבר באלהים אהלל דבר ביי' אהלל דבר זו מדה טובה באלהים אהלל דבר זו מדת פורענות ר' תנחום אמר מהכא כוס ישועות אשא ובשם יי' אקרא צרה ויגון אמצא ובשם יי' אקרא ורבנן אמרי מהכא יי' נתן ויי' לקח יהי שם יי' מבורך אמר רב הונא אמר רב משום רבי מאיר וכן תנא משמיה דרבי עקיבא לעולם יהא אדם רגיל לומר כל דעביד רחמנא לטב עביד כי הא דר' עקיבא דהוה קאזיל באורחא מטא לההיא מתא בעא אושפיזא לא יהבי ליה אמר כל דעביד רחמנא *לטב אזל ובת בדברא והוה בהדיה תרנגולא וחמרא ושרגא אתא זיקא כבייה לשרגא אתא שונרא אכליה לתרנגולא אתא אריא אכליה לחמרא אמר כל דעביד רחמנא לטב ביליא אתא גייסא שביה למתא אמר להו לאו אמרי לכו כל מה שעושה הקב"ה הכל

תורה אור

רש"י

התכבדו וכו'. אל המלאכים המלוים אותו הוא אומר שנאמר כי מלאכיו יצוה לך (תהלים צא). שאם יפתח. אחד מן החללים כגון הלב או הכרס או המעים: או אם יסתם אחד מהם. מן הנקבים הפתוחים כגון הפה או החוטם או פי הטבעת. יפתח קאי אחללים יסתם קאי אנקבים: קצירי. חולים: רופא כל בשר. כנגד הטילאה שהיא רפואת כל הגוף: ומפליא לעשות. כנגד שהגוף אצול כמו נאד והנאד הזה אם יש בו נקב אין הרוח עומד בתוכו והקב"ה ברא את האדם בחכמה וברא בו נקבים נקבים הרבה ואעפ"כ הרוח בתוכו כל ימי חייו וזו היא פליאה וחכמה: ותהא מטתי שלמה. שלא יהא פסול ורשע בזרעי: לשכוי. תרנגול דאיכא דוכתא דקרו לתרנגול שכוי כדאמרינן בר"ה (דף כו.): הכי גרסי'. אילימא כשם שמברך על הטובה הטוב והמטיב כן מברך על הרעה הטוב והמטיב והתנן על בשורו' טובות הטוב והמטיב ועל שמועות רעות אומר ברוך דיין האמת: לקבולינהו בשמחה. מברך על מדת פורענות בלבב שלם: אלהים. לשון דיין כמו עד האלהים יבא דבר שניהם (שמות כב): ובת בדברא. ולן בשדה: הוה בהדיה תרנגולא. להקיצו משנתו: הכל

תוספות

אשר יצר את האדם בחכמה. בתנחומא ויצר אלהים את האדם א"ר בון בחכמה שהתקין מזונותיו ואח"כ בראו היינו דאמר בסנהדרין בפ' אחד דיני ממונות (דף לח.) לכך נברא בע"ש כדי שיכנס לסעודה מיד וע"כ יסדו אשר יצר את האדם בחכמה:

מפליא לעשות. משום דאמרינן בב"ר כי גדול אתה ועושה נפלאות אתה אלהים לבדך אדם עושה נאד אפילו יש בו נקב א' מלא מחט סדקית הרוח יוצא ואינו יכול לשמור בו יין והקב"ה ברא נקבים נקבים באדם ושומר הרוח שאינו יוצא ממנו:

כי שמע קול תרנגולא אומר ברוך שנתן לשכוי בינה להבחין. והוא הדין אפילו כי לא שמע דאין ברכה זו אלא להבחנה על הנאת האורה שתרנגול מבחין והוא נהנה מן האור:

כי פריס סודרא על רישיה. וה"ה לכל כובע ולכל כסוי ודוקא כשנהנה אבל אם אינו נהנה כגון כשהוא שוכב על מטתו לא יברך לא זו ולא מלביש ערומים ולא ברכות כיוצא בהן כיון שלא נהנה כדמשמע בפרק שלישי דמגילה (דף כד:) גבי מי שלא ראה מאורות מימיו דכולי עלמא בעי שיהנה מן האורה:

אשר קדשנו במצותיו וצונו להניח תפילין. כיון דתחלת הנחתו בזרועו יש לו לברך להניח אבל בשל ראש מברך על מצות ולא להניח שכבר התחיל והניח אחד מהם. ובפ' הקומץ (דף לו. ושם) אמר לא שח מברך אחת שח מברך שתים פ"ה דעל שתי התפילין קאמר דמברך ברכה אחת על שתיהן בלא שח בנתים ודוחק לומר דלא הוצרכו שתי ברכות דלהניח ועל מצות אלא כששח ועבר עבירה לכן פר"ת דעל של ראש שהיא גמר מצוה ועיקר דיש בה ד' בתים וש"ן מברך על מצות אבל שח חוזר ומברך שתים על של ראש וכן בשימושא רבא דגאונים ולפר"ת גבי שח מברך שתים אם יניח של ראש לבד דאין מעכבין זה את זה מברך שתים על של ראש בלבד ומה שלא הזכיר הגמרא על של ראש בלבד מברך שתים לפי שאין כלל רגילות להניח זה בלא זה דתפילין בי בר חבו שכיחין (ב"מ דף כט:) וכן פי' ר"ת בתשובותיו וכן רבינו אלחנן בסדר תקון תפלה שלו כתב כן: וכל

עין משפט נר מצוה

סא א מיי' פ"ז מהלכות תפלה הלכה ה סמג עשין יט טוש"ע א"ח סי' ג סעיף א

סב ב ג ד מיי' וסמג שם טוש"ע א"ח סימן ו סעיף א

סג ה מיי' שם הלכה א ב וסמג שם טוש"ע א"ח סימן רלט סעיף א

סד ו מיי' שם הלכה ג ד וסמג שם טוש"ע א"ח סימן מו סעיף א

סה ח מיי' פ"ג מהלכות ציצית הלכה ח סמג שם טוש"ע א"ח סימן ח סעיף ה

סו ט מיי' פרק ד מהל' תפילין הלכ' ד סמג עשין כב טוש"ע א"ח סימן כה סעיף ה

סז י מיי' שם טוש"ע א"ח שם סעי' ט

סח כ מיי' פרק ז מהלכות תפלה הלכה ד סמג עשין יט טוש"ע א"ח סימן ד סעי' א וסימן מו סעי' א

סט ל מיי' פרק י מהלכות ברכות הלכה ג סמג עשין כז טוש"ע א"ח סימן רכב סעי' ג

ע מ טוש"ע א"ח סימן רל סעי' ה

מסורת הש"ס

[גי' הרי"ף ורא"ש פלוני' ועי' ב"י וד"מ]

[פירושו תמצא ברש"י לעיל מז. ד"ה אלו]

[ע' בהרא"ש פירושו]

[עמ"ש על הגליון בזבחים סב:]

[מנחות לו. מג:]

תהלי' קא

שם נו

שם קיו

איוב א

[תענית כא.]

[באלהים אהלל דבר בס' אהלל דבר כך איתא בקהלת וכן ברב אלפס העתיק על נכון]

[60b] On entering a privy one should say: 'Be honoured, ye honoured and holy ones[5] that minister to the Most High. Give honour to the God of Israel. Wait for me till I enter and do my needs, and return to you'. Abaye said: A man should not speak thus, lest they should leave him and go. What he should say is: 'Preserve me, preserve me, help me, help me, support me, support me, till I have entered and come forth, for this is the way of human beings'. When he comes out he says: 'Blessed is He who has formed man in wisdom and created in him many orifices and many cavities. It is fully known before the throne of Thy glory that if one of them should be [improperly] opened or one of them closed it would be impossible for a man to stand before Thee'. How does the blessing conclude? Rab said: '[Blessed art Thou] that healest the sick'. Said Samuel: Abba[6] has turned the whole world into invalids! No; what he says is, 'That healest all flesh'. R. Sheshet said: 'Who doest wonderfully'. R. Papa said: Therefore let
a us say both, 'Who healest all flesh and doest wonderfully'.[1]

On going to bed one says from *'Hear, oh Israel'* to *'And it shall come to pass if ye hearken diligently'*. Then he says: 'Blessed is He who causes the bands of sleep to fall upon my eyes and slumber on my eyelids, and gives light to the apple of the eye. May it be Thy will, O Lord, my God, to make me lie down in peace, and set my portion in Thy law and accustom me to the performance of religious duties, but do not accustom me to transgression; and bring me not into sin, or into iniquity, or into temptation, or into contempt. And may the good inclination have sway over me and let not the evil inclination have sway over me. And deliver me from evil hap and sore diseases, and let not evil dreams and evil thoughts disturb me, and may my couch be flawless before Thee, and enlighten mine eyes lest I sleep the sleep of death. Blessed art Thou, oh Lord, who givest light to the whole world in Thy glory.'[2]

When he wakes he says: 'My God, the soul which Thou hast placed in me is pure. Thou hast fashioned it in me, Thou didst breathe it into me, and Thou preservest it within me and Thou wilt one day take it from me and restore it to me in the time to come. So long as the soul is within me I give thanks unto Thee, O Lord, my God, and the God of my fathers, Sovereign of all worlds, Lord of all souls. Blessed art Thou, O Lord, who restorest souls to dead corpses'.[3] When he hears the cock crowing he should say: 'Blessed is He who has given to the cock understanding to distinguish between day and night'. When he opens his eyes he should say: 'Blessed is He who opens the eyes of the blind'. When he stretches himself and sits up, he should say: 'Blessed is He who looseneth the bound'. When he dresses he should say: 'Blessed is He who clothes the naked'. When he draws himself up he should say: 'Blessed is He who raises the bowed'. When he steps on to the ground he should say: 'Blessed is He who spread the earth on the waters'. When he commences to walk he should say: 'Blessed is He who makes firm the steps of man'. When he ties his shoes he should say: 'Blessed is He who has supplied all my wants'. When he fastens his girdle, he should say: 'Blessed is He who girds Israel with might'. When he spreads a kerchief over his head he should say: 'Blessed is He who crowns Israel with glory'. When he wraps himself with the fringed garment he should say: 'Blessed is He who hast sanctified us with His commandments and commanded us to enwrap ourselves in the fringed garment'. When he puts the *tefillin* on his arm he should say: 'Blessed is He who has sanctified us with His commandments and commanded us to put on *tefillin*'. [When he puts it] on his head he should say: 'Blessed is He who has sanctified us with His commandments and commanded us concerning the commandment of *tefillin*'. When he washes his hands he should say: 'Blessed is He who has sanctified us with His commandments and commanded us concerning the
b washing of hands'.[1] When he washes his face he should say: 'Blessed is He who has removed the bands of sleep from mine eyes and slumber from mine eyes. And may it be Thy will O Lord, my God, to habituate me to Thy law and make me cleave to Thy commandments, and do not bring me into sin, or into iniquity, or into temptation, or into contempt, and bend my inclination to be subservient unto Thee, and remove me far from a bad man and a bad companion, and make me cleave to the good inclination and to a good companion in Thy world, and let me obtain this day and every day grace, favour, and mercy in Thine eyes, and in the eyes of all that see me, and show lovingkindness unto me. Blessed art Thou, O Lord, who bestowest lovingkindness upon Thy people Israel'.[2]

IT IS INCUMBENT ON A MAN TO BLESS etc. What is meant by being bound to bless for the evil in the same way as for the good? Shall I say that, just as for good one says the benediction 'Who is good and bestows good', so for evil one should say the benediction 'Who is good and bestows good'? But we have learnt: FOR GOOD TIDINGS ONE SAYS, WHO IS GOOD AND BESTOWS GOOD: FOR EVIL TIDINGS ONE SAYS, BLESSED BE THE TRUE JUDGE?—Raba said: What it really means is that one must receive the evil with gladness. R. Aḥa said in the name of R. Levi: Where do we find this in the Scripture? *I will sing of mercy and justice, unto*
c *Thee, O Lord, will I sing praises;*[1] whether it is 'mercy' I will sing, or whether it is 'justice' I will sing. R. Samuel b. Naḥmani said: We learn it from here: *In the Lord I will praise His word, in God I will praise His word.*[2] *'In the Lord*[3] *I will praise His word'*: this refers to good dispensation; *'In God*[4] *I will praise His word'*: this refers to the dispensation of suffering. R. Tanḥum said: We learn it from here: *I will lift up the cup of salvation and call on the name of the Lord;*[5] *I found trouble and sorrow, but I called upon the name of the Lord.*[6] The Rabbis derive it from here: *The Lord gave and the Lord hath taken away; blessed be the name of the Lord.*[7]

R. Huna said in the name of Rab citing R. Meir, and so it was taught in the name of R. Akiba: A man should always accustom himself to say, 'Whatever the All-Merciful does is for good', [as exemplified in] the following incident. R. Akiba was once going along the road and he came to a certain town and looked for lodgings but was everywhere refused. He said 'Whatever the All-Merciful does is for good', and he went and spent the night in the open field. He had with him a cock, an ass and a lamp. A gust of wind came and blew out the lamp, a weasel came and ate the cock, a lion came and ate the ass. He said: 'Whatever the All-Merciful does is for good'. The same night some brigands came and carried off the inhabitants of the town. He said to them:[8] Did I not say to you, 'Whatever the All-Merciful does [61a] is all for good?[9]

(5) These words are addressed to the angels who are supposed to accompany a man to the privies, which were regarded as the haunt of evil spirits, v. *infra* 61a. (6) Rab.

a (1) *P.B.* p. 4. (2) Ibid. p. 293. (3) Ibid. p. 5.

b (1) For all these blessings v. *P.B.* p. 5f. These blessings are now no longer said after each act, but are all said together in the morning service. (2) Ibid. p. 6.

c (1) Ps. CI, 1. (2) Ibid. LVI, 11. In the M.T. the order of the divine names is reserved. (3) The name of the Attribute of Mercy. (4) The name of the Attribute of Justice. (5) Ibid. CXVI, 13. (6) Ibid. 3. (7) Job. I, 21. (8) Apparently to the men of the town, on a subsequent occasion; or perhaps to his disciples who accompanied him. (9) Because the lamp or the cock or the ass might have disclosed his whereabouts to the brigands.

R. Huna further said in the name of R. Meir: A man's words should always be few in addressing the Holy One, blessed be He, since it says, *Be not rash with thy mouth and let not thy heart be hasty to utter a word before God; for God is in heaven and thou upon earth;* a *therefore let thy words be few.*[1]

R. Naḥman b. R. Ḥisda expounded: What is meant by the text, *Then the Lord God formed* [wa-yiẓer] *man?*[2] [The word *wa-yiẓer*] is written with two *yods*,[3] to show that God created two inclinations, one good and the other evil. R. Naḥman b. Isaac demurred to this. According to this, he said, animals, of which it is not written *wa-yiẓer*,[4] should have no evil inclination, yet we see that they injure and bite and kick? In truth [the point of the two *yods*] is as stated by R. Simeon b. Pazzi; for R. Simeon b. Pazzi said: Woe is me because of my Creator [*yoẓri*],[5] woe is me because of my evil inclination [*yiẓri*]![6] Or again as explained by R. Jeremiah b. Eleazar; for R. Jeremiah b. Eleazar said: God created two countenances in the first man,[7] as it says, *Behind and before hast Thou formed me.*[8]

And the rib which the Lord God had taken from man made he a woman.[9] Rab and Samuel explained this differently. One said that [this '*rib*'] was a face, the other that it was a tail.[10] No objection can be raised against the one who says it was a face, since so it is written, '*Behind and before hast Thou formed me*'. But how does he who says it was a tail explain '*Behind and before hast Thou formed me*'?— As stated by R. Ammi; for R. Ammi said: '*Behind*' [i.e., last] in the work of creation, and '*before*' [i.e., first] for punishment. We grant you he was last in the work of creation, for he was not created till the eve of Sabbath. But when you say 'first for punishment', to what punishment do you refer? Do you mean the punishment in connection with the serpent? Surely it has been taught: Rabbi says, In conferring honour we commence with the greatest, in cursing with the least important. 'In conferring honour we commence with the greatest', as it is written, *And Moses spoke to Aaron and to Eleazar and to Ithamar his* b *sons that were left, Take the meal-offering that remaineth* etc.[1] 'In cursing we commence with the least'; first the serpent was cursed then Eve and then Adam![2] I must say then that the punishment of the Flood is meant, as it is written, *And He blotted out every living substance which was upon the face of the ground, both man and cattle.*[3]

No difficulty arises for the one who says that Eve was created from the face, for so it is written, *wa-yiẓer*, with two *yods*. But he who says it was a tail, what does he make of *wa-yiẓer?*—As explained by R. Simeon b. Pazzi? For R. Simeon b. Pazzi said: Woe is me because of my Creator [*yoẓri,*] woe is me because of my evil inclination [*yiẓri*]! No difficulty arises for one who says it was a face, for so it is written, *Male and female created He them.*[4] But he who says it was a tail, what does he make of '*male and female created He them*'?—As explained by R. Abbahu. For R. Abbahu contrasted two texts. It is written, '*Male and female created He* them', and it is also written, *For in the image of God made He* man.[5] How are these statements to be reconciled? At first the intention was to create two, but in the end only one was created. No difficulty arises for him who says it was a face, since so it is written, *He closed up the place with flesh instead thereof.*[6] But he who says it was a tail, how does he explain, '*he closed up the place with flesh instead thereof?*— R. Jeremiah, or as some say R. Zebid, or again as some say, R. Naḥman b. Isaac, replied: These words are meant to apply only to the place of the cut. No difficulty arises for the one who says it was a tail, for so it is written, *And God built.*[7] But he who says it was a face, what does he make of the words '*And God built*'?[8] As explained by R. Simeon b. Menasia. For R. Simeon b. Menasia expounded: What is meant by the words, '*And the Lord built the rib*'? It teaches that the Holy One, blessed be He, plaited Eve's hair and brought her to Adam; for in the seacoast towns 'plaiting' [*keli'atha*][9] is called, 'building' [*binyatha*]. Another explanation: R. Ḥisda said (some say, it was taught in a Baraitha): It teaches that [God] built Eve after the fashion of a storehouse. Just as a storehouse is narrow at the top and broad at the bottom so as to hold the produce [safely], so a woman is narrower above and broader c below so as to hold the embryo. *And he brought her to the man.*[1] R. Jeremiah b. Eleazar said: This teaches that [God] acted as best man[2] to Adam. Here the Torah teaches a maxim of behaviour, that a man of eminence should associate himself with a lesser man in acting as best man, and he should not take it amiss.

According to the one who says it was a face, which of the two faces went in front?—R. Naḥman b. Isaac answered: It is reasonable to suppose that the man's face went in front, since it has been taught: A man should not walk behind a woman on the road,[3] and even if his wife happens to be in front of him on a bridge he should let her pass on one side, and whoever crosses a river behind a woman will have no portion in the future world.[4]

Our Rabbis taught: If a man counts out money from his hand into the hand of a woman so as to have the opportunity of gazing at her, even if he can vie in Torah and good deeds with Moses our teacher, he shall not escape the punishment of Gehinnom, as it says, *Hand to hand, he shall not escape from evil,*[5] he shall not escape from the punishment of Gehinnom.

R. Naḥman said: Manoah was an *'am ha-areẓ*, since it is written, *And Manoah went after his wife.*[6] R. Naḥman b. Isaac demurred to this. According to this, [he said,] in the case of Elkanah when it says, 'And Elkanah went after his wife',[7] and in the case of Elisha when it says, *And he rose and went after her,*[8] are we to suppose that this means literally after her? No; it means, after her words and her advice. So here [in the case of Manoah] it means, after her words and her advice! Said R. Ashi: On the view of R. Naḥman that Manoah was an *'am ha'areẓ*, he cannot even have known as d much of Scripture as a schoolboy;[1] for it says, *And Rebekah arose and her damsels, and they rode upon the camels and followed the man,*[2] [after the man] and not in front of the man.

R. Joḥanan said: Better go behind a lion than behind a woman; better go behind a woman than behind an idol; better go behind an idol than behind the synagogue when the congregation are praying.[3] This, however, is the case only when he is not carrying a load; if he is carrying a load, there is no objection. And also this is the case only when there is no other entrance; but if there is another entrance there is no objection. And again this is the case only when he is not riding on an ass, but if he is riding on an ass, there is no objection. And again this is the case only when he is not wearing *tefillin;* but if he is wearing *tefillin* there is no objection.

Rab said: The evil inclination resembles a fly[4] and dwells between the two entrances of the heart, as it says, *Dead flies make the ointment of the perfumers fetid and putrid.*[5] Samuel said: It is a like a kind of wheat [*ḥiṭṭah*], as it says, *Sin* [ḥaṭṭath] *coucheth at the door.*[6]

Our Rabbis taught: Man has two kidneys, one of which prompts him to good, the other to evil; and it is natural to suppose that the good one is on his right side and the bad one on his left, as it is written, *A wise man's understanding is at his right hand, but a fool's understanding is at his left.*[7]

Our Rabbis taught: The kidneys prompt, the heart discerns, the tongue shapes [the words], the mouth articulates, the gullet takes in and lets out all kinds of food, the wind-pipe produces the

a (1) Eccl. V, 1. (2) Gen. II, 7. (3) וייצר. (4) In Gen. II, 19, *And the Lord God formed all the beasts of the field*, etc., the word *wa-yiẓer* is spelt with one *yod*. (5) If I follow my inclination. (6) If I combat it. (7) And out of one of them Eve was made. (8) Ps. CXXXIX, 5. E.V. '*Thou hdst hemmed me in*'. (9) Gen. II, 22. (10) I.e., projected like a tail.

b (1) Lev. X, 12. Aaron is mentioned first. (2) V. Gen. III, 14–20. (3) Ibid.

מסורת הש"ס הכל לטובה. אלו היה כל דלוק היה הגייס רואה אותי ואלו היה החמור נוער או התרנגול קורא היה הגייס בא ושובה אותי: והא קחזינן דמזקא. שוחקת: אוי לי מיצרי. אם אלך אחר יצרי ואם לא אלך אחריו אוי לי מיצרי המיגעני בהרהורים: דו פרצופין. שני פרצופין בראו תחלה אחד מלפניו ואחד מאחריו וחלקו לשנים ועשה מן האחד חוה: אחור וקדם צרתני. לשון צורה דהיינו שני פרצופין: זכר ונקבה בראם. משמע מתחלת בריאתם תרי הוו: היינו דכתיב ויבן. שהיה צריך בנין: מאי ויבן. והלא כבר נבנה: כדי לקבל את הפירות. שאם יהי' קצר מלמטה ורחב מלמעלה תהא התבואה דוחפת את הכתלים מלמעלה לכאן ולכאן שהמשא מכביד עליהם: שושבין. משתדל בחופתו ובזווגו: ולמ"ד פרצוף. ומתחלתו היה מצד אחד זכר ונקבה מצד אחר: הי מינייהו סגי ברישא. איזה פרצוף היה מהלך לפנים: אפילו היא אשתו. גנאי הדבר: נזדמנה לו על הגשר. אשת איש והיא לפניו: יסלקנה לצדדין. עד שיעבור לפניה: אחורי אשה בנהר. אחורי אשת איש מגבהת בגדיה מפני המים וזה מסתכל בה: יד ליד לא ינקה רע. אפילו כמשה רבינו שקבל תורה מימינו של הקב"ה לא ינקה רע וקרא באשה משתעי: עם הארץ. לא שמש תלמידי חכמים שלא למד משנה זו שהכינו לא יהלך אדם אחורי אשה ואפילו היא אשתו: ולמאי דקאמר רב נחמן. שהלך אחריה ממש אם כן אפילו בי רב עם תינוקות של בית רבן נמי לא קרא: בשעה שהצבור מתפללים. דכיון שאינו נכנס נראה כפורק עול ומבזה בית הכנסת: ואי דרי מידי. אין כאן גנאי דמוכחא מלתא דהאי דלא נכנס מפני המשוי: ואי איכא פתחא אחרינא. אין כאן בזוי דמאן דחזי סבר בפתחא אחרינא ליעול: יביע. לשון אבעבועות כלשה מבקה מסריח מעלה רתיחה ואבעבועות: חטאת. לשון חטה דרים ליה: כליות יועצות. את הלב עשה כן: והלב מבין. מה יש לו לעשות אם ישמע לעצת הכליות אם לאו ומנין שהכליות יועצות שנאמר (תהלים טז) אברך את יי' אשר יעצני אף לילות יסרוני כליותי ומנין שהלב מבין שנאמר (ישעיה ו) ולבבו יבין: לשון מחתך. הדבור להוציא מפיו: והפה. הם השפתים גומר ומוציאו:

שואבת

תורה אור

הכל לטובה: ואמר רב הונא אמר רב משום ר' מאיר לעולם יהיו דבריו של אדם מועטין לפני הקב"ה שנאמר °אל תבהל על פיך ולבך אל ימהר להוציא דבר לפני האלהים כי האלהים בשמים ואתה על הארץ על כן יהיו דבריך מעטים: דרש רב נחמן בר רב חסדא מאי דכתיב °וייצר יי' אלהים את האדם בשני יוד"ין שני יצרים ברא הקב"ה אחד יצר טוב ואחד יצר רע מתקיף לה רב נחמן בר יצחק אלא מעתה בהמה דלא כתיב בה וייצר לית לה יצרא והא קא חזינן דמזקא ונשכא ובעטא אלא כדר"ש בן פזי דאמר *ר"ש בן פזי אוי לי מיוצרי ואוי לי מיצרי אי נמי כדר' ירמיה בן אלעזר דא"ר ירמיה בן אלעזר דו פרצופין ברא הקב"ה באדם הראשון שנאמר °אחור וקדם צרתני: °ויבן יי' אלהים את הצלע *רב ושמואל חד אמר פרצוף וחד אמר זנב בשלמא למ"ד פרצוף היינו דכתיב אחור וקדם צרתני אלא למ"ד זנב מאי אחור וקדם צרתני כדר' אמי דא"ר אמי אחור למעשה בראשית וקדם לפורענות בשלמא אחור למעשה בראשית דלא אברי עד מעלי שבתא אלא וקדם לפורענות פורענות דמאי אילימא *פורענות דנחש והתניא *ר' אומר בגדולה מתחילין מן הגדול ובקללה מתחילין מן הקטן בגדולה מתחילין מן הגדול דכתיב °ויאמר משה אל אהרן ואל אלעזר ואל איתמר בניו *הנותרים קחו וגו' בקללה מתחילין מן הקטן בתחלה נתקלל נחש ולבסוף נתקללה חוה ולבסוף נתקלל אדם אלא פורענות דמבול דכתיב °וימח את כל היקום אשר על פני האדמה מאדם ועד בהמה ברישא אדם והדר בהמה בשלמא למ"ד פרצוף היינו דכתיב וייצר בשני יודי"ן אלא למ"ד זנב מאי וייצר כדר"ש בן פזי דאר"ש בן פזי אוי לי מיוצרי אוי לי מיצרי בשלמא למ"ד פרצוף היינו דכתי' °זכר ונקבה בראם אלא למ"ד זנב מאי זכר ונקבה בראם כדר' אבהו דר' אבהו *רמי כתיב זכר ונקבה בראם וכתיב °כי בצלם אלהים עשה את האדם הא כיצד בתחלה עלה במחשבה לבראת ב' ולבסוף לא נברא אלא אחד בשלמא למ"ד פרצוף היינו דכתיב °ויסגור בשר תחתנה אלא למ"ד זנב מאי ויסגור בשר תחתנה א"ר ירמיה ואיתימא רב זביד ואיתימא רב נחמן בר יצחק לא נצרכה אלא למקום חתך בשלמא למ"ד זנב היינו דכתיב ויבן אלא למ"ד פרצוף מאי ויבן לכדר"ש בן מנסיא *דדרש ר"ש בן מנסיא מאי דכתיב ויבן יי' את הצלע מלמד שקלעה הקב"ה לחוה והביאה לאדם הראשון שכן בכרכי הים קורין לקליעתא בנייתא דבר אחר ויבן א"ר חסדא ואמרי לה במתניתא תנא מלמד שבנאה הקב"ה לחוה כבנין אוצר מה אוצר זה קצר מלמעלה ורחב מלמטה כדי לקבל את הפירות אף אשה קצרה מלמעלה ורחבה מלמטה כדי לקבל את הולד. ויביאה אל האדם א"ר ירמיה בן אלעזר מלמד שנעשה הקב"ה שושבין לאדם הראשון מכאן למדה תורה ד"א שיחזור גדול עם קטן בשושבינות ואל ירע לו ולמאן דאמר פרצוף הי מינייהו סגי ברישא אמר רב נחמן בר יצחק מסתברא דגברא סגי ברישא דתניא *לא יהלך אדם אחורי אשה בדרך ואפילו אשתו נזדמנה לו על הגשר יסלקנה לצדדין וכל העובר אחורי אשה בנהר אין לו חלק לעולם הבא *ת"ר המרצה מעות לאשה מידו לידה כדי להסתכל בה אפילו יש בידו תורה ומעשים טובים כמשה רבינו לא ינקה מדינה של גיהנם שנאמר °יד *ליד לא ינקה רע לא ינקה מדינה של גיהנם אמר רב נחמן מנוח עם הארץ היה דכתיב °וילך מנוח אחרי אשתו מתקיף לה רב נחמן בר יצחק אלא מעתה גבי אלקנה דכתיב וילך אלקנה אחרי אשתו וגבי אלישע דכתיב °ויקם וילך אחריה הכי נמי אחריה ממש אלא אחרי דבריה ואחרי עצתה ה"נ אחרי דבריה ואחרי עצתה א"ר אשי ולמאי דקאמר רב נחמן מנוח ע"ה היה אפי' בי רב נמי לא קרא שנאמר °ותקם רבקה ונערותיה ותרכבנה על הגמלים ותלכנה אחרי האיש ולא לפני האיש א"ר יוחנן אחורי ארי ולא אחורי אשה אחורי אשה ולא אחורי ע"א אחורי ע"א *ולא אחורי בית הכנסת בשעה שהצבור מתפללין ולא אמרן אלא דלא דרי מידי ואי דרי מידי לית לן בה ולא אמרן אלא דליכא פתחא אחרינא ואי איכא פתחא אחרינא לית לן בה ולא אמרן אלא דלא רכיב חמרא אבל רכיב חמרא לית לן בה ולא אמרן אלא דלא מנח תפילי אבל מנח תפילי לית לן בה: א"ר יצר הרע דומה לזבוב ויושב בין שני מפתחי הלב שנאמר °זבובי מות יבאיש יביע שמן רוקח ושמואל אמר כמין חטה הוא דומה שנאמר °לפתח חטאת רובץ. ת"ר שתי כליות יש בו באדם אחת יועצתו לטובה ואחת יועצתו לרעה ומסתברא דטובה לימינו ורעה לשמאלו דכתיב °לב חכם לימינו ולב כסיל לשמאלו: ת"ר *כליות יועצות לב מבין לשון מחתך פה גומר ושט מכניס ומוציא כל מיני מאכל קנה מוציא קול

ריאה

וכל העובר אחורי אשה בנהר אין לו חלק לעולם הבא. פירוש אם רגיל בכך לפי שיבא לידי ניאוף וסופו יורד לגיהנם: אלא מעתה גבי אלקנה דכתיב וילך אלקנה אחרי אשתו וגו'. שבוש הוא שאין פסוק זה בכל המקרא ול"ג ליה*: רבי

עין משפט נר מצוה

עא
א מיי' פכ"א מה' איסורי ביאה הלכה כב סמג לאוין קכו טוש"ע א"ה סי' כא סעי' א

[עמ"ש בס"ד על הגליון בערכין יח.]

עיין במהרש"ל הגירסא שהביא בשם ילקוט פ' שופטים

עב
ב מיי' פ"י מהל' תפלה ה"א סמג עשין יט טוש"ע א"ח סי' צ סעיף ח

[מכאן עד ולבסוף נתקלל אדם ליתא בעירובין יח. וע"ש הגוסח' שבגמרא]

קהלת ה; בראשית ב; תהלים קלט; בראשית ב; ויקרא י; בראשית ז; בראשית ה; שם ט; שם ב

[עירובין יח.] [שם: ע"ש כמה שינויים] [תענית טז:] [בתענית ליתא] [כתובות ח. ע"ש ול"ע עירובין יח. ע"ש ול"ע] שבת לה. עירובין יח. נדה מה: ע"ש

כלה פ"א עירובין יח: משלי יא; שופטים יג; מלכים ב ד; בראשית כד; לעיל ח:; קהלת י; בראשית ד; קהלת י

[ע' תוס' עירובין יח: ד"ה יד] [חולין יא. שבת לג:]

VII, 23. Man is here mentioned before cattle. (4) Ibid. V, 2. (5) Ibid. IX, 6. (6) Ibid. II, 21. (7) Ibid. 22. E.V. '*made*'. (8) The face needed no 'building', since it was already there. (9) This word in Aramaic also means 'tents'.

c (1) Gen. II, 22. (2) Heb. *shoshbin*, the man who looks after the wedding arrangements; v. B.B., Sonc. ed., p. 618 n. 10. (3) To avoid unchaste thoughts. (4) Because the woman in crossing will naturally lift up her dress. (5) Prov. XI, 21. E.V. '*My hand upon it! The evil man shall not be unpunished!*' (6) Judg. XIII, 11. (7) This text is not found in the Scripture, and Tosaf. deletes the mention of Elkanah here; v. Rashal and Maharsha. (8) II Kings IV, 30.

d (1) Lit., he did not read Scripture in a schoolhouse'. (2) Gen. XXIV, 61. (3) V. *supra* 8*b*. (4) V. Suk. 52*b*. (5) Eccl. X, 1. (6) Gen. IV, 7. This is probably connected with the view that the forbidden fruit of which Adam ate was wheat; v. *supra* 40*a* (Maharsha).

תורה אור

ריאה שואבת כל מיני משקין כבד כועס מרה זורקת בו טפה ומניחתו טחול שוחק קרקבן טוחן קיבה ישנה אף נעור נעור הישן ישן הנעור נמוק והולך לו תנא אם שניהם ישנים או שניהם נעורים מיד מת תניא רבי יוסי הגלילי אומר צדיקים יצר טוב שופטן שנאמר °ולבי חלל בקרבי רשעים יצר רע שופטן שנאמר °נאם פשע לרשע בקרב לבי אין פחד אלהים לנגד עיניו בינונים זה וזה שופטן שנאמר °יעמוד לימין אביון להושיע משפטי נפשו אמר *רבא כגון אנו בינונים א"ל אביי לא שביק מר חיי לכל בריה ואמר רבא לא איברי עלמא אלא לרשיעי גמורי או לצדיקי גמורי אמר רבא לידע איניש בנפשיה אם צדיק גמור הוא אם לאו אמר רב לא איברי עלמא אלא לאחאב בן עמרי ולרבי חנינא בן דוסא לאחאב בן עמרי העולם הזה ולרבי חנינא בן דוסא העולם הבא: ואהבת את יי' אלהיך: *תניא רבי אליעזר אומר אם נאמר בכל נפשך למה נאמר בכל מאדך ואם נא' בכל מאדך למה נאמר בכל נפשך אלא אם יש לך אדם שגופו חביב עליו מממונו לכך נאמר בכל נפשך ואם יש לך אדם שממונו חביב עליו מגופו לכך נאמר בכל מאדך ר"ע *אומר בכל נפשך *אפילו נוטל את נפשך ת"ר פעם אחת גזרה מלכות יון שלא יעסקו ישראל בתורה בא פפוס בן יהודה ומצאו לרבי עקיבא שהיה מקהיל קהילות ברבים ועוסק בתורה אמר ליה עקיבא אי אתה מתירא מפני המלכות אמר לו אמשול לך משל למה הדבר דומה לשועל שהיה מהלך על גב הנהר וראה דגים שהיו מתקבצים ממקום למקום אמר להם מפני מה אתם בורחים אמרו לו מפני רשתות שמביאין עלינו בני אדם אמר להם רצונכם שתעלו ליבשה ונדור אני ואתם כשם שדרו אבותי עם אבותיכם אמרו לו אתה הוא שאומרין עליך פקח שבחיות לא פקח אתה אלא טפש אתה ומה במקום חיותנו אנו מתיראין במקום מיתתנו עאכ"ו אף אנחנו עכשיו שאנו יושבים ועוסקים בתורה שכתוב בה °כי הוא חייך וארך ימיך כך אם אנו הולכים ומבטלים ממנה עאכ"ו אמרו לא היו ימים מועטים עד שתפסוהו לר"ע וחבשוהו בבית האסורים ותפסו לפפוס בן יהודה וחבשוהו אצלו אמר לו פפוס מי הביאך לכאן א"ל אשריך ר"ע שנתפסת על דברי תורה אוי לו לפפוס שנתפס על דברים בטלים בשעה שהוציאו את ר"ע להריגה זמן ק"ש היה והיו סורקין את בשרו במסרקות של ברזל והיה מקבל עליו עול מלכות שמים אמרו לו *תלמידיו רבינו עד כאן אמר להם כל ימי הייתי מצטער על פסוק זה בכל נפשך אפילו נוטל את נשמתך אמרתי מתי יבא לידי ואקיימנו ועכשיו שבא לידי לא אקיימנו היה מאריך באחד עד שיצתה נשמתו באחד יצתה בת קול ואמרה אשריך ר"ע שיצאה נשמתך באחד אמרו מלאכי השרת לפני הקב"ה זו *תורה וזו שכרה °ממתים ידך יי' ממתים וגו' אמר להם חלקם בחיים יצתה בת קול ואמרה אשריך ר"ע *שאתה מזומן לחיי העה"ב: [ג]לא יקל אדם את ראשו כנגד שער המזרח שהוא מכוון כנגד בית קדשי הקדשים וכו': אמר רב יהודה אמר רב לא אמרו אלא מן הצופים ולפנים וברואה אתמר נמי א"ר אבא בריה דר' חייא בר אבא הכי א"ר יוחנן לא אמרו [ד]אלא מן הצופים ולפנים וברואה ובשאין גדר ובזמן שהשכינה שורה ת"ר הנפנה ביהודה לא יפנה מזרח ומערב אלא צפון ודרום ובגליל לא יפנה אלא מזרח ומערב ור' יוסי מתיר שהיה ר' יוסי אומר לא אסרו אלא ברואה ובמקום שאין שם גדר ובזמן שהשכינה שורה וחכמים אוסרים חכמים היינו ת"ק איכא בינייהו צדדין תניא אידך הנפנה ביהודה לא יפנה מזרח ומערב אלא צפון ודרום ובגליל צפון ודרום אסור מזרח ומערב מותר ור' יוסי מתיר שהיה ר' יוסי אומר לא אסרו אלא ברואה ר' יהודה אומר בזמן שב"ה קיים אסור בזמן שאין ב"ה קיים מותר ר"ע אוסר בכל מקום ר"ע היינו ת"ק איכא בינייהו ח"ל. רבה הוו שדיין ליה לבני מזרח ומערב אזל אביי שדנהו צפון ודרום על רבה תרצנהו אמר מאן האי דקמצער לי [ה]אנא כר"ע סבירא לי דאמר בכל מקום אסור:

תניא

ר"ע אוסר בכל מקום. מזרח אחוריו ופניו למערב ומשקי' אפילו בח"ל ומפרש בירושלמי ובלבד שאין שם כותל

רבא

שואבת כל מיני משקין. אע"פ שאין נכנסין בכבד דרך הושט הריאה מוללתן ושואבתן מעבר לדפני הכבד: זורקת בו טפה. מרה ומניחתו מן הכעס: שוחק. שחוק: קרקבן. בעוף הוא המסס בבהמה: טוחן. המאכל: אף. החוטם: נעור. מקיצו משנתו: נעור הישן וישן הנעור. שמתחלפה ובאה השינה מן האף והקיצה נעורת: נמוק והולך לו. מתמוגג והולך לו ונמשך למיתה. לשון אחר נעור הישן הקיבה ונמצאו קיבה ואף נעורים שאינו ישן כלל או ישן הנעור ונמצאו שניהם ישנים ואינו נעור כי אם בקושי: ולבי חלל בקרבי. יצר הרע הרי הוא כמת בקרבי שיש בידי לכופו: נאם פשע לרשע וגו'. אמר דוד בקרב לבי יש ואומר אני שהפשע נאם לרשע כלומר שיצר הרע אומר לרשע אל יהא פחד אלהים לנגד עיניך אלמא יצר הרע שופטו עד שמרחיקו שאינו מתפחד מיוצרו: כי יעמוד. הקב"ה: לימין אביון להושיע משופטי נפשו. ש"מ יש לך אדם שיש לנפשו שני שופטים: לא שבק מר חיי לכל בריה. אם אתה מן הבינונים אין לך צדיק גמור בעולם: לרשיעי גמורי. העולם הזה שאין להם בעולם הבא כלום וצריכים ליטול שכרן כאן כגון אחאב שהיה עשיר מאד דקאמר ליה בן הדד כספך וזהבך לי הוא (מ"א כ): לצדיקי גמורי העולם הבא. שאין להם בעולם הזה כלום כגון רבי חנינא בן דוסא שדי לו בקב חרובין מערב שבת לערב שבת (תענית כד.): לכך נאמר בכל מאדך. מן החביב עליך: והיה מקבל עליו עול מלכות שמים. קורא קרית שמע: ממתים ידך יי' ממתים. מידך היה לו למות ולא מידי בשר ודם: מן הצופים. מקום שיכולין לראות משם הר הבית ומשם והלאה אין יכולין לראותו: וברואה. שיכול לראות משם פרט אם מקום נמוך הוא: ובשאין גדר. מפסיק בינו להר הבית: ובזמן שהשכינה שורה. שבית המקדש קיים: הנפנה ביהודה לא יפנה מזרח ומערב. אחוריו למזרח ופניו למערב ולא אחוריו למערב ופניו למזרח מפני שירושלים בארץ יהודה היא בצפונה של ארץ יהודה בגבול שבין יהודה לבנימין ויש מארץ יהודה הימנה (למזרח) עד סוף ארץ ישראל והימנה למערב עד סוף ארץ ישראל שארץ יהודה על פני כל אורך ארץ ישראל היא מן המזרח למערב כדכתיב' ארוכה וקצרה ואם יפנה מזרח ומערב יהיה פרועו נגד ירושלים או פרועו שלפניו או פרועו שלאחריו אבל צפון ודרום יפנה ובלבד שלא יפנה כנגד ירושלים ממש בדרומה של ארץ יהודה: ובגליל. שהיא בצפונה של א"י לא יחזיר פניו לצפון ודרום אלא מזרח ומערב: ה"ג וחכמים אוסרים ולא גרסינן בכל מקום: חכמים היינו ת"ק. דאמר לא יפנה ולא מפליג בין רואה ללא רואה בין בזמן הבית בין בזמן הזה: איכא בינייהו צדדים. דיהודה וגליל שאינן כנגד ירושלים ממש לתנא קמא לדידהו אסירי דהא הנפנה ביהודה קאמר כל יהודה משמע ורבנן בתראי סברי כנגד ירושלי' ממש אסור אבל צדדין מותר דהא אדר' יוסי קיימי דאמר לא אסרו אלא ברואה אבל ברחוק לא ואפילו כנגד ירושלי' ממש ואתו רבנן למימר וחכמים אוסרים אפילו שלא ברואה ואפילו בזמן הזה ונהי נגד ירושלים לא: בדר' עקיבא גרסינן בכל מקום הלכך בחוצה לארץ נמי קאמר: הוו שדיין ליה לבני. לבנים שישב עליהם לפנות היו מתוקנות תקופות על צדיהן ראשן א' למזרח והשני למערב לבנה אחת לצפון ולבנה אחת לדרום והוא יושב על האחת ונפנה ביניהם נמצא הוא נפנה צפון ודרום ולא היה רוצה לפנות בגבול מזרח ומערב לפי שבבל במזרחה של ארץ ישראל עומדת שלא יהא פרועו לא מלפניו ולא מלאחריו נגד ארץ ישראל: אזל אביי שדנהו צפון ודרום. לראות אם יקפיד רבו על כך אי סבירא ליה כר"ע דאמר בח"ל נמי קפדינן עלה דמלתא:

אחר

עין משפט נר מצוה

עג א מיי' פ"ה מהל' יסודי התורה הלכה ז סמג עשין ג

עד ב מיי' פ"ז מה' בית הבחירה הל' ה

עה ג מיי' שם הלכ' ח

עו ד מיי' שם ה"ט טוש"ע א"ח סי' ג סעי' ה

מסורת הש"ס

תהלים קט

שם לו

שם קט

[בע"י וילקוט איתא רבה וכן הוא נכון לפמ"ש תוס' ערכין ה. ד"ה והא שלא אמר אביי מר לרבה מבינון]

פסחים כה. סנהדרין עד. יומא פב.

[בילקוט רמז תתל"ד איתא ר' עקיבא אומר אם נאמר בכל נפשך ק"ו בכל מאדך אלא בכל מדה ומדה שהוא מודד לך בין במדת הטוב בין במדת הפורענות]

דברים ל

(ירוש' הביא שאלתם על שם טורנוסרופוס שדן אותו)

תהלים יז

[מנחות כט:]

[ע' תוס' כתובו' קג: ד"ה מזומן וכו']

voice, [61b] the lungs absorb all kinds of liquids,[8] the liver is the seat of anger, the gall lets a drop fall into it and allays it, the milt produces laughter, the large intestine grinds [the food], the maw brings sleep and the nose awakens. If the awakener sleeps or the a sleeper rouses,[1] a man pines away. A Tanna taught: If both induce sleep or both awaken, a man dies forthwith.

It has been taught: R. Jose the Galilean says, The righteous are swayed[2] by their good inclination, as it says, *My heart*[3] *is slain within me*.[4] The wicked are swayed by their evil inclination, as it says, *Transgression speaketh to the wicked, methinks, there is no fear of God before his eyes*.[5] Average people are swayed by both inclinations, as it says, *Because He standeth at the right hand of the needy,*[6] *to save him from them that judge his soul*.[7] Raba said: People such as we are of the average. Said Abaye to him: The Master gives no one a chance to live![8] Raba further said: The world was created only for either the totally wicked or the totally righteous.[9] Raba said: Let a man know concerning himself whether he is completely righteous or not! Rab said: The world was created only for Ahab son of Omri and for R. Ḥanina b. Dosa; for Ahab son of Omri this world, and for R. Ḥanina b. Dosa the future world.

And thou shalt love the Lord thy God etc.[10] It has been taught: R. Eliezer says: If it says '*with all thy soul*', why should it also say, '*with all thy might*',[11] and if it says '*with all thy might*', why should it also say '*with all thy soul*'? Should there be a man who values his life more than his money, for him it says; '*with all thy soul*'; and should there be a man who values his money more than his life, for him it says, '*with all thy might*'. R. Akiba says: '*With all thy soul*': even if He takes away thy soul.[12]

Our Rabbis taught: Once the wicked Government[13] issued a decree forbidding the Jews to study and practise the Torah. Pappus b. Judah came and found R. Akiba publicly bringing gatherings together and occupying himself with the Torah. He said to him: Akiba, are you not afraid of the Government? He replied: I will explain to you with a parable. A fox was once walking alongside of a river, and he saw fishes going in swarms from one place to another. He said to them: From what are you fleeing? They replied: From the nets cast for us by men. He said to them: Would you like to come up on to the dry land so that you and I can live together in the way that my ancestors lived with your ancestors? They replied: Art thou the one that they call the cleverest of animals? Thou art not clever but foolish. If we are afraid in the element in which we live, how much more in the element in which we would die! So it is with us. If such is our condition when we sit and study the Torah, of which it is written, b *For that is thy life and the length of thy days*,[1] if we go and neglect it how much worse off we shall be! It is related that soon afterwards R. Akiba was arrested and thrown into prison, and Pappus b. Judah was also arrested and imprisoned next to him. He said to him: Pappus, who brought you here? He replied: Happy are you, R. Akiba, that you have been seized for busying yourself with the Torah! Alas for Pappus who has been seized for busying himself with idle things! When R. Akiba was taken out for execution, it was the hour for the recital of the *Shema'*, and while they combed his flesh with iron combs, he was accepting upon himself the kingship of heaven.[2] His disciples said to him: Our teacher, even to this point? He said to them: All my days I have been troubled by this verse, '*with all thy soul*', [which I interpret,] 'even if He takes thy soul'. I said: When shall I have the opportunity of[3] fulfilling this? Now that I have the opportunity shall I not fulfil it? He prolonged the word *eḥad*[4] until he expired while saying it. A *bath kol*[5] went forth and proclaimed: Happy art thou, Akiba, that thy soul has departed with the word *eḥad!* The ministering angels said before the Holy One, blessed be He: Such Torah, and such a reward? [He should have been] *from them that die by Thy hand, O Lord*.[6] He replied to them: *Their portion is in life*.[7] A *bath kol* went forth and proclaimed, Happy art thou, R. Akiba, that thou art destined for the life of the world to come.

ONE SHOULD AVOID SHOWING DISRESPECT TO THE EASTERN GATE BECAUSE IT IS IN A DIRECT LINE WITH THE HOLY OF HOLIES, etc. Rab Judah said in the name of Rab: These rules c apply only to this side of Mount Scopus[1] and to one who can see the Temple.[2] It has also been recorded: R. Abba the son of R. Ḥiyya b. Abba said: Thus said R. Joḥanan: These rules apply only to this side of Scopus and to one who can see [Jerusalem], and when there is no fence intervening, and at the time when the Divine Presence rests on it.[3]

Our Rabbis taught: One who consults nature in Judea should not do so east and west[4] but north and south. In Galilee he should do so only east and west.[5] R. Jose, however, allows it, since R. Jose said: The prohibition was meant to apply only to one in sight of the Temple and in a place where there is no fence intervening and at the time when the Divine Presence rests there. The Sages, however, forbid it. The Sages say the same as the First Tanna?—They differ with regard to the sides.[6] It has been taught elsewhere: One who consults nature in Judea should not do so east and west but south and north, and in Galilee north and south is forbidden, east and west is permitted. R. Jose, however, permits it, since R. Jose used to say: This prohibition was meant to apply only to one who is in sight [of Jerusalem]. R. Judah says: When the Temple is in existence it is forbidden, when the Temple is not in existence it is permitted. R. Akiba forbids it in all places. R. Akiba says the same as the First Tanna?—They differ in the matter of outside of Palestine. Rabbah had bricks placed for him east and west.[7] Abaye went and changed them round to north and south. Rabbah went in and readjusted them. He said, Who is this that is annoying me? I take the view of R. Akiba, who said that it is forbidden in every place.

(8) I.e., they absorb some moisture from the stomach.

a (1) I.e., if the nose induces sleep or the maw waking. (2) Lit., 'judged'. (3) I.e., evil promptings (4) Ps. CIX, 22. E.V. '*wounded*'. (5) Ibid. XXXVI, 2. (6) I.e., in good deeds. (7) I.e., his two inclinations. Ibid. CIX, 31. (8) If Raba is only average, what must other people be? (9) I.e., this world for the wicked and the next for the righteous. (10) Deut. VI, 5. (11) This word is interpreted by the Rabbis to mean money. (12) I.e., thy very self, thy life. (13) I.e., Roman.

b (1) Deut. XXX, 20. (2) I.e., recited the *Shema'*. V. *supra* 13a. (3) Lit., 'when will it come to my hands'. (4) 'One' in Hear, O Israel etc. (5) V. Glos. (6) Ps. XVII, 14. E.V. '*From men by thy hand, O Lord*'. (7) Ibid.

c (1) From the other side of Mount Scopus the Temple was no longer visible. (2) Even from this side of Scopus, not being in a hollow. (3) I.e., when the Temple is in existence. (4) So as not to turn his back to Jerusalem. (5) Galilee being north of Jerusalem. (6) I.e., those parts of Judea and Galilee which were not due east or due north of Jerusalem. The first Tanna prohibits even in these parts, since they speak of the whole of Judea, whereas the Sages permit, referring as they do only to R. Jose's statement. (7) So that he should not turn his back on Palestine.

[62*a*]. It has been taught: R. Akiba said: Once I went in after R. Joshua to a privy, and I learnt from him three things. I learnt that one does not sit east and west but north and south; I learnt that one evacuates not standing but sitting; and I learnt that it is proper to wipe with the left hand and not with the right. Said Ben 'Azzai to him: Did you dare to take such liberties with your master?—He replied: It was a matter of Torah, and I required to learn. It has been taught: Ben 'Azzai said: Once I went in after R. Akiba to a privy, and I learnt from him three things. I learnt that one does not evacuate east and west but north and south. I also learnt that one evacuates sitting and not standing. I also learnt it is proper to wipe with the left hand and not with the right. Said R. Judah to him: Did you dare to take such liberties with your master?—He replied: It was a matter of Torah, and I required to learn. R. Kahana once went in and hid under Rab's bed. He heard him chatting [with his wife] and joking and doing what he required. He said to him: One would think that Abba's mouth had never sipped the dish before! He said to him: Kahana,
a are you here? Go out, because it is rude.[1] He replied: It is a matter of Torah, and I require to learn.

Why should one wipe with the left hand and not with the right?—Raba said: Because the Torah was given with the right hand, as it says, *At His right hand was a fiery law unto them.*[2] Rabbah b. Ḥanah said: Because it is brought to the mouth.[3] R. Simeon b. Laḳish said: Because one binds the *tefillin* [on the left arm] with it. R. Naḥman b. Isaac said: Because he points to the accents in the scroll with it.[4] A similar difference of opinion is found among Tannaim. R. Eliezer says, because one eats with it; R. Joshua says, because one writes with it; R. Akiba says, because one points with it to the accents in the scroll.

R. Tanḥum b. Hanilai said: Whoever behaves modestly in a privy is delivered from three things: from snakes, from scorpions, and from evil spirits. Some say also that he will not have disturbing
b dreams.[1] There was a certain privy in Tiberias which if two persons entered together even by day, they came to harm. R. Ammi and R. Assi used to enter it separately, and they suffered no harm. The Rabbis said to them, Are you not afraid? They replied: We have learnt a certain tradition.[2] The tradition for [avoiding harm in] the privy is modesty and silence; the tradition relating to sufferings is silence[3] and prayer. The mother of Abaye trained for him a lamb to go with him into the privy.[4] She should rather have trained for him a goat?[5]—A satyr might be changed into a goat.[6] Before Raba became head of the Academy, the daughter of R. Ḥisda[7] used to rattle a nut in a brass dish.[8] After he became head, she made a window for him,[9] and put her hand on his head.[10]

'Ulla said: Behind a fence one may ease himself immediately; in an open field, so long as he can break wind without anyone hearing it. Issi b. Nathan reported thus: Behind a fence, as long as he can break wind without anyone hearing it; in a open field, as long as he cannot be seen by anyone. An objection was raised: [The watchers][11] may go out by the door of the olive press and ease themselves behind a fence [immediately] and they [the olives] remain clean!—For the sake of ritual purity they made a concession. Come and hear: How far can one go without affecting the cleanness [of the olive press]? Any distance as long as he can still see it![12]—The case of food-stuffs prepared in purity is different, as the Rabbis made a concession for them. R. Ashi said: What is meant by the words 'as long as he cannot be seen by anyone' used by Issi b. Nathan? As long as the exposed part of his body cannot be seen; but the man himself may be seen.

A certain funeral orator went down in the presence of R. Naḥman [to deliver an address] and said: This man was modest in all his ways. Said R. Naḥman to him: Did you ever follow him into a privy so that you should know whether he was modest or not? For it has been taught: A man is called modest only if he is such in the privy. And why was R. Naḥman so much concerned about
c it? Because it has been taught: Just as the dead are punished,[1] so the funeral orators are punished[2] and those who answer [Amen] after them.

Our Rabbis taught: Who is a modest man? One who eases himself by night in the place where he eased himself by day.[3] Is that so? Has not Rab Judah said in the name of Rab: A man should always accustom himself [to consult nature] in the early morning and in the evening[4] so that he may have no need to go a long distance? And again, in the day-time Raba used to go as far as a *mil*, but at night he said to his attendant, Clear me a spot in the street of the town, and so too R. Zera said to his attendant, See if there is anyone behind the Seminary as I wish to ease myself?—Do not read 'in the place', but read, 'in the same way as he eases himself by day'.[5] R. Ashi said, You may even retain the reading 'place', the reference being to a private corner.[6]

The [above] text [states:] 'Rab Judah said in the name of Rab: A man should always accustom himself to consult nature morning and evening so that he may have no need to go a long distance'. It has been taught similarly, Ben 'Azzai said: Go forth before dawn and after dark, so that you should not have to go far. Feel yourself before sitting, but do not sit and then feel yourself, for if one sits and then feels himself, should witchcraft be used
d against him even as far away as Aspamia,[1] he will not be immune from it. And if he forgets and does sit and then feels, what is his remedy?—When he rises he should say, thus: Not for me, not for me; not *taḥim* nor *taḥtim;*[2] not these nor any part of these;[3] neither the sorceries of sorcerers nor the sorceries of sorceresses!

a (1) Lit., 'it is not the way of the world'. (2) Deut. XXXIII, 2. (3) It was usual to bring food to the mouth with the right hand and not with the left. (4) Rashi explains: Because in chanting he makes corresponding movements with the right hand, this having been the custom of Palestinians in his day.
b (1) Lit., 'his dreams will be settled on him'. (2) Jastrow, with a slight change of reading (*kible*), renders 'charm'. (3) I.e., resignation. (4) As a protection against evil spirits. (5) Goats were associated by the ancients with evil spirits. (6) The Hebrew word *sa'ir* means both 'he-goat' and 'satyr'. (7) His wife. (8) To frighten away the evil spirits. (9) In the wall of the house, through which she could put her hand. (10) As a protection. After becoming head of the Academy, he was more exposed to danger from the evil spirits. (11) Men who watched the olive-oil press to see that no unclean person entered. (12) But not further, so that he would himself still be visible. This refutes Issi.
c (1) If they were sinners. (2) For uttering false eulogies. (3) I.e., a long way off. (4) I.e., before daylight and after dark. (5) I.e., modestly; v. *supra.* (6) To be used by night as well as by day.
d (1) A name given to several far-distant places, including Spain. (2) Words apparently used in incantations. (3) *Aliter:* 'Let not avail against me either the sorceries etc.'.

תורה אור

*תניא א"ר עקיבא פעם אחת נכנסתי אחר ר' יהושע לבית הכסא ולמדתי ממנו *ג' דברים למדתי שאין נפנין מזרח ומערב אלא צפון ודרום [א]ולמדתי שאין נפרעין מעומד אלא מיושב [ב]ולמדתי שאין מקנחין בימין אלא בשמאל א"ל בן עזאי עד כאן העזת פניך ברבך א"ל תורה היא וללמוד אני צריך תניא בן עזאי אומר פעם אחת נכנסתי אחר ר"ע לבית הכסא ולמדתי ממנו שלש' דברים למדתי שאין נפנין מזרח ומערב אלא צפון ודרום ולמדתי שאין נפרעין מעומד אלא מיושב ולמדתי שאין מקנחין בימין אלא בשמאל אמר לו ר' יהודה עד כאן העזת פניך ברבך אמר לו תורה היא וללמוד אני צריך רב כהנא על גנא תותי' פורייה דרב שמעיה דשח ושחק ועשה צרכיו אמר ליה *דמי פומיה דאבא כדלא שריף תבשילא א"ל כהנא הכא את פוק דלאו אורח ארעא א"ל תורה היא וללמוד אני צריך מפני מה אין מקנחין בימין אלא בשמאל אמר רבא מפני שהתורה ניתנה בימין שנאמר °מימינו אש דת למו רבה בר בר חנה אמר מפני שהיא קרובה לפה ור' שמעון בן לקיש אמר מפני שקושר בה תפילין רב נחמן בר יצחק אמר מפני שמראה בה טעמי תורה כתנאי ר' אליעזר אומר מפני שאוכל בה ר' יהושע אומר מפני שכותב בה ר"ע אומר מפני שמראה בה טעמי תורה א"ר תנחום בר חנילאי כל הצנוע בבי' הכסא נצול משלשה דברים מן הנחשים ומן העקרבים ומן המזיקין וי"א אף חלומותיו מיושבי' עליו ההוא בית הכסא דהוה בטבריא כי הוו עיילו ביה בי תרי אפי' בימָמא מתזקי רבי אמי ור' אסי הוו עיילו ביה חד וחד לחודיה ולא מתזקי אמרי להו רבנן לא מסתפיתו אמרי להו אנן קבלה גמירינן קבלה דבית הכסא צניעות' ושתיקותא קבלה דיסורי שתיקותא ומבעי רחמי אביי מרביא ליה אמרא למיעל בהדיה לבית הכסא ולרבי' ליה גדיא שעיר בשעיר מיחלף רבא מקמי דהוה רישא מקרקשא ליה בת רב חסדא אמגוזא בלקנא בתר דמלך עבדא ליה כוות' ומנחה ליה ידא ארישיה אמר עולא [ג]אחורי הגדר נפנה מיד ובבקעה כל זמן שמתעטש ואין חברו שומע איסי בר נתן מתני הכי אחורי הגדר כל זמן שמתעטש ואין חברו שומע [ד]ובבקעה כל זמן שאין חברו רואהו מתיבי *[ה]יוצאין מפתח בית הבד ונפנין לאחורי הגדר והן טהורין בטהרות הקלו תא שמע *[ו]כמה ירחקו ויהיו טהורין כדי שיהא רואהו שאני אוכלי טהרות דאקילו בהו רבנן רב אשי אמר [ז]מאי כל זמן שאין חברו רואהו דקאמר איסי בר נתן כל זמן שאין חברו רואה את פרועו אבל לדידיה חזי ליה ההוא ספדנא דנחית קמיה דרב נחמן אמר האי צנוע באורחותיו הוה א"ל רב נחמן את עיילת בהדיה לבית הכסא וידעת אי צנוע אי לא דתניא אין קורין צנוע אלא למי שצנוע בבית הכסא ורב נחמן מאי נפקא ליה מיניה משום דתני' *[ח]כשם שנפרעין מן המתים כך נפרעין מן הספדנים ומן העוני' אחריהן *ת"ר איזהו צנוע זה הנפנה בלילה במקום שנפנה ביום איני *והאמר רב יהודה אמר רב [ט]לעולם ינהיג אדם את עצמו שחרית וערבית כדי שלא יהא צריך להתרחק ותו רבא ביממ' הוה אזיל עד מיל ובליליא' א"ל לשמעי' פני לי דוכת' ברחובה דמתא וכן א"ל ר' זירא לשמעיה חזי מאן דאיכא אחורי בית חבריא דבעינא למפני לא תימא במקום אלא אימא [י]כדרך שנפנה ביום רב אשי אמר אפילו תימא במקום לא נצרכ' אלא לקרן זוית גופא אמר רב יהודה אמר רב לעולם ינהיג אדם עצמו שחרית וערבית כדי שלא יהא צריך להתרחק תנ"ה בן עזאי אומר השכם וצא הערב וצא כדי שלא תתרחק משמש ושב ואל תשב ותמשמש שכל היושב וממשמש אפי' עושין כשפים באספמיא באין עליו ואי אנשי ויתיב ואח"כ משמש מאי תקנתי' כי קאי לימ' הכי לא לי לא לי לא תחים ולא תחתים לא הני ולא מהני לא חרשי' דחרש' ולא חרשי דחרשתא

תניא

רש"י

אחר ר' יהושע וכו'. וביהודה הוה: עד כאן. כלומר כל זה העזת פניך בפני רבך שנסתכלת בכל אלו: דשח ושחק. עם אשתו שיחה בטלה של ריצוי תשמיש: ועשה צרכיו. ושימש מטתו: כדלא שריף תבשילא. כאדם רעב כמו שלא שמשת מעתך מעול' שאתה נוהג קלות ראש זה לתאותך: שריף. הו"מיל בלע"ז: שקרובה לפה. רגילין להושיטה לפה: שקושר בה תפילין. בזרוע שמאלו: טעמי תורה. נגינות טעמי מקרא של תורה נביאים וכתובים בין בניקוד של ספר בין בהגבהת קול ובצלצול נעימות הנגינה של פשטא ודרגא ושופר מהפך מוליך ידו לפי טעם הנגינה ראיתי בקוראים הבאים מארץ ישראל: מן הנחשים ומן העקרבים ומן המזיקין. דמתוך צניעתו מתנהג בנחת ובשתיקה ואין הנחשים מרגישי' להתקנאות בו ואף המזיקין חסין עליו: חלומותיו מיושבים עליו. שאין המזיקין מבהילין אותו: קבלה. מסורת ומנהג שקבלנו מרבותינו בבית הכסא: קבלה דיסורי שתיקותא. שלא יבעט ביסורין הבאים עליו: מרביא ליה אמרא. מגדלת לו שה ומלמדתו שהולך עמו תמיד: שעיר. שד של בית הכסא דומה לשעיר ועליהם נאמר (ישעיה יג) ושעירים ירקדו שם: אמגוזא בלקנא. נותנת אגוז בספל של נחשת ומקרקשת בו מבית והוא נפנה כנגדם מבחוץ: בתר דמלך. ונעשה ראש ישיבה צריך שימור טפי מפני המזיקים *שמתקנאי' השדים בתלמידי חכמים יותר משאר בני אדם: כוותא. חלון כנגד מקום שהוא נפנה שם אחורי הבית: אחורי הגדר נפנה מיד. ואין צריך להתרחק כלום: ובבקעה. צריך להתרחק כדי שלא ישמע חברו עטושי' של מטה אבל אין צריך להתרחק עד כדי שלא יראנו: רב אשי אמר וכו'. לא גרסי' עד לקמן דמוקי לדאיסי בר נתן בהכי: יוצאים מפתח בית הבד. משומרי טהרות של שמן בית הבד אם הולרכו לפנות יוצאי' מפתח בית הבד ונפנין לאחורי הגדר שלפני הפתח ואין חוששין שמא בתוך כך יכנס עם הארץ ויגע אלמא נפנים לאחורי הגד' מיד: בטהרות הקלו. בשביל שמיר' טהרות הקלו בבית הכסא: כמה ירחקו. שומרי טהרות: כדי שיהא רואהו. וכיון דאינו יכול להתרחק יותר על כרחך אם הולך לפנות יפנה תיובתא דאיסי דבעי שלא יראנו: דאקילו בהו רבנן. בשביל שמירתן הקלו בבית הכסא: אבל לדידיה חזי ליה. אבל הוא עצמו את חביריו יכול לראו' ולא ירחיק: במקום שנפנה ביום. מתרחק מבני אדם בלילה כביום: ינהיג אדם עצמו. לפנות: שחרית. קודם היום: וערבית. משחשכה: כדי שלא יהא צריך להתרחק. אלמא אין מתרחקין בלילה: פני לי דוכתא. מבני אדם: כדרך שנפנה ביום. לצנין פרוע טפח ועפחיים כדאמרינן בפרקי קמאי (פ"ג דף כג:) ומיושב כדאמרי' לעיל: לקרן זוית. אם יש קרן זוית סמוך צריך להסתלק שם בלילה כבי' ולא יפנה בגלוי: משמש. בצרור או בקיס' לפתוח נקבי' כדאמרי' במס' שבת (דף פב.) לשון אחר משמש המושב שלא יהא מלוכלך ולשון ראשון הגון דא"כ למה לי משום כשפי' תיפו' לי כיון שישב כבר מלוכלים בגדיו ומה יועיל משמושו: לא לי לא לי. לא תוכלי לי: לא תחים ולא תחתים. הם שמות הכשפים המעשיים ע"י תחתוניות: לא הני ולא מהני. לא כולן ולא מקצתן: לא חרשי דחרשא ולא דחרשתא. לא מכשפות מכשף זכר ולא מכשפות מכשפה נקבה לשון אחר לא הכי ולא מהכי לא יצלח ולא יועיל עוד מכשפות:

על

תוספות

רבא מקמי דהוה רישא כו' בתר דמלך עבדא כוותא ומנחא ליה ידא כו'. תימה דע"כ לא מלך רבא עד אחר פטירתו של אביי כדמשמע לעיל *בעובדא דבר הדי' [דף נו.] וכן בכתובות דקאמר חומה דביתהו דאביי אתיא לקמיה דרבא בסוף פרק אע"פ (דף סה.) והוו תימה דלעיל (דף נו.) משמע דראה בחלום פטירת' קודם פטירתו דאביי וי"ל מכל מקום לא נפטרה עד אחר אביי:

סליקו תוספות דמסכת ברכות

מסורת הש"ס

מס' ד"א פ"ז (ירושלמי מוסיף לא ישב עד שישפשף)

[מגילה כח.]

[אדר"כ פ"מ וכד"א פ"ז] חגיגה ה: [לעיל כד:]

דברי' לג

טהרות פ"י מ"ב שם

[ע"ז מז:] הוריות יג:

[פי' כשם שנפרעין מן המת אם הוא חוטא כך נפרעין מן הספדנין שאומרים עליו שהוא צדיק ערוך ערך ספד]

עין משפט נר מצוה

עז [א]מיי' פ"ה מהל' דעות הלכה ו טוש"ע א"ח סי' ג סעי' ב

עח [ב]מיי' שם טוש"ע א"ח שם סעי' י

עט [ג]מיי' שם טוש"ע א"ח שם סעיף ח

פ [ה]מיי' פי"ג מהלכות טומאת משכב ומושב הלכה ב

פא [ז]מיי' פ"ה מהלכו' דעות הלכה ו טוש"ע א"ח סי' ג סעי' ח

פב [ח]מיי' שם טוש"ע י"ד סי' שמד סעיף א

פג [ט]מיי' פ"ה מהלכות דיעות הל' ו טוש"ע א"ח סי' ב סעיף ו

פד [י]מיי' שם טוש"ע א"ח סי' ג סעי' יב

עין משפט נר מצוה

[ע' בערוך ערך אסטמ' ועי' עוד במוסף הערוך ערך שן ר' שפירש השתנה מלשון את שיניהם מלכים יט]

פה אבג מיי' פ"ה מהלכות תפלה הלכה יוד סמג עשין יט טוש"ע א"ח סי' קנא סעיף ה

פו ד מיי' פ"ז מהלכות בית הבחירה הל' ז סמג עשין קסד

פז ה מיי' שם הלכה ג

על כל מושב שב חוץ מן הקורה. שמא תפול: כאסטמא לפרזלא. אליי"ר בלעז שמועיל לברזל כך מועיל לגוף יציאה להפנות: אדכפנת אכול. שאם תשהא תעבור ממך תאות המאכל ואין המאכל מועיל: עד דרתחא קדרך שפוך. קודם שתצטרך משל הוא זה כשאתה צריך לנקביך שפוך ואל תשהא אותם: קרנא קריא ברומי. אם תשמע קול קרן ברומי הוא סימן למבקשי' תאנים לקנות ולהוליך למקום אחר: בר מזבין תאני דאבוך זבין. אם אין אביך בבית הזהר אתה בנו למכור תאניו בעוד שיש תובעים: בשבילי. שביל קטן שהולכים בו לשדות: נחר ליה אבבא. לידע אם יש שם אדם כמו טו"סיר בלעז: אמר ליה. ר' אבא לרב ספרא: עד כאן לא עיילת לשעיר. שאיכן לכוונן בבית הכסא: וגמרת לך מילי דשעיר. שאיכך לכוון: לאו הכי תנן. במסכת תמיד: מדורה היתה שם. בעזרה היסק גדול של אור להתחמם שם הכהנים המסיכים רגליהם בבית הכסא שצריכין טבילה כדתנן במסכת יומא (דף כח.) כל המסך רגליו טעון טבילה: ובית הכסא של כבוד. אלמא אין מספרים בבית הכסא ואת אמרת ליעול מר: והוא סבר. רב ספרא שאמר לומר ליעול מר סבר מסוכן הוא בעמוד החוזר אם ישוב לאחוריו ויחזור העמוד: הדרוקן. כרסו לבה: דרקונא

דרקונא. נחש: שמטי' לכרכשיה. האלולית שהרעי יוצא בו שקורין טנבחיא: ואמר להרגך ותחס עליך. דוד אמר לשאול כן באמתו מן המערה שנכנס בו לפנות וכרת דוד את כנף מעילו ואמר להרגך הקב"ה התיר לי להרגך: התורה אמרה וכו'. אם במחתרת ימצא הגנב וגו' (שמות כב) וכבר פירשנוהו למעלה במעשה דר' שילא (דף נח.): צניעות שראיתי בך. שנכנס למערה בשביל הצנע ואף שם נהג צניעות כדמפרש ואזיל: שסכך. רגליו בבגדיו כסוכה: שיש בו ליפרע כמה. שיש במיתתו כדי לכפר על כמה עונות: ובהשחית ראה יי' וינחם. מקרא הוא באותה פרשה בדברי הימים: כסף כפורים ראה. שנתן במנין ראשון של ישראל למשכן והוא כפר על מנין זה שהרי לזכרון נתן כדכתיב והיה לבני ישראל לזכרון לכפר ועכשיו הוצרכה כפרתו: כשמה. כמשמע' פי' שמה: אדמקיפנא אדרי איעול בהאי. בעוד שאני מקיף כל שורות הבתים הללו אכנס כאן לקצר דרכי. אדרי שורות: קפנדריא. טרי"א בלעז: מעיקרא. קודם שנבנה עליו בית הכנסת. נילף מקפנדריא. לאיסור' דתנן במסכת מגילה (דף כח.) אין עושין בית הכנסת קפנדריא. תנא יליף. רקיקה ממנעל: פונדתו. אזור חלול שנותנין בו מעות: ואימא

מסורת הש"ס

[בערוך ערך כפן פירש דברים אלו על דרך מוסר יפה ע"ש]

תמיד כז:

שם כו.

שם ולעיל כה. [בכורות מד:]

תורה אור

תניא בן עזאי אומר על כל משכב שכב חוץ מן הקרקע על כל מושב שב חוץ מן הקורה אמר שמואל שינה בעמוד השחר *כאסטמא לפרזלא יציאה בעמוד השחר כאסטמא לפרזלא בר קפר' הוה מזבן מילי בדינרי עד דכפנת אכול עד דצחית שתי עד דרתח' קדרך שפוך קרנא קריא ברומי בר מזבין תאני דאבוך זבין אמר להו אביי לרבנן כי עייליתו בשבילי דמחוזא למיפק ביה בחקלא לא תחזו לא להך גיס' ולא להך גיסא דילמא יתבי נשי ולאו אורח ארע' לאסתכולי בהו *רב ספרא על לבית הכסא אתא ר' אבא נחר ליה אבבא א"ל ליעול מר בתר דנפק א"ל עד השתא לא עיילת לשעיר וגמרת לך מילי דשעיר לאו הכי תנן *מדורה היתה שם ובית הכסא של כבוד וזה היה כבודו מצאו נעול בידוע שיש שם אדם מצאו פתוח בידוע שאין שם אדם אלמא לאו אורח ארע' הוא והוא סבר מסוכן הוא *דתניא רבן שמעון בן גמליאל אומר עמוד החוזר מביא את האדם לידי הדרוקן סלון החוזר מביא את האדם לידי ירקון רבי אלעזר על לבית הכסא אתא ההוא *פרסאה דחקיה קם רבי אלעזר ונפק אתא דרקונא שמטיה לכרכשיה קרי עליה רבי אלעזר °ואתן אדם תחתיך אל תקרי אדם אלא אדום: °ואמר להרגך ותחס ישעיה מג
עליך ואמר ואמרתי מיבעי ליה ותחס וחסתי מיבעי ליה א"ר אלעזר אמר לו דוד לשאול מן התורה בן הריגה אתה שמואל א כד
שהרי רודף אתה *והתורה אמרה בא להרגך השכם להרגו אלא צניעות שהיתה בך היא חסה עליך ומאי היא [לעיל כח. סנה' עב.]
דכתיב °ויבא אל גדרות הצאן על הדרך ושם מער' ויבא שאול להסך את רגליו תנא גדר לפנים מן גדר ומערה שם
לפנים ממערה להסך אמר ר' אלעזר מלמד שסכך עצמו כסוכה: °ויקם דוד ויכרת את כנף המעיל אשר שם
לשאול בלט אמר ר' יוסי ברבי חנינא כל המבזה את הבגדים סוף אינו נהנה מהם שנאמר °והמלך דוד זקן מלכים א א
בא בימים ויכסוהו בבגדים ולא יחם לו: °אם ה' הסיתך בי ירח מנחה א"ר אלעזר א"ל הקב"ה לדוד מסית שמואל א כו
קרית לי הרי אני מכשילך בדבר שאפי' תינוקות של בית רבן יודע' אותו דכתיב °כי תשא את ראש בני שמות ל
ישראל לפקודיהם ונתנו איש כפר נפשו וגו' מיד °ויעמוד שטן על ישראל וכתיב °ויסת את דוד בהם לאמר לך ד"ה א כא
מנה את ישראל וכיון דמנגהו לא שקל מנייהו כפר דכתיב °ויתן ה' דבר בישראל מהבקר ועד עת מועד מאי שמואל ב כד
עת מועד אמר שמואל סבא חתניה דר' חנינא משמיה דרבי חנינא משעת שחיטת התמיד עד שעת זריקתו שם
ר' יוחנן אמר עד חצות ממש: °ויאמר למלאך המשחית בעם רב א"ר אלעזר א"ל הקב"ה למלאך טול לי לרב שם
שבהם שיש בו ליפרע מהם כמה חובות באותו. שעה מת אבישי בן צרויה ששקול כרובה של סנהדרין:
°ובהשחית ראה ה' וינחם מאי ראה אמר רב ראה יעקב אבינו דכתיב °ויאמר יעקב כאשר ראם ושמואל אמר ד"ה א כא
אפרו של יצחק ראה שנאמר °אלהים יראה לו השה רבי יצחק נפחא אמר כסף כפורים ראה שנאמר °ולקחת בראשית לב
את כסף הכפורים מאת בני ישראל וגו' רבי יוחנן אמר בית המקדש ראה דכתיב °בהר ה' יראה פליגי בה שם כב
רבי יעקב בר אידי ורבי שמואל בר נחמני חד אמר כסף הכפורים ראה וחד אמר בה"מ ראה ומסתברא כמאן שמות ל
דאמר בה"מ ראה שנאמר °אשר יאמר היום בהר ה' יראה: לא יכנס אדם להר הבית במקלו וכו': *מאי בראשית כב
קפנדריא אמר רבא קפנדריא כשמה ורב חנא בר אדא משמיה דרב סמא בריה דרב מרי אמר כמאן דאמר שם
אניש אדמקיפנא אדרי איעול בהא א"ר נחמן אמר רבה בר אבוה *הנכנס לבית הכנסת על מנת שלא לעשותו מגילה כט. ע"ש
קפנדריא מותר לעשותו קפנדריא רבי אבהו אמר *אם היה שביל מעיקרו מותר א"ר חלבו א"ר הונא *הנכנס
לבית הכנסת להתפלל מותר לעשותו קפנדריא שנאמר °ובבא עם הארץ לפני ה' במועדים וגו': ורקיקה יחזקאל מו
מק"ו: אמר רב ביבי אמר ריב"ל *כל הרוקק בהר הבית בזמן הזה כאלו רוקק בבת עינו שנאמר °והיה עיני ולבי מלכים א ט
שם כל הימים אמר רבא רקיקה בבה"כ שריא מידי דהוה אמנעל מה מנעל בהר הבית אסור בבה"כ מותר אף
רקיקה בהר הבית הוא דאסור בבה"כ שרי א"ל רב פפא לרבא ואמרי לה רבינא לרבא ואמרי לה רב אדא בר
מתנא לרבא אדיליף ממנעל נילף מקפנדריא א"ל תנא יליף ממנעל ואת אמרת מקפנדריא מאי היא דתניא
*לא יכנס אדם להר הבית לא במקלו שבידו ולא במנעלו שברגלו *ולא במעות הצרורים לו בסדינו ובפונדתו [תוספתא פ"ז] [ע' תו" ב"מ כו. ד"ה בהל ותוס' פסחים ז. ד"ה כהל]
מופשלת לאחוריו ולא יעשנה קפנדריא ורקיקה מק"ו ממנעל ומה מנעל שאין בו דרך בזיון *אמרה תורה °של [ע' תוספות חגיגה ד: ד"ה כי תבואו]
נעליך מעל רגליך רקיקה שהיא דרך בזיון לא כל שכן רבי יוסי בר יהודה אומר אינו צריך הרי הוא אומר °כי שמות ג
אין לבא אל שער המלך בלבוש שק והלא דברים קל וחומר ומה שק שאינו מאוס לפני בשר ודם כך רקיקה אסתר ד
שהיא מאוסה לפני מלך מלכי המלכים לא כל שכן א"ל אנא הכי קאמינא נימא הכא לחומרא והכא
לחומרא ואימא

(5) Ibid. 16. (6) According to the dictum that the death of the righteous is an atonement. (7) I Chron. XXI, 15. (8) Gen. XXXII, 3. (9) So lit., E.V. '*provide*'. (10) Ibid. XXII, 8. (11) Ex. XXX, 16. (12) Adverting to the name of the mountain which is '*The Lord shall see*'. Gen. XXII, 14.

c (1) Representing as it does the Latin *compendiaria via*. Raba seems to imply that there is no need to try to interpret it as an Aramaic expression. (2) Before the synagogue was built. (3) Ezek. XLVI, 9. (4) When the Temple is no longer there. (5) I Kings IX, 3. (6) A synagogue may not be used as a short cut, v. Meg. 28*a*. (7) Ex. III, 5.

d (1) Esth. IV, 2. (2) Thus we see that the Tanna derives the rule regarding spitting from the analogy of a shoe.

[62*b*]. It has been taught: Ben 'Azzai says: Lie on anything but not on the ground;[4] sit on anything but not on a beam.[5]

Samuel said: Sleep[6] at dawn is like a steel edge to iron; evacuation at dawn is like a steel edge to iron. Bar Kappara used to sell sayings for *denarii*. 'While thou art still hungry, eat; while thou art still thirsty, drink; while thy pot is still hot, empty it out.[7] When the horn is sounded in [the market of] Rome, do you, O son of the fig-seller, sell thy father's figs'.[8] Abaye said to the Rabbis: When you go through the lanes of Mahoza to get to the fields, do not look to this side or to that, for perhaps women[9] are sitting there, and it is not proper to gaze at them.

R. Safra entered a privy. R. Abba came and cleared his throat at the entrance.[10] He said to him: Let the master enter. When he came out, he [R. Abba] said to him: You have not yet been turned into a satyr,[11] but you have learnt the manners of a satyr.[12] Have we not learnt as follows: There was a fire there,[13] and a superior privy. Its superiority lay in this: if one found it locked, he could be sure that someone was in there, but if he found it open, he could be sure that there was no one there. We see therefore, that it is not proper [for two to be in a privy].[14] He [R. Safra], however, was of opinion that it was dangerous [to keep him waiting], as it
a has been taught:[1] R. Simeon b. Gamaliel says: To keep back the fecal discharge causes dropsy; to keep back the urinary discharge causes jaundice.

R. Eleazar once entered a privy, and a Persian[2] came and thrust him away. R. Eleazar got up and went out, and a serpent came and tore out the other's gut.[3] R. Eleazar applied to him the verse, *Therefore will I give a man for thee*.[4] Read not *adam* [a man] but *edom* [an Edomite].

And he bade to kill thee, but he spared thee.[5] '*And* he *bade*'! It should be, '*And* I *bade*'![6] '*And* he *spared*'! It should be, '*And* I *spared*'! R. Eleazar said: David said to Saul: According to the law, you deserve to be slain, since you are a pursuer, and the Torah has said, If one comes to kill you, rise and kill him first.[7] But the modesty which you have shown has caused you to be spared. What is this? As it is written: *And he came to the fences*[8] *by the way, where was a cave; and Saul went in* le-hasek [*to cover his feet*].[9] It has been taught: There was a fence within a fence, and a cave within a cave. R. Eleazar says: It [the word *le-hasek*] teaches that he covered himself like a booth [*sukkah*].

Then David arose and cut off the skirt of Saul's robe privily.[10] R. Jose son of R. Hanina said: Whoever treats garments contemptuously will in the end derive no benefit from them; for it says, *Now King David was old and stricken in years; and they covered him with clothes, but he could get no heat*.[11]

If it be the Lord that hath stirred thee up against me, let Him accept an offering.[12] R. Eleazar said: Said the Holy One blessed be He, to David: Thou callest me a 'stirrer-up'. Behold, I will make thee stumble over a thing which even school-children know, namely, that which is written, *When thou takest the sum of the children of Israel according to their number, then shall they give every man a ransom*
b *for his soul unto the Lord .... [that there be no plague among them]* etc.[1] Forthwith, *Satan stood up against Israel;*[2] and it is further written, *He stirred up David against them saying, Go, number Israel*.[3] And when he did number them, he took no ransom from them and it is written, *So the Lord sent a pestilence upon Israel from the morning even to the time appointed*.[4] What is meant by '*the time appointed*'? Samuel the elder, the son-in-law of R. Hanina, answered in the name of R. Hanina: From the time of slaughtering the continual offering until the time of sprinkling the blood. R. Johanan said: Right up precisely to midday.

And He said to the Angel that destroyed the people, It is enough[5] [rab]. R. Eleazar said: The Holy One, blessed be He, said to the Angel: Take a great man [*rab*] among them, through whose death many sins can be expiated for them.[6] At that time there died Abishai son of Zeruiah, who was [singly] equal in worth to the greater part of the Sanhedrin.

And as he was about to destroy, the Lord beheld, and He repented Him.[7] What did He behold?—Rab said: He beheld Jacob our ancestor, as it is written, *And Jacob said when he beheld them*.[8] Samuel said: He beheld the ashes of [the ram of] Isaac, as it says, *God will see*[9] *for Himself the lamb*.[10] R. Isaac Nappaha said: He saw the money of the atonement, as it says, *And thou shalt take the atonement money from the children of Israel, and it shall be a memorial*[11] etc. R. Johanan said: He saw the Temple, as it is written, *In the mount where the Lord is seen*.[12] R. Jacob b. Iddi and R. Samuel b. Nahmani differed on the matter. One said that He saw the atonement money, the other that He saw the Temple. The more likely view is that of him who says that He saw the Temple, since it is written, *As it will be said on that day, in the mount where the Lord is seen*.

A MAN SHOULD NOT ENTER THE TEMPLE MOUNT WITH HIS STAFF etc. What is the meaning of *kappandaria?* Raba said: A short
c cut, as its name implies.[1] R. Hanah b. Adda said in the name of R. Sama the son of R. Meri: It is as if a man said, Instead of going round the blocks [*makkifna adari*], I will go in here. R. Nahman said in the name of Rabbah: If one enters a synagogue not intending to use it as a short cut, he may use it as a short cut. R. Abbahu said: If there was a path there originally,[2] it is permitted. R. Helbo said in the name of R. Huna: If one entered a synagogue to pray, he may use it as a short cut, as it says, *But when the people of the land shall come before the Lord in the appointed seasons [he that entereth by the north gate shall go forth by the south gate*, etc.].[3]

AND SPITTING [ON IT IS FORBIDDEN] A FORTIORI. R. Bibi said in the name of R. Simeon b. Lakish: If one spits in these times[4] on the Temple mount, it is as if he spat into the pupil of His eye, since it says: *And Mine eyes and My heart shall be there perpetually*.[5] Raba said: It is permitted to expectorate in the synagogue, this being on the same footing as wearing a shoe. Just as wearing a shoe is forbidden on the Temple mount but permitted in the synagogue, so spitting is forbidden in the Temple mount but permitted in the synagogue. Said R. Papa to Raba—according to others, Rabina said to Raba, while others again report that R. Adda b. Mattena said it to Raba, Instead of learning the rule from the analogy of a shoe, why not learn it from that of a short cut?[6]—He replied: The Tanna derives it from a shoe, and you want to derive it from a short cut! What is this [reference]? As it has been taught: 'A man should not enter the Temple mount either with his staff in his hand or his shoe on his foot, or with his money tied up in his cloth, or with his money bag slung over his shoulder, and he should not make it a short cut, and spitting [on it is forbidden] *a fortiori* from the case of the shoe: seeing that regarding a shoe, the wearing of which does not show contempt, the Torah has said, *Put off thy shoes from off thy feet*,[7] must not the rule all the more apply to spitting, which does show contempt? R. Jose b. Judah said: This reasoning is not necessary. For see,
d it says, *For none might enter within the king's gate clothed in sackcloth*.[1] Now have we not here an argument *a fortiori*: if such is the case with sackcloth which is not in itself disgusting, and before an earthly king, how much more so with spitting which is in itself disgusting, and before the supreme King of Kings!'[2] He [R. Papa] replied to him [Raba]: What I mean is this. Let us be stringent in

(4) For fear of serpents. (5) Lest it may break. (6) The Aruch renders the word *shinah* here 'Making water'. (7) The proverb is applied to relieving oneself. (8) And do not wait for thy father to come; an admonition against procrastination. (9) MS.M. 'men'. (10) To find out if anyone was within. (11) שְׂעִיר Lit., 'goat' v. *supra* 62*a*, n. b6. (12) Inviting me to come in, not in accordance with the rules of propriety. The meaning is not clear, Rashi seems to read שעיר (Seir), thus rendering: You have not yet entered Seir (Edom) and you have learnt the manners of (the people of) Seir, v. Maharsha. (13) In the Temple court, to keep the priests warm. (14) V. Strashun Glosses.

a (1) V. *supra* 25*a*. (2) This is obviously a censor's correction for 'Roman', v. MS.M. (3) Jast. renders 'his gut dropped', from fright. (4) Isa. XLIII, 4. (5) I Sam. XXIV, 11. (6) Since David is reporting his own action. (7) V. *supra* 58*a*. (8) E.V. '*sheepcotes*'. (9) Ibid. 4. (10) Ibid. 5. (11) I Kings I, 1. (12) I Sam. XXVI, 19.

b (1) Ex. XXX, 12. (2) 1 Chron. XXI, 1. (3) II Sam. XXIV, 1. (4) Ibid. 15.

both cases,[3] and reason thus: [63*a*] The rule [about spitting] for the Temple mount where the shoe is forbidden we may derive from the analogy of the shoe, but in the case of the synagogue where the shoe is permitted, instead of deriving the rule from the shoe and permitting it, let us rather derive it from the short cut and forbid it?—Rather, said Raba: [The synagogue is] on the same footing as a man's house. Just as a man objects to his house being made a short cut but does not object to the wearing of shoes or to spitting there, so in the case of the synagogue, the using it as a short cut is forbidden, but wearing the shoe and spitting in it is not forbidden.

AT THE CONCLUSION OF THE BENEDICTIONS SAID IN THE TEMPLE [THEY USED TO SAY, FOR EVER etc.]. Why all this?—Because the Amen response is not given in the Sanctuary. And whence do we know that the Amen response was not made in the Sanctuary?—Because it says, *Stand up and bless the Lord your God from everlasting to everlasting*,[4] and it goes on, *And let them say*,[5] *Blessed be Thy glorious name that is exalted above every*[6] *blessing and praise*. I might think that one praise would suffice for all the blessings.[7] It therefore says, '*Above every blessing and praise*', implying, for every blessing assign to Him praise.[8]

IT WAS LAID DOWN THAT GREETING SHOULD BE GIVEN IN [GOD'S] NAME etc. Why the further citation?—You might think
a that Boaz spoke thus on his own accord;[1] come and hear, therefore, [the other text] 'THE LORD IS WITH THEE, THOU MIGHTY MAN OF VALOUR'. You might still say that it was an angel who spoke thus to Gideon;[2] come and hear, therefore, the other text, 'DESPISE NOT THY MOTHER WHEN SHE IS OLD';[3] and it says, 'IT IS TIME TO WORK FOR THE LORD, THEY HAVE MADE VOID THY LAW.[4] Raba said: The first clause of this verse can be taken as explaining the second, and the second can be taken as explaining the first. 'The first clause may be taken as explaining the second', thus: It is time to work for the Lord.[5] Why? Because they have made void Thy law. 'The second clause may be taken as explaining the first', thus: They have made void Thy law.[6] Why? Because it is time to work for the Lord.

It was taught: Hillel the Elder said: When the scholars keep in [the teaching of] the Torah, do thou disseminate it,[7] and when they disseminate it do thou keep it in.[8] If thou seest a generation which is eager for the knowledge of the Torah, spread it abroad,[9] as it says, *There is that scattereth and yet increaseth*.[10] But if thou seest a generation which takes no interest in the Torah, keep it in to thyself, as it says, *When it is time to work for the Lord*,[11] *they make void Thy law*. Bar Ḳappara expounded: When goods are cheap, collect[12] [money] and buy. In a place where there is no man, there be a man. Abaye said: You may infer from this that in a place where there is a man [to teach the Torah], there you should not be a man. This is obvious?—It required to be stated for the case where the two are equal.[13]

Bar Ḳappara expounded: What short text is there upon which all the essential principles of the Torah depend? *In all thy ways*
b *acknowledge Him and He will direct thy paths*.[1] Raba remarked: Even for a matter of transgression.[2] Bar Ḳappara [further] expounded: A man should always teach his son a clean and not laborious trade. What, for example? R. Ḥisda said: Needle-stitching.[3]

It has been taught: Rabbi says, A man should not invite too many friends to his house, as it says, *There are friends that one hath to his own hurt*.[4] It has been taught: Rabbi says, A man should not appoint a steward over his house, for had not Potiphar appointed Joseph as steward over his house, he would not have fallen into such trouble as he did. It has been taught: Rabbi says, Why does the section of the Nazirite[5] follow immediately on that of the unfaithful wife?[6] To teach you that anyone who sees an unfaithful wife in her evil ways should completely abstain from wine. Hezekiah the son of R. Parnak said in the name of R. Joḥanan: Why does the section of the unfaithful wife follow immediately on one dealing with *terumoth*[7] and tithes?[8] To teach you that if one has *terumoth* and tithes and does not give them to the priest, in the end he will require the priest's services to deal with his wife. For so it says, *Every man's hallowed things shall be his*,[9] and immediately afterwards it says, *If any man's wife go aside*,[10] and later is it written, *And the man shall bring his wife*, etc.[11] Nay more, in the end he shall be in need of them,[12] as it says, '*Every man's hallowed things shall be his*'.[13] R. Naḥman b. Isaac said: If he does give, he will eventually become rich, as it says, *Whatever a man giveth the priest, he shall have*[14]—he shall have much wealth.

R. Huna b. Berekiah said in the name of R. Eleazar ha-Ḳappar: Whoever associates the name of heaven with his suffering[15] will have his sustenance doubled, as it says, *And the Almighty shall be*
c *in thy distress, and thou shalt have double silver*.[1] R. Samuel b. Naḥmani said: His sustenance shall fly to him like a bird, as it says, *And silver shall fly to thee*.[2]

R. Ṭabi said in the name of R. Josiah: Whoso is faint[3] in the study of the Torah will have no strength to stand in the day of trouble, as it says, *If thou art faint* [in the study of the Torah] *in the day of adversity thy strength will be small*.[4] R. Ammi b. Mattenah said in the name of Samuel: Even if only in the performance of a single precept, as it says, '*If thou faint*', in any case.

R. Safra said: R. Abbahu used to relate that when Ḥananiah the son of R. Joshua's brother went down to the Diaspora,[5] he began to intercalate the years and fix new moons outside Palestine. So they [the Beth din] sent after him two scholars, R. Jose b. Ḳippar and the grandson of R. Zechariah b. Ḳebuṭal. When he saw them, he said to them: Why have you come?—They replied: We have come to learn Torah [from you]. He thereupon proclaimed: These men are among the most eminent of the generation. They and their ancestors have ministered in the Sanctuary (as we have learnt: Zechariah b. Ḳebuṭal said: Several times I read to him[6] out of the book of Daniel). Soon they began to declare clean what he declared unclean and to permit what he forbade. Thereupon he proclaimed: These men are worthless, they are good for nothing. They said to him: You have already built and you cannot overthrow, you have made a fence and you cannot break it down.[7] He said to them: Why do you declare clean when I declare unclean, why do you permit when I forbid?—They replied: Because you intercalate years and fix new moons outside of Palestine. He said to them: Did not Akiba son of Joseph intercalate
d years and fix new moons outside of Palestine?[1]—They replied: Don't cite R. Akiba, who left not his equal in the Land of Israel. He said to them: I also left not my equal in the Land of Israel. They said to him: The kids which you left behind have become goats with horns, and they have sent us to you, bidding us, 'Go and tell him in our name. If he listens, well and good; if not, he will

(3) Of spitting on the Temple mount and in the synagogue. (4) Neh. IX, 5. (5) Those who made the response. (6) E.V. '*all*'. (7) I.e., that one response should be made at the end of all the blessings (Rashi). (8) V. Soṭ. (Sonc. ed.) p. 198, n. 2.

a (1) And his action need not be taken as a precedent. (2) Simply transmitting his message. (3) I.e., despise not the example of Boaz. (4) V. 54*a*, n. c4. (5) As much as to say, Boaz had good warrant for what he did. This rule apparently was cavilled at in certain quarters, and the Rabbis felt that some very strong justification was needed for it. (6) Like Elijah in sacrificing on Mount Carmel. (7) So that it should not be forgotten. Lit., 'scatter', like a sower scattering seed. (8) So as not to compete with them. (9) Lit., 'scatter'. Cf. n. 7. (10) Prov. XI, 24. (11) I.e., when disseminating the Torah would bring it into contempt. (12) The Aruch reads, 'make haste'. (13) For there is no question that a superior may displace an inferior.

b (1) Prov. III, 6. (2) Weigh the pros and cons of it. This must be linked with the foregoing principle which permits the violation of the law when the exigencies of the time demand it. (3) Lit., 'the stitching of furrows'. (4) Prov. XVIII, 24. (5) Num. VI. (6) Ibid. V, 11—31. (7) Plural of *terumah*, v. Glos. (8) Ibid. V, 5—10. (9) Ibid. 10. (10) Ibid. 12. The juxtaposition implies: 'If a man keeps his hallowed things to himself and does not give them to the priest, then this wife, etc.'. (11) Ibid. 15. (12) Since he will lose his money. (13) In the form of poor man's tithe. (14) Ibid. 10. E.V. '*it shall be his*'. (15) By blessing God for the evil, or praying.

c (1) Job XXII, 25. E.V. '*And the Almighty shall be thy treasure, and thou shalt have precious silver*. The word *to'afoth* (precious) is connected by the Rabbis with the Aramaic word '*af*, to double. (2) Here the word *to'afoth* is connected

מסורת הש"ס

ואימא הר הבית דאסור במנעל לילפא ממנעל אבל בית (*המקדש) דשרי במנעל אדיליף ממנעל ולהיתר נילף מקפנדריא ולאיסור אלא אמר רבא כי ביתו מה ביתו אקפנדריא קפיד איניש ארקיק' ומנעל לא קפיד איניש אף ב"ה *קפנדריא הוא דאסור רקיקה ומנעל שרי: כל חותמי ברכות שבמקדש וכו': כל כך למה לפי שאין עונין אמן במקדש *ומנין שאין עונין אמן במקדש שנאמר °קומו ברכו את אלהיכם מן העולם עד העולם ואומר °ויברכו (את) שם כבודך ומרומם על כל ברכה ותהלה יכול כל הברכות כולן תהא להן תהלה אחת ת"ל ומרומם על כל ברכה ותהלה על כל ברכה וברכה תן לו תהלה: התקינו שיהא אדם שואל בשלום חברו וכו': *מאי ואומר וכי תימא בועז מדעתי' דנפשיה קאמר ת"ש °ה' עמך גבור החיל וכי תימא מלאך הוא דקאמר ליה לגדעון ת"ש °אל תבוז כי זקנה אמך ואומר °עת לעשות לה' הפרו תורתך אמר רבא האי קרא *מרישי' לסיפי' מדריש מסיפי' לרישי' מדריש מרישי' לסיפיה מדריש עת לעשות לה' מאי טעם משום הפרו תורתך מסיפיה לרישיה מדרי' הפרו תורתך מ"ט משום עת לעשות לה' *תניא הלל הזקן אומר בשעת המכניסין פזר בשעת המפזרים כנס ואם ראית דור שהתורה חביבה עליו פזר שנאמר °יש מפזר ונוסף עוד ואם ראית דור שאין התור' חביבה עליו כנס שנאמר עת לעשות לה' הפרו תורתך דרש בר קפרא זלת *קבוץ קנה מינה באתר דלית גבר תמן הוי גבר אמר אביי ש"מ *באתר דאית גבר תמן לא תהוי גבר פשיטא לא נצרכ' אלא בששניהם שוין דרש בר קפרא איזוהי פרשה קטנה שכל גופי תורה תלוין בה °בכל דרכיך דעהו והוא יישר ארחותיך אמר רבא אפילו לדבר עבירה * *דרש בר קפרא לעולם ילמד אדם את בנו אומנות נקיה וקלה מה היא אמר רב חסדא מחטא דתלמיותא: תניא ר' אומר לעולם אל ירבה אדם ריעים בתוך ביתו שנאמר °איש רעים להתרועע תניא ר' אומר אל ימנה אדם אפוטרופוס בתוך ביתו שאלמלא לא מינה פוטיפר את יוסף אפוטרופוס בתוך ביתו לא בא לאותו דבר תניא *ר' אומר למה נסמכה פרשת נזיר לפרשת סוטה לומר לך שכל הרואה סוטה בקלקולה יזיר עצמו מן היין אמר חזקיה בריה דר' פרנך א"ר יוחנן למה נסמכה פרשת סוטה לפרשת תרומות ומעשרות לומר לך כל שיש לו תרומות ומעשרות ואינו נותנן לכהן סוף נצרך לכהן ע"י אשתו שנאמר °ואיש את קדשיו לו יהיו וסמיך ליה איש איש כי תשטה אשתו וכתיב והביא האיש את אשתו וגו' ולא עוד אלא סוף שנצרך להן שנאמר ואיש את קדשיו לו יהיו אמר רב נחמן בר יצחק ואם נתנן סוף מתעשר שנאמר °איש אשר יתן לכהן לו יהיה לו יהיה ממון הרבה: א"ר הונ' בר ברכיה משום ר' אלעזר הקפר כל המשתף שם שמים בצערו כופלין לו פרנסתו שנאמר °והיה שדי בצריך וכסף תועפות לך ר' שמואל בר נחמני אמר פרנסתו מעופפת לו כצפור שנא' וכסף תועפות לך א"ר טבי א"ר יאשיה כל המרפה עצמו מדברי תורה אין בו כח לעמוד ביום צרה שנא' °התרפית ביום צרה צר כחכה א"ר אמי בר מתנה אמר שמואל ואפי' מצוה אחת שנאמר התרפית מכל מקום אמר רב ספרא ר' אבהו הוה משתעי כשירד *חנינא בן אחי רבי יהושע לגולה היה מעבר שנים וקובע חדשים בחוצה לארץ שגרו אחריו שני ת"ח רבי יוסי בן כיפר ובן בנו של זכריה בן קבוטל כיון שראה אותם אמר להם למה באתם א"ל ללמוד תורה באנו הכריז עליהם אנשים הללו גדולי הדור הם ואבותיהם שמשו בבית המקדש כאותה ששנינו *זכריה בן קבוטל אומר הרבה פעמים קריתי לפניו בספר דניאל התחיל הוא מטמא והם מטהרים הוא אוסר והם מתירים הכריז עליהם אנשים הללו של שוא הם של תהו הם אמרו לו כבר בנית ואי אתה יכול לסתור כבר גדרת ואי אתה יכול לפרוץ אמר להם מפני מה אני מטמא ואתם מטהרים אני אוסר ואתם מתירים אמרו לו מפני שאתה מעבר שנים וקובע חדשים בח"ל אמר להם והלא עקיבא בן יוסף היה מעבר שנים וקובע חדשים בח"ל אמרו לו הנח ר"ע שלא הניח כמותו בארץ ישראל א"ל אף אני לא הנחתי כמותי בא"י אמרו לו גדיים שהנחת נעשו תישים בעלי קרניים והם שגרונו אצלך וכן אמרו לנו לכו ואמרו לו בשמנו אם שומע מוטב ואם לאו יהא בנדוי ואמרו

(margin references: תורה אור; נחמיה ט; שם; שופטים ו; משלי כג; תלים קיט; משלי יא; תענית יז:; סוטה מ:; [מכות כג:]; [לעיל ס. סנה' ע.]; [תוספתא פ"ו]; [ע' תו' סוט' דף כב: ד"ה בשין וכו' אריכת פירושי' בסוגיא דהכא]; שם ב; קדושין פב. ע"ש; משלי יח; במדבר ה; שם; איוב כב; משלי כד; יומא יח:)

רש"י

ואימא הר הבית דאסור במנעל. ילפי' רקיקה מיניה לאסורא בקל וחומר אבל בבית הכנסת דשרי במנעל לא נילף רקיקה להתירא דרקיקה מאיסא אלא ילפי' מקפנדריא לאיסורא: ויברכו את שם כבודך. בשכמל"ו עונים והמברך אומר ברוך ה' אלהי ישראל מן העולם ועד העולם מפרש בתוספתא שתקנו מן העולם ועד העולם להודיע שאין העה"ז לפני העה"ב כלום אלא כפרוזדור לפני הטרקלין כלומר השיגו ברכותיו בעה"ז כדי להיות רגילים לעה"ב שכולו ארוך: תהלה אחת. שיענו פעם אחת בשכמל"ו על כל הברכות בסוף ברכה אחרונה: וכי תימא. בועז מדעתיה עבד ולא גמרינן מיניה: תא שמע. דגמרינן ממלאך שאמר לגדעון: וכי תימא מלאך הוא דקאמר ליה לגדעון. כלומר לא שאל בשלומו ולא ברכו אלא בשליחות קאמר מאת המקום לבשרו שהשכינה עמו ולא גמרינן מיניה: תא שמע אל תבוז כי זקנה אמך. אל תבוז את בועז לאמר מדעתו עשה אלא למד מזקני ישראל כי יש לו על מי שיסמוך שנא' עת לעשות לה': מסיפיה לרישיה כו'. אם באת לדרשו למקרא זה יש לך לדרשו יפה בין בכתיבתו בין בהפוך: מרישיה לסיפיה. עת לעשות לה' משום הפרו. עתים שלה' לעשות משפט פורענות בעוברי רצונו משום דהפרו תורתך: מסיפיה לרישיה. הפרו תורתו עושי רצונו כגון אליהו בהר הכרמל (מלכים א יח) שהקריב בבמה בשעת איסור הבמות משום דעת לעשות סייג וגדר בישראל לשמו של הקב"ה: בשעת המכניסים. שאין חכמי הדור מרביצי' תורה לתלמידי': פזר. אתה לשנות לתלמידים: בשעת המפזרים. שהגדולים שבדור מרביצים תורה: כנס. אתה ולא תטול שררה עליהם דאף זו לכבוד שמים היא לאחוז במדת הענו' וכתיב עת לעשות לה' הפרו תורתך: ואם ראית דור שאין התורה חביבה עליו כנס. ואל תטיל דברי תורה לבזיון: הפרו תורתך. מלפזרה בשעה שהכנוס לשם שמים: הכי גרסינן זלת קבוץ קנה מינה. אם ראית פרקמטיא בזול קבוץ וקנה מינה ואסוף שסופה להתיקר: פשיטא. הא דאביי למה לי פשיטא שלא יורה אדם הלכה בפני רבו למה ליה לאביי למשמעה מכללא: בששניהן שוין. אם באת במקום תלמיד חכם ואינך גדול ממנו אל תטול עטרה לדרוש במקומו: בכל דרכיך. אפי' לעבור עבירה: דעהו. תן לב אם צורך מצוה הוא כגון אליהו בהר הכרמל עבור עליה: מחטא דתלמיותא. ברו"שיד בלע"ז שהתפירות עשויות שורות שורות כתלמי מענה: להתרועע. להתרוצץ: אפוטרופוס. מכניס ומוציא נכסיו: כל שיש לו תרומות ומעשרות ואינו נותנן לכהן סוף שנצרך לו על ידי אשתו. שנעשית סוטה: ה"ג ואיש את קדשיו לו יהיו וסמיך ליה איש כי תשטה אשתו וכתיב והביא האיש את אשתו: ואיש את קדשיו לו יהיו. שמעכב קדשיו אצלו ואינו נותנן לכהנים וללוים: סוף שנצרך להן. שנעשה עני וצריך לכך ליטול מעשר עני: לו יהיו. לעצמו יצטרכו: המשתף שם שמים בצערו. שמברך על הרעה דיין האמת אי נמי שמבקש רחמים מלפניו: בצריך. בצרתך: תועפות. לשון כפילה כדמתרגמי' וכפלת ותעיף (שמות כו): התרפית. מדברי תורה ביום צרה צר כחכה: אפילו מצוה אחת. אם נתרפה ממנה כשבאה לידו ולא חש להתעסק בה צר כחו: התרפית מ"מ. אף במצוה אחת משמע: מעבר שנים וכו'. ותנן אין מעברין את השנים אלא ביהודה דכתיב לשכנו תדרשו כל דרישות שאתה דורש לא יהו אלא בשכנו של מקום בפ"ק דסנהדרין (דף יא:): שגרו אחריו. למחות בידו: כבר בנית. שהגדלת שמכם לומר גדולי הדור הם: והלא עקיבא בן יוסף עשה כן. דתנן ביבמות אמר רבי עקיבא כשירדתי לנהרדעא לעבר שנים בפרק בתרא האשה שהלכו בעלה וצרתה (דף קכב.): ואמרו

עין משפט נר מצוה

פח א מיי' פ"א מהלכות תפלה הלכה ח סמג עשין יט טוש"ע א"ח סימן קנא סעיף ה

פט ב מיי' שם הלכה י טוש"ע א"ח שם סעיף ז וסימן ל סעיף יג

צ ג מיי' פרק ד' מהלכות תענית הלכה טו

צא ד מיי' פכ"ב מהלכות אסורי ביאה הלכ' טו סמג לאוין קכו טוש"ע אה"ע סימן כב סעיף י

[גי' הערוך בערך קפוץ ע"ש]

[אמר רב פפא היינו דאמרי אינשי גנבא אפום מחתרתא רחמנא קרי כך היא הגי' בע"י]

צ"ל חנניא ע' סוכה סוף פ"א רש"י ד"ה חנניא

with the Hebrew *'uf*, to fly. (3) I.e., is negligent. (4) Prov. XXIV, 10. E.V. *'If thou art faint in the day of adversity, thy strength shall be small indeed'.* (5) *Golah*, Babylon. Here the reference is to Pumbeditha. This was during the Hadrianic persecution following the Bar Kochebah Wars. V. *J.E.* VI, p. 207. (6) The High Priest. V. Yoma 18*b*. (7) I.e., you cannot take away from us the name you have conferred on us.

d (1) Yeb. 122*a*.

עין משפט נר מצוה

צב
א מוש"ע י"ד סימן רמב סעיף לח בה"גה

צג
ב מיי' פ"ג מה' ת"ת הלכה יב סמג עשין יב טוש"ע י"ד סי' רמו סעי' כא

[עירובין כה:]

ואמרו לאחינו שבגולה. שלא ישמעו לו: יעלו להר. לאחד ההרים להתנהג בחקות העמים לבנות במות: אחיה יבנה מזבח. אדם גדול היה ורא לבני הגולה: חנניא. הוא חנניה [בן] אחי ר' יהושע: ינגן בכנור. לפני הבמה לפי שחנניה לוי היה כדתנן במס' ערכין (דף יא:) ומעשה בר' יהושע בן חנניה שהלך לסייע את ר' יוחנן בן גודגדא בהגפת דלתות אמר לו חזור בך שאתה מן המשוררים ולא מן השוערים: לכרם. על שם שהיו יושבים שורות שורות ככרם זה הנטוע שורות שורו': בכבוד אכסניא. מכניסי אורחי' בבתים: ראש המדברים. במס' שבת מפרש לה בבמה מדליקין (לג:): שנים עשר מיל. ג' פרסאות מחנה ישראל מבית הישימות עד אבל השטים * תלתא פרסי: אמרה תורה כו'. כלומר קראו הכתוב מבקש יי': כשם שאני הסברתי לך פנים כך אתה הסבר פנים. והיינו דכתיב פנים בפנים: הרב בכעס. עליהם משום מעשה העגל: ותלמיד בכעס. וגם אתה מראה להם כעס שהרחקת אהלך ממחנה: אם אתה מחזיר האהל למקומו גרסינן: והיינו דכתיב ושב אל המחנה. השב האהל למחנה ואם לאו משרתך יהושע בן נון נער לא ימיש מתוכ' שישמש תחתיך ואף על פי שהשיבו לאחר שנתרצה הקב"ה לישראל והוקם המשכן לא יצא דבר לבטלה:

תורה אור

ואמרו לאחינו שבגולה אם שומעין מוטב ואם לאו יעלו להר אחיה יבנה מזבח חנניא ינגן בכנור ויכפרו כולם ויאמרו אין להם חלק באלהי ישראל מיד געו כל העם בבכי' ואמרו חס ושלום יש לנו חלק באלהי ישראל וכל כך למה משום שנאמר °כי מציון תצא תורה ודבר יי' מירושלים (ישעיה ב) בשלמא הוא מטהר והם מטמאין לחומרא אלא הוא מטמא והם מטהרין היכי הוי והא *תניא [א]חכם שטמא אין חברו רשאי לטהר אסר אין חברו רשאי להתיר קסברי כי היכי דלא נגררו בתריה: ת"ר כשנכנסו רבותינו לכרם ביבנה היו שם ר' יהודה ורבי יוסי ור' נחמיה ור' אלעזר בנו של רבי יוסי הגלילי פתחו כולם בכבוד אכסניא ודרשו פתח רבי יהודה ראש *המדברים בכל מקום בכבוד תורה ודרש °ומשה יקח את האהל ונטה לו מחוץ למחנ' (שמות לג) והלא דברי' קל וחומר ומה ארון יי' שלא היה מרוחק אלא שנים עשר מיל אמרה תורה °והיה כל מבקש יי' יצא אל אהל מועד (שם) תלמידי חכמי' שהולכי' מעיר לעיר וממדינה למדינה ללמוד תורה על אחת כמה וכמה: °ודבר יי' אל משה פנים אל פנים (שם) א"ר יצחק אמר לו הקב"ה למשה משה אני ואתה נסביר פנים בהלכה איכא דאמרי כך אמר לו הקב"ה למשה כשם שאני הסברתי לך פנים כך אתה הסבר פנים לישראל והחזר האהל למקומו: °ושב אל המחנה וגו' (שם) אמר ר' אבהו אמר לו הקב"ה למשה *עכשיו יאמרו הרב בכעס ותלמיד בכעס ישראל מה תהא עליהם אם אתה מחזיר האהל למקומו מוטב ואם לאו יהושע בן נון תלמידך משרת תחתך והיינו דכתיב ושב אל המחנה אמר רבא אף על פי כן לא יצא הדבר לבטלה שנאמר °ומשרתו יהושע בן נון נער לא ימיש מתוך האהל (שם): ועוד פתח ר' יהודה בכבוד תורה ודרש °הסכת ושמע ישראל היום הזה נהייתה לעם (דברים כז) וכי אותו היום נתנה תורה לישראל והלא אותו יום סוף ארבעים שנה היה אלא ללמדך שחביבה תור' על לומדיה בכל יום ויום כיום שנתנה מהר סיני א"ר תנחום בריה דר' חייא איש כפר עכו תדע שהרי אדם קורא קריאת שמע שחרית וערבית וערב אחד אינו קורא דומה כמי שלא קרא קריאת שמע מעולם הסכת עשו כתות כתות ועסקו בתורה לפי שאין התורה נקנית אלא בחבורה כדר' יוסי בר' חנינא *דא"ר יוסי בר' חנינא מאי דכתיב °חרב (*על) [אל] הבדי' ונואלו (ירמיה נ) חרב על שונאיהם של תלמידי חכמים שיושבים בד בבד ועוסקים בתורה ולא עוד אלא שמטפשים כתיב הכא ונואלו וכתיב התם °אשר נואלנו (במדבר יב) ולא עוד אלא שחוטאים שנאמר ואשר חטאנו איבעית אימא מהכא °נואלו שרי צוען (ישעיה יט) דבר אחר הסכת ושמע ישראל כתתו עצמכם על דברי תורה כדאמר ריש לקיש *דאמר ריש לקיש [ב]מנין שאין דברי תורה מתקיימין אלא במי שממית עצמו עליה שנאמר °זאת התורה אדם כי ימות באהל (במדבר יט) ד"א הסכת ושמע ישראל הס ואח"כ כתת כדרבא *דאמר רבא לעולם ילמוד אדם תורה ואח"כ יהגה אמרי דבי ר' ינאי מאי דכתיב °כי מיץ חלב יוציא חמאה ומיץ אף יוציא דם ומיץ אפים יוציא ריב (משלי ל) במי אתה מוציא חמאה של תורה במי שמקיא חלב שינק משדי אמו עליה ומיץ אף יוציא דם כל תלמיד שכועס עליו רבו פעם ראשונה ושותק זוכה להבחין בין דם טמא לדם טהור ומיץ אפים יוציא ריב כל תלמיד שכועס עליו רבו פעם ראשונה ושניה ושותק זוכה להבחין בין דיני ממונות לדיני נפשות *דתנן ר' ישמעאל אומר הרוצה שיתחכם יעסוק בדיני ממונות שאין לך מקצוע בתורה יותר מהן שהן כמעין נובע א"ר שמואל בר נחמני מאי דכתיב °אם *נבלת בהתנשא ואם זמות יד לפה (משלי ל) כל המנבל עצמו על דברי תורה סופו להתנשא ואם זמם יד לפה: פתח רבי נחמיה בכבוד אכסניא ודרש מאי דכתיב °ויאמר שאול אל הקיני לכו סורו רדו מתוך עמלקי פן אוסיפך עמו ואתה עשית חסד עם כל בני ישראל (שמואל א טו) והלא דברים קל וחומר ומה יתרו שלא קרב את משה אלא לכבוד עצמו כך המארח תלמיד חכם בתוך ביתו ומאכילו ומשקהו ומהנהו מנכסיו על אחת כמה וכמה: פתח רבי יוסי בכבוד אכסניא ודרש °לא תתעב אדומי כי אחיך הוא ולא תתעב מצרי כי גר היית בארצו (דברים כג) והלא דברים קל וחומר ומה מצריים שלא קרבו את ישראל אלא לצורך עצמן שנאמר °ואם ידעת ויש בם אנשי חיל ושמתם שרי מקנה על אשר לי (בראשית מז) כך המארח תלמיד חכם בתוך ביתו ומאכילו ומשקהו ומהנהו מנכסיו על אחת כמה וכמה: פתח ר' אלעזר בנו של ר' יוסי הגלילי בכבוד אכסניא ודרש °ויברך יי' את עובד אדום הגתי בעבור ארון האלהים (שמואל ב ו) והלא דברים ק"ו ומה ארון שלא אכל ושתה אלא כבד ורבץ לפניו כך המארח ת"ח בתוך ביתו ומאכילו ומשקהו ומהנהו מנכסיו על אחת כמה וכמה מאי היא ברכה שברכו אמר רב יהודה בר זבידא זו חמות וח' כלותיה שילדו ששה בכרס אחד שנאמר

[ז"ל הסטני במרוצת עכשיו וכו' ויש מכוסבין עכשיו ביזו וליס לכיך]

[אל]

[שבת פג: ברכות נ:] ... [מגילה ב] (marginal references)

מסורת הש"ס

לא גרסינן ומשרתו יהושע וגו': הסכת עשו כתות כתות. דריש הס כמו עשו: כתתו עצמיכם. ודרשו כמו הס כמו עשה עשו עצמיכם כתותים להצטער על דברי תורה: זאת התורה. היכן מצויה באדם שימות באהלי תורה: הס ואח"כ כתת. שתוק כמו ויהס כלב (במדבר יג) שתוק והאזן לשמוע עתך עד שתהא שגורה בפיך ואף על פי שאינה מיושבת לך ואח"כ כתתנה והקשה עליה מה שיש לך להקשות ותריץ תרוצין עד שתתיישב לך: יהגה. יעיין: מיץ חלב יוציא חמאה. המוציא את החלב שמלך משדי אמו על דברי תורה חמאה היא לו: ומיץ אף. המולך כעס רבו וסובלו יוציא הלכות דם לעומתם: דתנן. שדיני ממונות עמוקים הם והרוצה שיתחכם יעסוק בדיני ממונו' שאין מקצוע בתורה גדול מהם: המנבל עצמו. ששואל לרבו כל ספקותיו ואף ע"פ שיש בהם שחבריו מלעיגי' עליו: ואם זמות. שסתמת פיך ומלשאול לשון זמם טבעת של רצועה שתוחבים בחוטם בהמה שעסקיה רעים ונותנים אותו בשפתיה לתופרן יחד ולסותמן סופך שתתן יד לפה כשישאלוך ולא תדע להשיב: עשית חסד. שהאכילם שנאמר ויבא אהרן וכל זקני ישראל לאכל לחם וגו' (שמות יח): חמות. אשתו של עובד אדום: וח' כלותיה. שהיו לה ומ' בניה.

(עירובין נד. חולין מד: נדה כ:) [שבת לג: מנחות קנ:]

(10) Deut. XXVII, 9. (11) In Lower Galilee. (12) I.e., he feels as if.

b (1) Jer. L, 36. (2) Euphemism for the disciples themselves. (3) Num. XII, 11. In both texts the Hebrew word is *no'alu*. (4) Ibid. (5) Isa. XIX, 13. (6) Num. XIX, 14. 'Tent' is taken to mean a place of study. (7) I.e., first listen to the teacher, and then discuss what he has said. (8) Prov. XXX, 33. (9) I.e., who commences to learn in his earliest childhood. (10) Heb. *af*, which also means anger. (11) Heb. *appayim*, lit., 'two angers'. (12) I.e., to decide to which category an intricate case belongs.

c (1) Prov. XXX, 32. (2) I.e., is not ashamed to ask questions which may at first sound foolish. (3) He will be unable to answer questions put to him. (4) I Sam. XV, 6. (5) Who is called the Kenite, Judg. I, 16. (6) Deut. XXIII, 8. (7) Gen. XLVII, 6. (8) II Sam. VI, 12.

d (1) The wife of Obed-Edom.

be excommunicated. [63b] Tell also our brethren in the Diaspora [not to listen to him]. If they listen to you, well and good; if not, let them go up to the mountain, let Ahia[2] build an altar and let Ḥananiah play the harp,[3] and let them all become renegades and say that they have no portion in the God of Israel'. Straightway all the people broke out into weeping and cried, Heaven forbid, we have a portion in the God of Israel. Why all this to-do?—Because it says, *For out of Zion shall go forth the law, and the word of the Lord from Jerusalem.*[4] We can understand that if he declared clean they should declare unclean, because this would be more stringent. But how was it possible that they should declare clean what he declared unclean, seeing that it has been taught: If a Sage has declared unclean, his colleague is not permitted to declare clean?—They thought proper to act thus so that the people should not be drawn after him.

Our Rabbis have taught: When our teachers entered the vineyard at Jabneh,[5] there were among them R. Judah and R. Jose and R. Nehemiah and R. Eliezer the son of R. Jose the Galilean. They all spoke in honour of hospitality and expounded texts [for that purpose]. R. Judah, the head of the speakers in every place,[6] spoke in honour of the Torah and expounded the text, *Now Moses used to take the tent and pitch it without the camp.*[7] Have we not here, he said, an argument *a fortiori?* Seeing that the Ark of the Lord
a was never more than twelve *mil* distant[1] and yet the Torah says, *Everyone that sought the Lord went out unto the tent of meeting,*[2] how much more [is this title[3] applicable to] the disciples of the wise who go from city to city and from province to province to learn Torah!

And the Lord spoke unto Moses face to face.[4] R. Isaac said: The Holy One, blessed be He, said to Moses, Moses, I and thou will propound views[5] on the *halachah*. Some say that the Holy One, blessed be He, said thus to Moses: Just as I have turned upon thee a cheerful face, so do thou turn upon Israel a cheerful face and restore the tent to its place. *And he would return to the camp.*[6] R. Abbahu said: The Holy One, blessed be He, said to Moses: Now they will say, The Master[7] is angry and the disciple[8] is angry, what will happen to Israel? If thou wilt restore the tent to its place, well and good, but if not, Joshua son of Nun, the disciple, will minister in thy place. Therefore it is written, '*And he would return to the camp*'. Raba said: All the same [God's] word was not uttered in vain, since it says, *But his minister Joshua, the son of Nun, a young man, departed not out of the tent.*[9]

R. Judah spoke further in honour of the Torah, expounding the text, *Attend* [hasket] *and hear, O Israel: this day thou art become a people unto the Lord thy God.*[10] Now was it on that day that the Torah was given to Israel? Was not that day the end of the forty years [of the wandering]? It is, however, to teach thee that the Torah is as beloved every day to those that study it as on the day when it was given from Mount Sinai. R. Tanḥum the son of R. Ḥiyya, a man of Kefar Acco[11] said: The proof is that if a man recites the *Shema'* every morning and evening and misses one evening, it is as if[12] he had never recited the *Shema'*. The word '*hasket*' implies: Make yourselves into groups [*kittoth*] to study the Torah, since the knowledge of the Torah can be acquired only in association with others, as stated by R. Jose b. Ḥanina; for R. Jose b. Ḥanina said: What is the meaning of the text, *A
b sword is upon the boasters* [baddim] *and they shall become fools?*[1] A sword is upon the enemies of the disciples of the wise[2] who sit separately [*bad bebad*] and study the Torah. What is more, they become stupid. It is written here, '*and they shall become fools*', and it is written elsewhere, *For that we have done foolishly.*[3] What is more, they are sinners, as it says, *and we have sinned.*[4] If you prefer, I can learn the meaning from here: *The princes of Zoan are become fools* [no'alu].[5] Another explanation of '*Attend* [hasket] *and hear, Israel*'. Cut yourselves to pieces [*kattetu*] for words of Torah, as was said by Resh Lakish. For Resh Lakish said: Whence do we learn that words of Torah are firmly held by one who kills himself for it? Because it says, *This is the Torah, when a man shall die in the tent.*[6] Another explanation of '*Attend and hear, O Israel*': Be silent [*has*] and then analyse [*katteth*],[7] as stated by Raba; for Raba said: A man should always first learn Torah and then scrutinize it.

They said in the school of R. Jannai: What is meant by the verse, *For the churning of milk bringeth forth curd, and the wringing of the nose bringeth forth blood; so the forcing of wrath bringeth forth strife?*[8] With whom do you find the cream of the Torah? With him who spits out upon it the milk which he has sucked from the breasts of his mother.[9] '*The wringing of the nose*[10] *bringeth forth blood*'. Every student who is silent when his teacher is angry with him the first time will become worthy to distinguish between clean blood and unclean. '*The forcing of wrath*[11] *bringeth forth strife*': Every student who is silent when his teacher is angry with him a first and a second time will be worthy to distinguish between money cases and capital cases,[12] as we have learnt: R. Ishmael says, One who desires to be wise should occupy himself with money judgments, since no branch of the Torah surpasses them, for they are like a perpetual fountain [of instruction]. R. Samuel b. Naḥmani said: What is meant by the verse, *If thou hast done foolishly* [nobaltah] *in lifting up thyself, or if thou hast planned devices* [zammotah], *lay thy
c hand upon thy mouth?*[1] Whoever abases [*menabbel*] himself for words of Torah[2] will in the end be exalted, but if one muzzles [*zamam*] himself, his hand will be upon his mouth.[3]

R. Nehemiah began to speak in praise of hospitality, expounding the text, *And Saul said unto the Kenites, Go, depart, get you down from among the Amalekites, lest I destroy you with them; for ye showed kindness to all the children of Israel when they came up out of Egypt.*[4] Have we not here an argument *a fortiori*: if such was the reward of Jethro[5] who befriended Moses only for his own benefit, how much more will it be for one who entertains a scholar in his house and gives him to eat and drink and allows him the use of his possessions!

R. Jose began to speak in praise of hospitality, expounding the verse, *Thou shalt not abhor an Edomite, for he is thy brother; thou shalt not abhor an Egyptian, because thou wast a stranger in his land.*[6] Have we not here an argument *a fortiori?* If such was the reward of the Egyptians who befriended the Israelites only for their own purposes, as it says, *And if thou knowest any able men among them, then make them rulers over my cattle,*[7] how much more will it be for one who entertains a scholar in his house and gives him to eat and drink and allows him the use of his possessions!

R. Eliezer the son of R. Jose the Galilean began to speak in praise of hospitality, expounding the verse, *And the Lord blessed Obed-Edom and all his house .... because of the Ark of God.*[8] Have we not here an argument *a fortiori?* If such was the reward for attending to the ark which did not eat or drink, but before which he merely swept and laid the dust, how much more will it be for one who entertains a scholar in his house and gives him to eat and drink and allows him the use of his possessions! What was the blessing with which God blessed him [Obed-Edom]?—R. Judah b. Zebida
d says: This refers to Hamoth[1] and her eight daughters-in-law who

(2) The head of the community. (3) Ḥananiah was a Levite. (4) Isa. II, 3. (5) The Academy at Jabneh, so called either because it actually was in a vineyard, or because the disciples sat in rows like the vines in a vineyard. The incident is related in a somewhat different form in the Midrash Rabbah on Cant. II, 5. (6) V. Shab. 33b. (7) Ex. XXXIII, 7.
a (1) This being the extent of the Israelitish camp. (2) Ex. XXXIII, 7. (3) Of 'one who seeks the Lord'. (4) Ibid. 11. (5) Lit., 'faces'. (6) Ibid. (7) God. (8) Moses. (9) Ibid. This is taken to mean that he succeeded Moses.

each bore six children at a birth [64a], as it says, *Peullethai the eighth son*[2] *for God blessed him,*[3] and it is written, *All these were of the sons of Obed-Edom, they and their sons and their brethren, able men in the strength for the service, threescore and two of Obed-Edom.*[4]

R. Abin the Levite said: Whoever tries to force his [good] fortune will be dogged by [ill] fortune,[5] and whoever forgoes his [good] fortune will postpone his [ill] fortune.[6] This we can illustrate from the case of Rabbah and R. Joseph. For R. Joseph was 'Sinai'[7] and Rabbah was 'an uprooter of mountains'.[8] The time came when they were required [to be head of the Academy].[9] They [the collegiates] sent there [to Palestine] to ask, As between 'Sinai' and an 'uprooter of mountains', which should have the preference? They sent answer: Sinai, because all require the owner of wheat.[10] Nevertheless, R. Joseph would not accept the post, because the astrologers had told him that he would be head for only two years. Rabbah thereupon remained head for twenty-two years, and R. Joseph after him for two years and a half.[11] During all the time that Rabbah was head, R. Joseph did not so much as summon a cupper to come to his house.[12]

R. Abin the Levite further said: What is the point of the verse, *The Lord answer thee in the day of trouble, the name of the God of Jacob set thee up on high?*[13] The God of Jacob and not the God of Abraham and Isaac? This teaches that the owner of the beam should go in
a with the thickest part of it.[1]

R. Abin the Levite also said: If one partakes of a meal at which a scholar is present, it is as if he feasted on the effulgence of the Divine Presence, since it says, *And Aaron came and all the elders of Israel, to eat bread with Moses' father-in-law before God.*[2] Was it before God that they ate? Did not they eat before Moses? This tells you, however, that if one partakes of a meal at which a scholar is present, it is as if he feasted on the effulgence of the Divine Presence.

R. Abin the Levite also said: When a man takes leave of his fellow, he should not say to him, 'Go *in* peace', but 'Go *to* peace'. For Moses, to whom Jethro said, *Go* to *peace,*[3] went up and prospered, whereas Absalom to whom David said, *Go* in *peace,*[4] went away and was hung.

R. Abin the Levite also said: One who takes leave of the dead[5] should not say to him 'Go to peace', but 'Go in peace', as it says, *But thou shalt go to thy fathers* in *peace.*[6]

R. Levi b. Ḥiyya said: One who on leaving the synagogue goes into the House of Study and studies the Torah is deemed worthy to welcome the Divine Presence, as it says, *They go from strength to strength, every one of them appeareth before God in Zion.*[7]

R. Ḥiyya b. Ashi said in the name of Rab: The disciples of the wise have no rest either in this world or in the world to come,[8] as it says, *They go from strength to strength, every one of them appeareth before God in Zion'.*

R. Eleazar said in the name of R. Ḥanina: The disciples of the wise increase peace in the world, as it says, *And all thy children shall be taught of the Lord, and great shall be the peace of thy children.*[9] Read not *banayik* [thy children] but *bonayik* [thy builders].[10] *Great*
b *peace have they that love Thy law, and there is no stumbling for them.*[1] *Peace be within thy walls and prosperity within thy palaces.*[2] *For my brethren and companions' sake I will now say, Peace be within thee.*[3] *For the sake of the house of the Lord our God I will seek thy good.*[4] *The Lord will give strength unto His people, the Lord will bless His people with peace.*[5]

(2) Omitting with BaḤ: 'and it is written' inserted in cur. edd. (3) I Chron. XXVI, 5. This shows that he had eight sons. (4) Ibid. 8. The sixty-two are made up of the eight sons mentioned, six more to his wife at one birth, and six to each of his eight daughters-in-law. (5) Lit., 'whoever pushes his hour will be pushed by his hour'. (6) Lit., 'if one is pushed away from before his hour, his hour is pushed away from before him'. (7) I.e., possessed an encyclopaedic knowledge of the traditions. (8) I.e., exceptionally skilful in dialectic. (9) *Sc.* of Pumbeditha. (10) I.e., to know the authentic traditions. (11) Rabbah was head 309—330. R. Joseph who succeeded him died in 333. (12) But went instead to him, like any ordinary individual. On the whole passage v. Hor. (Sonc. ed.) p. 105 notes. (13) Ps. XX, 2.

a (1) He should put the thicker end in the ground so as to give better support. So the name of Jacob would be more efficacious in prayer because he was the more immediate ancestor of the Jewish people. (2) Ex. XVIII, 12. (3) Ibid. IV, 18. (4) II Sam. XV, 9. (5) On leaving the funeral procession. (6) Gen. XV, 15. (7) Ps. LXXXIV, 8. (8) Because they are always progressing in their spiritual strivings. (9) Isa. LIV, 13. (10) I.e., learned men.

b (1) Ps. CXIX, 165. (2) Ibid. CXXII, 7. (3) Ibid. 8. (4) Ibid. 9. (5) Ibid. XXIX, 11.

מסורת הש"ס

עין משפט נר מצוה

שנאמר פעלתי השמיני. בני עובד אדום קא חשיב בדברי הימים וקא חשיב תמניא והיא תשיעית כל אחת ילדה ששה הם חמשים ולרבע הוסיף עליהם שמנה בניה הראשונים הרי ששים ושנים לעובד אדום: הדוחק את השעה. כגון אבשלום שבקש למלוך בחזקה: אצטריכא להו שעתא. להיות אחד מהם ראש ישיבה אצטריכא להו גרסינן הוצרכו להם חכמים: סיני. היו קורין לרב יוסף שהיה בקי בברייתות הרבה: עוקר הרים. לרבה בר נחמני שהיה מחודד יותר בפלפול: למרי חטיא. למי שקבץ תבואה למכור כלומר למי שקבץ שמועות: דאמרי ליה כלדאי. לרב יוסף: מלכת תרתין שנין. אמר אם אמלוך תחלה אמות לסוף שנתים ודחה מפני שעה ולא אבה למלוך והשעה עמדה לו שלא העמיד שנותיו בכך: אומנא לביתיה לא קרא. לא נהג כל אותן השנים שום לד שררה וכשהיה צריך להקיז דם היה הולך לבית הרופא ולא היה שולח לבא אליו: שיאחוז בעובי הקורה. אם בא לטלטלה ממקום למקום לתתה בבנין כלומר יעקב שכל הבנים שלו וטרח בגידולם יבקש עליהם רחמים: הנפטר מן המת. כשהיו מוליכים ארונות ממקום למקום לקבורה היו מלוים אותו מעיר לעיר וחוזרים אלו ואחרים מלוים אותו משם והלאה והחוזרים קרי נפטרים נוטלין רשות להפטר ממנו: אין להם מנוחה. מישיבה לישיבה וממדרש למדרש:

הדרן עלך הרואה וסליקא לה מסכת ברכות

תורה אור

[ד"ה א כו] שנאמר °פעלתי השמיני וכתיב °כי ברכו אלהים °כל אלה *לעובד אדום המה [שם] בניהם ואחיהם *אנשי חיל בכח לעבודה ששים ושנים לעובד אדום: אמר ר' אבין הלוי *כל הדוחק את השעה שעה דוחקתו וכל הנדחה מפני השעה שעה נדחת מפניו מדרבה ורב יוסף *דרב יוסף סיני ורבה עוקר הרים אצטריכא להו שעתא *שלחו להתם סיני ועוקר הרים איזה מהם קודם שלחו להו סיני קודם *שהכל צריכין למרי חטיא אע"פ כן לא קבל עליו רב יוסף דאמרי ליה כלדאי מלכת תרתין שנין מלך רבה עשרין ותרתין שנין מלך רב יוסף תרתין שנין ופלגא כל הנך שני דמלך רבה אפי' אומנא לביתיה לא קרא: ואמר רבי אבין [תהלים כ] הלוי מאי דכתיב °יענך יי' ביום צרה ישגבך שם אלהי' יעקב אלהי יעקב ולא אלהי אברהם ויצחק מכאן לבעל הקורה שיכנס בעביה של קורה: ואמר רבי אבין הלוי כל הנהנה מסעודה שתלמיד חכם שרוי בתוכה כאלו נהנה מזיו [שמות יח] שכינה שנאמר °ויבא אהרן וכל זקני ישראל לאכל לחם עם חותן משה לפני האלהים וכי לפני אלהים אכלו והלא לפני משה אכלו אלא לומר לך כל הנהנה מסעודה שתלמיד חכם שרוי בתוכה כאלו נהנה מזיו שכינה: *ואמר רבי אבין הלוי הנפטר מחברו אל יאמר לו לך בשלום אלא לך לשלום [שם ד] [א] שהרי יתרו שאמר לו למשה °לך לשלום עלה והצליח דוד שאמר לו לאבשלום [שמואל ב טו] °לך בשלום הלך ונתלה ואמר רבי אבין הלוי הנפטר מן המת אל יאמר לו לך [בראשית טו] לשלום אלא לך בשלום שנאמר [ב] °ואתה תבא אל אבותיך בשלום: אמר רבי לוי בר חייא *היוצא מבית הכנסת ונכנס לבית המדרש ועוסק בתורה *זוכה ומקבל פני שכינה שנאמר °ילכו מחיל אל חיל יראה אל אלהים בציון: אמר רבי חייא בר אשי אמר רב *תלמידי חכמים אין להם מנוחה לא בעולם הזה ולא בעולם הבא שנאמר ילכו מחיל אל חיל יראה אל אלהים בציון: *אמר רבי אלעזר אמר ר' חנינא תלמידי חכמים מרבים שלום בעולם שנאמר °וכל בניך למודי יי' ורב שלום בניך אל תקרי בניך אלא בוניך °שלום רב לאוהבי תורתך ואין למו מכשול °יהי שלום בחילך שלוה בארמנותיך °למען אחי ורעי אדברה נא שלום בך °למען בית יי' אלהינו אבקשה טוב לך °יי' עז לעמו יתן יי' יברך את עמו בשלום:

מסורת הש"ס: מגילה [ב"ב קמא:] [ערכין יג:] [מ"ק יג.] הוריות יד. [ב"ב קמה:] [מ"ק כט. ע"ש] [שם ע"ש] שם תהלים פד יבמות קכב: נזיר סו: תמיד לב: כריתות כח: ישעיה כד תהלים קיט שם קכב שם כט

עין משפט נר מצוה: צד א טוש"ע א"ח סי' קנה סעי' א — [א] מג"א סי' ק"י סק"ט — [ב] רמב"ם פ"ד מהל' אבל ה"ד

הדרן עלך הרואה וסליקא לה מסכת ברכות

אחר השלמת המסכתא יאמר זה ויועיל לשכחה בעזרת השם יתברך

*הדרן עלך מסכת ברכות והדרך עלן דעתן עלך מסכת ברכות ודעתך עלן לא נתנשי מינך מסכת ברכות ולא תתנשי מינן לא בעלמא הדין ולא בעלמא דאתי:

[פי' הגון על זה ממלא בס' החיים שחיבר אחי הגאון מהר"ל מפראג בספ' זכיות ח"א פ"ג]

יאמר כן שלשה פעמים ואחר כך יאמר

יהי רצון מלפניך יי' אלהינו ואלהי אבותינו שתהא תורתך אומנותנו בעולם הזה ותהא עמנו לעולם הבא *חנינא בר פפא רמי בר פפא נחמן בר פפא אחאי בר פפא אבא מרי בר פפא רפרם בר פפא רכיש בר פפא סורחב בר פפא אדא בר פפא דרו בר פפא:

[בסיומא וסוף תשו' הרמ"א ז"ל וכן בסוף יש"ש בב"ק כתובים רמזים על הזכרת שמות הללו]

הערב נא יי' אלהינו את דברי תורתך בפינו ובפיפיות עמך בית ישראל ונהיה כולנו אנחנו וצאצאינו וצאצאי עמך בית ישראל יראי שמך ולומדי תורתך: מאויבי תחכמני מצותיך כי לעולם היא לי: יהי לבי תמים בחקיך למען לא אבוש: לעולם לא אשכח פקודיך כי בם חייתני: ברוך אתה ה' למדני חקיך: אמן אמן אמן סלה ועד:

מודים אנו לפניך יי' אלהינו ואלהי אבותינו ששמת חלקנו מיושבי בית המדרש ולא מיושבי קרנות שאנו משכימים והם משכימים אנו משכימים לדברי תורה והם משכימים לדברים בטלים אנו עמלים והם עמלים אנו עמלים ומקבלים שכר והם עמלים ואינם מקבלים שכר אנו רצים והם רצים הם רצים לבאר שחת ואנו רצים לחיי העולם הבא:

יהי רצון לפניך ה' אלהי כשם שעזרתני לסיים מסכת ברכות כן תעזרני להתחיל מסכתות וספרים אחרים ולסיימם ללמוד וללמד לשמור ולעשות ולקיים את כל דברי תלמוד תורתך באהבה וזכות כל התנאים ואמוראים ותלמידי חכמים תעמוד לי ולזרעי שלא תמוש התורה מפי ומפי זרעי וזרע זרעי עד עולם ויתקיים בי בהתהלכך תנחה אותך בשכבך תשמור עליך והקיצות היא תשיחך כי בי ירבו ימיך ויוסיפו לך שנות חיים ארך ימים בימינה עושר וכבוד בשמאלה ה' עז לעמו יתן ה' יברך את עמו בשלום:

ABBREVIATIONS

Alfasi	R. Isaac b. Jacob Alfasi (1013-1103).
Aruk	Talmudic Dictionary by R. Nathan b. Jehiel of Rome (d. 1106).
Asheri	R. Asher b. Jeḥiel (1250-1327).
A.Z.	‘Abodah Zarah.
b.	ben, bar: son of.
B.B.	Baba Bathra.
BaḤ.	Bayith Ḥadash, Glosses by R. Joel b. Samuel Sirkes (1561-1640).
Beḳ.	Beḳoroth.
Ber.	Berakoth.
B.Ḳ.	Baba Ḳamma.
B.M.	Baba Meẓi'a.
Cur. ed(d).	Current edition(s).
D.S.	*Diḳduḳe Soferim* by R. Rabbinowicz.
‘Ed.	‘Eduyyoth.
E.J.	*Encyclopaedia Judaica.*
‘Er.	‘Erubin.
E. V.	English Version.
Giṭ.	Giṭṭin.
Glos.	Glossary.
Ḥag.	Ḥagigah.
Hor.	Horayoth.
Ḥul.	Ḥullin.
J.E.	*Jewish Encyclopaedia.*
J.T.	*Jerusalem Talmud.*
Jast.	M. Jastrow's Dictionary of the Targumim, the Talmud Bible and Yerushalmi, and the Midrashic Literature.
Keth.	Kethuboth.
Ḳid.	Ḳiddushin.
Ma‘as.	Ma‘asroth.
Mak.	Makkoth.
Meg.	Megillah.
Men.	Menaḥoth.
MGWJ	*Monatsschrift für Geschichte und Wissenschaft des Judentums.*
M.Sh.	Ma‘aser Sheni.
MS.M.	Munich Codex of the Talmud.
Naz.	Nazir.
Ned.	Nedarim.
Nid.	Niddah.
Obermeyer	Obermeyer J., *Die Landschaft Babylonien.*
P.B.	*The Authorized Daily Prayer Book*, S. Singer.
Pes.	Pesaḥim.
R.	Rab, Rabban, Rabbenu, Rabbi.
Rashal	Notes and Glosses on the Talmud by R. Solomon Luria (d. 1573).
Rashi	Commentary of R. Isaac Yiẓḥaḳi (d. 1105).
R.H.	Rosh Hashannah.
R.V.	Revised version of the Bible.
Sanh.	Sanhedrin.
Shab.	Shabbath.
Sheḳ.	Sheḳalim.
Sonc. ed.	English Translation of the Babylonian Talmud, Soncino Press, London.
Soṭ.	Soṭah.
Suk.	Sukkah.
TA.	*Talmudische Archäologie*, by S. Krauss.
Ta‘an.	Ta‘anith.
Ter.	Terumoth.
Tosaf.	Tosafoth.
Tosef.	Tosefta.
Wilna Gaon	Notes by Elijah of Wilna (1720-1797) in the Wilna editions of the Talmud.
Yeb.	Yebamoth.
Zeb.	Zebaḥim.

TRANSLITERATION OF HEBREW LETTERS

א (in middle of word)	= ’
ב	= b
ו	= w
ח	= ḥ
ט	= ṭ
כ	= k
ע	= ‘
פ	= f
צ	= ẓ
ק	= ḳ
ת	= th or t

Full particulars regarding the method and scope of the translation are given in the Editor's Introduction.

GLOSSARY

'AM HA-AREẒ pl. *'amme ha-areẓ*, (lit., 'people of the land', 'country people'); the name given in Rabbinic literature to (*a*) a person who through ignorance was careless in the observance of the laws of Levitical purity and of those relating to the priestly and Levitical gifts. In this sense opposed to *ḥaber*, q.v.; (*b*) an illiterate or uncultured man, as opposed to *talmid ḥakam*, q.v.

'AMIDAH (Lit., 'standing'); the Eighteen Benedictions (seven on Sabbaths and Festivals) which the worshipper always recites in a standing posture.

BATH ḲOL (Lit., 'daughter of a voice'); (*a*) a reverberating sound; (*b*) a voice descending from heaven (cf. Dan. IV, 28) to offer guidance in human affairs, and regarded as a lower grade of prophecy.

'ERUB (Lit., 'mixture'); a quantity of food, enough for two meals, placed (*a*) 2000 cubits from the town boundary, so as to extend the Sabbath limit by that distance; (*b*) in a room or in a court-yard to enable all the residents to carry to and fro in the court-yard on Sabbath.

GEMARA (Lit., 'completion' or 'learning'). The traditions, discussions and rulings of the Amoras, based mainly on the Mishnah and forming (*a*) the Babylonian Talmud and (*b*) the Palestinian Talmud.

GEZERAH SHAWAH (Lit., 'equal cut'); the application to one subject of a rule already known to apply to another, on the strength of a common expression used in connection with both in the Scriptures.

HABDALAH (Lit., 'separation'); the blessing (usually made over wine) by which the Sabbath or any other holy day is ushered out.

ḤABER. 'Fellow', 'associate', opp. to *'am ha-areẓ* (q.v.); one scrupulous in the observance of the law, particularly in relation to ritual cleanness and the separation of the priestly and Levitical dues.

HALLEL (Lit., 'Praise'); Psalms CXIII—CXVIII, recited in the morning service on New Moons and Festivals.

HEFḲER. Property which has no owner: a renunciation of ownership in favour of all and sundry. When used in reference to a court of law, it denotes an act of transfer of property from one person to another, in virtue of the power of the court to declare property ownerless, after which it can assign it to another.

ISSAR. A small Roman coin.

KADDISH (Lit., 'holy'): a brief doxology (in Aramaic) recited at the close of each section of a public service.

KALLAH. Name given to an assembly at which the law was expounded to scholars, as well as to the half-yearly assemblies of the Babylonian Academies.

KARETH. 'Cutting off'; divine punishment for a number of sins for which no human penalty is specified. Sudden death is described as '*kerath* of days', premature death at sixty as '*kareth* of years'.

KAWANAH (Lit., 'aiming', 'concentration') (*a*) devotion (in prayer); (*b*) deliberate purpose (in the performance of a religious precept).

KERI (Lit., 'read'); the text of the Scripture as it is to be read in places where this is not correctly indicated by the text as written (*Ketib*).

ḲIDDUSH (Lit., 'sanctification'); the blessing (usually made over wine) by which the Sabbath or any other holy day is ushered in.

LABUD (Lit., 'joined'). A legal fiction whereby a horizontal gap of certain prescribed dimensions is deemed to be closed up (cf. ḤABUṬ).

LOG. A liquid measure equal to a quarter of a *ḳab* (q.v.), or the space occupied by six eggs, c. 549 cubic centimetres.

LULAB. The palm-branch used in the ceremony of the Feast of Tabernacles (v. Lev. XXIII, 40).

MEGILLAH (Lit., 'Scroll'); a term commonly applied to the Book of Esther.

MEZUZAH (Lit., 'doorpost'); a small case containing certain passages from the Scripture affixed to the post of a door (v. Deut. VI, 9).

MIN pl. *minim*, (lit., 'kind', 'species'); (*a*) a heretic, esp. (*b*) a member of the sect of the early Jewish Christians.

MINḤAH. The afternoon service, about two and a half hours before nightfall.

MINUTH. Heresy, the belief in more than one Power, especially Judeo-Christianity.

MISHNAH (rt. SHaNaH, 'to learn', 'to repeat'), (*a*) the collection of the statements, discussions and Biblical interpretations of the Tannaim in the form edited by R. Judah the Patriarch c. 200; (*b*) similar minor collections by previous editors; (*c*) a single clause or paragraph the author of which was a Tanna.

MI'UN (Lit., 'refusal'); a declaration by a fatherless girl who has been married off by her mother or brother under age, that she does not wish to live with her husband. Such a declaration made by her in the presence of a Beth din secures her freedom without the requirement of a *Geṭ*.

MU'AD (Lit., 'forewarned'); applied to an ox (or any other animal) that has gored or done injury on three successive occasions, so that the owner thus stands 'forewarned' and is liable to pay in full for any damage that has been done by his beast.

MUSAF (Lit., 'addition'); the additional *'Amidah* recited during the morning service on Sabbaths and Holy Days.

ONAN. A mourner while his dead relative is awaiting burial; opposite to *abel*, a mourner from the time of burial for a period of seven or thirty days.

SANHEDRIN (συνέδριον); the council of state and supreme tribunal of the Jewish people during the century or more preceding the fall of the Second Temple. It consisted of seventy-one members, and was presided over by the High Priest. A minor court (for judicial purposes only) consisting of twenty-three members was known as the 'Small Sanhedrin'.

SHECHINAH (Lit., 'abiding [of God]' 'Divine presence'); the spirit of the Omnipresent as manifested on earth.

SHEMA' (Lit., 'hear'); the biblical verse, *'Hear, O Israel'* etc. (Deut. VI, 4); also the three sections (Deut. VI, 5-9; Deut. XI, 13-20; and Num. XV, 37-41) which are recited after this verse in the morning and evening prayers.

SUKKAH. 'Booth'; esp. the festive booth for Tabernacles (Lev. XXIII, 34ff), the roof of which must be made of something that grows from the ground such as reeds, branches or leaves of a prescribed size, quantity and quality.

TALLITH. A garment, cloak, esp. the four-cornered shawl with fringes (*ẓiẓith*) at each corner, worn during the recital of certain prayers.

TALMID ḤAKAM (Lit., 'disciple of the wise'); scholar, student of the Torah.

TALMUD (Lit., 'teaching', 'learning') applies (*a*) to the Gemara (q.v.) or (*b*) generally to the Mishnah and Gemara combined.

TANNA (Lit., 'one who repeats' or 'teaches'); (*a*) a Rabbi quoted in the Mishnah or Baraitha (q.v.); (*b*) in the Amoraic period, a scholar whose special task was to memorize and recite Baraithas in the presence of expounding teachers.

TEFILLAH. Prayer, whether private or public; specifically, the *'Amidah'* prayer.

TEFILLIN. Phylacteries; small cases containing passages from the Scripture and affixed to the forehead and arm during the recital of morning prayers, in accordance with Deut. VI, 8.

TERUMAH. 'That which is lifted or separated'; the heave-offering given from the yields of the yearly harvests, from certain sacrifices, and from the *shekels* collected in a special chamber in the Temple (*terumath ha-lishkah*). *Terumah gedolah* (great offering): the first levy on the produce of the year given to the priest, (v. Num. XVIII, 8ff). Its quantity varied according to the generosity of the owner, who could give one-fortieth, one-fiftieth, or one-sixtieth of his harvest. *Terumath ma'aser* (heave offering of the tithe): the heave-offering given to the priest by the Levite from the tithes he receives (v. Num. XVIII, 25ff).

TORAH (Lit., 'teaching', 'learning', 'instruction'); (*a*) the Pentateuch (Written Law); (*b*) the Mishnah (Oral Law); (*c*) the whole body of Jewish religious literature.

TURGEMAN (Lit., 'interpreter', 'dragoman'). A public speaker who elaborated before a popular audience the heads of a discourse which he received from a Rabbi or scholar.

ZUZ. A coin of the value of a *denarius*, six *ma'ah*, or twelve *dupondia*.

PRINTED IN THE NETHERLANDS
BY JOH. ENSCHEDÉ EN ZONEN, HAARLEM

GLOSSARY

'AM HA-AREẒ pl. *'amme ha-areẓ*, (lit., 'people of the land', 'country people'); the name given in Rabbinic literature to (*a*) a person who through ignorance was careless in the observance of the laws of Levitical purity and of those relating to the priestly and Levitical gifts. In this sense opposed to *ḥaber*, q.v.; (*b*) an illiterate or uncultured man, as opposed to *talmid ḥakam*, q.v.

'AMIDAH (Lit., 'standing'); the Eighteen Benedictions (seven on Sabbaths and Festivals) which the worshipper always recites in a standing posture.

BATH ḲOL (Lit., 'daughter of a voice'); (*a*) a reverberating sound; (*b*) a voice descending from heaven (cf. Dan. IV, 28) to offer guidance in human affairs, and regarded as a lower grade of prophecy.

'ERUB (Lit., 'mixture'); a quantity of food, enough for two meals, placed (*a*) 2000 cubits from the town boundary, so as to extend the Sabbath limit by that distance; (*b*) in a room or in a court-yard to enable all the residents to carry to and fro in the court-yard on Sabbath.

GEMARA (Lit., 'completion' or 'learning'). The traditions, discussions and rulings of the Amoras, based mainly on the Mishnah and forming (*a*) the Babylonian Talmud and (*b*) the Palestinian Talmud.

GEZERAH SHAWAH (Lit., 'equal cut'); the application to one subject of a rule already known to apply to another, on the strength of a common expression used in connection with both in the Scriptures.

HABDALAH (Lit., 'separation'); the blessing (usually made over wine) by which the Sabbath or any other holy day is ushered out.

ḤABER. 'Fellow', 'associate', opp. to *'am ha-areẓ* (q.v.); one scrupulous in the observance of the law, particularly in relation to ritual cleanness and the separation of the priestly and Levitical dues.

HALLEL (Lit., 'Praise'); Psalms CXIII—CXVIII, recited in the morning service on New Moons and Festivals.

HEFḲER. Property which has no owner: a renunciation of ownership in favour of all and sundry. When used in reference to a court of law, it denotes an act of transfer of property from one person to another, in virtue of the power of the court to declare property ownerless, after which it can assign it to another.

ISSAR. A small Roman coin.

KADDISH (Lit., 'holy'): a brief doxology (in Aramaic) recited at the close of each section of a public service.

KALLAH. Name given to an assembly at which the law was expounded to scholars, as well as to the half-yearly assemblies of the Babylonian Academies.

KARETH. 'Cutting off'; divine punishment for a number of sins for which no human penalty is specified. Sudden death is described as *'kerath* of days', premature death at sixty as *'kareth* of years'.

KAWANAH (Lit., 'aiming', 'concentration') (*a*) devotion (in prayer); (*b*) deliberate purpose (in the performance of a religious precept).

KERI (Lit., 'read'); the text of the Scripture as it is to be read in places where this is not correctly indicated by the text as written (*Ketib*).

ḲIDDUSH (Lit., 'sanctification'); the blessing (usually made over wine) by which the Sabbath or any other holy day is ushered in.

LABUD (Lit., 'joined'). A legal fiction whereby a horizontal gap of certain prescribed dimensions is deemed to be closed up (cf. ḤABUṬ).

LOG. A liquid measure equal to a quarter of a *ḳab* (q.v.), or the space occupied by six eggs, c. 549 cubic centimetres.

LULAB. The palm-branch used in the ceremony of the Feast of Tabernacles (v. Lev. XXIII, 40).

MEGILLAH (Lit., 'Scroll'); a term commonly applied to the Book of Esther.

MEZUZAH (Lit., 'doorpost'); a small case containing certain passages from the Scripture affixed to the post of a door (v. Deut. VI, 9).

MIN pl. *minim*, (lit., 'kind', 'species'); (*a*) a heretic, esp. (*b*) a member of the sect of the early Jewish Christians.

MINḤAH. The afternoon service, about two and a half hours before nightfall.

MINUTH. Heresy, the belief in more than one Power, especially Judeo-Christianity.

MISHNAH (rt. SHaNaH, 'to learn', 'to repeat'), (*a*) the collection of the statements, discussions and Biblical interpretations of the Tannaim in the form edited by R. Judah the Patriarch c. 200; (*b*) similar minor collections by previous editors; (*c*) a single clause or paragraph the author of which was a Tanna.

MI'UN (Lit., 'refusal'); a declaration by a fatherless girl who has been married off by her mother or brother under age, that she does not wish to live with her husband. Such a declaration made by her in the presence of a Beth din secures her freedom without the requirement of a *Geṭ*.

MU'AD (Lit., 'forewarned'); applied to an ox (or any other animal) that has gored or done injury on three successive occasions, so that the owner thus stands 'forewarned' and is liable to pay in full for any damage that has been done by his beast.

MUSAF (Lit., 'addition'); the additional *'Amidah* recited during the morning service on Sabbaths and Holy Days.

ONAN. A mourner while his dead relative is awaiting burial; opposite to *abel*, a mourner from the time of burial for a period of seven or thirty days.

SANHEDRIN (συνέδριον); the council of state and supreme tribunal of the Jewish people during the century or more preceding the fall of the Second Temple. It consisted of seventy-one members, and was presided over by the High Priest. A minor court (for judicial purposes only) consisting of twenty-three members was known as the 'Small Sanhedrin'.

SHECHINAH (Lit., 'abiding [of God]' 'Divine presence'); the spirit of the Omnipresent as manifested on earth.

SHEMA' (Lit., 'hear'); the biblical verse, *'Hear, O Israel'* etc. (Deut. VI, 4); also the three sections (Deut. VI, 5-9; Deut. XI, 13-20; and Num. XV, 37-41) which are recited after this verse in the morning and evening prayers.

SUKKAH. 'Booth'; esp. the festive booth for Tabernacles (Lev. XXIII, 34ff), the roof of which must be made of something that grows from the ground such as reeds, branches or leaves of a prescribed size, quantity and quality.

TALLITH. A garment, cloak, esp. the four-cornered shawl with fringes (*ẓiẓith*) at each corner, worn during the recital of certain prayers.

TALMID ḤAKAM (Lit., 'disciple of the wise'); scholar, student of the Torah.

TALMUD (Lit., 'teaching', 'learning') applies (*a*) to the Gemara (q.v.) or (*b*) generally to the Mishnah and Gemara combined.

TANNA (Lit., 'one who repeats' or 'teaches'); (*a*) a Rabbi quoted in the Mishnah or Baraitha (q.v.); (*b*) in the Amoraic period, a scholar whose special task was to memorize and recite Baraithas in the presence of expounding teachers.

TEFILLAH. Prayer, whether private or public; specifically, the *'Amidah'* prayer.

TEFILLIN. Phylacteries; small cases containing passages from the Scripture and affixed to the forehead and arm during the recital of morning prayers, in accordance with Deut. VI, 8.

TERUMAH. 'That which is lifted or separated'; the heave-offering given from the yields of the yearly harvests, from certain sacrifices, and from the *shekels* collected in a special chamber in the Temple (*terumath ha-lishkah*). *Terumah gedolah* (great offering): the first levy on the produce of the year given to the priest, (v. Num. XVIII, 8ff). Its quantity varied according to the generosity of the owner, who could give one-fortieth, one-fiftieth, or one-sixtieth of his harvest. *Terumath ma'aser* (heave-offering of the tithe): the heave-offering given to the priest by the Levite from the tithes he receives (v. Num. XVIII, 25ff).

TORAH (Lit., 'teaching', 'learning', 'instruction'); (*a*) the Pentateuch (Written Law); (*b*) the Mishnah (Oral Law); (*c*) the whole body of Jewish religious literature.

TURGEMAN (Lit., 'interpreter', 'dragoman'). A public speaker who elaborated before a popular audience the heads of a discourse which he received from a Rabbi or scholar.

ZUZ. A coin of the value of a *denarius*, six *ma'ah*, or twelve *dupondia*.

PRINTED IN THE NETHERLANDS
BY JOH. ENSCHEDÉ EN ZONEN, HAARLEM